Annual Abstract
of Statistics

2003 edition
United Kingdom
No 139

Editor: Kevin Laverty

London: TSO

ISBN 0 11 621572 0

ISSN 0072–5730

A National Statistics publication

Official statistics bearing the National Statistics logo are produced to high professional standards set out in the National Statistics Code of Practice. They undergo regular quality assurance reviews to ensure that they meet customer needs. They are produced free from any political interference.

Contact points

For enquiries about this publication, contact the Editor, Kevin Laverty

Tel: 020 7533 5739

E-mail: kevin.laverty@ons.gov.uk

To order this publication, call TSO on **0870 600 5522.** See also back cover.

For general enquiries, contact the National Statistics Customer Enquiry Centre on **0845 601 3034** (minicom: 01633 812399)

E-mail: info@statistics.gov.uk

Fax: 01633 652747

Letters: Room D115, Government Buildings, Cardiff Road, Newport NP10 8XG

You can also find National Statistics on the internet - go to **www.statistics.gov.uk**

About the Office for National Statistics

The Office for National Statistics (ONS) is the government agency responsible for compiling, analysing and disseminating many of the United Kingdom's economic, social and demographic statistics, including the retail prices index, trade figures and labour market data, as well as the periodic census of the population and health statistics. The Director of ONS is also the National Statistician and the Registrar General for England and Wales, and the agency administers the statutory registration of births, marriages and deaths there.

CONTENTS

CONTENTS

CONTENTS

CONTENTS

CONTENTS

CONTENTS

15 National accounts

16 Prices

17 Government finance

CONTENTS

CONTENTS

CONTENTS

Banking, insurance etc 22

Service industry 23

UNITS OF MEASUREMENT

Length

1 millimetre (mm)		= 0.0393701 inch
1 centimetre (cm)	= 10 millimetres	= 0.393701 inch
1 metre (m)	= 1,000 millimetres	= 1.09361 yards
1 kilometre (km)	= 1,000 metres	= 0.621371 mile

1 inch (in.)		= 25.4 millimetres or 2.54 centimetres
1 foot (ft.)	= 12 inches	= 0.3048 metre
1 yard (yd.)	= 3 feet	= 0.9144 metre
1 mile	= 1,760 yards	= 1.60934 kilometres

Area

1 square millimetre (mm²)		= 0.00 55 square inch
1 square metre (m²)	= one million square millimetres	= 1.19599 square yards
1 hectare (ha)	= 10,000 square metres	= 2.47105 acres
1 square kilometre (km²)	= one million square metres	= 247.105 acres

1 square inch (sq. in.)		= 645.16 square millimetres or 6.4516 square centimetres
1 square foot (sq. ft.)	= 144 square inches	= 0.092903 square metre or 929.03 square centimetres
1 square yard (sq. yd.)	= 9 square feet	= 0.836127 square metres
1 acre	= 4,840 square yards	= 4,046.86 square metres or 0.404686 hectare
1 square mile (sq. mile)	= 640 acres	= 2.58999 square kilometres or 258.999 hectares

Volume

1 cubic centimetre (cm³)		= 0.0610237 cubic inch
1 cubic decimetre (dm³)	= 1,000 cubic centimetres	= 0.0353147 cubic foot
1 cubic metre (m³)	= one million cubic centimetres	= 1.30795 cubic yards

1 cubic foot (cu. ft.)		= 0.0283168 cubic metre or 28.3168 cubic decimetres
1 cubic yard (cu. yd.)	= 27 cubic feet	= 0.764555 cubic metre

Capacity

1 litre (l)	= 1 cubic decimetre	= 0.220 gallon
1 hectolitre (hl)	= 100 litres	= 22.0 gallons

1 pint		= 0.568 litre
2 pints	= 1 quart	= 1.137 litres
8 pints	= 1 gallon	= 4.54609 cubic decimetres or 4.546 litres
36 gallons (gal.)	= 1 bulk barrel	= 1.63656 hectolitres

Weight

1 gram (g)		= 0.0352740 ounce
1 hectogram (hg)	= 100 grams	= 3.5274 ounces or 0.220462 pound
1 kilogram (kg)	= 1,000 grams or 10 hectograms	= 2.20462 pounds
1 tonne (t)	= 1,000 kilograms	= 1.10231 short tons or 0.9842 long ton

1 ounce avoirdupois (oz.)		= 28.3495 grams
1 pound avoirdupois (lb.)	= 16 ounces	= 0.45359237 kilogram
1 hundredweight (cwt.)	= 112 pounds	= 50.8023 kilograms
1 short ton	= 2,000 pounds	= 907.18474 kilograms or 0.90718474 tonne
1 long ton (referred to as ton)	= 2,240 pounds	= 1,016.05 kilograms or 1.01605 tonnes

1 ounce troy	= 480 grains	= 31.1035 grams

Energy

British thermal unit (Btu)	= 0.252 kilocalorie (kcal) = 1.05506 kilojoule (kj)
Therm	= 100,000 British thermal units = 25,200 kcal = 105,506 kj
Megawatt (Mw)	= 10^6 watts
Gigawatt hour (GWh)	= 10^6 kilowatt hours = 34,121 therms

Food and drink

Butter	23,310 litres milk	= 1 tonne butter (average)
Cheese	10,070 litres milk	= 1 tonne cheese
Condensed milk	2,550 litres milk	= 1 tonne full cream condensed milk
	2,953 litres skimmed milk	= 1 tonne skimmed condensed milk
Milk	1 million litres	= 1,030 tonnes
Milk powder	8,054 litres milk	= 1 tonne full cream milk powder
	10,740 litres skimmed milk	= 1 tonne skimmed milk powder
Eggs	17,126 eggs	= 1 tonne (approximate)
Sugar	100 tonnes raw sugar	= 95 tonnes refined sugar
Beer	1 bulk barrel	= 36 gallons irrespective of gravity

Shipping

Gross tonnage	= The total volume of all the enclosed spaces of a vessel, the unit of measurement being a ton of 100 cubic feet.
Deadweight tonnage	= Deadweight tonnage is the total weight in tons of 2,240 lb. that a ship can legally carry, that is the total weight of cargo, bunkers, stores and crew.

ACKNOWLEDGEMENTS

The Editor would like to thank the following people for their help in producing this book:

Production team: Nicola Amaranayake

Karin Bosveld

Andrew Corris

Michael Crawley

Jonathan Elphick

Mark Nevill

David Penny

Matthew Richardson

Steve Whyman

Brian Yin

Contributors

The Editor also wishes to thank all his colleagues in the ONS, the rest of the Government Statistical Service and all contributors in other organisations for their generous support and helpful comments, without whose help this publication would not be possible.

INTRODUCTION

Welcome to the 2003 edition of the *Annual Abstract of Statistics*. This compendium draws together statistics from a wide range of official and other authoritative sources. Their help is gratefully acknowledged.

Regional information, supplementary to the national figures in this *Annual Abstract*, appears in *Regional Trends*. The 2002 edition is available electronically, free of charge, from the National Statistics website. This can be accessed from the *Regional Trends* entry under the Compendia and Reference theme, or directly at: www.statistics.gov.uk/statbase/product.asp?vlnk= 836. Previous editions are available via The Stationery Office (TSO).

The five Parts of the *Annual Abstract*, illustrated in the contents, align with their equivalents in *UK 2003: The Official Yearbook of Great Britain and Northern Ireland*, so that the two books can be consulted as complementary volumes, painting a picture of the UK in words and figures.

Current data for many of the series appearing in this *Annual Abstract* are contained in other ONS publications, such as *Economic Trends, Monthly Digest of Statistics, Population Trends, Health Statistics Quarterly* and *Financial Statistics*. All are published by TSO.

The name and telephone number of the organisation providing the statistics are shown under each table. In addition, a list of Sources is given at the back of the book, which sets out the official publications or other sources to which further reference can be made.

All the data series published in the *Annual Abstract* are contained on a database, and almost all are stored with a four letter identification code (eg LUJS). These codes appear at the start of most columns or rows of data and can be quoted if you contact us requiring any further information about the data.

Implications of the 2001 Census

The first results of the 2001 Census, published on 30 September 2002, showed that previous estimates of the total UK population were about 1 million too high. This was mainly due to the overestimation of the net flow of international migrants into the United Kingdom.

To assist users in the period before revised estimates are published, the ONS has produced national level interim revised population estimates for the period mid-1982 to mid-2000. These interim estimates have been used in this volume.

The interim population data has led to the Labour Force Survey (LFS) needing to reweight their estimates to the new population figures. Again, to assist users in the period before revised estimates are published, ONS has published interim reweighted LFS estimates for the UK, which have been used in this volume.

The ONS intend to release revised population estimates for mid-1982 to mid-2000 in February and March 2003. In addition, a full reweighting of the Labour Force Survey data should be complete by Summer 2003. The Annual Abstract datasets, available on the National Statistics website, (www.statistics.gov.uk/statbase/product.asp? vlnk=94) will be updated in late-Spring for the Population chapter and late-Summer for the Labour Market chapter. Please see the introductions to both these chapters for more information and details of which tables are affected.

Definitions and Classification

Time Series
So far as possible annual totals are given throughout, but quarterly or monthly figures are given where these are more suitable to the type of series.

Explanatory notes
Most sections are preceded by explanatory notes which should be read in conjunction with the tables. Definitions and explanatory notes for many of the terms occurring in the *Annual Abstract* are also given in the *Annual Supplement* to the *Monthly Digest of Statistics*, published annually in the January editions. Detailed notes on items which appear in both the *Abstract* and *Financial Statistics* are given in an annual supplement to the latter entitled *Financial Statistics: Explanatory Handbook*. The original sources listed in the Sources may also be consulted.

Standard Industrial Classification
A Standard Industrial Classification (SIC) was first introduced into the United Kingdom in 1948 for use in classifying business establishments and other statistical units by the type of economic activity in which they are engaged. The classification provides a framework for the collection, tabulation, presentation and analysis of data about economic activities. Its use promotes uniformity of data collected by various government departments and agencies.

Since 1948 the classification has been revised in 1958, 1968, 1980 and 1992. One of the principal objectives of the 1980 revision was to eliminate differences from the activity classification issued by the Statistical Office of the European Communities (Eurostat) and entitled 'Nomenclature générale des activités économiques dans les Communautés Européennes', usually abbreviated to NACE. In 1990, the European Communities introduced a new statistical classification of economic activities (NACE Rev 1) by regulation. The regulation made it obligatory for the UK to introduce a new Standard Industrial Classification SIC(92), based on NACE Rev 1.

UK SIC(92) is based exactly on NACE Rev 1 but, where it is thought necessary or helpful, a fifth digit

Introduction

has been added to form subclasses of the NACE 1 four digit system. There are 17 sections, 16 subsections, 60 divisions, 222 groups, 503 classes and 253 subclasses. Full details are available from *UK Standard Industrial Classification of Economic Activities 1992* (TSO 1997, price £25.00) and *Indexes to the UK Standard Industrial Classification of Economic Activities 1992* (TSO 1997, price £22.50).

Revisions to contents

Some of the figures, particularly for the latest year, are provisional and may be revised in a subsequent issue of the *Annual Abstract*.

Symbols and conventions used

Change of basis
Where consecutive figures have been compiled on different bases and are not strictly comparable, a footnote is added indicating the nature of the difference.

Units of measurement
The various units of measurement used are listed opposite the inside back cover.

Rounding of figures
In tables where figures have been rounded to the nearest final digit, the constituent items may not add up exactly to the total.

Symbols
The following symbols have been used throughout:

.. = not available or not applicable (also information suppressed to avoid disclosure).

- = nil or less than half the final digit shown.

National Statistics Online: www.statistics.gov.uk

Web-based access to time series, cross sectional data and metadata from across the Government Statistical Service (GSS), is available using the site search and index functions from the homepage. Download many datasets, in whole or in part, or consult directory information for all GSS statistical resources, including censuses, surveys, periodicals and enquiry services. Information is posted as PDF electronic documents or in XLS and CSV formats, compatible with most spreadsheet packages.

Complete copies of this publication are available to download free of charge on the following web page: www.statistics.gov.uk/statbase/product.asp?vlnk=94.

Contact point

The Editor welcomes any feedback on the content of the *Annual Abstract*, including comments on the format of the data and the selection of topics. Comments and requests for general information should be addressed to:

Kevin Laverty
Social Analysis and Reporting Division
Room B5/06
Office for National Statistics
1, Drummond Gate
London SW1V 2QQ

or

Email: annual.abstract@ons.gov.uk

January 2003

1 Area

Area

The United Kingdom comprises Great Britain and Northern Ireland. Great Britain comprises England, Wales and Scotland only.

Physical Features

The United Kingdom (UK) constitutes the greater part of the British Isles. The largest of the islands is Great Britain. The next largest comprises Northern Ireland and the Irish Republic. Western Scotland is fringed by the large island chain known as the Hebrides, and to the north east of the Scottish mainland are the Orkney and Shetland Islands. All these, along with the Isle of Wight, Anglesey and the Isles of Scilly, have administrative ties with the mainland, but the Isle of Man in the Irish Sea and the Channel Islands between Great Britain and France are largely self-governing, and are not part of the United Kingdom. The UK is one of the 15 member states of the European Union (EU).

With an area of about 243 000 sq km (94 000 sq miles), the United Kingdom is just under 1 000 km (about 600 miles) from the south coast to the extreme north of Scotland and just under 500 km (around 300 miles) across at the widest point.

- Highest mountain: Ben Nevis, in the highlands of Scotland, at 1 343 m (4 406 ft)

- Longest river: the Severn, 354 km (220 miles) long, which rises in central Wales and flows through Shrewsbury, Worcester and Gloucester in England to the Bristol Channel

- Largest lake: Lough Neagh, Northern Ireland, at 396 sq km (153 sq miles)

- Deepest lake: Loch Morar in the Highlands of Scotland, 310 m (1 017 ft) deep

- Highest waterfall: Eas a'Chual Aluinn, from Glas Bheinn, in the highlands of Scotland, with a drop of 200 m (660 ft)

- Deepest cave: Ogof Ffynnon Ddu, Wales, at 308 m (1 010 ft) deep

- Most northerly point on the British mainland: Dunnet Head, north-east Scotland

- Most southerly point on the British mainland: Lizard Point, Cornwall

- Closest point to mainland continental Europe: Dover, Kent. The Channel Tunnel, which links England and France, is a little over 50 km (31 miles) long, of which nearly 38 km (24 miles) are actually under the Channel.

1.1 Area of the United Kingdom, 2001

	sq km		sq km
		Worcestershire County	1 741
UNITED KINGDOM	242 513		
		Herefordshire and Worcestershire	3 920
GREAT BRITAIN	228 937	*Former county of Shropshire*	3 488
		Former county of Staffordshire	2 714
ENGLAND AND WALES	151 013		
		EAST	19 110
ENGLAND	130 281		
		Luton UA	43
NORTH EAST	8 573	Peterborough UA	343
		Southend-on-Sea UA	42
Darlington UA	197	Thurrock UA	163
Hartlepool UA	94		
Middlesbrough UA	54	Bedfordshire County	1 192
Redcar and Cleveland UA	245	Cambridgeshire County	3 046
Stockton-on-Tees UA	204	Essex County	3 465
		Hertfordshire	1 643
Durham County	2 226	Norfolk	5 371
Northumberland	5 013	Suffolk	3 801
Tyne and Wear (Met County)	540		
		Former county of Bedfordshire	1 235
Tees Valley	794	*Former county of Cambridgeshire*	3 390
Tees Valley less Darlington	597	*Former county of Essex*	3 670
Former county of Durham	2 424		
		LONDON	1 572
NORTH WEST	14 106		
		Inner London	319
Blackburn with Darwen UA	137	Outer London	1 253
Blackpool UA	35		
Halton UA	79	**SOUTH EAST**	19 069
Warrington UA	181		
		Bracknell Forest UA	109
Cheshire County	2 083	Brighton and Hove UA	83
Cumbria	6 768	Isle of Wight UA	380
Greater Manchester (Met County)	1 276	Medway UA	192
Lancashire County	2 903	Milton Keynes UA	309
Merseyside (Met County)	645	Portsmouth UA	40
		Reading UA	40
Former county of Cheshire	2 343	Slough UA	33
Former county of Lancashire	3 075	Southampton UA	50
		West Berkshire UA	704
YORKSHIRE AND THE HUMBER	15 408	Windsor and Maidenhead UA	197
		Wokingham UA	179
East Riding of Youkshire UA	2 408		
Kingston upon Hull, City of UA	71	Buckinghamshire County	1 565
North East Lincolnshire UA	192	East Sussex County	1 709
North Lincolnshire UA	846	Hampshire County	3 679
York UA	272	Kent County	3 544
		Oxfordshire	2 605
North Yorkshire County	8 038	Surrey	1 663
South Yorkshire (Met County)	1 552	West Sussex	1 991
West Yorkshire (Met County)	2 029		
		Former county of Berkshire	1 262
The Humber	3 517	*Former county of Buckinghamshire*	1 874
Former county of North Yorkshire	8 310	*Former county of East Sussex*	1 791
		Former county of Hampshire	3 769
EAST MIDLANDS	15 607	*Former county of Kent*	3 736
Derby UA	78	**SOUTH WEST**	23 837
Leicester UA	73		
Nottingham UA	75	Bath and North East Somerset UA	346
Rutland UA	382	Bournemouth UA	46
		Bristol, City of UA	110
Derbyshire County	2 547	North Somerset UA	374
Leicestershire County	2 083	Plymouth UA	80
Lincolnshire	5 921	Poole UA	65
Northamptonshire	2 364	South Gloucestershire UA	497
Nottinghamshire County	2 085	Swindon UA	230
		Torbay UA	63
Former county of Derbyshire	2 625		
Former county of Leicestershire	2 538	Cornwall and the Isles of Scilly	3 563
Former county of Nottinghamshire	2 159	Devon County	6 564
		Dorset County	2 542
WEST MIDLANDS	12 998	Gloucestershire	2 653
		Somerset	3 451
Herefordshire, County of UA	2 180	Wiltshire County	3 255
Stoke-on-Trent UA	93		
Telford and Wrekin UA	290	*Bristol/Bath area*	1 326
		Former county of Devon	6 707
Shropshire County	3 197	*Former county of Dorset*	2 653
Staffordshire County	2 620	*Former county of Wiltshire*	3 485
Warwickshire	1 975		
West Midlands (Met County)	902		

1.1 Area of the United Kingdom, 2001
continued

	sq km		sq km
WALES	20 732	Dumfries and Galloway	6 426
Blaenau Gwent	109	Dundee City	60
Bridgend	251	East Ayrshire	1 262
Caerphilly	278	East Dunbartonshire	175
Cardiff	139	East Lothian	679
Carmarthenshire	2 394		
		East Renfrewshire	174
Ceredigion	1 792	Edinburgh, City of	264
Conwy	1 126	Eilean Siar (Western Isles)	3 071
Denbighshire	837	Falkirk	297
Flintshire	438	Fife	1 325
Gwynedd	2 535		
		Glasgow City	175
Isle of Anglesey	711	Highland	25 659
Merthyr Tydfil	111	Inverclyde	160
Monmouthshire	849	Midlothian	354
Neath Port Talbot	441	Moray	2 238
Newport	190		
Pembrokeshire	1 589	North Ayrshire	885
		North Lanarkshire	470
Powys	5 181	Orkney Islands	990
Rhondda, Cynon, Taff	424	Perth and Kinross	5 286
Swansea	378	Renfrewshire	261
Torfaen	126	Scottish Borders	4 732
The Vale of Glamorgan	331		
Wrexham	504	Shetland Islands	1 466
		South Ayrshire	1 222
		South Lanarkshire	1 772
SCOTLAND	77 925	Stirling	2 187
		West Dunbartonshire	159
Aberdeen City	186	West Lothian	427
Aberdeenshire	6 313		
Angus	2 182		
Argyll and Bute	6 909	**NORTHERN IRELAND**	13 576
Clackmannanshire	159		

Source: Office for National Statistics

2 Parliamentary elections

Parliamentary elections

2.1 Parliamentary elections[1]

Thousands and percentages

	26 May 1955	8 Oct 1959	15 Oct 1964	31 Mar 1966	18 June 1970[1]	28 Feb 1974	10 Oct 1974	3 May 1979	9 June 1983	11 June 1987	9 April 1992	1 May 1997	7 June 2001
United Kingdom													
Electorate	34 852	35 397	35 894	35 957	39 615	40 256	40 256	41 573	42 704	43 666	43 719	43 846	44 403
Average-electors per seat	55.3	56.2	57.0	57.1	62.9	63.4	63.4	65.5	66.7	67.2	67.2	66.5	67.4
Valid votes counted	26 760	27 863	27 657	27 265	28 345	31 340	29 189	31 221	30 671	32 530	33 614	31 286	26 367
As percentage of electorate	76.8	78.7	77.1	75.8	71.5	77.9	72.5	75.1	71.8	74.5	76.7	71.4	59.4
England and Wales													
Electorate	30 591	31 109	31 610	31 695	34 931	35 509	35 509	36 695	37 708	38 568	38 648	38 719	39 228
Average-electors per seat	55.9	56.9	57.8	57.9	63.9	64.3	64.3	66.5	67.2	68.8	68.8	68.0	68.9
Valid votes counted	23 570	24 619	24 384	24 116	24 877	27 735	25 729	27 609	27 082	28 832	29 897	27 679	23 243
As percentage of electorate	77.0	79.1	77.1	76.1	71.2	78.1	72.5	75.2	71.8	74.8	77.5	71.5	59.3
Scotland													
Electorate	3 388	3 414	3 393	3 360	3 659	3 705	3 705	3 837	3 934	3 995	3 929	3 949	3 984
Average-electors per seat	47.7	48.1	47.8	47.3	51.5	52.2	52.2	54.0	54.6	55.5	54.6	54.8	55.3
Valid votes counted	2 543	2 668	2 635	2 553	2 688	2 887	2 758	2 917	2 825	2 968	2 931	2 817	2 313
As percentage of electorate	75.1	78.1	77.6	76.0	73.5	77.9	74.5	76.0	71.8	74.3	74.2	71.3	58.1
Northern Ireland													
Electorate	873	875	891	902	1 025	1 027	1 037	1 028	1 050	1 090	1 141	1 178	1 191
Average-electors per seat	72.8	72.9	74.2	75.2	85.4	85.6	86.4	85.6	61.8	64.1	67.1	65.4	66.2
Valid votes counted	647	576	638	596	779	718	702	696	765	730	785	791	810
As percentage of electorate	74.1	65.8	71.7	66.1	76.0	69.9	67.7	67.7	72.9	67.0	68.8	67.1	68.0
Members of Parliament elected: (Numbers)	630	630	630	630	630	635	635	635	650	650	651	659	659
Conservative	344	364	303	253	330	296	276	339	396	375	336	165	166
Labour	277	258	317	363	287	301	319	268	209	229	271	418	412
Liberal Democrat	6	6	9	12	6	14	13	11	17	17	20	46	52
Social Democratic Party	-	-	-	-	-	-	-	-	6	5	-	-	-
Scottish National Party	-	-	-	-	1	7	11	2	2	3	3	6	5
Plaid Cymru	-	-	-	-	-	2	3	2	2	3	4	4	4
Other[2]	3	2	1	2	6	15	13	13	18	18	17	20	20

1 The Representation of the People Act 1969 lowered the minimum voting age from 21 to 18 years with effect from 16 February 1970.
2 Including the Speaker.

Source: University of Plymouth for the Electoral Commission: 01752 233205

2.2 Parliamentary by-elections

	April 1992 - April 1997	General[1] Election April 1992	May 1997 - June 2001	General[1,2] Election May 1997	June 2001 - November 2002	General[1] Election June 2001
Numbers of by-elections	18		17		2	
Votes recorded						
By party (percentages)						
Conservative	21.4	40.1	27.0	25.1	20.0	22.0
Labour	39.5	36.2	29.7	40.1	46.8	56.0
Liberal Democrat	24.6	16.4	22.1	14.4	16.9	14.1
Scottish National Party	5.2	3.1	6.0	4.1	-	-
Plaid Cymru	0.5	0.2	2.5	2.3	8.4	6.2
Other	8.8	4.1	12.7	14.1	7.9	1.7
Total votes recorded						
(percentages)	100.0	100.0	100.0	100.0	100.0	100.0
(thousands)	625	808	435	723	46	69

1 Votes recorded in the same seats in the previous General Election.
2 Proportions of 'other' votes inflated by the fact that votes were cast for the retiring Speaker as 'The Speaker seeking re-election' and not as a party candidate.

Source: University of Plymouth for the Electoral Commission: 01752 233205

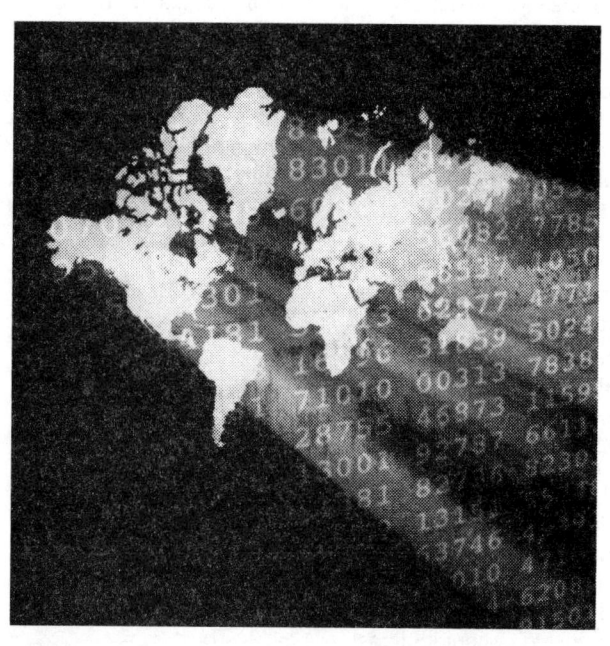

3 International development

International development

Overseas development assistance
(Tables 3.1 and 3.2)

The UK development assistance programme is administered by the Department for International Development (DFID) to promote the economic development and welfare of recipient countries. It is managed within financial years, the money being voted annually by Parliament. Since 1992 the statistics relating to the programme are also published on a financial year basis and on a calendar year basis for both international aid comparisons and for national purposes such as the balance of payments.

Aid flows can be measured before (gross) or after (net) deduction of repayments of principal on past loans. These tables show only the gross figures.

Assistance is provided in two main ways: *bilateral*, that is directly to recipient countries or to institutions in the United Kingdom for work on behalf of such countries, or *multilateral*, that is to international institutions for their development assistance programmes. Table 3.1 shows the main groups of multilateral agencies, the International Development Association being the largest in the World Bank Group.

Bilateral assistance takes various forms:

Project or sector aid is finance for investment schemes primarily designed to increase the physical capital of the recipient country, including contributions for local and recurrent costs.

Sector-wide programmes (typically in education, health or agriculture) comprise a combination of assistance including direct budget support, financial assistance in the form of projects and technical co-operation.

Programme aid is financial assistance to fund imports, sector support programmes or budgetary expenditure, usually as part of or in conjunction with a World Bank/IMF co-ordinated structural adjustment programme.

Technical co-operation is the provision of know-how in the form of personnel, training, research and associated costs.

Grants and other aid in kind are used to provide equipment and supplies, and support to the development work of UK and international voluntary organisations.

Humanitarian assistance comprises food aid and other disaster relief.

Aid and Trade Provision is a special allocation to soften the terms of credit to developing countries by mixing aid funds with private export credits. The ATP scheme lacked poverty elimination as its central focus and was closed in November 1997.

CDC Capital Partners (formerly The Commonwealth Development Corporation) invests in productive public or private sector projects in developing countries.

Other Government Departments' expenditure covers debt relief, drug-related assistance and support to the British Council or voluntary organisations.

Most of the expenditure not allocable by region in Table 3.2 is for assistance provided through organisations in the United Kingdom.

Fuller statistics of the UK's development assistance effort are published annually in *Statistics on International Development* (obtainable from Statistics Department, Abercrombie House, East Kilbride, Glasgow G75 8EA). International comparisons are available in the OECD Development Assistance Committee's annual report. The latest is *2001 Report: Development Co-operation* (available from The Stationery Office).

3.1 UK Gross public expenditure on aid (GPEX)[1]

£ Thousands

		1993/94	1994/95	1995/96	1996/97	1997/98	1998/99	1999/00	2000/01	2001/02
Bilateral Assistance										
DFID										
Project or Sector Aid	LUJS	119 832	121 812	121 456	106 361	96 448	128 870	176 215	185 544	255 989
Programme Aid	LUJW	121 027	113 510	83 494	96 299	84 784	133 574	140 372	251 597	248 519
Technical Co-operation Projects	LUOS	401 560	430 447	446 788	457 060	487 003	479 281	513 453	573 037	656 939
Grants & Other Aid in Kind	LUOT	171 688	149 556	184 315	191 152	172 665	187 714	168 089	175 983	137 857
Humanitarian Assistance	LUOU	179 601	205 368	141 410	121 886	94 680	116 058	226 208	179 775	165 495
Debt Relief	LUOV	23 698	28 144	27 337	23 529	23 161	25 659	23 140	21 188	18 322
Aid and Trade Provision	LUOW	84 700	59 987	71 988	61 978	60 711	56 898	37 790	27 645	23 094
CDC Investments	LUOX	183 354	215 295	279 986	189 082	249 062	166 716	269 052	194 194	132 412
Other Government Departments	LUOY	22 796	33 034	61 606	34 224	170 171	87 147	100 721	149 128	315 530
Total Bilateral Assistance	LUOZ	1 308 257	1 357 153	1 418 381	1 281 571	1 438 684	1 381 918	1 655 039	1 758 091	1 954 157
Multilateral Assistance										
European Community	LUPA	529 823	612 080	693 690	636 418	557 287	754 548	757 867	727 999	750 634
World Bank Group	LUPB	229 613	227 728	206 877	174 398	189 851	175 254	170 631	277 121	243 894
International Monetary Fund	LUPC	20 000	90 000	30 000	20 000	20 000	18 000	17 000	–	10 000
UN Agencies	LUPD	142 527	127 880	116 772	130 775	141 300	131 004	177 031	245 892	238 095
Regional Development Banks	LUPE	76 413	71 212	69 513	58 833	60 411	66 295	67 179	54 803	76 655
Other	LUPF	17 829	27 904	27 036	30 665	30 846	31 216	35 146	39 765	48 104
Total Multilateral Assistance	LUPG	1 016 205	1 156 804	1 143 887	1 051 089	999 695	1 176 317	1 224 854	1 345 580	1 367 382
Administrative Costs	LUPH	65 329	70 314	72 198	82 133	91 436	99 506	105 682	122 664	120 029
Total Gross Public Expenditure on Aid	LUPI	2 389 790	2 584 270	2 634 465	2 414 793	2 529 815	2 657 741	2 985 575	3 226 335	3 441 568

1 See chapter text.

Source: Department for International Development: 01355 843612

3.2 Total bilateral gross public expenditure on aid (GPEX): by main recipient countries and regions[1]

£ Thousands

		1993/94	1994/95	1995/96	1996/97	1997/98	1998/99	1999/00	2000/01	2001/02
Main recipients										
India	LUPJ	102 367	98 622	154 730	111 789	114 022	110 374	107 283	128 818	204 559
States of Former Yugoslavia[2]	ZBXN	51 803	43 511	38 905	42 639	20 669	4 033	84 100	32 176	7 784
Uganda	LUPN	40 551	46 615	40 590	49 207	59 325	64 261	90 286	97 572	68 724
Tanzania	LUPK	32 499	31 633	29 900	56 414	51 437	78 085	75 099	112 034	206 062
Bangladesh	LUPM	56 068	57 441	54 282	44 329	39 078	67 361	71 794	76 921	65 843
Mozambique	LUPV	34 744	25 068	22 026	26 610	48 311	28 902	70 630	43 304	134 671
Indonesia	LUPZ	34 885	51 404	57 265	38 472	48 689	25 420	58 714	28 324	18 350
Ghana	LUPL	26 190	23 530	26 305	28 474	30 428	62 907	52 032	75 215	54 619
Malawi	LUPP	27 015	41 174	35 720	44 876	30 651	52 629	49 337	57 499	49 067
South Africa	LUPT	14 504	15 706	17 666	23 214	28 372	35 110	47 838	36 755	44 344
Zambia	LUPO	47 752	56 629	58 915	40 529	46 742	33 511	46 677	93 406	59 226
Rwanda	LUQA	1 761	45 284	11 958	9 704	6 198	13 642	14 394	32 878	27 189
Nepal	LUQC	13 220	15 475	16 485	15 271	16 953	16 041	14 847	17 695	23 414
Kenya	LUPR	31 503	30 691	29 378	26 438	30 025	42 163	32 927	62 765	35 853
Sierra Leone	ZBXQ	4 003	8 345	8 963	10 841	3 293	9 153	30 044	35 148	37 177
Russian Federation	LUPW	20 749	32 753	30 884	32 205	33 617	30 887	27 728	26 114	25 405
China	LUPS	33 630	28 344	32 803	30 956	38 616	39 190	26 260	56 766	50 418
Pakistan	LUPY	48 197	63 487	60 234	59 365	32 654	26 904	23 471	16 345	44 911
Montserrat	LUPU	5 689	5 815	6 568	14 441	37 867	31 096	22 640	20 811	24 412
Zimbabwe	LUPX	41 390	35 394	20 191	21 007	13 715	29 394	17 363	14 716	15 726
Total Main Recipients	LUQD	668 520	756 921	753 768	726 781	730 662	801 063	963 464	1 065 262	1 197 754
Total Other Countries	LUQE	639 737	600 232	664 613	554 790	708 021	580 856	691 576	692 828	756 404
Regional Totals										
Africa	LUQF	457 991	475 626	437 146	445 153	450 076	574 303	634 686	786 942	884 010
America	LUQG	114 208	132 407	192 769	107 291	271 336	170 125	240 362	176 721	136 573
Asia	LUQH	410 387	415 812	465 945	401 402	391 763	349 943	381 896	418 043	550 020
Europe	LUQI	134 713	137 995	129 941	137 934	114 537	83 172	191 892	114 156	98 216
Pacific	LUQJ	14 935	16 291	14 053	12 458	26 890	20 251	7 248	4 760	7 790
World Unallocated[3]	LUQK	176 022	179 023	178 527	177 333	184 081	184 125	198 956	257 468	277 549
Total Bilateral GPEX	LUQL	1 308 257	1 357 153	1 418 381	1 281 571	1 438 683	1 381 919	1 655 040	1 758 090	1 954 158

1 See chapter text.
2 The totals for the period prior to 1998/99 include amounts for the successor states of the former Yugoslavia. The figures for 1999/00 and 2000/01 include humanitarian assistance to Kosovo.

3 World Unallocated comprises block grants to the British Council, VSO, CSOs, Research Institutions and Commonwealth Organisations based in the UK, and some ATP Technical Co-operation.

Source: Department for International Development: 01355 843612

4 Defence

Defence

This section includes figures on Defence expenditure, on the size and role of the Armed Forces and on related support activities.

Much of the material in this section can be found in *UK Defence Statistics 2002 (The Stationery Office).*

Formation of the armed forces *(Table 4.1)*
This table shows the number of units which comprise the "teeth" elements of the Armed Forces and excludes supporting units.

The aircraft and helicopters which comprise both the Joint Force Harrier squadrons and the Joint Helicopter Command squadrons are excluded.

The figures for the Royal Marines include two Artillery regiments and two Engineer regiments which are now also assigned to 3 Commando Brigade. The Infantry figures include two in role Parachute Battalions. One of the Infantry battalions are based in Great Britain as the Province Reserve Battalion. The Queen's Colour Squadron is part of the Field Squadrons, which since 1994 have had a war role.

Defence expenditure *(Table 4.2)*
Adjusted Defence Budget: These cash based defence budget figures are adjusted to take account of major definitional changes in defence spending and transfers of responsibility to and from other Government Departments. This is the basis upon which defence spending figures have been presented in the Ministry of Defence (MOD) Department Report, the Statement on the Defence Estimates and certain Treasury publications.

Up to 2000/01 all figures are calculated using cash accounting basis. From 2001/02, figures are calculated using the Resource Accounting and Budgeting technique. These are not directly comparable with previous years. Hence a break in series. It is planned to continue this model for future years. The individual headings consist of the following:-

Intangible Assets: comprise the development costs of major equipment projects and Intellectual Property Rights.

Assets in the Course of Construction: largely consist of major weapons platforms under construction in the Defence Procurement Agency (there is a smaller element of buildings under construction). Once construction is complete, those platforms will transfer to the relevant top level budget holder as Fighting Equipment.

Capital Spares: are items of repairable material used to replace parts of assets undergoing repair, refurbishment, and maintenance, servicing, modification, enhancement or conversion. Examples include aircraft engines and ships.

Other Expenditure: includes equipment support costs, stock consumption, research, estate management and maintenance, and general services.

Service personnel *(Tables 4.3 to 4.6 and 4.9)*
The Regular Forces consist entirely of volunteer members serving on a whole-time basis.

Locally Entered Personnel are recruited outside the United Kingdom for whole-time service in special formations with special conditions of service and normally restricted locations. The Brigade of Gurkhas is an example.

The Regular Forces are supported by Reserves and Auxiliary Forces. There are both regular and volunteer Reserves. Regular Reserves consist of former Service personnel with a Reserve liability. Volunteer Reserves are open to both former Service personnel and civilians. The call out liabilities of the various reserve forces differ in accordance with their roles.

All three Services run cadet forces for young people and the Combined Cadet Force, which is found in certain schools where education is continued to the age of 17 or above, may operate sections for any or all of the Services.

Service manpower strengths *(Table 4.3)*
This table excludes mobilised reservists and Naval Activated Reservists.

Full-Time Reserve Service personnel represent reserves serving full-time in regular posts. This was made possible by the Reserve Forces Act 1996. None existed before 1998.

Royal Air Force (RAF) Full-Time Reserve Service figures comprise Full Commitment, Limited Commitment and Home Commitment.

Home Service battalions of the Royal Irish Regiment. Up until 1 July 1992, this was the Ulster Defence Regiment.

The figures for the Territorial Army include Officer Training Corps and non-regular permanent staff.

The figures for cadet forces for each service include the Combined Cadet Force. Naval Service figures include officers and civilian instructors. The Army and Royal Air Force figures exclude officers and civilian instructors.

Deployment of Service personnel *(Table 4.6)*
The figures for Service personnel in England, Wales, Scotland and Northern Ireland are obtained from a different source from that used to compile the United Kingdom total. Consequently the sum of the national figures can differ from the United Kingdom total. The figures for Northern Ireland include all personnel who are serving on emergency tours of duty but exclude the former Ulster Defence Regiment, now the Home Services element of the Royal Irish Regiment. The figures for overseas countries include service personnel who are on loan to countries in the areas shown. Royal Navy and Royal Marines personnel on board ship are included in the United Kingdom figure if the ship was in home waters on the situation date or otherwise against the appropriate overseas area. All Defence Attaches and Advisers and their staffs are included under "Other Locations" and not identified within specific

areas. From 2001 the grouping of overseas locations has been changed to give a more relevant overview.

Family accommodation and defence land holdings (Table 4.7)
In November 1996 most of the MOD's housing stock in England and Wales was sold to a private company, Annington Homes. The homes retained for use by Service families were leased back, with the condition that the MOD release a certain number of houses each year for disposal by Annington. The proceeds of the sale are being used to upgrade the housing stock.

The table also presents statistics of land and foreshore in the United Kingdom owned or leased by the Ministry of Defence or over which it has limited rights under grants or licences. Land declared as surplus to Defence requirements is also included.

Civilian personnel (Table 4.8)
This table gives an analysis of the number of civilians employed in the various management areas. The attribution of civilian staff can change according to circumstances so that figures for successive years may not always be comparable. The figures include UK based civilians serving overseas. Other civilian staff are engaged overseas to work locally as circumstances demand.

Prior to April 1995 all part-timers were counted as half of full time. From that date they are counted as the number of hours worked as a proportion of normal conditioned hours. The average part timer works about 60% of full time.

The Centre includes all MOD Police. From 1991 it includes staff in the Meteorological Office (transferred from RAF), staff in the Chemical Defence Establishment (transferred from Procurement Executive), and all personnel serving overseas in support of the services (other than in British Army on the Rhine (BAOR) or RAF Germany). Communications staff are excluded after 1993 and the Meteorological staff after 1995. From 1996, those staff in the procurement executive are included in the Centre.

Prior to becoming Trading Funds the Defence Evaluation Agency and the Hydrographic Office were included in Procurement Executive.

As from 1 April 2000 a new top level budget was formed in the Centre called Defence Logistics Organisation, replacing the top level budgets CinC Fleet Support, Quarter Master General and RAF Logistics Command.

The Devonport and Rosyth Dockyards were contractorised with effect from 6 April 1987. The Atomic Weapons Establishment was contractorised with effect from 1 April 1992.

Health (Table 4.9)
The Services operate a number of hospitals in this country and in areas abroad where there is a significant British military presence. These hospitals take as patients, members of all three Services and their dependants; in addition, the hospitals in the United Kingdom take civilian patients under arrangements agreed with the National Health Service. Medical support is also supplied by Service medical staff at individual units, ships and stations.

UK regular forces - deaths (Table 4.10)
No further data on health indicators are currently available as the data are under review. This table will be revised in future if more data become available.

Deaths includes deaths occurring on or off duty. Rates per thousand have been calculated by taking the number of episodes in each year and dividing by the average strength for the year. These have then been standardised for age and sex. Standardised death rates for the Services are calculated using a fixed age and sex structure over the whole period, in this case that for 2002. This eliminates changes in death rates caused simply by changes in the age and sex structure of the Services, and reveals the true underlying picture.

Defence services and the civilian community (Table 4.11)
This table covers incidents in which Rescue Coordinating Centres (RCCs) in the United Kingdom coordinated search and rescue (SAR) action in which elements of the Armed Forces were involved. The table also includes urgent medical incidents in which the Forces SAR facilities gave assistance (eg inter-hospital transfers). More than one element of the SAR services are called to the same incident. Consequently, the number of callouts is likely to be greater than the number of incidents.

Persons rescued refers to civilian or military personnel who were removed from a hazardous environment or were transported from the scene by SAR Units in order to receive urgent medical attention. People assisted by Mountain Rescue Teams, but subsequently transported from the scene by helicopter, are credited as having been rescued by the helicopter unit concerned. The total incidents figure also includes any HM Coastguard incidents under the control of ARCC Kinloss.

The Ministry of Defence helps the civil community in a variety of ways, for example by providing assistance in time of natural disasters or other emergencies and by undertaking community projects which are of training value to the Services. In some cases facilities established primarily for defence purposes also provide benefits to the general public.

Service assistance may be provided during an industrial dispute at the request of the civil ministries in order to maintain services essential to the life of the community (eg maintenance of emergency fire services). Figures for the number of man weeks spent by service personnel are no longer collected, so this has been removed from the table.

The Royal Navy Fishery Protection squadron operates within the British fishery limits under contract to the Department for Environment, Food and Rural Affairs. Boardings carried out by vessels of the Executive Environment and Rural Affairs Department and the Department of Agriculture for Northern Ireland are not included.

Defence

4.1 Formation of the UK armed forces[1]
As at 1 April

Numbers

			1992	1993	1994	1995	1996	1997	1998	1999	2000	2001	2002
		Front Line Units											
Royal Navy[2]													
Submarines	KCGA	Vessels	23	23	23	16	15	15	15	15	16	16	16
Carriers and assault ships	KCGB	Vessels	5	5	5	5	5	5	5	6	6	6	4
Cruisers, Destroyers and Frigates	KCGC	Vessels	44	40	37	35	36	35	35	35	32	32	32
Mine counter-measure	KCGE	Vessels	34	35	18	18	18	18	19	20	21	23	22
Patrol ships and craft	KCGF	Vessels	25	25	34	32	32	34	28	24	24	23	23
Fixed wing aircraft[3]	KCGG	Squadrons	3	3	3	3	3	3	3	3	1	1	1
Helicopters[4]	KCGH	Squadrons	17	17	17	15	15	15	12	12	9	9	9
Royal Marines	KCGI	Commandos	3	3	3	3	3	3	3	3	3	3	3
Regular Army													
Royal Armoured Corps[5,6]	KCGJ	Regiments	19	14	12	11	11	11	11	11	11	10	10
Royal Artillery[5]	KCGK	Regiments	21	18	16	16	16	16	15	15	15	15	15
Royal Engineers[7]	KCGL	Regiments	13	13	12	10	10	10	10	10	11	11	11
Infantry	KCGM	Battalions	55	48	45	41	41	40	40	40	40	46	46
Special Air Service	KCGN	Regiments	1	1	1	1	1	1	1	1	1	1	1
Army Air Corps[4]	KCGO	Regiments	5	6	6	5	5	5	5	5	–	–	–
Royal Air Force													
Strike/attack	KCGP	Squadrons	9	8	6	6	6	6	6	5	5	5	5
Offensive support[3]	KCGQ	Squadrons	5	5	5	5	5	5	5	5	2	2	2
Air defence	KCGR	Squadrons	9	7	6	6	6	6	6	5	5	5	5
Maritime patrol	KCGS	Squadrons	4	3	3	3	3	3	3	3	3	3	3
Reconnaissance	KCGT	Squadrons	5	5	5	5	5	5	5	5	5	5	5
Airborne early warning[8]	KCGU	Squadrons	1	1	1	1	2	2	2	2	2	2	2
Air transport and tankers and helicopters[3]	KCGV	Squadrons	16	16	15	14	14	13	14	14	8	9	9
Search and rescue	KCGX	Squadrons	2	2	2	2	2	2	2	2	2	2	2
Ground based air defence	KCGY	Squadrons	6	5	5	5	6	6	6	4	4	4	4
Field	KCGZ	Squadrons	5	5	5	5	5	5	5	5	5	6	6

1 See chapter text.
2 Only active vessels are shown from 1995 onwards. All vessels are included before then.
3 From 2000 excludes aircraft transferred to the Joint Force Harrier squadron.
4 From 2000 excludes helicopters transferred to the Joint Helicopter command.
5 Figure for 1994 includes one training regiment.

6 From 2000 includes one Armoured Regiment which is committed to the new Joint Nuclear Biological and Chemical Regiment.
7 Figure for 2000 includes an additional Close Support Regiment formed as a result of the Stategic Defence Review.
8 Figure for 2001 includes an embedded Operational Conversion Unit at the Sentry Operation Establishments.

Source: Ministry of Defence/DASA (Tri-Service): 020 7218 0390

4.2 UK Defence expenditure[1]

£ millions

		1997/98	1998/99	1999/00	2000/01			2001[2]/02	2002[3]/03
Total expenditure at outturn prices[4]	KDAA	20 945	22 482	22 572	23 552	**Total defence budget[5,6]**	HGDS	24 457	24 597
of which:									
Expenditure on personnel	KDAB	8 293	8 556	8 530	8 768	**Expenditure on personnel**	HGDT	9 377	9 777
of the Armed Forces	KDAC	5 938	6 286	6 257	6 500	of the Armed Forces	HGDU	7 040	7 238
of civilian staff	KDAE	2 355	2 270	2 273	2 268	of civilian staff	HGDV	2 337	2 539
Expenditure on equipment[7]	KDAF	9 003	9 889	9 715	10 008	**Expenditure on categories of fixed assets[8]**	HGDW	5 552	5 732
Sea systems	KDAG	2 142	2 319	..	..	Intangible assets	HGEO	1 355	1 543
Land systems	KDAH	1 658	1 665	..	..	Land and buildings	HGEP	-123	-139
Air systems	KDAI	3 843	4 572	..	..	Fighting equipment	HGHH	-68	100
Other	KDAJ	1 360	1 333	..	..	Plant, machinery and vehicles	HGHQ	477	143
						IT and communications equipment	HGOH	230	92
Other expenditure	KDAK	3 649	4 037	4 327	4 776	Assets in the course of construction	HHAF	3 318	3 660
Works, buildings and land	KDAL	1 253	1 761	1 800	1 919	Capital spares	HHAK	363	333
Miscellaneous stores and services	KDAM	2 396	2 276	2 527	2 857				
Adjusted defence budget[9]									
at 2001/02 prices	GPWI	23 036	24 065	23 591	24 082	**Other expenditure**	HHAT	9 528	9 088

1 See chapter text.
2 Estimated outturn.
3 Planned.
4 Calculated using cash accounting basis.
5 Calculated using the Resource Accounting and Budgeting technique. These figures are not directly comparable with previous years.

6 Includes expenditure on conflict prevention activities.
7 The split between sea, land and air is no longer available, due to a change in accounting practice.
8 Includes disposal receipts for 2001/02 and planned disposals in 2002/03.
9 Adjusted to 2001/02 prices using the GDP deflator.

Source: Ministry of Defence/DASA (Procurement): 0117 913 4585

4.3 UK Defence: service manpower strengths[1]
As at 1 April

Thousands

		1992	1993	1994	1995	1996	1997	1998	1999	2000	2001	2002
UK service personnel												
Full-time trained strength	ZBTR	278.3	267.1	248.4	226.3	211.6	197.4	194.0	191.1	190.5	188.8	187.6
Trained Naval Service	ZBTS	55.8	55.3	52.4	48.2	45.6	41.7	40.5	39.3	38.9	38.5	37.5
UK regulars	ZBTT	55.8	55.3	52.4	48.2	45.6	41.7	40.4	39.1	38.3	38.0	36.8
Full-time reserve service	ZBTU	..	..	..	..	..	..	0.1	0.3	0.3	0.5	0.7
Trained Army	ZBTV	140.5	132.9	121.8	108.7	103.6	101.5	100.9	99.9	100.4	100.2	100.9
UK regulars	ZBTW	133.4	126.5	116.1	104.5	99.5	97.8	97.5	96.3	96.5	96.3	96.5
Full-time reserve service	ZBTX	..	..	..	..	..	..	..	0.2	0.5	0.6	0.9
Gurkhas	ZBTY	7.2	6.5	5.6	4.2	4.0	3.8	3.4	3.4	3.4	3.4	3.4
Trained Royal Air Force	ZBTZ	82.0	78.9	74.2	69.4	62.5	54.2	52.7	51.9	51.2	50.1	49.2
UK regulars	ZBUA	82.0	78.9	74.2	69.4	62.5	54.2	52.7	51.8	51.0	49.8	48.8
Full-time reserve service	ZBUB	..	..	..	..	..	..	..	0.1	0.2	0.3	0.3
Untrained UK regulars	ZBUC	22.3	14.2	11.8	11.2	14.3	17.2	19.7	21.5	21.9	21.5	22.5
Naval Service	ZBUD	6.4	4.1	3.4	2.7	2.8	3.5	4.1	4.6	4.6	4.4	4.9
Army	ZBUE	12.0	8.1	6.9	7.2	9.3	11.1	12.4	13.4	13.6	13.2	13.5
Royal Air Force	ZBUF	4.0	2.0	1.5	1.3	2.2	2.7	3.2	3.5	3.7	3.9	4.1
Locally Entered Personnel (excluding Gurkhas)	ZBUG	1.3	1.3	1.2	0.6	0.6	0.4	0.4	0.4	0.4	0.3	0.4
Royal Irish Regiment Home Service batallions	ZBUH	6.0	5.6	5.4	5.3	5.0	4.8	4.6	4.4	4.2	3.8	3.8
Reserve personnel	ZBUI	341.0	334.2	334.1	329.6	327.3	323.6	318.6	306.4	293.7	278.0	267.7
Regular Reserves	ZBUJ	260.8	258.3	262.2	264.1	264.6	259.5	254.7	247.5	241.3	234.7	224.6
Naval Services	ZBUK	27.5	22.0	23.3	23.3	23.9	24.1	24.8	24.7	24.2	23.5	23.5
Army	ZBUL	188.6	190.1	192.5	195.3	195.5	190.1	186.0	180.4	175.2	169.5	160.8
Royal Air Force	ZBUM	44.8	46.1	46.4	45.5	45.2	45.4	43.9	42.4	41.9	41.6	40.3
Volunteer Reserves	ZBUN	80.2	75.9	71.9	65.5	62.7	64.1	63.9	58.9	52.4	43.3	43.1
Royal Naval Reserve and Royal Marine Reserve[2]	ZBUO	7.0	5.6	4.6	3.7	3.5	4.3	4.4	4.5	4.8	4.8	5.0
Territorial Army	ZBUP	71.3	68.5	65.0	59.7	57.3	57.6	57.0	51.8	44.8	35.9	35.5
Royal Auxilliary Air Force	ZBUQ	1.8	1.8	2.3	2.1	1.9	2.2	2.5	2.6	2.7	2.6	2.6
Cadet Forces	ZBUR	137.2	135.9	135.7	133.9	134.7	133.1	132.0	132.9	136.4	142.1	143.3
Naval Service	ZBUS	28.8	27.1	26.7	26.5	26.9	26.3	25.9	24.5	24.1	23.8	23.8
Army	ZBUT	64.8	65.1	65.2	63.7	65.4	65.1	64.9	65.7	68.5	66.4	66.8
Royal Air Force	ZBUU	43.6	43.7	43.8	43.7	42.4	41.8	41.2	42.7	43.7	51.9	52.7

1 See chapter text.
2 Figures before 1997 do not include University Royal Navy Units.

Source: Ministry of Defence/DASA (Tri-Service): 020 7218 1546

4.4 Intake of UK regular forces from civilian life: by service[1]

Numbers

		1991 /92	1992 /93	1993 /94	1994 /95	1995 /96	1996 /97	1997 /98	1998 /99	1999 /00	2000 /01	2001 /02
All services:												
Male	KCJB	24 357	13 067	10 619	11 154	15 495	19 230	20 169	22 545	22 374	20 363	20 886
Female	KCJC	3 550	1 750	1 333	1 853	2 175	2 935	3 336	3 431	3 159	2 606	2 692
Total	KCJA	27 907	14 817	11 952	13 007	17 670	22 165	23 505	25 976	25 533	22 969	23 578
Naval service:												
Male	KCJE	5 570	1 888	1 275	961	2 007	3 397	3 966	4 106	4 250	3 990	4 270
Female	KCJF	1 013	384	260	340	353	562	634	661	703	633	743
Total	KCJD	6 583	2 272	1 535	1 301	2 360	3 959	4 600	4 767	4 953	4 623	5 013
Army:												
Male	KCJJ	15 544	10 289	8 764	9 491	11 510	13 583	13 374	14 988	14 740	13 396	13 549
Female	KCJK	1 594	1 098	812	1 193	1 376	1 939	2 005	1 975	1 743	1 318	1 233
Total	KCJI	17 138	11 387	9 576	10 684	12 886	15 522	15 379	16 963	16 483	14 714	14 782
Royal Air Force:												
Male	KCJM	3 243	890	580	702	1 978	2 250	2 829	3 451	3 384	2 977	3 067
Female	KCJN	943	268	261	320	446	434	697	795	713	655	716
Total	KCJL	4 186	1 158	841	1 022	2 424	2 684	3 526	4 246	4 097	3 632	3 783

1 See chapter text.

Source: Ministry of Defence/DASA (Tri-Service): 020 7218 0390

4.5 Outflow of UK regular forces: by service[1]

Numbers

		1991/92	1992/93	1993/94	1994/95	1995/96	1996/97	1997/98	1998/99	1999/00	2000/01	2001/02
All Services:												
Male	KDNA	30 057	31 138	29 699	31 046	25 746	29 325	21 775	24 459	23 767	22 415	22 249
Female	KDNB	2 748	2 517	2 429	2 994	3 118	3 675	2 483	2 976	2 739	2 419	2 342
Total	KDNC	32 805	33 655	32 128	34 040	28 864	33 000	24 258	27 435	26 506	24 834	24 591
Naval Service:												
Male	KDND	6 105	4 655	4 613	5 504	4 314	6 191	4 650	4 925	5 164	4 460	5 060
Female	KDNE	662	455	493	681	631	940	621	606	632	550	687
Total	KDNF	6 767	5 110	5 106	6 185	4 945	7 131	5 271	5 531	5 796	5 010	5 747
Army:												
Male	KDNI	18 304	20 993	19 633	20 234	13 935	13 758	13 103	15 282	14 520	13 816	13 226
Female	KDNJ	1 147	1 336	1 288	1 651	1 508	1 596	1 275	1 733	1 570	1 326	1 089
Total	KDNK	19 451	22 329	20 921	21 885	15 443	15 354	14 378	17 015	16 090	15 142	14 315
Royal Air Force:												
Male	KDNL	5 648	5 490	5 453	5 308	7 497	9 376	4 022	4 252	4 083	4 139	3 963
Female	KDNM	939	726	648	662	979	1 139	587	637	537	543	566
Total	KDNN	6 587	6 216	6 101	5 970	8 476	10 515	4 609	4 889	4 620	4 682	4 529

1 See chapter text. Comprises all those who left the Regular Forces and includes deaths.

Source: Ministry of Defence/DASA (Tri-Service): 020 7218 0390

4.6 Deployment of UK service personnel[1]
As at 1 July

Thousands

		1991	1992	1993	1994	1995	1996	1997	1998	1999	2000	2001
UK Service personnel, Regular Forces:												
UK distribution												
In United Kingdom[2,3]	KDOB	207.9	210.7	204.3	192.1	182.2	177.4	171.6	173.4	171.7	170.3	172.0
England[4]	KDOC	173.3	174.2	167.1	156.5	149.4	146.6	142.6	144.6	144.3	143.0	144.1
Wales[4]	KDOD	5.2	5.2	5.1	4.8	5.2	4.3	3.3	3.2	3.3	3.2	2.6
Scotland[4]	KDOE	18.2	18.8	19.4	18.4	16.9	15.5	13.9	14.2	14.9	15.1	14.5
Northern Ireland	KDOF	11.2	12.6	12.5	12.3	9.9	10.5	11.5	11.0	9.0	8.4	9.4
Global deployment												
United Kingdom[2]	MKCN	207.9	210.7	205.4	193.6	180.7	172.0	167.5	165.0	161.0	163.1	162.8
Overseas	KDOG	89.3	78.9	65.5	56.2	50.0	48.5	42.6	43.1	47.1	43.0	40.9
Mainland European States[5]	KDOI	–	–	–	–	–	11.7	6.2	6.9	15.2	8.2	8.6
Germany[6,7]	KDOH	69.7	60.0	45.6	37.2	33.4	20.8	21.2	20.3	18.0	19.5	17.3
Balkans	MKCO	..	..	..	..	..	..	..	..	..	..	..
Mediterranean[8]	KDOM	1.1	2.2	2.8	2.4	0.6	0.5	0.3	1.2	1.3	1.1	2.3
Gibraltar	KDOJ	1.0	1.0	1.3	1.5	0.6	0.6	0.5	0.5	0.6	0.6	0.5
Cyprus	KDOL	5.2	4.8	4.7	4.1	4.4	4.0	3.9	3.6	3.6	3.5	3.5
Far East/Asia[9]	MKCT	2.8	4.2	2.2	2.0	1.2	1.2	1.5	0.3	0.3	1.0	0.3
Africa	MKCP	..	..	..	..	..	..	..	..	..	..	–
North America	MKCQ	..	..	..	..	..	..	..	..	..	..	2.5
Central/South America	MKCR	..	..	..	..	..	..	..	..	..	..	–
Falkland Islands	MKCS	..	..	..	..	..	..	..	..	..	..	0.8
Other locations, including unallocated[4]	KDOQ	9.5	6.7	8.8	8.9	9.4	9.8	9.0	10.4	8.2	9.1	5.1
Locally entered service personnel:[10]												
United Kingdom	KDOS	1.4	1.3	1.4	1.5	1.8	1.7	2.1	2.1	2.0	2.1	2.3
Gibraltar	KDOT	0.1	0.2	0.2	0.2	0.2	0.2	0.2	0.4	0.4	0.3	0.4
Hong Kong	KDOV	5.5	5.2	4.4	3.7	1.8	1.6	0.7	..	..	..	..
Brunei	KDOW	0.8	0.8	0.8	0.7	0.9	0.7	1.0	0.9	0.8	0.8	0.8
India/Nepal	KDOX	1.3	1.3	1.2	0.2	0.5	0.7	0.9	0.5	0.5	0.5	0.4
Total	KDOK	9.1	8.8	7.9	7.1	5.1	4.9	4.7	4.0	3.7	3.7	3.9

1 See chapter text.
2 Figures for global deployment of service personnel are compiled using different methodologies to those for UK distribution. Comparison is therefore not possible between the two sets of UK personnel figures.
3 Includes personnel within the UK whose location is unknown on the 1st July.
4 Up to 1992 the England, Wales and Scotland national figures include personnel who were UK based but temporarily deployed in the South Atlantic. These have also been included in the Overseas numbers against 'Other locations'.
5 Includes the Balkans until 2001.

6 Prior to 1994, personnel serving in Northern Ireland on emergency tours of duty but remaining under the command of the Commander-in-Chief, British Army of the Rhine, are included in these numbers. Personnel serving on emergency tours of duty in other overseas areas are included in the numbers for that area.
7 Prior to 1996, figures for the Federal Republic of Germany and Mainland European States were combined.
8 Includes Med Near East and Middle East
9 Prior to 1997 figures include personnel serving in Hong Kong.
10 Including Gurkhas.

Source: Ministry of Defence/DASA (Tri-Service): 020 7218 1546

4.7 Family accommodation and defence land holdings[1]
As at 1 April

			1992	1993	1994	1995	1996	1997	1998	1999	2000	2001	2002
Family accommodation													
United Kingdom: total	KDPA	Thousands	72.3	71.8	71.1	69.7	72.1	68.6	67.3	65.5	64.8	59.2	55.8
Land holdings		Thousand hectares											
United Kingdom													
Land[2]	KDPF	"	225.4	224.1	223.5	221.0	222.6	221.0	220.0	220.2	219.9	224.3	222.4
Foreshore[2]	KDPH	"	18.0	18.4	18.5	18.4	18.5	18.6	18.6	18.6	18.6	18.6	18.6
Rights held	KDPJ	"	120.7	100.2	100.4	122.3	124.3	124.5	124.5	124.8	124.8	124.8	124.9
Defence land													
Used for agricultural purposes	KDPL	"	109.3	107.1	107.6	107.9	107.4	96.2	103.5	114.5	92.2	98.6	91.8
Used for grazing only	KDPM	"	62.6	62.4	61.3	61.8	60.7	51.9	59.6	65.5	50.3	66.6	60.0
Full agricultural use	KDPN	"	46.7	44.6	46.3	46.1	46.7	44.3	43.9	49.0	41.9	32.0	31.8

1 See chapter text.
2 Freehold and leasehold.

Sources: Ministry of Defence/Defence Housing Executive: 020 7305 3051;
Ministry of Defence/Defence Estates: 0121 311 3818

4.8 UK Defence civilian manpower strengths[1]
As at 1 April

Thousands: Full-time Equivalent

		1992	1993	1994	1995	1996	1997	1998	1999	2000	2001	2002
Ministry of Defence civilians												
Centre												
Non-industrial	KDQE	22.9	23.7	18.9	17.3	20.0	21.2	20.6	20.0	18.1	17.7	18.5
Industrial	KDQF	0.8	0.8	0.8	0.7	0.9	1.1	1.1	1.0	0.9	0.9	0.8
Defence Logistics Organisation												
Non-industrial	ZBTJ	..	..	..	..	..	..	..	..	19.0	17.0	16.5
Industrial	ZBTK	..	..	..	..	..	..	..	..	11.3	8.2	6.1
Naval Service												
Non-industrial	KYCW	14.9	15.5	15.8	15.2	13.7	12.6	12.2	11.6	3.6	3.5	3.6
Industrial	KYCX	15.2	14.1	13.0	12.0	9.7	9.0	8.0	6.8	2.7	2.6	2.3
Army												
Non-industrial	KDQK	21.2	22.0	22.5	22.1	21.4	20.7	20.5	20.3	15.4	15.5	14.9
Industrial	KDQL	17.0	15.1	14.9	14.5	13.7	13.2	11.8	10.3	5.7	5.6	5.4
Royal Air Force												
Non-industrial	KDQM	10.7	10.3	10.3	10.1	9.9	10.0	10.1	10.6	5.6	5.6	5.6
Industrial	KDQN	7.7	7.2	7.0	6.7	6.5	6.4	6.1	7.1	3.4	3.3	3.3
Procurement Executive												
Non-industrial	KDQO	21.0	16.4	15.3	15.1	–	–	–	–	–	–	–
Industrial	KDQP	8.1	4.1	3.1	2.5	–	–	–	–	–	–	–
Total UK based[2]	KDQB	139.5	129.2	121.6	116.1	109.9	109.2	104.0	100.9	100.3	80.0	77.1
Non-industrial	KDQC	90.7	87.9	82.8	79.8	77.1	77.9	75.7	74.5	75.2	59.4	59.1
Industrial	KDQD	48.8	41.3	38.8	36.3	32.7	31.3	28.3	26.4	25.1	20.6	18.0
Locally engaged overseas	KDQA	27.0	26.6	20.7	16.9	16.9	15.7	15.0	14.8	14.7	13.3	14.1
Non-industrial	KDQT	9.7	9.6	7.3	6.4	7.1	7.0	6.7	6.7	6.7	6.3	6.5
Industrial	KDQU	17.3	17.0	13.4	10.5	9.8	8.7	8.2	8.0	8.0	7.0	7.6
Total	KFHT	166.5	155.8	142.3	133.0	126.8	124.9	119.0	115.7	114.7	93.3	91.2
Trading funds[3]	GQHI	..	..	..	..	14.0	15.1	13.6	13.0	14.2	18.4	12.2
Non-industrial	KYCU	..	..	..	..	12.1	13.4	12.3	11.9	13.1	..	..
Industrial	KYCV	..	..	..	..	1.9	1.7	1.3	1.1	1.1	..	..

1 See chapter text. Individuals on temporary and geographic (T&G) promotion are classed as non-industrial. The figures refer to personnel above the line.
2 From 2001 does not include trading funds.
3 The split between industrial and non-industrial is no longer available.

Source: Ministry of Defence/DASA (Civilian): 020 7218 6019

4.9 Strength of uniformed UK medical staff[1]
As at 1 April

Numbers

		1992	1993	1994	1995	1996	1997	1998	1999	2000	2001	2002[2]
Qualified doctors:												
Naval Service	KDMA	263	270	268	262	238	211	209	209	211	215	225
Army	KDMB	530	522	490	473	431	434	431	437	452	459	475
Royal Air Force	KDMC	375	368	359	334	273	223	207	197	185	183	180
All Services	KDMD	1 168	1 160	1 117	1 069	942	868	847	843	848	857	880
Qualified dentists:												
Naval Services	KDME	75	76	75	73	62	65	64	65	60	62	60
Army	KDMF	183	178	168	154	145	139	140	141	144	149	140
Royal Air Force	KDMG	121	119	115	110	104	87	80	85	78	76	75
All Services	KDMH	379	373	358	337	311	291	284	291	282	287	275
Support staff:[3,4]												
Naval Services	KDMI	1 308	1 361	1 401	1 411	1 294	1 025	946	935	963	998	..
Nursing services	ZBTL	..	..	..	..	..	..	..	299	282	268	..
Support	ZBTM	..	..	..	..	..	..	..	636	681	730	..
Army	KDMJ	4 297	4 288	3 761	3 458	3 284	3 017	3 094	3 002	2 991	3 037	..
Nursing services	ZBTN	..	..	..	..	..	..	..	667	658	658	..
Support	ZBTO	..	..	..	..	..	..	..	2 335	2 333	2 379	..
Royal Air Force	KDMK	1 948	2 038	1 837	1 795	1 404	1 213	1 194	1 225	1 286	1 335	..
Nursing services	ZBTP	..	..	..	..	..	..	..	296	334	336	..
Support	ZBTQ	..	..	..	..	..	..	..	929	952	999	..
All Services	KDML	7 553	7 687	6 999	6 664	5 982	5 255	5 234	5 162	5 240	5 370	..

1 See chapter text. Includes staff employed at units (including ships) and in hospitals.
2 From April 2002, to comply with National Statistics guidelines, figures have been rounded.
3 Includes all members of the Nursing Services/Nursing Corps. From 1999, figures for support staff have been split so that nurses are separate from other support staff.

4 Data are not available for 2002 due to a review of the data. Back data will be available next year.

Source: Ministry of Defence/DASA (Tri- Service): 020 7218 1546

4.10 UK regular forces - deaths[1]

		1975	1980	1985	1990	1995	1996	1997	1998	1999	2000	2001
Deaths												
Total Number	LUIC	422	370	319	320	207	146	165	165	143	153	143
Male	LUID	414	367	314	314	198	144	156	157	140	149	140
Female	LUIE	8	3	5	6	9	2	9	8	3	4	3
Rates per thousand												
Tri-service	LUIF	1.24	1.11	0.96	1.03	0.88	0.65	0.79	0.78	0.68	0.73	0.70
Navy	LUIG	0.81	1.07	0.81	0.80	0.61	0.54	0.86	0.60	0.58	0.58	0.79
Army[2]	LUIH	1.45	1.16	0.90	1.10	0.99	0.77	0.87	0.91	0.76	0.85	0.75
RAF	LUII	1.21	1.05	1.18	1.06	0.82	0.48	0.47	0.66	0.50	0.60	0.52

1 See chapter text.
2 Includes Gurkhas, except for 1975.

Source: Ministry of Defence/DASA (Medical Statistics): 01225 472963

4.11 UK Defence services and the civilian community[1]

Numbers

		1992	1993	1994	1995	1996	1997	1998	1999	2000	2001
Search and rescue operations at home											
Call outs	GPYC	2 306	2 145	2 024	2 300	2 164	1 942	1 898	1 915	1 940	1 764
of Royal Navy helicopters	GPXO	544	606	560	667	512	495	463	499	499	503
of Royal Air Force helicopters	GPXP	1 475	1 260	1 215	1 393	1 392	1 258	1 257	1 238	1 278	1 115
of Contractorised and other helicopters	GPXQ	92	47	26	24	27	16	20	–	–	–
of Royal Air Force Nimrod aircraft	GPXR	64	73	74	78	69	79	71	65	71	54
of other fixed wing aircraft[2]	GPXS	1	2	3	6	1	2	1	–	–	1
of HM ships and auxilliary vessels[2]	KCMG	5	8	6	7	1	4	4	–	–	–
of Royal Air Force mountain rescue teams	KCMH	125	149	140	125	162	88	82	113	92	91
Persons rescued: total	KCMI	1 432	1 508	1 391	1 448	1 598	1 259	1 245	1 163	1 297	1 181
By rescue service											
Royal Navy helicopters	GPXT	318	406	369	426	371	358	285	343	348	390
Royal Air Force helicopters	GPXU	1 015	952	893	958	1 116	878	937	800	925	776
Royal Air Force mountain rescue teams	GPXV	23	97	49	44	101	16	12	20	24	15
Other	GPXW	76	53	80	20	10	7	11	–	–	–
By type of rescue											
Rescue	GPXX	365	479	464	275	307	219	317	302	272	281
Medrescue	GPXY	794	764	766	828	919	711	667	621	703	621
Medivac	GPXZ	193	194	123	220	275	224	209	201	236	226
Recovery	GPYA	29	32	25	44	38	54	43	31	29	36
Other	GPYB	51	39	13	81	59	51	9	8	57	17
Search and rescue incidents: Total	KCMM	1 976	1 856	1 775	2 011	1 900	1 738	1 687	1 707	1 779	1 607
Fishery protection											
Vessels boarded	KCMO	2 465	2 540	2 080	1 878	2 224	1 758	1 829	1 777	1 658	1 531

1 See chapter text.
2 Not permanently on stand-by.

Source: Ministry of Defence/DASA (Logistics): 01225 468769/467249

5 Population and vital statistics

Population and vital statistics

This section begins with a summary of population figures for the United Kingdom and constituent countries for 1851 to 2026 and for Great Britain from 1801 (Table 5.1). Table 5.2 analyses the components of population change. Table 5.3 gives details of the national sex and age structures for years up to the present date, with projected figures up to the year 2021. Legal marital condition of the population is shown in Table 5.4. The distribution of population at regional and local levels is summarised in Table 5.5.

In the main, historical series relate to census information, while mid-year estimates, which make allowance for under-enumeration in the census, are given for the recent past and the present (from 1961 onwards).

Implications of the 2001 Census
(Tables 5.1 to 5.5, 5.7 to 5.9, 5.12, 5.15, 5.17, 5.19 to 5.21)

The first results of the 2001 Census, published on 30 September 2002, showed that the previous mid-year estimates (MYEs) produced during the 1990s were overestimates of the population. The estimated population of the United Kingdom in mid-2001, based on these Census results was 58,837,000. This estimate is 919,000 lower than the estimated population at mid-2000. The difference was mainly due to the overestimation of the net flow of migrants into the United Kingdom.

To assist users in the period before revised estimates are published, the ONS has produced national level interim revised population estimates for the period mid-1982 to mid-2000. These interim estimates have been used in these tables (excluding table 5.4).

As is usual after a Census, ONS will revise the past intercensal MYEs to be consistent with the 2001 Census. The latest Census results also provide an opportunity to review the adjustments for under-enumeration that were made for the mid 1991 population estimates for England and Wales. As a result of these revisions it will also be necessary to revise the England and Wales population estimates for mid-1982 to mid-1990.

The revised population estimates for mid-1991 to mid-2000 are due to be published on 13 February 2003, while revised series for mid-1982 to mid-1990 should be available during March 2003. These Annual Abstract datasets, available on the National Statistics website (www.statistics.gov.uk), will be updated in late-Spring 2003.

Population *(Tables 5.1 - 5.3)*
Figures shown in these tables relate to the population enumerated at successive censuses, (up to 1951), mid-year estimates (from 1961 to 2001) and population projections (up to 2026). The population estimates for mid-2001 are the first in a new series based on the 2001 Census. The figures for earlier years from 1982-2000 are not consistent with them, apart from national estimates for the UK or for England and Wales combined where interim revised population estimates are available. The population estimates for 1982-2000 are

subject to revision in 2003, including the UK and England and Wales interim estimates.

Definition of resident population
The estimated population of an area includes all those usually resident in the area, whatever their nationality. HM Forces serving abroad are excluded from, but non-UK Armed Forces stationed here are included within the estimates of resident population. Students are taken to be resident at their term-time addresses.

The current series of estimates are updated annually. Starting with results of the 2001 Census of Population, which include allowance for estimated Census enumeration, the mid-2001 estimates are derived by taking account of births, deaths, net migration and ageing of the population since Census day.

The projections of the resident population of the United Kingdom and constituent countries are prepared by the Government Actuary, in consultation with the Registrars General, as a common framework for use in national planning in a number of different fields. New projections are made every second year on assumptions regarding future fertility, mortality and migration which seem most appropriate on the basis of the statistical evidence available at the time. The population projections in Tables 5.1 - 5.3 are based on the estimates of the population of the United Kingdom at mid-2001 made by the Registrars General.

Marital condition (de jure): estimated population *(Table 5.4)*
This table shows the population estimates by marital status. The 1991 figures for England and Wales have been rebased using 1991 Census results. Marital status population estimates for 2001 (based on the 2001 Census) will not be available until early 2003.

Geographical distribution of the population *(Table 5.5)*
The population enumerated in the censuses for 1911-1951, and the mid-year population estimates for later years, are provided for standard regions of the United Kingdom, for metropolitan areas, for broad groupings of local authority districts by type within England and Wales, and for some of the larger cities. Projections of future sub-national population levels are prepared from time to time by the Registrar General, but are not shown in this publication.

Migration into and out of the United Kingdom *(Tables 5.7 - 5.9)*
A migrant is defined as a person who changes his or her country of usual residence for a period of at least a year, so that the country of destination effectively becomes the country of usual residence.

The interim revised estimates in Table 5.7 are derived from three data sources and represent total international migration:

1. The International Passenger Survey (IPS) is a sample survey of all passengers travelling through major air and seaports of the United Kingdom. Routes to and from the Irish Republic are excluded from the survey as well as diplomats and military

personnel. The IPS data also exclude persons seeking asylum after entering the country and short-term visitors granted extensions of stay. Migration between the Channel Islands or the Isle of Man and the rest of the world was previously included in the total migration to the United Kingdom. From 1988 this has been excluded.

2.The Home Office provides data on people who entered the UK as asylum seekers, or as short-term visitors who were subsequently granted an extension of stay for a year or more, for example as asylum seekers, students or on the basis of marriage, plus an estimate of those asylum seekers that failed in their application and were subsequently removed.

3.Information on migration between the UK and the Irish Republic from the Irish Labour Force Survey and the National Health Service Central Register agreed between the Irish Central Statistics Office and the ONS.

Recent results from the 2001 Census have shown that, by combining data from these three sources, net inward migration to the UK has been overestimated. Therefore, an adjustment has been made to these data to take account of this known overestimation. This is approximately 76,000 each year, after allowing for the removal of failed asylum seekers. The international migration estimates presented in table 5.7 in this volume represent interim revised estimates and provide an indication of the extent of the revision to this component.

The estimates shown in tables 5.8 and 5.9 are derived from the IPS only. The ONS intends to publish revised data in Spring 2003. These Annual Abstract datasets, available on the National Statistics website (www.statistics.gov.uk), will be updated in late-Spring 2003.

Acceptances for settlement in the United Kingdom (Table 5.10)
This table presents in geographic regions, the statistics of individual nationalities, arranged alphabetically within each region. The figures are on a different basis from those derived from IPS (Tables 5.8 and 5.9) and relate only to people subject to immigration control. Persons accepted for settlement are allowed to stay indefinitely in the United Kingdom. They exclude temporary migrants such as students and generally relate only to non-EEA nationals. Settlement can occur several years after entry to the country.

Applications received for asylum in the United Kingdom, excluding dependants (Table 5.11)
This table shows statistics of applications for asylum in the United Kingdom. Figures are shown for the main applicant nationalities by geographic region. The basis of assessing asylum applications, and hence of deciding whether to grant asylum in the United Kingdom, is the 1951 United Nations Convention on Refugees.

Marriages (Table 5.12)
The figures in this table relate to marriages solemnised in the constituent countries of the UK. They take no account of the growing trend towards marrying abroad.

Divorces (Tables 5.13 and 5.14)
A marriage may be either *dissolved* following a petition for divorce and the granting of a decree absolute, or *annulled*, following a petition for nullity and the awarding of a decree of nullity. The first group of decrees are known as dissolutions of marriage and the second as annulments of marriage. In Table 5.13 the term 'divorce' includes *both* types of decrees, although strictly speaking, it should refer only to dissolutions.

Births (Tables 5.15 –5.17)
For Scotland and Northern Ireland the number of births relate to those registered during the year. For England and Wales the figures up to and including 1930-32 are for those **registered,** while later figures relate to births **occurring** in each year.

All data for England and Wales and for Scotland include births occurring in those countries to mothers not usually resident in them. Data for Northern Ireland, and hence UK, prior to 1981 include births occurring in Northern Ireland to non-resident mothers; from 1981, such births are excluded.

Deaths (Tables 5.19)
The figures relate to the number of deaths registered during each calendar year. However, from 1993 onwards, the figures for England and Wales represent occurrences. This change has little effect on annual totals.

Infant and maternal mortality (Table 5.20)
On 1 October 1992 the legal definition of a stillbirth was altered from baby born dead after 28 completed weeks gestation or more, to one born after 24 completed weeks of gestation or more. The 258 stillbirths of 24 to 27 weeks gestation which occurred between 1 October and 31 December 1992 are excluded from this table.

Life tables (Table 5.22)
The interim life tables are constructed from the estimated populations in 1998-2000 and the deaths occurring in those years for England and Wales and registered in those years for Scotland and Northern Ireland. These tables do not take account of the 2001 Census. The Government Actuary's Department will publish interim life tables for 1999-2001, once all the final revised population estimates based on the 2001 Census are available.

Adoptions (Tables 5.23 and 5.24)
The figures shown within these tables relate to the date the adoption was entered in the Adopted Children Register. Figures based on the date of court order are available for England and Wales from the volume *Marriage, divorce and adoption statistics 2000* (no. 28 in the FM2 series) available on the National Statistics website *www.statistics.gov.uk* or from the enquiry point in the ONS shown at the foot of the tables.

5.1 Population summary[1]

Thousands

	United Kingdom[2]			England and Wales[2]			Wales[3]	Scotland[4]			Northern Ireland[5]		
	Persons	Males	Females	Persons	Males	Females	Persons	Persons	Males	Females	Persons	Males	Females
Enumerated population: census figures													
1801	..	..	..	8 893	4 255	4 638	587	1 608	739	869	..	..	..
1851	22 259	10 855	11 404	17 928	8 781	9 146	1 163	2 889	1 376	1 513	1 442	698	745
1901	38 237	18 492	19 745	32 528	15 729	16 799	2 013	4 472	2 174	2 298	1 237	590	647
1911	42 082	20 357	21 725	36 070	17 446	18 625	2 421	4 761	2 309	2 452	1 251	603	648
1921[6]	44 027	21 033	22 994	37 887	18 075	19 811	2 656	4 882	2 348	2 535	1 258	610	648
1931[6]	46 038	22 060	23 978	39 952	19 133	20 819	2 593	4 843	2 326	2 517	1 243	601	642
1951	50 225	24 118	26 107	43 758	21 016	22 742	2 599	5 096	2 434	2 662	1 371	668	703
1961	52 709	25 481	27 228	46 105	22 304	23 801	2 644	5 179	2 483	2 697	1 425	694	731
Resident population: mid-year estimates													
	DYAY	BBAB	BBAC	BBAD	BBAE	BBAF	KGJM	BBAG	BBAH	BBAI	BBAJ	BBAK	BBAL
1966	54 643	26 511	28 132	47 967	23 296	24 671	2 702	5 201	2 496	2 704	1 476	719	757
1967	54 959	26 673	28 286	48 272	23 451	24 821	2 710	5 198	2 496	2 702	1 489	726	763
1968	55 214	26 784	28 429	48 511	23 554	24 957	2 715	5 200	2 498	2 702	1 503	733	770
1969	55 461	26 908	28 553	48 738	23 666	25 072	2 722	5 209	2 503	2 706	1 514	739	776
1970	55 632	26 992	28 641	48 891	23 738	25 153	2 729	5 214	2 507	2 707	1 527	747	781
1971	55 928	27 167	28 761	49 152	23 897	25 255	2 740	5 236	2 516	2 720	1 540	755	786
1972	56 097	27 259	28 837	49 327	23 989	25 339	2 755	5 231	2 513	2 717	1 539	758	782
1973	56 223	27 332	28 891	49 459	24 061	25 399	2 773	5 234	2 515	2 719	1 530	756	774
1974	56 236	27 349	28 887	49 468	24 075	25 393	2 785	5 241	2 519	2 722	1 527	755	772
1975	56 226	27 361	28 865	49 470	24 091	25 378	2 795	5 232	2 516	2 716	1 524	753	770
1976	56 216	27 360	28 856	49 459	24 089	25 370	2 799	5 233	2 517	2 716	1 524	754	770
1977	56 190	27 345	28 845	49 440	24 076	25 364	2 801	5 226	2 515	2 711	1 523	754	769
1978	56 178	27 330	28 849	49 443	24 067	25 375	2 804	5 212	2 509	2 704	1 523	754	770
1979	56 240	27 373	28 867	49 508	24 113	25 395	2 810	5 204	2 505	2 699	1 528	755	773
1980	56 330	27 411	28 919	49 603	24 156	25 448	2 816	5 194	2 501	2 693	1 533	755	778
1981	56 357	27 412	28 946	49 634	24 160	25 474	2 813	5 180	2 495	2 685	1 543	757	786
1982	56 298	27 370	28 928	49 587	24 123	25 464	2 806	5 167	2 490	2 677	1 545	757	788
1983	56 328	27 380	28 948	49 625	24 137	25 487	2 807	5 153	2 484	2 669	1 551	759	792
1984	56 423	27 429	28 993	49 720	24 186	25 534	2 806	5 146	2 482	2 664	1 557	761	796
1985	56 567	27 497	29 071	49 865	24 253	25 612	2 810	5 137	2 479	2 658	1 565	765	800
1986	56 699	27 550	29 149	50 003	24 307	25 696	2 820	5 123	2 474	2 649	1 574	768	805
1987	56 850	27 620	29 230	50 155	24 377	25 778	2 833	5 113	2 470	2 643	1 582	773	809
1988	56 970	27 676	29 294	50 291	24 441	25 850	2 854	5 093	2 461	2 632	1 585	774	812
1989	57 248	27 834	29 415	50 561	24 595	25 966	2 869	5 097	2 463	2 634	1 590	776	814
1990	57 436	27 942	29 494	50 738	24 698	26 040	2 878	5 102	2 466	2 636	1 596	778	818
1991	57 472	27 915	29 557	50 758	24 663	26 095	2 891	5 107	2 470	2 637	1 607	783	824
1992	57 593	27 968	29 625	50 859	24 703	26 155	2 899	5 111	2 473	2 638	1 623	792	831
1993	57 700	28 017	29 683	50 944	24 740	26 204	2 906	5 120	2 479	2 642	1 636	798	837
1994	57 825	28 071	29 755	51 049	24 783	26 267	2 913	5 132	2 486	2 646	1 644	802	842
1995	57 958	28 142	29 816	51 173	24 849	26 323	2 917	5 137	2 489	2 647	1 649	804	845
1996	58 076	28 207	29 869	51 286	24 910	26 376	2 921	5 128	2 486	2 642	1 662	810	851
1997	58 204	28 275	29 930	51 411	24 975	26 436	2 927	5 123	2 484	2 638	1 671	816	856
1998	58 349	28 347	30 002	51 551	25 044	26 507	2 933	5 120	2 484	2 636	1 678	819	859
1999	58 535	28 453	30 081	51 736	25 149	26 587	2 937	5 119	2 486	2 634	1 679	818	861
2000	58 654	28 492	30 162	51 913	25 244	26 669	2 946	5 058	2 428	2 630	1 683	820	862
2001[7]	58 837	28 611	30 225	52 084	25 355	26 730	2 903	5 064	2 434	2 630	1 689	824	865
Resident population: projections (mid-year)[8]													
2006	59 657	29 053	30 604	52 920	25 798	27 122	2 926	5 023	2 418	2 605	1 714	837	877
2011	60 524	29 487	31 037	53 806	26 241	27 565	2 947	4 983	2 398	2 585	1 735	847	888
2021	62 386	30 316	32 070	55 722	27 109	28 614	2 997	4 895	2 346	2 549	1 769	862	907
2026	63 156	30 609	32 547	56 553	27 442	29 112	3 012	4 828	2 305	2 523	1 775	862	912

1 See chapter text.
2 Interim revised population estimates are shown between 1982 and 2000 for the UK and England and Wales. The revised population estimates will be available in 2003.
3 The mid-1982 to mid-2000 have not yet been revised in light of the results of the 2001 Census. They are therefore not consistent with the mid-2001 estimates. The revised estimates will be available in 2003.
4 The mid-1982 to mid-1999 have not yet been revised in light of the results of the 2001 Census. They are not consistent with the mid-2001 estimates. Provisionally revised estimates for mid-2000 are shown.The revised estimates will be available in 2003.

5 Northern Ireland's population estimates between 1992 and 2000 have been re-based to take account of the 2001 Census.
6 Figures for Northern Ireland are estimated. The population at the Census of 1926 was 1 257 thousand (608 thousand males and 649 thousand females).
7 Population estimates for 2001 are based on the 2001 Census.
8 These projections are 2001-based. See chapter text for more detail.

Sources: Office for National Statistics: 01329 813233;
General Register Office for Scotland;
Northern Ireland Statistics and Research Agency;
Government Actuary's Department: 020 7211 2622

5.2 Population changes[1]

	Population[2] at start of period	Average annual change				
		Overall annual change	Births	Deaths[3]	Natural change	Net migration and other adjustments[4]
United Kingdom						
1901 - 1911	38 237	385	1 091	624	467	-82
1911 - 1921	42 082	195	975	689	286	-92
1921 - 1931	44 027	201	824	555	268	-67
1931 - 1951	46 038	213	793	603	190	22
1951 - 1961	50 225	258	839	593	246	12
1961 - 1971	52 807	312	962	638	324	-12
1971 - 1981	55 928	42	736	666	69	-27
1981 - 1991	56 357	111	757	655	103	9
1991 - 2001[5]	57 472	136	731	632	99	37
2011 - 2021[6]	62 382	211	704	628	76	135
England and Wales						
1901 - 1911	32 528	354	929	525	404	-50
1911 - 1921	36 070	182	828	584	244	-62
1921 - 1931	37 887	207	693	469	224	-17
1931 - 1951	39 952	193	673	518	155	38
1951 - 1961	43 758	244	714	516	197	47
1961 - 1971	46 196	296	832	560	272	23
1971 - 1981	49 152	48	638	585	53	-5
1981 - 1991	49 634	112	664	576	89	24
1991 - 2001[5]	50 758	133	648	557	91	42
2011 - 2021[6]	55 580	215	633	554	80	136
Scotland						
1901 - 1911	4 472	29	131	76	54	-25
1911 - 1921	4 761	12	118	82	36	-24
1921 - 1931	4 882	-4	100	65	35	-39
1931 - 1951	4 843	13	92	67	25	-12
1951 - 1961	5 096	9	95	62	34	-25
1961 - 1971	5 184	5	97	63	34	-30
1971 - 1981	5 236	-6	70	64	6	-11
1981 - 1991	5 180	-7	66	63	3	-10
1991 - 2001	5 107	-4	60	60	-1	-4
2011 - 2021[6]	5 034	-8	50	58	-8	0
Northern Ireland						
1901 - 1911	1 237	1	31	23	8	-6
1911 - 1921	1 251	1	29	22	7	-6
1921 - 1931	1 258	-2	30	21	9	-11
1931 - 1951	1 243	6	28	18	10	-4
1951 - 1961	1 371	6	30	15	15	-9
1961 - 1971	1 427	11	33	16	17	-6
1971 - 1981	1 540	0	28	17	11	-11
1981 - 1991	1 543	6	27	16	12	-5
1991 - 2001	1 607	8	24	15	9	0
2011 - 2021[6]	1 769	4	21	16	5	-1

1 See chapter text.
2 Census enumerated population up to 1951; mid-year estimates of resident population from 1961 to 2001 and mid-2000-based projections of resident population thereafter.
3 Including deaths of non-civilians and merchant seamen who died outside the country. These numbered 577 000 in 1911-1921 and 240 000 in 1931-1951 for England and Wales; 74 000 in 1911-1921 and 34 000 in 1931-1951 for Scotland; and 10 000 in 1911-1926 for Northern Ireland.
4 For the UK and England and Wales for 1981-1991 and 1991-2001 this column is not an estimate of migration and other changes. It has been derived by subtraction using interim revised population estimates based on the results of the 2001 Census and natural change. It will be revised in 2003 when the final revised population estimates become available that are consistent with the 2001 Census.

5 The population at the beginning of the period is an interim revised estimate. See chapter text.
6 These projections are 2000-based.

Sources: Government Actuary's Department: 020 7211 2622;
Office for National Statistics: 01329 813233;
General Register Office for Scotland;
Northern Ireland Statistics and Research Agency

5.3 Age distribution of the resident population[1]

Thousands

		Population enumerated in Census			Estimated mid-year resident population					Projected mid-year resident population[2]				
		1901	1931	1951	1961	1971	1981	1991[3]	2001[4]	2006	2011	2016	2021	2026
Persons: All ages	KGUA	38 237	46 038	50 225	52 807	55 928	56 357	57 472	58 837	59 657	60 524	61 459	62 386	63 156
Under 1[5]	KGUK	938	712	773	4 274	899	730	793	662	676	686	703	709	698
1 - 4	KABA	3 443	2 818	3 553	..	3 654	2 726	3 078	2 815	2 696	2 726	2 785	2 838	2 827
5 - 9	KGUN	4 106	3 897	3 689	3 819	4 684	3 677	3 660	3 729	3 497	3 393	3 433	3 509	3 569
10 - 14	KGUO	3 934	3 746	3 310	4 267	4 232	4 470	3 486	3 885	3 755	3 524	3 420	3 461	3 536
15 - 19	KGUP	3 826	3 989	3 175	3 748	3 862	4 735	3 708	3 673	3 950	3 821	3 590	3 487	3 528
20 - 29	KABB	6 982	7 865	7 154	6 570	7 968	8 113	9 133	7 400	7 478	7 979	8 127	7 770	7 439
30 - 44	KABC	7 493	9 717	11 125	10 529	9 797	10 956	12 133	13 291	12 996	12 133	11 644	11 997	12 370
45 - 59	KABD	4 639	7 979	9 558	10 605	10 202	9 540	9 500	11 144	11 735	12 223	12 868	12 582	11 760
60 - 64	KGUY	1 067	1 897	2 422	2 788	3 222	2 935	2 888	2 880	3 247	3 765	3 483	3 855	4 256
65 - 74	KBCP	1 278	2 461	3 689	3 977	4 764	5 195	5 067	4 940	5 033	5 501	6 339	6 552	6 698
75 - 84	KBCU	470	844	1 555	1 885	2 159	2 677	3 130	3 290	3 373	3 427	3 614	4 040	4 718
85 and over	KGVD	61	113	224	346	485	603	895	1 128	1 221	1 347	1 452	1 585	1 757
School ages (5-15)	KBWU	..	..	7 649	..	9 704	9 086	7 820	8 377	8 049	7 652	7 532	7 662	7 808
Under 18	KGUD	–	..	..	..	..	..	..	..	12 994	12 568	12 437	12 607	12 742
Pensionable ages[6]	KFIA	2 387	4 421	6 828	7 747	9 123	10 035	10 590	10 828	11 283	11 968	12 049	12 177	13 173
Males: All ages	KGWA	18 492	22 060	24 118	25 528	27 167	27 412	27 915	28 611	29 053	29 487	29 921	30 316	30 609
Under 1[5]	KGWK	471	361	397	2 194	461	374	406	338	346	351	360	363	357
1 - 4	KBCV	1 719	1 423	1 818	..	1 874	1 400	1 573	1 443	1 381	1 396	1 427	1 454	1 448
5 - 9	KGWN	2 052	1 967	1 885	1 956	2 401	1 889	1 874	1 911	1 789	1 736	1 757	1 796	1 826
10 - 14	KGWO	1 972	1 892	1 681	2 185	2 175	2 295	1 785	1 990	1 922	1 801	1 749	1 769	1 808
15 - 19	KGWP	1 898	1 987	1 564	1 897	1 976	2 424	1 893	1 877	2 020	1 953	1 833	1 780	1 801
20 - 29	KBCW	3 293	3 818	3 509	3 288	4 024	4 103	4 573	3 657	3 695	3 943	4 017	3 831	3 659
30 - 44	KBCX	3 597	4 495	5 461	5 237	4 938	5 513	6 053	6 544	6 360	5 901	5 642	5 812	5 993
45 - 59	KBUU	2 215	3 753	4 493	5 137	4 970	4 711	4 732	5 520	5 792	6 008	6 291	6 110	5 677
60 - 64	KGWY	490	894	1 061	1 250	1 507	1 376	1 390	1 409	1 591	1 838	1 695	1 871	2 054
65 - 74	KBWL	565	1 099	1 560	1 605	1 999	2 264	2 272	2 304	2 392	2 636	3 036	3 124	3 189
75 - 84	KBWM	196	335	617	675	716	922	1 150	1 306	1 396	1 479	1 603	1 815	2 122
85 and over	KGXD	23	36	70	105	126	141	214	312	368	443	513	591	674
School ages (5-15)	KBWV	–	..	3 895	..	4 982	4 666	4 003	4 292	4 120	3 914	3 851	3 919	3 994
Under 18	KGWD	–	..	6 753	..	8 108	7 430	6 713	6 838	6 654	6 433	6 364	6 451	6 520
Pensionable ages[6]	KFIB	785	1 471	2 247	2 385	2 841	3 327	3 637	3 922	4 156	4 558	5 152	5 530	5 985
Females: All ages	KGYA	19 745	23 978	26 107	27 279	28 761	28 946	29 557	30 225	30 604	31 037	31 538	32 070	32 547
Under 1[5]	KGYK	466	351	376	2 079	437	356	387	324	330	335	343	346	340
1 - 4	KBWN	1 724	1 397	1 735	..	1 779	1 327	1 505	1 372	1 315	1 330	1 358	1 384	1 379
5 - 9	KGYN	2 054	1 930	1 804	1 863	2 283	1 788	1 786	1 819	1 708	1 657	1 677	1 714	1 743
10 - 14	KGYO	1 962	1 854	1 629	2 083	2 057	2 175	1 701	1 895	1 832	1 722	1 672	1 691	1 728
15 - 19	KGYP	1 928	2 002	1 611	1 851	1 887	2 311	1 815	1 796	1 930	1 868	1 758	1 708	1 727
20 - 29	KBWO	3 690	4 047	3 644	3 282	3 945	4 009	4 560	3 742	3 783	4 036	4 111	3 940	3 780
30 - 44	KBWP	3 895	5 222	5 663	5 292	4 859	5 442	6 080	6 747	6 636	6 231	6 002	6 185	6 377
45 - 59	KBWR	2 424	4 226	5 065	5 467	5 231	4 829	4 769	5 624	5 943	6 214	6 578	6 472	6 083
60 - 64	KGYY	577	1 003	1 361	1 539	1 715	1 559	1 498	1 470	1 655	1 927	1 788	1 983	2 201
65 - 74	KBWS	713	1 361	2 127	2 372	2 765	2 931	2 795	2 636	2 641	2 865	3 303	3 428	3 509
75 - 84	KBWT	274	509	937	1 210	1 443	1 756	1 980	1 983	1 977	1 947	2 011	2 225	2 597
85 and over	KGZD	38	77	154	241	359	462	681	816	853	904	939	995	1 083
School ages (5-15)	KBWW	–	..	3 753	..	4 722	4 421	3 817	4 085	3 929	3 738	3 681	3 743	3 814
Under 18	KGYD	–	..	6 495	..	7 690	7 042	6 409	6 507	6 340	6 135	6 073	6 156	6 221
Pensionable ages[6]	KFIC	1 601	2 950	4 580	5 362	6 282	6 708	6 954	6 906	7 127	7 410	6 897	6 647	7 188

5.3 Age distribution of the resident population[1]
continued

Thousands

		England						Wales				
		Estimated mid-year resident population			Projected population[2]			Estimated mid-year resident population			Projected population[2]	
		1981	1991[7]	2001[4]	2011	2026		1981	1991[7]	2001[4]	2011	2026
Persons: All ages	KCCI	46 821	48 208	49 181	50 859	53 541	KERY	2 813	2 891	2 903	2 947	3 012
Under 1	KCCJ	598	663	557	583	600	KFAC	36	39	32	32	32
1 - 4	KCCK	2 235	2 574	2 362	2 311	2 424	KFBX	136	154	135	128	131
5 - 9	KCCL	3 011	3 035	3 116	2 868	3 045	KFCA	185	187	185	161	170
10 - 14	KCCM	3 666	2 880	3 233	2 957	3 007	KFCB	222	178	196	174	172
15 - 19	KCCN	3 897	3 083	3 040	3 197	2 994	KFCC	233	188	185	193	172
20 - 29	KCEG	6 734	7 790	6 211	6 711	6 353	KFCD	381	422	334	379	340
30 - 44	KCEH	9 175	10 231	11 147	10 281	10 552	KFCE	536	587	606	530	559
45 - 59	KCEQ	7 948	7 920	9 304	10 205	9 958	KFCF	485	486	571	595	537
60 - 64	KCEW	2 449	2 399	2 391	3 148	3 566	KFCG	158	154	153	201	209
65 - 74	KCGD	4 347	4 222	4 106	4 589	5 584	KFCH	272	284	264	298	345
75 - 84	KCJG	2 249	2 645	2 758	2 866	3 971	KFCI	139	165	183	181	253
85 and over	KCKJ	511	763	957	1 144	1 487	KFCK	29	47	59	74	93
School ages (5-15)	KCWX	7 451	6 473	6 981	6 441	6 649	KFCL	453	399	420	372	376
Under 18	KCWY	11 871	10 899	11 135	10 595	10 870	KFCM	721	665	662	608	607
Pensionable ages [6]	KEAA	8 403	8 870	9 038	10 015	11 042	KFEB	525	576	583	643	691
Males: All ages	KEAB	22 795	23 588	23 951	24 816	25 998	KFEI	1 365	1 407	1 404	1 425	1 444
Under 1	KEAC	306	340	285	298	307	KFEJ	18	20	16	16	16
1 - 4	KEAD	1 147	1 322	1 210	1 184	1 242	KFEK	70	79	69	66	67
5 - 9	KEAE	1 547	1 561	1 597	1 467	1 558	KFEL	95	96	95	82	87
10 - 14	KEAF	1 883	1 482	1 656	1 511	1 537	KFFA	113	92	101	89	88
15 - 19	KECA	1 996	1 588	1 556	1 634	1 528	KFFN	119	97	94	98	87
20 - 29	KECB	3 404	3 974	3 070	3 311	3 117	KFHA	193	214	165	188	168
30 - 44	KECC	4 623	5 148	5 502	5 015	5 117	KFHB	270	294	295	251	266
45 - 59	KECD	3 938	3 957	4 611	5 031	4 829	KFHW	240	242	282	290	251
60 - 64	KECE	1 154	1 159	1 174	1 538	1 730	KFQO	73	74	75	98	100
65 - 74	KECF	1 902	1 900	1 924	2 205	2 668	KFQV	118	128	124	144	164
75 - 84	KECG	777	975	1 101	1 245	1 792	KFUK	48	60	72	78	114
85 and over	KECH	119	183	267	377	573	KFUL	7	11	16	24	36
School ages (5-15)	KECI	3 827	3 330	3 577	3 293	3 400	KFUV	232	206	215	191	192
Under 18	KECJ	6 096	5 604	5 706	5 421	5 561	KFVE	370	342	339	311	310
Pensionable ages[6]	KECK	2 798	3 058	3 291	3 828	5 033	KFVF	173	199	212	246	313
Females: All ages	KEJV	24 026	24 620	25 231	26 043	27 543	KFVL	1 448	1 484	1 499	1 522	1 568
Under 1	KEJW	292	324	273	284	293	KFYW	18	19	15	16	15
1 - 4	KEJX	1 088	1 253	1 152	1 127	1 182	KFZJ	66	75	66	63	64
5 - 9	KEKP	1 464	1 474	1 519	1 401	1 487	KGCK	90	91	90	79	83
10 - 14	KEKQ	1 783	1 399	1 578	1 447	1 470	KGCM	109	86	95	85	84
15 - 19	KEKR	1 901	1 495	1 484	1 563	1 466	KGCN	114	91	92	95	84
20 - 29	KEKS	3 330	3 816	3 141	3 401	3 235	KGCO	189	208	169	191	172
30 - 44	KENR	4 553	5 083	5 645	5 266	5 436	KGCP	265	294	311	279	293
45 - 59	KEOQ	4 009	3 964	4 693	5 174	5 128	KGGZ	246	244	289	306	286
60 - 64	KEOZ	1 295	1 239	1 217	1 610	1 836	KGIY	85	80	78	103	109
65 - 74	KEQJ	2 445	2 323	2 182	2 384	2 916	KGKR	154	156	140	154	182
75 - 84	KEQK	1 472	1 670	1 657	1 621	2 180	KGTQ	91	105	110	103	139
85 and over	KEQL	392	580	691	766	914	KGTZ	22	36	43	50	57
School ages (5-15)	KEQM	3 625	3 143	3 405	3 148	3 249	KGVG	221	194	204	182	184
Under 18	KEQN	5 775	5 295	5 430	5 174	5 309	KGVH	351	323	323	297	296
Pensionable ages[6]	KEQO	5 605	5 812	5 747	6 187	6 009	KGVK	352	377	371	397	378

5.3 Age distribution of the resident population[1]
continued

Thousands

| | | Scotland | | | | | | Northern Ireland | | | | |
| | | Estimated mid-year resident population | | | Projected population[2] | | | Estimated mid-year resident population | | | Projected population[2] | |
		1981	1991[7]	2001[4]	2011	2026		1981	1991	2001[4]	2011	2026
Persons: All ages	KGVP	5 180	5 107	5 064	4 983	4 828	KIOY	1 543	1 607	1 689	1 735	1 775
Under 1	KHAQ	69	66	52	50	47	KIOZ	27	26	22	21	19
1 - 4	KHCT	249	259	224	202	191	KIPA	106	106	93	85	80
5 - 9	KHDN	348	321	306	256	248	KIPN	133	131	123	108	105
10 - 14	KHDQ	433	313	323	276	251	KIPP	148	129	132	117	107
15 - 19	KHDT	459	340	318	310	256	KIPQ	146	128	130	122	106
20 - 29	KHDU	771	834	630	649	546	KIPR	227	253	225	240	201
30 - 44	KHDV	971	1 088	1 163	973	912	KIPS	273	315	376	349	347
45 - 59	KHFK	880	853	979	1 080	927	KIPT	227	241	290	342	338
60 - 64	KHOZ	260	265	262	324	361	KIPU	68	70	74	93	120
65 - 74	KHTU	460	441	447	469	580	KIPV	116	120	123	144	189
75 - 84	KHUO	232	259	272	294	375	KIPW	57	69	77	85	119
85 and over	KHUQ	49	69	89	100	135	KIPX	14	19	23	30	43
School ages (5-15)	KHVV	871	698	694	590	549	KIPY	311	285	282	249	234
Under 18	KIMT	1 377	1 153	1 098	962	887	KIQL	504	467	451	403	377
Pensionable ages [6]	KIMU	882	910	944	1 010	1 090	KIQM	224	246	262	301	351
Males: All ages	KIMV	2 495	2 470	2 434	2 398	2 305	KIQN	757	783	824	847	862
Under 1	KIMW	35	34	26	26	24	KIQO	14	13	11	11	10
1 - 4	KIMX	128	133	115	103	98	KIQP	54	54	48	43	41
5 - 9	KIMY	178	164	156	131	127	KIQQ	69	67	63	55	54
10 - 14	KIMZ	222	161	166	142	129	KIQR	76	66	68	60	55
15 - 19	KINA	234	174	161	158	131	KIQS	75	66	66	63	54
20 - 29	KINB	390	423	311	323	272	KIQT	117	127	113	121	102
30 - 44	KINC	483	543	563	467	441	KIQU	137	156	185	169	170
45 - 59	KIND	424	415	483	520	436	KIQV	109	118	144	168	161
60 - 64	KINE	118	124	125	157	167	KIQW	32	32	35	45	57
65 - 74	KINR	194	192	200	219	268	KIRJ	50	53	56	68	90
75 - 84	KINS	77	91	103	121	164	KIRK	21	26	30	35	53
85 and over	KINT	11	16	23	32	50	KIRL	4	5	6	10	16
School ages (5-15)	KINU	446	358	356	303	282	KIRM	160	146	145	128	120
Under 18	KINV	706	591	562	493	455	KIRN	259	239	231	207	193
Pensionable ages[6]	KINW	282	299	327	371	481	KIRO	75	83	92	112	158
Females: All ages	KINX	2 685	2 637	2 630	2 585	2 523	KIRP	786	824	865	888	912
Under 1	KINY	33	32	26	25	23	KIRQ	13	13	10	10	9
1 - 4	KINZ	121	126	109	98	93	KIRR	52	52	45	41	39
5 - 9	KIOA	170	157	149	125	121	KIRS	65	64	60	53	51
10 - 14	KIOB	211	153	157	134	122	KIRT	72	63	65	57	52
15 - 19	KIOC	225	166	156	152	125	KIRU	70	62	64	59	51
20 - 29	KIOO	381	411	319	326	274	KISH	110	126	113	119	99
30 - 44	KIOP	488	545	600	506	471	KISI	137	159	191	180	177
45 - 59	KIOQ	456	437	496	560	492	KISJ	118	123	146	175	177
60 - 64	KIOR	142	141	137	167	193	KISK	37	38	38	48	63
65 - 74	KIOS	265	249	246	251	312	KISL	66	67	68	76	99
75 - 84	KIOT	155	168	169	174	212	KISM	37	44	47	50	67
85 and over	KIOU	38	53	66	68	85	KISN	10	14	17	21	27
School ages (5-15)	KIOV	424	340	339	287	267	KISO	151	139	138	121	114
Under 18	KIOW	671	562	536	468	432	KISP	245	228	220	196	184
Pensionable ages[6]	KIOX	600	611	617	638	609	KISQ	150	163	170	188	193

1 See chapter text.
2 2000-based projections are made as described in the introduction.
3 Interim revised population estimates are shown for 1991. These will be replaced by the final rebased estimates on 13 February 2003
4 The mid-2001 estimates are based on the 2001 Census.
5 1961 estimates are for ages 0 - 4.
6 The pensionable age population is that over state retirement age. The 2011 figures take account of planned changes in retirement age from 65 for men and 60 for women at present to 65 for both sexes. This change will be phased in between April 2010 and March 2020.

7 The mid-1991 population estimates of England, Wales and Scotland will be revised in light of the results of the 2001 Census. These are not consistent with the mid-2001 population estimates. The revised estimates will be published in February 2003. See chapter text.

Sources: Office for National Statistics: 01329 813233;
General Register Office for Scotland;
Northern Ireland Statistics and Research Agency;
Government Actuary's Department: 020 7211 2622

5.4 Marital condition (de jure): estimated population[1]

Thousands

| | | United Kingdom[2] | | | | | | | | England and Wales | | | | | | | |
| | | Males | | | | Females | | | | Males | | | | Females | | | |
		1971	1981	1991[3]		1971	1981	1991[3]		1971	1981	1991		1971	1981	1991	
All ages:																	
Single	KQCA	12 120	12 168	12 874	KQDP	11 131	10 860	11 231	KRPL	10 507	10 614	11 320	KUBS	9 584	9 424	9 829
Married	KQCB	14 067	13 791	13 237	KQDQ	14 130	13 856	13 364	KRPM	12 522	12 238	11 745	KVCC	12 566	12 284	11 838
Widowed	KQCC	779	793	828	KQDR	3 178	3 331	3 370	KRPN	682	698	731	KVCD	2 810	2 939	2 978
Divorced	KQCD	201	657	1 306	KQDS	321	897	1 598	KRPO	187	611	1 200	KVCE	296	828	1 459
Age groups:																	
0 - 14: Single	KQCE	6 912	5 956	5 683	KQDT	6 557	5 646	5 378	KRPP	5 984	5 181	4 991	KVCF	5 672	4 910	4 720
15 - 19: Single	KQCF	1 936	2 400	1 916	KQDU	1 726	2 203	1 778	KRPQ	1 677	2 095	1 677	KVCG	1 491	1 923	1 554
Married	KQCG	39	24	9	KQDV	160	107	36	KRPR	34	20	8	KVCH	142	93	32
Widowed	KQCH	–	–	–	KQDW	–	–	–	KRPS	–	–	–	KVCI	–	–	–
Divorced	KQCI	–	–	–	KQDX	–	–	–	KRPT	–	–	–	KVCJ	–	–	–
20 - 24: Single	KQCJ	1 376	1 618	2 004	KQDY	857	1 150	1 616	KRPU	1 211	1 420	1 764	KVCK	745	1 007	1 421
Married	KQCK	781	542	285	KQDZ	1 251	930	558	KRPV	689	466	249	KVCL	1 113	811	490
Widowed	KQCL	–	1	–	KQYZ	2	2	1	KRPW	–	1	–	KVCM	2	2	1
Divorced	KQCM	3	11	13	KQZA	10	30	32	KRPX	3	10	12	KVCN	9	27	29
25 - 34: Single	KQCN	722	1 020	1 925	KQZB	379	563	1 280	KRPY	637	906	1 718	KVCO	326	496	1 135
Married	KQCO	2 762	2 847	2 393	KQZC	2 980	3 160	2 831	KRPZ	2 450	2 508	2 100	KVCP	2 635	2 791	2 488
Widowed	KQCP	4	5	3	KQZD	14	16	9	KRQA	4	4	2	KVCQ	12	13	8
Divorced	KQCQ	41	163	270	KQZE	68	236	345	KRQB	38	151	245	KVCR	63	218	312
35 - 44: Single	KQCR	366	359	548	KQZF	242	198	322	KRQC	317	316	482	KVEH	201	170	280
Married	KQCS	2 838	2 845	3 002	KQZG	2 871	2 878	3 118	KRQD	2 513	2 519	2 658	KVEI	2 529	2 540	2 760
Widowed	KQCT	15	14	14	KQZH	57	49	41	KRQE	13	12	12	KVEJ	48	41	34
Divorced	KQCU	52	191	423	KQZI	72	240	487	KRQF	48	178	388	KVEK	66	222	444
45 - 54: Single	KQCV	326	293	287	KQZJ	298	203	168	KRQG	279	254	251	KVEL	248	169	144
Married	KQCW	2 924	2 640	2 648	KQZK	2 891	2 598	2 629	KUAR	2 605	2 338	2 347	KVEM	2 570	2 292	2 322
Widowed	KQCX	55	44	37	KQZL	218	176	138	KUBA	47	38	31	KVEN	187	150	118
Divorced	KQCY	50	144	315	KQZM	75	171	361	KUBB	46	134	290	KVEO	69	158	332
55 - 59: Single	KQCZ	140	149	116	KQZN	177	131	82	KUBC	118	128	101	KVEP	148	108	69
Married	KQDA	1 399	1 336	1 186	KQZO	1 293	1 267	1 114	KUBD	1 250	1 192	1 050	KVEQ	1 154	1 130	982
Widowed	KQDB	57	53	40	KQZP	247	216	159	KUBE	49	46	34	KVER	213	186	136
Divorced	KQDC	21	53	103	KQZQ	33	68	117	KUBF	20	49	95	KVES	31	63	107
60 - 64: Single	KQDD	125	115	120	KQZR	208	131	97	KUBG	105	98	104	KVET	174	109	80
Married	KQDE	1 276	1 149	1 121	KQZS	1 098	1 046	1 023	KUBH	1 140	1 029	997	KVEU	985	936	908
Widowed	KQDF	89	74	73	KQZT	382	328	289	KUBI	77	64	63	KVEV	332	284	250
Divorced	KQDG	17	38	76	KQZU	27	55	89	KUBJ	16	35	70	KVEW	25	51	82
65 - 74: Single	KQDH	159	178	177	KQZV	396	315	214	KUBK	132	149	150	KMGN	332	263	176
Married	KQDI	1 567	1 773	1 754	KQZW	1 254	1 431	1 464	KUBL	1 407	1 594	1 574	KMGO	1 133	1 291	1 317
Widowed	KQDJ	258	267	261	KQZX	1 087	1 112	1 002	KUBM	226	234	229	KMGP	959	978	879
Divorced	KQDK	15	46	80	KQZY	28	72	116	KUBN	14	43	74	KMGQ	26	68	107
75 and over: Single	KQDL	58	81	99	KQZZ	291	320	295	KUBO	47	67	81	KMGR	249	270	250
Married	KQDM	480	633	840	KRPI	332	440	592	KUBP	434	573	763	KMGS	304	401	541
Widowed	KQDN	301	336	401	KRPJ	1 172	1 433	1 731	KUBQ	266	300	360	KMGT	1 056	1 285	1 554
Divorced	KQDO	3	11	26	KRPK	7	24	50	KUBR	3	11	25	KMGU	6	23	46

5.4 Marital condition (de jure): estimated population[1]

continued

Thousands

		Scotland								Northern Ireland[2]							
		Males				Females				Males				Females			
		1971	1981	1991		1971	1981	1991		1971	1981	1991[3]		1971	1981	1991[3]	
All ages:																	
Single	KJPS	1 197	1 149	1 135	KJVG	1 155	1 066	1 029	KJWV	417	406	411	KJYK	392	370	373
Married	KJPT	1 227	1 227	1 159	KJVH	1 243	1 240	1 181	KJWW	318	327	339	KJYL	321	332	350
Widowed	KJPU	79	77	78	KJVI	297	317	306	KJWX	19	18	19	KJYM	71	75	80
Divorced	KJPV	13	42	97	KJVJ	24	62	122	KJWY	1	4	11	KJYN	2	6	18
Age groups:																	
0 - 14: Single	KJPW	695	563	492	KJRI	660	535	468	KJWZ	232	212	200	KJYO	224	201	191
15 - 19: Single	KJPX	195	230	173	KJVL	178	214	163	KJXA	64	75	66	KJYP	58	67	61
Married	KJPY	5	4	1	KJVM	15	11	2	KJXB	1	1	–	KJYQ	3	3	1
Widowed	KJPZ	–	–	–	KJVN	–	–	–	KJXC	–	–	–	KJYR	–	–	–
Divorced	KJQQ	–	–	–	KJVO	–	–	–	KJXD	–	–	–	KJYS	–	–	–
20 - 24: Single	KJQR	120	149	184	KJVP	81	109	151	KJXE	45	48	57	KJYT	31	34	46
Married	KJQS	75	60	26	KJVQ	111	93	49	KJXF	18	16	9	KJYU	27	26	16
Widowed	KJQT	–	–	–	KJVR	–	–	–	KJXG	–	–	–	KJYV	–	–	–
Divorced	KJQU	–	1	1	KJVS	1	3	2	KJXH	–	–	–	KJYW	–	–	–
25 - 34: Single	KJQV	61	87	160	KJVT	37	51	113	KJXI	25	27	43	KJYX	16	16	30
Married	KJQW	243	266	224	KJVU	267	290	259	KJXJ	70	73	73	KJYY	77	80	86
Widowed	KJQX	–	1	–	KJVV	2	2	1	KJXK	–	–	–	KJYZ	–	1	1
Divorced	KJQY	3	11	23	KJVW	5	17	29	KJXL	–	1	2	KJZA	–	2	5
35 - 44: Single	KJQZ	35	32	49	KJVX	30	21	32	KJXM	13	11	14	KJZB	11	8	9
Married	KJRW	259	252	265	KJVY	271	262	276	KJXN	67	74	81	KJZC	70	76	83
Widowed	KJRX	2	2	2	KJVZ	7	6	5	KJXO	–	–	–	KJZD	2	2	2
Divorced	KJRY	3	12	31	KJWA	6	17	38	KJXP	–	1	4	KJZE	–	2	6
45 - 54: Single	KJRZ	34	28	26	KJWB	37	25	18	KJXQ	13	10	10	KJZF	13	9	7
Married	KJTD	254	241	232	KJWC	255	244	237	KJXR	64	61	69	KJZG	65	63	70
Widowed	KJTE	6	5	4	KJWD	25	21	15	KJXS	1	1	1	KJZH	6	6	5
Divorced	KJTF	3	9	22	KJWE	6	12	26	KJXT	–	1	3	KJZI	1	1	4
55 - 59: Single	KJTG	16	15	11	KJWF	22	17	10	KJXU	6	5	4	KJZJ	7	6	4
Married	KJTH	120	116	107	KJWG	112	110	105	KJXV	29	28	28	KJZK	27	27	28
Widowed	KJTI	6	6	5	KJWH	27	23	18	KJXW	1	1	1	KJZL	6	6	5
Divorced	KJTJ	1	3	8	KJWI	2	5	9	KJXX	–	–	1	KJZM	–	–	1
60 - 64: Single	KJTK	15	12	11	KJWJ	26	16	12	KJXY	6	5	5	KJZN	8	6	5
Married	KJTL	109	96	99	KJWK	92	88	92	KJXZ	27	24	25	KJZO	21	22	24
Widowed	KJTM	10	8	8	KJWL	40	35	30	KJYA	2	2	2	KJZP	9	9	8
Divorced	KJTN	1	2	5	KJWM	2	4	7	KJYB	–	–	1	KJZQ	–	–	1
65 - 74: Single	KJUY	20	21	18	KJWN	50	39	27	KJYC	8	8	8	KJZR	14	13	10
Married	KJUZ	129	144	143	KJWO	98	113	119	KJYD	31	35	38	KJZS	23	27	31
Widowed	KJVA	27	27	26	KJWP	104	109	95	KJYE	6	6	6	KJZT	24	26	26
Divorced	KJVB	1	2	5	KJWQ	2	4	8	KJYF	–	–	1	KJZU	–	–	1
75 and over: Single	KJVC	7	10	11	KJWR	34	39	34	KJYG	4	4	4	KJZV	9	10	11
Married	KJVD	36	48	62	KJWS	22	31	43	KJYH	11	13	16	KJZW	6	8	10
Widowed	KJVE	28	29	33	KJWT	93	121	141	KJYI	7	7	8	KJZX	23	26	34
Divorced	KJVF	–	1	1	KJWU	–	1	3	KJYJ	–	–	–	KJZY	–	–	–

1 See chapter text.
2 Figures for Northern Ireland are more approximate than those for other countries: at each age/sex the proportions enumerated in the census in the various marital status groups have been applied to the estimated total (all statuses) population.
3 Mid-1991 population estimates by marital status for Northern Ireland are still provisional.

Sources: Office for National Statistics: 01329 813233;
General Register Office for Scotland;
Northern Ireland Statistics and Research Agency

5.5 Geographical distribution of the population[1]

Thousands

		Population enumerated in Census			Mid-year population estimates				
		1911	1931	1951	1961	1971	1981	1991[2]	2001[3]
United Kingdom	KIUR	42 082	46 074	50 225	52 807	55 928	56 357	57 472	58 837
Great Britain	KISR	40 831	44 795	48 854	51 380	54 388	54 815	55 865	57 149
England	KKOJ	33 650	37 359	41 159	43 561	46 412	46 821	48 208	49 181
Standard Regions									
North	KKNA	2 729	2 938	3 009	3 246	3 152	3 117	3 092	3 004
Yorkshire and Humberside	KKNB	3 896	4 319	4 567	4 630	4 902	4 918	4 983	4 967
East Midlands	KKNC	2 467	2 732	3 118	3 108	3 652	3 853	4 035	4 175
East Anglia	KKND	1 191	1 231	1 381	1 489	1 688	1 894	2 082	2 177
South East	KKNE	11 613	13 349	14 877	16 346	17 125	17 011	17 637	18 412
South West	KKNF	2 818	2 984	3 479	3 436	4 112	4 381	4 718	4 934
West Midlands	KKNG	3 277	3 743	4 423	4 762	5 146	5 187	5 265	5 267
North West	KKNH	5 659	6 062	6 305	6 545	6 634	6 459	6 396	6 244
Government Office Regions									
North East	JZBU	..	..	..	..	2 679	2 636	2 603	2 517
North West (including Merseyside)	JZBV	..	..	..	..	7 108	6 940	6 885	6 732
Yorkshire and The Humber	JZBX	..	..	..	..	4 902	4 918	4 983	4 967
East Midlands	JZBY	..	..	..	..	3 652	3 853	4 035	4 175
West Midlands	JZBZ	..	..	..	..	5 146	5 187	5 265	5 267
South West	JZCA	..	..	..	..	4 112	4 381	4 718	4 934
East	JZCB	..	..	..	..	4 454	4 854	5 150	5 395
London	JZCC	..	..	..	..	7 529	6 806	6 890	7 188
South East	JZCD	..	..	..	..	6 830	7 245	7 679	8 007
Wales	KKNI	2 421	2 593	2 599	2 635	2 740	2 813	2 891	2 903
Scotland	KGJB	4 761	4 843	5 096	5 184	5 236	5 180	5 107	5 064
Northern Ireland	KGJC	1 251	1 280[6]	1 371	1 427	1 540	1 543	1 607	1 689
Greater London	KKNJ	7 161	8 110	8 197	7 977	7 529	6 806	6 890	7 188
Inner London[4]	KISS	4 998	4 893	3 679	3 481	3 060	2 550	2 627	2 772
Outer London[4]	KITF	2 162	3 217	4 518	4 496	4 470	4 255	4 263	4 416
Metropolitan areas of England & Wales	KITG	9 716	10 770	11 365	11 686	11 862	11 353	11 166	10 822
Tyne and Wear	KGJN	1 105	1 201	1 201	1 241	1 218	1 155	1 130	1 076
West Yorkshire	KGJP	1 852	1 939	1 985	2 002	2 090	2 067	2 085	2 080
South Yorkshire	KGJO	963	1 173	1 253	1 298	1 331	1 317	1 302	1 266
West Midlands	KGJQ	1 780	2 143	2 547	2 724	2 811	2 673	2 629	2 554
Greater Manchester	KGJR	2 638	2 727	2 716	2 710	2 750	2 619	2 570	2 483
Merseyside	KGJS	1 378	1 587	1 663	1 711	1 662	1 522	1 450	1 362
Principal Metropolitan Cities[4]	KITH	3 154	3 906	3 915	4 204	3 910	3 550	3 451	3 297
Newcastle	KGJT	267	286	292	336	312	284	278	260
Leeds	KGJX	446	483	505	710	749	718	717	716
Sheffield	KGJV	455	512	513	581	579	548	529	513
Birmingham	KGKF	526	1 003	1 113	1 179	1 107	1 021	1 007	976
Manchester	KGKJ	714	766	703	657	554	463	439	393
Liverpool	KGKM	746	856	789	741	610	517	481	439
Other metropolitan districts[4]	KITI	6 562	6 864	7 450	7 482	7 952	7 803	7 716	7 525
Non-metropolitan districts of England & Wales	KITJ	19 194	21 072	24 196	26 533	29 761	31 475	33 043	34 075
Non-metropolitan cities[4,5]	KITK	..	..	..	4 670	4 715	4 617	4 676	..
Incl. Kingston-upon-Hull	KKNZ	278	314	299	302	288	274	267	..
Leicester	KKOA	227	239	285	286	285	283	285	..
Nottingham	KKNX	260	269	308	311	302	278	281	..
Bristol	KKNV	357	397	443	436	433	401	397	..
Plymouth	KITL	207	215	225	240	249	253	254	..
Stoke-on-Trent	KKOD	235	277	275	276	265	252	253	..
Cardiff	KKOB	182	224	244	289	291	281	294	..
Industrial districts[4,5]	KITM	..	..	..	6 004	6 486	6 713	6 852	..
New Towns[4,5]	KITN	..	..	..	1 552	1 895	2 194	2 382	..
Resort, port and retirement districts[4,5]	KITO	..	..	..	2 828	3 184	3 368	3 626	..
Urban and mixed urban/rural districts[4,5]	KITP	..	..	..	7 240	8 821	9 446	9 964	..
Remoter, mainly rural districts[4,5]	KITQ	..	..	..	4 239	4 661	5 137	5 544	..
City of Edinburgh local government district	KGKU	320	439	467	..	478	446	440	449
City of Glasgow local government district	KGKT	784	1 088	1 090	..	983	774	689	579
Belfast	KGKV	387	438[6]	444	..	..	315	294	277

1 See chapter text.
2 The mid-1991 population estimates for the UK and Great Britain are interim revised estimates which are consistent with the 2001 Census. No breakdown of these interim estimates is available below Engalnd & Wales level. Hence all other mid-1991 population estimates in this table are not consistent with the 2001 Census. These estimates, including interim estimates will be revised and published on 13 February 2003.
3 The mid-2001 estimates are the based on the 2001 Census.
4 Details of the classification by broad area type are given in recent issues of the ONS annual reference volume "Key Population and Vital Statistics; local and health authority areas" (Series VS). The ten broad area types include all local authorities in England and Wales.

5 The breakdown of non-metropolitan districts by area type has not been provided for the mid-2001 population. This is because the effect of boundary changes due to the major local government reorganisation on 1 April 1995 and 1 April 1996 (particularly in Wales) make the comparison of 1991 and 1996 data with data for earlier years invalid.
6 Figures for Northern Ireland and the City of Belfast relate to the 1937 Census.

Sources: Office for National Statistics: 01329 813233;
General Register Office for Scotland;
Northern Ireland Statistics and Research Agency

5.6 Population by age and ethnic group, United Kingdom
Average over the period Spring 2001 to Winter 2001/02

Percentages and thousands

	Age-group											All ages	
	0 to 4	5 to 9	10 to 14	15 to 19	20 to 24	25 to 29	30 to 34	35 to 44	45 to 59	60 to 74	75 and over	%	000's
Population:													
by ethnic group and age, 2001 - 02[1]													
White													
British	6	6	6	6	6	6	8	15	20	14	7	100	51312
Other	4	4	3	4	8	12	12	19	18	11	5	100	1690
Mixed													
White and Black Caribbean	20	18	19	11	6	6	6	8	4	..	..	100	271
White and Black African	20	14	21	10	..	..	..	9	..	..	..	100	65
White and Asian	22	14	13	11	7	6	5	8	9	..	..	100	145
Other Mixed	..	..	18	..	..	..	..	..	..	..	..	100	30
Asian													
Indian	7	7	8	8	8	8	9	18	17	8	2	100	956
Pakistani	11	11	12	11	11	8	8	13	10	5	1	100	728
Bangladeshi	13	11	11	12	11	9	9	10	8	5	..	100	261
Other Asian	7	7	6	8	8	9	11	19	16	7	..	100	250
Black													
Black Caribbean	8	8	8	7	6	5	9	23	13	11	3	100	618
Black African	12	10	8	8	9	9	12	19	10	3	..	100	506
Black Other	14	12	8	9	11	8	10	14	10	..	..	100	72
Chinese	8	6	7	9	12	7	9	21	15	6	..	100	180
Other	6	8	6	6	8	11	11	21	18	5	..	100	282
All[1]	6	6	7	6	6	7	8	16	19	13	7	100	59139

Note: These Labour Force Survey (LFS) estimates are not seasonally adjusted (NSA) and have not been adjusted to take account of the recent Census 2001 results. See chapter text for the labour market chapter for more details.

1 Includes ethnic group not stated. In some instances, sample too small for reliable estimates.

Source: Office for National Statistics, Labour Force Survey

5.7 Interim revised total international migration estimates[1]: citizenship 1992-2001
United Kingdom

Thousands

	All citizenships	British	Non-British	European Union[2]	Commonwealth		Other foreign[4]
					Old[3]	New	
Balance							
1992	-41.6	-72.2	30.6	-0.5	0.6	30.5	0.1
1993	-41.6	-73.2	31.6	-4.9	3.3	21.6	11.6
1994	31.6	-29.2	60.8	2.1	5.9	29.6	23.1
1995	30.7	-60.3	91.0	14.1	6.6	35.9	34.5
1996	13.8	-71.7	85.6	16.5	9.7	27.8	31.5
1997	10.8	-67.3	78.0	7.6	9.3	33.3	27.8
1998	96.3	-29.2	125.5	19.8	32.2	32.2	41.3
1999	100.5	-29.7	130.2	-2.1	20.6	45.0	66.6
2000	99.6	-65.6	165.1	0.1	21.9	63.1	80.0
2001	125.7	-56.3	182.1	4.0	26.3	64.4	87.4

1 These estimates represent interim revised migration estimates. Further revisions to the series, in the light of more detailed Census data, will be made available in Spring 2003. See chapter text.
2 Figures for all years show EU as it was constituted on 1 January 1995.
3 Includes estimates for South African citizenship for all years.
4 Figures for all years include Hong Kong.

Source: Office for National Statistics: 01329 813255

5.8 Estimates of migration into and out of the United Kingdom[1]

Analysis by usual occupation[2] and sex

Thousands

	Total			Professional and managerial			Manual and clerical			Not gainfully employed[3]		
	Persons	Males	Females	Persons	Males	Females	Persons	Males	Females	Persons	Males	Females
Inflow												
	KGOA	KGOB	KGOC	KGOD	KGOE	KGOF	KGOG	KGOH	KGOI	KGOJ	KGOK	KGOL
1990	267	135	132	93	61	32	53	26	27	121	48	72
1991	267	122	144	80	51	29	56	23	33	131	48	83
1992	216	99	117	62	39	23	44	17	27	111	43	68
1993	213	101	112	66	41	25	43	21	22	105	39	66
1994	253	126	127	82	49	34	56	31	25	115	46	68
1995	245	130	115	86	57	29	46	20	26	113	53	60
1996	272	130	143	89	53	36	57	25	33	125	52	74
1997	285	143	142	93	59	34	44	24	20	147	60	87
1998	332	167	165	117	68	49	74	37	37	142	63	79
1999	354	181	173	131	77	54	77	41	36	146	63	83
2000	364	191	173	163	98	65	64	34	30	137	60	77
Outflow												
	KGPA	KGPB	KGPC	KGPD	KGPE	KGPF	KGPG	KGPH	KGPI	KGPJ	KGPK	KGPL
1990	231	113	118	75	47	27	56	25	31	100	41	59
1991	239	120	119	82	48	34	50	28	21	108	44	63
1992	227	113	114	82	50	33	47	23	24	98	40	58
1993	216	113	103	70	38	32	45	24	20	101	51	50
1994	191	92	98	55	32	23	48	24	25	87	37	50
1995	192	102	90	62	42	20	42	23	19	88	38	50
1996	216	105	111	84	53	31	46	23	24	86	30	56
1997	225	121	103	86	57	29	48	23	25	91	42	50
1998	199	100	99	79	46	33	41	21	20	79	32	47
1999	245	132	114	97	60	38	70	32	37	79	41	39
2000	278	154	124	128	80	48	59	36	23	90	37	53
Balance												
	KGRA	KGRB	KGRC	KGRD	KGRE	KGRF	KGRG	KGRH	KGRI	KGRJ	KGRK	KGRL
1990	36	22	14	19	14	5	–3	1	–4	21	7	13
1991	28	2	26	–2	3	–5	6	–5	11	24	4	19
1992	–11	–14	3	–21	–11	–10	–4	–6	3	13	3	10
1993	–2	–12	10	–4	3	–8	–2	–4	2	3	–12	15
1994	62	34	28	27	17	11	8	8	–	27	9	18
1995	54	28	26	24	15	9	5	–3	7	25	16	9
1996	56	24	32	5	1	5	11	2	9	39	22	18
1997	60	22	38	8	2	5	–4	1	–5	56	18	38
1998	133	68	66	38	22	16	33	16	17	63	30	32
1999	109	49	60	33	17	16	8	9	–2	67	22	45
2000	87	38	49	35	18	17	5	–2	8	47	22	24

1 See chapter text.
2 Refers to regular occupation before migration.
3 Includes housewives, students, children and retired persons.

Source: Office for National Statistics: 01329 813255

5.9 Estimates of migration into and out of the United Kingdom[1]
Analysis by citizenship and country of last or next residence

Thousands

| | All migrants | British citizens | | | | | | European Union citizens[2] (excluding British) | | | |
| | | | Country of last/next residence | | | | | | Country of last/next residence | | |
	Total	Total	European[2] Union	Old[3] Common-wealth	New[4] Common-wealth	United States of America	Other countries	Total	European[2] Union	Other Europe	Other countries
Inflow											
	KEZR	KGLA	KGLB	KGLC	KGLD	KGLE	KGLF	KGLG	KGLH	KGLI	KGLJ
1990	267	106	30	29	22	10	15	37	33	–	4
1991	267	117	39	30	23	10	15	32	29	–	3
1992	216	99	47	22	13	8	10	24	23	–	2
1993	213	92	31	24	19	10	9	25	23	–	2
1994	253	118	45	22	21	16	14	31	27	1	3
1995	245	91	32	16	18	13	13	41	36	–	5
1996	272	104	33	21	22	14	13	54	49	1	4
1997	285	97	36	23	12	8	19	61	56	–	5
1998	332	111	29	33	16	17	17	68	63	–	5
1999	354	116	32	38	15	11	20	60	55	–	5
2000	364	103	29	29	19	8	19	59	53	–	6
Outflow											
	KEZS	KGMA	KGMB	KGMC	KGMD	KGME	KGMF	KGMG	KGMH	KGMI	KGMJ
1990	231	135	34	49	15	22	15	30	25	2	3
1991	239	137	46	42	19	13	18	32	23	2	6
1992	227	133	45	34	15	16	23	17	14	–	3
1993	216	127	45	34	16	16	16	23	21	–	3
1994	191	108	34	28	13	15	18	23	19	–	4
1995	192	118	38	34	13	17	16	20	16	–	4
1996	216	139	52	37	18	16	17	24	18	–	5
1997	225	131	40	37	12	15	26	32	27	1	4
1998	199	111	37	34	7	15	18	26	21	1	4
1999	245	115	37	41	8	14	15	47	41	–	6
2000	278	140	41	48	9	19	23	46	39	1	6
Balance											
	KEZT	KGNA	KGNB	KGNC	KGND	KGNE	KGNF	KGNG	KGNH	KGNI	KGNJ
1990	36	–30	–4	–20	7	–12	–1	7	8	–1	1
1991	28	–20	–7	–12	4	–3	–2	–	5	–2	–3
1992	–11	–34	2	–12	–3	–8	–13	8	9	–	–1
1993	–2	–35	–13	–10	2	–7	–7	2	2	–	–
1994	62	10	11	–6	8	1	–4	8	9	1	–2
1995	54	–27	–6	–17	5	–5	–4	21	21	–	1
1996	56	–36	–19	–16	4	–1	–3	30	31	1	–1
1997	60	–34	–5	–14	–1	–8	–7	29	29	–1	1
1998	133	–	–8	–2	9	2	–1	42	42	–1	1
1999	109	1	–6	–3	7	–3	6	13	14	–	–1
2000	87	–37	–13	–19	11	–12	–4	13	14	–1	–

5.9 Estimates of migration into and out of the United Kingdom[1]
Analysis by citizenship and country of last or next residence

continued

Thousands

	Commonwealth citizens										Other foreign citizens				
	Country of last/next residence										Country of last/next residence				
	Total	Aust-ralia	Canada	New Zealand	South Africa	Bangl-adesh, India, Sri Lanka	Pakistan	Other African Common-wealth	Carib-bean Common-wealth	Other count-ries	Total	Euro-pean[2] Union	Other Europe	United States of America	Other coun-tries
Inflow															
	KGLK	KGLL	KGLM	KGLN	KTDK	KGLO	KGLP	KGLQ	KGLR	KGLT	KGLU	KGLV	KGLW	KGLX	KGLY
1990	71	17	3	10	1	11	4	9	2	10	53	6	7	17	22
1991	68	12	4	7	1	10	7	9	2	14	50	6	7	14	23
1992	52	9	2	6	–	7	5	6	2	14	40	2	7	9	21
1993	53	11	3	5	2	9	4	5	–	10	44	2	12	12	18
1994	52	9	2	6	1	7	4	8	–	12	53	6	14	11	22
1995	63	12	5	7	2	8	3	4	–	19	50	2	10	11	26
1996	64	15	3	7	4	8	7	6	1	10	50	–	7	16	27
1997	80	15	5	7	5	16	5	7	1	19	47	–	7	12	28
1998	94	25	5	14	12	10	4	11	2	12	59	4	8	19	28
1999	99	26	2	12	12	14	6	14	3	10	79	3	19	15	42
2000	115	23	6	11	14	21	9	13	1	16	87	2	11	13	61
Outflow															
	KGMK	KGML	KGMM	KGMN	KTDL	KGMO	KGMP	KGMQ	KGMR	KGMT	KGMU	KGMV	KGMW	KGMX	KGMY
1990	31	8	3	5	2	1	1	4	1	5	34	–	4	18	12
1991	34	7	4	5	–	2	2	3	–	10	36	1	3	16	16
1992	29	6	2	5	1	2	1	2	1	7	48	1	11	19	17
1993	32	8	2	4	1	3	1	3	1	7	34	2	3	16	14
1994	29	5	2	4	1	2	3	2	1	7	31	1	9	8	13
1995	27	6	1	4	1	1	1	2	1	6	27	–	5	8	14
1996	29	7	2	3	2	2	–	2	–	8	24	1	6	5	11
1997	34	6	1	5	4	2	2	2	1	12	28	2	5	8	12
1998	29	8	1	3	4	2	1	2	–	6	33	2	6	9	16
1999	38	11	2	6	4	1	–	1	–	13	45	–	9	14	22
2000	44	12	3	8	5	2	2	2	1	9	48	3	11	9	24
Balance															
	KGNK	KGNL	KGNM	KGNN	KTDM	KGNO	KGNP	KGNQ	KGNR	KGNT	KGNU	KGNV	KGNW	KGNX	KGNY
1990	40	9	–	5	–1	10	3	4	2	5	19	6	4	–1	10
1991	34	6	–	2	1	7	5	6	2	4	14	4	4	–2	7
1992	23	4	–	1	–1	5	4	3	1	7	–8	1	–4	–10	4
1993	21	3	1	1	1	6	3	2	–	2	10	–	9	–4	4
1994	23	4	–	2	–	5	1	6	–1	5	22	4	5	4	9
1995	36	6	4	3	1	7	3	2	–1	13	23	2	6	3	12
1996	35	8	1	5	2	6	7	4	1	1	27	–1	1	11	16
1997	46	8	4	3	1	14	4	4	–	8	20	–2	2	4	16
1998	65	17	3	11	7	8	3	9	1	5	26	2	1	11	12
1999	61	15	–	6	8	13	6	13	3	–3	34	3	10	2	19
2000	71	11	3	3	9	19	8	11	–	7	40	–1	–	4	36

1 See chapter text.
2 Figures for the European Union have been revised for all the years in this
  table to show the Union as it was constituted on 1 January 1995. This includes Austria, Finland and Sweden.
3 Figures for all years include South Africa in the Old Commonwealth.
4 Figures for all years include Pakistan in the New Commonwealth.

Source: Office for National Statistics: 01329 813255

5.10 Acceptances for settlement by nationality[1]
United Kingdom

Number of persons

Geographical region and nationality		All acceptances for settlement			Geographical region and nationality		All acceptances for settlement		
		1999	2000	2001			1999	2000	2001
All nationalities	KGFA	97 115	125 090	106 820	**Africa(continued)**				
					Somalia	KGHG	3 180	12 285	8 290
Europe[1]					South Africa	KGHH	2 955	4 300	4 755
					Sudan	KGHI	545	1 520	600
Bulgaria	KGFW	275	295	310	Tanzania	KGHJ	235	415	280
Cyprus	KGFN	425	510	240	Tunisia	KGHK	160	125	190
Former Czechoslovakia	KGFX	505	760	910	Uganda	KGHL	1 400	3 435	740
Of which,					Zambia	KGHM	235	440	345
Czech Republic[2]	LQLS	270	415	480	Zimbabwe	KGHN	435	955	980
Slovakia	LQLT	230	345	430	Other Africa	KOSU	1 570	2 065	1 950
Hungary	KGFZ	190	250	215					
Malta	KGFP	60	75	95	Africa	KGHO	27 025	44 460	31 430
Poland	KGGA	615	830	945					
Romania	KGGB	290	310	355	**Asia**				
Switzerland	KGFS	220	220	220					
Turkey	KGFT	5 225	5 205	3 240	**Indian sub-continent**				
Former USSR	KGGC	1 395	2 075	1 995	Bangladesh	KGHP	3 285	3 680	4 050
Of which,					India	KGHQ	6 295	8 045	7 280
Estonia	LQLU	25	25	40	Pakistan	KGHR	11 865	11 005	11 535
Latvia	LQLV	35	60	70					
Lithuania	LQLW	110	130	120	Indian sub-continent	KGHS	21 440	22 735	22 860
Russia[3]	LQLX	870	1 185	1 020					
Ukraine	LQLY	200	385	405	**Middle East**				
Other former USSR	LQLZ	160	300	340	Iran	KGHT	1 560	1 915	1 460
Former Yugoslavia	KGFU	6 650	4 440	5 020	Iraq	KGHU	2 210	2 715	1 640
Of which,					Israel	KGHV	260	365	320
Croatia	LQMA	315	650	665	Jordan	KGHW	145	255	175
Slovenia	LQMB	20	20	10	Kuwait	KGHX	60	60	15
Yugoslavia[4]	LQMC	5 760	2 640	2 780	Lebanon	KGHY	760	990	265
Other former Yugoslavia	LQMD	550	1 130	1 565	Saudi Arabia	KGHZ	55	50	45
Other Europe	KOSO	130	135	250	Syria	KGIA	140	245	175
					Yemen	KOSV	260	290	370
Europe[1]	KOSP	15 980	15 105	13 795	Other Middle East	KOSW	145	205	130
Americas					Middle East	KGIB	5 590	7 090	4 595
Argentina	KGGF	60	80	120					
Barbados	KGGG	65	95	115	**Remainder of Asia**				
Brazil	KGGH	405	460	575	China	KGIC	1 525	1 710	1 510
Canada	KGGI	1 010	1 325	1 320	Hong Kong[6]	KOSX	485	795	605
Chile	KGGJ	55	80	75	Indonesia	KGID	200	210	205
Colombia	KGGK	650	805	745	Japan	KGIE	1 590	1 720	1 695
Guyana	KGGM	135	200	205	Malaysia	KGIF	510	780	705
Jamaica	KGGN	1 060	2 095	2 850	Philippines	KGIG	1 190	1 910	1 355
Mexico	KGGO	90	125	130	Singapore	KGIH	170	230	225
Peru	KGGP	140	160	150	South Korea	KOTE	305	485	480
Trinidad and Tobago	KGGQ	280	490	365	Sri Lanka	KGII	5 365	7 530	4 040
USA	KGGR	3 760	4 580	4 385	Taiwan	KOSY	120	175	165
Venezuela	KGGT	65	80	85	Thailand	KGIJ	830	955	1 255
Other Americas	KOSR	750	935	785	Other Asia	KOSZ	775	1 225	3 645
Americas	KGGU	8 515	11 520	11 895	Remainder of Asia	KGIL	13 060	17 720	15 885
Africa					Asia	KGIM	40 090	47 540	43 340
Algeria	KGGV	1 130	1 010	775					
Angola	KOSS	520	305	275	**Oceania**				
Congo (Dem. Rep.)[5]	KOST	2 575	910	735	Australia	KGIN	2 410	2 925	3 205
Egypt	KGGW	385	485	405	New Zealand	KGIO	1 670	1 920	2 185
Ethiopia	KGGX	2 165	2 730	455	Other Oceania	KOTA	40	55	60
Ghana	KGGY	3 475	3 135	2 440					
Kenya	KGHA	760	1 120	990	Oceania	KGIP	4 120	4 900	5 450
Libya	KGHB	160	370	370					
Mauritius	KGHC	460	675	375	British Overseas citizens	KGIQ	560	630	515
Morocco	KGHD	430	590	575	Stateless	KGIS	815	930	385
Nigeria	KGHE	3 185	6 520	5 040					
Sierra Leone	KGHF	1 060	1 075	875	**All nationalities**	KGFA	97 115	125 090	106 820

1 Excluding European Economic Area nationals
2 Includes Czechoslovakian passport holders.
3 Includes Soviet Union passport holders.

4 Includes holders of passports of the former Yugoslavia.
5 Formerly known as Zaire.
6 Includes Hong Kong stateless persons.

Source: Home Office: 020 8760 8289

5.11 Applications[1] received for asylum, excluding dependants, by nationality
United Kingdom

Number of principal applicants

Nationality		1993	1994	1995	1996	1997	1998	1999[2]	2000[2]	2001[3]
Europe										
Albania	LQME	70	75	110	105	445	560	1 310	1 490	1 065
Czech Republic	LQMF	5	5	15	55	240	515	1 790	1 200	880
FYR	ZAFA	..	..	..	400	1 865	7 395	11 465	6 070	3 190
Macedonia	PTDW	..	..	..	15	20	50	90	65	745
Poland	DMLX	155	360	1 210	900	565	1 585	1 860	1 015	630
Romania	KEAV	370	355	770	455	605	1 015	1 985	2 160	1 415
Russia	ZAEQ	..	..	..	205	180	185	685	1 000	455
Turkey	KEAW	1 480	2 045	1 820	1 495	1 445	2 015	2 850	3 990	3 700
Ukraine	ZAER	..	..	..	235	490	370	775	770	440
Other Former USSR	ZAES	385	595	795	960	1 345	2 260	2 640	2 505	1 335
Other Former Yugoslavia	ZAET	1 830	1 385	1 565	620	375	535	2 625	2 200	90
Europe Other	ZAEU	245	535	770	1 035	1 575	1 260	200	415	360
Europe Total	KEAZ	4 535	5 360	7 050	6 475	9 145	17 745	28 280	22 880	14 305
Americas										
Colombia	KEBZ	380	405	525	1 005	1 330	425	1 000	505	360
Ecuador	KYDB	60	105	250	435	1 205	280	610	445	245
Jamaica	PTDX	55	110	150	125	130	105	180	310	480
Americas Other	PTDY	250	265	415	205	165	165	240	155	175
Americas Total	KECT	745	890	1 340	1 765	2 825	975	2 025	1 420	1 260
Africa										
Algeria	KOTB	275	995	1 865	715	715	1 260	1 385	1 635	1 145
Angola	KECU	320	605	555	385	195	150	545	800	1 025
Burundi	PTDZ	10	50	95	60	85	215	780	620	615
Congo	PTEA	15	40	80	75	90	150	450	485	520
Congo (Dem. Rep.)	KEEH	635	775	935	680	690	660	1 240	1 030	1 395
Eritrea	PTEC	20	110	245	135	125	345	565	505	620
Ethiopia	KECW	615	730	585	205	145	345	455	415	610
Gambia	DMMA	25	140	1 170	245	125	45	30	50	65
Ghana	KECX	1 785	2 035	1 915	780	350	225	195	285	200
Ivory Coast	DMLZ	330	705	245	125	70	95	190	445	280
Kenya	KOTC	630	1 130	1 395	1 170	605	885	485	455	310
Nigeria	KECY	1 665	4 340	5 825	2 900	1 480	1 380	945	835	870
Rwanda	ZAEV	10	100	135	80	90	280	820	760	540
Sierra Leone	KOTD	1 050	1 810	855	395	815	565	1 125	1 330	1 930
Somalia	KECZ	1 465	1 840	3 465	1 780	2 730	4 685	7 495	5 020	6 465
Sudan	KEEE	300	330	345	280	230	250	280	415	390
Tanzania	DMMC	110	205	1 535	225	90	80	80	60	80
Uganda	KEEG	595	360	365	215	220	210	420	740	475
Zimbabwe	GRFS	40	55	105	130	60	80	230	1 010	2 115
Africa Other	PTEB	395	605	835	705	600	470	710	1 025	1 060
Africa Total	KEEJ	10 295	16 960	22 545	11 290	9 515	12 380	18 435	17 920	20 710
Middle East										
Iran	KEEK	365	520	615	585	585	745	1 320	5 610	3 415
Iraq	KEEL	495	550	930	965	1 075	1 295	1 800	7 475	6 705
Middle East Other	ZAEX	655	910	755	600	675	745	1 045	1 330	1 095
Middle East Total	KEGY	1 520	1 985	2 295	2 150	2 335	2 785	4 165	14 415	11 215
Asia										
Afghanistan	DMLY	315	325	580	675	1 085	2 395	3 975	5 555	9 000
Bangladesh	ZAEY	155	310	685	645	545	460	530	795	500
China	KEGZ	215	425	790	820	1 945	1 925	2 625	4 000	2 390
India	KEIL	1 275	2 030	3 255	2 220	1 285	1 030	1 365	2 120	1 850
Nepal	PTED	75	95	100	70	55	105	230	640	640
Pakistan	KEIM	1 125	1 810	2 915	1 915	1 615	1 975	2 615	3 165	2 860
Sri Lanka	KEIN	1 965	2 350	2 070	1 340	1 830	3 505	5 130	6 395	5 510
Asia Other	PTEE	60	170	290	205	210	550	995	565	800
Asia Total	KEJO	5 175	7 515	10 685	7 885	8 570	11 940	17 465	23 230	23 550
Grand Total	KEJQ	22 370	32 830	43 965	29 640	32 500	46 015	71 160	80 315	71 365

1 Figures rounded to the nearest 5.
2 May exclude some cases lodged at Local Enforcement Offices between
   January 1999 and March 2000.
3 Provisional figures.

Source: Home Office: 020 8760 8297

5.12 Marriages[1]

Numbers

		1990	1991	1992	1993	1994	1995	1996	1997	1998	1999	2000
United Kingdom[2]												
Marriages	KKAA	375 410	349 739	356 013	341 608	331 232	322 251	317 514	310 218	304 797	301 083	305 912
Persons marrying per 1,000 resident population	KKAB	13.1	12.2	12.4	11.8	11.5	11.1	10.9	10.7	10.4	10.3	10.4
Previous marital status												
Bachelors	KKAC	276 512	256 538	258 567	245 996	236 619	227 717	221 826	216 237	214 005	211 820	213 777
Divorced men	KKAD	88 199	83 069	87 419	85 824	85 261	85 743	87 113	85 625	82 977	81 750	84 771
Widowers	KKAE	10 699	10 132	10 027	9 788	9 352	8 791	8 575	8 356	7 815	7 513	7 364
Spinsters	KKAF	279 442	259 084	260 252	248 063	237 241	228 462	221 697	216 776	215 399	213 246	215 865
Divorced women	KKAG	85 608	81 224	86 361	84 268	85 220	85 396	87 618	85 648	82 016	80 816	83 166
Widows	KKAH	10 360	9 431	9 400	9 277	8 771	8 393	8 199	7 794	7 382	7 021	6 881
First marriage for both partners	KMGH	240 729	222 369	222 142	210 567	200 910	192 078	185 293	181 135	180 404	178 759	180 020
First marriage for one partner	KMGI	74 496	70 884	74 535	72 925	72 040	72 023	72 937	70 743	68 596	67 548	69 602
Remarriage for both partners	KMGJ	60 185	56 486	59 336	58 116	58 282	58 150	59 284	58 340	55 797	54 776	56 290
Males												
Under 21 years	KKAI	15 930	13 271	11 031	8 767	7 091	6 302	5 497	5 126	5 173	5 234	5 019
21-24	KKAJ	92 270	79 877	74 458	65 129	56 877	49 432	42 488	36 875	32 723	29 390	28 467
25-29	KKAK	122 800	115 637	118 255	114 101	111 108	105 218	101 647	97 345	94 696	90 412	85 870
30-34	KKAL	56 966	56 970	62 470	63 848	65 490	68 245	69 867	70 904	71 096	72 129	73 809
35-44	KKAM	49 984	48 147	51 125	50 553	51 310	53 350	56 513	58 292	59 838	62 114	68 019
45-54	KKAN	21 996	20 915	23 290	23 841	24 136	24 786	26 252	26 472	26 118	26 581	28 791
55 and over	KKAO	15 464	14 922	15 384	15 369	15 220	14 918	15 250	15 204	15 153	15 223	15 937
Females												
Under 21 years	KKAP	45 626	38 305	32 618	26 839	22 903	20 643	18 485	17 254	16 793	16 082	15 938
21-24	KKAQ	119 037	105 505	102 494	93 125	84 171	75 071	66 191	59 549	54 645	50 350	48 578
25-29	KKAR	103 209	99 851	105 223	104 517	102 803	100 644	99 651	97 932	97 181	94 703	92 753
30-34	KKAS	42 794	43 617	48 514	49 546	52 359	54 819	57 752	58 589	59 349	60 446	62 478
35-44	KKAT	38 983	37 582	40 075	40 090	41 213	43 115	45 969	47 267	47 721	50 136	54 697
45-54	KKAU	16 825	16 473	18 504	18 800	19 280	19 720	21 025	21 038	20 708	20 822	22 621
55 and over	KKAV	8 936	8 406	8 585	8 691	8 503	8 239	8 441	8 589	8 400	8 544	8 847
England and Wales[2]												
Marriages	KKBA	331 150	306 756	311 564	299 197	291 069	283 012	278 975	272 536	267 303	263 515	267 961
Persons marrying per 1,000 resident population	KKBB	13.1	12.1	12.3	11.7	11.4	11.1	10.9	10.6	10.4	10.2	10.3
Previous marital status												
Bachelors	KKBC	241 274	222 823	224 152	213 476	206 077	198 208	193 306	188 268	186 329	184 266	186 113
Divorced men	KKBD	80 282	74 860	78 473	76 986	76 633	76 967	78 003	76 839	74 029	72 617	75 378
Widowers	KKBE	9 594	9 073	8 939	8 735	8 359	7 837	7 666	7 429	6 945	6 632	6 470
Spinsters	KKBF	243 825	224 812	225 608	214 987	206 332	198 603	192 707	188 457	187 391	185 328	187 717
Divorced women	KKBG	77 994	73 408	77 542	75 904	76 857	76 869	78 939	77 098	73 330	71 971	74 092
Widows	KKBH	9 331	8 536	8 414	8 306	7 880	7 540	7 329	6 981	6 582	6 216	6 152
First marriage for both partners	KMGK	209 043	192 238	191 732	181 956	174 200	166 418	160 680	156 907	156 539	155 027	156 140
First marriage for one partner	KMGL	67 013	63 159	66 296	64 551	64 009	63 975	64 653	62 911	60 642	59 540	61 550
Remarriage for both partners	KMGM	55 094	51 359	53 536	52 690	52 860	52 619	53 642	52 718	50 122	48 948	50 271
Males												
Under 21 years	KKBI	13 772	11 416	9 471	7 540	6 175	5 520	4 877	4 574	4 608	4 629	4 536
21-24	KKBJ	79 818	68 547	63 932	55 963	49 073	42 711	36 713	31 907	28 389	25 424	24 764
25-29	KKBK	107 784	100 891	102 942	99 314	96 862	91 607	88 338	84 644	82 135	78 364	74 367
30-34	KKBL	50 600	50 403	55 012	56 129	57 848	60 014	61 582	62 265	62 323	63 212	64 611
35-44	KKBM	45 038	43 013	45 364	44 863	45 514	47 330	50 038	51 654	52 812	54 528	59 834
45-54	KKBN	19 991	18 929	20 925	21 440	21 794	22 349	23 661	23 688	23 385	23 676	25 470
55 and over	KKBO	14 147	13 557	13 918	13 948	13 803	13 481	13 766	13 804	13 651	13 682	14 379
Females												
Under 21 years	KKBP	40 022	33 428	28 541	23 469	20 250	18 343	16 510	15 439	15 065	14 379	14 421
21-24	KKBQ	103 653	91 338	88 553	80 470	72 937	65 126	57 296	51 766	47 446	43 691	42 265
25-29	KKBR	90 629	87 244	91 735	91 134	89 941	87 680	86 838	85 352	84 399	82 250	80 312
30-34	KKBS	38 032	38 425	42 675	43 559	46 119	48 216	50 799	51 405	51 982	52 721	54 649
35-44	KKBT	35 315	33 755	35 660	35 662	36 651	38 367	40 889	41 838	42 245	44 199	48 245
45-54	KKBU	15 290	14 891	16 619	16 969	17 409	17 791	18 992	18 938	18 575	18 572	20 083
55 and over	KKBV	8 209	7 675	7 781	7 934	7 762	7 489	7 651	7 798	7 591	7 703	7 986

5.12 Marriages[1]
continued

		1991	1992	1993	1994	1995	1996	1997	1998	1999	2000	2001
Scotland												
Marriages	KKCA	33 762	35 057	33 366	31 480	30 663	30 242	29 611	29 668	29 940	30 367	29 621
Persons marrying per 1,000 resident population	KKCB	*13.2*	*13.7*	*13.0*	*12.3*	*11.9*	*11.8*	*11.6*	*11.6*	*11.7*	*12.0*	*11.7*
Previous marital status												
Bachelors	KKCC	25 549	26 106	24 609	23 004	22 126	21 454	20 994	20 987	21 052	21 201	20 737
Divorced men	KKCD	7 344	8 027	7 879	7 654	7 741	8 048	7 845	7 934	8 142	8 427	8 238
Widowers	KKCE	869	924	878	822	796	740	772	747	746	739	646
Spinsters	KKCF	25 979	26 274	25 103	23 248	22 410	21 799	21 303	21 241	21 308	21 608	21 223
Divorced women	KKCG	7 048	7 935	7 469	7 487	7 542	7 718	7 621	7 754	7 949	8 141	7 825
Widows	KKCH	735	848	794	745	711	725	687	673	683	618	573
First marriage for both partners	KEZV	22 401	22 588	21 214	19 644	18 822	18 071	17 751	17 677	17 680	17 864	17 468
First marriage for one partner	KEZW	6 726	7 204	7 284	6 964	6 892	7 111	6 795	6 874	7 000	7 081	7 024
Remarriage for both partners	KEZX	4 635	5 265	4 868	4 872	4 949	5 060	5 065	5 117	5 260	5 422	5 129
Males												
Under 21 years	KKCI	1 378	1 172	902	680	577	452	406	421	490	364	371
21-24	KKCJ	8 572	7 958	6 870	5 693	4 915	4 191	3 494	3 147	2 853	2 720	2 489
25-29	KKCK	11 244	11 587	11 266	10 812	10 209	10 056	9 495	9 439	9 031	8 536	7 949
30-34	KKCL	5 290	6 022	6 214	6 176	6 574	6 574	6 911	6 988	7 179	7 419	7 464
35-44	KKCM	4 383	4 950	4 803	4 864	5 021	5 412	5 649	5 945	6 470	7 018	7 215
45-54	KKCN	1 733	2 083	2 093	2 050	2 124	2 288	2 459	2 412	2 575	2 960	2 816
55 and over	KKCO	1 162	1 285	1 218	1 205	1 243	1 269	1 197	1 316	1 342	1 350	1 317
Females												
Under 21 years	KKCP	3 589	3 060	2 461	1 959	1 728	1 423	1 302	1 289	1 322	1 171	1 111
21-24	KKCQ	10 735	10 503	9 506	8 291	7 264	6 474	5 568	5 248	4 778	4 581	4 343
25-29	KKCR	9 771	10 457	10 368	9 895	9 904	9 818	9 574	9 764	9 539	9 495	8 994
30-34	KKCS	4 331	4 822	5 002	5 145	5 401	5 675	5 927	6 036	6 433	6 463	6 618
35-44	KKCT	3 333	3 847	3 774	3 917	4 025	4 378	4 722	4 726	5 150	5 633	5 712
45-54	KKCU	1 386	1 673	1 606	1 648	1 689	1 794	1 844	1 900	1 994	2 279	2 147
55 and over	KKCV	617	695	649	625	652	680	674	705	724	745	696
Northern Ireland												
Marriages	KKDA	9 221	9 392	9 045	8 683	8 576	8 297	8 071	7 826	7 628	7 584	7 281
Persons marrying per 1,000 resident population	KKDB	*11.5*	*11.6*	*11.1*	*10.6*	*10.4*	*10.0*	*9.7*	*9.3*	*9.1*	*9.0*	*8.6*
Previous marital status												
Bachelors	KKDC	8 166	8 309	7 911	7 538	7 383	7 066	6 975	6 689	6 502	6 463	6 232
Divorced men	KKDD	865	919	959	974	1 035	1 062	941	1 014	991	966	936
Widowers	KKDE	190	164	175	171	158	169	155	123	135	155	113
Spinsters	KKDF	8 293	8 370	7 973	7 661	7 449	7 191	7 016	6 767	6 610	6 540	6 319
Divorced women	KKDG	768	884	895	876	985	961	929	932	896	933	862
Widows	KKDH	160	138	177	146	142	145	126	127	122	111	100
First marriage for both partners	KEZY	7 730	7 822	7 397	7 066	6 838	6 542	6 477	6 188	6 052	6 016	5 802
First marriage for one partner	KEZZ	999	1 035	1 090	1 067	1 156	1 173	1 037	1 080	1 008	971	947
Remarriage for both partners	KFBI	492	535	558	550	582	582	557	558	568	597	532
Males												
Under 21 years	KKDI	477	388	325	236	205	168	146	144	115	119	94
21-24	KKDJ	2 758	2 568	2 296	2 111	1 806	1 584	1 474	1 187	1 113	983	915
25-29	KKDK	3 502	3 726	3 521	3 434	3 402	3 253	3 206	3 122	3 017	2 967	2 804
30-34	KKDL	1 277	1 436	1 505	1 466	1 657	1 711	1 728	1 785	1 738	1 779	1 784
35-44	KKDM	751	811	887	932	999	1 063	989	1 081	1 116	1 167	1 155
45-54	KKDN	253	282	308	292	313	303	325	321	330	361	357
55 and over	KKDO	203	181	203	212	194	215	203	186	199	208	172
Females												
Under 21 years	KKDP	1 288	1 017	909	694	572	552	513	439	381	346	296
21-24	KKDQ	3 432	3 438	3 149	2 943	2 681	2 421	2 215	1 951	1 881	1 732	1 598
25-29	KKDR	2 836	3 031	3 015	2 967	3 060	2 995	3 006	3 018	2 914	2 946	2 854
30-34	KKDS	861	1 017	985	1 095	1 202	1 278	1 257	1 331	1 292	1 366	1 376
35-44	KKDT	494	568	654	645	723	702	707	750	787	819	825
45-54	KKDU	196	212	225	223	240	239	256	233	256	259	241
55 and over	KKDV	114	109	108	116	98	110	117	104	117	116	91

1 Mid-year population estimates for England and Wales, United Kingdom, Scotland and Northern Ireland are based on the 2001 Census. See chapter text.
2 2001 data for UK /England and Wales will be available in February 2003

Sources: Office for National Statistics: 01329 813339;
General Register Office for Scotland;
Northern Ireland Statistics and Research Agency

5.13 Divorce

		1991	1992	1993	1994	1995	1996	1997	1998	1999	2000	2001
United Kingdom												
Decrees absolute granted[1,2]:												
Number	ZBRL	173 454	175 144	180 018	173 611	170 050	171 729	161 087	160 057	158 746	154 628	156 814
Duration of marriage:												
0-4 years	ZBRM	40 123	39 191	39 530	37 978	36 594	37 016	33 719	33 087	31 047	28 933	28 306
5-9 years	ZBRN	46 884	47 990	50 883	49 215	48 309	48 670	45 040	44 243	43 357	41 621	42 360
10-14 years	ZBRO	31 773	32 261	33 221	31 177	30 257	30 159	29 085	29 706	30 270	30 166	30 849
15-19 years	ZBRP	22 233	22 179	22 324	21 336	21 040	21 379	20 211	20 078	20 147	19 902	20 568
20 years and over	ZBRQ	32 422	33 516	34 055	33 898	33 840	34 487	33 020	32 935	33 916	34 000	34 729
Not stated	ZBRR	19	7	5	7	10	18	12	8	9	6	2
Age of wife at marriage:												
16-19 years	ZBRS	45 356	44 347	43 368	38 464	35 145	33 590	28 987	27 627	25 440	23 505	22 558
20-24 years	ZBRT	80 969	81 574	83 806	80 594	78 341	78 075	72 971	71 416	69 509	66 215	66 282
25-29 years	ZBRU	25 813	27 109	29 213	30 576	31 611	33 634	33 452	34 195	35 585	36 009	37 418
30-34 years	ZBRV	10 180	10 582	11 272	11 716	12 322	13 122	12 968	13 719	14 420	14 892	15 842
35-39 years	ZBRW	5 300	5 531	6 018	5 979	6 172	6 470	6 155	6 571	6 848	6 993	7 417
40-44 years	ZBRX	2 897	3 017	3 260	3 247	3 335	3 507	3 375	3 360	3 557	3 568	3 778
45 years and over	ZBRY	2 877	2 933	3 004	2 952	3 052	3 239	3 094	3 086	3 291	3 352	3 429
Not stated	ZBRZ	62	51	77	83	72	92	85	83	96	94	90
Age of wife at divorce:												
16-24 years	ZBSA	16 150	14 604	13 895	11 845	10 517	9 298	7 371	6 758	5 671	5 115	4 874
25-29 years	ZBSB	39 059	38 186	38 632	35 824	33 354	32 808	28 814	26 968	24 120	21 280	19 635
30-34 years	ZBSC	36 434	38 220	39 879	39 456	38 839	39 497	37 257	36 795	36 052	34 356	34 194
35-39 years	ZBSD	28 097	29 044	30 746	30 000	30 280	31 497	30 641	31 688	32 605	32 588	33 997
40-44 years	ZBSE	23 928	23 756	23 943	22 847	22 791	22 843	22 246	22 810	23 614	23 879	25 579
45 years and over	ZBSF	29 705	31 276	32 841	33 549	34 187	35 684	34 662	34 947	36 578	37 311	38 442
Not stated	ZBSG	81	58	82	90	82	102	96	91	106	99	93
Divorces in which there were:												
No children aged under 16[3]	ZBSH	78 694	77 709	78 803	78 913	78 844	..	..	..	..	..	..
One or more children aged under 16[3]	ZBSI	94 760	97 435	101 215	94 698	91 206	..	..	..	..	..	..
England and Wales												
Decrees absolute granted[1]:												
Number	KKEA	158 745	160 385	165 018	158 175	155 499	157 107	146 689	145 214	144 556	141 135	143 818
Rate per 1,000 married couples	KKEB	*13.5*	*13.7*	*14.2*	*13.7*	*13.6*	*13.8*	*13.0*	*12.9*	*13.0*	*12.7*	*13.0*
Duration of marriage:												
0-4 years	KKEC	37 779	36 898	37 252	35 695	34 507	34 924	31 767	31 136	29 307	27 474	26 987
5-9 years	KKED	42 735	43 745	46 536	44 769	44 304	44 609	41 260	40 239	39 676	38 206	39 079
10-14 years	KKEE	28 791	29 285	30 156	28 073	27 365	27 332	26 215	26 698	27 384	27 459	28 176
15-19 years	KKEF	20 127	20 160	20 233	19 200	18 943	19 321	18 027	17 934	18 072	17 870	18 603
20 years and over	KKEG	29 294	30 290	30 836	30 431	30 370	30 912	29 408	29 199	30 108	30 120	30 971
Not stated	KKEH	19	7	5	7	10	9	12	8	9	6	2
Age of wife at marriage:												
16-19 years	KKEI	40 594	39 734	38 811	34 069	31 322	29 927	25 579	24 276	22 486	20 930	20 218
20-24 years	KKEJ	74 050	74 701	76 853	73 291	71 360	71 123	66 167	64 453	62 853	59 874	60 211
25-29 years	KKEK	24 025	25 173	27 178	28 360	29 441	31 396	31 022	31 533	32 867	33 282	34 759
30-34 years	KKEL	9 608	9 939	10 593	11 007	11 585	12 335	12 094	12 788	13 507	13 972	14 890
35-39 years	KKEM	5 024	5 200	5 673	5 615	5 800	6 051	5 767	6 153	6 432	6 562	6 956
40-44 years	KKEN	2 727	2 872	3 091	3 064	3 121	3 254	3 156	3 135	3 331	3 378	3 559
45 years and over	KKEO	2 717	2 766	2 819	2 769	2 870	3 021	2 904	2 876	3 080	3 137	3 225
Age of wife at divorce:												
16-24 years	KKEP	14 960	13 482	12 924	10 956	9 783	8 615	6 871	6 298	5 318	4 839	4 643
25-29 years	KKEQ	35 582	34 853	35 362	32 608	30 563	30 075	26 435	24 586	22 173	19 650	18 231
30-34 years	KKER	33 195	34 901	36 300	35 848	35 538	36 274	33 967	33 446	32 837	31 420	31 489
35-39 years	KKES	25 661	26 577	28 162	27 195	27 550	28 727	27 715	28 605	29 663	29 820	31 164
40-44 years	KKET	21 979	21 783	21 891	20 765	20 739	20 774	20 125	20 521	21 325	21 469	23 190
45 years and over	KKEU	27 349	28 782	30 374	30 796	31 316	32 633	31 564	31 750	33 231	33 931	35 099
Not stated	KKEV	19	7	5	7	10	9	12	8	9	6	2
Divorces in which there were:												
No children aged under 16[3]	ZBSJ	70 399	68 960	70 103	69 684	69 632	70 174	66 019	64 738	65 258	64 359	64 541
One or more children aged under 16[3]	ZBSK	88 346	91 425	94 915	88 491	85 867	86 933	80 670	80 476	79 298	76 776	79 277

5.13 Divorce

continued

Numbers

		1991	1992	1993	1994	1995	1996	1997	1998	1999	2000	2001
Scotland												
Decrees absolute granted[1]												
Number	**KKFA**	12 399	12 479	12 787	13 133	12 249	12 308	12 222	12 384	11 864	11 143	10 631
Rate per 1,000 married couples	**KKFB**	*10.6*	*10.8*	*11.1*	*11.5*	*10.8*	*10.9*	*11.0*	*11.2*	*10.8*	*10.3*	*9.8*
Duration of marriage:												
0-4 years	**KKFC**	2 142	2 085	2 092	2 095	1 908	1 914	1 793	1 766	1 588	1 304	1 159
5-9 years	**KKFD**	3 508	3 610	3 722	3 790	3 399	3 432	3 224	3 360	3 095	2 890	2 721
10-14 years	**KKFE**	2 484	2 454	2 539	2 592	2 407	2 310	2 385	2 456	2 368	2 168	2 163
15-19 years	**KKFF**	1 718	1 675	1 745	1 786	1 698	1 709	1 804	1 729	1 686	1 622	1 562
20 years and over	**KKFG**	2 547	2 655	2 689	2 870	2 837	2 934	3 016	3 073	3 127	3 159	3 026
Not stated	**ZBSL**	–	–	–	–	–	9	–	–	–	–	–
Age of wife at marriage:												
16-19 years	**ZBSM**	3 894	3 755	3 768	3 641	3 091	2 939	2 749	2 654	2 374	2 043	1 839
20-24 years	**ZBSN**	5 845	5 821	5 890	6 197	5 845	5 822	5 714	5 744	5 453	5 142	4 873
25-29 years	**KKFJ**	1 545	1 685	1 812	1 926	1 887	1 933	2 151	2 314	2 333	2 318	2 233
30-34 years	**KKFK**	514	575	612	628	654	697	791	824	829	805	827
35-39 years	**KKFL**	249	301	312	329	338	393	360	382	379	378	401
40-44 years	**KKFM**	148	138	152	163	196	234	199	198	208	170	193
45 years and over	**KKFN**	142	153	164	166	166	198	173	185	192	193	175
Not stated	**KKFO**	62	51	77	83	72	92	85	83	96	94	90
Age of wife at divorce:												
16-24 years	**KKFP**	1 038	963	844	767	622	583	426	377	301	232	182
25-29 years	**KKFQ**	2 932	2 807	2 775	2 750	2 353	2 269	2 021	1 957	1 597	1 330	1 109
30-34 years	**KKFR**	2 741	2 785	3 037	3 045	2 747	2 708	2 736	2 767	2 642	2 381	2 215
35-39 years	**KKFS**	2 037	2 092	2 212	2 390	2 290	2 307	2 469	2 562	2 450	2 298	2 311
40-44 years	**KKFT**	1 665	1 685	1 771	1 788	1 734	1 761	1 819	1 951	1 929	1 999	1 963
45 years and over	**KKFU**	1 924	2 096	2 071	2 310	2 431	2 587	2 667	2 687	2 848	2 810	2 760
Not stated	**KKFV**	62	51	77	83	72	93	84	83	97	93	91
Divorces in which there were:												
No children aged under 16[3]	**KKFW**	6 521	6 927	6 951	7 390	7 515	..	..	..	..	..	..
One or more children under 16[3]	**KKFX**	5 878	5 552	5 836	5 743	4 734	..	..	..	..	..	..
Northern Ireland												
Decrees absolute granted[1,2]:												
Number	**ZBSO**	2 310	2 280	2 213	2 303	2 302	2 314	2 176	2 459	2 326	2 350	2 365
Duration of marriage:												
0-4 years	**ZBSP**	202	208	186	188	179	178	159	185	152	155	160
5-9 years	**ZBSQ**	641	635	625	656	606	629	556	644	586	525	560
10-14 years	**ZBSR**	498	522	526	512	485	517	485	552	518	539	510
15-19 years	**ZBSS**	388	344	346	350	399	349	380	415	389	410	403
20 years and over	**ZBST**	581	571	530	597	633	641	596	663	681	721	732
Age of wife at marriage:												
16-19 years	**ZBSU**	868	858	789	754	732	724	659	697	580	532	501
20-24 years	**ZBSV**	1 074	1 052	1 063	1 106	1 136	1 130	1 090	1 219	1 203	1 199	1 198
25-29 years	**ZBSW**	243	251	223	290	283	305	279	348	385	409	426
30-34 years	**ZBSX**	58	68	67	81	83	90	83	107	84	115	125
35-39 years	**ZBSY**	27	30	33	35	34	26	28	36	37	53	60
40-44 years	**ZBSZ**	22	7	17	20	18	19	20	27	18	20	26
45 years and over	**ZBTA**	18	14	21	17	16	20	17	25	19	22	29
Age of wife at divorce:												
16-24 years	**ZBTB**	152	159	127	122	112	100	74	83	52	44	49
25-29 years	**ZBTC**	545	526	495	466	438	464	358	425	350	300	295
30-34 years	**ZBTD**	498	534	542	563	554	515	554	582	573	555	490
35-39 years	**ZBTE**	399	375	372	415	440	463	457	521	492	470	522
40-44 years	**ZBTF**	284	288	281	294	318	308	302	338	360	411	426
45 years and over	**ZBTG**	432	398	396	443	440	464	431	510	499	570	583
Divorces in which there were:												
No children aged under 16[3]	**ZBTH**	1 774	1 822	1 749	1 839	1 697	1 676	1 573	1 807	1 649	1 051	1 054
One or more children aged under 16[3]	**ZBTI**	536	458	464	464	605	638	603	652	677	1 299	1 311

1 Includes decrees of nullities.
2 Marital estimates are not available for Northern Ireland - no divorce rate for UK/Northern Ireland.
3 Children of the family as defined by the Matrimonial Causes Act 1973.

Sources: Office for National Statistics: 01329 813339;
General Register Office for Scotland;
Northern Ireland Statistics and Research Agency

5.14 Divorce proceedings

Numbers

United Kingdom

		1991	1992	1993	1994	1995	1996	1997	1998	1999	2000	2001
Dissolution of marriage[1]												
Decree absolute/decree granted	ZBXR	172 997	174 718	179 539	173 178	169 621	171 309	160 733	159 688	158 418	154 273	156 563
On grounds of:												
Adultery	ZBXS	46 161	45 458	45 759	42 743	41 313	41 127	38 652	37 302	35 545	34 082	33 452
Behaviour	ZBXT	77 294	77 648	78 686	75 029	71 733	72 581	68 546	68 685	67 851	65 687	66 818
Desertion	ZBXU	1 185	1 096	1 193	1 185	1 196	1 101	956	828	748	722	718
Separation (2 years and consent)	ZBXV	36 041	37 955	41 002	41 144	41 969	42 265	39 398	39 627	40 368	39 763	40 699
Separation(5 years)	ZBXW	11 528	11 806	12 183	12 317	12 699	13 547	12 552	12 697	13 389	13 653	14 575
Combination of more than one ground and other	ZBXX	788	755	716	760	711	688	629	549	517	366	301
Decree absolute/decree granted to:												
the wife	ZBXY	124 472	125 833	128 797	123 256	118 869	119 570	111 912	111 556	109 828	106 958	107 346
the husband	ZBXZ	48 136	48 509	50 407	49 507	50 268	51 247	48 393	47 764	48 236	47 069	49 015
both	ZBYA	393	379	345	423	490	493	430	369	358	247	202
Nullity of marriage[2]												
Decree absolute/decree granted	ZBYB	457	426	479	433	429	420	354	369	328	355	251

England and Wales

		1991	1992	1993	1994	1995	1996	1997	1998	1999	2000	2001
Dissolution of marriage												
Petitions filed	KKGA	179 103	189 329	184 471	175 510	173 966	177 970	163 769	165 870	162 137	157 809	161 580
Decree nisi granted	KKGM	153 258	149 126	160 625	154 241	155 739	157 588	148 310	144 231	143 106	143 729	146 932
Decree absolute granted	KKGN	158 301	159 967	164 556	157 756	155 076	156 692	146 339	144 851	144 233	140 783	143 568
On grounds of:												
Adultery	KKGB	44 737	44 128	44 466	41 449	40 178	40 012	37 592	36 319	34 584	33 310	32 839
Behaviour	KKGC	73 266	73 906	74 583	70 932	68 168	68 986	65 047	65 257	64 816	63 182	64 768
Desertion	KKGD	1 082	1 021	1 118	1 062	1 108	1 030	912	790	713	680	689
Separation (2 years and consent)	KKGE	29 414	30 995	34 144	33 996	35 030	35 422	32 638	32 394	33 482	32 820	33 703
Separation(5 years)	KKGF	9 031	9 181	9 556	9 589	9 930	10 626	9 592	9 616	10 193	10 498	11 355
Combination of more than one ground and other	ZBYC	771	736	689	728	662	616	558	475	445	293	214
Decree absolute granted to[2]												
the wife	ZBYD	113 947	115 393	118 127	112 415	108 764	109 489	102 173	101 583	100 469	98 227	98 992
the husband	ZBYE	43 961	44 195	46 084	44 918	45 823	46 712	43 739	42 902	43 413	42 311	44 378
both	ZBYF	393	379	345	423	489	491	427	366	351	245	198
Nullity of marriage												
Petitions filed	KKGO	619	535	634	822	881	702	485	505	549	452	657
Decree nisi granted	KKGR	508	369	365	705	425	332	248	281	495	274	297
Decree absolute granted	KKGS	444	418	462	419	423	415	350	363	323	352	250
Judicial separation												
Petitions filed	KKGT	2 588	2 434	2 251	4 358	3 349	2 795	1 078	916	882	650	535
Decrees granted	KKGW	1 747	1 452	1 413	1 350	1 543	1 199	589	519	696	540	925

5.14 Divorce proceedings
continued

		Scotland										
		1991	1992	1993	1994	1995	1996	1997	1998	1999	2000	2001
Dissolution of marriage[1]												
Decree granted	ZBYG	12 395	12 476	12 777	13 125	12 243	12 307	12 220	12 383	11 860	11 142	10 631
On grounds of:												
Adultery	ZBYH	1 198	1 136	1 092	1 099	956	943	909	832	770	610	473
Behaviour	ZBYI	3 688	3 407	3 757	3 711	3 203	3 184	3 081	3 005	2 611	2 099	1 639
Desertion	ZBYJ	82	58	56	103	72	61	33	28	18	34	24
Separation (2 years and consent)	ZBYK	5 508	5 823	5 800	6 078	5 846	5 835	5 773	6 121	5 908	5 878	5 943
Separation(5 years)	ZBYL	1 919	2 052	2 072	2 134	2 166	2 284	2 424	2 397	2 553	2 521	2 552
Decree granted to[2]												
the wife	ZBYM	8 930	8 865	9 190	9 278	8 545	8 559	8 266	8 329	7 774	7 191	6 775
the husband	ZBYN	3 469	3 614	3 597	3 855	3 704	3 749	3 956	4 055	4 090	3 952	3 856
Nullity of marriage												
Decree granted	ZBYO	4	3	10	8	6	1	2	1	4	1	–

		Northern Ireland										
		1991	1992	1993	1994	1995	1996	1997	1998	1999	2000	2001
Dissolution of marriage												
Petitions filed	ZBYP	2 591	2 597	2 610	2 875	2 875	2 695	2 808	2 760	2 414	3 005	2 869
Decree nisi granted	ZBYQ	2 344	2 386	2 384	2 535	2 535	2 419	2 532	2 904	2 393	2 456	2 615
Decree absolute granted	ZBYR	2 301	2 275	2 206	2 297	2 302	2 310	2 174	2 454	2 325	2 348	2 364
On grounds of:												
Adultery	ZBYS	226	194	201	195	179	172	151	151	191	162	140
Behaviour	ZBYT	340	335	346	386	362	411	418	423	424	406	411
Desertion	ZBYU	21	17	19	20	16	10	11	10	17	8	5
Separation (2 years and consent)	ZBYV	1 119	1 137	1 059	1 072	1 093	1 010	991	1 112	978	1 065	1 053
Separation(5 years)	ZBYW	578	573	555	594	603	637	536	684	643	634	668
Combination of more than one ground and other	ZBYX	17	19	26	30	49	70	67	74	72	73	87
Decree absolute granted to:												
the wife	ZBYY	1 595	1 575	1 480	1 563	1 560	1 522	1 473	1 644	1 585	1 540	1 579
the husband	ZBYZ	706	700	726	734	741	786	698	807	733	806	781
both	ZBZA	–	–	–	–	1	2	3	3	7	2	4
Nullity of marriage												
Petitions filed	ZBZB	5	1	2	5	5	5	7	2	4	3	6
Decree nisi granted	ZBZC	10	3	2	3	5	5	2	6	2	5	2
Decree absolute granted	ZBZD	9	5	7	6	–	4	2	5	1	2	1
Judicial separation												
Petitions filed	ZBZE	23	17	44	57	84	63	70	64	50	54	40
Decrees granted	ZBZF	13	22	6	15	30	22	34	40	31	23	25

1 The terms Petition filed, Decree nisi granted, Decree absolute and Judicial separation are not used in Scotland. Decree absolute granted to 'both' and 'Combination of more than one ground and other' are not procedures used in Scotland.
2 Information on Decree granted for the wife or husband for Scotland includes nullities (these are identified separately under 'Nullity of marriage'); figures excluding nullities are not available.

Sources: Office for National Statistics: 01329 813339;
General Register Office for Scotland;
Northern Ireland Statistics and Research Agency;
The Court Service (E&W and NI);
Scottish Courts Administration

Population and vital statistics

5.15 Births[1]
Annual averages or calendar years

	Live births				Rates				
	Total	Male	Female	Sex ratio[2]	Crude birth rate[3]	General fertility rate[4]	TFR[5]	Still-births[6]	Still-birth rate[6]
United Kingdom[7,8]									
1900 - 02	1 095	558	537	1 037	28.6	115.1	..	..	..
1910 - 12	1 037	528	508	1 039	24.6	99.4	..	..	..
1920 - 22	1 018	522	496	1 052	23.1	93.0	..	..	..
1930 - 32	750	383	367	1 046	16.3	66.5	..	..	..
1940 - 42	723	372	351	1 062	15.0	..	1.89	..	..
1950 - 52	803	413	390	1 061	16.0	73.7	2.21	..	..
1960 - 62	946	487	459	1 063	17.9	90.3	2.80	18.6	19.2
1970 - 72	880	453	427	1 064	15.8	82.5	2.36	11.3	12.7
1980 - 82	735	377	358	1 053	13.0	62.5	1.83	5.0	6.8
1990 - 92	790	405	385	1 051	13.8	63.7	..	3.6	4.6
	BBCA	KBCZ	KBCY	KMFW	KBCT	KBCS	KBCR	KBCQ	KMFX
1985	751	385	365	1 053	13.3	61.4	1.79	4.2	5.6
1986	755	387	368	1 053	13.3	61.0	1.78	4.1	5.3
1987	775	398	378	1 053	13.6	62.3	1.81	3.9	5.0
1988	787	403	384	1 049	13.8	63.1	1.82	3.9	4.9
1989	777	398	379	1 051	13.6	62.1	1.79	3.7	4.7
1990	798	409	390	1 049	13.9	64.0	1.83	3.7	4.6
1991	792	406	386	1 052	13.8	63.6	1.81	3.7	4.7
1992	781	400	381	1 052	13.6	63.4	1.79	3.4	4.4
1993	762	391	371	1 054	13.2	62.4	1.75	4.4	5.7
1994	750	385	365	1 054	13.0	61.6	1.74	4.4	5.8
1995	732	375	357	1 052	12.6	60.1	1.70	4.1	5.6
1996	733	376	357	1 055	12.6	60.2	1.72	4.1	5.5
1997	727	372	354	1 051	12.5	59.6	1.72	3.9	5.3
1998	717	367	350	1 052	12.3	58.8	1.71	3.9	5.4
1999	700	359	341	1 056	12.0	57.3	1.68	3.7	5.3
2000	679	348	331	1 051	11.6	55.4	1.64	3.6	5.3
2001	669	343	326	1 050	11.4	54.5	1.63	3.6	5.3
England and Wales[8]									
1900 - 02	932	475	458	1 037	28.6	114.7	..	..	..
1910 - 12	884	450	433	1 040	24.5	98.6	..	..	..
1920 - 22	862	442	420	1 051	22.8	91.1	..	..	..
1930 - 32	632	323	309	1 047	15.8	64.4	..	27.0	..
1940 - 42	607	312	295	1 057	15.6	61.3	1.81	22.0	..
1950 - 52	683	351	332	1 058	15.6	72.1	2.16	16.0	..
1960 - 62	812	418	394	1 061	17.6	88.9	2.77	15.6	18.9
1970 - 72	764	394	371	1 061	15.6	81.4	2.31	9.7	12.5
1980 - 82	639	328	311	1 053	12.9	61.8	1.81	4.3	6.7
1990 - 92	698	358	340	1 051	13.8	64.0	..	3.2	4.5
	BBCB	KMFY	KMFZ	KMGA	KMGB	KMGC	KMGD	KMGE	KMGF
1985	656	337	320	1 054	13.2	61.0	1.78	3.6	5.5
1986	661	339	322	1 052	13.2	60.6	1.77	3.5	5.3
1987	682	350	332	1 053	13.6	62.0	1.81	3.4	5.0
1988	694	355	339	1 048	13.8	63.0	1.82	3.4	4.9
1989	688	352	335	1 051	13.6	62.5	1.80	3.2	4.7
1990	706	361	345	1 048	14.0	64.2	1.84	3.3	4.6
1991	699	358	341	1 052	13.8	63.6	1.82	3.3	4.6
1992	690	354	336	1 053	13.6	63.6	1.80	3.0	4.3
1993	673	346	328	1 056	13.2	62.6	1.76	3.9	5.7
1994	665	341	323	1 055	13.0	62.0	1.75	3.8	5.7
1995	648	332	316	1 051	12.7	60.5	1.71	3.6	5.5
1996	649	333	316	1 055	12.7	60.6	1.73	3.5	5.4
1997	643	330	314	1 051	12.5	60.0	1.73	3.4	5.3
1998	636	326	310	1 051	12.3	59.2	1.72	3.4	5.3
1999	622	319	303	1 055	12.0	57.8	1.70	3.3	5.3
2000	604	310	295	1 050	11.6	55.9	1.65	3.2	5.3
2001	595	305	290	1 050	11.4	54.8	1.64	3.2	5.3

5.15 Births[1]
Annual averages or calendar years
continued

Thousands

	Live births				Rates				
	Total	Male	Female	Sex ratio[2]	Crude birth rate[3]	General fertility rate[4]	TFR[5]	Still-births[6]	Still-birth rate[6]
Scotland[8]									
1900 - 02	132	67	65	1 046	29.5	120.6	..	..	..
1910 - 12	123	63	60	1 044	25.9	107.4	..	..	..
1920 - 22	125	64	61	1 046	25.6	105.9	..	..	..
1930 - 32	93	47	45	1 040	19.1	78.8	..	..	..
1940 - 42	89	46	43	1 051	18.5	73.7	..	4.0	..
1950 - 52	91	47	44	1 060	17.9	81.4	2.41	2.0	..
1960 - 62	102	53	50	1 060	19.7	97.8	2.98	2.2	20.8
1970 - 72	84	43	41	1 057	16.1	83.3	2.46	1.1	13.5
1980 - 82	68	35	33	1 051	13.1	62.2	1.80	0.4	6.3
1990 - 92	66	34	32	1 052	13.0	59.1	1.68	0.4	5.7
	BBCD	KMEU	KMEV	KMEW	KMEX	KMEY	KMEZ	KMFM	KMFN
1985	67	34	33	1 048	13.0	59.5	1.70	0.4	5.5
1986	66	34	32	1 061	12.9	58.5	1.67	0.4	5.8
1987	66	34	32	1 053	13.0	58.8	1.67	0.3	5.1
1988	66	34	32	1 059	13.0	59.1	1.68	0.4	5.4
1989	63	33	31	1 049	12.5	56.8	1.61	0.3	5.0
1990	66	34	32	1 057	12.9	58.8	1.66	0.3	5.3
1991	67	34	33	1 056	13.1	59.8	1.69	0.4	5.5
1992	66	34	32	1 044	12.9	59.3	1.68	0.4	5.4
1993	63	32	31	1 046	12.4	57.4	1.61	0.4	6.4
1994	62	31	30	1 038	12.0	56.0	1.58	0.4	6.1
1995	60	31	29	1 043	11.7	54.5	1.55	0.4	6.6
1996	59	31	29	1 061	11.6	54.0	1.55	0.4	6.4
1997	59	31	29	1 055	11.6	54.3	1.58	0.3	5.3
1998	57	29	28	1 060	11.2	52.6	1.55	0.4	6.1
1999	55	28	27	1 050	10.8	50.8	1.51	0.3	5.2
2000	53	27	26	1 051	10.5	49.1	1.48	0.3	5.6
2001	53	27	26	1 041	10.4	48.8	1.49	0.3	5.7
Northern Ireland[7,8]									
1900 - 02	..	..	..	..	..	..	..	..	..
1910 - 12	..	..	..	..	..	..	..	..	..
1920 - 22	31	16	15	1 048	24.2	105.9	..	..	..
1930 - 32	26	13	12	1 047	20.5	78.8	..	..	..
1940 - 42	27	14	13	1 078	20.8	73.7	..	..	..
1950 - 52	29	15	14	1 066	20.9	81.4	..	..	..
1960 - 62	31	16	15	1 068	22.5	111.5	3.47	0.7	22.0
1970 - 72	31	16	15	1 074	20.4	105.7	3.13	0.5	14.3
1980 - 82	28	14	13	1 048	18.0	87.5	2.59	0.2	8.4
1990 - 92	26	13	13	1 051	16.0	74.8	2.15	0.1	4.6
	BBCE	KMFO	KMFP	KMFQ	KMFR	KMFS	KMFT	KMFU	KMFV
1985	27	14	13	1 054	17.5	82.1	2.45	0.2	6.4
1986	28	15	13	1 076	17.8	82.7	2.44	0.1	4.4
1987	28	14	13	1 055	17.5	81.2	2.39	0.2	6.1
1988	28	14	13	1 056	17.4	80.6	2.35	0.1	5.0
1989	26	13	13	1 063	16.2	75.5	2.19	0.1	5.1
1990	26	13	13	1 049	16.5	76.5	2.21	0.1	4.4
1991	26	13	13	1 066	16.2	75.1	2.16	0.1	4.7
1992	25	13	12	1 040	15.6	72.7	2.09	0.1	4.9
1993	25	13	12	1 025	15.1	70.3	2.01	0.1	5.2
1994	24	12	12	1 053	14.7	68.0	1.95	0.2	6.3
1995	24	12	11	1 078	14.4	66.6	1.91	0.1	6.1
1996	24	12	12	1 032	14.7	67.8	1.96	0.2	6.2
1997	24	12	12	1 048	14.4	66.4	1.93	0.1	5.4
1998	24	12	12	1 039	14.1	65.0	1.90	0.1	5.1
1999	23	12	11	1 084	13.7	62.9	1.86	0.1	5.7
2000	22	11	10	1 070	12.8	58.7	1.75	0.1	4.3
2001	22	11	11	1 058	13.0	59.7	1.80	0.1	5.1

1 See chapter text.
2 Males per 1,000 females (in whole numbers).
3 Rate per 1,000 population and produced using whole numbers.
4 Rate per 1,000 women aged 15 - 44.
5 Total period fertility rate is the average number of children which would be born to a woman if she experienced the age-specific fertility rates of the period in question throughout her child-bearing life span. UK figures for the years 1970-72 and earlier are estimates.
6 On 1 October 1992 the legal definition of a stillbirth was changed from a baby born dead after 28 completed weeks gestation or more to one born dead after 24 completed weeks gestation or more. Between 1 October and 31 December 1992 in the UK there were 258 babies born dead between 24 and 27 completed weeks gestation (216 in England and Wales, 35 in

Scotland and 7 in Northern Ireland). If these babies were included in the still-birth figures given, the stillbirth rate would be 4.7 for the UK and England and Wales, while Scotland and Northern Ireland stillbirth rate would remain as stated.
7 From 1981, data for the United Kingdom and Northern Ireland exclude births in Northern Ireland to non-residents of Northern Ireland.
8 Mid-year population estimates for England & Wales, United Kingdom, Scotland and Northern Ireland 2001 are based on the 2001 Census. See chapter text.

Sources: Office for National Statistics: 020 7533 5113;
General Register Office for Scotland;
Northern Ireland Statistics and Research Agency

5.16 Birth occurrence inside and outside marriage by age of mother

Thousands

	Inside marriage						Outside marriage					
	All ages	Under 20	20 - 24	25 - 29	Over 30	Mean[1] age (Years)	All ages	Under 20	20 - 24	25 - 29	Over 30	Mean[1] age (Years)
United Kingdom[2]												
	KKEY	KKEZ	KKFY	KKFZ	KKGX	KKGY	KKGZ	KKIC	KKID	KKIE	KKIF	KKIG
1961	890	55	273	280	282	27.7	54	13	17	10	13	25.5
1971	828	70	301	271	185	26.4	74	24	25	13	12	23.8
1981	640	36	193	231	180	27.3	91	30	33	16	13	23.4
1986	596	21	159	231	185	27.9	158	45	60	31	22	23.7
1987	598	18	153	235	192	28.1	178	48	68	37	26	23.9
1988	589	16	144	234	195	28.2	198	51	76	42	29	24.1
1989	570	14	130	228	198	28.4	207	49	79	46	32	24.3
1990	576	13	121	233	209	28.6	223	51	83	53	37	24.5
1991	556	10	109	224	213	28.9	236	50	87	58	41	24.8
1992	540	9	98	216	218	29.1	241	46	86	62	46	25.1
1993	520	8	87	204	221	29.3	242	44	84	64	50	25.4
1994	510	7	78	194	231	29.6	240	41	80	65	55	25.7
1995	486	6	69	180	232	29.8	246	42	79	66	60	25.9
1996	473	6	61	170	237	30.1	260	45	80	69	66	26.0
1997	460	6	55	159	240	30.3	267	47	79	71	71	26.1
1998	447	6	51	149	243	30.5	270	49	77	70	74	26.2
1999	428	6	47	136	239	30.7	272	49	77	68	77	26.3
2000	411	5	44	126	237	30.9	268	47	77	66	78	26.4
2001	401	5	44	116	236	30.9	268	45	77	64	82	26.7
Great Britain												
	KKIH	KKII	KKIJ	KKIK	KKIL	KKIM	KKIN	KKIO	KKIP	KKIQ	KKIR	KKIS
1961	859	53	264	270	272	27.7	53	13	17	10	13	25.5
1971	797	68	293	261	176	26.4	73	24	25	13	12	23.8
1981	614	34	186	223	171	27.2	89	29	32	16	13	23.3
1986	572	20	153	222	177	27.9	155	44	59	30	22	22.9
1987	574	17	147	227	184	28.0	174	46	66	36	25	23.4
1988	566	16	138	226	186	28.2	194	49	74	42	29	23.6
1989	549	13	125	220	190	28.4	202	48	77	45	32	24.2
1990	554	12	116	225	201	28.6	218	49	81	52	36	24.6
1991	535	10	105	216	205	28.9	231	48	85	57	41	24.8
1992	520	9	94	208	210	29.1	235	45	84	61	46	25.1
1993	500	7	84	196	213	29.3	236	42	82	62	49	25.4
1994	492	7	75	188	222	29.6	235	41	78	63	53	25.7
1995	468	6	66	173	223	29.8	240	40	77	65	59	25.9
1996	455	6	59	163	227	30.1	254	44	78	68	65	26.0
1997	442	6	53	152	231	30.3	261	46	76	69	69	26.2
1998	430	6	49	143	233	30.5	263	48	74	68	73	26.3
1999	412	6	46	131	230	30.7	265	48	74	67	76	26.4
2000	396	5	43	121	228	30.9	261	46	74	65	77	26.5
2001	386	5	43	112	227	30.9	261	44	75	62	80	26.6

1 The mean ages presented in this table do not take into account the changing population distribution of women.
2 From 1981, data for the United Kingdom exclude births in Northern Ireland to non-residents of Northern Ireland.

Sources: Office for National Statistics: 01329 813339; General Register Office for Scotland; Northern Ireland Statistics and Research Agency

5.17 Live births by age of mother[1]

Numbers

All live births - United Kingdom[2,3]

Age-group:	Under 20	20 - 24	25 - 29	30 - 34	35 - 39	40 - 44	45 and over	All ages
	KMDV	KMDW	KMDX	KMDY	KMDZ	KMES	KMET	KMBZ
1991	59 702	196 193	282 069	182 637	60 539	10 449	577	792 269
1992	54 922	184 359	277 315	189 020	63 768	10 802	553	780 799
1993	51 463	171 096	267 413	193 565	66 235	11 123	582	761 526
1994	47 874	157 468	259 367	202 880	70 871	11 432	536	750 480
1995	47 646	147 056	246 017	204 601	73 945	12 008	585	731 882
1996	50 793	141 090	238 857	210 490	78 335	12 832	638	733 163
1997	52 851	133 257	229 429	212 162	84 508	13 731	618	726 622
1998	54 822	127 230	218 072	212 876	88 729	14 453	640	716 888
1999	54 921	124 036	204 808	208 986	91 272	15 210	695	699 976
2000	52 060	120 304	191 583	202 893	95 400	16 032	708	679 029
2001	50 157	121 664	179 776	202 017	97 379	17 271	831	669 123

Age-specific fertility rates - United Kingdom[2,3]

Age-group:	Under 20	20 - 24	25 - 29	30 - 34	35 - 39	40 - 44	45 and over	All ages
	KMBR	KMBS	KMBT	KMBU	KMBV	KMBW	KMBX	KMBY
1991	32.9	88.9	119.9	86.5	32.0	5.0	0.3	63.6
1992	31.8	85.5	117.5	87.0	33.2	5.5	0.3	63.4
1993	30.9	81.7	114.0	86.8	34.0	5.8	0.3	62.4
1994	28.9	78.1	111.7	88.4	35.6	6.0	0.3	61.6
1995	28.4	75.5	108.0	87.1	36.3	6.4	0.3	60.1
1996	29.8	75.9	106.1	88.5	37.3	6.8	0.3	60.2
1997	30.3	75.0	103.9	88.8	39.2	7.2	0.3	59.6
1998	30.9	73.7	101.1	89.6	40.1	7.4	0.3	58.6
1999	30.9	71.9	97.8	88.8	40.1	7.7	0.4	57.3
2000	29.4	68.8	93.7	87.6	41.0	7.8	0.4	55.4
2001	27.9	68.2	91.8	88.2	41.4	8.2	0.4	54.5

All live births - England and Wales

Age-group:	Under 20	20 - 24	25 - 29	30 - 34	35 - 39	40 - 44	45 and over	All ages
	KGSA	KGSB	KGSC	KGSD	KGSE	KGSF	KGSG	KGSH
1991	52 396	173 356	248 727	161 259	53 644	9 316	519	699 217
1992	47 861	163 311	244 798	166 839	56 650	9 696	501	689 656
1993	45 121	151 975	235 961	171 061	58 824	9 986	539	673 467
1994	42 026	140 240	229 102	179 568	63 061	10 241	488	664 726
1995	41 938	130 744	217 418	181 202	65 517	10 779	540	648 138
1996	44 667	125 732	211 103	186 377	69 503	11 516	587	649 485
1997	46 372	118 589	202 792	187 528	74 900	12 332	582	643 095
1998	48 285	113 537	193 144	188 499	78 881	12 980	575	635 901
1999	48 375	110 722	181 931	185 311	81 281	13 617	635	621 872
2000	45 846	107 741	170 701	180 113	84 974	14 403	663	604 441
2001	44 189	108 844	159 926	178 920	86 495	15 499	761	594 634

Age-specific fertility rates - England and Wales

Age-group:	Under 20	20 - 24	25 - 29	30 - 34	35 - 39	40 - 44	45 and over	All ages
	KGSI	KGSJ	KGSK	KGSL	KGSM	KGSN	KGSO	KGSP
1991	33.0	89.3	119.4	86.7	32.1	5.1	0.3	63.6
1992	31.8	86.1	117.2	87.2	33.5	5.5	0.3	63.5
1993	31.1	82.6	113.8	86.9	34.3	5.9	0.3	62.6
1994	29.1	79.2	111.6	88.6	36.0	6.1	0.3	62.0
1995	28.7	76.5	108.0	87.3	36.6	6.5	0.3	60.5
1996	30.0	77.2	106.2	88.5	37.7	6.9	0.3	60.6
1997	30.4	76.1	103.9	88.7	39.5	7.4	0.3	60.0
1998	31.1	75.0	101.2	89.7	40.5	7.6	0.3	59.2
1999	31.1	73.1	98.0	89.0	40.6	7.8	0.4	57.8
2000	29.5	70.1	94.0	87.8	41.3	8.0	0.4	55.9
2001	28.0	69.3	91.9	88.2	41.6	8.4	0.5	54.8

5.17 Live births by age of mother[1]
continued

Numbers

All live births - Scotland[2]

Age-group:	Under 20	20 - 24	25 - 29	30 - 34	35 - 39	40 - 44	45 and over	All ages
	KGTA	KGTB	KGTC	KGTD	KGTE	KGTF	KGTG	KGTH
1991	5 523	16 723	24 163	15 206	4 589	686	31	67 024
1992	5 206	15 405	23 571	15 973	4 877	674	23	65 789
1993[1]	4 750	13 923	22 758	16 088	5 049	697	23	63 337
1994	4 303	12 637	21 851	16 705	5 346	736	26	61 656
1995	4 280	11 913	20 395	16 803	5 799	811	26	60 051
1996	4 544	11 026	19 511	17 038	6 126	891	32	59 296
1997	4 835	10 607	18 782	17 455	6 740	936	19	59 440
1998	4 802	9 804	17 477	17 207	6 893	1 027	43	57 319
1999	4 755	9 440	16 011	16 722	7 034	1 096	41	55 147
2000	4 599	8 962	14 676	16 233	7 395	1 133	29	53 076
2001	4 444	9 121	13 763	16 206	7 701	1 224	40	52 527

Age-specific fertility rates - Scotland[2]

Age-group:	Under 20	20 - 24	25 - 29	30 - 34	35 - 39	40 - 44	45 and over	All ages
	KGTI	KGTJ	KGTK	KGTL	KGTM	KGTN	KGTO	KGTP
1991	33.3	82.3	116.5	78.3	26.8	4.0	0.2	59.8
1992	33.1	77.6	113.6	80.7	27.8	4.1	0.1	59.3
1993	31.2	72.4	109.7	79.7	28.0	4.3	0.1	57.4
1994	28.4	68.2	106.1	81.2	28.9	4.5	0.2	56.0
1995	28.1	66.7	100.8	80.5	30.5	5.0	0.2	54.5
1996	29.6	64.6	97.9	81.6	31.4	5.4	0.2	54.0
1997	30.9	65.5	97.0	83.5	33.9	5.5	0.1	54.3
1998	30.4	62.7	94.2	82.6	34.1	6.0	0.3	52.6
1999	30.0	60.7	90.4	81.3	34.2	6.2	0.2	50.8
2000	29.3	57.6	86.5	81.4	35.9	6.0	0.2	49.2
2001	28.4	57.8	85.1	82.2	36.9	6.3	0.2	48.8

All live births - Northern Ireland[3]

Age-group:	Under 20	20 - 24	25 - 29	30 - 34	35 - 39	40 - 44	45 and over	All ages
	KMDF	KMDG	KMDH	KMDI	KMDJ	KMDK	KMDL	KMDM
1991	1 783	6 114	9 179	6 172	2 306	447	27	26 028
1992	1 855	5 643	8 946	6 208	2 241	432	29	25 354
1993	1 592	5 198	8 694	6 416	2 362	440	20	24 722
1994	1 545	4 591	8 414	6 607	2 464	455	22	24 098
1995	1 428	4 399	8 204	6 596	2 629	418	19	23 693
1996	1 582	4 332	8 243	7 075	2 706	425	19	24 382
1997	1 644	4 061	7 855	7 179	2 868	463	17	24 087
1998	1 735	3 889	7 451	7 170	2 955	446	22	23 668
1999	1 791	3 874	6 866	6 953	2 957	497	19	22 957
2000	1 615	3 601	6 206	6 547	3 031	496	16	21 512
2001	1 524	3 699	6 087	6 891	3 183	548	30	21 962

Age-specific fertility rates - Northern Ireland[3]

Age - group:	Under 20	20 - 24	25 - 29	30 - 34	35 - 39	40 - 44	45 and over	All ages
	KMDN	KMDO	KMDP	KMDQ	KMDR	KMDS	KMDT	KMDU
1991	28.7	97.2	146.4	105.3	45.8	9.0	0.6	75.1
1992	30.2	90.2	141.3	103.1	43.0	8.8	0.6	72.7
1993	26.1	83.3	136.1	104.3	43.9	8.9	0.4	70.3
1994	25.4	75.0	131.2	104.9	44.3	9.2	0.4	68.0
1995	23.4	73.5	129.1	102.7	45.5	8.4	0.4	66.6
1996	25.7	73.8	129.4	108.3	45.4	8.4	0.4	67.8
1997	26.4	71.1	124.2	109.2	46.6	8.8	0.3	66.4
1998	27.8	69.6	119.0	108.4	47.2	8.2	0.4	65.0
1999	28.6	70.6	112.3	105.6	46.1	8.9	0.4	62.9
2000	25.6	66.0	103.9	100.4	46.2	8.5	0.3	58.7
2001	23.9	67.5	105.1	106.0	48.0	9.1	0.6	59.7

1 2001 mid-year population estimates for England & Wales, United Kingdom, Scotland and Northern Ireland are based on the 2001 Census. See chapter text.

2 The 'All ages' figure for Scotland includes births to mothers whose age was not known. There were 65 such births in 1990, 103 in 1991, 60 in 1992, 49 in 1993, 52 in 1994, 24 in 1995, 128 in 1996, 66 in 1997, 66 in 1998, 48 in 1999 and 49 in 2000 and 28 in 2001.

3 Data for the United Kingdom and Northern Ireland exclude births in Northern Ireland to non-residents of Northern Ireland.

Sources: Office for National Statistics: 01329 813339;
General Register Office for Scotland;
Northern Ireland Statistics and Research Agency

5.18 Legal abortions
Total by age for residents

Numbers

	All ages	Under 15	15	16 - 19	20 - 24	25 - 29	30 - 34	35 - 39	40 - 44	45 and over	Not stated
England and Wales											
1986	147 619	924	2 970	33 819	45 316	28 656	18 005	12 977	4 521	409	22
1987	156 191	907	2 858	35 167	49 256	31 243	18 960	12 639	4 757	390	14
1988	168 298	859	2 709	37 928	54 067	34 584	20 000	12 681	5 047	412	11
1989	170 463	803	2 580	36 182	54 880	36 604	21 284	12 713	5 020	388	9
1990	173 900	873	2 549	35 520	55 281	38 770	22 431	12 956	5 104	404	12
1991	167 376	886	2 272	31 130	52 678	38 611	23 445	13 035	4 901	408	10
1992	160 501	905	2 095	27 589	49 052	38 430	23 870	13 252	4 844	452	12
1993	157 846	964	2 119	25 806	46 846	38 139	24 690	13 885	4 889	494	14
1994	156 539	1 080	2 166	25 223	44 871	38 081	25 507	14 156	5 008	440	7
1995	154 315	946	2 324	24 945	43 394	37 254	25 759	14 352	4 868	457	16
1996	167 916	1 098	2 547	28 790	46 356	39 311	28 228	16 118	5 027	428	13
1997	170 145	1 020	2 414	29 947	44 960	40 159	28 892	16 858	5 413	482	-
1998	177 871	1 103	2 656	33 236	45 766	40 366	30 449	18 174	5 576	511	34
1999	173 701	1 066	2 537	32 807	45 004	38 492	29 139	18 341	5 755	502	58
2000	175 542	1 048	2 700	33 218	47 099	37 852	28 735	18 589	5 794	459	48
2001	176 364	1 066	2 592	33 431	48 267	36 506	28 782	19 146	6 094	456	24
Scotland											
1986	9 628	74	236	2 529	2 985	1 744	1 081	708	249	22	
1987	9 460	70	210	2 417	2 996	1 729	1 082	697	242	17	
1988	10 128	65	218	2 529	3 304	1 970	1 107	663	257	15	
1989	10 209	53	209	2 561	3 202	1 968	1 229	706	266	15	
1990	10 219	54	186	2 539	3 242	2 063	1 161	700	253	21	
1991	11 068	77	203	2 571	3 486	2 253	1 445	743	262	28	
1992	10 818	73	174	2 377	3 389	2 291	1 444	799	254	17	
1993	11 076	92	193	2 300	3 368	2 447	1 492	891	264	29	
1994	11 392	78	215	2 312	3 486	2 431	1 648	877	315	30	
1995	11 143	79	233	2 169	3 399	2 438	1 609	887	296	33	
1996	11 978	87	236	2 362	3 571	2 603	1 801	960	331	27	
1997	12 109	85	204	2 431	3 444	2 651	1 854	1 093	322	25	
1998	12 485	73	213	2 707	3 426	2 749	1 807	1 149	339	22	
1999	12 167	69	182	2 635	3 354	2 553	1 810	1 180	361	23	
2000	11 995	93	181	2 610	3 355	2 403	1 768	1 176	381	28	
2001	12 052	66	210	2 706	3 439	2 308	1 806	1 120	374	23	

Sources: Office for National Statistics;
Scottish Executive

5.19 Deaths: analysis by age and sex[1]
Annual averages or calendar years

Numbers

United Kingdom

	All ages[2]	Under 1 year	1-4	5-9	10-14	15-19	20-24	25-34	35-44	45-54	55-64	65-74	75-84	85 and over
Males														
1900 - 02	340 664	87 242	37 834	8 429	4 696	7 047	8 766	19 154	24 739	30 488	37 610	39 765	28 320	6 563
1910 - 12	303 703	63 885	29 452	7 091	4 095	5 873	6 817	16 141	21 813	28 981	37 721	45 140	29 397	7 283
1920 - 22	284 876	48 044	19 008	6 052	3 953	5 906	6 572	13 663	19 702	29 256	40 583	49 398	34 937	7 801
1930 - 32	284 249	28 840	11 276	4 580	2 890	5 076	6 495	12 327	16 326	29 376	47 989	63 804	45 247	10 022
1940 - 42	314 643	24 624	6 949	3 400	2 474	4 653	4 246	11 506	17 296	30 082	57 076	79 652	59 733	12 900
1950 - 52	307 312	14 105	2 585	1 317	919	1 498	2 289	5 862	11 074	27 637	53 691	86 435	79 768	20 131
1960 - 62	318 850	12 234	1 733	971	871	1 718	1 857	3 842	8 753	26 422	63 009	87 542	83 291	26 605
1970 - 72	335 166	9 158	1 485	1 019	802	1 778	2 104	3 590	7 733	24 608	64 898	105 058	82 905	30 027
1980 - 82	330 495	4 829	774	527	652	1 999	1 943	3 736	6 568	19 728	54 159	105 155	98 488	31 936
1990 - 92	312 521	3 315	623	372	396	1 349	2 059	4 334	6 979	15 412	40 424	87 849	106 376	43 032
	KHUA	KHUB	KHUC	KHUD	KHUE	KHUF	KHUG	KHUH	KHUI	KHUJ	KHUK	KHUL	KHUM	KHUN
1981	329 145	4 759	771	517	666	2 008	1 919	3 761	6 544	19 740	53 770	104 950	97 881	31 859
1982	329 971	4 555	760	456	632	1 966	1 971	3 661	6 462	18 867	53 531	103 426	101 281	32 403
1983	328 824	4 230	695	469	609	1 834	1 899	3 601	6 537	18 238	54 493	100 469	103 038	32 712
1984	321 095	3 995	725	423	580	1 708	1 999	3 595	6 425	17 647	53 715	95 420	102 513	32 350
1985	331 562	4 003	728	393	583	1 612	2 031	3 452	6 728	17 316	52 502	97 458	109 241	35 515
1986	327 160	4 219	653	384	444	1 676	2 067	3 668	6 712	16 814	50 352	95 987	108 123	36 061
1987	318 282	4 105	657	377	470	1 612	2 125	3 776	6 793	15 950	47 675	93 348	105 773	35 621
1988	319 119	4 110	680	433	460	1 525	2 160	3 983	6 860	16 016	46 001	91 893	107 082	37 916
1989	320 193	3 799	699	414	398	1 537	2 118	3 968	6 832	15 560	43 693	90 304	109 450	41 421
1990	314 601	3 614	674	376	406	1 487	2 197	4 354	6 991	15 507	41 983	88 458	107 451	41 103
1991	314 427	3 377	636	395	404	1 417	2 049	4 270	7 102	15 493	40 256	88 014	107 416	43 598
1992	308 535	2 954	559	346	377	1 144	1 932	4 379	6 845	15 236	39 033	87 075	104 261	44 394
1993[1]	317 796	2 746	582	325	401	1 072	1 907	4 442	6 672	15 631	38 734	90 160	105 693	49 431
1994	303 333	2 660	497	319	400	1 041	1 829	4 741	6 661	14 983	36 469	86 896	98 982	47 855
1995	310 722	2 595	447	314	388	1 115	1 810	4 748	6 754	15 644	36 068	85 459	103 324	52 056
1996	305 323	2 562	489	267	352	1 104	1 693	4 746	6 789	15 796	35 033	81 333	102 090	53 069
1997	300 414	2 391	456	300	364	1 111	1 712	4 583	6 667	15 689	33 707	77 870	101 365	54 199
1998	300 160	2 327	463	283	343	1 058	1 539	4 684	6 902	15 825	33 778	75 718	101 468	55 772
1999	300 368	2 318	456	257	319	1 085	1 553	4 516	6 946	15 849	33 338	73 736	101 795	58 200
2000	290 186	2 120	380	253	326	1 042	1 491	4 397	7 081	15 470	32 556	69 499	98 075	57 496
2001	286 760	2 042	347	223	330	1 061	1 508	4 262	7 156	15 515	32 005	66 111	97 816	58 384
Females														
1900 - 02	322 058	68 770	36 164	8 757	5 034	6 818	8 264	18 702	21 887	25 679	34 521	42 456	34 907	10 099
1910 - 12	289 608	49 865	27 817	7 113	4 355	5 683	6 531	15 676	19 647	24 481	32 813	46 453	37 353	11 828
1920 - 22	274 772	35 356	17 323	5 808	4 133	5 729	6 753	14 878	18 121	24 347	34 026	48 573	45 521	14 203
1930 - 32	275 336	21 072	9 995	3 990	2 734	4 721	5 931	12 699	15 373	24 695	39 471	59 520	56 250	18 886
1940 - 42	296 646	17 936	5 952	2 743	2 068	4 180	5 028	11 261	14 255	23 629	42 651	70 907	71 377	24 658
1950 - 52	291 597	10 293	2 098	880	625	1 115	1 717	5 018	8 989	18 875	37 075	75 220	92 848	36 844
1960 - 62	304 871	8 887	1 334	627	522	684	811	2 504	6 513	16 720	36 078	73 118	105 956	51 117
1970 - 72	322 968	6 666	1 183	654	459	718	900	2 110	5 345	15 594	36 177	75 599	109 539	68 024
1980 - 82	330 269	3 561	585	355	425	733	772	2 099	4 360	12 206	32 052	72 618	117 760	82 743
1990 - 92	328 218	2 431	485	259	255	520	714	1 989	4 340	9 707	25 105	61 951	115 467	104 994
	KIUA	KIUB	KIUC	KIUD	KIUE	KIUF	KIUG	KIUH	KIUI	KIUJ	KIUK	KIUL	KIUM	KIUN
1981	328 829	3 402	599	352	424	738	737	2 083	4 309	12 275	31 625	72 476	117 458	82 351
1982	332 830	3 342	561	304	410	689	767	2 057	4 312	11 759	32 183	71 705	119 362	85 379
1983	330 277	3 126	568	318	374	719	698	1 914	4 318	11 384	32 197	69 266	118 940	86 455
1984	323 824	3 005	537	304	344	665	722	1 932	4 269	10 947	32 262	66 432	116 649	85 756
1985	339 094	3 027	574	314	355	626	729	1 852	4 397	10 581	32 010	68 505	122 445	93 679
1986	333 575	2 961	561	275	307	635	769	1 882	4 387	10 211	29 954	67 313	120 663	93 657
1987	326 060	2 972	550	265	288	614	733	1 974	4 454	10 177	29 037	65 570	117 266	92 160
1988	330 059	2 951	552	264	251	612	745	1 915	4 615	9 887	28 154	65 020	117 731	97 362
1989	337 540	2 743	551	271	268	598	773	1 955	4 506	9 834	27 324	64 575	120 975	103 167
1990	327 198	2 658	489	249	273	534	700	1 967	4 463	9 718	26 350	62 019	116 357	101 421
1991	331 754	2 448	512	280	264	538	738	2 005	4 295	9 699	24 952	62 200	116 924	106 899
1992	325 703	2 187	455	249	228	489	704	1 994	4 262	9 705	24 013	61 635	113 119	106 663
1993[1]	340 685	2 084	436	239	283	465	659	2 121	4 204	9 973	23 900	63 767	114 905	117 649
1994	324 303	1 989	410	205	232	406	626	2 053	4 285	10 081	22 401	62 069	106 816	112 730
1995	334 771	1 931	370	224	250	449	592	2 140	4 203	10 389	22 093	60 988	110 247	120 895
1996	330 701	1 904	355	214	224	493	589	2 140	4 215	10 301	21 406	57 889	109 578	121 393
1997	329 332	1 862	333	215	239	487	574	1 960	4 323	10 412	20 999	55 687	108 276	123 965
1998	329 012	1 752	347	213	215	486	568	1 971	4 289	10 430	20 874	54 200	107 135	126 532
1999	331 694	1 727	338	195	240	473	553	1 924	4 372	10 430	21 045	52 240	106 841	131 316
2000	318 180	1 671	277	177	203	449	535	1 961	4 509	10 459	20 533	48 994	101 711	126 701
2001	315 508	1 622	297	208	207	439	552	1 821	4 385	10 287	20 481	46 964	100 907	127 338

5.19 Deaths: analysis by age and sex[1]
Annual averages or calendar years
continued

Numbers

	All ages[2]	Under 1 year	1-4	5-9	10-14	15-19	20-24	25-34	35-44	45-54	55-64	65-74	75-84	85 and over
Males														
1900 - 02	288 886	76 095	32 051	7 066	3 818	5 611	7 028	15 869	21 135	26 065	31 600	33 568	23 835	5 144
1910 - 12	257 253	54 678	24 676	5 907	3 348	4 765	5 596	13 603	18 665	24 820	32 217	38 016	24 928	6 036
1920 - 22	240 605	39 796	15 565	5 151	3 314	4 901	5 447	11 551	17 004	25 073	34 639	42 025	29 685	6 455
1930 - 32	243 147	23 331	9 099	3 844	2 435	4 354	5 580	10 600	14 041	25 657	41 581	54 910	39 091	8 624
1940 - 42	268 876	19 393	5 616	2 834	2 051	3 832	3 156	9 484	14 744	25 983	50 058	68 791	51 779	11 158
1950 - 52	266 879	11 498	2 131	1 087	778	1 248	1 947	4 990	9 489	23 815	46 948	75 774	69 496	17 677
1960 - 62	278 369	10 157	1 444	812	742	1 523	1 624	3 278	7 524	22 813	54 908	77 000	73 180	23 364
1970 - 72	293 934	7 818	1 259	860	677	1 524	1 788	3 079	6 637	21 348	56 667	92 389	73 365	26 522
1980 - 82	290 352	4 168	657	452	555	1 716	1 619	3 169	5 590	16 909	47 144	92 485	87 338	28 551
1990 - 92	275 550	2 926	545	325	338	1 157	1 757	3 717	6 057	13 258	34 977	77 063	94 672	38 757
	KHVA	KHVB	KHVC	KHVD	KHVE	KHVF	KHVG	KHVH	KHVI	KHVJ	KHVK	KHVL	KHVM	KHVN
1981	289 022	4 119	651	447	573	1 734	1 576	3 181	5 535	16 889	46 858	92 189	86 714	28 496
1982	290 166	3 914	652	391	546	1 669	1 668	3 122	5 526	16 144	46 521	91 079	89 940	28 994
1983	289 419	3 654	604	391	514	1 580	1 635	3 071	5 581	15 632	47 315	88 622	91 531	29 289
1984	282 357	3 443	610	348	501	1 484	1 728	3 033	5 512	15 113	46 904	83 728	90 983	28 970
1985	292 327	3 510	638	328	503	1 374	1 738	2 953	5 776	14 838	45 704	85 695	97 362	31 908
1986	287 894	3 724	573	325	380	1 429	1 746	3 104	5 767	14 370	43 637	84 437	96 201	32 201
1987	280 177	3 637	578	309	404	1 389	1 811	3 218	5 823	13 678	41 367	82 021	94 060	31 882
1988	280 931	3 649	587	374	402	1 279	1 802	3 367	5 855	13 701	39 791	80 870	95 306	33 948
1989	281 290	3 368	606	371	337	1 325	1 782	3 380	5 947	13 407	37 680	79 012	97 027	37 048
1990	277 336	3 207	593	333	338	1 295	1 889	3 714	6 060	13 342	36 405	77 604	95 539	37 017
1991	277 582	2 966	554	341	354	1 208	1 760	3 687	6 160	13 316	34 853	77 227	95 815	39 341
1992	271 732	2 606	487	302	322	969	1 621	3 751	5 952	13 117	33 674	76 357	92 662	39 912
1993[1]	279 561	2 407	510	276	340	912	1 596	3 813	5 784	13 416	33 347	78 881	93 754	44 525
1994	267 555	2 367	432	278	331	843	1 550	4 065	5 769	12 923	31 320	76 270	88 230	43 177
1995	274 449	2 305	391	269	340	910	1 533	4 043	5 880	13 487	30 973	74 970	92 291	47 057
1996	268 682	2 272	441	236	291	925	1 409	4 064	5 843	13 565	30 066	71 046	90 708	47 816
1997	264 865	2 137	412	267	325	947	1 442	3 940	5 707	13 484	28 907	68 024	90 207	49 066
1998	264 707	2 070	413	240	291	875	1 292	4 013	5 895	13 595	29 052	66 099	90 450	50 422
1999	264 299	2 075	405	218	275	902	1 270	3 847	5 934	13 620	28 689	64 296	90 431	52 337
2000	255 547	1 886	335	217	284	872	1 224	3 755	6 048	13 367	27 898	60 593	87 126	51 942
2001	252 426	1 808	318	185	281	882	1 266	3 633	6 065	13 271	27 469	57 492	87 013	52 743
Females														
1900 - 02	269 432	60 090	30 674	7 278	4 010	5 265	6 497	15 065	18 253	21 474	28 424	35 307	29 118	7 977
1910 - 12	242 079	42 642	23 335	5 883	3 519	4 522	5 256	12 742	16 363	20 611	27 571	38 489	31 363	9 782
1920 - 22	229 908	29 178	14 174	4 928	3 456	4 719	5 533	12 244	15 142	20 580	28 633	41 010	38 439	11 871
1930 - 32	233 915	16 929	8 013	3 338	2 293	3 969	5 039	10 716	13 022	21 190	33 798	50 844	48 531	16 234
1940 - 42	253 702	14 174	4 726	2 265	1 695	3 426	4 198	9 470	12 093	20 413	36 814	60 987	61 891	21 550
1950 - 52	252 176	8 367	1 727	732	520	893	1 365	4 131	7 586	16 161	31 875	65 087	81 154	32 579
1960 - 62	266 849	7 409	1 103	527	444	591	700	2 147	5 576	14 389	31 083	63 543	93 548	45 789
1970 - 72	284 181	5 677	1 020	562	396	620	806	1 814	4 585	13 417	31 222	65 817	96 952	61 293
1980 - 82	290 026	3 064	511	301	365	635	670	1 821	3 740	10 420	27 606	63 023	103 676	74 194
1990 - 92	288 851	2 161	420	227	217	455	625	1 718	3 765	8 347	21 466	53 783	101 752	93 914
	KIVA	KIVB	KIVC	KIVD	KIVE	KIVF	KIVG	KIVH	KIVI	KIVJ	KIVK	KIVL	KIVM	KIVN
1981	288 868	2 902	529	302	368	650	642	1 821	3 742	10 513	27 211	62 762	103 554	73 872
1982	291 695	2 861	485	253	353	588	672	1 781	3 708	9 990	27 751	62 221	104 745	76 287
1983	290 189	2 727	489	269	332	629	597	1 655	3 708	9 786	27 792	59 913	104 844	77 448
1984	284 524	2 594	454	260	302	575	621	1 676	3 658	9 343	27 764	57 813	102 744	76 720
1985	298 407	2 631	497	260	308	544	630	1 583	3 803	9 111	27 664	59 285	108 099	83 992
1986	293 309	2 589	491	248	272	562	674	1 646	3 834	8 761	25 785	58 360	106 463	83 624
1987	286 817	2 635	489	237	246	525	639	1 708	3 897	8 774	25 000	56 858	103 354	82 455
1988	290 477	2 621	498	232	218	542	650	1 670	4 025	8 448	24 104	56 567	103 666	87 236
1989	295 582	2 440	472	241	226	531	650	1 678	3 925	8 406	23 336	55 932	106 000	91 745
1990	287 510	2 357	434	220	230	472	616	1 702	3 875	8 337	22 511	53 770	102 440	90 546
1991	292 462	2 192	439	248	222	462	644	1 729	3 703	8 369	21 303	54 156	103 268	95 727
1992	286 581	1 933	387	214	199	432	615	1 722	3 717	8 336	20 585	53 423	99 548	95 470
1993[1]	299 238	1 835	374	194	246	394	575	1 802	3 625	8 614	20 423	55 245	100 947	104 964
1994	285 639	1 753	364	187	204	357	535	1 771	3 669	8 688	19 039	53 921	94 197	100 954
1995	295 234	1 677	333	196	210	382	502	1 859	3 644	9 001	18 891	52 987	97 162	108 390
1996	291 453	1 687	320	175	196	430	507	1 852	3 658	8 852	18 244	50 195	96 679	108 658
1997	290 416	1 663	297	177	209	426	490	1 718	3 737	9 016	17 949	48 293	95 508	110 933
1998	290 308	1 555	309	177	189	407	480	1 724	3 678	9 066	17 927	46 894	94 713	113 189
1999	291 819	1 546	300	168	215	385	470	1 668	3 786	9 029	18 031	45 100	93 878	117 243
2000	280 117	1 491	246	156	179	384	466	1 688	3 874	9 090	17 635	42 174	89 310	113 424
2001	277 947	1 432	270	188	178	378	467	1 591	3 768	8 917	17 610	40 465	88 808	113 875

England and Wales

5.19 Deaths: analysis by age and sex[1]
Annual averages or calendar years
continued

Numbers

	All ages[2]	Under 1 year	1-4	5-9	10-14	15-19	20-24	25-34	35-44	45-54	55-64	65-74	75-84	85 and over
Males														
1900 - 02	40 224	9 189	4 798	1 083	672	1 069	1 292	2 506	2 935	3 591	4 597	4 531	3 117	834
1910 - 12	35 981	7 510	3 935	962	595	826	910	1 969	2 469	3 325	4 356	5 113	3 182	813
1920 - 22	34 649	6 757	2 847	710	489	747	791	1 616	2 128	3 314	4 785	5 624	3 928	911
1930 - 32	32 476	4 426	1 771	610	365	568	706	1 352	1 848	2 979	5 095	6 906	4 839	1 010
1940 - 42	36 384	3 973	1 011	449	321	668	888	1 643	2 090	3 348	5 728	8 556	6 317	1 337
1950 - 52	32 236	1 949	349	175	105	200	265	693	1 267	3 151	5 574	8 544	8 094	1 871
1960 - 62	32 401	1 578	222	121	102	146	185	456	1 013	2 986	6 682	8 505	7 980	2 425
1970 - 72	32 446	944	168	119	93	178	233	396	875	2 617	6 641	10 176	7 383	2 624
1980 - 82	31 723	451	80	56	71	206	233	423	776	2 280	5 601	10 152	8 804	2 591
1990 - 92	29 421	287	57	34	40	137	230	485	744	1 730	4 402	8 611	9 311	3 353
	KHWA	KHWB	KHWC	KHWD	KHWE	KHWF	KHWG	KHWH	KHWI	KHWJ	KHWK	KHWL	KHWM	KHWN
1981	31 700	435	71	50	66	208	250	439	816	2 330	5 506	10 193	8 788	2 548
1982	31 801	436	77	53	69	220	225	410	733	2 195	5 669	10 015	9 052	2 647
1983	31 196	380	67	53	65	185	178	406	764	2 131	5 769	9 414	9 204	2 580
1984	30 731	389	87	53	65	172	202	429	696	2 017	5 493	9 337	9 222	2 569
1985	31 147	342	57	49	58	174	208	390	759	1 959	5 486	9 339	9 569	2 757
1986	31 111	334	66	44	49	177	238	436	757	1 967	5 354	9 169	9 574	2 946
1987	30 384	331	54	46	47	163	212	415	779	1 870	5 131	9 058	9 383	2 895
1988	30 195	324	64	39	42	181	246	475	808	1 915	4 997	8 763	9 314	3 027
1989	31 025	331	62	24	45	150	246	445	719	1 721	4 889	9 028	9 922	3 443
1990	29 617	297	62	31	50	138	240	502	745	1 734	4 512	8 635	9 499	3 172
1991	29 312	299	59	42	34	150	211	441	757	1 741	4 382	8 657	9 209	3 330
1992	29 334	265	51	28	36	123	238	511	731	1 716	4 313	8 541	9 225	3 556
1993[1]	30 504	240	50	39	37	107	225	490	725	1 817	4 375	9 031	9 470	3 898
1994	28 416	212	42	27	48	133	212	538	715	1 684	4 114	8 575	8 446	3 670
1995	28 791	197	37	30	30	152	195	563	698	1 746	4 144	8 449	8 604	3 946
1996	29 223	206	41	23	46	139	212	556	755	1 845	4 087	8 259	8 926	4 128
1997	28 305	186	32	22	27	114	208	521	788	1 794	3 876	7 909	8 791	4 037
1998	28 132	183	37	34	39	134	200	524	843	1 796	3 828	7 746	8 585	4 183
1999	28 605	161	31	23	33	138	215	545	818	1 820	3 773	7 569	8 908	4 571
2000	27 511	173	33	24	28	115	198	512	842	1 716	3 789	7 224	8 523	4 334
2001	27 324	155	22	27	35	131	179	510	902	1 820	3 751	6 950	8 433	4 409
Females														
1900 - 02	39 891	7 143	4 477	1 162	747	1 058	1 246	2 625	2 732	3 130	4 485	5 273	4 305	1 508
1910 - 12	36 132	5 854	3 674	981	618	836	910	2 149	2 473	2 909	3 960	5 636	4 588	1 552
1920 - 22	34 449	5 029	2 602	687	489	711	889	1 947	2 266	2 828	4 157	5 587	5 443	1 814
1930 - 32	32 377	3 319	1 602	527	339	568	666	1 508	1 812	2 731	4 380	6 630	6 178	2 117
1940 - 42	33 715	2 852	921	373	283	595	656	1 382	1 672	2 528	4 630	7 674	7 613	2 536
1950 - 52	31 525	1 432	284	115	84	185	293	714	1 127	2 188	4 204	8 157	9 310	3 431
1960 - 62	30 559	1 107	170	80	63	72	87	287	762	1 897	4 115	7 752	9 991	4 177
1970 - 72	30 978	694	118	69	46	73	74	231	608	1 769	4 036	7 823	10 112	5 324
1980 - 82	32 326	337	49	37	44	74	73	213	493	1 456	3 565	7 781	11 333	6 871
1990 - 92	31 747	190	45	20	29	49	72	218	458	1 093	2 966	6 630	11 079	8 898
	KIWA	KIWB	KIWC	KIWD	KIWE	KIWF	KIWG	KIWH	KIWI	KIWJ	KIWK	KIWL	KIWM	KIWN
1981	32 128	345	46	35	43	68	69	213	453	1 414	3 556	7 935	11 144	6 807
1982	33 221	317	50	35	45	78	60	203	479	1 444	3 552	7 735	11 867	7 356
1983	32 258	266	51	33	33	67	76	201	504	1 317	3 568	7 558	11 340	7 244
1984	31 614	283	62	32	37	72	78	205	475	1 320	3 703	6 979	11 134	7 234
1985	32 820	282	55	37	34	63	76	207	481	1 179	3 563	7 449	11 604	7 790
1986	32 356	247	50	16	24	50	77	188	441	1 181	3 372	7 251	11 476	7 983
1987	31 630	232	44	21	34	60	70	195	429	1 160	3 301	7 032	11 262	7 790
1988	31 762	219	33	22	21	54	63	197	470	1 115	3 250	6 879	11 361	8 078
1989	33 992	223	56	23	27	54	104	224	470	1 156	3 279	7 052	12 100	9 224
1990	31 910	213	32	16	34	46	68	204	468	1 099	3 109	6 685	11 233	8 703
1991	31 729	174	54	22	31	57	74	225	463	1 070	2 974	6 542	11 059	8 984
1992	31 603	184	50	23	21	45	73	225	442	1 109	2 816	6 663	10 944	9 008
1993[1]	33 545	172	45	34	27	55	60	258	460	1 089	2 793	6 918	11 330	10 304
1994	30 912	170	29	11	19	33	74	229	495	1 102	2 723	6 617	10 008	9 402
1995	31 709	178	26	16	26	50	70	231	435	1 100	2 601	6 449	10 452	10 075
1996	31 448	159	24	31	21	49	67	218	453	1 172	2 573	6 206	10 256	10 219
1997	31 189	130	23	28	21	43	71	199	496	1 128	2 480	5 985	10 164	10 421
1998	31 032	137	26	28	19	55	68	198	485	1 106	2 416	5 955	9 913	10 626
1999	31 676	115	26	20	17	65	58	201	467	1 128	2 431	5 837	10 198	11 113
2000	30 288	132	20	10	21	46	56	222	510	1 086	2 324	5 512	9 875	10 474
2001	30 058	135	20	16	21	47	71	189	480	1 111	2 361	5 235	9 695	10 677

Scotland

5.19 Deaths: analysis by age and sex[1]
Annual averages or calendar years
continued

Numbers

	All ages[2]	Under 1 year	1-4	5-9	10-14	15-19	20-24	25-34	35-44	45-54	55-64	65-74	75-84	85 and over
							Northern Ireland							
Males														
1900 - 02	11 554	1 958	985	280	206	367	446	779	669	832	1 413	1 666	1 368	585
1910 - 12	10 469	1 697	841	222	152	282	311	569	679	836	1 148	2 011	1 287	434
1920 - 22	9 622	1 491	596	191	150	258	334	496	570	869	1 159	1 749	1 324	435
1930 - 32	8 626	1 083	406	126	90	154	209	375	437	740	1 313	1 988	1 317	388
1940 - 42	9 383	1 258	322	117	102	153	202	379	462	751	1 290	2 305	1 637	405
1950 - 52	8 197	658	105	55	36	50	77	179	318	671	1 169	2 117	2 178	583
1960 - 62	8 080	499	67	38	27	49	48	108	216	623	1 419	2 037	2 131	816
1970 - 72	8 786	396	58	40	32	76	83	115	221	643	1 590	2 493	2 157	881
1980 - 82	8 420	211	37	20	26	77	92	144	202	539	1 414	2 518	2 346	795
1990 - 92	7 550	102	21	13	18	55	73	132	178	423	1 044	2 175	2 393	922
	KHXA	KHXB	KHXC	KHXD	KHXE	KHXF	KHXG	KHXH	KHXI	KHXJ	KHXK	KHXL	KHXM	KHXN
1981	8 423	205	49	20	27	66	93	141	193	521	1 406	2 568	2 319	815
1982	8 004	205	31	12	17	77	78	129	203	528	1 341	2 332	2 289	762
1983	8 209	196	24	25	30	69	86	124	192	475	1 409	2 433	2 303	843
1984	8 007	163	28	22	14	52	69	133	217	517	1 318	2 355	2 308	811
1985	8 088	151	33	16	22	64	85	109	193	519	1 312	2 424	2 310	850
1986	8 155	161	14	15	15	70	83	128	188	477	1 361	2 381	2 348	914
1987	7 721	137	25	22	19	60	102	143	191	402	1 177	2 269	2 330	844
1988	7 993	137	29	20	16	65	112	141	197	400	1 213	2 260	2 462	941
1989	7 878	100	31	19	16	62	90	143	166	432	1 124	2 264	2 501	930
1990	7 648	110	19	12	18	54	68	138	186	431	1 066	2 219	2 413	914
1991	7 533	112	23	12	16	59	78	142	185	436	1 021	2 130	2 392	927
1992	7 469	83	21	16	19	52	73	117	162	403	1 046	2 177	2 374	926
1993[1]	7 731	99	22	10	24	53	86	139	163	398	1 012	2 248	2 469	1 008
1994	7 362	81	23	14	21	65	67	138	177	376	1 035	2 051	2 306	1 008
1995	7 482	93	19	15	18	53	82	142	176	411	951	2 040	2 429	1 053
1996	7 418	84	7	8	15	40	72	126	191	386	880	2 028	2 456	1 125
1997	7 244	68	12	11	12	50	62	122	172	411	924	1 937	2 367	1 096
1998	7 321	74	13	9	13	49	47	147	164	434	898	1 873	2 433	1 167
1999	7 464	82	20	16	11	45	68	124	194	409	876	1 871	2 456	1 292
2000	7 128	61	12	12	14	55	69	130	191	387	869	1 682	2 426	1 220
2001	7 010	79	7	11	14	48	63	119	189	424	785	1 669	2 370	1 232
Females														
1900 - 02	12 735	1 537	1 013	317	277	495	521	1 012	902	1 075	1 612	1 876	1 484	614
1910 - 12	11 397	1 369	808	249	218	325	365	785	811	961	1 282	2 328	1 402	494
1920 - 22	10 415	1 149	547	193	188	299	331	687	713	939	1 236	1 976	1 639	518
1930 - 32	9 044	824	380	125	102	184	226	475	539	774	1 293	2 046	1 541	535
1940 - 42	9 229	910	305	105	90	159	174	409	490	688	1 207	2 246	1 873	572
1950 - 52	7 896	494	87	33	21	37	59	173	276	526	996	1 976	2 384	834
1960 - 62	7 463	371	61	20	15	21	24	70	175	434	880	1 823	2 417	1 151
1970 - 72	7 809	295	45	23	17	25	20	65	152	408	919	1 959	2 475	1 407
1980 - 82	7 917	160	26	17	17	23	29	65	127	329	881	1 813	2 752	1 678
1990 - 92	7 620	80	20	12	9	16	17	53	117	267	672	1 538	2 636	2 182
	KIXA	KIXB	KIXC	KIXD	KIXE	KIXF	KIXG	KIXH	KIXI	KIXJ	KIXK	KIXL	KIXM	KIXN
1981	7 833	155	24	15	13	20	26	49	114	348	858	1 779	2 760	1 672
1982	7 914	164	26	16	12	23	35	73	125	325	880	1 749	2 750	1 736
1983	7 830	133	28	16	9	23	25	58	106	281	837	1 795	2 756	1 763
1984	7 685	128	21	12	5	18	23	51	136	284	795	1 640	2 770	1 802
1985	7 867	114	22	17	13	19	23	62	113	291	783	1 771	2 742	1 897
1986	7 910	125	20	11	11	23	18	48	112	269	797	1 702	2 724	2 050
1987	7 613	105	17	7	8	29	24	71	128	243	736	1 680	2 650	1 915
1988	7 820	111	21	10	12	16	32	48	120	324	800	1 574	2 704	2 048
1989	7 966	80	23	7	15	13	19	53	111	272	709	1 591	2 875	2 198
1990	7 778	88	23	13	9	16	16	61	120	282	730	1 564	2 684	2 172
1991	7 563	82	19	10	11	19	20	51	129	260	675	1 502	2 597	2 188
1992	7 519	70	18	12	8	12	16	47	103	260	612	1 549	2 627	2 185
1993[1]	7 902	77	17	11	10	16	24	61	119	270	684	1 604	2 628	2 381
1994	7 752	66	17	7	9	16	17	53	121	291	639	1 531	2 611	2 374
1995	7 828	76	11	12	14	17	20	50	124	288	601	1 552	2 633	2 430
1996	7 800	58	11	8	7	14	15	70	104	277	589	1 488	2 643	2 516
1997	7 727	69	13	10	9	18	13	43	90	268	570	1 409	2 604	2 611
1998	7 672	60	12	8	7	24	20	49	126	258	531	1 351	2 509	2 717
1999	8 199	66	12	7	8	23	25	55	119	273	583	1 303	2 765	2 960
2000	7 775	48	11	11	3	19	13	51	125	283	574	1 308	2 526	2 803
2001	7 503	55	7	4	8	14	14	41	137	259	510	1 264	2 404	2 786

1 See chapter text.
2 In some years the totals include a small number of persons whose age was not stated.

Sources: Office for National Statistics: 01329 813223;
General Register Office for Scotland;
Northern Ireland Statistics and Research Agency

55

5.20 Infant and maternal mortality[1]

	Deaths of Infants under 1 year of age per thousand live births												Maternal deaths per thousand live births[3]			
	United Kingdom			England and Wales[2]			Scotland			Northern Ireland			United Kingdom	England and Wales	Scotland	Northern Ireland
	Total	Males	Females	Total	Males	Females	Total	Males	Females	Total	Males	Females				
1900 - 02	142	156	128	146	160	131	124	136	111	113	123	103	4.71	4.67	4.74	6.03
1910 - 12	110	121	98	110	121	98	109	120	97	101	110	92	3.95	3.67	5.65	5.28
1920 - 22	82	92	71	80	90	69	94	106	82	86	95	77	4.37	4.03	6.36	5.62
1930 - 32	67	75	58	64	72	55	84	94	73	75	83	66	4.54	4.24	6.40	5.24
1940 - 42	59	66	51	55	62	48	77	87	66	80	89	70	3.29	2.74	4.50	3.79
1950 - 52	30	34	26	29	33	25	37	42	32	40	45	36	0.88	0.79	1.09	1.09
1960 - 62	22	25	19	22	24	19	26	30	22	27	30	24	0.36	0.36	0.37	0.43
1970 - 72	18	20	16	18	20	15	19	22	17	22	24	20	0.17	0.17	0.17	0.12
1980 - 82	12	13	10	11	13	10	12	13	10	13	15	12	0.09	0.09	0.14	0.06
1990 - 92	7	8	6	7	8	6	7	8	6	7	8	6	0.07	0.07	0.10	-
	KKAW	KKAX	KKAY	KKAZ	KKBW	KKBX	KKBY	KKBZ	KKCW	KKCX	KKCY	KKCZ	KKDW	KKDX	KKDY	KKDZ
1980	12.2	13.4	10.6	12.0	13.3	10.7	12.1	13.6	10.4	13.4	15.1	11.5	0.11	0.11	0.15	0.07
1981	11.2	12.7	9.5	11.1	12.6	9.4	11.3	12.3	10.2	13.2	14.7	11.6	0.09	0.09	0.19	0.04
1982	11.0	12.3	9.5	10.8	12.2	9.4	11.4	12.9	9.8	13.6	14.8	12.4	0.07	0.07	0.09	0.07
1983	10.1	11.3	8.9	10.1	11.3	8.9	9.9	11.3	8.5	12.1	13.9	10.1	0.09	0.09	0.12	0.15
1984	9.6	10.7	8.4	9.5	10.6	8.3	10.3	11.7	8.9	10.5	11.4	9.6	0.09	0.08	0.12	0.11
1985	9.4	10.4	8.3	9.4	10.4	8.2	9.4	10.0	8.7	9.6	10.6	8.5	0.07	0.07	0.13	0.07
1986	9.5	10.9	8.1	9.6	11.0	8.0	8.8	9.9	7.7	10.2	11.0	9.2	0.07	0.07	0.11	–
1987	9.1	10.3	7.9	9.2	10.4	7.9	8.5	9.7	7.2	8.7	9.6	7.7	0.06	0.07	0.03	0.04
1988	9.0	10.2	7.7	9.0	10.3	7.7	8.2	9.5	6.8	8.9	9.6	8.2	0.06	0.06	0.12	0.07
1989	8.4	9.5	7.2	8.4	9.6	7.3	8.7	10.2	7.2	6.9	7.4	6.3	0.08	0.08	0.06	–
1990	7.9	8.8	6.8	7.9	8.9	6.8	7.7	8.8	6.6	7.5	8.1	6.8	0.08	0.08	0.06	–
1991	7.4	8.3	6.3	7.4	8.3	6.4	7.1	8.7	5.3	7.4	8.3	6.4	0.07	0.06	0.13	0.04
1992	6.6	7.4	5.7	6.6	7.4	5.8	6.8	7.9	5.7	6.0	6.4	5.6	0.07	0.07	0.11	–
1993	6.3	7.0	5.6	6.3	7.0	5.6	6.5	7.4	5.6	7.1	7.8	6.3	0.06	0.05	0.11	–
1994	6.2	6.9	5.4	6.2	6.9	5.4	6.2	6.8	5.6	6.1	6.5	5.6	0.08	0.08	0.15	–
1995	6.2	6.9	5.4	6.1	6.9	5.3	6.2	6.4	6.1	7.1	7.5	6.6	0.07	0.07	0.10	–
1996	6.1	6.8	5.4	6.1	6.9	5.4	6.2	6.7	5.5	5.8	6.7	4.8	0.07	0.07	0.10	0.04
1997	5.8	6.4	5.3	5.9	6.5	5.3	5.3	6.1	4.5	5.6	5.5	5.8	0.06	0.06	0.07	–
1998	5.7	6.3	5.0	5.7	6.4	5.0	5.6	6.2	4.9	5.6	6.1	5.1	0.07	0.07	0.09	0.04
1999	5.8	6.4	5.1	5.8	6.5	5.1	5.0	5.7	4.3	6.4	6.8	5.9	0.05	0.05	0.13	–
2000	5.6	6.1	5.0	5.6	6.1	5.1	5.7	6.4	5.1	5.1	5.5	4.6	0.07	0.06	0.15	–
2001	5.5	6.0	5.0	5.4	5.9	4.9	5.5	5.8	5.2	6.1	7.0	5.2	0.07	0.07	0.11	0.09

5.20 Infant and maternal mortality[1]
continued

Deaths per thousand live births

							Analysis by sex of infant							
		1988	1989	1990	1991	1992	1993	1994	1995	1996	1997	1998	1999	2000	2001
Total															
United Kingdom:															
Stillbirths[4]	KHNQ	4.9	4.7	4.6	4.7	4.3	5.7	5.8	5.6	5.5	5.3	5.4	5.3	5.3	5.3
Perinatal[4]	KHNR	8.8	8.3	8.1	8.1	7.7	9.0	8.9	8.9	8.7	8.3	8.3	8.2	8.1	8.0
Neonatal	KHNS	4.9	4.7	4.5	4.4	4.3	4.2	4.1	4.2	4.1	3.9	3.8	3.9	3.9	3.6
Post neonatal	KHNT	4.1	3.7	3.3	3.0	2.3	2.2	2.1	2.0	2.0	2.0	1.9	1.9	1.7	1.8
England and Wales:															
Stillbirths[4]	KHNU	4.9	4.7	4.6	4.6	4.3	5.7	5.7	5.5	5.4	5.3	5.3	5.3	5.3	5.3
Perinatal[4]	KHNV	8.7	8.3	8.1	8.0	7.6	8.9	8.9	8.7	8.6	8.3	8.2	8.2	8.2	8.0
Neonatal	KHNW	4.9	4.8	4.6	4.4	4.3	4.2	4.1	4.1	4.1	3.9	3.8	3.9	3.9	3.6
Post neonatal	KHNX	4.1	3.7	3.3	3.0	2.3	2.1	2.1	2.0	2.0	2.0	1.9	1.9	1.7	1.9
Scotland:															
Stillbirths[4]	KHNY	5.4	5.0	5.3	5.5	4.9	6.4	6.1	6.6	6.4	5.3	6.1	5.2	5.6	5.7
Perinatal[4]	KHNZ	8.9	8.7	8.7	8.6	8.5	9.6	9.0	9.6	9.2	7.8	8.7	7.6	8.4	8.5
Neonatal	KHOA	4.5	4.7	4.4	4.4	4.6	4.0	4.0	4.0	3.9	3.2	3.6	3.3	4.0	3.8
Post neonatal	KHOB	3.7	4.0	3.3	2.7	2.2	2.5	2.2	2.2	2.2	2.1	2.0	1.7	1.8	1.7
Northern Ireland:															
Stillbirths[4]	KHOC	5.0	5.1	4.4	4.7	4.9	5.2	6.3	6.1	6.3	5.4	5.1	5.7	4.3	5.1
Perinatal[4]	KHOD	9.3	8.2	7.6	8.4	8.2	8.8	9.7	10.4	9.4	8.2	8.1	10.0	7.3	8.5
Neonatal	KHOE	5.4	4.0	4.0	4.6	4.1	4.9	4.2	5.5	3.7	4.2	3.9	4.8	3.8	4.5
Post neonatal	KHOF	3.6	2.9	3.5	2.8	1.9	2.1	1.9	1.6	2.0	1.4	1.7	1.6	1.3	1.6
Males															
United Kingdom:															
Perinatal[4]	KHOG	9.5	9.3	8.8	8.7	8.3	9.7	9.6	9.4	9.1	8.7	8.8	8.7	8.7	8.6
Neonatal	KHOH	5.5	5.4	5.0	4.9	4.8	4.7	4.6	4.6	4.6	4.2	4.2	4.3	4.2	4.0
Infant mortality	KHOI	10.2	9.5	8.8	8.3	7.4	7.0	6.9	6.9	6.8	6.4	6.3	6.4	6.1	6.0
England and Wales:															
Perinatal[4]	KHOK	9.4	9.2	8.8	8.6	8.1	9.5	9.6	9.3	9.0	8.7	8.8	8.6	8.7	8.5
Neonatal	KHOL	5.5	5.4	5.1	4.8	4.7	4.6	4.6	4.6	4.6	4.2	4.3	4.3	4.2	3.9
Infant mortality	KHOM	10.3	9.6	8.9	8.3	7.4	7.0	6.9	6.9	6.9	6.5	6.4	6.5	6.1	5.9
Scotland:															
Perinatal[4]	KHOO	9.7	10.0	9.1	9.8	9.8	10.8	9.6	10.1	10.0	8.1	9.6	8.4	9.5	9.2
Neonatal	KHOP	5.3	5.3	4.7	5.5	5.5	4.5	4.4	4.1	4.3	3.4	4.0	3.8	4.5	4.0
Infant mortality	KHOQ	9.5	10.2	8.8	8.7	7.9	7.4	6.8	6.4	6.7	6.1	6.2	5.7	6.4	5.8
Northern Ireland:															
Perinatal[4]	KHOS	10.9	8.7	8.7	7.9	8.6	10.3	10.4	10.4	10.1	8.5	8.9	10.5	8.0	9.8
Neonatal	KHOT	6.0	4.5	4.8	5.5	4.5	5.9	4.3	5.7	4.3	4.3	4.4	5.5	4.2	5.3
Infant mortality	KHOU	9.6	7.4	8.1	8.3	6.4	7.8	6.5	7.5	6.7	5.5	6.1	6.8	5.5	7.0
Females															
United Kingdom:															
Perinatal[4]	KHOW	8.0	7.4	7.4	7.5	7.0	8.2	8.2	8.3	8.2	7.9	7.7	7.8	7.5	7.4
Neonatal	KHOX	4.3	4.0	4.0	3.8	3.8	3.6	3.6	3.7	3.6	3.5	3.3	3.4	3.5	3.3
Infant mortality	KHOY	7.7	7.2	6.8	6.3	5.7	5.6	5.4	5.4	5.4	5.3	5.0	5.1	5.0	5.0
England and Wales:															
Perinatal[4]	KHPA	8.0	7.4	7.4	7.5	7.0	8.3	8.1	8.1	8.2	7.9	7.7	7.8	7.6	7.3
Neonatal	KHPB	4.3	4.0	4.0	3.9	3.9	3.6	3.6	3.6	3.6	3.6	3.3	3.5	3.5	3.2
Infant mortality	KHPC	7.7	7.3	6.8	6.4	5.8	5.6	5.4	5.3	5.4	5.3	5.0	5.1	5.1	4.9
Scotland:															
Perinatal[4]	KHPE	8.1	7.3	8.2	7.4	7.1	8.3	8.4	9.2	8.4	7.5	7.9	6.7	7.2	7.8
Neonatal	KHPF	3.7	4.1	4.1	3.2	3.7	3.5	3.6	3.9	3.5	2.9	3.2	2.8	3.5	3.5
Infant mortality	KHPG	6.8	7.2	6.6	5.3	5.7	5.6	5.6	6.1	5.5	4.5	4.9	4.3	5.1	5.2
Northern Ireland:															
Perinatal[4]	KHPI	7.6	7.6	6.4	9.0	7.9	7.2	8.9	10.5	8.6	8.0	7.3	9.5	6.5	7.0
Neonatal	KHPJ	4.7	3.5	3.2	3.7	3.6	3.9	4.1	5.2	3.1	4.0	3.4	4.1	3.4	3.6
Infant mortality	KHPK	8.2	6.3	6.8	6.4	5.6	6.3	5.6	6.6	4.8	5.8	5.1	5.9	4.6	5.2

1 See chapter text.
2 From 1937 to 1956 death rates are based on the births to which they relate
  in the current and preceding years.
3 Deaths in pregnancy and childbirth.
4 Deaths per 1,000 live and stillbirths.

Sources: Office for National Statistics: 01329 813758;
General Register Office for Scotland;
Northern Ireland Statistics and Research Agency

5.21 Death rates per 1,000 population[1]
United Kingdom
Analysis by age and sex

	All ages	0-4	5-9	10-14	15-19	20-24	25-34	35-44	45-54	55-64	65-74	75-84	85 and over
Males													
1900 - 02	18.4	57.0	4.1	2.4	3.7	5.0	6.6	11.0	18.6	35.0	69.9	143.6	289.6
1910 - 12	14.9	40.5	3.3	2.0	3.0	3.9	5.0	8.0	14.9	29.8	62.1	133.8	261.5
1920 - 22	13.5	33.4	2.9	1.8	2.9	3.9	4.5	6.9	11.9	25.3	57.8	131.8	259.1
1930 - 32	12.9	22.3	2.3	1.5	2.6	3.3	3.5	5.7	11.3	23.7	57.9	134.2	277.0
1940 - 42	..	..	..	..	..	..	..	..	..	..	..	..	..
1950 - 52	12.6	7.7	0.7	0.5	0.9	1.4	1.6	3.0	8.5	23.2	55.2	127.6	272.0
1960 - 62	12.5	6.4	0.5	0.4	0.9	1.1	1.1	2.5	7.4	22.2	54.4	123.4	251.0
1970 - 72	12.4	4.6	0.4	0.4	0.9	1.0	1.0	2.4	7.3	20.9	52.9	116.3	246.1
1980 - 82	12.1	3.2	0.3	0.3	0.8	0.9	0.9	1.9	6.3	18.2	46.7	107.1	224.9
1990 - 92	11.3	2.0	0.2	0.2	0.7	0.9	1.0	1.8	4.6	14.2	38.6	92.8	200.5
	KHZA	KHZB	KHZC	KHZD	KHZE	KHZF	KHZG	KHZH	KHZJ	KHZK	KHZL	KHZM	KHZN
1980	12.1	3.4	0.3	0.3	0.8	0.9	0.9	2.0	6.5	18.7	47.2	108.6	227.0
1981	12.3	3.2	0.3	0.3	0.9	0.9	1.0	2.0	6.4	18.4	47.5	110.6	239.5
1982	12.1	2.9	0.3	0.3	0.8	0.9	0.9	1.8	6.1	17.9	46.4	106.2	226.0
1983	12.0	2.7	0.3	0.3	0.8	0.8	0.9	1.8	5.9	18.0	46.3	104.4	226.1
1984	11.7	2.6	0.2	0.3	0.7	0.9	0.9	1.7	5.7	17.5	45.0	100.6	219.0
1985	12.1	2.6	0.2	0.3	0.7	0.9	0.9	1.8	5.6	17.5	44.9	104.4	232.8
1986	11.9	2.6	0.2	0.2	0.7	0.9	0.9	1.7	5.5	17.0	43.5	101.6	227.8
1987	11.5	2.5	0.2	0.3	0.7	0.9	0.9	1.7	5.2	16.4	41.8	96.8	204.8
1988	11.5	2.5	0.2	0.3	0.7	0.9	1.0	1.7	5.1	15.9	41.1	96.1	205.9
1989	11.5	2.3	0.2	0.2	0.7	0.9	0.9	1.7	4.9	15.3	40.2	96.4	212.5
1990	11.3	2.2	0.2	0.2	0.7	1.0	1.0	1.8	4.8	14.8	39.3	93.7	201.4
1991	11.3	2.0	0.2	0.2	0.7	0.9	1.0	1.8	4.7	14.2	38.7	93.4	203.4
1992	11.0	1.8	0.2	0.2	0.6	0.9	1.0	1.8	4.4	13.8	37.9	91.2	196.6
1993	11.3	1.7	0.2	0.2	0.6	0.9	1.0	1.7	4.4	13.7	38.6	94.6	206.2
1994	10.8	1.6	0.2	0.2	0.6	0.9	1.0	1.7	4.2	12.8	36.8	90.2	193.0
1995	11.0	1.6	0.2	0.2	0.6	0.9	1.0	1.8	4.3	12.7	36.7	90.0	201.1
1996	10.8	1.6	0.1	0.2	0.6	0.9	1.1	1.7	4.2	12.4	35.2	86.0	198.7
1997	10.6	1.5	0.2	0.2	0.6	1.0	1.0	1.7	4.1	11.8	33.8	83.3	196.5
1998	10.6	1.5	0.1	0.2	0.6	0.9	1.1	1.7	4.2	11.7	33.0	81.9	193.8
1999	10.6	1.5	0.1	0.2	0.6	0.9	1.0	1.7	4.2	11.2	32.2	81.0	196.3
2000	10.2	1.4	0.1	0.2	0.6	0.9	1.1	1.7	4.0	10.8	30.3	76.9	188.8
2001	10.0	1.3	0.1	0.2	0.6	0.9	1.0	1.6	4.0	10.4	28.7	74.9	187.1
Females													
1900 - 02	16.3	47.9	4.3	2.6	3.5	4.3	5.8	9.0	14.4	27.9	59.3	127.0	262.6
1910 - 12	13.3	34.0	3.3	2.1	2.9	3.4	4.4	6.7	11.5	23.1	50.7	113.7	234.0
1920 - 22	11.9	26.9	2.8	1.9	2.8	3.4	4.1	5.6	9.3	19.2	45.6	111.5	232.4
1930 - 32	11.5	17.7	2.1	1.5	2.4	2.9	3.3	4.6	8.3	17.6	43.7	110.1	246.3
1940 - 42	..	..	..	..	..	..	..	..	..	..	..	..	..
1950 - 52	11.2	6.0	0.5	0.4	0.7	1.0	1.4	2.3	5.3	12.9	35.5	98.4	228.8
1960 - 62	11.2	4.9	0.3	0.3	0.4	0.5	0.8	1.8	4.5	11.0	30.8	87.3	218.5
1970 - 72	11.3	3.6	0.3	0.2	0.4	0.4	0.6	1.6	4.5	10.5	27.5	76.7	196.1
1980 - 82	11.4	2.3	0.2	0.2	0.3	0.4	0.5	1.3	3.9	9.9	24.8	67.2	179.5
1990 - 92	11.1	1.6	0.1	0.2	0.3	0.3	0.4	1.1	2.9	8.4	22.1	58.5	154.4
	KHZO	KHZP	KHZQ	KHZR	KHZS	KHZT	KHZU	KHZV	KHZW	KHZX	KHZY	KHZZ	KHZI
1980	11.4	2.7	0.2	0.2	0.3	0.4	0.5	1.3	4.0	10.0	25.0	67.7	181.3
1981	11.6	2.5	0.2	0.2	0.3	0.4	0.5	1.3	3.9	10.0	25.5	70.4	190.6
1982	11.5	2.3	0.2	0.2	0.3	0.4	0.5	1.2	3.8	9.9	24.9	66.7	178.8
1983	11.4	2.1	0.2	0.2	0.3	0.3	0.5	1.2	3.6	9.8	24.7	65.0	176.0
1984	11.2	2.0	0.2	0.2	0.3	0.3	0.5	1.2	3.5	9.8	24.3	62.4	168.8
1985	11.7	2.0	0.2	0.2	0.3	0.3	0.5	1.2	3.4	9.9	24.6	64.5	177.1
1986	11.4	2.0	0.2	0.2	0.3	0.3	0.5	1.1	3.3	9.5	23.9	63.0	170.7
1987	11.2	2.0	0.2	0.2	0.3	0.3	0.5	1.1	3.3	9.4	23.2	60.5	158.1
1988	11.3	1.9	0.2	0.2	0.3	0.3	0.5	1.2	3.2	9.2	23.1	60.1	160.4
1989	11.5	1.8	0.2	0.2	0.3	0.3	0.5	1.1	3.1	9.1	23.0	61.0	162.7
1990	11.1	1.7	0.1	0.2	0.3	0.3	0.4	1.1	3.0	8.8	22.2	58.5	154.8
1991	11.2	1.6	0.2	0.2	0.3	0.3	0.4	1.1	2.9	8.4	22.3	59.1	157.1
1992	11.0	1.4	0.1	0.1	0.3	0.3	0.4	1.1	2.8	8.1	21.9	57.9	151.4
1993	11.5	1.3	0.1	0.2	0.3	0.3	0.5	1.1	2.8	8.1	22.5	60.5	160.9
1994	10.9	1.3	0.1	0.1	0.3	0.3	0.4	1.1	2.8	7.6	21.7	57.6	151.2
1995	11.2	1.2	0.1	0.1	0.3	0.3	0.5	1.1	2.8	7.5	21.8	57.8	158.6
1996	11.1	1.2	0.1	0.1	0.3	0.3	0.5	1.1	2.7	7.3	21.0	56.4	157.5
1997	11.0	1.2	0.1	0.1	0.3	0.3	0.4	1.1	2.7	7.1	20.5	55.1	159.1
1998	11.0	1.2	0.1	0.1	0.3	0.3	0.4	1.0	2.7	7.0	20.2	54.3	159.5
1999	11.0	1.2	0.1	0.1	0.3	0.3	0.4	1.0	2.7	6.9	19.7	54.2	164.1
2000	10.5	1.1	0.1	0.1	0.3	0.3	0.4	1.0	2.7	6.6	18.5	51.6	156.0
2001	10.4	1.1	0.1	0.1	0.2	0.3	0.4	1.0	2.6	6.4	17.8	50.9	156.0

1 The figures for 1980 incorporate the revised intercensal estimates for England and Wales and Northern Ireland. The figures for 1982 to 2000 have been revised using interim population estimates. See chapter text.

Sources: Office for National Statistics: 01329 813223; General Register Office for Scotland; Northern Ireland Statistics and Research Agency

5.22 Life tables[1]

	Interim life tables, 1998-00							
	United Kingdom				**England and Wales**			
	Males		Females		Males		Females	
	l_x	e^0_x	l_x	e^0_x	l_x	e^0_x	l_x	e^0_x
Age(x)								
0 years	100 000	75.1	100 000	80.0	100 000	75.4	100 000	80.2
5 years	99 258	70.7	99 408	75.5	99 256	70.9	99 406	75.7
10 years	99 193	65.7	99 357	70.5	99 193	66.0	99 357	70.7
15 years	99 110	60.8	99 299	65.5	99 112	61.0	99 298	65.7
20 years	98 832	55.9	99 168	60.6	98 849	56.2	99 174	60.8
25 years	98 416	51.2	99 010	55.7	98 457	51.4	99 019	55.9
30 years	97 964	46.4	98 827	50.8	98 025	46.6	98 841	51.0
35 years	97 464	41.6	98 579	45.9	97 542	41.8	98 597	46.1
40 years	96 840	36.9	98 199	41.1	96 939	37.1	98 223	41.3
45 years	95 909	32.2	97 560	36.3	96 041	32.4	97 602	36.5
50 years	94 442	27.7	96 557	31.7	94 615	27.9	96 627	31.9
55 years	92 113	23.3	94 991	27.2	92 368	23.5	95 092	27.3
60 years	88 241	19.2	92 512	22.8	88 616	19.3	92 675	23.0
65 years	82 134	15.4	88 624	18.7	82 664	15.6	88 882	18.9
70 years	72 744	12.1	82 463	14.9	73 437	12.2	82 864	15.0
75 years	59 174	9.2	72 740	11.5	59 961	9.3	73 275	11.6
80 years	42 306	6.9	58 972	8.6	43 064	7.0	59 608	8.7
85 years	24 577	5.1	41 096	6.3	25 151	5.2	41 735	6.3
90 years	10 424	3.9	21 940	4.6	10 753	3.9	22 419	4.7

	Interim life tables, 1998-00							
	Scotland				**Northern Ireland**			
	Males		Females		Males		Females	
	l_x	e^0_x	l_x	e^0_x	l_x	e^0_x	l_x	e^0_x
Age(x)								
0 years	10 000	72.8	10 000	78.2	10 000	74.5	10 000	79.6
5 years	9 928	68.4	9 944	73.7	9 927	70.0	9 938	75.1
10 years	9 920	63.4	9 938	68.7	9 917	65.1	9 931	70.1
15 years	9 910	58.5	9 932	63.7	9 908	60.1	9 927	65.2
20 years	9 871	53.7	9 915	58.8	9 870	55.4	9 909	60.3
25 years	9 810	49.0	9 895	53.9	9 819	50.6	9 892	55.4
30 years	9 744	44.3	9 873	49.1	9 773	45.9	9 874	50.5
35 years	9 677	39.6	9 843	44.2	9 719	41.1	9 852	45.6
40 years	9 592	34.9	9 797	39.4	9 659	36.4	9 818	40.7
45 years	9 467	30.4	9 718	34.7	9 564	31.7	9 749	36.0
50 years	9 283	25.9	9 591	30.1	9 407	27.2	9 645	31.4
55 years	8 966	21.7	9 403	25.7	9 164	22.8	9 484	26.9
60 years	8 461	17.9	9 097	21.4	8 768	18.7	9 226	22.5
65 years	7 712	14.4	8 624	17.5	8 127	15.0	8 830	18.4
70 years	6 635	11.3	7 882	13.9	7 144	11.7	8 207	14.6
75 years	5 199	8.6	6 783	10.7	5 767	8.9	7 248	11.2
80 years	3 550	6.5	5 317	7.9	4 041	6.6	5 831	8.3
85 years	1 962	4.8	3 546	5.6	2 241	4.9	3 959	6.0
90 years	776	3.5	1 777	3.8	856	4.0	2 056	4.2

Note Column l_x shows the number who would survive to exact **age(x)**, out of 100,000 or 10,000 born, who were subject throughout their lives to the death rates experienced in the three-year period indicated. Column e^0_x is 'the expectation of life', that is, the average future lifetime which would be lived by a person aged exactly x if likewise subject to the death rates experienced in the three-year period indicated.

1 See chapter text.

Source: Government Actuary's Department: 020 7211 2622

5.23 Adoptions by date of entry in Adopted Children Register: by age and sex

	All ages		Under 1		1-4		5-9		10-14		15-17	
	Numbers	Percentages	Numbers	Percentages	Numbers	Percentages	Numbers	Percentages	Numbers	Percentages	Numbers	Percentages
Great Britain **Persons**												
	GQSF	GQSG	GQSH	GQSI	GQSJ	GQSK	GQSL	GQSM	GQSN	GQSO	GQSP	GQSQ
1996[1]	6 547	100	302	5	1 729	26	2 541	39	1 581	24	393	6
1997	5 778	100	251	4	1 743	30	2 106	36	1 353	23	325	6
1998	4 877	100	211	4	1 615	33	1 743	36	1 066	22	242	5
1999	4 805	100	230	5	1 762	37	1 653	34	919	19	241	5
2000	5 333	100	275	5	2 158	40	1 673	31	993	19	234	4
2001[2]	6 450	100	264	4	2 824	44	2 007	31	1 076	17	278	4
Males												
	GQSR	GQSS	GQST	GQSU	GQSV	GQSW	GQSX	GQSY	GQSZ	GQTA	GQTB	GQTC
1996	3 290	100	160	5	892	27	1 319	40	741	23	178	5
1997	2 840	100	139	5	888	31	1 017	36	656	23	140	5
1998	2 449	100	108	4	838	34	849	35	549	22	105	4
1999	2 361	100	113	5	887	38	803	34	443	19	115	5
2000	2 662	100	140	5	1 097	41	830	31	477	18	118	4
2001	3 252	100	135	4	1 463	45	988	30	534	16	132	4
Females												
	GQTD	GQTE	GQTF	GQTG	GQTH	GQTI	GQTJ	GQTK	GQTL	GQTM	GQTN	GQTO
1996[1]	3 257	100	142	4	837	26	1 222	38	840	26	215	7
1997	2 938	100	112	4	855	29	1 089	37	697	24	185	6
1998	2 428	100	103	4	777	32	894	37	516	21	137	6
1999	2 444	100	117	5	875	36	850	35	476	19	126	5
2000	2 671	100	135	5	1 061	40	843	32	516	19	116	4
2001[2]	3 198	100	129	4	1 361	43	1 019	32	542	17	146	5
England and Wales **Persons**												
	GQTP	GQTQ	GQTR	GQTS	GQTT	GQTU	GQTV	GQTW	GQTX	GQTY	GQTZ	GQUA
1996	5 962	100	253	4	1 598	27	2 310	39	1 435	24	366	6
1997	5 307	100	225	4	1 606	30	1 914	36	1 265	24	297	6
1998	4 387	100	195	4	1 489	34	1 545	35	938	21	220	5
1999	4 316	100	196	5	1 627	38	1 477	34	802	19	214	5
2000	4 942	100	251	5	2 018	41	1 550	31	908	18	215	4
2001[2]	5 982	100	246	4	2 648	44	1 846	31	984	16	257	4
Males												
	GQUB	GQUC	GQUD	GQUE	GQUF	GQUG	GQUH	GQUI	GQUJ	GQUK	GQUL	GQUM
1996	2 988	100	143	5	822	28	1 184	40	674	23	165	6
1997	2 610	100	122	5	824	32	917	35	619	24	128	5
1998	2 214	100	100	5	775	35	755	34	489	22	95	4
1999	2 114	100	96	5	816	39	712	34	389	18	101	5
2000	2 452	100	127	5	1 022	42	759	31	434	18	110	4
2001	3 011	100	124	4	1 370	45	905	30	494	16	118	4
Females												
	GQUN	GQUO	GQUP	GQUQ	GQUR	GQUS	GQUT	GQUU	GQUV	GQUW	GQUX	GQUY
1996	2 974	100	110	4	776	26	1 126	38	761	26	201	7
1997	2 697	100	103	4	782	29	997	37	646	24	169	6
1998	2 173	100	95	4	714	33	790	36	448	21	125	6
1999	2 202	100	100	5	811	37	765	35	413	19	113	5
2000	2 490	100	124	5	996	40	791	32	474	19	105	4
2001[2]	2 971	100	122	4	1 278	43	941	32	490	16	139	5

5.23 continued — Adoptions by date of entry in Adopted Children Register: by age and sex

	All ages		Under 1		1-4		5-9		10-14		15-17	
	Numbers	Percentages	Numbers	Percentages	Numbers	Percentages	Numbers	Percentages	Numbers	Percentages	Numbers	Percentages
Scotland **Persons**												
	GQUZ	GQVA	GQVB	GQVC	GQVD	GQVE	GQVF	GQVG	GQVH	GQVI	GQVJ	GQVK
1996[1]	585	100	49	8	131	22	231	39	146	25	27	5
1997	471	100	26	6	137	29	192	41	88	19	28	6
1998	490	100	16	3	126	26	198	40	128	26	22	4
1999	489	100	34	7	135	28	176	36	117	24	27	6
2000	391	100	24	6	140	36	123	31	85	22	19	5
2001	468	100	18	4	176	38	161	34	92	20	21	4
Males												
	GQVL	GQVM	GQVN	GQVO	GQVP	GQVQ	GQVR	GQVS	GQVT	GQVU	GQVV	GQVW
1996	302	100	17	6	70	23	135	45	67	22	13	4
1997	230	100	17	7	64	28	100	43	37	16	12	5
1998	235	100	8	3	63	27	94	40	60	26	10	4
1999	247	100	17	7	71	29	91	37	54	22	14	6
2000	210	100	13	6	75	36	71	34	43	20	8	4
2001	241	100	11	5	93	39	83	34	40	17	14	6
Females												
	GQVX	GQVY	GQVZ	GQWA	GRFK	GRFL	GRFM	GRFN	GRFO	GRFP	GRFQ	GRFR
1996[1]	283	100	32	11	61	22	96	34	79	28	14	5
1997	241	100	9	4	73	30	92	38	51	21	16	7
1998	255	100	8	3	63	25	104	41	68	27	12	5
1999	242	100	17	7	64	26	85	35	63	26	13	5
2000	181	100	11	6	65	36	52	29	42	23	11	6
2001	227	100	7	3	83	37	78	34	52	23	7	3

1 Includes one female with age not stated.
2 Includes one case where age was greater then 17.

Sources: Office for National Statistics: 01329 813339;
General Register Office for Scotland

5.24 — Adoptions by date of entry in Adopted Children Register

Numbers

		1991	1992	1993	1994	1995	1996	1997	1998	1999	2000	2001
United Kingdom	**GRFT**	8 207	8 400	7 851	7 096	6 600	6 711	5 927	4 998	4 949	5 505	6 589
England and Wales	**GRFU**	7 170	7 341	6 854	6 240	5 797	5 962	5 307	4 387	4 316	4 942	5 982
Scotland	**GRFV**	815	823	805	664	640	585	471	490	489	391	468
Northern Ireland	**GRFW**	222	236	192	192	163	169	150	121	144	172	139

Sources: Office for National Statistics: 01329 813339;
General Register Office for Scotland;
Northern Ireland Statistics and Research Agency

6 Education

Education

Educational establishments in the United Kingdom are administered and financed in several ways. Most schools are controlled by local education authorities (LEAs), which are part of the structure of local government, but some are 'assisted', receiving grants direct from central government sources and being controlled by governing bodies which have a substantial degree of autonomy. Completely outside the public sector are non-maintained schools run by individuals, companies or charitable institutions.

For the purposes of UK education statistics, schools fall under the following broad categories:

Mainstream state schools
(Grant-aided mainstream schools in Northern Ireland)
These schools work in partnership with other schools and local education authorities and they receive funding from LEAs. Since 1 September 1999, the categories (typically in England) are:

Community - schools formerly known as 'county' plus some former Grant-maintained (GM) schools;

Foundation - most former GM schools;

Voluntary Aided - schools formerly known as 'aided' and some former GM schools;

Voluntary Controlled - schools formerly known as 'controlled'.

Non-maintained mainstream schools consisting of

(a) Independent schools
Schools which charge fees and may also be financed by individuals, companies or charitable institutions. These include Direct Grant schools, where the governing bodies are assisted by Departmental grants and a proportion of the pupils attending them do so free or under an arrangement by which local education authorities meet tuition fees. City technology colleges (applicable in England only) are also included as independent schools.

(b) Non-maintained schools
Run by voluntary bodies who may receive some grant from central government for capital work and for equipment, but their current expenditure is met primarily from the fees charged to the LEAs for pupils placed in schools.

Special schools
Provide education for children with special educational needs (SEN) who cannot be educated satisfactorily in an ordinary school. Maintained special schools are run by LEAs, while non-maintained special schools are financed as shown at (b) above.

Pupil Referral Units
Pupil Referral Units (PRUs) operate in England and Wales and provide education outside of a mainstream or special school setting, to meet the needs of difficult or disruptive children.

Schools in Scotland are categorised as Education Authority, Grant-Aided, Opted-out/Self-governing (these three being grouped together as 'Publicly funded' schools), Independent schools and Partnership schools.

The home Government Departments dealing with education statistics are:

Department for Education and Skills (DfES);

National Assembly for Wales (NAfW);

Scottish Executive (SE);

Northern Ireland Department of Education (DENI);

Northern Ireland Department for Employment and Learning (DELNI).

Each of the home Education Departments in Great Britain, along with the Northern Ireland Department of Education, have overall responsibility for funding the schools sectors in their own country.

Up to March 2001, further education (FE) courses in FE sector colleges in England and in Wales were largely funded through grants from the respective Further Education Funding Councils. In April 2001, however, the Learning and Skills Council (LSC) took over the responsibility for funding the FE sector in England, and the National Council for Education and Training for Wales (part of Education and Learning Wales – ELWa) did so for Wales. The LSC in England is also responsible for funding provision for FE and some non-prescribed higher education in FE sector colleges; it also funds some FE provided by LEA maintained and other institutions referred to as 'external institutions'. In Wales, the National Council – ELWa, funds FE provision made by FE institutions via a third party or sponsored arrangements. The Scottish Further Education Funding Council (SFEFC) funds FE colleges in Scotland, while the Department for Employment and Learning funds FE colleges in Northern Ireland.

Higher education courses in higher education establishments are largely publicly funded through block grants from the HE funding councils in England and Scotland, the Higher Education Council – ELWa in Wales, and the Department of Employment and Learning in Northern Ireland. In addition, some designated HE (mainly HND/HNC Diplomas and Certificates of HE) is also funded by these sources. The FE sources mentioned above fund the remainder.

Statistics for the separate systems obtained in England, Wales, Scotland and Northern Ireland are collected and processed separately in accordance with the particular needs of the responsible Departments. Since 1994/95 the Higher Education Statistics Agency (HESA) has undertaken the data collection for all higher education institutions (HEIs) in the UK. This includes the former Universities Funding Council (UFC) funded

UK universities previously collected by the Universities Statistical Record. There are some structural differences in the information collected for schools, further and higher education in each of the four home countries and in some tables the GB/UK data presented are amalgamations from sources that are not entirely comparable.

Stages of education

There are five stages of education: foundation, primary, secondary, further and higher education, and education is compulsory for all children between the ages of five (four in Northern Ireland) and sixteen. The non-compulsory fourth stage, further education, covers non-advanced education, which can be taken at both further (including tertiary) education colleges, higher education institutions and increasingly in secondary schools. The fifth stage, higher education, is study beyond A levels and their equivalent which, for most full-time students, takes place in higher education institutions.

Foundation education

In recent years there has been a major expansion of pre-school education, and in England, the National Curriculum has been extended to include the Foundation stage and covers children's education from the age of three to the end of reception year, when most are just five and some almost six years old. Children under five attend a variety of settings including state nursery schools, nursery classes within primary schools and, in England and Wales, reception classes within primary schools, as well as settings outside the state sector such as voluntary pre-schools or privately run nurseries.

Primary education

The primary stage covers three age ranges: nursery (under 5), infant (5 to 7 or 8) and junior (up to 11 or 12) but in Scotland and Northern Ireland there is generally no distinction between infant and junior schools. Most public sector primary schools take both boys and girls in mixed classes. It is usual to transfer straight to secondary school at age 11 (in England, Wales and Northern Ireland) or 12 (in Scotland), but in England some children make the transition via middle schools catering for various age ranges between 8 and 14. Depending on their individual age ranges middle schools are classified as either primary or secondary.

Secondary education

Public provision of secondary education in an area may consist of a combination of different types of school, the pattern reflecting historical circumstance and the policy adopted by the local education authority. Comprehensive schools largely admit pupils without reference to ability or aptitude and cater for all the children in a neighbourhood, but in some areas they co-exist with grammar, secondary modern or technical schools. In 2001/02, 88 per cent of pupils in England attended comprehensive schools while all secondary schools in Wales are comprehensive schools. The majority of education authority secondary schools in Scotland are compre-hensive in character and offer six years of secondary education; however in remote areas there are several two-year and four-year secondary schools. In Northern Ireland, post primary education is provided by secondary intermediate and grammar schools.

Special schools

Special schools (day or boarding) provide education for children who require specialist support to complete their education, for example because they have physical or other difficulties. Many pupils with special educational needs are educated in main-stream schools. All children attending special schools are offered a curriculum designed to overcome their learning difficulties and to enable them to become self-reliant.

Further education

The term further education may be used in a general sense to cover all non-advanced courses taken after the period of compulsory education, but more commonly it excludes those staying on at secondary school and those in higher education, i.e. courses in universities and colleges leading to qualifications above GCE A Level, SCE H Grade, GNVQ/NVQ level 3, and their equivalents. Since 1 April 1993 sixth form colleges have been included in the further education sector.

Higher education

Higher education is defined as courses that are of a standard that is higher than GCE A level, the Higher Grade of the Scottish Certificate of Education, GNVQ/NVQ level 3 or the Edexcel (formerly BTEC) or SQA National Certificate/Diploma. There are three main levels of HE course: (i) postgraduate courses are those leading to higher degrees, diplomas and certificates (including postgraduate certificates of education and professional qualifications) which usually require a first degree as entry qualification; (ii) first degrees which includes first degrees, first degrees with qualified teacher status, enhanced first degrees, first degrees obtained concurrently with a diploma, and intercalated first degrees; (iii) other undergraduate courses which includes all other higher education courses, for example HND's and Diplomas in HE. As a result of the 1992 Further and Higher Education Act, former polytechnics and some other higher education institutions were designated as universities in 1992/93. Students normally attend HE courses at higher education institutions, but some attend at further education colleges. Some also attend institutions which do not receive public grant (such as the University of Buckingham) and these numbers are excluded from the tables.

6.1 Number of schools or departments[1] by type and establishments of further and higher education

Academic years

		1990/91	1995/96	1997/98	1998/99	1999[2]/00	2000[2]/01	2001[3]/02
United Kingdom:								
Public sector mainstream								
Nursery[4,5]	KBFK	1 364	1 486	1 681	2 369	2 864	3 228	3 216
Primary[6]	KBFA	24 135	23 441	23 230	23 125	23 036	22 902	22 800
Secondary[7]	KBFF	4 790	4 463	4 434	4 418	4 405	4 337	4 306
of which 6th form colleges	KPGM	116	..	..	..	..	..	..
Non-maintained mainstream[1]	KBFU	2 508	2 436	2 499	2 482	2 457	2 414	2 409
Special - all	KBFP	1 830	1 565	1 517	1 522	1 523	1 498	1 483
maintained	KPVX	..	1 456	1 419	1 428	1 426	1 401	1 387
non maintained	KPGO	..	109	98	94	97	97	96
Pupil referral units	KXEP	..	315	332	325	325	338	340
Universities (including Open University)[8]	KAHG	48	89	88	88	88	90	89
All other further and higher education institutions	KJPQ	588	609	596	581	574	549	546
Higher education institutions	KPVY	..	66	63	58	58	58	63
Further education institutions	KSNY	..	543	533	523	516	491	483
of which 6th form colleges	KPGP	..	110	108	107	105	103	84
England:								
Public sector mainstream								
Nursery	KBAK	566	547	533	520	514	506	494
Primary	KBAA	19 047	18 480	18 312	18 234	18 158	18 069	17 985
Secondary[7]	KBAF	3 897	3 594	3 567	3 560	3 550	3 481	3 457
of which 6th form colleges	KPGS	114	..	..	..	..	..	..
Non-maintained	KBAU	2 289	2 266	2 244	2 231	2 204	2 205	2 206
Special - all	KBAP	1 380	1 263	1 229	1 209	1 197	1 175	1 161
maintained	KPGT	..	1 191	1 164	1 148	1 134	1 113	1 098
non maintained	KPGU	..	72	65	61	63	62	63
Pupil referral units	KXEQ	..	291	309	298	295	308	312
Universities (including Open University)[8]	KAHM	37	72	71	70	70	72	72
All other further and higher education institutions	KJPR	460	503	491	482	458	449	447
Higher education institutions	KPXA	..	50	48	47	47	46	51
Further education institutions	KPWC	..	453	443	435	411	403	396
of which 6th form colleges	KPGV	..	110	108	107	105	103	84
Wales:								
Public sector mainstream								
Nursery	KBBK	54	52	47	46	42	41	40
Primary	KBBA	1 717	1 681	1 673	1 660	1 644	1 631	1 624
Secondary[7]	KBBF	230	228	228	229	228	229	227
of which 6th form colleges	KPGY	2	..	..	..	..	..	..
Non-maintained	KBBU	71	62	57	54	55	54	56
Special (Maintained)	KBBP	61	54	50	48	47	45	44
Pupil referral units	KZBF	..	24	23	27	30	30	28
Universities[8]	KAHS	1	2	2	2	2	2	2
All other further and higher education institutions	KJQP	38	31	30	28	28	28	28
Higher education institutions	KSNZ	..	5	4	4	4	4	4
Further education institutions	KPGZ	..	26	26	24	24	24	24
Scotland:								
Public sector mainstream								
Nursery[5]	KBDK	659	796	1 010	1 712	2 213	2 586	2 586
Primary	KBDA	2 372	2 332	2 300	2 291	2 293	2 278	2 271
Secondary	KBDF	424	405	401	392	389	389	387
Non-maintained[1]	KBDU	131	87	176	175	176	129	122
Special - all	KBDP	343	201	191	218	229	230	230
maintained	KYCZ	343	164	158	185	195	195	197
non-maintained	KYDA	..	37	33	33	34	35	33
Universities[8]	KAHX	8	13	13	14	14	14	13
All other further and higher education institutions	KJRA	64	56	56	52	52	53	52
Higher education institutions	KPWE	..	9	9	5	5	6	6
Further education institutions	KPHB	..	47	47	47	47	47	46
Northern Ireland:								
Grant aided mainstream								
Nursery[4]	KBEK	85	91	91	91	95	95	96
Primary[6]	KBEA	999	948	945	940	941	924	920
Secondary	KBEF	239	236	238	237	238	238	235
Non-maintained	KBEU	17	21	22	22	22	26	25
Special (Maintained)	KBEP	46	47	47	47	50	48	48
Universities	KIAD	2	2	2	2	2	2	2
Colleges of education	KIAE	2	2	2	2	2	2	2
Further education colleges	KIAG	24	17	17	17	17	17	17

1 See chapter text. From 1997/98 to 1999/00 non-maintained schools in Scotland with more than one department have been counted once for each department, eg a school with nursery, primary and secondary departments has been counted 3 times. Subsequent figures show primary and secondary only.

2 Includes revised data.

3 Provisional. Includes 2000/01 nursery schools data for Scotland.

4 Excludes voluntary and private pre-school education centres in Northern Ireland (360 in total in 2001/02).

5 Nursery schools figures for Scotland prior to 1998/99 only include data for Local Authority pre-schools. Data thereafter include partnership pre-schools.

6 From 1995/96, includes Preparatory Departments in Northern Ireland Grammar Schools (21 in total in 2001/02).

7 From 1993/94 excludes sixth form colleges in England and Wales which were reclassified as further education colleges on 1 April 1993.

8 From 1993/94 includes former polytechnics and colleges which became universities as a result of the Further and Higher Education Act 1992.

Source: Education Departments: 01325 392756

6.2 Full-time and part-time pupils in school[1] by age and sex
United Kingdom

		1992	1993	1994	1995	1996[2]	1997[2]	1998[2]	1999[2]	2000	2001	2002[3]
Age at previous 31 August[4]												
Number (thousands)												
England[5]	KBIA	7 712	7 842	7 883	8 013	8 110	8 195	8 261	8 310	8 346	8 374	8 369
Wales	KBIB	487	493	498	504	508	510	513	513	512	512	511
Scotland[6]	KBIC	826	832	841	845	846	848	850	844	874	882	876
Northern Ireland[7]	KBID	343	346	349	351	353	354	352	352	349	348	346
United Kingdom	KBIE	9 368	9 513	9 571	9 714	9 816	9 907	9 975	10 020	10 081	10 116	10 102
Boys and girls												
2 - 4[8]	KBIF	1 045	1 082	1 103	1 135	1 146	1 148	1 149	1 154	1 184	1 187	1 181
5 - 10	KBIG	4 356	4 392	4 462	4 517	4 583	4 628	4 668	4 661	4 629	4 597	4 537
11	KBIH	735	727	713	718	717	744	746	762	783	771	783
12 - 14	KBII	2 021	2 112	2 179	2 179	2 157	2 151	2 182	2 211	2 256	2 297	2 320
15	KBIK	664	638	651	700	722	716	701	706	705	732	737
16	KBIL	308	313	259	259	279	289	288	283	285	287	298
17	KBIM	206	215	180	181	191	206	217	218	213	219	223
18 and over	KBIN	34	35	23	24	22	22	24	25	27	27	23
Boys												
14	KBIO	332	338	367	376	370	365	368	367	381	384	391
15	KBIP	341	327	333	358	368	365	358	361	359	374	377
16	KBIQ	151	154	128	127	137	141	140	137	138	139	145
17	KBIR	100	104	88	88	92	100	104	104	101	105	107
18 and over	KBIS	18	18	12	13	12	12	13	13	14	15	13
Girls												
14	KBIT	314	322	347	358	355	349	350	352	364	365	373
15	KBIU	323	311	318	342	354	351	343	345	346	358	360
16	KBIV	156	159	131	132	143	148	149	146	147	148	154
17	KBIW	106	111	92	93	99	107	113	114	111	114	116
18 and over	KBIX	16	16	11	11	10	10	11	11	13	12	11

1 From 1 April 1993 excludes 6th form colleges in England and Wales which were reclassified as further education colleges. Schools in England and Northern Ireland as at January; in Wales and Scotland as at previous September.
2 Includes revised figures.
3 Provisional.
4 1 July for Northern Ireland and 31 December for Scotland.

5 Figures for independent schools in England include pupils aged less than 2.
6 Figures for Scotland are estimates using the stage rolls.
7 In Northern Ireland, a split is not collected by age but is available by year group and so this is used as a proxy.
8 Includes the so-called "rising 5s" (i.e. those pupils who become 5 during the autumn term).

Source: Education Departments: 01325 392756

6.3 Number of pupils and teachers: pupil/teacher ratios[1] by school type
United Kingdom

		1997	1998	1999	2000[2]	2001[2]	2002[2,3]
All schools or departments							
Total							
Pupils (thousands)							
Full-time and full-time							
equivalent of part-time	KBCA	9 663.7	9 741.3	9 782.6	9 828.3	9 867.7	9 860.1
Teachers[4] (thousands)	KBCB	533.0	533.6	540.4	545.6	553.1	557.7
Pupils per teacher[4]:							
United Kingdom	KBCC	18.1	18.2	18.2	18.1	17.9	17.8
England	KBCD	18.3	18.5	18.4	18.3	18.1	18.0
Wales	KBCE	18.8	19.1	18.8	18.7	18.4	18.1
Scotland	KBCF	15.8	15.8	15.4	15.4	15.6	15.5
Northern Ireland	KBCG	17.1	17.1	17.1	16.9	16.6	16.4
Public sector mainstream schools or departments							
Nursery							
Pupils (thousands)							
Full-time and full-time							
equivalent of part-time	KBFM	61.5	61.7	61.1	75.3	88.8	87.6
Teachers[4] (thousands)	KBFN	2.9	3.0	3.0	3.1	3.4	3.4
Pupils per teacher[4]	KBFO	21.3	20.7	20.6	24.2	26.5	25.9
Primary[5]							
Pupils (thousands)							
Full-time and full-time							
equivalent of part-time	KBFB	5 184.9	5 213.8	5 202.5	5 167.9	5 130.5	5 083.4
Teachers[4] (thousands)	KBFD	227.0	225.4	226.7	228.0	229.6	231.4
Pupils per teacher[4]	KBFE	22.8	23.1	22.9	22.7	22.3	22.0
Secondary[6]							
Pupils (thousands)							
Full-time and full-time							
equivalent of part-time	KBFG	3 742.7	3 741.1	3 793.3	3 859.0	3 915.5	3 948.0
Teachers[4] (thousands)	KBFH	228.5	228.7	230.4	232.9	237.0	241.0
Pupils per teacher[4]	KBFI	16.2	16.4	16.5	16.6	16.5	16.4
Special schools							
Pupils (thousands)							
Full-time and full-time							
equivalent of part-time							
all	KBFQ	114.2	114.5	..	..	..	..
maintained	KPGE	107.8	108.4	108.5	107.4	106.5	105.4
non-maintained[7]	KPGF	6.4	6.0	..	..	..	..
Teachers[4] (thousands)							
all	KBFS	18.3	18.1	..	..	..	..
maintained	KPGG	16.8	16.7	16.9	17.0	17.0	17.0
non-maintained[7]	KPGH	1.4	1.4	..	..	..	..
Pupils per teacher[4]							
all	KBFT	6.2	6.3	..	..	..	..
maintained	KPGI	6.4	6.5	6.4	6.3	6.3	6.2
non-maintained[7]	KPGJ	4.4	4.4	..	..	..	..

1 See chapter text. 'All schools' pupil/teacher ratios exclude Pupil Referral Units and non-maintained special schools. Figures at January for England and Northern Ireland and at the previous September for Wales and Scotland.
2 Nursery schools for Scotland refer to pre-school education centres and are not therefore directly comparable with earlier years.
3 Provisional.
4 Figures of teachers and of pupil/teacher ratios take account of the full-time equivalent of part-time teachers.
5 Includes preparatory departments attached to grammar schools in Northern Ireland.
6 Includes voluntary grammar schools in Northern Ireland.
7 England and Scotland only.

Source: Education Departments: 01325 392756

6.4 Full-time and part-time pupils with special educational needs (SEN)[1], 2001/02[2]
United Kingdom
By type of school

Thousands and percentages

	United Kingdom	England[3]	Wales	Scotland	Northern Ireland
All schools					
Total pupils	10 097.1	8 369.1	510.6	865.6	351.8
SEN pupils with statements	292.4	249.0	16.9	17.1	9.4
Incidence (%)[4]	2.9	3.0	3.3	2.0	2.7
Maintained schools[5]					
Nursery[6]					
Total pupils	144.8	42.4	2.2	88.8	11.4
SEN pupils with statements	1.1	0.5	-	0.4	0.1
Incidence (%)[4]	0.7	1.3	0.6	0.5	0.6
Placement (%)[7]	0.4	0.2	0.1	2.6	0.7
Primary[8]					
Total pupils	5 245.5	4 363.3	282.6	420.5	179.0
SEN pupils without statements	922.8	834.1	73.5	15.2	..
SEN pupils with statements	84.0	70.7	6.2	4.3	2.8
Pupils with statements - incidence (%)[4]	1.6	1.6	2.2	1.0	1.6
Pupils with statements - placement (%)[7]	28.7	28.4	36.5	25.1	30.2
Secondary					
Total pupils	3 949.3	3 264.1	212.0	317.7	155.5
SEN pupils without statements	563.1	519.1	32.9	11.1	..
SEN pupils with statements	92.7	78.6	6.7	5.0	2.5
Pupils with statements - incidents (%)[4]	2.3	2.4	3.1	1.6	1.6
Pupils with statements - placement (%)[7]	31.7	31.6	39.4	29.0	26.6
Special[9,10]					
Total pupils	106.4	89.8	3.7	8.2	4.7
SEN pupils with statements	100.3	85.8	3.6	6.9	4.0
Incidence (%)[4]	94.2	95.6	97.2	83.9	84.6
Placement (%)[7]	34.3	34.5	21.5	40.1	42.5
Pupil referral units[9,11]					
Total pupils	10.4	10.0	0.5	..	..
SEN pupils with statements	2.0	1.8	0.1	..	..
Incidence (%)[4]	19.0	18.5	30.0	..	..
Placement (%)[7]	0.7	0.7	0.9	..	..
Other schools					
Independent					
Total pupils	635.0	594.9	9.6	29.4	1.1
SEN pupils with statements	7.3	7.0	0.3	..	..
Incidence (%)[4]	1.1	1.2	3.0	0.1	..
Placement (%)[7]	2.5	2.8	1.7	0.1	..
Non-maintained special[9]					
Total pupils	5.7	4.7	..	1.0	..
SEN pupils with statements	5.0	4.5	..	0.5	..
Incidents (%)[4]	87.9	96.0	..	51.3	..
Placement (%)[7]	1.7	1.8	..	3.1	..

1 See chapter text. For Scotland, pupils with a Record of Needs.
2 Provisional.
3 Includes new codes for recording SEN status following the introduction of a new SEN Code of Practice from January 2002. Data are therefore not directly comparable with earlier years.
4 Incidence of pupils - the number of pupils with statements within each school type expressed as a proportion of the total number of pupils on roll in each school type.
5 Grant-aided schools in Northern Ireland.
6 Includes pupils in Voluntary and Private Pre-School Centres in Northern Ireland funded under the Pre-School Expansion Programme which began in 1998/99. Nursery school figures for Scotland are for 1999/00.

7 Placement of pupils - the number of pupils with statements within each school type expressed as a proportion of the number of pupils with statements in all schools.
8 Includes nursery classes (except for Scotland, where they are included with Nursery Schools) and reception classes in primary schools.
9 England and Wales figures exclude dually registered pupils.
10 Including general and hospital special schools.
11 England and Wales only.

Source: Education Departments: 01325 392756

6.5 GCE, GCSE and SCE[1] qualifications obtained at a typical age[2,3], and GCE, GCSE, SCE and GNVQ/GSVQ qualifications obtained by students of all ages

United Kingdom

Percentages and thousands

	Pupils in their last year of compulsory education[2]					Pupils/students in education[3]			
						% achieving GCE A Levels and equivalent			Population aged 17 (thousands)
	5 or more grades A*-C[4]	1-4 grades A*-C[4]	Grades D-G[5] only	No graded results	Total (=100%) (Thousands)	2 or more passes[6,7]	1 pass[8]	1 or more passes	
Students at a typical age (percentages and thousands)									
1996/97									
All	46.2	25.5	20.9	7.4	713.3	29.6	7.4	37.0	723.5
Males	41.4	25.3	24.9	8.5	363.5	26.5	6.7	33.2	372.4
Females	51.3	25.7	16.7	6.3	349.7	33.0	8.1	41.1	351.0
1997/98									
All	47.5	25.2	21.1	6.5	698.4	33.5	6.5	40.1	751.0
Males	42.3	25.4	24.9	7.5	356.1	29.9	6.0	35.9	384.9
Females	52.8	25.0	17.1	5.3	342.3	37.4	7.2	44.5	366.1
1998/99									
All	49.1	24.8	20.3	5.9	703.6	33.7	6.7	40.3	744.2
Males	43.8	25.2	24.1	6.9	359.6	30.1	6.1	36.2	381.4
Females	54.6	24.3	16.3	4.8	344.0	37.4	7.3	44.7	362.8
1999/00									
All	50.4	24.5	19.7	5.5	703.7	34.5	6.5	41.0	732.2
Males	45.0	25.0	23.6	6.4	357.7	30.5	6.0	36.6	376.0
Females	55.9	23.9	15.7	4.5	346.0	38.6	7.1	45.6	356.3
2000/01									
All	51.0	24.1	19.4	5.5	729.7	37.2	4.7	41.9	735.4
Males	45.7	24.6	23.1	6.5	372.1	32.9	4.5	37.4	378.5
Females	56.5	23.6	15.5	4.4	357.6	41.7	4.9	46.6	356.9

	GCSE and SCE S Grade/Standard Grade (SG)				GCE A Level and SCE/NQ Higher Grade		
	5 or more grades A*-C[4,9]	1-4 grades A*-C[4,9]	Grades D-G[5,10] only	No graded results[11]	2 or more passes[6,7]	1 pass[8]	Total 1 or more passes
Students of all ages (thousands)							
1996/97							
All	333.6	358.7	240.5	41.8	219.3	76.6	295.9
Males	152.3	169.6	133.5	20.7	101.2	33.2	134.3
Females	181.0	189.1	107.0	21.2	118.1	43.4	161.6
1997/98							
All	335.3	336.4	233.9	37.4	260.4	70.3	330.6
Males	152.8	162.3	129.5	18.3	119.2	30.5	149.7
Females	182.5	174.1	104.5	19.2	141.2	39.8	181.0
1998/99							
All	341.0	323.7	229.8	31.2	257.9	69.9	327.8
Males	162.3	150.6	128.1	15.6	118.4	30.6	149.0
Females	178.7	173.2	101.7	15.6	139.5	39.3	178.8
1999/00							
All	357.7	311.6	224.4	30.3	258.8	65.6	324.4
Males	162.8	150.9	125.3	15.2	118.0	28.7	146.6
Females	194.9	160.7	99.1	15.1	140.9	36.9	177.7
2000/01							
All	375.1	335.0	227.3	31.8	280.8	64.2	345.1
Males	171.8	164.1	127.3	16.0	128.4	29.1	157.5
Females	203.3	170.9	100.1	15.8	152.4	35.2	187.6

1 From 1999/00 National Qualifications (NQ) were introduced in Scotland but not all are shown until 2000/01. NQs include Standard Grades, Intermediate 1 & 2 and Higher Grades. The figures for Higher Grades combine the new NQ Higher and the old SCE Higher and include Advanced Higher.

2 Pupils aged 15 at the start of the academic year, pupils in year S4 in Scotland.

3 Up to 1999/00, pupils in schools and students in further education institutions aged 16-18 at the start of the academic year in England, Wales and Northern Ireland as a percentage of the 17 year old population. For 2000/01 pupils in schools and students in further education institutions aged 17-18 at the start of the academic year in England, aged 17 in Wales and aged 16-18 in Northern Ireland, as a percentage of the 17 year old population. Figures for England and Wales are not directly comparable with earlier years. Pupils in Scotland generally sit Highers one year earlier and the figures relate to the results of pupils in year S5/S6.

4 Standard Grades 1-3/Intermediate 2 A-C/Intermediate 1 A-B in Scotland.

5 Grades D-G at GCSE and Scottish Standard Grades 4-6/Intermediate 1 (C)/ Access 3 (pass).

6 3 or more SCE/NQ Higher Grades/ 2 or more Advanced Highers/ 1 Advanced Higher with more than 2 Higher passes in Scotland.

7 Includes Advanced level GNVQ/GSVQ which is equivalent to 2 GCE A Levels or AS equivalents/3 SCE/NQ Higher grades. Includes VCE Single awards in Nothern Ireland.

8 2 AS levels or 2 Highers/ 1 Advanced or 1 each in Scotland, count as 1 A Level pass. Includes those with 1.5 A level passes.

9 Includes GNVQ/GSVQ Intermediate Part 1, Full and Language unit which are equivalent to 2, 4 and 0.5 GCSE grades A*-C/SCE Standard grades 1-3 respectively. Figures include those with 4.5 GCSEs.

10 Includes GNVQ/GSVQ Foundation Part 1, Full and Language unit which are equivalent to 2, 4 and 0.5 GCSE grades D-G/SCE Standard grades 4-7 respectively.

11 Figures for Scotland include students in Year S4 only.

Source: Education Departments: 01325 392756

6.6 Students in further education[1] by country, mode of study[2], sex and age,[3] during 2000/01[4]

United Kingdom (home and overseas students)

Thousands

	United Kingdom		England[5]		Wales		Scotland[6]		Northern Ireland[7]	
	Full-time	Part-time	Full-time	Part-time	Full-time	Part-time	Full-time	Part-time	Full-time	Part-time
All										
Age under 16	12.5	87.5	9.9	50.1	0.7	4.6	1.7	30.2	0.1	2.6
16	257.7	86.0	227.5	61.2	13.7	3.8	9.0	15.0	7.4	6.1
17	217.4	97.0	191.5	72.8	11.3	4.3	7.8	15.2	6.9	4.7
18	112.4	98.9	97.3	80.2	5.5	5.0	5.5	10.7	4.0	3.0
19	53.6	89.0	47.5	72.8	2.3	4.6	2.7	9.3	1.1	2.3
20	34.8	82.4	31.6	69.2	1.2	4.3	1.6	7.2	0.4	1.7
21	25.9	77.4	23.8	66.1	0.8	4.0	1.1	5.9	0.2	1.5
22	20.2	72.8	18.6	62.5	0.6	3.5	0.9	5.4	0.1	1.3
23	17.3	72.2	16.0	62.2	0.5	3.4	0.8	5.2	0.1	1.4
24	16.3	74.6	15.2	64.8	0.5	3.3	0.6	5.2	0.1	1.3
25	15.3	77.0	14.3	67.3	0.4	3.4	0.6	5.1	-	1.3
26	14.6	79.2	13.6	69.3	0.4	3.6	0.6	5.0	-	1.2
27	14.6	82.9	13.6	72.6	0.4	3.7	0.5	5.4	-	1.2
28	14.2	86.8	13.3	76.0	0.4	4.0	0.5	5.4	-	1.3
29	14.2	91.0	13.3	79.8	0.4	4.2	0.5	5.8	-	1.2
30+	240.8	2 583.4	228.2	2 257.2	5.5	123.6	6.9	177.8	0.2	24.8
Unknown	4.3	65.3	4.1	62.0	0.1	2.9	-	-	-	0.4
All ages	1 086.0	3 903.4	979.3	3 346.1	44.6	186.2	41.3	313.8	20.7	57.3
Males										
Age under 16	7.1	45.8	5.5	27.0	0.4	2.7	1.0	14.5	0.1	1.6
16	126.8	44.5	110.9	33.1	6.7	2.0	5.3	6.6	4.0	2.7
17	106.2	51.8	93.2	39.9	5.5	2.4	4.0	7.4	3.4	2.1
18	58.7	53.2	51.0	42.9	2.8	2.9	2.7	6.0	2.1	1.5
19	29.5	45.0	26.2	36.1	1.2	2.5	1.4	5.3	0.7	1.0
20	19.0	38.4	17.3	31.6	0.6	2.2	0.9	4.0	0.2	0.6
21	13.6	33.1	12.6	27.8	0.4	1.8	0.6	2.9	0.1	0.6
22	10.4	29.7	9.6	25.3	0.3	1.5	0.4	2.4	-	0.5
23	8.8	28.8	8.2	24.7	0.2	1.4	0.3	2.2	-	0.5
24	8.3	29.6	7.7	25.6	0.2	1.4	0.3	2.3	-	0.4
25	7.7	30.4	7.2	26.6	0.2	1.3	0.3	2.1	-	0.4
26	7.3	31.1	6.9	27.2	0.1	1.4	0.2	2.1	-	0.3
27	7.3	32.4	6.9	28.5	0.1	1.4	0.2	2.2	-	0.3
28	6.9	33.9	6.6	29.8	0.1	1.5	0.2	2.1	-	0.4
29	6.9	35.1	6.6	30.8	0.1	1.6	0.2	2.3	-	0.4
30+	116.7	941.1	112.5	820.3	1.7	46.0	2.5	67.5	0.1	7.2
Unknown	2.3	24.0	2.3	22.5	-	1.3	-	-	-	0.1
All ages	543.4	1 527.8	491.2	1 299.7	20.8	75.2	20.6	132.1	10.8	20.7
Females										
Age under 16	5.4	41.7	4.3	23.1	0.3	2.0	0.7	15.6	-	1.0
16	130.8	41.5	116.6	28.0	7.0	1.8	3.7	8.3	3.5	3.3
17	111.2	45.2	98.2	32.9	5.8	1.9	3.7	7.8	3.5	2.6
18	53.7	45.7	46.3	37.4	2.8	2.1	2.8	4.7	1.9	1.6
19	24.1	44.0	21.3	36.7	1.1	2.1	1.3	4.1	0.5	1.2
20	15.8	44.0	14.4	37.7	0.6	2.1	0.7	3.2	0.1	1.0
21	12.3	44.4	11.2	38.3	0.4	2.2	0.6	3.0	0.1	0.9
22	9.9	43.1	9.0	37.2	0.3	2.0	0.5	3.0	-	0.9
23	8.5	43.4	7.8	37.5	0.3	2.0	0.4	3.0	-	1.0
24	8.0	44.9	7.4	39.2	0.3	1.9	0.3	2.9	-	0.9
25	7.7	46.6	7.1	40.7	0.2	2.1	0.3	2.9	-	0.9
26	7.3	48.1	6.7	42.1	0.2	2.2	0.3	2.9	-	0.9
27	7.3	50.5	6.7	44.0	0.2	2.4	0.3	3.2	-	0.9
28	7.3	52.9	6.7	46.2	0.3	2.5	0.3	3.3	-	0.9
29	7.4	55.9	6.8	49.0	0.3	2.6	0.3	3.5	-	0.9
30+	124.1	1 642.3	115.7	1 436.9	3.8	77.6	4.4	110.3	0.2	17.5
Unknown	1.9	41.3	1.9	39.4	-	1.6	-	-	-	0.3
All ages	542.6	2 375.6	488.1	2 046.4	23.8	111.0	20.7	181.8	10.0	36.5

1 Further education (FE) figures are whole year counts exept for Northern Ireland, which are on a snapshot basis. FE figures differ from the higher education tables which use annual snapshots (apart from Scottish FE college data, which is all finalised data).

2 Full-time includes sandwich. Part-time comprises both day and evening, including block release and open/distance learning.

3 Ages as at 31 August 2000 (1 July in Northern Ireland and 31 December in Scotland).

4 All data are provisional.

5 FE institution figures for England include external institutions and specialist designated colleges and are not directly comparable with previous years.

6 Figures for Scotland FE colleges are enrolments rather than headcounts.

7 Data for Northern Ireland FE institutions refer to 1999/00.

Source: Education Departments: 01325 392756

6.7 Students in further education[1] by country, mode of study[2], sex and subject group, during 2000/01[3]

United Kingdom - Home and overseas students

Thousands

	United Kingdom		England		Wales		Scotland		Northern Ireland	
	Full-time	Part-time	Full-time	Part-time	Full-time	Part-time	Full-time	Part-time	Full-time	Part-time
All persons										
Subject group										
Medicine & Dentistry	-	-	-	-	-	-	-	-	-	-
Allied Medicine	132.0	259.5	129.4	246.2	-	-	1.2	11.6	1.4	1.8
Biological Sciences	7.8	9.8	7.6	6.8	-	-	0.2	2.9	-	-
Agriculture	22.1	55.7	20.6	45.0	-	-	1.4	10.2	0.1	0.5
Physical Sciences	4.8	5.4	4.8	4.2	-	-	-	1.0	-	0.3
Mathematical and Computing Sciences	34.1	114.1	29.3	24.8	-	-	3.2	78.5	1.6	10.8
Engineering & Technology	66.7	164.6	59.3	141.7	-	-	5.5	18.8	1.9	4.0
Architecture	31.7	108.0	26.0	99.2	-	-	3.2	7.1	2.6	1.6
Social Sciences	46.6	337.5	39.8	309.5	-	-	6.0	25.5	0.7	2.6
Business & Financial	78.5	452.1	67.0	398.8	-	-	6.4	40.5	5.1	12.7
Documentation	78.5	614.7	77.4	603.1	-	-	0.7	11.2	0.4	0.4
Languages	137.6	179.1	136.8	160.2	-	0.2	0.9	16.8	-	1.9
Humanities	24.5	109.9	24.3	109.0	-	-	0.2	1.0	-	-
Creative arts	101.5	230.9	93.1	206.3	0.1	-	5.8	21.4	2.5	3.3
Education[4]	3.2	21.2	-	1.1	-	0.2	2.5	17.3	0.6	2.5
Other subjects[5]	166.7	705.4	158.5	636.0	0.3	4.5	4.1	50.0	3.8	14.8
Unknown	149.7	535.4	105.5	354.2	44.2	181.2	-	-	-	-
All subjects	1 086.0	3 903.4	979.3	3 346.1	44.6	186.2	41.3	313.8	20.7	57.3
Males										
Subject group										
Medicine and Dentistry	-	-	-	-	-	-	-	-	-	-
Allied Medicine	55.5	87.0	55.3	81.4	-	-	0.2	5.4	0.1	0.2
Biological Sciences	2.8	3.0	2.7	1.7	-	-	0.1	1.3	-	-
Agriculture	10.8	26.0	9.9	20.9	-	-	0.8	4.8	-	0.3
Physical Sciences	3.1	2.6	3.1	2.0	-	-	-	0.4	-	0.1
Mathematical and Computing Sciences	19.0	43.0	15.5	9.4	-	-	2.2	30.0	1.3	3.5
Engineering & Technology	59.4	144.7	52.4	124.8	-	-	5.1	16.2	1.8	3.6
Architecture	29.9	98.9	24.3	91.2	-	-	3.0	6.2	2.6	1.6
Social Sciences	20.3	98.0	19.3	92.8	-	-	0.9	5.0	0.1	0.2
Business & Financial	33.8	154.0	30.0	135.1	-	-	2.0	15.6	1.7	3.3
Documentation	44.3	243.0	43.7	238.4	-	-	0.3	4.6	0.2	0.1
Languages	67.7	65.3	67.3	57.8	-	0.1	0.4	6.8	-	0.7
Humanities	10.4	36.9	10.3	36.5	-	-	0.1	0.4	-	-
Creative arts	44.4	62.7	41.7	57.0	-	-	1.9	5.2	0.8	0.4
Education[4]	2.0	8.9	-	0.2	-	0.1	1.6	7.7	0.4	0.9
Other subjects[5]	69.7	262.6	65.8	232.8	0.1	1.6	1.9	22.5	1.8	5.8
Unknown	70.4	191.2	49.8	117.7	20.6	73.5	-	-	-	-
All subjects	543.4	1 527.8	491.2	1 299.7	20.8	75.2	20.6	132.1	10.8	20.7
Females										
Subject group										
Medicine & Dentistry	-	-	-	-	-	-	-	-	-	-
Allied Medicine	76.5	172.6	74.1	164.8	-	-	1.1	6.2	1.3	1.6
Biological Sciences	5.1	7.1	4.9	5.2	-	-	0.1	1.7	0.1	0.3
Agriculture	11.3	29.4	10.6	24.1	-	-	0.6	5.4	-	-
Physical Sciences	1.7	2.8	1.7	2.2	-	-	-	0.5	-	0.1
Mathematical and Computing Sciences	15.0	71.1	13.8	15.4	-	-	0.9	48.4	0.3	7.2
Engineering & Technology	7.3	19.9	6.9	16.9	-	-	0.3	2.6	0.1	0.4
Architecture	1.8	9.0	1.7	8.0	-	-	0.1	1.0	-	0.1
Social Sciences	26.3	239.5	20.5	216.7	-	-	5.1	20.5	0.7	2.4
Business & Financial	44.7	298.1	36.9	263.8	-	-	4.4	24.9	3.4	9.5
Documentation	34.2	371.7	33.7	364.7	-	-	0.3	6.7	0.2	0.3
Languages	69.9	113.8	69.5	102.4	-	0.1	0.5	10.1	-	1.3
Humanities	14.1	73.1	14.0	72.5	-	-	0.2	0.6	-	-
Creative arts	57.1	168.2	51.4	149.2	-	-	3.9	16.1	1.7	2.9
Education[4]	1.2	12.3	-	0.9	-	0.1	1.0	9.6	0.2	1.6
Other subjects[5]	97.0	442.7	92.7	403.2	0.2	2.9	2.2	27.5	2.0	9.0
Unknown	79.3	344.2	55.7	236.5	23.6	107.7	-	-	-	-
All subjects	542.6	2 375.6	488.1	2 046.4	23.8	111.0	20.7	181.8	10.0	36.5

1 Further education (FE) figures are whole year counts except for Northern Ireland, which are collected on a snapshot basis. FE figurs differ from the education tables which use annual snapshots (apart from Scottish FE college data, which is finalised data).

2 Full-time excludes sandwich, short full-time. Part-time comprises both day and evening, including block release and open/distance learning.

3 Provisional. FE institution data for Northern Ireland refer to 1999/00. Due to a change in methodology, FE institution figures for England are not directly comparable with previous years. Figures also include external institutions and specialist designated colleges. Figures for Scotland FE colleges are enrolments rather than headcounts. Due to a reclassification of subject grouping, subject categories for Scotland cannot be directly compared with previous years.

4 Includes ITT and INSET.

5 Includes combined and general categories plus for England FE institutions Hotel and Catering and Basic Education.

Source: Education Departments: 01325 392756

6.8 Students in higher education[1] by level, mode of study[2], sex and age[3], 2001/02[4,5]
United Kingdom (home and overseas students)

Thousands

| | Postgraduate level | | | | | | First degree | | Other undergraduate | | Total higher education[6] | |
| | PHD's and equivalent | | Masters and others | | Total postgraduate | | | | | | | |
	Full-time	Part-time	Full-time	Part-time	Full-time	Part-time	Full-time	Part-time	Full-time	Part-time	Full-time	Part-time
All Persons												
Age under 16	-	-	-	-	-	-	-	-	-	0.2	-	0.3
16	-	-	-	-	-	-	0.4	-	1.1	0.5	1.4	0.5
17	-	-	-	-	-	-	10.2	0.1	4.8	1.1	15.0	1.2
18	-	-	0.1	-	0.1	-	151.4	1.1	23.6	5.7	175.2	6.8
19	-	-	0.1	-	0.1	-	204.6	3.7	31.3	10.3	236.2	14.1
20	-	-	1.1	0.1	1.2	0.1	212.7	6.1	26.6	12.1	240.6	18.4
21	0.8	-	13.7	1.1	14.5	1.2	144.4	7.3	18.5	12.5	177.5	21.1
22	2.8	0.1	19.8	4.2	22.6	4.3	65.6	6.7	12.8	12.0	101.0	23.0
23	4.5	0.3	16.9	6.4	21.4	6.7	31.5	5.3	9.1	11.5	62.0	23.5
24	4.9	1.1	13.1	7.2	17.9	8.3	18.2	4.4	6.9	11.4	43.1	24.2
25	3.8	2.4	10.0	7.9	13.8	10.3	12.6	3.9	5.5	11.8	31.9	26.0
26	3.2	2.4	8.0	8.0	11.2	10.4	9.7	3.7	4.7	11.9	25.6	26.0
27	2.7	2.1	6.6	8.4	9.3	10.5	7.8	3.5	4.0	12.1	21.2	26.2
28	2.3	2.1	5.4	8.8	7.7	10.9	6.8	3.6	3.7	13.1	18.2	27.6
29	1.9	2.1	4.7	9.1	6.6	11.2	6.0	3.5	3.5	13.2	16.2	27.9
30+	12.7	28.9	32.5	162.8	45.2	191.6	59.6	62.3	40.6	312.5	145.7	567.0
Unknown	-	3.9	0.3	21.6	0.3	25.5	0.4	8.4	0.4	61.1	1.1	95.1
All ages	39.6	45.4	132.3	245.6	172.0	291.0	942.0	123.7	197.1	513.0	1 311.8	928.9
Males												
Age under 16	-	-	-	-	-	-	-	-	-	0.1	-	0.1
16	-	-	-	-	-	-	0.1	-	0.3	0.2	0.4	0.3
17	-	-	-	-	-	-	4.5	-	2.1	0.6	6.6	0.6
18	-	-	-	-	-	-	68.4	0.5	11.0	3.4	79.5	4.0
19	-	-	0.1	-	0.1	-	94.2	2.1	14.7	6.4	109.0	8.5
20	-	-	0.5	-	0.5	-	98.2	3.4	11.9	6.6	110.7	10.1
21	0.4	-	5.6	0.4	6.0	0.4	70.7	4.0	7.9	6.2	84.7	10.6
22	1.7	-	8.8	1.7	10.5	1.7	34.5	3.6	5.4	5.2	50.5	10.5
23	2.6	0.1	7.8	2.6	10.3	2.7	16.8	2.8	3.9	4.7	31.1	10.2
24	2.8	0.6	6.1	2.9	8.9	3.5	9.8	2.1	2.8	4.5	21.6	10.2
25	2.1	1.4	4.9	3.4	6.9	4.7	6.5	1.7	2.2	4.6	15.6	11.1
26	1.7	1.3	3.8	3.2	5.5	4.5	4.8	1.6	1.7	4.6	12.0	10.8
27	1.4	1.2	3.2	3.4	4.7	4.6	3.8	1.4	1.4	4.9	9.9	11.0
28	1.3	1.2	2.8	3.9	4.0	5.1	3.1	1.5	1.3	5.4	8.5	11.9
29	1.1	1.2	2.4	4.2	3.5	5.4	2.8	1.5	1.2	5.5	7.6	12.4
30+	7.5	16.5	17.0	77.5	24.5	94.0	21.2	20.5	11.4	122.7	57.2	237.6
Unknown	-	2.5	0.2	10.9	0.2	13.4	0.2	4.1	0.2	20.2	0.6	37.7
All ages	22.6	26.0	63.1	114.2	85.7	140.2	439.6	50.9	79.6	205.9	605.3	397.6
Females												
Age under 16	-	-	-	-	-	-	-	-	-	0.1	-	0.1
16	-	-	-	-	-	-	0.2	-	0.8	0.2	1.0	0.2
17	-	-	-	-	-	-	5.7	-	2.7	0.6	8.4	0.6
18	-	-	-	-	-	-	83.0	0.5	12.6	2.2	95.6	2.8
19	-	-	0.1	-	0.1	-	110.4	1.6	16.6	4.0	127.1	5.6
20	-	-	0.6	0.1	0.7	0.1	114.5	2.7	14.6	5.5	129.8	8.3
21	0.4	-	8.2	0.7	8.5	0.8	73.7	3.4	10.6	6.3	92.8	10.5
22	1.1	0.1	11.0	2.5	12.1	2.6	31.1	3.1	7.3	6.7	50.5	12.4
23	1.9	0.1	9.1	3.8	11.0	4.0	14.7	2.5	5.2	6.9	30.9	13.3
24	2.1	0.5	6.9	4.3	9.0	4.8	8.5	2.3	4.0	6.9	21.5	14.0
25	1.7	1.0	5.1	4.5	6.9	5.5	6.1	2.2	3.4	7.1	16.3	14.9
26	1.5	1.0	4.2	4.8	5.7	5.8	4.9	2.1	3.0	7.3	13.6	15.3
27	1.2	1.0	3.4	4.9	4.6	5.9	4.1	2.1	2.6	7.1	11.3	15.2
28	1.0	1.0	2.7	4.9	3.7	5.8	3.6	2.1	2.4	7.7	9.7	15.7
29	0.9	0.9	2.3	4.9	3.1	5.8	3.2	2.0	2.3	7.7	8.7	15.6
30+	5.2	12.4	15.5	85.3	20.7	97.6	38.5	41.7	29.2	189.8	88.5	329.5
Unknown	-	1.5	0.1	10.7	0.1	12.2	0.2	4.3	0.2	40.9	0.5	57.4
All ages	17.0	19.3	69.2	131.5	86.3	150.8	502.3	72.8	117.5	307.1	706.4	531.4

1 Includes Open University students. Part-time figures include dormant modes, those writing up at home and on sabbaticals, which are not included in HESA SFR 56.
2 Full-time includes sandwich. Part-time comprises both day and evening, including block release and open/distance learning.
3 Ages as at 31 August 2001 (1 July in Northern Ireland and 31 December in Scotland).
4 Figures for students (other than in Scotland further education colleges) are snapshots counted at a particular point in the year. (December for UK HE institutions and FE institutions in Wales, November for FE institutions in England and Northern Ireland.) Students starting courses after these dates will not therefore be counted. Figures for Scotland, however, are whole year (not snapshot) enrolments (rather than headcounts) for 2000/01.
5 Provisional. Figures for HE students in FE institutions in Wales and Northern Ireland and FE colleges in Scotland relate to 2000/01.
6 Includes data for HE education students in FE institutions in Wales which cannot be split by level.

Source: Education Departments: 01325 392756

6.9 Students in higher education[1] by type of course, mode of study[2], sex and subject group, 2001/02[3,4]

United Kingdom - Home and overseas students

Thousands

	Postgraduate level						First degree		Other undergraduate		Total higher education[5]	
	PHD's & equivalent		Masters and others		Total postgraduate							
	Full-time	Part-time	Full-time	Part-time	Full-time	Part-time	Full-time	Part-time	Full-time	Part-time	Full-time[5]	Part-time[5]
All persons												
Subject group												
Medicine & Dentistry	2.5	2.1	2.9	4.6	5.5	6.7	31.1	0.1	0.3	0.2	36.9	6.9
Allied Medicine	1.8	1.2	3.4	17.2	5.2	18.4	57.7	25.3	61.0	43.3	123.9	87.0
Biological Sciences	6.2	1.8	4.2	4.1	10.4	5.9	65.8	3.2	2.4	1.8	78.6	11.0
Agriculture	0.9	0.2	1.2	1.2	2.1	1.4	10.6	0.5	4.4	2.7	17.1	4.6
Physical Sciences	6.4	0.9	4.6	2.5	11.0	3.4	42.8	1.6	1.3	2.3	55.1	7.4
Mathematical and Computing Sciences	2.7	0.8	11.1	7.5	13.7	8.3	78.7	6.0	15.2	16.5	107.6	30.8
Engineering & Technology	5.9	1.8	9.8	9.0	15.7	10.8	72.4	7.3	11.4	25.4	99.5	43.5
Architecture	0.5	0.4	3.9	4.9	4.4	5.3	19.5	6.0	3.2	11.1	27.1	22.4
Social Sciences	4.1	2.7	23.6	18.5	27.8	21.2	113.9	11.5	12.5	22.7	154.1	55.4
Business & Financial	1.4	1.6	21.1	39.7	22.5	41.4	110.1	13.5	30.5	70.9	163.2	125.8
Documentation	0.2	0.2	3.2	2.8	3.4	3.0	20.4	0.9	5.1	5.8	29.0	9.6
Languages	2.3	1.3	4.7	3.5	7.0	4.7	55.3	2.9	4.7	18.8	66.9	26.4
Humanities	2.3	1.7	3.9	5.9	6.2	7.6	32.6	3.1	1.3	14.4	40.2	25.1
Creative arts	0.7	0.7	5.9	3.2	6.6	3.9	85.5	4.4	22.6	9.5	114.7	17.8
Education[6]	0.9	3.4	26.2	38.0	27.1	41.4	44.3	5.2	2.5	15.2	73.9	61.9
Other subjects[7]	0.7	0.5	2.7	22.8	3.4	23.3	99.8	10.6	18.3	182.8	121.5	216.7
Unknown[5]	-	24.0	-	60.2	-	84.2	1.3	21.4	0.5	69.6	2.5	176.5
All subjects	39.6	45.4	132.3	245.6	172.0	291.0	942.0	123.7	197.1	513.0	1 311.8	928.9
Males												
Subject group												
Medicine and Dentistry	1.0	1.2	1.3	2.1	2.3	3.3	13.7	0.1	0.1	0.1	16.1	3.4
Allied Medicine	0.8	0.4	1.0	4.3	1.8	4.8	13.1	3.0	9.0	4.6	24.0	12.4
Biological Sciences	2.6	0.8	1.6	1.3	4.2	2.0	24.0	1.2	1.1	0.7	29.3	3.9
Agriculture	0.4	0.1	0.6	0.6	1.1	0.7	3.8	0.2	1.9	1.4	6.7	2.3
Physical Sciences	4.2	0.6	2.6	1.5	6.8	2.1	26.0	0.9	0.8	1.4	33.6	4.4
Mathematical and Computing Sciences	2.1	0.6	7.9	4.9	10.0	5.5	60.2	4.5	11.9	9.2	82.1	19.2
Engineering & Technology	4.6	1.6	7.8	7.7	12.5	9.3	61.0	6.8	9.9	23.4	83.4	39.5
Architecture	0.3	0.3	2.3	3.1	2.6	3.4	13.9	4.7	2.5	9.2	19.1	17.4
Social Sciences	2.2	1.4	10.3	7.3	12.5	8.7	45.0	4.3	3.5	5.5	61.0	18.5
Business & Financial	0.9	1.1	11.6	21.0	12.4	22.0	52.0	5.9	13.2	26.9	77.6	54.9
Documentation	0.1	0.1	1.1	1.0	1.2	1.1	8.0	0.3	3.5	3.6	12.7	5.0
Languages	1.0	0.5	1.5	1.1	2.5	1.7	15.3	0.8	1.4	7.0	19.2	9.6
Humanities	1.3	1.0	1.9	2.7	3.2	3.6	15.3	1.2	0.5	5.1	19.0	9.9
Creative arts	0.3	0.4	2.5	1.3	2.8	1.7	34.3	1.6	11.0	3.5	48.0	6.7
Education[6]	0.4	1.5	7.8	11.0	8.2	12.6	10.4	1.2	1.2	4.2	19.9	18.0
Other subjects[7]	0.3	0.2	1.4	13.0	1.7	13.3	42.8	3.8	7.8	77.1	52.3	94.1
Unknown[5]	-	14.3	-	30.3	-	44.6	0.7	10.2	0.2	23.2	1.3	78.6
All subjects	22.6	26.0	63.1	114.2	85.7	140.2	439.6	50.9	79.6	205.9	605.3	397.6
Females												
Subject group												
Medicine & Dentistry	1.5	0.9	1.7	2.5	3.2	3.4	17.4	-	0.2	0.1	20.8	3.5
Allied Medicine	1.0	0.7	2.3	12.9	3.3	13.6	44.6	22.3	51.9	38.7	99.9	74.6
Biological Sciences	3.7	1.0	2.6	2.9	6.3	3.9	41.8	2.1	1.2	1.1	49.2	7.1
Agriculture	0.5	0.1	0.6	0.6	1.0	0.7	6.8	0.2	2.5	1.3	10.3	2.3
Physical Sciences	2.1	0.3	2.0	1.1	4.2	1.4	16.9	0.7	0.5	0.9	21.5	3.0
Mathematical and Computing Sciences	0.6	0.2	3.1	2.6	3.7	2.8	18.5	1.6	3.2	7.3	25.5	11.6
Engineering & Technology	1.3	0.3	1.9	1.3	3.2	1.6	11.4	0.5	1.6	2.0	16.2	4.1
Architecture	0.2	0.1	1.6	1.8	1.8	1.9	5.6	1.2	0.6	1.9	7.9	5.0
Social Sciences	1.9	1.3	13.4	11.2	15.3	12.5	68.9	7.2	9.0	17.3	93.1	37.0
Business & Financial	0.6	0.6	9.6	18.8	10.1	19.3	58.1	7.6	17.3	44.0	85.6	70.9
Documentation	0.1	0.1	2.1	1.8	2.2	1.9	12.5	0.5	1.7	2.2	16.3	4.6
Languages	1.3	0.7	3.2	2.3	4.6	3.1	39.9	2.1	3.2	11.7	47.7	16.9
Humanities	1.0	0.7	2.0	3.3	3.0	4.0	17.4	1.9	0.8	9.3	21.2	15.2
Creative arts	0.4	0.3	3.4	1.9	3.8	2.2	51.3	2.8	11.6	6.0	66.7	11.1
Education[6]	0.5	1.9	18.4	27.0	18.9	28.9	33.9	4.0	1.3	11.1	54.0	44.0
Other subjects[7]	0.3	0.3	1.3	9.7	1.7	10.0	57.0	6.8	10.5	105.6	69.2	122.5
Unknown[5]	-	9.7	-	29.9	-	39.6	0.6	11.2	0.2	46.5	1.2	98.0
All subjects	17.0	19.3	69.2	131.5	86.3	150.8	502.3	72.8	117.5	307.1	706.4	531.4

1 Higher education institutions include Open University students. Part-time figures include dormant modes, those writing up at home and on sabbaticals, which are not included in HESA SFR56.

2 Full-time includes sandwich. Part-time comprises both day and evening, including block release and open/distance learning.

3 Provisional. Figures for HE students in FE institutions in Wales and Northern Ireland and FE colleges in Scotland relate to 2000/01.

4 Figures for students (other than Scotland FE institutions) are snapshots counted at a particular point in the year (December for UK HE institutions and FE institutions in Wales, November for FE institutions in England and Northern Ireland). Students starting courses after these dates will not therefore be counted. Figures for Scotland, however are whole year (not snapshot) enrolments (rather than headcounts) for 2000/01.

5 Includes data for HE students in FE institutions in Wales which cannot be split by level. Figures for home, part-time UK HE institution dormant modes, those writing up at home, and on sabbaticals, which cannot be identified by subject are also included in the 'Unknown' row, throughout the levels.

6 Including ITT and INSET.

7 Includes combined and general categories, plus for England FE institutions, Hotel and Catering and Basic Education.

Source: Education Departments: 01325 392756

6.10 Students[1] obtaining higher education qualifications[2] by type of course, sex and subject group, 2000/01

United Kingdom

Thousands

			Postgraduate			
	Sub-degree[3]	First degree	PHD's and equivalent	Other	Total	Total higher education
All persons						
Subject group						
Medicine & Dentistry	-	6.0	1.0	2.0	3.0	9.0
Subjects Allied to Medicine	22.9	19.5	0.6	4.9	5.5	47.9
Biological Sciences	1.1	18.6	1.7	3.0	4.7	24.4
Vet. Science, Agriculture & related	1.4	2.9	0.3	0.8	1.1	5.3
Physical Sciences	0.7	13.0	1.8	2.5	4.2	18.0
Mathematical & Computer Sciences	5.4	16.7	0.6	5.7	6.3	28.5
Engineering & Technology	4.4	19.8	1.7	6.6	8.3	32.4
Architecture, Building & Planning	1.9	6.2	0.1	3.3	3.4	11.5
Social Sciences[4]	5.1	32.0	1.1	17.2	18.3	55.4
Business & Financial Studies	9.0	32.6	0.4	23.3	23.7	65.3
Librarianship & Info Science	0.4	4.5	0.1	2.5	2.5	7.5
Languages	2.0	16.6	0.7	3.0	3.7	22.3
Humanities	1.0	9.9	0.7	2.5	3.2	14.1
Creative Arts & Design	2.8	22.2	0.1	4.4	4.5	29.5
Education[5]	4.8	11.8	0.5	28.4	28.8	45.4
Combined, gen.	13.9	33.1	0.2	6.7	6.9	53.9
All subjects	76.9	265.3	11.5	116.5	128.1	470.3
Males						
Subject group						
Medicine and Dentistry	-	2.8	0.5	0.9	1.3	4.2
Subjects Allied to Medicine	2.4	3.9	0.3	1.2	1.5	7.8
Biological Sciences	0.6	6.6	0.8	1.0	1.8	9.0
Vet. Science, Agriculture & related	0.7	1.1	0.2	0.4	0.6	2.4
Physical Sciences	0.5	7.9	1.2	1.4	2.6	11.0
Mathematical & Computer Sciences	3.8	12.3	0.5	3.8	4.3	20.4
Engineering & Technology	3.9	16.7	1.4	5.3	6.7	27.3
Architecture, Building & Planning	1.4	4.6	0.1	2.1	2.2	8.1
Social Sciences[4]	1.4	12.4	0.6	7.4	8.0	21.8
Business & Financial Studies	3.8	14.8	0.3	12.7	13.0	31.6
Librarianship & Info Science	0.2	1.6	-	0.8	0.8	2.6
Languages	0.7	4.5	0.3	0.9	1.2	6.4
Humanities	0.4	4.5	0.4	1.1	1.6	6.5
Creative Arts & Design	1.3	8.7	0.1	1.8	1.8	11.8
Education[5]	1.4	2.7	0.2	7.9	8.1	12.2
Combined, gen.	5.0	13.6	0.1	3.8	3.9	22.6
All subjects	27.5	118.9	6.9	52.6	59.5	205.9
Females						
Subject group						
Medicine & Dentistry	-	3.2	0.5	1.2	1.7	4.9
Subjects Allied to Medicine	20.5	15.5	0.3	3.6	4.0	40.0
Biological Sciences	0.5	11.9	1.0	2.0	2.9	15.3
Vet. Science, Agriculture & related	0.7	1.7	0.1	0.4	0.5	2.9
Physical Sciences	0.2	5.2	0.5	1.0	1.6	7.0
Mathematical & Computer Sciences	1.6	4.4	0.1	1.9	2.0	8.1
Engineering & Technology	0.5	3.1	0.3	1.2	1.6	5.1
Architecture, Building & Planning	0.5	1.6	-	1.2	1.2	3.4
Social Sciences[4]	3.7	19.6	0.5	9.8	10.3	33.6
Business & Financial Studies	5.2	17.8	0.1	10.6	10.7	33.7
Librarianship & Info Science	0.2	2.9	-	1.7	1.7	4.8
Languages	1.3	12.1	0.4	2.1	2.5	15.8
Humanities	0.6	5.4	0.3	1.3	1.6	7.6
Creative Arts & Design	1.5	13.5	0.1	2.6	2.7	17.7
Education[5]	3.3	9.1	0.2	20.5	20.8	33.2
Combined, gen.	8.9	19.5	0.1	2.9	2.9	31.3
All subjects	49.4	146.5	4.6	64.0	68.6	264.4

1 Includes students on Open University courses.
2 Includes higher education in higher education institutions in the UK only. Excludes qualifications from the private sector and higher education qualifications in further education institutions (approximately 6% of the total number of students).

3 Excludes students who successfully completed courses for which formal qualifications are not awarded.
4 Includes Law.
5 Includes ITT and INSET.

Source: Education Departments: 01325 392756

6.11 Qualified teachers: by type of school and sex

Thousands

	Public sector mainstream schools		Non-maintained mainstream schools	All special schools	Total
	Nursery and primary	Secondary[1]			
All full-time teachers					
Great Britain					
1990/91	200.3	223.2	44.9	18.2	486.6
1995/96	203.3	212.2	48.6	16.6	480.6
1996/97	202.8	211.4	48.2	16.3	478.7
1997/98	201.3	209.8	49.1	16.0	476.2
United Kingdom					
1998/99	210.8	221.7	50.5	16.7	499.7
1999/00[2]	211.1	223.0	51.2	16.6	502.0
2000/01[3,4]	211.9	225.6	52.3	16.6	506.3
of which:					
England and Wales[5]	181.8	193.2	49.7	13.7	438.4
Scotland[4]	21.6	22.6	2.5	2.1	48.8
Northern Ireland[3]	8.6	9.7	0.1	0.8	19.1
Full-time male teachers					
Great Britain					
1990/91	35.8	116.0	20.6	5.8	178.2
1995/96	33.8	103.4	21.1	5.3	163.5
1996/97	33.0	101.7	20.6	5.1	160.4
1997/98	31.9	99.4	20.7	5.0	157.1
United Kingdom					
1998/99	33.0	103.4	20.8	5.1	162.4
1999/00[2]	32.6	102.9	21.1	5.0	161.6
2000/01[3,4]	32.1	102.9	21.3	5.0	161.3
of which:					
England and Wales[5]	29.1	88.2	20.3	4.4	142.0
Scotland[4]	1.5	10.8	1.0	0.4	13.7
Northern Ireland[3]	1.5	3.9	..	0.1	5.6
Full-time female teachers					
Great Britain					
1990/91	164.5	107.1	24.3	12.4	308.4
1995/96	169.5	108.8	27.4	11.3	317.0
1996/97	169.8	109.7	27.6	11.2	318.3
1997/98	169.3	110.3	28.5	11.0	319.1
United Kingdom					
1998/99	177.8	118.3	29.6	11.6	337.8
1999/00[2]	178.5	120.1	30.2	11.6	340.4
2000/01[3,4]	179.8	122.7	30.9	11.6	345.1
of which:					
England and Wales[5]	152.7	105.1	29.4	9.4	296.5
Scotland[4]	20.1	11.9	1.5	1.6	35.1
Northern Ireland[3]	7.1	5.8	0.1	0.6	13.6
All part-time teachers[5]					
Great Britain					
1990/91	..	..	..	..	30.0
1995/96	18.7	17.6	8.9	1.5	46.7
1996/97	17.8	15.7	9.4	1.4	44.3
1997/98	18.0	16.2	10.7	1.4	46.4
United Kingdom					
1998/99	19.7	16.8	9.8	1.5	47.8
1999/00[2]	20.0	17.3	10.2	1.6	49.0
2000/01[3,4]	22.8	17.3	10.5	1.6	52.2

1 From 1993/94 excludes sixth form colleges in England and Wales which were reclassified as further education colleges on 1 April 1993.
2 Includes 1998/99 data for Northern Ireland.
3 Provisional. Includes 2000/01 data for Northern Ireland.
4 Nursery figures for Scotland are for 1999/00 as figures for 2000/01 are not yet available.

5 A gender breakdown of public sector teachers in England and Wales is only available from the Database of Teachers Records (DTR) where some in service teachers may be shown as not in service because their service details are not recorded. Complete coverage of teachers in England and Wales is available from the Form 618G survey, and published in "Statistics of Education: Teachers England and Wales".

Source: Education Departments: 01325 392756

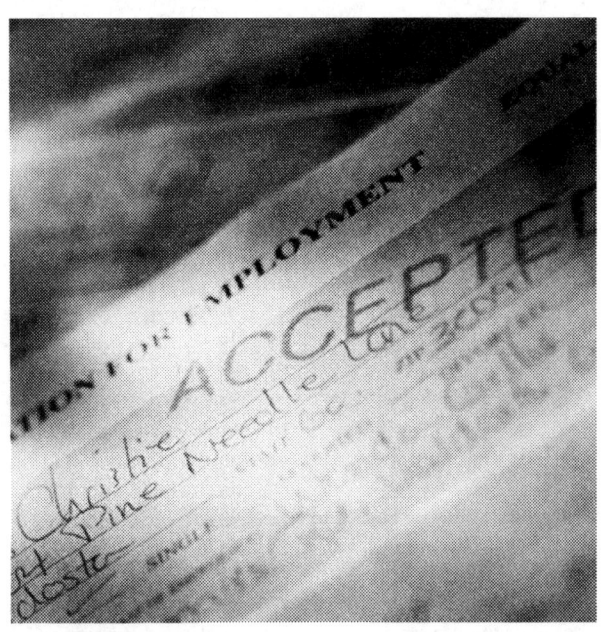

7 Labour market

Labour market

The impact of Census 2001 on Labour Force Survey data (Tables 7.1 to 7.3, 7.6, 7.9 to 7.10, 7.15 to 7.17)

The first results of the 2001 Census, published on 30 September 2002, showed that previous estimates of the total UK population were 919,000 too high. Please see the introduction for more details. Estimates of employment and unemployment levels from the LFS released before 30 October 2002 are therefore too high, with rates also affected. This has led to the Labour Force Survey (LFS) needing to reweight their estimates to the new population figures.

ONS has published interim reweighted LFS estimates for the UK, which have been used in this chapter. The interim reweighted figures only cover top-level seasonally adjusted series published in the Labour Market Statistics First Release. The non-seasonally adjusted series, used in previous editions of the Annual Abstract, were not available in time for this publication.

Future editions of the Annual Abstract will continue to show seasonally adjusted data for these tables, in line with other headline publications. These figures are not directly comparable to the non-seasonally adjusted figures previously published in the Annual Abstract.

A full set of 2001 population mid-year estimates will be available in Spring 2003, which will enable the full reweighting of all LFS series and databases to be completed in Summer 2003. The Annual Abstract datasets, available on the National Statistics website (www.statistics.gov.uk), will be updated in late-Summer 2003.

(Tables 7.12 and 5.6)

Interim reweighted figures for table 7.12, and table 5.6 in the population chapter, are not yet available and have been produced from unrevised not seasonally adjusted data. They are based on the old population estimates and are not in line with the results of the 2001 Census. Future editions of the Annual Abstract will show seasonally adjusted data for table 7.12, in line with the rest of the chapter.

Labour Force Survey
(Tables 7.1 to 7.3, 7.6, 7.9, 7.10, 7.12 and 7.15 to 7.17)

Background

The LFS is the largest regular household survey in the United Kingdom. LFS interviews are conducted continuously throughout the year. In any 3-month period, a nationally representative sample of approximately 120,000 people aged 16 or over in around 61,000 households are interviewed. Each household is interviewed five times, at 3 monthly intervals. The initial interview is done face-to-face by an interviewer visiting the address. The other interviews are done by telephone wherever possible. The survey asks a series of questions about respondents' personal circumstances and their labour market activity. Most questions refer to activity in the week before the interview.

The concepts and definitions used in the LFS are agreed by the International Labour Organisation (ILO) - an agency of the United Nations. The definitions are used by European Union member countries and members of the Organisation for Economic Co-operation and Development (OECD).

The Labour Force Survey was carried out every two years from 1973 to 1983. The ILO definition was first used in 1984. This was also the first year in which the survey was conducted on an annual basis with results available for every spring quarter (representing an average of the period from March to May). The survey moved to a continuous basis in spring 1992 in Great Britain and in winter 1994/5 in Northern Ireland, with average quarterly results published 4 times a year for seasonal quarters: spring (March to May), summer (June to August), autumn (September to November) and winter (December to February). From April 1998, results are published 12 times a year for the average of 3 consecutive months.

The LFS collects information on a sample of the population. To convert this information to give estimates for the population the data must be grossed. This is achieved by calculating weighting factors (often referred to simply as weights) which can be applied to each sampled individual in such a way that the weighted-up results match estimates or projections of the total population in terms of age distribution, sex, and region of residence.

Strengths and limitations of the LFS

The LFS produces coherent labour market information on the basis of internationally standard concepts and definitions. It is a rich source of data on a wide variety of labour market and personal characteristics. It is the most suitable source for making comparisons between countries. The LFS is designed so that households interviewed in each three month period constitute a representative sample of UK households. The survey covers those living in private households and nurses in National Health Service accommodation. Students living in halls of residence have been included since 1992 as information about them is collected at their parents' address.

However the LFS has its limitations. It is a sample survey and is therefore subject to sampling variability. The survey does not include people living in institutions such as hostels or residential homes. 'Proxy' reporting (when members of the household are not present at the interview, another member of the household answers the questions on their behalf) can affect the quality of information on topics such as earnings, hours worked, benefit receipt and qualifications. Around one third of interviews are conducted 'by proxy', usually by a spouse or partner but sometimes by a parent or other near relation.

Sampling Variability

Survey estimates are prone to *sampling variability*. The easiest way to explain this concept is by example. In the September to November 1997 period, ILO unemployment in Great Britain (seasonally adjusted) stood at 1,847,000. If we drew another sample for the same period we could get a different result, perhaps 1,900,000 or 1,820,000.

In theory, we could draw many samples, and each would give a different result. This is because each sample would be made up of different people who would give different answers to the questions. The spread of these results is the sampling variability. Sampling variability is determined by a number of factors including the sample size, the variability of the population from which the sample is drawn and the sample design. Once we know the sampling variability we can calculate a range of values about the sample estimate that represents the expected variation with a given level of assurance. This is called a confidence interval. For a 95% confidence interval we expect that in 95% of the samples (19 times out of 20) the confidence interval will contain the true value that would be obtained by surveying the entire population. For the example given above, we can be 95% confident that the true value was in the range 1,791,000 to 1,903,000.

Unreliable estimates
Very small estimates have relatively wide confidence intervals making them unreliable. For this reason, the ONS does not publish LFS estimates below 10,000.

Non-Response
Non-response can introduce bias to a survey, particularly if the people not responding have characteristics that are different from those who do respond. The LFS has a response rate of around 80 per cent to the first interview, and over 90 per cent of those who are interviewed once go on to complete all five interviews. These are relatively high levels for a household survey. Any bias from non-response is minimised by *weighting* the results.

Weighting (or grossing) converts sample data to represent the full population. In the LFS, the data are weighted separately by age, sex and area of residence to population estimates based on the Census. Weighting also adjusts for people not in the survey and thus minimises non-response bias.

Labour Force Survey Concepts and Definitions

Discouraged workers - a sub-group of the economically inactive population, defined as those neither in employment nor unemployed (on the ILO measure) who said they would like a job and whose main reason for not seeking work was because they believed there were no jobs available.

Economically active - people aged 16 and over who are either in employment or ILO unemployed.

Economic activity rate - the percentage of people aged 16 and over who are economically active.

Economically inactive - people who are neither in employment nor unemployed. This group includes, for example, all those who were looking after a home or retired.

Employment - people aged 16 or over who did at least one hour of paid work in the reference week (whether as an employee or self-employed); those who had a job that they were temporarily away from (on holiday, for example); those on Government-supported training and employment programmes (from spring 1983); and those doing unpaid family work (from spring 1992).

Employees - the division between employees and self-employed is based on survey respondents' own assessment of their employment status.

Full Time - the classification of employees, self-employed and unpaid family workers in their main job as full-time or part-time is on the basis of self-assessment. Up until autumn 1995, people who were on government work-related training programmes are classified as full-time or part-time according to whether their usual hours of work per week were over 30 or 30 and under; from winter 1995/96 onwards, the full-time/part-time classification for this group has been changed to self-assessment, in line with the other groups outlined above. People on Government-supported training and employment programmes who are at college in the survey reference week are classified, by convention, as part-time.

Government-supported training and employment programmes - comprise all people aged 16 and over participating in one of the Government's employment and training programmes (Youth Training, Training for Work and Community Action), together with those on similar programmes administered by Training and Enterprise Councils in England and Wales, or Local Enterprise Companies in Scotland.

Hours worked - respondents to the LFS are asked a series of questions enabling the identification of both their usual hours and their actual hours. Total hours include overtime (paid and unpaid) and exclude lunchbreaks.

Unemployment – Unemployment figures from the Labour Force Survey (LFS), which are based upon the International Labour Organisation (ILO) definition, were re-labelled 'unemployment' rather than 'ILO unemployment' in January 2003. This emphasises that the LFS figures provide the official and only internationally comparable measure of unemployment in the UK. For more details see the National Statistics website at www.statistics.gov.uk/cci/nugget.asp?id=251

The International Labour Office (ILO) measure of unemployment used throughout this supplement refers to people without a job who were available to start work in the two weeks following their LFS interview and who had either looked for work in the four weeks prior to interview or were waiting to start a job they had already obtained. This definition of unemployment is in accordance with that adopted by the 13th International Conference of Labour Statisticians, further clarified at the 14th ICLS, and promulgated by the ILO in its publications.

Labour market

Unemployment (rate) - the percentage of economically active people who are unemployed on the ILO measure.

Unemployment (duration) - defined as the shorter of the following two periods: (a) duration of active search for work; and (b) length of time since employment.

Part-Time - see full-time

Second jobs - jobs which LFS respondents hold in addition to a main full-time or part -time job.

Self-employment - See Employees

Temporary employees - in the LFS these are defined as those employees who say that their main job is non permanent in one of the following ways: fixed period contract; agency temping; casual work; seasonal work; other temporary work.

Unpaid Family Workers - the separate identification from spring 1992 of this group in the LFS is in accordance with international recommendations. The group comprises persons doing unpaid work for a business they own or for a business that a relative owns.

Distribution of workforce *(Table 7.4)*

Claimant unemployed - those people who were claiming unemployment-related benefits (Unemployment Benefit, Income Support or National Insurance credits) at Employment service local offices on the day of the monthly count. The seasonally adjusted claimant unemployment series allows for all relevant changes which, unless adjusted for, would distort comparisons over time.

**Workforce jobs (formerly workforce in *employment)* - comprises employee jobs, self-employment jobs (from the Labour Force Survey), HM Forces and government supported trainees.

HM Forces (provided by Ministry of Defence) - represent the total number of UK service personnel, male and female, in HM Regular Forces, wherever serving and including those on leave.

Self-employed jobs - estimates are based on the results of the Labour Force Survey. The Northern Ireland estimates are not seasonally adjusted.

Government-supported trainees - include all participants on government training and employment programmes who are receiving some work experience on their placement but who do not have a contract of employment (those with a contract are included in the employee jobs series). The numbers are not subject to seasonal adjustment.

Persons employed in local authorities *(Table 7.8)*

The full-time equivalents for local authorities are derived by applying factors to the numbers of part-time workers in three groups based on average hours worked in each group nationally.

Jobseekers allowance claimant count *(Tables 7.13 and 7.14)*

This is a count of all those people who are claiming unemployment-related benefits at Employment Service local offices and who have declared that they are unemployed, capable of, available for, and actively seeking work during the week in which their claim is made. All people claiming unemployment-related benefits on the day of the monthly count are included in the claimant count, irrespective of whether they are actually receiving benefits.

Labour disputes *(Table 7.18)*

These figures exclude details of stoppages involving fewer than ten workers or lasting less than one day except any in which the aggregate number of working days lost is 100 or more. There may be some under-recording of small or short stoppages; this would have much more effect on the total of stoppages than of working days lost. Some stoppages which affected more than one industry group have been counted under each of the industries but only once in the totals. Stoppages have been classified using *Standard Industrial Classification (SIC) 1992*.

The figures for working days lost and workers involved have been rounded and consequently the sum of the constituent items may not agree with the totals. Classifications by size are based on the full duration of stoppages where these continue into the following year. Working days lost per thousand employees are based on the latest available mid-year (June) estimates of employee jobs.

Earnings *(Tables 7.19 to 7.23, 7.25)*

The total gross remuneration employees receive before any statutory deductions (tax, national insurance). Income in kind and pension funds are excluded.

Average earnings index *(Tables 7.21 and 7.22)*

The Average Earnings Index (AEI) is designed to measure changes in the level of earnings, i.e. wage inflation in Great Britain. Average earnings are calculated as the total wages and salaries paid by firms, divided by the number of employees paid. Like all indices, changes are measured against a base year, whose index value is set to 100. The current base year is 1995 for Table 7.21 and July 1999 for Table 7.22.

Users should note that the data contained in table 7.22 are not comparable with those previously published in Annual Abstract. The ONS has withdrawn the old set of 26 industry sectors and has a new set of 20 industries that better reflect the current state of the economy. The new series are available in the format of excluding bonus index, including bonus index, and an annual percentage change for including and excluding bonuses. An article covering the reasons for the change can be found on our website www.statistics.gov.uk/labour.

The reference period of July 1999 has been chosen as this is the first period for which these data are available. However, growth rates are comparable with other AEI series. Data from July 1999 can be found in the Monthly Digest of Statistics and Labour Market Trends, also on the website.

The AEI is published monthly in the Labour Market Statistics First Release. The main indicator of growth, the headline rate, is based on the annual change in the seasonally adjusted index values for the latest 3 months compared with the same period a year ago. The use of a 3-month average reduces the level of volatility seen in the data on a month-on-month basis.

Strengths of the AEI
The AEI, based on monthly survey data, is a timely indicator of changes in the level of earnings.

Limitations of the AEI
The index is not adjusted for any changes in the composition of the workforce such as changes in the share of full-time and part-time workers, or in the share of skilled and unskilled workers. Similarly, the index does not account for changes in the number of hours worked, or any temporary factors that affect earnings.

The sample of the Monthly Wages and Salaries Survey on which the AEI is based is not designed to provide information on the level of earnings. The sample is not completely representative of the economy as firms with fewer than 20 employees are excluded, as are the earnings of self employed persons.

The AEI only covers earnings in Great Britain as earnings information is not collected for Northern Ireland and regional data are not available.

Earnings (Table 7.24)
Those whose pay in the survey period was not affected by absence. Weekly earnings figures refer to April in each year and are gross before deductions, generally excluding the value of incomes in kind but including bonus, overtime and commission payments for the pay period.

Trade unions (Table 7.26)
The statistics relate to all organisations of employees known to Certification Officer with head offices in the United Kingdom that fall within the appropriate definition of a trade union in the 1992 Trade Union and Labour Relations Act. Included in the data are home and overseas membership figures of contributory and non-contributory members. Employment status of members is not provided and the figures may therefore include some people who are self-employed, unemployed or retired.

The membership part of this table was revised in 2001, so that statistics presented here are on a consistent basis with the GB table produced by the Certification Officer in his Annual Report and with tables produced in the annual Labour Market Trends Trade Union article. There is a break in the time series for the figures in this table between the years 1988 (contained within previous publications) and 1989. GB data for 1989-95 are DTI analyses of annual returns, with 1996-1999 as published in the Certification Officer's Annual Report. Data for Northern Ireland for 1989-1991 are DTI analyses of annual returns, with 1992-1999 from the Certification Officer's Annual Report.

Vacancies at jobcentres (Table 7.27)
Publication of the jobcentre vacancy statistics has been deferred. This publication contains vacancy data only up to April 2001 because the figures from May 2001 are affected by the introduction of Employer Direct. This major change involves transferring the vacancy taking process from local Jobcentres to regional Customer Service Centres, as part of modernising the Employment Service. ONS and the Employment Service will continue to monitor and review the data with the aim of publishing the series as soon as it is possible to produce a consistent measure. Vacancies notified to and placings made by jobcentres do not represent the total number of vacancies/engagements in the economy. Latest estimates suggest that about a third of all vacancies are notified to jobcentres: and about a quarter of all engagements are made through jobcentres. Inflow, outflow and placings figures are collected for four or five-week periods between count dates; the figures in this table are converted to a standard 4 1 / 3 week month. Table excludes vacancies on government programmes except vacancies on Enterprise Ulster and Action for Community Employment (ACE) which are included in the seasonally adjusted figures for Northern Ireland. The latest national seasonally adjusted vacancy figures are provisional and subject to revision in the following month.

Vacancy - This is a job opportunity notified by an employer to a Jobcentre.

Unfilled vacancy - (also known as "Stock of vacancies")
This is the number of vacancies which have not been filled or cancelled on the count date.

Inflow of vacancy - (also known as "Notified vacancies")
This is the number of job opportunities notified by employers to Jobcentres in the period between two successive count dates.

Outflow of vacancy - This is a derived statistic which represents the total of vacancies filled plus cancelled between count dates. This concept can also be expressed as "vacancy stock" at the beginning of the period plus notified vacancies (inflows) minus "vacancy stock" at the end of the period.

Placings - This is the number of Jobseekers placed into employment by individual Jobcentres.

7.1 Summary for United Kingdom labour force[1]
Spring each year. Seasonally adjusted.

Thousands

| | All aged 16+[2] | All aged 16 and over | | | | Economic activity rate 16-59/64 (%)[3] | Employment rate - all aged 16+ (%)[4] | Employment rate 16-59/64 (%)[5] | Unemployment rate (%)[6] |
		Total economically active	Total in employment	Total unemployed	Economically inactive				
All									
	MGSL	MGSF	MGRZ	MGSC	MGSI	MGSO	MGSR	MGSU	MGSX
1992	44 990	28 397	25 606	2 791	16 593	79.1	56.9	71.2	9.8
1993	44 994	28 192	25 245	2 947	16 803	78.6	56.1	70.3	10.5
1994	45 013	28 138	25 393	2 745	16 875	78.4	56.4	70.6	9.8
1995	45 099	28 113	25 648	2 465	16 986	78.2	56.9	71.2	8.8
1996	45 223	28 237	25 899	2 339	16 986	78.4	57.3	71.7	8.3
1997	45 350	28 370	26 334	2 036	16 980	78.4	58.1	72.7	7.2
1998	45 491	28 354	26 579	1 775	17 136	78.2	58.4	73.2	6.3
1999	45 668	28 659	26 900	1 759	17 008	78.6	58.9	73.7	6.1
2000	45 877	28 910	27 274	1 636	16 967	78.9	59.4	74.3	5.7
2001	46 127	28 939	27 510	1 428	17 188	78.5	59.6	74.6	4.9
2002	46 383	29 183	27 659	1 524	17 199	78.6	59.6	74.4	5.2
Men									
	MGSM	MGSG	MGSA	MGSD	MGSJ	MGSP	MGSS	MGSV	MGSY
1992	21 595	15 960	14 108	1 852	5 635	86.7	65.3	76.5	11.6
1993	21 589	15 736	13 771	1 965	5 853	85.9	63.8	75.0	12.5
1994	21 587	15 654	13 851	1 802	5 934	85.5	64.2	75.5	11.5
1995	21 629	15 607	14 020	1 588	6 022	85.0	64.8	76.2	10.2
1996	21 692	15 595	14 075	1 520	6 097	84.9	64.9	76.5	9.7
1997	21 754	15 584	14 306	1 278	6 171	84.6	65.8	77.6	8.2
1998	21 823	15 525	14 456	1 069	6 298	84.1	66.2	78.3	6.9
1999	21 919	15 650	14 579	1 072	6 268	84.4	66.5	78.5	6.8
2000	22 029	15 748	14 773	975	6 281	84.5	67.1	79.2	6.2
2001	22 174	15 713	14 866	847	6 461	84.0	67.0	79.4	5.4
2002	22 322	15 795	14 886	909	6 526	83.8	66.7	79.0	5.8
Women									
	MGSN	MGSH	MGSB	MGSE	MGSK	MGSQ	MGST	MGSW	MGSZ
1992	23 395	12 437	11 498	939	10 959	70.9	49.1	65.4	7.5
1993	23 405	12 456	11 474	982	10 949	70.9	49.0	65.2	7.9
1994	23 425	12 484	11 541	943	10 941	70.9	49.3	65.4	7.6
1995	23 470	12 506	11 629	878	10 964	70.9	49.5	65.8	7.0
1996	23 531	12 642	11 824	819	10 889	71.4	50.2	66.7	6.5
1997	23 595	12 786	12 028	758	10 809	71.8	51.0	67.4	5.9
1998	23 668	12 830	12 123	707	10 838	72.0	51.2	67.9	5.5
1999	23 749	13 009	12 321	687	10 740	72.5	51.9	68.6	5.3
2000	23 848	13 162	12 501	662	10 686	72.9	52.4	69.1	5.0
2001	23 953	13 226	12 644	581	10 727	72.8	52.8	69.5	4.4
2002	24 061	13 388	12 773	615	10 673	73.0	53.1	69.6	4.6

1 See chapter text.
2 Population in private households and student halls of residence.
3 Economically active of working age as a percentage of all persons of working age.
4 Total employed as a percentage of all persons 16 and over.

5 Total employed of working age as a percentage of all persons of working age (men 16-64, women 16-59).
6 Total unemployment as a percentage of all economically active.

Source: Labour Force Survey, Office for National Statistics

7.2 Employment status, full-time/part-time, second jobs, temporary employees[1]
United Kingdom
Spring each year. Seasonally adjusted.

Thousands

	All in employment[2]					Total employment[2]		Employees[2]		Self-employed[2]		Workers with second jobs[4]	Temporary employees
	Total	Employees	Self employed	Unpaid family workers	Government supported training and employment programmes[3]	Full-time	Part-time	Full-time	Part-time	Full-time	Part-time		
All													
	MGRZ	MGRN	MGRQ	MGRT	MGRW	YCBE	YCBH	YCBK	YCBN	YCBQ	YCBT	YCBW	YCBZ
1992	25 606	21 872	3 184	179	372	19 605	6 001	16 733	5 139	2 639	545	965	1 293
1993	25 245	21 614	3 132	149	350	19 177	6 068	16 422	5 191	2 555	578	1 031	1 343
1994	25 393	21 684	3 237	144	329	19 173	6 219	16 359	5 325	2 632	605	1 135	1 473
1995	25 648	21 945	3 287	138	279	19 385	6 263	16 547	5 398	2 664	622	1 275	1 607
1996	25 899	22 309	3 220	125	244	19 406	6 493	16 662	5 648	2 580	640	1 277	1 644
1997	26 334	22 737	3 263	117	216	19 700	6 634	16 960	5 777	2 584	679	1 236	1 757
1998	26 579	23 116	3 190	100	173	19 895	6 684	17 287	5 829	2 483	707	1 166	1 710
1999	26 900	23 523	3 123	100	154	20 130	6 771	17 581	5 942	2 443	681	1 255	1 673
2000	27 274	23 961	3 065	108	140	20 391	6 883	17 909	6 052	2 379	686	1 164	1 686
2001	27 510	24 194	3 074	96	146	20 567	6 944	18 042	6 153	2 425	649	1 158	1 684
2002	27 659	24 339	3 124	95	102	20 650	7 009	18 150	6 189	2 429	694	1 124	1 546
Men													
	MGSA	MGRO	MGRR	MGRU	MGRX	YCBF	YCBI	YCBL	YCBO	YCBR	YCBU	YCBX	YCCA
1992	14 108	11 415	2 398	54	241	13 130	978	10 769	647	2 219	179	437	552
1993	13 771	11 166	2 335	42	227	12 768	1 003	10 503	663	2 136	199	461	594
1994	13 851	11 170	2 420	48	213	12 780	1 071	10 456	715	2 211	209	497	647
1995	14 020	11 322	2 478	42	178	12 899	1 121	10 545	777	2 251	226	530	739
1996	14 075	11 488	2 394	41	152	12 882	1 193	10 628	860	2 164	230	533	728
1997	14 306	11 735	2 401	37	132	13 038	1 267	10 786	949	2 158	243	537	799
1998	14 456	11 996	2 321	28	111	13 180	1 276	11 042	953	2 061	260	505	756
1999	14 579	12 147	2 296	34	101	13 260	1 318	11 145	1 002	2 048	248	522	786
2000	14 773	12 442	2 212	35	83	13 432	1 341	11 421	1 021	1 951	261	482	767
2001	14 866	12 490	2 247	34	95	13 519	1 347	11 443	1 047	2 008	239	465	768
2002	14 886	12 507	2 292	28	58	13 486	1 400	11 428	1 079	2 014	278	455	711
Women													
	MGSB	MGRP	MGRS	MGRV	MGRY	YCBG	YCBJ	YCBM	YCBP	YCBS	YCBV	YCBY	YCCB
1992	11 498	10 457	786	125	131	6 475	5 023	5 965	4 492	420	366	529	742
1993	11 474	10 448	797	106	123	6 409	5 065	5 919	4 529	418	379	570	749
1994	11 541	10 513	816	96	116	6 393	5 148	5 903	4 610	421	395	638	826
1995	11 629	10 623	809	96	101	6 486	5 142	6 002	4 622	413	396	745	868
1996	11 824	10 821	826	84	93	6 524	5 299	6 034	4 787	416	410	743	916
1997	12 028	11 002	862	79	84	6 661	5 367	6 174	4 828	426	436	698	959
1998	12 123	11 121	869	72	62	6 716	5 408	6 244	4 876	422	447	661	954
1999	12 321	11 375	827	65	53	6 869	5 452	6 435	4 940	395	432	733	887
2000	12 501	11 519	853	72	57	6 960	5 541	6 488	5 031	429	424	682	919
2001	12 644	11 704	827	61	51	7 048	5 596	6 598	5 106	417	410	693	916
2002	12 773	11 832	831	66	43	7 164	5 609	6 722	5 110	415	417	669	835

1 See chapter text.
2 People whose main job is full or part-time.
3 Those on employment and training programmes are classified as in employment. Some of those on programmes may consider themselves to be employees or self employed so appear in other categories.

4 Second jobs reported in LFS in addition to person's main full or part-time job.

Source: Labour Force Survey, Office for National Statistics

7.3 Employment[1]
United Kingdom
By age and sex. At Spring each year. Seasonally adjusted.

Thousands and percentages.

	All aged 16 and over	16-59/64	16-17	18-24	16-24	25-34	35-49	50-64 (m) 50-59 (f)	65+ (m) 60+ (f)
All	**Thousands**								
	MGRZ	YBSE	YBTO	YBTR	PXLA	YBTU	YBTX	MGUW	MGUZ
1994	25 393	24 614	582	3 426	4 008	6 734	9 193	4 678	779
1995	25 648	24 854	604	3 321	3 926	6 826	9 311	4 791	794
1996	25 899	25 130	657	3 274	3 930	6 846	9 460	4 894	769
1997	26 334	25 534	697	3 220	3 918	6 980	9 500	5 136	800
1998	26 579	25 807	693	3 182	3 875	6 941	9 613	5 378	772
1999	26 900	26 084	675	3 187	3 862	6 892	9 767	5 563	816
2000	27 274	26 443	671	3 246	3 916	6 819	9 992	5 715	831
2001	27 510	26 691	664	3 281	3 944	6 660	10 165	5 922	819
2002	27 659	26 768	649	3 364	4 013	6 455	10 309	5 990	891
Men									
	MGSA	YBSF	YBTP	YBTS	PXLB	YBTV	YBTY	MGUX	MGVA
1994	13 851	13 587	296	1 791	2 087	3 730	4 934	2 836	264
1995	14 020	13 731	304	1 745	2 049	3 773	5 017	2 892	288
1996	14 075	13 809	333	1 703	2 036	3 760	5 050	2 963	266
1997	14 306	14 037	341	1 693	2 034	3 809	5 079	3 115	268
1998	14 456	14 183	343	1 669	2 013	3 796	5 143	3 232	272
1999	14 579	14 292	333	1 671	2 005	3 735	5 214	3 338	287
2000	14 773	14 486	334	1 706	2 040	3 695	5 349	3 403	287
2001	14 866	14 600	331	1 722	2 053	3 606	5 415	3 526	266
2002	14 886	14 593	321	1 759	2 080	3 487	5 482	3 544	293
Women									
	MGSB	YBSG	YBTQ	YBTT	PXLC	YBTW	YBTZ	MGUY	MGVB
1994	11 541	11 026	286	1 635	1 921	3 004	4 259	1 842	515
1995	11 629	11 123	301	1 576	1 877	3 053	4 294	1 899	505
1996	11 824	11 321	324	1 570	1 894	3 086	4 409	1 930	503
1997	12 028	11 496	357	1 527	1 884	3 171	4 420	2 021	532
1998	12 123	11 624	349	1 512	1 862	3 145	4 470	2 147	499
1999	12 321	11 792	342	1 515	1 857	3 157	4 552	2 225	529
2000	12 501	11 957	336	1 540	1 876	3 124	4 643	2 313	544
2001	12 644	12 091	333	1 559	1 891	3 054	4 750	2 396	553
2002	12 773	12 175	328	1 605	1 933	2 968	4 828	2 446	598
All	**Rates[2]**								
	MGSR	MGSU	YBUA	YBUD	PXLD	YBUG	YBUJ	YBUM	YBUP
1994	56.4	70.6	45.0	63.7	60.1	74.5	79.0	62.4	7.7
1995	56.9	71.2	45.1	64.2	60.2	75.4	79.3	63.0	7.8
1996	57.3	71.7	46.4	65.8	61.5	75.6	79.6	63.5	7.5
1997	58.1	72.7	47.9	66.5	62.2	77.7	79.9	64.5	7.8
1998	58.4	73.2	47.7	66.5	62.1	78.3	80.6	65.5	7.5
1999	58.9	73.7	46.8	66.6	62.0	79.3	81.0	66.2	7.9
2000	59.4	74.3	46.7	67.6	62.8	80.1	81.6	66.7	8.1
2001	59.6	74.6	45.4	67.4	62.3	80.1	81.8	68.0	7.9
2002	59.6	74.4	43.2	68.0	62.2	79.7	81.8	67.9	8.6
Men									
	MGSS	MGSV	YBUB	YBUE	PXLE	YBUH	YBUK	YBUN	YBUQ
1994	64.2	75.5	44.8	66.2	62.0	83.7	85.5	64.4	7.4
1995	64.8	76.2	44.4	67.1	62.4	84.6	86.3	65.0	8.0
1996	64.9	76.5	46.0	68.2	63.2	84.6	85.9	65.9	7.3
1997	65.8	77.6	46.0	69.9	64.3	86.4	86.4	67.3	7.3
1998	66.2	78.3	46.4	69.8	64.3	87.5	87.3	67.9	7.4
1999	66.5	78.5	45.2	70.0	64.2	87.8	87.5	68.6	7.7
2000	67.1	79.2	45.5	71.2	65.2	88.8	88.5	68.8	7.7
2001	67.0	79.4	44.3	70.9	64.6	88.8	88.3	70.3	7.0
2002	66.7	79.0	41.7	71.2	64.2	88.1	88.2	69.9	7.6
Women									
	MGST	MGSW	YBUC	YBUF	PXLF	YBUI	YBUL	YBUO	YBUR
1994	49.3	65.4	45.2	61.1	58.1	65.6	72.6	59.5	7.8
1995	49.5	65.8	45.9	61.2	58.1	66.4	72.4	60.3	7.7
1996	50.2	66.7	46.7	63.3	59.7	67.0	73.5	60.2	7.7
1997	51.0	67.4	50.0	63.2	60.2	69.2	73.6	60.6	8.1
1998	51.2	67.9	49.1	63.1	59.9	69.5	74.1	62.1	7.6
1999	51.9	68.6	48.5	63.2	59.8	71.1	74.6	62.8	8.1
2000	52.4	69.1	47.9	63.9	60.3	71.7	74.9	63.9	8.3
2001	52.8	69.5	46.6	63.9	60.0	71.8	75.4	64.8	8.4
2002	53.1	69.6	44.8	64.8	60.3	71.6	75.6	65.1	9.1

1 See chapter text.
2 Total in employment as a percentage of all persons in the relevant group.

Source: Labour Force Survey, Office for National Statistics

7.4 Distribution of the workforce[1]

At mid-June each year

Thousands, seasonally adjusted

		1992	1993	1994	1995	1996	1997	1998	1999	2000	2001	2002
United Kingdom												
Claimant unemployed	KAMO	2 711	2 902	2 625	2 294	2 135	1 572	1 344	1 263	1 095	967	953
Males	KAMP	2 084	2 235	2 016	1 756	1 625	1 208	1 028	969	837	737	722
Females	KAMQ	627	667	609	538	509	364	317	294	259	231	231
Workforce jobs	DYDC	27 249	26 865	27 016	27 350	27 778	28 272	28 489	28 974	29 299	29 516	29 519
Males	KAMS	14 698	14 340	14 398	14 578	14 660	15 041	15 199	15 515	15 655	15 867	15 838
Females	KAMT	12 551	12 525	12 618	12 772	13 119	13 231	13 290	13 459	13 644	13 649	13 681
HM Forces	KAMU	290	271	250	230	222	210	210	209	207	204	204
Males	KAMV	270	252	232	214	206	195	194	192	190	188	187
Females	KAMW	20	19	18	16	16	15	16	16	17	17	17
Self-employment jobs	DYZN	3 441	3 446	3 550	3 616	3 625	3 620	3 499	3 521	3 441	3 442	3 500
Males	KAMZ	2 573	2 537	2 633	2 686	2 681	2 632	2 534	2 559	2 492	2 505	2 548
Females	KANA	868	910	917	930	943	989	964	962	948	937	952
Employees jobs	BCAJ	23 178	22 821	22 900	23 264	23 738	24 270	24 649	25 114	25 533	25 769	25 718
Males	KANC	11 642	11 348	11 334	11 523	11 654	12 109	12 394	12 684	12 900	13 113	13 045
Females	KAND	11 536	11 473	11 566	11 741	12 085	12 161	12 255	12 430	12 634	12 656	12 673
of whom												
Total, production and construction industries	KANF	5 573	5 243	5 221	5 266	5 292	5 398	5 525	5 382	5 341	5 223	5 040
Total, all manufacturing industries	KANG	4 146	3 960	3 975	4 076	4 138	4 191	4 209	4 060	3 967	3 838	3 671
Government-supported trainees	KANH	340	326	317	240	194	171	131	131	119	101	97
Males	KANI	213	203	199	156	119	105	76	81	73	62	59
Females	KANJ	128	124	118	84	75	66	55	50	46	38	38
Great Britain												
Claimant unemployed	KANN	2 607	2 798	2 527	2 207	2 048	1 510	1 287	1 212	1 054	928	916
Males	KANO	2 004	2 155	1 940	1 687	1 559	1 159	983	929	805	707	694
Females	KANP	603	643	587	519	489	351	304	283	249	221	222
Workforce jobs	KANQ	26 600	26 218	26 357	26 668	27 098	27 569	27 773	28 251	28 555	28 764	28 760
Males	KANR	14 339	13 982	14 035	14 206	14 293	14 662	14 811	15 127	15 252	15 462	15 431
Females	KANS	12 261	12 236	12 322	12 462	12 805	12 907	12 962	13 124	13 303	13 302	13 328
HM Forces	BCAH	290	271	250	230	222	210	210	209	207	204	204
Males	KANU	270	252	232	214	206	195	194	192	190	188	187
Females	KANV	20	19	18	16	16	15	16	16	17	17	17
Self-employment jobs	KANW	3 354	3 362	3 464	3 525	3 539	3 529	3 411	3 435	3 347	3 347	3 405
Males	KANX	2 501	2 464	2 558	2 609	2 610	2 558	2 461	2 490	2 414	2 425	2 468
Females	KANY	853	898	906	915	930	971	950	946	933	921	937
Employee jobs	KANZ	22 635	22 275	22 342	22 689	23 159	23 672	24 036	24 487	24 892	25 119	25 060
Males	KAOA	11 368	11 074	11 055	11 237	11 368	11 812	12 089	12 372	12 581	12 792	12 722
Females	KAOB	11 267	11 201	11 286	11 452	11 791	11 860	11 946	12 115	12 310	12 327	12 338
of whom												
Total, production and construction industries	KAOC	5 425	5 091	5 069	5 115	5 158	5 256	5 383	5 240	5 198	5 081	4 902
Total, all manufacturing industries	KAOD	4 046	3 853	3 868	3 968	4 034	4 083	4 102	3 954	3 863	3 736	3 573
Government-supported trainees	KAOE	322	310	301	224	178	157	117	119	109	94	90
Males	KAOF	201	192	189	145	109	96	67	73	66	57	54
Females	KAOG	121	118	112	79	69	61	50	47	43	36	36

Note: Because the figures have been rounded independently totals may differ from the sum of the components. Also the totals may include some employees whose industrial classification could not be ascertained.

1 The data in this table have not been adjusted to reflect the 2001 Census population data. See chapter text.

Source: Earnings and Employment Division, Office for National Statistics: 01633 812318

7.5 Employee jobs[1]
Analysis by industry based on the Standard Industrial Classification 1992
At June in each year

Thousands, not seasonally adjusted

		SIC 1992	United Kingdom							Great Britain					
			1997	1998	1999	2000	2001	2002		1997	1998	1999	2000	2001	2002
All sections	KAOH	A - Q	24 174	24 569	25 045	25 469	25 707	25 661	LMAB	23 578	23 957	24 421	24 829	25 059	25 005
Index of production and construction industries	KAOI	C - F	5 372	5 504	5 366	5 328	5 213	5 031	LMAH	5 231	5 363	5 224	5 186	5 071	4 893
Index of production industries	KAOJ	C - E	4 395	4 406	4 256	4 146	4 012	3 845	LMAF	4 282	4 294	4 145	4 037	3 906	3 743
of which, manufacturing industries	KAOK	D	4 176	4 197	4 051	3 961	3 834	3 668	KAPQ	4 069	4 090	3 946	3 857	3 732	3 571
Service industries	KAOL	G - Q	18 488	18 743	19 362	19 835	20 216	20 375	LMAJ	18 049	18 289	18 895	19 354	19 724	19 872
Agriculture, hunting and forestry and fishing	KAOM	A/B	314	322	318	306	279	255	KAPS	298	306	302	290	264	240
Agriculture hunting and forestry	KPHI	A	304	311	305	295	270	246	KOVW	288	295	290	279	255	231
Agriculture hunting & related activities	KPHJ	01	295	303	297	288	259	235	KOVX	279	287	282	273	245	221
Fishing	KPHK	B	10	12	13	11	9	9	KOVY	10	11	12	11	9	9
Mining and quarrying	KPHL	C	77	75	74	73	75	75	KOVZ	75	73	72	71	73	73
Mining and quarrying of energy producing materials	KPHM	CA	47	46	46	44	45	44	KOWA	47	46	45	44	44	44
Mining	KAPG	10/12	..	..	..	..	..	..	KOWB	15	13	14	13	13	13
Extraction of crude petroleum	KPHN	11	..	..	..	..	..	..	KOWC	32	33	31	31	31	31
Mining and quarrying except of energy producing materials	KPHO	CB(13/14)	30	29	28	29	30	31	KOWD	28	27	27	27	29	29
Energy and water supply industries	KAOO	C/E	219	209	205	185	179	177	LMAM	213	204	199	179	174	172
Manufacturing	KPHP	D	4 176	4 197	4 051	3 961	3 834	3 668	LMAD	4 069	4 090	3 946	3 857	3 732	3 571
Manufacture of food products Beverages and tobacco	KPHQ	DA	491	502	499	494	489	487	LMAN	471	482	480	475	470	467
Of food	KPHR	151 to 158	..	..	..	..	..	..	KOWH	420	428	425	421	415	412
Of beverages and tobacco	KPHS	159/16	..	..	..	..	..	..	KOWI	51	54	54	54	54	55
Manufacture of textiles and textile products	KPHT	DB	347	336	294	259	229	209	KOWJ	324	314	275	242	216	197
Of textiles	KPHU	17	184	178	162	149	138	126	KOWK	173	167	152	141	130	120
Of made-up textile articles except apparel	KPHV	174	..	..	..	..	..	..	KOWL	34	36	34	34	34	33
Of textiles excluding made-up textile	KPHW	Rest of 17	..	..	..	..	..	..	KOWM	140	132	118	106	97	87
Of wearing apparel,dressing and dyeing of fur	KPHX	18	163	159	133	109	91	83	KOWN	150	147	123	102	85	78
Manufacture of leather and leather products including footwear	KPHY	DC	39	35	30	26	22	19	KOWO	38	34	30	26	21	19
Of leather and leather goods	KPHZ	191/192	..	..	..	..	..	..	KOWP	12	12	11	10	9	8
Of footwear	KPIA	193	..	..	..	..	..	..	KOWQ	26	22	19	16	12	11
Manufacture of wood and wood products	KPIB	DD(20)	89	87	84	83	81	81	LMAP	85	84	81	80	77	78
Manufacture of pulp paper and paper products,publishing and printing	KPIC	DE	465	473	469	465	451	442	LMAQ	458	466	463	458	444	436
Of pulp paper and paper products	KPID	21	111	110	104	100	95	90	KOWT	109	107	102	98	94	88
Publishing printing and reproduction of recorded media	KPIE	22	353	363	365	365	355	352	KOWU	349	359	361	360	351	347
Manufacture of coke refined petroleum products and nuclear fuel	KPIF	DF(23)	26	24	26	27	31	31	KOWV	26	24	26	27	31	31
Manufacture of chemicals,chemical products and man-made fibres	KPIG	DG(24)	252	258	249	239	235	229	LMAR	248	254	246	236	232	225
Manufacture of rubber and plastics	KPIH	DH(25)	251	253	244	238	227	222	LMAS	244	246	237	231	220	215
Manufacture of other non-metallic mineral products	KPII	DI(26)	149	146	140	140	136	132	KOWZ	144	141	135	135	131	126
Manufacture of basic metals and fabricated metal products	KPIJ	DJ	571	553	534	521	497	475	KOXA	565	548	528	515	490	468
Of basic metals	KPIK	27	134	133	124	117	110	102	KOXB	133	133	124	117	109	101
except machinery	KPIL	28	437	420	410	404	387	373	KOXC	432	415	405	398	381	367

7.5
Employee jobs[1]
Analysis by industry based on the Standard Industrial Classification 1992
continued   At June in each year

Thousands, not seasonally adjusted

		SIC 1992	United Kingdom							Great Britain					
			1997	1998	1999	2000	2001	2002		1997	1998	1999	2000	2001	2002
Manufacture of Machinery and Equipment not elsewhere classified	KPIM	DK(29)	388	389	368	357	352	337	LMAU	381	382	361	351	345	331
Manufacture of electrical and optical equipment	KPIN	DL	509	519	497	495	478	419	LMAV	499	508	486	482	465	408
Of office machinery and computers	KPIO	30	41	49	51	53	52	44	KOXF	40	47	49	51	49	41
Of electrical machinery and apparatus	KPIP	31	184	191	181	179	168	148	KOXG	182	188	179	175	165	145
Of electric motors etc control apparatus and insulated cable	KPIQ	311 to 313	..	..	..	..	..	..	KOXH	99	104	103	102	94	82
Of accumulators, primary cells, batteries, lamps and electrical equipment	KPIR	314 to 316	..	..	..	..	..	..	KOXI	83	85	76	74	70	63
Radio television and communication equipment	KPIS	32	134	133	125	129	124	98	KOXJ	129	127	120	123	118	94
Of electronic components	KPIT	321	..	..	..	..	..	..	KOXK	54	52	50	45	39	32
Of radio TV and telephone apparatus, sound and video recorders	KPIU	322/323	..	..	..	..	..	..	KOXL	75	75	70	78	79	62
Of medical precision and optical equipment, watches	KPIV	33	150	146	140	134	134	128	KOXM	148	145	138	132	133	127
Manufacture of transport equipment	KPIW	DM	393	411	403	401	388	376	LMAW	381	399	390	388	375	363
Of motor vehicles and trailers	KPIX	34	239	245	232	226	214	211	KOXO	235	241	228	222	209	206
Of other transport equipment	KPIY	35	154	166	171	174	174	165	KOXP	146	158	163	166	166	157
Manufacturing not elsewhere classified	KPIZ	DN(36/37)	208	211	211	216	217	210	KOXQ	204	208	207	212	213	206
Electricity gas and water supply	KPJA	E	142	134	131	112	104	102	KOXR	122	127	125	127	128	125
Electricity gas steam and hot water supply	KPJB	40	..	..	..	..	..	..	KOXS KOXT	138 102	131 98	127 97	108 90	101 91	99 90
Collection purification and distribution of water	KPJC	41	..	..	..	..	..	..	KOXU	35	32	30	19	10	9
Construction	KPJD	F(45)	976	1 098	1 110	1 183	1 200	1 186	LMAY	949	1 069	1 079	1 149	1 165	1 150
Services	KPJE	G - Q	18 488	18 743	19 362	19 835	20 216	20 375	KOXX	18 049	18 289	18 895	19 354	19 724	19 872
Wholesale and retail trade; Repair of motor vehicles, motorcycles and personal household goods	KPJF	G (50 - 52)	4 251	4 301	4 325	4 365	4 427	4 466	LMAZ	4 158	4 202	4 223	4 260	4 320	4 355
Sale maintenance and repair of motor vehicles,retail of automotive fuel	KPJG	50	583	577	576	574	552	554	KOXZ	570	563	562	559	536	539
Sale of motor vehicles, motorcycles and parts,motorcycle repair and sale of automotive fuel	KPJH	501/503 - 505	..	..	..	..	..	..	KOYA	405	412	405	391	381	384
Maintenance and repair of motor vehicles	KPJI	502	..	..	..	..	..	..	KOYB	165	151	158	169	156	155
Wholesale trade and commission trade except motor vehicles	KPJJ	51	1 148	1 141	1 167	1 184	1 179	1 160	KOYC	1 127	1 119	1 144	1 161	1 156	1 138
Wholesale on a fee of contract basis	KPJK	511	..	..	..	..	..	..	KOYD	46	49	58	60	65	62
Wholesale agricultural raw materials and live animals	KPJL	512	..	..	..	..	..	..	KPLD	22	24	24	23	24	23
Wholesale food beverages & tobacco	KPJM	513	..	..	..	..	..	..	KPLE	218	208	206	206	193	190
Wholesale household goods	KPJN	514	..	..	..	..	..	..	KPLF	243	243	254	263	273	270
Wholesale of non-agricultural intermediate products waste & scrap	KPJO	515	..	..	..	..	..	..	KPLG	231	230	239	245	236	237
Wholesale machinery eqpt. & supplies	KPJP	516	..	..	..	..	..	..	KPLH	248	258	256	255	253	245
Other wholesale	KPJQ	517	..	..	..	..	..	..	KPLI	119	106	107	110	111	110
Retail trade except of motor vehicles and motorcycles;repair of personal and household goods	KPJR	52	2 520	2 583	2 582	2 607	2 696	2 751	KPLJ	2 460	2 519	2 517	2 539	2 627	2 678
Non-specialised stores selling mainly food beverages & tobacco	KPJS	5211/5221-4,5227	..	..	..	..	..	..	KPLK	889	956	968	977	1 031	1 063
Other non-specialised stores second hand shops & sales not in stores	KPJT	5212/525-526	..	..	..	..	..	..	KPLL	332	367	381	379	391	398

7.5 Employee jobs[1]
Analysis by industry based on the Standard Industrial Classification 1992

continued   At June in each year

Thousands, not seasonally adjusted

		SIC 1992	United Kingdom							Great Britain					
			1997	1998	1999	2000	2001	2002		1997	1998	1999	2000	2001	2002
Alcoholic & other beverages, tobacco	KPJU	5225 to 5226	..	..	..	..	..	..	KPLM	85	87	70	70	69	65
Pharmaceutical & medical goods cosmetics & toilet articles	KPJV	523	..	..	..	..	..	..	KPLN	132	98	88	92	79	83
Clothing footwear & leather goods	KPJW	5242/5243	..	..	..	..	..	..	KPLO	309	337	339	353	358	363
Textile furniture lighting equipment electrical household appliances radio and TV paints glass hardware and household goods not elsewhere classified	KPJX	5241/5244-46	..	..	..	..	..	..	KPLP	314	279	266	275	286	295
Books newspapers and stationery, other retail in specialised stores	KPJY	5247/5248	..	..	..	..	..	..	KPLQ	384	378	384	372	390	390
Repair of personal and household goods	KPJZ	527	..	..	..	..	..	..	KPLR	15	17	20	21	23	22
Hotels and restaurants	KPKA	H	1 551	1 571	1 649	1 690	1 676	1 696	LMBA	1 521	1 537	1 613	1 652	1 637	1 657
Hotels camp sites short-stay accom.	KPKB	551/552	..	..	..	..	..	..	KPLT	328	342	371	370	381	389
Restaurants	KPKC	553	..	..	..	..	..	..	KPLU	438	465	478	493	488	489
Bars	KPKD	554	..	..	..	..	..	..	KPLV	503	517	534	559	515	518
Canteens and catering	KPKE	555	..	..	..	..	..	..	KPLW	253	213	229	229	253	261
Transport, storage and communication	KPKF	I	1 387	1 416	1 459	1 516	1 557	1 524	KPLX	1 364	1 392	1 434	1 490	1 530	1 497
Land transport, transport via pipelines	KPKG	60	495	515	519	528	518	527	KPLY	485	504	508	516	507	516
Transport via railways	KPKH	601	..	..	..	..	..	..	KPLZ	46	50	49	50	49	51
Other land transport and via pipelines	KPKI	602/603	..	..	..	..	..	..	KPMA	439	455	460	467	458	464
Water transport	KPKJ	61	23	20	20	19	17	16	KPMB	22	20	20	18	16	15
Air transport	KPKK	62	73	82	89	94	98	92	KPMC	72	81	88	94	98	91
Supporting and auxiliary transport activities, activities of travel agents	KPKL	63	339	335	354	377	391	376	KPMD	335	331	349	372	386	371
Travel agencies and tour operators	KPKM	633	..	..	..	..	..	..	KPME	104	105	115	121	128	121
Post and telecommunications	KPKN	64	458	464	477	499	532	514	LMBC	449	456	469	490	523	504
National post and courier activities	KPKO	641	..	..	..	..	..	..	KPMG	258	277	276	279	291	282
National post activities	KPKP	6411	..	..	..	..	..	..	KPMH	220	221	216	214	222	218
Courier activities	KPKQ	6412	..	..	..	..	..	..	KPMI	38	56	60	65	69	64
Telecommunications	KPKR	6420	..	..	..	..	..	..	KPMJ	192	180	193	211	232	221
Financial intermediation	KPKS	J	1 036	1 046	1 074	1 068	1 068	1 062	LMBD	1 022	1 032	1 059	1 053	1 052	1 045
Financial intermediation except insurance and pension funding	KPKT	65	600	596	618	600	603	600	KPML	591	587	609	590	593	589
Insurance and pension funding except compulsory social security	KPKU	66	228	232	232	228	229	227	KPMM	226	230	230	226	227	225
Activities auxiliary to financial intermediation	KPKV	67	208	218	223	239	236	234	KPMN	206	216	220	236	233	231
Except insurance and pension funding	KPKW	671	..	..	..	..	..	..	KPMO	60	71	79	91	100	96
Auxiliary to insurance and pension funding	KPKX	672	..	..	..	..	..	..	KPMP	146	145	141	145	133	136
Real estate renting & business activities	KPKY	K	3 300	3 423	3 572	3 699	3 905	3 907	KPMQ	3 265	3 383	3 526	3 650	3 853	3 854
Real estate activities	KPKZ	70	291	292	313	345	368	373	LMBE	288	289	310	341	364	369
Activities with own property, letting of own property	KPLA	701/702	..	..	..	..	..	..	KPMS	166	174	187	214	224	227
Activities on a fee or contract basis	KPLB	703	..	..	..	..	..	..	KPMT	122	115	122	128	141	143

7.5
continued

Employee jobs[1]
Analysis by industry based on the Standard Industrial Classification 1992
At June in each year

Thousands, not seasonally adjusted

		SIC 1992	United Kingdom							Great Britain					
			1997	1998	1999	2000	2001	2002		1997	1998	1999	2000	2001	2002
Renting of machinery and equipment without operator & of personal & household goods	KPLC	71	131	133	148	155	156	162	KPMU	129	131	146	153	154	160
Construction and civil engineering machinery	KOUU	7132	..	..	..	..	..	..	KPMV	35	39	39	41	44	43
All other goods and equipment	KOUV	Rest of 71	..	..	..	..	..	..	KPMW	94	92	108	112	110	117
Computer and related equipment	KOUW	72	302	354	418	437	490	491	KPMX	300	351	415	432	484	486
Research and development	KOUX	73	93	96	97	100	94	89	KPMY	92	95	96	99	92	87
Other business activities	KOUY	74	2 483	2 548	2 595	2 662	2 797	2 792	KPMZ	2 456	2 516	2 560	2 625	2 758	2 751
Legal, accounting,book-keeping & auditing activities	KOUZ	741	..	..	..	..	..	..	KPNA	579	620	663	690	726	729
Legal activities	KOVA	7411	..	..	..	..	..	..	KPNB	225	232	233	238	241	249
Accounting, book-keeping auditing, tax consultancy	KOVB	7412	..	..	..	..	..	..	KPNC	141	164	190	202	217	215
Market research business and consultancy activities	KOVC	7413/7414	..	..	..	..	..	..	KPND	183	190	202	218	235	234
Management activities of holding companies	KOVD	7415	..	..	..	..	..	..	KPNE	30	34	38	32	33	31
Architectural engineering activities and related technical consultancy, technical testing	KOVE	742/743	..	..	..	..	..	..	KPNF	342	319	324	323	334	335
Advertising	KOVF	744	..	..	..	..	..	..	KPNG	76	77	83	83	94	90
Industrial cleaning	KOVG	747	..	..	..	..	..	..	KPNH	545	478	445	424	427	415
Public administration and defence, compulsory social security	KOVH	L(75)	1 366	1 399	1 400	1 408	1 408	1 443	LMBG	1 307	1 341	1 342	1 349	1 349	1 382
Education	KOVI	M(80)	1 872	1 852	2 044	2 126	2 140	2 183	LMBH	1 808	1 788	1 979	2 059	2 073	2 116
Health and social work	KOVJ	N	2 580	2 582	2 600	2 683	2 742	2 796	LOJV	2 488	2 489	2 506	2 588	2 646	2 698
Human health, veterinary activities	KOVK	851/852	..	..	..	..	..	..	KPNL	1 585	1 584	1 600	1 693	1 737	1 786
Social work activities	KOVL	853	..	..	..	..	..	..	KPNM	903	906	906	895	909	912
Other community social and personal service activities,private households with employed persons, extra-territorial organisations and bodies	KOVM	O - Q	1 145	1 152	1 240	1 282	1 293	1 298	LMBK	1 118	1 126	1 213	1 254	1 264	1 268
Sewage and refuse disposal; sanitation	KOVN	90	96	106	110	97	86	82	KPNO	94	103	107	94	84	79
Activities of membership organisations	KOVO	91	208	210	212	221	224	229	KPNP	199	203	205	214	216	220
Recreational cultural and sporting activities	KOVP	92	581	568	625	659	672	672	KPNQ	568	555	612	646	658	657
Motion picture video radio TV news agencies and entertainment activities	KOVQ	921 to 924	..	..	..	..	..	..	KPNR	179	175	203	218	207	209
Library archives museums and other cultural activities	KOVR	925	..	..	..	..	..	..	KPNS	74	73	74	85	79	79
Sporting activities and other recreational activities	KOVS	926/927	..	..	..	..	..	..	KPNT	315	307	335	343	372	368
Other service activities,private households with employed persons, extra territorial organisations	KOVT	93/95/99	260	269	293	304	311	316	KPNU	256	265	289	300	307	312
Washing, dry cleaning of textile and fur products	KOVU	9301	..	..	..	..	..	..	KPNV	40	44	46	43	48	46
Hairdressing, other beauty treatment, physical and well-being activities	KOVV	9302/9304	..	..	..	..	..	..	KPNW	84	92	97	99	102	103

1 The data in this table have not been adjusted to reflect the 2001 Census population data. See chapter text.

Sources: Department of Manpower Services (Northern Ireland); Earnings and Employment Division, ONS: 01633 812318

7.6 Weekly hours worked[1,2]
United Kingdom
At Spring each year. Seasonally adjusted.

Hours

	All workers' weekly hours[3]		Average actual weekly hours of work		
	Total (millions)	Average	Full-time employment[3,4]	Part-time employment[4]	Second jobs[5]
All					
	YBUS	YBUV	YBUY	YBVB	YBVE
1992	843.5	33.1	38.2	14.8	
1993	826.5	32.9	38.1	14.7	10.5
1994	838.3	33.2	38.4	15.0	9.7
1995	853.4	33.4	38.7	15.1	8.9
1996	857.4	33.2	38.7	15.1	9.1
					8.8
1997	873.9	33.3	38.7	15.2	9.4
1998	880.4	33.2	38.6	15.2	9.1
1999	882.2	32.9	38.2	15.3	9.0
2000	887.9	32.6	37.9	15.4	8.9
2001	900.1	32.8	38.0	15.7	9.4
2002	900.2	32.6	37.8	15.6	9.4
Men					
	YBUT	YBUW	YBUZ	YBVC	YBVF
1992	542.0	38.7	40.0	14.3	11.8
1993	528.5	38.6	40.0	14.3	10.7
1994	536.0	38.9	40.4	14.8	9.5
1995	546.6	39.2	40.8	14.6	9.9
1996	546.5	39.0	40.7	14.8	9.6
1997	555.1	38.9	40.7	14.8	10.7
1998	559.7	38.8	40.7	15.0	9.7
1999	556.0	38.2	40.1	15.1	9.7
2000	559.3	37.9	39.8	15.1	9.3
2001	564.3	38.0	39.9	15.7	10.2
2002	560.2	37.7	39.6	15.1	10.3
Women					
	YBUU	YBUX	YBVA	YBVD	YBVG
1992	301.5	26.3	34.5	14.9	9.4
1993	298.0	26.1	34.2	14.7	8.9
1994	302.3	26.3	34.5	15.0	8.5
1995	306.7	26.4	34.4	15.2	8.5
1996	310.9	26.4	34.6	15.1	8.2
1997	318.8	26.6	34.7	15.3	8.4
1998	320.7	26.5	34.6	15.3	8.7
1999	326.1	26.5	34.5	15.3	8.5
2000	328.6	26.3	34.1	15.5	8.6
2001	335.8	26.6	34.4	15.7	8.9
2002	340.1	26.7	34.4	15.8	8.8

1 See chapter text.
2 Average hours actually worked in the reference week which includes hours worked in second jobs.
3 Main and second job.

4 People whose main job is full-time or part-time.
5 Second jobs reported in the LFS in addition to persons' main full time job.

Source: Labour Force Survey, Office for National Statistics

7.7 Civil Service staff
Analysis by ministerial responsibility[1,2]
At 1 April each year

Full-time equivalents (thousands)[3]

		1992	1993	1994	1995	1996	1997	1998	1999	2000	2001	2002
Agriculture, Fisheries and Food	BCDA	11.0	11.0	11.0	10.6	10.8	10.1	10.8	11.7	10.8	11.4	–
Cabinet Office	BBGD	2.0	6.0	12.0	11.7	12.3	7.8	7.7	7.6	6.9	6.9	6.9
Chancellor of the Exchequer's Departments:												
Customs and Excise	BCDC	27.0	25.0	25.0	24.1	23.2	23.1	23.4	22.5	21.9	21.7	21.8
Inland Revenue	BCDD	70.0	68.0	64.0	59.1	56.5	54.4	53.4	61.3	66.3	66.9	68.2
Department for National Savings	BCDE	6.0	6.0	6.0	5.4	4.7	4.3	4.1	0.1	0.1	0.1	0.1
Treasury and others	BCDF	10.0	5.0	5.0	4.3	6.0	5.1	5.1	5.0	5.5	5.5	5.6
Total	BCDB	113.0	105.0	99.0	92.9	90.3	86.8	86.0	89.0	93.8	94.2	95.7
Culture, Media and Sport	DMTC	–	–	–	–	–	–	0.6	0.6	0.6	0.6	0.7
Education	BCDG	3.0	3.0	2.0	2.5	–	–	–	–	–	–	–
Education and Employment	BBFT	–	–	–	–	40.8	34.1	33.6	34.6	36.5	38.3	–
Education and Skills	LNFW	–	–	–	–	–	–	–	–	–	–	7.2
Environment	BCDJ	23.0	18.0	10.0	9.4	10.9	9.6	–	–	–	–	–
Environment, Food and Rural Affairs	LNFX	–	–	–	–	–	–	–	–	–	–	14.6
Environment, Transport and the Regions	CKUZ	–	–	–	–	–	–	21.2	21.8	23.2	25.4	–
Foreign and Commonwealth	BCDK	10.0	10.0	8.0	7.5	7.1	6.6	5.4	5.5	5.5	5.5	5.7
Health	BAKR	7.0	7.0	7.0	6.2	4.8	4.7	4.6	4.8	7.0	7.2	5.1
Home	BCDL	50.0	52.0	51.0	51.4	50.8	50.4	50.7	50.0	53.6	60.1	61.0
International Development	DMUA	–	–	–	–	–	–	1.1	1.2	1.2	1.3	1.5
Legal Departments	BBGE	29.0	30.0	29.0	28.7	27.8	26.3	25.4	25.5	24.9	25.0	26.9
National Heritage	BBGF	1.0	1.0	1.0	1.0	1.0	1.0	–	–	–	–	–
Northern Ireland	BBGG	–	–	–	0.2	0.2	0.2	0.2	0.2	0.2	0.2	0.2
Scotland	BCDN	13.0	14.0	13.0	12.1	11.7	11.8	12.0	12.5	13.6	13.7	14.3
Social Security	BAKS	81.0	86.0	90.0	89.2	91.5	93.1	87.2	81.6	83.5	81.9	–
Trade and Industry	BCDQ	13.0	13.0	12.0	11.1	11.2	10.3	10.4	10.5	11.0	11.4	12.0
Transport	BCDR	15.0	15.0	14.0	12.9	11.3	11.4	–	–	–	–	–
Transport, Local Government and the Regions	LNFZ	–	–	–	–	–	–	–	–	–	–	23.9
Welsh Office	BCDS	2.0	3.0	2.0	2.2	2.1	2.2	2.1	2.3	2.7	3.2	3.5
Work and Pensions	LNGA	–	–	–	–	–	–	–	–	–	–	122
Total civil departments	BCDU	431.0	431.0	418.0	400.8	384.6	366.3	359.1	359.1	375.1	384.4	401.2
Defence	BCDW	140.0	130.0	122.0	116.1	109.9	109.2	104.2	100.9	100.3	98.3	89.0
Total all departments	BCDX	571.0	560.0	540.0	516.9	494.5	475.6	463.3	460.0	475.4	482.7	490.2
of which												
Non-industrial staff	BCDY	509.0	509.0	494.0	474.1	458.7	439.6	430.5	429.2	446.0	453.8	462.9
Industrial staff	BCDZ	61.0	52.0	46.0	42.0	35.9	36.0	32.8	30.8	29.4	28.9	27.3

1 The figures include non-industrial and industrial staff but exclude casual or seasonal staff and employees of the Northern Ireland Civil Service.
2 A comprehensive list of Machinery of Government changes is listed on the Cabinet Office's web site at: www.civil-service.gov.uk/statistics

3 Figures included are measured as 'full-time equivalent' staff. Part-time staff are recorded as a proportion of full-time employees according to the proportion of a full week that they work.

Source: Cabinet Office: 020 7276 1532

7.8 Persons employed in local authorities[1]

Thousands (Full-time equivalents)[2]

		1992	1993	1994	1995	1996	1997	1998	1999	2000	2001	2002
England												
Education	ATAM	835.8	712.1	692.8	698.4	691.8	691.8	693.9	707.3	731.5	768.2	781.7
Construction	BCHC	77.1	70.9	67.4	63.5	58.8	55.0	51.9	52.3	51.2	48.7	40.8
Transport	BCHD	1.5	1.4	1.4	1.4	1.4	1.4	1.4	1.4	..	..	..
Social services	BCHE	232.3	225.8	233.3	234.3	230.6	227.3	221.3	215.9	213.0	213.3	206.6
Public libraries and museums	BCHF	32.4	31.9	31.8	32.7	31.5	31.4	31.1	31.5	31.1	32.3	32.0
Recreation, parks and baths	BCHG	72.7	68.6	67.2	65.2	63.6	60.7	59.8	58.1	57.2	59.8	59.0
Environmental health	BCHH	19.6	19.0	18.5	17.4	17.2	17.4	16.9	17.2	17.7	17.9	18.5
Refuse collection and disposal	BCHS	23.6	21.8	20.5	25.1	24.5	24.6	24.0	23.7	21.8	21.8	21.2
Housing	BCHT	65.4	65.5	65.7	68.0	66.8	65.5	64.7	65.4	65.0	66.5	68.1
Town and country planning	BCHU	23.1	22.5	22.2	25.9	27.1	27.3	26.8	27.7	27.7	28.4	28.9
Fire service												
regulars	BAIV	34.3	34.2	33.9	33.8	33.6	33.3	33.1	34.0	33.8	34.5	35.2
others	BAIW	5.8	5.7	5.7	5.8	5.7	5.6	5.6	6.3	6.2	6.4	6.5
Other services[3]	BCHM	238.0	226.7	217.0	191.3	183.8	177.9	173.1	178.1	177.8	182.2	190.0
Total of above	BCHN	1 661.6	1 506.1	1 477.4	1 462.8	1 436.4	1 419.2	1 403.6	1 417.5	1 434.0	1 480.0	1 488.5
Police Service												
police: all ranks	BCHO	120.8	121.4	121.0	118.8	118.4	118.5	119.2	119.2	117.0	118.6	120.1
cadets	BAIX	0.3	0.2	0.1	0.1	0.3	0.3	0.1	–	..	..	..
traffic wardens	BAIY	4.9	4.9	4.7	4.5	4.3	4.1	3.5	3.3	2.8	2.6	2.2
civilians	BAIZ	44.9	46.7	46.9	48.1	49.8	50.0	50.3	50.5	50.8	51.1	53.0
Magistrates courts	BAJA	10.0	10.0	9.9	10.0	9.9	9.2	8.9	9.0	8.9	9.1	9.3
Probation staff												
officers	BAJB	6.9	7.1	7.2	7.2	6.9	6.9	6.2	6.8	7.1	7.2	7.2
others	BAJC	7.5	7.9	8.0	8.5	7.2	7.1	5.4	7.1	7.5	8.0	8.0
Total law and order	BAJD	195.3	198.2	197.8	197.2	196.8	196.1	193.6	195.9	194.1	196.6	199.8
Agency staff	BAJE	1.1	1.4	1.6	0.9	0.8	0.8	0.8	–	..	..	..
Total (excluding special employment and training measures)	BCHR	1 858.0	1 705.7	1 676.8	1 660.9	1 634.0	1 616.1	1 598.0	1 613.4	1 628.1	1 676.6	1 688.3

		1992	1993	1994	1995	1996	1997	1998	1999	2000	2001	2002
Wales												
Education	ATAN	53.8	48.2	47.9	48.7	50.6	49.5	49.9	51.6	51.7	52.8	53.9
Construction	BCGC	6.5	5.9	5.8	5.9	6.0	5.5	5.5	5.7	5.6	5.1	5.1
Transport	BCGD	–	–	–	–	–	–	..	..	..	..	..
Social services	BCGE	16.0	16.0	17.0	18.3	18.5	19.0	18.8	19.2	19.3	18.9	18.9
Public libraries and museums	BCGF	1.7	1.7	1.7	1.7	1.5	1.6	1.5	1.6	1.6	1.8	1.8
Recreation, parks and baths	BCGG	5.8	6.0	6.0	6.3	5.8	6.4	6.1	6.1	6.2	6.5	6.5
Environmental health	BCGH	1.5	1.5	1.5	1.5	1.6	1.5	1.3	1.4	1.5	1.6	1.4
Refuse collection and disposal	BCGI	1.6	1.6	1.5	2.2	2.9	2.9	2.9	2.8	2.6	2.6	2.7
Housing	BCGJ	3.0	3.1	3.1	3.4	3.3	3.6	3.6	3.8	3.6	..	..
Town and country planning	BCGK	1.7	1.8	1.8	2.2	1.9	2.0	2.0	2.1	2.1	2.0	2.0
Fire service												
regulars	BAKT	1.8	1.8	1.8	1.8	1.9	1.9	1.9	1.9	1.9	1.9	1.8
others	BAKU	0.4	0.4	0.4	0.3	0.3	0.3	0.3	0.4	0.4	..	..
Other services	BCGM	18.7	23.5	19.8	15.6	14.2	14.6	14.0	15.1	15.2	15.6	14.6
Total of above	BCGN	112.5	111.5	108.1	107.9	108.5	108.8	107.8	111.7	111.9	112.9	112.8
Police Service												
police: all ranks	BCGO	6.6	6.6	6.5	6.4	6.4	6.6	6.6	6.6	6.6	6.9	7.1
cadets	BAKV	–	–	–	–	–	–	..	..	..	..	..
traffic wardens	BAKW	0.2	0.2	0.2	0.2	0.2	0.2	0.2	0.2	0.2	0.1	0.2
civilians	BAKX	2.1	2.1	2.2	2.2	2.5	2.4	2.4	2.8	2.7	2.9	3.1
Magistrates courts	BAKY	0.6	0.7	0.7	0.7	0.6	0.6	0.6	0.7	0.7	0.6	0.6
Probation staff												
officers	BAKZ	0.4	0.4	0.4	0.4	0.4	0.4	0.3	0.4	0.4	0.4	0.4
others	BALA	0.4	0.4	0.4	0.4	0.4	0.4	0.3	0.4	0.4	0.5	0.5
Total law and order	BALB	10.3	10.4	10.4	10.3	10.5	10.6	10.4	10.3	10.2	10.5	11.0
Agency staff	BALC	–	–	–	–	–	–	..	..	..	..	..
Total (excluding special employment and training measures)	BCGR	122.8	121.9	118.5	118.2	119.0	119.4	118.2	122.0	122.1	123.4	123.8

7.8 Persons employed in local authorities[1]

continued

Thousands (Full-time equivalents)[4]

		1991	1992	1993	1994	1995	1996	1997	1998	1999	2000	2001
Scotland												
Education	ATAO	87.1	87.5	80.0	77.1	77.6	74.7	73.6	75.5	76.7	79.2	80.5
Construction	BCMC	23.5	23.1	22.9	22.0	21.7	20.7	20.6	20.5	20.4	20.6	20.6
Transport	BCMD	0.8	0.8	0.8	0.9	0.9	0.9	0.9	0.9	0.9	0.9	0.9
Social Services	BCME	36.2	36.8	37.3	38.3	39.1	38.4	37.9	37.0	34.6	36.4	37.0
Public libraries and museums	BCMF	4.4	4.5	4.6	4.7	4.7	4.2	4.2	4.2	4.1	4.0	4.1
Recreation, leisure and tourism	BCMG	13.6	13.3	13.7	13.9	13.9	11.4	11.4	11.3	11.3	11.4	11.4
Environmental health	BCMH	2.5	2.5	2.7	2.7	2.6	3.4	3.4	3.3	3.1	3.0	3.9
Cleansing	BCMI	8.2	8.1	8.2	8.1	8.0	7.3	7.2	7.2	7.2	7.2	7.3
Housing	BCMJ	7.3	7.2	7.4	7.8	7.9	7.9	8.4	8.5	8.5	8.6	8.9
Physical planning	BCMK	2.0	2.1	2.2	2.2	2.2	3.7	3.4	3.3	3.3	3.4	3.4
Fire service	BCML	5.2	5.2	5.3	5.3	5.2	5.8	5.6	5.7	5.7	5.7	5.5
Other services[3]	BCMM	46.8	48.1	48.0	52.1	51.5	40.7	40.7	38.5	39.0	37.2	33.8
Total of above	BCMN	237.6	239.2	233.1	235.1	235.3	219.1	217.3	215.9	214.8	217.6	217.3
Police service												
police (all ranks)	BCMO	13.9	13.9	14.2	14.2	14.4	13.7	14.2	14.3	14.4	14.2	14.6
others[5]	BCMP	4.6	4.8	5.1	5.2	5.2	5.2	5.3	5.4	5.4	5.3	5.5
Administration of district courts	BCMQ	0.2	0.1	0.2	0.2	0.2	0.2	0.2	0.2	0.2	0.2	0.2
Total (excluding special employment and training measures)	BCMR	256.3	258.0	252.6	254.7	255.1	238.2	237.0	235.8	234.8	237.3	237.6

1 Figures are based on surveys undertaken on behalf of central and local government by the ONS and the Scottish Executive and the Convention of Scottish Local Authorities (COSLA).
2 Based on the following factors to convert part-time employees to approximate full-time equivalents: for teachers and lecturers in further education, 0.295; teachers in primary and secondary education and all other non-manual employees, 0.53; manual employees, 0.41.
3 Including civil/central services departments (eg engineers and finance) and all services not shown separately.
4 Based on the following factors to convert part-time employees to approximate full-time equivalents: for lecturers and teachers, 0.40; non-manual staff (excluding teachers), 0.58; manual employees, 0.46.

5 Includes civilian employees of police forces and traffic wardens.

Sources: Office for National Statistics: 0117 987 8675;
Home Office;
Scottish Executive;
Scottish Joint Staffing Watch.

7.9 Duration of unemployment[1]
United Kingdom

At Spring each year. Seasonally adjusted.

Thousands

		1992	1993	1994	1995	1996	1997	1998	1999	2000	2001	2002
All												
All unemployed	MGSC	2 791	2 947	2 745	2 465	2 339	2 036	1 775	1 759	1 636	1 428	1 524
Duration of unemployment												
Less than 6 months	YBWF	1 232	1 137	1 062	1 020	1 039	971	964	998	962	848	970
6 months & less than 1 year	YBWG	577	568	458	395	394	303	247	262	238	213	223
1 year or more	YBWH	982	1 243	1 225	1 051	905	763	564	499	436	367	331
1 year or more as % of total	YBWI	*35.2*	*42.2*	*44.6*	*42.6*	*38.7*	*37.4*	*31.8*	*28.4*	*26.7*	*25.7*	*21.7*
Men												
All unemployed	MGSD	1 852	1 965	1 802	1 588	1 520	1 278	1 069	1 072	975	847	909
Duration of unemployment												
Less than 6 months	MGYK	735	682	598	562	585	532	510	552	520	455	528
6 months & less than 1 year	MGYM	390	365	293	249	250	183	159	162	138	129	149
1 year or more	MGYO	727	918	912	777	685	563	399	358	317	263	232
1 year or more as % of total	YBWJ	*39.2*	*46.7*	*50.6*	*48.9*	*45.1*	*44.0*	*37.3*	*33.4*	*32.5*	*31.0*	*25.5*
Women												
All unemployed	MGSE	939	982	943	878	819	758	707	687	662	581	615
Duration of unemployment												
Less than 6 months	MGYL	496	455	465	458	454	439	454	446	442	393	442
6 months & less than 1 year	MGYN	187	202	165	146	144	120	87	101	100	84	75
1 year or more	MGYP	255	325	313	274	220	200	165	141	120	105	99
1 year or more as % of total	YBWK	*27.2*	*33.1*	*33.2*	*31.2*	*26.9*	*26.4*	*23.4*	*20.5*	*18.1*	*18.0*	*16.0*

1 See chapter text.

Source: Labour Force Survey, Office for National Statistics

7.10 Unemployment[1]
United Kingdom
By age group and sex. At Spring each year. Seasonally adjusted.

Thousands and percentages

	All aged 16 and over	16-59/64	16-17	18-24	16-24	25-34	35-49	50-64 (m) 50-59 (w)	65+ (m) 60+ (w)
All	**Thousands**								
	MGSC	YBSH	YBVH	YBVN	PXLG	PXLJ	PXLM	PXLP	PXLS
1993	2 947	2 913	136	770	906	783	742	482	34
1994	2 745	2 718	145	667	812	744	703	459	27
1995	2 465	2 446	145	604	749	669	644	384	19
1996	2 339	2 318	166	555	721	636	605	356	21
1997	2 036	2 012	169	485	653	513	529	316	24
1998	1 775	1 755	158	434	592	463	432	267	21
1999	1 759	1 739	171	424	595	420	456	268	20
2000	1 636	1 619	178	402	579	367	412	260	17
2001	1 428	1 413	147	373	520	322	381	190	15
2002	1 524	1 503	164	392	556	343	387	217	22
Men									
	MGSD	YBSI	YBVI	YBVO	PXLH	PXLK	PXLN	PXLQ	PXLT
1993	1 965	1 952	74	501	575	510	493	375	13
1994	1 802	1 792	77	432	509	487	447	348	11
1995	1 588	1 579	80	382	463	427	399	290	9
1996	1 520	1 508	98	359	457	392	389	269	12
1997	1 278	1 266	91	303	394	318	328	226	12
1998	1 069	1 059	85	260	345	271	250	193	9
1999	1 072	1 062	102	252	353	239	276	194	9
2000	975	968	96	240	336	210	236	185	7
2001	847	840	84	222	307	183	211	139	7
2002	909	899	90	244	334	195	226	144	10
Women									
	MGSE	YBSJ	YBVJ	YBVP	PXLI	PXLL	PXLO	PXLR	PXLU
1993	982	961	62	270	332	273	248	108	21
1994	943	927	68	235	303	256	256	112	16
1995	878	867	64	222	287	242	245	94	10
1996	819	810	68	196	264	243	216	87	9
1997	758	746	78	182	260	195	201	90	12
1998	707	695	73	174	247	192	182	74	11
1999	687	677	69	172	241	180	180	75	11
2000	662	651	82	161	243	157	176	75	10
2001	581	573	62	151	213	139	170	51	8
2002	615	603	73	148	221	148	161	73	12
All	**Rates[2]**								
	MGSX	YBTI	YBVK	YBVQ	PXLV	PXLY	PXMB	PXME	PXMH
1993	10.5	10.6	19.2	17.7	17.9	10.6	7.5	9.5	4.3
1994	9.8	9.9	19.9	16.3	16.8	9.9	7.1	8.9	3.3
1995	8.8	9.0	19.3	15.4	16.0	8.9	6.5	7.4	2.3
1996	8.3	8.4	20.2	14.5	15.5	8.5	6.0	6.8	2.6
1997	7.2	7.3	19.5	13.1	14.3	6.9	5.3	5.8	2.9
1998	6.3	6.4	18.6	12.0	13.3	6.3	4.3	4.7	2.6
1999	6.1	6.3	20.2	11.7	13.3	5.7	4.5	4.6	2.4
2000	5.7	5.8	20.9	11.0	12.9	5.1	4.0	4.4	2.0
2001	4.9	5.0	18.1	10.2	11.6	4.6	3.6	3.1	1.8
2002	5.2	5.3	20.1	10.4	12.2	5.0	3.6	3.5	2.4
Men									
	MGSY	YBTJ	YBVL	YBVR	PXLW	PXLZ	PXMC	PXMF	PXMI
1993	12.5	12.6	20.5	21.3	21.2	12.1	9.2	11.8	4.9
1994	11.5	11.6	20.7	19.4	19.6	11.6	8.3	10.9	4.0
1995	10.2	10.3	20.9	18.0	18.4	10.2	7.4	9.1	3.0
1996	9.7	9.8	22.7	17.4	18.3	9.5	7.2	8.3	4.3
1997	8.2	8.3	21.0	15.2	16.2	7.7	6.1	6.8	4.3
1998	6.9	6.9	19.9	13.5	14.6	6.7	4.6	5.6	3.3
1999	6.8	6.9	23.4	13.1	15.0	6.0	5.0	5.5	3.1
2000	6.2	6.3	22.3	12.3	14.2	5.4	4.2	5.2	2.4
2001	5.4	5.4	20.3	11.4	13.0	4.8	3.7	3.8	2.7
2002	5.8	5.8	22.0	12.2	13.9	5.3	4.0	3.9	3.3
Women									
	MGSZ	YBTK	YBVM	YBVS	PXLX	PXMA	PXMD	PXMG	PXMJ
1993	7.9	8.1	17.7	13.6	14.2	8.5	5.6	5.7	3.9
1994	7.6	7.8	19.1	12.6	13.6	7.9	5.7	5.7	3.0
1995	7.0	7.2	17.7	12.4	13.2	7.4	5.4	4.7	2.0
1996	6.5	6.7	17.3	11.1	12.2	7.3	4.7	4.3	1.8
1997	5.9	6.1	17.9	10.6	12.1	5.8	4.4	4.3	2.2
1998	5.5	5.6	17.4	10.3	11.7	5.8	3.9	3.3	2.2
1999	5.3	5.4	16.8	10.2	11.5	5.4	3.8	3.2	2.0
2000	5.0	5.2	19.5	9.5	11.5	4.8	3.7	3.1	1.8
2001	4.4	4.5	15.8	8.8	10.1	4.3	3.5	2.1	1.4
2002	4.6	4.7	18.3	8.4	10.3	4.7	3.2	2.9	1.9

1 See chapter text.
2 Total unemployment as a percentage of all economically active persons in the relevant age group.

Source: Labour Force Survey, Office for National Statistics

7.11 Claimant count[1] by age and duration
Computerised claims
United Kingdom

Thousands, not seasonally adjusted

		1996	1997	1998	1999	2000	2001
Annual averages							
Males							
All ages							
All durations	GEZG	1 601.0	1 216.3	1 031.0	954.6	834.0	740.6
Up to 6 months	GEZH	667.1	569.4	541.1	530.6	488.8	455.9
Over 6 and up to 12 months	GEZI	300.6	200.6	188.5	166.8	143.2	125.9
All over 12 months	GEZJ	633.4	446.3	301.4	257.1	202.0	158.8
All over 24 months	GEZK	372.7	269.7	169.8	128.9	102.4	77.5
Aged 18 to 24							
All durations	GEZL	378.1	284.6	237.5	205.2	182.2	167.8
Up to 6 months	GEZM	203.8	172.5	159.8	160.9	149.6	141.3
Over 6 and up to 12 months	GEZN	81.0	53.2	44.2	34.3	28.3	23.4
All over 12 months	GEZO	93.5	58.9	33.5	10.0	4.4	3.1
All over 24 months	GEZP	35.3	22.1	10.7	2.3	0.5	0.3
Aged 25 to 49							
All durations	IACI	957.7	729.1	619.4	582.9	506.2	446.0
Up to 6 months	IACK	363.5	313.7	303.2	291.3	266.9	248.2
Over 6 and up to 12 months	IACN	173.7	118.2	117.3	107.4	92.8	83.1
All over 12 months	IACQ	420.6	297.2	198.9	184.3	146.5	114.7
All over 24 months	IACT	257.5	185.6	112.4	88.0	70.5	52.4
Aged 50 and over							
All durations	IACW	255.6	193.0	165.8	158.0	137.7	119.8
Up to 6 months	IACZ	91.2	74.3	70.3	70.6	65.0	59.8
Over 6 and up to 12 months	IADC	45.1	28.6	26.6	24.6	21.6	18.9
All over 12 months	IADF	119.2	90.1	69.0	62.8	51.1	41.0
All over 24 months	IADI	80.0	62.0	46.7	38.6	31.5	24.8
Females							
All ages							
All durations	GEZR	506.9	373.5	321.8	296.3	260.6	233.7
Up to 6 months	GEZS	267.4	216.3	203.0	195.5	177.9	165.8
Over 6 and up to 12 months	GEZT	102.1	62.1	54.5	48.1	41.3	35.4
All over 12 months	GEZU	137.4	95.2	64.2	52.7	41.4	32.5
All over 24 months	GEZV	67.0	48.9	30.9	22.9	18.2	13.9
Aged 18 to 24							
All durations	GEZW	164.9	121.8	101.5	88.9	79.2	73.4
Up to 6 months	GEZX	100.1	80.1	72.4	71.1	65.6	62.1
Over 6 and up to 12 months	GEZY	33.6	21.6	17.3	14.0	11.7	9.8
All over 12 months	GEZZ	31.1	20.1	11.8	3.8	1.9	1.4
All over 24 months	GEYU	9.9	6.6	3.3	0.8	0.2	0.2
Aged 25 to 49							
All durations	IACJ	253.3	181.7	157.4	147.1	127.9	113.4
Up to 6 months	IACL	127.8	100.8	96.1	90.3	80.7	74.4
Over 6 and up to 12 months	IACO	52.3	29.9	27.0	24.7	21.3	18.6
All over 12 months	IACR	73.3	51.1	34.3	32.1	25.9	20.4
All over 24 months	IACU	37.2	27.5	16.9	13.4	10.9	8.2
Aged 50 and over							
All durations	IACX	81.5	62.8	56.7	54.0	47.5	41.3
Up to 6 months	IADA	33.0	28.6	28.6	28.2	26.0	23.9
Over 6 and up to 12 months	IADD	15.6	10.2	9.9	9.1	7.9	6.7
All over 12 months	IADG	32.9	23.9	18.1	16.7	13.6	10.7
All over 24 months	IADJ	20.0	14.9	10.7	8.7	7.1	5.5

1 Count of claimants of unemployment-related benefits; computerised claims
  only.

Sources: Jobcentre Plus administrative system;
Office for National Statistics: 020 7533 6094

7.12 Unemployment rates[1]
At Spring each year. Not seasonally adjusted.

Percentages

		1992	1993	1994	1995	1996	1997	1998	1999	2000	2001	2002
North East	BENU	11.9	12.0	12.5	11.4	10.8	9.8	8.1	10.1	9.1	7.4	6.9
North West	BENV	10.1	10.8	10.3	9.0	8.4	6.8	6.6	6.2	5.3	5.1	5.4
Yorkshire and Humber	BENY	10.1	10.0	9.9	8.7	8.1	8.0	7.0	6.5	6.0	4.9	5.3
East Midlands	BENZ	8.8	9.1	8.3	7.4	7.4	6.3	4.9	5.2	5.1	4.9	4.2
West Midlands	BEOA	10.7	11.8	10.0	8.9	9.2	6.8	6.3	6.8	6.2	5.0	5.4
East	BEOB	7.7	9.2	8.2	7.5	6.1	5.8	5.0	4.1	3.5	3.6	3.4
London	BEOC	12.0	13.2	13.1	11.5	11.3	9.1	8.2	7.6	7.0	5.8	6.5
South East	BEOD	7.8	8.0	7.1	6.4	6.0	5.2	4.3	3.6	3.3	3.0	3.9
South West	BEOE	9.1	9.2	7.5	7.8	6.3	5.2	4.5	4.7	4.1	3.5	3.5
Wales	BEOG	8.9	9.6	9.4	8.8	8.3	8.3	6.7	7.0	6.1	5.7	6.0
Scotland	BEOH	9.5	10.2	10.0	8.4	8.7	8.5	7.4	7.4	7.6	5.7	6.8
Northern Ireland	BEOI	12.3	12.5	11.6	11.0	9.5	7.5	7.2	7.2	7.0	6.2	5.4

1 See chapter text.

Source: Labour Force Survey, Office for National Statistics

7.13 Claimant count rates[1]
Seasonally adjusted annual averages

Percentages

		1991	1992	1993	1994	1995	1996	1997	1998	1999	2000	2001
United Kingdom	BCJE	7.6	9.2	9.7	8.8	7.6	7.0	5.3	4.5	4.2	3.6	3.2
North East	DPDM	10.5	11.3	12.1	11.7	10.8	10.0	8.1	7.2	7.0	6.3	5.5
North West	IBWC	8.6	9.8	10.0	9.3	8.1	7.5	5.9	5.1	4.6	4.1	3.7
Yorkshire and the Humber	DPBI	8.2	9.4	9.7	9.1	8.1	7.6	6.1	5.4	5.0	4.4	4.0
East Midlands	DPBJ	6.9	8.6	9.0	8.3	7.1	6.5	4.7	4.0	3.7	3.5	3.2
West Midlands	DPBN	8.0	9.8	10.3	9.4	7.7	6.9	5.3	4.6	4.5	4.0	3.7
East	DPDP	6.0	8.1	8.8	7.6	6.2	5.7	4.0	3.2	2.9	2.5	2.1
London	DPDQ	7.6	9.9	10.9	10.1	8.9	8.2	6.2	5.0	4.5	3.8	3.3
South East	DPDR	5.4	7.4	8.1	6.9	5.6	4.9	3.3	2.6	2.3	1.9	1.6
South West	DPBM	6.5	8.7	9.0	7.7	6.5	5.9	4.2	3.4	3.1	2.5	2.1
England	VASQ	7.3	9.1	9.7	8.7	7.5	6.8	5.1	4.3	3.9	3.4	3.0
Wales	DPBP	8.5	9.5	9.8	8.9	8.1	7.7	6.2	5.4	5.0	4.4	3.9
Scotland	DPBQ	8.2	8.9	9.2	8.7	7.5	7.3	6.2	5.5	5.1	4.6	4.2
Northern Ireland	DPBR	12.9	13.7	13.6	12.6	11.2	10.7	8.1	7.3	6.4	5.3	5.0
Great Britain	DPAJ	7.5	9.1	9.6	8.7	7.5	6.9	5.3	4.4	4.1	3.6	3.2

1 The number of unemployment-related benefit claimants as a percentage of the estimated total workforce (the sum of claimants, employee jobs, self-employed, participants on work-related government training programmes and HM Forces) at mid-year. Excluded are claimants under 18, consistent with current coverage. See chapter text.

Sources: Jobcentre Plus administrative system;
Office for National Statistics: 020 7533 6094

7.14 Claimant count[1]
Analysis by Government Office Regions
Seasonally adjusted

Thousands

	North East	North West	Yorkshire and the Humber	East Midlands	West Midlands	East	London	South East	South West	England	Wales	Scotland	Great Britain	Northern Ireland	United Kingdom
	DPDG	IBWA	DPAX	DPAY	DPBC	DPDJ	DPDK	DPDL	DPBB	IBWK	DPBE	DPBF	DPAG	DPBG	BCJD
1988 Jan	164.7	363.6	237.6	150.7	256.1	138.3	313.7	171.7	150.4	1 943.7	132.9	294.6	2 374.3	114.3	2 488.6
Apr	158.8	347.1	229.2	143.1	241.4	124.0	299.8	154.6	140.1	1 835.6	128.7	283.5	2 250.3	112.1	2 362.4
Jul	151.7	328.4	216.1	134.1	224.4	110.8	277.6	140.1	129.6	1 713.8	120.9	270.4	2 104.1	110.3	2 214.4
Oct	146.2	319.0	207.0	127.2	210.0	101.4	265.4	130.8	122.3	1 629.0	117.1	265.0	2 011.4	108.6	2 120.0
1989 Jan	140.3	301.4	192.6	116.8	190.9	89.5	242.3	114.6	109.2	1 495.9	108.1	254.2	1 859.9	107.4	1 967.3
Apr	132.3	283.0	178.6	106.6	171.9	80.2	221.3	103.4	99.9	1 375.7	99.4	238.9	1 715.5	105.1	1 820.6
Jul	124.4	269.7	171.3	101.7	163.0	78.4	216.1	100.6	95.5	1 322.0	93.2	226.3	1 640.2	102.8	1 743.0
Oct	118.0	256.5	164.5	97.8	155.9	76.8	204.8	99.7	91.5	1 265.2	88.5	217.7	1 571.7	100.0	1 671.7
1990 Jan	112.5	243.7	159.5	93.8	151.1	74.3	199.4	95.5	86.5	1 215.7	84.4	207.9	1 508.6	97.3	1 605.9
Apr	109.3	238.0	154.0	92.7	145.0	75.3	194.7	95.1	86.5	1 189.9	82.8	200.8	1 474.2	96.0	1 570.2
Jul	109.1	237.7	156.1	96.1	147.1	83.8	203.9	107.2	94.1	1 234.7	83.2	194.3	1 512.6	94.4	1 607.0
Oct	112.3	248.0	165.0	104.8	157.3	98.2	226.6	127.5	106.4	1 345.5	88.7	197.3	1 632.1	93.8	1 725.9
1991 Jan	116.7	261.8	176.4	113.1	171.0	112.5	255.8	149.7	122.2	1 478.8	95.0	200.9	1 775.1	96.0	1 871.1
Apr	126.2	285.9	197.5	132.0	203.5	138.5	303.2	190.5	146.9	1 723.9	108.8	212.7	2 045.7	97.9	2 143.6
Jul	130.5	305.4	211.9	145.5	225.4	158.9	342.3	221.3	165.7	1 906.8	115.5	220.1	2 242.5	98.8	2 341.3
Oct	133.2	318.2	219.6	154.5	240.0	172.4	368.9	240.9	178.6	2 025.9	119.3	224.0	2 369.6	100.5	2 470.1
1992 Jan	133.9	325.4	222.7	160.4	250.6	183.3	389.8	258.4	188.4	2 112.6	121.3	228.0	2 462.2	102.2	2 564.4
Apr	135.7	332.8	227.6	168.0	260.0	196.0	409.6	277.7	199.0	2 205.5	123.4	231.8	2 561.6	103.4	2 665.0
Jul	136.7	335.2	232.4	172.1	266.1	205.1	426.2	288.9	206.6	2 268.9	124.1	235.2	2 628.6	104.6	2 733.2
Oct	141.4	343.6	240.2	178.8	277.4	218.6	448.0	308.4	215.3	2 371.1	129.2	242.4	2 743.3	105.1	2 848.4
1993 Jan	146.2	348.3	247.5	185.2	286.2	229.5	464.6	325.2	222.6	2 454.4	131.4	245.3	2 832.0	105.5	2 937.5
Apr	148.0	345.2	246.5	183.6	285.1	228.2	469.5	321.4	220.0	2 446.6	130.3	243.2	2 821.0	104.5	2 925.5
Jul	148.5	338.0	240.9	180.8	278.7	223.5	466.3	314.0	214.4	2 404.4	129.3	241.2	2 775.6	102.5	2 878.1
Oct	147.5	331.1	237.8	177.8	271.5	216.6	460.4	306.6	208.4	2 356.8	127.8	236.6	2 722.1	101.8	2 823.9
1994 Jan	145.6	325.1	233.7	174.7	262.3	210.0	451.4	296.7	203.6	2 302.3	126.7	236.0	2 665.8	100.2	2 766.0
Apr	141.6	314.5	227.4	170.7	252.0	200.4	440.4	280.9	194.5	2 221.7	123.3	231.7	2 577.4	98.9	2 676.3
Jul	139.1	304.2	222.7	166.3	242.3	191.0	428.1	268.1	188.1	2 148.8	119.0	227.4	2 496.3	97.2	2 593.5
Oct	136.0	291.7	215.9	160.1	230.5	180.5	415.4	251.1	178.9	2 059.0	112.9	218.1	2 391.1	93.8	2 484.9
1995 Jan	133.0	280.1	210.6	153.2	218.5	172.3	401.4	237.9	171.4	1 977.5	108.3	209.3	2 296.0	91.3	2 387.3
Apr	130.0	270.8	206.8	148.1	211.0	167.1	395.0	229.7	166.0	1 923.8	106.2	200.3	2 231.0	88.6	2 319.6
Jul	128.2	266.1	204.6	145.3	206.9	165.0	390.2	225.1	162.5	1 892.8	106.7	195.3	2 195.9	87.6	2 283.5
Oct	126.4	260.9	200.7	142.3	201.3	160.7	383.2	219.1	159.4	1 852.7	105.4	193.5	2 152.9	85.8	2 238.7
1996 Jan	123.1	255.8	197.0	140.0	196.5	157.2	376.8	213.3	155.6	1 814.6	104.0	193.2	2 112.5	85.9	2 198.4
Apr	121.7	254.9	195.7	137.7	194.2	153.5	367.9	207.6	152.3	1 785.1	104.6	194.9	2 085.0	86.1	2 171.1
Jul	116.9	248.2	188.8	131.8	187.6	146.8	357.5	198.9	146.8	1 722.5	101.8	191.9	2 017.0	86.4	2 103.4
Oct	110.5	238.4	181.1	124.9	177.8	138.5	341.6	185.5	137.9	1 635.0	98.2	186.3	1 920.7	81.7	2 002.4
1997 Jan	101.0	218.5	166.4	111.8	160.1	123.5	312.6	163.3	126.0	1 483.2	90.3	173.8	1 747.3	71.1	1 818.4
Apr	95.2	201.3	154.7	102.4	147.3	110.6	284.9	144.4	112.1	1 352.9	82.5	162.2	1 597.6	65.0	1 662.6
Jul	92.4	188.9	148.2	95.0	138.0	102.5	264.3	131.0	100.7	1 261.0	78.1	153.6	1 492.7	61.4	1 554.1
Oct	90.4	177.6	142.0	87.6	131.7	94.3	246.4	120.4	93.0	1 183.4	73.6	146.5	1 403.5	60.6	1 464.1
1998 Jan	87.6	170.6	137.2	82.8	126.1	88.5	234.3	112.3	88.7	1 128.1	70.9	141.6	1 340.6	59.9	1 400.5
Apr	84.1	165.4	134.1	79.9	122.3	85.2	229.4	108.0	85.1	1 093.5	69.3	138.7	1 301.5	57.9	1 359.4
Jul	81.8	163.7	133.3	80.0	121.4	83.7	225.2	105.5	84.1	1 078.7	68.6	139.4	1 286.7	57.3	1 344.0
Oct	82.1	160.9	130.9	79.9	121.4	82.0	219.3	102.5	81.8	1 060.8	68.1	136.9	1 265.8	56.1	1 321.9
1999 Jan	82.6	159.5	129.5	79.0	122.6	80.3	214.5	101.2	81.2	1 050.4	67.8	135.6	1 253.8	55.9	1 309.7
Apr	82.5	157.2	127.0	78.2	123.1	79.1	207.8	98.8	78.4	1 032.1	67.1	133.9	1 233.1	55.0	1 288.1
Jul	80.3	153.8	122.4	75.9	120.2	76.6	202.2	94.4	74.9	1 000.7	63.8	130.2	1 194.7	50.0	1 244.7
Oct	76.7	150.0	118.3	73.6	115.9	73.6	196.5	91.1	71.4	967.1	61.0	126.1	1 154.2	46.5	1 200.7
2000 Jan	75.6	145.6	114.4	73.1	112.1	70.0	188.9	87.0	68.1	934.8	59.3	123.1	1 117.2	44.1	1 161.3
Apr	73.9	140.1	109.2	70.2	108.5	67.2	181.9	81.6	63.9	896.5	57.9	119.5	1 073.9	42.5	1 116.4
Jul	72.2	135.6	105.2	68.8	107.5	63.0	172.5	78.1	61.2	864.1	57.1	115.0	1 036.2	41.2	1 077.4
Oct	69.6	131.3	102.7	67.8	106.6	60.8	165.0	74.3	58.2	836.3	56.5	111.9	1 004.7	41.3	1 046.0
2001 Jan	66.1	127.2	99.6	66.3	103.9	56.6	157.1	69.1	54.8	800.7	54.8	108.6	964.1	40.8	1 004.9
Apr	63.2	124.8	97.7	65.1	101.1	55.1	152.5	66.6	53.5	779.6	52.4	105.4	937.4	39.9	977.3
Jul	61.6	121.8	95.5	63.2	97.7	54.5	151.7	65.8	52.3	764.1	50.1	102.3	916.5	39.3	955.8
Oct	61.5	121.9	93.7	62.0	95.9	54.3	156.1	65.9	51.5	762.8	49.3	104.7	916.8	38.6	955.4
2002 Jan	60.6	120.7	90.7	59.9	95.2	54.5	161.2	67.7	50.6	761.1	47.8	103.5	912.4	38.0	950.4
Apr	59.1	118.8	89.1	59.0	93.6	56.0	165.6	70.7	50.5	762.6	47.4	104.1	914.1	37.5	951.6
Jul	58.4	118.1	88.7	58.4	93.1	57.6	167.7	72.4	50.3	764.9	47.0	101.9	913.6	36.0	949.7
Oct	55.9	116.6	87.7	58.0	93.3	57.1	167.9	72.4	49.5	758.4	46.5	100.5	905.4	35.1	940.5

1 The figures are based on the number of claimants receiving unemployment related benefits and are adjusted for seasonality and discontinuities to be consistent with current coverage. See chapter text. The latest national and regional seasonally adjusted claimant count figures are provisional and subject to revision in the following month.

Sources: Jobcentre Plus administrative system; Office for National Statistics: 020 7533 6094

7.15 Economic activity: by age and sex[1]
United Kingdom
At Spring each year. Seasonally adjusted.

Thousands and percentages

	All aged 16 and over	16-59/64	16-17	18-24	16-24	25-34	35-49	50-64 (m) 50-59 (w)	65+ (m) 60+ (w)
All	**Thousands**								
	MGSF	YBSK	YBZL	YBZO	PXMK	YBZR	YBZU	YBZX	YCAD
1994	28 138	27 332	727	4 093	4 820	7 478	9 896	5 138	806
1995	28 113	27 301	749	3 926	4 675	7 496	9 955	5 175	813
1996	28 237	27 448	822	3 829	4 651	7 482	10 065	5 249	790
1997	28 370	27 546	866	3 705	4 571	7 493	10 029	5 452	824
1998	28 354	27 562	851	3 615	4 467	7 405	10 045	5 645	793
1999	28 659	27 823	846	3 611	4 457	7 312	10 223	5 831	836
2000	28 910	28 062	848	3 647	4 496	7 186	10 404	5 976	848
2001	28 939	28 104	810	3 653	4 464	6 982	10 546	6 112	834
2002	29 183	28 270	813	3 756	4 569	6 798	10 696	6 207	913
Men									
	MGSG	YBSL	YBZM	YBZP	PXML	YBZS	YBZV	YBZY	YCAE
1994	15 654	15 379	373	2 223	2 596	4 218	5 381	3 184	275
1995	15 607	15 310	384	2 127	2 511	4 200	5 416	3 182	297
1996	15 595	15 317	430	2 063	2 493	4 152	5 440	3 232	278
1997	15 584	15 303	431	1 997	2 428	4 127	5 407	3 341	280
1998	15 525	15 243	428	1 929	2 358	4 068	5 393	3 425	282
1999	15 650	15 354	435	1 923	2 358	3 974	5 490	3 532	296
2000	15 748	15 454	430	1 946	2 376	3 905	5 585	3 588	294
2001	15 713	15 440	415	1 944	2 360	3 789	5 626	3 665	273
2002	15 795	15 492	411	2 004	2 414	3 682	5 708	3 688	303
Women									
	MGSH	YBSM	YBZN	YBZQ	PXMM	YBZT	YBZW	YBZZ	YCAF
1994	12 484	11 953	354	1 870	2 224	3 260	4 515	1 954	530
1995	12 506	11 991	365	1 799	2 164	3 295	4 538	1 993	516
1996	12 642	12 130	392	1 766	2 158	3 329	4 625	2 017	512
1997	12 786	12 243	435	1 709	2 144	3 366	4 622	2 111	544
1998	12 830	12 319	423	1 686	2 109	3 337	4 652	2 221	511
1999	13 009	12 469	411	1 688	2 099	3 338	4 733	2 299	540
2000	13 162	12 608	418	1 701	2 119	3 281	4 819	2 388	554
2001	13 226	12 665	395	1 709	2 104	3 193	4 920	2 447	561
2002	13 388	12 778	402	1 753	2 155	3 116	4 989	2 519	610
All	**Rates[2]**								
	MGWG	MGSO	YCAG	YCAJ	PXMN	YCAM	YCAP	MGWP	MGWS
1994	62.5	78.4	56.2	76.1	72.2	82.7	85.0	68.5	7.9
1995	62.3	78.2	55.9	75.8	71.7	82.7	84.8	68.1	8.0
1996	62.4	78.4	58.1	77.0	72.8	82.7	84.7	68.1	7.7
1997	62.6	78.4	59.5	76.5	72.6	83.4	84.4	68.5	8.1
1998	62.3	78.2	58.7	75.5	71.6	83.5	84.2	68.7	7.7
1999	62.8	78.6	58.7	75.4	71.5	84.1	84.8	69.3	8.1
2000	63.0	78.9	59.1	75.9	72.0	84.4	85.0	69.7	8.2
2001	62.7	78.5	55.4	75.1	70.5	84.0	84.9	70.2	8.1
2002	62.9	78.6	54.1	75.9	70.8	83.9	84.9	70.4	8.8
Men									
	MGWH	MGSP	YCAH	YCAK	PXMO	YCAN	YCAQ	MGWQ	MGWT
1994	72.5	85.5	56.4	82.2	77.2	94.6	93.3	72.3	7.7
1995	72.2	85.0	56.2	81.8	76.5	94.2	93.1	71.5	8.2
1996	71.9	84.9	59.5	82.6	77.4	93.4	92.5	71.8	7.6
1997	71.6	84.6	58.2	82.4	76.7	93.6	92.0	72.2	7.6
1998	71.1	84.1	57.9	80.7	75.3	93.7	91.5	72.0	7.6
1999	71.4	84.4	59.1	80.5	75.5	93.5	92.2	72.6	8.0
2000	71.5	84.5	58.6	81.2	75.9	93.9	92.4	72.5	7.8
2001	70.9	84.0	55.6	80.1	74.3	93.3	91.8	73.1	7.2
2002	70.8	83.8	53.4	81.0	74.5	93.0	91.8	72.8	7.9
Women									
	MGWI	MGSQ	YCAI	YCAL	PXMP	YCAO	YCAR	MGWR	MGWU
1994	53.3	70.9	55.9	69.9	67.2	71.2	76.9	63.1	8.1
1995	53.3	70.9	55.7	69.8	66.9	71.6	76.6	63.2	7.9
1996	53.7	71.4	56.5	71.2	68.0	72.3	77.1	62.9	7.8
1997	54.2	71.8	60.9	70.7	68.5	73.5	76.9	63.3	8.3
1998	54.2	72.0	59.4	70.4	67.9	73.8	77.1	64.3	7.8
1999	54.8	72.5	58.3	70.3	67.6	75.1	77.5	64.9	8.2
2000	55.2	72.9	59.5	70.6	68.1	75.3	77.7	65.9	8.5
2001	55.2	72.8	55.3	70.1	66.8	75.1	78.2	66.2	8.6
2002	55.6	73.0	54.8	70.8	67.2	75.1	78.1	67.1	9.3

1 See chapter text.
2 Total economically active as a percentage of all persons in the relevant age group.

Source: Labour Force Survey, Office for National Statistics

7.16 Economically inactive: by age and sex[1]
United Kingdom
At Spring each year. Seasonally adjusted.

Thousands and percentages

	All aged 16 and over	16-59/64	16-17	18-24	16-24	25-34	35-49	50-64 (m) 50-59 (w)	65+ (m) 60+ (w)
All	**Thousands**								
	MGSI	YBSN	YCAS	YCAV	PXMQ	YCAY	YCBB	MGWA	MGWD
1994	16 875	7 517	567	1 287	1 854	1 561	1 742	2 360	9 358
1995	16 986	7 620	590	1 252	1 841	1 563	1 788	2 428	9 365
1996	16 986	7 580	594	1 147	1 741	1 568	1 814	2 457	9 407
1997	16 980	7 588	589	1 136	1 724	1 496	1 858	2 510	9 392
1998	17 136	7 682	600	1 171	1 771	1 460	1 883	2 569	9 455
1999	17 008	7 571	596	1 177	1 773	1 383	1 839	2 577	9 437
2000	16 967	7 510	588	1 157	1 744	1 331	1 841	2 594	9 457
2001	17 188	7 677	651	1 213	1 864	1 332	1 881	2 600	9 511
2002	17 199	7 707	689	1 191	1 880	1 306	1 907	2 614	9 492
Men									
	MGSJ	YBSO	YCAT	YCAW	PXMR	YCAZ	YCBC	MGWB	MGWE
1994	5 934	2 615	288	481	769	240	388	1 219	3 318
1995	6 022	2 699	300	473	773	259	399	1 269	3 323
1996	6 097	2 727	293	434	726	293	440	1 267	3 370
1997	6 171	2 776	310	428	738	282	471	1 286	3 394
1998	6 298	2 880	311	462	773	273	500	1 334	3 418
1999	6 268	2 842	302	465	767	277	466	1 332	3 426
2000	6 281	2 826	304	449	753	254	458	1 361	3 455
2001	6 461	2 943	332	484	816	271	505	1 351	3 518
2002	6 526	2 989	358	469	826	275	508	1 379	3 537
Women									
	MGSK	YBSP	YCAU	YCAX	PXMS	YCBA	YCBD	MGWC	MGWF
1994	10 941	4 902	279	806	1 085	1 321	1 355	1 141	6 039
1995	10 964	4 921	290	779	1 069	1 304	1 389	1 159	6 042
1996	10 889	4 853	302	713	1 015	1 275	1 374	1 190	6 036
1997	10 809	4 812	279	708	987	1 214	1 388	1 223	5 997
1998	10 838	4 802	289	709	998	1 187	1 383	1 235	6 036
1999	10 740	4 729	294	711	1 006	1 105	1 373	1 245	6 011
2000	10 686	4 684	284	707	991	1 076	1 383	1 234	6 002
2001	10 727	4 734	319	729	1 048	1 061	1 375	1 250	5 993
2002	10 673	4 718	331	722	1 053	1 031	1 398	1 235	5 955
All	**Rates[2]**								
	YBTC	YBTL	LWEX	LWFA	PXNF	LWFD	LWFG	LWFJ	LWFM
1994	37.5	21.6	43.8	23.9	27.8	17.3	15.0	31.5	92.1
1995	37.7	21.8	44.1	24.2	28.3	17.3	15.2	31.9	92.0
1996	37.6	21.6	41.9	23.0	27.2	17.3	15.3	31.9	92.3
1997	37.4	21.6	40.5	23.5	27.4	16.6	15.6	31.5	91.9
1998	37.7	21.8	41.3	24.5	28.4	16.5	15.8	31.3	92.3
1999	37.2	21.4	41.3	24.6	28.5	15.9	15.2	30.7	91.9
2000	37.0	21.1	40.9	24.1	28.0	15.6	15.0	30.3	91.8
2001	37.3	21.5	44.6	24.9	29.5	16.0	15.1	29.8	91.9
2002	37.1	21.4	45.9	24.1	29.2	16.1	15.1	29.6	91.2
Men									
	YBTD	YBTM	LWEY	LWFB	PXNG	LWFE	LWFH	LWFK	LWFN
1994	27.5	14.5	43.6	17.8	22.8	5.4	6.7	27.7	92.3
1995	27.8	15.0	43.8	18.2	23.5	5.8	6.9	28.5	91.8
1996	28.1	15.1	40.5	17.4	22.6	6.6	7.5	28.2	92.4
1997	28.4	15.4	41.8	17.6	23.3	6.4	8.0	27.8	92.4
1998	28.9	15.9	42.1	19.3	24.7	6.3	8.5	28.0	92.4
1999	28.6	15.6	40.9	19.5	24.5	6.5	7.8	27.4	92.0
2000	28.5	15.5	41.4	18.8	24.1	6.1	7.6	27.5	92.2
2001	29.1	16.0	44.4	19.9	25.7	6.7	8.2	26.9	92.8
2002	29.2	16.2	46.6	19.0	25.5	7.0	8.2	27.2	92.1
Women									
	YBTE	YBTN	LWEZ	LWFC	PXNH	LWFF	LWFI	LWFL	LWFO
1994	46.7	29.1	44.1	30.1	32.8	28.8	23.1	36.9	91.9
1995	46.7	29.1	44.3	30.2	33.1	28.4	23.4	36.8	92.1
1996	46.3	28.6	43.5	28.8	32.0	27.7	22.9	37.1	92.2
1997	45.8	28.2	39.1	29.3	31.5	26.5	23.1	36.7	91.7
1998	45.8	28.0	40.6	29.6	32.1	26.2	22.9	35.7	92.2
1999	45.2	27.5	41.7	29.7	32.4	24.9	22.5	35.1	91.8
2000	44.8	27.1	40.5	29.4	31.9	24.7	22.3	34.1	91.5
2001	44.8	27.2	44.7	29.9	33.2	24.9	21.8	33.8	91.4
2002	44.4	27.0	45.2	29.2	32.8	24.9	21.9	32.9	90.7

1 See chapter text.
2 Total economically inactive as a percentage of all persons in the relevant age group.

Source: Labour Force Survey, Office for National Statistics

7.17 Economically inactive: by reason[1]
United Kingdom
At Spring each year. Seasonally adjusted.

Thousands

| | Total economically inactive | Does not want job[2] | Wants job[2] but not seeking in last 4 weeks | | | | | | | | Wants job[2] and seeking work but not available to start[3] | | |
| | | | Total | Availability to start work in next 2 weeks | | Discouraged workers | Long term sick/ disabled | Looking after family/ home | Students | Other | All | Students | Other |
				Available	Not available[3]								
All[4]													
	YBSN	YBVZ	YCFF	YCFI	YCFL	YCFO	YCFR	YCFU	YCFX	YCGA	YCGD	YCGG	YCGJ
1995	7 620	5 357	2 026	919	1 108	108	518	770	237	393	237	119	117
1996	7 580	5 284	2 113	888	1 225	103	572	773	259	407	182	85	98
1997	7 588	5 218	2 166	775	1 391	88	682	743	264	389	205	91	114
1998	7 682	5 310	2 155	727	1 429	70	738	739	245	363	217	92	125
1999	7 571	5 269	2 091	680	1 411	67	739	676	238	371	212	91	121
2000	7 510	5 211	2 111	664	1 447	62	756	652	237	403	188	78	110
2001	7 677	5 498	1 985	615	1 371	33	718	632	248	354	194	72	122
2002	7 707	5 464	2 061	630	1 432	33	751	632	255	390	182	74	108
Men													
	YBSO	YBWA	YCFG	YCFJ	YCFM	YCFP	YCFS	YCFV	YCFY	YCGB	YCGE	YCGH	YCGK
1995	2 699	1 867	724	315	408	63	321	50	126	163	108	57	51
1996	2 727	1 844	798	333	465	59	354	68	138	179	84	40	44
1997	2 776	1 856	827	266	560	50	410	68	134	165	94	52	42
1998	2 880	1 916	858	272	587	43	460	73	127	155	105	54	52
1999	2 842	1 919	834	266	567	39	450	70	119	155	90	43	47
2000	2 826	1 903	845	257	588	33	456	63	113	179	78	40	38
2001	2 943	2 036	815	250	566	22	435	66	124	169	92	41	51
2002	2 989	2 045	862	267	596	20	457	65	132	188	82	36	46
Women													
	YBSP	YBWB	YCFH	YCFK	YCFN	YCFQ	YCFT	YCFW	YCFZ	YCGC	YCGF	YCGI	YCGL
1995	4 921	3 490	1 303	603	699	45	196	720	111	230	128	62	67
1996	4 853	3 439	1 315	555	760	44	217	705	121	228	99	44	54
1997	4 812	3 362	1 339	509	830	38	272	674	131	225	111	39	72
1998	4 802	3 394	1 297	455	842	27	278	666	118	208	111	39	73
1999	4 729	3 350	1 257	414	843	28	289	606	119	216	122	47	75
2000	4 684	3 308	1 266	407	859	29	300	588	124	224	110	38	72
2001	4 734	3 462	1 170	365	805	12	282	567	124	185	102	31	71
2002	4 718	3 418	1 199	363	836	13	293	568	123	202	100	38	62

1 See chapter text.
2 According to responses to LFS question.
3 Not available to start work in next two weeks, including a few people who could not state whether or not they were available.

4 All persons of working age (men 16-64, women 16-59).

Source: Labour Force Survey, Office for National Statistics

7.18 Labour disputes[1]
United Kingdom

		1995	1996	1997	1998	1999	2000	2001
SIC 1992								
Working days lost through all stoppages in progress: total	**KBBZ**	415	1 303	235	282	242	499	525
Analysis by industry								
Mining, quarrying, electricity, gas and water	DMME	1	2	2	..	..	3	25
Manufacturing	BBFX	65	97	86	34	57	52	43
Construction	DMMG	10	8	17	13	49	49	10
Transport, storage and communication	BBFY	120	884	36	139	50	97	107
Public administration and defence	BBFZ	95	158	29	28	35	50	216
Education	BBGA	67	128	28	6	25	50	43
Health and social work	BBGB	16	8	7	16	5	122	73
Other community, social and personal services	DMML	23	3	5	30	7	36	4
All other industries and services	DMMM	16	15	25	15	12	40	4
Analysis by number of working days lost in each stoppage								
Under 250 days	KBFC	11	14	12	8	11	12	9
250 and under 500 days	KBFJ	10	13	6	11	13	9	11
500 and under 1,000 days	KBFL	19	13	17	11	16	21	15
1,000 and under 5,000 days	KBFY	82	61	72	48	69	71	59
5,000 and under 25,000 days	KBFZ	195	123	101	118	133	85	140
25,000 and under 50,000 days	KBGS	29	54	26	..	..	..	72
50,000 days and over	KBGT	68	1 025	..	86	..	301	220
Working days lost per 1 000 employees all industries and services	**KBHA**	18	55	10	11	10	20	20
Workers directly and indirectly involved: total	**KBHB**	174	364	130	93	141	183	180
Analysis by industry								
Mining, quarrying, electricity, gas and water	DMMN	2	1	..	1	..	1	3
Manufacturing	DMMO	33	34	28	14	31	28	17
Construction	DMMP	2	3	13	2	18	16	3
Transport, storage and communications	DMMQ	54	146	24	39	42	39	69
Public administration and defence	DMMR	28	32	20	4	17	29	46
Education	DMMS	30	122	15	4	28	17	34
Health and social work	DMMT	4	5	5	2	..	28	6
Other community, social and personal services	DMMU	10	2	1	22	2	13	1
All other industries and services	DMMV	11	21	23	4	2	12	1
Analysis by duration of stoppage								
Not more than 5 days	KBHM	142	208	108	57	129	82	98
Over 5 but not more than 10 days	KBHN	11	133	7	32	8	9	43
Over 10 but not more than 20 days	KBJQ	2	4	14	1	3	8	4
Over 20 but not more than 30 days	KBJR	2	3	..	..	..	..	..
Over 30 but not more than 50 days	KBJS	10	16	1	1	..	83	6
Over 50 days	KBJT	7	1	..	1	..	1	30
Numbers of stoppages in progress: total	**KBLG**	235	244	216	166	205	212	194
Analysis by industry								
Mining, quarrying, electricity, gas and water	DMMW	5	6	1	1	..	3	3
Manufacturing	DMMX	68	67	53	36	37	38	32
Construction	DMMY	9	11	11	13	20	16	9
Transport, storage and communications	DMMZ	56	72	68	57	91	116	94
Public administration and defence	DMNA	26	22	23	10	17	7	22
Education	DMNB	27	35	35	19	21	18	16
Health and social work	DMNC	17	9	7	6	4	10	12
Other community, social and personal services	DMND	19	12	8	17	8	13	10
All other industries and services	DMNE	14	11	12	7	8	5	9
Analysis of number of stoppages by duration								
Not more than 5 days	KBNH	199	196	184	130	179	187	162
Over 5 but not more than 10 days	KBNI	12	20	15	21	8	14	15
Over 10 but not more than 20 days	KBNJ	9	7	8	3	9	5	7
Over 20 but not more than 30 days	KBNK	6	6	2	4	4	1	1
Over 30 but not more than 50 days	KBNL	2	10	6	3	3	3	4
Over 50 days	KBNM	7	5	1	5	2	2	5

1 See chapter text.

Source: Labour Market Statistics, Office for National Statistics: 01633 819205

7.19 Average earnings[1] and hours of manual employees by industry division
Full time employees on adult rates: pay unaffected by absence: Great Britain
At April

	Agriculture, Hunting and Forestry	Fishing	Mining and Quarrying	Manufacturing	Electricity, Gas and Water Supply	Construction	Wholesale and Retail Trade; repair of motor vehicles, cycles, personal and household goods
Standard Industrial Classification: Revised 1992							
Full-time manual men							
Weekly earnings							
	KOTK	KOTL	KOTM	KOTN	KOTO	KOTP	KOTQ
1998	260.3	..	408.3	352.6	418.6	342.3	292.2
1999	272.4	..	396.0	354.6	440.5	351.3	299.4
2000	273.2	..	398.4	365.4	453.8	371.5	305.7
2001	284.8	..	416.1	378.5	464.1	393.9	318.8
2002	310.0	..	427.1	388.0	489.1	411.1	335.5
Hours worked							
	KOTZ	KPFV	KOUA	KOUB	KOUC	KOUD	KOUE
1998	47.0	..	50.1	44.3	42.5	46.9	44.3
1999	47.5	..	51.7	43.5	42.8	46.4	43.9
2000	45.8	..	49.5	43.6	41.4	46.6	43.8
2001	45.6	..	49.4	43.5	42.3	46.6	43.7
2002	47.4	..	47.4	43.1	42.6	45.7	43.9
Hourly earnings							
	KOUN	KPFW	KOUO	KOUP	KOUQ	KOUR	KOUS
1998	5.54	..	8.14	7.96	9.85	7.29	6.59
1999	5.75	..	7.66	8.15	10.30	7.56	6.84
2000	5.91	..	8.08	8.35	10.93	7.92	7.03
2001	6.25	..	8.61	8.69	11.02	8.50	7.25
2002	6.56	..	9.04	9.01	11.49	8.97	7.63
Full-time manual women							
Weekly earnings							
	KOYL	KPFX	KOYM	KOYN	KOYO	KOYP	KOYQ
1998	185.7	..	..	224.2	..	..	203.6
1999	199.0	..	..	231.7	..	..	215.3
2000	224.7	..	..	241.0	..	..	216.2
2001	227.3	..	..	251.4	..	..	230.3
2002	..	..	..	260.5	..	..	238.2
Hours worked							
	KOYZ	KPFY	KOZA	KOZB	KOZC	KOZD	KOZE
1998	42.0	..	..	40.7	..	..	40.3
1999	41.8	..	..	40.4	..	..	39.9
2000	41.9	..	..	40.5	..	..	39.2
2001	41.1	..	..	40.4	..	..	39.5
2002	..	..	..	40.2	..	..	39.7
Hourly earnings							
	KOZN	KOZO	KOZP	KOZQ	KOZR	KOZS	KOZT
1998	4.43	..	..	5.52	..	..	5.06
1999	4.74	..	..	5.74	..	..	5.44
2000	5.37	..	..	5.94	..	..	5.45
2001	5.67	..	..	6.22	..	..	5.81
2002	..	..	..	6.48	..	..	5.99
Full-time manual adults							
Weekly earnings							
	KPBO	KPFZ	KPBP	KPBQ	KPBR	KPBS	KPBT
1998	251.7	..	403.8	329.9	416.2	340.9	280.3
1999	264.1	..	392.5	333.7	439.5	350.9	287.7
2000	265.6	..	392.3	343.5	452.8	368.6	295.2
2001	280.1	..	..	357.8	..	393.8	305.4
2002	305.6	..	..	368.7	..	410.3	322.2
Hours worked							
	KPCT	KPGA	KPCU	KPCV	KPCW	KPCX	KPCY
1998	46.4	..	49.9	43.7	42.4	46.9	43.8
1999	46.8	..	51.6	43.0	42.7	46.4	43.4
2000	45.4	..	48.7	43.1	41.4	46.5	43.2
2001	45.2	..	49.0	43.0	42.4	46.4	43.2
2002	46.8	..	..	42.6	..	45.7	43.3
Hourly earnings							
	KPDV	KPGB	KPDW	KPDX	KPDY	KPDZ	KPFA
1998	5.42	..	8.07	7.56	9.81	7.27	6.40
1999	5.65	..	7.61	7.77	10.29	7.56	6.66
2000	5.86	..	8.06	7.98	10.93	7.92	6.84
2001	6.20	..	8.56	8.32	11.01	8.49	7.07
2002	6.55	..	..	8.64	..	8.97	7.42

7.19 continued

Average earnings[1] and hours of manual employees by industry division
Full time employees on adult rates: pay unaffected by absence: Great Britain
At April

	Hotels and restaurants	Transport, Storage and Communication	Financial Inter-mediation	Real Estate, Renting and Business	Public Administration and Defence; compulsory social security	Education	Health and Social work	Other community, social and personal service activities
Standard Industrial Classification: Revised 1992								
Full-time manual men								
Weekly earnings								
	KOTR	KOTS	KOTT	KOTU	KOTV	KOTW	KOTX	KOTY
1998	227.0	344.0	394.8	302.7	289.0	277.9	264.4	289.0
1999	230.5	359.6	377.9	312.3	307.5	285.2	267.7	300.8
2000	242.2	368.8	394.3	322.0	310.7	293.5	284.9	301.9
2001	249.3	386.7	417.1	340.8	329.8	305.1	295.3	315.9
2002	262.1	381.5	420.1	346.6	333.5	324.4	308.2	340.8
Hours worked								
	KOUF	KOUG	KOUH	KOUI	KOUJ	KOUK	KOUL	KOUM
1998	42.5	48.0	42.5	46.4	41.9	41.7	42.1	44.8
1999	42.1	47.5	39.9	45.5	42.2	40.8	41.8	44.8
2000	41.8	47.4	39.5	45.1	41.3	40.2	42.0	43.5
2001	42.0	46.9	41.2	45.6	41.2	40.3	42.4	43.4
2002	42.3	45.8	41.6	45.5	40.8	40.3	42.2	43.7
Hourly earnings								
	KOUT	KOYE	KOYF	KOYG	KOYH	KOYI	KOYJ	KOYK
1998	5.34	7.17	9.28	6.53	6.90	6.67	6.26	6.47
1999	5.48	7.56	9.46	6.86	7.30	7.00	6.41	6.72
2000	5.74	7.75	9.72	7.20	7.56	7.22	6.91	6.95
2001	5.99	8.28	9.93	7.51	7.83	7.68	7.01	7.26
2002	6.25	8.34	10.10	7.63	8.18	8.06	7.31	7.81
Full-time manual women								
Weekly earnings								
	KOYR	KOYS	KOYT	KOYU	KOYV	KOYW	KOYX	KOYY
1998	170.8	292.7	..	211.9	232.2	203.7	187.2	178.1
1999	180.5	311.5	..	221.5	232.3	223.0	199.5	197.4
2000	187.5	323.9	..	234.5	240.1	228.4	204.5	207.8
2001	196.5	336.9	..	250.7	246.9	235.5	221.5	215.5
2002	209.1	340.0	..	252.7	275.3	250.7	230.1	228.4
Hours worked								
	KOZF	KOZG	KOZH	KOZI	KOZJ	KOZK	KOZL	KOZM
1998	39.4	42.0	..	41.4	39.6	38.3	39.3	39.6
1999	39.3	41.5	..	40.4	38.6	38.0	39.1	39.8
2000	39.4	41.8	..	40.6	38.5	38.0	39.3	39.4
2001	39.4	41.5	..	40.9	38.6	37.6	39.6	39.4
2002	39.7	40.5	..	40.5	38.2	37.8	39.3	39.2
Hourly earnings								
	KOZU	KOZV	KOZW	KOZX	KOZY	KOZZ	KPBN	KTDJ
1998	4.30	6.98	..	5.08	5.89	5.32	4.75	4.50
1999	4.55	7.52	..	5.48	6.09	5.86	5.10	4.94
2000	4.72	7.69	..	5.82	6.38	6.00	5.24	5.25
2001	4.99	8.10	..	6.16	6.79	6.27	5.52	5.41
2002	5.29	..	..	6.27	..	6.64	5.84	5.83
Full-time manual adults								
Weekly earnings								
	KPBU	KPBV	KPBW	KPBX	KPBY	KPBZ	KPCR	KPCS
1998	203.6	340.0	367.3	289.1	280.7	254.8	218.9	258.3
1999	210.3	355.7	353.6	298.2	296.9	266.0	227.8	273.8
2000	217.1	363.3	359.6	308.7	301.3	270.3	237.2	274.1
2001	227.4	381.0	..	326.3	312.7	287.1	252.2	285.1
2002	240.5	377.6	..	331.9	325.4	303.2	262.2	309.1
Hours worked								
	KPCZ	KPDO	KPDP	KPDQ	KPDR	KPDS	KPDT	KPDU
1998	41.2	47.6	41.6	45.6	41.6	40.7	40.5	43.3
1999	41.0	47.0	39.7	44.7	41.7	40.0	40.2	43.5
2000	40.7	46.9	39.5	44.1	40.8	39.5	40.0	42.2
2001	40.9	46.2	40.9	44.8	40.7	39.6	40.9	42.4
2002	41.2	45.3	..	44.7	40.4	39.6	40.5	42.4
Hourly earnings								
	KPFB	KPFC	KPFD	KPFE	KPFF	KPFG	KPFT	KPFU
1998	4.93	7.16	8.84	6.33	6.76	6.27	5.40	5.97
1999	5.12	7.56	8.92	6.67	7.15	6.66	5.66	6.29
2000	5.33	7.74	9.11	7.00	7.41	6.86	5.95	6.51
2001	5.58	8.26	9.86	7.31	7.69	7.27	6.15	6.74
2002	5.87	8.35	..	7.44	8.05	7.67	6.46	..

1 See chapter text.

Source: New Earnings Survey, Office for National Statistics: 01633 819024

7.20 Average weekly and hourly earnings[1] and hours of full-time employees on adult rates: Great Britain

At April

	All Industries				Manufacturing industries			
			Average hourly earnings				Average hourly earnings	
	Average weekly earnings[2]	Average hours	including overtime	excluding overtime	Average weekly earnings	Average hours	including overtime	excluding overtime
	£		£	£	£		£	£
All adults								
	BAPY	BAQM	BAPZ	BAQA	BAPM	BAQJ	BAPN	BAPO
1998	384.5	40.2	9.53	9.54	384.5	41.8	9.17	9.10
1999	400.1	40.0	10.01	10.03	395.3	41.4	9.55	9.49
2000	419.7	39.8	10.53	10.51	412.5	41.4	9.96	9.86
2001	444.3	39.8	11.15	11.18	435.5	41.3	10.53	10.49
2002	464.7	39.6	11.69	11.73	455.8	41.0	11.10	11.08
All men								
	BAQC	BAQN	BAQD	BAQE	BAPQ	BAQK	BAPR	BAPS
1998	427.1	41.7	10.20	10.26	416.8	42.6	9.75	9.72
1999	442.4	41.4	10.68	10.75	424.6	42.0	10.10	10.06
2000	464.1	41.2	11.24	11.26	441.7	42.0	10.49	10.40
2001	490.5	41.2	11.90	11.97	463.9	42.0	11.04	11.02
2002	513.8	40.9	12.50	12.59	484.1	41.6	11.62	11.61
Manual men								
	KFHX	KFHY	KIWU	KIWV	KFJT	KFJU	KIWW	KIWX
1998	328.5	45.0	7.30	7.10	352.6	44.3	7.96	7.71
1999	335.0	44.4	7.54	7.36	354.6	43.5	8.15	7.92
2000	344.8	44.3	7.79	7.54	365.4	43.6	8.35	8.07
2001	359.9	44.3	8.14	7.92	378.5	43.5	8.69	8.44
2002	368.2	43.9	8.39	8.21	388.0	43.1	9.01	8.76
Non-manual men								
	KFJX	KFJY	KIWY	KIWZ	KFMU	KFMV	KIXO	KIXP
1998	506.1	39.1	12.90	12.94	525.9	39.8	13.17	13.23
1999	525.5	39.0	13.49	13.52	541.6	39.6	13.68	13.73
2000	550.9	38.9	14.14	14.14	562.1	39.6	13.92	14.18
2001	582.4	39.0	14.95	14.99	592.4	39.7	14.97	14.99
2002	610.4	38.9	15.62	15.68	615.5	39.5	15.54	15.61
All women								
	BAQG	BAQO	BAQH	BAQI	BAPU	BAQL	BAPV	BAPW
1998	309.6	37.6	8.23	8.22	274.5	39.2	7.01	6.97
1999	326.5	37.5	8.71	8.70	292.1	39.0	7.49	7.46
2000	343.7	37.4	9.17	9.13	307.9	38.9	7.91	7.86
2001	366.8	37.5	9.77	9.76	333.4	38.9	8.56	8.54
2002	383.4	37.5	10.21	10.22	351.8	38.7	9.08	9.06
Manual women								
	KFMY	KFMZ	KIXU	KIXV	KFPS	KFPT	KIXW	KIXX
1998	210.8	40.2	5.23	5.14	224.2	40.7	5.52	5.39
1999	221.9	39.9	5.56	5.48	231.7	40.4	5.74	5.62
2000	229.1	39.9	5.76	5.65	241.0	40.5	5.94	5.81
2001	241.8	39.9	6.06	5.97	251.4	40.4	6.22	6.07
2002	251.0	39.7	6.33	6.26	260.5	40.2	6.48	6.37
Non-manual women								
	KFRY	KFRZ	KIXY	KIYA	KFUY	KFUZ	KIYB	KIYC
1998	330.1	37.0	8.90	8.89	317.2	37.9	8.38	8.36
1999	346.9	37.0	9.37	9.36	341.5	37.9	9.02	9.01
2000	364.5	37.0	9.85	9.80	358.4	37.8	9.34	9.46
2001	388.8	37.1	10.48	10.47	389.5	37.9	10.14	10.27
2002	405.2	37.1	10.91	10.91	408.1	37.8	10.78	10.78

1 See chapter text.
2 Excluding those whose pay was affected by absence.

Source: New Earnings Survey, Office for National Statistics: 01633 819024

7.21 Average earnings index[1]: all employees: main industrial sectors
Great Britain
Analyses by industry based on Standard Industrial Classification 1992

1995 = 100

Unadjusted

	Annual averages	January	February	March	April	May	June	July	August	September	October	November	December
Whole economy (Divisions 01 - 93)													
LNMM													
2000	124.4	123.2	125.3	129.3	122.5	122.4	123.4	123.6	122.5	122.3	122.8	124.0	131.3
2001	129.8	128.7	133.9	134.8	128.5	127.7	129.3	128.9	127.8	127.6	128.2	128.6	134.1
2002	..	132.4	137.5	139.2	133.4	132.5	134.1	133.9	132.2	132.2	..	..	..
Manufacturing industries (Divisions 15 - 37)													
LNMN													
2000	123.8	121.8	122.1	126.1	122.8	122.7	122.4	124.0	121.8	122.6	123.9	125.8	129.6
2001	129.1	126.3	128.3	132.7	129.0	128.4	128.2	129.3	127.4	128.0	128.8	129.4	132.9
2002	..	130.1	131.6	136.7	133.4	132.8	132.9	134.2	132.2	132.1	..	..	..
Production industries (Divisions 10 - 41)													
LNMO													
2000	122.9	121.2	121.6	125.4	122.0	121.9	121.8	123.0	120.9	121.6	122.8	124.7	128.4
2001	128.0	125.4	127.9	131.8	128.1	127.3	127.5	128.1	126.3	126.8	127.6	128.1	131.6
2002	..	129.1	130.5	136.3	132.3	131.6	132.3	133.0	131.1	131.2	..	..	..
Service industries (Divisions 50 - 93)													
LNMP													
2000	124.5	123.7	126.5	130.2	122.4	122.3	123.5	123.6	122.9	122.0	122.3	123.3	131.8
2001	130.0	129.5	136.0	135.5	128.2	127.3	129.3	128.7	127.7	127.2	127.8	128.1	134.3
2002	..	133.1	139.4	139.5	133.2	132.4	134.1	133.6	132.1	131.9	..	..	..
Private sector services (unadjusted) (Divisions 50-99)													
JJGF													
2000	127.2	123.7	126.5	130.2	122.4	122.3	123.5	123.6	122.9	122.0	122.3	123.3	131.8
2001	132.4	129.5	136.0	135.5	128.2	127.3	129.3	128.7	127.7	127.2	127.8	128.1	134.3
2002	..	133.1	139.4	139.5	133.2	132.4	134.1	133.6	132.1	131.9	..	..	..

Seasonally adjusted

	Annual averages	January	February	March	April	May	June	July	August	September	October	November	December
Whole economy (Divisions 01 - 93)													
LNMQ													
2000	124.5	123.2	122.1	123.4	122.8	123.2	123.5	124.1	125.0	125.4	125.9	126.7	128.7
2001	130.0	128.4	129.9	128.7	128.8	129.0	129.6	129.6	130.4	130.9	131.4	131.5	131.5
2002	..	132.1	133.0	133.2	133.8	134.1	134.5	134.9	135.1	135.7	..	..	..
Manufacturing industries (Divisions 15 - 37)													
LNMR													
2000	123.7	122.3	121.5	121.8	122.1	123.1	122.9	123.6	123.9	124.8	125.3	126.4	127.2
2001	129.1	127.0	128.0	128.2	128.5	128.8	129.0	129.2	129.6	130.1	130.2	130.0	130.5
2002	..	130.9	131.3	132.1	132.8	133.2	133.7	134.0	134.4	134.5	..	..	..
Production industries (Divisions 10 - 41)													
LNMS													
2000	122.9	121.7	121.0	120.9	121.2	122.3	122.1	122.6	123.0	123.8	124.3	125.4	126.0
2001	128.0	125.9	127.4	127.1	127.4	127.7	128.0	128.1	128.5	129.0	129.0	128.9	129.2
2002	..	129.8	130.2	131.4	131.7	132.1	132.7	132.9	133.4	133.4	..	..	..
Service industries (Divisions 50 - 93)													
LNMT													
2000	124.7	123.3	122.2	123.8	123.1	123.4	123.7	124.4	125.5	125.6	126.1	126.8	129.0
2001	130.2	128.8	130.6	129.0	128.9	128.9	129.6	129.6	130.5	131.0	131.7	131.9	131.7
2002	..	132.4	133.4	133.2	134.0	134.3	134.7	135.1	135.2	135.9	..	..	..
Private sector services (seasonally adjusted) (Divisions 50-93)													
JJGH													
2000	127.4	123.3	122.2	123.8	123.1	123.4	123.7	124.4	125.5	125.6	126.1	126.8	
2001	132.6	128.8	130.6	129.0	128.9	128.9	129.6	129.6	130.5	131.0	131.7	131.9	
2002	..	132.4	133.4	133.2	134.0	134.3	134.7	135.1	135.2	135.9	..	..	

1 See chapter text.

Source: Office for National Statistics: 01633 819002

7.22 Average earnings index[1] : all employee jobs: by industry (not seasonally adjusted)
Great Britain

July 1999 = 100

Excluding bonuses

	Agriculture, forestry and fishing	Mining and quarrying	Food products, beverages and tobacco	Textiles, leather and clothing	Chemicals and man-made fibres	Basic metals and metal products	Engineering and allied industries	Other manufacturing	Electricity, gas and water supply	Construction
SIC 1992	(A,B)	(C)	(DA)	(DB,DC)	(DG)	(DJ)	(DK, DL,DM)	(DD,DE,DF, DH,DI,DN)	(E)	(F)
	JVUZ	JVVA	JVVB	JVVC	JVVD	JVVE	JVVF	JVVG	JVVH	JVVI
2000	104.1	103.1	104.4	100.2	104.1	101.7	105.0	104.2	99.3	105.8
2001	110.4	106.1	108.6	104.4	108.8	106.0	110.1	109.3	101.8	112.4
2000 Feb	97.5	102.5	102.6	99.8	102.4	100.2	102.7	102.2	99.0	103.9
Mar	104.1	102.7	103.9	98.3	103.5	99.9	103.9	102.7	97.6	105.0
Apr	103.6	102.5	106.7	98.1	104.1	100.2	104.3	102.7	98.6	104.3
May	105.0	102.1	105.8	98.9	103.2	101.4	104.3	103.7	99.4	104.5
Jun	106.1	102.5	104.7	100.1	103.6	101.4	105.4	104.0	99.4	106.1
Jul	102.2	103.5	103.1	100.4	104.3	104.2	105.7	104.2	98.6	107.0
Aug	101.6	102.7	103.3	99.8	103.9	101.2	105.1	104.4	99.2	104.9
Sep	111.7	103.1	104.2	101.8	103.9	101.5	105.5	106.0	98.5	105.9
Oct	107.9	104.2	103.7	102.0	104.7	103.6	106.5	105.8	98.4	107.5
Nov	106.2	105.5	105.4	103.4	105.3	103.9	107.3	106.5	99.8	108.8
Dec	104.6	103.4	106.5	102.2	106.8	102.3	107.5	106.6	101.3	108.7
2001 Jan	104.6	103.6	105.5	102.7	107.5	103.3	107.8	106.7	100.8	109.8
Feb	101.0	105.2	106.0	103.7	107.1	103.3	108.5	106.7	100.6	109.6
Mar	107.3	105.3	107.3	103.6	109.0	104.3	109.1	107.1	99.4	111.1
Apr	108.0	105.4	108.9	103.2	107.8	106.1	110.2	108.9	101.0	111.1
May	112.2	106.1	109.6	104.5	107.7	106.9	110.1	109.2	101.1	111.9
Jun	107.1	106.1	109.7	104.1	109.6	107.7	110.5	109.5	101.5	113.6
Jul	108.4	107.3	108.4	104.6	109.8	107.4	110.9	109.6	102.3	114.0
Aug	114.2	105.3	109.1	104.1	108.8	106.5	110.0	109.4	104.5	111.2
Sep	119.0	105.7	108.9	105.2	109.2	106.4	110.6	110.7	101.5	113.4
Oct	114.8	108.5	108.9	106.6	109.2	107.6	110.6	111.2	101.8	114.5
Nov	114.3	106.8	110.0	105.9	109.9	106.6	111.1	111.8	102.4	115.0
Dec	114.1	107.9	111.4	104.8	110.1	105.3	112.1	111.3	104.7	114.1
2002 Jan	112.1	107.4	110.4	105.1	110.1	106.4	111.9	111.2	101.0	114.1
Feb	112.5	107.5	109.8	105.4	109.8	106.5	112.5	111.6	102.6	116.0
Mar	117.9	106.8	111.9	106.4	110.3	106.6	113.2	111.9	101.4	116.2
Apr	115.0	109.6	112.4	108.2	112.8	109.4	114.0	113.7	102.2	116.7
May	113.9	109.7	113.0	107.0	113.1	108.3	114.4	114.8	100.8	116.9
Jun	115.1	111.2	114.0	108.2	113.1	108.5	115.4	114.2	102.5	117.8
Jul	114.8	110.2	112.5	111.3	114.1	109.5	115.9	114.4	103.2	118.3
Aug	119.6	111.1	113.8	108.1	112.8	107.7	114.9	114.0	103.0	115.7
Sep	124.4	111.5	113.8	109.7	113.8	108.8	114.7	115.2	104.1	117.7

Percentage change on the year

	JVVT	JVVU	JVVV	JVVW	JVVX	JVVY	JVVZ	JVWA	JVWB	JVWC
2001 Feb	3.5	2.6	3.3	3.9	4.6	3.1	5.6	4.3	1.6	5.5
Mar	3.0	2.6	3.3	5.4	5.3	4.4	5.0	4.3	1.8	5.9
Apr	4.2	2.9	2.1	5.1	3.5	5.8	5.7	6.0	2.4	6.5
May	6.9	3.9	3.6	5.7	4.3	5.4	5.5	5.3	1.7	7.1
Jun	1.0	3.5	4.8	4.1	5.7	6.2	4.8	5.3	2.1	7.1
Jul	6.0	3.6	5.2	4.2	5.2	3.1	5.0	5.2	3.7	6.6
Aug	12.4	2.6	5.7	4.3	4.7	5.2	4.8	4.9	5.4	6.0
Sep	6.5	2.5	4.5	3.3	5.1	4.9	4.9	4.4	3.1	7.1
Oct	6.4	4.1	5.0	4.5	4.3	3.8	3.9	5.1	3.5	6.5
Nov	7.6	1.2	4.4	2.4	4.4	2.6	3.6	4.9	2.6	5.7
Dec	9.1	4.4	4.6	2.5	3.1	2.9	4.3	4.4	3.4	4.9
2002 Jan	7.2	3.6	4.6	2.3	2.4	3.0	3.8	4.1	0.2	3.9
Feb	11.4	2.2	3.6	1.6	2.5	3.2	3.7	4.6	2.0	5.9
Mar	10.0	1.4	4.3	2.6	1.2	2.2	3.7	4.4	2.0	4.5
Apr	6.5	4.0	3.2	4.9	4.6	3.2	3.4	4.4	1.2	5.0
May	1.5	3.4	3.1	2.4	5.0	1.3	4.0	5.2	−0.3	4.4
Jun	7.5	4.7	4.0	3.9	3.2	0.8	4.4	4.3	1.0	3.7
Jul	5.9	2.7	3.8	6.4	3.9	1.9	4.5	4.3	0.9	3.7
Aug	4.7	5.4	4.3	3.8	3.6	1.1	4.4	4.1	−1.5	4.0
Sep	4.5	5.5	4.5	4.3	4.2	2.2	3.6	4.1	2.6	3.8

7.22 continued Average earnings index[1] : all employee jobs: by industry (not seasonally adjusted)
Great Britain

July 1999 = 100

	Wholesale trade	Retail trade and repairs	Hotels and restaurants	Transport, storage and communication	Financial interm-ediation	Real estate renting and business activities	Public admini-stration	Education	Health and social work	Other services
Excluding bonuses										
SIC 1992	(G:51)	(G:50,52)	(H)	(I)	(J)	(K)	(L)	(M)	(N)	(O)
	JVVJ	JVVK	JVVL	JVVM	JVVN	JVVO	JVVP	JVVQ	JVVR	JVVS
2000	103.8	102.4	105.0	102.9	104.5	104.5	103.7	102.2	104.9	105.9
2001	107.0	105.4	109.7	107.7	110.3	110.8	108.6	107.6	111.4	108.4
2000 Feb	102.7	101.0	102.7	100.6	102.0	103.0	105.2	99.5	102.9	107.1
Mar	102.6	100.9	101.7	100.7	102.8	102.8	102.2	99.1	102.9	103.9
Apr	103.5	101.6	106.4	101.2	102.8	102.9	102.6	101.4	104.4	104.7
May	103.8	103.8	103.7	102.0	104.1	104.3	102.1	101.2	105.2	105.2
Jun	103.7	103.0	104.6	103.1	104.1	103.9	103.2	102.3	105.7	106.5
Jul	103.8	102.8	105.6	102.7	104.6	104.9	102.9	103.4	105.1	106.4
Aug	103.5	102.9	107.6	103.1	104.5	104.7	103.0	105.2	105.2	107.4
Sep	104.6	104.1	105.3	103.7	104.9	104.7	103.8	104.6	105.1	105.5
Oct	105.0	101.9	106.1	104.4	105.9	105.7	104.4	103.5	105.5	105.4
Nov	105.1	101.4	105.3	104.3	106.5	106.7	106.8	103.2	106.2	105.3
Dec	105.3	102.0	108.2	105.3	107.6	107.7	105.9	103.5	107.4	107.3
2001 Jan	105.1	103.9	104.8	105.4	108.0	109.1	106.1	102.8	108.4	107.0
Feb	105.4	102.6	105.8	105.7	108.7	109.3	106.8	103.1	107.7	107.6
Mar	106.1	103.1	106.6	107.7	110.0	109.3	106.4	103.6	107.9	106.4
Apr	106.9	105.4	109.0	107.7	110.5	110.2	107.7	107.3	111.3	105.5
May	106.5	106.2	108.9	108.4	111.0	110.5	107.6	106.6	112.5	107.3
Jun	107.2	106.7	110.0	107.8	110.5	111.1	108.4	108.1	112.4	108.2
Jul	107.2	105.7	111.0	108.0	110.9	110.6	108.7	111.1	112.0	108.9
Aug	107.6	107.1	111.8	107.1	111.3	110.7	109.0	111.5	112.3	110.7
Sep	107.7	107.2	112.2	107.6	110.0	110.9	110.4	110.5	112.3	109.3
Oct	107.9	106.1	111.1	108.5	110.2	112.2	110.4	109.2	113.0	109.6
Nov	108.3	105.4	111.0	109.3	111.0	112.2	110.5	108.4	113.4	109.8
Dec	108.4	105.6	114.6	109.4	111.3	112.9	111.6	109.1	113.7	110.1
2002 Jan	107.7	107.0	111.6	109.4	111.8	113.9	110.9	108.0	115.1	111.1
Feb	108.8	105.9	112.5	108.9	113.0	114.4	111.1	108.1	113.9	110.7
Mar	109.7	107.9	115.9	110.7	112.0	114.9	111.1	108.3	114.5	111.2
Apr	109.8	109.2	115.1	110.2	113.1	115.6	112.4	110.5	118.2	110.5
May	110.0	109.2	116.6	110.6	112.9	116.1	111.8	110.8	118.4	111.2
Jun	109.5	111.9	117.8	111.7	112.8	116.2	112.2	111.4	119.6	112.3
Jul	109.4	110.3	118.4	111.5	113.0	116.1	112.3	111.9	120.8	112.6
Aug	109.5	111.0	119.2	110.5	112.9	115.1	111.7	113.6	119.0	112.6
Sep	109.2	111.1	116.8	112.5	113.1	115.5	112.2	114.1	119.3	109.9
Percentage change on the year										
	JVWD	JVWE	JVWF	JVYJ	JVYK	JVYL	JVYM	JVYN	JVYO	JVYP
2001 Feb	2.7	1.6	3.1	5.1	6.6	6.1	1.6	3.5	4.7	0.5
Mar	3.4	2.2	4.8	6.9	7.0	6.3	4.2	4.5	4.9	2.4
Apr	3.3	3.7	2.4	6.5	7.4	7.1	4.9	5.8	6.6	0.8
May	2.6	2.3	5.0	6.3	6.7	5.9	5.4	5.3	7.0	2.1
Jun	3.4	3.5	5.1	4.5	6.1	6.9	5.1	5.6	6.4	1.6
Jul	3.3	2.8	5.1	5.1	6.0	5.4	5.6	7.4	6.5	2.4
Aug	3.9	4.1	3.9	3.9	6.6	5.8	5.9	5.9	6.7	3.1
Sep	3.0	3.0	6.5	3.8	4.8	5.9	6.3	5.6	6.8	3.6
Oct	2.8	4.0	4.7	3.9	4.0	6.2	5.7	5.5	7.0	3.9
Nov	3.1	3.9	5.4	4.8	4.2	5.2	3.5	5.1	6.8	4.2
Dec	3.0	3.5	5.9	3.9	3.5	4.8	5.5	5.4	5.9	2.6
2002 Jan	2.5	3.0	6.5	3.7	3.5	4.4	4.5	5.0	6.1	3.9
Feb	3.3	3.2	6.3	3.0	3.9	4.7	4.0	4.9	5.7	2.8
Mar	3.4	4.6	8.7	2.8	1.8	5.1	4.4	4.5	6.2	4.5
Apr	2.7	3.6	5.6	2.3	2.4	4.9	4.4	3.0	6.2	4.8
May	3.3	2.9	7.1	2.0	1.7	5.1	3.8	3.9	5.2	3.6
Jun	2.2	4.9	7.1	3.6	2.1	4.6	3.5	3.1	6.4	3.7
Jul	2.1	4.3	6.6	3.3	1.9	5.0	3.3	0.7	7.8	3.4
Aug	1.7	3.6	6.6	3.2	1.4	3.9	2.5	1.9	6.0	1.7
Sep	1.4	3.6	4.1	4.6	2.9	4.2	1.7	3.2	6.2	0.5

7.22
continued

Average earnings index[1] : all employee jobs: by industry (not seasonally adjusted)
Great Britain

July 1999 = 100

	Agriculture, forestry and fishing	Mining and quarrying	Food products, beverages and tobacco	Textiles, leather and clothing	Chemicals and man-made fibres	Basic metals and metal products	Engineering and allied industries	Other manufacturing	Electricity, gas and water supply	Construction
Including bonuses										
SIC 1992	(A,B)	(C)	(DA)	(DB,DC)	(DG)	(DJ)	(DK, DL,DM)	(DD,DE,DF, DH,DI,DN)	(E)	(F)
	JVUF	JVUG	JVUH	JVUI	JVUJ	JVUK	JVUL	JVUM	JVUN	JVUO
2000	102.9	102.1	104.9	103.1	109.4	101.0	104.6	103.9	99.5	106.3
2001	108.9	108.2	108.0	106.5	114.5	105.7	109.2	108.4	100.4	112.5
2000 Feb	95.4	106.4	103.2	102.3	108.6	98.7	103.1	102.7	101.7	105.0
Mar	106.3	105.0	106.0	103.2	116.4	101.9	108.1	103.6	104.4	109.8
Apr	102.1	102.7	106.3	101.6	109.5	100.4	103.6	102.1	97.8	104.0
May	102.9	99.6	105.2	101.8	109.1	99.9	103.3	103.1	100.4	104.1
Jun	104.3	99.8	103.3	102.0	107.0	99.9	103.4	103.2	103.7	106.4
Jul	100.1	100.2	103.4	102.5	106.8	104.7	104.5	104.2	98.2	106.2
Aug	99.4	99.5	103.2	101.2	106.9	99.4	102.8	102.6	96.6	103.6
Sep	110.3	100.4	103.0	102.9	106.8	99.3	103.5	104.0	96.4	106.0
Oct	105.9	101.9	103.1	104.8	106.4	103.0	104.7	104.5	95.8	106.0
Nov	104.6	102.3	106.1	107.6	108.2	101.5	107.2	105.6	98.0	108.6
Dec	106.1	103.6	111.9	106.4	118.8	102.1	109.2	108.9	100.2	113.0
2001 Jan	102.6	105.0	105.4	104.7	113.8	103.3	107.1	105.4	100.0	108.4
Feb	99.5	121.7	107.6	106.4	118.3	101.6	109.6	106.7	101.1	108.9
Mar	106.5	115.4	110.8	108.2	126.6	106.9	112.0	110.2	104.3	113.4
Apr	107.0	111.2	107.9	104.5	116.1	106.7	108.7	108.4	99.4	110.8
May	110.2	105.8	109.8	105.3	112.0	105.7	108.5	107.5	99.6	111.7
Jun	105.1	104.4	107.1	105.1	111.7	106.3	108.3	108.1	107.5	115.4
Jul	106.3	105.5	107.5	106.2	110.9	108.1	109.9	108.5	98.8	114.1
Aug	112.9	102.3	107.4	105.2	110.8	104.9	108.0	106.9	100.2	111.4
Sep	116.4	107.2	106.9	106.5	109.9	104.8	108.2	108.6	97.3	113.0
Oct	112.4	105.9	105.1	107.7	110.2	107.9	108.8	109.5	97.8	112.6
Nov	112.5	104.8	106.7	107.7	111.7	106.3	109.8	109.6	97.9	114.1
Dec	115.8	108.7	113.4	109.9	122.0	105.9	111.8	111.7	101.2	116.0
2002 Jan	111.1	108.4	108.5	106.8	113.7	106.4	110.8	109.3	101.9	111.3
Feb	110.1	108.9	110.1	107.6	121.5	105.4	111.6	110.1	101.6	114.2
Mar	116.6	129.8	118.1	111.8	132.1	106.9	114.4	114.2	110.5	121.5
Apr	113.3	115.0	109.0	108.5	121.0	109.6	113.4	111.8	101.5	116.4
May	112.3	114.4	110.3	107.4	116.1	105.9	113.4	112.7	99.9	115.0
Jun	112.2	114.6	110.9	109.2	114.9	106.8	113.7	112.1	110.3	116.6
Jul	111.3	111.6	110.2	110.5	118.0	110.0	114.5	112.7	101.8	117.1
Aug	116.2	112.7	110.6	107.8	119.2	105.1	113.0	110.8	101.2	114.1
Sep	121.5	116.8	110.4	108.9	114.1	106.5	112.3	112.2	100.9	116.4
Percentage change on the year										
	JVYQ	JVYR	JVYS	JVYT	JVYU	JVYV	JVYW	JVYX	JVYY	JVYZ
2001 Feb	4.3	14.4	4.2	4.0	8.9	3.0	6.3	3.9	−0.6	3.7
Mar	0.1	9.9	4.5	4.9	8.8	4.9	3.6	6.4	−0.1	3.2
Apr	4.8	8.3	1.5	2.9	6.1	6.3	4.9	6.2	1.7	6.6
May	7.1	6.3	4.4	3.4	2.7	5.7	5.1	4.3	−0.8	7.3
Jun	0.8	4.6	3.7	3.1	4.4	6.5	4.7	4.7	3.7	8.5
Jul	6.2	5.3	3.9	3.6	3.8	3.2	5.2	4.1	0.6	7.4
Aug	13.6	2.8	4.1	4.0	3.7	5.5	5.1	4.1	3.8	7.6
Sep	5.6	6.8	3.8	3.5	2.9	5.5	4.6	4.3	0.9	6.6
Oct	6.2	3.9	2.0	2.8	3.6	4.8	3.9	4.7	2.0	6.2
Nov	7.5	2.4	0.5	−	3.2	4.8	2.4	3.8	−0.1	5.0
Dec	9.2	4.8	1.3	3.3	2.7	3.8	2.3	2.6	1.0	2.7
2002 Jan	8.3	3.2	2.9	2.0	−0.1	3.0	3.5	3.6	1.9	2.7
Feb	10.7	−10.5	2.3	1.1	2.7	3.7	1.9	3.2	0.5	4.8
Mar	9.5	12.4	6.6	3.4	4.3	−	2.2	3.6	6.0	7.2
Apr	6.0	3.4	1.0	3.8	4.2	2.8	4.3	3.2	2.0	5.0
May	1.8	8.0	0.4	2.0	3.6	0.3	4.4	4.8	0.3	2.9
Jun	6.7	9.8	3.5	3.9	2.8	0.4	5.0	3.8	2.6	1.0
Jul	4.7	5.8	2.5	4.1	6.4	1.8	4.2	3.9	3.0	2.6
Aug	2.9	10.2	3.0	2.4	7.6	0.1	4.6	3.6	0.9	2.5
Sep	4.4	9.0	3.3	2.3	3.9	1.6	3.7	3.4	3.7	3.0

7.22 Average earnings index[1] : all employee jobs: by industry (not seasonally adjusted)

continued Great Britain

July 1999 = 100

	Wholesale trade	Retail trade and repairs	Hotels and restaurants	Transport, storage and communication	Financial interm-ediation	Real estate renting and business activities	Public admini-stration	Education	Health and social work	Other services
Including bonuses										
SIC 1992	(G:51)	(G:50,52)	(H)	(I)	(J)	(K)	(L)	(M)	(N)	(O)
	JVUP	JVUQ	JVUR	JVUS	JVUT	JVUU	JVUV	JVUW	JVUX	JVUY
2000	102.3	102.7	105.2	103.5	110.3	103.2	103.8	102.1	105.0	107.3
2001	106.0	105.7	112.0	107.8	116.0	107.7	108.3	107.4	111.4	110.2
2000 Feb	105.9	101.4	104.8	101.5	130.7	103.1	105.1	99.3	102.9	107.9
Mar	113.5	103.4	102.1	103.0	148.7	106.1	102.2	99.4	103.0	109.6
Apr	100.8	103.0	105.3	100.5	105.2	101.0	102.7	101.3	104.7	103.9
May	99.1	103.6	103.8	102.8	97.3	102.9	102.1	101.1	105.7	106.5
Jun	99.9	104.8	103.8	107.7	98.3	102.7	103.3	102.2	105.7	107.5
Jul	101.3	102.6	105.6	101.7	100.4	103.7	102.9	103.5	105.2	110.3
Aug	100.0	102.3	107.7	102.1	97.2	102.2	103.1	105.0	105.2	107.9
Sep	98.0	102.9	104.1	102.0	94.9	101.9	103.8	104.3	105.0	106.2
Oct	101.8	101.5	105.2	103.7	96.1	100.9	104.4	103.6	105.7	106.0
Nov	102.3	101.2	106.1	104.0	98.1	102.4	106.9	102.9	106.2	107.1
Dec	105.1	102.5	111.7	109.9	142.8	108.1	106.2	103.4	107.5	109.8
2001 Jan	104.0	104.0	105.5	105.1	136.3	105.6	106.0	103.0	108.3	107.3
Feb	107.1	104.2	106.8	107.2	179.3	106.8	106.7	102.8	107.6	112.5
Mar	117.7	105.2	109.5	108.6	150.4	113.6	106.2	103.4	107.9	109.5
Apr	104.6	106.2	111.0	107.0	108.3	106.7	107.3	107.0	111.5	107.0
May	103.9	107.1	111.3	109.4	98.2	106.4	107.2	106.3	112.5	108.5
Jun	103.5	107.5	113.6	111.4	103.6	108.6	108.1	107.6	112.5	109.4
Jul	103.7	105.4	113.7	107.3	101.7	107.7	108.2	110.8	112.0	110.1
Aug	103.5	105.9	113.9	106.0	98.4	105.5	108.7	111.2	112.2	111.2
Sep	103.2	106.1	113.6	105.5	96.9	105.0	109.9	110.3	112.2	109.7
Oct	103.2	105.9	112.3	107.1	96.0	107.0	109.9	108.9	112.9	112.5
Nov	105.4	105.6	114.1	107.8	96.5	107.3	110.0	108.1	113.4	111.4
Dec	111.8	105.5	118.1	111.2	126.2	111.6	111.2	108.9	113.8	113.7
2002 Jan	106.7	106.9	113.5	107.5	129.7	109.5	110.3	107.9	115.1	113.5
Feb	108.0	108.1	116.1	110.7	170.3	111.8	110.6	108.1	113.9	114.9
Mar	120.0	110.3	118.6	111.5	151.5	113.8	110.8	108.0	114.8	114.9
Apr	106.3	110.9	117.9	110.4	112.0	110.5	111.9	110.3	118.5	110.8
May	108.1	110.0	120.6	111.8	100.4	111.1	111.2	110.5	118.4	111.1
Jun	106.4	114.6	120.2	116.5	100.3	112.7	111.9	111.2	119.6	112.6
Jul	106.5	110.2	121.6	110.5	104.8	111.9	111.8	111.7	120.9	114.1
Aug	105.5	110.7	122.2	109.3	99.0	109.3	111.2	113.4	119.2	112.8
Sep	103.8	111.3	119.0	110.6	98.4	109.4	116.6	113.8	119.4	110.0
Percentage change on the year										
	JVZA	JVZB	JVZC	JVZD	JVZE	JVZF	JVZG	JVZH	JVZI	JVZJ
2001 Feb	1.1	2.7	2.0	5.6	37.2	3.6	1.6	3.5	4.6	4.3
Mar	3.6	1.8	7.3	5.4	1.1	7.1	3.8	4.0	4.8	−0.2
Apr	3.8	3.1	5.4	6.5	3.0	5.7	4.5	5.6	6.5	3.0
May	4.8	3.4	7.2	6.4	0.9	3.4	5.0	5.2	6.5	1.8
Jun	3.6	2.5	9.5	3.5	5.4	5.8	4.6	5.4	6.4	1.8
Jul	2.3	2.7	7.7	5.5	1.3	3.8	5.2	7.1	6.5	−0.1
Aug	3.5	3.5	5.8	3.8	1.2	3.3	5.5	5.9	6.7	3.1
Sep	5.3	3.1	9.2	3.5	2.1	3.1	5.9	5.7	6.8	3.3
Oct	1.3	4.3	6.8	3.3	−0.1	6.1	5.3	5.2	6.8	6.1
Nov	3.1	4.4	7.5	3.7	−1.6	4.8	2.9	5.1	6.8	4.1
Dec	6.3	3.0	5.8	1.2	−11.6	3.3	4.7	5.3	5.9	3.5
2002 Jan	2.6	2.7	7.5	2.2	−4.8	3.7	4.1	4.8	6.3	5.8
Feb	0.9	3.8	8.6	3.2	−5.0	4.7	3.6	5.2	5.8	2.1
Mar	2.0	4.8	8.3	2.7	0.7	0.1	4.3	4.4	6.3	5.0
Apr	1.7	4.4	6.2	3.1	3.3	3.5	4.3	3.1	6.3	3.5
May	4.0	2.8	8.4	2.2	2.2	4.4	3.7	3.9	5.3	2.5
Jun	2.8	6.6	5.8	4.5	−3.2	3.8	3.5	3.3	6.4	2.9
Jul	2.7	4.5	7.0	2.9	3.0	3.9	3.3	0.8	8.0	3.6
Aug	1.9	4.6	7.3	3.1	0.7	3.6	2.3	2.0	6.2	1.4
Sep	0.6	4.9	4.7	4.8	1.6	4.2	1.6	3.1	6.4	0.2

1 See chapter text.

Source: Office for National Statistics: 01633 819024

7.23 Gross weekly and hourly earnings[1] of full-time adult employees
Great Britain
At April

	Gross weekly earnings					Gross hourly earnings				
	Lowest decile	Lower quartile	Median	Upper quartile	Highest decile	Lowest decile	Lower quartile	Median	Upper quartile	Highest decile
	£	£	£	£	£	£	£	£	£	£
All men										
	KBYD	KBYE	KBYF	KBYG	KBYH	KIYD	KIYE	KIYF	KIYG	KIYH
1994	179.9	231.1	312.8	427.3	581.7	4.33	5.44	7.39	10.51	14.96
1995	182.0	237.1	323.2	442.7	600.8	4.33	5.55	7.60	10.90	15.60
1996	189.0	245.2	334.9	460.7	632.0	4.50	5.75	7.91	11.40	16.32
1997	198.6	256.4	349.7	480.0	656.9	4.71	6.00	8.24	11.89	17.01
1998	203.9	265.3	362.8	499.0	685.1	4.88	6.24	8.57	12.34	17.75
1999	211.1	274.5	374.3	517.3	711.6	5.09	6.50	8.92	12.96	18.63
2000	220.0	284.7	389.7	537.7	745.2	5.30	6.74	9.31	13.55	19.51
2001	229.5	296.6	407.7	567.5	799.6	5.54	7.06	9.74	14.29	20.96
2002	238.0	305.5	420.0	585.7	836.6	5.77	7.30	10.08	14.85	21.94
Manual men										
	KFZY	KFZZ	KGAK	KGAL	KGAM	KIYN	KIYO	KIYP	KIYQ	KIYR
1994	165.9	206.1	261.8	331.6	414.2	3.99	4.82	5.95	7.46	9.10
1995	166.9	211.1	271.8	347.1	437.5	3.97	4.86	6.09	7.66	9.43
1996	173.8	218.4	280.0	358.9	452.5	4.11	5.01	6.32	7.99	9.83
1997	182.4	228.8	292.5	373.9	472.8	4.32	5.25	6.60	8.28	10.17
1998	190.0	238.0	305.0	392.7	494.2	4.50	5.48	6.87	8.67	10.72
1999	194.9	244.8	312.8	399.0	500.6	4.68	5.69	7.11	8.95	11.04
2000	200.2	251.8	321.2	413.0	512.7	4.86	5.88	7.30	9.23	11.42
2001	209.7	262.0	336.1	431.3	536.1	5.05	6.11	7.66	9.63	11.90
2002	219.6	271.1	342.4	437.2	543.8	5.27	6.34	7.88	9.89	12.22
Non-manual men										
	KGAS	KGAT	KGAU	KGAV	KGAW	KIYX	KIYY	KIYZ	KIZA	KIZB
1994	200.4	274.4	376.0	503.9	688.5	5.03	6.90	9.67	13.30	18.20
1995	204.1	280.1	384.6	519.5	712.7	5.11	7.06	9.93	13.83	19.07
1996	211.1	287.9	399.4	544.0	752.4	5.28	7.28	10.28	14.38	19.87
1997	220.7	301.0	415.9	565.8	780.8	5.49	7.60	10.72	14.94	20.81
1998	225.5	309.1	430.7	586.1	823.4	5.62	7.79	11.09	15.54	21.74
1999	233.5	321.1	449.1	612.2	862.6	5.90	8.14	11.59	16.24	22.90
2000	243.8	334.3	463.9	634.6	902.1	6.14	8.42	12.03	16.86	23.88
2001	252.1	345.5	485.7	671.8	962.4	6.35	8.72	12.61	17.85	25.78
2002	259.8	355.4	500.4	695.6	1 011.3	6.54	8.97	12.99	18.44	26.95

As percentages of the corresponding median

	Gross weekly earnings					Gross hourly earnings				
All men										
	KBZH	KBZI	KBZJ	KBZK	KBZL	KBZM	KBZN	KBZO	KBZP	KBZQ
1994	57.5	73.9	100.0	136.6	186.0	58.6	73.6	100.0	142.2	202.4
1995	56.3	73.4	100.0	137.0	185.9	57.0	73.0	100.0	143.4	205.3
1996	56.4	73.2	100.0	137.5	188.7	56.9	72.7	100.0	144.2	206.3
1997	56.8	73.3	100.0	137.3	187.8	57.2	72.8	100.0	144.3	206.4
1998	56.2	73.1	100.0	137.6	188.8	56.9	72.7	100.0	143.9	207.1
1999	56.4	73.3	100.0	138.2	190.1	57.1	72.9	100.0	145.3	208.8
2000	56.5	73.1	100.0	138.0	191.2	57.0	72.4	100.0	145.5	209.5
2001	56.3	72.7	100.0	139.2	196.1	56.8	72.4	100.0	147.2	215.1
2002	56.7	72.7	100.0	139.5	199.2	57.3	72.5	100.0	147.3	217.6
Manual men										
	KGBS	KGBT	KGBU	KGBV	KGBW	KGBX	KGBY	KGBZ	KGCH	KGCI
1994	63.4	78.7	100.0	126.7	158.2	67.1	81.0	100.0	125.4	152.9
1995	61.4	77.7	100.0	127.7	161.0	65.2	79.8	100.0	125.8	154.8
1996	62.1	78.0	100.0	128.2	161.6	65.0	79.3	100.0	126.4	155.6
1997	62.4	78.2	100.0	127.8	161.6	65.5	79.5	100.0	125.5	154.1
1998	62.3	78.0	100.0	128.8	162.0	65.5	79.8	100.0	126.2	156.1
1999	62.3	78.3	100.0	127.6	160.0	65.9	80.0	100.0	125.8	155.2
2000	62.3	78.4	100.0	128.6	159.6	66.6	80.6	100.0	126.4	156.5
2001	62.4	77.9	100.0	128.3	159.5	66.0	79.7	100.0	125.7	155.6
2002	64.1	79.2	100.0	127.7	158.8	66.9	80.5	100.0	125.5	155.1
Non-manual men										
	KGCJ	KGCQ	KGCR	KGCS	KGCT	KGCU	KGCV	KGCW	KGCX	KGCY
1994	53.3	73.0	100.0	134.0	183.1	52.0	71.4	100.0	137.5	188.2
1995	53.1	72.8	100.0	135.1	185.3	51.5	71.1	100.0	139.3	192.0
1996	52.9	72.1	100.0	136.2	188.4	51.3	70.8	100.0	139.9	193.2
1997	53.1	72.4	100.0	136.0	187.7	51.2	70.9	100.0	139.4	194.1
1998	52.4	71.8	100.0	136.1	191.2	50.7	70.2	100.0	140.1	196.0
1999	52.0	71.5	100.0	136.3	192.1	50.9	70.2	100.0	140.0	197.5
2000	52.6	72.1	100.0	136.8	194.5	51.0	69.9	100.0	140.1	198.4
2001	51.9	71.1	100.0	138.3	198.1	50.3	69.2	100.0	141.4	204.1
2002	51.9	71.0	100.0	139.0	202.1	50.4	69.0	100.0	141.9	207.4

7.23
continued

Gross weekly and hourly earnings[1] of full-time adult employees
Great Britain
At April

	Gross weekly earnings					Gross hourly earnings				
	Lowest decile	Lower quartile	Median	Upper quartile	Highest decile	Lowest decile	Lower quartile	Median	Upper quartile	Highest decile
	£	£	£	£	£	£	£	£	£	£
All women										
	KCBK	KCBL	KCBM	KCBN	KCBO	KIZC	KIZD	KIZE	KIZF	KIZG
1994	139.1	174.6	229.4	320.1	417.8	3.66	4.58	6.02	8.39	11.59
1995	141.1	179.5	237.2	332.5	430.7	3.70	4.69	6.24	8.87	12.30
1996	146.7	186.8	248.1	347.3	449.4	3.84	4.87	6.55	9.31	12.97
1997	154.5	196.1	260.5	364.7	472.1	4.03	5.11	6.84	9.79	13.54
1998	161.0	203.6	270.0	379.1	493.5	4.22	5.32	7.10	10.20	14.16
1999	169.5	213.3	284.0	398.2	521.2	4.47	5.59	7.47	10.75	14.98
2000	177.3	223.6	296.7	417.6	546.1	4.66	5.85	7.79	11.24	15.65
2001	185.8	233.9	313.2	446.4	584.7	4.90	6.14	8.23	12.00	16.73
2002	195.0	243.6	326.9	464.5	614.2	5.12	6.41	8.60	12.51	17.40
Manual women										
	KGCZ	KGDA	KGDB	KGDC	KGDD	KIZM	KIZN	KIZO	KIZP	KIZQ
1994	114.1	134.7	165.4	212.0	272.0	3.05	3.51	4.20	5.23	6.39
1995	114.8	137.4	171.0	222.1	282.6	3.02	3.56	4.32	5.37	6.61
1996	119.0	142.8	178.7	230.8	291.4	3.15	3.68	4.49	5.61	6.85
1997	122.4	148.7	185.4	237.3	300.0	3.25	3.83	4.66	5.81	7.16
1998	128.9	156.3	193.9	248.6	312.5	3.43	4.02	4.87	6.08	7.44
1999	140.4	164.7	201.4	260.9	327.8	3.73	4.27	5.08	6.37	7.93
2000	144.9	171.2	210.1	268.1	335.7	3.86	4.44	5.27	6.58	8.14
2001	151.0	179.3	220.0	280.0	360.1	4.01	4.65	5.55	6.94	8.64
2002	161.3	186.3	229.2	290.0	365.0	4.30	4.86	5.76	7.21	8.93
Non-manual women										
	KGDJ	KGDK	KGDL	KGDM	KGDN	KIZW	KIZX	KIZY	KIZZ	KJAN
1994	152.0	188.9	247.0	342.5	430.3	4.06	5.05	6.52	9.04	12.25
1995	155.6	194.7	256.2	355.6	445.3	4.13	5.22	6.83	9.61	13.09
1996	161.7	203.0	268.7	372.2	471.1	4.31	5.44	7.16	10.08	13.75
1997	171.4	212.8	283.3	390.7	495.1	4.53	5.68	7.53	10.61	14.38
1998	176.2	219.3	291.5	405.6	513.5	4.68	5.86	7.77	11.01	14.88
1999	184.0	230.3	305.0	422.3	540.9	4.92	6.14	8.16	11.52	15.78
2000	192.0	239.2	317.9	442.5	567.8	5.10	6.40	8.47	12.08	16.41
2001	200.9	249.8	335.9	472.6	613.3	5.35	6.67	8.94	12.86	17.57
2002	209.5	259.1	349.2	492.6	639.0	5.56	6.93	9.31	13.33	18.27

As percentages of the corresponding median

All women										
	KGEO	KGEP	KGEQ	KGER	KGES	KGET	KGEU	KGEV	KGEW	KGEX
1994	60.6	76.1	100.0	139.5	182.1	60.8	76.1	100.0	139.4	192.5
1995	59.5	75.6	100.0	140.2	181.5	59.3	75.2	100.0	142.1	197.1
1996	59.1	75.3	100.0	140.0	181.1	58.6	74.4	100.0	142.2	198.1
1997	59.3	75.3	100.0	140.0	181.2	58.9	74.7	100.0	143.1	198.0
1998	59.6	75.4	100.0	140.4	182.8	59.4	74.9	100.0	143.6	199.4
1999	59.7	75.1	100.0	140.2	183.5	59.8	74.8	100.0	143.9	200.4
2000	59.8	75.4	100.0	140.7	184.1	59.8	75.0	100.0	144.3	200.8
2001	59.3	74.7	100.0	142.5	186.7	59.5	74.5	100.0	145.8	203.1
2002	59.6	74.5	100.0	142.1	187.9	59.5	74.5	100.0	145.5	202.2
Manual women										
	KGDT	KGDU	KGDV	KGDW	KGDX	KGDY	KGDZ	KGEA	KGEB	KGEC
1994	69.0	81.4	100.0	128.2	164.4	72.6	83.6	100.0	124.5	152.1
1995	67.1	80.3	100.0	129.9	165.2	69.9	82.4	100.0	124.3	153.0
1996	66.5	79.9	100.0	129.1	163.0	70.2	82.0	100.0	125.1	152.6
1997	66.0	80.2	100.0	128.0	161.8	69.7	82.2	100.0	124.7	153.6
1998	66.5	80.6	100.0	128.2	161.2	70.4	82.6	100.0	124.9	152.7
1999	69.7	81.8	100.0	129.5	162.8	73.4	84.0	100.0	125.4	156.1
2000	69.0	81.5	100.0	127.6	159.8	73.3	84.2	100.0	124.8	154.4
2001	68.6	81.5	100.0	127.3	163.7	72.2	83.7	100.0	125.1	155.7
2002	70.3	81.3	100.0	126.5	159.2	74.6	84.3	100.0	125.1	155.0
Non-manual women										
	KGED	KGEE	KGEF	KGEG	KGEH	KGEI	KGEJ	KGEK	KGEL	KGEM
1994	61.5	76.5	100.0	138.7	174.2	62.3	77.5	100.0	138.7	187.9
1995	60.7	76.0	100.0	138.8	173.8	60.5	76.4	100.0	140.7	191.7
1996	60.2	75.6	100.0	138.5	175.3	60.2	76.0	100.0	140.7	192.1
1997	60.5	75.1	100.0	137.9	174.8	60.2	75.4	100.0	140.9	191.0
1998	60.4	75.2	100.0	139.1	176.2	60.2	75.5	100.0	141.7	191.5
1999	60.3	75.5	100.0	138.4	177.3	60.3	75.3	100.0	141.2	193.4
2000	60.4	75.2	100.0	139.2	178.6	60.2	75.5	100.0	142.5	193.7
2001	59.8	74.4	100.0	140.7	182.6	59.8	74.5	100.0	143.9	196.2
2002	60.0	74.2	100.0	141.1	183.0	59.7	74.4	100.0	143.1	196.1

1 See chapter text.

Source: New Earnings Survey, Office for National Statistics: 01633 819024

7.24 Gross weekly and hourly earnings[1] of full-time adults
Northern Ireland

April of each year

	Gross weekly earnings					Gross hourly earnings				
	Lowest decile	Lower quartile	Median	Upper quartile	Highest decile	Lowest decile	Lower quartile	Median	Upper quartile	Highest decile
	£	£	£	£	£	p	p	p	p	p
All men										
	KCIF	KCIG	KCIH	KCII	KCIJ	KCIK	KCIL	KCIM	KCIN	KCIO
1995	161.0	205.3	285.6	419.4	548.5	394.6	491.2	674.6	1 043.5	1 371.6
1996	163.0	213.7	296.9	424.0	549.8	399.4	512.3	695.7	1 073.9	1 402.8
1997	171.1	222.2	307.1	449.6	575.8	414.8	522.1	724.4	1 106.2	1 452.0
1998	175.4	227.4	322.1	455.1	596.1	435.8	548.8	763.0	1 137.2	1 497.5
1999	183.9	237.0	328.9	467.7	607.6	457.0	572.3	778.4	1 167.1	1 545.9
2000	190.1	247.3	342.4	491.3	636.3	476.3	601.0	799.8	1 204.6	1 596.9
2001	194.2	250.0	352.6	500.2	668.6	491.0	614.8	828.5	1 257.3	1 678.4
2002	208.7	261.2	360.5	516.4	701.4	522.4	644.1	854.4	1 282.2	1 752.7
Manual men										
	KCIP	KCIQ	KCIR	KCIS	KCIT	KCIU	KCIV	KCIW	KCIX	KCIY
1995	149.7	181.5	230.9	299.4	383.3	359.7	435.5	527.0	664.6	826.5
1996	150.6	187.2	240.7	310.1	389.9	369.9	448.0	563.7	684.6	860.6
1997	158.4	192.9	249.4	321.4	402.7	385.0	460.0	570.5	709.5	882.0
1998	165.0	200.9	262.9	340.5	422.8	408.3	487.3	595.3	767.3	940.7
1999	175.6	216.4	270.4	355.0	454.6	435.5	515.0	624.5	786.0	994.7
2000	180.0	225.5	279.8	363.9	457.0	445.0	535.7	650.0	814.5	987.3
2001	182.5	229.0	292.8	380.7	475.7	463.6	550.0	677.3	842.0	1 059.9
2002	196.0	237.0	296.3	380.1	471.0	494.0	576.7	700.0	862.0	1 062.0
Non-manual men										
	KCIZ	KCJO	KCJP	KCJQ	KCJR	KCJS	KCJT	KCJU	KCJV	KCJW
1995	183.4	260.7	383.4	511.0	628.9	470.3	660.6	987.7	1 292.8	1 601.8
1996	192.5	268.4	387.1	506.4	617.2	482.4	682.5	1 013.0	1 322.7	1 612.2
1997	198.3	277.4	403.0	533.1	666.6	491.4	690.9	1 048.2	1 363.0	1 638.2
1998	200.5	284.2	418.4	543.8	685.9	500.0	715.7	1 074.7	1 404.5	1 739.5
1999	200.0	296.8	424.0	546.8	680.6	502.8	740.4	1 103.6	1 461.9	1 779.4
2000	209.1	306.0	456.6	580.0	730.8	543.3	767.7	1 165.1	1 519.9	1 917.3
2001	220.6	317.9	459.8	609.5	788.4	555.6	800.3	1 188.9	1 583.6	2 017.6
2002	245.7	340.7	486.4	646.2	863.6	647.5	892.0	1 270.4	1 656.6	2 195.1

As percentages of the corresponding median

All men										
	KCJX	KCJY	KCJZ	KCKA	KCKB	KCKC	KCKD	KCKE	KCKF	KCKG
1995	56.4	71.9	100.0	146.8	192.1	58.5	72.8	100.0	154.7	203.3
1996	54.9	72.0	100.0	142.8	185.2	57.4	73.6	100.0	154.4	201.6
1997	55.7	72.4	100.0	146.4	187.5	57.3	72.1	100.0	152.7	200.4
1998	54.5	70.6	100.0	141.3	185.1	57.1	71.9	100.0	149.0	196.3
1999	55.9	72.0	100.0	142.2	184.7	58.7	73.5	100.0	149.9	198.6
2000	55.5	72.2	100.0	143.5	185.9	59.5	75.1	100.0	150.6	199.6
2001	55.1	70.9	100.0	141.9	189.6	59.3	74.2	100.0	151.7	202.6
2002	57.9	72.4	100.0	143.2	194.6	61.1	75.4	100.0	150.1	205.1
Manual men										
	KCKH	KCKI	KCKT	KCKK	KCKL	KCKM	KCKN	KCKO	KCKP	KCKR
1995	64.8	78.6	100.0	129.7	166.0	68.3	82.6	100.0	126.1	156.8
1996	62.6	77.8	100.0	128.8	162.0	65.6	79.5	100.0	121.4	152.7
1997	63.5	77.3	100.0	128.9	161.5	67.5	80.6	100.0	124.4	154.6
1998	62.8	76.4	100.0	129.5	160.8	68.6	81.9	100.0	128.9	158.0
1999	64.9	80.0	100.0	131.3	168.1	69.7	82.5	100.0	125.9	159.3
2000	64.3	80.6	100.0	130.1	163.4	68.5	82.4	100.0	125.3	151.9
2001	62.4	78.2	100.0	130.0	162.5	68.5	81.2	100.0	124.3	156.5
2002	66.2	80.0	100.0	128.3	159.0	70.6	82.4	100.0	123.1	151.7
Non-manual men										
	KCKQ	KCKS	KFZW	KCKU	KCKV	KCKW	KCKX	KCKY	KCKZ	KCLA
1995	47.8	68.0	100.0	133.3	164.0	47.6	66.9	100.0	130.9	162.2
1996	49.7	69.3	100.0	130.8	159.4	47.6	67.4	100.0	130.6	159.2
1997	49.2	68.8	100.0	132.3	165.4	46.9	65.9	100.0	130.0	156.3
1998	47.9	67.9	100.0	130.0	163.9	46.5	66.6	100.0	130.7	161.9
1999	47.2	70.0	100.0	129.0	160.5	45.6	67.1	100.0	132.5	161.2
2000	45.8	67.0	100.0	127.0	160.1	46.6	65.9	100.0	130.4	164.6
2001	48.0	69.1	100.0	132.6	171.5	46.7	67.3	100.0	133.2	169.7
2002	50.5	70.1	100.0	132.9	177.6	51.0	70.2	100.0	130.4	172.8

7.24
continued

Gross weekly and hourly earnings[1] of full-time adults
Northern Ireland
April of each year

	Gross weekly earnings					Gross hourly earnings				
	Lowest decile	Lower quartile	Median	Upper quartile	Highest decile	Lowest decile	Lower quartile	Median	Upper quartile	Highest decile
	£	£	£	£	£	p	p	p	p	p
All women										
	KCDS	KCDT	KCDU	KCDV	KCDW	KCDX	KCDY	KCDZ	KCFF	KCFG
1995	130.2	162.9	217.4	320.5	423.2	345.1	424.3	583.8	885.5	1 203.8
1996	133.3	165.5	226.2	331.9	434.8	354.5	431.0	595.8	893.6	1 256.9
1997	137.5	170.0	231.3	334.4	450.9	360.0	441.6	602.6	906.2	1 285.5
1998	148.1	181.4	243.9	348.0	465.2	390.2	471.5	652.5	950.9	1 304.5
1999	151.3	191.9	257.8	374.3	485.9	404.3	494.7	683.3	1 026.6	1 410.6
2000	162.9	203.9	271.8	400.4	512.5	435.3	536.5	713.4	1 091.7	1 440.2
2001	173.2	211.8	287.9	412.7	517.4	456.6	560.4	748.4	1 106.1	1 462.8
2002	180.5	221.3	297.1	438.2	561.6	475.0	580.0	792.2	1 185.3	1 650.4
Manual women										
	KCFH	KCFI	KCFJ	KCFK	KCFL	KCFM	KCFN	KCFO	KCFP	KCFQ
1995	109.1	131.5	161.0	193.7	247.7	287.6	343.0	401.7	483.0	616.2
1996	110.9	132.5	161.1	197.1	248.7	293.9	345.7	408.0	496.2	599.7
1997	113.4	138.3	160.0	201.8	250.8	308.3	354.4	413.7	500.0	593.0
1998	120.0	146.5	172.9	213.6	258.4	309.0	385.7	440.0	549.0	631.2
1999	136.1	151.3	175.1	219.0	275.8	360.0	397.2	451.3	546.8	633.8
2000	144.0	163.7	195.0	240.1	282.3	395.1	435.5	509.7	592.9	713.9
2001	152.2	176.2	209.2	254.6	309.8	396.2	457.6	536.4	635.4	750.3
2002	155.0	179.4	212.5	258.4	325.6	423.8	471.6	553.5	663.7	775.9
Non-manual women										
	KCFR	KCFS	KCFT	KCFU	KCFV	KCFW	KCFX	KCFY	KCFZ	KCHA
1995	139.1	176.9	241.4	346.3	435.8	375.2	473.9	650.1	943.0	1 269.6
1996	145.3	182.5	253.0	364.7	437.0	385.0	490.2	675.6	997.3	1 302.6
1997	149.7	188.6	254.0	364.3	451.3	389.0	501.6	679.4	996.7	1 342.9
1998	156.6	200.2	270.9	383.8	475.5	412.8	530.7	725.0	1 028.2	1 373.9
1999	167.4	211.5	289.3	409.2	500.9	442.1	569.7	773.3	1 137.8	1 459.0
2000	174.3	219.9	299.1	426.8	517.4	458.7	590.2	793.3	1 170.2	1 507.1
2001	183.4	231.2	311.6	448.6	521.2	487.7	620.6	838.7	1 212.8	1 507.1
2002	192.7	244.6	331.4	469.0	574.3	516.9	655.0	886.1	1 272.1	1 700.2

As percentages of the corresponding median

	Gross weekly earnings					Gross hourly earnings				
All women										
	KCHB	KCHC	KCHD	KCHE	KCHF	KCHG	KCHH	KCHI	KCHJ	KCHK
1995	59.9	74.9	100.0	147.4	194.7	59.1	72.7	100.0	151.7	206.2
1996	58.9	73.2	100.0	146.7	192.2	59.5	72.3	100.0	150.0	211.0
1997	59.4	73.5	100.0	144.6	194.9	59.7	73.3	100.0	150.4	213.3
1998	60.7	74.4	100.0	142.7	190.7	59.8	72.3	100.0	145.7	199.9
1999	58.7	74.5	100.0	145.2	188.5	59.2	72.4	100.0	150.2	206.5
2000	59.9	75.0	100.0	147.3	188.6	61.0	75.2	100.0	153.0	201.9
2001	60.2	73.6	100.0	143.4	179.7	61.0	74.9	100.0	147.8	195.4
2002	60.8	74.5	100.0	147.5	189.0	60.0	73.2	100.0	149.6	208.3
Manual women										
	KCHL	KCHM	KCHN	KCHO	KCHP	KCHQ	KCHR	KCHS	KCHT	KCHU
1995	67.8	81.7	100.0	120.3	153.9	71.6	85.4	100.0	120.2	153.4
1996	68.8	82.2	100.0	122.3	154.4	72.0	84.7	100.0	121.6	147.0
1997	70.9	86.4	100.0	126.1	156.8	74.5	85.7	100.0	120.9	143.3
1998	69.4	84.7	100.0	123.5	149.4	70.2	87.7	100.0	124.8	143.5
1999	77.7	86.4	100.0	125.1	157.5	79.8	88.0	100.0	121.2	140.4
2000	73.9	84.0	100.0	123.1	144.8	77.5	85.4	100.0	116.3	140.1
2001	72.8	84.2	100.0	121.7	148.1	73.9	85.3	100.0	118.5	139.9
2002	73.0	84.4	100.0	121.6	153.2	76.6	85.2	100.0	119.9	140.2
Non-manual women										
	KCHV	KCHW	KCHX	KCHY	KCHZ	KCIA	KCIB	KCIC	KCID	KCIE
1995	57.6	73.3	100.0	143.5	180.5	57.7	72.9	100.0	145.1	195.3
1996	57.4	72.1	100.0	144.2	172.7	57.0	72.6	100.0	147.6	192.8
1997	58.9	74.3	100.0	143.4	177.7	57.3	73.8	100.0	146.7	197.7
1998	57.8	73.9	100.0	141.7	175.5	56.9	73.2	100.0	141.8	189.5
1999	57.9	73.1	100.0	141.5	173.2	57.2	73.7	100.0	147.1	188.7
2000	58.3	73.5	100.0	142.7	173.0	57.8	74.4	100.0	147.5	190.0
2001	58.9	74.2	100.0	143.9	167.3	58.1	74.0	100.0	144.6	179.7
2002	58.1	73.8	100.0	141.5	173.3	58.3	73.9	100.0	143.6	191.9

1 See chapter text.

Sources: Department of Enterprise, Trade and Investment (Northern Ireland);
028 9052 9897

7.25 Average earnings by age group of full-time employees whose pay for the survey pay period was not affected by absence[1]: Great Britain

At April 2001

	Gross weekly earnings								Average weekly hours		Average hourly earnings excluding overtime pay
	Average		As a percentage of the median			As a percentage of the median		Percentage earning under £250			
	Total	Overtime pay	Lowest decile	Lower quartile	Median	Upper quartile	Highest decile		Total	Overtime	
	£	£	per cent	per cent	£	per cent	per cent				£
All males											
Under 18	168.3	9.6	61.1	80.2	157.4	122.4	156.2	91.4	40.5	1.7	4.09
18 to 20	240.9	14.7	70.4	82.9	220.8	123.8	152.2	66.1	40.7	1.9	5.83
21 to 24	334.5	19.0	66.0	80.0	294.1	129.5	165.9	32.0	40.6	2.0	8.03
25 to 29	442.0	22.8	60.0	75.1	383.5	132.7	178.2	14.8	40.7	2.1	10.86
30 to 39	533.8	27.1	58.1	73.6	441.5	136.8	195.7	8.6	41.0	2.4	13.08
40 to 49	573.7	28.1	56.3	72.9	472.3	137.6	198.3	7.6	40.9	2.5	14.16
50 to 59	540.5	25.2	56.6	72.4	436.3	142.0	202.1	10.6	41.0	2.4	13.25
60 to 64	429.8	26.3	60.7	77.7	345.5	134.7	194.4	20.1	42.0	2.8	10.11
All ages	509.2	25.5	55.9	72.4	415.7	139.9	200.0	13.3	40.9	2.4	12.48
Manual males											
Under 18	160.9	10.8	56.0	80.5	155.0	122.5	151.5	92.1	41.2	2.0	3.84
18 to 20	238.5	18.0	69.6	82.6	215.1	125.8	156.2	67.5	41.9	2.4	5.59
21 to 24	304.3	30.6	65.7	79.3	283.7	126.6	156.6	35.5	43.1	3.3	6.89
25 to 29	347.8	36.9	64.4	79.1	326.3	126.4	156.6	22.1	43.6	3.8	7.81
30 to 39	383.0	46.0	66.2	79.9	354.7	128.0	158.6	13.6	44.1	4.5	8.50
40 to 49	393.0	49.3	65.1	79.7	367.1	126.6	155.6	12.5	44.1	4.7	8.72
50 to 59	370.1	43.4	65.9	80.2	345.5	126.1	157.3	16.3	44.0	4.4	8.26
60 to 64	328.2	37.7	64.8	80.0	308.1	126.1	152.7	26.2	43.9	4.1	7.31
All ages	364.3	42.7	62.8	78.7	339.4	127.9	159.5	19.4	43.9	4.3	8.13
Non-manual males											
Under 18	..	..	..	..	..	..	..	..	..	..	..
18 to 20	243.7	10.7	71.9	83.4	226.8	121.5	149.7	64.4	39.3	1.4	6.12
21 to 24	353.8	11.6	66.4	79.4	302.1	130.1	171.8	29.8	39.1	1.2	8.81
25 to 29	493.4	15.1	58.3	75.0	423.2	133.9	185.0	10.8	39.0	1.2	12.63
30 to 39	626.9	15.5	55.7	73.6	517.0	137.3	198.6	5.6	39.0	1.1	16.07
40 to 49	688.5	14.7	54.0	74.3	569.5	135.1	200.9	4.5	38.8	1.0	17.83
50 to 59	666.6	11.8	51.4	71.8	550.0	138.1	199.5	6.4	38.8	0.9	17.21
60 to 64	564.4	11.1	55.4	73.1	430.1	141.7	223.1	11.9	39.4	1.0	14.11
All ages	606.8	14.0	51.3	70.5	499.0	138.7	201.9	9.2	38.9	1.1	15.59
All females											
Under 18	171.3	3.7	64.6	82.2	162.5	116.9	139.5	75.3	37.9	0.6	4.49
18 to 20	216.5	5.3	74.0	85.0	206.3	117.7	139.7	34.6	38.3	0.7	5.62
21 to 24	293.8	7.0	66.5	79.7	274.1	126.1	153.1	12.5	38.0	0.8	7.68
25 to 29	379.9	7.3	61.5	76.5	344.6	129.5	167.1	5.5	37.6	0.7	10.10
30 to 39	428.1	7.9	57.9	73.6	365.0	140.3	186.6	5.6	37.5	0.7	11.41
40 to 49	402.8	7.4	58.0	72.8	341.7	146.8	188.2	7.9	37.3	0.8	10.80
50 to 59	374.6	6.7	60.0	74.8	318.7	148.9	188.9	9.7	37.1	0.7	10.04
60 to 64	324.8	6.0	66.2	80.2	269.0	135.6	200.3	14.8	37.5	0.7	8.60
All ages	381.1	7.2	59	74.2	325.7	142.0	188.2	9.2	37.5	0.7	10.15
Manual females											
Under 18	162.7	5.5	69.8	85.6	154.4	126.2	156.4	73.7	39.2	1.0	4.12
18 to 20	196.4	5.5	74.6	84.8	187.7	117.4	142.0	52.7	39.3	0.9	4.99
21 to 24	236.0	11.2	72.7	81.2	217.5	127.9	150.3	33.9	39.8	1.4	5.87
25 to 29	267.4	14.8	65.7	77.1	249.2	127.1	161.9	23.5	39.8	1.8	6.67
30 to 39	268.9	13.8	68.0	80.5	247.8	127.2	156.6	20.4	39.7	1.7	6.72
40 to 49	253.0	16.3	70.5	81.4	231.3	126.6	159.8	26.0	39.9	2.0	6.26
50 to 59	243.5	13.7	71.8	82.9	223.7	126.1	156.4	28.3	39.5	1.7	6.08
60 to 64	231.3	9.7	75.7	85.7	213.0	121.8	148.8	32.0	39.0	1.4	5.90
All ages	249.8	13.6	70.0	81.2	193.6	126.7	159.3	27.8	39.7	1.7	6.23
Non-manual females											
Under 18	174.2	3.1	62.4	83.4	163.2	115.9	136.4	75.9	37.5	0.5	4.63
18 to 20	221.8	5.2	74.2	86.2	211.5	117.7	139.2	29.8	38.0	0.7	5.79
21 to 24	301.9	6.4	67.9	80.4	282.2	125.8	151.4	9.5	37.7	0.7	7.96
25 to 29	391.9	6.5	62.8	77.3	355.1	129.4	166.1	3.6	37.3	0.6	10.48
30 to 39	451.2	7.1	59.0	74.3	387.4	138.1	183.0	3.4	37.2	0.6	12.12
40 to 49	428.7	5.8	57.8	72.3	369.4	142.3	182.2	4.7	36.8	0.5	11.64
50 to 59	401.6	5.2	60.1	74.6	347.5	146.1	181.6	5.8	36.6	0.5	10.91
60 to 64	357.6	4.7	65.8	80.4	297.2	136.8	191.6	8.8	36.9	0.5	9.61
All ages	402.8	6.2	59.6	74.3	261.7	141.4	183.5	6.1	37.1	0.6	10.84

1 See chapter text.

Source: New Earnings Survey, Office for National Statistics: 01633 819024

7.26 Trade unions[1]
United Kingdom
At end of year

Percentages

		1990	1991	1992	1993	1994	1995	1996	1997	1998	1999	2000
Number of trade unions	KCLB	327	306	315	302	281	271	261	257	243	241	230
Analysis by number of members:												
Under 100 members	KCLC	17.7	15.7	14.3	15.9	16.4	15.5	13.0	16.0	16.9	18.7	22.2
100 and under 500	KCLD	22.3	23.2	22.9	24.8	23.1	23.2	27.2	22.2	21.4	20.3	17.8
500 and under 1,000	KCLE	7.6	6.9	9.8	7.6	8.9	10.0	8.0	12.1	10.7	9.5	9.6
1,000 and under 2,500	KCLF	15.6	17.0	17.1	15.2	15.3	15.1	17.2	14.8	13.2	14.1	12.2
2,500 and under 5,000	KCLG	9.5	9.5	8.9	8.9	9.3	8.9	7.7	7.8	9.5	9.5	9.1
5,000 and under 10,000	KCLH	5.2	5.9	6.0	6.3	6.4	5.9	5.7	5.8	6.2	5.4	5.7
10,000 and under 15,000	KCLI	2.1	1.6	1.6	2.0	2.1	3.0	2.7	2.7	2.1	1.7	1.7
15,000 and under 25,000	KCLJ	3.4	3.3	3.8	3.0	2.8	2.6	2.3	2.3	2.9	4.1	5.2
25,000 and under 50,000	KCLK	7.6	7.2	6.3	7.0	7.1	7.4	7.7	7.4	8.2	7.9	7.0
50,000 and under 100,000	KCLL	1.8	2.3	2.9	3.0	2.5	2.6	1.9	2.3	2.5	2.1	2.6
100,000 and under 250,000	KCLM	4.3	4.6	3.5	3.3	3.6	3.0	3.1	3.1	2.5	2.1	2.2
250,000 and over	KCLN	2.8	2.9	2.9	3.0	2.5	3.0	3.4	3.5	4.1	4.6	4.8
All sizes	KCLP	100	100	100	100	100	100	100	100	100	100	100
Membership												
Analysis by size of union:												
Under 100 members	KCLQ	–	–	–	–	–	–	–	–	–	–	–
100 and under 500	KCLR	0.2	0.2	0.2	0.2	0.2	0.2	0.3	0.2	0.2	0.2	0.2
500 and under 1,000	KCLS	0.2	0.2	0.2	0.2	0.2	0.2	0.2	0.3	0.2	0.2	0.2
1,000 and under 2,500	KCLT	0.8	0.9	1.0	0.9	0.9	0.9	0.9	0.8	0.7	0.7	0.6
2,500 and under 5,000	KCLU	1.1	1.1	1.1	1.1	1.1	1.1	0.9	0.9	1.1	1.1	0.9
5,000 and under 10,000	KCLV	1.2	1.3	1.5	1.5	1.6	1.4	1.3	1.3	1.4	1.2	1.2
10,000 and under 15,000	KCLW	0.8	0.6	0.6	0.8	0.9	1.3	1.2	1.1	0.9	0.7	0.6
15,000 and under 25,000	KCLX	2.0	1.8	2.3	1.8	1.7	1.5	1.3	1.3	1.6	2.3	2.8
25,000 and under 50,000	KCLY	9.0	8.3	8.0	8.6	8.9	9.1	8.8	8.1	8.4	8.2	7.1
50,000 and under 100,000	KCLZ	4.3	4.9	7.0	7.3	5.9	5.9	3.9	4.5	4.5	3.8	4.6
100,000 and under 250,000	KCMA	22.3	22.9	18.6	18.2	19.3	16.3	15.2	15.3	11.9	9.9	9.8
250,000 and over	KCMB	58.1	57.8	59.4	59.2	59.3	62.0	66.0	66.1	69.1	71.7	72.0
All sizes	KCMC	100	100	100	100	100	100	100	100	100	100	100
Total membership (thousands)	KCMD	9 960	9 555	9 171	8 848	8 297	8 111	7 982	7 841	7 894	7 940	7 823

1 See chapter text.

Source: Department of Trade and Industry: 020 7215 5780

7.27 Vacancies at jobcentres in the United Kingdom[1]
Seasonally adjusted

Thousands

	January	February	March	April	May	June	July	August	September	October	November	December
Numbers of vacancies remaining unfilled DPCB												
1991	140.0	138.9	133.9	119.8	110.2	105.6	106.0	109.2	112.5	109.6	111.8	117.4
1992	117.0	118.2	118.2	117.1	118.8	119.8	120.2	118.6	113.1	112.9	114.4	117.0
1993	119.0	120.3	124.3	123.6	125.9	124.8	129.2	129.8	129.5	133.2	136.3	138.2
1994	140.4	142.7	143.4	146.2	149.1	154.9	158.8	165.0	165.4	175.3	176.9	177.6
1995	175.2	174.3	177.5	186.0	185.4	182.9	181.8	181.7	184.5	181.7	185.2	186.7
1996	190.4	189.3	196.9	201.2	209.2	220.7	233.0	238.8	247.4	248.7	257.5	265.5
1997	272.6	279.2	279.6	279.4	277.3	283.9	288.0	295.2	297.2	293.7	275.2	278.2
1998	275.0	285.0	286.3	288.2	298.1	300.1	302.8	302.7	301.5	302.9	304.4	303.2
1999	305.3	300.8	298.5	295.7	304.6	305.6	307.8	315.8	314.7	336.5	338.5	347.4
2000	340.3	341.7	344.6	355.7	354.3	357.2	362.9	361.6	365.6	364.5	374.3	376.5
2001	395.7	391.6	394.9	387.8	..	..	..	..	..	..	..	..
Inflow of vacancies DRYW												
1991	185.4	167.8	168.0	182.8	182.2	163.9	165.6	168.7	170.7	168.3	164.9	167.1
1992	166.4	166.9	171.7	166.0	166.2	176.4	173.3	164.0	167.1	171.3	164.7	173.8
1993	180.2	175.9	181.5	179.3	180.2	183.5	190.5	183.4	191.5	189.6	193.9	197.2
1994	199.2	199.5	199.1	203.7	205.2	212.2	208.3	223.6	216.6	219.1	223.1	226.8
1995	218.2	219.5	215.2	205.4	227.7	223.1	225.6	230.9	226.5	231.9	232.9	222.1
1996	228.9	222.2	219.8	231.7	221.4	219.5	224.4	223.1	221.7	203.4	230.2	232.8
1997	202.9	239.3	242.9	239.1	236.2	226.2	226.4	220.8	227.6	222.6	217.9	216.2
1998	184.2	218.5	219.2	216.3	218.2	225.0	222.0	221.4	221.8	229.9	223.1	219.4
1999	237.7	222.8	221.8	229.6	224.4	226.2	231.2	234.0	230.2	235.0	235.3	236.7
2000	227.9	226.1	228.8	225.3	213.2	222.3	220.6	219.0	225.6	221.3	220.2	222.8
2001	224.9	233.2	232.8	237.6	..	..	..	..	..	..	..	..
Outflow of vacancies DRZL												
1991	176.4	168.7	172.4	197.5	197.1	168.3	165.0	164.9	168.7	170.2	159.9	160.8
1992	169.7	165.6	170.5	168.4	168.6	174.1	172.5	164.1	170.5	169.8	160.8	170.6
1993	178.8	173.6	176.6	180.1	181.0	184.0	185.6	182.0	189.8	186.4	191.0	195.3
1994	196.8	196.7	198.3	202.3	203.4	205.8	202.8	217.1	214.8	210.8	221.6	227.0
1995	219.0	220.6	214.1	195.1	229.0	225.0	224.6	230.4	225.5	237.1	229.7	219.2
1996	225.6	222.1	213.8	222.7	212.9	211.1	214.3	218.4	213.9	200.9	220.9	229.8
1997	208.5	232.1	238.0	236.8	234.1	220.9	225.0	215.0	216.8	224.2	232.5	219.9
1998	207.2	208.7	213.1	214.0	209.0	222.3	219.3	221.2	218.5	228.7	220.4	223.5
1999	236.9	224.4	220.9	232.3	219.4	225.2	227.6	226.5	229.0	219.6	233.6	231.1
2000	240.6	223.6	224.1	218.9	213.9	218.6	214.6	219.2	221.8	217.1	211.8	220.4
2001	212.1	237.6	226.1	241.1	..	..	..	..	..	..	..	..
Number of placings DTQR												
1991	129.4	122.5	127.6	148.4	148.4	123.9	123.2	120.9	122.1	122.7	114.8	115.9
1992	124.6	119.7	123.6	122.6	123.0	126.5	126.5	119.6	125.9	127.6	120.6	130.2
1993	134.3	132.1	131.7	134.0	134.9	136.3	139.0	136.1	144.1	140.6	146.4	148.2
1994	149.5	150.6	151.5	156.6	157.7	161.9	157.7	169.6	166.4	162.3	170.3	173.2
1995	166.2	169.1	164.6	145.8	179.8	173.6	174.4	178.5	172.5	183.5	179.7	167.4
1996	176.1	164.6	151.5	152.8	151.6	148.2	149.7	153.6	148.9	135.4	150.4	159.3
1997	147.9	157.7	163.6	164.0	151.8	143.1	138.6	127.1	126.4	123.1	120.2	116.9
1998	109.0	113.9	115.5	114.1	110.5	115.9	115.8	116.4	117.8	121.4	118.0	117.2
1999	119.8	120.3	116.7	126.5	118.1	121.0	123.0	121.8	122.7	120.3	123.1	122.6
2000	121.1	116.4	115.7	111.4	108.1	109.5	107.3	109.9	111.3	109.9	107.1	108.4
2001	110.2	108.6	109.1	117.5	..	..	..	..	..	..	..	..

1 See chapter text.

Sources: Jobcentre Plus administrative system;
Office for National Statistics: 020 7533 6094

8 Personal income, expenditure and wealth

Personal income, expenditure and wealth

Average incomes of households *(Table 8.1)*
Original income is the total income in cash of all the members of the household before the deduction of taxes or the addition of state benefits. It includes income from employment, self-employment, investment income, etc. The addition of cash benefits (retirement pensions, child benefit, etc) and the deduction of income tax, council tax, water charges, domestic rates and employees' national insurance contributions give disposable income. By further allowing for taxes paid on goods and services purchased, such as VAT, an estimate of "post-tax" income is derived. These income figures are derived from estimates made by the Office for National Statistics, based largely on information from the Expenditure and Food Survey (EFS), and published each year in *Economic Trends,* and, from 2002, available on the National Statistics website.

A retired household is defined as one where the combined income of retired members amounts to at least half the total gross income of the household, where a retired person is defined as anyone who describes themselves as "retired" or anyone over the minimum NI pension age describing themselves as "unoccupied" or "sick or injured but not intending to seek work."

Children are defined as persons aged under 16 or aged between 16 and 18, unmarried and receiving full-time non-advanced further education.

Distribution of total incomes *(Table 8.2)*
The information shown in Table 8.2 comes from the Survey of Personal Incomes for the financial years 1997/98, 1998/99, 1999/00 & 2000/01. This is an annual survey that covers approximately 200,000 individuals across the whole of the UK. It is based on administrative data held by Inland Revenue offices on individuals who could be liable to tax.

The table relates only to those individuals who are taxpayers. The distributions cover only incomes as computed for tax purposes and above a level which for each year corresponds approximately to the single person's allowance. Incomes below these levels are not shown because the information about them is incomplete.

Investment income from which tax has been deducted at source is not always known to local tax offices. Estimates of missing bank and building society interest and dividends from United Kingdom companies are included in these tables. The missing investment income is distributed, in a manner consistent with information from the Expenditure and Food Survey and the National Accounts, to individuals for whom there is no investment income already reported by the tax office.

Superannuation contributions are estimated and included in total income. They have been distributed among earners in the Survey of Personal Incomes sample by a method consistent with information about the number of employees who are contracted in or out of the State Earnings Related Pension Scheme and the proportion of their earnings contributed.

When comparing results of these surveys across years, it should be noted that the Survey of Personal Incomes is not a longitudinal survey. However, sample sizes have increased in recent years to increase precision.

Estimates of self employment income in the annual surveys for 1996-97 to 1999-00 are incomplete due to the absence of data from a limited number of sole trader sources. The deficiency is estimated to be worth about ½ per cent of total income. Estimates of income from employment and share of partnership profits are believed to be under-recorded in the 1999-00 survey. The extent of the deficiency is under investigation.

Expenditure and Food Survey *(Tables 8.3 - 8.5)*
The Expenditure and Food Survey (formerly the Family Expenditure Survey), introduced in 1957, covers all types of private households in the United Kingdom. It is a continuous survey with fieldwork carried out in every month of the year. In 2001-02 around 7,500 households in the UK provided information. The main purpose of the survey is to provide a source for the weighting pattern for the Index of Retail Prices, so it is primarily concerned with household expenditure on goods and services. However, it does have several other important uses.

Although the survey is primarily concerned with the expenditure of private households, much additional information is collected about income and the characteristics of co-operating households. Consequently, the survey provides a unique fund of important economic and social data.

Like all surveys based on a sample of the population, its results are subject to sampling error, and to some bias due to non-response.

The results of the survey are published in an annual report, the latest being *'Family Spending 2001-2002'.* The report includes a list of definitions used in the survey, items on which information is collected and a brief account of the fieldwork procedure.

8.1 Average incomes of households before and after taxes and benefits[1], 2000/01
United Kingdom

	Retired households		Non-retired households								
	1 adult	2 or more adults	1 adult	2 adults	3 or more adults	1 adult with children	2 adults with 1 child	2 adults with 2 children	2 adults with 3 or more children	3 or more adults with children	All house-holds
Number of households in the population (thousands)	3 416	2 988	4 077	5 151	2 124	1 288	1 819	2 227	927	1 013	25 030
Average per household (£ per year)											
Original income	4 045	10 390	16 286	32 643	40 854	8 456	32 734	36 241	30 222	35 745	23 234
Disposable income	8 195	15 223	13 946	26 583	34 916	12 698	26 904	30 181	27 380	31 947	21 242
Post-tax income	6 756	11 750	11 160	21 233	27 382	9 868	21 397	24 310	21 818	24 354	16 855

1 See chapter text. Redistribution of Income, included in the Effects of taxes and benefits on household income, 2000/01, analysis published on the National Statistics website *(www.statistics.gov.uk/taxesbenefits)* and in the May 2002 edition of *Economic Trends.*

Source: Office for National Statistics: 020 7533 5772

8.2 Distribution of total incomes before and after tax
United Kingdom
Years ended 5 April

| | 1997/98 Annual Survey | | | | | 1998/99 Annual Survey | | | |
| | Number of individuals (000s) | £ million | | | | Number of individuals (000s) | £ million | | |
		Total income before tax	Total tax	Total income after tax			Total income before tax	Total tax	Total income after tax
Lower limit of range of income					**Lower limit of range of income**				
All incomes[1]	26 200	461 000	79 500	381 100	All incomes[1]	26 900	498 000	88 000	409 000
Income before tax £					Income before tax £				
4 045	509	2 170	21	2 150	4 195	322	1 400	9	1 390
4 500	560	2 660	74	2 580	4 500	552	2 620	57	2 560
5 000	678	3 580	127	3 450	5 000	580	3 050	112	2 930
5 500	841	4 840	190	4 650	5 500	873	5 030	183	4 850
6 000	1 640	10 700	600	10 100	6 000	1 640	10 600	561	10 100
7 000	1 540	11 600	820	10 800	7 000	1 560	11 700	821	10 900
8 000	3 050	27 400	2 440	25 000	8 000	3 120	28 000	2 400	25 600
10 000	2 850	31 200	3 520	27 700	10 000	2 730	30 000	3 290	26 700
12 000	3 530	47 500	6 270	41 200	12 000	3 650	49 100	6 290	42 800
15 000	4 260	73 800	11 100	62 700	15 000	4 460	77 200	11 400	65 800
20 000	4 260	102 700	17 200	85 500	20 000	4 460	107 600	17 900	89 700
30 000	1 730	63 700	13 100	50 600	30 000	2 060	75 900	15 300	60 600
50 000	582	38 400	10 600	27 700	50 000	702	46 400	12 800	33 600
100 000	135	18 000	5 850	12 100	100 000	160	21 300	6 940	14 300
200 000 and over	51	22 400	7 560	14 900	200 000 and over	62	27 600	9 980	17 700
Income after tax £					Income after tax £				
4 045	629	2 710	33	2 680	4 195	394	1 730	14	1 710
4 500	683	3 350	112	3 240	4 500	701	3 420	91	3 330
5 000	812	4 470	186	4 280	5 000	725	3 990	175	3 810
5 500	1 000	6 050	281	5 770	5 500	1 010	6 060	260	5 800
6 000	1 960	13 600	885	12 700	6 000	1 990	13 700	839	12 900
7 000	1 900	15 600	1 270	14 300	7 000	1 840	15 000	1 210	13 800
8 000	3 750	37 600	3 840	33 800	8 000	3 740	37 100	3 630	33 500
10 000	3 230	40 500	5 100	35 400	10 000	3 280	41 000	5 010	36 000
12 000	3 760	58 800	8 390	50 400	12 000	3 940	61 600	8 610	53 000
15 000	4 030	82 800	13 300	69 500	15 000	4 220	86 400	13 600	72 800
20 000	3 070	89 100	15 900	73 200	20 000	3 390	98 800	17 500	81 300
30 000	1 030	50 100	12 300	37 900	30 000	1 250	60 400	14 500	45 900
50 000	291	27 700	8 460	19 200	50 000	352	33 400	10 200	23 200
100 000	63	12 800	4 350	8 420	100 000	76	15 400	5 290	10 100
200 000 and over	23	15 500	5 150	10 400	200 000 and over	28	19 300	7 060	12 300

8.2
continued Distribution of total incomes before and after tax
United Kingdom
Years ended 5 April

| | 1999/00 Annual Survey | | | | | 2000/01 Annual Survey | | | |
| | Number of individuals (000s) | £ million | | | | Number of individuals (000s) | £ million | | |
		Total income before tax	Total tax	Total income after tax			Total income before tax	Total tax	Total income after tax
Lower limit of range of income					**Lower limit of range of income**				
All incomes[1]	27 000	527 400	92 000	435 400	All incomes[1]	29 300	594 700	105 600	489 100
Income before tax £					Income before tax £				
4 335	736	3 440	24	3 420	4 385	786	3 690	23	3 660
5 000	1 070	5 920	113	5 810	5 000	1 360	7 470	139	7 330
6 000	3 120	21 800	930	20 900	6 000	3 270	22 800	986	21 800
8 000	2 980	26 800	2 090	24 800	8 000	2 960	26 700	2 070	24 600
10 000	2 780	30 700	3 100	27 600	10 000	2 740	30 200	3 030	27 100
12 000	2 450	31 700	3 770	28 000	12 000	2 590	33 600	3 950	29 700
14 000	2 170	32 500	4 240	28 200	14 000	2 340	35 100	4 540	30 500
16 000	1 940	32 900	4 590	28 300	16 000	2 040	34 600	4 730	29 900
18 000	1 570	29 700	4 450	25 300	18 000	1 750	33 300	4 850	28 400
20 000	4 760	115 300	18 700	96 600	20 000	5 400	131 000	20 800	110 200
30 000	2 390	88 200	17 000	71 200	30 000	2 780	103 500	19 700	83 800
50 000	800	52 900	14 100	38 800	50 000	961	63 500	16 900	46 600
100 000	178	23 700	7 550	16 200	100 000	216	28 800	9 150	19 600
200 000 and over	69	31 700	11 400	20 400	200 000 and over	88	40 600	14 700	25 900
Income after tax £					Income after tax £				
4 335	802	3 780	28	3 750	4 385	891	4 220	30	4 190
5 000	1 250	7 060	155	6 900	5 000	1 490	8 390	175	8 210
6 000	3 820	28 100	1 470	26 600	6 000	3 980	29 300	1 540	27 800
8 000	3 600	35 600	3 220	32 300	8 000	3 560	35 200	3 160	32 000
10 000	3 320	41 100	4 670	36 400	10 000	3 370	41 700	4 730	37 000
12 000	2 730	40 700	5 330	35 300	12 000	2 940	43 800	5 650	38 100
14 000	2 360	41 100	5 810	35 300	14 000	2 490	43 300	6 020	37 300
16 000	1 870	37 400	5 680	31 700	16 000	2 060	41 100	6 080	35 000
18 000	1 470	33 100	5 220	27 900	18 000	1 630	36 500	5 640	30 800
20 000	3 740	108 400	18 500	88 900	20 000	4 410	127 500	21 300	106 200
30 000	1 530	72 600	16 500	56 120	30 000	1 820	86 400	19 500	66 900
50 000	414	38 500	11 400	27 140	50 000	502	46 500	13 800	32 800
100 000	86	17 200	5 780	11 500	100 000	105	21 200	7 100	14 100
200 000 and over	32	22 800	8 300	14 500	200 000 and over	43	29 700	10 900	18 900

1 See chapter text. All figures have been independently rounded.

Source: Board of Inland Revenue: 020 7438 4335

Personal income, expenditure and wealth

8.3 Sources of gross household income[1]
United Kingdom

		1991	1992	1993	1994 /95	1995 /96	1996 /97	1997 /98	1998[2] /99	1999[2] /00	2000[2] /01	2001[2] /02
Number of households supplying data	KPDA	7 056	7 418	6 979	6 853	6 797	6 415	6 409	6 630	7 097	6 637	7 473
Average weekly household income by source (£)												
Wages and salaries	KPCB	222.00	222.70	228.30	237.90	245.00	256.30	280.20	309.20	315.40	336.70	377.40
Self-employment	KPCC	29.70	29.60	29.20	35.30	32.90	37.50	32.90	37.20	46.00	44.50	47.70
Investments	KPCD	23.70	20.80	18.00	16.20	18.10	17.80	18.70	18.80	21.80	20.00	19.70
Annuities and pensions (other than social security benefits)	KPCE	17.30	19.60	21.90	23.50	26.00	26.00	28.90	30.30	32.80	35.00	36.10
Social security benefits	KPCF	40.10	45.00	48.90	49.90	52.40	54.10	55.00	55.80	58.00	60.10	63.20
Other sources	KPCH	5.30	5.20	6.70	6.50	6.60	5.30	5.20	5.70	5.90	6.20	6.80
Total	KPCI	362.70	342.90	353.00	369.30	380.90	396.90	420.80	457.00	479.90	502.50	551.00
Sources of household income as a percentage of total household income												
Wages and salaries	KPCJ	61	65	65	64	64	65	67	68	66	67	69
Self-employment	KPCK	8	9	8	10	9	9	8	8	10	9	9
Investments	KPCL	7	6	5	4	5	5	4	4	5	4	4
Annuities and pensions (other than social security benefits)	KPCM	5	6	6	6	7	7	7	7	7	7	7
Social security benefits	KPCN	11	13	14	14	14	14	13	12	12	12	11
Other sources	KPCP	2	2	2	2	2	1	1	1	1	1	1
Total	KPCQ	100	100	100	100	100	100	100	100	100	100	100

1 See chapter text.
2 Income based on weighted data.

Source: Expenditure and Food Survey, Office for National Statistics: 020 7533 5755

8.4 Availability in households of certain durable goods[1]
United Kingdom

Percentage

		1991	1992	1993	1994 /95	1995 /96	1996 /97	1997 /98	1998[2] /99	1999[2] /00	2000[2] /01	2001[2] /02
Number of households supplying data	KPDA	7 056	7 418	6 979	6 853	6 797	6 415	6 409	6 630	7 097	6 637	7 473
Car	KPDB	68	68	69	69	70	69	70	72	71	72	74
One	KPDC	45	45	46	45	47	43	44	44	43	44	44
Two	KPDD	19	19	19	20	19	22	21	23	21	22	24
Three or more	KPDE	4	4	4	4	4	5	5	5	6	6	6
Central heating, full or partial	KPDF	81	82	83	84	85	87	89	89	90	91	92
Washing machine	KPDG	87	88	89	89	91	91	91	92	91	92	93
Refrigerator or fridge/freezer	KPDH	98	99	99	99	99	..	..	..	..	..	..
Fridge/freezer or deep freezer	KPDI	82	84	87	86	87	91	90	92	91	94	95
Refrigerator	KPDJ	..	..	..	..	..	49	51	52	53	..	..
Dishwasher	GPTL	..	..	..	18	20	20	22	23	23	25	27
Television	KPDK	98	98	..	..	..	..	..	..	..	..	..
Telephone	KPDL	88	88	90	91	92	93	94	95	95	93	94
Home computer	KPDM	18	19	..	..	..	27	29	33	38	44	49
Video recorder	KPDN	65	69	73	76	79	82	84	85	86	87	90
Internet access	ZBUZ	..	..	..	..	..	..	..	10	19	32	40

1 See chapter text.
2 Percentages based on grossed number of households.

Source: Expenditure and Food Survey, Office for National Statistics: 020 7533 5755

8.5 Households and their expenditure at current prices[1]
United Kingdom

		1991	1992	1993	1994 /95	1995 /96	1996 /97	1997[2] /98	1998[2,3] /99	1999[2,3] /00	2000[2,3] /01	2001[2,3] /02
Number of households supplying data	KPDA	7 056	7 418	6 979	6 853	6 797	6 415	6 409	6 630	7 097	6 637	7 473
Average weekly household expenditure on commodities and services (£)												
Housing	KPEV	50.20	47.40	44.90	46.40	48.30	49.10	51.50	57.20	57.00	63.90	66.70
Fuel and power	KPEW	12.30	13.00	13.20	13.00	12.90	13.40	12.70	11.70	11.30	11.90	11.70
Food	KPEX	46.10	47.70	50.00	50.40	52.90	55.20	55.90	58.90	59.60	61.90	62.20
Alcoholic drink	KPEY	10.80	11.10	12.00	12.30	11.40	12.40	13.30	14.00	15.30	15.00	14.60
Tobacco	KPEZ	5.20	5.40	5.60	5.60	5.80	6.10	6.10	5.80	6.00	6.10	5.60
Clothing and footwear	KCWC	15.80	16.40	17.40	17.10	17.20	18.30	20.00	21.70	21.00	22.00	22.40
Household goods	KCWH	20.10	21.90	23.10	22.70	23.50	26.70	26.90	29.60	30.70	32.60	33.10
Household services	KCWI	13.00	13.40	15.40	15.10	15.10	16.40	17.90	18.90	18.90	22.00	23.70
Personal goods and services	KCWJ	10.00	10.20	11.00	10.80	11.60	11.60	12.50	13.30	13.90	14.70	14.80
Motoring expenditure	KCWK	34.10	35.70	36.30	36.20	37.00	41.20	46.60	51.70	52.60	55.10	58.30
Fares and other travel costs	KCWL	5.60	7.20	7.00	6.60	6.20	7.50	8.10	8.30	9.20	9.50	9.50
Leisure goods	KCWM	12.10	13.30	13.30	13.90	13.20	15.20	16.40	17.80	18.50	19.70	19.90
Leisure services	KCWN	22.20	27.60	25.60	31.20	32.10	34.00	38.80	41.90	43.90	50.60	52.30
Miscellaneous	KCWO	1.60	1.80	2.10	2.30	2.40	2.20	2.00	1.20	1.40	0.70	1.90
Total	KCWP	259.00	271.80	276.70	283.60	289.90	309.10	328.80	352.20	359.40	385.70	396.80

		1991	1992	1993	1994 /95	1995 /96	1996 /97	1997[2] /98	1998[2,3] /99	1999[2,3] /00	2000[2,3] /01	2001[2,3] /02
Expenditure on commodity or service as a percentage of total expenditure												
Housing	KPFH	19	17	16	16	17	16	16	16	16	17	17
Fuel and power	KPFI	5	5	5	5	5	4	4	3	3	3	3
Food	KPFJ	18	18	18	18	18	18	17	17	17	16	16
Alcoholic drink	KPFK	4	4	4	4	4	4	4	4	4	4	4
Tobacco	KPFL	2	2	2	2	2	2	2	2	2	2	1
Clothing and footwear	KPFM	6	6	6	6	6	6	6	6	6	6	6
Household goods	KCWQ	8	8	8	8	8	9	8	8	9	8	8
Household services	KCWR	5	5	6	5	5	5	5	5	5	6	6
Personal goods and services	KCWS	4	4	4	4	4	4	4	4	4	4	4
Motoring expenditure	KCWT	13	13	13	13	13	13	14	15	15	14	15
Fares and other travel costs	KCWU	2	3	3	2	2	2	3	2	3	2	2
Leisure goods	KCWV	5	5	5	5	5	5	5	5	5	5	5
Leisure services	KCWW	9	10	9	11	11	11	12	12	12	13	13
Miscellaneous	KPFR	1	1	1	1	1	1	1	–	–	–	–
Total	KPFS	100	100	100	100	100	100	100	100	100	100	100

1 See chapter text.
2 Rented unfurnished includes Local Authority and Housing Association (furnished and unfurnished) and privately rented (unfurnished). Rented furnished only includes privately rented (furnished) Owner-occupied includes shared owners (who part own and part rent).

3 Averages based on grossed number of households. Expenditure based on weighted data and including children's expenditure.

Source: Expenditure and Food Survey, Office for National Statistics: 020 7533 5755

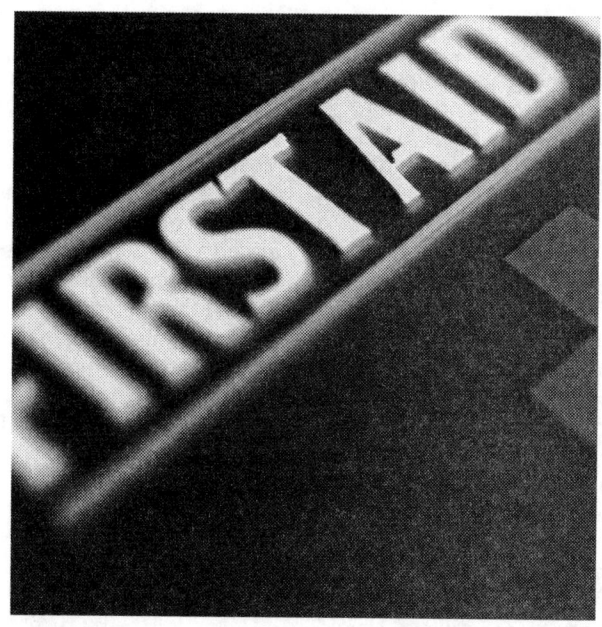

9 Health

Health

Hospital and family health services *(Table 9.1)*

The courses of treatment are for the General Dental Services (GDS). A course of treatment is complete when the treatment that is required – or such of it that the patient is willing to undergo – has been carried out. A dentist in accepting a patient for continuing care (adults) or capitation (children), undertakes to provide the care and treatment necessary to secure and maintain oral health.

Deaths: analysed by cause *(Table 9.5)*

All figures in this table for England and Wales represent the number of deaths **occurring** in each calendar year. All data for Scotland and Northern Ireland relate to the number of deaths **registered** during each calendar year.

Bridge coding exercise

From 2001, all three constituent countries of the United Kingdom are coding their causes of death using the latest, tenth, revision of the International Statistical Classification of Diseases and Related Health Problems (ICD-10). All cause of death information for 2001 (also for 2000 for Scotland) presented in this table is based on the revised classification. To assist users in assessing any discontinuities arising from the introduction of the revised classification, bridge-coding exercises were carried out on all deaths registered in 1999 in England and Wales and also in Scotland and, for this reason, data for that year are presented in the table on both ICD-9 and ICD-10 bases for Scotland. No bridge-coding exercise has been conducted for Northern Ireland.

For further information about ICD-10 and the bridge-coding carried out by The Office for National Statistics, see the ONS Report: Results of the ICD-10 bridge-coding study, England and Wales, 1999. *Health Statistics Quarterly* 14 (2002), pages 75-83 or log on to the National Statistics website at: www.statistics.gov.uk. For information on the Scottish bridge-coding exercise, consult the Annual Report of the General Register Office for Scotland or log on to their website at: www.gro-scotland.gov.uk.

Neonatal deaths and homicide and assault

For England and Wales, neonatal deaths (those at age under 28 days) are included in the number of total deaths but excluded from the cause figures. This has particular impact on the totals shown for the chapters covered by the ranges P and Q, 'Conditions originating in the perinatal period' and 'Congenital malformations, deformations and chromosomal abnormalities'. These are considerably lower than the actual number of deaths because it is not possible to assign an underlying cause of death from the neonatal death certificate used in England and Wales.

Also, for England and Wales only, the total number shown for Homicide and assault, X85-Y09, will not be a true representation because the registration of these deaths is often delayed by adjourned inquests.

Occupational ill health *(Tables 9.7 and 9.8)*

There are a number of sources of data on the extent of occupational or work-related ill health in Great Britain. For some potentially severe lung diseases caused by exposures which are highly unlikely to be found in a non-occupational setting, it is useful to count the number of death certificates issued each year. This is also true for mesothelioma, a cancer affecting the lining of the lungs and stomach, for which the number of cases with non-occupational causes is likely to be larger (although still a minority). **Table 9.8** shows the number of deaths for *mesothelioma* and *asbestosis* (linked to exposure to asbestos), *pneumoconiosis* (linked to coal dust or silica), *byssinosis* (linked to cotton dust) and some forms of *allergic alveolitis* (including farmer's lung). For asbestos-related diseases the figures are derived from a special register maintained by HSE.

Most conditions which can be caused or made worse by work can also arise from other factors. The remaining sources of data on work-related ill health rely on *attribution* of individual cases of illness to work causes. In the Occupational Disease Intelligence Network (ODIN), this is done by specialist doctors - either occupational physicians or those working in particular disease specialisms (covering musculoskeletal, psychological, respiratory, skin, audiological and infectious disease). **Table 9.7** presents data from ODIN for the last three years. It should be noted that not all cases of occupational disease will be seen by participating specialists; for example, the number of deaths due to mesothelioma (shown in Table 9.8) is known to be greater than the number of cases reported to ODIN.

Injuries at work *(Table 9.9)*

The appropriate 'responsible person' is required to report injuries arising from workplace activities to HSC or the local authority under the Reporting of Injuries, Diseases and Dangerous Occurrences Regulations 1995 (RIDDOR 95). This includes fatal injuries, non-fatal major injuries, as defined by the Regulations, and other injuries causing incapacity for work for more than 3 days. As of 1 April 2001, cases could be alternatively reported to an Incident Contact Centre (ICC), based at Caerphilly.

HSE gets to know about virtually all workplace fatalities. However, it is known that employers and others do not report all non-fatal reportable injuries. To estimate the level of under-reporting by employers, HSE place questions each year with the Labour Force Survey (LFS), asking respondents if they have suffered a workplace injury in the past year.

The results from the LFS show that in Great Britain employers now report 44% of reportable injuries. Although the reporting level is higher now than in 1990, LFS results are indicating that the rate of improvement in non-fatal injury rates is slowing more recently. The self-employed report fewer that 1 in 20 reportable injuries.

9.1 Hospital and family health services
England and Wales

			England					Wales				
			1997	1998	1999	2000	2001	1997	1998	1999	2000	2001
Hospital services[1]												
Average daily number of available beds	KNMY	Thousands	194	190	186	186	.. KNHY	15.2	14.9	14.7	14.6	14.4
Average daily occupation of beds:												
All departments	KNMX	"	157	157	154	156	.. KNHX	12.0	11.8	11.8	11.7	11.7
Psychiatric departments	KNMW	"	39	37	34	34	.. KNGZ	2.9	2.7	2.6	2.5	2.5
Persons waiting for admission at 31 March[2]	KNMV	"	1 158	1 298	1 037	1 007	1 035 KNGY	69.9	61.8	75.5	61.1	65.6
Finished consultant episodes	KNLZ		..	..	..	..	..					
Day case admissions	KNLY	"	3 071	3 421	3 593	3 620	.. KNBZ	121.5	126.2	121.9	133.4	130.0
Ordinary admissions	KIBS	"	8 459	8 563	8 604	8 645	.. KNEO	521.1	522.7	515.1	513.8	509.4
Out-patients												
New cases	KNLX	"	11 529	11 778	12 136	12 466	12 714 KNBY	693.3	691.4	694.1	698.9	697.1
Total attendances	KNLW	"	41 635	42 154	43 041	43 569	44 008 KNBX	2 653.3	2 678.4	2 706.2	2 736.8	2 761.9
Accident and Emergency:												
New cases	KOTH	"	12 794	12 811	13 167	12 953	12 853 KTCO	826.6	831.0	868.0	853.7	877.7
Total attendances	KOTI	"	14 364	14 280	14 629	14 293	14 044 KTCP	997.9	982.0	1 026.4	986.2	1 009.8
Ward attendances	KOTJ	"	1 034	1 068	1 073	1 078	1 089 KTCQ	..	..	..	..	..
Family health services[3]												
Medical services:												
Doctors on the list[4]	KNKX	Numbers	..	..	..	..	.. KNBR	1 753	1 749	1 761	1 775	1 785
Number of UPEs[5]	LQZZ		27 099	27 392	27 591	27 704	27 843 ZCMA	1 756	1 751	1 767	1 880	1 796
Number of patients per doctor	KNKW	"	1 878	1 866	1 845	1 853	1 841 KNBQ	1 706	1 713	1 694	1 695	1 685
Paid to doctors[6]	KNKV	£ millions	3 131	3 242	3 348	..	.. KNBP	179	186	201	213	222
Pharmaceutical services:[7,8]												
Number of prescription forms	KWUK	Millions	287	291	294	300	315					
Number of prescription items	KWUL	"	500	513	530	552	587 KNBO	40	41	42	44	47
Total cost	KWUM	£ millions	4 920	5 231	5 620	5 966	6 494 KNBN	352	373	404	434	472
Average total cost per prescription	KWUN	£	9.80	10.20	10.60	11.00	11.10 KNBK	8.89	9.17	9.60	9.92	10.00
Income from patients	KWUO	£ millions	321	341	367	387	408 KNBM	19	20	22	23	23
General Dental service[9]:												
Principals on an FHSA/HA list at 30 September[10]	KIAZ	Numbers	15 509	15 820	16 089	16 276	16 451 KIBG	863	879	913	928	931
Number of adult courses of treatments[11]	KIBA	Thousands	25 268	26 171	25 915	26 353	26 318 KIBH	1 446	1 514	1 525	1 557	1 564
Number of adult patients accepted into continuing care provision at 30 September[12]	KIBB	"	19 383	16 721	16 649	16 813	16 793 KIBI	1 184	1 043	1 055	1 074	1 063
Number of children accepted into capitation at 30 September[12]	KIBC	"	7 367	6 775	6 821	6 845	6 784 KIBJ	434	405	408	411	403
Gross expenditure[13]	KIBD	£ thousands	1 347 577	1 437 727	1 477 423	1 554 885	1 627 817 KIBK	76 816	82 262	86 093	91 498	95 222
Paid by patients[13]	KIBE	"	388 436	419 621	431 189	453 062	468 578 KIBL	20 665	22 293	23 456	24 634	24 374
Paid out of public funds[13]	KIBF	"	959 141	1 018 106	1 046 234	1 101 823	1 159 239 KIBM	56 151	59 969	62 637	66 864	70 848
General ophthalmic services:												
Sight tests[11,14]	KNJL	Thousands	6 991	6 992	9 399	9 567	9 807 KNBD	477	477	631	659	668
Pairs of spectacles for which NHS vouchers redeemed[11]	KNJK	"	3 935	3 777	3 662	3 575	3 607 KNBC	300	288	275	273	273
Cost of services (gross)	KNJJ	£ millions	241	240	281	292	302 KNBA	18	18	20	21	22
Paid out of public funds:												
For sight testing	KNJH	"	102.8	103.5	146.1	156.1	162.6 KMZZ	7	7	10	10	11
For cost of vouchers[11]	KNHZ	"	138.6	136.0	134.4	135.9	138.9 KMZX	10	10	9	10	10

1 Data shown reflect data for the financial year commencing the year in the heading (for example, the figures under 1999 represent 1999/2000 data). Out-patient figures do not include accident and emergency figures or ward attenders which are given separately. Information on general practitioner maternity clinics is not collected separately in England but is included for Wales.

2 People awaiting elective admission at NHS Trusts in England and Wales, as an inpatient or a day case.

3 Welsh FHS expenditure and income is based upon cash payments and receipts in each financial year, as accrued gross expenditure is not available in a common format for all years shown in this series.

4 For Wales, Principals providing unrestricted services as at 1 October

5 UPE's include Unrestricted Principals, PMS Contracted GP's and PMS salaried GP's. UPE data are at 1 October.

6 For Wales, includes PFMA but excludes GPFH drugs and payments to providers.

7 Welsh data are based on pricing bureau totals of prescriptions dispensed in a calendar year and paid during the financial year. Data shown reflect data for the financial year commencing the year in the heading (for example, the figures under 1999 represent 1999/2000 data).

8 The data cover all prescription items dispensed by community pharmacists and appliance contractors, dispensing doctors and prescriptions submitted by prescribing doctors for items personally administered. Total cost refers to the cost of the drug less discounts and includes on cost allowance, dispensing fees, container allowance, oxygen payments and VAT. The figures for income from patients are for financial years. Figures include charges retained by pharmacists, received by dispensing doctors, income from pre-payment certificates, and recoveries from patients.

9 See chapter text. Welsh Dental Service data excludes refunds of dental charges

10 Principals only. Assistants and vocational trainees are not included. Some dentists may have a contract with more than one Family Health Service /Health Authority. These dentists have been counted once only.

11 Data shown reflect data for the financial year commencing the year in the heading (for example, the figures under 1999 represent 1999/2000 data).

12 Figures for 1998 onwards are affected by the shortening of the registration period to 15 months.

13 Figures for England are for the financial year and are based on provisional outturn figures.

14 Number of NHS sight tests paid for by FHSAs/HAs in the period.

Sources: Department of Health;
National Assembly for Wales: 029 2082 5080

9.2 Hospital and primary care services
Scotland

	Unit	1991	1992	1993	1994	1995	1996	1997	1998	1999	2000	2001
Hospital and community services												
In-patients[1,2]:												
Average available staffed beds	KDEA	Thousands	50.6	48.7	46.7	44.2	42.4	40.6	38.4	36.8	35.2	33.5	32.1
Average occupied beds:												
All departments	KDEB	"	41.2	39.5	38.1	35.9	34.3	32.8	30.9	29.5	28.2	26.9	25.8
Psychiatric and learning disability	KDEC	"	16.3	15.5	14.6	13.2	12.6	11.7	10.8	10.0	9.1	8.3	7.6
Discharges or deaths[3]	KDED	"	912	920	942	952	960	973	965	978	977	965	957
Outpatients:[2,4]												
New cases	KDEE	"	2 403	2 426	2 457	2 503	2 577	2 666	2 675	2 715	2 734	2 766	2 744
Total attendances	KDEF	"	5 971	6 005	6 086	6 145	6 241	6 338	6 272	6 331	6 424	6 451	6 382
Medical and dental staff:[5]	JYXO	Numbers	7 890	8 069	8 078	8 317	8 524	8 774	9 098	9 157	9 367	9 325	9 702
Whole-time	KDEG	"	5 481	5 625	5 767	5 937	6 102	6 433	6 707	7 052	7 202	6 896	7 250
Part-time	KDEH	"	1 862	1 883	1 730	1 827	1 854	1 819	1 886	1 613	1 685	1 966	2 010
Honorary	JYXN	"	547	561	582	563	579	534	522	506	495	495	472
Professional and technical staff[6]:												
Whole-time	KDEI	"	9 387	9 759	9 953	10 062	10 452	10 584	10 740	10 884	11 261	11 261	11 705
Part-time	KDEJ	"	2 782	3 127	3 434	3 753	4 075	4 370	4 738	4 928	5 218	5 483	5 852
Nursing and midwifery staff[7]:												
Whole-time	KDEK	"	34 302	34 053	33 284	32 956	32 693	32 560	32 218	32 156	32 356	32 401	33 334
Part-time	KDEL	"	29 887	30 709	30 459	30 532	30 580	29 917	29 736	29 178	29 242	29 131	29 004
Administrative and clerical staff[8]:												
Whole-time	KDEM	"	13 718	14 447	15 125	15 723	15 815	15 155	14 707	14 564	14 541	14 710	15 361
Part-time	KDEN	"	5 276	5 815	6 113	6 624	7 005	6 986	7 174	7 265	7 456	7 677	8 075
Domestic, transport, etc, staff[9]:												
Whole-time	KDEO	"	11 622	10 805	10 205	9 574	9 037	8 596	8 187	8 090	7 972	7 848	7 625
Part-time	KDEP	"	16 167	15 753	15 403	14 464	14 105	13 554	13 082	12 716	12 424	12 272	11 522
Cost of services (gross)[10]	KDEQ	£ millions	2 503.6	2 768.0	2 940.5	3 050.5	3 269.5	3 430.6	3 610.3	3 856.0	4 309.7	4 862.6	5 378.6
Payments by patients[10]	KDER	"	1.5	2.0	2.3	0.4	–	–	–	–	–	–	–
Payments out of public funds[10]	KDES	"	2 502.1	2 766.0	2 938.2	3 050.1	3 269.5	3 430.6	3 610.3	3 855.9	4 309.7	4 862.6	5 378.6
Primary care services												
Medical services												
Doctors on the list[11]:												
Principals[12]	KDET	Numbers	3 379	3 421	3 456	3 490	3 524	3 573	3 625	3 660	3 698	3 707	3 756
Assistants	KDEU	"	24	31	22	25	28	22	22	27	19	25	39
Average number of patients per principal doctor[13]	KDEV	"	1 580	1 556	1 542	1 524	1 506	1 488	1 468	1 450	1 441	1 425	1 409
Payments to doctor[14]	KDEW	£ millions	247.2	263.8	275.3	291.7	311.9	333.2	356.4	365.9	377.5	404.7	429.6
Pharmaceutical services[15]												
Prescriptions dispensed	KDEX	Millions	44.31	46.10	48.18	49.27	51.08	54.62	56.64	58.52	60.36	62.34	65.56
Payments to pharmacists (gross)	KDEY	£ millions	329.8	370.2	406.1	434.9	474.2	543.4	588.4	627.2	693.7	731.0	788.6
Average gross cost per prescription	KDEZ	£	7.44	8.03	8.43	8.83	9.28	9.95	10.39	10.72	11.49	11.73	12.03
Dental services[16]												
Dentists on list[17]	KDFA	Numbers	1 676	1 702	1 772	1 763	1 764	1 772	1 798	1 854	1 833	1 831	1 866
Number of courses of treatment completed	KDFB	Thousands	2 485	2 569	2 647	2 723	2 711	2 825	3 406	3 349	3 406	3 395	3 390
Payments to dentists (gross)[18]	KDFC	£ millions	132.8	133.6	128.4	136.1	137.3	139.2	154.9	157.5	160.6	162.9	165.1
Payments by patients	KDFD	"	41.6	40.5	40.0	42.2	41.7	41.4	45.9	47.4	48.8	50.6	52.3
Payments out of public funds[18]	KDFE	"	91.3	93.2	88.4	93.9	95.6	97.8	109.0	110.1	111.8	112.3	112.9
Average gross cost per course	KDFF	£	40.0	39.0	37.0	38.0	38.0	40.1	36.5	38.0	38.0	37.0	38.0
General ophthalmic services												
Number of sight tests given[19]	KDFG	Thousands	477	537	568	614	618	635	656	657	850	861	877
Number of pairs of glasses supplied[20]	KDFH	"	374	404	463	473	461	474	488	485	494	439	462
Payments out of public funds for sight testing and dispensing	KDFK	£ millions	16.4	19.7	22.2	24.4	25.8	27.7	29.1	29.8	32.0	33.1	38.6

1 Excludes joint user and contractual hospitals.
2 In year to 31 March.
3 Includes transfers out and emergency inpatients treated in day bed units.
4 Including attendances at accident and emergency consultant clinics.
5 At 30 September. Figures exclude officers holding honorary locum appointments. There is an element of double counting of "heads" in this table as doctors can hold more than one contract. For example, they may hold contracts of different type, eg part time and honorary. Doctors holding two or more contracts of the same type, eg part time, are not double counted. Doctors, whose sum of contracts amounts to whole time, are classed as such.
6 At 30 September. Comprises Scientific and Professional, Professions Allied to Medicine and Technical staff
7 At 30 September. Excludes nurse teachers, nurses in training and students on '1992' courses. Between 1992 and 1993 the criterion for excluding nursing staff on low hours was changed from 0.25 hours to 2 hours. This partially accounts for any decrease in staff numbers between these two years.
8 At 30 September. Comprises Senior Management and Administrative and Clerical staff.
9 At 30 September. Comprises Ambulance, Works, Ancillary, Trades and Health Care Assistant staff.

10 These figures are for Health Boards only and do not include the 2 NHS Trusts in 1992/93, 17 in 1993/94, 39 in 1994/95 and 47 in 1995/96. Estimated from financial years.
11 At 1 October.
12 Unrestricted principals in post.
13 Unrestricted principals: establishment.
14 Data relate to financial year, eg 1997 data are for year ending 31 March 1998. As 1994/95 data are unavailable for Dumfries & Galloway Health Board, 1993/94 data have been substituted for that board only.
15 For prescriptions dispensed in calendar year by all community pharmacists (including stock orders), dispensing doctors and appliance suppliers.
16 Data refer to financial year (eg 1991 data are for year ending 31 March 1992).
17 Comprises principals only.
18 Includes capitation, continuing care, weighted entry and item of service fees.
19 This figure represents sight tests paid for by health boards and GOS(s) ST(v) claimants. From 1994, data refer to financial years (eg 1994 data are for year ending 31 March 1995).
20 Includes hospital eye service. From 1994, data refer to financial years (eg 1994 data are for year ending 31 March 1995).

Source: Common Services Agency and The Scottish Executive: 0131 551 8899

9.3 Hospital and general health services
Northern Ireland

		Unit	1992	1993	1994	1995	1996	1997	1998	1999	2000	2001
Hospital services[1]												
In-patients:												
Beds available[2]	KDGA	Numbers	11 712	10 878	10 356	10 054	9 475	9 007	8 819	8 639	8 571	8 419
Average daily occupation of beds	KDGB	*Per cent*	*77.8*	*77.9*	*78.1*	*77.7*	*78.9*	*80.8*	*81.9*	*81.5*	*82.0*	*83.0*
Discharges or deaths[3]	KDGC	Thousands	275	290	298	304	300	306	338	332	333	328
Out-patients[4]:												
New cases	KDGD	"	819	836	873	937	933	952	962	980	994	997
Total attendances	KDGE	"	1 969	1 967	2 051	2 087	2 072	2 083	2 091	2 106	2 113	2 131
General health services												
Medical services[1]												
Doctors (principals) on the list[5,6]	KDGF	Numbers	935	953	991	1 005	1 028	1 039	1 042	1 054	1 066	1 073
Number of patients per doctor	KDGG	"	1 808	1 779	1 743	1 731	1 698	1 690	1 693	1 679	1 662	1 651
GrossPayments to doctors[7]	KDGH	£ thousand	56 529	60 975	62 849	65 130	67 872	69 889	71 385	78 604	82 471	84 664
Pharmaceutical services[8]												
Prescription forms dispensed	KDGI	Thousands	10 498	11 291	11 152	12 017	12 802	12 855	13 116	13 453	13 666	14 277
Number of prescriptions	KDGJ	"	17 496	18 660	18 560	19 893	21 203	22 047	22 754	23 249	23 985	24 705
Gross cost	KDGK	£ thousand	146 925	165 638	173 064	197 579	219 978	236 746	248 845	266 535	278 405	303 489
Charges	KDGL	"	5 582	6 175	6 299	6 255	6 028	6 607	6 853	8 183	8 499	9 074
Net Cost	KDGM	"	141 343	159 463	166 764	191 324	213 950	230 139	241 992	258 353	269 906	294 415
Average gross cost per prescription	KDGN	£	8.40	8.90	9.44	9.93	10.36	10.73	10.91	11.46	11.61	12.28
Dental services[8,9]												
Dentists on the list[5]	KDGO	Numbers	523	541	568	581	596	609	634	660	674	689
Number of courses of paid treatment	KDGP	Thousands	780	801	825	832	928	1 053	1 088	1 097	1 128	1 147
Gross cost[10]	KDGQ	£ thousand	47 701	43 904	46 318	48 780	51 512	53 733	56 835	58 712	61 251	63 529
Patients[10]	KDGR	"	11 036	10 378	11 231	11 530	11 870	12 433	13 686	14 358	15 078	16 041
Contributions (Net cost)[10]	KDGS	"	36 665	33 525	35 086	37 250	39 642	41 300	43 149	44 354	46 173	47 489
Average gross cost per paid treatment	KDGT	£	61	55	56	59	56	51	52	54	54	55
Ophthalmic services[8]												
Number of sight tests given[11]	KDGU	Thousands	142	169	182	196	212	227	237	298	305	326
Number of optical appliances supplied[12]	KDGV	"	114	133	139	146	153	159	161	157	160	166
Cost of service (gross)[13]	KDGW	£ thousand	5 555	7 363	7 127	8 568	9 555	10 271	10 452	11 365	11 975	12 490
Health and social services[14]												
Medical and dental staff:												
Whole-time	KDGZ	Numbers	2 226	2 209	2 358	2 053	2 107	2 156	2 196	2 231	2 224	2 281
Part-time	KDHA	"	511	554	694	1 154	1 094	1 041	1 009	1 014	580	597
Nursing and midwifery staff:												
Whole-time	KDHB	"	12 381	11 445	11 047	10 896	10 578	10 114	10 117	10 135	9 926	9 828
Part-time	KDHC	"	7 417	7 952	8 662	9 169	8 943	9 015	8 287	8 813	7 591	7 814
Administrative and clerical staff:												
Whole-time	KDHD	"	6 573	6 696	7 006	7 078	7 055	6 915	7 019	7 230	7 373	7 536
Part-time	KDHE	"	1 924	2 050	2 186	2 306	2 518	2 708	2 776	2 910	2 972	3 136
Professional and technical staff:												
Whole-time	KDHF	"	2 695	2 695	2 786	2 862	2 939	2 933	3 014	3 177	3 642	3 762
Part-time	KDHG	"	636	710	804	921	985	1 060	1 146	1 226	1 283	1 369
Social services staff(excluding casual home helps):												
Whole-time	KDHH	"	3 607	3 550	3 480	3 470	3 441	3 349	3 262	3 319	3 017	3 127
Part-time	KDHI	"	1 707	1 766	1 933	2 110	2 250	2 394	2 241	2 358	868	911
Ancillary and other staff:												
Whole-time	KDHJ	"	4 954	4 679	4 364	3 982	3 812	3 569	3 423	3 426	3 506	3 472
Part-time	KDHK	"	4 862	4 767	4 609	3 685	3 558	3 482	3 558	3 913	4 508	4 925
Cost of services (gross)[15]	KDHL	£ thousand	947 354	1 002 326	1 043 745	1 111 507	1 120 563	1 153 741	1 292 348	1 422 920	1 576 657	1 639 283
Payments by recipients	KDHM	"	12 569	13 189	20 629	32 685	40 725	49 498	59 484	65 533	71 411	78 478
Payments out of public funds	KDHN	"	934 785	989 137	1 023 116	1 078 822	1 079 838	1 104 243	1 232 864	1 357 387	1 505 246	1 560 805

1 Financial Year.
2 Average available beds in wards open overnight during the year.
3 Includes transfers to other hospitals.
4 Includes consultant outpatient clinics and Accident and Emergency departments.
5 At beginning of period.
6 Doctors include assistants.
7 These costs refer to the majority of non-cash limited services: further expenditure under GMS is allocated through HSS Boards on a cash limited basis.
8 From 1995 onwards figures are taken from financial year.
9 Due to changes in the Dental Contract which came into force in October 1990 dentists are paid under a combination of headings relating to Capitation and Continuing Care patients.
10 Prior to 1992, headings read 'Payments to Dentists (Gross)', 'Payments by Patients', 'Payments out of Public Funds'.
11 Excluding sight tests given in hospitals and under the school health service and in the home.

12 Relates to the number of vouchers supplied and excludes repair/replace spectacles.
13 Gross cost is defined as net ingredient costs plus on-cost, fees and other payments.
14 Workforce figures until 1999 refer to 31st December and are taken from the Trust and Board payroll system. Figures from 2000 onwards are at 30th September and are taken from the Trust and Board Human Resource Management Systems. Figures for 2000 onwards exclude all home helps and all agency/bank staff but include Ambulance and Works staff in the Ancillary & Other Staff category. As a result, backward comparison of the workforce is not advisable as definitions differ. Some figures for 2000 have been revised.
15 Figures relate to the costs of the hospital, community health and personal social services, and have been estimated from financial year data.

Sources: Central Service Agency Northern Ireland: 028 9032 4431; Dept of Health, Social Services & Public Safety Northern Ireland: 028 9052 2509;
(Figures on Hospital Services: 028 9052 2800)

9.4 Health and personal social services: workforce summary
Great Britain

Numbers or whole-time equivalent

		1992	1993	1994	1995	1996	1997	1998	1999	2000	2001
Health service staff and practitioners at 30 Sep:											
Medical staff: total	KDBC	53 987	55 632	56 736	60 172	62 176	64 316	67 408	69 089	70 939	73 206
Hospital medical staff: total	KDBD	50 793	52 476	53 787	57 299	59 592	61 937	65 088	66 812	68 767	71 107
Consultant	KDBE	17 846	18 251	18 808	20 246	21 066	21 699	23 139	24 250	25 067	26 106
Staff grade	KADJ	819	1 230	1 536	2 037	2 440	2 785	3 458	3 868	4 423	4 720
Associate specialist	KDBF	960	1 032	1 013	1 128	1 223	1 340	1 439	1 527	1 572	1 609
Registrar group[1]	KWUG	..	..	..	..	11 898	12 435	12 863	13 299	13 372	13 826
Senior registrar	KDBG	3 994	4 130	4 281	4 540	..	..	..	..	..	..
Registrar	KDBH	7 132	7 103	7 273	7 294	..	..	..	..	..	..
Senior house officer	KDBI	13 863	14 586	14 942	15 661	16 616	17 353	17 760	17 518	17 945	18 377
House officer	KADK	3 798	3 792	3 781	4 003	4 025	4 163	4 287	4 364	4 518	4 560
Hospital practitioner	KDBL	183	183	178	197	212	198	220	230	231	223
Clinical assistant	KDBM	2 189	2 162	1 964	2 182	2 094	1 924	1 907	1 744	1 638	1 684
Other staff[2]	KDBK	10	8	11	11	18	38	16	11	1	1
Community health medical staff[3]	KDBN	3 194	3 156	2 948	2 873	2 584	2 379	2 320	2 278	2 172	2 100
Dental staff: total	KDBO	2 971	2 973	2 947	3 070	3 127	3 078	3 193	3 147	3 107	3 149
Hospital dental staff: total	KDBP	1 546	1 573	1 597	1 687	1 737	1 696	1 807	1 816	1 781	1 816
Consultant	KDBQ	541	521	537	549	556	524	570	581	580	578
Staff grade	KADL	13	24	39	54	67	86	99	113	118	135
Associate specialist	KDBR	70	69	62	69	65	62	68	70	73	74
Registrar group[1]	LQMZ	..	..	..	..	..	..	309	314	295	311
Senior registrar	KDBS	122	135	124	123	138	169	..	..	..	..
Registrar	KDBT	188	184	178	186	183	125	..	..	..	..
Senior house officer	KDBU	300	353	394	446	490	491	531	496	497	513
Dental house officer	KDBV	143	126	101	86	68	58	59	68	60	61
Hospital practitioner	KDBX	15	17	20	17	23	22	21	23	21	18
Clinical assistant	KDBY	154	142	141	158	145	152	144	146	136	126
Other staff[2]	KDBW	2	2	2	–	3	6	5	6	–	–
Community health dental staff[3]	KDBZ	1 425	1 400	1 350	1 383	1 390	1 382	1 386	1 331	1 326	1 332
Non-medical staff[4]: total	KWUH	906 236	899 234	876 630	804 148	856 732	849 426	855 305	870 921	890 282	927 831
Nursing and midwifery staff:[5,6] (excluding agency): total	KDCA	467 723	446 056	429 214	387 441	410 692	407 762	409 041	415 788	423 733	437 417
qualified	KSBR	300 698	295 245	291 070	282 202	300 371	298 485	299 652	303 645	309 678	320 685
unqualified	KSBS	115 431	116 360	116 138	99 946	106 182	106 313	106 777	109 690	111 932	114 532
learners	KSBT	44 879	27 560	13 945	4 582	2 805	2 357	2 177	1 962	2 054	2 201
unknown	KSBV	6 714	6 891	8 061	710	1 334	607	435	491	69	–
All Professional and Technical staff (excluding works)	KSBM	107 367	109 463	111 597	106 544	118 403	120 439	123 902	128 116	131 943	138 348
Health care assistants	KWUI	..	..	..	13 090	18 025	19 268	22 026	22 746	24 919	30 047
Support staff	KWUJ	..	..	..	74 540	75 836	72 608	71 043	69 883	68 449	69 245
Ancillary, Works and Maintenance	KSBN	123 100	118 867	110 577	29 466	27 603	26 037	25 131	24 468	23 962	23 013
Administrative and Clerical staff	KSBO	179 300	180 820	186 446	172 948	183 049	183 112	184 711	190 421	197 327	209 004
Ambulance staff	KSBP	21 744	21 424	21 379	16 744	18 655	18 751	18 382	18 552	19 209	19 888
Others	KSBQ	7 165	639	1 250	3 180	4 159	1 079	906	780	746	711

9.4 Health and personal social services: workforce summary
Great Britain
continued

Numbers or whole-time equivalent

		1992	1993	1994	1995	1996	1997	1998	1999	2000	2001
Family Health services:[7]											
General medical practitioners at 1 Oct:											
All practitioners: total	GPYL	..	..	..	..	..	..	..	37 125	37 572	38 164
All practitioners (excluding GP Retainers)	LQZN	33 834	34 134	34 421	34 594	34 825	35 205	35 611	35 952	36 225	36 753
Unrestricted Principals & equivalents (UPE's)	LQZO	31 065	31 447	31 767	31 945	32 164	32 477	32 801	33 050	33 186	33 383
of which GMS UP's	LQZP	31 065	31 447	31 767	31 945	32 164	32 477	32 414	32 140	31 869	29 474
PMS contracted	LQZQ PTKJ	..	..	..	..	..	..	324	837	1 046	3 909
PMS salaried	GRGB	..	..	..	..	..	..	63	71	271	
Restricted principals	LQZS	152	161	156	137	126	111	106	97	94	102
Assistants	LQZT	521	539	626	684	890	891	750	690	671	533
GP Registrars[8]	LQZU	2 067	1 956	1 841	1 790	1 605	1 678	1 830	1 903	2 028	2 278
of which GMS[7]	LQZV	2 067	1 956	1 841	1 790	1 605	1 678	1 796	1 825	1 920	1 956
Salaried Doctors	LQZW	..	..	..	..	..	..	60	118	159	160
PMS Other[9]	LQZX	..	..	..	..	..	..	12	46	37	251
Associates	LQZY	29	31	31	38	40	48	52	50	51	49
GP Retainers	GPYM	..	..	..	..	..	..	..	1 181	1 347	1 408
General dental practitioners: total[10]	KDCQ	18 019	18 467	18 600	18 736	19 139	19 598	20 216	20 840	21 316	21 929
General Dental Service	GPYN	18 019	18 467	18 600	18 736	19 139	19 598	20 216	20 750	21 124	21 462
Personal Dental Service	GPYO	..	..	..	..	..	..	..	90	192	467
Ophthalmic medical practitioners[11]	KDCT	837	789	735	752	766	830	855	814	765	754
Ophthalmic opticians[11]	KDCU	6 997	7 124	7 179	7 445	7 652	7 847	8 160	8 422	8 359	8 692
Personal Social Services staff: total[12]	KDDE	235 240	232 911	237 752	233 861	233 655	229 439	223 500	221 700	217 200	212 000
Management, administration and ancillary staff[13]	KADS	29 433	..	..	..	..	..	..	..	..	..
Home help service	KSBU	58 004	57 593	59 391	56 961	55 430	53 573	50 417	47 227	42 583	40 200
Field Social Workers[14]	KSBX	26 509	28 850	29 820	31 926	32 140	32 990	33 400	33 900	34 700	35 200
Day care establishments staff	KADV	28 596	30 221	31 270	31 109	31 605	30 839	30 300	30 800	30 800	29 500
Residential care staff	KADW	78 918	74 038	72 155	68 651	67 975	65 422	62 100	59 200	56 600	53 800
All other staff[13]	KADX	5 049	..	..	..	..	..	..	..	..	..

1 Includes Specialist Registrar (SpR), Senior Registrar and Registrar. The SpR grade was introduced formally on 1 April 1996.
2 Figures include Senior Hospital Medical/Dental Officers (SHMO) without an allowance and other ungraded staff.
3 Whole-time equivalent. Figures exclude locums and occasional seasonal staff.
4 1995 data do not include Wales. A new system for classifying NHS non-medical staff was used for the first time in September 1995 non-medical workforce census classifying staff according to what they do (known as new occupation codes). Data for years prior to 1995 for all classes of non-medical staff are incomparable.
5 Excludes bank nurses for Wales.
6 Nursing total includes qualified, unqualified and others only.
7 GP Registrars in GMS Partnerships.
8 GP Registrars were formerly referred to as Trainees.

9 PMS other includes 2 Salaried Restricted Principals who are working in salaried GP's in Scotland.
10 Includes principals, assistants and Vocational Dental Practioners and PDS dentists not working in the GDS. Some dentists may have a contract with more than one Health Authority. These dentists have been counted only once. PDS pilots are only in operation in England and not the whole of Great Britian.
11 Figures for England and Wales relate to 31 December. Figures for Scotland relate to 31 March of the following year. OMPs and OOs holding contracts with FHSAs/HAs and/or Scottish Health Boards to carry out NHS sight tests. OOs with contracts with more than one Health Board and/or a Health Board and a FHSA/HA will be counted more than once.
12 Figures are for England only.
13 Breakdown for England not available in this form from 1993.
14 Includes care managers from 1993.

Sources: Scottish Health Service Common Services Agency;
Department of Health;
National Assembly for Wales

9.5 Deaths: analysed by cause
International Statistical Classification of Diseases, Injuries and Causes of Death
Ninth Revision 1979 and Tenth Revision 1999.

Numbers

	ICD-9 code	England and Wales				
		1996	1997	1998	1999	2000
Total deaths		560 135	555 281	555 015	556 118	535 664
Deaths from natural causes	001-799	541 429	536 453	536 396	537 166	516 803
Certain infectious and parasitic diseases	001-139	3 637	3 496	3 410	3 613	3 767
Intestinal infectious diseases	001-009	339	384	418	476	547
Respiratory and other tuberculosis including late effects	010-018,137	476	437	453	437	427
Meningococcal infection	036	235	242	210	217	199
Viral hepatitis	070	150	165	173	179	200
AIDS (HIV - disease)	042-044	491	259	163	155	182
Neoplasms	140-239	139 459	137 618	138 306	136 181	134 793
Malignant neoplasms	140-208	137 459	135 647	136 329	134 135	132 686
Malignant neoplasm of oesophagus	150	5 835	5 855	5 952	6 040	6 061
Malignant neoplasm of stomach	151	6 756	6 613	6 442	6 139	5 779
Malignant neoplasm of colon	153	10 492	10 448	10 170	9 911	9 554
Malignant neoplasm of rectum and anus	154.1-154.8	4 451	4 177	4 182	4 059	4 024
Malignant neoplasm of pancreas	157	5 848	5 782	5 801	5 956	6 105
Malignant neoplasm of trachea, bronchus and lung	162	30 810	29 976	30 199	29 493	29 029
Malignant neoplasm of skin	172	1 361	1 378	1 468	1 476	1 536
Malignant neoplasm of breast	174-175	12 246	12 047	11 835	11 670	11 433
Malignant neoplasm of cervix uteri	180	1 315	1 225	1 158	1 107	1 106
Malignant neoplasm of prostate	185	8 742	8 523	8 573	8 533	8 293
Leukaemia	204-208	3 464	3 587	3 551	3 680	3 570
Diseases of the blood and blood-forming organs and certain disorders involving the immune mechanism	279-289	2 058	2 056	1 978	1 907	1 829
Endocrine, nutritional and metabolic diseases	240-278	7 430	7 335	7 501	7 508	7 209
Diabetes mellitus	250	5 994	5 890	5 938	5 963	5 773
Mental and behavioural disorders	290-319	9 295	9 725	10 430	11 173	10 865
Vascular and unspecified dementia	290	6 592	6 731	7 124	7 654	7 173
Alcohol abuse (inc. alcoholic psychosis)	291,303	264	344	350	347	331
Drug dependence and non-dependent abuse of drugs	292,304-305	683	736	895	935	1 049
Diseases of the nervous system and sense organs	320-389	9 772	9 772	10 035	10 192	9 632
Meningitis (including meningococcal)	320-322	245	224	216	182	206
Alzheimer's disease	331.0	2 141	2 185	2 374	2 406	2 182
Diseases of the circulatory system	390-459	237 669	228 446	226 677	219 087	207 228
Ischaemic heart diseases	410-414	129 047	122 432	121 037	115 119	108 418
Cerebrovascular diseases	430-438	59 723	57 747	57 516	56 051	52 516
Diseases of the respiratory system	460-519	88 630	92 517	90 192	97 755	92 461
Influenza	487	179	347	129	585	509
Pneumonia	480-486	54 137	56 719	54 631	59 273	56 329
Bronchitis, emphysema and other chronic obstructive pulmonary diseases	490-492,496	24 799	25 097	24 878	26 114	23 538
Asthma	493	1 349	1 439	1 366	1 364	1 272
Diseases of the digestive system	520-579	19 946	20 406	21 025	21 698	22 134
Gastric and duodenal ulcer	531-533	4 111	3 959	3 935	4 011	4 007
Chronic liver disease	571	3 789	4 107	4 494	4 718	4 770
Diseases of the skin and subcutaneous tissue	680-709	1 075	1 025	1 070	1 152	1 266
Diseases of the musculo-skeletal system and connective tissue	710-739	3 517	3 559	3 566	3 554	3 407
Rheumatoid arthritis and juvenile arthritis	714	789	797	778	697	675
Osteoporosis	733.0-733.1	1 184	1 282	1 273	1 335	1 268
Diseases of the genito-urinary system	580-629	6 752	6 757	6 946	7 299	7 270
Diseases of the kidney and ureter	580-594	4 012	3 767	3 803	3 844	3 799
Complications of pregnancy, childbirth and the puerperium	630-676	41	35	43	30	38
Certain conditions originating in the perinatal period (excludng neonatals)[1]	760-779	149	131	124	116	83
Congenital malformations, deformations and chromasomal abnormalities (excluding neonatals)[1]	740-759	1 227	1 283	1 247	1 194	1 165
Congenital malformations of the nervous system	740-742	123	121	124	104	116
Congenital malformations of the circulatory system	745-747	640	689	643	621	617
Symptoms, signs and abnormal clinical and laboratory findings not elsewhere classified	780-799	10 772	12 292	13 846	14 707	13 656
Senility without mention of psychosis (old age)	797	9 632	11 028	12 615	13 473	12 458
Sudden infant death syndrome	798.0	345	327	236	222	180
Deaths from external causes	E800-E999	16 061	16 311	16 201	16 517	16 526
All accidents	E800-E929	10 479	10 661	10 351	10 625	10 771
Land transport accidents	E800-E829	3 302	3 291	3 023	3 098	2 985
Accidental falls	E880-E888	3 637	3 885	3 865	3 993	4 281
Accidental poisonings	E850-E869	1 089	1 058	1 045	1 030	1 064
Suicide and intentional self-harm	E950-E959	3 445	3 424	3 614	3 690	3 480
Homicide and assault[2]	E960-E969	313	290	285	293	380
Event of undetermined intent	E980-E989	1 798	1 914	1 931	1 886	1 872

9.5 Deaths: analysed by cause
continued International Statistical Classification of Diseases, Injuries and Causes of Death
Ninth Revision 1979 and Tenth Revision 1999.

Numbers

			England and Wales		
				Registration-based bridge-coding exercise[3]	
	ICD-9 code	ICD-10 code	2001	1999	1999
			ICD-10	ICD-9	ICD-10
Total deaths			530 373	553 532	553 532
Deaths from natural causes	001-799	A00-R99	511 667	534 188	534 155
Certain infectious and parasitic diseases	001-139	A00-B99	4 253	3 611	3 902
Intestinal infectious diseases	001-009	A00-A09	777	478	620
Respiratory and other tuberculosis including late effects	010-018,137	A15-A19,B90	446	442	457
Meningococcal infection	036	A39	201	216	218
Viral hepatitis	070	B15-B19	196	176	191
AIDS (HIV - disease)	042-044	B20-B24	180	154	179
Neoplasms	140-239	C00-D48	139 135	135 791	140 281
Malignant neoplasms	140-208	C00-97	135 839	133 749	136 861
Malignant neoplasm of oesophagus	150	C15	6 107	6 031	6 076
Malignant neoplasm of stomach	151	C16	5 606	6 133	6 208
Malignant neoplasm of colon	153	C18	9 436	9 880	10 038
Malignant neoplasm of rectum and anus	154.1-154.8	C20-C21	3 927	4 049	4 102
Malignant neoplasm of pancreas	157	C25	6 011	5 926	5 931
Malignant neoplasm of trachea, bronchus and lung	162	C33-C34	28 728	29 406	29 283
Malignant neoplasm of skin	172	C43	1 470	1 474	1 416
Malignant neoplasm of breast	174-175	C50	11 638	11 613	11 928
Malignant neoplasm of cervix uteri	180	C53	1 039	1 106	1 103
Malignant neoplasm of prostate	185	C61	8 912	8 502	8 827
Leukaemia	204-208	C91-C95	3 781	3 674	3 877
Diseases of the blood and blood-forming organs and certain disorders involving the immune mechanism	279-289	D50-D89	1 000	1 907	1 076
Endocrine, nutritional and metabolic diseases	240-278	E00-E90	7 711	7 485	7 816
Diabetes mellitus	250	E10-E14	6 119	5 949	6 204
Mental and behavioural disorders	290-319	F00-F99	14 143	11 145	13 461
Vascular and unspecified dementia	290	F01,F03	12 572	7 605	11 894
Alcohol abuse (inc. alcoholic psychosis)	291,303	F10	477	338	465
Drug dependence and non-dependent abuse of drugs	292,304-305	F11-F16,F18-F19	798	983	802
Diseases of the nervous system and sense organs	320-389	G00-H95	14 732	10 164	14 795
Meningitis (including meningococcal)	320-322	G00-G03	189	184	183
Alzheimer's disease	331.0	G30	4 579	2 396	4 679
Diseases of the circulatory system	390-459	I00-I99	211 842	218 062	226 438
Ischaemic heart diseases	410-414	I20-I25	105 895	114 467	115 130
Cerebrovascular diseases	430-438	I60-I69	58 517	55 867	61 734
Diseases of the respiratory system	460-519	J00-J99	67 391	96 453	74 831
Influenza	487	J10-J11	38	561	553
Pneumonia	480-486	J12-J18	31 636	58 449	36 241
Bronchitis, emphysema and other chronic obstructive pulmonary diseases	490-492,496	J40-J44	23 700	25 820	26 734
Asthma	493	J45-J46	1268	1 356	1 386
Diseases of the digestive system	520-579	K00-K93	23 386	21 606	21 998
Gastric and duodenal ulcer	531-533	K25-K27	3 802	3 997	3 981
Chronic liver disease	571	K70,K73-K74	5 234	4 675	4 735
Diseases of the skin and subcutaneous tissue	680-709	L00-L99	1 291	1 146	1 142
Diseases of the musculo-skeletal system and connective tissue	710-739	M00-M99	4 588	3 567	4 969
Rheumatoid arthritis and juvenile arthritis	714	M05-M06,M08	970	699	1114
Osteoporosis	733.0-733.1	M80-M81	1 542	1 343	1 710
Diseases of the genito-urinary system	580-629	N00-N99	7 682	7 279	7 255
Diseases of the kidney and ureter	580-594	N00-N29	3 848	3 833	3 900
Complications of pregnancy, childbirth and the puerperium	630-676	O00-O99	42	31	34
Certain conditions originating in the perinatal period (excluding neonatals)[1]	760-779	P00-P96	200	115	137
Congenital malformations, deformations and chromosomal abnormalities (excluding neonatals)[1]	740-759	Q00-Q99	1 280	1 175	1 328
Congenital malformations of the nervous system	740-742	Q00-Q07	119	104	131
Congenital malformations of the circulatory system	745-747	Q20-Q28	592	609	628
Symptoms, signs and abnormal clinical and laboratory findings not elsewhere classified	780-799	R00-R99	13 351	14 651	14 692
Senility without mention of psychosis (old age)	797	R54	11 900	13 407	13 321
Sudden infant death syndrome	798.0	R95	195	222	225
Deaths from external causes	E800-E999	V01-Y89	16 569	16 905	16 938
All accidents	E800-E929	V01-X59,Y85,Y86	10 733	10 901	10 526
Land transport accidents	E800-E829	V01-V89	2 949	3 149	3 149
Accidental falls	E880-E888	W00-W19	2 617	4 056	2 253
Accidental poisonings	E850-E869	X40-X49	1 037	1 101	1 109
Suicide and intentional self-harm	E950-E959	X60-X84,Y87.0	3 264	3 685	3 684
Homicide and assault[2]	E960-E969	X85-Y09,Y87.1	386	292	300
Event of undetermined intent	E980-E989	Y10-Y34, Y87.2	1 803	2 004	2 029

9.5

Deaths: analysed by cause
International Statistical Classification of Diseases, Injuries and Causes of Death
Ninth Revision 1979 and Tenth Revision 1999.

Numbers

	ICD-9 code	ICD-10 code	Scotland						
			1996	1997	1998	1999[3] ICD-9	1999[3] ICD-10	2000	2001
Total deaths			60 654	59 494	59 164	60 281	60 281	57 799	57382
Deaths from natural causes	001-799	A00-R99	58 157	57 121	56 785	57 831	57 803	55 415	54 961
Certain infectious and parasitic diseases	001-139	A00-B99	493	431	486	498	601	476	558
Intestinal infectious diseases	001-009	A00-A09	22	19	34	31	29	51	65
Respiratory and other tuberculosis including late effects	010-018,137	A15-A19,B90	53	71	58	65	64	66	54
Meningococcal infection	036	A39	12	12	20	14	14	18	12
Viral hepatitis	070	B15-B19	15	15	22	17	14	14	6
AIDS (HIV - disease)	042-044	B20-B24	79	41	32	23	28	23	33
Neoplasms	140-239	C00-D48	15 414	15 054	14 907	14 966	15 327	15 255	15 475
Malignant neoplasms	140-208	C00-C97	15 171	14 889	14 752	14 789	15 008	14 958	15 196
Malignant neoplasm of oesophagus	150	C15	723	734	730	776	780	708	752
Malignant neoplasm of stomach	151	C16	699	710	680	650	657	649	678
Malignant neoplasm of colon	153	C18	1 189	1 065	996	1 018	1 017	1 052	1 062
Malignant neoplasm of rectum and anus	154.1-154.8	C20-21	428	477	448	474	479	400	405
Malignant neoplasm of pancreas	157	C25	560	556	607	574	570	633	595
Malignant neoplasm of trachea, bronchus and lung	162	C33-34	4 125	4 106	3 984	3 961	3 906	3 948	3 915
Malignant neoplasm of skin	172	C43	119	118	144	131	127	115	145
Malignant neoplasm of breast	174-175	C50	1 200	1 161	1 147	1 136	1 165	1 122	1 150
Malignant neoplasm of cervix uteri	180	C53	138	144	145	122	120	117	113
Malignant neoplasm of prostate	185	C61	743	708	677	769	790	773	777
Leukaemia	204-208	C91-C95	319	291	329	313	337	325	350
Diseases of the blood and blood-forming organs and certain disorders involving the immune mechanism	279-289	D50-D89	181	200	222	204	129	114	124
Endocrine, nutritional and metabolic diseases	240-278	E00-E90	721	727	797	870	911	828	891
Diabetes mellitus	250	E10-E14	525	510	574	670	700	616	695
Mental and behavioural disorders	290-319	F00-F99	1 595	1 611	1 725	1 901	2 330	2 309	2 425
Vascular and unspecified dementia	290	F01,F03	654	700	690	783	1 697	1 684	1 809
Alcohol abuse (inc. alcoholic psychosis)	291,303	F10	271	292	329	358	334	330	341
Drug dependence and non-dependent abuse of drugs	292,304-305	F11-F16,F18-F19	183	143	182	230	230	245	238
Diseases of the nervous system and sense organs	320-389	G00-H95	852	900	894	971	1 393	1 315	1 243
Meningitis (including meningococcal)	320-322	G00-G03	14	17	6	19	21	15	16
Alzheimer's disease	331.0	G30	105	121	142	140	355	329	324
Diseases of the circulatory system	390-459	I00-I99	26 723	25 911	25 153	24 787	25 284	23 657	22 666
Ischaemic heart diseases	410-414	I20-I25	14 647	14 013	13 419	13 337	13 368	12 412	11914
Cerebrovascular diseases	430-438	I60-I69	7 128	6 959	6 900	6 785	7 183	6 803	6 621
Diseases of the respiratory system	460-519	J00-J99	7 859	7 891	8 011	8 870	6 881	6 547	6 435
Influenza	487	J10-J11	45	83	12	62	62	131	5
Pneumonia	480-486	J12-J18	4 155	4 028	4 064	4 526	2 490	2 312	2 370
Bronchitis, emphysema and other chronic obstructive pulmonary diseases	490-492,496	J40-J44	2 508	2 596	2 662	2 941	3 071	2 825	2 836
Asthma	493	J45-J46	122	113	120	119	117	131	101
Diseases of the digestive system	520-579	K00-K93	2 438	2 428	2 578	2 787	2 829	2 922	3 063
Gastric and duodenal ulcer	531-533	K25-K27	344	306	314	337	321	348	308
Chronic liver disease	571	K70,K73-K74	722	767	806	896	855	956	1 061
Diseases of the skin and subcutaneous tissue	680-709	L00-L99	75	87	94	90	94	89	90
Diseases of the musculo-skeletal system and connective tissue	710-739	M00-M99	252	268	284	295	398	405	357
Rheumatoid arthritis and juvenile arthritis	714	M05-M06,M08	81	89	86	87	121	126	125
Osteoporosis	733.0-733.1	M80-M81	43	40	46	53	63	58	56
Diseases of the genito-urinary system	580-629	N00-N99	839	904	890	936	961	844	969
Diseases of the kidney and ureter	580-594	N00-N29	613	652	644	619	657	563	638
Complications of pregnancy, childbirth and the puerperium	630-676	O00-O99	6	4	5	7	8	8	6
Certain conditions originating in the perinatal period	760-779	P00-P96	181	140	165	137	129	170	167
Congenital malformations, deformations and chromasomal abnormalities	740-759	Q00-Q99	192	182	176	157	163	154	172
Congenital malformations of the nervous system	740-742	Q00-Q07	21	24	23	13	13	25	16
Congenital malformations of the circulatory system	745-747	Q20-Q28	97	84	81	59	56	56	65
Symptoms, signs and abnormal clinical and laboratory findings not elsewhere classified	780-799	R00-R99	336	383	398	355	365	322	320
Senility without mention of psychosis (old age)	797	R54	75	95	111	185	183	161	172
Sudden infant death syndrome	798.0	R95	43	52	37	41	41	33	32
Deaths from external causes	E800-E999	V01-Y89	2 497	2 373	2 379	2 450	2 478	2 384	2 421
All accidents	E800-E929	V01-X59,Y85,Y86	1 371	1 299	1 303	1 359	1 407	1 341	1 350
Land transport accidents	E800-E829	V01-V89	368	387	394	326	326	338	367
Accidental falls	E880-E888	W00-W19	624	620	613	713	714	675	626
Accidental poisonings	E850-E869	X40-X49	20	30	38	30	30	34	50
Suicide and intentional self-harm	E950-E959	X60-X84,Y87.0	597	599	649	637	637	648	609
Homicide and assault	E960-E969	X85-Y09,Y87.1	129	86	94	121	121	93	92
Event of undetermined intent	E980-E989	Y10-Y34, Y87.2	249	275	229	237	251	230	278

9.5
continued

Deaths: analysed by cause
International Statistical Classification of Diseases, Injuries and Causes of Death
Ninth Revision 1979 and Tenth Revision 1999.

Numbers

	ICD-9 code	ICD-10 code	Northern Ireland					
			1996	1997	1998	1999	2000 ICD-9	2001 ICD-10
Total deaths			15 218	14 971	14 993	15 663	14 903	14 513
Deaths from natural causes	001-799	A00-R99	14 620	14 378	14 424	15 054	14 296	13 968
Certain infectious and parasitic diseases	001-139	A00-B99	54	61	53	47	73	117
Intestinal infectious diseases	001-009	A00-A09	1	-	-	1	4	7
Respiratory and other tuberculosis including late effects	010-018,137	A15-A19,B90	12	11	6	7	7	6
Meningococcal infection	036	A39	5	4	6	4	9	4
Viral hepatitis	070	B15-B19	-	2	1	2	6	-
AIDS (HIV - disease)	042-044	B20-B24	4	1	1	2	1	-
Neoplasms	140-239	C00-D48	3 715	3 672	3 769	3 654	3 647	3 802
Malignant neoplasms	140-208	C00-C97	3 623	3 589	3 648	3 552	3 541	3 696
Malignant neoplasm of oesophagus	150	C15	142	144	154	161	150	155
Malignant neoplasm of stomach	151	C16	200	172	215	187	180	174
Malignant neoplasm of colon	153	C18	309	308	329	303	301	271
Malignant neoplasm of rectum and anus	154.1-154.8	C20-C21	109	94	98	95	84	100
Malignant neoplasm of pancreas	157	C25	155	161	154	142	159	176
Malignant neoplasm of trachea, bronchus and lung	162	C33-C34	816	773	775	781	792	782
Malignant neoplasm of skin	172	C43	29	26	28	33	31	37
Malignant neoplasm of breast	174-175	C50	309	267	299	286	289	316
Malignant neoplasm of cervix uteri	180	C53	45	26	33	36	30	24
Malignant neoplasm of prostate	185	C61	211	208	220	195	213	214
Leukaemia	204-208	C91-C95	92	107	93	104	91	87
Diseases of the blood and blood-forming organs and certain disorders involving the immune mechanism	279-289	D50-D89	23	21	24	24	24	32
Endocrine, nutritional and metabolic diseases	240-278	E00-E90	80	105	85	118	122	200
Diabetes mellitus	250	E10-E14	49	77	55	93	89	145
Mental and behavioural disorders	290-319	F00-F99	100	137	145	190	207	381
Vascular and unspecified dementia	290	F01,F03	44	41	58	75	66	298
Alcohol abuse (inc. alcoholic psychosis)	291,303	F10	35	55	35	46	46	75
Drug dependence and non-dependent abuse of drugs	292,304-305	F11-F16,F18-F19	13	20	11	25	38	2
Diseases of the nervous system and sense organs	320-389	G00-H95	236	236	240	285	245	467
Meningitis (including meningococcal)	320-322	G00-G03	7	8	4	3	6	9
Alzheimer's disease	331.0	G30	70	65	80	98	81	211
Diseases of the circulatory system	390-459	I00-I99	6 633	6 506	6 367	6 422	5 776	5 829
Ischaemic heart diseases	410-414	I20-I25	3 856	3 764	3 654	3 568	3 234	3 148
Cerebrovascular diseases	430-438	I60-I69	1 653	1 646	1 602	1 679	1 469	1 531
Diseases of the respiratory system	460-519	J00-J99	2 749	2 665	2 627	3 161	3 019	1 975
Influenza	487	J10-J11	6	8	2	5	39	-
Pneumonia	480-486	J12-J18	1 817	1 775	1 727	2 130	2 027	1 028
Bronchitis, emphysema and other chronic obstructive pulmonary diseases	490-492,496	J40-J44	671	637	627	704	610	584
Asthma	493	J45-J46	31	32	44	38	33	38
Diseases of the digestive system	520-579	K00-K93	483	446	499	507	531	556
Gastric and duodenal ulcer	531-533	K25-K27	102	95	80	80	89	76
Chronic liver disease	571	K70,K73-K74	88	68	104	92	101	133
Diseases of the skin and subcutaneous tissue	680-709	L00-L99	29	25	36	27	21	24
Diseases of the musculo-skeletal system and connective tissue	710-739	M00-M99	35	44	30	54	40	94
Rheumatoid arthritis and juvenile arthritis	714	M05-M06,M08	10	14	6	13	26	31
Osteoporosis	733.0-733.1	M80-M81	9	5	4	11	5	12
Diseases of the genito-urinary system	580-629	N00-N99	254	242	265	242	292	278
Diseases of the kidney and ureter	580-594	N00-N29	191	187	184	173	201	192
Complications of pregnancy, childbirth and the puerperium	630-676	O00-O99	1	-	1	-	-	2
Certain conditions originating in the perinatal period	760-779	P00-P96	68	67	64	69	62	63
Congenital malformations, deformations and chromasomal abnormalities	740-759	Q00-Q99	72	59	70	93	57	83
Congenital malformations of the nervous system	740-742	Q00-Q07	17	5	9	9	14	16
Congenital malformations of the circulatory system	745-747	Q20-Q28	22	20	17	32	19	24
Symptoms, signs and abnormal clinical and laboratory findings not elsewhere classified	780-799	R00-R99	88	92	149	161	180	65
Senility without mention of psychosis (old age)	797	R54	36	36	105	122	146	37
Sudden infant death syndrome	798.0	R95	15	8	4	3	-	2
Deaths from external causes	E800-E999	V01-Y89	598	593	569	609	607	545
All accidents	E800-E929	V01-X59,Y85,Y86	402	428	381	430	364	361
Land transport accidents	E800-E829	V01-V89	125	157	131	134	142	148
Accidental falls	E880-E888	W00-W19	148	137	127	161	131	52
Accidental poisonings	E850-E869	X40-X49	38	38	36	38	25	13
Suicide and intentional self-harm	E950-E959	X60-X84,Y87.0	124	120	126	121	163	141
Homicide and assault	E960-E969	X85-Y09,Y87.1	50	24	36	24	56	20
Event of undetermined intent	E980-E989	Y10-Y34, Y87.2	19	18	24	33	22	17

1 See chapter text re: neonatal deaths.
2 See chapter text re: late registrations.
3 See chapter text re: Bridge coding exercise.

Sources: Office for National Statistics;
General Register Office, Scotland;
Northern Ireland Statistics and Research Agency

9.6 Notifications of infectious diseases

Numbers

		1991	1992	1993	1994	1995	1996	1997	1998	1999	2000	2001
United Kingdom												
Measles	KHQD	11 723	12 318	12 018	23 517	9 017	6 866	4 844	4 540	2 951	2 865	2 661
Mumps	KWNN	3 836	3 169	2 726	3 143	2 400	2 182	2 264	1 917	2 000	3 367	3 433
Rubella	KWNO	9 702	9 150	12 300	9 650	7 674	11 720	4 205	4 064	2 575	2 064	1 782
Whooping cough	KHQE	6 279	2 750	4 718	4 837	2 399	2 721	3 669	1 902	1 461	866	1 059
Scarlet fever	KHQC	6 876	5 978	7 341	8 031	6 863	6 101	4 639	4 708	2 956	2 544	2 320
Dysentery	KHQG	11 527	20 620	7 577	7 538	5 498	2 643	2 427	1 934	1 630	1 613	1 495
Food poisoning	KHQH	59 497	72 139	76 711	91 128	92 604	94 923	105 579	105 060	96 866	98 076	95 752
Typhoid and Paratyphoid fevers	KHQB	288	298	277	390	386	291	249	252	278	205	254
Hepatitis	KWNP	9 856	9 616	6 142	4 285	3 823	2 876	3 601	3 781	4 365	4 530	4 419
Tuberculosis	KHQI	6 078	6 442	6 565	6 230	6 176	6 238	6 367	6 605	6 701	7 100	7 231
Malaria	KWNQ	1 652	1 253	1 281	1 219	1 363	1 743	1 549	1 163	1 038	1 166	1 118
England and Wales[1]												
Measles	KHRD	9 680	10 268	9 612	16 375	7 447	5 614	3 962	3 728	2 438	2 378	2 250
Mumps	KWNR	2 924	2 412	2 153	2 494	1 936	1 747	1 914	1 587	1 691	2 162	2 741
Rubella	KWNS	7 174	6 212	9 724	6 326	6 196	9 081	3 260	3 208	1 954	1 653	1 483
Whooping cough	KHRE	5 201	2 309	4 091	3 964	1 869	2 387	2 989	1 577	1 139	712	888
Scarlet fever	KHRC	5 217	4 645	5 855	6 193	5 296	4 873	3 569	3 339	2 086	1 933	1 756
Dysentery	KHRG	9 935	16 960	6 841	6 956	4 651	2 312	2 274	1 813	1 538	1 494	1 388
Food poisoning	KHRB	52 543	63 347	68 587	81 833	82 041	83 233	93 901	93 932	86 316	86 528	85 468
Typhoid and Paratyphoid fevers	KHRB	281	282	268	370	370	276	241	243	276	204	250
Viral hepatitis	KWNT	8 860	8 993	5 557	3 722	3 296	2 437	3 186	3 183	3 424	3 541	3 388
Tuberculosis[2]	KHRJ	5 436	5 799	5 921	5 591	5 608	5 654	5 859	6 087	6 144	6 572	6 714
Malaria	KWNU	1 553	1 189	1 198	1 139	1 300	1 659	1 476	1 110	1 005	1 128	1 081
Total meningitis	KHRO	2 760	2 571	2 082	1 800	2 285	2 686	2 345	2 072	2 094	2 432	2 623
Meningococcal meningitis	KHRP	1 117	1 067	1 053	938	1 146	1 164	1 220	1 152	1 145	1 164	1 020
Meningococcal septicaemia	KWNV	273	277	398	430	707	1 129	1 440	1 509	1 822	1 614	1 238
Ophthalmia neonatorum	KHRI	433	424	340	268	245	246	224	198	163	176	115
Scotland												
Measles	KHSE	1 701	1 747	1 911	6 192	1 307	1 055	762	700	434	395	315
Mumps	KWNW	723	601	458	546	371	368	282	251	216	199	155
Rubella	KWNX	2 171	2 645	2 048	2 916	1 258	2 449	818	745	548	349	234
Whooping cough	KHSF	838	236	493	639	399	186	545	225	214	93	106
Scarlet fever	KHSD	1 084	808	911	1 319	1 065	750	645	883	438	301	281
Dysentery	KHSH	1 526	3 486	607	446	575	176	124	103	82	95	85
Food poisoning[3]	KHSI	6 318	7 877	7 170	8 291	9 297	10 234	10 144	9 186	8 517	9 263	8 640
Typhoid and Paratyphoid fevers	KHSB	7	15	7	18	16	14	6	6	2	1	3
Viral hepatitis	KWNY	556	319	290	296	405	360	359	490	863	943	1 008
Tuberculosis[4]	KHSL	546	559	554	546	478	509	433	457	496	469	469
Malaria	KWUC	91	50	75	74	58	70	57	30	20	27	24
Meningococcal infection	KWUD	178	207	207	201	190	201	271	313	329	301	256
Erysipelas	KHSC	155	128	130	118	125	84	95	66	64	41	39
Northern Ireland												
Measles	KHTD	342	303	495	950	263	197	120	112	79	92	96
Mumps	KHTR	189	156	115	103	93	67	68	79	93	1 006	537
Rubella	KHTQ	357	293	528	408	220	190	127	111	73	62	65
Whooping cough	KHTE	240	205	134	234	131	148	135	100	108	61	65
Scarlet fever	KHTC	575	525	575	519	502	478	425	486	432	310	283
Dysentery	KHTG	66	174	129	136	272	155	29	18	10	24	22
Food poisoning	KHTH	636	915	954	1 004	1 266	1 456	1 534	1 942	2 033	2 285	1 644
Typhoid and Paratyphoid fevers	KHTB	–	1	2	2	–	1	2	3	–	–	1
Infective hepatitis	KHTO	440	304	295	267	122	79	56	108	78	46	23
Tuberculosis	KHTI	96	84	90	93	90	75	75	61	61	59	48
Malaria	KWUE	8	14	8	6	5	14	16	23	13	11	13
Acute encephalitis/meningitis	KHTM	172	118	122	144	116	105	91	64	99	129	97
Meningococcal septicaemia	KWUF	23	27	34	39	42	67	56	87	145	123	90
Gastro-enteritis (children under 2 years)	KHTP	1 091	1 070	1 379	888	1 072	745	896	1 371	1 121	1 205	1 106

1 The figures show the corrected number of notifications, incorporating revisions of diagnosis, either by the notifying medical practitioner or by the medical superintendent of the infectious diseases hospital. Cases notified in Port Health Authorities are included.

2 Formal notifications of new cases only. The figures exclude chemoprophylaxis.

3 Scotland's food poisoning includes 'otherwise ascertained' for the first time in 1995.

4 Figures include cases of tuberculosis not notified before death.

Sources: Information and Statistics Division, NHS in Scotland;
General Register Office (Northern Ireland);
PHLS Communicable Diseases Surveillance Centre: 020 8200 6868

9.7 Estimated number of cases of work-related disease reported by specialist physicians to ODIN[1]

Great Britain

	All physicians			Disease specialist			Occupational physicians		
	1999	2000	2001	1999	2000	2001	1999	2000	2001
Musculoskeletal disorders				(MOSS)			(OPRA)		
Upper limb	5 174	5 055	4 882	1 872	1 752	1 824	3 302	3 303	3 058
Spine/ back	2 715	2 305	2 270	768	636	432	1 947	1 669	1 838
Lower limb	626	372	516	168	144	84	458	228	432
Other	300	216	360	120	48	84	180	168	276
Total number of diagnoses	8 815	7 948	8 028	2 928	2 580	2 424	5 887	5 368	5 604
Total number of individuals[2]	8 635	7 816	7 787	2 844	2 568	2 328	5 791	5 248	5 459
Mental ill health				(SOS-) (MI)			(OPRA)		
Stress/ anxiety/ depression	5 523	6 327	6 735	3 024	2 820	2 268	2 499	3 507	4 467
Other	1 464	912	1 212	1 224	756	888	240	156	324
Total number of diagnoses	6 987	7 239	7 947	4 248	3 576	3 156	2 739	3 663	4 791
Total number of individuals[2]	6 566	6 555	7 419	3 996	3 420	3 048	2 570	3 135	4 371
Respiratory disease				(SWO-) (RD)			(OPRA)		
Asthma	1 129	785	650	663	482	415	466	303	235
Malignant mesothelioma	1 018	936	972	991	881	965	27	55	7
Benign pleural disease	1 242	1 064	866	1 204	1 040	854	38	24	12
Other	1 029	1 021	939	688	730	709	341	291	230
Total number of diagnoses	4 418	3 806	3 427	3 546	3 133	2 943	872	673	484
Total number of individuals[2]	4 298	3 725	3 354	3 474	3 052	2 870	824	673	484
Skin disease				(EPI-) (DERM)			(OPRA)		
Contact dermatitis	3 933	3 410	2 782	2 291	2 063	1 771	1 642	1 337	1 011
Skin neoplasia	339	503	545	339	491	545	-	12	-
Other	678	518	414	288	241	244	390	277	170
Total number of diagnoses	4 950	4 431	3 741	2 918	2 805	2 560	2 032	1 626	1 181
Total number of individuals[2]	4 850	4 355	3 717	2 830	2 729	2 536	2 020	1 626	1 181
Audiological disease				(OSSA)			(OPRA)		
Sensorineural hearing loss	714	627	323	436	279	131	278	348	192
Other	289	170	115	265	170	67	24	-	48
Total number of diagnoses	1 003	797	438	701	449	198	302	348	240
Total number of individuals[2]	756	648	377	454	300	137	302	348	240
Infections[3]				(SI-) (DAW)					
Diarrhoeal diseases	..	..	..	481	374	539	..	..	..
Other	..	..	..	141	187	155	..	..	..
Total number of diagnoses	..	..	..	622	561	694	..	..	..
Total number of individuals[2]	..	..	..	622	561	694	..	..	..

1 See chapter text. ODIN is the Occupational Disease Intelligence Network and comprises of the following schemes: OPRA: Occupational Physicians Reporting Activity; MOSS: Musculoskeletal Occupational Surveillance Scheme; SOSMI: Surveillance of Occupational Stress and Mental Illness; SWORD: Surveillance of Work-related and Occupational Respiratory Disease; EPIDERM: Occupational Skin Disease Surveillance by Dermatologists; OSSA: Occupational Surveillance Scheme for Audiologists; SIDAW: Surveillance of Infectious Disease at Work.
2 Individuals may have more than one diagnosis.
3 Infections are not covered by OPRA.

Source: Health and Safety Executive: 0151 951 4556

9.8 Deaths due to occupationally related lung disease[1]
Great Britain

		1990	1991	1992	1993	1994	1995	1996	1997	1998	1999	2000
Asbestosis (without mesothelioma)[2]	KADY	164	163	150	173	174	166	196	191	165	171	186
Mesothelioma[2]	KADZ	895	1 023	1 097	1 152	1 246	1 317	1 322	1 367	1 541	1 613	1 628
Pneumoconiosis (other than asbestosis)	KAEA	328	287	274	281	276	287	223	230	268	321	279
Byssinosis	KAEB	19	16	21	11	7	6	3	5	5	6	4
Farmer's lung and other occupational allergic alveolitis	KAEC	6	8	4	12	10	10	1	5	8	9	7
Total	KAED	1 412	1 497	1 546	1 629	1 713	1 786	1 745	1 798	1 987	2 120	2 104

1 See chapter text.
2 By definition every case of asbestosis is due to asbestos; the association with mesothelioma is also very strong, though there is thought to be a low natural background incidence.

Sources: Office for National Statistics; Health and Safety Executive: 0151 951 4540

9.9 Injuries to workers by industry and severity of injury[1]
Great Britain

As reported to all enforcing authorities

				Fatal				Major				Over 3 Days[2]			
		Section	SIC (92)	1998/99	1999/00	2000/01		1998/99	1999/00	2000/01		1998/99	1999/00	2000/01	
Agriculture, hunting, forestry and fishing[3]	KSYS	A,B	01,02,05	46	36	46	KSZN	679	726	655	KTAZ	1 298	1 456	1 398	
Energy and water supply industries[4]	KSYT	C,E	10-14,40/41	11	7	8	KSZO	555	506	472	KTBH	2 974	2 511	2 375	
Mining and quarrying[4]	KSYU	C	10-14	7	5	8	KSZP	346	313	296	KTBI	1 773	1 503	1 481	
Mining and quarrying of energy producing materials[4]	KSON	CA	10-12	5	3	3	KSZQ	213	189	174	KTBJ	1 238	1 029	1 040	
Mining and quarrying except energy producing materials	KSOO	CB	13/14	2	2	5	KSZR	133	124	122	KTBK	535	474	441	
Electricity, gas and water supply	KSOP	E	40/41	4	2	–	KSZS	209	193	176	KTBL	1 201	1 008	894	
Manufacturing	KSOQ	D	15-37	69	41	50	KSZT	8 233	8 038	7 459	KTBM	39 264	39 460	38 187	
of food products; beverages and tobacco	KSOR	DA	15/16	7	1	4	KSZU	1 525	1 536	1 344	KTBN	9 589	9 796	9 417	
of textile and textile products	KSOS	DB	17/18	–	1	4	KSZV	290	262	252	KTBO	1 524	1 341	1 131	
of leather and leather products	KSOT	DC	19	–	1	–	KSZW	25	38	22	KTBP	140	132	161	
of wood and wood products	KSOU	DD	20	4	1	4	KSZX	346	361	349	KTBQ	1 026	1 064	1 060	
of pulp, paper and paper products; publishing and printing	KSOV	DE	21/22	2	3	–	KSZY	503	493	466	KTBR	2 496	2 547	2 544	
of coke, refined petroleum products and nuclear fuel	KSOW	DF	23	–	–	–	KSZZ	38	48	42	KTBS	132	121	115	
of chemicals, chemical products and man-made fibres	KSOX	DG	24	4	2	–	KTAE	424	428	395	KTBT	1 782	1 936	1 846	
of rubber and plastic products	KSOY	DH	25	5	2	5	KTAF	651	653	619	KTBU	3 437	3 535	3 306	
of other non-metallic mineral products	KSOZ	DI	26	6	1	5	KTAG	426	428	417	KTBV	2 076	2 095	2 052	
of basic metals and fabricated metal products	KSYV	DJ	27/28	22	17	19	KTAH	1 656	1 556	1 534	KTBW	6 144	6 119	6 070	
of machinery and equipment not elsewhere classified	KSYW	DK	29	5	4	4	KTAI	685	638	629	KTBX	2 913	2 859	2 876	
of electrical and optical equipment	KSYX	DL	30-33	–	–	2	KTAJ	481	473	428	KTBY	2 198	2 284	2 321	
of transport equipment	KSYY	DM	34/35	5	2	1	KTAK	770	721	654	KTBZ	4 342	4 100	3 799	
Manufacturing not elsewhere classified	KSYZ	DN	36/37	9	6	2	KTAL	413	403	308	KTCA	1 465	1 531	1 489	
Construction	KSZA	F	45	65	81	105	KTAM	4 656	4 749	4 708	KTCB	9 576	10 504	9 796	
Total service industries	KSZB	G-Q	50-99	62	55	83	KTAN	14 930	15 296	14 860	KTCC	80 032	82 182	83 064	
Wholesale and retail trade, and repairs	KSZC	G	50-52	15	15	15	KTAO	3 158	3 221	3 045	KTCD	15 695	15 568	15 154	
Hotel and restaurants	KSZD	H	55	1	1	4	KTAP	924	874	754	KTCE	3 434	3 439	3 358	
Transport, storage and communication[5]	KSZE	I	60-64	25	19	40	KTAQ	2 879	2 978	3 061	KTCF	18 626	20 603	22 596	
Financial intermediation	KSZF	J	65-67	–	–	1	KTAR	153	159	152	KTCG	653	579	586	
Real estate, renting and business activities	KSZG	K	70-74	13	10	7	KTAS	1 050	1 134	1 031	KTCH	3 981	3 879	3 474	
Public administration and defence	KSZH	L	75	2	3	2	KTAT	2 001	2 227	2 165	KTCI	14 266	14 908	15 067	
Education	KSZI	M	80	1	–	2	KTAU	1 548	1 475	1 462	KTCJ	4 680	4 767	4 682	
Health and social work	KSZJ	N	85	–	–	2	KTAV	1 930	1 863	1 857	KTCK	14 148	13 825	13 400	
Other community, social and personal services activities	KSZK	O-Q	90-99	5	11	10	KTAW	1 287	1 365	1 333	KTCL	4 549	4 614	4 747	
Unclassified	KSZL			–	–	–	KTAX	–	–	–	KTCM	–	–	–	
All industries	KSZM			253	220	292	KTAY	29 053	29 315	28 154	KTCN	133 144	136 113	134 820	

1 See chapter text.
2 Injuries causing incapacity for normal work for more than 3 days.
3 Excludes sea fishing.
4 Includes the number of injuries in the oil and gas industry collected under offshore installations safety legislation.
5 Injuries arising from shore based services only. Excludes incidents reported under merchant shipping legislation.

Source: Health and Safety Executive (HSE): 0151 951 4842

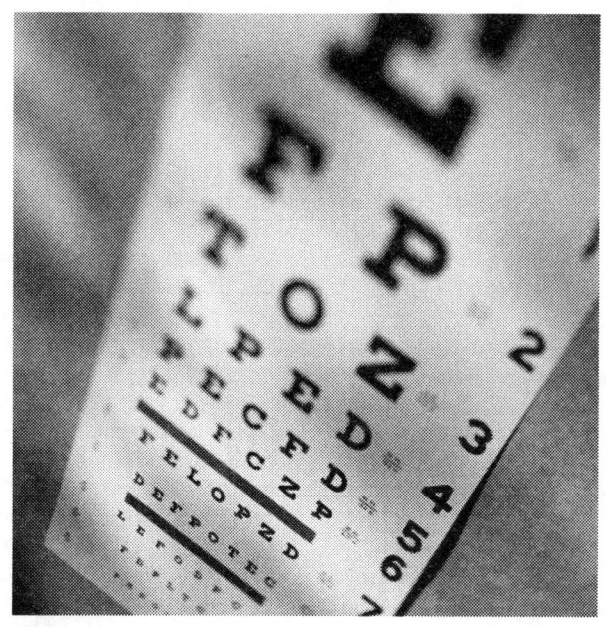

10 Social protection

Social protection

Social security
(Tables 10.2 - 10.8, 10.10, 10.11 and 10.13 to 10.16)

Tables 10.2 to 10.6 and 10.10 to 10.16 give details of contributors and beneficiaries under the National Insurance and Industrial Injury Acts, supplementary benefits and war pensions.

There are three types of contributor:

Class 1   Employed people, that is, people working for employers. Their contributions are paid partly by themselves and partly by their employers. They are covered for all benefits.

Class 2   Self-employed people, that is, people working on their own account. They are covered for all benefits other than unemployment and industrial injuries.

Class 3   Non-employed people, that is, people who do not work for gain. These people pay contributions on a voluntary basis. They are covered for benefits other than unemployment, sickness, industrial injuries and maternity allowances.

Class 4   Payable, in addition to Class 2 by self-employed people, and the amount payable is proportionate to profits or gains between a lower and upper limit in any one year.

An employer must pay a contribution for every employee whose earnings exceed a base level. Most employed people pay the full employee's contribution, but retirement pensioners working for an employer do not, and some married women and some widows who are working need not, unless they so wish, contribute except for industrial injuries benefit. Thus the total numbers in the analysis by benefit for which the contributions were payable are less than the total numbers in the analysis by class of contributor.

Unemployment benefit and jobseekers allowance
(Table 10.6)

Jobseeker's allowance replaced unemployment benefit and Income Support for unemployed claimants on 7 October 1996. It is a unified benefit with two routes of entry: contribution-based which depends mainly upon national insurance contributions and income-based which depends mainly upon a means test. Some claimants can qualify by either route. In practice they receive income-based JSA but have an underlying entitlement to the contribution-based element.

Sickness benefit, Invalidity benefit and Incapacity benefit (Tables 10.7 and 10.8)

Incapacity Benefit replaced Sickness Benefit and Invalidity Benefit from 13 April 1995. The first condition for entitlement to these contributory benefits is that the claimants are incapable of work because of illness or disablement. Secondly, that they satisfy the contribution conditions which depend on contributions paid as an employed (Class 1) or self-employed person (Class 2). Under Sickness and Invalidity Benefits the contribution conditions were automatically treated as satisfied if a person was incapable of work because of an industrial accident or prescribed disease. Under Incapacity Benefit those who do not satisfy the contribution conditions in this case do not have them treated as satisfied. Class 1A contributions paid by employers are in respect of the benefit of cars provided for the private use of employees, and the free fuel provided for private use. These contributions do not provide any type of benefit cover.

Since 6 April 1983, most people working for an employer and paying National Insurance contributions as employed persons, receive Statutory Sick Pay (SSP) from their employer when they are off work sick. SSP was payable for a maximum of 8 weeks until 5 April 1986, and 28 weeks thereafter. People who do not work for an employer, and employees who are excluded from the SSP scheme, or those who have run out of SSP before reaching the maximum of 28 weeks and are still sick can claim benefit. Any period of SSP is excluded from the tables.

Spells of incapacity of 3 days or less do not count as periods of interruption of employment, and are excluded from the tables. Exceptions are where people are receiving regular weekly treatment by dialysis, or treatment by radiotherapy, chemotherapy or plasmapheresis where 2 days in any 6 consecutive days make up a period of interruption of employment, and those whose incapacity for work ends within 3 days of the end of SSP entitlement.

At the beginning of a period of incapacity, benefit is subject to 3 waiting days, except where there was an earlier spell of incapacity of more than 3 days in the previous 8 weeks. Employees entitled to SSP for less than 28 weeks and who are still sick can get Sickness Benefit or Incapacity Benefit Short Term (Low) until they reach a total of 28 weeks provided they satisfy the conditions. After 28 weeks SSP and/or Sickness Benefit (SB), Invalidity Benefit (IVB) was payable up to pension age for as long as the incapacity lasts. From pension age Invalidity Benefit was paid at the person's Retirement Pension rate, until entitlement ceases when RP is paid or at deemed pension age (70 for a man, 65 for a woman). For people on Incapacity Benefit under State pension age there are two short-term rates: the lower rate is paid for the first 28 weeks of sickness and the higher rate for weeks 29 to 52. From week 53 the Long Term rate Incapacity Benefit is payable. The Short Term rate Incapacity Benefit is based on Retirement Pension entitlement for people over State pension age and is paid for up to a year if incapacity began before pension age.

The long-term rate of Incapacity Benefit applies to people under State pension age who have been sick for more than a year. People with a terminal illness or who are receiving the higher rate care component of Disability Living Allowance will get the Long Term rate. The Long Term rate is not paid for people over pension age.

Under Incapacity Benefit, for the first 28 weeks of incapacity, people previously in work will be assessed on the 'own occupation' test - the claimant's ability to do their own job. Otherwise, incapacity will be based on a new 'all work' test which will assess ability to carry out a range of work-related activities. The test will apply after 28 weeks of incapacity or from the start of the claim for people who did not previously have a job. Certain people will be exempted from this test.

The tables exclude all men aged over 65 and women aged over 60 who are in receipt of Retirement Pension, and all people over deemed pension age (70 for a man and 65 for a woman), members of the Armed Forces, mariners while at sea, and married women and certain widows who have chosen not to be insured for Sickness Benefit. In addition, employees of the Post Office are excluded prior to 29 March 1986, and the remainder of Civil Service Departments, British Telecom and fringe bodies prior to 25 August 1986. The tables include a number of individuals who were unemployed prior to incapacity.

The Short Term (Higher) and Long Term rates of Incapacity Benefit are treated as taxable income.

There were transitional provisions for people who were on Sickness or Invalidity Benefit on 12 April 1995. They were automatically transferred to Incapacity Benefit, payable on the same basis as before. Former IVB recipients continue to get Additional Pension entitlement, but frozen at 1994 levels. Also their IVB is not subject to tax. If they were over State pension age on 12 April 1995 they may get Incapacity Benefit for up to 5 years beyond pension age.

Family Credit/ Working Families' Tax Credit (Table 10.12)
Working Families' Tax Credit (WFTC) replaced Family Credit from 5 October 1999.

Family Credit was, and Working Families' Tax Credit is, available to families with at least one adult in remunerative work for at least 16 hours per week and who is responsible for at least one child under 16 (under 19 if in full time education up to A-level or equivalent standard). The rate of payment of WFTC depends on the number of such children and expenditure incurred on eligible childcare. It is also higher if the worker works for at least 30 hours per week, or if there are disabled children or severely disabled adults in the family. It is tapered away above an income threshold. Further details can be obtained from the Inland Revenue.

Government expenditure on social services and housing (Table 10.17 - 10.22)
The tables of general government expenditure on social services and housing in the United Kingdom comprise a summary table followed by separate tables for each of the social services and housing. The definition of government expenditure used in these tables follows that in Table 9.4 of the *Blue Book 2002 Edition*, and covers both current and capital expenditure of the central government (including the National Insurance Fund) and local authorities. The housing table also includes the capital expenditure of public corporations concerned with housing. As in the *Blue Book*, government expenditure is measured after deducting

fees and charges for services. Expenditure on administration includes the cost of common services (accommodation, stationery and printing, superannuation, etc) some of which is not directly borne by the departments administering each service. Transfers from one part of government to another have been eliminated to avoid double counting. The figures relate to years ended 31 March.

It should be noted that the figures no longer include imputed rents for the use of fixed assets owned and used by general government. In the *Blue Book*, imputed rents have been replaced by capital consumption. Capital consumption, however, cannot be allocated to individual services and is therefore not included in these tables.

The following notes give brief descriptions of each of the main services shown in the tables.

Education (Table 10.18)
This covers expenditure by the Education Departments, local education authorities and the University Grants Committee on education in schools, training colleges, technical institutions and universities. It includes expenditure on school meals.

National Health Service (Table 10.19)
This covers expenditure by central government on hospital and community health, family practitioner and other health services. The expenditure by local authorities on the provision of health centres, health visiting, home nursing, ambulance services, vaccination and immunisation, etc, was transferred to central government on 1 April 1974. Only the net costs of providing these services are included in total government expenditure, receipts from patients being shown separately.

Personal social services (Table 10.20)
This covers local authority expenditure on the aged, handicapped and homeless, child care, care of mothers and young children, mental health, domestic help, etc. Also included are central government grants to voluntary approved schools.

Welfare foods (Table 10.20)
This covers the cost of providing welfare foods at reduced prices to children and expectant mothers. Only the net costs of providing these services are included in the total government expenditure, payments by the recipients of the services being shown separately.

Social security (Table 10.21)
This comprises both benefits under the Social Security schemes and non-contributory benefits and allowances, administered by the Department for Work and Pensions. The analysis by type of Income Support is not exact; the estimates are derived from average numbers in receipt of benefit and average amounts paid. Unified housing benefit (rent rebates and allowances) is also included as social security expenditure and not as housing expenditure. This is now mainly administered by local authorities who receive grants from central government.

Social protection

Housing *(Table 10.22)*

The table shows, in addition to government expenditure on housing, the capital expenditure of public corporations and the total expenditure of the public sector on housing. The government expenditure figures cover subsidies paid by the housing departments towards the provision of housing by local authorities, new town development corporations and housing associations; subsidies by local authorities to their housing revenue accounts; rent rebates for tenants of housing owned by local authorities and new towns; rent allowances for tenants of privately-owned housing; grants to persons for the reduction of mortgage interest payments; capital expenditure on the provision of houses for letting; capital grants to housing associations; grants by local authorities towards the cost of conversion and improvement of privately-owned houses; net lending by the central government and local authorities for private house purchase; and improvement and loans for first time purchasers. The public corporations' figures cover capital expenditure on the provision of houses for letting and lending by the Housing Corporation to housing associations.

10.1 National Insurance Fund
United Kingdom
Years ended 31 March

£ thousands

		1992 /93	1993 /94	1994 /95	1995 /96	1996 /97	1997 /98	1998 /99	1999 /00	2000 /01
Receipts										
Opening balance	KJFB	8 637 595	3 577 671	4 672 345	7 042 118	8 044 941	7 869 121	9 763 346	12 624 962	14 909 008
Contributions		34 331 672	35 872 925	38 712 218	40 874 579	42 806 429	46 754 687	50 023 377	51 851 720	55 664 741
Grant from Consolidated Fund	KOTF	..	7 785 000	6 445 000	3 680 000	1 951 560	966 250	3 430	2 200	..
Compensation for SSP/SMP	KJQM	1 124 500	1 158 289	563 400	474 700	541 800	600 500	576 400	624 906	687 694
Transfers from GB	KOTG	40 000	40 000	145 000	125 000	75 000	150 000	315 000	230 000	200 000
Income from investments	KJFE	970 862	488 484	365 096	459 217	488 728	474 296	667 261	724 145	884 070
Other receipts	KJFF	24 813	41 989	60 625	76 487	85 126	97 206	92 292	126 728	111 577
Redundancy receipts	KIBQ	26 942	25 688	25 288	23 899	26 193	24 720	21 210	20 874	23 108
Total		45 156 384	48 990 046	50 988 972	52 756 000	54 019 777	56 936 780	61 462 316	66 205 535	72 480 198
Expenditure										
Total benefits		39 823 984	42 366 510	42 270 821	43 198 045	44 517 872	45 321 626	46 822 291	49 550 870	50 510 781
Unemployment	KJFH	1 800 589	1 689 604	1 330 922	1 131 373	605 095	148	..	..	..
Sickness[1]	KJFI	378 136	378 407	350 700	14 711	..	..	..	..	..
Invalidity[1]	KJFJ	6 452 717	7 341 161	8 009 286	599 829	..	..	..	..	..
Incapacity[1]	JYXL	..	..	..	7 622 940	7 992 748	7 739 556	7 574 276	7 205 700	6 981 951
Maternity	KETY	32 660	34 230	28 230	29 897	34 283	36 715	39 329	40 412	45 995
Widows' pensions	KEWU	1 044 397	1 075 990	1 057 395	1 050 693	1 016 822	1 020 813	1 007 653	1 019 916	1 008 042
Guardians' allowances and Child's special allowance[2]	KJFK	2 091	1 111	1 111	1 842	1 569	1 637	1 834	1 823	1 611
Retirement pensions[3]		29 995 404	31 720 928	31 366 872	32 619 571	34 735 720	36 396 421	38 071 687	41 156 649	42 349 778
Pensioners' lump sum payments	KAAW	117 990	125 079	126 305	127 189	131 635	126 336	127 512	126 370	123 404
Other payments	KAAZ	10 523	35 045	8 879	14 174	17 392	19 037	18 305	19 159	21 274
Administration	KABE	1 379 212	1 604 510	1 323 631	1 218 772	1 065 338	1 073 350	1 052 820	847 386	1 197 417
Transfers to Northern Ireland	KABF	40 000	40 000	145 000	125 000	75 000	150 000	315 000	230 000	200 000
Redundancy payments	KIBR	324 994	271 636	198 523	155 068	133 621	119 961	140 075	173 988	195 281
Jobseeker's allowance (Contributory)[4]	LUQW	..	..	..	..	341 433	489 460	488 863	475 124	449 282
Total		41 578 713	44 317 701	43 946 854	44 711 059	46 150 656	47 173 434	48 837 354	51 296 527	52 574 035
Accumulated funds		3 577 671	4 672 345	7 042 118	8 044 941	7 869 121	9 763 346	12 624 962	14 909 008	19 906 163

1 Incapacity Benefit replaced Sickness Benefit and Invalidity Benefit from April 1995.
2 Including figures of Child's special allowance for Northern Ireland.
3 Includes figures for Personal Pensions.
4 Jobseeker's Allowance (Contributory) was introduced in October 1996 and replaced Unemployment Benefit.

Sources: Department for Work and Pensions: 01253 856123 Ext 62436; Department of Health, Social Services and Public Safety (Northern Ireland); 028 9052 2062

10.2 Persons who paid National Insurance contributions in a tax year[1]
United Kingdom

Millions

		Total				Men				Women		
		1998 /99	1999 /00	2000 /01		1998 /99	1999 /00	2000 /01		1998 /99	1999 /00	2000 /01
Total[2]	KABI	26.82	27.35	27.95	KEYF	15.13	15.31	15.58	KEYP	11.69	12.04	12.36
Class 1	KABJ	24.26	24.82	25.36	KEYG	13.16	13.39	13.62	KEYQ	11.10	11.43	11.74
Not contracted out[3]	KABK	14.90	15.49	15.99	KEYH	8.23	8.56	8.86	KEYR	6.67	6.93	7.13
Contracted out	KABL	7.65	7.63	7.60	KEYI	4.21	4.11	4.00	KEYS	3.45	3.53	3.59
Mixed contracted in/out[4]	KABM	1.49	1.52	1.63	KEYJ	0.72	0.72	0.76	KEYT	0.77	0.80	0.87
Class 1 Reduced rate (including standard rate)	KABO	0.21	0.17	0.14	KEYL	..	..	..	KEYV	0.21	0.17	0.14
Class 2 exclusively	KABP	2.03	1.98	2.02	KEYM	1.61	1.56	1.58	KEYW	0.42	0.42	0.44
Mixed Class 1 and Class 2	KABQ	0.38	0.41	0.46	KEYN	0.27	0.29	0.32	KEYX	0.11	0.12	0.14
Class 3 exclusively[5]	KABR	0.15	0.13	0.10	KEYO	0.08	0.07	0.06	KEYY	0.07	0.06	0.05

1 See chapter text. The tax year commences on 6 April and ends on 5 April of the following year.
2 Not all figures agree because of rounding.
3 Includes those persons with an Appropriate Personal Pension (such persons pay contributions at the not contracted out rate but then receive a rebate).
4 Not included in the above rows
5 Persons who paid a mixture of Class 3 contributions and others are not included in this category.

Source: Board of Inland Revenue 020 7438 6234

10.3 Weekly rates of principal social security benefits[1]
Great Britain

£

		1990 Apr	1991 Apr	1992 Apr	1993 Apr	1994 Apr	1995 Apr	1996 Apr	1997 Apr	1998 Apr	1999 Apr	2000 Apr	2001 Apr	2002 Apr
Unemployment benefit:[2,3]														
Men and women	KJNA	37.35	41.40	43.10	44.65	45.45	46.45	48.25	..	..	..	..	..	..
Jobseeker's allowance:[3]														
Personal allowances														
Single														
Aged under 18(Depending	KXDH	..	..	..	..	..	..	..	29.60	30.30	30.95	31.45	31.95	32.50
on their circumstances)	KXDI	..	..	..	..	..	..	..	38.90	39.85	40.70	41.35	42.00	42.70
Aged 18 - 24	KXDJ	..	..	..	..	..	..	..	38.90	39.85	40.70	41.35	42.00	42.70
Aged 25 or over	KXDK	..	..	..	..	..	..	..	49.15	50.35	51.40	52.20	53.05	53.95
Couple														
Both aged under 18[4]	KXDL	..	..	..	..	..	..	..	58.70	30.30	30.95	31.45	31.95	32.50
Both aged 18 or over	KXDM	..	..	..	..	..	..	..	77.15	79.00	80.65	81.95	83.25	84.65
Dependant children and young people														
Aged under 11	KXDN	..	..	..	..	..	..	..	16.90	17.30	20.20	26.60	31.45	33.50
Aged 11 - 16	KXDO	..	..	..	..	..	..	..	24.75	25.35	25.90	26.60	31.45	33.50
Aged 16 - 18	KXDP	..	..	..	..	..	..	..	29.60	30.30	30.95	31.75	32.25	34.30
Sickness benefit:[2,5]														
Men and women	KJNB	35.70	39.60	41.20	42.70	43.45	..	..	..	..	..	..	..	..
Invalidity benefit:[5]														
Invalidity pension	KJNC	46.90	52.00	54.15	56.10	57.60	..	..	..	..	..	..	..	..
Invalidity allowance:[5]														
High rate	KJND	10.00	11.10	11.55	11.95	12.15	12.40	12.90	13.15	13.60	14.05	14.20	14.65	14.90
Middle rate	KJNE	6.20	6.90	7.20	7.50	7.60	7.80	8.10	8.30	8.60	8.90	9.00	9.30	9.50
Low rate	KJNF	3.10	3.45	3.60	3.75	3.80	3.90	4.05	4.15	4.30	4.45	4.50	4.65	4.75
Increase for dependants:[5]														
Adult	KJNG	28.20	31.25	32.55	33.70	34.50	35.25	36.60	37.35	38.70	39.95	40.40	41.75	42.45
Each child	KJNH	9.65	10.70	10.85	10.95	11.00	11.05	11.15	11.20	11.30	11.35	11.35	11.35	11.35
Incapacity benefit:														
Short term (Lower) Under pension age	KOSB	..	..	..	..	..	44.40	46.15	47.10	48.80	50.35	50.90	52.60	53.50
Increase for adult dependant	KOSC	..	..	..	..	..	27.50	28.55	29.15	30.20	31.15	31.50	32.55	33.10
Short term (Lower) Over pension age	KOSD	..	..	..	..	..	56.45	58.65	59.90	62.05	64.05	64.75	66.90	68.05
Increase for adult dependant	KOSE	..	..	..	..	..	33.85	35.15	35.90	37.20	38.40	38.80	40.10	42.45
Short term (Higher)	KOSF	..	..	..	..	..	52.50	54.55	55.70	57.70	59.55	60.20	62.20	63.25
Increase for dependants:														
Adult	KOSG	..	..	..	..	..	27.50	28.55	29.15	30.20	31.15	31.50	32.55	33.10
Child[6]	KOSH	..	..	..	..	..	11.05	11.15	11.20	11.30	11.35	11.35	11.35	11.35
Long term	KOSI	..	..	..	..	..	58.85	61.15	62.45	64.70	66.75	67.50	69.75	70.95
Increase for dependants:														
Adult	KOSJ	..	..	..	..	..	35.25	36.60	37.35	38.70	39.95	40.40	41.75	42.45
Child[5]	KOSK	..	..	..	..	..	11.05	11.15	11.20	11.30	11.35	11.35	11.35	11.35
Incapacity age addition:[7]														
Higher rate	KOSL	..	..	..	..	..	12.40	12.90	13.15	13.60	14.05	14.20	14.65	14.90
Lower rate	KOSM	..	..	..	..	..	6.20	6.45	6.60	6.80	7.05	7.10	7.35	7.45
Attendance allowance:														
Higher rate	KJNI	37.55	41.65	43.35	44.90	45.70	46.70	48.50	49.50	51.30	52.95	53.55	55.30	56.25
Lower rate	KJNJ	25.05	27.10	28.95	30.00	30.55	31.20	32.40	33.10	34.30	35.40	35.80	37.00	37.65
Mobility allowance[8]	KJNK	26.25	29.80	..	..	..	..	..	..	..	..	..	..	..
Disability living allowance:														
care component														
Higher rate	KXDC	..	..	43.35	44.90	45.70	46.70	48.50	49.50	51.30	52.95	53.55	55.30	56.25
Middle rate	KXDD	..	..	28.95	30.00	30.55	31.20	32.40	33.10	34.30	35.40	35.80	37.00	37.65
Lower rate	KXDE	..	..	11.55	11.95	12.15	12.40	12.90	13.15	13.60	14.05	14.20	14.65	14.90
mobility component														
Higher rate	KXDF	..	..	30.30	31.40	31.95	32.65	33.90	34.60	35.85	37.00	37.40	38.65	39.30
Lower rate	KXDG	..	..	11.55	11.95	12.15	12.40	12.90	13.15	13.60	14.05	14.20	14.65	14.90

10.3 Weekly rates of principal social security benefits[1]
Great Britain
continued

£

		1990 Apr	1991 Apr	1992 Apr	1993 Apr	1994 Apr	1995 Apr	1996 Apr	1997 Apr	1998 Apr	1999 Apr	2000 Apr	2001 Apr	2002 Apr
Maternity benefit:														
Maternity allowances for insured women[9]														
Higher rate	KOSN	..	..	..	..	..	52.50	54.55	55.70	57.70	59.55	60.20	..	..
Lower rate[10]	KJNL	35.70	40.60	42.25	43.75	44.55	45.55	47.35	48.35	50.10	51.70	52.25	..	..
Standard rate[11]	GPTJ	..	..	..	..	..	..	..	..	..	..	..	62.20	75.00
Threshold[12]	GPTK	..	..	..	..	..	..	..	..	..	..	..	30.00	30.00
Guardian's allowance	KJNN	9.65	10.70	10.85	10.95	11.00	11.05	11.15	11.20	11.30	11.35	11.35	11.35	11.35
Widow's benefit:														
Widow's pension	KJNO	46.90	52.00	54.15	56.10	57.60	58.85	61.15	62.45	64.70	66.75	67.50	72.50	75.50
Widowed mother's allowance	KJNP	46.90	52.00	54.15	56.10	57.60	58.85	61.15	62.45	64.70	66.75	67.50	72.50	75.50
Addition for each child	KJNQ	9.65	10.70	10.85	10.95	11.00	11.05	11.15	11.20	11.30	11.35	11.35	11.35	11.35
Retirement pension:[13]														
Single person	KJNR	46.90	52.00	54.15	56.10	57.60	58.85	61.15	62.45	64.70	66.75	67.50	72.50	75.50
Married couple	KJNS	75.10	83.25	86.70	89.80	92.10	94.10	97.75	99.80	103.40	106.70	107.90	115.90	120.70
Non-contributory retirement pension:														
Man or woman	KJNT	28.20	31.25	32.55	33.70	34.50	35.25	36.60	37.35	38.70	39.95	40.40	43.40	45.20
Married woman	KJNU	16.85	18.70	19.45	20.15	20.65	21.10	21.90	22.35	23.15	23.90	24.15	24.95	27.00
Industrial injuries benefit														
Disablement pension at 100 per cent rate	KJNW	76.60	84.90	88.40	91.60	93.20	95.30	99.00	101.10	104.70	108.10	109.30	112.90	114.80
Widow's or widower's pension	KJNX	46.90	52.00	54.15	56.10	57.60	58.85	61.15	62.45	..	..	..	..	..
Increase for dependants:[14]														
Adult	KJNY	23.05	25.55	26.60	27.55	28.05	28.65	29.75	..	..	..	..	..	..
Child benefit:[15]														
First child	KJOA	7.25	8.25	9.65	10.00	10.20	10.40	10.80	11.05	11.45	14.40	15.00	15.50	15.75
Subsequent children	KETZ	..	..	7.80	8.10	8.25	8.45	8.80	9.00	9.30	9.60	10.00	10.35	10.55
Family Credit[16]														
(maximum awards payable):[17]														
Families with 1 child														
Birth to September following 11th birthday	KJOB	44.60	48.00	51.40	53.25	55.15	56.50	58.20	59.70	61.15	64.95	..	..	..
From September following 11th birthday to September following 16th birthday	KJOC	50.50	54.40	58.25	60.35	62.45	64.00	65.90	67.60	69.25	70.70	..	..	..
From September following 16th birthday to day before 19th birthday	KJOD	54.15	58.35	62.45	64.70	67.00	68.55	70.60	72.45	74.20	75.95	..	..	..
Increase for each additional child														
Birth to September following 11th birthday	KJOF	8.25	9.70	10.40	10.75	11.15	11.40	11.75	12.05	12.35	15.15	..	..	..
From September following 11th birthday to September following 16th birthday	KJOG	14.15	16.10	17.25	17.85	18.45	18.90	19.45	19.95	20.45	20.90	..	..	..
From September following 16th birthday to day before 19th birthday	KJOH	17.80	20.05	21.45	22.20	23.00	23.45	24.15	24.80	25.40	25.95	..	..	..
War pension:														
Ex-private (100 per cent assessment)	KJOJ	76.60	84.90	89.00	97.20	98.90	101.10	105.00	107.20	111.10	114.70	116.00	119.80	121.80
War widow	KJOK	60.95	67.60	70.35	72.90	74.70	76.35	79.35	81.00	83.90	86.60	87.55	90.45	92.00

10.3 Weekly rates of principal social security benefits[1]
Great Britain

continued

£

		1990 Apr	1991 Apr	1992 Apr	1993 Apr	1994 Apr	1995 Apr	1996 Apr	1997 Apr	1998 Apr	1999 Apr	2000 Apr	2001 Apr	2002 Apr
Income Support:														
Personal allowances[18]														
Single														
aged 16-17 either[19] or depending on their circumstances[19]	KJOW	21.90	23.65	25.55	26.45	27.50	28.00	28.85	29.60	30.30	30.95	31.45	31.95	32.50
	KABS	28.80	31.15	33.60	34.80	36.15	36.80	37.90	38.90	39.85	40.70	41.35	42.00	42.70
aged 18-24	KJOX	28.80	31.15	33.60	34.80	36.15	36.80	37.90	38.90	39.85	40.70	41.35	42.00	42.70
aged 25 or over	KJOY	36.70	39.65	42.45	44.00	45.70	46.50	47.90	49.15	50.35	51.40	52.20	53.05	53.95
Couple														
both aged under 18[4]	KJOZ	43.80	47.30	50.60	52.40	54.55	55.55	57.20	58.70	60.10	61.90	..	..	..
one or both 18 or over	KJPA	57.60	62.25	66.60	69.00	71.70	73.00	75.20	77.15	79.00	80.65	81.95	83.25	84.65
Lone parent														
aged 16-17 either or depending on their circumstances[20]	KJPB	21.90	23.65	25.55	26.45	27.50	28.00	28.85	29.60	30.30	30.95	31.45	31.95	32.50
	KABT	28.80	31.15	33.60	34.80	36.15	36.80	37.90	38.90	39.85	40.70	41.35	42.00	42.70
aged 18 or over	KJPC	36.70	39.65	42.45	44.00	45.70	46.50	47.90	49.15	50.35	51.40	52.20	53.05	53.95
Dependant children and young people[16]														
aged under 11[21]	KJPD	12.35	13.35	14.55	15.05	15.65	15.95	16.45	..	..	..	..	..	..
aged 11-15	KJPE	18.25	19.75	21.40	22.15	23.00	23.40	24.10	..	..	..	..	..	..
aged 16-17	KJPF	21.90	23.65	25.65	26.45	27.50	28.00	28.85	..	..	..	..	..	..
aged 18	KABU	28.80	31.15	33.60	34.80	36.15	36.80	37.90	..	..	..	..	..	..
Birth to September following 11th birthday	KXDQ	..	..	..	..	..	..	..	16.90	17.30	20.20			
From September following 11th birthday to September following 16th birthday	ZBXM											26.60	31.45	33.50
	KXDR	..	..	..	..	..	..	..	24.75	25.35	25.90			
From September following 16th birthday to day before 19th birthday	KXDS	..	..	..	..	..	..	..	29.60	30.30	30.95	31.75	32.25	34.30

1 See chapter text
2 Persons under the age of 18 are entitled to the appropriate adult rate.
3 Jobseeker's allowance, introduced 7 October 1996, replaced unemployment benefit and income support for the unemployed.
4 From 12 April 1999 the personal allowance for couples where both members are not yet 18 or one of the couples is aged 18 or over depends on the couple's circumstances. They may be entitled to a couple allowance or a single person's allowance dependant on certain criteria.
5 Incapacity benefit introduced from 13 April 1995, has replaced sickness benefit and invalidity benefit.
6 For the first child only the Child Dependency increase is from 1994, reduced by £1.30 to £9.90 because of child benefit.
7 The rate of age addition depends on age at date of onset of incapacity: higher rate for under age 35 and lower rate for age 35-44.
8 Disability living allowance replaced Mobility allowance from April 1992.
9 Following a EU Directive, employee's maternity benefit is aligned with the state benefit they would receive if off work sick.
10 Women who were either not employed or self-employed received the lower rate.

11 New Standard rate introduced from April 2000.
12 MA Earnings Threshold introduced April 2000.
13 Retirement pensioners over 80 receive 25p addition.
14 An allowance for one adult dependent was payable, where appropriate, with unemployment benefit, sickness benefit, retirement pension, injury benefit and maternity allowance.
15 From October 1991 the first child receives £9.25 and each subsequent child £7.50
16 Age bandings for children's personal allowances were revised on 7 April 1997. Some children have protected rights. Further information is available from the Department for Work and Pensions.
17 Maximum award does not include the 30 hour credit.
18 In addition to personal allowances, a claimant may also be entitled to premiums. The types of premiums are family, lone parent, pensioner, higher pensioner, disability, severe disability and disabled child.
19 From October 1991 the rate is £23.90
20 From October 1991 the rate is £31.40
21 From October 1991 each rate increased by 25p.

Source: Department for Work and Pensions: 0191 225 7373

10.4 National Insurance contributions[1]

	Employee's standard contributions (%)[2]		Employer's standard contributions (%)[2]	
	not contracted-out rate	contracted-out rate[3]	not contracted-out rate	contracted-out rate[4]
Class 1				
Weekly earnings				
1997/98				
Below 62.00 (LEL)	-	-	-	-
62.00-109.99	2% on first £62.00;	2% on first £62.00;	3.0	-
110.00-154.99	10% on balance	8.4% on balance	5.0	2.0
155.00-209.99			7.0	4.0
210.00-465.00			10.0	7.0
Above 465.00 (LEL)	£41.54	£35.09	10.0	10.0
1998/99				
Below 64.00 (LEL)	-	-	-	-
64.00-109.99	2% on first £64.00;	2% on first £64.00;	3.0	-
110.00-154.99	10% on balance	8.4% on balance	5.0	2.0
155.00-209.99			7.0	4.0
210.00-485.00			10.0	7.0
Above 485.00 (UEL)	£43.38	£36.64	10.0	10.0
1999/00				
Below 66.00 (LEL)	-	-	-	-
66.00-83.00	10.0%	8.4%	-	-
83.00-500.00	10.0%	8.4%	12.2	9.2
Above 500.00 (UEL)	£43.40	£36.46	12.2	12.2
2000/01				
Below 67.00 (LEL)	-	-	-	-
67.00-76.00 (PT)	-	See note 5	-	See note 6
76.00-84.00 (ST)	10.0%		-	
84.00-535.00 (UEL)	10.0%		12.2	
Above 535.00 (UEL)	£45.90	£38.41	12.2	12.2
2001/02				
Below 72.00 (LEL)	-	-	-	-
72.00-87.00 (PT/ST)	10.0%	See note 5	-	See note 6
87.00-575.00 (UEL)	10.0%		11.9	
Above 575.00 (UEL)	£48.80	£40.75	11.9	11.9
2002/03				
Below 75.00 (LEL)	-	-	-	-
75.00-89.00 (PT/ST)	10.0%	See note 5	-	See note 7
89.00-585.00 (UEL)	10.0%		11.8	
Above 585.00 (UEL)	£49.60	£41.44	11.8	11.8

	1997/98	1998/99	1999/00	2000/01	2001/02	2002/03
Class 2						
Flat rate weekly	£6.15	£6.35	£6.55	£2.00	£2.00	£2.00
Small earnings exception[8] (per annum)	£3,480	£3,590	£3,770	£3,825	£3,955	£4,025
Class 3						
Flat-rate voluntary weekly contributions	£6.05	£6.25	£6.45	£6.55	£6.75	£6.85
Class 4 (Self-employed; profit-related)						
Rate on profits between LPL and UPL	6.0%	6.0%	6.0%	7.0%	7.0%	7.0%
Lower profits limit (LPL)	£7,010	£7,310	£7,530	£4,385	£4,535	£4.615
Upper profits limit (UPL)	£24,180	£25,220	£26,000	£27,820	£29,900	£30,420

Note: LEL: Lower Earnings Limit; UEL: Upper Earnings Limit. PT: Primary Threshold; ST: Secondary Threshold.

1 See chapter text.

2 Married women opting to pay contributions at the reduced rate (3.85%) earn no entitlement to contributory National Insurance benefits as a result of these contributions. No women have been allowed to exercise this option since 1977, but around 200,000 women who have been continually married or widowed and in the labour market since that time have retained their right to pay the reduced rate.

3 The contracted-out rebate for employees' contributions is applied only between LEL and UEL. Earnings below LEL are charged at the appropriate not contracted-out rate (which depends on total earnings). Earnings above the UEL are not subject to employee NICs.

4 The rates shown only apply to Contracted-Out Salary Related schemes. (COSR). Earnings below the LEL and above the UEL are charged at the appropriate not-contracted out rate. The employers' contracted-out rate applies only between the LEL and the UEL.

5 The contracted-out rebate for primary contributions in 2000/01 is 1.6 per cent of earnings between the LEL and the UEL for all forms of contracting-out.

6 The contracted-out rebate for secondary contributions is 3 per cent of earnings between the LEL and the UEL.

7 The contracted out rate for secondary contributions is 3.5 per cent of earnings between the LEL and the UEL.

8 If earnings from self-employment are below this annual limit and the contributor applies for and is granted a small earnings exception Class 2 contributions need not be paid. Class 2 or 3 contributions may be paid voluntarily.

Source: Board of Inland Revenue: 020 7438 4335

10.5 Social Security Acts: number of persons receiving benefit[1]
Great Britain
At any one time

Thousands

		1992	1993	1994	1995	1996	1997	1998	1999	2000	2001	2002
Persons receiving:												
Unemployment benefit[2]	KJHA	685.2	671.9	553.5	426.5	397.8	..	..	..	..	..	..
Jobseeker's allowance[2,3]	JYXM	..	..	..	..	..	1 406.3	1 181.2	1 105.8	972.7	848.3	827.5
Sickness and Invalidity benefit[4,5]	KJHB	1 577.3	1 727.0	1 808.6	1 894.1	..	..	..	..	..	..	..
Incapacity benefit[6]	KXDT	..	..	..	..	1 812.8	1 749.2	1 671.2	1 557.1	1 504.3	1 515.2	1 496.9
Attendance allowance[7]	KXDU	1 059.0	890.0	962.0	1 046.0	1 120.6	1 183.2	1 225.6	1 243.8	1 249.6	1 290.0	1 291.4
Disability living allowance[8]	KXDW	..	1 200.6	1 343.2	1 541.4	1 729.2	1 886.5	1 995.9	2 061.3	2 130.5	2 240.5	2 322.8
Guardians' allowances[9]	KJHE	1.9	2.0	2.1	2.1	2.2	2.3	2.3	2.3	2.5	2.1	2.3
Widows' benefits[10]	KJHF	351.0	345.3	335.0	323.1	311.6	284.6	277.6	263.7	261.0	255.5	226.4
National Insurance retirement pensions[5]:												
Males[10]	KJHH	3 613.7	3 623.6	3 657.5	3 728.7	3 836.6	3 926.7	4 010.6	4 015.3	4 039.4	4 083.9	4 141.5
Females[10]	KJHL	6 683.0	6 680.0	6 727.1	6 777.2	6 948.5	6 983.2	7 031.1	6 925.4	6 928.0	6 959.7	6 982.5
Total[10]	KJHG	10 296.8	10 303.6	10 384.7	10 505.9	10 785.1	10 909.9	11 041.9	10 940.7	10 967.4	11 043.6	11 124.0
Non-contributory retirement pensions[5]:												
Males[10]	KJHI	6.1	6.1	6.1	6.5	6.1	5.9	5.7	5.1	5.2	5.1	5.0
Females[10]	KJHJ	25.7	24.9	24.1	24.5	23.5	22.5	21.3	18.7	18.3	18.3	18.3
Total[10]	KJHK	31.8	31.0	30.2	31.0	29.6	28.3	27.0	23.8	23.4	23.5	23.3
Industrial Injuries disablement pensions assessments[11]	KJHN	204.3	212.4	225.6	235.2	249.2	257.8	269.1	278.2	280.8	280.4	..
Reduced earnings allowance/ Retirement allowance assessments[11]	KEYC	159.7	156.0	154.3	152.1	154.9	155.6	152.8	153.5	153.5	152.3	..
Child benefit[5]												
Families receiving benefit[9]	KJHO	7 078.3	6 913.0	6 954.7	6 996.0	7 024.1	6 956.1	6 976.1	6 989.4	7 107.8	7 065.9	7 066.4
Family Credit[12]	ZCGF	397	488	551	608	693	748	767	791	..	..	..
Income Support[13]	KABV	5 292.9	5 858.4	5 693.7	5 670.2	5 548.9	3 958.1	3 853.1	3 814.4	3 810.5	3 927.9	3 929.8
Housing Benefit and Council Tax Benefit												
Rent rebate	KABY	3 033.9	3 052.5	3 016.1	2 964.3	2 898.3	2 792.7	2 664.1	2 518.5	2 287.8	2 133.5	2 037.6
Rent allowance[14]	KABZ	1 291.6	1 480.6	1 633.9	1 770.1	1 877.6	1 847.5	1 810.6	1 794.6	1 745.5	1 740.9	1 775.0
Council tax benefit[15]	KJPO	..	5 251.8	5 496.5	5 623.9	5 611.2	5 500.3	5 326.2	5 166.1	4 830.1	4 673.4	4 601.7
War pensions[5]	KJHR	260.1	292.9	309.2	315.4	327.5	320.7	302.0	306.0	295.7	284.3	272.7

1 See chapter text. Caseload counts at a specific date in the year which varies from benefit to benefit.
2 Figures are given at May each year.
3 Jobseeker's Allowance introduced 7 October 1996, replacing unemployment benefit.
4 A relatively small number of claims do not result in the payment of benefit but are included here because they indicate notified incapacity for work.
5 Includes overseas cases.
6 Incapacity Benefit replaced Sickness Benefit and Invalidity Benefit from 13 April 1995. Figures are taken at the last day in February.
7 Attendance Allowance figures are based at 31 March until 1995 then at the end of May. 2002 figures as at February.
8 Figures for 1993-2001 as at May. Figures for 2002 as at February.
9 Figure for 1999 as at November. Figure for 2000 as at August. Figures for 2001 and 2002 as at May.

10 Figure for 1999 as at September. Figure for 2000 as at March. Figure for 2001 as at February. Figure for 2002 as at March.
11 Industrial injuries disablement pension, reduced earnings allowance, retirement allowance assessments starting first Monday in April. Includes an allowance for late returns.
12 Family Credit was replaced by Working Families' Tax Credit from October 1999. See table 10.12 for latest figures.
13 From 9 October 1996 Income Support for the unemployed was replaced by Income-based Jobseeker's Allowance. Figures in this table up to and including 1996 include unemployed Income Support claimants. Figures from 1997 exclude unemployed who will be counted in the Jobseeker's Allowance claims.
14 Rent Allowance figures include housing association tenants.
15 Figure excludes Second Adult Rebate Claims.

Source: Department for Work and Pensions: 0191 225 7373

10.6 Unemployed benefit/jobseekers allowance[1] claimants analysed by benefit entitlement

Great Britain

Thousands

		Jobseekers Allowance November 1996	Jobseekers Allowance May 1997	Jobseekers Allowance May 1998	Jobseekers Allowance May 1999	Jobseekers Allowance May 2000	Jobseekers Allowance May 2001	Jobseekers Allowance May 2002
All Persons								
All with benefit - total	KXDX	1 643.2	1 406.3	1 181.2	1 105.2	972.7	848.3	827.5
Contribution-based JSA only	KXDY	293.5	181.1	154.2	158.2	148.2	147.0	162.6
Contribution based JSA & income-based JSA	KXDZ	41.5	28.3	23.5	27.1	19.0	18.3	19.4
Income-based JSA only payment	KXEA	1 308.2	1 196.8	1 003.6	920.4	805.5	683.1	645.5
No benefit in payment	KXEB	158.7	156.2	114.5	118.7	94.6	93.7	91.1
Total	KXEC	1 801.9	1 562.4	1 295.8	1 224.5	1 067.3	942.0	918.5
Males								
All with benefit - total	KXED	1 264.8	1 096.9	918.2	862.3	755.0	659.4	634.6
Contribution-based JSA only	KXEE	189.6	119.5	101.6	109.0	104.2	104.5	116.0
Contribution based JSA & income-based JSA	KXEF	37.1	25.4	20.7	24.4	17.2	16.7	17.5
Income-based JSA only payment	KXEG	1 038.1	952.0	795.9	728.9	633.6	538.2	501.1
No benefit in payment	KXEH	105.6	106.8	75.5	79.2	63.4	61.9	62.3
Total	KXEI	1 370.4	1 203.7	993.7	941.5	818.4	721.3	696.9
Females								
All with benefit - total	KXEJ	378.5	309.4	263.0	243.4	217.7	188.9	192.9
Contribution-based JSA only	KXEK	104.0	61.6	52.6	49.2	44.0	42.5	46.6
Contribution based JSA & income-based JSA	KXEL	4.5	3.0	2.8	2.7	1.8	1.5	1.9
Income-based JSA only payment	KXEM	270.0	244.8	207.7	191.5	171.9	144.9	144.4
No benefit in payment	KXEN	53.0	49.4	39.1	39.5	31.2	31.8	28.8
Total	KXEO	431.5	358.8	302.1	283.0	248.9	220.7	221.7

10.6 Unemployed benefit/jobseekers allowance[1] claimants analysed by benefit entitlement

continued

Great Britain

Thousands

		Unemployment Benefit[2]										
		1985	1986	1987	1988	1989	1990	1991	1992	1993	1994	1995
All Persons												
Unemployment benefit in payment - total	KJIB	872.0	955.0	676.0	521.6	304.4	356.1	641.7	671.1	598.3	471.6	386.5
Unemployment benefit only	KJIC	679.0	768.0	549.0	402.2	220.3	294.0	520.2	548.3	495.6	333.6	266.3
Unemployment benefit and Income Support[3]	KJIF	193.0	187.0	127.0	119.3	82.1	62.0	121.5	122.8	102.7	138.0	120.2
Income Support only in payment[3]	KJIG	1 690.0	1 715.0	1 407.0	1 143.0	995.5	1 044.4	1 464.0	1 746.8	1 823.1	1 714.2	1 515.0
Neither Unemployment benefit nor Income Support in payment[3]	KJIH	461.0	500.0	425.0	347.3	252.0	252.9	306.6	374.2	316.9	250.1	215.7
Total	KJIA	3 023.0	3 170.0	2 508.0	2 012.8	1 551.9	1 653.3	2 412.3	2 792.1	2 738.3	2 435.9	2 117.1
Males												
Unemployment benefit in payment - total	KJIJ	541.0	596.0	442.0	328.2	200.5	254.1	472.1	488.4	425.8	326.0	265.4
Unemployment benefit only	KJIK	375.0	435.0	331.0	227.5	128.9	197.3	362.0	378.6	335.3	212.8	168.2
Unemployment benefit and Income Support[3]	KJIN	166.0	161.0	111.0	100.7	71.6	56.9	110.1	109.8	90.5	113.1	97.3
Income Support only in payment[3]	KJIO	1 281.0	1 308.0	1 140.0	886.0	778.2	825.4	1 171.7	1 410.3	1 465.1	1 366.3	1 198.8
Neither Unemployment benefit nor Income Support in payment[3]	KJIP	252.0	275.0	279.0	209.9	157.6	166.8	205.3	255.3	215.2	167.0	144.5
Total	KJII	2 074.0	2 179.0	1 861.0	1 424.1	1 136.3	1 246.3	1 849.4	2 154.0	2 106.1	1 859.2	1 608.7
Females												
Unemployment benefit in payment - total	KJIR	331.0	359.0	250.0	278.0	103.9	101.9	169.7	182.7	172.6	145.8	121.1
Unemployment benefit only	KJIS	304.0	333.0	231.0	174.8	92.5	96.8	158.1	169.8	160.4	120.8	98.2
Unemployment benefit and Income Support[3]	KJIV	27.0	26.0	19.0	18.6	11.5	5.1	11.5	12.9	12.2	25.0	22.9
Income Support only in payment[3]	KJIW	409.0	407.0	354.0	258.0	217.3	219.0	291.9	336.5	358.0	347.9	316.2
Neither Unemployment benefit nor Income Support in payment[3]	KJIX	209.0	225.0	184.0	138.3	95.4	86.1	101.4	119.0	101.8	83.1	71.2
Total	KJIQ	949.0	991.0	788.0	588.7	416.7	407.0	562.9	638.1	632.4	576.7	508.4

1 See chapter text. Jobseeker's Allowance replaced Unemployment Benefit and Income Support for unemployed claimants on 7 October 1996. It is a unified benefit with two routes of entry: contribution-based which depends mainly upon national insurance contributions and income-based which depends mainly on a means test. Some claimants can qualify by either route. In practice they receive income-based JSA but have an underlying entitlement to the contribution-based element. Figures quoted at May of each year apart from 1996 which is at November.

2 At November each year.
3 Income Support replaced Supplementary Benefit from April 1988.

Source: Department for Work and Pensions: 0191 225 7373

10.7 Sickness benefit, invalidity benefit and incapacity benefit[1] claimants, by age and duration of spell

Great Britain at end of statistical year[2]

Thousands

		1992	1993	1994	1995[3]	1996	1997	1998	1999	2000	2001	2002
Age at 31 March[4]												
Males												
All durations: All ages	KJJA	1 327.1	1 468.0	1 544.4	1 629.9	1 627.0	1 577.9	1 530.1	1 458.4	1 432.0	1 458.5	1 454.7
Under 20	KJJB	6.2	7.1	6.8	7.8	8.7	8.8	10.7	10.7	11.2	10.2	12.7
20-29	KJJC	75.7	86.2	97.2	106.0	119.3	118.8	119.1	115.0	114.2	119.1	123.1
30-39	KJJD	125.2	145.7	160.4	189.7	202.6	208.5	216.6	217.6	222.5	234.8	236.4
40-49	KJJE	194.5	228.1	245.2	260.4	274.3	272.4	271.4	271.0	277.0	285.2	291.7
50-59	KJJF	386.6	426.1	441.7	468.7	475.4	473.4	474.1	467.3	469.8	473.5	468.9
60-64	KJJG	319.7	344.7	356.6	362.5	352.1	349.7	344.2	336.0	334.2	334.3	321.9
65 and over	KJJH	219.2	230.1	236.5	234.8	194.6	146.2	94.0	40.7	3.1	1.4	–
Over six months: All ages	KJJI	1 148.5	1 273.8	1 361.5	1 442.1	1 440.9	1 385.7	1 349.2	1 287.0	1 344.8	1 293.4	1 299.6
Under 20	KJJJ	2.9	2.8	2.9	3.0	3.9	3.6	4.7	4.9	7.4	4.7	5.6
20-29	KJJK	50.2	59.6	65.7	74.3	86.4	83.1	84.5	81.4	97.8	87.8	91.9
30-39	KJJL	94.5	112.9	126.5	152.1	165.1	166.8	177.2	181.2	203.9	197.6	201.6
40-49	KJJM	159.6	184.8	208.6	219.7	235.9	232.3	234.0	237.6	260.0	253.6	261.8
50-59	KJJN	331.7	367.2	389.2	418.2	426.5	423.8	428.2	423.8	446.8	431.6	431.7
60-64	KJJO	291.1	317.1	332.6	340.2	329.7	330.4	326.8	317.6	325.8	316.7	307.0
65 and over	KJJP	218.5	229.4	236.0	234.6	193.3	145.6	93.7	40.6	3.1	1.4	–
Females												
All durations: All ages	KJJQ	570.2	646.1	704.7	776.5	779.1	795.1	810.8	815.5	827.5	865.9	883.0
Under 20	KJJR	9.3	9.5	11.0	12.0	12.5	12.3	13.0	14.1	13.7	13.7	13.7
20-29	KJJS	70.8	75.9	74.9	79.4	88.6	89.0	87.8	85.3	84.6	85.1	87.3
30-39	KJJT	86.7	95.5	108.5	122.4	134.6	137.6	144.7	149.4	153.5	159.1	163.3
40-49	KJJU	140.6	162.6	176.0	200.7	201.9	206.5	209.7	217.2	221.0	232.0	237.1
50-59	KJJV	213.1	244.6	266.6	290.7	285.1	303.3	323.1	333.2	349.9	371.5	381.3
60 and over	KJJW	49.7	58.0	67.7	71.3	56.3	46.4	32.5	16.3	4.8	4.6	0.3
Over six months: All ages	KJJX	483.1	552.9	611.4	673.1	672.9	686.6	701.7	707.9	776.2	768.2	790.0
Under 20	KJJY	3.4	3.6	4.7	4.2	6.2	4.8	5.7	6.1	9.9	6.8	6.0
20-29	KJJZ	47.3	54.0	55.9	60.3	66.3	66.1	65.8	64.2	73.9	66.7	68.9
30-39	KJKA	70.5	79.3	92.3	103.2	113.2	117.5	120.9	126.3	142.4	139.4	143.6
40-49	KJKB	120.0	138.4	151.8	170.8	176.4	179.6	183.3	190.1	208.8	207.2	215.1
50-59	KJKC	193.0	220.8	239.9	263.7	256.6	273.1	294.1	305.2	336.5	343.5	356.4
60 and over	KJKD	48.9	56.8	66.8	70.9	54.3	45.4	31.9	16.0	4.6	4.5	0.1

1 See chapter text. Figures are based on a 1 per cent sample up to 1995 and 5% sample thereafter.
2 The end of the statistical year up to 1993/94 was the Saturday before the first Monday in April.

3 The statistical year for 1994/95 was extended to 12 April 1995, the day before the introduction of the new Incapacity Benefit which replaced Sickness and Invalidity Benefit from 13 April 1995.
4 Until 1995/96 then at 1 March. From 1995/96 the duration is taken on the the last day of February.

Source: Department for Work and Pensions: 0191 225 7373

10.8 Sickness, invalidity and incapacity benefit: days of certified incapacity

Great Britain analysis by age at end of period[1]

Years starting on first Monday in April[2]

Millions

		1990/91	1991/92	1992/93	1993/94	1994[3]/95	1995/96	1996/97	1997/98	1998/99	1999/00	2000/01
Age at 31 March[4]												
Males: All ages	KJKH	356.0	402.7	445.5	468.8	507.9	596.2	576.3	563.5	538.6	526.7	531.7
Under 20	KJKI	1.6	1.7	1.5	1.6	1.8	3.4	3.1	3.5	3.7	3.3	2.6
20 - 29	KJKJ	16.9	21.6	24.5	27.0	30.4	43.7	42.4	43.2	41.7	38.3	38.9
30 - 39	KJKK	28.1	36.1	41.4	46.6	56.0	72.3	73.9	77.7	78.2	75.8	81.3
40 - 49	KJKL	49.2	57.1	64.6	72.7	78.9	98.5	98.5	97.7	97.6	98.0	103.9
50 - 59	KJKM	100.8	112.8	121.7	129.8	141.4	172.0	170.7	172.2	170.0	161.9	165.9
60 - 64	KJKN	89.3	96.1	102.4	107.3	112.6	127.9	127.8	126.7	124.3	126.0	125.8
65 and over	KJKO	70.1	77.4	80.4	83.9	86.8	78.4	59.9	41.7	23.0	23.4	13.3
Females: All ages	KJKP	147.0	170.8	190.7	211.4	237.5	279.5	285.8	292.8	294.8	315.0	325.1
Under 20	KJKQ	2.3	2.2	2.1	2.4	2.6	4.8	4.1	4.4	4.5	4.0	3.5
20 - 29	KJKR	16.7	19.7	22.1	22.1	23.9	31.9	32.0	32.1	31.3	30.7	30.3
30 - 39	KJKS	21.7	25.6	28.5	32.7	37.6	48.0	49.8	51.4	53.4	54.9	58.9
40 - 49	KJKT	34.9	41.2	46.6	51.5	58.9	72.1	74.0	75.8	77.1	79.1	82.8
50 - 59	KJKU	56.7	63.8	71.3	79.1	88.4	101.0	107.5	115.3	120.0	134.3	142.2
60 and over	KJKV	14.6	18.2	20.1	23.6	26.1	21.7	18.4	13.8	8.4	12.0	7.3

1 See chapter text. The end of the statistical year up to 1993/94 was the Saturday before the first Monday in April.
2 Up to and including 1994/95 years start first Monday in April. The 1995/96 year started 13 April and ended 31 March. From 1996/97 years start 1 April

3 The statistical year for 1994/95 was extended to 12 April 1995, the day before the introduction of the new Incapacity Benefit which replaced Sickness and Invalidity Benefit from 13 April 1995.
4 Until 1995/96 then at 1 March.

Source: Department for Work and Pensions: 0191 225 7373

10.9 Widows' benefit (excluding widows' payment[1])
Great Britain
Number in payment analysed by type of benefit and age of widow

Thousands

		September										
		1992	1993	1994	1995	1996	1997	1998	1999	2000	2001[2]	2002
All widows' benefit (excluding widows' allowance)												
All ages	KJGA	351.0	345.3	335.0	323.1	311.6	293.2	277.6	263.7	261.0	255.5	226.4
Under 30	KJGB	2.1	2.0	1.9	1.6	1.4	1.2	1.1	1.6	1.5	1.3	0.6
30 - 39	KJGC	15.9	15.0	14.5	13.9	13.5	13.0	12.3	10.8	11.0	10.2	8.9
40 - 49	KJGD	57.8	56.0	53.0	52.8	50.1	44.9	41.3	38.5	38.1	37.2	31.1
50 - 59	KJGE	224.2	219.9	216.7	206.9	202.5	197.3	187.7	181.8	182.2	179.1	158.4
60 and over	KJGF	51.1	52.5	48.8	47.8	44.0	36.8	35.2	31.1	28.4	27.7	27.2
Widowed mothers' allowance - with dependant children												
All ages	KJGG	53.2	53.2	53.3	52.8	51.7	49.5	47.1	44.9	47.0	46.6	40.4
Under 30	KJGH	2.0	1.9	1.7	1.6	1.4	1.2	1.1	1.6	1.4	1.2	0.6
30 - 39	KJGI	14.5	13.8	13.9	13.3	12.9	12.4	11.8	10.4	10.6	9.8	8.9
40 - 49	KJGJ	25.8	27.1	26.9	27.5	26.7	24.6	23.3	22.5	23.3	23.7	20.1
50 - 59	KJGK	10.6	10.2	10.7	10.1	10.2	10.7	10.5	10.3	11.6	11.5	10.8
60 and over	KJGL	0.2	0.2	0.2	0.4	0.3	0.3	0.2	0.2	0.2	0.4	0.3
Widowed mothers' allowance - without dependant children												
All ages	KJGM	10.7	8.3	6.7	6.2	5.6	4.6	3.4	3.1	2.9	2.5	2.2
Under 30	KJGN	0.1	–	0.1	0.1	–	–	–	–	–	–	0.1
30 - 39	KJGO	1.3	1.1	0.8	0.6	0.6	0.5	0.5	0.4	0.4	0.4	0.4
40 - 49	KJGP	5.1	3.9	3.4	3.3	2.8	2.3	1.9	1.4	1.2	1.1	1.0
50 - 59	KJGQ	4.0	2.9	2.2	1.9	2.1	1.7	1.0	1.2	1.1	1.0	0.8
60 and over	KJGR	0.2	0.2	0.2	0.1	0.1	0.1	–	0.1	0.1	–	–
Widows' pension												
All ages	KJGS	134.4	122.8	108.1	95.1	84.3	71.9	63.4	57.1	54.5	53.0	42.3
40 - 49	KJGT	–	–	–	–	–	–	–	–	–	–	–
50 - 59	KJGU	89.1	76.5	65.8	54.6	48.4	43.0	37.1	35.7	35.6	34.8	25.5
60 and over	KJGV	45.3	46.3	42.1	40.5	36.0	28.9	26.3	21.4	18.9	18.2	16.6
Age-related widows' pension[3]												
All ages	KJGW	152.7	161.0	166.9	168.9	170.0	167.1	163.7	158.6	156.6	153.4	141.5
40 - 49	KJGX	27.0	25.0	22.7	21.9	20.4	17.8	16.0	14.6	13.5	12.4	9.9
50 - 59	KJGY	120.4	130.3	137.9	140.2	141.9	141.6	139.0	134.6	133.8	131.9	121.3
60 and over	KJGZ	5.2	5.7	6.3	6.8	7.6	7.6	8.7	9.4	9.3	9.2	10.3

1 This is an especially high rate of benefit which is payable for the first 26 weeks of widowhood, provided that the widow is under pensionable age (age 60) or, if she is over that age, provided that her husband was not entitled to retirement pension.

2 Figures as at March.
3 Figures for widows' basic pension are included in age-related widows' pension.

Source: Department for Work and Pensions: 0191 225 7874

10.10 Child benefits[1]
Great Britain
At 31 December

Thousands

		1992	1993	1994	1995	1996	1997[2]	1998[2]	1999[3]	2000[4]	2001[5]	2002[5]
Families receiving allowances:												
Total	KJMU	6 857	6 913	6 955	6 996	7 024	6 956	6 976	6 989	7 108	7 066	7 066
With 1 child	KJMV	2 906	2 920	2 941	2 970	2 983	..	..	3 007	3 037	3 042	3 061
2 children	KJMW	2 752	2 772	2 781	2 783	2 794	..	..	2 759	2 815	2 790	2 786
3 children	KJMX	894	908	920	928	929	..	..	916	938	924	913
4 children	KJMY	226	231	228	231	236	..	..	231	238	233	229
5 or more children	KJMZ	79	81	84	84	82	..	..	76	80	78	77

1 See chapter text.
2 Figures provided by Child Benefit Centre Management Information Statistics as a new scan was being developed.

3 Figures for 1999 are as at November.
4 Figures for 2000 are as at August.
5 Figures for 2001 and 2002 are as at May.

Source: Department for Work and Pensions: 0191 225 7373

10.11 Contributory and non-contributory retirement pensions[1]
Great Britain
Numbers in payment analysed by age-group

Thousands (percentages in italics)

						At 30 September						
		1992	1993	1994	1995	1996	1997	1998	1999	2000	2001[2]	2002
Men:												
Age-groups:												
65-69	KJSB	1 095.5	1 063.9	1 053.6	1 079.1	1 142.5	1 200.5	1 249.9	1 267.9	1 288.8	1 287.5	1 293.6
Percentage	KJSC	*30.3*	*29.3*	*28.8*	*28.9*	*29.8*	*30.5*	*31.1*	*31.5*	*31.9*	*31.5*	*31.3*
70-74	KJSD	1 104.0	1 155.3	1 196.2	1 155.0	1 146.6	1 138.2	1 131.1	1 115.4	1 117.5	1 125.9	1 134.1
Percentage	KJSE	*30.5*	*31.8*	*32.7*	*31.0*	*29.9*	*28.9*	*28.2*	*27.7*	*27.6*	*27.5*	*27.4*
75-79	KJSF	738.5	706.3	681.8	748.8	787.3	831.3	876.6	889.3	867.4	860.5	862.0
Percentage	KJSG	*20.4*	*19.5*	*18.6*	*20.1*	*20.5*	*21.1*	*21.8*	*22.1*	*21.5*	*21.0*	*20.8*
80-84	KJSH	448.9	458.2	468.0	477.4	481.8	471.2	454.5	433.6	457.7	493.6	524.3
Percentage	KJSI	*12.4*	*12.6*	*12.8*	*12.8*	*12.6*	*12.0*	*11.3*	*10.8*	*11.3*	*12.1*	*12.6*
85-89	KJSJ	180.5	189.6	197.4	204.4	209.4	217.2	225.0	231.6	231.1	237.0	234.0
Percentage	KJSK	*5.0*	*5.2*	*5.4*	*5.5*	*5.5*	*5.5*	*5.6*	*5.8*	*5.7*	*5.8*	*5.6*
90 and over	KJSL	53.8	57.2	60.6	64.5	69.4	75.3	79.3	82.6	82.1	84.6	90.4
Percentage	KJSM	*1.5*	*1.6*	*1.7*	*1.7*	*1.8*	*1.9*	*2.0*	*2.1*	*2.0*	*2.1*	*2.2*
Total all ages	KJSA	3 621.3	3 630.4	3 657.5	3 729.2	3 837.0	3 933.8	4 016.3	4 020.4	4 044.6	4 089.0	4 146.5
Women:												
Age-groups:												
60-64	KJSO	1 121.1	1 099.1	1 090.6	1 094.3	1 200.6	1 245.0	1 296.2	1 310.5	1 332.2	1 339.4	1 346.2
Percentage	KJSP	*16.7*	*16.4*	*16.2*	*16.1*	*17.3*	*17.8*	*18.4*	*18.9*	*19.2*	*19.2*	*19.2*
65-69	KJSQ	1 472.7	1 447.0	1 436.6	1 437.6	1 461.2	1 458.9	1 442.8	1 398.8	1 396.5	1 392.4	1 396.6
Percentage	KJSR	*21.9*	*21.5*	*21.4*	*21.2*	*21.0*	*20.8*	*20.5*	*20.1*	*20.2*	*20.0*	*20.0*
70-74	KJSS	1 403.8	1 469.3	1 515.9	1 447.3	1 423.7	1 398.6	1 379.6	1 341.5	1 339.8	1 341.9	1 331.0
Percentage	KJST	*20.9*	*21.9*	*22.5*	*21.3*	*20.5*	*20.0*	*19.6*	*19.3*	*19.3*	*19.2*	*19.1*
75-79	KJSU	1 126.0	1 068.0	1 023.0	1 100.6	1 148.7	1 197.2	1 255.7	1 267.3	1 227.9	1 196.0	1 179.1
Percentage	KJSV	*16.8*	*15.9*	*15.2*	*16.2*	*16.5*	*17.1*	*17.8*	*18.3*	*17.7*	*17.1*	*16.8*
80-84	KJSW	868.0	873.9	882.0	892.9	888.4	861.0	814.6	762.9	786.4	843.3	878.3
Percentage	KJSX	*12.9*	*13.0*	*13.1*	*13.2*	*12.8*	*12.3*	*11.6*	*11.0*	*11.4*	*12.1*	*12.5*
85-89	KJSY	499.2	514.1	521.9	534.3	542.2	545.9	552.3	548.9	539.7	543.5	537.8
Percentage	KJSZ	*7.4*	*7.7*	*7.8*	*7.9*	*7.8*	*7.8*	*7.8*	*7.9*	*7.8*	*7.8*	*7.7*
90 and over	KJTA	231.0	244.9	256.8	271.9	285.3	300.4	311.4	314.1	305.5	321.6	330.1
Percentage	KJTB	*3.4*	*3.6*	*3.8*	*4.0*	*4.1*	*4.3*	*4.4*	*4.5*	*4.4*	*4.6*	*4.7*
Total all ages	KJSN	6 721.7	6 716.3	6 727.1	6 779.0	6 950.2	7 006.8	7 052.5	6 944.1	6 928.0	6 978.0	7 008.1

1 See chapter text. Including pensions payable to persons residing overseas.
2 Figures are at 31 March.

Source: Department for Work and Pensions: 0191 225 7874

10.12 Family Credit/ Working Families' Tax Credit[1]

Thousands

		Great Britain As at 31 December							United Kingdom As at 30 December		
		1993	1994	1995	1996	1997	1998		1999	2000	2001
Families in receipt:											
Total	KJTO	518.3	578.0	646.5	716.7	751.4	779.7	ZCMK	965.3	1 167.8	1 293.7
Two-parent families: total	KJTP	291.0	324.6	356.9	390.2	388.0	383.4	ZCML	467.6	565.9	617.2
With 1 child	KJTQ	73.3	80.1	89.7	98.6	96.6	95.4	ZCMM	116.8	144.8	151.6
2 children	KJTR	110.1	122.4	135.1	146.1	144.4	141.7	ZCMN	178.4	220.1	243.5
3 children	KJTS	66.9	76.4	83.4	91.1	91.4	89.1	ZCMO	107.8	129.2	142.9
4 children or more children	ZIYM	40.7	45.8	48.6	54.4	55.6	57.3	ZCMP	64.6	71.8	79.2
One-parent families: total	KJTW	227.3	253.4	289.6	326.5	363.4	396.3	ZIYI	497.8	601.8	676.5
With 1 child	KJTX	117.8	133.8	152.2	170.4	189.3	203.4	ZIYJ	259.6	313.7	349.5
2 children	KJTY	79.2	86.0	99.1	111.2	121.8	136.1	ZIYK	169.6	207.6	238.7
3 or more children	KJTZ	30.4	33.5	38.3	45.0	52.3	56.9	ZIYL	68.6	80.5	88.3

1 See chapter text. Family Credit was replaced by Working Families Tax Credit in October 1999. The WFTC figures for December 1999 include Family Credit awards made before October 1999 and still current (both FC and WFTC awards last for 26 weeks).

Sources: Board of Inland Revenue: 020 7438 6275; Department for Work and Pensions: 0191 225 7373

10.13 Income support: number of claimants receiving weekly payment[1]
Great Britain
On a day in May

Thousands

		1994	1995	1996	1997	1998	1999	2000	2001	2002
All income support	KACC	3 689	3 889	3 963	3 958	3 853	3 814	3 811	3 928	3 930
All aged 60 and over	KACD	1 749	1 770	1 753	1 720	1 659	1 624	1 615	1 717	1 746
Retirement pensioners	KACE	1 407	1 417	1 404	1 383	1 338	1 308	1 305	1 406	1 428
In receipt of other NI benefit[2]	KACF	81	92	89	81	74	67	64	65	75
Others	KACG	261	261	260	256	248	249	246	246	243
All under 60	KACH	1 940	2 120	2 211	2 238	2 194	2 190	2 196	2 211	2 184
Disabled with contributory benefit[2]	KACK	113	146	161	180	195	196	207	210	236
Disabled without contributory benefit[2]	KFBJ	481	570	604	646	685	718	755	807	831
Lone parent premium not in other groups[3]	KACL	1 017	1 040	1 044	1 013	961	936	910	888	856
Others	KACM	328	363	402	398	353	341	324	306	261

1 See chapter text. Data are extracted from the Quarterly Statistical Enquiries. From 1997 figures exclude unemployed claimants who transferred to Jobseeker's Allowance from 7 October 1996.
2 Contributory/NI benefits other than Retirement pension are Incapacity Benefit (previously IVB & Sickness Benefit), Widows Pension and Widowed Mothers Allowance.

3 Figures relate to one-parent families headed by a man or a woman, where the claimant is not receiving a pensioner or disability premium.

Source: Department for Work and Pensions: 0191 225 7373

10.14 Income support[1]
Great Britain
On a day in May

Thousands

		1994	1995	1996	1997	1998	1999	2000	2001	2002
Number of regular weekly payments	KACN	3 689	3 889	3 963	3 958	3 853	3 814	3 811	3 928	3 930
Total number of persons provided for	KACO	6 465	6 858	7 004	6 973	6 769	6 689	6 666	6 782	6 749
Number of dependants	KACP	2 296	2 440	2 494	2 464	2 379	2 344	2 317	2 289	2 242
Partners	KACQ	480	528	546	551	537	531	539	565	577
Total children under 16 years	KACR	2 156	2 292	2 340	2 303	2 224	2 188	2 158	2 123	2 074
Under 11	KACS	1 623	1 708	1 728	1 685	1 605	1 557	1 524	1 489	1 441
11 - 15 years	KACT	533	584	612	618	618	631	634	634	633
16 - 17 years	KACU	112	119	129	134	129	128	131	138	138
Other dependants										
18 years and over	KACV	28	28	25	28	26	28	28	28	30

1 See chapter text. Data are extracted from the the Quarterly Statistical Enquires. Figures exclude unemployed claimants in receipt of Income Support prior to the introduction of Jobseeker's Allowance in October 1996.

Source: Department for Work and Pensions: 0191 225 7373

10.15 Income support: average weekly amounts of benefit[1]
Great Britain
May

Thousands

		1994	1995	1996	1997	1998	1999	2000	2001	2002
All income support	**KACW**	56.16	56.29	57.26	58.03	58.72	61.42	65.72	70.21	69.64
All aged 60 and over	**KJUB**	42.45	41.18	41.69	42.24	42.29	45.30	48.18	50.73	49.69
Retirement pensioners	**KACX**	36.14	34.61	34.66	34.90	34.50	36.99	39.50	41.20	40.35
In receipt of other NI benefit[2]	**KJUD**	27.83	27.28	29.17	30.73	32.42	35.58	40.76	47.31	47.08
Others	**KACY**	80.97	81.72	83.99	85.57	87.29	91.70	96.20	106.10	105.25
All under 60	**KACZ**	68.51	68.91	69.61	70.17	71.14	73.36	78.61	85.34	85.60
Disabled with contributory benefit[2]	**KADC**	29.54	31.96	33.05	33.87	33.56	34.40	36.85	41.78	41.01
Disabled without contributory benefit[2]	**KADD**	64.14	66.84	68.55	70.38	72.86	75.88	79.25	84.29	87.11
Lone parent premium not in other groups[3]	**KADE**	74.93	76.63	78.19	79.21	79.67	82.01	91.21	101.44	105.39
Others	**KADF**	68.44	64.92	63.59	63.24	65.38	66.71	68.37	71.26	56.16

1 See chapter text. Data are extracted from the Quarterly Statistical Enquiries. From 1997 figures exclude unemployed claimants who transferred to Jobseeker's Allowance from 7 October 1996.

2 Contributory/NI benefits other than Retirement pension are Incapacity Benefit (previously IVB & Sickness Benefit), Widows Pension and Widowed Mothers Allowance.

3 Figures relate to one-parent families headed by a man or a woman, where the claimant is not receiving a pensioner or disability premium.

Source: Department for Work and Pensions: 0191 225 7373

10.16 War pensions: Estimated number of pensioners[1]
Great Britain
At 31 March in each year

Thousands

		1992	1993	1994	1995	1996	1997	1998	1999	2000	2001	2002
Total	**KADG**	249.95	266.92	296.30	309.84	323.74	324.64	317.65	306.06	295.67	284.33	272.73
Disablement	**KADH**	196.19	214.53	245.44	260.30	265.37	264.59	259.16	248.93	240.76	231.62	222.25
Widows and dependants	**KADI**	53.76	52.39	50.86	49.54	58.37	60.05	58.49	55.85	54.92	52.71	50.48

1 See chapter text. From 1914 war; 1939 war and later service.

Source: Department for Work and Pensions: 0191 225 7373

10.17 Summary of government expenditure on social services and housing[1]

Years ended 31 March

£ millions

		1992 /93	1993 /94	1994 /95	1995 /96	1996 /97	1997 /98	1998 /99	1999 /00	2000 /01	2001 /02
Education[2]	KJAA	31 576	33 544	35 367	36 810	37 953	39 078	38 761	40 921	..	..
National health service	KJAB	35 413	37 259	39 879	40 691	42 383	43 878	47 194	48 362	53 039	..
Welfare services	CSWL	6 683	7 700	9 016	10 312	11 521	11 713	11 984	12 168	12 995	..
Social security benefits	KJAE	78 846	85 805	87 941	90 534	92 217	92 146	93 929	95 859	96 012	43 222
Housing	KJAF	6 984	5 919	5 634	5 445	4 593	3 415	3 605	2 825	2 947	2 973
Total government expenditure	KJAG	159 502	170 227	177 837	183 792	188 667	190 230	195 147	200 254	..	..
Current expenditure	KJAH	151 010	163 289	171 277	177 667	183 842	182 500	191 383	198 404	..	..
Capital expenditure	KJAI	8 492	6 938	6 560	6 125	4 825	3 590	4 090	3 628	..	..
Total government expenditure	KJAG	159 502	170 227	177 837	183 792	188 667	190 230	195 147	200 254	..	..
Central government	KJAK	116 304	126 371	130 819	134 954	137 487	142 133	155 290	160 041	..	..
Local authorities	KJAL	43 198	43 856	47 018	48 838	51 180	48 102	40 183	40 213	..	..
Total government expenditure	KJAG	159 502	170 227	177 837	183 792	188 667	190 230	195 147	200 254	..	..
Total government expenditure on social services and housing as a percentage of GDP[3]		25.86	26.11	25.72	25.22	24.41	23.08	22.44	21.89	..	..

1 See chapter text.
2 Includes school meals.
3 GDP adjusted to take account of change from rates to community charge.

Source: Office for National Statistics: 020 7533 5990

10.18 Government expenditure on education[1]
Years ended 31 March

£ millions

			1990 /91	1991 /92	1992 /93	1993 /94	1994 /95	1995 /96	1996 /97	1997 /98	1998 /99	1999 /00
Current expenditure												
Nursery schools	KEZN	KJBA	6 458	7 247	8 262	8 712	9 094	9 352	9 697	10 405	..	..
Primary schools		KJBB										
Secondary schools	KJBC		7 147	7 787	8 347	8 615	8 875	8 844	9 194	9 322	..	..
Special schools	KJBD		1 121	1 245	1 354	1 420	1 451	1 493	1 578	1 655	..	..
Universities[2]	KJBG		2 265	2 437	3 361	..	..	..	..	..	..	..
Other Higher, Further and adult education[3]	KJBE		4 128	4 454	4 136	..	..	..	..	..	..	..
Higher Education Funding Council[3,4]	CSWM		..	..	..	4 908	5 192	5 472	5 729	5 693	4 757	5 232
Further Education Funding Council[5]	CSWO		..	..	..	3 072	3 200	3 392	3 694	3 718	5 108	4 499
Continuing Education	CSWP		..	..	..	380	294	1 801	1 891	1 960	..	..
Other education expenditure	KJBH		1 325	1 361	1 009	905	963	948	1 277	1 355	4 690	5 429
Related current expenditure:												
School welfare[6]	KJBJ		155	214	270	346	359	328	336	372	..	..
School meals[7]	KJBK		506	556	161	149	147	148	147	138	..	..
Youth service and physical training	KJBL		348	360	393	392	401	396	389	389	..	..
Maintenance grants and allowances to pupils and students[8]	KJBM		1 028	1 379	1 705	1 972	2 204	1 660	1 440	1 289	..	..
Transport of pupils	KJBN		393	442	417	444	486	507	526	584	..	..
Miscellaneous expenditure	KJBO		2	3	8	10	31	31	49	45	..	..
Total current expenditure[9]	KJBQ		24 876	27 485	29 424	31 325	32 697	34 372	35 947	36 925	37 250	39 151
Capital expenditure												
Nursery schools	KEZP	KJBR	353	376	384	414	517	497	482	546	..	..
Primary schools		KJBS										
Secondary schools	KJBT		465	493	518	485	565	482	515	601	..	..
Special schools	KJBU		36	35	32	31	37	51	52	44	..	..
Universities[2]	KJBX		211	231	236	..	..	..	..	..	..	..
Other Higher, Further and adult education[3]	KJBV		230	293	285	..	..	..	..	..	..	..
Higher Education Funding Council[3,4]	CSWQ		..	..	..	406	412	424	74	61	31	..
Further Education Funding Council[5]	CSWR		..	..	..	194	201	187	33	29	44	..
Continuing Education	CSWS		..	..	..	6	8	8	5	–	–	–
Other education expenditure	KJBY		39	33	25	12	45	25	24	30	57	..
Related capital expenditure	KJBZ		26	20	17	23	25	17	20	24	..	..
Total capital expenditure[9]	KJCA		1 359	1 481	1 496	1 571	1 810	1 691	1 205	1 335	1 511	1 770
VAT refunds to local authorities	KJBP		493	584	656	648	860	747	801	818	816	906
Total expenditure												
Central government	KJCB		4 582	4 288	4 722	8 186	9 490	10 853	11 388	12 167	11 202	13 000
Local authorities	KJCC		22 146	25 261	26 853	25 354	25 900	25 954	26 562	26 910	27 559	27 961
Total government expenditure on education[10]	KJAA		26 728	29 550	31 576	33 544	35 367	36 810	37 953	39 078	38 761	40 921
Total government education expenditure as a percentage of GDP[11]			4.72	4.98	5.12	5.15	5.11	5.05	4.91	4.74	4.46	4.47

1 See chapter text. From 1998/99 figures have been taken from HM Treasury Public Expenditure Statistical Analyses. They are not comparable with earlier years which used different sources.
2 Includes expenditure on University departments of Education for England and Wales
3 Includes tuition fees.
4 Includes expenditure on Higher Education Institutions in Northern Ireland.
5 Includes expenditure on Further Education Institutions in Northern Ireland.
6 Expenditure on the school health service is included in the National Health Service.
7 Expenditure on school meals in England has been recharged across other expenditure headings.
8 Excludes the secondment of teachers on further training. Includes student loans expenditure.
9 Due to rounding constituent figures may not sum to totals.
10 Excludes additional adjustment to allow for Capital consumption made for National Accounts purposes. From 1995/96, figures include expenditure on training programmes in England (such as Work Based Training for Young People) reclassified as education. Therefore the figures are not comparable with earlier years.
11 GDP includes adjustments to remove the distortion caused by the abolition of domestic rates.

Sources: Department for Education and Skills;
Office for National Statistics: 020 7533 5990

10.19 Government expenditure on the National Health Service[1]
Years ended 31 March

£ millions

		1990 /91	1991 /92	1992 /93	1993 /94	1994 /95	1995 /96	1996 /97	1997 /98	1998 /99	1999 /00	2000 /01
Current expenditure												
Central government:												
Hospitals and Community Health Services[2] and Family Health Services[3]	KJQA	25 276	29 061	32 195	35 567	37 698	38 514	39 425	40 993	43 600	48 275	52 599
Administration[4]	KJQB	979	1 119	1 258	–	–	–	–	–	–	–	–
less Payments by patients:												
Hospital services	KJQC	–510	–540	–505	–368	–111	–42	–42	–48	–84	–138	–138
Pharmaceutical services	KJQD	–247	–270	–297	–324	–342	–383	–376	–396	–391	–405	–425
Dental services	KJQE	–441	–477	–470	–440	–464	–494	–447	–475	–470	–483	–506
Total	KJQG	–1 198	–1 287	–1 272	–1 132	–917	–919	–865	–919	–945	–1 026	–1 068
Departmental administration	KJQH	268	293	319	270	256	242	265	245	227	231	324
Other central services	KJQI	738	865	1 301	1 651	2 304	2 538	3 124	3 242	4 980	1 601	..
Total current expenditure	KJQJ	26 063	30 051	33 801	36 356	39 341	40 375	41 949	43 561	46 910	48 055	52 707
Capital expenditure												
Central government	KJQK	1 848	1 791	1 612	903	538	316	434	317	284	307	332
Total government NHS Expenditure												
Central government	KJAB	27 911	31 842	35 413	37 259	39 879	40 691	42 383	43 878	47 194	48 362	53 039
Total NHS expenditure as a percentage of GDP[5]		4.93	5.37	5.74	5.72	5.77	5.58	5.48	5.32	5.43	5.29	5.51

1 See chapter text.
2 Including the school health service.
3 General Medical Services have been included in the expenditure of the Health Authorities. Therefore, Hospitals and Community Health Services and Family Practitioner Services (now Family Health Services) are not identifiable separately.

4 Administration costs are not separately identifiable from 1993/94.
5 GDP adjusted to take account of change from rates to community charge.

Source: Office for National Statistics: 020 7533 5990

10.20 Government expenditure on welfare services[1]
Years ended 31 March

£ millions

		1990 /91	1991 /92	1992 /93	1993 /94	1994 /95	1995 /96	1996 /97	1997 /98	1998 /99	1999 /00	2000 /01
Personal social services												
Central government current expenditure	KJCG	163	190	202	216	197	140	101	73	53	50	49
Local authorities current expenditure:												
Running expenses	CTKQ	5 022	5 725	6 122	7 113	8 400	9 716	10 947	11 131	11 378	11 563	12 048
Capital expenditure	KJCI	227	200	189	190	235	229	210	204	199	145	128
Total	KJAC	5 626	4 732	6 513	7 519	8 832	10 085	11 258	11 408	11 630	11 758	12 226
Welfare foods service												
Central government current expenditure on welfare foods (including administration)	KJCK	120	142	171	182	185	228	264	306	355	411	411
less Receipts from the public	KJCL	–1	–1	–1	–1	–1	–1	–1	–1	–1	–1	–2
Total	KJAD	119	141	170	181	184	227	263	305	354	410	409
Total government expenditure	CSWL	5 745	4 873	6 683	7 700	9 016	10 312	11 521	11 713	11 984	12 168	12 995
Total government expenditure as a percentage of GDP[2]		1.02	0.82	1.08	1.18	1.30	1.41	1.49	1.42	1.38	1.33	1.35

1 See chapter text.
2 GDP adjusted to take account of change from rates to community charge.

Source: Office for National Statistics: 020 7533 5990

10.21 Government expenditure on social security benefits[1]
Years ended 31 March

£ millions

		1990 /91	1991 /92	1992 /93	1993 /94	1994 /95	1995 /96	1996 /97	1997 /98	1998 /99	1999 /00	2000 /01	2001 /02
Government current expenditure													
National insurance fund:													
Retirement pensions	EKXK	22 725	25 691	27 076	28 481	28 925	30 162	32 146	33 643	35 782	37 918	39 361	43 222
Lump sums to pensioners	KJDB	114	114	115	122	123	124	129	118	120	123	128	134
Widows and guardians allowances	CSDH	893	884	1 014	1 041	1 034	1 018	974	992	973	990	982	1 113
Unemployment benefit	CSDI	892	1 627	1 761	1 623	1 277	1 099	588	1	–	–1	–1	–
Jobseeker's allowance[2]	CJTJ	–	–	–	–	–	–	379	590	474	462	435	441
Sickness benefit	CSDJ	222	278	365	294	426	12	–	–	–	–	–	–
Invalidity benefit	CSDK	4 544	5 461	6 198	7 146	8 042	271	–	–	–	–	–	–
Incapacity benefit[3]	CUNL	–	–	–	–	–	7 615	7 668	7 471	7 295	6 897	6 677	6 836
Maternity benefit	CSDL	35	40	42	32	17	28	32	36	39	40	52	56
Statutory sick pay	CSDQ	966	725	688	688	24	24	24	28	28	28	36	32
Statutory maternity pay	GTKZ	344	396	416	440	498	476	500	516	552	585	611	652
Total	ACHH	31 323	35 216	37 675	39 867	40 366	40 829	42 440	43 395	45 192	46 853	47 547	52 776
Redundancy Fund	GTKN	130	276	321	110	208	128	108	88	116	148	196	194
Social Fund	GTLQ	123	130	175	189	183	216	203	200	360	920	1 957	1 859
Non-contributory benefits:													
War pensions	KJDP	688	844	976	913	1 083	1 247	1 352	1 284	1 262	1 254	1 201	1 182
Family benefits:													
Child benefit	KJDQ	4 840	5 433	5 950	6 347	6 294	6 332	6 645	7 095	7 327	8 212	8 528	8 685
One parent benefit	KJDR	227	249	275	282	289	310	317	9	–	–	–	–
Family credit	KAAA	466	626	929	1 208	1 441	1 739	2 084	2 338	2 430	1 927	–788	–
Income support/Supplementary benefits:													
Income support	KAAB	9 106	12 325	15 578	16 997	16 387	16 650	14 438	11 998	11 793	12 227	13 076	14 222
Other non-contributory benefits:													
Old persons' pensions	KJDX	38	36	36	36	35	36	30	29	29	28	28	27
Lump sums to pensioners	KJDY	8	11	13	14	13	15	15	17	17	17	17	17
Attendance allowance	KJDZ	1 698	1 706	1 553	1 795	1 963	2 194	2 393	2 640	2 682	2 834	2 957	3 121
Invalid care allowance	KJEA	229	285	345	442	526	617	736	745	783	814	849	924
Mobility allowance	KJEB	895	1 063	68	–	–	–	–	–	–	–	–	–
Disability living allowance	EKXL	–	–	1 973	2 772	3 125	3 802	4 498	5 018	5 367	5 653	6 021	6 567
Disability working allowance	EKYE	–	–	3	7	11	19	34	44	49	40	–	–
Severe disablement allowance	KJEC	407	596	640	703	776	820	906	1 007	984	1 016	1 024	1 034
Industrial injury benefits	EKXM	142	655	668	687	706	731	744	754	–	–	–	–
Housing benefit	KJED	4 735	6 053	7 670	9 163	10 345	10 773	11 276	11 315	11 311	11 247	11 616	11 688
Administration	KJEE	3 206	3 617	3 998	4 273	4 190	4 076	3 998	4 170	4 349	3 737	3 936	3 986
Total government benefit expenditure	KJAE	58 261	69 121	78 846	85 805	87 941	90 534	92 217	92 146	93 929	95 859	96 012	43 222
Total government benefit expenditure as a percentage of GDP[4]		10.30	11.65	12.78	13.16	12.72	12.42	11.93	11.18	10.80	10.48	9.98	4.33

1 See chapter text.
2 Jobseeker's allowance was introduced in October 1996 to replace Unemployment benefit and Income Support for the unemployed.

3 Sickness benefit and Invalidity benefit were replaced by a single incapacity benefit in 1995.
4 GDP adjusted to take account of change from rates to community charge.

Source: Office for National Statistics: 020 7533 5990

10.22 Government and other public sector expenditure on housing[1]
Years ended 31 March

£ millions

		1991 /92	1992 /93	1993 /94	1994 /95	1995 /96	1996 /97	1997 /98	1998 /99	1999 /00	2000 /01	2001 /02
Government expenditure												
Current expenditure												
Central government												
housing subsidies:												
to local authorities	CTMN	1 144	992	874	814	687	717	711	737	466	438	976
to public corporations	ADVA	260	208	214	228	228	236	244	218	132	152	156
to housing associations	KJRC	40	135	180	207	235	215	216	−22	−111	252	−302
grants to housing associations	KJRD	117	59	13	3	1	1	–	–	–	–	–
Local authorities												
housing subsidies	KJVK	–	1	–	–	3	1	1	1	3	3	–
Administration, etc	KGVL	373	394	364	405	402	447	509	575	590	573	576
Total current expenditure	KJRH	1 934	1 789	1 645	1 657	1 556	1 617	1 681	1 509	1 178	1 398	1 406
Capital expenditure												
Investment in housing by local authorities	KGVM	822	913	780	842	1 009	937	−52	59	−729	−368	−280
Capital grants to housing associations	KJRJ	2 045	2 583	2 136	1 774	1 329	1 393	1 102	1 021	975	1 900	925
Improvement grants	ADCE	1 152	1 240	1 287	1 105	846	980	1 157	779	766	920	1 181
Net lending for house purchase	KJRL	−782	−211	−402	−141	−136	−719	−816	−168	−82	−84	−80
Capital grants to public corporations	KJRM	482	631	439	387	837	386	400	415	431	450	467
Net lending to public corporations	KJRN	−104	39	34	10	7	−1	−57	−10	−10	−11	−11
Total capital expenditure	KJRO	3 613	5 195	4 274	3 977	3 889	2 976	1 734	2 096	1 351	2 807	2 202
Total expenditure												
Central government	KJRP	3 697	4 595	3 839	3 409	3 313	2 362	1 962	2 359	2 276	2 287	2 292
Local authorities	KJRQ	1 850	2 389	2 080	2 225	2 132	2 231	1 453	1 246	549	660	681
Total government expenditure	KJAF	5 547	6 984	5 919	5 634	5 445	4 593	3 415	3 605	2 825	2 947	2 973
Public corporations' capital expenditure												
Investment in housing	KGVN	673	549	568	560	580	574	452	424	420	400	400
Net lending to private sector	AAFR	−4	3	1	−1	−5	−1	−1	–	–	–	–
Total	KJRU	669	552	569	559	575	569	451	424	420	400	400
Total public sector housing expenditure[2]	KJRV	5 838	6 866	6 015	5 796	5 176	4 777	3 523	3 624	2 824	3 116	2 917
Total public sector housing expenditure as a percentage of GDP[3]		0.98	1.11	0.92	0.84	0.71	0.62	0.43	0.42	0.31	0.32	0.29

1 See chapter text.
2 Total government expenditure *less* grants and loans to public corporations *plus* public corporations' capital expenditure.
3 GDP adjusted to take account of change from rates to community charge.

Source: Office for National Statistics: 020 7533 5990

11 Crime and justice

Crime and justice

There are differences in the legal and judicial systems of England and Wales, Scotland and Northern Ireland which make it impossible to provide tables covering the United Kingdom as a whole in this section. These differences concern the classification of offences, the meaning of certain terms used in the statistics, the effects of the several Criminal Justice Acts, and recording practices.

Recorded crime statistics *(Table 11.1)*
Crimes recorded by the police provide a measure of the amount of crime committed. The statistics are based on counting rules, revised with effect from 1 April 1998, which are standard for all the police forces in England and Wales and now include all indictable and triable-either-way offences together with a few summary offences which are closely linked to these offences. The new rules have changed the emphasis of measurement more towards one crime per victim, and have also increased the coverage of offences. These changes have particularly impacted on the offence groups of violence against the person, fraud and forgery, drugs offences and other offences.

For a variety of reasons many offences are either not reported to the police or not recorded by them. The changes in the number of offences recorded do not necessarily provide an accurate reflection of changes in the amount of crime committed.

In order to further improve the consistency of recorded crime statistics, and to take a more victim oriented approach to crime recording, the National Crime Recording Standard was introduced in England and Wales from 1 April 2002. It is anticipated that this will increase significantly the numbers of recorded crimes counted. Some police forces adopted the principles of the Standard in advance of this date, so that there has already been an increase in the number of crimes counted. For 2001/02 as a whole, for example, it has been calculated that this has inflated the total number of crimes counted by 5%, although the impact will differ for each offence group.

Further information is available from the Home Office: *Crime in England and Wales 2001/2002*, Jon Simmons and colleagues.

Court proceedings and police cautions
(Tables 11.3 - 11.7, 11.13 - 11.17, 11.20 - 11.22)
The statistical basis of the tables of court proceedings is broadly similar in England and Wales, Scotland and Northern Ireland; the tables show the number of persons found guilty, recording a person under the heading of the principal offence of which he is found guilty, excluding additional findings of guilt at the same proceedings. A person found guilty at a number of separate court proceedings is included more than once.

The statistics on offenders cautioned in England and Wales cover only those who, on admission of guilt, were given a formal caution by, or on the instructions of, a senior police officer as an alternative to prosecution. Written warnings by the police for motor offences and persons paying fixed penalties for certain motoring offences are excluded. Formal cautions are not issued in Scotland. There are no statistics on cautioning available for Northern Ireland.

The Crime and Disorder Act 1998 created provisions in relation to reprimands and final warnings, new offences and orders which have been implemented nationally since 1 June 2000. They replace the system of cautioning for offenders aged under 18. Reprimands can be given to first-time offenders for minor offences. Any further offending results in either a final warning or a charge.

For persons proceeded against in Scotland, the statistics relate to the High Court of Justiciary, the Sheriff Court and the District Court. The High Court deals with serious solemn (ie Jury) cases and has unlimited sentencing power. The Sheriff Court is limited to imprisonment of 3 years for solemn cases, or 3 months (6 months when specified in legislation for second or subsequent offences and 12 months for certain statutory offences) for summary (ie non-Jury) cases. The District Court deals only with summary cases and is limited to 60 days imprisonment and level 4 fines. Stipendiary Magistrates sit in Glasgow District Court and have the summary sentencing powers of a Sheriff.

In England and Wales, indictable offences are offences which are:

(a) *Triable only on indictment*. These offences are the most serious breaches of the criminal law and must be tried at the Crown Court. 'Indictable-only' offences include murder, manslaughter, rape and robbery.

(b) *Triable either way*. These offences may be tried at the Crown Court or Magistrates' Court.

The Criminal Justice Act 1991 led to the following main changes in the sentences available to the courts in England and Wales:

(a) introduction of combination orders,

(b) introduction of the "unit fine scheme" at Magistrates' courts,

(c) abolishing the sentence of detention in a young offender institution for 14 year old boys and changing the minimum and maximum sentence lengths for 15 to 17 year olds to 10 and 12 months respectively, and

(d) abolishing partly suspended sentences of imprisonment and restricting the use of a fully suspended sentence.

The Criminal Justice Act 1993 abolished the "Unit Fine Scheme" in Magistrates' courts which had been introduced under the Criminal Justice Act 1991.

A *charging standard for assault* was introduced in England and Wales on 31 August 1994 with the aim to promote consistency between the police and prosecution on the appropriate level of charge to be brought.

The Criminal Justice and Public Order Act 1994 created several new offences in England and Wales, mainly in the area of Public Order, but also including male rape (there is no statutory offence of 'male rape' in Scotland, although such a crime may be charged as serious assault). The Act also:

(a) extended the provisions of section 53 of the Children and Young Persons Act 1993 for 10 to 13 year olds,

(b) increased the maximum sentence length for 15 to 17 year olds to 2 years,

(c) increased the upper limit from £2,000 to £5,000 for offences of criminal damage proceeded against as if triable only summarily,

(d) introduced provisions for the reduction of sentences for early guilty pleas, and

(e) increased the maximum sentence length for certain firearm offences.

Provisions within the Crime (Sentences) Act 1997 (as amended by the Powers of Criminal Courts Sentencing Act 2000), in England and Wales, and the Crime and Punishment (Scotland) Act 1997, in Scotland, included:

a) an automatic life sentence for a second serious violent or sexual offence unless there are exceptional circumstances (this provision has not been enacted in Scotland);

b) a minimum sentence of seven years for an offender convicted for a third time of a class A drug trafficking offence unless the court considers this to be unjust in all the circumstances, and, in England and Wales,

c) the new section 38A of the Magistrates' Courts' Act 1980 extending the circumstances in which a magistrates' court may commit a person convicted of an offence triable either way to the Crown Court for sentence - it was implemented in conjunction with section 49 of the Criminal Procedure and Investigations Act 1996, which involves the magistrates' courts in asking defendants to indicate plea before the mode of trial decision is taken and compels the court to sentence or commit for sentence any defendant who indicates a guilty plea.

Under the Criminal Justice and Court Service Act 2000 new terms were introduced for certain orders. Community rehabilitation order is the new name for a probation order. A community service order is now known as a community punishment order. Finally, the new term for a combination order is community punishment and rehabilitation order. In April 2000 the secure training order was replaced by the detention and training order. Section 53 of the Children and Young Persons Act 1993 was repealed on 25 August 2000 and its provisions were transferred to Sections 90-92 of the Powers of Criminal Courts (Sentencing) Act 2000. These changes are now reflected in Table 11.7.

The system of Magistrates' courts and Crown Courts in Northern Ireland operates in a similar way to that in England and Wales. A particularly significant statutory development, however, has been the Criminal Justice (NI) Order 1996 which introduces a new sentencing regime into Northern Ireland, largely replicating that which was introduced into England and Wales by the Criminal Justice Acts of 1991 and 1993. The order makes many changes to both community and custodial sentences, while introducing new orders such as the combination order, the custody probation order and orders for release on licence of sexual offenders.

**Previous convictions of prisoners
(Tables 11.8 and 11.9)**
Standard list offences consist of all the indictable offences plus some of the more serious summary offences. From 1 January 1996 a number of summary motoring offences became standard list offences. Excluding the new standard lists from the analysis presented in the table would slightly alter the percentages with previous convictions.

Information on previous convictions of prisoners published prior to 1995 was based upon Prison Service records. However, details of a prisoner's previous conviction were often not recorded (eg. this information was missing for 44 per cent of the 1990 male receptions under sentence). To overcome this problem the Home Office Offenders Index (a computerised database containing details of convictions for standard list offences) is now being used to provide information on prisoners' previous convictions. Unfortunately, this means that the most up-to-date information on previous convictions is not directly comparable with that previously published. Standard list offences include indictable offences and some of the more serious summary offences so the coverage is not as complete. The published information also does not relate to 'prison receptions' but to those sentenced to immediate custody for standard list offences (which accounted for 82 per cent of those sentenced to custody in 1993).

The problems with non-availability of previous history information are much less acute using the Offenders Index data source. Previous convictions were found for 95 per cent of the 1993 prison population sample. Some of the cases where information is missing would be accounted for by prisoners who are not sentenced for a standard list offence and have no previous record for such offences.

**Previous convictions of prisoners
(Table 11.19)**

The results shown in this table are reported on a cash basis for financial years 1991-92 to 2000-01 in line with funding arrangements. Financial year 2001-02 is reported on a resource accounting basis in line with the introduction of Resource Budgeting.

11.1 Recorded crime statistics[1]
England and Wales

Thousands

		Old counting rules								New counting rules			
		1991	1992	1993	1994	1995	1996	1997	1998[2] /99		1998 /99	1999 /00	2000 /01	2001 /02
Violence against the person	BEAB	190.3	201.8	205.1	218.4	212.6	239.3	250.8	230.8	LQMP	502.8	581.0	600.9	650.2
Sexual offences	BEAC	29.4	29.5	31.3	32.0	30.3	31.4	33.2	34.9	LQMQ	36.2	37.8	37.3	41.4
Burglary	BEAD	1 219.5	1 355.3	1 369.6	1 256.7	1 239.5	1 164.6	1 015.1	951.9	LQMR	953.2	906.5	836.0	878.5
Robbery	BEAE	45.3	52.9	57.8	60.0	68.1	74.0	63.1	66.2	LQMS	66.8	84.3	95.2	121.4
Theft and handling stolen goods	BEAF	2 761.1	2 851.6	2 751.9	2 564.6	2 452.1	2 383.9	2 165.0	2 126.7	LQMT	2 191.4	2 223.6	2 145.4	2 267.1
Fraud and forgery	BEAG	174.7	168.6	162.8	145.3	133.0	136.2	134.4	173.7	LQMU	279.5	334.8	319.3	317.4
Criminal damage	BEAH	821.1	892.6	906.7	928.3	914.0	951.3	877.0	834.4	LQMV	879.6	945.7	960.1	1 064.5
Drug offences[3]	LQMO	..	..	..	..	..	..	..	21.3	LQYT	135.9	121.9	113.5	121.3
Other offences[3]	BEAI	23.2	39.4	41.0	47.7	29.4	33.6	36.6	42.0	LQYU	63.6	65.7	63.2	65.3
Total	BEAA	5 276.2	5 591.7	5 526.3	5 253.0	5 100.2	5 036.6	4 598.3	4 481.8	LQYV	5 109.1	5 301.2	5 170.8	5 527.1

1 See chapter text.
2 Estimates.
3 Prior to 1 April 1998 the offence of drug trafficking was included in the "Other offences" group. From 1 April 1999, under the new counting rules, drug trafficking became part of a new "Drug offences" group which, with the expanded coverage, now includes possession and other drug offences. For 1998/99, under the old counting rules, drug trafficking - the only drugs offence counted - has been listed under drugs offences.

Source: Home Office: 020 7273 2583

11.2 Police forces: strength
End of year

		1991	1992	1993	1994	1995[1]	1996[1]	1997[1]	1998[1]	1999[1]	2000[1]	2001[1]
England and Wales												
Regular police												
Strength:												
Men	KERB	110 396	111 027	108 967	108 030	107 022	106 549	105 691	104 606	103 083	101 683	103 156
Women	KERC	14 898	15 841	16 571	17 263	17 688	18 501	19 124	19 659	19 967	20 519	21 794
Seconded:[2]												
Men	KERD	1 670	1 766	1 938	1 881	1 896	1 864	1 814	2 007	2 158	2 077	1 967
Women	KERE	163	167	182	184	202	209	233	232	256	307	294
Additional officers:[3]												
Men	KERF	73	68	63	97	105	111	200	267	324	361	493
Women	KERG	3	3	12	17	22	57	158	514	582	519	509
Special constables												
Enrolled strength:												
Men	KERH	11 592	12 251	13 240	12 772	12 751	12 594	12 483	11 331	10 667	9 120	8 238
Women	KERI	6 480	6 992	7 326	7 060	6 904	6 857	6 680	5 965	5 060	4 367	3 816
Scotland												
Regular police												
Strength[4]:												
Men	KERK	12 566	12 629	12 580	12 634	12 341	12 347	12 495	12 479	12 258	12 058	12 033
Women	KERL	1 357	1 465	1 559	1 679	1 665	1 856	2 019	2 202	2 098	2 115	2 363
Central service:[4,5]												
Men	KERM	64	70	73	79	96	94	85	85	88	95	131
Women	KERN	6	5	5	4	7	8	4	6	9	13	14
Seconded:[4,6]												
Men	KERO	103	120	109	110	108	105	101	101	85	130	49
Women	KERP	6	10	16	16	16	16	13	10	12	18	5
Additional regular police:												
Strength	KERR	93	90	58	91	90	72	72	97	91	84	88
Special constables												
Strength:												
Men	KERS	1 436	1 454	1 466	1 518	1 411	1 336	1 286	1 289	1 229	981	827
Women	KERT	342	393	431	474	467	450	437	444	422	355	309
Northern Ireland												
Regular police[7]												
Strength:												
Men	KERU	7 510	7 687	7 646	7 640	7 528	7 531	7 562	7 527	7 406	6 916	6 058
Women	KERV	707	791	818	853	887	897	923	933	987	978	918
Reserve[8]												
Strength:												
Men	KERW	4 069	4 060	4 027	4 052	3 976	3 727	3 587	3 469	3 199	2 959	2 620
Women	KERX	491	533	545	638	709	675	719	705	641	606	554

1 Figures for England and Wales are as at 30 September. Figures for Scotland are as at 31 December. From 1999, figures for Northern Ireland reflect the position at the end of the financial year, i.e. 1999 and 2000 figures are as at 31 March 2000 and 31 March 2001 respectively. Prior to this, the figures were as at 31 December.
2 NCS, NCIS, other inter-force units and officers in central service.
3 Includes Police Officers on loan to organisations outside the British Police Service such as the Royal Hong Kong police, those on career breaks, and those on maternity leave.

4 'Strength' includes central service and seconded police.
5 Instructors at Training Establishments, etc, formerly shown as secondments.
6 Scottish Crime Squad, officers on courses, etc.
7 Does not include officers on secondment.
8 Includes Part-Time Reserve, 1,000 at 31 March 2002 (643 males and 357 females).

Sources: Home Office: 020 7273 2583;
The Scottish Executive Justice Department: 0131 244 2225;
The Police Service of Northern Ireland: 028 9065 0222 ext 24135

11.3 Offenders found guilty[1]: by offence group
Magistrates' courts and the Crown Court
England and Wales

Thousands

		1991	1992	1993	1994	1995	1996	1997	1998	1999	2000	2001
All ages[2]												
Indictable offences												
Violence against the person:	KJEJ	47.2	43.6	38.9	37.6	29.1	30.0	34.6	35.7	34.4	34.0	35.3
Murder	KESB	0.2	0.2	0.2	0.2	0.2	0.3	0.3	0.3	0.3	0.3	0.3
Manslaughter	KESC	0.2	0.3	0.2	0.2	0.2	0.3	0.3	0.3	0.3	0.3	0.3
Wounding	KESD	45.5	42.0	37.4	36.1	27.4	28.3	32.7	35.2	33.9	33.5	33.5
Other offences of violence against the person	KESE	1.2	1.1	1.0	1.0	1.2	1.2	1.3	1.3	1.3	1.3	1.2
Sexual offences	KESF	5.5	5.0	4.3	4.5	4.7	4.4	4.5	4.6	4.3	3.9	3.8
Burglary	KESG	46.1	44.3	40.3	38.0	35.3	32.2	31.7	30.8	29.3	26.2	24.8
Robbery	KESH	4.8	5.1	5.1	4.9	5.2	5.9	5.6	5.5	5.6	6.0	6.8
Theft and handling stolen goods	KESI	133.5	127.9	121.6	121.6	116.1	114.5	118.4	125.7	131.2	128.0	127.0
Fraud and forgery	KESJ	21.2	20.0	17.5	18.4	17.2	16.3	17.0	19.8	20.3	19.2	18.3
Criminal damage	KESK	10.2	9.8	9.4	10.0	9.6	9.8	10.5	10.9	10.9	10.2	10.7
Drugs	KBWX	23.5	22.7	21.9	27.8	31.6	34.1	40.7	48.8	48.7	44.6	45.6
Other offences (excluding motoring)	KESL	34.4	36.0	37.8	39.4	42.2	43.5	47.6	49.6	47.9	44.5	44.2
Motoring offences	KESM	11.3	10.7	10.8	12.0	11.2	9.9	9.5	9.0	8.1	7.6	7.7
Total	KESA	337.6	324.9	307.6	314.1	302.2	300.6	320.1	341.7	342.0	325.5	324.2
Summary offences[3]												
Assaults[4]	KESO	16.5	18.0	19.0	21.9	29.3	30.0	32.0	35.3	37.5	37.4	37.7
Betting and gaming	KESP	–	–	–	–	–	–	–	–	–	–	–
Offences with pedal cycles	KBWY	1.9	1.4	1.2	1.0	1.1	1.3	1.5	2.1	1.3	0.8	0.6
Other Highways Acts offences	KBWZ	5.9	4.5	3.6	3.4	2.6	2.8	3.2	3.1	2.9	2.7	2.4
Breach of local or other regulations	KESQ	8.5	8.2	10.5	9.4	6.7	5.9	6.4	5.8	6.5	5.0	4.3
Intoxicating Liquor Laws: Drunkenness	KESR	29.4	23.8	18.8	20.2	19.8	24.2	28.8	30.8	28.7	27.2	26.2
Other offences	KESS	1.5	1.2	0.8	0.7	0.7	0.5	0.6	0.6	0.5	0.4	0.3
Education Acts	KEST	2.8	2.0	2.3	2.8	3.1	3.5	3.7	5.0	5.1	5.1	5.6
Game Laws	KESU	1.0	0.8	0.6	0.6	0.4	0.4	0.3	0.4	0.3	0.2	0.2
Labour Laws	KESV	0.1	0.1	0.1	0.1	0.1	–	0.1	0.1	0.1	0.1	–
Summary offences of criminal damage and malicious damage	KESW	28.5	24.6	21.6	22.7	22.6	23.4	24.7	26.5	27.9	28.0	26.9
Offences by prostitutes	KESX	10.9	9.8	8.2	7.7	6.8	6.6	6.6	6.0	4.0	4.1	3.7
Railway offences	KESY	5.4	4.7	4.0	5.6	6.2	9.1	11.4	12.6	15.2	17.4	22.6
Revenue Laws[3]	KESZ	115.6	121.6	123.0	126.2	123.8	139.1	143.5	174.7	165.8	175.0	146.9
Vagrancy Acts	KETB	2.1	1.8	1.7	1.9	1.6	2.0	2.0	2.2	2.7	3.3	3.2
Wireless Telegraphy Acts[3]	KETC	138.7	170.3	168.7	162.9	113.8	164.9	77.0	76.6	55.8	105.7	83.8
Other summary offences	KETD	85.6	78.9	69.0	67.8	71.5	74.7	74.7	80.9	79.3	78.1	77.8
Motoring offences (summary)[3]	KETA	713.1	723.1	664.7	638.7	642.4	649.0	649.3	665.2	632.9	607.5	583.3
Total	KESN	1 167.5	1 194.8	1 117.7	1 093.5	1 052.4	1 137.4	1 065.8	1 128.0	1 066.5	1 098.2	1 025.5
Persons aged 10 to under 18[3,5]												
Indictable offences												
Violence against the person:	KETF	5.6	5.2	5.1	5.8	4.7	5.3	5.9	5.9	6.2	6.4	6.9
Murder	KBXA	–	–	–	–	–	–	–	–	–	–	–
Manslaughter	KBXB	–	–	–	–	–	–	–	–	0.2	–	–
Wounding	KBXC	5.5	5.2	5.1	5.7	4.7	5.3	5.8	5.9	5.9	6.3	6.8
Other offences of violence against the person	KCAA	0.1	–	–	–	–	–	0.1	0.1	–	0.1	0.1
Sexual offences	KETG	0.4	0.4	0.4	0.4	0.4	0.4	0.5	0.5	0.5	0.5	0.5
Burglary	KETH	10.4	9.5	8.7	8.9	9.1	8.6	8.6	8.5	7.8	6.8	6.3
Robbery	KETI	1.4	1.4	1.5	1.7	2.0	2.4	2.3	2.2	2.0	2.2	2.8
Theft and handling stolen goods	KETJ	17.0	15.2	14.1	14.4	18.2	19.0	19.6	21.9	22.7	21.0	20.6
Fraud and forgery	KETK	0.8	0.6	0.4	0.5	0.6	0.7	0.8	1.0	1.1	1.0	1.0
Criminal damage	KETL	1.8	1.6	1.7	2.0	2.1	2.2	2.3	2.3	2.7	2.6	2.9
Drugs	KCAB	1.2	1.0	0.8	1.1	1.3	1.6	1.8	2.7	3.1	3.7	4.3
Other offences (excluding motoring)	KETM	2.8	2.7	2.4	2.8	3.3	3.8	4.2	4.2	4.3	4.4	4.4
Motoring	KETN	0.7	0.5	0.3	0.3	0.4	0.4	0.4	0.4	0.4	0.6	0.7
Total	KETE	42.0	38.1	35.4	37.9	42.2	44.4	46.4	49.7	50.6	49.2	50.3
Summary offences[3]												
Offences with pedal cycles	KETP	0.3	0.2	0.1	0.1	0.2	0.2	0.2	0.3	0.3	0.2	0.2
Breach of local or other regulations	KETR	0.3	0.2	0.1	0.1	0.2	0.3	0.2	0.2	0.2	0.2	0.2
Summary offences of criminal damage and malicious damage	KETS	2.9	2.5	2.2	2.9	3.4	3.9	4.4	5.2	6.1	6.7	6.9
Railway offences	KETT	0.3	0.2	0.2	0.3	0.4	0.4	0.5	0.5	0.5	0.4	0.4
Other summary offences	KETU	14.1	11.3	8.3	9.7	7.2	8.8	10.1	12.1	11.7	11.3	11.6
Motoring offences (summary)[3]	KCAC	13.7	10.8	8.9	8.6	9.3	10.8	10.8	11.3	12.6	14.5	16.7
Total	KETO	31.6	25.2	19.9	21.7	25.6	30.3	22.0	36.8	39.6	42.2	45.2

1 See chapter text.
2 Includes 'Companies', etc.
3 It is estimated that in 1995 there was a shortfall of 75,100 offenders found guilty for certain summary offences.

4 A new charging standard was introduced for assault in 1994.
5 Figures for persons aged 10 to under 18 are included in the totals above.

Source: Home Office: 020 8760 8270

11.4 Offenders cautioned: by offence group[1]
England and Wales

Thousands

		1991	1992	1993	1994	1995	1996	1997	1998	1999	2000	2001
All ages[2]												
Indictable offences												
Violence against the person	KELB	19.4	23.5	24.1	23.6	20.4	21.8	23.6	23.5	21.2	19.9	19.5
Murder	KCAD	–	–	–	–	–	–	–	–	–	–	–
Manslaughter	KCAE	–	–	–	–	–	–	–	–	–	–	–
Wounding	KCAF	19.1	23.2	23.8	23.2	20.1	21.4	23.3	22.9	20.6	19.3	18.9
Other offences of violence against the person	KCAG	0.2	0.3	0.3	0.3	0.3	0.4	0.4	0.6	0.6	0.6	0.6
Sexual offences	KELC	3.3	3.4	3.3	3.0	2.3	2.0	1.9	1.7	1.5	1.3	1.2
Burglary	KELD	13.3	14.4	12.8	11.5	10.5	10.2	9.4	8.4	7.7	6.6	6.4
Robbery	KELE	0.6	0.6	0.7	0.6	0.6	0.6	0.7	0.6	0.6	0.6	0.5
Theft and handling stolen goods	KELF	108.5	130.3	117.2	104.8	104.9	93.6	82.8	83.6	75.4	67.6	63.5
Fraud and forgery	KELG	5.6	7.5	8.1	7.6	7.9	7.5	7.2	7.4	7.2	6.2	5.8
Criminal damage	KELH	3.8	4.0	4.1	4.3	3.8	3.1	2.8	2.7	3.0	3.2	3.4
Drugs	KCAI	21.2	27.6	35.1	44.4	48.2	47.5	56.0	58.7	49.4	41.1	39.4
Other offences (excluding motoring)	KELI	4.1	4.8	4.2	4.0	4.0	4.4	5.0	5.0	4.6	4.4	4.2
Motoring[3]	KCAJ	..	..	..	..	..	..	..	..	..	..	..
Total	KELA	179.9	216.2	209.6	209.8	202.6	190.8	189.4	191.7	170.6	150.9	143.9
Summary offences												
Assaults[4]	KELK	1.6	2.4	3.1	4.2	8.1	9.1	9.1	–	17.0	17.2	18.2
Betting and gaming	KELL	–	–	–	–	–	–	–	–	–	–	–
Offences with pedal cycles	KCAK	1.7	1.4	0.9	0.8	0.8	0.9	0.9	0.8	0.6	0.3	0.2
Other Highways Acts offences	KCAL	1.2	1.2	1.0	0.9	0.9	0.8	0.8	0.8	0.7	0.4	0.3
Breach of local or other regulations	KELM	1.3	1.5	1.1	1.1	0.9	0.8	0.9	0.9	0.7	0.5	0.3
Intoxicating Liquor Laws:												
Drunkenness	KELN	46.0	45.0	41.1	37.7	22.9	25.9	25.7	22.8	20.3	18.1	16.6
Other offences	KELO	1.7	1.7	1.2	1.0	1.0	0.9	0.9	0.7	0.4	0.2	0.3
Education Acts	KELP	–	–	–	–	–	–	–	–	–	–	–
Game Laws	KELQ	0.2	0.1	0.2	0.1	0.1	0.1	0.1	0.1	0.1	–	–
Labour Laws	KELR	–	–	–	–	–	–	–	–	–	–	–
Summary offences of criminal damage and malicious damage	KELS	17.3	20.5	22.1	23.1	25.1	27.7	27.6	28.3	28.7	26.8	26.7
Offences by prostitutes	KELT	4.1	4.2	4.0	3.6	3.3	3.5	3.5	3.5	2.1	1.3	1.0
Railway offences	KELU	0.3	0.3	0.2	0.2	0.3	0.2	0.1	–	–	–	–
Revenue Laws	KELV	0.7	0.8	0.5	0.2	0.2	0.1	0.1	0.1	0.1	–	–
Vagrancy Acts	KELX	0.7	1.3	1.5	1.0	1.0	0.6	0.6	1.2	0.8	0.4	0.3
Wireless Telegraphy Acts	KELY	–	–	–	–	–	–	–	–	–	–	–
Other summary offences	KELZ	22.1	25.0	24.9	24.6	24.2	24.7	22.3	37.0	24.1	22.5	21.9
Motoring offences[3]	KCAM	..	..	..	..	..	..	..	..	..	..	..
Total	KELJ	98.9	105.1	101.8	98.7	88.7	95.4	92.7	96.2	95.6	88.1	85.9
Persons aged 10 to under 18[5]												
Indictable offences												
Violence against the person	KEMB	9.2	10.8	10.8	11.1	9.4	9.4	9.6	9.5	8.5	8.3	8.7
Murder	KCAN	–	–	–	–	–	–	–	–	–	–	–
Manslaughter	KCAO	–	–	–	–	–	–	–	–	–	–	–
Wounding	KCAP	9.2	10.7	10.8	11.1	9.4	9.4	9.6	9.4	8.4	8.2	8.6
Other offences of violence against the person	KCCE	–	–	–	–	–	–	–	–	–	0.1	0.1
Sexual offences	KEMC	1.4	1.3	1.1	1.1	0.8	0.7	0.7	0.6	0.6	0.5	0.5
Burglary	KEMD	11.7	12.0	10.3	9.6	8.5	8.2	7.5	6.7	6.1	5.4	5.3
Robbery	KEME	0.6	0.6	0.6	0.6	0.5	0.6	0.6	0.5	0.5	0.5	0.5
Theft and handling stolen goods	KEMF	62.3	69.8	58.9	58.6	57.4	48.2	40.9	44.0	39.6	36.9	35.2
Fraud and forgery	KEMG	1.5	1.7	1.5	1.4	1.6	1.5	1.4	1.6	1.7	1.5	1.3
Criminal damage	KEMH	2.6	2.6	2.6	2.8	2.4	2.0	1.8	1.7	1.9	2.1	2.3
Drugs	KCCF	5.0	5.4	6.7	8.5	8.7	7.9	9.7	11.0	9.6	7.9	8.5
Other offences (excluding motoring)	KEMI	1.2	1.4	1.4	1.4	1.3	1.3	1.5	1.5	1.4	1.3	1.3
Motoring[3]	KCCG	..	..	..	..	..	..	..	..	..	..	..
Total	KEMA	95.5	105.6	94.1	95.1	90.6	79.9	73.7	77.2	69.8	64.3	63.5
Summary offences												
Offences with pedal cycles	KEMK	0.9	0.7	0.4	0.5	0.4	0.5	0.5	0.4	0.3	0.2	0.1
Breach of local or other regulations	KEMM	0.5	0.6	0.3	0.4	0.3	0.3	0.3	0.3	0.2	0.2	0.1
Summary offences of criminal damage and malicious damage	KEMN	10.1	10.7	11.4	12.5	12.8	13.8	13.5	14.2	14.7	14.4	15.2
Railway offences	KEMO	0.1	0.1	0.1	0.1	0.1	0.1	0.1	–	–	–	–
Other summary offences	KEMP	15.5	16.0	15.3	15.6	10.3	10.8	9.1	13.8	9.9	9.2	9.5
Motoring offences[3]	KCCH	..	..	..	..	..	..	..	..	..	..	..
Total	KEMJ	27.1	28.1	27.5	29.2	30.0	33.2	30.8	32.5	34.2	33.2	34.5

1 See chapter text.
2 Includes 'Companies', etc.
3 Not applicable as motoring offences may attract written warning.
4 A new charging standard was introduced for assault in 1994.
5 Figures for persons aged 10 to under 18 are included in the totals above.

Source: Home Office: 020 8760 8270

11.5 Offenders found guilty of offences[1]: by age and sex
England and Wales
Magistrates' courts and the Crown Court

Thousands

		1991	1992	1993	1994	1995	1996	1997	1998	1999	2000	2001
Males												
Indictable offences												
All ages	KEFA	293.5	282.8	268.2	273.2	263.2	261.1	276.5	292.9	291.7	276.5	275.5
10 and under 15 years	KEFB	5.1	4.9	5.5	6.9	7.1	6.6	7.1	8.1	8.9	8.7	9.0
15 and under 18 years	KEFC	32.3	28.9	26.2	28.7	30.2	32.5	33.6	35.2	35.1	33.8	34.4
18 and under 21 years	KEFD	65.3	58.9	53.0	50.3	47.4	46.3	48.4	51.8	52.6	49.9	48.2
21 years and over	KEFE	190.8	190.1	183.4	187.4	178.6	175.6	187.3	197.9	195.0	184.0	183.9
Summary offences[2]												
All ages	KEFF	956.3	959.6	892.0	871.0	862.0	903.6	880.9	929.0	886.6	881.0	826.6
10 and under 15 years	KEFG	1.8	1.8	1.8	2.3	2.9	2.8	3.0	3.9	5.1	5.8	6.2
15 and under 18 years	KEFH	21.7	21.7	16.8	17.7	20.5	24.6	25.9	28.5	30.3	32.2	34.5
18 and under 21 years	KEFI	109.8	97.6	85.7	82.9	84.0	88.4	91.0	96.3	94.8	93.0	92.2
21 years and over	KEFJ	816.9	838.5	787.7	768.2	754.6	787.9	761.0	800.3	756.5	750.0	693.6
Females												
Indictable offences												
All ages	KEFK	41.9	40.0	37.8	39.5	37.5	38.0	42.2	47.3	49.0	47.7	47.4
10 and under 15 years	KEFL	0.6	0.6	0.7	1.0	1.0	1.0	1.0	1.4	1.4	1.5	1.6
15 and under 18 years	KEFM	4.0	3.6	3.1	3.8	4.0	4.2	4.6	5.1	5.2	5.2	5.3
18 and under 21 years	KEFN	8.1	7.3	6.3	6.2	5.7	5.7	6.3	7.1	7.6	7.5	7.0
21 years and over	KEFO	29.2	28.5	27.7	28.6	26.8	27.2	30.4	33.7	34.7	33.5	33.5
Summary offences[2]												
All ages	KEFP	194.1	219.0	213.3	211.5	180.5	222.9	174.9	188.3	171.0	208.3	190.2
10 and under 15 years	KEFQ	0.1	0.1	0.2	0.2	0.4	0.4	0.5	0.6	0.8	0.9	0.9
15 and under 18 years	KEFR	2.0	1.7	1.2	1.5	1.8	2.6	3.4	3.8	3.4	3.3	3.6
18 and under 21 years	KEFS	12.1	11.2	10.0	9.6	10.4	12.1	11.1	12.1	10.8	11.8	11.1
21 years and over	KEFT	179.8	206.0	201.9	200.2	167.9	207.9	160.0	171.7	155.4	192.3	174.7
Companies, etc												
Indictable offences	KEFU	2.2	2.1	1.7	1.4	1.5	1.5	1.3	1.5	1.3	1.3	1.3
Summary offences[2]	KEFV	17.2	16.2	12.5	10.9	9.9	10.9	10.0	10.7	8.9	8.8	8.6

1 See chapter text.
2 It is estimated that in 1995 there was a shortfall of 75,100 offenders found guilty for certain summary offences.

Source: Home Office: 020 8760 8270

11.6 Persons cautioned by the police[1]: by age and sex
England and Wales

Thousands

		1991	1992	1993	1994	1995	1996	1997	1998	1999	2000	2001
Males												
Indictable offences												
All ages	KEGA	131.4	155.0	153.6	153.6	149.3	142.6	143.3	142.9	126.1	109.7	103.8
10 and under 15 years	KEGB	33.0	35.0	31.4	32.3	29.2	25.1	22.9	23.7	22.0	20.3	19.7
15 and under 18 years	KEGC	38.5	41.1	37.1	35.5	35.3	33.0	32.0	32.0	28.7	25.0	24.5
18 and under 21 years	KEGD	18.4	23.8	24.5	25.0	24.8	24.3	25.2	25.7	22.7	20.1	18.5
21 years and over	KEGE	41.4	55.1	60.6	60.7	60.0	60.2	63.2	61.5	52.7	44.3	41.2
Summary offences												
All ages	KEGF	85.3	90.0	86.3	83.6	73.8	79.2	75.7	76.9	76.1	69.6	68.0
10 and under 15 years	KEGG	8.9	9.3	9.4	10.5	10.1	10.3	9.9	10.6	11.7	12.0	12.7
15 and under 18 years	KEGH	14.8	15.1	14.4	14.7	15.4	18.0	16.1	16.1	16.1	14.9	15.2
18 and under 21 years	KEGI	9.7	11.3	11.4	11.3	11.1	13.0	12.9	13.2	13.0	11.9	11.0
21 years and over	KEGJ	51.9	54.3	51.0	47.0	37.1	37.9	36.9	37.0	35.3	30.9	29.0
Females												
Indictable offences												
All ages	KEGK	48.5	61.1	55.9	56.2	53.3	48.2	46.0	48.8	44.5	41.2	40.1
10 and under 15 years	KEGL	11.0	14.3	12.8	15.2	14.0	10.8	9.2	11.1	9.8	10.0	10.1
15 and under 18 years	KEGM	13.1	15.2	12.8	12.4	12.2	10.9	9.5	10.3	9.3	9.0	9.3
18 and under 21 years	KEGN	5.5	7.3	6.7	6.1	6.0	5.6	5.7	5.9	5.7	5.2	4.9
21 years and over	KEGO	19.0	24.4	23.6	22.4	21.1	20.9	21.5	21.4	19.6	17.0	15.9
Summary offences												
All ages	KEGP	13.6	15.1	18.5	15.1	14.8	16.2	17.0	19.2	9.4	18.5	18.0
10 and under 15 years	KEGQ	1.0	1.2	1.3	1.5	1.7	1.8	1.7	2.1	2.5	2.8	2.9
15 and under 18 years	KEGR	2.4	2.5	2.3	2.5	2.7	3.2	3.2	3.7	3.9	3.7	3.8
18 and under 21 years	KEGS	1.9	2.0	2.1	1.9	1.9	2.1	2.3	2.6	2.7	2.5	2.3
21 years and over	KEGT	8.3	9.5	9.8	9.2	8.6	9.1	9.9	10.8	10.3	9.6	9.0

1 See chapter text.

Source: Home Office: 020 8760 8270

11.7 Sentence or order passed on offenders sentenced for indictable offences[1]: by sex
England and Wales

Magistrates' courts and the Crown Court

Percentages

		1991	1992	1993	1994	1995	1996	1997	1998	1999	2000	2001
Males												
Sentence or order												
Absolute discharge	KEJB	0.7	0.8	0.9	0.8	0.8	0.8	0.7	0.7	0.6	0.6	0.6
Conditional discharge	KEJC	16.1	18.0	18.6	17.4	16.2	15.6	15.5	15.3	15.0	14.1	13.4
Community rehabilitation order	KEJD	9.3	9.1	9.3	10.2	10.0	9.9	10.0	10.0	10.1	10.1	10.7
Supervision order	KEJE	1.4	1.4	2.0	2.4	2.7	2.9	2.7	2.7	2.7	2.4	2.3
Fine	KEJF	36.0	34.2	33.8	31.8	30.0	28.6	28.2	28.4	27.7	25.7	24.5
Community punishment order	KEJG	9.5	10.3	11.4	11.1	10.6	9.9	9.5	9.3	9.3	9.5	9.0
Attendance centre order	KEJH	1.9	1.8	1.9	2.0	2.0	1.9	1.8	1.7	1.8	1.5	1.2
Community punishment and rehabilitation order	KIJW	..	0.3	2.1	2.7	3.0	3.5	3.7	3.8	3.7	3.6	2.6
Curfew order	LUJP	..	..	..	..	..	0.1	0.1	0.2	0.3	0.5	0.7
Care order	KEJJ	–	..	..	..	..	..	..	..	..	..	..
Sec 90-92	LUJQ	–	–	0.1	0.1	0.1	0.2	0.3	0.2	0.2	0.2	0.2
Young offender institution	KEJK	4.6	4.3	0.8	4.9	5.6	6.1	6.1	6.0	6.2	5.2	4.5
Detention and training order	LUJR	..	..	..	..	..	..	..	–	0.1	–	1.9
Imprisonment												
Fully suspended	KEJL	6.4	5.4	0.9	0.7	0.7	0.8	0.8	0.7	0.6	0.7	0.6
Partly suspended[1]	KAFN	0.3	0.2	..	..	..	..	..	..	..	..	..
Unsuspended	KEJM	11.4	11.6	12.0	13.6	16.0	17.2	17.9	18.2	18.7	21.3	20.0
Other sentence or order	KEJN	2.2	2.5	2.5	2.3	2.2	2.4	3.0	2.6	3.1	4.7	3.4
Total number of offenders (thousands) = 100 per cent	KEJA	291.9	282.5	267.5	272.6	262.9	260.8	275.4	292.4	291.3	277.1	274.6
Females												
Sentence or order												
Absolute discharge	KEKB	0.9	1.0	0.9	0.9	0.8	0.9	0.8	0.7	0.7	0.6	0.6
Conditional discharge	KEKC	35.9	37.5	35.4	34.4	32.4	30.6	29.4	28.7	26.9	24.9	23.9
Community rehabilitation order	KEKD	17.0	15.9	15.4	17.5	18.0	19.0	19.1	19.1	19.4	19.6	19.1
Supervision order	KEKE	1.1	1.3	1.8	2.4	2.7	2.9	2.9	3.1	2.9	2.8	2.7
Fine	KEKF	27.2	26.2	29.2	25.6	24.1	22.5	21.8	21.3	20.8	20.1	18.6
Community punishment order	KEKG	4.6	5.3	6.1	6.4	6.6	6.5	6.5	6.5	7.1	7.5	7.3
Attendance centre order	KEKH	0.4	0.4	0.5	0.8	1.0	1.0	1.0	0.9	0.9	0.8	0.6
Community punishment and rehabilitation order	KIJX	..	0.2	1.4	2.1	2.4	3.0	3.2	3.4	3.3	3.0	2.1
Curfew order	LUJT	..	..	..	..	..	–	0.1	0.1	0.3	0.4	0.6
Care order	KEKJ	–	..	..	..	..	..	..	..	..	..	..
Sec 90-92	LUJU	–	–	–	–	0.1	0.1	0.1	–	0.1	0.1	0.1
Young offender institution	KEKK	0.9	0.8	1.1	1.1	1.5	1.8	1.9	2.2	2.4	2.2	2.0
Detention and training order	LUJV	..	..	..	..	..	..	..	–	–	–	0.8
Imprisonment												
Fully suspended	KEKL	5.9	4.8	1.2	1.1	1.4	1.5	1.6	1.5	1.3	1.3	1.2
Partly suspended[2]	KAFP	0.3	0.2	..	..	..	..	..	..	..	..	..
Unsuspended	KEKM	4.1	4.4	5.0	5.9	7.4	8.4	9.4	10.0	11.0	12.2	12.1
Other sentence or order	KEKN	1.8	2.2	1.9	1.7	1.8	2.0	2.2	2.5	3.0	4.7	3.5
Total number of offenders (thousands) = 100 per cent	KEKA	41.9	40.0	37.7	39.5	37.5	38.0	42.1	47.2	49.0	47.8	47.3

1 See chapter text.
2 Abolished October 1992.

Source: Home Office: 020 8760 8270

11.8 Offenders sentenced to immediate custody for standard list offences[1]
England and Wales

Between 1997 and 2000: by gender and number of previous convictions

Percentages and numbers[2]

| | | Number of previous convictions[3] | | | | | |
Year and gender	Nil	1 - 2	3 - 6	7 - 10	11 and over	Total sentenced for standard list offences	Total sentenced to custody for all offences
1997							
Males	16	16	23	16	29	85 580	87 620
Females	31	18	22	12	17	5 345	5 473
Total	17	16	23	16	28	90 934	93 093
1998							
Males	20	14	20	15	30	91 800	94 000
Females	37	16	18	10	18	6 400	6 600
Total	22	14	20	15	29	98 200	100 600
1999							
Males	32	22	19	10	17	95 500	97 800
Females	49	23	15	6	7	7 300	7 500
Total	34	22	19	9	16	102 800	105 300
2000							
Males	30	17	14	11	28	95 700	98 300
Females	40	17	15	10	17	7 700	7 900
Total	31	17	14	11	27	103 400	106 200

1 See chapter text.
2 The percentages are based on samples of 6 994, 7 562, 6 096 and 17 771 males and 379, 459, 426 and 1 361 females in the years 1997, 1998, 1999 and 2000 respectively. Percentages are rounded and therefore may not add to 100.

3 Counting one conviction per court appearance.

Source: Home Office: 020 7273 4122

11.9 Population in Prison Service establishments under sentence[1]
England and Wales

On 30 June each year: by gender and number of previous convictions

Percentages and numbers[2]

| | | Number of previous convictions[3] | | | | | |
Year and gender	Previous convictions not found[3]	Nil	1 - 2	3 - 6	7 - 10	11 and over	Number of prisoners
1997							
Males	9	15	16	20	15	24	46 611
Females	15	36	16	15	8	11	2 063
Total	9	16	16	20	15	24	48 674
1998							
Males	5	16	14	19	15	31	49 793
Females	11	35	17	17	8	13	2 366
Total	5	17	14	19	14	30	52 159
1999							
Males	8	12	15	21	15	28	47 989
Females	16	27	18	17	9	13	2 486
Total	9	13	15	21	15	27	50 475
2000							
Males	9	14	15	19	14	29	50 437
Females	10	32	15	17	10	14	2 633
Total	9	15	15	19	14	28	53 070

1 Excludes fine defaulters.
2 The percentages are based on samples of 11 800, 12 303, 12 341 and 12 833 males and 2 032, 2 291, 2 472 and 2 633 females in the years 1997, 1998, 1999 and 2000 respectively. Percentages are rounded and therefore may not add to 100.

3 In some cases it was not possible to find details on previous convictions. This can happen when a prisoner is not sentenced for a standard list offence and has no previous record for such offences. See chapter text.

Source: Home Office: 020 7273 4122

11.10 Receptions and average population in custody
England and Wales

Numbers

		1991	1992	1993	1994	1995	1996	1997	1998	1999	2000	2001[1]
Receptions												
Type of inmate:												
Untried	KEDA	54 676	49 869	53 565	57 079	55 287	58 888	62 066	64 697	64 572	54 892	53 467
Convicted, unsentenced	KEDB	19 927	21 250	30 098	34 563	32 039	34 987	36 424	43 387	45 893	43 889	46 851
Sentenced	KEDE	72 313	69 832	72 966	83 657	89 173	82 861	87 168	91 282	93 965	93 671	91 978
Immediate custodial sentence	KEDF	53 340	50 006	50 563	61 188	69 016	74 306	80 832	85 908	90 238	91 195	90 523
Young offenders	KEDG	15 028	13 174	13 205	14 956	16 244	17 593	18 743	19 599	21 020	21 322	20 969
Up to 18 months	KEDH	12 447	10 862	11 114	12 739	13 783	14 156	14 893	15 965	17 338	17 158	17 475
Over 18 months up to 4 years	KEDJ	2 270	1 982	1 752	1 882	2 129	2 913	3 254	3 153	3 171	3 447	2 895
Over 4 years (including life)	KEDL	311	330	339	335	332	524	596	481	511	717	599
Adults	KFBO	38 312	36 832	37 358	46 232	52 772	56 713	62 089	66 309	69 218	69 873	69 554
Up to 18 months	KEDV	27 159	25 872	27 643	35 520	40 638	42 673	46 727	50 844	53 814	54 147	53 559
Over 18 months up to 4 years	KEDW	8 199	7 967	6 864	7 744	8 811	10 119	10 972	11 126	10 892	11 199	11 071
Over 4 years (including life)	KEDX	2 954	2 993	2 851	2 968	3 323	3 921	4 390	4 339	4 512	4 527	4 924
Committed in default of payment of a fine	KEDY	18 973	19 826	22 403	22 469	20 157	8 555	6 336	5 374	3 727	2 476	1 455
Young offenders	KEEA	4 209	4 282	3 353	3 268	2 846	885	555	568	366	216	138
Adults	KAFQ	14 764	15 544	19 050	19 201	17 311	7 670	5 781	4 806	3 361	2 260	1 317
Non-criminal prisoners	KEDM	2 791	3 109	5 073	4 507	3 789	3 128	3 204	3 290	3 271	3 153	4 630
Immigration Act 1971	KEDN	1 225	1 272	1 837	1 641	1 825	1 857	2 122	2 348	2 443	2 455	4 451
Others	KEDO	1 566	1 837	3 236	2 866	1 964	1 271	1 082	942	828	698	179
Average population												
Total in custody	KEDP	45 897	45 817	44 565	48 794	51 047	55 281	61 114	65 298	64 771	64 602	66 301
Total in prison service establishments	KFBQ	44 809	44 718	44 551	48 621	50 962	55 281	61 114	65 298	64 771	64 602	66 301
Police cells[2]	KFBN	1 088	1 098	14	173	85	–	–	–	–	–	–
Untried	KEDQ	7 545	7 387	7 960	9 047	8 352	8 374	8 453	8 157	7 947	7 098	6 924
Convicted, unsentenced	KEDR	1 930	1 987	2 700	3 181	2 954	3 238	3 678	4 411	4 571	4 177	4 314
Remanded for medical examination[3]	KEDS	17	14	12	15	9	6	8	9	8	..	40
Others	KEDT	1 913	1 973	2 688	3 166	2 945	3 232	3 670	4 402	4 563	..	4 274
Sentenced	KEDU	35 034	35 037	33 317	35 753	39 040	43 043	48 413	52 176	51 691	52 685	54 051
Immediate custodial sentence	KFBR	34 665	34 707	32 825	35 308	38 636	42 863	48 272	52 045	51 596	52 620	54 006
Young offenders	KFBS	5 754	5 382	5 054	5 258	5 752	6 700	7 820	8 490	8 344	8 435	8 559
Up to 18 months	KFBU	3 095	2 808	2 671	2 736	2 911	2 930	3 267	3 507	3 394	3 987	4 194
Over 18 months up to 4 years	KFBV	2 033	1 999	1 800	1 902	2 159	2 606	3 019	3 155	3 158	3 373	3 241
Over 4 years (including life)	KFBW	623	575	583	620	682	1 164	1 534	1 828	1 792	1 075	1 124
Adults	KFCO	28 911	29 326	27 771	30 050	32 884	36 162	40 451	43 556	43 343	44 186	45 447
Up to 18 months	KFCP	7 194	7 170	7 054	8 051	8 845	8 199	9 724	10 308	9 441	9 851	9 825
Over 18 months up to 4 years	KFCQ	9 333	9 416	8 445	9 164	10 184	10 320	10 777	11 707	11 322	14 267	14 750
Over 4 years (including life)	KFCR	12 384	12 740	12 272	12 835	13 855	17 644	19 950	21 541	22 580	20 068	20 872
Committed in default of payment of a fine	KFCS	369	330	492	446	403	180	141	131	95	64	45
Young offenders	KFEW	85	65	77	62	54	22	13	15	9	4	6
Adults	KFEX	284	265	415	384	349	158	128	116	86	60	39
Non-criminal prisoners	KEEB	300	308	574	640	615	626	571	554	558	641	1 012
Immigration Act 1971	KEEC	222	227	431	487	483	516	485	476	485	576	955
Others	KEED	78	81	143	153	132	111	87	78	73	63	57

1 Provisional.
2 Mostly untried prisoners.
3 Under Section 30, Magistrates' Courts Act 1980.

Source: Home Office: 020 7217 5567

11.11 Prison population serving sentences: analysis by age and offence[1]
England and Wales

Numbers

		Age in years							
	Total	15 - 17	18 - 20	21 - 24	25 - 29	30 - 39	40 - 49	50 - 59	60 and over
At 30 June 1996									
Offences									
Males									
Total	41 323	1 262	5 101	7 569	8 719	11 259	4 723	2 002	688
Violence against the person	9 236	177	937	1 547	1 986	2 747	1 174	501	167
Sexual offences	3 939	32	120	246	437	1 175	946	628	355
Burglary	6 351	373	1 287	1 753	1 484	1 199	202	49	4
Robbery	5 594	268	978	1 171	1 316	1 445	350	62	4
Theft, handling, fraud and forgery	4 709	180	540	798	893	1 311	678	266	43
Drugs offences	5 273	11	293	746	1 239	1 787	850	286	61
Other offences	4 729	119	600	1 050	1 102	1 248	419	160	31
Offence not known	1 492	102	346	258	262	347	104	50	23
Females									
Total	1 732	57	195	263	373	534	223	77	10
Violence against the person	355	16	51	55	60	89	57	22	5
Sexual offences	12	-	2	3	1	2	4	-	-
Burglary	80	5	23	25	12	11	4	-	-
Robbery	124	17	28	23	32	20	3	1	-
Theft, handling, fraud and forgery	433	7	29	48	115	141	62	27	4
Drugs offences	486	-	35	65	106	192	68	19	1
Other offences	166	5	23	31	32	52	16	7	-
Offence not known	76	7	4	13	15	27	9	1	-
At 30 June 1997									
Offences									
Males									
Total	46 739	1 620	6 078	8 472	9 939	12 503	5 046	2 299	782
Violence against the person	10 045	216	1 039	1 631	2 181	3 014	1 234	549	181
Sexual offences	4 069	39	121	232	465	1 169	934	726	383
Burglary	7 983	448	1 574	2 184	1 938	1 515	245	71	8
Robbery	6 278	437	1 227	1 352	1 370	1 471	337	73	11
Theft, handling, fraud and forgery	5 052	167	605	865	1 020	1 417	638	272	68
Drugs offences	6 486	29	356	892	1 494	2 242	1 027	371	75
Other offences	1 746	142	437	296	324	321	141	64	21
Offence not known	5 080	142	719	1 020	1 147	1 354	490	173	35
Females									
Total	2 066	53	198	372	449	615	271	91	17
Violence against the person	391	18	43	72	61	105	62	22	8
Sexual offences	8	-	1	1	1	3	2	-	-
Burglary	101	4	13	29	31	17	6	1	-
Robbery	161	18	50	29	29	28	5	2	-
Theft, handling, fraud and forgery	455	3	25	78	100	148	71	25	5
Drugs offences	691	4	43	111	173	237	88	31	4
Other offences	68	-	8	12	15	25	4	4	-
Offence not known	191	6	15	40	39	52	33	6	-
At 30 June 1998									
Offences									
Males									
Total	49 902	1 627	5 807	8 780	10 590	14 109	5 485	2 608	896
Violence against the person	10 530	235	1 028	1 670	2 215	3 239	1 345	594	204
Sexual offences	4 781	51	140	224	560	1 366	1 113	872	455
Burglary	8 541	432	1 502	2 256	2 179	1 799	298	65	10
Robbery	6 452	449	1 244	1 319	1 427	1 587	350	61	15
Theft, handling, fraud & forgery	5 193	190	556	906	1 071	1 535	587	300	48
Drugs offences	7 103	38	308	944	1 616	2 569	1 092	441	95
Other offences	5 277	137	690	1 087	1 132	1 461	509	215	46
Offence not known	2 025	95	339	374	390	553	191	60	23
Females									
Total	2 367	62	210	425	501	709	332	116	12
Violence against the person	420	11	44	68	80	116	68	27	6
Sexual offences	16	1	1	1	2	5	5	1	-
Burglary	118	6	17	27	32	28	6	2	-
Robbery	177	24	45	33	36	28	8	3	-
Theft, handling, fraud & forgery	514	6	36	97	107	169	72	26	1
Drugs offences	794	3	32	134	181	267	131	44	2
Other offences	218	8	22	42	41	65	30	8	2
Offences not known	110	3	13	23	22	31	12	5	1

11.11
continued

Prison population serving sentences: analysis by age and offence[1]
England and Wales

Numbers

| | Total | Age in years | | | | | | | |
		15 - 17	18 - 20	21 - 24	25 - 29	30 - 39	40 - 49	50 - 59	60 and over
At 30 June 1999									
Offences									
Males									
Total	48 956	1 643	5 633	8 245	10 080	14 072	5 552	2 678	1 053
Violence against the person	10 435	250	1 070	1 548	2 033	3 260	1 428	608	238
Sexual offences	4 930	48	99	236	485	1 448	1 133	935	546
Burglary	8 626	447	1 441	2 207	2 230	1 899	322	73	7
Robbery	6 175	410	1 126	1 384	1 272	1 556	353	58	16
Theft, handling, fraud and forgery	5 027	208	585	886	1 065	1 418	529	279	57
Drugs offences	7 303	36	338	866	1 614	2 720	1 132	476	121
Other offences	5 224	185	742	968	1 120	1 422	541	197	49
Offence not known	1 236	59	232	150	261	349	114	52	19
Females									
Total	2 436	67	224	427	491	798	301	108	20
Violence against the person	429	17	65	50	77	125	63	25	7
Sexual offences	17	-	2	1	-	5	7	1	1
Burglary	158	7	27	37	38	41	6	2	-
Robbery	158	15	24	36	33	41	6	3	-
Theft, handling, fraud and forgery	502	11	33	113	99	159	58	24	5
Drugs offences	875	2	50	131	184	340	129	35	4
Other offences	220	13	9	45	43	68	26	16	-
Offence not known	77	2	14	14	17	19	6	2	3
At 30 June 2000									
Offences									
Males									
Total	50 514	1 788	5 911	8 691	10 060	14 454	5 720	2 749	1 140
Violence against the person	10 807	256	1 092	1 658	1 964	3 440	1 480	690	226
Sexual offences	5 070	58	139	261	460	1 424	1 157	937	635
Burglary	8 824	453	1 426	2 165	2 291	2 040	359	77	13
Robbery	6 158	399	1 087	1 343	1 315	1 556	387	57	14
Theft, handling, fraud & forgery	5 422	312	798	1 006	1 118	1 419	483	233	53
Drugs offences	7 526	43	405	949	1 591	2 765	1 188	480	106
Other offences	5 909	225	818	1 180	1 161	1 616	598	236	76
Offence not known	797	43	148	131	160	194	67	38	16
Females									
Total	2 666	65	266	457	563	863	335	102	15
Violence against the person	410	22	46	56	71	122	62	26	6
Sexual offences	20	-	1	1	1	7	5	2	2
Burglary	158	10	24	33	45	40	5	1	-
Robbery	195	13	43	39	39	50	10	1	-
Theft, handling, fraud & forgery	638	7	61	117	154	196	74	24	4
Drugs offences	947	6	58	151	200	354	141	34	2
Other offences	229	5	26	47	40	70	31	9	1
Offence not known	69	2	7	13	12	23	7	5	-
At 30 June 2001[2]									
Offences									
Males									
Total	51 313	1 918	5 864	9 051	9 964	14 538	6 044	2 723	1 211
Violence against the person	11 347	343	1 180	1 810	1 997	3 432	1 631	702	252
Sexual offences	5 048	53	145	265	406	1 368	1 172	953	686
Burglary	8 410	383	1 176	2 039	2 190	2 158	389	61	15
Robbery	6 449	429	1 191	1 436	1 309	1 652	360	60	12
Theft, handling, fraud & forgery	5 370	318	742	1 086	1 080	1 362	510	217	55
Drugs offences	7 980	47	423	1 126	1 686	2 828	1 278	479	113
Other offences	5 868	285	840	1 146	1 163	1 541	616	213	66
Offence not known	841	61	165	143	133	196	90	40	13
Females									
Total	2 899	63	305	493	589	906	406	119	18
Violence against the person	441	18	63	55	72	123	81	24	6
Sexual offences	25	-	2	1	1	7	10	2	2
Burglary	153	9	29	44	29	36	5	2	-
Robbery	248	10	53	63	54	55	13	1	-
Theft, handling, fraud & forgery	594	12	53	100	155	178	64	29	4
Drugs offences	1 130	3	72	183	215	411	193	49	4
Other offences	249	8	27	40	50	82	32	9	2
Offence not known	59	3	7	8	14	14	9	4	-

1 Includes persons committed in default of payment of a fine.
2 Provisional.

Source: Home Office: 020 7217 5567

173

11.12 Expenditure on prisons
England and Wales
Operating cost and total capital employed, years ending 31 March

£ thousand

		1995 /96	1996 /97	1997 /98	1998 /99	1999 /00	2000 /01	2001 /02
Expenditure								
Staff costs	KWUV	895 700	948 700	939 700	995 200	1 044 700	1 094 500	1 138 400
Accommodation costs	KXCO	122 400	113 900	116 200	163 400	149 300	153 700	193 100
Other operating costs	KXCP	369 000	373 900	472 600	538 800	584 300	654 200	706 100
Depreciation	KXCQ	159 300	123 600	160 200	146 100	115 700	117 200	128 100
Cost of capital	KXCR	211 500	225 500	231 300	262 500	254 900	259 900	284 900
Total expenditure	KXCS	1 757 900	1 785 600	1 920 000	2 106 000	2 148 900	2 279 500	2 450 600
Income								
Contributions from industries	KXCT	−6 400	−6 600	−7 900	−8 300	−10 400	−10 600	−11 600
Other operating income	KXCU	−4 900	−5 300	−8 500	−8 500	−9 600	−10 300	−13 100
Income from other Government Departments[1]	GDPM	..	..	..	..	..	−123 900	−180 600
Total income	KXCV	−11 300	−11 900	−16 400	−16 800	−20 000	−144 800	−205 300
Net operating costs	KXCW	1 746 600	1 773 700	1 903 600	2 089 200	2 128 900	2 134 700	2 245 300
Total capital employed	KXCX	3 580 700	3 920 900	4 116 900	4 345 100	4 382 600	4 726 200	4 859 600

1 Income from the Youth Justice Board (a non-departmental public body of the
Home Office) for the provision of juvenile custody within the Prison Service
and Department for Education and Skills for the provision of education services.

Source: Home Office: 020 7217 5567

11.13 Crimes and offences recorded by the police[1]
Scotland

Thousands

		1991	1992	1993	1994	1995	1996	1997	1998	1999	2000	2001
Non-sexual crimes of violence												
against the person	BEBC	21.7	23.3	19.4	19.8	21.1	21.5	19.2	21.1	23.4	23.3	23.8
Serious assault, etc	KAFS	7.0	7.7	6.5	6.7	6.9	7.0	6.1	6.6	7.2	7.0	7.3
Handling offensive weapons	KAFT	6.2	6.5	5.2	5.3	6.5	6.8	6.0	6.7	7.9	8.2	8.7
Robbery	KAFU	6.2	6.8	5.6	5.3	5.3	5.3	4.5	5.0	5.1	4.4	4.2
Other	KAFV	2.4	2.2	2.1	2.5	2.4	2.5	2.6	2.8	3.3	3.8	3.6
Crimes involving indecency	BEBD	5.8	6.2	6.0	6.0	5.5	5.7	7.1	7.4	6.0	5.8	6.0
Rape and attempted rape[2]	OXBQ	0.5	0.5	0.5	0.6	0.6	0.6	0.7	0.8	0.8	0.7	0.8
Indecent assault[2]	OXBR	0.9	1.1	1.1	1.0	1.0	1.1	1.2	1.4	1.2	1.1	1.2
Lewd and indecent behaviour	KAFY	2.6	2.6	2.7	2.7	2.4	2.5	3.0	3.0	2.4	2.3	2.4
Other	KAFZ	1.8	2.0	1.7	1.7	1.5	1.5	2.2	2.3	1.7	1.6	1.7
Crimes involving dishonesty	BEBE	430.2	415.0	374.9	350.3	321.2	295.4	267.2	275.4	276.2	260.9	239.9
Housebreaking	KAGB	116.1	113.2	97.8	88.4	74.2	64.5	55.5	56.6	53.8	48.7	44.9
Theft by opening lockfast places	KAGC	102.8	92.2	84.8	74.9	66.5	60.5	51.1	51.8	50.2	45.0	39.7
Theft of a motor vehicle	KAGD	44.3	47.4	42.8	42.0	37.5	34.2	28.6	28.4	29.8	26.2	23.2
Shoplifting	KAGE	30.1	29.7	26.7	26.6	28.0	26.9	26.3	29.6	32.0	32.3	31.6
Other theft	KAGF	104.6	98.8	93.3	88.9	87.7	82.6	79.6	80.1	81.1	78.1	74.7
Fraud	KAGG	22.0	22.6	19.1	17.7	17.1	16.1	15.7	18.6	18.6	21.2	17.4
Other	KAGH	10.3	11.1	10.3	12.0	10.2	10.8	10.3	10.2	10.6	9.4	8.4
Fire-raising, vandalism, etc	BEBF	89.7	92.2	84.2	88.5	86.5	89.0	81.0	79.2	79.6	83.2	94.9
Fire-raising	KAGJ	4.8	4.7	4.1	3.6	3.3	3.3	2.8	2.5	2.3	2.4	2.8
Vandalism, etc	KAGK	84.9	87.6	80.1	85.0	83.2	85.7	78.2	76.6	77.2	80.8	92.2
Other crimes	BEBG	25.5	28.2	32.7	35.4	41.3	40.3	46.1	48.5	50.5	49.9	56.5
Crimes against public justice	KAGM	13.3	14.4	14.5	16.0	16.4	16.1	16.6	16.9	18.5	18.4	20.3
Drugs	KAGN	12.0	13.6	18.0	19.3	24.8	24.0	29.4	31.5	31.9	31.4	36.2
Other	KAGO	0.2	0.2	0.2	0.2	0.2	0.1	0.1	0.1	0.1	0.1	0.1
Total crimes	KAGQ	572.9	564.9	517.2	500.1	475.7	452.0	420.6	431.6	435.7	423.2	421.0
Miscellaneous offences	BEBH	122.3	127.5	126.6	133.2	134.4	146.1	155.9	153.7	151.0	153.8	162.5
Petty assault	KAGS	41.0	42.5	41.3	45.1	46.6	47.6	50.1	51.0	54.0	54.8	54.9
Breach of the peace	KAGT	55.3	60.0	61.4	65.5	66.1	70.8	73.1	71.7	71.0	70.0	72.6
Drunkenness	KAGU	10.4	10.4	10.1	10.3	9.7	9.6	9.7	8.5	7.8	7.8	7.9
Other	KAGV	15.6	14.6	13.7	12.3	11.9	18.0	23.1	22.6	18.2	21.3	27.1
Motor vehicle offences	BEBI	305.6	306.4	315.1	330.7	317.5	305.9	331.0	362.1	353.4	345.8	362.1
Dangerous and careless driving	KAGX	23.1	22.5	20.0	21.1	18.7	17.3	16.3	15.8	14.0	12.3	12.0
Drunk driving	KAGY	11.0	11.3	10.9	10.8	10.7	11.8	11.2	10.6	10.8	10.7	11.4
Speeding	KAGZ	100.1	93.6	85.4	85.8	85.1	82.4	91.9	115.5	125.3	116.8	123.2
Unlawful use of a motor vehicle	KAHA	75.7	79.9	85.8	88.7	83.4	79.1	79.1	75.5	77.8	85.2	88.1
Vehicle defect offences	KAHB	46.8	47.8	51.4	56.9	56.3	53.5	60.1	63.6	52.9	48.3	47.3
Other	KAHC	48.9	51.5	61.7	67.4	63.2	61.8	72.3	81.2	72.5	72.5	80.1
Total offences	KAHD	427.9	433.9	441.7	463.9	451.9	452.0	486.9	515.8	504.5	499.6	524.6
Total crimes and offences	BEBB	1 000.8	998.8	959.0	964.0	927.6	903.9	907.5	947.3	940.2	922.8	945.7

1 See chapter text.
2 The category of "sexual assault" was split into "rape and attempted rape" and "indecent assault with effect from 2001, allowing the police Statutory Performance Indicator of serious violent crime to be readily calculated. The statutory Performance Indicator of serious violent crime includes all "non-sexual crimes", excluding "handling an offensive weapon", and includes "rape and attempted rape".

Source: The Scottish Executive Justice Department: 0131 244 2225

11.14 Persons proceeded against[1]
Scotland

Number of persons

		1990	1991	1992	1993	1994	1995	1996	1997	1998	1999	2000
Non-sexual crimes of violence	KEHC	3 965	3 965	4 717	4 948	4 622	4 867	5 682	5 601	5 248	5 467	5 497
Homicide	KEHD	100	106	148	150	122	157	159	119	104	110	100
Serious assault, etc	KEHE	1 084	1 032	1 120	1 212	1 218	1 194	1 355	1 445	1 397	1 503	1 480
Handling offensive weapons	KEHF	1 427	1 504	2 028	2 208	2 001	2 357	2 946	2 882	2 664	2 741	2 900
Robbery	KEHG	846	885	949	1 006	990	855	933	852	763	825	758
Other violence	KEHH	508	438	472	372	291	304	289	303	320	288	259
Crimes of indecency	KEHI	1 825	1 660	1 563	1 683	1 587	1 452	1 154	1 379	1 496	1 083	835
Sexual assault	KEHJ	233	200	203	229	195	182	194	212	207	184	171
Lewd and libidinous practices	KEHK	440	429	363	370	399	350	376	399	400	408	319
Other indecency	KEHL	1 152	1 031	997	1 084	993	920	584	768	889	491	345
Crimes of dishonesty	KEHM	39 409	40 037	40 152	37 678	35 719	33 948	32 528	31 073	29 815	27 912	25 166
Housebreaking	KEHN	7 418	7 269	7 115	6 379	6 135	5 457	4 642	4 058	3 709	3 662	3 213
Theft by opening lockfast places	KEHO	3 576	3 895	3 688	3 631	3 556	3 106	2 903	2 661	2 299	2 104	1 964
Theft of motor vehicle	KEHP	3 226	3 476	3 688	3 480	3 494	3 449	3 497	3 259	2 849	2 531	2 299
Shoplifting	KEHQ	7 098	7 921	8 469	8 262	7 260	7 185	7 840	7 959	8 357	8 424	8 255
Other theft	KEHR	10 765	9 944	9 485	8 565	7 532	7 485	7 170	7 113	6 761	6 198	5 314
Fraud	KEHS	2 833	2 710	2 528	2 592	2 884	2 720	2 399	2 344	2 400	2 045	1 836
Other dishonesty	KEHT	4 493	4 822	5 179	4 769	4 858	4 546	4 077	3 679	3 440	2 948	2 285
Fire-raising, vandalism, etc	KEHU	6 757	6 593	6 651	6 029	5 644	5 808	6 198	5 917	5 475	4 893	4 765
Fire-raising	KEHV	214	192	213	188	203	177	173	149	150	137	134
Vandalism, etc	KEHW	6 543	6 401	6 438	5 841	5 441	5 631	6 025	5 768	5 325	4 756	4 631
Other crime	KEHX	10 749	11 990	12 126	13 751	15 108	16 018	17 243	15 515	14 414	13 940	12 985
Crime against public justice	KFBK	7 272	7 537	7 377	8 407	8 892	9 424	9 748	7 248	6 224	6 218	6 508
Drugs offences	KFBL	3 436	4 413	4 713	5 313	6 185	6 556	7 454	8 219	8 153	7 689	6 458
Other	KFBM	41	40	36	31	31	38	41	48	37	33	19
Total crimes	KEHB	62 705	64 245	65 209	64 089	62 680	62 093	62 805	59 485	56 448	53 295	49 248
Miscellaneous offences	KEHZ	62 128	60 081	61 811	55 799	49 978	52 235	53 940	52 727	48 179	40 234	39 056
Simple assault	KEIA	16 417	15 507	15 139	14 831	14 250	14 911	15 636	15 907	15 207	13 832	13 111
Breach of the peace	KEIB	23 483	21 955	21 148	20 353	19 102	20 613	22 377	22 336	20 732	16 589	15 432
Drunkenness	KEIC	2 930	2 376	2 253	1 803	1 483	1 364	1 160	983	783	523	463
Other miscellaneous offences	KEID	19 298	20 243	23 271	18 812	15 143	15 347	14 767	13 501	11 457	9 290	10 050
Motor vehicle offences	KEIE	73 784	76 566	72 055	64 580	66 009	62 840	58 712	60 344	54 605	53 312	48 722
Dangerous and careless driving	KEIF	8 862	7 840	7 177	5 883	5 162	5 273	5 193	5 150	4 199	3 742	3 131
Drunk driving	KEIG	8 997	8 679	8 314	7 812	7 601	7 798	8 313	8 900	7 527	7 236	7 071
Speeding	KEIH	18 203	21 811	19 519	15 405	16 787	15 160	12 648	11 806	12 557	14 324	11 405
Unlawful use of vehicle	KEII	20 881	21 742	22 033	21 951	22 947	21 528	21 124	22 213	20 062	18 597	19 080
Vehicle defect offences	KEIJ	5 035	4 489	4 111	3 308	3 560	3 683	3 548	3 775	2 960	2 363	1 869
Other motor vehicle offences	KEIK	11 806	12 005	10 901	10 221	9 952	9 398	7 886	8 500	7 300	7 050	6 166
Total offences	KEHY	135 912	136 647	133 866	120 379	115 987	115 075	112 652	113 071	102 784	93 546	87 778
Total crimes and offences	KEHA	198 617	200 892	199 075	184 468	178 667	177 168	175 457	172 556	159 232	146 841	137 026

1 See chapter text.

Source: Scottish Executive Justice Department: 0131 244 2229

11.15 Persons proceeded against in court[1]
Scotland

Number of persons

		1990	1991	1992	1993	1994	1995	1996	1997	1998	1999	2000
Court procedure												
High Court[2]	KEIQ	1 099	1 227	1 419	1 601	1 228	1 390	1 420	1 356	1 225	1 357	1 196
Sheriff Court	KEIU	101 673	100 028	100 108	96 391	97 579	98 304	100 928	98 867	92 519	89 266	85 481
District Court	KEIV	83 596	87 186	84 705	74 920	68 183	66 039	62 485	61 648	57 182	49 020	44 899
Stipendiary Magistrate Court	KEIW	11 300	11 522	11 732	10 472	10 893	10 649	9 973	9 943	7 794	6 689	5 081
Total called to court[3]	KEIZ	197 722	200 017	198 038	183 674	178 067	176 423	174 844	171 932	158 815	146 474	136 772

1 See chapter text.
2 Including cases remitted to the High Court from the Sheriff Court.
3 Includes court type not known.

Source: Scottish Executive Justice Department: 0131 244 2229

11.16 Persons with charge proved: by main penalty[1]
Scotland

Number of persons

Main penalty		1990	1991	1992	1993	1994	1995	1996	1997	1998	1999	2000
Restriction of liberty order[2]	ZBRE	..	..	..	..	..	..	..	..	71	206	215
Supervised attendance order[3]	ZBRF	..	..	..	..	..	..	8	73	68	107	75
Drug treatment and testing order[4]	OEWA	..	..	..	..	..	..	..	..	..	..	80
Absolute discharge	KEXA	869	887	967	989	839	939	1 000	1 064	957	985	967
Admonition or caution	KEXB	16 558	17 137	17 441	16 976	16 243	15 857	15 859	15 039	13 893	12 914	11 801
Probation	KEXC	4 268	4 877	5 385	5 722	6 145	6 145	6 435	6 814	7 144	7 340	7 360
Remit to children's hearing	KEXD	52	81	72	83	124	172	193	219	177	136	106
Community service order	KEXE	4 739	5 190	5 473	5 079	5 320	5 339	5 711	5 707	5 246	4 888	4 684
Fine	KEXF	135 273	135 479	131 842	116 918	112 748	110 337	105 384	103 861	94 917	83 479	76 237
Compensation order	KEXG	1 678	1 591	1 575	1 578	1 535	1 527	1 415	1 304	1 298	1 154	1 111
Insanity, hospital, guardianship order	KYAN	152	148	133	138	133	136	159	162	129	135	108
Prison	KEXI	8 796	9 222	10 085	10 832	11 583	11 561	12 134	11 621	11 447	11 591	10 936
Young offenders' institution	KEXJ	4 150	4 318	4 488	4 461	4 472	4 646	4 744	4 557	4 459	4 483	4 318
Detention of child	KEXM	23	35	22	30	36	48	45	29	20	17	11
Total persons with charge proved	KEXO	176 558	178 965	177 483	162 806	159 178	156 707	153 087	150 450	139 826	127 435	118 009

1 See chapter text.
2 A community sentence introduced by Section 5 of the Crime and Punishment (Scotland) Act 1995 and available on a pilot basis to 3 Scottish sheriff courts since August 1998. This sentence was made available to High Court, Sheriff Courts and Stipendiary Magistrates court from 1 May 2002.
3 The pilot scheme under the Criminal Procedure (Scotland) Act 1995, where fines for 16 & 17 year olds were replaced by supervised attendance orders, was discontinued in December 1999. The majority of supervised attendance orders recorded in the year 2000 were disposals relating to breaches of an existing order.

4 Drug treatment and testing orders are new measures made available on a pilot basis to courts in Fife and Glasgow since February 2000.

Source: Scottish Executive Justice Department: 0131 244 2229

11.17 Persons with charge proved[1]: by age and sex
Scotland

Number of persons

		1990	1991	1992	1993	1994	1995	1996	1997	1998	1999	2000
Males	KEWA	150 107	150 482	147 693	136 127	136 533	133 330	130 961	129 461	120 482	110 326	101 208
Under 16	KEWB	173	189	138	138	171	180	149	137	135	75	54
16 to 20	KEWC	39 720	38 284	36 494	32 589	30 708	30 113	31 704	31 310	29 311	26 927	24 338
21 to 30	KEWD	59 114	59 532	59 561	56 052	56 519	54 184	52 218	50 684	46 121	41 667	38 523
Over 30	KEWE	48 392	49 802	49 094	45 701	47 788	47 648	45 799	46 281	44 047	40 786	37 548
Age not known	KEWF	2 708	2 675	2 406	1 647	1 347	1 205	1 091	1 049	868	871	745
Females	KEWG	24 400	26 340	28 051	25 405	21 650	22 412	21 308	20 246	18 667	16 539	16 366
Under 16	KEWH	11	18	9	6	8	17	12	11	5	6	9
16 to 20	KEWI	3 904	3 927	3 885	3 589	2 939	3 098	3 302	3 424	3 361	3 273	3 050
21 to 30	KEWJ	10 077	10 958	11 998	10 557	9 190	9 284	8 461	8 095	7 456	6 494	6 283
Over 30	KEWK	9 507	10 519	11 409	10 611	9 002	9 439	8 894	8 266	7 531	6 494	6 765
Age not known	KEWL	901	918	750	642	511	574	639	450	314	272	259
Males and Females	KEWM	174 507	176 822	175 744	161 532	158 183	155 742	152 269	149 707	139 149	126 865	117 574
Under 16	KEWN	184	207	147	144	179	197	161	148	140	81	63
16 to 20	KEWO	43 624	42 211	40 379	36 178	33 647	33 211	35 006	34 734	32 672	30 200	27 388
21 to 30	KEWP	69 191	70 490	71 559	66 609	65 709	63 468	60 679	58 779	53 577	48 161	44 806
Over 30	KEWQ	57 899	60 321	60 503	56 312	56 790	57 087	54 693	54 547	51 578	47 280	44 313
Age not known	KEWR	3 609	3 593	3 156	2 289	1 858	1 779	1 730	1 499	1 182	1 143	1 004
Companies	KEWS	2 024	2 126	1 717	1 263	991	961	812	737	675	551	399
Total persons with charge proved[2]	KEWT	176 558	178 965	177 483	162 806	159 178	156 707	153 087	150 450	139 826	127 435	118 009

1 See chapter text.
2 Includes sex unknown.

Source: Scottish Executive Justice Department: 0131 244 2229

11.18 Penal establishments: average daily population and receptions
Scotland

Numbers

		1991	1992	1993	1994	1995	1996	1997	1998	1999	2000	2001
Average daily population												
Male	KEPB	4 696	5 099	5 466	5 408	5 451	5 673	5 900	5 825	5 817	5 666	5 889
Female	KEPC	143	158	171	177	175	189	184	193	212	203	249
Total	KEPA	4 839	5 257	5 637	5 585	5 626	5 862	6 084	6 018	6 029	5 869	6 137
Analysis by type of custody												
Remand	KEPD	770	876	948	1 015	998	1 000	947	938	1 012	894	960
Persons under sentence: total	KEPE	4 056	4 375	4 686	4 569	4 624	4 861	5 134	5 077	5 016	4 974	5 176
Adult prisoners[1]	KEPF	3 322	3 552	3 795	3 785	·3 823	4 026	4 345	4 362	4 318	4 319	4 526
Young offenders[1]	KEPI	684	769	819	720	719	770	789	715	697	654	650
Persons recalled from supervision/licence	KEPN	39	32	40	37	44	46	46	72	93	129	193
Others	KEPO	12	21	32	28	38	18	20	17	28	31	47
Persons sentenced by court martial	KEPP	12	6	2	1	3	–	1	2	1	–	–
Civil prisoners	KEPQ	1	1	1	1	–	1	1	1	1	1	1
Receptions to penal establishments												
Remand	KEPR	13 127	13 546	13 412	14 922	14 253	14 977	14 826	15 098	15 291	13 945	15 433
Male	KEPS	12 360	12 722	12 478	13 985	13 377	13 976	13 850	13 979	14 090	12 916	14 166
Female	KEPT	767	824	934	937	876	1 001	976	1 119	1 201	1 029	1 267
Persons under sentence: total	KEPU	18 226	19 966	22 157	21 111	19 030	22 155	23 202	22 269	20 741	18 916	19 247
Male	KEPV	17 033	18 856	20 741	19 697	17 737	20 869	21 936	20 862	19 465	17 739	18 035
Female	KEPW	1 193	1 110	1 416	1 414	1 293	1 286	1 266	1 407	1 276	1 177	1 212
Imprisoned: Adults:												
directly	KEPX	7 951	8 543	9 444	9 349	8 730	10 040	9 698	9 959	9 484	8 713	9 617
in default of fine	KEPY	6 336	6 603	7 956	7 377	6 299	7 432	8 873	7 866	7 154	6 542	6 088
in default of compensation order[2]	KEPZ	6	40	41	26	13	..	..	..	..	..	..
Sentenced to young offenders' institution:												
directly	KEQA	2 356	3 041	3 052	2 855	2 772	3 111	2 784	2 844	2 687	2 500	2 414
in default of fine	KEQB	1 573	1 736	1 660	1 498	1 210	1 567	1 847	1 593	1 411	1 161	1 128
in default of compensation order[2]	KEQC	2	2	4	6	4	..	..	..	..	..	..
Persons recalled from supervised release orders	JYYD	2	1	–	–	2	5	11	7	5	–	–
Persons sentenced by court martial	KEQH	1	2	7	5	4	4	4	5	3	2	1
Civil prisoners[3]	KEQI	25	34	37	27	25	32	23	10	14	12	9

1 Figures for 1998 have been revised to reflect improved treatment of missing data.

2 From 1996 compensation orders are included in the figures for default of fine.

3 For 1995 and 1996 data are estimated.

Source: The Scottish Executive Justice Department: 0131 244 2225

11.19 Expenditure on penal establishments[1]
Scotland
Years ended 31 March

£ thousands

		1991/92	1992/93	1993/94	1994/95	1995/96	1996/97	1997/98	1998/99	1999/00	2000/01	2001/02
Departmental Expenditure												
Manpower and Associated Services	KPHC	124 898	129 597	135 301	140 009	135 941	143 107	137 890	144 660	170 347	160 242	172 490
Prisoner and Associated Costs	KPHD	8 504	10 274	10 795	11 679	12 373	13 377	16 313	18 891	22 930	23 501	24 652
Capital Expenditure	KPHE	13 032	13 681	11 845	15 636	15 377	22 577	22 136	23 697	28 918	24 283	24 955
Gross Expenditure	KPHF	146 434	153 552	157 941	167 324	163 691	179 061	176 339	187 248	222 195	208 026	222 097
Less Receipts	KPHG	3 711	3 542	3 598	3 042	2 800	2 600	2 810	8 160	6 668	8 380	8 194
Net Departmental Expenditure	KPHH	142 723	150 010	154 343	164 282	160 891	176 461	173 529	179 088	215 527	200 746	213 903
Plus Annually Managed Expenditure Capital Charges	DSJI	..	..	..	..	..	..	..	..	..	..	31 341
Total Net Expenditure	DSNX	142 723	150 010	154 343	164 282	160 891	176 461	173 529	179 088	215 527	200 746	245 244

1 See chapter text.

Source: The Scottish Executive Justice Department: 0131 244 8544

11.20 Recorded crime statistics
Northern Ireland

Thousands

		Old counting rules								New counting rules			
		1992	1993	1994	1995	1996	1997	1998/99		1998/99	1999/00	2000/01	2001/02
Violence against the person	RVCP	4.1	4.6	4.8	5.2	5.6	5.2	6.6	RVCQ	18.5	21.4	21.4	26.1
Sexual offences	RVCR	1.0	1.2	1.3	1.7	1.7	1.4	1.5	RVCS	1.6	1.3	1.2	1.4
Burglary	RVCT	17.1	15.7	16.9	16.5	16.1	14.3	15.5	RVCU	15.5	16.1	15.8	17.1
Robbery	RVCV	1.9	1.7	1.6	1.5	1.7	1.7	1.4	RVCW	1.4	1.4	1.8	2.2
Theft	RVCX	34.3	33.2	33.2	33.5	32.8	29.5	34.6	RVCY	35.4	37.0	36.9	41.7
Fraud and forgery	RVCZ	5.5	5.6	5.1	4.9	4.1	3.8	5.3	RVDA	6.8	7.9	8.0	8.6
Criminal damage	RVDB	2.5	2.9	3.1	3.8	4.8	4.7	9.8	RVDC	27.7	31.2	32.3	40.0
Offences against the state	RVDD	0.5	0.4	0.4	0.3	0.4	0.5	0.5	RVDE	0.6	0.7	0.8	1.2
Other notifiable offences	RVDF	0.8	1.0	1.4	1.5	1.2	1.1	1.5	RVDG	1.7	2.1	1.7	1.4
of which drug offences	RVDH	0.6	0.8	1.3	1.4	1.1	1.0	1.4	RVDI	1.4	1.7	1.5	1.1
Total	RVDR	67.5	66.2	67.9	68.8	68.5	62.2	76.6	RVDS	109.1	119.1	119.9	139.8

Source: The Police Service of Northern Ireland

11.21 Persons found guilty at all courts by offence group
Northern Ireland

Numbers

		1989	1990	1991	1992	1993	1994	1995	1996	1997	1998	1999
Violence against the person	KYCT	1 424	1 750	1 634	1 558	1 674	1 498	1 685	1 597	1 594	1 596	1 699
Sexual offences	KEVG	226	275	193	184	126	148	182	184	130	128	90
Burglary	KYBW	1 363	1 362	1 208	1 149	1 114	979	951	801	715	647	703
Robbery	KYBX	273	220	162	202	159	168	195	161	166	134	129
Theft	KYBY	3 298	3 399	3 429	3 158	3 254	3 044	3 128	2 765	2 596	2 342	1 995
Fraud and forgery	KYBZ	783	699	648	683	633	568	533	467	491	426	476
Criminal damage	KYCA	939	1 054	1 019	967	1 145	1 134	1 008	1 076	1 163	1 043	931
Offences against the state	KYCB	216	233	195	187	184	137	166	147	165	198	178
Other indictable	KYCC	380	287	368	448	606	669	863	899	739	936	943
Total indictable[1]	KYCD	8 902	9 279	8 856	8 536	8 895	8 345	8 711	8 097	7 759	7 450	7 144
Summary	KYCE	5 113	4 293	4 278	4 115	4 307	4 369	4 137	4 402	4 435	4 062	3 598
Motoring[2]	KYCF	26 116	27 248	20 169	20 808	21 882	21 502	20 124	18 177	18 770	15 369	15 782
All offences	KYCG	40 131	40 820	33 303	33 459	35 084	34 216	32 972	30 676	30 964	26 881	26 524

1 Excludes indictable motoring offences
2 Includes indictable motoring offences

Source: Northern Ireland Office: 028 9052 7534

11.22 Juveniles found guilty at all courts by offence group[1]
Northern Ireland

Numbers

		1989	1990	1991	1992	1993	1994	1995	1996	1997	1998	1999
Violence against the person	KYCH	33	44	38	46	43	49	51	75	49	97	73
Sexual offences	KAHF	14	17	8	11	7	8	7	4	8	12	12
Burglary	KYCI	228	232	194	165	155	180	170	137	124	108	117
Robbery	KYCJ	11	10	7	8	4	9	22	13	18	4	7
Theft	KYCK	308	329	328	247	280	283	345	338	334	304	227
Fraud and forgery	KYCL	10	10	10	16	14	14	21	14	11	4	10
Criminal damage	KYCM	119	90	92	82	94	117	116	121	136	139	102
Offences against the state	KYCN	14	6	5	6	1	8	9	6	10	11	12
Other indictable	KYCO	15	10	11	8	2	6	14	24	10	20	17
Total indictable[2]	KYCP	752	748	693	589	600	674	755	732	700	699	577
Summary	KYCQ	186	138	111	113	125	131	180	182	198	187	163
Motoring[3]	KYCR	81	92	71	40	44	74	74	58	57	98	97
All offences	KYCS	1 019	978	875	742	769	879	1 009	972	955	984	837

1 Juveniles are aged 10 - 16 years inclusive.
2 Excludes indictable motoring offences.
3 Includes indictable motoring offences.

Source: Northern Ireland Office: 028 9052 7534

11.23 Disposals given to those convicted by court
Northern Ireland

Numbers

		1989	1990	1991	1992	1993	1994	1995	1996	1997	1998	1999
Magistrates court - all offences												
Prison	KYAO	1 006	1 009	960	830	1 027	945	1 046	1 003	989	993	1 277
Young offenders centre	KYAP	368	370	502	588	575	499	483	443	430	326	243
Training school	KYAQ	168	153	177	120	125	193	169	147	148	136	13
Juvenile Justice Centre order	OEUX	..	..	..	..	..	..	..	..	..	..	22
Custody-probation order	OEUY	..	..	..	..	..	..	..	..	..	3	1
Total immediate custody	KYAR	1 542	1 532	1 639	1 538	1 727	1 637	1 698	1 593	1 567	1 458	1 556
Prison suspended	KYAS	1 544	1 513	1 379	1 420	1 529	1 558	1 674	1 722	1 506	1 025	1 080
YOC suspended	KYAT	319	310	432	507	447	447	385	444	461	139	104
Attendance centre	KYAU	108	118	90	66	94	89	101	91	66	55	14
Probations/supervision	KYAV	778	854	742	849	881	1 017	1 137	1 134	1 155	1 473	1 246
Community supervision order	KYAW	435	575	547	464	536	551	547	591	561	622	678
Combination order	OEUZ	..	..	..	..	..	..	..	..	..	38	7
Fine	KYAX	26 306	26 644	19 569	23 418	25 166	24 390	22 726	20 612	21 313	17 955	18 076
Recognizance	KYAY	412	399	514	713	858	961	1 001	1 203	1 267	1 134	1 089
Conditional discharge	KYAZ	2 022	1 982	2 102	1 965	2 021	1 830	1 928	1 679	1 597	1 538	1 439
Absolute discharge	KYBA	1 305	1 274	845	732	690	661	608	509	424	303	223
Penalty points	OEVA	..	..	..	..	..	..	..	..	..	44	105
Disqualification	KYBB	4 106	4 335	4 211	640	6	6	2	5	2	57	97
Other	KYBC	20	28	24	12	7	11	8	10	6	23	19
Total	KYBD	38 897	39 564	32 094	32 324	33 962	33 158	31 815	29 593	29 925	25 864	25 733
Crown court - all offences												
Prison	KYBE	472	493	493	447	555	471	533	469	475	345	334
Young offenders centre	KYBF	111	106	125	119	130	87	76	106	111	63	67
Training school	KYBG	10	4	13	5	2	5	6	–	4	2	–
Custody-probation order	ZAEO	..	..	..	..	..	..	..	..	..	175	52
Total immediate custody	KYBH	593	603	631	571	687	563	615	575	590	585	453
Prison suspended	KYBI	318	295	238	249	211	277	265	253	220	199	185
YOC suspended	KYBJ	73	78	46	63	37	43	63	71	60	49	41
Combination order	ZAEP	..	..	..	..	..	..	..	..	..	13	6
Attendance centre	KYBK	2	–	–	–	–	1	–	–	–	–	–
Probation/supervision	KYBL	72	85	103	95	73	58	60	49	47	70	43
Community supervision order	KYBM	71	105	89	79	48	59	60	54	37	33	24
Fine	KYBN	39	33	23	17	33	23	27	39	40	25	20
Recognizance	KYBO	3	8	7	9	5	16	–	7	10	7	–
Conditional discharge	KYBR	51	37	53	36	19	15	64	30	31	23	17
Absolute discharge	KYBS	1	2	5	8	3	2	1	–	1	6	–
Disqualification	KYBT	8	10	6	2	–	–	–	–	–	1	–
Other	KYBU	3	–	8	6	6	1	2	3	3	6	2
Total	KYBV	1 234	1 256	1 209	1 135	1 122	1 058	1 157	1 081	1 039	1 017	791

Source: Northern Ireland Office: 028 9052 7534

11.24 Prisons and Young Offenders Centres
Northern Ireland
Receptions and average population

		1991	1992	1993	1994	1995	1996	1997	1998	1999	2000	2001
Receptions:												
Reception of untried prisoners	**KEOA**	1 851	1 987	2 045	2 043	2 003	2 292	2 188	2 284	2 497	2 197	1 922
Reception of sentenced prisoners:												
Imprisonment under sentence of immediate custody[1]	**KEOB**	974	941	1 135	1 029	1 070	1 070	1 062	949	963	1 001	791
Imprisonment in default of payment of a fine	**KEOC**	1 282	1 352	1 221	1 190	1 248	1 374	1 513	1 530	1 423	1 261	1 090
Total	**KEOD**	2 256	2 293	2 356	2 219	2 318	2 444	2 575	2 479	2 386	2 262	1 881
Reception into Young Offender Centres:												
Detention under sentence of immediate custody	**KEOE**	348	371	416	346	371	362	331	347	346	282	252
Detention in default of payment of a fine	**KEOF**	356	364	353	276	351	373	366	385	417	389	303
Total	**KEOG**	704	735	769	622	722	735	697	732	763	671	555
Other receptions:												
Civil committals	**KEOI**	17	10	21	13	45	27	42	70	38	56	58
Total	**KEOL**	17	10	21	13	45	27	42	70	38	56	58
Daily average population:												
Total	**KEOM**	1 796	1 810	1 934	1 899	1 762	1 639	1 632	1 507	1 244	1 068	910
Unconvicted[2]	**KEON**	350	414	427	440	322	337	376	383	377	317	272
Convicted[3]	**KEOP**	1 446	1 396	1 507	1 459	1 440	1 302	1 256	1 124	867	751	638

1 Includes those detained under Section 73 of the Children and Young Persons (NI) Act 1968.
2 Prisoners on remand or awaiting trial and prisoners committed by civil process.
3 Includes those sentenced to immediate custody and fine defaulters.

Source: Northern Ireland Office: 028 9052 7534

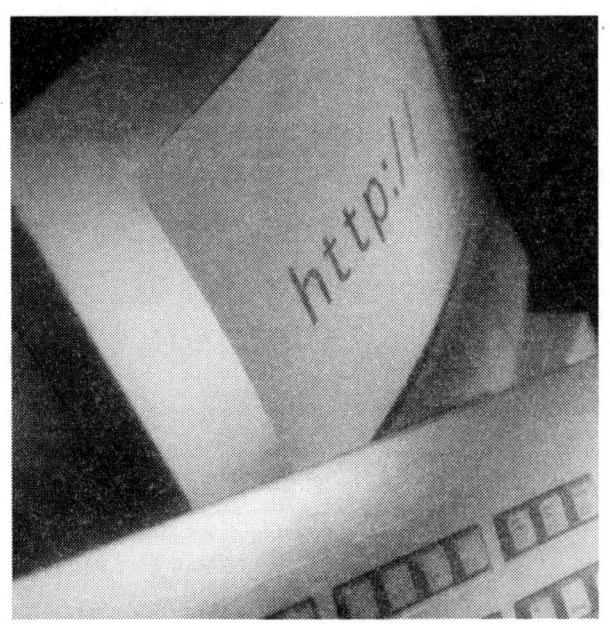

12 Lifestyles

Lifestyles

Expenditure by the Department for Culture, Media and Sport *(Table 12.1)*

The figures in this table are taken from the Department's Annual Report and are outturn figures for each of the headings shown (later figures are the estimated outturn). The Department's planned expenditure for future years is also shown.

Cinema statistics *(Table 12.3)*

These estimates represent the motion picture projection activity for all individual legal units (i.e. companies, sole proprietorships, partnerships etc.) whose main activity is motion picture projection (i.e. heading 92.13 of the UK Standard Industrial Classification 1992). However, where such activity can be identified, the estimates also include the film exhibition activity of a number of legal units where motion picture projection is not their main activity. The Office for National Statistics does not maintain registers of all sites where film exhibition takes place so the estimates will not be completely comprehensive. It is believed, however, that the estimates cover the great majority of units engaged in cinema activity in Great Britain (i.e. England, Scotland and Wales but not Northern Ireland, the Isle of Man or the Channel Islands).

These figures are produced by combining information obtained by grossing data from a voluntary quarterly panel with estimates derived from the larger sample approached in the annual inquiry to the service trades.

All financial figures are exclusive of Value Added Tax.

Tourist attractions *(Table 12.5)*

The figures in this table are compiled using data from the Visits to Visitor Attraction Survey. The tourist attractions included within the headings shown are as follows: -

Country parks: Country parks and forest parks.

Farms: Farms, rare breeds, shire horse centres and farm animals.

Gardens: Gardens, arboretums and botanical gardens.

Historic properties: Historic houses, palaces, castles, forts, historic monuments, archaeological sites, historic ships and other historic properties.

Leisure and theme parks: Leisure parks and theme parks.

Museums and art galleries: Museums and/or art galleries and science centres.

Steam and heritage railways: Steam railways and heritage railways.

Visitor and heritage centres: Visitor and heritage centres.

Wildlife attractions: Nature reserves, wetlands, wildlife trips, safari parks, zoos, aquariums and aviaries.

Workplaces: Distilleries, vineyards, breweries and industrial or craft premises.

Tourism *(Table 12.6)*

The figures in this table are compiled using data from the International Passenger Survey, the United Kingdom Tourism Survey, the Visits to Visitor Attraction Survey and the British National Travel Survey.

Gambling *(Table 12.7)*

The National Lottery figures in this table are the latest expenditure figures at the time of going to press which have been released by OFLOT - the National Lottery regulator, and represent ticket sales for each of the games which comprise the lottery. The figures have been adjusted to real terms using the Retail Prices Index.

The National Lottery commenced on the 19 November 1994, with the first instant ticket being sold in March 1995. Various other games have been started since, the latest being the Lottery Extra game. The sum of the individual games may not agree exactly with the figures for total sales, and also includes the Easy Play games which commenced in 1998, but were dropped in 1999.

The other gambling figures in this table are obtained from the Gaming Board for Great Britain Annual Report. The figures have been adjusted to real terms using the Retail Prices Index.

The money spent at casinos represents the money recorded as having been exchanged for chips. The money spent at bingo clubs refers to licensed clubs only. Prior to 1994-95 the figures for bingo clubs relate to the year ending August.

12.1 Expenditure by the Department for Culture, Media and Sport[1]

£ millions

	Museums, galleries and libraries[2]	The arts (England)	Sports (UK)	Historic buildings, monuments, and sites (England)	The Royal Parks (UK)	Tourism (UK)	Broadcasting and media (UK)	Administration research and other research	National Lottery Commission	Gaming Board	Queen's Golden Jubilee	European regional development fund	Commemorative services and royal funerals	Spaces for sports and arts	Culture online
	GQIF	KWFP	KWFQ	KWFR	LQYY	KWFS	KWFT	GQIG	LQYZ	GYPK	GYPL	JYXQ	JYXP	GQIH	GQII
1991/92	333	212	47	..	..	44	22	8	..	—	..	..	—	..	..
1992/93	350	235	50	..	..	46	79	17	..	—	..	..	—	..	..
1993/94	335	235	54	164	23	46	85	22	2	—	..	..	—	..	..
1994/95	372	195	53	164	24	44	93	21	—	—	..	..	3	..	..
1995/96	399	200	54	164	25	45	98	20	—	—	..	6	3	..	..
1996/97	336	195	52	162	23	46	97	21	—	—	..	16	—	..	..
1997/98	321	196	50	156	22	45	43	21	—	—	..	26	3	..	..
1998/99	303	198	49	144	21	45	99	23	—	—	..	28	—	..	..
1999/00[3]	328	232	52	146	26	47	104	27	—	—	..	38	1	..	..
2000/01[3]	325	240	53	150	23	47	103	31	—	—	..	55	—	13	1
2001/02[4]	373	253	69	141	25	67	105	35	1	2	3	31	—	60	2
2002/03[5]	388	296	111	148	24	72	112	33	1	3	4	31	—	—	—
2003/04[5]	395	336	102	154	24	51	114	32	1	2	—	31	—	—	—

1 See chapter text.
2 Includes museums and galleries (England), libraries (UK) and museums library archives (UK).
3 Outturn.
4 Data are estimated outturn.
5 Data are plans.

Source: Department for Culture, Media and Sport: 020 7211 2189

12.2 Employment in tourism related industries
Great Britain
At June in each year

Thousands, not seasonally adjusted

	Hotels and other tourist accommodation	Restaurants, cafes etc.	Bars, public houses and nightclubs	Travel agents, tour operators	Libraries, museums and other cultural activities	Sport and other recreation activities	All tourism related industries		
							All	Of which:	
								Employee jobs	Self-employment jobs
	KWFV	KWFW	KWFX	KWFY	KWFZ	KWGA	LQZA	KWGB	KWGC
1992	311.0	303.0	414.2	69.2	74.8	320.8	1 671.0	1 493.0	178.0
1993	317.6	298.0	370.6	69.3	75.6	316.5	1 643.6	1 447.6	196.0
1994	375.3	372.2	399.1	83.7	75.6	355.7	1 663.3	1 455.5	207.8
1995	385.8	386.2	445.1	90.7	77.3	363.5	1 751.6	1 536.6	215.0
1996	399.1	487.9	506.4	104.0	73.9	352.1	1 923.4	1 706.3	217.0
1997	371.0	505.1	553.9	115.8	75.4	359.2	1 980.3	1 762.1	218.2
1998	385.0	520.8	555.3	111.0	74.8	347.1	1 994.0	1 809.0	185.0
1999	409.9	535.1	555.6	123.2	76.2	367.3	2 067.3	1 906.7	160.6
2000	406.2	555.2	576.1	131.4	88.9	385.6	2 143.5	1 971.6	171.9
2001	410.2	550.8	533.0	141.7	80.0	406.7	2 122.5	1 962.5	160.0
2002	418.0	545.4	535.9	133.6	81.4	412.9	2 127.2	1 964.0	163.2

Source: Department for Culture, Media and Sport: 020 7211 2189

12.3 Cinema exhibitor statistics[1]
Great Britain

	Sites	Screens	Total no. of admissions	Gross box office takings	Amount paid out for films	Revenue per admission	Revenue per screen
	number	number	millions	£ million	£ million	£	£ thousand
	CKNU	CKNV	CKQE	CKQF	CKQG	CKQH	CKQI
1991	537	1 544	88.9	229.7	78.5	2.58	152.4
1992	480	1 547	89.4	243.7	81.9	2.73	153.6
1993	495	1 591	99.3	271.3	95.9	2.73	171.0
1994	505	1 619	105.9	293.5	104.6	2.77	183.5
1995	475	1 620	96.9	286.5	96.3	2.96	176.7
1996	483	1 738	118.7	373.5	144.9	3.15	215.5
1997	504	1 886	128.2	443.2	165.9	3.46	255.0
1998	512	2 168	127.1	437.1	159.1	3.43	201.6
1999	539	2 492	133.8	479.4	175.3	3.58	192.4
2000	509	2 560	137.1	507.1	187.4	3.70	198.1
2001	440	2 509	141.0	550.1	209.0	3.90	219.3

1 See chapter text.

Source: Office for National Statistics: 01633 812264

12.4 Films
United Kingdom

	Production of UK films		Expenditure on feature films				
	Films produced in the UK	Production costs	UK box office	Video rental	Video retail	Subscriptions to movie channels	Box office, video, subscription channels
	number	£ million 1998 prices	£ million current prices	£ million current prices	£ million current prices	£ million current prices	£ million current prices
	KWGD	KWGE	KWHU	KWHV	KWHW	KWHX	KWHY
1991	59	285.3	295	407	440	121	1 263
1992	47	208.6	291	389	506	283	1 469
1993	67	214.0	319	350	643	350	1 662
1994	84	436.0	364	339	698	540	1 941
1995	78	421.0	385	351	789	721	2 246
1996	128	726.0	426	382	803	1 319	2 930
1997	116	558.0	506	369	858	..	1 733
1998	88	487.0	515	437	940	..	1 892
1999	100	570.0	606	408	882	..	1 896
2000	98	792.5	628	444	1 104	..	2 176
2001	96	..	692	465	1 490	..	..

Source: Department for Culture, Media and Sport: 020 7211 2189

12.5 Visits to tourist attractions[1]
United Kingdom

Index 1989 = 100

	Country Parks	Farms	Gardens	Historic properties	Leisure and theme parks	Museums and art galleries	Steam and heritage railways	Visitor and heritage centres	Wildlife attractions and zoos	Workplaces	All attractions
	MKDZ	MKEA	LQZC	LQZB	MKEB	LQZD	MKEC	MKED	LQZE	MKEE	LQZG
1989	100	100	100	100	100	100	100	100	100	100	100
1990	105	117	102	102	102	106	101	103	101	102	103
1991	108	123	106	98	100	107	99	100	95	101	102
1992	106	127	105	98	99	110	95	103	87	101	102
1993	107	141	111	100	103	109	98	106	89	106	104
1994	110	148	116	99	106	110	98	108	87	108	105
1995	118	153	122	103	106	108	100	112	86	106	107
1996	118	160	125	106	106	111	107	117	90	112	110
1997	122	165	127	108	106	111	108	117	92	115	112
1998	117	165	118	107	103	112	108	116	92	113	110
1999	120	176	122	106	106	111	112	115	94	113	111
2000	119	162	120	101	105	108	115	114	92	108	109
2001	112	122	124	94	110	110	112	109	88	105	107

1 See chapter text.

Source: The National Tourist Boards: 020 8563 3011

12.6 Tourism[1]

	Visits to the UK by overseas residents	Spending in the UK by overseas residents	Spending in the UK by overseas residents	Visits overseas by UK residents	Spending overseas by UK residents	Spending overseas by UK residents
	Thousands	£ million current prices	£ million constant 1995 prices	Thousand	£ million current prices	£ million constant 1995 prices
	GMAA	GMAK	CQPR	GMAF	GMAM	CQPS
1991	17 125	7 386	8 627	30 809	9 951	11 775
1992	18 533	7 892	8 784	33 832	11 243	12 678
1993	19 863	9 487	10 188	36 720	12 972	13 184
1994	20 794	9 786	10 050	39 630	14 365	14 852
1995	23 537	11 763	11 763	41 345	15 386	15 386
1996	25 163	12 290	11 954	42 050	16 223	15 897
1997	25 515	12 244	11 542	45 957	16 931	18 652
1998	25 745	12 671	11 573	50 872	19 489	21 847
1999	25 394	12 498	11 133	53 881	22 020	24 676
2000	25 209	12 805	11 102	56 837	24 251	27 281
2001	22 835	11 306	9 528	58 281	25 332	27 710

International tourism (heading spanning the above six columns)

UK Domestic tourism: one or more nights

	Number of trips	Number of nights spent	Expenditure at current prices	Average nights spent	Average expenditure per trip
	Millions	Millions	£ million	Numbers	£
	GQGY	GQGZ	GQHA	GQHB	GQHC
1995	147.8	526.0	20 072	3.6	135.8
1996	154.2	532.8	22 041	3.5	142.9
1997	162.2	555.3	24 137	3.4	148.8
1998	148.8	515.9	22 814	3.5	153.3
1999	173.1	568.6	25 635	3.3	148.1
2000	175.4	576.4	26 133	3.3	150.0
2001	163.1	529.6	26 094	3.2	160.0

1 See chapter text.

Sources: Office for National Statistics: 020 7533 5765;
The National Tourist Boards: 020 8563 3011

12.7 Gambling[1]
United Kingdom

£ millions at 2001/02 prices[2]

		1993 /94	1994 /95	1995 /96	1996 /97	1997 /98	1998 /99	1999 /00	2000 /01	2001 /02
Money spent on gambling										
National Lottery - Total[3]	GYRX	..	1 351	6 100	5 335	6 025	5 511	5 250	4 989	4 859
On-line	GYRY	..	1 339	4 315	4 353	5 156	4 798	4 454	4 157	3 902
Instants	GYRZ	..	12	1 785	982	869	705	594	534	583
Thunderball	GYSA	..	..	..	..	..	..	201	252	247
Lottery Extra	GYSB	..	..	..	..	..	..	..	47	126
Lotteries (excluding the National Lottery)[4]	GYSC	53	46	92	130	137	171	108	109	109
Casinos[4]	GYSD	2 741	2 943	2 952	2 941	2 979	2 834	3 249	3 366	3 582
Bingo clubs[4]	GYSF	997	1 009	1 050	1 094	1 116	1 105	1 124	1 135	1 164

1 See chapter text.
2 Adjusted to real terms using the Retail Prices Index.
3 Includes Easy Play tickets which are not shown separately.
4 Great Britain only.

Sources: Department for Culture, Media and Sport: 020 7211 2189;
Gaming Board for Great Britain: 020 7306 6253

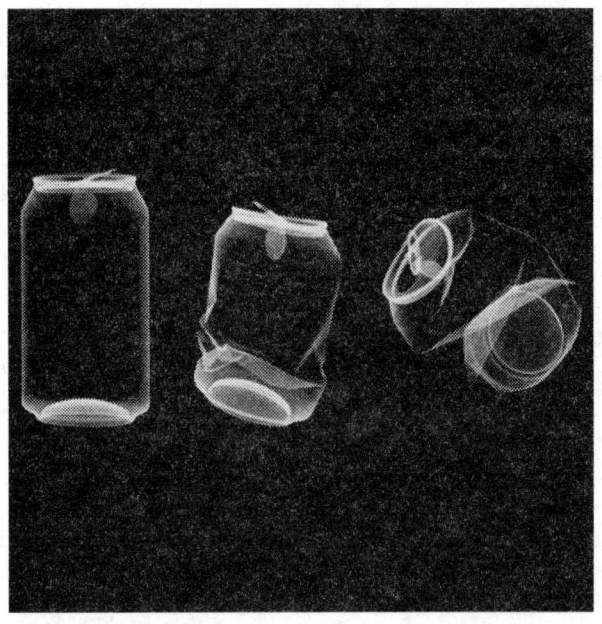

13 Environment, water and housing

Environment, water and housing

Air Emissions *(Table 13.1 to 13.7)*

Emissions of air pollutants arise from a wide variety of sources. The National Atmospheric Emissions Inventory (NAEI) is prepared annually for the Government and the devolved administrations by the National Environmental Technology Centre (NETCEN), with the work being co-ordinated by DEFRA. Information is available for a range of point sources, including the most significant polluters. However, a different approach has to be taken for diffuse sources such as transport and domestic emissions where this type of information could not be available and estimates for these are derived from statistical information and from research on emission factors for stationary and mobile sources. Although for any given year considerable uncertainties surround the emission estimates for each pollutant, trends over time are likely to be more reliable.

UK national emission estimates are updated annually and any developments in methodology are applied retrospectively to earlier years. Adjustments in the methodology are made to accommodate new technical information and to improve international comparability.

Three different classification systems are used in the tables presented here: a National Accounts basis (Table 13.1); the format required by the Inter-governmental Panel on Climate Change (IPCC) (Table 13.2); and the EMEP format used by the United Nations Economic Commission for Europe (UNECE) (Tables 13.3-13.7).

In January 2002 a new format (UNECE/EMEP) for classifying sources of emissions was introduced for reporting emissions to the UNECE, the 'Nomenclature for Reporting' (NFR). The EMEP source categories are detailed below, together with details of the main sources of these emissions.

Power stations: Public power plants, including power generation from waste incineration.

Refineries: Petroleum refineries combustion.

Combustion in fuel extraction and transformation: Combustion in smokeless fuel plant, collieries, oil and gas plant, offshore industry (not flaring).

Domestic combustion: Combustion in residential plant, including domestic boilers and fires.

Commercial, public and agricultural combustion: Commercial and institutional plants; plants in agriculture, forestry and aquaculture.

Power generation within industry: Boilers, gas turbines and other stationary engines for power generation within industry, including iron and steel industry.

Other iron and steel combustion: Iron and steel reheating furnaces, sinter plant, foundries.

Other industrial combustion: Industrial combustion plants, furnaces, industrial production.

Production processes: Processes in petroleum, iron and steel, non-ferrous metal, chemical, wood, food, drink and other industries.

Extraction and distribution of fossil fuels: Extraction of solid, liquid and gaseous fossil fuels, including off-shore activities (apart from gas flaring); liquid fuel, gasoline and gas distribution.

Solvent use: Paint application; degreasing; chemical products manufacturing or processing; other use of solvents.

Road transport: Passenger cars, light and heavy duty vehicles, mopeds, motorcycles; gasoline evaporation from vehicles, tyre and brake wear.

Military: Military aircraft and naval vessels, military machinery (military road vehicles are included in road transport).

Railways: Railway locomotives.

Shipping: Inland waterways boats; domestic navigation, fishing vessels.

Civil aircraft: Domestic and international ground movement and take off and landing cycles up to 1 km from the airport.

Other mobile sources: Agricultural machinery; gardening, construction and aircraft support equipment; mobile industrial equipment powered by diesel or petrol engines.

Waste treatment and disposal: Treatment of domestic, industrial and other waste, including landfill, but excluding incineration with energy recovery; off-shore gas flaring.

Agriculture: Culture with and without fertilisers; stubble straw burning; enteric fermentation and manure management of animals; managed forests.

Forests: Volatile organic compounds emissions from managed and unmanaged forests only.

The EMEP source categories used in tables 13.3 to 13.7 are effectively the same as the CORINAIR94 categories used previously in *Annual Abstract,* except for the following changes:-

Power generation within industry: Includes emissions which were formerly classified to either 'Iron and steel combustion' or 'Other industrial combustion'.

Other iron and steel combustion: Excludes emissions from power generation within iron and steel industry, but includes some combustion previously classified as 'Other industrial combustion'.

Other industrial combustion: Excludes power generation within industry, and some combustion re-classified to 'Other iron and steel combustion'.

Production processes: Excludes some processes now classified as 'Solvent use'.

Solvent use: Includes some processes previously classified as 'Production processes'.

In tables 13.3 and 13.5, the figures on emissions from individual large combustion plants (LCPs) for 1991 onwards are totals of those reported by the Environment Agency to DEFRA. For 1970-1990, estimates are made assuming all power station emissions from coal, fuel oil and orimulsion stations are included, plus 79 per cent of refineries' emissions, 12 per cent of iron and steel emissions and 38 per cent of other (Table 13.3), and 88 per cent of refineries' emissions, 11 per cent of iron and steel emissions and 40 per cent of other industrial combustions in fuel extraction and transformation (Table 13.5). It is not possible to calculate LCP figures from the categories presented in these tables as refineries and other industrial combustion are both included in more than one category.

Estimated atmospheric emissions on a National Accounts basis *(Table 13.1)*
The National Accounts figures in Table 13.1 differ from those on an IPCC basis in that they include estimated emissions from fuels purchased by UK residents either at home or abroad, including emissions from UK international shipping and aircraft operators and exclude emissions in the UK resulting from the activities of non-residents.

Greenhouse gases include carbon dioxide, methane, nitrous oxide, hydro-fluorocarbons, perfluorocarbons and sulphur hexafluoride which are expressed in thousand tonnes of carbon dioxide equivalent.

Acid rain precursors include sulphur dioxide, nitrogen oxides and ammonia which are expressed as thousand tonnes of sulphur dioxide equivalent.

PM^{10} are carbon particles in the air arising from incomplete combustion.

Estimated total emissions of greenhouse gases on a IPCC basis *(Table 13.2)*
The IPCC classification is used to report greenhouse gas emissions and includes land use change and all emissions from domestic aviation and shipping, but excludes international marine and aviation bunker fuels. Estimates of the relative contribution to global warming of the main greenhouse gases, or classes of gases, is presented weighted by their global warming potential.

Emissions of PM^{10} *(Table 13.4)*
Emissions of PM^{10} includes particles which pass through a size selective inlet with a 50 per cent efficiency cut-off at 10μm aerodynamics diameter.

Emissions of nitrogen oxides *(Table 13.5)*
Most of the figures in this table are based on a single NO_x emission factor for each fuel which is held constant over time. Emissions are expressed as nitrogen dioxide equivalent.

Emissions of carbon monoxide *(Table 13.6)*
Most of the figures in this table are based on a single carbon monoxide emission factor for each fuel held constant over time.

Emissions of volatile organic compounds *(Table 13.7)*
Most of the figures in this table are based on a single volatile organic compound emission factor for each source held constant over time.

Water industry expenditure *(Table 13.8)*
The table is informed by the annual and regulatory accounts of water and sewerage companies and water companies of England and Wales. Figures are given based on current cost rather than historical cost accounting principles. The elements which make up operating expenditure are as follows: manpower costs, other costs of employment, power, agencies, associated companies, Environment Agency charges, bulk supply imports, general and support, customer services, scientific services, other business activities, local authority rates, water charges, local authority sewerage agencies, materials and consumables, hired and contracted services, charge for bad and doubtful debts, depreciation, infrastructure renewals expenditure, infrastructure renewals accrual, exceptional items and other operating costs. Capital expenditure figures are the addition to tangible fixed assets including management and general expenditure but excluding infrastructure renewals expenditure. Adopted assets at nil cost are also included.

Biological and chemical quality of rivers and canals *(Tables 13.9 and 13.10)*
The chemical quality of river and canal waters in the UK is monitored in a series of separate national surveys in England and Wales and Northern Ireland. The General Quality Assessment (GQA) Scheme used in the surveys provides a rigorous and objective method for assessing the basic chemical quality of rivers and canals based on three determinants – dissolved oxygen, biochemical oxygen demand (BOD), and ammoniacal nitrogen. The GQA grades river stretches into six categories (A-F) of chemical quality and these in turn have been grouped into four broader groups – good (classes A and B), fair (C and D), poor (E) and bad (F).

To provide a more comprehensive picture of the health of rivers and canals, biological testing has also been carried out. The biological grading is based on the monitoring of tiny animals (invertebrates) which live in or on the bed of the river. Research has shown that there is a relationship between species composition and water quality. Using a procedure known as the River Invertebrate Prediction and Classification System (RIVPACS), species groups recorded at a site were compared with those which would be expected to be present in the absence of pollution, allowing for the different environmental characteristics in different parts of the country. Two different summary statistics (known as ecological quality indices (EQI)) were calculated and then the biological quality was assigned to one of six bands based on a combination of these two statistics.

Environment, water and housing

River length stretches were allocated to Government Office Regions using a 1995 digitised map. This provides consistently smaller total river lengths for local areas than the equivalent Environment Agency figures. This is because of differences between stretch lengths used by the Environment Agency and those calculated using the map, and because it was not possible to link all stretch codes to the map, so some stretches were excluded. It should be noted that the monitoring network only covers stretches the Environment Agency are required to monitor, that is rivers and streams with a flow greater than 1m³ / second. On this basis 40,000km of river network are monitored in England and Wales out of an estimated total river length of 150,000km. No canals are classified in Northern Ireland. The figures in table 13.9 are rounded to the nearest 10km and may not sum to totals.

In Scotland, water quality is based upon the Scottish River Classification Scheme of 20 June 1997 which combines chemical, biological, nutrient and aesthetic quality using the following classes: excellent (A1), good (A2) fair (B), poor (C) and seriously polluted (D). The figures in table 13.10 are also rounded to the nearest 10km and may not sum to totals.

Water pollution incidents (Table 13.11)
The Environment Agency responds to complaints and reported incidents of pollution in England and Wales. Each incident is then logged and categorised according to its severity. The category describes the impact of each incident on our water, land and air. The impact of an incident on each medium is considered and reported separately. If no impact has occurred for a particular medium, the incident is reported as a Category 4. Before 1999, the reporting system was used only for water pollution incidents, thus the total number of substantiated incidents was lower as it did not include incidents not relating to the water environment.

Bathing waters (Table 13.12)
Under the EC Bathing Water Directive 76/160/EEC, eleven physical, chemical and microbiological parameters are measured including total and faecal coliforms which are generally considered to be the most important indicators of the extent to which water is contaminated by sewage. The mandatory value for total coliforms is 10,000 per 100 ml, and for faecal coliforms 2,000 per 100 ml. For a bathing water to comply with the coliform standards, the Directive requires that at least 95 per cent of samples taken for each of these parameters over the bathing season are less than or equal to the mandatory values. In the UK a minimum of 20 samples are normally taken at each site. In practice this means that where 20 samples are taken, a maximum of only one sample may exceed the mandatory value for the bathing water to comply, and where less than 20 samples are taken none may exceed the mandatory value for the bathing water to comply.

The bathing water season is from mid-May to end-September in England and Wales, but shorter in Scotland and Northern Ireland. Bathing waters which are closed for the season are excluded for that year.

The table shows Environment Agency (EA) regions for England and Wales. The boundaries of which are based on river catchment areas and not county borders. In particular, the figures shown for Wales are the EA Welsh Region, the boundary of which does not coincide with the boundary of Wales.

The following changes have occurred to these regions:-

North East: Up to 1998 includes Alnmouth which has been undesignated since. Earls Dyke was closed for the 2001 season, but re-opened in 2002.

North West: In 1997 West Kirby was reclassified from the Welsh to the North West region. West Kirby data are presented in the North West region for all years for consistency.

Anglian: A new bathing water was designated in this region in 2002, this is Sea Palling.

Thames: Two new bathing waters were designated in this region in 2001, these are Shoeburyness and Three Shells

South West: Bathing waters closed for both the 2001 and 2002 seasons were Redgate, Dartmouth Castle and Sugary Cove. Bathing waters closed for just the 2002 season were Beacon Cove, Gunwalloe and West Bay West. Two new bathing waters were designated in this region in 2002, these are Trebarwith Strand and Crackington Haven.

Surface and groundwater abstractions (Table 13.13)
From 1991 data were collected on a different basis. Figures are therefore not strictly comparable with those in previous years. Some regions report licensed and actual abstracts for financial rather than calendar years. As figures represent an average for the whole year expressed as daily amounts, differences between amounts reported for financial and calendar years are small.

The following changes have occurred in the classification of individual sources:-

Public water supply: The 1991 figures include some private water supply.

Spray irrigation: This category includes small amounts of non-agricultural spray irrigation.

Mineral washing: Included for the first time as a separate category in 1991 survey, but no longer reported from 1999.

Private water supply: was shown as separate category from 1992 and includes private abstractions for domestic use and individual households.

Fish farming, cress growing, amenity ponds: Includes amenity ponds, but excludes miscellaneous from 1991.

Other: was included for the first time as a separate category in 1991 survey. The figure for 1991 included some private domestic water supply wells and boreholes, public water supply transfer licences and frost protection use.

Annual waste arisings *(Table 13.14)*
Agriculture: The estimate is derived from a survey of agricultural waste commissioned by DEFRA and relates to Great Britain. It includes all waste streams, eg excreta from all livestock (both housed and grazing animals) and other wastes including straw, plastics and packaging, animal carcasses and slurries.

Mining and quarrying: The minerals waste estimate is based on ratios of waste to product.

Sewage sludge: The estimate of sewage sludge arisings has been made on the basis of dry weight (wet weight can be estimated on the basis of 4 per cent solid content on average - giving a total of 26,450,000 tonnes).

Dredged material: The data for dredged material are for all UK waters.

Municipal waste: The UK estimate for municipal waste is based on returns made by Waste Disposal Authorities in England and Wales to a DEFRA/National Assembly for Wales survey.

Commercial and industrial: The figures for these sectors only cover England and Wales, and are estimated from a EA survey.

Demolition and construction: These provisional estimates only cover England and Wales, and are estimated from a DEFRA/EA survey.

Radioactive wastes *(Table 13.15)*
Solid radioactive wastes are not discharged to the environment but stored and conditioned by processes such as supercompaction, cementation or turning into glass. Such wastes cover a wide range of materials and can be classified, according to the nature and quantity of radioactivity associated with them, as high level wastes (HLW), intermediate level wastes (ILW) or low level wastes (LLW). HLW result from the reprocessing of nuclear fuel and are highly radioactive. They contain over 95 per cent of all the radioactivity in wastes from nuclear establishments. Although small in volume, HLW have a high heat output as a result of the energy from radioactive decay. ILW include the irradiated metal cladding for nuclear reactor fuel, reactor components, and chemical process residues and filters. They have a lower radioactivity and heat output than HLW but their radioactivity content exceeds the upper limits for LLW.

The table shows recent trends in the volume of radioactive waste stocks for particular groups of nuclear sites. Data for HLW and ILW are presented in two physical states – as stored and conditioned. "As stored" is the form in which the waste is currently stored. "Conditioned" is the form of waste suitable for long-term storage and ultimate disposal to deep underground repositories when these become available. There is no simple relationship between as-stored and conditioned

volumes of waste, since the effects of conditioning can vary with different wastes. Estimates of conditioned wastes are indicative only and should be interpreted with care.

LLW include concrete, rubble and soil from building demolition, discarded protective clothing and worn out or damaged plant and equipment. Unlike HLW and ILW, LLW do not normally require shielding against radiation emissions during handling and transport. The table reports LLW volumes in the form in which the wastes will be disposed of in existing facilities or a future repository.

The table excludes waste from defence establishments prior to 1991. Such ILW and LLW will add no more than 20 per cent to the volumes of radioactive waste from civil sources before 1991.

Recycling *(Table 13.16)*
The ratios shown reflect the amount of secondary material (scrap) used in the UK in a year as a proportion of consumption in that year. This gives some indication of the extent to which secondary material is displacing raw materials from the feedstock. This definition takes no account of the lifetime of the article being recovered, ie that material which is being recycled now and related to current consumption might originally have been delivered to an end market some years ago.

Designated areas *(Table 13.17)*
National Parks, Areas of Outstanding Natural Beauty (AONB's) in England, Wales and Northern Ireland and National Scenic Areas in Scotland are the major areas which have been designated to protect their landscape importance. National Scenic Areas in Scotland are the equivalent of AONB's in England, Wales and Northern Ireland.

Some areas may be in more than one category. All areas shown in the table are at December 2000, except for Green Belt land which relates to 1 January 1997.

The area for Green Belt land is based on a new methodology in which the extent of Green Belt land is captured in digital form. This approach provides much more reliable figures than those previously published in earlier years.

Noise complaints *(Table 13.18)*
The table shows trends in the number of complaints received by local authority Environmental Health Officers. The figures are from those authorities making returns and are calculated per million people based on the population of the authorities making returns.

Most complaints about traffic noise are usually addressed to highways authorities or Department for Transport (DfT) Regional Directors, and will not necessarily be included in the figures. Similarly, complaints about noise from civil aircraft are generally received by aircraft operators, the airport companies, the DfT or Civil Aviation Authority. Complaints about military flying are dealt with either by Station Commanding Officers or by Ministry of Defence headquarters. The figures in this table will not necessarily include these complaints.

Over time some of the categories shown in this table have changed. These have included:- Up until 1996/97 Section 62 of the *Control of Pollution Act 1974* covered noise in the streets - it primarily included the chimes of ice-cream vendors and the use of loudspeakers other than for strictly defined purposes. From 1997/98 all complaints about noise in the street are included with 'vehicles machinery and equipment in streets'. From 1997/98 complaints about road works are included with 'vehicles machinery and equipment in streets'.

Material Flows *(Table 13.19)*

Economy-wide material flow accounts record the total mass of natural resources and products that are used by the UK economy, either directly in the production and distribution of products and services, or indirectly through the movement of materials which are displaced in order for production to take place.

The direct movement of materials into the economy derives primarily from domestic extraction, that is from biomass (agricultural harvest, timber, fish and animal grazing), fossil fuel extraction (such as coal, crude oil and natural gas) and mineral extraction (metal ores, industrial minerals such as pottery clay, and construction material such as crushed rock, sand and gravel). This domestic extraction is supplemented by the imports of products, which may be of raw materials such as unprocessed agricultural products, but can also be semi-manufactured or finished products. In a similar way the UK produces exports of raw materials, semi-manufactured and finished goods which can be viewed as inputs to the production and consumption of overseas economies.

Indirect flows of natural resources consist of the unused material resulting from domestic extraction such as mining and quarrying overburden and the soil removed during construction and dredging activities. They also include the movement of used and unused material overseas which is associated with the production and delivery of imports. Water – except for that included directly in products – is excluded from the accounts.

There are three main indicators used to measure inputs. The **Direct Material Input (DMI)** measures the input of used materials into the economy, that is all materials which are of economic value and are used in production and consumption activities (including the production of exports). **Domestic material consumption (DMC)** measures the total amount of material directly used in the economy, ie it includes imports but excludes exports. The **Total Material Requirement (TMR)** measures the total material basis of the economy, that is the total primary resource requirements of all the production and consumption activities. It includes not only the direct use of resources for producing exports, but also indirect flows from the production of imports and the indirect flows associated with domestic extraction. Although TMR is widely favoured as a resource use indicator, the estimates of indirect flows are less reliable than those for materials directly used by the economy, and the indicator therefore needs to be considered alongside other indicators.

Further details regarding tables 13.2 to 13.7 and 13.9 to 13.18 can be found in DEFRA's annual *Digest of Environmental Statistics*. If you would like to discuss the tables, Adrian Redfern can be contacted at DEFRA on 020 7944 6497.

Permanent dwellings *(Table 13.20)*

Local housing authorities include the Commission for the New Towns and New Towns Development Corporations, Communities Scotland, the Northern Ireland Housing Trust and the Northern Ireland Housing Executive. The figures shown for housing associations include dwellings provided by housing associations other than the Communities Scotland and the Northern Ireland Housing Trust and provided or authorised by government departments for the families of police, prison staff, the Armed Forces and certain other services.

13.1 Estimated atmospheric emissions 2000 on National Accounts basis[1]
United Kingdom

Thousand tonnes

	Greenhouse gases[2]	Acid rain precursors[3]	PM$_{10}$	Carbon monoxide	Volatile organic compounds[4]	Benzene	Butadiene	Lead (Tonnes)	Cadmium (Tonnes)	Mercury (Tonnes)
					Emissions affecting air quality					
Agriculture	54 200	530	20.1	60.8	147.7	0.2	0.2	3.8	0.01	-
Mining and quarrying	31 400	70	23.2	43.9	196.1	0.4	-	0.4	0.04	0.02
Manufacturing	133 000	440	37.9	780.6	439.4	3.4	0.9	132.8	3.42	4.17
Electricity, gas and water supply	165 900	1 060	22.4	68.4	75.0	0.3	-	17.5	0.41	1.44
Construction	3 700	10	5.4	51.4	53.8	0.2	0.1	0.5	0.01	-
Wholesale and retail trade	19 800	40	6.2	186.7	131.1	0.9	0.4	17.7	0.04	0.01
Transport and communication	82 000	560	17.4	366.3	128.8	2.4	2.5	21.9	0.25	0.03
Financial intermediation	14 900	30	4.2	183.1	24.0	0.5	0.2	17.9	0.03	-
Public administration	10 000	60	1.4	21.4	5.6	0.3	-	1.4	0.01	0.04
Education, health and social work	11 600	20	1.9	40.8	6.3	0.1	-	4.9	0.02	0.08
Other services	19 900	40	1.3	23.9	15.2	0.1	0.1	5.7	0.66	2.24
Domestic	150 000	360	37.0	2 521.5	476.5	9.8	2.7	277.7	0.47	0.53
Total	**696 400**	**3 220**	**178.4**	**4 348.8**	**1 699.4**	**18.5**	**7.1**	**502.3**	**5.36**	**8.56**
Of which, emissions from road transport	123 600	480	32.2	2 915.5	414.2	7.8	4.7	329.2	0.38	-

1 See chapter text.
2 Thousand tonnes of carbon dioxide equivalent.
3 Thousand tonnes of sulphur dioxide equivalent.
4 Excluding methane, but including benzene and 1,3-butadiene.

Sources: National Environmental Technology Centre;
Office for National Statistics: 020 7533 5904

13.2 Estimated total emissions[1] of greenhouse gases on IPCC basis[2]
United Kingdom

Million tonnes (Carbon dioxide equivalent[3])

		1990	1991	1992	1993	1994	1995	1996	1997	1998	1999	2000
Carbon dioxide	JZCK	603.1	606.8	592.1	576.6	572.6	563.6	583.5	559.0	561.6	552.9	557.7
Methane	GXDO	76.5	75.4	73.6	70.4	63.9	63.6	62.2	59.9	57.2	54.4	51.0
Nitrous oxide	GXDP	67.9	66.0	59.1	55.4	59.8	57.1	59.1	60.8	58.0	44.9	43.8
Hydrofluorocarbons	JZCN	11.37	11.86	12.35	12.90	13.81	15.21	16.29	18.45	20.18	8.60	9.32
Perfluorocarbons	JZCO	2.28	1.79	0.96	0.81	0.98	1.09	0.91	0.66	0.65	0.68	0.67
Sulphur hexafluoride	JZCP	0.72	0.78	0.83	0.89	1.06	1.13	1.27	1.26	1.48	1.51	1.54
Total	**GXDQ**	**762**	**763**	**739**	**717**	**712**	**702**	**723**	**700**	**699**	**663**	**664**
1990 Baseline[4]	GXJK	765	..	..	..	..	..	..	..	..	..	..
Percentage change from 1990 baseline	GXDR	..	−0.3	−3.4	−6.3	−6.9	−8.3	−5.4	−8.5	−8.6	−13.3	−13.2

1 Weighted by global warming potential. Emissions inventories based on the the methodology developed by the Intergovernmental Panel on Climate Change (IPCC) are used to report UK emissions to the Climate Change Convention.
2 See chapter text.
3 12 tonnes of carbon is equivalent to 44 tonnes of carbon dioxide.

4 The 1990 baseline, used for comparison with the Kyoto target, is the sum of 1990 totals for carbon dioxide, methane and nitrous oxide and 1995 totals for hydrofluorocarbons, perfluorocarbons and sulphur hexafluoride.

Sources: National Environmental Technology Centre;
for Department for Environment, Food and Rural Affairs 020 7944 6497

13.3 Estimated emissions of sulphur dioxide (SO$_2$) by source[1]
United Kingdom

Thousand tonnes

By source category (UNECE/EMEP)		Percentage of total in 2000	1970	1980	1990	1991	1992	1993	1994	1995	1996	1997	1998	1999	2000
Power stations	JZCR	71	2 913	3 007	2 723	2 535	2 434	2 083	1 762	1 591	1 320	1 025	1 072	776	826
Refineries	GPKK	6	242	262	153	161	146	148	135	142	144	134	98	93	72
Combustion in fuel extraction and transformation	JZCT	1	231	25	8	8	6	5	4	3	3	6	7	9	8
Domestic	JZCU	4	522	226	108	115	103	113	92	67	71	63	53	52	44
Commercial, public and agricultural combustion	JZCV	1	451	218	93	88	90	95	81	60	57	47	34	27	17
Power generation within industry	ESYA	7	1 719	834	374	392	452	451	379	288	240	210	158	107	81
Other iron and steel combustion	ESYB	1	35	10	18	17	18	18	16	17	17	17	15	15	11
Other industrial combustion	ESYC	3	94	76	52	43	40	39	43	47	38	44	42	41	34
Production processes	GPLN	3	115	88	61	57	52	49	46	45	44	41	41	37	31
Extraction and distribution of fossil fuels	GPKD	-	5	5	16	6	7	5	6	6	7	6	6	1	1
Road transport	JZCZ	1	44	42	63	58	62	59	63	51	37	27	23	14	6
Military	GPKX	1	9	9	9	10	9	8	8	8	8	8	6	6	6
Railways	GPUX	-	14	7	3	3	3	2	2	2	2	1	1	1	1
Shipping	GPUY	2	35	25	27	30	29	30	29	29	30	27	25	22	20
Civil Aircraft	GPUZ	-	–	–	–	–	–	–	–	–	–	–	–	–	–
Other mobile sources	GPLD	-	35	19	8	8	8	8	7	5	5	5	5	5	4
Waste treatment and disposal	GPVA	-	4	5	5	5	4	3	3	3	2	1	2	4	3
Total	JZDC	100	6 468	4 859	3 721	3 534	3 462	3 115	2 676	2 363	2 025	1 665	1 588	1 210	1 165
Emissions from large combustion plants															
Large plants	ZBZK		3 660	3 490	2 930	2 747	2 674	2 329	1 969	1 756	1 468	1 107	1 207	894	899
Index (1980=100)	ZBZL		105	100	84	79	77	67	56	50	42	32	35	26	26

1 See chapter text.

Sources: National Environmental Technology Centre; Environment Agency; for Department for Environment, Food and Rural Affairs 020 7944 6497

13.4 Estimated emissions of PM$_{10}$ by source[1]
United Kingdom

Thousand tonnes

By source category (UNECE/EMEP)		Percentage of total in 2000	1970	1980	1990	1991	1992	1993	1994	1995	1996	1997	1998	1999	2000
Power stations	JZDN	13	67	76	70	70	66	55	49	38	35	24	25	20	22
Refineries	GQOZ	1	5	5	3	4	4	4	4	4	4	4	4	3	3
Combustion in fuel extraction and transformation	GQPA	-	16	2	–	–	–	–	–	–	–	–	–	–	–
Domestic	GQPB	16	222	102	52	55	51	53	43	33	35	33	33	34	28
Commercial, public & agricultural combustion	JZDP	3	22	11	8	8	8	7	7	6	6	7	6	5	5
Power generation within industry	EUID	6	68	29	22	24	26	24	23	21	19	17	14	13	10
Other iron and steel combustion	EVNZ	2	17	8	8	7	7	7	7	7	6	6	5	4	4
Other industrial combustion	EVPN	4	11	10	10	9	8	8	9	8	8	8	8	8	7
Production processes in industry	GQPE	7	14	12	14	14	14	14	14	13	14	13	13	12	11
Construction, mining and quarrying	GQPF	15	30	25	34	30	28	29	31	29	27	27	27	25	25
Road transport	JZDS	18	46	56	63	62	60	58	56	52	49	44	40	37	31
Other transport and mobile sources	GQPG	6	15	13	13	13	12	12	12	11	12	12	11	11	10
Waste treatment and disposal	GQPH	1	1	4	3	3	2	2	3	2	2	1	1	1	1
Agriculture	GQPI	8	11	12	12	13	12	12	12	12	13	13	14	14	14
Total	JZGA	100	546	365	313	311	299	285	270	238	230	209	201	188	172

1 See chapter text.

Sources: National Environmental Technology Centre; for Department for Environment, Food and Rural Affairs 020 7944 6497

13.5 Estimated emissions of nitrogen oxides (NOx) by source[1]
United Kingdom

Thousand tonnes

By source category (UNECE/EMEP)		Percentage of total in 2000	1970	1980	1990	1991	1992	1993	1994	1995	1996	1997	1998	1999	2000
Power stations	JZGB	24	812	861	781	683	671	567	527	495	449	372	364	338	358
Refineries	JZGC	2	43	42	40	41	40	37	36	35	35	33	39	32	28
Combustion in fuel extraction and transformation	JZGD	3	56	42	61	62	63	65	75	47	47	47	50	53	52
Domestic	JZGE	5	62	64	64	71	69	72	69	66	75	69	71	71	72
Commercial, public and agricultural combustion	JZGF	2	74	46	38	41	40	38	38	38	39	36	34	34	32
Power generation within industry	GWDV	7	295	185	131	134	135	132	132	124	122	120	113	110	105
Other iron and steel combustion	GWDW	1	20	6	10	10	10	10	13	13	13	14	13	14	13
Other industrial combustion	GWEL	3	95	83	84	71	66	67	74	67	61	66	63	52	46
Production processes	JZGI	-	13	14	11	9	9	8	7	4	4	4	4	4	4
Extraction and distribution of fossil fuels	GQRZ	-	–	–	1	1	1	–	1	1	1	1	1	1	1
Road transport	JZGJ	42	771	990	1 305	1 274	1 224	1 147	1 084	997	956	881	788	716	629
Military	GQSB	1	32	32	35	34	31	29	28	28	28	28	22	23	22
Railways	GQSC	1	25	15	21	21	19	18	14	15	14	12	12	12	11
Shipping	GQSD	4	62	66	72	75	72	71	66	64	69	66	62	56	55
Civil aircraft	GQSE	-	1	2	3	3	3	3	3	3	3	3	4	4	4
Other mobile sources	GQSA	5	120	104	89	92	92	90	88	85	89	87	88	81	78
Waste treatment and disposal	JZGL	-	6	12	9	8	8	6	8	8	7	4	4	3	3
Agriculture	JZGM	-	10	15	9	8	6	–	–	–	–	–	–	–	–
Total	JZGO	100	2 499	2 580	2 763	2 637	2 558	2 361	2 263	2 088	2 014	1 844	1 732	1 604	1 512

Emissions from large combustion plants

			1970	1980	1990	1991	1992	1993	1994	1995	1996	1997	1998	1999	2000
Large plants	ZBZM		933	957	846	749	742	636	572	524	471	371	369	333	341
Index (1980=100)	ZBZN		97	100	88	78	78	66	60	55	49	39	39	35	36

1 See chapter text.

Sources: National Environmental Technology Centre; Environment Agency;
for Department for Environment, Food and Rural Affairs 020 7944 6497

13.6 Estimated emissions of carbon monoxide (CO) by source[1]
United Kingdom

Thousand tonnes

By source category (UNECE/EMEP)		Percentage of total in 2000	1970	1980	1990	1991	1992	1993	1994	1995	1996	1997	1998	1999	2000
Power stations	JZGP	1	117	121	114	113	110	99	106	104	102	71	73	61	60
Refineries	GPVW	-	8	8	7	7	7	8	7	8	8	8	8	7	6
Combustion in fuel extraction and transformation	JZGQ	1	45	24	22	22	20	20	20	22	23	23	26	27	28
Domestic	JZGR	5	1 237	608	345	369	347	369	324	260	268	246	239	244	215
Commercial, public and agricultural combustion	JZGS	-	46	26	23	23	21	21	20	19	19	19	18	18	18
Power generation within industry	HFLY	1	106	43	39	41	45	42	42	41	37	35	30	27	21
Other iron and steel combustion	HFLZ	6	757	215	385	364	377	378	342	348	347	353	339	343	241
Other industrial combustion	HFMA	3	130	93	91	84	81	83	84	85	79	84	75	113	118
Production processes	GPVZ	3	180	142	184	177	167	167	172	175	180	182	166	145	139
Extraction and distribution of fossil fuels	GPWA	-	2	2	7	3	3	2	3	3	3	3	3	1	1
Road transport	GPWB	69	5 409	5 367	5 240	5 076	4 858	4 528	4 271	4 003	3 966	3 728	3 508	3 290	2 881
Military	GPWD	-	11	11	13	11	10	10	10	10	10	9	8	8	7
Railways	GPWE	-	9	6	6	6	6	5	4	4	4	3	3	3	3
Shipping	GPWF	-	8	9	9	10	9	9	9	8	9	9	8	7	7
Civil aircraft	GPWG	-	1	2	3	3	3	3	3	3	4	4	4	4	4
Other transport and mobile sources	GPWC	10	584	512	428	445	453	439	428	407	408	407	407	406	405
Waste treatment and disposal	GPWH	-	3	45	31	28	27	27	35	24	25	20	21	17	16
Agriculture	JZGY	-	288	449	266	228	165	4	–	–	–	–	–	–	–
Total	JZHA	100	8 941	7 684	7 214	7 008	6 711	6 214	5 880	5 525	5 490	5 205	4 937	4 721	4 171

1 See chapter text.

Sources: National Environmental Technology Centre;
for Department for Environment, Food and Rural Affairs 020 7944 6497

13.7 Estimated emissions of volatile organic compounds[1] by source[2]
United Kingdom

Thousand tonnes

By source category (UNECE/EMEP)		Percentage of total in 2000	1970	1980	1990	1991	1992	1993	1994	1995	1996	1997	1998	1999	2000
Power stations	JZHB	-	7	8	7	7	7	7	8	8	9	8	6	8	8
Refineries	GQJF	-	1	1	1	1	1	1	1	1	1	1	1	1	1
Combustion in fuel extraction and transformation	GQJG	-	2	2	2	2	3	3	3	1	1	1	1	1	1
Domestic	JZHC	2	292	128	63	66	61	61	48	37	40	37	38	41	32
Commercial, public and agricultural combustion	GQJH	-	4	3	3	4	4	4	4	4	4	4	4	4	4
Power generation within industry	GWEO	-	6	5	4	4	4	4	5	5	5	5	5	5	5
Other iron and steel combustion	GWEP	-	1	-	-	-	-	-	1	1	1	1	1	1	1
Other industrial combustion	GWEQ	-	11	9	5	4	3	3	3	3	3	3	3	2	3
Production processes	GQJL	12	291	307	340	331	330	321	314	320	307	283	262	215	207
Extraction and distribution of fossil fuels	GQJM	18	82	237	334	337	326	326	346	335	348	377	344	301	303
Solvent use	GQJN	27	588	575	666	628	591	582	579	541	524	513	503	462	445
Road transport[3]	JZHG	24	644	772	938	916	880	817	763	699	651	592	524	474	408
Military	GQJP	-	2	2	2	2	2	2	2	2	2	2	1	1	1
Railways	GQJQ	-	4	3	3	3	3	3	2	2	2	2	2	2	2
Shipping	GQJR	-	2	2	3	3	3	3	2	2	3	2	2	2	2
Civil aircraft	GQJJ	-	-	-	1	1	1	1	1	1	1	1	1	1	1
Other transport and mobile sources	GQJO	3	70	64	58	59	59	58	58	56	57	56	57	56	55
Waste treatment and disposal	JZHI	1	10	56	43	40	38	38	45	37	36	31	29	24	21
Agriculture	JZHJ	-	37	58	35	30	22	-	-	-	-	-	-	-	-
Forests[4]	JZHK	11	178	178	178	178	178	178	178	178	178	178	178	178	178
Total	JZHM	100	2 231	2 410	2 686	2 616	2 516	2 411	2 362	2 232	2 170	2 097	1 962	1 778	1 676

1 Excluding methane.
2 See chapter text.
3 Includes evaporative emissions from the petrol tank and carburettor of petrol-engined vehicles.

4 An order of magnitude estimate of natural emissions from managed and unmanaged forests.

Sources: National Environmental Technology Centre; Environment Agency; for Department for Environment, Food and Rural Affairs 020 7944 6497

13.8 Water industry expenditure[1]
England and Wales

£ millions

		1991 /92	1992 /93	1993 /94	1994 /95	1995 /96	1996 /97	1997 /98	1998 /99	1999 /00	2000 /01	2001 /02
Operating expenditure												
Water supply	KQQX	1 953.8	2 024.4	2 108.0	2 209.0	2 347.0	2 304.2	2 331.0	2 386.1	2 426.8	2 403.3	2 428.3
Sewerage services	KQQY	1 580.9	1 635.4	1 757.9	1 755.0	1 763.0	1 780.7	1 856.1	1 971.4	2 069.9	2 087.6	2 167.6
Capital expenditure												
Water supply	KQSX	1 307.0	1 358.2	1 386.7	1 081.0	1 074.5	1 314.3	1 467.2	1 294.1	1 290.0	935.0	1 132.5
Sewerage	KQSY	559.0	455.3	410.7	381.0	375.6	479.9	455.2	507.5	488.5	352.0	362.4
Sewage treatment and disposal	KQSZ	968.0	906.0	735.3	763.0	773.0	959.4	1 296.3	1 374.5	1 440.8	1 040.9	996.0

1 See chapter text.

Source: Office of Water Services: 0121 625 1312

13.9 Biological[1] and chemical[2] quality of rivers and canals[3]
England, Wales and Northern Ireland

	Years	Good A	Good B	Fair C	Fair D	Poor E	Bad F	Total	Good or fair	Poor or bad
									Percentage of total	
Biological quality										
North East	1990	530	740	260	160	150	50	1 890	90	10
	2000	870	740	210	140	30	10	2 010	98	2
North West	1990	410	1 030	650	320	570	750	3 730	64	36
	2000	670	1 390	1 210	690	660	90	4 720	84	16
Yorkshire and the Humber	1990	780	480	300	270	230	260	2 320	79	21
	2000	1 120	910	760	360	310	100	3 560	88	12
East Midlands	1990	220	550	1 040	500	260	120	2 690	86	14
	2000	790	1 080	1 010	220	100	30	3 230	96	4
West Midlands	1990	400	580	470	360	220	150	2 160	83	17
	2000	930	970	850	340	180	30	3 300	94	6
East	1990	360	990	1 040	370	170	60	2 990	92	8
	2000	1 580	1 220	510	110	30	-	3 450	99	1
London	1990	-	20	70	40	100	40	280	49	51
	2000	20	100	110	90	60	-	380	84	16
South East	1990	850	1 210	780	300	130	50	3 320	95	5
	2000	1 850	1 450	820	190	40	-	4 360	99	1
South West	1990	2 150	2 150	880	280	150	80	5 690	96	4
	2000	3 480	1 990	540	230	80	10	6 340	99	1
England[4]	1990	6 080	8 190	5 970	2 760	2 120	1 690	26 800	86	14
	2000	11 550	10 210	6 580	2 710	1 730	320	33 100	94	6
Wales	1990	1 170	1 320	520	180	80	20	3 290	97	3
	2000	1 450	1 890	840	150	70	10	4 400	98	2
Northern Ireland	1991	710	950	410	100	10	-	2 190	100	-
	2000	1 230	1 930	1 300	550	120	20	5 140	97	3
	2001	1 010	1 560	1 740	650	180	10	5 140	97	3
Chemical quality										
North East	1990	230	560	170	70	70	30	1 130	92	8
	2001	610	1 110	240	70	50	10	2 090	97	3
North West	1990	660	590	520	440	610	200	3 030	73	27
	2001	2 050	1 170	1 210	570	370	70	5 430	92	8
Yorkshire and the Humber	1990	590	1 050	400	370	610	160	3 180	76	24
	2001	1 130	1 180	940	420	360	20	4 050	91	9
East Midlands	1990	50	560	1 120	710	550	80	3 070	79	21
	2001	630	1 680	760	330	140	10	3 560	96	4
West Midlands	1990	190	1 150	840	610	540	80	3 420	82	18
	2001	810	1 800	770	300	240	20	3 930	94	6
East	1990	50	690	1 350	790	570	70	3 510	82	18
	2001	550	1 410	970	440	210	10	3 590	94	6
London	1990	-	50	120	110	110	10	390	71	29
	2001	10	140	90	130	50	-	420	88	12
South East	1990	330	1 380	1 350	590	610	60	4 320	84	16
	2001	950	1 890	1 020	360	260	-	4 480	94	6
South West	1990	1 590	2 320	1 280	720	380	60	6 360	93	7
	2001	2 970	2 370	840	190	180	-	6 550	97	3
England[4]	1990	4 200	9 160	7 670	4 640	4 300	770	30 750	83	17
	2001	10 430	13 480	7 200	2 980	1 960	120	36 170	94	6
Wales	1990	1 830	1 210	270	130	60	30	3 520	98	2
	2001	2 990	1 230	220	50	60	10	4 570	98	2
Northern Ireland	1991	100	640	680	170	60	20	1 680	95	5
	2001	220	1 190	590	300	110	-	2 400	95	5

Column headings (span): Length surveyed (kms) — Good: A, B; Fair: C, D; Poor E; Bad F; Total. Percentage of total — Good or fair; Poor or bad.

1 Based on the River Invertebrate Prediction and Classification System (RIVPACS).
2 Based on the General Quality Assessment (GQA) chemical classification system.
3 See chapter text.
4 Figures for the English regions will not add to the national figure for England because a small amount of river lengths which are located along the border between England and Wales are counted in both the national figures figures for England and Wales.

Sources: Environment Agency; Environment and Heritage Service

13.10 Biological and chemical quality of rivers and canals[1]
Scotland

	Year	Length surveyed (kms)						Percentage of total	
		Excellent A1	Good A2	Fair B	Poor C	Seriously polluted D	Total	Good or fair[2]	Poor or seriously polluted
Scottish Environment Protection Agency Regions									
North[3]	1996	20 060	1 840	380	160	50	22 490	99	1
	1997	19 370	2 310	600	160	60	22 490	99	1
	1998	19 450	2 210	630	160	40	22 490	99	1
	1999	19 370	2 210	770	120	20	22 490	99	1
	2000	15 150	2 490	730	110	10	22 490	99	1
East	1996	8 770	2 060	800	590	50	12 270	95	5
	1997	8 730	2 200	710	590	50	12 270	95	5
	1998	8 500	2 510	750	470	40	12 270	96	4
	1999	8 450	2 450	870	470	30	12 270	96	4
	2000	8 480	2 420	950	380	40	12 270	97	3
West	1996	8 900	4 290	1 830	440	40	15 490	97	3
	1997	8 970	4 050	2 030	410	40	15 490	97	3
	1998	8 320	4 250	2 360	530	30	15 490	96	4
	1999	8 430	4 550	1 880	590	40	15 490	96	4
	2000	8 850	4 490	1 740	380	30	15 490	97	3
Scotland	1996	37 740	8 190	3 010	1 180	140	50 250	97	3
	1997	37 060	8 550	3 340	1 160	140	50 250	97	3
	1998	36 270	8 970	3 740	1 160	110	50 250	97	3
	1999	36 250	9 210	3 530	1 180	90	50 250	97	3
	2000	36 480	9 400	3 420	870	80	50 250	98	2

1 See chapter text.
2 Classes A1, A2 and B.
3 Excludes islands.

Source: Scottish Environmental Protection Agency

13.11 Water pollution incidents[1]
United Kingdom

		1992	1993	1994	1995	1996	1997	1998		1999[2]	2000[2]	2001[2]
Categories 1 to 3												
Environment Agency Regions												
North West	JZIA	3 270	3 656	3 532	3 717	2 818	2 160	2 201	MKDB	1 668	1 757	1 734
North East	JZIB	3 059	3 642	3 243	2 576	2 143	2 404	1 993	MKDC	1 828	1 822	1 952
Midlands	JZKR	4 420	4 876	4 895	4 259	4 305	4 411	4 061	MKDD	2 804	3 106	2 862
Anglian	JZKS	2 462	2 625	2 819	2 156	2 417	2 411	2 163	MKDE	1 726	1 369	1 606
Thames	JZKT	1 955	2 071	2 006	1 972	1 959	1 917	1 819	MKDF	1 208	1 379	1 510
Southern	JZKU	1 089	1 355	1 316	1 235	1 189	1 174	1 138	MKDG	1 317	1 540	1 585
South West	JZKV	4 278	4 129	4 340	4 558	3 042	2 847	2 603	MKDH	2 463	2 294	2 292
Welsh	JZKW	2 798	2 945	3 264	2 990	2 285	2 247	1 885	MKDI	1 360	1 395	1 475
England and Wales	JZKX	23 331	25 299	25 415	23 463	20 158	19 571	17 863	MKDJ	14 374	14 662	15 016
Scotland[3]	JZKY	3 020	3 081	3 170	2 752	2 878	3 356	2 329	MKDK	2 306	2 345	1 829
Northern Ireland	JZKZ	..	..	..	..	2 063	1 824	1 644	MKDL	1 510	1 701	1 546
By category in England and Wales												
Category 1	MKCW	388	331	229	199	156	194	128	MKDM	90	77	118
Category 2	MKCX	..	6 768	6 567	2 194	1 510	1 354	1 238	MKDN	863	758	860
Category 3	MKCY	..	18 200	18 619	21 070	18 492	18 023	16 497	MKDO	13 421	13 827	14 038
Category 4[2,4]	MKCZ	..	..	..	..	..	..	..	MKDP	16 548	21 744	18 706
Total substantiated incidents[4]	MKDA	23 331	25 299	25 415	23 463	20 158	19 571	17 863	MKDQ	30 922	36 406	33 722

1 See chapter text. Substantiated incidents to water, unless otherwise specified.
2 From 1999, categories 1-3 do not include all substantiated incidents to water. An additional category (Category 4) was introduced which includes all incidents which were substantiated, but which had no impact on the water environment. Therefore, data are not comparable to previous years
3 Data for all years refer to financial years.

4 Category 4 and Total substantiated incidents include incidents to other media (air, land), which did not involve the water environment.

Sources: Environment Agency;
Scottish Environment Protection Agency;
Environment and Heritage Service

13.12 Bathing water surveys[1]
United Kingdom

		Compliance with EC Bathing Water Directive coliform standards during the bathing season												
		Identified bathing waters						Numbers complying						Percentage complying
		1998	1999	2000	2001	2002		1998	1999	2000	2001	2002		2002
Environment Agency Regions														
United Kingdom	GPKA	496	535	545	546	547	GPKN	440	489	514	520	533	GPLA	97
North East	GPKB	56	55	56	55	56	GPKO	47	52	51	55	55	GPLB	98
North West	GPKC	34	34	34	34	34	GPKP	21	23	28	30	33	GPLC	97
Anglian	GPKE	36	36	37	37	38	GPKR	36	34	37	36	38	GPLE	100
Thames	GPKF	3	3	3	5	5	GPKS	3	3	3	5	5	GPLF	100
Southern	GPKG	77	79	79	79	79	GPKT	75	74	77	78	78	GPLG	99
South West	GPKH	183	184	187	187	186	GPKU	167	167	179	184	183	GPLH	98
England	GPKI	389	391	396	397	398	GPKV	349	353	375	388	392	GPLI	98
Wales	GPKJ	68	70	75	75	75	GPKW	64	69	74	70	75	GPLJ	100
Scotland	GPKL	23	58	58	58	58	GPKY	12	51	49	49	51	GPLL	88
Northern Ireland	GPKM	16	16	16	16	16	GPKZ	15	16	16	13	15	GPLM	94

1 See chapter text.

Sources: Environment Agency;
Scottish Environment Protection Agency;
Environment and Heritage Service, Northern Ireland

13.13 Estimated abstractions from all surface and groundwater sources by purpose[1]
England and Wales

Megalitres per day

		1990	1991	1992	1993	1994	1995	1996	1997	1998	1999	2000
Public water supply	JZLA	18 337	17 562	17 953	16 651	16 735	17 346	17 453	16 820	16 765	16 255	17 052
Spray irrigation	JZLB	377	366	269	164	283	352	369	292	282	325	291
Agriculture (excl spray irrigation)	JZLC	128	131	129	139	115	103	136	108	111	142	152
Electricity supply industry[2]	JZLD	30 768	30 359	37 693	26 581	27 732	25 805	31 294	33 307	34 587	26 515	31 543
Other industry	JZLE	9 275	5 469	5 326	6 017	4 292	7 513	4 960	4 352	4 964	5 428	5 385
Mineral washing	JZLF	..	173	213	198	222	262	250	297	223	..	..
Fish farming, cress growing, amenity ponds	JYXG	1 323	3 882	4 479	3 818	3 985	4 268	4 338	4 211	5 495	4 867	4 904
Private water supply	JZLG	..	..	53	81	82	98	171	162	175	91	102
Other	JZLH	..	1 254	1 794	93	194	223	531	408	289	526	559
Total	JZLI	60 208	59 196	67 909	53 742	53 640	55 970	59 503	59 957	62 891	54 148	59 989

1 See chapter text.
2 In South West region in 1991 and 1992, Hydroelectric licences were classified as "Other", in 1993 they were classified as "Other industry" and from 1994 they were classified correctly as "Electricity supply".

Source: Environment Agency

13.14 Estimated total annual waste arisings by sector[1]
United Kingdom

Sector	Annual arisings (million tonnes)	Date of estimate	Status[2]	Source	Percentage of total arisings
Agriculture	87	1999	NC	DEFRA	20
Minerals (Mining and quarrying)[3]					
Colliery[3]	15	1997	NC	DTLR	3
Coal[3]	9	1997	NC	DTLR	2
China clay[3]	26	1997	NC	DTLR	6
Clay[3]	14	1997	NC	DTLR	3
Slate[3]	7	1997	NC	DTLR	2
Quarrying[3]	47	1997	NC	DTLR	11
Sewage sludge	1	1998/89	C	Water UK[4]	-
Dredged material	33	1997	C	DEFRA	8
Municipal waste	30	2000/01	C	DEFRA	7
of which household	29	2000/01	C	DEFRA	6
Commercial	28	1998/99	C	EA	6
Industrial	55	1998/99	C	EA	13
Demolition and construction	80	2000	C	EA	19
Total	430				100

1 See chapter text.
2 NC = Not classed as a controlled waste under the terms of the Environmental Protection Act (Controlled Waste Regulations) 1992; C = controlled wastes under the terms of the Environmental Protection Act (Controlled Waste Regulation) 1992.

3 1997 estimate used, as 1998 estimate is still provisional.
4 Formerly Water Services Association and Water Companies Association.

Sources: Department for Environment, Food and Rural Affairs 020 7944 6497; Environment Agency; Water UK

13.15 Radioactive waste stocks and arisings
Great Britain

m^3

	Stocks						
	1/1/1986	1/1/1987	1/1/1988	1/1/1989	1/1/1991	1/4/1994	1/4/1998
High level waste							
As stored	1 351	1 430	1 463	1 575	1 686	1 639	1 804
Conditioned	436	517	594	674	681	653	717
Intermediate level waste							
As stored	41 887	43 602	47 783	45 313	51 558	61 494	70 948
Conditioned	56 211	59 479	66 020	81 762	78 512	66 102	74 131
Low level waste							
As stored	2 429	2 343	1 002	13 752	6 252	7 882	7 983

Source: Electrowatt Engineering Services (UK) Ltd

13.16 Recycling[1] of selected materials[2]
United Kingdom

Scrap reused as a percentage of consumption

		1985	1986	1987	1988	1989	1990	1991	1992	1993	1994	1995	1996	1997	1998
Ferrous	JYWQ	39	36	38	34	36	38	36	45	42	42	40	44	45	35
Aluminium	JYWR	40	34	34	41	44	39	41	39	29	39	53	44	40	43
Copper	JYWS	43	44	47	49	49	50	49	35	35	32	34	36	37	38
Lead	JYWT	69	66	77	73	71	67	62	64	67	74	71	73	69	66
Zinc	JYWU	22	24	24	24	23	24	24	21	21	20	20	19	19	18
Paper & board	JYWV	28	27	27	27	28	32	34	34	32	34	37	38	38	38
Newsprint	GEKY	..	..	..	..	..	26	26	31	31	33	35	44	47	52
Glass cullet	JYWW	9	..	10	11	12	15	17	20	22	22	22	22	21	22
Plastics	ZBZJ	..	..	..	..	..	..	2	2	2	2	3	3	3	3

1 The ratios shown reflect the amount of secondary material used (scrap collected less exported scrap plus imported scrap) in the UK in a year as a proportion of consumption in that year.
2 See chapter text.

Sources: Iron and Steel Statistics Bureau; Aluminium Federation; Customs and Excise; World Bureau of Metal Statistics; British Paper and Board Industry Federation; The Paper Federation of Great Britain; British Glass Manufacturers Confederation; British Plastics Federation

13.17 Designated areas[1]

	National Parks		Areas of Outstanding Natural Beauty[2]		Green Belt Land		Defined Heritage Coasts length (km)
	Area (thousand hectares)	Percentage of total area in region	Area (thousand hectares)	Percentage of total area in region	Area (thousand hectares)	Percentage of total area in region	
North East	111	13	147	17	53	6	138
North West	261	18	157	11	252	18	6
Yorkshire and the Humber	315	21	92	6	264	17	80
East Midlands	92	6	52	3	80	5	-
West Midlands	20	2	127	10	267	21	-
East	30	2	112	6	237	12	121
London	-	-	-	-	36	22	-
South East	-	-	641	31	356	19	74
South West	165	7	712	30	106	4	638
England	994	7	2 040	16	1 650	13	1 057
Wales	413	20	83	4	-	-	496
Scotland	187	2	1 002	13	155	2	-
Northern Ireland	-	-	285	20	227	16	-

1 See chapter text.
2 The South East includes London.

Source: Department for Environment, Food and Rural Affairs 020 7944 6497

13.18 Noise complaints received by Environmental Health Officers[1]

Number per million people

		1990 /91	1991 /92	1992 /93	1993 /94	1994 /95	1995 /96	1996 /97	1997 /98	1998 /99	1999 /00	2000 /01
England and Wales												
Not controlled by the Environmental Protection Act 1990:												
Road traffic	JZLJ	46	65	59	59	60	66	62	52	39	38	44
Aircraft	JZLK	34	72	73	64	111	48	58	92	109	121	26
Other	JZLL	60	99	105	84	91	90	74	229	..	..	..
Total	JZLM	140	236	237	207	262	204	194	373	..	..	..
Controlled by the Environmental Protection Act 1990:												
Industrial/commercial premises	JZLN	913	1 037	1 108	1 120	1 320	1 466	1 455	1 647	1 280	1 368	1 381
Road works, construction and demolition	JZLO	252	148	191	168	300	229	242	285	248	292	325
Domestic premises	JZLP	2 264	2 627	3 137	3 468	3 949	4 895	5 051	5 050	4 330	5 149	5 001
Controlled by the Noise and Statutory Nuisance Act 1993:												
Vehicles, machinery and equipment in streets	JZLQ	..	..	..	..	249	225	206	300	252	269	365
Total	JZLR	3 429	3 812	4 436	4 756	5 818	6 815	6 954	7 282	6 110	7 078	7 072
Controlled by Section 62 of the Control and Pollution Act 1974:												
Noise in streets	JZLS	75	100	76	92	89	109	111	..	..	..	..
Total complaints received	JZLT	3 644	4 148	4 749	5 055	6 169	7 128	7 259	..	..	..	..

		1990	1991	1992[2] /93	1993 /94	1994 /95	1995 /96	1996 /97	1997 /98	1998 /99	1999 /00	2000 /01
Scotland												
Not controlled by the Environmental Protection Act 1990:												
Road traffic	JZLU	54	51	35	..	..	..	24	21	..	..	..
Aircraft	JZLV	17	8	14	..	..	..	14	7	..	..	..
Other	JZLW	87	128	172	..	..	..	304	229	..	..	..
Total	JZLX	158	187	221	..	..	..	342	257	..	..	..
Controlled by the Environmental Protection Act 1990:												
Industrial/commercial premises	JZLY	537	519	560	..	..	..	845	504	..	..	..
Road works, construction and demolition	JZLZ	162	177	89	..	..	..	206	177	..	..	..
Domestic premises	JYWN	210	302	431	..	..	..	754	787	..	..	..
Vehicles, machinery and equipment in streets	JYXH	..	..	..	..	..	..	12	41	..	..	..
Total	JYWO	909	998	1 080	..	..	..	1 817	1 509	..	..	..
Controlled by Section 62 of the Control and Pollution Act 1974:												
Noise in streets	JYXI	25	61	33	..	..	..	27	22	..	..	..
Total complaints received	JYWP	1 092	1 246	1 334	..	..	..	2 186	1 788	..	..	..

1 See chapter text.
2 1992/93 figures cover a period of 15 months from January 1992 to March 1993 due to the change from calendar year to financial year in order to come into line with England and Wales.

Sources: The Chartered Institute of Environmental Health; Royal Environmental Health Institute of Scotland

13.19 Material flows[1]
United Kingdom

Million tonnes

		1970	1975	1980	1985	1990	1995	1996	1997	1998	1999	2000
Domestic extraction												
Biomass												
Agricultural harvest	GYVR	42	38	47	47	46	47	54	53	51	52	51
Timber	GYVS	3	3	4	5	6	8	7	7	7	7	7
Animal grazing	GYVU	49	49	49	48	46	44	44	45	44	43	43
Fish	GYVV	1	1	1	1	1	1	1	1	1	1	1
Total biomass	GYVW	96	92	101	100	100	100	106	107	103	104	103
Minerals												
Ores	GYVX	12	5	1	1	–	–	16	–	16	–	–
Clay	GYVY	38	33	25	23	21	18	16	15	16	15	16
Other industrial minerals	GYVZ	14	12	11	11	11	10	10	10	9	8	8
Sand and gravel	GYWA	122	131	110	112	128	106	101	103	103	105	102
Crushed stone	GYWC	156	169	150	160	212	200	181	182	182	179	168
Total minerals	GYWD	342	350	298	307	373	334	308	310	310	308	295
Fossil fuels												
Coal	GYWE	149	129	130	94	94	53	50	48	41	37	32
Natural gas	GYWF	11	37	39	37	43	71	84	86	90	99	108
Crude oil	GYWG	–	2	80	128	92	130	130	128	133	137	127
Total fossil fuels	GYWI	161	168	249	259	229	255	265	263	265	274	268
Total domestic extraction	GYWJ	598	609	648	666	701	689	679	680	678	686	665
Imports												
Biomass	GYWK	40	35	32	34	41	43	43	44	45	45	46
Minerals	GYWL	30	32	24	34	41	51	48	51	53	49	49
Fossil fuels	GYWM	123	111	74	76	89	73	77	79	76	70	83
Other products	GYWN	3	5	11	12	17	21	24	25	26	24	30
Total imports	GYWR	197	183	140	156	187	187	191	200	201	189	208
Exports												
Biomass	GYWS	3	6	8	12	14	16	16	19	18	17	18
Minerals	GYWT	17	20	26	22	25	39	41	43	42	41	44
Fossil fuels	GYWU	23	19	60	102	67	103	99	106	103	108	115
Other products	GYWW	4	6	7	10	11	16	17	18	17	18	19
Total exports	GYWX	47	51	101	146	117	174	174	185	181	184	196
Indirect flows												
From domestic extraction[2], excluding soil erosion	GYWY	579	597	665	653	720	666	675	671	637	644	612
Of which:												
Unused biomass	GYWZ	16	16	22	25	27	27	31	31	30	29	30
Fossil fuels	GYXB	189	228	327	313	355	318	317	323	288	298	267
Minerals and ores	GYXC	177	158	121	115	135	117	110	110	112	110	108
Soil excavation and dredging	GYXD	198	197	195	200	204	204	216	207	207	207	207
From production of imports	GYXE	394	395	368	423	457	527	514	541	597	549	614
Summary aggregates												
Direct material input (Domestic extraction + imports)	GYXF	795	792	788	821	888	876	871	880	879	875	873
Domestic material consumption (Domestic extraction + imports - exports)	GYXG	748	741	687	676	771	702	697	694	698	691	677
Total material requirement (Direct material input + indirect flows)	GYXI	1 768	1 784	1 821	1 897	2 065	2 069	2 059	2 093	2 113	2 067	2 099

1 See chapter text.
2 Indirect flows from domestic extraction relate to unused material which is
 moved during extraction, such as overburden from mining and quarrying.

Sources: Wuppertal Institute;
Office for National Statistics: 020 7533 5904

13.20 Permanent dwellings completed[1]

Numbers

	United Kingdom				England and Wales			
	All dwellings	Local authorities[2]	Private enterprise	Registered Social Landlords[3]	All dwellings	Local authorities[2]	Private enterprise	Registered Social Landlords[3]
	KAAD	KAAE	KAAF	KAAG	KAAH	KAAI	KAAJ	KAAK
1976	324 836	146 444	155 296	23 096	278 727	125 565	138 544	14 618
1977	314 160	139 537	143 972	30 651	276 078	122 742	128 755	24 581
1978	288 689	110 165	152 233	26 291	254 068	97 779	134 645	21 644
1979	251 823	86 316	144 121	21 386	220 788	78 125	125 372	17 291
1980	241 999	88 534	131 989	21 476	214 723	78 328	116 179	20 216
1981	206 632	68 340	118 590	19 702	179 628	58 253	104 012	17 363
1982	182 853	40 091	129 022	13 740	159 298	33 435	113 893	11 970
1983	209 018	39 161	153 038	16 819	181 196	31 430	134 901	14 865
1984	220 414	37 573	165 555	17 286	190 957	31 183	145 263	14 511
1985	207 465	30 420	163 395	13 650	178 201	24 276	142 020	11 905
1986	216 544	25 377	178 008	13 159	187 584	20 370	156 056	11 158
1987	226 234	21 833	191 250	13 151	198 730	17 433	169 895	11 402
1988	242 359	21 448	207 423	13 488	214 155	16 920	185 733	11 502
1989	221 463	19 323	187 542	14 598	190 926	15 268	163 344	12 314
1990	203 388	17 862	167 473	18 053	175 099	14 625	144 849	15 625
1991	191 635	11 229	159 536	20 870	165 197	8 544	138 839	17 814
1992	179 362	5 709	147 322	26 331	154 087	3 649	127 020	23 418
1993	186 040	3 371	146 673	35 996	157 592	1 603	123 255	32 734
1994	193 383	2 882	153 334	37 167	165 210	1 321	130 066	33 823
1995	199 716	3 440	157 233	39 043	166 953	974	132 549	33 430
1996	188 877	1 758	154 014	33 105	159 436	576	129 278	29 582
1997	191 065	1 543	161 204	28 318	158 384	291	135 003	23 090
1998	179 663	1 111	154 414	24 138	149 266	289	127 563	21 414
1999	182 105	361	157 311	24 433	148 235	84	129 747	18 404
2000	179 199	379	154 995	23 825	144 403	207	126 180	18 016
2001	175 989	505	152 737	22 747	138 626	408	122 478	15 740

	Scotland				Northern Ireland			
	All dwellings	Local authorities[2]	Private enterprise	Registered Social Landlords[3]	All dwellings	Local authorities[2]	Private enterprise	Registered Social Landlords[3]
	BLFI	BAEZ	BLFK	BLFO	BLGI	BAFA	BLGK	BLGO
1976	36 527	14 361	13 704	8 462	9 582	6 518	3 048	16
1977	27 320	9 119	12 132	6 069	10 762	7 676	3 085	1
1978	25 778	6 705	14 443	4 630	8 843	5 681	3 145	17
1979	23 782	4 755	15 175	3 852	7 253	3 436	3 574	243
1980	20 611	7 488	12 242	881	6 398	2 451	3 568	379
1981	20 011	7 062	11 021	1 928	6 604	2 636	3 557	411
1982	16 423	3 733	11 523	1 167	6 805	2 596	3 606	603
1983	17 929	3 492	13 166	1 271	9 649	3 995	4 971	683
1984	18 838	2 647	14 115	2 076	10 458	3 582	6 177	699
1985	18 411	2 828	14 435	1 148	10 768	3 231	6 940	597
1986	18 637	2 301	14 870	1 466	10 197	2 580	7 082	535
1987	17 707	2 634	13 904	1 169	9 795	1 764	7 451	580
1988	18 272	2 815	14 179	1 278	9 928	1 709	7 511	708
1989	20 190	2 283	16 287	1 620	10 283	1 708	7 911	664
1990	20 362	1 938	16 461	1 963	7 927	1 299	6 163	465
1991	19 529	1 732	15 533	2 264	6 909	953	5 164	792
1992	17 620	1 010	14 389	2 221	7 654	1 049	5 913	692
1993	21 221	958	17 711	2 552	7 209	792	5 707	710
1994	21 203	661	17 753	2 789	6 970	900	5 515	555
1995	24 325	1 161	18 310	4 854	8 438	1 305	6 374	759
1996	20 950	292	18 092	2 566	8 491	890	6 644	957
1997	22 539	177	17 855	4 507	10 142	1 075	8 346	721
1998	20 320	139	18 270	1 911	10 077	683	8 581	813
1999	24 373	81	19 381	4 911	9 497	196	8 183	1 118
2000	23 384	95	18 395	4 894	11 412	77	10 420	915
2001	23 713	72	18 139	5 502	13 650	25	12 120	1 505

1 see Chapter text.
2 Including the Commission for the New Towns Development Corporations, Communities Scotland, the Northern Ireland Housing Executive.
3 Dwellings provided by housing associations other than Communities Scotland and the Northern Ireland Housing Trust and provided or authorised by government departments for families of police, prison staff, the armed forces and certain other services.

Sources: Office of the Deputy Prime Minister 0117 372 8055;
Scottish Executive;
National Assembly for Wales;
Department for Social Development, Northern Ireland

13.21 Stock of dwellings: Estimated annual gains and losses
England

Thousands of dwellings

		1992 /93	1993 /94	1994 /95	1995 /96	1996 /97	1997 /98	1998 /99	1999 /00	2000 /01	2001 /02
Dwelling stock at start of financial year	GRWM	19 829	19 974	20 120	20 279	20 435	20 583	20 732	20 875	21 016	21 142
Gains to dwelling stock:											
Housebuilding completions	GRWN	142.5	147.7	158.0	154.6	146.2	149.6	138.6	141.8	133.7	130.3
Conversions (net gain)[1]	GRWO	8.3	7.5	9.9	8.9	8.6	2.8	4.2	3.5	2.8	5.1
Change of use	GRWP	..	..	..	..	..	11.6	15.9	13.9	10.1	16.1
Non-permanent dwellings additions	GRWQ	..	..	..	..	..	0.2	0.2	0.3	0.3	0.3
Losses from dwelling stock:											
Slum clearance (non LA owned dwelling demolished)	GRWR	2.0	3.9	3.0	2.7	2.9	1.3	1.3	1.4	1.7	1.6
Other demolitions[1]	GRWS	4.3	5.2	5.8	4.8	4.1	12.8	13.2	15.8	18.3	24.7
Change of use	GRWT	..	..	..	..	..	0.7	1.4	0.8	0.7	0.8
Non-permanent dwelling losses	GRWU	..	..	..	..	..	0.1	0.2	0.1	0.3	0.3
New gain in year	GRWV	144.5	146.2	159.0	156.0	147.8	149.3	143.0	141.3	125.9	124.4
Dwelling stock at end of financial year	GRWW	19 974	20 120	20 279	20 435	20 583	20 732	20 875	21 016	21 142	21 266

1 Figures prior to 1997/98 include change of use, and zero for net non-permanent dwellings.

Source: Office of the Deputy Prime Minister: 0117 372 8055

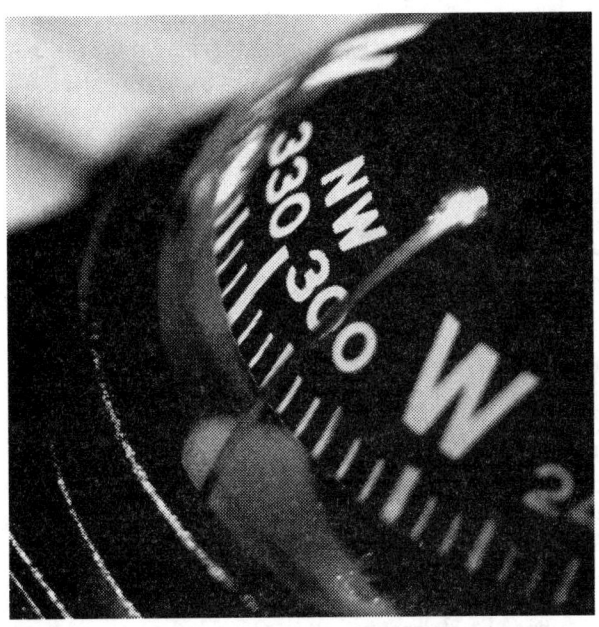

14 Transport and communications

Transport and communications

Road data (Tables 14.1, 14.5, 14.6 and 14.7)

Figures for 1999, 2000 and 2001have been produced on a new basis and are not directly comparable with earlier figures. For time-series tables, the 1999 values are shown on both the original and the new basis. The reasons for the changes are described below.

In 2000/2001, steps were taken to improve the quality of DfT's major road network database used in producing traffic estimates. This was done using a geographical information system (GIS), together with Ordnance Survey (OS) data. One result of this work was that it identified inconsistencies in the road length data supplied by local authorities. Preliminary checks showed that this was mainly due to the variety of methods used by them to calculate road lengths. However, local authorities have useful local knowledge of their roads, particularly recent changes to their classification. Therefore, once the network data had been compiled, it was sent to each local authority for final checking. In some instances, this led to discussions with Government Regional Offices and the Highways Agency in order to establish the correct, up-to-date classification of roads. The end result of this extensive work was a much-improved road network database for the whole of Great Britain. It was decided to use this GIS-based information, rather than data supplied by local authorities, for grossing-up average traffic flows, in order to produce traffic estimates.

The road network data was further refined by information collected by DfT traffic count contractors on the location of relevant speed limit signs. This enabled DfT to be more confident about the built-up and non built-up lengths of each section of road. The net result of both these improvements has been a reduction in the estimates of principal road traffic, particularly on built-up roads.

Furthermore, DfT began a review of the expansion factors used to convert the occasional, 12-hour manual count data to estimates of annual average daily flows. Highways Agency data strongly suggested that the expansion factors for some motorways, particularly the busiest ones in the South East and Midlands regions, were too low. Temporary adjustments to the factors have been made and these adjustments have led to a general upward revision to 1999, 2000 and 2001 motorway traffic estimates. Further work will need to be done to refine these estimates over the coming year.

One final change to the figures is that the estimates of minor road lengths are also now based on OS data, rather than local authority returns. This has led to an upward revision of minor road lengths of about five per cent. It is believed that the increase in length is mainly due to the inclusion in the OS coding of public road lengths that are surfaced, but unadopted. It may also be due to OS's practice of measuring road lengths from the centre of one junction to the next junction, rather than purely the length that is wholly attributable to one road class. Overall the change is not thought to have much implication for the minor road traffic estimates and so the adjustments to the minor roads traffic estimates for 1999 and 2000 are minimal.

The net result of these improvements has been little change to the estimates of *total* motor vehicle traffic for Great Britain for 1999, 2000 and 2001, but some changes to the composition of the overall figure. In general, the new motorway traffic estimates are now higher than before, whilst those for other major roads are lower than before.

The new figures for 1999,2000 and 2001 are already considerably more accurate than those produced for earlier years. In the time available, it has not been possible to consider the changes that ought to be made to estimates prior to 1999.

14.1 Passenger transport[1]: by mode
Great Britain

	Road					Rail[3]	Air	All modes[4]
	Buses and coaches[2]	Cars, vans and taxis	Motor cycles	Pedal cycles	All road			
Billion passenger kilometres								
	KCTP	KCTQ	KCTR	KCTS	ZCBD	KCTN	KCTM	KCTT
1991	44	582	6	5	637	39	4.8	681
1992	43	583	5	5	635	38	4.8	678
1993	44	584	4	4	636	37	5.1	678
1994	44	591	4	5	643	35	5.5	684
1995	44	596	4	4	648	37	5.9	691
1996	44	606	4	4	658	39	6.3	703
1997	44	614	4	4	666	42	6.8	715
1998	45	618	4	4	671	44	7.0	722
1999	45	617	5	4	671	46	7.3	725
	GRXK	GRXG	GRXH	GRXI	GRXJ			GRXM
1999	45	613	5	4	667	46	7.3	721
2000	45	618	5	4	672	47	7.6	726
2001	46	624	5	4	679	47	7.7	734
Percentages								
	ZCBE	ZCBF	ZCBG	ZCBH	ZCBI	ZCBJ	ZCBK	ZCBL
1991	6	86	1	1	94	6	0.7	100
1992	6	86	1	1	94	6	0.7	100
1993	6	86	1	1	94	5	0.8	100
1994	6	86	1	1	94	5	0.8	100
1995	6	86	1	1	94	5	0.9	100
1996	6	86	1	1	94	6	0.9	100
1997	6	86	1	1	93	6	0.9	100
1998	6	86	1	1	93	6	1.0	100
1999	6	85	1	1	93	6	1.0	100
	GRXN	GRXO	GRXP	GRXQ	GRXR			GRXU
1999	6	85	1	1	93	6	1.0	100
2000	6	85	1	1	92	7	1.1	100
2001	6	85	1	1	93	6	1.0	100

1 Data for 1999, 2000 and 2001 have been produced on a new basis and are not directly comparable with earlier figures. 1999 values are shown on both the original and new basis. See chapter text.
2 Data for 2001 are provisional.
3 Financial years. Former British Rail companies and Urban Rail systems.

4 Excluding travel by water within the United Kingdom (including the Channel Islands), estimated at 0.7 billion passenger kilometres in 2000.

Source: Department for Transport

14.2 Trips per person per year by main mode[1] and purpose, 1999/2001
Great Britain

Numbers

	Walk	Bicycle	Car/van driver	Car/van passenger	Motor-cycle	Other private	Buses in London
Commuting	18	6	89	18	2	1	3
Business	3	-	25	3	-	-	-
Education	30	1	3	18	-	3	2
Escort education	20	-	20	6	-	-	-
Shopping	60	2	81	49	-	-	4
Other escort	9	-	48	23	-	-	-
Other personal business	27	1	44	24	-	1	1
Visiting friends at home	27	2	50	43	-	-	1
Visiting friends elsewhere	14	-	12	14	-	-	-
Social/entertainment	9	1	25	22	-	1	-
Holidays/day trips	2	2	9	12	-	-	-
Other, including just walk	43	-	1	-	-	-	-
All purposes	263	16	407	231	3	8	13

	Other local bus	Non-local bus	LT Under-ground	Surface rail	Taxi/ minicab	Other public	All modes
Commuting	9	-	3	6	2	-	156
Business	-	-	-	1	-	-	35
Education	8	-	-	1	-	-	67
Escort education	-	-	-	-	-	-	47
Shopping	13	-	-	1	2	-	214
Other escort	1	-	-	-	-	-	82
Other personal business	4	-	-	1	1	-	105
Visiting friends at home	4	-	-	1	2	-	133
Visiting friends elsewhere	2	-	-	-	3	-	46
Social/entertainment	2	-	-	-	1	-	62
Holidays/day trips	-	-	-	-	-	-	29
Other, including just walk	-	-	-	-	-	-	44
All purposes	44	2	7	13	12	2	1 019

1 Main mode is that used for the longest part of the trip.

Source: Department for Transport 020 7944 3097

14.3 Retail Prices Index: real changes in the cost of transport and disposable income
Great Britain

Constant prices

Index 1974=100

	Petrol/oil	All motoring	Rail	Bus and coach fares	Disposable income
	ZCFV	ZCFW	ZCFX	ZCFY	ZCFZ
1975	109.5	104.3	109.1	104.8	100.7
1976	99.9	101.2	124.3	115.0	100.3
1977	92.5	99.9	125.0	114.1	98.3
1978	81.2	99.6	132.0	119.4	105.6
1979	94.1	104.0	128.7	118.3	111.5
1980	102.2	103.8	135.6	127.0	113.4
1981	108.5	103.9	138.5	125.6	112.8
1982	107.4	101.0	146.4	133.2	112.6
1983	109.8	103.3	148.5	134.6	115.3
1984	108.2	100.7	142.0	131.0	119.5
1985	108.5	99.4	142.3	128.9	123.6
1986	91.3	94.7	147.0	135.1	128.9
1987	88.4	96.3	148.3	137.3	133.6
1988	83.4	95.9	151.2	140.1	140.6
1989	82.9	93.9	153.1	140.1	146.7
1990	84.6	90.9	152.1	135.0	152.2
1991	85.9	92.3	158.7	145.5	154.5
1992	85.2	95.0	164.1	150.1	160.2
1993	90.5	97.6	172.9	154.3	165.1
1994	92.4	98.5	176.3	154.5	167.2
1995	93.9	97.0	178.0	154.9	171.6
1996	96.3	97.5	180.3	156.9	175.3
1997	102.7	99.6	178.9	157.5	181.9
1998	104.2	99.3	180.0	157.3	182.1
1999	111.3	100.2	183.8	160.6	188.6
2000	122.4	101.0	181.6	162.3	196.7
2001	114.0	98.7	185.3	166.1	206.7

Source: Office for National Statistics

14.4 Domestic freight transport: by mode
Great Britain

		1991	1992	1993	1994	1995	1996	1997	1998	1999	2000	2001
Goods moved												
(Billion tonnes kilometres)												
Petroleum products												
Road[1]	ZBZP	4.9	4.5	5.0	5.1	5.7	6.1	5.8	5.1	4.9	6.3	5.8
Rail	ZBZQ	2.0	2.0	1.9	1.8	1.8	..	..	1.6[3]	1.5	1.4	1.2
Water[2]	ZBZR	46.0	42.7	41.7	43.0	42.5	45.9	38.3	45.2	48.6	54.8	..
of which: coastwise	ZBZS	31.2	29.4	28.9	28.9	31.4	38.7	33.8	36.4	33.3	27.6	..
Pipeline	ZBZT	11.1	11.0	11.6	12.0	11.1	11.6	11.2	11.7	11.6	11.4	11.5
All modes	ZBZU	64.0	60.2	60.2	61.9	61.1	63.6[4]	55.3[4]	63.6	66.6	..	..
Coal and coke												
Road[1]	ZBZV	3.7	3.5	3.1	2.9	2.7	2.5	2.7	2.0	2.2	1.5	2.1
Rail	ZBZW	5.0	5.4	3.9	3.3	3.6	3.9	4.4	4.5[3]	4.8	4.8	6.2
Water[2]	ZBZX	1.8	1.8	1.5	1.4	2.3	0.6	0.6	0.5	0.5	0.2	..
All modes	ZBZY	10.5	10.7	8.5	7.6	8.6	6.9	7.7	7.0	7.5	..	..
Other traffic												
Road[1]	ZBZZ	121.4	118.5	126.4	135.7	141.2	145.3	148.6	152.4	149.6	150.2	149.0
Rail	ZCAA	8.3	8.1	7.9	7.9	7.9	11.2	12.5	11.2[3]	11.9	11.9	12.3
Water[2]	ZCAB	9.9	10.4	8.0	7.8	8.3	8.7	9.2	11.2	9.6	12.4	..
All modes	ZCAC	139.6	137.0	142.3	151.4	157.4	165.3	170.3	174.8	171.1	..	..
All traffic												
Road[1]	KCTA	130.0	126.5	134.5	143.7	149.6	153.9	157.1	159.5	156.7	158.0	156.9
Rail	KCTB	15.3	15.5	13.8	13.0	13.3	15.1	16.9	17.3[3]	18.2	18.1	19.7
Water[2]	ZCAD	57.7	54.9	51.2	52.2	53.1	55.3	48.1	56.9	58.7	67.4	..
Pipeline	KCTE	11.1	11.0	11.6	12.0	11.1	11.6	11.2	11.7	11.6	11.4	11.5
All modes	KCTF	214.1	207.9	211.1	220.9	227.1	235.9	233.3	245.4	245.2	..	..
Percentage of all traffic												
Road[1]	ZCAE	61	61	64	65	66	65	67	65	64	..	..
Rail	ZCAF	7	7	7	6	6	6	7	7[3]	7	..	..
Water[2]	ZCAG	27	26	24	24	23	23	21	23	24	..	..
Pipeline	ZCAH	5	5	5	5	5	5	5	5	5	..	..
All modes	ZCAI	100	100	100	100	100	100	100	100	100	..	..

		1991	1992	1993	1994	1995	1996	1997	1998	1999	2000	2001
Goods lifted (Million tonnes)												
Petroleum products												
Road[1]	ZCAJ	73	63	67	68	71	75	73	61	61	74	74
Rail	ZCAK	10	10	9	8	6	..	..	..	..	..	..
Water[2]	ZCAL	67	66	64	70	72	71	69	76	72	68	..
of which: coastwise	ZCAM	44	43	42	43	47	54	52	55	52	43	..
Pipeline	ZCAN	105	106	125	161	168	157	148	153	155	151	151
All modes	ZCAO	255	245	265	307	317	303[4]	290[4]	290[4]	288[4]	..	..
Coal and coke												
Road[1]	ZCAP	57	55	48	42	34	32	37	22	28	22	21
Rail	ZCAQ	75	68	49	43	45	52	50	45	44	46	46
Water[2]	ZCAR	6	6	5	4	4	3	4	3	3	3	..
All modes	ZCAS	138	129	102	89	83	87	91	70	75	..	..
Other traffic												
Road[1]	ZCAT	1 470	1 437	1 500	1 579	1 596	1 623	1 630	1 646	1 572	1 593	1 565
Rail	ZCAU	51	45	45	47	50	50	55	57	48[5]	50	48
Water[2]	ZCAV	71	68	65	66	67	67	69	70	70	66	..
All modes	ZCAW	1 592	1 550	1 610	1 692	1 713	1 740	1 754	1 773	1 690	..	..
All traffic												
Road[1]	KCTG	1 600	1 555	1 615	1 689	1 701	1 730	1 740	1 727	1 661	1 689	1 660
Rail	KCTH	136	122	103	97	101	102	105	102	92[5]	95	94
Water[2]	ZCAX	144	140	134	140	143	142	142	149	144	137	..
Pipeline	KCTK	105	106	125	161	168	157	148	153	155	151	151
All modes	KCTL	1 985	1 923	1 977	2 087	2 113	2 131	2 135	2 131	2 052	..	..
Percentage of all traffic												
Road[1]	ZCAY	81	81	82	81	80	81	81	81	81	..	..
Rail	ZCAZ	7	6	5	5	5	5	5	5	4[5]	..	..
Water[2]	ZCBA	7	7	7	7	7	7	7	7	7	..	..
Pipeline	ZCBB	5	6	6	8	8	7	7	7	8	..	..
All modes	ZCBC	100	100	100	100	100	100	100	100	100	..	..

1 All goods vehicles, including those under 3.5 tonnes gross vehicle weight.
These estimates were revised following a survey in 1993.
2 Figures for water are for UK traffic.
3 Figures for goods moved by rail is a new series from 1998.

4 Excludes rail.
5 Figures for goods lifted by rail have been revised from 1999.

Source: Department for Transport

213

14.5 Public road length[1]: by road type
Great Britain

Kilometres

		1991	1992	1993	1994	1995	1996	1997	1998	1999		1999	2000	2001
Trunk motorway	ZCBM	3 033	3 063	3 061	3 092	3 118	3 181	3 250	3 295	3 316	GSMX	3 404	3 421	3 428
Principal motorway	ZCBN	68	71	78	76	72	45	45	45	42	GSMY	44	44	44
Non built-up major roads:														
Trunk	ZCBO	10 867	10 865	10 803	10 767	10 811	11 046	10 955	10 791	10 837	GSMZ	10 483	10 458	10 461
Principal	ZCBP	23 005	23 014	23 034	23 054	23 207	22 896	22 884	22 954	22 897	GSNA	22 319	22 364	22 259
Total	ZCBQ	33 872	33 879	33 837	33 821	34 019	33 941	33 839	33 745	33 734	GSNB	32 802	32 822	32 720
Built-up major roads														
Trunk	ZCBR	1 455	1 431	1 400	1 344	1 297	1 313	1 314	1 344	1 313	GSNC	1 285	1 284	1 264
Principal	ZCBS	12 575	12 627	12 681	12 737	12 750	12 961	12 950	13 048	13 147	GSND	12 444	12 458	12 566
Total	ZCBT	14 030	14 058	14 081	14 081	14 047	14 274	14 264	14 392	14 460	GSNE	13 729	13 742	13 830
Minor non built-up roads:														
B roads	ZCBU	22 290	22 161	22 093	21 872	21 686	21 293	21 169	21 149	20 952	GSNF	20 828	20 740	20 564
C roads	ZCBV	67 360	67 350	67 448	66 980	67 509	66 903	66 472	66 571	65 811	GSNG	65 811	66 004	66 589
Unclassified	ZCBW	81 773	81 108	80 973	79 450	78 944	78 390	77 318	77 083	76 572	GSNH	83 613	82 958	81 540
All	ZCBX	171 424	170 618	170 514	168 302	168 139	166 585	164 958	164 804	163 335	GSNI	170 252	169 702	168 693
Minor built-up roads:														
B roads	ZCBY	7 816	8 066	8 215	8 475	8 567	8 903	9 195	9 129	9 353	GSNJ	9 264	9 317	9 416
C roads	ZCBZ	13 713	13 984	14 376	15 125	15 065	15 626	16 435	16 582	16 989	GSNK	16 989	17 267	18 387
Unclassified	ZCCA	116 010	118 572	120 050	121 995	123 974	126 267	127 881	129 553	130 684	GSNL	143 159	145 391	145 890
All	ZCCB	137 538	140 622	142 641	145 594	147 606	150 795	153 511	155 264	157 026	GSNM	169 412	171 976	173 692
All minor roads	ZCCC	308 962	311 241	313 155	313 897	315 744	317 380	318 470	320 068	320 361	GSNN	339 664	341 678	342 386
All roads	KCTY	359 966	362 310	364 212	364 966	366 999	368 821	369 867	371 543	371 914	GSNO	389 643	391 707	392 408

1 Figures for 1999, 2000 and 2001 have been produced on a new basis and are not directly comparable with earlier figures. 1999 values are shown on both the original and new basis. See chapter text.

Source: Department for Transport 020 7944 3095

14.6 Road traffic[1]: by type of vehicle
Great Britain

Billion vehicle kilometres

		1990	1991	1992	1993	1994	1995	1996	1997	1998	1999		1999	2000	2001
Cars and taxis	KCWA	335.9	335.2	338.0	338.5	345.7	353.2	362.4	370.9	375.6	380.1	GSNP	378.4	378.7	383.7
Motor cycles etc.	KCWB	5.6	5.4	4.5	4.1	4.2	4.1	4.2	4.1	3.9	4.6	GSNQ	4.5	4.4	4.8
Larger buses and coaches	KDZS	4.6	4.8	4.6	4.6	4.7	4.7	4.8	4.9	4.9	5.0	GSNR	5.0	4.8	4.9
Light vans[2]	KDZT	39.9	41.7	41.2	41.1	42.5	43.8	45.1	45.6	48.1	49.2	GSNS	49.4	50.5	51.1
Goods vehicles:															
2 axles rigid	ZCCD	11.6	11.5	11.4	11.3	12.1	11.4	11.4	11.7	10.9	11.7	GSNT	11.8	11.7	11.7
3 axles rigid	ZCCE	1.6	1.5	1.4	1.3	1.4	1.5	1.5	1.8	1.9	1.7	GSNU	1.7	1.6	1.6
4 or more axles rigid	ZCCF	1.7	1.5	1.4	1.5	1.5	1.5	1.4	1.4	1.4	1.5	GSNV	1.5	1.5	1.5
3 and 4 axles artic.	ZCCG	4.6	4.3	3.9	3.4	3.4	3.3	3.5	3.4	3.1	3.0	GSNW	3.1	2.9	2.9
5 axles artic.	ZCCH	4.1	4.3	4.3	4.8	5.3	5.6	6.1	6.5	6.7	6.9	GSNX	7.4	7.2	7.2
6 or more axles artic.	ZCCI	1.3	1.4	1.4	1.5	1.7	1.8	2.1	2.4	2.6	3.2	GSNY	3.3	4.4	4.3
All	KDZV	24.9	24.5	23.8	23.8	25.5	25.1	26.0	27.1	26.7	28.1	GSNZ	28.8	29.3	29.2
All motor vehicles	KCVZ	410.8	411.6	412.1	412.2	422.6	430.9	442.5	452.5	459.2	467.0	GSOA	466.0	467.7	473.7
Pedal cycles	KDZW	5.3	5.2	4.7	4.5	4.5	4.5	4.3	4.1	3.9	4.2	GSOB	4.1	4.0	4.0

1 Data for 1999, 2000 and 2001 have been produced on a new basis and are not directly comparable with earlier figures. 1999 values are shown on both the original and new basis. See chapter text.
2 Not exceeding 3,500 kgs gross vehicle weight.

Source: Department for Transport 020 7944 3095

14.7
Motor vehicle traffic[1]: by road class
Great Britain

Billion vehicle kilometres

		1991	1992	1993	1994	1995	1996	1997	1998	1999		1999	2000	2001
Motorways	ZCEF	61.0	61.5	63.9	66.7	70.9	73.7	77.9	81.3	83.6	GRXF	93.4	94.1	95.4
Non built-up major roads														
Trunk	ZCEG	59.5	58.9	59.3	59.8	61.3	63.2	64.8	65.5	68.9	GRXL	67.0	66.7	68.3
Principal	ZCEH	57.5	58.2	58.9	60.0	61.2	62.5	64.2	66.3	65.9	GRXS	61.8	62.1	61.8
All	ZCEI	117.0	117.0	118.1	119.9	122.5	125.8	128.9	131.8	134.9	GRXT	128.9	128.8	130.1
Built-up major roads[2]														
Trunk	ZCEJ	9.9	9.8	9.4	10.0	9.1	9.4	9.3	9.5	9.7	GRXV	9.4	9.4	9.4
Principal	ZCEK	69.5	69.7	68.6	70.1	70.0	71.6	70.4	70.1	70.1	GRXW	66.3	66.3	67.6
All	ZCEL	79.4	79.5	78.0	80.2	79.1	81.1	79.7	79.6	79.8	GRXX	75.7	75.7	77.1
Minor roads														
Minor non built-up roads	ZCEM	50.7	49.7	45.5	44.9	44.8	46.3	48.3	48.5	48.4	GRXY	48.2	48.1	48.2
Minor built-up roads	ZCEN	103.4	104.4	106.8	110.9	113.6	115.7	117.7	118.1	120.4	GRXZ	119.8	121.0	122.9
All	ZCEO	154.2	154.1	152.2	155.9	158.4	161.9	166.0	166.6	168.8	GRYA	168.0	169.1	171.1
All roads	KCVZ	411.6	412.1	412.2	422.6	430.9	442.5	452.5	459.2	467.0	GRYB	466.0	467.7	473.7

1 Figures for 1999, 2000 and 2001 have been produced on a new basis and are not directly comparable with earlier figures. 1999 values are shown on both the original and the new basis. See chapter text.
2 Built-up roads are those with a speed limit of 40 mph or less, irrespective of whether there are buildings or not.

Source: Department for Transport: 020 7944 3095

14.8
Motor vehicles currently licenced at end of year
Great Britain

Thousands

	Private and light goods					Special machines/				Body type cars	
	Body type cars	Other vehicles	Motor cycles, scooters and mopeds	Public transport vehicles[1]	Goods vehicles	special conces-sionary	Other vehicles	Crown & exempt vehicles	Special vehicles group	All vehicles	All	Company cars (%)
	BMBJ	BMBK	BMBB	BMBE	BMBD	KSBY	BMBF	BMBL	KSBZ	BMBI	ZCGR	ZCGS
1991	19 737	2 215	750	109	449	346	65	840	..	24 511	20 253	12.0
1992[2]	19 870	2 198	684	107	432	324	59	903	..	24 577	20 444	11.1
1993	20 102	2 187	650	107	428	318	55	979	..	24 826	20 755	10.7
1994	20 479	2 192	630	107	434	309	50	1 030	..	25 231	21 199	10.4
1995[3]	20 505	2 217	594	74	421	274	44	1 169	28	25 369[4]	21 394	10.4
1996	21 172	2 267	609	77	413	254	40	1 424	48	26 302	22 238	10.3
1997	21 681	2 317	626	79	414	249	38	1 522	48	26 974	22 832	10.5
1998	22 115	2 362	684	80	412	243	37	1 558	47	27 538	23 293	10.4
1999	22 785	2 427	760	84	415	241	36	1 573	47	28 368	23 975	10.0
2000	23 196	2 469	825	86	418	233	34	1 590	46	28 898	24 406	10.3
2001	23 899	2 544	882	89	422	233	33	1 602	45	29 747	25 126	9.7

1 Includes taxis for years up to 1994. Taxation group now restricted to only vehicles with 9 or more seats.
2 New methods of estimating vehicle stock were introduced in 1992.
3 The vehicle taxation system was subject to substantial revision from 1 July 1995.
4 Contains 44,000 vehicles still taxed in classes abolished from 1 July 1995.

Source: Department for Transport 020 7944 6386

14.9 New vehicle registrations by taxation class
Great Britain

Thousands

		1991	1992	1993	1994	1995	1996	1997	1998	1999	2000	2001
Total[1]	BBKD	1 921.5	1 901.8	2 073.9	2 249.0	2 306.5	2 410.1	2 597.7	2 740.3	2 765.8	2 870.9	3 137.7
Private and light goods												
Private cars	BMAA	1 536.6	1 528.0	1 694.6	1 809.1	1 828.3	1 888.4	2 015.9	2 123.5	2 100.4	2 174.9	2 431.8
Other vehicles	BMAE	171.9	166.4	158.8	182.6	195.7	205.0	228.4	244.5	241.6	254.9	277.9
Total	BMAK	1 708.5	1 694.4	1 853.4	1 991.7	2 024.0	2 093.4	2 244.3	2 368.0	2 342.0	2 429.8	2 709.7
Motor cycles, etc:												
Up to 50c.c.	KCUH	13.1	9.1	6.5	6.9	6.3	8.9	14.2	22.6	36.2	49.4	45.6
Other	KCUI	63.6	56.5	51.9	57.7	62.6	80.7	107.1	120.7	132.2	133.5	131.5
Total	BMAL	76.5	65.6	58.4	64.6	68.9	89.6	121.3	143.3	168.4	182.9	177.1
Public road passenger vehicles												
Buses, coaches, taxis, etc												
Not over 8 seats[2]	KCUJ	2.2	2.0	1.8	2.5	1.3	..	..	..	..	..	..
Over 8 seats	KCUK	3.0	3.1	3.6	4.2	5.2	6.5	6.6	7.4	8.0	7.5	6.8
Total	BBJZ	5.2	5.1	5.4	6.7	6.5	6.5	6.6	7.4	8.0	7.5	6.8
Heavy general goods and farmers[3]												
Goods vehicles: by weight	BBJY	28.6	28.7	32.8	41.1	48.0	45.5	41.8	49.1	48.3	50.4	48.6
Privately owned agricultural tractors and engines[4]	BMAH	26.1	24.1	30.0	35.3	33.3	25.7	21.7	15.2	24.9	24.0	26.7
Special concession group[5]	BBKA	..	..	..	..	33.0	25.7	21.7	15.2	17.3	16.9	19.8
Other licensed vehicles[6]	KCUM	0.7	1.6	1.4	1.3	1.0	1.0	1.5	1.5	1.5	1.2	1.2
Special vehicles group[7]	DMNR	..	..	..	..	3.3	8.1	8.6	7.6	7.6	6.5	7.0
Exempt from license duty												
Crown vehicles	KCUN	3.2	3.7	3.1	4.1	3.3	1.2	0.7	1.1	1.1	1.0	1.0
All other exempt vehicles[1,8]	KCUO	72.6	78.7	89.4	104.3	118.1	139.1	150.7	146.6	170.4	173.9	166.5
Total	KCUP	75.8	82.3	92.4	108.4	121.4	140.3	151.4	147.7	171.6	174.9	167.5

1 Including personal and direct export vehicles.
2 From 1 July 1995 separate taxation of public transport vehicles with 8 or fewer seats was abolished. After this date new vehicles of this type were registered as PLG.
3 Owned by a farmer and available for hauling produce and requisites for his own farm.
4 Agricultural tractors are excluded unless driven on public roads
5 Various revisions to the vehicle taxation system were introduced on 1 July 1995 and on 29 November 1995. Separate taxation classes for farmers' goods vehicles were abolished on 1 July 1995; after this date new vehicles of this type were registered as HGVs. The total includes 5,900 vehicles registered between 1 January and 30 June in the (now abolished) agricultural and special machines group in classes which were not eligible to register in the special concession group. The old agricultural and special machines taxation group was abolished at end June 1995.

The group includes agricultural and mowing machines, snow ploughs and gritting vehicles. Electric vehicles are also included in this group and are no longer exempt from Vehicle Excise Duty (VED). Steam propelled vehicles were added to this group from November 1995.
6 Includes three wheelers, pedestrian controlled vehicles, general haulage and showmen's tractors and recovery vehicles. Recovery vehicle tax class introduced January 1988.
7 The special vehicles group was created on 1 July 1995 and consists of various vehicle types over 3.5 tonnes gross weight but not required to pay VED as heavy goods vehicles. The group includes mobile cranes, works trucks, digging machines, road rollers and vehicles previously taxed as showman's goods and haulage. Figure shown for 1995 covers period from 1 July to 31 December only.
8 Between 1980 and 30 June 1995 electric vehicles were exempt from duty. From 1 July 1995 electric vehicles pay VED as part of the special concession group.

Source: Department for Transport: 020 7944 3077

14.10 Private motoring: full car driving licence holders by age and sex
Great Britain

	Age							Estimated number of licence holders (millions)
	17-20	21-29	30-39	40-49	50-59	60-69	70 or over	
All adults								
1975/76	28	59	67	60	50	35	15	19.4
1985/86	33	63	74	71	60	47	27	24.4
1989/91	43	72	77	78	67	54	32	28.0
1992/94	48	75	82	79	72	57	33	29.0
1996/98	43	73	82	82	76	64	38	31.0
1999/01[1]	36	73	83	84	78	71	44	32.3
Males								
1975/76	36	78	85	83	75	58	32	13.4
1985/86	37	73	86	87	81	72	51	15.3
1989/91	52	82	88	89	85	78	58	16.9
1992/94	54	83	91	88	88	81	59	17.1
1996/98	48	79	89	90	88	82	64	17.7
1999/01[1]	41	81	89	91	88	86	69	18.4
Females								
1975/76	20	43	48	37	24	15	4	6.0
1985/86	29	54	62	56	41	24	11	9.2
1989/91	35	64	67	66	49	33	15	11.2
1992/94	42	68	73	70	57	37	16	12.1
1996/98	38	68	75	73	63	48	20	13.4
1999/01[1]	31	66	77	77	69	57	25	14.2

1 Data are provisional.

Source: Department for Transport: 020 7944 3097

14.11 Private motoring: households with regular use of cars
Great Britain

Percentages

	No car	One car	Two cars	Three or more cars	Total (millions)
	ZCGA	ZCGB	ZCGC	ZCGD	ZCGE
1990	33	44	19	4	22.1
1991	32	45	19	4	22.4
1992	32	45	20	4	22.6
1993	31	45	20	4	22.9
1994	32	45	20	4	23.1
1995	30	45	21	4	23.3
1996	30	45	21	4	23.5
1997	30	45	21	4	23.7
1998	28	44	23	5	23.9
1999	28	44	22	5	24.1
2000	27	45	23	5	..

	No car	One car	Two or more cars	Total
Government Office Regions, 2000				
Great Britain	27	45	28	100
North East	39	43	18	100
North West	30	45	25	100
Yorkshire and the Humber	32	44	24	100
East Midlands	26	43	31	100
West Midlands	25	46	29	100
East	18	46	35	100
London	37	44	19	100
South East	17	46	37	100
South West	20	47	33	100
England	27	45	28	100
Wales	30	45	25	100
Scotland	34	44	22	100

	No car	One car	Two or more cars	Total
Area type, 1998/00				
London	36	45	19	100
Metropolitan areas	36	42	22	100
Other urban areas with population:				
Over 250,000	32	46	22	100
25,000 - 250,000	29	46	25	100
10,000 - 25,000	25	45	31	100
3,000 - 10,000	18	48	34	100
Rural areas	16	43	40	100
Great Britain	28	45	26	100

Sources: Office for National Statistics;
Department for Transport

14.12 Vehicles with licences current[1]
Northern Ireland

Numbers

		1991	1992	1993	1994	1995	1996[2]	1997	1998	1999	2000	2001[3]
Private cars, etc	KNKA	498 471	516 194	515 185	514 760	521 610	540 083	575 923	584 706	608 316	615 180	644 968
Cycles and tricycles	KNKB	9 684	9 023	8 634	8 775	9 142	10 026	10 932	11 663	13 087	14 116	15 205
Public road passenger vehicles:												
Taxis up to 4 seats	KNKD	656	494	462	623	739	..	..	..	..	..	..
Buses, coaches, over 4 seats	KNKE	2 231	2 250	2 217	2 455	1 353	2 090	2 144	2 175	2 204	2 266	2 315
Total	KNKC	2 887	2 744	2 679	3 078	2 092	2 090	2 144	2 175	2 204	2 266	2 315
General (HGV) goods vehicles:	KNKF	13 907	14 286	14 576	14 810	16 338	17 401	18 172	18 312	17 075	17 864	19 415
Farmers' goods vehicles[4]	KNKJ	4 994	5 315	5 498	5 904	..	..	..	..	..	..	..
Agricultural tractors and engines, etc[4]	KNKM	7 199	6 892	7 201	7 317	9 074	5 911	6 378	5 906	5 505	5 048	4 901
Other	KNKN	403	343	329	354	1 257	1 019	1 188	1 193	1 446	1 287	1 366
Vehicles exempt from duty:												
Government owned	KNKP	5 120	5 004	4 828	4 818	3 872	3 753	3 705	3 785	4 032	3 822	6 427
Other:												
Ambulances	KNKQ	98	97	101	104	250	371	389	425	417	452	318
Fire engines	KNKR	250	251	205	194	301	292	291	285	286	290	181
Other exempt[5]	KNKS	15 305	18 163	27 089	35 837	47 626	58 340	64 447	66 981	68 277	70 405	72 209
Total	KNKO	20 773	23 515	32 223	40 953	52 049	62 756	68 832	71 476	73 012	74 969	79 135
Total	KNKT	558 318	578 312	586 325	595 951	611 562	639 286	683 569	695 431	720 645	730 730	767 305

1 Licences current at any time during the quarter ended December.
2 Due to a revision of taxation classes, 1996 data are not directly comparable with previous years.
3 Due to a revision of taxation classes, 2001 data are not directly comparable with previous years.
4 Owned by a farmer and available for hauling produce and requisites for his farm. From 1 July 1995 farmers goods taxation classes have been abolished

5 Changes in the Mobility Allowance (DSS) have contributed to the increase in Other exempt.

Source: Department of the Environment, Northern Ireland: 028 9054 0801

14.13 New vehicles registrations
Northern Ireland

Numbers

		1991	1992	1993	1994	1995	1996	1997	1998	1999	2000	2001
Private cars, etc	KNLA	63 739	62 777	65 360	70 765	73 718	77 817	83 968	91 141	89 078	84 973	88 592
Cycles and tricycles	KNLB	2 218	1 993	1 885	1 943	2 362	2 803	3 376	4 307	5 310	6 010	5 591
Public road passenger vehicles	KNLC	620	551	466	1 143	622	724	714	486	568	565	451
Goods vehicles:												
General haulage vehicles:												
Unladen weight:												
Under 3.5 tonnes	LDRZ	6 273	6 236	6 468	6 908	7 357	7 232	8 468	10 107	11 054	12 617	13 274
3.5 tonnes and over	LDSA	2 619	2 471	2 593	2 668	2 935	3 492	3 521	3 572	3 697	3 502	4 534
Agricultural tractors[1]	KNLM	1 177	1 184	1 658	1 558	1 619	1 292	1 364	971	987	1 313	301
Vehicles exempt from duty:												
Ambulances	KGVE KNLO	330	..	..	..	..	..	..	..	..	..	..
Fire engines	KNLP											
Road construction vehicles	KNLQ	..	..	..	..	..	..	..	..	..	..	..
Other exempt	KNLR	2 006	2 463	4 550	6 423	8 333	10 520	10 885	10 718	11 083	10 789	12 126
Total	KNLN	..	..	..	..	..	..	..	..	..	..	..
Total	KNLS	78 982	77 675	82 980	91 408	96 946	103 880	112 296	121 302	121 777	119 769	124 869

1 Agricultural tractors driven on public roads. From April 2001 tractors are exempt.

Source: Department of the Environment, Northern Ireland: 028 9054 0801

14.14 Local bus services: passenger journeys by area

Millions

		1990 /91	1991 /92	1992 /93	1993 /94	1994 /95	1995 /96	1996 /97	1997 /98	1998 /99	1999 /00	2000 /01
London	KILS	1 178	1 149	1 129	1 117	1 167	1 205	1 242	1 294	1 279	1 307	1 359
English metropolitan areas	KILT	1 547	1 478	1 383	1 337	1 331	1 292	1 246	1 232	1 195	1 162	1 166
English shire counties	KILU	1 396	1 333	1 307	1 274	1 277	1 265	1 265	1 247	1 246	1 263	1 236
England	ZCER	4 120	3 961	3 819	3 727	3 775	3 762	3 753	3 773	3 719	3 732	3 761
Scotland	KILV	585	571	532	525	513	494	467	438	413	434	436
Wales	KILW	145	133	129	133	132	127	130	120	116	114	113
All outside London	ZCES	3 672	3 516	3 351	3 268	3 253	3 178	3 108	3 036	2 969	2 973	2 950
Great Britain	ZCET	4 850	4 665	4 480	4 385	4 420	4 383	4 350	4 330	4 248	4 281	4 309

Source: Department for Transport 020 7944 3076

14.15 Local bus services: fare indices by area
Current prices

Index 1995=100

		1991 /92	1992 /93	1993 /94	1994 /95	1995 /96	1996 /97	1997 /98	1998 /99	1999 /00	2000 /01	2001 /02
London	KNEP	78.2	84.2	90.9	96.2	101.1	105.4	109.3	113.7	117.2	117.2	115.5
English metropolitan areas	KILD	82.9	88.6	92.9	96.4	101.5	106.9	113.3	118.7	124.5	129.9	137.4
English shire counties	KILE	86.6	90.4	93.1	97.0	101.1	106.0	111.5	116.7	121.9	128.6	135.1
England	ZCEP	83.6	88.3	92.5	96.7	101.2	106.1	111.4	116.5	121.4	125.9	130.3
Scotland	KILF	82.5	88.2	91.3	96.9	100.8	108.0	116.5	121.8	125.3	129.9	131.8
Wales[1]	KILG	..	90.4	93.8	97.4	100.7	104.4	110.1	116.3	122.2	127.5	133.5
All outside London	ZCEQ	84.8	89.4	92.8	96.8	101.2	106.6	112.8	118.2	123.3	129.2	135.3
Great Britain	KNEU	83.6	88.4	92.4	96.7	101.2	106.3	112.0	117.1	121.9	126.4	130.6
Retail Prices Index	KNEV	90.5	93.3	94.9	97.5	100.7	103.1	106.5	109.9	111.6	114.9	116.6

1 Figures for Wales before 1992/93 are omitted as insufficient fares data were available.

Source: Department for Transport 020 7944 3076

14.16 Road accident casualties : by road user type and severity
Great Britain

Numbers

		1991	1992	1993	1994	1995	1996	1997	1998	1999	2000	2001
Child pedestrians:												
Killed	ZCDH	225	180	165	160	132	131	138	103	107	107	107
KSI	KIJS	5 097	4 901	4 231	4 610	4 400	4 132	3 954	3 737	3 457	3 226	3 144
All severities	ZCDI	20 708	20 124	18 250	19 263	18 590	18 510	18 407	17 971	16 876	16 184	15 819
Adult pedestrians:												
Killed	ZCDJ	1 263	1 163	1 072	953	897	858	835	803	760	750	719
KSI	KIJT	9 733	9 125	8 260	8 114	7 716	7 300	6 925	6 592	6 221	6 112	5 920
All severities	ZCDK	32 229	30 354	28 750	28 129	27 178	26 827	26 223	25 827	24 806	24 481	24 758
Child pedal cyclists:												
Killed	ZCDL	50	48	37	42	48	54	33	32	36	27	25
KSI	KIJU	1 345	1 195	1 146	1 234	1 249	1 231	1 016	915	950	758	674
All severities	ZCDM	8 182	7 725	7 386	8 075	8 133	8 217	7 899	6 930	7 920	6 260	5 451
Adult pedal cyclists:												
Killed	ZCDN	192	156	148	129	164	148	150	126	135	98	113
KSI	KIJV	2 800	2 752	2 598	2 710	2 673	2 517	2 542	2 345	2 172	1 954	2 004
All severities	ZCDO	16 201	16 488	16 115	16 097	16 140	15 778	16 181	15 326	14 834	13 630	13 663
Motorcyclists[1] and passengers:												
Killed	ZCDP	548	469	427	444	445	440	509	498	547	605	569
KSI	ZCDQ	8 502	7 338	6 882	6 666	6 615	6 208	6 446	6 442	6 908	7 374	6 595
All severities	BMDH	30 751	26 891	25 094	24 354	23 524	23 133	24 492	24 610	26 192	28 212	24 164
Car drivers and passengers:												
Killed	ZCDS	2 053	1 978	1 760	1 764	1 749	1 806	1 795	1 696	1 687	1 665	1 749
KSI	ZCDT	25 395	25 124	22 833	23 892	23 461	24 048	23 191	21 676	20 368	19 719	19 424
All severities	ZCDU	179 383	185 662	187 479	195 154	194 027	205 336	211 448	210 474	205 735	206 799	202 802
Bus/coach drivers and passengers:												
Killed	ZCDV	25	19	35	21	35	11	14	18	11	15	14
KSI	KCUZ	725	655	725	815	836	695	601	631	611	578	562
All severities	ZCDW	8 875	9 103	9 307	10 090	9 278	9 345	9 439	9 839	10 252	10 088	9 884
LGV drivers and passengers:												
Killed	ZCDX	119	117	91	64	69	61	64	67	65	66	64
KSI	ZCDY	1 427	1 308	1 082	1 101	1 106	989	928	949	867	813	811
All severities	ZCDZ	8 673	8 129	7 420	7 558	7 200	7 215	7 476	7 672	7 124	7 007	7 304
HGV drivers and passengers:												
Killed	ZCEA	65	70	59	41	57	63	45	60	52	55	54
KSI	ZCEB	695	659	635	571	635	555	573	560	540	571	500
All severities	ZCEC	3 603	3 326	3 333	3 370	3 331	3 245	3 302	3 444	3 484	3 597	3 388
All road users:[2]												
Killed	BMDC	4 568	4 229	3 814	3 650	3 621	3 598	3 599	3 421	3 423	3 409	3 450
KSI	ZCEE	56 186	53 485	48 834	50 190	49 154	48 097	46 583	44 255	42 545	41 564	40 560
All severities	BMDA	311 368	310 753	306 135	315 359	310 687	320 578	327 803	325 212	320 310	320 283	313 309

Note: KSI = Killed or seriously injured.
1 Includes mopeds and scooters.
2 Includes other motor or non-motor vehicle users, and unknown road user type and casualty age.

Source: Department for Transport 020 7944 3078

14.17 Freight transport by road: goods moved by goods vehicles over 3.5 tonnes[1]
Great Britain

Billion tonne-kilometres

		1991	1992	1993	1994	1995	1996	1997	1998	1999	2000	2001
By mode of working												
Mainly public haulage	KNND	85.8	86.4	93.2	100.8	106.5	109.1	112.2	114.3	110.9	113.0	114.7
Mainly own account	KNNC	38.8	34.9	35.4	37.0	37.2	37.7	37.4	37.6	38.3	37.5	34.7
All modes	KNNB	124.6	121.3	128.6	137.8	143.7	146.8	149.6	151.9	149.2	150.5	149.4
By gross weight of vehicle												
Rigid vehicles:												
3.5-17 tonnes	ZCIL	20.1	19.0	18.7	19.9	18.7	19.5	19.2	17.8	17.9	15.8	13.1
17-25 tonnes	ZCIM	7.1	6.5	6.6	6.1	5.6	5.3	4.7	4.2	4.3	4.8	5.7
25 tonnes and over	ZCIN	11.3	10.7	11.3	12.4	13.3	13.5	14.3	14.7	15.3	15.4	15.6
All rigids	ZCIO	38.5	36.2	36.5	38.4	37.5	38.3	38.1	36.6	37.5	36.0	34.5
Articulated vehicles:												
3.5-33 tonnes	ZCIP	18.6	16.7	16.5	16.9	15.9	15.9	14.3	14.4	14.0	14.0	12.8
33 tonnes and over	ZCIQ	67.6	68.4	75.6	82.5	90.2	92.6	97.1	100.9	97.7	100.4	102.1
All articulated vehicles	ZCIR	86.1	85.0	92.1	99.4	106.1	108.5	111.4	115.3	111.7	114.4	114.9
All vehicles												
3.5-25 tonnes	ZCIS	28.0	26.3	25.9	26.6	24.7	25.3	24.3	22.5	22.7	21.3	19.3
25 tonnes and over	KNNG	96.6	95.0	102.7	111.2	119.0	121.5	125.2	129.4	126.5	129.2	130.1
All weights	ZCIT	124.6	121.3	128.6	137.8	143.7	146.8	149.6	151.9	149.2	150.5	149.4
By commodity												
Food, drink and tobacco	ZCIU	32.7	33.2	35.9	36.5	37.5	39.3	40.8	42.5	41.5	44.3	41.4
Wood, timber and cork	ZCIV	2.7	2.6	3.1	3.3	3.2	3.8	3.5	3.6	3.8	3.7	3.9
Fertiliser	ZCIW	1.5	1.4	1.5	1.3	1.4	1.5	1.3	1.2	1.4	1.2	1.2
Crude minerals	ZCIX	13.0	12.7	12.6	14.1	13.5	13.5	13.6	13.3	12.7	12.4	13.0
Ores	ZCIY	1.3	1.2	1.6	1.4	1.5	1.3	1.7	1.1	1.3	1.2	1.2
Crude materials	ZCIZ	1.7	2.0	1.7	2.0	1.9	2.1	2.1	2.6	2.6	2.6	2.3
Coal and coke	ZCJA	3.7	3.5	3.1	2.9	2.7	2.5	2.7	2.0	2.2	1.5	2.1
Petrol and petroleum products	ZCJB	4.9	4.5	5.0	5.1	5.7	6.1	5.8	5.2	5.0	6.4	5.8
Chemicals	ZCJC	7.3	6.8	7.2	8.1	7.4	7.7	8.2	7.9	7.4	6.8	7.2
Building materials	ZCJD	8.7	8.0	9.3	10.0	10.7	9.6	11.1	10.7	10.6	10.6	11.7
Iron and steel products	ZCJE	6.9	6.5	6.4	6.7	7.8	7.2	7.9	7.7	6.8	6.8	5.7
Other metal products[2]	ZCJF	1.9	2.0	1.9	2.0	1.7	1.7	1.5	1.7	1.7	1.7	1.4
Machinery and transport equipment	ZCJG	5.9	6.0	5.7	6.8	7.4	7.7	8.4	9.1	8.7	9.1	8.9
Miscellaneous manufactures[2]	ZCJH	12.4	12.0	12.4	13.4	13.3	14.2	14.2	15.9	15.7	15.1	15.4
Miscellaneous transactions[3]	ZCJI	20.0	19.0	21.3	24.3	27.8	28.4	26.8	27.5	27.9	27.1	28.2
All commodities	ZCJJ	124.6	121.3	128.6	137.8	143.7	146.8	149.6	151.9	149.2	150.5	149.4

1 Rigid vehicles or articulated vehicles (tractive unit and trailer) with gross vehicle weight over 3.5 tonnes.
2 Includes not elsewhere specified.
3 Includes not elsewhere specified and commodity not known.

Source: Department for Transport 020 7944 3093

14.18
Freight transport by road: goods lifted by goods vehicles over 3.5 tonnes[1]
Great Britain

Million tonnes

		1991	1992	1993	1994	1995	1996	1997	1998	1999	2000	2001
By mode of working												
Mainly public haulage	ZCJK	862	843	911	980	987	1 011	1 044	1 041	991	1 038	1 052
Mainly own account	ZCJL	643	620	612	618	622	618	599	589	576	556	529
All modes	ZCJM	1 505	1 463	1 523	1 597	1 609	1 628	1 643	1 630	1 567	1 593	1 581
By gross weight of vehicle												
Rigid vehicles:												
3.5-17 tonnes	ZCJN	331	315	322	317	298	306	294	268	254	229	203
17-25 tonnes	ZCJO	236	219	211	202	162	133	120	106	86	87	86
25 tonnes and over	ZCJP	289	282	307	332	373	371	380	401	408	424	443
All rigids	ZCJQ	857	817	840	852	833	811	793	776	748	741	733
Articulated vehicles:												
3.5-33 tonnes	ZCJR	165	142	144	142	139	138	124	125	113	107	97
33 tonnes and over	ZCJS	484	505	540	604	637	679	726	729	706	746	751
All articulated vehicles	ZCJT	648	646	683	746	776	817	850	854	819	852	848
All vehicles												
3.5-25 tonnes	ZCJU	578	544	541	527	467	447	419	382	346	325	294
25 tonnes and over	ZCJV	927	919	982	1 070	1 142	1 181	1 224	1 248	1 221	1 268	1 287
All weights	ZCJW	1 505	1 463	1 523	1 597	1 609	1 628	1 643	1 630	1 567	1 593	1 581
By commodity												
Food, drink and tobacco	ZCJX	291	290	300	302	308	326	342	346	333	346	321
Wood, timber and cork	ZCJY	21	20	25	24	24	27	26	27	28	26	28
Fertiliser	ZCJZ	13	13	12	10	11	13	10	9	11	10	9
Crude minerals	ZCKA	298	327	310	355	319	320	329	327	297	308	298
Ores	ZCKB	14	15	21	18	18	18	25	18	20	16	16
Crude materials	ZCKC	15	17	14	16	16	18	17	20	20	18	20
Coal and coke	ZCKD	57	55	48	42	34	32	37	26	28	22	21
Petrol and petroleum products	ZCKE	73	63	67	68	71	75	73	61	61	75	74
Chemicals	ZCKF	45	42	47	51	50	51	53	53	47	49	50
Building materials	ZCKG	155	136	153	156	161	142	156	161	159	165	165
Iron and steel products	ZCKH	50	46	45	47	54	52	55	54	48	49	44
Other metal products[2]	ZCKI	16	18	20	17	17	15	16	18	17	16	14
Machinery and transport equipment	ZCKJ	46	47	46	57	61	59	71	73	67	69	70
Miscellaneous manufactures[2]	ZCKK	80	75	81	84	85	88	90	96	91	97	97
Miscellaneous transactions[3]	ZCKL	331	300	332	351	379	393	343	342	340	328	353
All commodities	ZCKM	1 505	1 463	1 523	1 597	1 609	1 628	1 643	1 630	1 567	1 593	1 581

1 Rigid vehicles or articulated vehicles (tractive unit and trailer) with gross vehicle weight over 3.5 tonnes.
2 Includes not elsewhere specified.
3 Includes not elsewhere specified and commodity not known.

Source: Department for Transport 020 7944 3093

14.19 Rail systems summary

		1991 /92	1992 /93	1993 /94	1994 /95	1995 /96	1996 /97	1997 /98	1998 /99	1999[1] /00	2000[1] /01	2001[1] /02
Passenger journeys (Millions)												
National Rail network[2]	ZCKN	792	770	740	735	761	801	846	892	931	957	960
London Underground	KNOE	751	728	735	764	784	772	832	866	927	970	953
Docklands Light Railway	ZCKO	8	7	8	12	14	17	21	28	31	38	41
Glasgow Underground	ZCKP	14	14	14	15	14	14	14	15	15	14	14
Tyne and Wear Metro	ZCKQ	41	39	39	37	36	35	35	34	33	33	33
West Midlands Metro[3]	ZCKR	..	..	..	..	..	..	..	..	5	5	5
Croydon Tramlink[4]	GEOE	..	..	..	..	..	..	..	..	..	15	18
Manchester Metrolink[5]	ZCKS	..	8	11	12	13	13	14	13	14	17	18
Stagecoach Supertram (Sheffield)	ZCKT	..	..	..	2	5	8	9	10	11	11	11
All rail	ZCKU	1 605	1 566	1 547	1 577	1 627	1 660	1 771	1 858	1 967	2 061	2 054
of which: light rail[6]	GENZ	49	54	58	63	68	73	79	85	94	120	127
Passenger receipts (£ million at current prices)												
National Rail network[2]	KNDL	2 117	2 154	2 193	2 171	2 379	2 573	2 821	3 089	3 368	3 414	3 548
London Underground	KNOA	559	589	637	718	765	797	899	977	1 058	1 129	1 151
Docklands Light Railway	ZCKV	3	3	5	6	9	12	14	20	22	29	32
Glasgow Underground	ZCKW	6	6	7	7	8	8	9	9	10	11	10
Tyne and Wear Metro	ZCKX	18	19	19	19	20	21	22	23	24	24	25
West Midlands Metro[3]	ZCKY	..	..	..	..	..	..	..	..	..	3	4
Croydon Tramlink[4]	GEOF	..	..	..	..	..	..	..	..	..	12	13
Manchester Metrolink[5]	ZCKZ	..	7	10	10	11	13	14	..	..	18	20
Stagecoach Supertram (Sheffield)	ZCLA	..	..	..	2	4	5	6	6	7	7	8
All rail	ZCLB	2 703	2 778	2 871	2 933	3 196	3 429	3 785	..	..	4 647	4 810
of which: light rail[6]	GEOA	21	29	34	37	44	51	56	..	..	93	102
Passenger kilometres (Millions)												
National Rail network[2]	KNDZ	32 500	31 700	30 400	28 700	30 000	32 100	34 700	36 300	38 454	39 218	39 104
London Underground	KNOI	5 895	5 758	5 814	6 051	6 337	6 153	6 479	6 716	7 171	7 470	7 451
Docklands Light Railway	ZCLC	32	33	39	55	70	86	103	144	172	200	207
Glasgow Underground	ZCLD	39	39	41	43	41	40	45	47	49	46	44
Tyne and Wear Metro	ZCLE	277	271	273	271	261	254	249	238	230	229	238
West Midlands Metro[3]	ZCLF	..	..	..	..	..	..	..	..	50	56	50
Croydon Tramlink[4]	GEOG	..	..	..	..	..	..	..	..	..	96	99
Manchester Metrolink[5]	ZCLG	..	53	73	79	81	86	88	117	126	152	161
Stagecoach Supertram (Sheffield)	ZCLH	..	..	..	8	20	29	34	35	37	38	39
All rail	ZCLI	38 744	37 854	36 640	35 206	36 810	38 748	41 698	43 597	46 289	47 505	47 394
of which: light rail[6]	GEOB	310	357	385	412	432	455	474	534	615	771	795
Route kilometres open for passenger traffic (Numbers)												
National Rail network[2]	ZCLJ	14 291	14 317	14 357	14 359	15 002	15 034	15 024	15 038	15 038	15 042	15 042
London Underground	ZCLK	394	394	394	392	392	392	392	392	408	408	408
Docklands Light Railway	ZCLM	14	14	14	22	22	22	22	22	27	27	27
Glasgow Underground	ZCLN	11	11	11	11	11	11	11	11	11	11	11
Tyne and Wear Metro	ZCLO	59	59	59	59	59	59	59	59	59	59	77
West Midlands Metro[3]	ZCLP	..	..	..	..	..	..	..	..	21	20	20
Croydon Tramlink[4]	GEOH	..	..	..	..	..	..	..	..	..	28	28
Manchester Metrolink[5]	ZCLQ	..	31	31	31	31	31	31	31	39	39	39
Stagecoach Supertram (Sheffield)	ZCLR	..	..	7	22	29	29	29	29	29	29	29
All rail	ZCLS	14 769	14 826	14 873	14 896	15 546	15 578	15 568	15 582	15 632	15 663	15 682
of which: light rail[6]	GEOC	73	104	111	134	141	141	141	141	175	202	221
Stations served (Numbers)												
National Rail network[2]	ZCLT	2 468	2 482	2 493	2 489	2 497	2 498	2 495	2 499	2 503	2 508	2 508
London Underground	KNOO	246	246	245	245	245	245	245	246	253	253	253
Docklands Light Railway	ZCLU	15	16	27	27	28	28	29	29	34	34	34
Glasgow Underground	ZCLV	15	15	15	15	15	15	15	15	15	15	15
Tyne and Wear Metro	ZCLW	46	46	46	46	46	46	46	46	46	46	58
West Midlands Metro[3]	ZCLX	..	..	..	..	..	..	..	..	23	23	23
Croydon Tramlink[4]	GEOI	..	..	..	..	..	..	..	..	..	38	38
Manchester Metrolink[5]	ZCLY	..	26	26	26	26	26	26	26	36	36	36
Stagecoach Supertram (Sheffield)	ZCLZ	..	..	9	37	45	45	46	47	47	47	48
All rail	ZCLL	2 790	2 831	2 861	2 885	2 902	2 903	2 902	2 908	2 957	3 000	3 013
of which: light rail[6]	GSOC	61	88	108	136	145	145	147	148	186	224	237

1 National Rail passenger journeys and passenger kilometres revised by the Strategic Rail Authority.
2 Franchised train operating companies from February 1996 following rail privatisation.
3 West Midlands Metro opened in 1999.
4 Croydon tramlink opened in 2000.
5 Transfer of 20 stations from the national rail network to Manchester Metrolink.
6 Light rail excludes London Underground and Glasgow Underground.

Sources: Railtrack; Strategic Rail Authority; Transport for London; Passenger Transport Executives and operators

14.20 National railways freight[1]
Great Britain

Billion tonne-kilometres

		1991 /92	1992 /93	1993 /94	1994 /95	1995 /96	1996 /97	1997 /98	1998 /99	1999 /00	2000 /01	2001 /02
Freight moved by commodity												
Coal	ZCGG	5.0	5.4	3.9	3.3	3.6	3.9	4.4	4.5	4.8	4.8	6.2
Metals	ZCGH	2.4	2.3	2.1	1.7	1.7	..	..	2.1	2.2	2.1	2.4
Construction	ZCGI	2.5	2.5	2.3	2.5	2.3	..	..	2.1	2.0	2.4	2.8
Oil and petroleum	ZCGJ	2.0	2.0	1.9	1.8	1.8	..	..	1.6	1.5	1.4	1.2
Other traffic	ZCGK	3.4	3.3	3.5	3.8	3.9	11.3	12.5	7.1	7.6	7.4	7.0
All traffic	KCTB	15.3	15.5	13.8	13.0	13.3	15.1	16.9	17.3	18.2	18.1	19.7

		1991 /92	1992 /93	1993 /94	1994 /95	1995 /96	1996 /97	1997 /98	1998 /99	1999 /00	2000 /01	2001 /02
Freight lifted by commodity												
Coal	ZCGL	75.1	67.9	48.9	42.5	45.2	52.2	50.3	45.3	44.3	45.7	46.1
Metals	ZCGM	17.8	15.9	15.8	16.9	15.1	..	..	..	..	..	..
Construction	ZCGN	17.7	15.8	16.1	16.8	11.5	..	..	..	..	..	..
Oil and petroleum	ZCGO	10.0	9.5	9.0	8.1	6.3	..	..	..	..	..	..
Other traffic	ZCGP	15.3	13.2	13.4	13.0	22.6	49.6	55.1	56.8	47.6	49.7	48.3
All traffic	KCTH	135.8	122.4	103.2	97.3	100.7	101.8	105.4	102.1	91.9	95.4	94.4

1 Because of changes in the way freight traffic has been estimated following privatisation, figures since 1996/97 are not strictly comparable with those for previous years. The series calculation was revised again from 1998/99 and from 1999/00 due to revisions from freight operators.

Source: Department for Transport: 020 7944 3094

14.21 Railways: permanent way and rolling stock
Northern Ireland

At end of year

Numbers

		1991	1992	1993	1994	1995	1996	1997	1998	1999	2000	2001
Length of road open for traffic[1] (km)	KNRA	332	332	330	331	333	335	335	335	335	356	334
Length of track open for traffic (km)												
Total	KNRB	553	553	504	503	506	506	505	526	526	547	480
Running lines	KNRC	500	500	463	462	464	464	464	484	484	505	464
Sidings (as single track)	KNRD	53	53	41	41	42	42	42	42	42	42	16
Locomotives												
Diesel-electrics	KNRE	9	9	9	11	11	8	6	5	6	6	6
Passenger carrying vehicles												
Total	KNRF	115	114	112	112	112	112	112	120	108	108	106
Rail motor vehicles:												
Diesel-electric, etc	KNRG	30	30	30	30	30	30	30	28	30	30	29
Trailer carriages:												
Total locomotive hauled	KNRH	28	28	28	28	28	28	28	38	21	21	25
Ordinary coaches	KNRI	26	26	26	26	26	26	26	36	19	19	23
Restaurant cars	KNRJ	2	2	2	2	2	2	2	2	2	2	2
Rail car trailers	KNRK	56	56	54	54	54	54	54	54	54	54	52
Rolling stock for maintenance and repair	KNRT	55	36	42	41	41	41	41	26	18	18	18

1 The total length of railroad open for traffic irrespective of the number of tracks comprising the road.

Source: Department for Regional Development, Northern Ireland: 028 9054 0801

14.22 Operating statistics of railways
Northern Ireland

		Unit	1991	1992	1993	1994	1995	1996	1997	1998	1999	2000	2001
Maintenance of way and works														
Material used:														
Ballast	KNSA	Thousand m^2	22.5	30.2	16.0	33.2	22.5	27.0	51.3	38.5	40.0	47.0	80.0
Rails	KNSB	Thousand tonnes	1.68	2.26	2.00	1.80	1.76	2.12	0.37	2.50	3.00	3.50	2.50
Sleepers	KNSC	Thousands	23.20	31.23	14.60	22.40	22.90	27.50	5.10	32.00	30.00	40.00	50.00
Track renewed	KNSD	Km	10.40	14.00	16.00	12.00	16.00	20.00	2.40	22.50	7.00	29.00	15.00
New Track laid	KPGD	Km	..	..	..	3.2	2.5	–	–	–	–	21.0	–
Engine kilometres														
Total[1]	KNSE	Thousand Km	3 200	3 540	3 640	3 640	4 000	4 100	4 100	4 100	4 100	4 100	4 056
Train kilometres:														
Total	KNSF	"	3 410	3 210	3 210	3 210	3 570	3 670	3 670	3 670	3 670	3 670	3 626
Coaching	KNSG	"	3 406	3 206	3 206	3 206	3 566	3 666	3 666	3 666	3 666	3 666	3 622
Freight	KNSH	"	4	4	4	4	4	4	4	4	4	4	4

1 Including shunting, assisting, light, departmental, maintenance and repair.

Source: Department for Regional Development, Northern Ireland: 028 9054 0801

14.23 Main output[1] of United Kingdom airlines

		1991	1992	1993	1994	1995	1996	1997	1998	1999	2000	2001
All services: total	KNTA	20 166	23 145	25 144	27 714	29 904	32 210	35 538	40 021	42 002	43 379	42 370
Percentage growth on previous year	KNTB	–1.0	14.8	8.5	10.2	7.4	7.7	10.3	12.5	5.0	3.6	–2.4
Scheduled services: total	KNTC	15 188	17 065	18 605	20 360	22 016	23 793	26 504	29 756	31 815	32 938	31 866
Percentage growth on previous year	KNTD	–0.6	12.4	9.0	9.4	8.1	8.1	11.4	12.3	6.9	3.5	–3.3
Non-scheduled services: total	KNTE	4 978	6 079	6 510	7 265	7 695	8 044	9 034	10 265	10 186	10 440	10 505
Percentage growth on previous year	KNTF	–2.5	22.0	7.1	13.0	5.9	4.5	7.3	13.3	–0.7	4.1	0.6

1 Available tonne kilometres (millions).

Source: Civil Aviation Authority: 020 7453 6246

14.24 Air traffic between the United Kingdom and abroad[1]
Aircraft flights and passengers carried

Thousands

		1991	1992	1993	1994[2]	1995	1996	1997	1998	1999	2000	2001
Flights												
United Kingdom airlines												
Scheduled services	KNUA	250.5	283.0	290.8	325.8	342.1	373.0	410.3	443.7	480.9	520.3	536.7
Non-scheduled services	KNUB	202.6	236.2	215.2	195.0	204.8	198.0	208.2	218.7	212.6	216.2	208.5
Overseas airlines[3]												
Scheduled services	KNUC	300.4	328.0	336.2	351.3	363.3	390.0	399.6	426.4	467.6	467.6	496.8
Non-scheduled services	KNUD	34.6	33.9	38.0	35.1	31.5	31.3	32.5	34.8	31.7	31.7	26.0
Total	KNUE	788.1	881.1	880.2	907.2	941.7	992.3	1 050.6	1 123.6	1 192.8	1 235.8	1 268.0
Passengers carried												
United Kingdom airlines												
Scheduled services	KNUF	23 271.6	27 138.8	29 798.2	32 578.0	34 934.7	37 902.2	41 854.7	46 747.7	50 148.5	54 522.8	53 591.7
Non-scheduled services	KNUG	19 715.2	23 347.6	24 777.1	19 501.0	20 484.5	26 304.4	28 699.5	31 616.6	32 603.8	33 185.9	34 009.1
Overseas airlines[3]												
Scheduled services	KNUH	26 719.4	29 240.9	31 163.4	35 134.5	34 568.5	36 992.1	39 900.7	42 554.5	46 628.0	46 627.9	51 107.8
Non-scheduled services	KNUI	3 078.8	3 222.6	3 638.0	3 509.5	4 244.2	4 416.3	4 413.0	4 569.7	4 156.5	4 156.5	3 966.1
Total	KNUJ	72 785.0	82 949.9	89 376.7	90 723.0	94 231.9	105 615.0	114 867.9	125 488.5	133 536.8	138 493.1	142 674.7

1 Excludes travel to and from the Channel Islands.
2 Due to the introduction of European licencing, off shore helicopter movements are no longer included in this figure.

3 Includes airlines of overseas UK Territories.

Source: Civil Aviation Authority: 020 7453 6246

14.25 Operations and traffic on scheduled services: revenue traffic
United Kingdom airlines[1]

		Unit	1991	1992	1993	1994	1995	1996	1997	1998	1999	2000	2001
All services													
Aircraft stage flights:													
Number	KNFA	Numbers	568 122	601 500	601 620	621 272	658 958	702 492	749 806	797 682	835 031	878 582	921 556
Average length	KNFB	Kilometres	876	916	971	1 023	1 032	1 047	1 079	1 111	1 134	1 156	1 138
Aircraft-kilometres flown	KNFC	Millions	497.7	551.2	584.3	663.2	679.9	735.3	809.2	886.3	946.9	1 016.3	1 048.6
Passengers uplifted	KNFD	"	34.6	38.2	40.1	43.9	47.5	51.1	56.3	61.7	65.4	70.3	69.7
Seat-kilometres used	KNFE	"	74 615.4	86 731.4	94 670.1	104 294.5	115 347.1	124 846.5	136 388.2	151 969.1	160 336.4	170 469.0	158 650.7
Cargo uplifted:[2]													
Total	KNFF	Tonnes	466 622	507 356	541 986	618 067	643 181	690 806	782 855	831 436	860 291	897 184	742 705
Tonne-kilometres used:		Millions											
Passenger	KNFH	"	7 007.9	8 135.2	8 905.3	9 789.2	11 171.5	12 189.6	13 287.2	14 754.9	15 517.7	16 507.0	15 258.0
Freight	KNFI	"	2 379.9	2 644.1	2 919.6	3 378.1	3 567.3	3 831.9	4 454.0	4 663.3	4 924.9	5 159.9	4 548.3
Mail	KNFJ	"	182.6	161.1	141.5	147.3	151.1	176.0	172.2	177.7	153.0	179.2	101.9
Total	KNFG	"	9 570.5	10 940.5	11 966.4	13 314.6	14 889.9	16 197.5	17 913.4	19 595.9	20 595.6	21 846.1	19 908.2
Domestic services													
Aircraft stage flights:													
Number	KNFK	Numbers	285 346	299 893	300 416	301 652	318 884	331 109	336 218	352 936	354 864	353 525	365 881
Average length	KNFL	Kilometres	301.0	305.7	311.3	314.8	317.0	320.0	330.0	333.1	337.0	343.5	350.3
Aircraft-kilometres flown	KNFM	Millions	86.0	91.6	93.5	94.9	101.1	105.8	111.0	117.6	119.6	121.4	128.2
Passengers uplifted	KNFN	"	11.6	11.6	12.1	13.0	14.0	15.0	15.9	16.6	17.1	18.0	18.2
Seat-kilometres used	KNFO	"	4 663.7	4 728.2	4 933.8	5 334.0	5 753.6	6 204.3	6 645.7	6 947.5	7 183.9	7 541.8	7 644.5
Cargo uplifted:[2]													
Total	KNFP	Tonnes	37 739	35 420	30 660	32 670	33 659	35 432	30 679	31 879	25 964	24 644	19 498
Tonne-kilometres used:		Millions											
Passenger	KNFR	"	382.3	387.4	405.2	417.3	485.0	527.8	568.9	592.6	609.9	640.2	648.5
Freight	KNFS	"	6.7	6.6	5.6	6.3	6.9	7.4	6.1	6.0	6.0	5.8	4.1
Mail	KNFT	"	7.4	7.0	6.5	6.7	6.6	6.4	6.0	6.0	4.0	3.7	3.5
Total	KNFQ	"	396.5	401.1	417.3	430.3	498.5	541.6	581.0	604.7	619.9	649.7	656.1
International services													
Aircraft stage flights:													
Number	KNFU	Numbers	282 776	301 607	301 204	319 620	339 714	371 400	413 588	444 746	480 167	525 057	555 675
Average length	KNFV	Kilometres	1 456	1 523	1 629	1 693	1 703	1 695	1 688	1 729	1 723	1 704	1 656
Aircraft-kilometres flown	KNFW	Millions	411.7	459.5	490.8	541.4	578.8	629.5	698.2	768.8	827.3	894.9	920.5
Passengers uplifted	KNFX	"	22.9	26.5	28.0	30.9	33.5	36.1	40.4	45.1	48.2	52.2	51.5
Seat-kilometres used	KNFY	"	69 951.7	82 003.1	89 736.3	98 960.5	109 593.4	118 642.2	129 742.5	145 021.6	153 152.5	162 927.2	151 005.5
Cargo uplifted:[2]													
Total	KNFZ	Tonnes	428 883	471 936	511 326	585 397	609 522	655 374	752 176	799 557	834 327	872 540	723 206
Tonne-kilometres used:		Millions											
Passenger	KNJX	"	6 625.6	7 747.8	8 500.1	9 352.3	10 686.4	11 661.9	12 718.2	14 162.3	14 908.0	13 611.1	14 609.5
Freight	KNJY	"	2 373.2	2 637.4	2 914.0	3 371.8	3 560.4	3 824.5	4 448.0	4 657.2	4 919.0	5 154.1	4 544.3
Mail	KNJZ	"	175.2	154.0	135.0	140.5	144.4	169.5	166.3	171.7	149.0	175.5	98.3
Total	KNJW	"	9 174.0	10 539.3	11 549.1	12 864.6	14 391.2	15 655.9	17 332.5	18 991.2	19 976.0	18 940.7	19 252.1

1 Includes services of British Airways and other UK private companies.
2 Cargo has been re-defined as freight and mail.

Source: Civil Aviation Authority: 020 7453 6246

14.26 Accidents on scheduled fixed wing passenger-carrying services[1]
United Kingdom airlines

	Passenger casualties			Crew casualties		Thousand aircraft stage flights per fatal accident	Million aircraft-kms. flown per fatal accident	Thousand passengers carried per passenger killed	Million passenger kms. flown per passenger killed	Fatal accidents		Passengers killed per hundred million passenger-kms.
	Number of fatal accidents	Killed	Seriously injured	Killed	Seriously injured					per 100 000 aircraft stage flights	per hundred million aircraft-kms.	
1950-54	7	194	9	28	4	107.4	61.8	46.1	50.0	0.93	1.62	1.99
1955-59	7	123	28	29	8	158.3	92.1	155.2	158.5	0.63	1.09	0.63
1960-64	5	104	35	21	6	303.7	182.3	373.4	390.6	0.33	0.55	0.25
1965-69	6	273	2	32	2	282.7	194.9	222.2	255.2	0.35	0.52	0.39
1970-74	2	167	5	14	2	897.4	737.6	466.3	657.7	0.11	0.14	0.15
1975-79	1	54	6	9	-	1 797.2	1 481.6	1 697.0	3 240.0	0.06	0.07	0.03
1980-84	-	-	4	-	1	-	-	-	-	-	-	-
1985-89	2	47	79	1	8	1 220.0	1 014.5	3031.0	6 262.9	0.08	0.10	0.02
1990-94	-	-	1	-	9	-	-	-	-	-	-	-
1995-99	1	9	1	3	3	3 700.0	4 026.0	31 265.6	76 539.4	0.03	0.02	0.001
	KCVN	KCVO	KCVP	KCVQ	KCVR							
2000	-	-	1	-		-	-	-	-	-	-	-
2001	-	-	-	-		-	-	-	-	-	-	-

1 Excluding accidents involving the deaths of third parties only.

Source: Civil Aviation Authority: 01293 573346

14.27 Activity at civil aerodromes
United Kingdom[1]

		1991	1992	1993	1994	1995	1996	1997	1998	1999	2000	2001
Movement of civil aircraft (Thousands)												
Commercial Transport	KNQC	1 365	1 448	1 487	1 552	1 615	1 686	1 764	1 871	1 959	2 045	2 095
Other[2]	KNQD	115	112	109	112	124	128	143	162	159	159	150
Total	KNQB	1 481	1 561	1 596	1 664	1 739	1 814	1 907	2 033	2 118	2 204	2 245
Non-commercial[3]	KNQE	1 466	1 321	1 523	1 684	1 809	1 281	1 330	1 343	1 263	1 186	1 207
Total	KNQA	2 947	2 881	3 119	3 348	3 548	3 095	3 237	3 376	3 381	3 390	3 452
Passengers handled												
Terminal	KNQG	95 770	106 123	112 277	122 159	129 369	135 810	146 657	158 856	168 363	179 885	181 231
Transit	KNQH	1 552	1 681	1 620	1 565	1 490	1 486	1 405	1 226	1 156	1 167	1 087
Total	KNQF	97 322	107 804	113 897	123 724	130 859	137 296	148 062	160 082	169 519	181 052	182 318
Commercial freight handled[4] (Tonnes)												
Set down	KNQJ	600 043	658 185	696 056	788 995	849 226	886 507	981 861	1 072 127	1 135 065	1 174 635	1 093 142
Picked up	KNQK	525 757	580 213	680 256	799 793	854 267	885 080	960 859	1 008 358	1 053 902	1 139 292	1 052 379
Total	KNQI	1 125 800	1 238 398	1 376 312	1 588 788	1 703 493	1 771 587	1 942 720	2 080 485	2 188 967	2 313 927	2 145 521
Mail handled												
Set down	KNQM	77 083	78 411	85 806	70 776	72 376	80 937	88 366	88 766	92 974	101 743	98 690
Picked up	KNQN	93 392	95 468	101 097	89 780	93 700	105 964	115 066	113 993	114 752	123 352	117 389
Total	KNQL	170 475	173 879	186 903	160 556	166 076	186 901	203 432	202 759	207 726	225 095	216 079

1 Figures exclude Channel Islands airports.
2 Local pleasure flights and non-transport charter flights for reward (for example: aerial survey work, crop dusting and delivery of empty aircraft).
3 Test and training flights, scheduled service positioning flights, private, aeroclub and official flights, and Business Aviation etc.

4 With effect from 2001, passengers, freight and mail handled; excludes traffic carried on air taxi operations.

Source: Civil Aviation Authority: 020 7453 6258

14.28 United Kingdom ports: foreign, coastwise and one-port traffic

Thousand tonnes

		1990	1991	1992	1993	1994	1995	1996	1997	1998	1999	2000
Inwards:												
Foreign												
Bulk fuel	HHEJ	76 434	79 783	78 921	81 458	73 530	69 311	72 493	76 512	79 013	71 489	87 293
Other traffic	HHEK	107 027	102 329	103 665	107 999	116 557	120 991	120 209	129 484	130 572	132 381	133 391
All traffic	HHEL	183 461	182 112	182 586	189 457	190 087	190 302	192 702	205 996	209 585	203 870	220 684
Coastwise												
Bulk fuel	HHEM	45 309	45 558	41 560	43 159	46 647	51 421	53 478	50 250	51 731	48 340	37 265
Other traffic	HHEN	15 545	16 135	16 634	16 274	16 632	16 477	16 439	16 956	18 700	18 338	20 890
All traffic	HHEO	60 854	61 693	58 194	59 433	63 279	67 898	69 917	67 206	70 431	66 678	58 155
One-port												
Bulk fuel	HHEP	13 859	13 446	14 107	10 063	13 725	10 848	10 861	6 871	10 587	20 220	24 866
Other traffic	HHEQ	20 239	16 397	14 871	13 739	14 852	15 878	14 244	14 973	15 498	16 196	12 639
All traffic	HHER	34 098	29 843	28 978	23 802	28 577	26 726	25 105	21 844	26 085	36 416	37 505
Total inwards												
Bulk fuel	HHES	135 602	138 787	134 589	134 680	133 902	131 580	136 831	133 633	141 330	140 049	149 423
Other traffic	HHET	142 811	134 861	135 169	138 012	148 041	153 346	150 893	161 413	164 770	166 914	166 921
All traffic	HHEU	278 413	273 648	269 758	272 692	281 943	284 926	287 724	295 046	306 100	306 963	316 344
Outwards:												
Foreign												
Bulk fuel	HHEV	80 343	84 698	88 828	94 130	112 106	109 587	103 917	102 533	103 651	106 414	115 265
Other traffic	HHEW	55 821	58 464	61 368	63 360	66 882	69 214	71 873	76 765	78 010	77 953	77 805
All traffic	HHEX	136 164	143 162	150 196	157 490	178 988	178 801	175 790	179 298	181 661	184 367	193 070
Coastwise												
Bulk fuel	HHEY	46 598	46 930	45 446	45 844	48 662	54 699	58 400	54 266	53 202	52 397	42 738
Other traffic	HHEZ	14 861	15 823	15 343	16 183	16 137	17 435	16 916	17 738	18 744	18 677	19 157
All traffic	HHFA	61 459	62 753	60 789	62 027	64 799	72 134	75 316	72 004	71 946	71 074	61 895
One-port												
Bulk fuel[1]	HHFB	..	..	..	..	..	..	..	..	..	..	128
Other traffic	HHFC	15 932	15 068	14 908	14 015	12 400	12 369	12 413	12 181	8 794	3 210	1 612
All traffic	HHFD	15 932	15 068	14 908	14 015	12 400	12 369	12 413	12 181	8 794	3 210	1 740
Total outwards												
Bulk fuel	HHFE	126 941	131 628	134 274	139 973	160 768	164 286	162 317	156 799	156 853	158 811	158 131
Other traffic	HHFG	86 613	89 355	91 619	93 559	95 419	99 018	101 202	106 685	105 549	99 840	98 575
All traffic	HHFH	213 554	220 983	225 893	233 532	256 187	263 304	263 519	263 484	262 402	258 651	256 706
Total goods handled	HHFI	491 968	494 631	495 651	506 224	538 130	548 230	551 243	558 530	568 502	565 614	573 050

1 For years to 1999, outward bulk fuel movements to offshore installations were included in 'other traffic - outwards'.

Source: Department for Transport; 020 7944 3087

14.29 Roll-on/roll-off ferry and Channel Tunnel traffic; road goods vehicles outward to mainland Europe: by country of registration

Thousands

		1991	1992	1993	1994	1995	1996	1997	1998	1999	2000	2001
Powered vehicles:												
United Kingdom	ZCGT	360.2	373.7	398.0	453.1	486.0	531.1	543.2	544.3	562.7	544.8	514.6
Austria	ZCGU	..	..	..	..	9.7	8.6	5.4	10.2	14.9	17.0	42.0
Belgium/Luxembourg	ZCGV	33.8	37.2	29.4	37.1	45.7	41.0	53.6	74.5	96.7	114.1	119.3
Denmark	ZCGW	6.5	6.9	4.9	5.0	4.5	4.6	5.5	7.3	8.7	9.5	12.0
Finland	ZCGX	..	..	..	..	0.3	0.2	0.8	0.6	0.7	0.9	3.1
Germany	ZCGY	29.8	30.8	27.7	28.1	28.0	30.4	39.3	52.4	73.1	111.5	132.0
France	ZCGZ	128.7	141.2	144.0	163.2	154.9	181.7	234.2	272.4	319.1	338.8	352.4
Greece	ZCHA	2.3	2.2	1.5	1.3	1.8	2.1	2.6	1.9	2.6	2.9	2.6
Irish Republic	ZCHB	24.3	24.7	35.6	32.4	31.0	30.1	32.3	38.8	44.7	48.5	46.6
Italy	ZCHC	13.7	13.5	13.0	22.7	29.3	28.8	30.4	35.3	45.8	67.8	91.1
Netherlands	ZCHD	69.0	71.9	73.3	76.3	84.6	87.2	107.0	125.4	153.3	185.1	187.5
Spain	ZCHE	25.3	32.4	29.5	35.2	38.4	39.4	45.1	56.3	67.7	81.8	93.9
Sweden	ZCHF	..	..	..	..	0.7	0.9	8.9	10.3	1.0	1.4	1.8
Portugal	ZCHG	2.5	3.4	3.3	3.7	3.4	3.1	5.1	6.7	9.2	10.7	10.2
European Union (excluding UK)	ZCHH	335.8	364.2	362.2	405.2	432.2	458.1	569.5	692.1	837.3	990.0	1 094.5
Non-European Union	ZCHI	27.1	29.8	30.2	34.2	29.0	26.3	28.0	33.6	47.4	52.9	82.3
Unknown	ZCHJ	2.4	2.1	5.8	4.0	4.0	2.2	5.7	4.5	6.3	17.7	20.5
All countries	ZCHK	725.5	769.8	796.2	896.5	950.2	1 017.7	1 146.4	1 274.5	1 453.7	1 605.4	1 711.9
Unaccompanied trailers	ZCHL	601.2	629.3	593.4	701.6	677.4	626.4	740.0	737.5	737.8	712.9	686.4
Powered vehicles and unaccompanied trailers	ZCHM	1 326.7	1 399.1	1 389.6	1 598.1	1 627.6	1 644.1	1 886.4	2 012.3	2 191.4	2 318.3	2 398.3

Source: Department for Transport; 0117 987 8484

14.30 United Kingdom international passenger movements by air and sea
Arrivals plus departures

Thousands

		1991	1992	1993	1994	1995	1996	1997	1998	1999	2000	2001
By air												
EC Europe[1]	ZCDD	43 094	48 640	51 506	58 042	59 987	60 949	66 089	73 360	79 003	84 930	87 534
Other Western Europe[2]	ZCDE	6 726	8 103	8 507	8 797	9 364	9 473	10 385	11 089	11 246	11 897	12 062
Rest of the world	ZCDF	22 039	25 455	27 335	28 915	31 542	34 499	37 594	40 263	42 619	45 293	42 591
All air passenger movements	KMUP	71 859	82 198	87 348	95 754	100 893	104 921	114 068	124 712	132 868	142 120	142 187
By sea												
Irish Republic, European continent and Mediterranean Sea area[3]	ZCDG	31 419	32 882	34 685	36 733	34 321	34 543	36 258	33 226	31 381	28 516	27 754
Rest of the world	BMMF	34	27	37	34	33	24	29	23	26	26	27
Pleasure cruises[4,5]	KMRQ	172	138	193	236	207	233	–	–	445	461	470
All sea passenger movements[5]	KMUO	31 625	33 046	34 915	37 002	34 562	34 792	36 288[6]	33 249[6]	31 852	29 003	28 250

1 Includes Azores, Madeira, Canary and Cape Verde Islands. Austria, Finland, and Sweden joined the EC in 1995, but are included in the EC section for all years to show a consistent time series.
2 Includes Iceland and the Faroe Islands.
3 Prior to 1992, includes passengers between the Isle of Man and the Irish Republic.

4 Cruise passengers, like other passengers are included at both departure and arrival if their journeys begin and end at United Kingdom seaports.
5 Figure for 2001 is provisional.
6 Excluding cruise passengers.

Sources: Civil Aviation Authority;
Department for Transport

14.31 Postal services and television licences
United Kingdom
Years ended 31 March[1]

		1992	1993	1994	1995	1996	1997	1998	1999	2000	2001	2002
Letters, etc posted[2](millions)	KMRA	16 038	16 364	16 651	17 468	18 322	18 101	18 350	18 878	19 711	20 076	20 648
of which:												
Registered and insured	KMRB	20.7	21.5	21.8	21.5	23.5	25.6	28.7	31.6	30.2	32.3	36.1
Airmail (Commonwealth and foreign)[3]	KMRC	544.5	534.4	545.0	567.1	655.1	684.5	658.4	693.2	672.3	659.2	600.7
Business reply and freepost items[4]	KMRD	428.9	481.3	482.9	477.6	493.1	505.8	524.7	503.6	475.3	487.4	486.2
Postal orders												
Total issued (thousands)[5]	KMRH	39 867	38 401	39 089	37 901	35 542	33 404	31 907	30 289	30 153	30 931	29 150
Television licences (thousands)												
in force on 31 March	KMQL	19 631	20 067	20 413	20 732	21 105	21 305	21 723	22 240	22 625	22 839	23 157
of which:												
Colour	KMQM	18 426	19 031	19 524	19 957	20 505	20 849	21 344	21 944	22 413	22 684	23 040

1 Years ended 31 March for letters, postal orders and telegrams sent. For all other items figures relate to 31 March in each year.
2 Including printed papers, newspapers, postcards and sample packets.
3 Including letters without special charge for air transport.
4 Business reply and Freepost is now known as Response Services.
5 Excluding those issued on HM ships, in many British possessions and in other places abroad. For 1992 to 1998 includes Postal Orders issued Overseas and by Ministry of Defence.

Sources: Royal Mail: 01246 547012;
Capita Business Services Limited: 01179 219384;
Post Office Counters Limited: 020 7921 9384

15 National accounts

National accounts

National accounts *(Tables 15.1 to 15.22)*
The tables which follow are based on those in the *Blue Book 2002 Edition*. Some of the figures are provisional and may be revised later; this applies particularly to the figures for 2000 and 2001.

The accounts are based on the European System of Accounts 1995 (ESA95). The *Blue Book* contains an introduction to the system of the UK accounts outlining some of the main concepts and principles of measurement used. It explains how key economic indicators are derived from the sequence of accounts and how the figures describing the whole economy are broken down by sector and by industry. A detailed description of the structure for the accounts is provided in a separate ONS publication *United Kingdom National Accounts: Concepts, Sources and Methods* (TSO 1998). Further information on the financial accounts is given in the *Financial Statistics Explanatory Handbook.*

In the tables in this chapter on national income, analyses by industry are based, as far as possible, on the Standard Industrial Classification Revised 1992. The principal aggregate measured in these tables is the **Gross domestic product** (GDP). This is a concept of the value of the total economic activity taking place in UK territory. It can be viewed as incomes earned, as expenditures incurred, or as production. Adding all primary incomes received from the rest of the world and deducting all primary incomes payable to non-residents produces **Gross national income** (previously known as gross national product). This is a concept of the value of all incomes earned by UK residents.

ESA95, the internationally compatible accounting framework, provides a systematic and detailed description of the UK economy. It includes the sector accounts which provide, by institutional sector, a description of the different stages of the economic process from production through income generation, distribution and use of income to capital accumulation and financing; and the input-output framework, which describes the production process in more detail. It contains all the elements required to compile such aggregate measures as GDP, gross national income (GNI) and saving.

Gross domestic product and national income *(Tables 15.1, 15.2, 15.3)*
Table 15.1 shows the main national accounts aggregates, at current prices and at constant 1995 prices.

Table 15.2 shows the various money flows which generate the gross domestic product and gross national income. The output approach to GDP shows the total output of goods and services, the use of goods and services in the production process (intermediate consumption) and taxes and subsidies on products. The expenditure approach to GDP shows consumption expenditure by households and government, gross capital formation and expenditure on UK exports by overseas purchasers. The sum of these items overstates the amount of income generated in the United Kingdom by the value of imports of goods and services; this item is therefore subtracted to produce gross domestic product at market prices. The income approach to GDP shows gross operating surplus, mixed income and compensation of employees (previously known as income from employment). Taxes are added and subsidies are deducted to produce the total of the income-based components at market prices.

Table 15.2 also shows the primary incomes received from the rest of the world, which are added to GDP and primary incomes payable to non-residents, which are deducted from GDP, to arrive at **Gross national income.** Primary income comprises compensation of employees, taxes *less* subsidies on production and property and entrepreneurial income.

Table 15.3 shows the expenditure approach to GDP at constant 1995 prices. When looking at the change in the economy over time the main concern is usually whether more goods and services are actually being produced now than at some time in the past. Over time changes in current price GDP show changes in the monetary value of the components of GDP and, as these changes in value can reflect changes in both price and volume, it is difficult to establish how much of an increase in the series is due either to increased activity in the economy or to an increase in the price level. As a result, when looking at the real growth in the economy over time it is useful to look at volume (or constant price) estimates of GDP. In constant price series, for all years the transactions are re-valued to a constant price level using the average prices of a selected year, known as the base year, presently 1995.

Industrial analysis *(Tables 15.4, 15.5)*
The analysis of gross value added by industry at current prices shown in Table 15.4 reflects the estimates based on the Standard Industrial Classification, Revised 1992 (SIC92). The table is based on current price data reconciled through the input-output process for 1992 to 2000. The estimates are valued at basic prices, that is, the only taxes included in the price will be taxes paid as part of the production process, such as business rates, and not any taxes specifically levied on the production of a unit of output, for example VAT.

Table 15.5 shows constant price estimates of gross value added at basic prices by industry. Constant price gross value added (output approach) provides the lead indicator of economic change in the short term. The output analysis of gross value added is estimated in terms of change and expressed in index number form. It is therefore inappropriate to show as a statistical adjustment any divergence of an output measure of GDP derived from it from other measures of GDP. Such an adjustment does, however, exist implicitly.

Sector analysis - Distribution of income accounts and capital account *(Tables 15.6-15.13)*
The new national accounts accounting framework includes the sector accounts which provide, by institutional sector, a description of the different stages of the economic process from production through income generation, distribution and use of income to capital accumulation and financing.

Tables 15.6-15.12 show the allocation of primary income account and the secondary distribution of income account for the non-financial corporations, financial corporations, government and households sectors. Additionally, Table 15.12 shows the use of income account for the households sector and Table 15.13 provides a summary of the capital account. The full sequence of accounts is shown in the *Blue Book.*

The allocation of primary income account shows the resident units and institutional sectors as recipients rather than producers of primary income. It demonstrates the extent to which operating surpluses are distributed to the owners of the enterprises. The resources side of the allocation of primary income accounts includes the components of the income approach to measurement of GDP. The balance of this account is the gross balance of primary income (B.5g) for each sector, and if the gross balance is aggregated across all sectors of the economy the result is **gross national income.**

The secondary distribution of income account describes how the balance of income for each sector is allocated by redistribution; through transfers such as taxes on income, social contributions and benefits and other current transfers. The balancing item of this account is gross disposable income (B.6g). For the households sector, gross disposable income at constant prices is shown as real household disposable income.

Table 15.12 shows, for the households sector, the use of disposable income where the balancing item is saving (B.8g). For the non-financial corporations sector the balancing item of the secondary distribution of income account, gross disposable income (B.6g) is equal to saving (B.8g).

The summary capital account *(Table 15.13)* brings together the saving and investment of the several sectors of the economy. It shows saving, capital transfers, gross capital formation and net acquisition of non-financial assets for each of the four sectors.

Household and non-profit institutions serving households (NPISH) consumption expenditure at current and constant prices *(Tables 15.14-15.17)*
Household and NPISH consumption expenditure is a major component of the expenditure measure of gross domestic product at current prices *(Table 15.2)* and at constant prices *(Table 15.3)*.

Household final consumption expenditure includes the value of income-in-kind and imputed rent of owner-occupied dwellings but excludes business expenditure allowed as deductions in computing income for tax purposes. It includes expenditure on durable goods, for instance motor cars, which from the point of view of the individual might more appropriately be treated as capital expenditure. The only exceptions are the purchase of land and dwellings and costs incurred in connection with the transfer of their ownership and expenditure on major improvements by occupiers, which are treated as personal capital expenditure.

The estimates of household consumption expenditure include purchases of second-hand as well as new goods, *less* the proceeds of sales of used goods.

The most detailed figures are published quarterly in *Consumer Trends* (available as a web-only publication on the National Statistics website www.statistics.gov.uk).

Change in inventories (previously known as value of physical increase in stocks and work in progress) *(Table 15.18)*
This table gives a broad analysis by industry, and, for manufacturing industry, by asset, of the value of entries *less* withdrawals and losses of inventories (stocks).

Gross fixed capital formation *(Tables 15.19-15.22)*
Gross fixed capital formation comprises expenditure on the replacement of, and additions to, fixed capital assets located in the United Kingdom, including all ships and aircraft of UK ownership.

15.1 UK national and domestic product[1]
Main aggregates: index numbers and values
At current and constant 1995 prices

		1993	1994	1995	1996	1997	1998	1999	2000	2001
INDICES (1995=100)										
VALUES AT CURRENT PRICES										
Gross domestic product at current market prices ("money GDP")	YBEU	89.3	94.8	100.0	106.0	112.8	119.5	125.5	132.1	137.4
Gross value added at current basic prices	YBEX	89.9	95.1	100.0	106.2	112.6	119.2	124.4	130.9	136.6
VALUES AT 1995 PRICES										
Gross domestic product at 1995 market prices	YBEZ	92.9	97.2	100.0	102.6	106.2	109.3	111.9	115.3	117.6
Gross national disposable income at 1995 market prices	YBFP	94.0	98.4	100.0	103.0	108.2	113.1	114.6	119.2	121.9
Gross value added at 1995 basic prices	CGCE	92.8	97.3	100.0	102.7	106.0	109.5	111.8	115.3	117.2
PRICES										
Implied deflator of GDP at market prices (expenditure based, "total home costs per unit of output")	YBGB	96.2	97.5	100.0	103.3	106.2	109.4	112.1	114.6	116.8
VALUES AT CURRENT PRICES (£ million)										
Gross measures (before deduction of fixed capital consumption) at current market prices										
Gross Domestic Product ("money GDP")	YBHA	642 327	681 327	719 176	762 214	811 067	859 384	902 459	950 415	988 014
Employment, property and entrepreneurial income from the rest of the world (receipts *less* payments)	YBGG	−191	3 348	2 101	1 204	3 906	12 558	2 536	9 312	9 162
Subsidies (receipts) *less* taxes (payments) on products from/to the rest of the world	-QZOZ	−4 725	−3 349	−5 220	−4 141	−2 811	−3 683	−2 563	−4 072	−3 704
Other subsidies on production from/to the rest of the world	-IBJL	215	286	293	253	206	246	309	292	298
Gross National Income (GNI)	ABMX	637 626	681 612	716 350	759 530	812 368	868 505	902 741	955 947	993 770
Current transfers from the rest of the world (receipts *less* payments)	-YBGF	−734	−2 309	−2 649	−1 902	−3 209	−4 790	−4 435	−6 256	−3 753
Gross National Disposable Income	NQCO	636 892	679 303	713 701	757 628	809 159	863 715	898 306	949 691	990 017
Adjustment to current basic prices										
Gross Domestic Product (at current market prices)	YBHA	642 327	681 327	719 176	762 214	811 067	859 384	902 459	950 415	988 014
Adjustment to current basic prices (*less* taxes *plus* subsidies on products)	-NQBU	−66 866	−72 587	−79 268	−82 594	−90 375	−97 021	−106 186	−112 350	−113 787
Gross Value Added (at current basic prices)	ABML	575 461	608 740	639 908	679 620	720 692	762 363	796 273	838 065	874 227
Net measures (after deduction of fixed capital consumption) at current market prices	-NQAE	−83 522	−85 161	−86 959	−89 639	−93 531	−96 074	−99 502	−106 099	−111 275
Net domestic product	NHRK	558 805	596 166	632 217	672 575	717 536	763 310	802 957	844 316	876 739
Net national income	NSRX	554 104	596 451	629 391	669 891	718 837	772 431	803 239	849 848	882 495
Net national disposable income	NQCP	553 370	594 142	626 742	667 989	715 628	767 641	798 804	843 592	878 742
VALUES AT 1995 PRICES (£ million)										
Gross measures (before deduction of fixed capital consumption) at 1995 market prices										
Gross Domestic Product	ABMI	667 804	698 915	719 176	738 046	763 459	785 777	804 713	829 517	845 552
Terms of trade effect ("Trading gain or loss")	YBGJ	7 950	4 835	−	2 610	10 677	16 671	19 480	24 670	24 817
Real gross domestic income	YBGL	675 753	703 750	719 176	740 656	774 136	802 448	824 193	854 187	870 369
Real employment, property and entrepreneurial income from the rest of the world (receipts *less* payments)	YBGI	−201	3 459	2 101	1 170	3 727	11 758	2 327	8 420	8 130
Subsidies (receipts) *less* taxes (payments) on production from/to the rest of the world	-QZPB	−3 695	−2 679	−5 220	−5 181	−2 576	−3 082	−4 990	−6 428	−5 192
Other subsidies on production from/to the rest of the world	-IBJN	212	287	293	248	198	242	357	353	353
Gross National Income (GNI)	YBGM	672 069	704 817	716 350	736 893	775 486	811 362	821 887	856 529	873 660
Real current transfers from the rest of the world (receipts *less* payments)	-YBGP	−773	−2 385	−2 649	−1 848	−3 062	−4 485	−4 069	−5 656	−3 330
Gross National Disposable Income	YBGO	671 298	702 432	713 701	735 045	772 424	806 877	817 818	850 873	870 330
Adjustment to 1995 basic prices										
Gross Domestic Product (at 1995 market prices)	ABMI	667 804	698 915	719 176	738 046	763 459	785 777	804 713	829 517	845 552
Adjustment to 1995 basic prices (*less* taxes *plus* subsidies on products)	-NTAQ	−73 672	−76 491	−79 268	−80 984	−85 193	−85 098	−88 860	−91 820	−95 427
Gross Value Added (at 1995 basic prices)	ABMM	594 215	622 424	639 908	657 062	678 266	700 679	715 853	737 697	750 125
Net measures (after deduction of fixed capital consumption) at 1995 market prices	-CIHA	−89 913	−88 882	−86 959	−87 148	−89 072	−90 126	−92 497	−96 480	−98 646
Net national income at 1995 market prices	YBET	581 642	615 935	629 391	649 745	686 414	721 236	729 390	760 049	775 014
Net national disposable income at 1995 market prices	YBEY	580 889	613 550	626 742	647 897	683 352	716 751	725 321	754 393	771 684

1 See chapter text.

Source: Office for National Statistics: 020 7533 6031

15.2 UK gross domestic product and national income[1]
Current prices

£ million

		1993	1994	1995	1996	1997	1998	1999	2000	2001
GROSS DOMESTIC PRODUCT										
Gross domestic product: output approach										
Gross value added, at basic prices										
Output of goods and services, at basic prices	NQAF	1 172 054	1 270 951	1 363 534	1 455 417	1 539 888	1 633 840	1 722 481	1 823 416	1 872 565
less intermediate consumption, at purchasers' prices	-NQAJ	-596 593	-662 211	-723 626	-775 797	-819 196	-871 477	-926 208	-985 351	-998 338
Total Gross Value Added	ABML	**575 461**	**608 740**	**639 908**	**679 620**	**720 692**	**762 363**	**796 273**	**838 065**	**874 227**
Value added taxes (VAT) on products	QYRC	42 429	46 117	48 424	51 389	55 454	57 055	62 124	64 917	68 081
Other taxes on products	NSUI	30 815	33 450	37 995	39 724	43 003	46 933	50 512	54 086	52 418
less subsidies on products	-NZHC	-6 378	-6 980	-7 151	-8 519	-8 082	-6 967	-6 450	-6 653	-6 712
Gross Domestic Product at market prices	YBHA	**642 327**	**681 327**	**719 176**	**762 214**	**811 067**	**859 384**	**902 459**	**950 415**	**988 014**
Gross domestic product: expenditure approach										
Final consumption expenditure										
Actual individual consumption										
Household final consumption expenditure	ABPB	401 970	422 397	443 367	473 800	503 374	536 235	569 481	603 557	631 010
Final consumption expenditure of NPISH	ABNV	13 981	15 287	16 481	18 385	19 602	21 117	22 150	23 027	24 255
Individual government final consumption expenditure	NNAQ	74 549	77 545	81 093	84 968	87 551	92 271	100 774	107 859	117 941
Total actual individual consumption	NQEO	490 500	515 229	540 941	577 153	610 527	649 623	692 405	734 443	773 206
Collective government final consumption expenditure	NQEP	56 985	58 710	59 938	61 811	61 596	62 610	65 840	69 942	72 722
Total final consumption expenditure	ABKW	547 485	573 939	600 879	638 964	672 123	712 233	758 245	804 385	845 928
Households and NPISH	NSSG	415 951	437 684	459 848	492 185	522 976	557 352	591 631	626 584	655 265
Central government	NMBJ	81 566	84 385	86 791	90 396	92 190	95 298	100 422	106 808	115 767
Local government	NMMT	49 968	51 870	54 240	56 383	56 957	59 583	66 192	70 993	75 945
Gross capital formation										
Gross fixed capital formation	NPQX	101 027	108 314	117 448	125 762	134 163	150 842	153 501	158 918	162 244
Changes in inventories	ABMP	329	3 708	4 512	1 771	4 621	5 026	6 060	5 595	1 441
Acquisitions less disposals of valuables	NPJO	-29	113	-121	-158	-26	430	231	5	363
Total gross capital formation	NQFM	101 327	112 135	121 839	127 375	138 758	156 298	159 792	164 518	164 048
Exports of goods and services	KTMW	163 640	180 508	203 509	223 091	231 622	228 801	236 609	265 135	267 979
less imports of goods and services	-KTMX	-170 125	-185 255	-207 051	-227 216	-231 436	-237 948	-252 187	-283 623	-290 912
External balance of goods and services	KTMY	-6 485	-4 747	-3 542	-4 125	186	-9 147	-15 578	-18 488	-22 461
Statistical discrepancy between expenditure components and GDP	RVFD	–	–	–	–	–	–	–	–	499
Gross Domestic Product at market prices	YBHA	**642 327**	**681 327**	**719 176**	**762 214**	**811 067**	**859 384**	**902 459**	**950 415**	**988 014**
Gross domestic product: income approach										
Operating surplus, gross										
Non-financial corporations										
Public non-financial corporations	NRJT	8 188	9 111	10 987	10 856	9 758	10 216	9 477	9 137	9 388
Private non-financial corporations	NRJK	116 282	133 037	142 165	157 745	168 871	174 261	177 652	186 764	187 455
Financial corporations	NQNV	17 726	20 708	17 838	17 135	14 806	18 436	15 785	17 113	13 788
Adjustment for financial services	-NSRV	-19 569	-23 119	-23 215	-22 580	-22 396	-27 998	-30 121	-37 949	-39 367
General government	NMXV	5 870	5 991	6 447	6 876	7 316	7 534	7 707	7 929	8 257
Households and non-profit institutions serving households	QWLS	33 026	35 354	38 165	40 160	43 147	48 023	52 161	55 050	59 104
Total operating surplus, gross	ABNF	161 523	181 082	192 387	210 192	221 502	230 472	232 661	238 044	238 625
Mixed income	QWLT	42 340	44 319	46 647	49 011	50 461	50 537	54 116	57 440	60 073
Compensation of employees	HAEA	357 662	369 645	386 718	405 469	432 960	465 058	492 724	524 890	556 371
Taxes on production and imports	NZGX	88 310	94 288	101 633	107 042	115 143	121 275	130 292	137 484	140 447
less subsidies	-AAXJ	-7 508	-8 007	-8 209	-9 500	-8 999	-7 958	-7 334	-7 443	-7 884
Statistical discrepancy between income components and GDP	RVFC	–	–	–	–	–	–	–	–	382
Gross domestic product at market prices	YBHA	**642 327**	**681 327**	**719 176**	**762 214**	**811 067**	**859 384**	**902 459**	**950 415**	**988 014**

15.2 UK gross domestic product and national income[1]
Current prices
continued

		1993	1994	1995	1996	1997	1998	1999	2000	2001
GROSS NATIONAL INCOME at market prices										
Gross Domestic Product at market prices	YBHA	642 327	681 327	719 176	762 214	811 067	859 384	902 459	950 415	988 014
Compensation of employees										
receipts from the rest of the world	KTMN	595	681	887	911	1 007	840	960	1 014	1 049
less payments to the rest of the world	−KTMO	−560	−851	−1 183	−818	−924	−850	−759	−871	−869
Total	KTMP	35	−170	−296	93	83	−10	201	143	180
less Taxes on products paid to the rest of the world										
plus Subsidies received from the rest of the world	−QZOZ	−4 725	−3 349	−5 220	−4 141	−2 811	−3 683	−2 563	−4 072	−3 704
Other subsidies on production	−IBJL	215	286	293	253	206	246	309	292	298
Property and entrepreneurial income										
receipts from the rest of the world	HMBN	72 333	73 702	87 132	91 621	95 337	102 945	99 865	134 223	138 831
less payments to the rest of the world	−HMBO	−72 559	−70 184	−84 735	−90 510	−91 514	−90 377	−97 530	−125 054	−129 849
Total	HMBM	−226	3 518	2 397	1 111	3 823	12 568	2 335	9 169	8 982
Gross National Income at market prices	ABMX	637 626	681 612	716 350	759 530	812 368	868 505	902 741	955 947	993 770

1 See chapter text.

Source: Office for National Statistics: 020 7533 6031

15.3 UK gross domestic product[1]
Constant (1995) prices

£ million

		1993	1994	1995	1996	1997	1998	1999	2000	2001
GROSS DOMESTIC PRODUCT										
Gross domestic product: expenditure approach										
Final consumption expenditure										
Actual individual consumption										
Household final consumption expenditure	ABPF	422 273	435 350	443 367	460 760	478 738	496 231	519 222	545 751	567 897
Final consumption expenditure of non-profit institutions serving households	ABNU	14 723	15 900	16 481	16 691	17 055	18 265	18 239	19 514	20 398
Individual government final consumption expenditure	NSZK	78 616	78 479	81 093	83 112	84 808	86 244	88 274	89 947	92 206
Total actual individual consumption	YBIO	515 535	529 729	540 941	560 563	580 601	600 740	625 735	655 212	680 501
Collective government final consumption expenditure	NSZL	58 579	60 145	59 938	59 590	57 971	58 747	61 145	62 577	63 674
Total final consumption expenditure	ABKX	574 114	589 874	600 879	620 153	638 572	659 487	686 880	717 789	744 175
Gross capital formation										
Gross fixed capital formation	NPQR	108 887	113 961	117 448	122 976	131 436	148 260	149 143	151 986	151 326
Changes in inventories	ABMQ	360	4 836	4 512	1 830	3 980	4 794	6 282	5 983	377
Acquisitions less disposals of valuables	NPJP	−9	115	−121	−182	−52	399	214	31	340
Total gross capital formation	NPQU	109 629	118 912	121 839	124 624	135 364	153 453	155 639	158 000	152 043
Gross domestic final expenditure	YBIK	682 932	708 786	722 718	744 777	773 936	812 940	842 519	875 789	896 218
Exports of goods and services	KTMZ	170 875	186 655	203 509	220 268	238 492	245 761	258 863	285 124	289 225
Gross final expenditure	ABME	853 767	895 441	926 227	965 045	1 012 428	1 058 701	1 101 382	1 160 913	1 185 443
less imports of goods and services	−KTNB	−186 015	−196 526	−207 051	−226 999	−248 969	−272 924	−296 669	−331 396	−340 318
Statistical discrepancy between expenditure components and GDP	GIXS	−	−	−	−	−	−	−	−	427
Gross Domestic Product at 1995 market prices	ABMI	667 804	698 915	719 176	738 046	763 459	785 777	804 713	829 517	845 552
of which External balance of goods and services	KTNC	−15 140	−9 871	−3 542	−6 731	−10 477	−27 163	−37 806	−46 272	−51 093

1 See chapter text.

Source: Office for National Statistics: 020 7533 6031

15.4 Gross value added at current basic prices: by industry[1,2]

£ million

		1993	1994	1995	1996	1997	1998	1999	2000	2001
Agriculture, hunting, forestry and fishing	EWSH	10 544	10 617	11 766	11 735	10 145	9 628	9 478	8 801	8 241
Production										
Mining and quarrying										
Mining and quarrying of energy producing materials										
Mining of coal	QTOQ	1 472	1 048	1 223	1 045	987	825	644	613	598
Extraction of mineral oil and natural gas	QTOR	10 892	12 493	13 704	17 124	15 435	13 203	15 044	22 883	23 379
Other mining and quarrying	QTOS	1 162	1 247	1 443	1 599	1 693	1 650	1 715	1 813	1 689
Total mining and quarrying	EWSL	13 526	14 788	16 369	19 768	18 116	15 677	17 402	25 308	25 665
Manufacturing										
Food; beverages and tobacco	QTOU	18 086	18 230	18 260	19 894	20 322	20 030	20 219	20 520	21 102
Textiles and textile products	QTOV	6 258	6 452	6 821	7 266	7 696	6 922	6 368	5 992	5 076
Leather and leather products	QTOW	1 019	1 018	946	892	843	802	755	672	702
Wood and wood products	QTOX	1 582	1 746	1 918	2 026	2 236	2 285	2 209	2 286	2 368
Pulp, paper and paper products; publishing and printing	QTOY	15 480	16 214	17 582	18 154	18 377	18 947	19 834	20 678	21 242
Coke, petroleum products and nuclear fuel	QTOZ	2 542	2 688	2 923	2 530	2 381	2 575	2 666	2 737	3 258
Chemicals, chemical products and man-made fibres	QTPA	13 005	13 908	15 311	15 726	15 322	15 049	15 165	15 457	16 419
Rubber and plastic products	QTPB	6 048	6 321	6 789	7 221	7 977	8 196	7 898	7 789	7 512
Other non-metal mineral products	QTPC	3 892	4 697	5 158	5 189	5 181	5 004	4 971	5 125	5 228
Basic metals and fabricated metal products	QTPD	13 146	14 243	16 124	16 410	17 050	17 653	16 612	16 295	15 906
Machinery and equipment not elsewhere classified	QTPE	9 813	11 052	12 273	12 469	13 364	13 550	12 696	12 324	12 708
Electrical and optical equipment	QTPF	14 544	16 523	17 757	18 593	19 980	20 111	20 774	21 818	19 732
Transport equipment	QTPG	11 856	13 258	13 067	14 318	15 589	16 051	15 919	15 608	15 242
Manufacturing not elsewhere classified	QTPH	3 717	4 417	4 857	5 394	5 983	6 226	6 319	6 368	6 635
Total manufacturing	EWSP	120 989	130 767	139 789	146 079	152 299	153 408	152 402	153 671	153 132
Electricity, gas and water supply	EWST	16 271	16 158	15 586	16 280	16 141	15 960	15 968	15 731	15 713
Total production	QTPK	150 786	161 713	171 744	182 127	186 557	185 042	185 771	194 710	194 510
Construction	EWSX	29 166	31 216	33 005	34 587	36 879	39 097	41 516	44 047	47 327
Service industries										
Wholesale and retail trade (including motor trade); repair of motor vehicles, personal and household goods	QTPM	68 324	71 537	74 612	79 668	86 747	93 503	99 144	102 333	106 766
Hotels and restaurants	QTPN	15 738	16 855	18 252	20 138	22 383	24 331	26 098	28 296	29 359
Transport, storage and communication										
Transport and storage	QTPO	28 990	31 391	33 045	34 879	37 380	39 729	40 950	43 159	43 092
Communication	QTPP	17 420	18 180	18 295	18 594	20 032	22 500	24 146	25 683	27 158
Total	EWTF	46 408	49 572	51 340	53 473	57 412	62 230	65 096	68 842	70 252
Financial intermediation	QTPR	39 289	42 358	40 089	40 912	40 585	45 313	43 190	45 784	46 034
Adjustment for financial services	-NSRV	−19 569	−23 119	−23 215	−22 580	−22 396	−27 998	−30 121	−37 949	−39 367
Real estate, renting and business activities										
Letting of dwellings including imputed rent of owner occupiers	QTPS	40 003	42 366	45 083	46 716	50 273	55 715	60 088	63 312	66 968
Other real estate, renting and business activities	QTPT	62 711	68 131	73 970	82 060	93 013	107 563	118 229	130 651	142 871
Total	QTPU	102 715	110 496	119 052	128 777	143 286	163 278	178 319	193 963	209 837
Public administration and defence (PAD)	EWTN	39 988	39 597	39 756	39 709	39 659	39 751	39 372	40 848	42 096
Education	QTPW	31 428	32 771	34 208	36 541	38 802	41 354	45 417	49 162	52 659
Health and social work	QTPX	37 108	39 495	42 051	44 567	46 892	49 570	52 783	56 496	61 410
Other social and personal services, private households with employees and extra-territorial organisations	EWTV	23 535	25 634	27 247	29 966	33 743	37 261	40 209	42 731	45 101
Total service industries	QTPZ	384 965	405 194	423 393	451 172	487 112	528 593	559 507	590 507	624 149
All industries	ABML	575 461	608 740	639 908	679 620	720 692	762 363	796 273	838 065	874 227

1 See chapter text. Components may not sum to totals as a result of rounding.
2 Because of differences in the annual and monthly production inquiries, estimates of current price output and value added by industry derived from the current price input-output supply-use balances are not consistent with the equivalent measures of constant price growth given in Table 15.5. These differences do not affect GDP totals. For further information see "Experimental Constant Price Input-Output Supply-Use Balances: An approach to improving the quality of the national accounts" Nadim Ahmad, *Economic Trends*, July 1999 (No. 548).

Source: Office for National Statistics: 020 7533 6031

15.5 Gross value added at 1995 basic prices: by industry[1,2,3]
Index numbers

Indices 1995=100

	Weight per 1000[1]										
	1995		1993	1994	1995	1996	1997	1998	1999	2000	2001
Agriculture, hunting, forestry and fishing	18.4	GDQA	102.5	101.2	100.0	99.1	98.2	99.9	103.1	99.8	88.2
Production											
Mining and quarrying											
Mining and quarrying of energy producing materials											
Mining of coal	1.9	CKZP	142.3	94.6	100.0	95.5	90.3	76.5	69.1	59.3	59.1
Extraction of mineral oil and natural gas	21.4	CKZO	77.5	96.1	100.0	105.6	104.7	107.5	112.2	110.7	105.2
Other mining and quarrying	2.3	CKZQ	105.6	105.3	100.0	88.7	87.3	97.0	103.6	110.8	103.1
Total mining and quarrying	25.6	CKYX	84.2	96.8	100.0	103.3	102.1	104.3	108.2	106.9	101.6
Manufacturing											
Food; beverages and tobacco	28.5	CKZA	99.2	101.7	100.0	100.9	103.2	101.5	100.8	99.6	101.2
Textiles and textile products	10.7	CKZB	101.3	103.6	100.0	98.2	95.9	89.0	81.9	78.3	67.3
Leather and leather products	1.5	CKZC	99.1	98.6	100.0	98.6	103.5	89.5	86.6	79.3	79.0
Wood and wood products	3.0	CKZD	100.0	107.8	100.0	98.1	95.5	94.6	89.7	91.7	90.2
Pulp, paper and paper products; publishing and printing	27.5	CKZE	96.0	98.5	100.0	98.0	98.2	98.9	99.1	98.9	97.2
Coke, petroleum products and nuclear fuel	4.6	CKZF	89.0	89.8	100.0	91.8	93.8	88.3	79.4	83.3	79.6
Chemicals, chemical products and man-made fibres	23.9	CKZG	90.4	95.1	100.0	100.6	102.4	104.0	107.4	111.8	116.2
Rubber and plastic products	10.6	CKZH	88.8	97.9	100.0	98.8	98.5	101.6	100.9	99.9	95.7
Other non-metallic mineral products	8.1	CKZI	99.1	102.7	100.0	96.6	99.3	96.9	95.7	95.9	96.5
Basic metals and fabricated metal products	25.2	CKZJ	95.0	97.3	100.0	99.9	101.1	99.2	95.2	95.6	92.7
Machinery and equipment not elsewhere classified	19.2	CKZK	94.6	99.8	100.0	98.0	95.7	95.8	90.1	90.2	91.1
Electrical and optical equipment	27.8	CKZL	83.4	93.5	100.0	104.9	108.1	114.8	126.1	144.5	132.6
Transport equipment	20.4	CKZM	98.1	100.8	100.0	107.7	112.1	118.2	120.2	115.5	112.4
Manufacturing not elsewhere classified	7.6	CKZN	98.6	101.7	100.0	102.0	104.0	105.3	106.6	104.7	103.8
Total manufacturing	218.5	CKYY	94.1	98.5	100.0	100.7	102.0	102.8	103.1	105.2	102.8
Electricity, gas and water supply	24.4	CKYZ	96.8	97.7	100.0	105.1	105.7	107.5	109.4	111.4	114.1
Total production	268.4	CKYW	93.3	98.3	100.0	101.3	102.4	103.4	104.2	105.9	103.7
Construction	51.6	GDQB	96.3	100.0	100.0	102.7	105.7	107.0	107.8	109.7	113.7
Service industries											
Wholesale and retail trade (including motor trade); repair of motor vehicles, personal and household goods	116.6	GDQC	92.8	97.8	100.0	106.1	110.9	115.6	119.3	122.9	127.1
Hotels and restaurants	28.5	GDQD	98.1	100.8	100.0	101.2	101.1	101.8	102.7	100.4	96.6
Transport, storage and communication											
Transport and storage	51.6	GDQF	89.9	96.9	100.0	99.7	104.6	111.3	113.1	117.6	117.1
Communication	28.6	GDQG	83.5	90.5	100.0	112.7	128.9	139.4	157.6	181.5	199.0
Total	80.2	GDQH	87.6	94.6	100.0	104.3	113.3	121.3	129.0	140.4	146.3
Financial intermediation	65.8	GDQI	95.5	96.5	100.0	103.8	109.3	114.2	117.0	121.4	126.0
Adjustment for financial services	−39.4	GDQJ	88.4	92.5	100.0	106.9	116.2	125.0	127.6	135.7	144.4
Real estate, renting and business activities											
Letting of dwellings, including imputed rent of owner occupiers	70.5	GDQL	96.1	97.4	100.0	101.2	103.2	105.8	107.8	108.7	110.2
Other real estate, renting and business activities	115.6	GDQK	84.1	92.8	100.0	107.0	117.5	129.3	135.1	143.6	153.7
Total	186.0	GDQM	88.9	94.5	100.0	104.8	112.1	120.4	124.8	130.4	137.2
Public administration and defence (PAD)	61.0	GDQO	102.5	100.9	100.0	98.8	98.1	98.0	97.8	98.8	100.0
Education	55.5	GDQP	95.0	98.7	100.0	101.3	102.4	102.9	105.2	106.7	108.3
Health and social work	64.7	GDQQ	93.5	95.9	100.0	103.2	106.5	110.2	112.9	114.8	118.3
Other social and personal services, private households with employees and extra-territorial organisations	42.6	GDQR	90.5	96.1	100.0	105.4	107.3	112.7	116.4	121.2	125.9
Total service industries	661.6	GDQS	92.5	96.9	100.0	103.6	108.1	112.9	116.6	120.8	124.8
All industries	1 000.0	CGCE	92.8	97.3	100.0	102.7	106.0	109.5	111.8	115.3	117.2

1 See chapter text. The weights are in proportion to total gross value added in 1995. The GVA for sections L, M, and N in this table follows the SIC(92) and differs from that shown in Table 15.4, which is based on Input- Output groups. Central government expenditure on teachers' pay is included in Education in Table 15.5 but in PAD in Table 15.4. The administration costs of the NHS are included in PAD in Table 15.5 but are included in Health and social work in Table 15.4.

2 The output analysis of gross value added is estimated in terms of change and expressed in index number form. It is therefore inappropriate to show as a statistical adjustment any divergence of an output measure of GDP derived from it from other measures of GDP. Such an adjustment does, however, exist implicitly.

3 See footnote 2 to Table 15.4.

Source: Office for National Statistics: 020 7533 6031

15.6 Non-financial corporations[1]
Allocation of primary income account
ESA95 sector S.11

£ million

		1993	1994	1995	1996	1997	1998	1999	2000	2001
ALLOCATION OF PRIMARY INCOME ACCOUNT before deduction of fixed capital consumption										
Resources										
Operating surplus, gross	NQBE	124 470	142 148	153 152	168 601	178 629	184 477	187 129	195 901	196 843
Property income, received										
Interest	EABC	7 596	7 566	9 337	9 660	9 874	13 940	10 978	14 105	14 143
Distributed income of corporations	EABD	14 281	16 446	22 367	22 919	26 548	25 086	21 501	26 631	36 868
Reinvested earnings on direct foreign investment	HDVR	7 748	12 138	11 376	13 417	11 747	10 979	16 214	20 036	18 619
Attributed property income of insurance policy-holders	FAOF	470	338	395	423	386	463	338	489	280
Rent	FAOG	106	108	110	114	118	118	117	117	117
Total	FAKY	30 201	36 596	43 585	46 533	48 673	50 586	49 148	61 378	70 027
Total resources	FBXJ	154 671	178 744	196 737	215 134	227 302	235 063	236 277	257 279	266 870
Uses										
Property income, paid										
Interest	EABG	23 247	23 243	26 575	26 047	27 738	33 025	33 217	39 548	39 949
Distributed income of corporations	NVCS	53 461	60 304	71 532	76 136	80 805	78 299	87 100	83 202	100 810
Reinvested earnings on direct foreign investment	HDVB	2 004	4 310	4 662	6 117	5 187	3 117	2 776	7 258	8 061
Rent	FBXO	734	693	719	815	756	584	564	1 319	1 896
Total	FBXK	79 446	88 550	103 488	109 115	114 486	115 025	123 657	131 327	150 716
Balance of primary incomes, gross	NQBG	**75 225**	**90 194**	**93 249**	**106 019**	**112 816**	**120 038**	**112 620**	**125 952**	**116 154**
Total uses	FBXJ	154 671	178 744	196 737	215 134	227 302	235 063	236 277	257 279	266 870
After deduction of fixed capital consumption	-DBGF	-55 907	-56 632	-57 527	-58 526	-60 356	-60 844	-62 119	-65 833	-69 071
Balance of primary incomes, net	FBXQ	19 318	33 562	35 722	47 493	52 460	59 194	50 501	60 119	47 083

1 See chapter text.   *Source: Office for National Statistics: 020 7533 6031*

15.7 Non-financial corporations[1]
Secondary distribution of income account
ESA95 sector S.11

£ million

		1993	1994	1995	1996	1997	1998	1999	2000	2001
Resources										
Balance of primary incomes, gross	NQBG	**75 225**	**90 194**	**93 249**	**106 019**	**112 816**	**120 038**	**112 620**	**125 952**	**116 154**
Social contributions										
Imputed social contributions	NSTJ	2 966	2 884	3 329	3 209	3 173	3 801	3 983	4 504	5 191
Current transfers other than taxes, social contributions and benefits										
Non-life insurance claims	FCBP	6 044	4 031	4 716	5 508	4 190	4 849	4 151	4 456	4 565
Miscellaneous transfers	NRJY	256	420	494	537	557	595	611	622	619
Total	NRJB	6 300	4 451	5 210	6 045	4 747	5 444	4 762	5 078	5 184
Total resources	FCBR	84 491	97 529	101 788	115 273	120 736	129 283	121 365	135 534	126 529
Uses										
Current taxes on income, wealth etc.										
Taxes on income	FCBS	13 536	15 234	19 005	22 417	27 557	25 590	23 090	26 464	26 134
Social benefits other than social transfers in kind	NSTJ	2 966	2 884	3 329	3 209	3 173	3 801	3 983	4 504	5 191
Current transfers other than taxes, social contributions and benefits										
Net non-life insurance premiums	FCBY	6 044	4 031	4 716	5 508	4 190	4 849	4 151	4 456	4 565
Miscellaneous current transfers	FDBI	272	311	343	1 455	402	363	373	393	411
Total, other current transfers	FCBX	6 316	4 342	5 059	6 963	4 592	5 212	4 524	4 849	4 976
Gross Disposable Income	NRJD	**61 673**	**75 069**	**74 395**	**82 684**	**85 414**	**94 680**	**89 768**	**99 717**	**90 228**
Total uses	FCBR	84 491	97 529	101 788	115 273	120 736	129 283	121 365	135 534	126 529
After deduction of fixed capital consumption	-DBGF	-55 907	-56 632	-57 527	-58 526	-60 356	-60 844	-62 119	-65 833	-69 071
Disposable income, net	FCCF	5 766	18 437	16 868	24 158	25 058	33 836	27 649	33 884	21 157

1 See chapter text.   *Source: Office for National Statistics: 020 7533 6031*

15.8 General government[1]
Allocation of primary income account
ESA95 sector S.13 Unconsolidated

£ million

		1993	1994	1995	1996	1997	1998	1999	2000	2001
Resources										
Operating surplus, gross	NMXV	5 870	5 991	6 447	6 876	7 316	7 534	7 707	7 929	8 257
Taxes on production and imports, received										
Taxes on products										
Value added tax (VAT)	NZGF	37 958	42 996	43 579	46 918	52 057	52 827	58 313	60 713	64 506
Taxes and duties on imports excluding VAT										
Import duties	NMXZ	–	–	–	–	–	–	–	–	–
Taxes on imports excluding VAT and import duties	NMBT	–	–	–	–	–	–	–	–	–
Taxes on products excluding VAT and import duties	NMYB	28 586	31 218	35 482	37 380	40 621	44 815	48 442	51 956	50 318
Total taxes on products	NVCC	66 544	74 214	79 061	84 298	92 678	97 642	106 755	112 669	114 824
Other taxes on production	NMYD	15 066	14 721	15 214	15 929	16 686	17 287	17 656	18 481	19 948
Total taxes on production and imports, received	NMYE	81 610	88 935	94 275	100 227	109 364	114 929	124 411	131 150	134 641
less Subsidies, paid										
Subsidies on products	-NMYF	–4 403	–4 976	–5 013	–5 845	–5 114	–4 304	–3 132	–4 391	–4 741
Other subsidies on production	-LIUF	–915	–741	–765	–728	–711	–745	–575	–498	–874
Total	-NMRL	–5 318	–5 717	–5 778	–6 573	–5 825	–5 049	–3 707	–4 889	–6 224
Property income, received										
Total Interest	NMYL	7 996	8 385	8 553	9 031	8 575	9 236	9 352	9 316	8 918
Distributed income of corporations	NMYM	6 601	6 754	6 915	6 882	6 527	7 450	7 101	7 161	7 541
Property income attributed to insurance policy holders	NMYO	28	30	32	28	33	48	33	48	28
Rent										
from sectors other than general government	NMYR	699	658	684	780	721	547	528	1 283	1 859
Total	NMYU	15 324	15 827	16 184	16 721	15 856	17 281	17 014	17 808	18 346
Total resources	NMYV	97 486	105 036	111 128	117 251	126 711	134 695	145 425	151 998	155 760
Uses										
Property income, paid										
Total interest	NRKB	24 056	26 804	30 077	31 905	33 809	34 874	30 649	30 617	28 027
Total	NMYY	24 056	26 804	30 077	31 905	33 809	34 874	30 649	30 617	28 027
Balance of primary incomes, gross	NMZH	**73 430**	**78 232**	**81 051**	**85 346**	**92 902**	**99 821**	**114 776**	**121 381**	**127 733**
Total uses	NMYV	97 486	105 036	111 128	117 251	126 711	134 695	145 425	151 998	155 760
After deduction of fixed capital consumption	-NMXO	–5 870	–5 991	–6 447	–6 876	–7 316	–7 534	–7 707	–7 929	–8 257
Balance of primary incomes, net	NMZI	67 560	72 241	74 604	78 470	85 586	92 287	107 069	113 452	119 476

1 See chapter text.

Source: Office for National Statistics: 020 7533 6031

15.9 General government[1]
Secondary distribution of income account
ESA95 sector S.13 Unconsolidated

£ million

		1993	1994	1995	1996	1997	1998	1999	2000	2001
Resources										
Balance of primary incomes, gross	NMZH	73 430	78 232	81 051	85 346	92 902	99 821	114 776	121 381	127 733
Current taxes on income, wealth etc.										
Taxes on income	NMZJ	78 313	85 348	95 042	99 310	107 647	124 060	129 483	140 153	147 504
Other current taxes	NVCM	10 551	11 140	11 937	12 795	13 820	14 993	16 197	17 225	18 103
Total	NMZL	88 864	96 488	106 979	112 105	121 467	139 053	145 680	157 378	165 607
Social contributions										
Actual social contributions										
Employers' actual social contributions	NMZM	24 670	24 913	25 917	27 344	29 038	31 391	32 164	36 086	38 147
Employees' social contributions	NMZN	17 235	19 649	21 091	21 700	24 121	25 690	25 893	27 745	29 402
Social contributions by self- and non-employed persons	NMZO	1 472	1 469	1 541	1 771	1 848	1 760	1 784	2 006	2 255
Total	NMZP	43 377	46 031	48 549	50 815	55 007	58 841	59 841	65 837	69 804
Imputed social contributions	NMZQ	5 396	5 419	5 279	5 299	5 356	5 880	5 823	5 935	6 318
Total	NMZR	48 773	51 450	53 828	56 114	60 363	64 721	65 664	71 772	76 122
Other current transfers										
Non-life insurance claims	NMZS	361	363	377	371	349	499	410	440	448
Current transfers within general government	NMZT	55 891	57 736	58 587	59 458	59 506	60 421	64 775	66 416	71 753
Current international cooperation	NMZU	2 558	1 752	1 233	2 424	1 739	1 384	3 176	2 084	4 561
Miscellaneous current transfers from sectors other than general government	NMZX	296	414	461	420	468	382	259	280	−27
Other current transfers	NNAA	59 106	60 265	60 658	62 673	62 062	62 686	68 620	69 220	76 735
Total resources	NNAB	270 173	286 435	302 516	316 238	336 794	366 281	394 740	419 751	446 197
Uses										
Social benefits other than social transfers in kind	NNAD	102 965	106 295	110 409	113 124	116 934	117 549	120 806	126 258	137 060
Other current transfers										
Net non-life insurance premiums	NNAE	361	363	377	371	349	499	410	440	448
Current transfers within general government	NNAF	55 891	57 736	58 587	59 458	59 506	60 421	64 775	66 416	71 753
Current international cooperation	NNAG	1 961	2 007	2 224	1 814	1 700	1 705	1 667	2 418	2 253
Miscellaneous current transfers to sectors other than general government	NNAI	8 467	10 440	10 614	12 549	13 916	15 803	17 280	18 602	19 225
Of which: GNP based fourth own resource	NMFH	1 558	2 071	1 826	2 454	2 458	3 920	4 632	4 379	3 858
Other current transfers	NNAN	66 680	70 546	71 802	74 192	75 471	78 428	84 132	87 876	93 344
Gross Disposable Income	NNAO	100 528	109 594	120 305	128 922	144 389	170 304	189 802	205 617	215 793
Total uses	NNAB	270 173	286 435	302 516	316 238	336 794	366 281	394 740	419 751	446 197
After deduction of fixed capital consumption	−NMXO	−5 870	−5 991	−6 447	−6 876	−7 316	−7 534	−7 707	−7 929	−8 257
Disposable income, net	NNAP	94 658	103 603	113 858	122 046	137 073	162 770	182 095	197 688	207 536

1 See chapter text.

Source: Office for National Statistics: 020 7533 6031

15.10

Households and non-profit institutions serving households[1]
Allocation of primary income account
ESA95 sectors S.14 and S.15

£ million

		1993	1994	1995	1996	1997	1998	1999	2000	2001
ALLOCATION OF PRIMARY INCOME ACCOUNT before deduction of fixed capital consumption										
Resources										
Operating surplus, gross	QWLS	33 026	35 354	38 165	40 160	43 147	48 023	52 161	55 050	59 104
Mixed income, gross	QWLT	42 340	44 319	46 647	49 011	50 461	50 537	54 116	57 440	60 073
Compensation of employees										
Wages and salaries	QWLW	311 615	322 179	336 973	352 285	376 926	403 121	426 569	451 242	477 746
Employers' social contributions	QWLX	46 082	47 296	49 449	53 277	56 117	61 927	66 356	73 791	78 805
Total	QWLY	357 697	369 475	386 422	405 562	433 043	465 048	492 925	525 033	556 551
Property income										
Interest	QWLZ	23 503	22 240	26 454	23 826	26 585	30 081	24 221	28 404	27 100
Distributed income of corporations	QWMA	25 225	28 582	32 544	33 777	37 164	37 613	39 388	41 714	45 581
Attributed property income of insurance policy holders	QWMC	35 437	37 301	42 358	47 807	52 144	55 587	54 774	55 463	59 645
Rent	QWMD	96	97	99	103	105	105	105	105	105
Total	QWME	84 261	88 220	101 455	105 513	115 998	123 386	118 488	125 686	132 431
Total resources	QWMF	517 324	537 368	572 689	600 246	642 649	686 994	717 690	763 209	808 159
Uses										
Property income										
Interest	QWMG	36 235	36 965	40 288	38 442	42 042	51 513	47 682	53 206	53 590
Rent	QWMH	195	198	202	210	216	216	215	215	215
Total	QWMI	36 430	37 163	40 490	38 652	42 258	51 729	47 897	53 421	53 805
Balance of primary incomes, gross	QWMJ	**480 894**	**500 205**	**532 199**	**561 594**	**600 391**	**635 265**	**669 793**	**709 788**	**754 354**
Total uses	QWMF	517 324	537 368	572 689	600 246	642 649	686 994	717 690	763 209	808 159
After deduction of fixed capital consumption	-QWLL	-17 143	-18 049	-18 922	-20 255	-21 957	-23 602	-25 868	-28 094	-30 291
Balance of primary incomes, net	QWMK	463 751	482 156	513 277	541 339	578 434	611 663	643 925	681 694	724 063

1 See chapter text.

Source: Office for National Statistics: 020 7533 6031

15.11

Households and non-profit institutions serving households[1]
Secondary distribution of income account

ESA95 sectors S.14 and S.15

£ million

		1993	1994	1995	1996	1997	1998	1999	2000	2001
Resources										
Balance of primary incomes, gross	QWMJ	**480 894**	**500 205**	**532 199**	**561 594**	**600 391**	**635 265**	**669 793**	**709 788**	**754 354**
Imputed social contributions	RVFH	438	425	455	429	410	478	450	373	405
Social benefits other than social transfers in kind	QWML	136 084	142 229	149 151	156 612	165 695	170 931	179 126	189 890	201 170
Other current transfers										
Non-life insurance claims	QWMM	12 496	13 272	14 123	19 360	14 004	15 224	13 762	14 905	15 212
Miscellaneous current transfers	QWMN	15 481	17 013	17 722	20 027	20 478	21 146	22 031	24 142	24 807
Total	QWMO	27 977	30 285	31 845	39 387	34 482	36 370	35 793	39 047	40 019
Total resources	QWMP	645 393	673 144	713 650	758 022	800 978	843 044	885 162	939 098	995 948
Uses										
Current taxes on income, wealth etc										
Taxes on income	QWMQ	65 153	69 530	74 590	75 137	75 914	91 076	96 263	105 396	111 928
Other current taxes	NVCO	10 551	11 140	11 937	12 795	13 820	14 993	16 197	17 225	18 103
Total	QWMS	75 704	80 670	86 527	87 932	89 734	106 069	112 460	122 621	130 031
Social contributions										
Actual social contributions										
Employers' actual social contributions	QWMT	36 850	38 146	39 934	43 916	46 773	51 297	55 652	62 489	66 407
Employees' social contributions	QWMU	45 415	49 615	53 747	59 900	66 890	71 182	71 553	73 784	72 182
Social contributions by self and non-employed	QWMV	1 472	1 469	1 541	1 771	1 848	1 760	1 784	2 006	2 255
Total	QWMW	83 737	89 230	95 222	105 587	115 511	124 239	128 989	138 279	140 844
Imputed social contributions	QWMX	9 232	9 150	9 515	9 361	9 344	10 630	10 704	11 302	12 398
Total	QWMY	92 969	98 380	104 737	114 948	124 855	134 869	139 693	149 581	153 242
Social benefits other than social transfers in kind	QWMZ	897	880	925	899	880	950	922	845	880
Other current transfers										
Net non-life insurance premiums	QWNA	12 496	13 272	14 123	19 360	14 004	15 224	13 762	14 905	15 212
Miscellaneous current transfers	QWNB	7 618	8 108	8 279	8 190	9 059	9 293	9 616	10 273	10 181
Total	QWNC	20 114	21 380	22 402	27 550	23 063	24 517	23 378	25 178	25 393
Gross Disposable Income	QWND	**455 709**	**471 834**	**499 059**	**526 693**	**562 446**	**576 639**	**608 709**	**640 873**	**686 402**
Total uses	QWMP	645 393	673 144	713 650	758 022	800 978	843 044	885 162	939 098	995 948
After deduction of fixed capital consumption	-QWLL	-17 143	-18 049	-18 922	-20 255	-21 957	-23 602	-25 868	-28 094	-30 291
Disposable income, net	QWNE	438 566	453 785	480 137	506 438	540 489	553 037	582 841	612 779	656 111

1 See chapter text.

Source: Office for National Statistics: 020 7533 6031

15.12 Households and non-profit institutions serving households[1]
Use of disposable income account

£ million

		1993	1994	1995	1996	1997	1998	1999	2000	2001
Resources										
Disposable income, gross	QWND	455 709	471 834	499 059	526 693	562 446	576 639	608 709	640 873	686 402
Adjustment for the change in net equity of households in pension funds	NSSE	10 742	10 577	11 690	14 824	15 131	16 105	15 027	13 455	12 219
Total resources	NSSF	466 451	482 411	510 749	541 517	577 577	592 744	623 736	654 328	697 762
Uses										
Final consumption expenditure Individual consumption expenditure	NSSG	415 951	437 684	459 848	492 185	522 976	557 352	591 631	626 584	655 265
Saving, gross	NSSH	50 500	44 727	50 901	49 332	54 601	35 392	32 105	27 744	43 356
Total uses	NSSF	466 451	482 411	510 749	541 517	577 577	592 744	623 736	654 328	697 762
Saving ratio (per cent)	RVGL	10.8	9.3	10.0	9.1	9.5	6.0	5.1	4.2	6.2

1 See chapter text.

Source: Office for National Statistics: 020 7533 6031

15.13 The sector accounts: Key economic indicators[1]

£ million

		1993	1994	1995	1996	1997	1998	1999	2000	2001
Net lending/borrowing by:										
Non-financial corporations	EABO	4 099	12 941	4 276	6 957	−2 192	−3 921	−13 361	−3 986	−10 919
Financial corporations	NHCQ	4 202	4 473	2 814	−2 086	−4 298	−5 231	−11 917	−21 421	−23 269
General government	NNBK	−50 823	−45 835	−41 438	−33 662	−17 723	1 992	10 322	15 629	7 668
Households and NPISH's	NSSZ	30 912	21 686	25 866	20 818	23 297	2 819	−3 830	−7 607	6 598
Rest of the world	NHRB	11 610	6 735	8 482	7 973	916	4 341	18 786	17 385	18 954
Private non-financial corporations										
Gross trading profits Continental shelf profits	CAGJ	9 375	10 776	12 124	15 702	13 978	11 696	13 864	21 458	20 397
Others	CAED	100 167	117 450	125 151	133 508	145 693	150 975	154 154	154 855	152 454
Rental of buildings	FCBW	9 132	8 641	9 379	9 493	9 561	10 837	11 435	12 510	12 999
less Holding gains of inventories	−DLQZ	−2 392	−3 830	−4 489	−958	−361	753	−1 801	−2 059	1 605
Gross operating surplus	NRJK	116 282	133 037	142 165	157 745	168 871	174 261	177 652	186 764	187 455
Households and NPISH										
Household gross disposable income	QWND	455 709	471 834	499 059	526 693	562 446	576 639	608 709	640 873	686 402
Implied deflator of household and NPISH individual consumption expenditure index 1995=100[2]	YBFS	95.2	97.0	100.0	103.1	105.5	108.3	110.1	110.9	111.4
Real household disposable income: £ million at 1995 prices	RVGK	478 766	486 458	499 059	510 926	533 211	532 300	552 975	578 156	616 250
Index 1995=100	OSXR	95.9	97.5	100.0	102.4	106.8	106.7	110.8	115.8	123.5
Gross saving	NSSH	50 500	44 727	50 901	49 332	54 601	35 392	32 105	27 744	43 356
Households total resources	NSSJ	541 000	559 956	591 842	626 485	665 128	685 015	724 510	762 187	816 562
Saving ratio, per cent	RVGL	10.8	9.3	10.0	9.1	9.5	6.0	5.1	4.2	6.2

1 See chapter text.
2 Rounded to one decimal place

Source: Office for National Statistics: 020 7533 6031

15.14 Household final consumption expenditure: classified by purpose[1]
At current market prices

£ million

		1993	1994	1995	1996	1997	1998	1999	2000	2001
FINAL CONSUMPTION EXPENDITURE OF HOUSEHOLDS										
Durable goods										
Furnishings, household equipment and routine maintenance of the house	LLIJ	11 995	12 776	13 508	14 321	15 250	15 873	16 566	17 648	18 865
Health	LLIK	1 139	1 432	1 401	1 453	1 549	1 717	1 878	2 057	2 159
Transport	LLIL	20 847	22 657	23 588	26 469	29 444	30 851	31 734	32 618	35 488
Communication	LLIM	262	291	244	276	282	440	512	542	580
Recreation and culture	LLIN	8 249	8 332	9 388	10 592	11 920	12 853	14 262	15 281	15 991
Miscellaneous goods and services	LLIO	2 788	2 787	2 963	3 094	3 295	3 320	3 398	3 479	3 451
Total durable goods	UTIA	45 280	48 275	51 092	56 205	61 740	65 054	68 350	71 625	76 534
Semi-durable goods										
Clothing and footwear	LLJL	24 344	26 314	27 426	28 865	30 270	31 540	32 561	34 334	36 796
Furnishings, household equipment and routine maintenance of the house	LLJM	7 355	7 758	7 990	8 429	9 091	9 751	10 529	11 414	12 079
Transport	LLJN	1 994	2 022	2 165	2 293	2 529	2 925	2 983	2 759	2 607
Recreation and culture	LLJO	9 847	10 909	11 770	12 887	14 724	17 292	18 910	20 926	22 157
Miscellaneous goods and services	LLJP	1 312	1 406	1 497	1 581	1 700	1 816	1 926	2 032	2 103
Total semi-durable goods	UTIQ	44 852	48 409	50 848	54 055	58 314	63 324	66 909	71 465	75 742
Non-durable goods										
Food & drink	ABZV	47 171	47 855	49 790	53 025	53 832	55 192	56 625	57 719	60 262
Alcohol & tobacco	ADFL	17 697	18 359	18 776	20 381	21 420	22 376	24 276	24 916	25 361
Housing, water, electricity, gas and other fuels	LLIX	20 339	20 876	21 357	22 757	22 656	22 094	21 800	22 542	22 753
Furnishings, household equipment and routine maintenance of the house	LLIY	2 410	2 387	2 374	2 433	2 495	2 505	2 657	2 703	2 736
Health	LLIZ	2 209	2 362	2 518	2 746	2 828	2 975	3 084	3 160	3 265
Transport	LLJA	11 525	11 968	11 986	12 767	13 818	14 396	15 200	16 717	15 395
Recreation and culture	LLJB	9 102	9 920	10 408	11 192	11 788	12 136	12 526	13 013	13 004
Miscellaneous goods and services	LLJC	5 767	6 464	7 257	8 014	8 383	8 727	9 121	9 626	10 009
Total non-durable goods	UTII	116 220	120 191	124 466	133 315	137 220	140 401	145 289	150 396	152 785
Total goods	UTIE	206 352	216 875	226 406	243 575	257 274	268 779	280 548	293 486	305 061
Services										
Clothing and footwear	LLJD	543	547	604	620	631	698	714	742	559
Housing, water, electricity, gas and other fuels	LLJE	53 551	56 502	60 055	63 173	67 558	74 103	79 911	84 871	89 964
Furnishings, household equipment and routine maintenance of the house	LLJF	2 049	2 258	2 415	2 545	2 686	2 873	3 048	3 384	3 514
Health	LLJG	2 639	2 874	2 916	3 048	3 189	3 389	3 531	3 654	4 032
Transport	LLJH	22 305	23 323	24 994	26 929	29 667	32 115	33 738	36 185	38 314
Communication	LLJI	7 611	8 352	8 823	9 083	9 732	10 607	11 493	12 757	13 247
Recreation and culture	LLJJ	15 479	16 391	19 509	20 737	21 539	22 967	23 747	24 683	25 602
Education	ADIE	5 182	5 487	6 197	6 405	7 440	7 814	8 943	9 634	10 012
Restaurants and hotels	ADIF	46 170	48 394	50 383	54 395	56 960	61 144	64 459	68 426	70 686
Miscellaneous goods and services	LLJK	38 946	39 496	40 612	42 951	45 793	49 377	53 971	58 786	59 976
Total services	UTIM	194 475	203 624	216 508	229 886	245 195	265 087	283 555	303 122	315 906
Final consumption expenditure in the UK by resident and non-resident households (domestic concept)	ABQI	400 827	420 499	442 914	473 461	502 469	533 866	564 103	596 608	620 967
Final consumption expenditure outside the UK by UK resident households	ABTA	11 890	13 058	13 721	14 377	14 942	16 913	19 690	21 662	22 948
Less Final consumption expenditure in the UK by households resident in the rest of the world	CDFD	−10 747	−11 160	−13 268	−14 038	−14 037	−14 544	−14 312	−14 713	−12 905
Final consumption expenditure by UK resident households in the UK and abroad (national concept)	ABPB	401 970	422 397	443 367	473 800	503 374	536 235	569 481	603 557	631 010

1 See chapter text. Additional detail is published in *Consumer Trends* and table A7 of *UK Economic Accounts*, available from the ONS website (http//:www. statistics.gov.uk/products/p242.asp).

Source: Office for National Statistics: 020 7533 6031

15.15 Household final consumption expenditure: classified by purpose[1]
At 1995 market prices

£ million at 1995 prices

		1993	1994	1995	1996	1997	1998	1999	2000	2001
FINAL CONSUMPTION EXPENDITURE OF HOUSEHOLDS										
Durable goods										
Furnishings, household equipment and routine maintenance of the house	LLME	12 341	13 255	13 508	13 815	14 545	14 962	15 563	16 781	17 822
Health	LLMF	1 351	1 616	1 401	1 313	1 259	1 195	1 120	1 093	1 041
Transport	LLMG	21 878	23 192	23 588	25 664	27 493	28 845	30 289	32 264	36 288
Communication	LLMH	248	283	244	280	319	532	708	804	884
Recreation and culture	LLMI	7 754	8 096	9 388	10 640	12 220	14 630	18 651	22 383	26 807
Miscellaneous goods and services	LLMJ	2 969	2 833	2 963	3 053	3 223	3 148	3 119	3 112	3 173
Total durable goods	UTIC	46 614	49 275	51 092	54 765	59 059	63 312	69 450	76 437	86 015
Semi-durable goods										
Clothing and footwear	LLNG	24 351	26 315	27 426	29 072	30 300	31 656	33 661	36 969	41 540
Furnishings, household equipment and routine maintenance of the house	LLNH	7 484	7 866	7 990	8 318	8 928	9 493	10 307	11 414	12 126
Transport	LLNI	2 018	2 041	2 165	2 193	2 349	2 649	2 649	2 423	2 317
Recreation and culture	LLNJ	9 865	10 941	11 770	12 658	14 371	16 736	18 923	21 750	23 144
Miscellaneous goods and services	LLNK	1 276	1 380	1 497	1 606	1 735	1 844	1 956	2 088	2 147
Total semi-durable goods	UTIS	44 981	48 543	50 848	53 847	57 683	62 378	67 496	74 644	81 274
Non-durable goods										
Food & drink	ADIP	49 262	49 744	49 790	51 405	52 347	52 983	54 102	55 610	56 135
Alcohol & tobacco	ADIS	19 255	19 268	18 776	19 449	19 695	19 553	20 203	20 164	20 171
Housing, water, electricity, gas and other fuels	LLMS	21 602	21 462	21 357	22 440	22 602	22 418	22 134	22 953	23 116
Furnishings, household equipment and routine maintenance of the house	LLMT	2 432	2 443	2 374	2 413	2 521	2 478	2 586	2 671	2 728
Health	LLMU	2 401	2 467	2 518	2 637	2 619	2 677	2 711	2 718	2 744
Transport	LLMV	12 484	12 437	11 986	12 262	12 204	12 165	11 926	11 646	11 315
Recreation and culture	LLMW	9 502	10 335	10 408	10 681	11 053	11 137	11 287	11 416	11 231
Miscellaneous goods and services	LLMX	6 128	6 809	7 257	7 695	7 763	7 643	7 849	8 501	8 786
Total non-durable goods	UTIK	123 050	124 965	124 466	128 982	130 804	131 054	132 798	135 679	136 226
Total goods	UTIG	214 323	222 783	226 406	237 594	247 546	256 744	269 744	286 760	303 515
Services										
Clothing and footwear	LLMY	585	569	604	601	589	620	604	615	451
Housing, water, electricity, gas and other fuels	LLMZ	59 241	59 280	60 055	60 737	61 592	62 429	63 061	64 041	64 575
Furnishings, household equipment and routine maintenance of the house	LLNA	2 175	2 334	2 415	2 445	2 473	2 510	2 526	2 615	2 564
Health	LLNB	2 877	3 013	2 916	2 916	2 932	2 952	2 926	2 898	3 105
Transport	LLNC	23 369	23 913	24 994	25 922	27 210	28 363	29 691	30 346	31 093
Communication	LLND	6 932	8 022	8 823	9 266	10 158	11 204	12 438	14 382	16 232
Recreation and culture	LLNE	16 471	17 007	19 509	20 147	20 281	20 889	20 928	21 208	21 969
Education	ADMJ	5 856	5 763	6 197	6 147	6 793	6 756	7 310	7 448	7 299
Restaurants and hotels	ADMK	49 267	50 211	50 383	52 648	53 225	54 556	55 194	56 139	55 522
Miscellaneous goods and services	LLNF	41 431	40 422	40 612	41 918	42 820	43 679	45 714	47 941	47 577
Total services	UTIO	207 794	210 534	216 508	222 747	228 073	233 958	240 392	247 633	250 387
Final consumption expenditure in the UK by resident and non-resident households (domestic concept)	ABQJ	421 707	433 317	442 914	460 341	475 619	490 702	510 136	534 393	553 902
Final consumption expenditure outside the UK by UK resident households	ABTC	12 093	13 490	13 721	14 077	16 357	18 813	21 837	24 118	24 877
Less Final consumption expenditure in the UK by households resident in the rest of the world	CCHX	−11 524	−11 457	−13 268	−13 658	−13 238	−13 284	−12 751	−12 760	−10 882
Final consumption expenditure by UK resident households in the UK and abroad (national concept)	ABPF	422 273	435 350	443 367	460 760	478 738	496 231	519 222	545 751	567 897

1 See chapter text. Additional detail is published in *Consumer Trends* and table A7 of *UK Economic Accounts*, available from the ONS website (http//:www.statistics.gov.uk/products/p242.asp).

Source: *Office for National Statistics: 020 7533 6031*

15.16 Individual consumption expenditure at current market prices by households, non-profit institutions serving households and general government[1]

Classified by function (COICOP/COPNI/COFOG)[2]

£ million

		1993	1994	1995	1996	1997	1998	1999	2000	2001
FINAL CONSUMPTION EXPENDITURE OF HOUSEHOLDS										
Food and non-alcoholic beverages	ABZV	47 171	47 855	49 790	53 025	53 832	55 192	56 625	57 719	60 262
Food	ABZW	42 133	42 665	44 324	47 323	47 996	49 134	50 304	51 051	52 717
Non-alcoholic beverages	ADFK	5 038	5 190	5 466	5 702	5 836	6 058	6 321	6 668	7 545
Alcoholic beverages and tobacco	ADFL	17 697	18 359	18 776	20 381	21 420	22 376	24 276	24 916	25 361
Alcoholic beverages	ADFM	6 938	7 426	7 257	8 116	8 772	9 013	9 984	10 385	10 627
Tobacco	ADFN	10 759	10 933	11 519	12 265	12 648	13 363	14 292	14 531	14 734
Clothing and footwear	ADFP	24 887	26 861	28 030	29 485	30 901	32 238	33 275	35 076	37 355
Clothing	ADFQ	20 853	22 587	23 711	25 158	26 500	27 799	28 932	30 640	32 594
Footwear	ADFR	4 034	4 274	4 319	4 327	4 401	4 439	4 343	4 436	4 761
Housing, water, electricity, gas and other fuels	ADFS	73 890	77 378	81 412	85 930	90 214	96 197	101 711	107 413	112 717
Actual rentals for housing	ADFT	16 222	17 379	17 906	18 784	19 821	21 155	22 584	24 239	25 219
Imputed rentals for housing	ADFU	32 546	34 591	37 479	39 548	42 426	47 336	51 503	54 433	58 399
Maintenance and repair of the dwelling	ADFV	6 836	6 458	6 526	6 943	7 920	8 396	8 650	9 281	9 430
Water supply and miscellaneous dwelling services	ADFW	3 667	4 051	4 290	4 558	4 772	4 961	5 201	4 928	5 004
Electricity, gas and other fuels	ADFX	14 619	14 899	15 211	16 097	15 275	14 349	13 773	14 532	14 665
Furnishings, household equipment and routine maintenance of the house	ADFY	23 809	25 179	26 287	27 728	29 522	31 002	32 800	35 149	37 194
Furniture, furnishings, carpets and other floor coverings	ADFZ	8 459	9 287	9 843	10 471	11 072	11 667	12 437	13 359	14 239
Household textiles	ADGG	2 802	2 843	3 020	3 227	3 404	3 676	3 972	4 292	4 528
Household appliances	ADGL	4 177	4 195	4 405	4 609	4 997	5 080	5 038	5 268	5 319
Glassware, tableware and household utensils	ADGM	2 554	2 751	2 767	2 887	3 159	3 410	3 722	4 059	4 360
Tools and equipment for house and garden	ADGN	1 773	1 889	1 911	1 998	2 179	2 332	2 538	2 788	3 098
Goods and services for routine household maintenance	ADGO	4 044	4 214	4 341	4 536	4 711	4 837	5 093	5 383	5 650
Health	ADGP	5 987	6 668	6 835	7 247	7 566	8 081	8 493	8 871	9 456
Medical products, appliances and equipment	ADGQ	3 348	3 794	3 919	4 199	4 377	4 692	4 962	5 217	5 424
Out-patient services	ADGR	1 586	1 754	1 781	1 825	1 893	2 005	2 091	2 125	2 490
Hospital services	ADGS	1 053	1 120	1 135	1 223	1 296	1 384	1 440	1 529	1 542
Transport	ADGT	56 671	59 970	62 733	68 458	75 458	80 287	83 655	88 279	91 804
Purchase of vehicles	ADGU	20 847	22 657	23 588	26 469	29 444	30 851	31 734	32 618	35 488
Operation of personal transport equipment	ADGV	22 362	22 977	23 861	25 556	28 044	29 826	31 122	33 232	33 047
Transport services	ADGW	13 462	14 336	15 284	16 433	17 970	19 610	20 799	22 429	23 269
Communication	ADGX	7 873	8 643	9 067	9 359	10 014	11 047	12 005	13 299	13 827
Postal services	CDEF	916	961	967	960	951	1 064	899	848	723
Telephone & telefax equipment	ADWO	262	291	244	276	282	440	512	542	580
Telephone & telefax services	ADWP	6 695	7 391	7 856	8 123	8 781	9 543	10 594	11 909	12 524
Recreation and culture	ADGY	42 677	45 552	51 075	55 408	59 971	65 248	69 445	73 903	76 754
Audio-visual, photographic and information processing equipment	ADGZ	9 633	9 620	10 862	11 974	13 501	15 032	16 232	17 393	18 405
Other major durables for recreation and culture	ADHL	1 617	1 818	2 133	2 548	2 854	3 089	3 582	4 049	4 212
Other recreational items and equipment; flowers, garden and pets	ADHZ	9 710	10 646	11 284	12 758	14 488	16 237	17 630	19 115	19 913
Recreational and cultural services	ADIA	14 265	15 251	18 241	19 246	20 005	21 357	22 118	23 033	23 897
Newspapers, books and stationery	ADIC	7 452	8 217	8 555	8 882	9 123	9 533	9 883	10 313	10 327
Package holidays[3]	ADID	–	–	–	–	–	–	–	–	–
Education										
Education services	ADIE	5 182	5 487	6 197	6 405	7 440	7 814	8 943	9 634	10 012
Restaurants and hotels	ADIF	46 170	48 394	50 383	54 395	56 960	61 144	64 459	68 426	70 686
Catering services	ADIG	39 327	41 040	42 182	45 766	48 026	52 008	55 316	59 085	61 849
Accommodation services	ADIH	6 843	7 354	8 201	8 629	8 934	9 136	9 143	9 341	8 837
Miscellaneous goods and services	ADII	48 813	50 153	52 329	55 640	59 171	63 240	68 416	73 923	75 539
Personal care	ADIJ	8 526	9 353	10 378	11 361	11 887	12 574	13 229	14 032	14 397
Personal effects not elsewhere classified	ADIK	3 615	3 657	3 898	4 083	4 351	4 490	4 673	4 860	4 904
Social protection	ADIL	8 430	8 413	8 187	8 220	8 241	8 332	8 446	8 824	9 418
Insurance	ADIM	16 477	16 408	16 306	16 520	17 841	19 513	21 789	23 613	24 409
Financial services not elsewhere classified	ADIN	5 326	5 705	5 853	6 966	7 935	8 582	9 856	11 554	11 021
Other services not elsewhere classified	ADIO	6 439	6 617	7 707	8 490	8 916	9 749	10 423	11 040	11 390
Final consumption expenditure in the UK by resident and non-resident households (domestic concept)	ABQI	400 827	420 499	442 914	473 461	502 469	533 866	564 103	596 608	620 967
Final consumption expenditure outside the UK by UK resident households	ABTA	11 890	13 058	13 721	14 377	14 942	16 913	19 690	21 662	22 948
less Final consumption expenditure in the UK by households resident in the rest of the world	CDFD	−10 747	−11 160	−13 268	−14 038	−14 037	−14 544	−14 312	−14 713	−12 905
Final consumption expenditure by UK resident households in the UK and abroad (national concept)	ABPB	401 970	422 397	443 367	473 800	503 374	536 235	569 481	603 557	631 010

15.16
continued

Individual consumption expenditure at current market prices by house-holds, non-profit institutions serving households and general government[1]
Classified by function (COICOP/COPNI/COFOG)[2]

£ million

		1993	1994	1995	1996	1997	1998	1999	2000	2001
CONSUMPTION EXPENDITURE OF UK RESIDENT HOUSEHOLDS										
Final consumption expenditure of UK resident households in the UK and abroad	ABPB	401 970	422 397	443 367	473 800	503 374	536 235	569 481	603 557	631 010
FINAL INDIVIDUAL CONSUMPTION EXPENDITURE OF NPISH										
Final individual consumption expenditure of NPISH	ABNV	13 981	15 287	16 481	18 385	19 602	21 117	22 150	23 027	24 255
FINAL INDIVIDUAL CONSUMPTION EXPENDITURE OF OF GENERAL GOVERNMENT										
Health	QYOT	35 441	37 272	38 981	41 466	42 657	45 391	50 108	53 843	59 494
Recreation and culture	QYSU	3 547	3 246	3 172	3 173	3 089	3 486	3 838	4 060	4 149
Education	QYSE	23 487	24 202	25 291	25 798	26 692	27 960	29 692	31 793	35 406
Social protection	QYSP	12 074	12 825	13 649	14 531	15 113	15 434	17 136	18 163	18 892
Housing	QYXO	–	–	–	–	–	–	–	–	–
Final individual consumption expenditure of general government	NNAQ	74 549	77 545	81 093	84 968	87 551	92 271	100 774	107 859	117 941
Total, individual consumption expenditure/ actual individual consumption	NQEO	490 500	515 229	540 941	577 153	610 527	649 623	692 405	734 443	773 206

1 See chapter text.
2 "Purpose" or "function" classifications are designed to indicate the "socio-economic objectives" that institutional units aim to achieve through various kinds of outlays. COICOP is the Classification of Individual Consumption by Purpose and applies to households. COPNI is the Classification of the Purposes of Non-profit Institutions Serving Households and COFOG the Classification of the Functions of Government. The introduction of ESA95 coincides with the redefinition of these classifications and data will be available on a consistent basis for all European Union member states.
3 Package holidays data are dispersed between components (transport etc).

Source: Office for National Statistics: 020 7533 6031

15.17 Individual consumption expenditure at 1995 market prices by households, non-profit institutions serving households and general government[1]

Classified by function (COICOP/COPNI/COFOG)[2]

£ million at 1995 prices

		1993	1994	1995	1996	1997	1998	1999	2000	2001
FINAL CONSUMPTION EXPENDITURE OF HOUSEHOLDS										
Food and non-alcoholic beverages	ADIP	49 262	49 744	49 790	51 405	52 347	52 983	54 102	55 610	56 135
Food	ADIQ	44 178	44 339	44 324	45 939	46 859	47 469	48 499	49 464	49 217
Non-alcoholic beverages	ADIR	5 102	5 405	5 466	5 466	5 488	5 514	5 603	6 146	6 918
Alcoholic beverages and tobacco	ADIS	19 255	19 268	18 776	19 449	19 695	19 553	20 203	20 164	20 171
Alcoholic beverages	ADIT	7 066	7 600	7 257	7 928	8 508	8 520	9 311	9 591	9 980
Tobacco	ADIU	12 357	11 668	11 519	11 521	11 187	11 033	10 892	10 573	10 191
Clothing and footwear	ADIW	24 923	26 884	28 030	29 673	30 889	32 276	34 265	37 584	41 991
Clothing	ADIX	20 859	22 593	23 711	25 259	26 274	27 561	29 578	32 733	36 761
Footwear	ADIY	4 068	4 291	4 319	4 414	4 615	4 715	4 687	4 851	5 230
Housing, water, electricity, gas and other fuels	ADIZ	80 872	80 742	81 412	83 177	84 194	84 847	85 195	86 994	87 691
Actual rentals for housing	ADJA	17 685	18 177	17 906	18 069	18 123	18 076	18 048	18 446	18 481
Imputed rentals for housing	ADJB	36 186	36 359	37 479	38 085	38 765	39 716	40 490	40 776	41 318
Maintenance and repair of the dwelling	ADJC	7 098	6 642	6 526	6 655	7 229	7 347	7 435	7 713	7 613
Water supply and miscellaneous dwelling services	ADJD	4 162	4 292	4 290	4 329	4 350	4 264	4 262	4 295	4 356
Electricity, gas and other fuels	ADJE	15 526	15 272	15 211	16 039	15 727	15 444	14 960	15 764	15 923
Furnishings, household equipment and routine maintenance of the house	ADJF	24 426	25 898	26 287	26 991	28 467	29 443	30 982	33 481	35 240
Furniture, furnishings, carpets and other floor coverings	ADJG	8 910	9 767	9 843	9 957	10 240	10 559	11 164	11 979	12 529
Household textiles	ADJH	2 848	2 882	3 020	3 158	3 325	3 548	3 860	4 320	4 566
Household appliances	ADJI	4 089	4 210	4 405	4 630	5 103	5 223	5 222	5 653	5 856
Glassware, tableware and household utensils	ADJJ	2 641	2 827	2 767	2 829	3 077	3 284	3 594	3 976	4 278
Tools and equipment for house and garden	ADJK	1 764	1 883	1 911	1 986	2 150	2 310	2 537	2 816	3 175
Goods and services for routine household maintenance	ADJL	4 148	4 329	4 341	4 431	4 572	4 519	4 605	4 737	4 836
Health	ADJM	6 678	7 096	6 835	6 866	6 810	6 824	6 757	6 709	6 890
Medical products, appliances and equipment	ADJN	3 801	4 083	3 919	3 950	3 878	3 872	3 831	3 811	3 785
Out-patient services	ADJO	1 777	1 863	1 781	1 726	1 696	1 648	1 595	1 536	1 766
Hospital services	ADJP	1 100	1 150	1 135	1 190	1 236	1 304	1 331	1 362	1 339
Transport	ADJQ	59 690	61 583	62 733	66 041	69 256	72 022	74 555	76 679	81 013
Purchase of vehicles	ADJR	21 878	23 192	23 588	25 664	27 493	28 845	30 289	32 264	36 288
Operation of personal transport equipment	ADJS	23 736	23 645	23 861	24 503	25 212	25 736	25 446	24 715	24 846
Transport services	ADJT	14 147	14 746	15 284	15 874	16 551	17 441	18 820	19 700	19 879
Communication	ADJU	7 181	8 305	9 067	9 546	10 477	11 736	13 146	15 186	17 116
Postal services	CCGZ	948	964	967	938	910	1 012	854	790	668
Telephone & telefax equipment	ADQF	248	283	244	280	319	532	708	804	884
Telephone & telefax services	ADQG	6 006	7 058	7 856	8 328	9 248	10 192	11 584	13 592	15 564
Recreation and culture	ADJV	43 583	46 379	51 075	54 126	57 925	63 392	69 789	76 757	83 151
Audio-visual, photographic and information processing equipment	ADJW	9 028	9 306	10 862	12 088	13 921	16 886	21 218	25 562	30 074
Other major durables for recreation and culture	ADJX	1 740	1 910	2 133	2 410	2 607	2 760	2 986	3 237	3 554
Other recreational items and equipment; flowers, gardens and pets	ADJY	9 808	10 740	11 284	12 523	14 101	15 762	17 465	19 374	20 365
Recreational and cultural services	ADJZ	15 158	15 827	18 241	18 706	18 860	19 467	19 556	19 888	20 657
Newspapers, books and stationery	ADKM	7 790	8 596	8 555	8 399	8 436	8 517	8 564	8 696	8 501
Package holidays[3]	ADMI	–	–	–	–	–	–	–	–	–
Education										
Education services	ADMJ	5 856	5 763	6 197	6 147	6 793	6 756	7 310	7 448	7 299
Restaurants and Hotels	ADMK	49 267	50 211	50 383	52 648	53 225	54 556	55 194	56 139	55 522
Catering services	ADML	42 272	42 727	42 182	44 190	44 763	46 293	47 237	48 463	48 652
Accommodation services	ADMM	7 033	7 484	8 201	8 458	8 462	8 263	7 957	7 676	6 870
Miscellaneous goods and services	ADMN	51 726	51 444	52 329	54 272	55 541	56 314	58 638	61 642	61 683
Personal care	ADMO	9 080	9 805	10 378	10 937	11 015	11 023	11 289	12 038	12 153
Personal effects not elsewhere classified	ADMP	3 761	3 685	3 898	4 040	4 287	4 323	4 392	4 501	4 652
Social protection	ADMQ	9 433	8 822	8 187	7 852	7 483	7 218	6 923	6 749	6 955
Insurance	ADMR	16 725	16 270	16 306	16 584	17 160	17 744	18 954	19 313	18 453
Financial services not elsewhere classified	ADMS	5 637	5 818	5 853	6 672	7 267	7 356	8 252	10 163	10 647
Other services not elsewhere classified	ADMT	7 177	7 044	7 707	8 187	8 329	8 650	8 828	8 878	8 823
Final consumption expenditure in the UK by resident and non-resident households (domestic concept)	ABQJ	421 707	433 317	442 914	460 341	475 619	490 702	510 136	534 393	553 902
Final consumption expenditure outside the UK by UK resident households	ABTC	12 093	13 490	13 721	14 077	16 357	18 813	21 837	24 118	24 877
less Final consumption expenditure in the UK by households resident in the rest of the world	CCHX	−11 524	−11 457	−13 268	−13 658	−13 238	−13 284	−12 751	−12 760	−10 882
Final consumption expenditure by UK resident households in the UK and abroad (national concept)	ABPF	422 273	435 350	443 367	460 760	478 738	496 231	519 222	545 751	567 897

15.17
continued

Individual consumption expenditure at 1995 market prices by households, non-profit institutions serving households and general government[1]
Classified by function (COICOP/COPNI/COFOG)[2]

£ million at 1995 prices

		1993	1994	1995	1996	1997	1998	1999	2000	2001
CONSUMPTION EXPENDITURE OF UK RESIDENT HOUSEHOLDS										
Final consumption expenditure of UK resident households in the UK and abroad	ABPF	422 273	435 350	443 367	460 760	478 738	496 231	519 222	545 751	567 897
FINAL INDIVIDUAL CONSUMPTION EXPENDITURE OF NPISH										
Final individual consumption expenditure of NPISH	ABNU	14 723	15 900	16 481	16 691	17 055	18 265	18 239	19 514	20 398
FINAL INDIVIDUAL CONSUMPTION EXPENDITURE OF GENERAL GOVERNMENT										
Health	EMOA	36 360	37 372	38 981	40 172	41 069	42 171	43 208	44 382	45 786
Recreation and culture	QYXK	3 892	3 333	3 172	3 200	3 287	3 206	3 575	3 686	3 685
Education	EMOB	25 201	24 986	25 291	25 565	25 811	26 037	26 254	26 434	26 848
Social protection	QYXM	13 068	12 788	13 649	14 175	14 641	14 830	15 237	15 445	15 887
Housing	QYXN	–	–	–	–	–	–	–	–	–
Final individual consumption expenditure of general government	NSZK	78 616	78 479	81 093	83 112	84 808	86 244	88 274	89 947	92 206
Total, individual consumption expenditure/ actual individual consumption	YBIO	515 535	529 729	540 941	560 563	580 601	600 740	625 735	655 212	680 501

1 See chapter text.
2 "Purpose" or "function" classifications are designed to indicate the "socieconomic objectives" that institutional units aim to achieve through various kinds of outlays. COICOP is the Classification of Individual Consumption by Purpose and applies to households. COPNI is the Classification of the Purposes of Non-profit Institutions Serving Households and COFOG the Classification of the Functions of Government. The introduction of ESA95 coincides with the redefinition of these classifications and data will be available on a consistent basis for all European Union member states.
3 Package holidays data are dispersed between components (transport etc).

Source: Office for National Statistics: 020 7533 6031

15.18 Change in inventories at constant prices[1,2]

£ million

	Mining and quarrying	Manufacturing industries				Electricity, gas and water supply	Distributive trades		Other industries[4]	Change in inventories
		Materials and fuel	Work in progress	Finished goods	Total		Wholesale[3]	Retail[3]		
Value of stocks held at end-December 2000	..	..	..	..	..	..	..	..	..	..
	FADO	FBID	FBIE	FBIF	DHBH	FADP	FAJM	FBYH	DLWV	ABMQ
1991	170	−861	−1 358	−1 346	−3 565	200	−612	−404	−420	−5 349
1992	66	−211	−1 124	−47	−1 382	−100	117	216	−616	−1 962
1993	−45	20	−981	−320	−1 281	−270	802	368	738	360
1994	−267	433	639	548	1 620	−661	1 332	884	1 928	4 836
1995	−123	514	1 144	998	2 656	−205	597	811	776	4 512
1996	−47	−105	−217	6	−316	15	681	638	859	1 830
1997	55	403	−1 332	340	−589	103	1 717	799	1 895	3 980
1998	257	721	−588	367	500	−154	550	987	2 654	4 794
1999	−215	683	−120	−474	89	−159	1 762	1 474	3 331	6 282
2000	−158	994	605	555	2 154	405	1 126	1 198	1 258	5 983

1 See chapter text. Estimates are given to the nearest £ million but cannot be regarded as accurate to this degree.
2 Components may not sum to totals due to rounding.
3 Wholesaling and retailing estimates exclude the motor trades.
4 Quarterly alignment adjustment included in this series.

Source: Office for National Statistics 020 7533 6031

15.19
Gross fixed capital formation at current purchasers' prices
Analysis by broad sector and type of asset[1,2]
Total economy

£ million

		1993	1994	1995	1996	1997	1998	1999	2000	2001
Private sector										
New dwellings, excluding land	DFDF	17 124	18 285	18 860	20 149	22 018	23 321	23 950	25 648	25 180
Other buildings and structures	EQBU	16 252	16 430	18 023	20 752	25 224	28 386	31 001	30 534	30 579
Transport equipment	EQBV	8 115	10 112	10 224	11 316	12 087	15 251	14 274	12 762	14 525
Other machinery and equipment and cultivated assets	EQBW	32 441	35 586	42 157	47 110	49 787	57 816	56 204	59 680	57 607
Intangible fixed assets	EQBX	3 122	2 982	3 179	3 278	3 395	3 555	3 624	4 004	4 320
Costs associated with the transfer of ownership of non-produced assets	EQBY	5 089	5 208	5 173	6 695	7 646	7 452	9 860	11 071	12 615
Total	EQBZ	82 143	88 603	97 616	109 300	120 157	135 781	138 913	143 699	144 826
Public non-financial corporations										
New dwellings, excluding land	DEER	150	139	162	151	123	49	8	1	–
Other buildings and structures	DEES	3 416	3 492	3 781	3 397	2 671	2 465	2 720	2 878	3 145
Transport equipment	DEEP	516	512	354	225	190	171	154	160	157
Other machinery and equipment and cultivated assets	DEEQ	720	761	857	765	705	758	964	823	776
Intangible fixed assets	DLXJ	279	374	496	585	595	605	625	640	655
Costs associated with the transfer of ownership of non-produced assets	DLXQ	376	349	126	133	267	352	–8	53	16
Total	FCCJ	5 457	5 627	5 776	5 256	4 551	4 400	4 463	4 555	4 749
General government										
New dwellings, excluding land	DFHW	2 618	2 809	2 642	2 148	1 788	1 856	1 771	1 790	2 357
Other buildings and structures	EQCH	9 757	10 118	10 039	8 693	7 556	8 172	7 943	8 907	10 113
Transport equipment	EQCI	684	771	717	672	675	693	610	626	745
Other machinery and equipment and cultivated assets	EQCJ	2 155	1 879	1 998	1 852	1 452	1 283	1 467	1 356	1 694
Intangible fixed assets	EQCK	247	257	264	273	259	387	396	367	334
Costs associated with the transfer of ownership of non-produced assets	EQCL	–2 034	–1 750	–1 604	–2 432	–2 275	–1 730	–2 062	–2 382	–2 574
Total	NNBF	13 427	14 084	14 056	11 206	9 455	10 661	10 125	10 664	12 669
Total gross fixed capital formation	NPQX	101 027	108 314	117 448	125 762	134 163	150 842	153 501	158 918	162 244

1 See chapter text.
2 Components may not sum to totals due to rounding.

Source: Office for National Statistics: 020 7533 6031

15.20
Gross fixed capital formation at current purchasers' prices
Analysis by type of asset[1,2]
Total economy

£ million

		1993	1994	1995	1996	1997	1998	1999	2000	2001
Tangible fixed assets										
New dwellings, excluding land	DFDK	19 892	21 233	21 664	22 448	23 929	25 226	25 729	27 439	27 537
Other buildings and structures	DLWS	29 425	30 040	31 843	32 842	35 451	39 023	41 664	42 319	43 837
Transport equipment	DLWZ	9 315	11 395	11 295	12 213	12 952	16 115	15 038	13 548	15 427
Other machinery and equipment and cultivated assets	DLXI	35 316	38 226	45 012	49 727	51 944	59 857	58 635	61 859	60 077
Total	EQCQ	93 948	100 894	109 814	117 230	124 276	140 221	141 066	145 165	146 878
Intangible fixed assets	DLXP	3 648	3 613	3 939	4 136	4 249	4 547	4 645	5 011	5 309
Costs associated with the transfer of ownership of non-produced assets	DFBH	3 431	3 807	3 695	4 396	5 638	6 074	7 790	8 742	10 057
Total gross fixed capital formation	NPQX	101 027	108 314	117 448	125 762	134 163	150 842	153 501	158 918	162 244

1 See chapter text.
2 Components may not sum to totals due to rounding.

Source: Office for National Statistics: 020 7533 6031

15.21 Gross fixed capital formation at 1995 purchasers' prices[1,2,3]
Analysis by broad sector and type of asset
Total economy

£ million at 1995 prices

		1993	1994	1995	1996	1997	1998	1999	2000	2001
Private sector										
New dwellings, excluding land	DFDP	18 353	19 076	18 860	19 607	20 824	20 967	20 258	20 560	19 234
Other buildings and structures	EQCU	18 018	18 018	18 023	19 776	23 802	25 703	26 727	25 580	24 865
Transport equipment	EQCV	8 978	10 666	10 224	10 951	11 690	15 030	13 458	11 903	13 832
Other machinery and equipment and cultivated assets	EQCW	33 758	36 169	42 157	47 089	51 542	63 841	65 768	70 442	68 373
Intangible fixed assets	EQCX	3 154	2 997	3 179	3 298	3 288	3 249	3 196	3 514	3 623
Costs associated with the transfer of ownership of non-produced assets	EQCY	5 821	5 705	5 173	6 094	6 199	5 507	5 486	5 399	5 624
Total	EQCZ	82 261	92 631	97 616	106 815	117 345	134 297	134 893	137 398	135 551
Public non-financial corporations										
New dwellings, excluding land	DEEW	169	150	162	147	119	46	7	1	–
Other buildings and structures	DEEX	4 391	3 847	3 781	3 154	2 508	2 225	2 366	2 446	2 590
Transport equipment	DEEU	459	529	354	223	180	159	141	149	144
Other machinery and equipment and cultivated assets	DEEV	639	766	857	768	731	801	1 031	878	820
Intangible fixed assets	EQDE	294	387	496	571	553	554	553	548	542
Costs associated with the transfer of ownership of non-produced assets	EQDF	368	355	126	151	288	363	−1	18	−16
Total	EQDG	5 932	6 031	5 776	5 014	4 379	4 148	4 097	4 040	4 080
General government										
New dwellings, excluding land	DFID	2 932	3 041	2 642	2 114	1 728	1 733	1 561	1 509	1 920
Other buildings and structures	EQDI	10 963	11 287	10 039	8 431	7 391	7 267	6 891	7 502	7 942
Transport equipment	EQDJ	745	804	717	659	693	637	555	588	708
Other machinery and equipment and cultivated assets	EQDK	2 184	1 857	1 998	1 834	1 464	1 344	1 568	1 433	1 777
Intangible fixed assets	EQDL	231	247	264	293	262	353	348	316	282
Costs associated with the transfer of ownership of non-produced assets	EQDM	−2 344	−1 937	−1 604	−2 184	−1 826	−1 519	−770	−800	−934
Total	EQDN	14 721	15 300	14 056	11 147	9 712	9 815	10 153	10 548	11 695
Total gross fixed capital formation	NPQR	108 887	113 961	117 448	122 976	131 436	148 260	149 143	151 986	151 326

1 See chapter text.
2 For 1993, the total differs from the sum of the components.
3 Components may not sum to totals due to rounding.

Source: Office for National Statistics: 020 7533 6031

15.22 Gross fixed capital formation at 1995 purchasers' prices[1,2,3]
Analysis by type of asset
Total economy

£ million at 1995 prices

		1993	1994	1995	1996	1997	1998	1999	2000	2001
Tangible fixed assets										
New dwellings, excluding land	DFDV	21 492	22 267	21 664	21 868	22 671	22 746	21 826	22 070	21 154
Other buildings and structures	EQDP	32 779	33 151	31 843	31 361	33 701	35 195	35 984	35 528	35 397
Transport equipment	DLWJ	10 281	11 998	11 295	11 833	12 563	15 826	14 154	12 640	14 684
Other machinery and equipment and cultivated assets	DLWM	36 679	38 791	45 012	49 691	53 737	65 986	68 367	72 753	70 970
Total	EQDS	101 456	106 207	109 814	114 753	122 672	139 753	140 331	142 991	142 205
Intangible fixed assets	EQDT	3 679	3 631	3 939	4 162	4 103	4 156	4 097	4 378	4 447
Costs associated with the transfer of ownership of non-produced assets	DFDW	3 889	4 123	3 695	4 061	4 661	4 351	4 715	4 617	4 674
Total gross fixed capital formation	NPQR	108 887	113 961	117 448	122 976	131 436	148 260	149 143	151 986	151 326

1 See chapter text.
2 For 1993, the total differs from the sum of the components.
3 Components may not sum to totals due to rounding.

Source: Office for National Statistics: 020 7533 6031

16 Prices

Prices

Producer price index numbers *(Tables 16.1 and 16.2)*

The producer price indices were published for the first time in August 1983, replacing the former wholesale price indices. Full details of the differences between the two indices were given in an article published in *British Business*, 15 April 1983. The producer price indices are calculated using the same general methodology as that used by the wholesale price indices.

The high level index numbers in Tables 16.1 and 16.2 are constructed on a net sector basis. That is to say, they are intended to measure only transactions between the sector concerned and other sectors. Within sector transactions are excluded. Index numbers for the whole of manufacturing are thus not weighted averages of sector index numbers.

The index numbers for selected industries in Tables 16.1 and 16.2 are constructed on a gross sector basis i.e. all transactions are included in deriving the weighting patterns, including sales within the same industry.

All the index numbers are compiled exclusive of value-added tax. Excise duties on cigarettes, manufactured tobacco and alcoholic liquor are included, as is the duty on hydrocarbon oils.

The indices relate to the average prices for a year. The movement in these prices are weighted to reflect the relative importance of the composite products in a chosen year (known as the base year), currently 1995.

Since July 1995, PPIs have been published fully reclassified to the 1992 version of the Standard Industrial Classification (SIC). From 1998, high level PPIs on the 1980 SIC will also be shown in Tables 16.1 and 16.2.

Further details are available from the National Statistics website: www.statistics.gov.uk/ppi.

Purchasing power of the pound *(Table 16.3)*

Changes in the internal purchasing power of a currency may be defined as the 'inverse' of changes in the levels of prices; when prices go up, the amount which can be purchased with a given sum of money goes down. Movements in the internal purchasing power of the pound are based on the consumers' expenditure deflator (CED) prior to 1962 and on the General index of retail prices (RPI) from January 1962 onwards. The CED shows the movement in prices implied by the national accounts estimates of consumers' expenditure valued at current and at constant prices, whilst the RPI is constructed directly by weighting together monthly movements in prices according to a given pattern of household expenditure derived from the Expenditure and Food Survey. If the purchasing power of the pound is taken to be 100p in a particular month (quarter, year), the comparable purchasing power in a subsequent month (quarter, year) is:

$$100 \quad \text{x} \quad \frac{\text{earlier period price index}}{\text{later period price index}}$$

where the price index used is the CED for years 1946-1961 and the RPI for periods after 1961.

Index of retail prices *(Table 16.4)*

The retail prices index measures the change from month to month in the average level of prices of goods and services purchased by most households in the United Kingdom. The expenditure pattern on which the index is based is revised each year using information from the Family Expenditure Survey, and its successor, the Expenditure and Food Survey introduced in April 2001. The expenditure of certain higher income households and households of retired people dependent mainly on social security benefits is excluded.

The index covers a large and representative selection of more than 650 separate goods and services, for which price movements are regularly measured in 147 locations throughout the country. Around 130,000 separate price quotations are used in compiling the index.

The index of retail prices replaced the interim index from January 1956 (indices of the interim index of retail prices for the period 1952 to January 1956 were last published in *Annual Abstract of Statistics* No 103, 1965). A new set of weights was introduced, based on expenditure in 1953-54, valued at January 1956 prices. Between January 1962 and 1974 the weights have been revised each January on the basis of expenditure in the three years ended in the previous June, valued at prices obtained at the date of revision. From 1975 the weights have been revised on expenditure for the latest available year.

Following the recommendations of the Retail Prices Index Advisory Committee, the index has been re-referenced to make January 13, 1987 = 100. Calculations of price changes which involve periods spanning the new reference date are made as follows:

$$\% \text{ change} = \frac{\text{Index for later month}}{\text{Index for earlier month (Jan 1974 = 100)}} \text{ x } \frac{\text{Index for Jan 1987}}{\text{(Jan 1974 = 100)}} - 100$$

Further details are available from the National Statistics website: www.statistics.gov.uk/rpi

Tax and price index (TPI) *(Table 16.5)*

The purpose and methodology of the TPI were described in an article in the August 1979 issue (No 310) of *Economic Trends* (The Stationery Office). The TPI measures the change in *gross* taxable income needed for taxpayers to maintain their purchasing power, allowing for changes in retail prices. The TPI thus takes account of the changes to direct taxes (and employees' National Insurance contributions) facing representative cross-section of taxpayers as well as changes in the retail prices index (RPI).

When direct taxation or employees' National Insurance contributions change, the TPI will rise by less than or more than the RPI according to the type of changes made. Between Budgets, the monthly increase in the TPI is normally slightly larger than that in the RPI, since all the extra income needed to offset any rise in retail prices is fully taxed.

Index numbers of agricultural prices
(Tables 16.6 and 16.7)

The indices of agricultural prices for the United Kingdom are based on the calendar year 1995 and designed to provide an indication of movements in the purchase prices of the means of agricultural production and of the prices received by producers for their agricultural products. The methodology is comparable with that used for the other member states of the European Community and enables the compilation of indices for the Fifteen, which appear in the Communities Eurostat series of publications.

16.1

Producer price index numbers of materials and fuels purchased
All manufacturing and selected industries SIC(92)[1]

United Kingdom

1995 = 100

			Annual averages							
			1994	1995	1996	1997	1998	1999	2000	2001
Net sector										
Materials and fuel purchased by manufacturing industry[2]	RNNK	6292000050	91.9	100.0	98.8	90.6	82.5	83.7	93.3	93.0
Materials	PLKX	6292000010	90.3	100.0	99.7	90.9	81.6	83.0	94.2	92.8
Fuels[2]	RNNL	6292000060	104.6	100.0	91.7	88.3	89.2	89.1	86.7	94.6
Materials and fuels purchased by manufacturing industry-seasonally adjusted[2]	RNPE	6292008950	91.9	100.0	98.7	90.6	82.4	83.7	93.5	93.0
Materials and fuels purchased by manufacturing industry other than food, beverages, petroleum and tobacco[2]	RNNQ	6292990050	91.3	100.0	95.7	89.7	85.9	83.1	85.8	87.0
Materials purchased by manufacturing industry other than food, drink and tobacco	RWCJ	6292990010	88.5	100.0	96.6	90.0	85.2	81.9	85.6	85.4
Fuel purchased by manufacturing industry other than food and beverages[2]	RNNS	6292990060	104.6	100.0	91.7	88.2	89.1	89.0	86.6	94.4
Materials and fuels purchased by manufacturing industries other than food, beverages, petroleum and tobacco-seasonally adjusted[2]	RNPF	6292998950	91.3	100.0	95.8	89.7	85.8	83.2	85.8	87.0
Gross sector[3]										
All manufacturing	RBBO	6192000000	94.0	100.0	100.3	96.9	93.2	92.5	96.8	96.3
Other mining and quarrying products	RABE	6112140000	95.7	100.0	101.9	102.9	103.9	105.1	108.2	108.8
Manufacture of food products	RBBQ	6192151600	94.2	100.0	99.8	94.2	90.3	88.9	89.1	91.1
Food products and beverages	RABF	6112150000	94.2	100.0	100.9	96.6	93.3	91.6	91.8	93.8
Tobacco products	RABG	6112160000	90.7	100.0	100.9	95.7	91.0	88.7	91.5	92.1
Manufacture of textiles	RBBR	6192171800	92.1	100.0	99.2	96.3	93.2	89.1	90.1	90.5
Textiles	RABH	6112170000	91.6	100.0	99.1	95.8	92.4	88.4	89.8	90.1
Wearing apparel	RABI	6112180000	92.9	100.0	99.5	97.0	94.6	90.2	90.6	91.2
Manufacture of leather	RBBS	6192190000	94.0	100.0	101.0	98.2	94.9	93.2	95.1	97.3
Manufacture of wood and wood products	RBBT	6192200000	93.7	100.0	99.0	98.1	95.3	93.6	94.6	94.4
Manufacture of pulp, paper, publishing and printing	RBBU	6192212200	88.4	100.0	99.2	93.1	90.4	88.9	92.4	93.1
Pulp and paper products	RABL	6112210000	88.3	100.0	99.1	93.1	90.5	89.0	92.3	93.0
Printed matter and recording material	RABM	6112220000	88.4	100.0	99.3	93.1	90.3	88.9	92.6	93.2
Manufacture of coke	RBBV	61922300000	94.7	100.0	118.1	107.4	78.9	103.5	161.0	147.0
Manufacture of chemical products	RBBW	6192240000	93.5	100.0	98.6	95.9	94.2	93.3	96.0	96.7
Manufacture of rubber products	RBBX	6192250000	87.4	100.0	94.7	90.2	84.2	82.2	87.3	86.3
Manufacture of other non-metallic mineral products	RBBY	6192260000	97.0	100.0	100.6	100.3	100.6	101.1	103.6	104.4
Manufacture of basic metals	RBBZ	6192272800	92.8	100.0	99.3	97.3	94.9	90.8	95.6	94.8
Basic metals	RABV	6112270000	92.2	100.0	98.8	96.3	93.3	88.5	94.4	93.2
Fabricated metal products	RABW	6112280000	93.5	100.0	99.9	98.5	96.8	93.7	97.1	96.7
Manufacture of machinery and equipment not elsewhere classified	RBCA	6192290000	95.2	100.0	100.8	100.4	99.5	97.7	99.3	99.6
Manufacture of electrical and optical equipment	RBCB	6192303300	98.0	100.0	97.5	92.9	88.0	84.7	84.9	83.9
Office machinery and computers	RABY	6112300000	102.6	100.0	94.4	85.4	77.0	72.3	70.7	68.1
Electrical machinery and apparatus not elsewhere classified	RACB	6112310000	94.0	100.0	99.4	97.6	95.0	92.5	95.3	95.2
Radio, television and communication equipment	RACC	6112320000	97.3	100.0	98.4	95.0	91.2	88.2	88.2	87.7
Medical, precision, optical instruments and clocks	RACD	6112330000	96.7	100.0	98.8	95.8	92.4	89.9	90.4	90.0
Manufacture of transport equipment	RBCC	6192343500	95.7	100.0	101.9	102.0	102.3	102.0	101.9	101.2
Motor vehicles, trailers and semi-trailers	RACE	6112340000	95.4	100.0	101.9	101.9	101.8	100.4	99.6	98.2

16.1
continued

Producer price index numbers of materials and fuels purchased
All manufacturing and selected industries SIC(92)[1]
United Kingdom

1995 = 100

			Annual averages							
			1994	1995	1996	1997	1998	1999	2000	2001
Other transport equipment	RACF	6112350000	96.5	100.0	101.9	102.3	103.8	106.2	108.5	109.7
Manufacturing not elsewhere classified	RBCD	6192363700	93.1	100.0	99.9	98.8	96.8	94.7	97.1	97.2
Electricity incl.CCL	RNOD	4010990050	103.8	100.0	96.6	90.7	90.6	90.5	84.2	81.2
Gas incl.CCL	RNOH	4020990050	107.1	100.0	76.4	79.1	83.3	82.8	90.1	126.9
Collected and purified water	PQNB	4100000000	96.8	100.0	104.9	109.6	115.3	119.7	115.3	116.6
Construction materials	ROGG	6101451800	94.4	100.0	100.5	102.1	102.9	101.6	103.8	105.7
House building materials	ROGH	6101452800	94.6	100.0	100.7	102.2	103.0	102.1	104.1	106.2

SIC (80) Net sector

Materials and fuels purchased by manufacturing industry	DZBR	6200000000	91.7	100.0	96.4	89.0	84.1	82.0	83.9	85.2

1 See chapter text.
2 These indices include the Climate Change Levy which was introduced in April
3 The Climate Change Levy is excluded from the detailed industry input index.

Source: Office for National Statistics: 01633 812106

16.2

Producer price index numbers of output[1]
All manufacturing and selected industries SIC(92)
United Kingdom

1995 = 100

			Annual averages							
			1994	1995	1996	1997	1998	1999	2000	2001
Net sector										
Output of manufactured products	PLLU	7209200000	96.1	100.0	102.6	103.5	104.1	105.3	108.0	108.2
All manufacturing excluding duty	PVNP	7209200010	96.2	100.0	102.3	102.4	102.0	102.1	103.9	104.4
All manufacturing excluding duty - seasonally adjusted	PVNQ	7209200890	96.2	100.0	102.3	102.4	102.0	102.1	103.9	104.4
Products of manufacturing industries other than the food, beverages, petroleum and tobacco manufacturing industries -unadjusted	PLLV	7209299000	96.0	100.0	101.9	102.1	102.0	101.6	102.4	102.6
All manufacturing excluding food, beverages, tobacco and petroleum - seasonally adjusted	PLLW	7209299890	96.0r	100.0r	101.9	102.1	102.0	101.6	102.4	102.6
Gross sector										
Manufactured product	POKE	7109200000	96.6	100.0	102.0	101.3	99.0	99.6	105.0	104.3
Manufactured products excluding food, drink, tobacco and petroleum	POKF	7109299000	95.8	100.0	101.3	100.6	99.9	99.0	99.7	99.7
Other mining and quarrying products	POKW	7112140000	94.3	100.0	105.0	108.1	111.2	112.3	113.6	118.0
Food products, beverages and tobacco	POKH	7111151600	96.3	100.0	103.1	103.0	102.7	102.6	102.5	104.2
Food products, beverages and tobacco including duty	RBGA	7111151680	96.6	100.0	103.3	103.9	104.7	106.4	107.8	110.1
Food products and beverages	POKX	7112150000	96.8	100.0	103.1	102.9	102.3	102.0	101.5	102.8
Food products excluding beverages	RBGD	7112159900	97.3	100.0	103.1	102.1	101.0	100.8	100.0	101.5
Tobacco products	POKY	7112160000	83.5	100.0	101.2	105.6	114.5	121.6	132.7	145.9
Textiles and textile products	POKI	7111171800	95.9 B	100.0 B	102.6	104.7	105.7	104.9	105.4	104.8
Textiles	POKZ	7112170000	95.5 B	100.0 B	102.3	104.1	104.9	103.5	103.6	103.2
Wearing apparel: Furs	POLA	7112180000	97.0 B	100.0 B	103.3	106.2	107.7	108.5	109.7	108.9
Leather and leather products	POKJ	7111190000	97.4	100.0	102.7	103.3	102.8	101.6	102.3	103.5
Wood and wood products	POKK	7111200000	94.0 B	100.0 B	98.8	100.3	98.9	96.4	95.9	95.8
Pulp, paper and paper products, recorded media and printing services	POKL	7111212200	92.9	100.0	103.4	102.0	102.5	102.9	105.6	107.4
Pulp, paper and paper products	POLD	7112210000	85.6	100.0	101.7	97.0	95.8	95.1	98.3	99.2
Printed matter and recorded media	POLE	7112220000	96.6	100.0	104.3	104.6	106.0	106.9	109.4	111.7
Chemicals, chemical, products and manmade fibres	POKN	7111240000	93.4	100.0	98.9	97.3	94.0	92.8	95.3	95.8
Rubber and plastic products	POKO	7111250000	92.3	100.0	101.4	100.8	98.4	96.3	96.4	96.5
Other non-metallic mineral products	POKP	7111260000	95.9	100.0	101.1	103.5	106.5	108.3	110.8	113.4
Base metals and fabricated metal products	POKQ	7111272800	93.6	100.0	101.4	100.7	100.1	96.8	99.0	98.8
Base metals	POLJ	712270000	90.0	100.0	98.8	96.0	93.0	87.3	92.7	91.0
Fabricated metal products, except machinery and equipment	POLK	7112280000	96.0 B	100.0 B	103.1	104.0	105.0	103.4	103.3	104.0
Machinery and equipment not elsewhere classified	POKR	7111290000	97.5 B	100.0 B	102.9	105.7	106.7	107.8	109.3	110.7
Electrical and optical equipment	POKS	7111343500	103.8	100.0	97.2	90.9	85.3	81.4	78.6	76.0
Office machinery and computers	POLM	7112300000	115.5	100.0	90.9	74.5	62.1	54.4	47.3	39.3
Electrical machinery and apparatus not elsewhere classified	POLN	7112310000	96.1 B	100.0 B	101.6	102.2	101.4	99.1	98.5	98.9
Radio, television and communication equipment and apparatus	POLO	7112320000	100.2	100.0	95.8	90.1	83.2	79.2	78.1	76.5
Medical precision and optical instruments, watches and clocks	POLP	7112330000	99.2 B	100.0 B	104.1	104.9	106.1	107.1	107.0	108.1

16.2 continued — Producer price index numbers of output[1]
All manufacturing and selected industries SIC(92)
United Kingdom

							Annual averages			
			1994	1995	1996	1997	1998	1999	2000	2001
Gross sector continued										
Transport equipment	POKT	7111343500	96.5	100.0	103.0	104.4	106.4	108.0	106.7	104.8
Motor vehicles, trailers and semi-trailers	POLQ	7112340000	96.2	100.0	103.0	104.3	105.9	106.2	103.5	100.6
Other transport	POLR	7112350000	97.4 B	100.0 B	102.9	104.9	108.2	114.7	117.8	119.9
Furniture: other manufactured goods not elsewhere classified	POLS	7112360000	96.9 B	100.0 B	103.7	105.1	107.3	108.0	107.8	108.5
SIC (80) Net sector										
Output of manufactured products	DZCV	7200000000	96.3	100.0	102.3	102.7	103.2	103.6	104.7	105.6

1 See chapter text. B = These index values are considered less reliable due to lack of market coverage.

Source: Office for National Statistics: 01633 812106

16.3 — Internal purchasing power of the pound (based on RPI)[1,2,3]
United Kingdom

Pence

								Year in which purchasing power was 100p											
	1982	1983	1984	1985	1986	1987	1988	1989	1990	1991	1992	1993	1994	1995	1996	1997	1998	1999	2000	2001
	BAMO	BAMP	BAMQ	BAMR	BAMS	BAMT	BAMU	BAMV	BAMW	BASX	CZVM	CBXX	DOFX	DOHR	DOLM	DTUL	CDQG	JKZZ	ZMHO	IKHI
1983	96	100	105	111	115	120	126	136	148	157	163	166	170	176	180	185	192	195	200	204
1984	91	95	100	106	110	114	120	129	141	150	155	158	162	167	171	177	183	185	191	194
1985	86	90	94	100	103	108	113	122	133	141	146	149	152	158	161	166	172	175	180	183
1986	83	87	91	97	100	104	109	118	129	136	142	144	147	152	156	161	167	169	174	177
1987	80	83	88	93	96	100	105	113	124	131	136	138	141	146	150	155	160	162	167	170
1988	76	79	83	88	92	95	100	108	118	125	130	132	135	139	143	147	152	155	159	162
1989	70	74	77	82	85	88	93	100	109	116	120	122	125	129	133	137	141	144	148	150
1990	64	67	71	75	78	81	85	91	100	106	110	112	114	118	121	125	129	131	135	137
1991	61	64	67	71	73	76	80	86	94	100	104	105	108	112	114	118	122	124	128	130
1992	59	61	64	68	71	74	77	83	91	96	100	102	104	108	110	114	118	119	123	125
1993	58	60	63	67	70	72	76	82	90	95	98	100	102	106	109	112	116	118	121	123
1994	56	59	62	66	68	71	74	80	88	93	96	98	100	103	106	109	113	115	118	120
1995	54	57	60	63	66	68	72	77	85	90	93	94	97	100	102	106	109	111	114	116
1996	53	56	58	62	64	67	70	75	83	87	91	92	94	98	100	103	107	108	112	113
1997	52	54	57	60	62	65	68	73	80	85	88	89	92	95	97	100	103	105	108	110
1998	50	52	55	58	60	63	66	71	77	82	85	86	88	92	94	97	100	102	105	106
1999	49	51	54	57	59	62	65	70	76	81	84	85	87	90	92	95	98	100	103	105
2000	48	50	52	56	57	60	63	68	74	78	81	83	85	88	90	92	96	97	100	102
2001	47	49	51	55	56	59	62	66	73	77	80	81	83	86	88	91	94	95	98	100

1 See chapter text.
2 To find the purchasing power of the pound in 1995, given that it was 100 pence in 1990, select the column headed 1990 and look at the 1995 row. The result is 85 pence.

3 These figures are calculated by taking the inverse ratio of the respective annual averages of the Retail Prices Index.

Source: Office for National Statistics: 020 7533 5874

16.4 Retail Prices Index[1]
United Kingdom

13 January 1987=100

| | ALL ITEMS (RPI) | All items excluding | | | | | Food and catering | Alcohol and tobacco | Housing and household expenditure | Personal expenditure | Travel and leisure | Consumer durables | All items excluding mortgage interest payments & indirect taxes (RPIY)[4] |
		mortgage interest payments (RPIX)	mortgage interest payments and depreciation[2]	housing	food	seasonal food[3]							
Weights													
	CZGU	CZGY	DOGZ	CZGX	CZGV	CZGW	CBVV	CBVW	CBVX	CBVY	CBVZ	CBWA	
1994	1 000	956	956	842	858	980	187	111	326	95	281	127	
1995	1 000	958	928	813	861	978	184	111	356	93	256	123	
1996	1 000	958	929	810	857	978	191	113	353	92	251	116	
1997	1 000	961	932	814	864	981	185	114	351	96	254	122	
1998	1 000	955	923	803	870	982	178	105	359	95	263	121	
1999	1 000	958	928	807	872	980	179	100	358	95	268	127	
2000	1 000	960	924	805	882	982	170	95	355	101	279	126	
2001	1 000	954	914	795	884	982	169	97	362	96	276	125	
2002	1 000	964	924	801	886	980	166	99	363	94	278	126	
Annual averages													
	CHAW	CHMK	CHON	CHAZ	CHAY	CHAX	CHBS	CHBT	CHBU	CHBV	CHBW	CHBY	CBZW
1993	140.7	140.5	140.5	138.4	142.6	141.4	136.1	155.1	141.2	129.5	141.8	115.9	139.0
1994	144.1	143.8	143.8	141.6	146.5	144.8	138.5	161.4	144.4	131.9	145.7	115.5	141.3
1995	149.1	147.9	148.0	145.4	151.4	149.6	143.9	169.0	150.8	133.6	148.4	116.2	144.5
1996	152.7	152.3	152.3	149.3	154.9	153.4	148.9	175.9	153.0	135.1	152.8	117.1	148.2
1997	157.5	156.5	156.4	152.9	160.5	158.5	150.4	183.2	158.4	137.7	159.0	117.3	151.5
1998	162.9	160.6	160.3	156.2	166.5	163.8	153.4	192.3	166.2	139.9	162.8	115.9	154.5
1999	165.4	164.3	163.6	158.9	169.4	166.5	155.4	202.6	167.7	139.6	165.6	112.3	157.1
2000	170.3	167.7	166.4	161.3	175.1	171.4	156.7	210.3	176.2	137.2	170.3	108.0	159.9
2001	173.3	171.3	169.5	163.7	178.0	174.3	162.2	216.9	180.0	135.7	172.0	105.0	163.7
Monthly figures													
1999 Aug	165.5	164.5	163.8	158.9	169.7	166.8	154.7	204.5	167.6	138.3	166.6	110.5	157.2
Sep	166.2	165.2	164.4	159.6	170.6	167.4	154.6	204.5	168.5	141.6	166.5	112.7	157.8
Oct	166.5	165.4	164.4	159.6	171.0	167.7	154.6	204.7	169.2	140.8	167.1	111.6	158.1
Nov	166.7	165.6	164.6	159.7	171.1	167.8	155.1	204.3	170.0	141.1	166.6	112.3	158.3
Dec	167.3	165.9	164.9	160.1	171.8	168.4	155.3	204.0	171.7	140.3	166.8	113.2	158.6
2000 Jan	166.6	165.2	164.1	159.1	171.0	167.8	155.5	205.0	170.8	134.4	167.7	106.3	157.9
Feb	167.5	165.8	164.7	159.7	172.0	168.7	155.6	205.7	171.9	137.1	167.8	108.4	158.6
Mar	168.4	166.4	165.3	160.5	173.2	169.7	155.0	206.0	173.2	138.5	169.2	109.6	159.2
Apr	170.1	167.5	166.4	161.3	175.3	171.5	155.1	210.4	175.9	139.2	170.4	110.0	159.4
May	170.7	168.0	166.8	161.7	175.7	171.9	156.3	211.1	176.3	139.4	170.7	110.1	160.0
Jun	171.1	168.4	167.1	162.0	176.1	172.3	156.6	211.5	176.7	138.7	171.7	109.3	160.4
Jul	170.5	167.7	166.4	161.2	175.2	171.5	157.7	211.4	176.7	133.1	171.5	104.5	159.7
Aug	170.5	167.6	166.2	160.9	175.4	171.7	156.9	212.0	177.1	134.6	170.5	105.6	159.6
Sep	171.7	168.9	167.4	162.2	176.8	172.9	157.2	212.7	178.5	137.5	171.3	108.0	160.9
Oct	171.6	168.7	167.2	162.0	176.6	172.8	157.5	212.9	178.6	137.7	170.6	107.4	160.7
Nov	172.1	169.2	167.7	162.5	177.1	173.2	158.1	212.8	179.0	138.4	171.2	108.2	161.2
Dec	172.2	169.3	167.7	162.5	177.1	173.2	158.4	212.3	179.8	137.7	170.8	108.6	161.3
2001 Jan	171.1	168.1	166.5	161.1	175.8	172.1	158.8	213.3	178.5	132.9	170.3	102.8	160.2
Feb	172.0	169.0	167.3	162.0	176.9	173.0	159.0	214.1	179.2	135.5	170.9	104.9	161.1
Mar	172.2	169.6	168.0	162.7	176.9	173.2	160.4	215.4	178.7	137.1	170.5	106.7	162.1
Apr	173.1	170.8	169.1	163.2	177.9	174.1	160.9	216.6	180.2	136.7	171.5	105.7	162.9
May	174.2	172.1	170.4	164.7	178.6	174.8	163.9	216.9	180.3	137.1	173.0	106.4	164.4
Jun	174.4	172.5	170.8	165.1	178.7	174.9	164.7	217.3	179.8	137.2	173.6	106.3	164.9
Jul	173.3	171.4	169.5	163.6	177.9	174.2	162.9	217.4	179.6	132.3	173.3	102.4	163.9
Aug	174.0	172.0	170.0	164.1	178.7	175.0	162.8	217.7	180.7	134.2	173.3	103.8	164.6
Sep	174.6	172.8	170.7	164.9	179.4	175.6	162.8	218.3	181.7	136.6	173.3	105.6	165.4
Oct	174.3	172.6	170.5	164.7	179.0	175.2	163.2	219.0	180.9	136.2	172.6	104.6	165.2
Nov	173.6	172.2	170.2	164.3	178.3	174.6	163.1	218.8	180.5	136.4	171.0	105.2	164.8
Dec	173.4	172.5	170.5	164.5	177.9	174.3	163.8	218.2	180.0	136.1	170.6	106.1	165.0
2002 Jan	173.3	172.4	170.3	164.2	177.6	174.0	164.9	219.2	179.5	132.3	171.7	101.1	165.0
Feb	173.8	172.8	170.7	164.7	178.1	174.6	164.9	219.6	179.9	133.0	172.2	102.0	165.4
Mar	174.5	173.5	171.4	165.5	178.9	175.2	165.3	220.2	180.8	134.1	172.7	103.7	166.1
Apr	175.7	174.7	172.7	166.1	180.4	176.6	165.1	220.9	182.7	134.2	174.8	102.7	166.9
May	176.2	175.2	173.0	166.4	181.0	177.2	165.0	222.3	183.6	134.4	174.8	103.1	167.3
Jun	176.2	175.1	172.7	166.1	181.2	177.3	164.4	222.6	184.2	133.6	174.7	102.2	167.2
Jul	175.9	174.8	172.1	165.4	180.9	177.0	164.3	223.6	184.8	129.5	174.6	99.5	167.0
Aug	176.4	175.3	172.4	165.7	181.5	177.6	164.4	223.5	185.6	130.7	174.8	100.1	167.6

1 See chapter text.
2 This series has been constructed using the index for all items excluding mortgage interest payments prior to February 1995.

3 Seasonal food is defined as items of food the prices of which show significant seasonal variations. These are fresh fruit and vegetables, fresh fish, eggs and home-killed lamb.
4 There are no weights available for RPIY.

Source: Office for National Statistics: 020 7533 5874

16.5 Tax and Price Index[1]
United Kingdom

Tax and Price Index: January 1987 = 100

DQAB

	1987	1988	1989	1990	1991	1992	1993	1994	1995	1996	1997	1998	1999	2000	2001	2002
January	100.0	101.4	107.1	113.9	123.6	128.1	128.7	132.1	137.2	141.6	143.6	147.1	150.5	152.7	156.7	156.5
February	100.5	101.8	108.0	114.7	124.3	128.8	129.6	132.9	138.2	142.3	144.2	147.9	150.8	153.7	157.6	157.0
March	100.7	102.3	108.5	115.9	124.9	129.3	130.2	133.4	138.8	143.0	144.6	148.4	151.2	154.6	157.8	157.7
April	99.7	101.4	109.8	118.2	125.4	129.6	131.3	135.3	140.3	141.7	143.8	149.7	151.2	155.7	156.3	158.5
May	99.8	101.9	110.5	119.4	125.8	130.2	131.8	135.8	141.0	142.0	144.4	150.6	151.7	156.3	157.4	159.0
June	99.8	102.3	110.9	119.9	126.5	130.2	131.7	135.8	141.2	142.1	145.0	150.5	151.7	156.7	157.6	159.0
July	99.7	102.4	111.1	120.0	126.2	129.6	131.4	135.1	140.4	141.5	145.0	150.1	151.1	156.1	156.5	158.7
August	100.0	103.7	111.4	121.4	126.5	129.7	132.1	135.8	141.3	142.2	146.0	150.8	151.5	156.1	157.2	159.2
September	100.4	104.3	112.2	122.7	127.0	130.3	132.7	136.1	142.0	143.0	146.9	151.5	152.3	157.3	157.8	160.4
October	100.9	105.4	111.7	123.8	127.5	130.8	132.6	136.4	141.2	143.0	147.1	151.6	152.6	157.2	157.5	..
November	101.5	106.0	112.8	123.4	128.1	130.6	132.4	136.5	141.2	143.1	147.2	151.5	152.8	157.7	156.8	..
December	101.4	106.3	113.1	123.3	128.2	130.1	132.7	137.2	142.1	143.6	147.6	151.5	153.4	157.8	156.6	..

Retail Prices Index: January 1987 = 100

CHAW

	1987	1988	1989	1990	1991	1992	1993	1994	1995	1996	1997	1998	1999	2000	2001	2002
January	100.0	103.3	111.0	119.5	130.2	135.6	137.9	141.3	146.0	150.2	154.4	159.5	163.4	166.6	171.1	173.3
February	100.4	103.7	111.8	120.2	130.9	136.3	138.8	142.1	146.9	150.9	155.0	160.3	163.7	167.5	172.0	173.8
March	100.6	104.1	112.3	121.4	131.4	136.7	139.3	142.5	147.5	151.5	155.4	160.8	164.1	168.4	172.2	174.5
April	101.8	105.8	114.3	125.1	133.1	138.8	140.6	144.2	149.0	152.6	156.3	162.6	165.2	170.1	173.1	175.7
May	101.9	106.2	115.0	126.2	133.5	139.3	141.1	144.7	149.6	152.9	156.9	163.5	165.6	170.7	174.2	176.2
June	101.9	106.6	115.4	126.7	134.1	139.3	141.0	144.7	149.8	153.0	157.5	163.4	165.6	171.1	174.4	176.2
July	101.8	106.7	115.5	126.8	133.8	138.8	140.7	144.0	149.1	152.4	157.5	163.0	165.1	170.5	173.3	175.9
August	102.1	107.9	115.8	128.1	134.1	138.9	141.3	144.7	149.9	153.1	158.5	163.7	165.5	170.5	174.0	176.4
September	102.4	108.4	116.6	129.3	134.6	139.4	141.9	145.0	150.6	153.8	159.3	164.4	166.2	171.7	174.6	..
October	102.9	109.5	117.5	130.3	135.1	139.9	141.8	145.2	149.8	153.8	159.5	164.5	166.5	171.6	174.3	..
November	103.4	110.0	118.5	130.0	135.6	139.7	141.6	145.3	149.8	153.9	159.6	164.4	166.7	172.1	173.6	..
December	103.3	110.3	118.8	129.9	135.7	139.2	141.9	146.0	150.7	154.4	160.0	164.4	167.3	172.2	173.4	..

Percentage changes on one year earlier

	1988	1989	1990	1991	1992	1993	1994	1995	1996	1997	1998	1999	2000	2001	2002
Tax and Price Index															
January	1.4	5.6	6.3	8.5	3.6	0.5	2.6	3.9	3.2	1.4	2.4	2.3	1.5	2.6	-0.1
February	1.3	6.1	6.2	8.4	3.6	0.6	2.5	4.0	3.0	1.3	2.6	2.0	1.9	2.5	-0.4
March	1.6	6.1	6.8	7.8	3.5	0.7	2.5	4.0	3.0	1.1	2.6	1.9	2.2	2.1	-0.1
April	1.7	8.3	7.7	6.1	3.3	1.3	3.0	3.7	1.0	1.5	4.1	1.0	3.0	0.4	1.4
May	2.1	8.4	8.1	5.4	3.5	1.2	3.0	3.8	0.7	1.7	4.3	0.7	3.0	0.7	1.0
June	2.5	8.4	8.1	5.5	2.9	1.2	3.1	4.0	0.6	2.0	3.8	0.8	3.3	0.6	0.9
July	2.7	8.5	8.0	5.2	2.7	1.4	2.8	3.9	0.8	2.5	3.5	0.7	3.3	0.3	1.4
August	3.7	7.4	9.0	4.2	2.5	1.9	2.8	4.1	0.6	2.7	3.3	0.5	3.0	0.7	1.3
September	3.9	7.6	9.4	3.5	2.6	1.8	2.6	4.3	0.7	2.7	3.1	0.5	3.3	0.3	..
October	4.5	6.0	10.8	3.0	2.6	1.4	2.9	3.5	1.3	2.9	3.1	0.7	3.0	0.2	..
November	4.4	6.4	9.4	3.8	2.0	1.4	3.1	3.4	1.3	2.9	2.9	0.9	3.2	-0.6	..
December	4.8	6.4	9.0	4.0	1.5	2.0	3.4	3.6	1.1	2.8	2.6	1.3	2.9	-0.8	..
Retail Prices Index															
January	3.3	7.5	7.7	9.0	4.1	1.7	2.5	3.3	2.9	2.8	3.3	2.4	2.0	2.7	1.3
February	3.3	7.8	7.5	8.9	4.1	1.8	2.4	3.4	2.7	2.7	3.4	2.1	2.3	2.7	1.0
March	3.5	7.9	8.1	8.2	4.0	1.9	2.3	3.5	2.7	2.6	3.5	2.1	2.6	2.3	1.3
April	3.9	8.0	9.4	6.4	4.3	1.3	2.6	3.3	2.4	2.4	4.0	1.6	3.0	1.8	1.5
May	4.2	8.3	9.7	5.8	4.3	1.3	2.6	3.4	2.2	2.6	4.2	1.3	3.1	2.1	1.1
June	4.6	8.3	9.8	5.8	3.9	1.2	2.6	3.5	2.1	2.9	3.7	1.3	3.3	1.9	1.0
July	4.8	8.2	9.8	5.5	3.7	1.4	2.3	3.5	2.2	3.3	3.5	1.3	3.3	1.6	1.5
August	5.7	7.3	10.6	4.7	3.6	1.7	2.4	3.6	2.1	3.5	3.3	1.1	3.0	2.1	1.4
September	5.9	7.6	10.9	4.1	3.6	1.8	2.2	3.6	2.1	3.6	3.2	1.1	3.3	1.7	..
October	6.4	7.3	10.9	3.7	3.6	1.4	2.4	3.2	2.7	3.7	3.1	1.2	3.1	1.6	..
November	6.4	7.7	9.7	4.3	3.0	1.4	2.6	3.1	2.7	3.7	3.0	1.4	3.2	0.9	..
December	6.8	7.7	9.3	4.5	2.6	1.9	2.9	3.2	2.5	3.6	2.8	1.8	2.9	0.7	..

1 See chapter text.

Source: Office for National Statistics: 020 7533 5874

16.6 Index of purchase prices of the means of agricultural production[1]
United Kingdom
Annual averages

1995 = 100

		Weights	1991	1992	1993	1994	1995	1996	1997	1998	1999	2000	2001
Goods and services currently consumed	BYEA	100	89.3	91.6	96.1	96.5	100.0	104.5	99.8	94.8	93.5	95.7	100.4
Seeds	BYEB	4.0	92.9	100.5	83.5	85.2	100.0	100.7	89.4	91.7	83.2	76.3	82.4
Energy, lubricants	BYED	6.0	94.5	97.2	100.6	101.6	100.0	103.4	103.4	94.5	102.6	127.6	122.9
Fuels for heating	KVBA	0.7	107.7	97.4	105.8	96.5	100.0	120.4	111.7	89.9	101.6	154.8	148.0
Motor fuel	KVBB	3.3	89.1	91.2	97.6	101.9	100.0	102.3	105.8	96.7	109.4	144.6	139.0
Electricity	KVBC	1.9	99.1	108.1	104.3	103.2	100.0	99.5	96.1	91.8	90.2	87.7	85.0
Lubricants	KVBD	0.1	99.5	96.9	97.4	99.4	100.0	99.3	101.1	103.4	113.5	117.2	118.4
Fertilisers and soil improvers	BYEE	9.7	92.7	86.6	81.7	88.7	100.0	107.2	97.3	86.2	83.4	87.9	102.1
Straight nitrogen	EDOZ	3.9	96.1	89.7	81.7	88.7	100.0	110.7	95.1	79.2	75.6	91.1	117.6
Compound fertilisers	KVBF	5.3	90.7	84.3	80.9	88.0	100.0	104.7	98.2	89.2	86.8	83.5	90.1
Other fertiliser (mainly lime and chalk)	KVBG	0.4	88.8	90.8	93.8	98.4	100.0	107.9	109.7	112.5	113.5	117.3	118.0
Plant protection products	BYEF	6.2	93.4	95.9	97.2	100.6	100.0	106.0	105.7	98.0	96.4	89.9	87.7
Animal feedstuffs	BYEG	32.0	93.6	97.3	103.4	97.7	100.0	107.9	97.1	83.0	77.1	77.5	83.0
Feed wheat	KVBI	2.6	103.6	105.1	106.4	93.0	100.0	101.4	80.3	68.4	66.6	60.0	66.8
Whole barley	KVBJ	2.9	102.0	103.2	107.9	96.4	100.0	99.6	77.6	67.1	69.2	62.4	63.9
Whole oats	KVBL	0.2	109.3	117.8	134.6	108.8	100.0	108.3	85.1	68.5	73.8	69.3	69.1
Maize glutten feed	ZBUW	0.4	97.1	96.2	97.2	96.6	100.0	111.4	81.7	66.0	69.4	69.3	76.2
Oilcake	KVBM	2.0	92.0	96.7	110.6	101.7	100.0	129.7	124.8	86.2	77.4	94.0	102.8
White fish meal	KVBN	0.6	92.1	94.6	88.7	86.9	100.0	127.9	120.4	132.6	89.6	96.2	110.6
Other straight feedstuffs	ZBUX	3.4	85.2	91.1	95.2	93.4	100.4	107.1	93.6	77.3	70.3	77.3	86.2
All straight feedstuffs	KVBH	12.3	95.8	99.3	104.3	95.2	100.1	108.4	92.6	76.7	71.2	72.7	79.3
Feedstuffs non-concentrates	EDPA	0.6	96.0	98.8	103.6	95.0	99.8	108.4	92.5	76.3	71.1	72.9	79.8
Compound feedstuffs for:	KVBP	19.1	92.0	96.0	102.9	99.4	100.0	107.6	100.2	87.3	81.1	80.7	85.4
Cattle and calves	ZBUY	7.7	91.6	96.8	105.4	100.8	100.0	107.9	100.9	87.0	82.7	82.7	87.9
Pigs	KVBS	4.9	91.8	95.6	102.6	98.2	100.0	106.6	98.0	85.2	77.0	75.5	79.8
Poultry	KVBT	5.3	95.1	97.1	101.4	99.1	100.0	108.1	99.8	89.0	82.4	81.8	87.0
Sheep	KVBU	1.2	82.2	86.8	94.3	97.7	100.0	108.2	106.0	90.7	82.1	84.0	85.8
Maintenance and repair of plant	BYEI	7.5	84.1	90.5	95.7	97.7	100.0	104.9	109.3	112.5	116.6	120.9	126.2
Maintenance and repair of buildings	BYEJ	3.9	87.1	87.7	90.3	94.5	100.0	100.9	102.6	103.8	102.8	105.3	107.3
Veterinary services	BYEK	3.0	98.0	98.9	99.4	99.5	100.0	100.9	102.3	103.5	103.8	102.8	101.6
General expenses	BYEL	18.0	85.0	85.4	95.9	98.7	100.0	98.7	99.9	105.5	109.4	112.4	118.6
Goods and services contributing to investment in agriculture	BYEM	100	89.6	93.0	95.9	97.7	100.0	103.9	107.0	109.0	109.7	109.7	108.6
Machinery and other equipment	BYEN	74.0	90.2	94.1	97.2	98.5	100.0	104.8	107.6	109.0	109.4	107.8	104.9
Machinery and plant for cultivation	KVBV	8.4	90.3	92.7	95.3	97.1	100.0	110.0	114.5	119.8	121.5	122.6	122.1
Machinery and plant for harvesting	KVBW	15.2	89.5	94.1	96.9	96.9	100.0	103.0	106.2	108.0	109.7	109.7	101.3
Farm machinery and installations	KVBX	6.4	92.5	94.3	95.6	98.0	100.0	101.3	103.2	106.6	108.3	111.3	118.6
Tractors	KVBY	30.2	89.7	93.9	99.1	100.1	100.0	105.7	108.4	109.0	109.8	107.3	103.9
Other vehicles	KVBZ	13.7	91.0	95.4	95.5	97.7	100.0	103.2	105.5	104.7	101.0	96.1	94.5
Buildings	BYEO	26.0	88.0	90.0	92.2	95.4	100.0	101.2	105.1	109.0	110.8	115.2	118.9
Farm buildings	KVCA	17.8	87.6	89.1	91.5	95.2	100.0	102.0	105.9	109.1	110.8	115.1	119.3
Engineering and soil improvement operations	KVCB	8.2	88.8	91.8	93.8	95.8	100.0	99.4	103.3	108.9	110.8	115.2	118.0

Note: The sum of the Percentages of categories included in "Goods and Services currently consumed" does not add up to 100% due to the exclusion of some minor categories.

1 See chapter text.

Source: Department for Environment, Food and Rural Affairs: 01904 455253

16.7 Index of producer prices of agricultural products[1]
United Kingdom
Annual averages

1995 = 100

		Weights	1991	1992	1993	1994	1995	1996	1997	1998	1999	2000	2001
All products	BYEP	100	84.8	86.0	92.1	92.6	100.0	98.0	85.7	78.6	76.3	74.9	80.5
All crop products	BYEQ	37.6	88.5	84.3	87.1	89.0	100.0	90.0	76.4	77.2	75.5	71.2	79.3
Cereals	BYER	13.7	100.0	103.6	105.3	93.7	100.0	99.7	79.3	68.3	66.5	59.9	64.6
Wheat for:													
breadmaking	KVDA	1.6	104.8	110.3	113.4	96.2	100.0	103.0	87.3	76.8	70.7	62.8	68.8
other milling	KVDB	0.9	107.6	108.9	106.5	93.1	100.0	101.3	82.1	71.2	68.1	61.6	66.0
feeding	KVDC	6.4	101.2	104.3	106.8	92.9	100.0	100.2	81.2	68.3	66.2	59.8	66.9
Barley for:													
feeding	KVDD	2.5	100.8	103.7	108.7	96.4	100.0	97.9	76.9	67.9	62.3	64.3	63.8
malting	KVDE	1.9	86.1	90.3	84.5	88.7	100.0	95.7	67.7	60.5	52.6	55.1	55.1
Oats for:													
milling	KVDF	0.2	105.2	115.3	123.3	103.2	100.0	101.7	81.3	66.2	63.3	68.5	68.7
feeding	KVDG	0.2	105.0	116.2	127.0	102.2	100.0	105.4	74.8	63.3	71.7	66.1	65.8
Root crops	BYES	7.9	54.0	48.6	45.8	67.7	100.0	59.4	39.0	56.3	57.9	44.1	56.0
Potatoes:													
early	KVDH	0.4	71.3	61.0	61.7	115.2	100.0	70.8	50.3	70.8	63.5	68.9	104.1
main crop	KVDI	5.5	40.1	31.7	25.5	54.9	100.0	42.6	21.5	48.6	52.1	33.9	46.3
Sugar beet	KVDJ	2.0	87.6	91.0	96.5	92.8	100.0	101.6	83.2	74.2	72.4	66.6	72.4
Fresh vegetables	BYET	6.2	91.0	83.2	90.9	93.4	100.1	96.6	90.9	96.8	90.6	94.9	104.3
Cauliflowers	KVDK	0.4	98.2	94.7	97.3	103.1	100.0	96.8	85.8	95.2	89.3	108.2	112.6
Lettuce	KVDL	0.8	95.6	100.4	107.1	105.1	100.2	84.1	101.7	85.7	91.4	85.9	114.1
Tomatoes	KVDM	0.4	107.3	105.6	103.9	94.1	100.0	117.0	90.8	94.5	91.1	105.1	95.4
Carrots	KVDN	0.6	74.9	50.6	64.0	77.1	100.0	92.0	61.9	88.1	83.8	76.6	106.8
Cabbage	KVDO	0.4	84.9	84.4	91.4	80.0	100.0	99.2	83.7	95.5	94.5	102.1	120.9
Beans	KVDP	0.1	95.9	88.3	110.0	124.2	100.0	100.8	103.4	132.3	101.1	194.5	132.2
Onions	KVDQ	0.5	89.6	68.8	98.2	118.9	100.0	73.0	83.4	109.4	72.2	70.0	87.1
Mushrooms	KVDR	0.9	89.9	83.2	91.5	90.1	100.0	102.7	92.0	91.9	91.1	92.9	84.6
Fresh fruit	BYEU	1.5	114.5	90.6	90.9	91.4	99.9	102.0	105.6	99.6	93.8	101.7	97.3
Dessert apples	KVDS	0.3	125.2	93.9	77.5	83.9	99.9	108.8	103.7	89.5	83.3	82.7	85.7
Dessert pears	KVDT	0.1	114.1	100.9	88.2	90.5	100.0	101.0	97.3	90.9	89.5	82.3	103.1
Cooking apples	KVDU	0.2	110.4	84.2	83.7	96.8	100.0	116.8	125.7	127.9	95.8	95.1	100.5
Strawberries	KVDV	0.4	150.9	122.8	114.4	112.8	100.0	102.3	106.6	93.4	102.1	99.4	94.2
Raspberries	KVDW	0.2	81.8	53.8	78.0	71.3	100.0	90.2	100.4	82.2	88.7	97.1	100.7
Seeds	BYEV	0.5	93.1	98.5	76.7	81.6	100.0	93.5	78.9	77.4	67.2	56.3	65.0
Flowers and plants	BYEW	3.7	94.2	93.8	93.6	99.1	100.0	100.8	103.9	104.0	107.4	103.6	107.6
Other crop products	BYEX	4.0	97.6	78.0	94.5	99.7	100.0	92.2	81.2	85.7	82.8	87.4	106.7
Animals and animal products	BYEY	56.4	85.0	91.2	99.5	97.1	100.0	103.7	91.3	76.2	74.2	78.2	79.2
Animals for slaughter	BYEZ	33.1	86.0	90.1	105.8	100.0	100.0	87.0	76.6	68.6	70.0	68.4	69.2
Calves	KVDX	0.5	75.9	90.2	118.8	115.3	100.0	90.9	74.5	62.0	47.8	41.5	39.1
Clean cattle	KVDY	9.7	87.3	89.2	103.8	99.4	100.0	85.3	77.9	69.1	74.0	72.7	73.3
Cows and bulls	KVDZ	2.4	82.7	93.7	111.4	99.4	100.0	92.9	71.8	68.0	58.6	58.6	58.6
Clean pigs	KVEA	6.6	86.1	96.6	86.8	83.7	100.0	115.4	92.9	67.7	65.9	79.1	81.9
Sows and boars	KVEB	0.3	85.3	101.0	76.1	78.9	100.0	109.1	85.3	44.0	44.0	54.4	58.3
Sheep	KVEC	4.4	60.6	76.4	89.9	97.6	100.0	118.5	108.7	80.4	74.9	83.0	84.5
Ewe and ram	KVED	0.4	71.2	88.3	106.2	101.3	100.0	138.4	144.9	84.8	59.3	73.1	111.3
Poultry	KVEE	7.9	96.3	96.1	104.7	103.5	100.0	111.1	101.9	93.5	90.0	91.7	90.1
Chickens	KVEF	5.5	97.8	99.3	109.4	105.9	100.0	112.1	104.2	91.1	87.1	85.9	86.0
Turkeys	KVEG	2.1	92.7	88.2	93.8	98.4	100.0	109.0	95.0	97.1	95.7	106.3	100.4
Cows' milk	BYFA	20.0	77.6	81.6	88.0	89.0	100.0	100.3	88.7	77.7	73.6	67.9	77.2
Eggs	BYFB	2.2	111.6	90.7	106.7	108.4	100.0	113.1	94.6	83.3	74.1	75.9	80.8
Other animal products:													
Wool (clip)	BYFC	0.3	88.2	85.2	66.3	101.5	100.0	91.8	79.4	52.1	49.4	52.9	46.0

Note: The sum of the Percentages of categories included in "All products" does not add up to 100% due to the exclusion of some minor categories.

1 See chapter text.

Source: Department for Environment, Food and Rural Affairs: 01904 455253

Prices

16.8 Commodity price trends[1]
United Kingdom
Calendar years

			1990	1991	1992	1993	1994	1995	1996	1997	1998	1999	2000
Wheat £ per tonne	KVAA	Average ex-farm price[2,3]	109.8	116.5	120.5	124.2	106.4	115.6	112.5	91.8	77.8	75.4	67.9
Barley £ per tonne	KVAB	Average ex-farm price[2,3]	108.8	107.8	113.9	113.6	105.4	107.6	103.7	86.3	79.2	74.2	69.9
Oats £ per tonne	KVAC	Average ex-farm price[2,3]	106.4	105.9	115.1	128.8	108.4	101.4	107.4	82.3	66.4	71.1	64.1
Rye £ per tonne	KVAD	Average ex-farm price[2]	114.60	118.50	115.20	113.40	112.80	107.90	113.90	..	..	..	..
Hops £ per tonne	KVAE	Average farm-gate price	2 922	3 211	3 208	3 357	4 005	3 595	3 360	3 550	3 676	4 033	3 820
Potatoes £ per tonne	KVAF	Average farm-gate price[4]	98.70	93.00	75.20	64.10	125.80	187.70	100.50	66.00	121.60	120.50	..
Sugar beet £ per tonne	KVAG	Producer price[5]	31.50	31.40	38.00	36.50	34.70	38.30	37.70	32.90	31.90	..	..
Oilseed rape	KVAH	Average market price[6]	280.00	248.00	133.00	153.00	185.40	177.70	186.90	160.20	164.30	..	..
Apples £ per tonne	KPUE	Dessert average farm-gate price[7]	501.7	561.2	315.4	297.7	391.4	437.3	493.6	525.0	476.1	405.0	359.8
	KVAI	Dessert average market price	500.0	589.0	414.0	370.0	447.4	465.7	474.7	538.1	..	..	..
	KVAJ	Culinary average market price	408.0	420.0	312.0	327.0	446.4	405.9	462.8	558.4	..	..	..
	KPUJ	Culinary average farm-gate price	269.6	281.3	189.5	230.8	232.3	248.2	286.8	335.1	297.3	209.9	236.0
Pears £ per tonne	KPUG	Average farm-gate price	474.9	546.9	430.9	368.4	466.2	425.1	446.2	432.3	404.0	393.5	264.0
	KVAK	Average market price	485.0	468.0	461.0	380.0	408.3	447.5	441.7	433.1	394.2	..	..
Tomatoes £ per tonne	LQMH	Average farm-gate price[7]	605.5	520.8	426.5	528.9	613.5	505.0	641.2	478.4	513.7	499.6	667.6
	KVAL	Average market price[7]	694.0	604.0	494.0	552.8	675.2	624.0	700.1	655.6	..	..	..
Cauliflowers £ per tonne	KPUI	Average farm-gate price[7]	238.5	246.3	201.5	218.6	222.1	283.3	237.8	225.5	215.4	217.4	242.3
	KVAM	Average market price[7]	296.0	292.0	253.0	296.9	323.5	394.9	442.6	372.0	..	..	..
Cattle (rearing)	KVAN	1st quality Hereford/cross bull calves[8,9]	128.00	119.92	145.44	185.95	182.06	166.32	131.81	146.95	107.86	88.24	79.52
£ per head	KVAO	1st quality beef/ cross yearling steers[9]	397.00	397.30	419.49	478.00	471.00	475.00	445.00	427.00	369.00	382.00	400.05
Cattle (fat) p per kg liveweight	KVAP	Clean cattle[10]	106.30	106.92	109.58	128.04	121.71	123.15	105.52	96.89	86.10	92.12	89.68

16.8
Commodity price trends[1]
United Kingdom
Calendar years

			1991	1992	1993	1994	1995	1996	1997	1998	1999	2000	2001
Sheep (store) £ per head	KVAQ	1st quality lambs, hoggets and tegs[8]	35.50	37.90	35.56	40.02	44.46	46.83	53.42	31.28	28.66	34.50	..
Sheep (fat) p per kg estimated dressed carcase weight	KVAR KVAS	Great Britain[11] Northern Ireland[12]	148.16 179.41	182.12 172.37	218.96 199.50	236.88 221.95	236.40 214.41	283.13 260.46	239.02 228.23	192.46 179.06	180.27 165.71	196.44 182.67	.. ..
Pigs £ per kg deadweight	KVAT	Average price clean pigs	102.42	115.12	103.02	99.57	118.84	137.73	110.83	80.65	78.55	94.35	..
Broilers p per kg carcass weight	KVAU	Average producer price	81.0	82.7	86.8	86.5	83.8	90.7	85.9	76.6	71.8	..	..
Milk p per litre	KVAV	Average net return to producers[13]	19.82	20.94	22.68	23.19	24.96	25.01	22.31	19.44	18.55	17.34	20.04
Eggs p per dozen	KVAW	Average producer price[14]	36.30	36.60	41.90	42.40	38.20	45.70	39.80	36.20	34.00		..
Wool p per kg	KHWQ	Average producer price for clip paid to producers by the British Wool Marketing Board	83.40	80.90	62.00	98.90	95.00	86.90	74.90	48.00	46.60	51.30	..

1 This table gives indications of the movement in commodity prices at the first point of sale. The series do not always show total receipts by farmers; for some commodities additional premiums or deficiency payments are made to achieve support price levels.

2 Weighted average ex-farm prices of United Kingdom cereals.

3 Data from 1997 onwards have been revised and are not directly comparable with earlier years.

4 Weighted average price paid to growers for early and main crop potatoes in the United Kingdom (includes all potatoes and a value for sacks).

5 Returns to growers figures since 1986 prices per 'adjusted' tonne at 16% sugar content.

6 Typical contract price adjusted to delivered basis and 40 per cent oil content.

7 Weighted average wholesale prices for England and Wales. Average farmgate price for England and Wales, crop year (June-May).

8 Average prices at representative markets in England and Wales.

9 Category change 1988: formerly 1st quality yearling steers beef/dairy cross, now consists of Hereford/cross, Charolais/cross, Limousin/cross, Simmental/cross, Belgian/cross, other continental cross, other beef/dairy cross, other beef/beef cross.

10 Based on Meat and Livestock Commission all clean cattle prices.

11 Average of Great Britain weekly market prices as used to determine the level of ewe premium.

12 Average of Northern Ireland weekly market prices used to determine the level of ewe premium.

13 Derived by dividing total value of output by the total quantity of output available for human consumption.

14 Average price of all Class A eggs weighted according to quantity in each grade.

Source: Department for Environment, Food and Rural Affairs: 01904 455332

17 Government finance

Government finance

Public sector *(Tables 17.1 to 17.3 and 17.5)*
In Table 17.1 the term public sector describes the consolidation of central government, local government and public corporations. General government is the consolidated total of central government and local government. The table shows details of the key public sector finances' indicators, consistent with the European System of Accounts 1995 (ESA95), by sub sector.

The concepts in Table 17.1 are consistent with the format for public finances in the *Economic and Fiscal Strategy Report (EFSR),* published by HM Treasury 11 June 1998, and The Budget. The public sector surplus on current budget is equivalent to net saving in national accounts plus capital tax receipts. Net investment is gross capital formation, plus payments less receipts of investment grants, less depreciation. Net borrowing is net investment less surplus on current budget. Net borrowing differs from the net cash requirement (see below) in that it is measured on an accruals basis whereas the net cash requirement is mainly a cash measure which includes some financial transactions.

Table 17.2 shows the Public sector key fiscal balances. The table shows the component detail of the public sector key fiscal balance by economic category. The tables are consistent with table C22 published in *Budget 2002.*

Table 17.3 shows public sector net debt. Public sector net debt consists of the public sector's financial liabilities at face value minus its liquid assets - mainly foreign currency exchange reserves and bank deposits. General government gross debt (consolidated) in table 17.3 is consistent with the definition of general government gross debt reported to the European Commission under the requirements of the Maastricht Treaty.

More information on the concepts in table 17.1, 17.2 and 17.3 can be found in a guide to monthly public sector finance statistics, *GSS Methodology Series No 12,* the ONS First Releases *Public Sector Finances* and *Public Sector Accounts* and *Financial Statistics Explanatory Handbook.*

Table 17.5 shows the taxes and national insurance contributions paid to central government, local government, and to the institutions of the European Union. The table is the same as table 11.1 of the Blue Book. More information on the data and concepts in the table can be found in Chapter 11 of the Blue Book.

Consolidated Fund and National Loans Fund *(Tables 17.4, 17.6 and 17.7)*
The central government embraces all bodies for whose activities a Minister of the Crown, or other responsible person, is accountable to Parliament. It includes, in addition to the ordinary government departments, a number of bodies administering public policy but without the substantial degree of financial independence which characterises the public corporations; it also includes certain extra-budgetary funds and accounts controlled by departments.

The government's financial transactions are handled through a number of statutory funds, or accounts. The most important of these is the Consolidated Fund which is the government's main account with the Bank of England. Up to 31 March 1968 the Consolidated Fund was virtually synonymous with the term 'Exchequer' which was then the government's central cash account. From 1 April 1968 the National Loans Fund, with a separate account at the Bank of England, was set up by the National Loans Act, 1968. The general effect of this Act was to remove from the Consolidated Fund most of the government's domestic lending and the whole of the government's borrowing transactions and to provide for them to be brought to account in the National Loans Fund.

Revenue from taxation and miscellaneous receipts, including interest and dividends on loans made from Votes, continue to be paid into the Consolidated Fund. After meeting the ordinary expenditure on Supply Services and the Consolidated Fund Standing Services, the surplus or deficit of the Consolidated Fund (Table 17.4), is payable into or met by the National Loans Fund.

Table 17.4 also provides a summary of the transactions of the National Loans Fund. The service of the National Debt, previously borne by the Consolidated Fund, is now met from the National Loans Fund which receives (a) interest payable on loans to the nationalised industries, local authorities and other bodies, whether the loans were made before or after 1 April 1968 and (b) the profits of the Issue Department of the Bank of England, mainly derived from interest on government securities, which were formerly paid into the Exchange Equalisation Account. The net cost of servicing the National Debt after applying these interest receipts and similar items is a charge on the Consolidated Fund as part of the standing services. Details of National Loans Fund loans outstanding are shown in Table 17.7.

Details of borrowing and repayments of debt, other than loans from the National Loans Fund, are shown in Table 17.6.

Income tax *(Table 17.10)*
Following the introduction of Independent Taxation from 1990-91 the married couple's allowance was introduced. It is payable in addition to the personal allowance and between 1990-91 and 1992-93 went to the husband unless the transfer condition was met. The condition was that the husband was unable to make full use of the allowance himself and in that case he could transfer only part or all of the married couple's allowance to his wife. In 1993-94 all or half of the allowance could be transferred to the wife if the couple had agreed beforehand. The wife has the right to claim half the allowance. The married couple's allowance, and allowances linked to it, were restricted to 20 per cent in 1994-95 and to 15 per cent from 1995-96.

The age allowance replaces the single allowance, provided the taxpayer's income is below the limits shown in the table. From 1989-90, for incomes in excess of the limits, the allowance is reduced by £1 for each additional £2 of income until the ordinary limit is reached (before it was £2 for each £3 of additional income). The relief is due where the taxpayer is aged 65 or over in the year of assessment.

The additional personal allowance could be claimed by a single parent (or by a married man if his wife was totally incapacitated) who maintained a resident child at his or her own expense. Widow's bereavement allowance was due to a widow in the year of her husband's death and in the following year provided the widow had not remarried before the beginning of that year. Both the additional personal allowance and the widow's bereavement allowance were abolished from April 2000.

The blind person's allowance may be claimed by blind persons (in England and Wales, registered as blind by a local authority) and surplus blind person's allowance may be transferred to a husband or wife. Relief on life assurance premiums is given by deduction from the premium payable. From 1984-85, it is confined to policies made before 14 March 1984.

Rateable values *(Table 17.12)*
Major changes to local government finance in England and Wales took effect from 1 April 1990. These included the abolition of domestic rating - replaced by the community charge (replaced in 1993 by the council tax), the revaluation of all non-domestic properties, and the introduction of the Uniform Business Rate. Also in 1990, a new classification scheme was introduced which has resulted in differences in coverage. Further differences are caused by legislative changes which have changed the treatment of certain types of property.

There was little change in the total rateable value of non-domestic properties when all these properties were revalued in April 1995. Rateable values for offices fell and there was a rise for all other property types shown in the table.

With effect from 1 April 2000 all non-domestic properties were revalued. Overall there was an increase in rateable values of over 25% compared to the end of the 1995 list. The largest proportionate increase was for offices and cinemas, with all property types given in the table showing rises.

17.1 Sectoral analysis of key fiscal balances[1]
United Kingdom
Not seasonally adjusted

£ millions[2]

		1991 /92	1992 /93	1993 /94	1994 /95	1995 /96	1996 /97	1997 /98	1998 /99	1999 /00	2000 /01	2001 /02
Surplus on current budget[3]												
Central Government	ANLV	−7 331	−32 187	−39 143	−30 568	−23 208	−22 010	−362	11 347	23 681	24 395	9 821
Local government	NMMX	389	2 627	2 768	2 016	425	553	136	289	−1 812	−1 244	−421
General Government	ANLW	−6 942	−29 560	−36 375	−28 552	−22 783	−21 457	−226	11 636	21 869	23 151	9 400
Public corporations	FDDP	−4 479	−4 682	−4 225	−4 261	−1 890	−1 676	−1 375	−1 514	−1 826	−1 836	−1 738
Public sector	ANMU	−11 421	−34 242	−40 600	−32 813	−24 673	−23 133	−1 601	10 122	20 043	21 315	7 662
Net investment[4]												
Central government	−ANNS	13 415	19 253	13 100	14 165	13 693	9 073	7 229	7 172	7 103	8 319	11 009
Local government	−ANNT	1 847	−3 044	1 208	2 157	−50	−297	53	423	−778	−1 421	89
General Government	−ANNV	15 262	16 209	14 308	16 322	13 643	8 776	7 282	7 595	6 325	6 898	11 098
Public corporations	−ANNU	−4 289	−3 853	−3 950	−5 931	−3 384	−3 504	−2 393	−1 580	−1 940	−1 519	−2 270
Public sector	−ANNW	10 973	12 356	10 358	10 391	10 259	5 272	4 889	6 015	4 385	5 379	8 828
Net borrowing[5]												
Central government	−NMFJ	20 746	51 440	52 243	44 733	36 901	31 083	7 591	−4 175	−16 578	−16 076	1 188
Local government	−NMOE	1 458	−5 671	−1 560	141	−475	−850	−83	134	1 034	−177	510
General Government	−NNBK	22 204	45 769	50 683	44 874	36 426	30 233	7 508	−4 041	−15 544	−16 253	1 698
Public corporations	−CPCM	190	829	275	−1 670	−1 494	−1 828	−1 018	−66	−114	317	−532
Public sector	−ANNX	22 394	46 598	50 958	43 204	34 932	28 405	6 490	−4 107	−15 658	−15 936	1 166
Net cash requirement												
Central government[6]	RUUX	11 830	42 312	48 850	39 057	35 628	24 995	2 650	−6 170	−10 592	−37 143	3 911
Local government	ABEG	1 590	−5 735	−2 780	−961	−1 139	−843	−820	−404	979	−611	−402
General Government	RUUS	13 420	36 577	46 070	38 096	34 489	24 152	1 830	−6 574	−9 613	−37 754	3 489
Public corporations	ABEM	436	−317	61	−1 408	−3 004	−1 424	−718	−386	1 018	533	99
Public sector	RURQ	13 856	36 260	46 131	36 688	31 485	22 728	1 112	−6 960	−8 595	−37 221	3 608
Public sector debt												
Public sector net debt (£ billion)	RUTN	166.1	202.3	249.4	289.3	321.3	348.5	352.9	348.7	340.1	305.9	310.9
Public sector net debt as % GDP	RUTO	27.4	32.0	37.2	40.7	42.7	43.7	41.6	39.2	36.2	31.3	30.4

1 National accounts entities as defined under the European System of Accounts 1995 (ESA95) consistent with the latest national accounts. See chapter text.
2 Unless otherwise stated
3 Net saving, plus capital taxes.
4 Gross capital formation, plus payments less receipts, of investment grants less depreciation.

5 Net borrowing = net investment minus surplus on current budget. A version of General government net borrowing is reported to the European Commision under the requirements of the Maastricht Treaty.
6 Central government net cash requirement (own account).

Source: Office for National Statistics: 020 7533 5984

17.2

Public sector transactions and fiscal balances[1]
United Kingdom

£ millions

		1991 /92	1992 /93	1993 /94	1994 /95	1995 /96	1996 /97	1997 /98	1998 /99	1999 /00	2000 /01	2001 /02
Current receipts												
Taxes on income and wealth	ANSO	83 105	78 270	78 585	87 845	96 450	102 308	114 825	123 869	133 711	143 941	145 088
Taxes on production	NMYE	79 524	79 891	83 091	90 389	96 307	101 009	111 322	117 155	126 795	131 402	136 437
Other current taxes[2]	NVCM	9 376	10 688	10 535	11 312	12 127	13 013	14 064	15 337	16 407	17 496	18 308
Taxes on capital	NMGI	1 300	1 211	1 335	1 409	1 518	1 558	1 684	1 805	2 054	2 238	2 372
Social contributions	ANBO	36 687	36 972	40 136	42 832	45 007	47 219	51 617	55 067	57 161	62 245	63 485
Gross operating surplus	ANBP	12 427	12 504	14 440	15 392	18 124	17 418	17 473	17 739	17 146	17 110	17 719
Interest and dividends from private sector and RoW	ANBQ	5 978	5 030	4 275	4 133	4 435	4 363	4 468	5 072	4 481	6 063	4 719
Interest and dividends (net) from public sector												
Rent and other current transfers[3]	ANBS	1 146	914	1 287	1 577	1 629	1 880	1 622	1 360	1 535	2 449	2 549
Total current receipts	ANBT	229 543	225 480	233 684	254 889	275 597	288 768	317 075	337 404	359 290	382 942	390 665
Current expenditure												
Current expenditure on goods and services[4]	GZSN	123 905	130 500	131 829	138 140	142 732	146 774	149 368	157 844	168 794	181 376	197 780
Subsidies	NMRL	4 986	5 768	4 712	5 537	5 744	6 695	5 912	4 525	4 509	5 016	6 027
Social benefits	ANLY	78 813	87 717	95 259	97 756	100 688	104 995	106 722	107 628	111 310	116 621	125 091
Net current grants abroad[5]	GZSI	−1 996	112	−371	553	458	−751	102	−847	−253	−146	−1 850
Current grants (net) within general government												
Other current grants	NNAI	4 612	4 675	10 108	9 739	10 907	13 571	14 441	16 163	16 957	19 313	19 934
Interest and dividends paid to private sector and RoW	ANLO	18 297	19 045	20 764	23 489	26 765	28 118	29 722	29 354	25 284	26 403	22 601
Total current expenditure	ANLT	228 617	247 817	262 301	275 214	287 294	299 402	306 267	314 667	326 601	348 583	369 583
Saving, gross plus capital taxes	ANSP	926	−22 337	−28 617	−20 325	−11 697	−10 634	10 808	22 737	32 689	34 359	21 082
Depreciation	−ANNZ	−12 347	−11 905	−11 983	−12 488	−12 976	−12 499	−12 409	−12 615	−12 646	−13 044	−13 420
Surplus on current budget	ANMU	−11 421	−34 242	−40 600	−32 813	−24 673	−23 133	−1 601	10 122	20 043	21 315	7 662
Net investment												
Gross fixed capital formation[6]	ANSQ	18 350	19 347	17 905	19 114	19 135	14 312	13 472	13 955	13 178	15 089	15 920
Less depreciation	−ANNZ	−12 347	−11 905	−11 983	−12 488	−12 976	−12 499	−12 409	−12 615	−12 646	−13 044	−13 420
Increase in inventories and valuables	ANSR	155	−165	−224	−662	21	56	138	231	−452	−211	49
Capital grants (net) within public sector												
Capital grants to private sector and RoW	ANSS	5 268	5 418	5 153	4 854	4 432	3 885	4 204	4 811	4 732	4 301	7 218
Capital grants from private sector and RoW	−ANST	−453	−339	−493	−427	−353	−482	−516	−367	−427	−756	−939
Total net investment	−ANNW	10 973	12 356	10 358	10 391	10 259	5 272	4 889	6 015	4 385	5 379	8 828
Net borrowing[7]	−ANNX	22 394	46 598	50 958	43 204	34 932	28 405	6 490	−4 107	−15 658	−15 936	1 166
Financial transactions determining net cash requirement												
Net lending to private sector and RoW	ANSU	−899	–	133	−1 167	−1 749	−655	−224	267	2 036	2 768	2 177
Net acquisition of UK company securities	ANSV	−7 766	−7 909	−5 194	−6 374	−2 344	−3 992	−1 642	423	−504	835	−693
Accounts receivable/payable	ANSW	1 084	−1 633	917	70	3 127	−992	−671	297	5 658	−21 170	732
Adjustment for interest on gilts	ANSX	−1 254	−1 255	−791	−1 036	−1 895	−382	−2 349	−2 446	−1 295	−2 630	−377
Other financial transcations[8]	ANSY	297	459	108	1 991	−586	344	−492	−1 394	1 168	−1 088	603
Public sector net cash requirement	RURQ	13 856	36 260	46 131	36 688	31 485	22 728	1 112	−6 960	−8 595	−37 221	3 608

1 See chapter text.
2 Includes domestic rates, council tax, community charge, motor vehicle duty paid by household, and some licence fees.
3 ESA95 transactions D44, D45, D74, D75 and D72-D71: includes rent of land, oil royalties, other property income, and fines.
4 Includes non-trading capital consumption.

5 Net of current grants received from abroad.
6 Including net acquisition of land.
7 Net borrowing equals net investment minus surplus on current budget.
8 Includes statistical discrepancy, finance leasing and similar borrowing, insurance technical reserves and some other minor adjustments.

Source: Office for National Statistics: 020 7533 5984

17.3 Public sector net debt[1]
United Kingdom

£ millions

		1993 /94	1994 /95	1995 /96	1996 /97	1997 /98	1998 /99	1999 /00	2000 /01	2001 /02
Cental government sterling gross debt:										
British government stock										
Conventional gilts	BKPK	168 414	186 666	208 943	231 869	232 292	223 105	218 687	204 285	200 833
Index linked gilts	BKPL	34 854	39 207	46 133	51 535	58 729	62 289	65 740	70 316	70 417
Total	BKPM	203 268	225 872	255 075	283 404	291 021	285 394	284 427	274 601	271 250
Sterling Treasury bills	BKPJ	3 483	8 051	10 781	4 996	2 106	4 721	4 453	3 521	9 700
National savings	ACUA	48 330	51 843	56 965	61 754	63 271	63 620	62 546	62 161	62 440
Tax instruments	ACRV	2 133	1 612	1 222	852	705	574	535	491	478
Other sterling debt[2]	BKSK	15 045	25 773	26 758	26 571	25 312	26 152	26 773	28 244	26 280
Central government sterling gross debt total	BKSL	272 259	313 151	350 801	377 578	382 416	380 461	378 734	369 018	370 148
Central government foreign currency gross debt:										
US$ bonds	BKPG	4 651	4 241	4 524	4 294	4 180	4 338	4 388	4 924	2 107
DM bonds[3]	EYST	2 018	2 245	2 219	1 828	–	–	–	–	–
ECU bonds	EYSJ	1 945	2 045	2 059	1 777	1 606	1 672	1 500	–	–
ECU/euro Treasury notes	EYSV	3 890	4 499	4 118	3 199	2 891	3 010	2 701	2 486	1 225
ECU/euro Treasury bills	EYSN	2 723	2 863	2 883	2 488	2 249	2 341	–	–	–
Other foreign currency debt	BKPH	1 632	1 018	982	752	537	456	365	291	243
Central government foreign currency gross debt total	BKPI	16 860	16 912	16 785	14 338	11 463	11 816	8 954	7 701	3 575
Central government gross debt total	BKPW	289 119	330 063	367 586	391 916	393 879	392 277	387 688	376 719	373 723
Local government gross debt total	EYKP	50 239	50 229	50 552	51 599	51 933	52 742	53 437	52 333	52 165
less										
Central government holdings of local government debt	-EYKZ	–40 977	–40 707	–41 266	–42 555	–43 397	–45 273	–46 771	–48 026	–47 762
Local government holdings of central government debt	-EYLA	–124	–149	–153	–155	–170	–273	–254	–31	–29
General government gross debt (consolidated)	BKPX	298 257	339 436	376 719	400 805	402 245	399 473	394 100	380 995	378 097
Public corporations gross debt	EYYD	23 867	26 916	26 595	26 158	26 044	26 775	26 812	27 740	26 668
less:										
Central government holdings of public corporations debt	-EYXY	–22 951	–26 279	–25 980	–25 664	–25 668	–26 440	–26 453	–27 181	–26 335
Local government holdings of public corporations debt	-EYXZ	–69	–3	–	–1	–	–4	–1	–124	–122
Public corporations holdings of central government debt	-BKPZ	–2 854	–3 503	–5 723	–7 125	–7 485	–6 529	–6 301	–6 363	–5 096
Public corporations holdings of local government debt	-EYXV	–1 620	–1 586	–890	–805	–810	–779	–812	–106	–65
Public sector gross debt (consolidated)	BKQA	294 630	334 981	370 721	393 368	394 326	392 496	387 345	374 961	373 147
Public sector liquid assets:										
Official reserves	AIPD	28 908	28 330	30 463	25 547	21 293	22 147	21 498	30 423	28 055
Central government deposits[4]	BKSN	1 775	1 816	1 808	2 067	2 292	1 762	1 879	2 797	2 846
Other central government	BKSN	1 250	–	–	–	–	–	4 756	15 663	10 734
Local government deposits[4]	BKSO	8 762	9 335	10 229	11 276	11 790	12 275	11 758	11 514	11 584
Other local government short term assets	BKQG	2 424	2 621	2 826	3 256	3 693	4 334	4 754	5 772	5 966
Public corporations deposits[4]	BKSP	1 353	2 622	3 089	1 778	1 469	2 029	1 455	1 633	1 895
Other public corporations short term assets	BKSQ	790	943	1 054	964	937	1 300	1 128	1 212	1 180
Public sector liquid assets total	BKQJ	45 262	45 667	49 469	44 888	41 474	43 847	47 228	69 014	62 260
Public sector net debt	BKQK	249 368	289 314	321 252	348 480	352 852	348 649	340 117	305 947	310 887
as percentage of GDP[5]	RUTO	37.2	40.7	42.7	43.7	41.6	39.2	36.2	31.3	30.4

1 See chapter text.
2 Including overdraft with Bank of England.
3 Matured on 28 October 1997.
4 Bank and building society deposits.
5 Gross domestic product at market prices from 12 months centred on the end of the month.

Source: Office for National Statistics: 020 7533 5984

17.4 Consolidated Fund and National Loans Fund[1]: revenue and expenditure; receipts and payments

United Kingdom   Years ending 31 March

£ millions

		1992 /93	1993 /94	1994 /95	1995 /96	1996 /97	1997 /98	1998 /99	1999 /00	2000 /01	2001 /02
Consolidated Fund											
Revenue											
Inland Revenue	KCWZ	76 345.9	77 270.6	87 230.4	97 100.9	103 892.4	117 632.8	128 249.8	139 384.0	149 084.8	149 112.4
Customs and Excise	KCXA	63 398.0	66 885.5	72 485.6	76 668.6	82 351.6	89 839.6	94 018.3	97 291.5	102 168.0	104 854.8
Motor vehicle duties	KCXB	3 196.0	3 752.3	3 805.9	4 043.6	4 217.5	4 543.0	4 666.3	4 893.0	4 642.1	4 402.3
National Non-Domestic Rates	KPOI	..	..	11 469.8	13 373.4	14 269.3	14 036.9	15 878.3	13 403.8	15 482.0	16 009.8
Miscellaneous receipts	KCXE	30 101.2	22 150.2	16 280.3	10 289.3	12 634.6	14 176.6	10 737.1	8 799.0	29 329.4	7 796.2
Total revenue	KCXF	173 041.2	170 058.6	191 272.0	201 475.8	217 365.4	240 228.9	253 549.8	263 771.3	300 706.3	282 175.5
Expenditure											
Supply services	KCXG	189 961.6	204 376.1	207 465.8	211 403.3	214 226.0	209 440.8	213 439.2	226 989.6	241 685.1	271 998.6
Debt interest[2]	KCXH	10 675.1	13 459.6	16 039.8	18 423.1	20 702.3	21 605.7	21 320.8	18 535.3	16 629.2	15 325.6
Payments to Northern Ireland	KCXI	2 632.1	3 090.3	4 052.6	3 903.5	3 685.2	4 581.5	4 709.3	3 104.4	–	–
Payments to the European Communities, etc	KCXJ	4 867.1	6 079.5	5 258.2	7 650.7	6 875.3	7 039.9	8 060.7	7 001.8	8 417.1	4 785.8
Other expenditure[3]	KCXL	117.7	−453.3	271.6	−14.0	876.2	−53.8	−62.1	223.7	170.1	257.9
Total expenditure	KCXM	208 253.6	226 552.2	233 088.0	241 366.5	246 365.0	242 614.1	247 467.9	255 854.8	266 901.5	292 367.9
Deficit met from the National Loans Fund	KCXN	35 212.4	56 493.6	41 816.0	39 890.7	28 999.6	2 385.2	−6 081.9	−7 916.5	−33 804.8	−10 192.4
National Loans Fund											
Receipts											
Profits of the Issue Department of the Bank of England - income[4]	KZAW	1 350.8	996.6	955.2	1 275.5	1 200.9	1 604.8	1 600.9	1 327.3	1 603.0	1 362.9
Other miscellaneous receipts	KZAX	66.7	106.6	4.8	4.4	3.6	5.0	5.0	4.4	6.0	7.3
Interest on loans	KCXO	5 100.7	4 695.2	4 564.5	4 598.7	4 393.5	5 103.6	4 409.7	4 533.3	6 215.4	5 901.2
Service of the National Debt - balance met from the Consolidated Fund	KCXP	10 675.1	13 459.6	16 039.8	18 423.2	20 702.3	21 605.7	21 320.8	18 535.3	16 629.2	15 325.6
Gilt Edged Official Operations Account Net Income	KJDO	..	2.0	–	–	–		–	127.5	–	–
Total	KCXQ	17 193.3	19 260.0	21 564.3	24 301.8	26 300.3	28 319.1	27 336.4	24 527.8	24 453.6	22 597.0
Exchange Equalisation Account- sterling capital	KCXR	3 574.5	400.0	1 250.0	2 750.0	2 150.0	3 650.0	1 880.0	975.0	−5 205.0	4 849.0
Net borrowing[5]	KCXS	25 907.6	58 939.5	39 848.1	37 688.8	27 547.9	–	–	4 997.3	–	4 884.8
International Monetary Fund- maintenance of sterling holdings	KCXT	47.6	–	–	–	82.1	707.0	181.2	–	–	–
Profits of the Issue Department of the Bank of England: capital appreciation	KZAY	..	..	..	..	18.8	21.2	19.3	1.7	2.5	6.4
Reduction of National Debt Commissioners' Liability in respect of the National Savings Bank Investment Account	KCXU	–	–	–	–	–	–	–	–	–	–
Change in balances and other items	KCXV	–	–	–	–	–	–	–	–	–	–
NILO Gilt-Edged operations A/C	KJDL	–	2 500.0	2 500.0	2 500.0	2 000.0	2 500.0	2 500.0	5 000.0	–	–
Debt Management Account	GPJW	–	–	–	–	–	–	–	–	20 000.0	–
Total	KCXW	46 723.0	81 099.5	65 162.4	67 240.6	58 099.1	35 197.3	31 916.9	35 501.8	39 251.1	32 337.2
Payments											
Service of the National Debt:											
Interest	KJDM	17 009.5	19 107.0	21 334.7	24 004.0	25 942.5	27 877.8	26 792.1	24 073.7	23 855.8	22 041.2
Management and expenses	KCXY	183.8	153.0	229.6	297.8	357.8	441.3	544.3	454.1	597.8	555.8
Total	KCXZ	17 193.3	19 260.0	21 564.3	24 301.8	26 300.3	28 319.1	27 336.4	24 527.8	24 453.6	22 597.0
Consolidated Fund deficit met from the National Loans Fund	KCYA	35 212.4	56 493.6	41 816.0	39 890.7	28 999.6	2 385.2	−6 081.9	−7 916.5	−33 804.8	10 192.6
Net repayment[5]	KCYB	–	–	–	–	–	2 482.1	3 558.2	–	7 083.4	–
Net lending[6]	KCYC	−6 787.0	−286.6	−974.8	334.1	280.6	−4.2	1 766.3	1 255.9	1 496.5	−786.2
International Monetary Fund- maintenance of value of sterling holding	KCYD	1 104.3	632.5	226.2	202.1	–	–	–	126.1	21.2	315.2
International Monetary Fund- additional subscription	KCYE	–	–	–	–	–	–	2 826.5	–	–	–
NILO Gilt-Edged Operations A/C	KJDN	–	5 000.0	2 500.0	2 500.0	2 500.0	2 000.0	2 500.0	2 500.0	–	–
Discharge of Treasury Liability to the Bank of England Issue Department	KPUK	−·	–	30.7	11.9	18.6	15.1	11.4	8.5	1.2	18.6
Debt Management Account	ZAFB	..	..	..	..	..	..	..	..	15 000.0	40 000.0	–
Total	KCYF	46 723.0	81 099.5	65 162.4	67 240.6	58 099.1	35 197.3	31 916.9	35 501.8	39 251.1	32 337.2

1 See chapter text.
2 Payment to National Loans Fund representing its payments for the service of the National Debt *less* its receipts of interest on loans outstanding, etc.
3 Includes net issues to Contingencies Fund.
4 Prior to 1996-97, receipts from the Bank of England for appreciation of the assets of the Issue Department were included in the total ammount for the profits of the Issue Department.

5 See Table 17.6.
6 Minus sign indicates a net issue repayment.

Source: HM Treasury: 020 7270 1586

17.5 Taxes paid by UK residents to general government and the European Union[1]

Total economy sector S.1

£ million

		1992 /93	1993 /94	1994 /95	1995 /96	1996 /97	1997 /98	1998 /99	1999 /00	2000 /01	2001 /02
GENERATION OF INCOME											
Uses											
Taxes on production and imports												
Taxes on products and imports												
Value added tax (VAT)											
Paid to central government	NZGF	37 050	39 389	43 686	44 598	46 995	52 454	54 281	59 309	61 529	66 009
Paid to the European Union	FJKM	4 224	4 276	3 220	4 942	4 661	3 531	4 105	3 451	4 172	3 592
Total	QYRC	41 274	43 665	46 906	49 540	51 656	55 985	58 386	62 760	65 701	69 601
Taxes and duties on imports excluding VAT											
Paid to CG: import duties[2]	NMBS	–	–	–	–	–	–	–	–	–	–
Paid to EU: import duties	FJWE	1 994	2 169	2 185	2 468	2 290	2 261	2 042	2 049	2 103	2 024
Total	QYRB	1 994	2 169	2 185	2 468	2 290	2 261	2 042	2 049	2 103	2 024
Taxes on products excluding VAT and import duties											
Paid to central government											
Customs & excise revenue											
Beer	GTAM	2 402	2 481	2 527	2 637	2 631	2 699	2 733	2 848	2 798	2 907
Wines, cider, perry & spirits	GTAN	2 787	2 893	3 017	2 983	2 999	3 057	3 301	3 652	3 814	4 067
Tobacco	GTAO	6 052	6 385	6 952	7 405	7 701	7 622	7 551	7 796	7 638	7 639
Hydrocarbon oils	GTAP	11 440	12 736	14 251	15 679	17 171	19 451	21 553	22 510	22 630	21 916
Car tax	GTAT	385	–2								
Betting, gaming & lottery	CJQY	1 025	1 106	1 233	1 591	1 460	1 539	1 527	1 500	1 517	1 437
Air passenger duty	CWAA	–	–	89	354	359	522	845	882	956	803
Insurance premium tax	CWAD	–	–	259	648	685	1 179	1 248	1 511	1 751	1 924
Landfill tax	BKOF	–	–	–	–	113	364	322	456	475	513
Other	ACDN	9	–	–	–	–	–	–	–	–	–
Fossil fuel levy	CIQY	1 346	1 327	1 379	1 272	880	256	164	84	52	92
Gas levy	GTAZ	290	149	211	171	199	188	–44	–	–	–
Stamp duties	GTBC	1 268	1 736	1 799	2 018	2 414	3 456	4 623	6 898	8 165	7 101
Levies on exports (Third country trade)	CUDF	1	–	–	–	–	–	–	–	–	–
Camelot payments to National Lottery											
Distribution Fund	LIYH	–	–	319	1 527	1 263	1 572	1 665	1 593	1 542	1 520
Purchase Tax	EBDB	–	–	–	–	–	–	–	–	–	–
Hydro-benefit	LITN	20	23	24	28	31	32	32	38	44	44
Other taxes and levies	GCSP	–	–	–	–	–	–	–	–	–	–
Total paid to central government	NMBV	27 025	28 834	32 060	36 313	37 906	41 937	45 520	49 768	51 382	49 963
Paid to the European Union											
Sugar levy	GTBA	47	61	116	36	37	72	44	46	43	27
European Coal & Steel Community levy	GTBB	4	1	–	–	–	–	–	–	–	–
Total paid to the European Union	FJWG	51	62	116	36	37	72	44	46	43	27
Total taxes on products excluding VAT & import duties	QYRA	27 076	28 896	32 176	36 349	37 943	42 009	45 564	49 814	51 425	49 990
Total taxes on products and imports	NZGW	70 344	74 730	81 267	88 357	91 889	100 255	105 992	114 623	119 229	121 615
Production taxes other than on products											
Paid to central government											
Consumer Credit Act fees	CUDB	173	160	153	166	113	168	158	140	98	105
National non-domestic rates	CUKY	14 085	13 090	12 785	13 481	14 166	14 858	15 200	15 442	16 717	17 885
Old style non-domestic rates	NSEZ	76	110	124	127	149	158	130	123	132	131
Levies paid to CG levy-funded bodies	LITK	120	131	130	134	147	162	171	241	207	177
Selective employment tax	CSAH	–	–	–	–	–	–	–	–	–	–
National insurance surcharge	GTAY	–	–	–	–	–	–	–	–	–	–
London regional transport levy	GTBE	–	–	–	–	–	–	–	–	–	–
IBA levy	GTAL	48	–	–	–	–	–	–	–	–	–
Motor vehicle duties paid by businesses	EKED	1 188	1 218	1 290	1 331	1 365	1 404	1 503	1 559	1 115	1 343
Regulator fees	GCSQ	54	71	69	57	54	57	61	69	72	62
Climate change levy	LSNT	–	–	–	–	–	–	–	–	–	831
Total	NMBX	15 744	14 780	14 551	15 296	15 994	16 807	17 223	17 574	18 341	20 534
Paid to local government											
Old style non-domestic rates	NMYH	72	88	92	100	114	124	131	144	150	161
Total production taxes other than on products	NMYD	15 816	14 868	14 643	15 396	16 108	16 931	17 354	17 718	18 491	20 695
Total taxes on production and imports, paid											
Paid to central government	NMBY	79 819	83 003	90 297	96 207	100 895	111 198	117 024	126 651	131 252	136 506
Paid to local government	NMYH	72	88	92	100	114	124	131	144	150	161
Paid to the European Union	FJWB	6 269	6 507	5 521	7 446	6 988	5 864	6 191	5 546	6 318	5 643
Total	NZGX	86 160	89 598	95 910	103 753	107 997	117 186	123 346	132 341	137 720	142 310

17.5
continued

**Taxes paid by UK residents
to general government and the European Union[1]**

Total economy sector S.1

£ million

		1992 /93	1993 /94	1994 /95	1995 /96	1996 /97	1997 /98	1998 /99	1999 /00	2000 /01	2001 /02
SECONDARY DISTRIBUTION OF INCOME											
Uses											
Current taxes on income, wealth etc											
Taxes on income											
Paid to central government											
Household income taxes	DRWH	66 838	66 805	71 689	77 221	78 710	84 572	90 870	97 746	107 114	108 946
Petroleum revenue tax	DBHA	68	359	711	968	1 729	963	502	853	1 518	1 307
Windfall tax	EYNK	–	–	–	–	–	2 610	2 614	–	–	–
Other corporate taxes	BMNX	11 526	11 595	15 744	18 529	22 243	27 059	30 115	35 386	35 415	35 003
Total	NMCU	78 432	78 759	88 144	96 718	102 682	115 204	124 101	133 985	144 047	145 256
Other current taxes											
Paid to central government											
Motor vehicle duty paid by households	CDDZ	2 076	2 410	2 556	2 686	2 802	3 046	3 116	3 296	3 155	2 871
Old style domestic rates	NSFA	61	73	80	76	81	93	114	117	108	109
Licences	NSNP	5	7	9	11	10	11	8	8	2	–
Total	NMCV	2 142	2 490	2 645	2 773	2 893	3 150	3 238	3 421	3 265	2 980
Paid to local government											
Old style domestic rates	NMHK	64	57	56	60	61	64	62	68	76	80
Community charge	NMHL	8 482	–	–	–	–	–	–	–	–	–
Council tax	NMHM	–	7 988	8 611	9 294	10 059	10 850	12 037	12 918	14 155	15 248
Total	NMIS	8 546	8 045	8 667	9 354	10 120	10 914	12 099	12 986	14 231	15 328
Total	NVCM	10 688	10 535	11 312	12 127	13 013	14 064	15 337	16 407	17 496	18 308
Total current taxes on income, wealth etc											
Paid to central government	NMCP	80 574	81 249	90 789	99 491	105 575	118 354	127 339	137 406	147 312	148 236
Paid to local government	NMIS	8 546	8 045	8 667	9 354	10 120	10 914	12 099	12 986	14 231	15 328
Total	NMZL	89 120	89 294	99 456	108 845	115 695	129 268	139 438	150 392	161 543	163 564
Social contributions											
Actual social contributions											
Paid to central government											
(National Insurance Contributions)											
Employers' compulsory contributions	CEAN	21 600	23 478	23 334	24 533	25 950	27 709	29 987	31 732	35 175	35 740
Employees' compulsory contributions	GCSE	14 062	15 183	17 974	18 889	19 611	22 049	23 338	23 621	24 998	25 500
Self- and non-employed persons' compulsory contributions	NMDE	1 310	1 475	1 524	1 585	1 658	1 859	1 742	1 808	2 072	2 316
Total	AIIH	36 972	40 136	42 832	45 007	47 219	51 617	55 067	57 161	62 245	63 556
CAPITAL ACCOUNT											
Changes in liabilities and net worth											
Other capital taxes											
Paid to central government											
Inheritance tax	GILF	1 167	1 307	1 383	1 484	1 517	1 649	1 764	2 016	2 183	2 341
Tax on other capital transfers	GILG	44	28	26	34	41	35	41	38	55	31
Development land tax and other	GCSV	–	–	–	–	–	–	–	–	–	–
Total	NMGI	1 211	1 335	1 409	1 518	1 558	1 684	1 805	2 054	2 238	2 372
TOTAL TAXES AND COMPULSORY SOCIAL CONTRIBUTIONS											
Paid to central government	GCSS	198 576	205 723	225 327	242 223	255 247	282 853	301 235	323 272	343 047	350 670
Paid to local government	GCST	8 618	8 133	8 759	9 454	10 234	11 038	12 230	13 130	14 381	15 489
Paid to the European Union	FJWB	6 269	6 507	5 521	7 446	6 988	5 864	6 191	5 546	6 318	5 643
Total	GCSU	213 463	220 363	239 607	259 123	272 469	299 755	319 656	341 948	363 746	371 802
Total taxes and social contributions as percentage of GDP	GDWM	34.6	33.8	34.6	35.5	35.3	36.3	36.7	37.3	37.8	37.2

1 See chapter text.
2 These taxes existed before the UK's entry into the EEC in 1973

17.6 Borrowing and repayment of debt[1]
United Kingdom
Years ending 31 March

£ millions

		1992 /93	1993 /94	1994 /95	1995 /96	1996 /97	1997 /98	1998 /99	1999 /00	2000 /01	2001 /02
Borrowing											
Government securities: new issues	KQGA	33 601.1	55 959.2	32 137.5	34 150.3	40 800.8	28 484.4	12 048.0	26 426.5	25 789.8	43 433.4
National savings securities:											
National savings certificates	KQGB	3 453.4	3 381.5	2 187.9	3 425.9	3 695.5	4 435.2	3 028.7	1 962.7	3 086.2	2 580.7
Capital bonds	KQGC	524.8	556.2	521.5	504.8	450.8	619.0	469.6	35.4	29.0	40.9
Income bonds	KQGD	1 251.2	1 940.8	1 255.7	780.7	1 272.7	1 043.4	1 371.7	653.4	760.5	625.6
Deposit bonds	KQGE	–	–	–	–	–	–	–	–	–	–
British savings bonds	KQGF	–	–	–	–	–	–	–	–	–	–
Premium savings bonds	KQGG	378.6	931.5	1 837.2	2 040.6	2 552.5	3 158.8	3 652.8	3 449.4	3 296.0	3 859.6
Save As You Earn	KQGH	85.3	76.4	66.5	50.8	34.1	20.7	11.4	5.0	0.3	–
Yearly plan	KQGI	109.9	112.4	116.5	94.1	–	–	5.2	–	–	–
National savings stamps and gift tokens	KQGJ	–	–	–	–	–	–	–	–	–	–
National Savings Bank Investments	KQGK	1 227.9	1 370.5	1 368.1	1 312.1	1 478.7	1 282.3	1 085.0	901.6	955.3	864.9
Children's Bonus Bonds	KGVO	95.5	91.2	118.9	144.9	352.4	255.3	205.0	58.5	53.4	45.0
First Option Bonds	KIAR	859.4	1 026.0	812.0	826.4	1 139.8	1 152.9	1 001.8	34.3	–	–
Pensioners Guaranteed Income Bond	KJDW	..	786.1	1 190.3	2 104.2	2 863.8	1 126.9	201.0	590.7	687.2	603.5
Treasurer's account	KWNF	..	..	..	..	21.1	39.9	17.1	13.6	12.5	15.2
Individual Savings Account	ZAFC	..	..	..	..	..	..	–	257.8	265.9	397.8
Fixed Rate Savings Bonds	ZAFD	..	..	..	..	..	..	–	175.9	284.7	192.7
Guaranteed Equity Bonds	ECPU	..	..	..	..	..	..	..	..	..	27.2
Certificate of tax deposit	KQGL	607.2	470.6	91.2	76.2	109.4	84.1	66.4	121.4	76.5	77.6
Nationalised industries', etc temporary deposits	KQGM	19 350.0	28 700.9	29 294.0	36 870.6	53 198.2	46 375.9	39 962.4	40 343.3	56 106.6	62 150.0
British Gas corporation deposits	KQGN	–	–	–	–	–	–	–	–	–	–
Sterling Treasury bills (net receipt)	KQGO	–	–	5 196.1	2 606.1	–	–	3 546.2	–	–	–
ECU Treasury bills (net receipt)	KQGP	–	–	–	–	–	–	–	–	–	–
ECU Treasury notes (net receipt)	KDZZ	1 396.0	2 073.2	429.8	–	–	–	–	721.1	–	–
Ways and means (net receipt)	KQGQ	–	9 007.0	8 891.7	1 162.3	511.1	–	183.6	5 599.0	12 126.0	12 095.3
Other debt : payable in sterling :											
Interest free notes	KQGR	1 045.6	796.6	382.6	247.4	99.2	32.4	2 130.9	373.5	972.7	1 427.2
Other debt : payable in external currencies	KHCY	33 147.7	9 243.9	–	–	2 565.2	–	–	–	–	–
Total receipts	KHCZ	97 133.6	116 524.0	85 897.5	86 397.4	111 145.3	88 111.2	68 986.8	81 723.1	104 502.6	128 436.6
Repayment of debt											
Government securities: redemptions	KQGS	8 351.8	7 390.5	9 333.3	4 652.7	14 488.4	20 678.9	18 575.5	19 815.8	33 722.2	43 642.3
Statutory sinking funds	KQGT	2.5	2.4	2.3	2.2	2.2	2.1	2.0	2.0	2.0	1.9
Terminable annuities:											
National Debt Commissioners	KQGU	–									
National savings securities:											
National savings certificates	KQGV	1 092.5	2 208.0	1 612.6	2 258.4	3 263.7	4 058.5	3 449.0	2 405.2	4 546.8	4 177.7
Capital bonds	KQGW	21.1	398.0	647.7	509.0	698.3	1 160.5	888.3	324.2	375.0	175.9
Income bonds	KQGX	955.2	1 000.7	1 181.8	1 256.9	1 394.0	1 148.9	880.8	1 686.3	857.0	933.8
Deposit bonds	KQGY	80.9	71.8	72.3	72.5	64.8	72.6	84.2	70.2	71.1	45.4
Yearly Plan	KQGZ	99.8	88.9	77.0	101.9	96.3	113.2	120.0	141.8	18.4	4.5
British savings bonds	KQHA	–	–	–	–	–	–	–	–	–	–
Premium savings bonds	KQHB	153.4	181.0	333.0	590.1	869.3	1 203.1	1 398.4	1 923.8	1 872.6	1 942.9
Save As You Earn	KQHC	116.9	96.3	92.3	98.7	70.1	68.2	37.1	34.5	22.9	8.0
National savings stamps and gift tokens	KQHD	–	0.7	–	–	–	–	–	–	–	–
National Savings Bank Investments (repayments)	KQHE	2 039.0	1 646.3	1 745.3	1 755.8	1 837.0	2 175.7	2 027.0	1 886.3	1 654.1	1 415.8
Children's Bonus Bonds	KGVQ	1.0	1.2	4.3	0.1	257.8	187.9	183.2	69.3	95.0	114.5
First Option Bonds	KIAS	4.6	1 085.1	969.9	732.7	833.9	1 283.0	1 055.5	298.1	225.2	111.6
Pensioners Guaranteed Income Bond	KPOB	–	–	57.0	104.5	185.0	318.8	897.8	935.3	2 003.8	1 640.4
Treasurer's account	KWNG	..	..	..	..	1.2	11.8	13.7	16.4	13.9	16.5
Individual Savings Account	ZAFE	..	..	..	..	..	..	..	12.3	39.9	70.3
Fixed Rate Savings Bonds	ZAFF	..	..	..	..	..	..	..	2.8	62.1	110.1
Certificates of tax deposit	KQHF	936.9	722.6	612.1	466.0	478.9	229.0	199.9	159.9	120.1	91.4
Tax reserve certificates	KQHG	–	–	–	–	–	–	–	–	–	–
Nationalised industries', etc temporary deposits	KQHH	18 477.0	28 098.5	28 557.8	35 263.1	51 979.3	46 835.7	41 776.9	41 089.4	56 004.0	63 127.9
Debt to the Bank of England	KPOC	–	–	11.0	–	–	–	–	–	–	–
British Gas Corporation (Repayment of Deposits)	KQHI	–	–	–	–	–	–	–	–	–	–
Sterling Treasury bills (net repayment)	KQHJ	4 882.1	1 547.5	–	–	4 009.6	1 928.5	–	3 014.8	6 194.2	–
ECU Treasury bills (net repayment)	KJEG	..	73.3	–	–	–	–	–	2 492.9	–	–
ECU Treasury notes (net repayment)	KSPA	..	..	..	439.1	318.3	3.3	13.2	–	1 391.9	1 359.6
Ways and means (net repayment)	KQHK	6 786.3				–	5 815.4				
Other debt: payable in sterling :											
Interest free notes	KQHL	155.8	101.3	225.2	301.3	87.6	1 215.5	850.5	246.4	458.2	1 723.3
Other	KQHM										
Other debt : payable in external currencies	KQHN	27 068.7	12 870.4	514.5	103.6	2 661.7	2 082.7	92.0	98.1	1 835.6	2 838.1
Total payments	KQHO	71 226.0	57 584.5	46 049.4	48 708.6	83 597.4	90 593.3	72 545.0	76 725.8	111 586.0	123 551.9
Net borrowing	KQHP	25 907.6	58 939.5	39 848.1	37 688.8	27 547.9	–	–	4 997.3	–	4 884.7
Net repayment	KHDD	–	–	–	–	–	2 482.1	3 558.2	–	7 083.4	–

1 See chapter text.

Source: HM Treasury: 020 7270 1586

17.7 Consolidated Fund and National Loans Fund: assets and liabilities[1]
United Kingdom
At 31 March in each year

£ millions

		1992	1993	1994	1995	1996	1997	1998	1999	2000	2001
Consolidated Fund											
Total estimated assets	KQIA	19 852.9	18 872.0	26 914.5	33 992.4	33 809.0	36 177.4	36 061.0	36 148.0	33 932.1	35 649.7
Subscriptions and contributions to international financial organisations	KQIB	4 315.2	5 009.2	5 438.2	5 898.1	6 470.8	6 528.9	6 660.8	7 059.7	6 903.6	7 298.4
International Bank for Reconstruction and Development	KQIC	236.3	259.8	274.5	265.2	271.6	265.0	262.5	266.0	267.1	279.2
International Finance Corporation	KQID	39.4	53.1	60.9	62.0	73.1	74.9	72.9	75.6	76.5	85.8
International Development Association	KQIE	2 343.3	2 576.0	2 785.4	3 005.5	3 205.8	3 372.7	3 562.2	3 733.3	3 900.0	4 134.0
African Development Bank	KQIF	91.2	108.1	127.9	141.2	148.3	162.9	180.0	199.1	215.7	229.8
Asian Development Bank	KQIG	173.0	180.9	188.9	201.5	214.6	240.4	272.5	304.6	339.3	365.5
Caribbean Development Bank	KQIH	27.5	29.4	31.2	32.6	34.2	34.1	34.6	36.8	40.7	41.9
European Investment Bank	KQII	1 252.8	1 588.9	1 713.7	1 876.4	2 166.6	2 036.5	1 840.7	2 083.1	1 706.6	1 767.3
European Bank for Reconstruction and Development	KPOD	22.3	61.3	99.4	146.3	189.4	175.6	164.2	179.2	170.0	187.4
Inter-American Development Bank	KQIJ	89.4	109.8	112.5	107.2	119.6	117.5	219.3	127.8	130.6	145.7
International Fund for Agricultural Development	KQIK	36.9	38.5	40.2	42.7	44.2	46.1	48.8	51.0	53.7	56.4
Multilateral Investment Guarantee Agency	KQIL	3.0	3.5	3.5	3.2	3.4	3.2	3.1	3.2	3.3	5.4
Amounts due from overseas governments	KQIM	–	–	–	–	–	–	–	–	–	–
War of 1939-45	KQIN	–	–	–	–	–	–	–	–	–	–
Other	KQIO	–	–	–	–	–	–	–	–	–	–
Loans from Votes	KQIP	4 047.3	6 709.2	11 057.4	13 599.7	12 967.0	13 684.7	14 050.0	11 546.3	3 970.3	5 113.7
Issues of public dividend capital:	KQIQ	1 642.7	4 920.0	7 979.2	11 467.0	12 161.1	12 424.8	13 157.1	16 238.5	21 338.3	20 083.6
British Airways Board	KQIR	–	–	–	–	–	–	–	–	–	–
British Steel Corporation	KQIS	–	–	–	–	–	–	–	–	–	–
Royal Ordnance Factories	KQIT	–	–	–	–	–	–	–	–	–	–
National Enterprise Board	KQIU	–	–	–	–	–	–	–	–	–	–
Royal Mint	KQIV	7.0	7.0	7.0	7.0	7.0	7.0	7.0	7.0	7.0	7.0
Post Office	KQIW	–	–	–	–	–	–	–	–	–	–
Scottish Development Agency	KQIX	–	–	–	–	–	–	–	–	–	–
Welsh Development Agency	KQIY	13.5	12.6	11.6	10.9	9.8	8.9	8.8	8.6	9.1	9.1
British Aerospace	KQIZ	–	–	–	–	–	–	–	–	–	–
British Shipbuilders[2]	KQJA	1 597.4	1 598.3	1 598.3	1 598.3	1 598.3	1 598.5	1 598.3	50.0	21.0	21.0
Patent Office	KIAT	6.3	6.3	6.3	6.3	6.3	6.3	6.3	6.3	6.3	6.3
NHS Trusts	KIAU	1 325.8	3 279.6	6 336.2	9 603.1	10 173.8	10 349.7	11 078.0	14 158.7	19 216.6	19 539.2
Companies House	KIAV	16.9	15.9	15.9	15.9	15.9	15.9	15.9	15.9	15.9	15.9
Central Office of Information	KIAW	0.3	0.3	0.3	0.3	0.3	0.3	0.3	0.3	0.3	0.3
Chessington Computer Centre	KPOE	–	–	3.5	3.5	3.5	–	–	–	–	–
Buying Agency	KWNH	..	..		0.1	0.4	0.4	0.4	0.4	0.4	0.4
Defence Evaluation and Research Agency	KWNI	..	..	..	128.8	253.0	274.5	274.5	275.4	275.4	275.4
Fire Service College	KWNJ	..	..	..	16.7	16.7	16.7	16.7	16.7	16.7	16.7
Forensic Science Service	GPVB	..	..	..	..	..	..	..	–	18.0	18.0
Hydrographic Office	GPVC	..	..	..	..	..	..	..	..	13.3	13.3
Land Registry	KWNK	..	..	..	55.4	55.4	61.5	61.5	61.5	61.5	61.5
Medicines Control Agency	KWNL	..	..	..	1.6	1.6	1.6	1.6	1.6	1.6	1.6
Meteorological Office	KZAZ	..	..	..	..	..	58.9	58.9	58.9	58.9	58.9
NHS Estates	GPVD	..	..	..	..	..	..	..	..	0.4	0.4
Registers of Scotland	KZBA	..	..	..	..	..	4.3	4.3	4.3	–	–
Vehicle Inspectorate	KWNM	..	..	..	19.1	19.1	20.3	20.3	20.3	20.3	20.3
Driving Standards Agency	LQMI	..	..	..	..	..	..	3.5	3.5	3.5	3.5
Ordnance Survey	GPVE	..	..	..	..	..	..	..	..	14.0	14.0
Queen Elizabeth II Conference Centre	LQMJ							0.8	0.8	0.8	0.8
Contingencies Fund - capital	KQJB	1 097.0	947.0	347.0	447.0	297.0	977.0	577.0	277.0	277.0	277.0
Balance on revenue accounts	KQJC	725.2	477.6	358.7	1 433.6	1 096.1	954.9	1 546.0	1 026.5	1 442.9	1 299.7
Privatisation receipts	KIAX	6 701.0	809.0	1 734.0	1 147.0	817.0	1 607.1	70.1	–	–	–
Total liabilities	KQJD	–	–	–	–	333 927.9	364 803.0	364 950.8	363 625.5	354 807.7	327 180.6
Liability to balance National Loans Fund	KQJE	142 306.7	182 102.2	240 351.0	286 055.9	331 164.9	362 506.5	362 582.5	361 065.3	351 626.3	324 336.7
Payment from Votes:	KQJF	66.9	66.1	65.2	64.3	63.4	62.4	61.3	60.2	59.0	57.7
Married quarters for Armed Forces	KQJG	66.9	66.1	65.2	64.3	63.4	62.4	61.3	60.2	59.0	57.7
Liability to Post Office Superannuation Fund	KQJH	–	–	–	–	–	–	–	–	–	–
Post-war credits outstanding and interest due - estimated	KQJI	46.1	46.0	46.0	46.0	45.9	45.9	45.9	45.9	45.8	45.8
Revenue paid over in advance of collection	KQJJ	8.3	–	83.7	37.0	–	28.2	13.8	177.9	259.7	626.5
Inland Revenue	KQJK	–	–	–	–	–	–	–	177.9	259.7	626.5
Customs and Excise	KQJL	–	–	–	–	–	28.2	–	–	–	–
Broadcast receiving licences	KQJM	–	–	–	–	–	–	–	–	–	–
Vehicle Excise Duty	KQJN	8.3	–	83.7	37.0	–	–	13.8	–	–	–

17.7
continued

Consolidated Fund and National Loans Fund: assets and liabilities[1]
United Kingdom
At 31 March in each year

£ millions

		1992	1993	1994	1995	1996	1997	1998	1999	2000	2001
Consolidated Fund (*continued*)											
Promissory notes issued by											
Minister of Overseas Development	KQJQ	770.3	979.5	1 002.6	996.7	1 005.8	1 021.9	822.1	963.1	783.1	939.9
International Development Association	KQJR	489.4	673.1	670.5	656.5	663.2	673.6	484.0	612.3	445.6	553.1
African Development Fund	KQJS	92.1	100.7	106.6	93.2	86.2	95.3	95.2	105.6	89.1	141.6
Asian Development Bank	KQJT	0.1	–	–	–	–	–	–	–	1.9	2.5
Asian Development Fund	KQJU	92.1	108.7	131.8	140.5	127.6	136.0	120.5	105.4	87.8	78.6
Caribbean Development Bank	KQJV	0.1	0.1	1.2	1.3	1.4	1.3	1.3	1.3	1.3	1.5
Special Development Fund	KQKC	8.3	6.9	8.0	9.5	10.6	13.2	15.8	16.4	16.9	15.9
European Community/International Development Association Special Action Account	KQJW	–	–	–	–	–	–	–	–	–	–
European Investment Bank	KQJX	–	–	–	–	–	–	–	–	–	–
Inter-American Development Bank	KQJY	1.7	2.6	2.2	1.3	2.0	1.8	1.9	1.0	2.0	1.4
Fund for special operations	KQJZ	22.5	15.4	16.4	13.1	11.3	8.8	6.3	2.6	2.1	1.1
International Fund for Agricultural Development	KQKA	17.8	16.1	18.2	15.8	14.2	12.3	14.2	16.5	18.4	15.6
International Bank for Reconstruction and Development	KQKB	31.9	30.2	24.2	39.2	60.7	71.7	81.9	94.3	105.9	112.5
European Bank for Reconstruction and Development	KIAY	14.3	20.4	19.9	20.9	21.0	6.1	–	7.7	12.1	16.1
United Nations Environment Programme	KJEH	–	5.3	3.6	5.4	7.6	1.8	1.0	–	–	–
Other contributions and instalments due in respect of international subscriptions, etc	KQYX	2 125.1	1 520.7	2 165.8	1 499.6	1 647.9	1 138.1	1 425.2	1 313.1	1 669.2	1 174.0
National Loans Fund											
Total assets	KQKD	214 527.6	248 643.5	306 872.6	349 159.5	390 681.8	419 548.9	418 444.7	421 635.7	426 239.2	425 956.9
Total National Loans Fund loans outstanding	KQKE	55 492.8	48 705.9	48 470.8	47 496.1	46 600.9	46 746.8	46 742.6	48 513.6	49 788.8	51 037.6
Loans to Public Corporations::											
Consignia PLC (previously Post Office)	KQKF	–	–	–	–	–	–	–	–	–	500.0
British Coal	KQKG	257.7	180.0	–	–	–	–	–	–	–	–
Electricity Council	KQKH	–	–	–	–	–	–	–	–	–	–
North of Scotland Hydro-Electric Board	KQKI	–	–	–	–	–	–	–	–	–	–
Scottish Hydro-Electric	KQKJ	–	–	–	–	–	–	–	–	–	–
South of Scotland Electricity Board	KQKK	–	..	..	–	–	–	–	–	–	–
Scottish Power	KQKL	–	–	–	–	–	–	–	–	–	–
Scottish Nuclear Ltd	KQKM	201.3	199.2	196.8	194.1	96.1	–	–	–	–	–
British Gas Corporation	KQKN	–	–	–	–	–	–	–	–	–	–
British Steel Corporation	KQKO	–	–	–	–	–	–	–	–	–	–
British Airways Board	KQKP	–	–	–	–	–	–	–	–	–	–
Railtrack	KTCR	..	..	..	1 287.7	–	–	–	–	–	–
European Passenger Services	KTCS	..	..	..	99.0	761.2	..	–	–	–	–
Civil Aviation Authority	KQKQ	271.2	311.9	403.7	453.3	476.1	447.5	420.9	365.7	342.5	92.5
British Airports Authority	KQKR	–	–	–	–	–	–	–	–	–	–
British Railways Board	KQKS	1 040.8	1 923.9	2 445.6	749.2	718.3	601.2	573.7	546.2	518.7	481.3
British Transport Docks Board	KQKT	–	–	–	–	–	–	–	–	–	–
British Waterways Board	KQKU	20.0	19.2	18.6	18.3	18.2	18.2	18.2	18.2	18.2	16.7
National Freight Corporation	KQKV	–	–	–	–	–	–	–	–	–	–
National Bus Company	KQKW	–	–	–	–	–	–	–	–	–	–
Scottish Transport Group	KQKX	–	–	–	–	–	–	–	–	–	–
British National Oil Corporation	KQKY	–	–	–	–	–	–	–	–	–	–
British Aerospace	KQKZ	–	–	–	–	–	–	–	–	–	–
British Shipbuilders	KQLA	–	–	–	–	–	–	–	–	–	–
British Telecommunications	KQLB	–	–	–	–	–	–	–	–	–	–
Regional Water Authorities	KQLC	–	–	–	–	–	–	–	–	–	–
New Towns - Development Corporations and Commission	KQLD	1 441.5	1 303.9	1 130.1	1 008.8	314.3	122.2	36.2	8.0	8.0	8.0
Scottish Special Housing Association	KQLE	–	–	–	–	–	–	–	–	–	–
Scottish Homes	KQLF	654.5	401.2	399.4	397.3	395.0	392.5	259.8	190.9	179.0	161.6
Housing Corporation (Scotland)	KQLG	–	–	–	–	–	–	–	–	–	–
Housing Corporation (England)	KQLH	1 021.4	986.0	899.0	869.9	926.3	848.7	4.0	4.0	3.0	3.0
Housing for Wales	KQLI	96.6	86.7	86.4	69.2	59.0	–	–	–	–	–
Covent Garden Market Authority	KQLJ	–	–	–	–	–	–	–	–	–	–
National Enterprise Board	KQLK	–	–	–	–	–	–	–	–	–	–
Land Authority for Wales	KQLL	8.8	10.3	6.2	3.2	3.2	1.3	1.3	–	–	–
Scottish Enterprise	KQLM	4.6	2.7	1.9	1.3	0.6	0.5	0.1	–	–	–
Welsh Development Agency	KQLN	1.8	1.5	1.2	0.9	1.1	1.2	1.2	0.9	0.6	0.3
Land Registry Trading Fund	KPOF	–	–	54.9	–	–	–	–	–	–	–
Development Board for Rural Wales	KQLO	8.8	8.8	8.8	8.8	7.9	4.1	4.0	4.0	4.0	4.0
Royal Mint	KQLP	–	–	–	–	–	–	–	–	2.0	5.0
Royal Ordnance Factories	KQLQ	–	–	–	–	–	–	–	–	–	–
The Crown Suppliers	KQLR	–	–	–	–	–	–	–	–	–	–
Crown Agents	KQLS	2.5	2.3	2.1	2.0	1.9	–	–	–	–	–
Her Majesty's Stationery Office	KQLT	10.6	6.7	3.3	–	7.0	–	–	–	–	–
Urban Development Corporations	KQLU	0.8	0.7	1.0	–	–	–	–	–	–	–
Harbour Authorities	KQLV	33.4	7.1	1.5	0.8	0.7	0.6	0.5	0.4	0.2	0.1
Commonwealth Development Corporation	KQLW	–	–	–	–	–	–	–	–	–	–
UK Atomic Energy Authority	KQLX	111.0	149.8	125.0	147.3	141.0	–	–	–	–	–
Ordnance Survey	GPVF	..	..	..	..	..	..	..	..	15.5	13.9

17.7 Consolidated Fund and National Loans Fund: assets and liabilities[1]
continued
United Kingdom
At 31 March in each year

£ millions

		1992	1993	1994	1995	1996	1997	1998	1999	2000	2001
Loans to public corporations: (*continued*)											
Loans to other public corporations: (*continued*)											
Central Office of Information	KJEI	1.3	1.0	0.8	0.5	0.3	–	–	–	–	–
Registers of Scotland	KZBB	..	..	..	..	..	6.4	5.6	5.1	4.5	4.0
East of Scotland Water Authority	KZBC	..	..	..	..	..	163.0	229.0	288.0	283.0	268.0
North of Scotland Water Authority	KZBD	..	..	..	..	..	155.0	189.2	242.0	236.5	236.5
West of Scotland Water Authority	KZBE	..	..	..	..	..	185.0	304.9	425.6	412.4	412.4
Loans to local authorities	KQLY	48 742.3	41 464.6	40 979.2	40 440.7	40 969.2	42 134.0	42 951.1	44 742.7	46 099.2	47 239.1
Loans to private sector:											
Shipbuilding Industry Board	KQLZ	–	–	–	–	–	–	–	–	–	–
Shipowners (Ship credit scheme)	KGVR	–	–	–	–	–	–	–	–	–	–
Housing associations	KGVS	14.6	14.1	13.8	13.2	12.7	0.5	0.5	0.5	0.5	0.5
Building societies	KGVT	–	–	–	–	–	–	–	–	–	–
British Nuclear Fuels Ltd	KGVU	–	–	–	–	–	–	–	–	–	–
British Aerospace plc	KGVV	–	–	–	–	–	–	–	–	–	–
Loans within central government:											
Northern Ireland Exchequer	KGVW	1 480.3	1 558.3	1 626.2	1 666.3	1 627.4	1 602.5	1 681.1	1 611.2	1 602.0	1 533.1
Married quarters for Armed Forces	KGVX	66.9	66.1	65.2	64.3	63.4	62.4	61.3	60.2	59.0	57.7
Redundancy Fund	KGVY	–	–	–	–	–	–	–	–	–	–
Other assets:											
Exchange Equalisation Account - capital	KGVZ	10 774.5	7 200.0	6 800.0	5 550.0	2 800.0	650.0	–	–	475.0	5 680.0
Subscriptions and contributions to international financial organisations:											
International Monetary Fund	KGXE	4 885.3	6 893.0	7 066.4	7 172.2	7 102.6	6 241.2	5 895.6	9 048.1	9 067.4	9 496.6
Gilt-Edged Official Operations Account -advances outstanding	KPUF	–	–	2 500.0	2 500.0	2 500.0	3 000.0	2 500.0	2 500.0	–	–
-surplus not paid to the National Loans Fund	KPUH	–	–	2.0	–	–	–	141.6	190.8	–	–
Borrowing included in national debt but not brought to account by 31 March	KGXF	1 068.2	3 742.5	1 682.4	385.2	513.4	404.7	568.6	317.9	281.6	405.9
Debt Management Account -advances outstanding	GPVG	..	..	..	..	..	..	..	..	15 000.0	35 000.0
National Debt Commissioners' liability in respect of the National Savings Bank's Investment Fund	KCYG	–	–	–	–	–	–	–	–	–	–
Other	KCYH	–	–	–	–	–	–	–	–	–	–
Consolidated Fund liability	KCYI	142 306.7	182 102.2	240 351.0	286 055.9	331 164.9	362 506.2	362 596.4	361 065.3	351 626.3	324 336.7
Total liabilities											
National Loans Fund - national debt outstanding	KCYJ	214 527.6	248 643.5	306 872.6	349 159.5	390 681.8	419 548.9	418 444.7	421 635.7	426 239.2	425 956.9

1 See chapter text.
2 PDC of £1,548.3m was cancelled in the financial year ending 1999.

Source: HM Treasury: 020 7270 1586

17.8 British government and government guaranteed marketable securities[1]
Nominal values of official and market holdings by maturity[2,3]
At 31 March in each year

£ millions

		1992	1993	1994	1995	1996	1997	1998	1999	2000	2001	2002
Total holdings	KQMO	133 121	162 642	209 507	232 486	262 262	290 259	297 366	291 788	290 629	285 915	278 808
Up to 5 years	KQMP	40 363	46 019	58 437	69 011	81 122	90 357	86 094	95 112	95 131	92 090	92 780
Over 5 and up to 15 years	KQMQ	61 239	72 612	94 308	101 960	111 510	125 401	131 758	124 603	116 910	120 101	106 044
Over 15 years (including undated)	KQMR	31 520	44 010	56 762	61 515	69 630	74 501	79 515	72 074	78 587	73 724	79 984
Official holdings:[3]												
Total	HHAW	8 799	4 138	6 239	6 614	7 186	6 858	6 345	6 394	6 204	8 210	7 558
Up to 5 years	HHAY	3 478	1 434	1 685	2 007	2 345	2 850	2 499	2 600	2 849	4 652	3 928
Over 5 and up to 15 years	HHAZ	4 323	1 826	3 194	3 700	3 774	3 041	2 726	2 989	2 567	3 009	2 844
Over 15 years (including undated)	HHBA	998	879	1 359	907	1 068	967	1 120	805	788	549	786
Market holdings:												
Total	HHBB	124 323	158 503	203 268	225 872	255 075	283 402	291 021	285 394	284 425	277 705	271 250
Up to 5 years	HHBD	36 885	44 585	56 751	67 004	78 777	87 508	83 595	92 512	92 282	87 438	88 852
Over 5 and up to 15 years	HHBE	56 916	70 786	91 115	98 260	107 736	122 360	129 032	121 614	114 343	117 092	103 200
Over 15 years (including undated)	HHBF	30 522	43 131	55 403	60 608	68 562	73 536	78 395	71 269	77 800	73 175	79 198

1 The government guaranteed securities of nationalised industries only. A relatively small amount of other government guaranteed securities is excluded.

2 Securities with optional redemption dates are classified according to the final redemption date. The nominal value of index-linked British Government Stock has been raised by the amount of accrued capital uplift.

3 Official holdings were changed following the introduction of the central bank sector in the UK national accounts. These holdings now principally include those of the Debt Management Office and other government departments. The Issue and Banking Departments of the Bank of England are classified within the central bank sector and are therefore part of market holdings.

Source: Bank of England: 020 7601 3598

17.9 National savings
Year ending 31 March

£ millions

		1991 /92	1992 /93	1993 /94	1994 /95	1995 /96	1996 /97	1997 /98	1998 /99	1999 /00	2000 /01	2001 /02
Department for National Savings												
Receipts												
Total	KQNA	7 704.7	8 485.5	10 336.2	9 246.9	11 596.9	13 353.5	12 565.6	10 212.9	9 156.1	11 004.5	11 794.3
Capital bonds	KQNB	338.3	476.6	566.4	511.2	500.5	482.7	583.6	238.1	75.7	137.9	126.2
National Savings Certificates:												
5yr Fixed Interest	KQNC	2 119.6	1 894.7	1 929.1	1 083.6	1 519.8	1 805.9	1 753.4	1 174.4	704.2	507.2	739.8
5yr Index-linked	KQND	1 500.8	1 600.0	1 434.9	1 083.2	1 949.8	1 871.8	2 640.4	1 734.1	552.0	427.7	654.1
2yr Fixed Interest	YZZZ	..	..	..	..	..	..	..	..	437.9	1 074.0	1 048.0
2yr Index Linked	ZCEZ	..	..	..	..	..	..	..	..	285.5	1 267.5	998.8
Yearly Plan	KQNE	89.3	115.7	118.2	117.5	97.0	0.7	–	–	–	–	0.2
Save As You Earn Total	KQNF	94.1	85.5	76.9	66.7	49.9	33.4	20.3	11.2	5.1	0.4	0.8
Income bonds	KQNH	1 355.9	1 241.2	1 948.9	1 228.9	802.4	1 263.6	1 044.1	1 365.4	642.2	767.8	619.7
First Option bonds	KHYZ	–	885.0	247.0	95.6	194.3	398.3	149.2	110.1	32.7	27.0	23.6
Investment Account	KQNI	1 247.7	1 107.4	1 392.9	1 393.1	1 299.2	1 478.3	1 270.1	1 045.4	1 249.4	1 292.7	1 268.6
Premium Savings bonds	KQNJ	257.5	384.5	998.2	1 826.2	2 075.7	2 578.1	3 199.6	3 622.9	3 384.1	3 355.7	3 832.9
Ordinary Account	KQNK	566.0	604.4	636.1	635.6	627.3	643.1	653.0	622.3	656.1	691.9	670.4
Children's Bonus bonds	KHCU	135.5	90.5	92.6	116.8	144.9	124.3	109.7	73.4	83.4	128.0	123.5
5yr Pensioners' bonds	KJRB	..	..	895.0	1 088.5	2 336.1	2 651.4	1 104.2	199.1	234.7	72.8	288.6
3yr Pensioners' bonds	ELIU	..	..	..	..	..	..	..	..	–	–	–
2yr Pensioners' bonds	ZCFA	..	..	..	..	..	..	..	..	373.6	432.7	362.0
1yr Pensioners' bonds	EUIC	..	..	..	..	..	..	..	..	–	196.2	314.2
Treasurer's Account	KXCY	–	–	–	–	–	21.9	38.0	16.5	13.2	15.3	19.2
ISA's	ZCFB	..	..	..	..	..	..	..	..	257.9	302.4	404.2
Fixed Rate Savings Bond	ZCFC	..	..	..	..	..	..	..	..	168.7	307.3	258.9
Guaranteed equity bond	GWEM	..	..	..	..	..	..	..	..	–	–	40.6
Repayments												
Total	KQNO	6 495.7	5 853.8	8 051.0	7 759.8	8 756.9	11 048.5	13 201.7	11 665.7	10 988.1	12 464.0	11 748.8
Capital bonds	KQNP	14.9	21.8	345.3	678.3	453.1	776.6	1 143.5	649.7	325.1	377.1	179.3
National Savings Certificates:												
5yr Fixed Interest - Principal	KQNQ	1 193.4	647.9	1 292.6	843.0	840.1	1 838.8	2 256.2	1 934.3	1 182.2	..	..
- Accrued Interest	KQNR	738.7	417.4	670.9	437.2	474.8	937.0	1 021.4	645.6	391.6	..	..
Total	GQRJ	..	..	..	..	..	..	..	..	..	1 982.3	1 907.7
5yr Index-linked - Principal	KQNS	418.8	448.2	913.5	761.7	1 419.7	1 432.7	1 803.5	1 520.1	1 200.5	..	..
- Accrued Interest/ Index-linking, etc.	KQNT	396.6	378.5	598.1	425.8	672.0	613.6	703.1	527.5	373.7	..	..
Total	GQRK	..	..	..	..	..	..	..	..	..	2 477.7	2 040.6
2yr Fixed Interest - Principal	ZCFD	..	..	..	..	..	..	..	..	3.1	..	..
- Accrued Interest	ZCFE	..	..	..	..	..	..	..	..	–	..	..
Total	GQRL	..	..	..	..	..	..	..	..	..	20.1	169.4
2yr Index-linked - Principal	ZCFF	..	..	..	..	..	..	..	..	1.5	..	..
- Accrued Interest/ Total	GQRM	..	..	..	..	..	..	..	..	..	17.4	121.3
Yearly Plan:												
Principal	KQNU	106.5	98.4	89.5	77.0	102.0	96.3	119.5	111.8	118.4	–	..
Interest	KQNV	40.9	35.7	30.3	26.2	42.1	39.2	43.6	30.6	32.6	–	..
Total repayment	GQRN	..	..	..	..	..	..	..	..	..	38.2	3.8
Save As You Earn:												
Fixed Interest - Principal	KQNW	74.4	88.7	86.1	85.0	96.7	69.1	67.4	35.9	35.2	..	..
- Accrued Interest	KQNX	16.0	18.2	18.1	19.2	21.9	17.9	18.5	9.1	7.9	..	..
Index-linked - Principal	KQNY	29.4	26.5	9.3	7.4	1.8	0.9	0.8	0.6	0.5	..	..
- Accrued Interest/ Index-linking	KQNZ	38.5	38.9	14.3	12.2	3.3	1.6	1.5	1.2	1.0	..	..
Total repayments	GQRO	..	..	..	..	..	..	..	..	..	22.8	7.9
Income bonds	KQOA	719.9	956.0	1 000.3	1 180.1	1 256.2	1 392.0	1 141.9	880.7	1 685.1	855.2	941.9
First Option bonds	KHYY	–	4.8	375.8	288.4	126.5	139.1	335.2	205.5	283.8	216.9	103.7
Investment Account	KQOB	1 803.9	1 780.0	1 677.1	1 777.2	1 797.2	1 856.0	2 177.1	1 981.6	1 888.2	1 624.3	1 434.2
Premium Savings bonds	KQOC	153.7	153.4	181.0	333.0	590.4	869.0	1 203.1	1 398.4	1 683.0	1 888.2	1 943.2
Ordinary Account	KQOD	663.7	658.1	674.7	676.8	676.5	692.3	703.4	684.6	676.4	661.9	654.2
Children's Bonus bonds	KHCV	0.1	0.9	1.2	1.8	2.6	30.8	39.8	52.4	69.5	95.1	115.7
5yr Pensioners' bonds	KJRE	..	..	..	56.7	104.8	172.5	331.4	903.1	922.1	1 959.2	1 614.3
3yr Pensioners' bonds	GWDU	..	..	..	..	..	..	..	..	..	..	–
2yr Pensioners' bonds	ZCFH	..	..	..	..	..	..	..	..	8.4	30.2	163.1
1yr Pensioners' bonds	GQRP	..	..	..	..	..	..	..	..	..	3.9	79.2
Deposit bonds	KQOE	85.3	79.8	72.4	72.2	73.5	65.5	76.6	79.0	67.1	72.3	46.8
Indexed-income bonds	KQOF	1.0	0.6	0.5	0.6	1.7	6.5	2.6	–	–	–	–
Treasurer's Account	KXCZ	–	–	–	–	–	1.1	11.6	14.0	15.8	13.9	16.5
ISA's	ZCFI	..	..	..	..	..	..	..	..	12.4	40.6	70.7
Fixed Rate Savings Bond	ZCFJ	..	..	..	..	..	..	..	..	3.0	66.7	135.3

17.9 National savings
Year ending 31 March
continued

£ millions

		1991/92	1992/93	1993/94	1994/95	1995/96	1996/97	1997/98	1998/99	1999/00	2000/01	2001/02
Department for National Savings												
Gross Accrued Interest												
Capital bonds	KQOO	76.8	130.8	223.1	218.8	214.6	249.9	172.0	146.9	126.6	102.0	82.8
National Savings Certificates:												
5yr Fixed Interest	KQOP	443.3	521.2	604.2	622.2	703.7	787.6	557.8	485.3	432.5	342.5	307.2
5yr Index-linked	KQOQ	351.7	267.8	303.9	458.5	655.2	671.9	690.3	502.7	344.1	500.0	309.7
2yr Fixed Interest	ZCFK	..	..	..	..	..	..	..	..	1.1	39.8	71.7
2yr Index-linked	ZCFL	..	..	..	..	..	..	..	..	1.0	39.8	69.9
Yearly Plan	KQOR	36.7	32.5	30.5	34.1	37.5	38.0	28.3	17.2	16.0	2.6	0.8
Save As You Earn:												
Fixed Interest (1st, 2nd and 4th issues)	KQOS	18.3	18.8	18.3	18.0	18.3	14.6	11.7	5.7	4.9	..	..
Index-linked (3rd issue)	KQOT	8.8	1.1	0.3	0.9	0.4	0.5	0.5	0.5	0.1	..	..
Total	GQRQ	..	..	..	..	..	..	..	..	..	1.4	0.4
Premium Bonds	GQRR	..	..	..	..	..	..	..	..	..		
First Option bonds	KIAJ	–	–	70.7	40.4	31.8	40.4	54.8	48.4	40.1	24.9	21.3
Investment Account	KQOU	864.4	657.7	541.8	529.1	518.5	509.0	497.8	464.5	335.7	374.1	287.1
Ordinary Account	KQOV	58.2	57.3	44.6	42.8	35.5	36.2	29.4	30.6	15.7	23.0	11.7
Childrens Bonus bonds	KHCW	–	9.3	14.4	19.2	27.0	98.9	73.7	66.6	72.0	75.3	70.0
Deposit Bonds	KQOW	77.9	59.8	46.4	41.4	39.4	38.3	37.2	31.5	22.9	21.0	17.5
Treasurer's Account	KXDA	–	–	–	–	–	–	–	–	6.2	1.5	2.6
ISA's	ZCFM	..	..	..	..	..	..	..	..	6.0	31.5	35.8
Fixed Rate Savings Bond	ZCFN	..	..	..	..	..	..	..	..	1.2	15.6	22.5
Total	KQOX	1 936.1	1 756.3	1 898.2	2 025.4	2 281.9	2 485.3	2 153.5	1 799.9	1 426.1	1 595.0	1 311.0
Amounts remaining invested												
Capital bonds	KQOY	1 094.9	1 680.5	2 124.7	2 176.4	2 438.4	2 394.4	2 006.5	1 741.8	1 572.5	1 325.0	1 371.1
National Savings Certificates												
5yr Fixed Interest - Principal	KQOZ	6 046.8	7 293.6	7 930.1	8 170.7	8 850.4	8 817.5	8 314.7	7 554.8	7 076.7	..	..
- Accrued Interest	KQPA	1 898.0	2 001.8	1 935.1	2 120.1	2 349.0	2 199.6	1 736.0	1 575.7	1 616.6	..	..
Total	GQRS	..	..	..	..	..	..	..	..	..	7 681.0	6 483.2
5yr Index-linked - Principal	KQPB	5 095.5	6 247.3	6 768.7	7 090.2	7 620.3	8 059.4	8 896.3	9 110.3	8 461.7	..	..
- Accrued Interest, Index-linking, etc.	KQPC	1 455.2	1 344.5	1 050.3	1 083.0	1 066.2	1 124.5	1 111.7	1 086.9	1 057.3	..	..
Total	GQRT	..	..	..	..	..	..	..	..	..	7 972	6 535
2yr Fixed interest - Principal	ZCFO	..	..	..	..	..	..	..	..	434.9	..	..
- Accrued Interest	ZCFP	..	..	..	..	..	..	..	..	1.0	..	..
Total	GQRU	..	..	..	..	..	..	..	..	..	1 506.0	2 405.3
2yr Index-linked - Principal	ZCFQ	..	..	..	..	..	..	..	..	284.1	..	..
- Accrued Interest/ Index-linking, etc.	ZCFR	..	..	..	..	..	..	..	..	1.0	..	..
Total	GQRV	..	..	..	..	..	..	..	..	..	1 563.0	2 461.5
Yearly Plan:												
Principal	KQPD	423.9	441.2	469.9	510.4	505.4	409.8	290.3	178.5	61.0	..	..
Interest	KQPE	68.9	65.7	65.9	73.8	69.2	68.0	52.7	39.3	20.0	..	..
Total	GQRW	..	..	..	..	..	..	..	..	..	45.0	32.5
Save As You Earn:												
Fixed Interest - Principal	KQPF	228.5	225.3	216.1	197.8	151.0	115.3	68.2	43.5	16.1	..	..
- Accrued Interest	KQPG	24.8	25.4	25.6	24.4	20.8	17.5	10.7	7.3	4.4	..	..
Index-linked - Principal	KQPH	62.6	36.1	26.8	19.4	17.6	16.7	15.9	15.3	13.5	..	..
- Accrued Interest/ Index-linking, etc.	KQPI	78.3	40.5	26.5	15.2	12.3	11.2	10.2	9.5	9.2	..	..
Total	GQRX	..	..	..	..	..	..	..	..	..	22.0	15.5
Register (DNS only)	KQPJ	1 026.2	1 180.3	1 198.6	1 392.7	1 530.7	1 541.1	1 468.5	–	–	–	–
Income bonds	KQPK	9 599.2	9 884.4	10 833.0	10 881.8	10 428.0	10 299.6	10 205.2	10 689.9	9 647.0	9 560.0	9 279.4
First Option bonds	KIAK	–	880.2	822.1	669.7	769.3	1 068.9	937.7	890.7	672.1	480.0	407.6
Investment Account	KQPL	8 934.7	8 919.8	9 177.4	9 322.4	9 342.9	9 474.2	9 065.0	8 593.3	7 959.4	7 628.0	7 442.1
Premium Savings bonds	KQPM	2 430.1	2 661.2	3 478.4	4 971.6	6 456.9	8 166.0	10 162.5	12 387.0	13 847.0	15 312.0	17 315.7
Ordinary Account	KQPN	1 434.8	1 438.4	1 444.4	1 446.0	1 432.3	1 419.3	1 398.3	1 366.6	1 347.6	1 380.0	1 381.0
Children's Bonus bonds	KHCX	135.4	234.3	340.1	474.3	643.6	836.0	979.6	1 067.2	1 127.0	1 158.0	1 213.0
5yr Pensioners' bonds	KJRG	–	–	895.0	1 926.8	4 158.1	6 637.0	7 409.8	6 705.8	6 016.9	4 132.0	2 804.8
3yr Pensioners' bonds	GWEN	–	–	–	–	–	–	–	–	–		
2yr Pensioners' bonds	ZCFS	..	..	..	..	..	..	..	..	365.2	767.0	966.1
1yr Pensioners'bonds	GQRY	..	..	..	..	..	..	..	..	–	192.0	427.2
Deposit bonds	KQPO	730.0	710.0	684.0	653.2	619.1	591.9	552.5	505.0	460.8	410.5	379.7
Indexed-income bonds	KQPP	15.9	15.3	14.8	14.2	12.5	6.0	–	–	–		
National Savings stamps and gift tokens	KQPR	1.8	1.8	1.7	1.7	1.6	1.6	1.6	1.6	1.6	1.6	1.6
Treasurer's Account	KXDB	–	–	–	–	–	20.8	47.2	49.7	53.3	54.9	62.0
ISA's	ZCFT	..	..	..	..	..	..	..	..	249.6	534.0	882.7
Fixed Rate Savings Bond	ZCFU	..	..	..	..	..	..	..	..	170.5	439.0	544.6
Guaranteed equity bond	GXDD	..	..	..	..	..	..	..	..	..	..	40.7
Total administered by DNS	KQPS	40 785.5	45 327.6	49 529.2	53 235.8	58 495.6	63 296.3	64 741.1	63 619.7	62 548.0	62 163.0	62 452.3

Source: Department for National Savings: 020 7605 9314

17.10 Income tax: allowances and reliefs[1]
United Kingdom

£

		1992/93	1993/94	1994/95	1995/96	1996/97	1997/98	1998/99	1999/00	2000/01	2001/02	2002/03
Personal allowances												
Personal allowance	KDZP	3 445	3 445	3 445	3 525	3 765	4 045	4 195	4 335	4 385	4 535	4 615
Married couples allowance	KDZR	1 720	1 720	1 720	1 720	1 790	1 830	1 900	1 970	..	..	..
Age allowance:												
Personal (aged 65-74)	KSOH	4 200	4 200	4 200	4 630	4 910	5 220	5 410	5 720	5 790	5 990	6 100
Personal (aged 75 or over)	KSOI	4 370	4 370	4 370	4 800	5 090	5 400	5 600	5 980	6 050	6 260	6 370
Married couple's (either partner between 65-74 but neither partner 75 or over)[2]	KEDI	2 465	2 465	2 665	2 995	3 115	3 185	3 305	5 125	5 185	5 365	5 465
Married couples (either partner 75 or over)	KEIY	2 505	2 505	2 705	3 035	3 155	3 225	3 345	5 195	5 255	5 435	5 535
Income limit	KEOO	14 200	14 200	14 200	14 600	15 200	15 600	16 200	16 800	17 000	17 600	17 900
Marginal fraction		1/2	1/2	1/2	1/2	1/2	1/2	1/2	1/2	1/2	1/2	1/2
Additional personal allowance	KEPG	1 720	1 720	1 720	1 720	1 790	1 830	1 900	1 970	..	..	..
Widow's bereavement allowance	KEPH	1 720	1 720	1 720	1 720	1 790	1 830	1 900	1 970	..	..	..
Blind person's allowance												
Single or married (one spouse blind)	KSOJ	1 080	1 080	1 200	1 200	1 250	1 280	1 330	1 380	1 400	1 450	1 480
Married (both spouses blind)	KSOK	2 160	2 160	2 400	2 400	2 500	2 560	2 660	2 760	2 800	2 900	2 960
Life Assurance Relief												
(Percentage of gross premium)	KFDR	12.5 or Nil	12.5 or Nil	12.5 or Nil	12.5 or Nil	12.5 or Nil	12.5 or Nil	12.5 or Nil	12.5 or Nil	12.5 or Nil	12.5 or Nil	12.5 or Nil

1 See chapter text.
2 At least one of the partners must be aged 65 before April 2000 to be entitled to the MCA. This means that only people born before 6 April 1935 are entitled to MCA

Source: Board of Inland Revenue: 020 7438 4335

17.11 Rates of Income tax
United Kingdom

	1993/94		1994/95		1995/96		1996/97		1997/98	
	Bands of taxable income (£)[1]	Rate of tax (%)	Bands of taxable income (£)[1]	Rate of tax (%)	Bands of taxable income (£)[1]	Rate of tax (%)	Bands of taxable income (£)[1]	Rate of tax (%)	Bands of taxable income (£)[1]	Rate of tax (%)
Lower rate	1 - 2 500	20	1 - 3 000	20	1 - 3 200	20	1 - 3 900	20	1 - 4 100	20
Basic rate	2 501 - 23 700	25[2]	3 001 - 23 700	25[2]	3 201 - 24 300	25[2]	3 901 - 25 500	24[3]	4 101 - 26 100	23[3]
Higher rate	over 23 700	40	over 23 700	40	over 24 300	40	over 25 500	40	over 26 100	40

	1998/99		1999/00		2000/01		2001/02		2001/02	
	Bands of taxable income (£)[1]	Rate of tax (%)	Bands of taxable income (£)[1]	Rate of tax (%)	Bands of taxable income (£)[1]	Rate of tax (%)	Bands of taxable income (£)[1]	Rate of tax (%)	Bands of taxable income (£)[1]	Rate of tax (%)
Lower rate	1 - 4 300	20	1 - 1 500	10[4]	1 - 1 520	10[4]	1 - 1 880	10[4]	1 - 1 920	10[4]
Basic rate	4 301 - 27 100	23[3]	1 501 - 28 000	23[5]	1 520 - 28 400	22[5]	1 880 - 29 400	22[5]	1 920 - 29 900	22[5]
Higher rate	over 27 100	40	over 28 000	40[6]	over 28 400	40[6]	over 29 400	40[6]	over 29 900	40[6]

1 Taxable income is defined as gross income for income tax purposes less any allowances and reliefs available at the taxpayer's marginal rate.
2 The basic rate of tax on dividend income is 20%.
3 The basic rate of tax on dividends and savings income is 20%.
4 The starting rate also applies to savings.
5 The basic rate of tax on dividends is 10% and savings income is 20%
6 The higher rate of tax on dividends is 32.5%.

Source: Board of Inland Revenue: 020 7438 4335

17.12 Rateable values[1]
England and Wales
At 1 April in each year

		Unit	1992	1993	1994	1995	1996	1997	1998	1999	2000	2001	2002
Number of properties		Thousands											
Total - all classes	KMIH	"	1 734	1 737	1 734	1 723	1 726	1 725	1 719	1 720	1 729	1 740	1 745
Commercial: total	KMIN	"	1 227	1 230	1 227	1 223	1 228	1 225	1 223	1 219	1 223	1 230	1 234
Shops and cafes	KMIO	"	570	567	565	562	497	491	488	484	478	476	473
Offices	KMIP	"	243	248	251	252	255	255	257	258	261	269	273
Other	KMIQ	"	413	415	411	409	476	479	478	477	484	485	487
On-licensed premises: total	KMIR	"	55	55	55	60	59	59	59	60	61	61	60
Entertainment and recreational: total	KMIS	"	94	93	92	87	87	87	81	80	79	79	80
Cinemas	KMIT	"	1	1	1	1	1	1	1	1	1	1	1
Theatres and music-halls	KMIU	"	1	1	1	1	1	1	1	1	1	1	1
Other	KMIV	"	93	92	91	86	85	86	80	79	76	76	77
Public utility: total	KMIW	"	15	15	15	9	8	8	9	9	8	8	8
Educational and cultural: total	KMIX	"	42	42	41	41	41	41	41	41	41	42	42
Miscellaneous: total	KMIY	"	59	58	58	56	55	55	56	61	67	70	70
Industrial: total	KMIZ	"	241	244	247	248	249	249	250	250	250	251	250
Value of assessments		£ million											
Total - all classes	KMHA	"	35 608	35 263	34 129	33 912	34 245	34 299	33 909	33 649	42 985	43 626	44 136
Commercial: total	KMHG	"	21 440	21 336	20 662	19 626	19 822	19 859	19 733	19 652	26 320	27 255	27 622
Shops and cafes	KMHH	"	7 472	7 335	7 068	7 780	6 094	5 959	5 860	5 840	6 801	6 972	6 953
Offices	KMHI	"	8 093	8 239	8 027	5 587	5 630	5 641	5 624	5 575	8 625	9 191	9 388
Other	KMHJ	"	5 876	5 762	5 568	6 260	8 098	8 259	8 249	8 237	10 894	11 092	11 281
On-licensed premises: total	KMHK	"	698	679	642	968	969	970	980	997	1 311	1 347	1 345
Entertainment and recreational: total	KMHL	"	1 025	1 022	988	1 009	1 018	1 033	1 040	1 045	1 310	1 369	1 430
Cinemas	KMHM	"	24	25	24	32	32	36	39	45	79	92	104
Theatres and music-halls	KMHN	"	22	21	19	21	21	21	21	20	24	25	26
Other	KMHO	"	979	975	946	956	965	975	979	980	1 207	1 252	1 300
Public utility: total	KMHP	"	3 518	3 505	3 424	3 455	3 469	3 488	3 380	3 361	3 828	3 411	3 460
Educational and cultural: total	KMHQ	"	1 970	1 883	1 813	1 873	1 883	1 894	1 773	1 672	1 829	1 872	1 902
Miscellaneous: total	KMHR	"	1 375	1 367	1 319	1 429	1 500	1 494	1 464	1 439	2 142	2 172	2 220
Industrial: total	KMHS	"	5 583	5 470	5 280	5 550	5 584	5 561	5 540	5 463	6 249	6 202	6 157

1 See chapter text.

Source: Board of Inland Revenue: 020 7438 6314

Government finance

17.13 Local authorities: gross loan debt outstanding[1]
At 31 March in each year

£ millions

		1992	1993	1994	1995	1996	1997	1998	1999	2000	2001	2002
United Kingdom												
Total debt	KQBR	56 331	55 943	55 869	..	..	..	..	..	..	..	..
Public Works Loan Board	KQBS	48 717	41 447	40 803	40 388	40 445	41 683	42 901	44 701	46 044	47 073	46 867
Northern Ireland Consolidated Fund	KQBT	93	109	126	138	157	175	220	..	..	..	..
Other debt	KQBU	..	..	..	..	..	..	..	..	..	..	..
England and Wales												
Total debt	KQBV	48 187	47 357	46 695	..	..	..	..	..	..	..	..
of which Public Works Loan Board	KQBW	41 501	34 082	33 132	32 448	32 617	33 660	34 606	36 049	37 172	38 013	37 627
Scotland												
Total debt[2]	KQBX	8 005	8 429	8 999	9 984	10 850	..	..	..	..	..	..
of which Public Works Loan Board	KQBY	7 216	7 365	7 671	7 940	7 828	8 023	8 295	8 652	8 872	9 060	9 241
Northern Ireland												
Total debt	KQBZ	139	157	175	186	183	211	225	250	..	..	..

1 The sums shown exclude inter-authority loans and debt transfers, and temporary loans and overdrafts obtained for the purpose of providing for current expenses. No deduction has been made in respect of sums held in sinking funds for the repayment of debt.
2 Data for 1996 are before transfer of responsibility for Water & Sewerage and the Scottish Childrens Reporters Administration.

Sources: Office of the Deputy Prime Minister: 020 7944 4163; Public Works Loan Board: 020 7270 3874; Department of the Environment for Northern Ireland: 028 9054 0707; Chartered Institute of Public Finance and Accountancy

17.14 Revenue expenditure of local authorities

	1999/00 outturn £m	2000/01 outturn £m	2001/02 budget[1] £m	2001/02 adjusted budget[2,3] £m	2002/03 budget £m	Difference 2002/03 over 2001/02 adjusted budget £m	%
England							
Education	22 164	23 747	25 813	24 543	26 144	1 601	6.5
Personal social services	10 050	10 703	11 076	11 749	12 672	923	7.9
Police	7 034	7 282	7 861	7 732	8 288	556	7.2
Fire	1 473	1 524	1 615	1 615	1 713	98	6.1
Highway maintenance	1 645	1 783	1 842	1 842	2 020	178	9.7
EPC services	15 505	16 509	16 865	16 875	18 399	1 524	9.0
Comprising:							
Civil defence and other Home office	594	569	105	91	109	18	20
Magistrates courts	316	323	324	324	332	8	2.4
Parking and public transport	669	817	972	980	1 125	145	14.8
Housing benefit	5 263	5 354	5 642	5 642	6 034	392	6.9
Council tax administration and housing benefit administration	494	545	525	525	573	48	9.1
Non-HRA housing	420	426	434	434	456	22	5.1
Libraries and art galleries	1 056	1 144	1 201	1 201	1 285	84	7.0
Sports and recreation centres	563	593	557	557	575	18	3.1
Local environmental services	3 850	4 417	4 696	4 702	5 153	451	9.6
Other	2 280	2 322	2 410	2 420	2 757	337	13.9
Net current expenditure	57 872	61 548	65 073	64 357	69 239	4 882	7.6
Capital charges	1 927	1 904	2 050	2 050	2 057	7	0.6
CERA[3]	628	623	699	699	698	-1	6.2
Interest receipts	-877	-1 112	-809	-809	697	1 506	2.7
Other non-current[4]	2 223	2 286	2 378	2 378	2 447	69	1.2
Gross revenue expenditure[5]	61 774	65 249	69 390	68 674	73 720	5 046	7.1
Specific grants outside AEF	-8 122	-7 920	-8 119	-7 980	-8 468	-488	3.0
Revenue expenditure	53 651	57 329	61 270	60 693	65 252	4 559	7.7
Specific and special grants inside AEF	-2 921	-4 671	-5 431	-6 401	-7 618	-1 217	48.5
Net revenue expenditure	50 730	52 658	55 839	54 292	57 634	3 342	4.9
Other adjustments	-35	-36	-25	-25	-55	-30	-21.0
Use of reserves	-157	201	-479	-479	-435	44	-13.0
Budget requirement	50 539	52 823	55 336	53 789	57 144	3 355	5.1
SSA reduction grant	-68	-18	-2	-2	-	2	-89.7
Police grant	-3 505	-3 627	-3 798	-3 798	-3 808	-10	4.7
Revenue support grant	-19 875	-19 437	-21 086	-19 540	-19 889	-349	9.5
Central Support Protection Grant	-51	-34	-1	-1	-	1	-96.0
Council Tax Benefit Subsid Limitation Scheme	31	54	83	83	-	-83	53.1
Non-domestic rates	-13 612	-15 400	-15 143	-15 143	-16 626	-1 483	-1.7
Greater London Authority Grant	-	-22	-23	-23	-28	-5	4.9
Other items	-181	-139	-119	-119	-145	-26	-9.7
Precepts/demand on collection fund	13 278	14 200	15 245	15 244	16 648	1 404	7.4
Scotland							
Net revenue expenditure on general fund	7 023	7 271	..	..	..	..	..

17.14 Revenue expenditure of local authorities
continued

£ millions

	1997/98 outturn	1998/99 outturn	1999/00 outturn	2000/01 outturn	2001/02 budget	2002/03 budget
Wales[6]						
Education	1 328.4	1 385.1	1 407.1	1 516.7	1 586.4	1694.5
Personal social services	560.5	595.1	631.8	681.1	716.5	836.4
Council fund housing, including housing benefit[7]	260.2	258.7	266.0	274.0	280.4	290.9
Local environmental services[8]	183.7	186.4	197.6	216.9	221.6	255.1
Roads and transport	160.6	162.5	163.3	176.6	197.4	228.3
Libraries, culture, heritage, sport and recreation	88.5	102.0	107.0	112.4	122.8	140.6
Planning, economic development, community development and tourism	38.8	47.5	49.6	62.1	68.0	72.0
Magistrates', coroners' and other courts	50.6	53.1	47.8	52.9	24.1	26.9
Council tax benefit and administration[9]	12.3	12.0	13.6	14.9	14.4	16.7
Local tax collection	13.4	12.4	13.3	15.4	15.6	14.9
Debt financing costs: counties	237.3	242.0	242.8	239.9	249.2	259.6
Central administrative and other revenue expenditure: counties[10,11]	145.9	134.0	161.3	136.8	185.9	206.1
Total county and county borough council expenditure	3 080.2	3 190.9	3 301.1	3 499.8	3 682.4	4 042.0
Police operational expenditure	..	..	..	..	..	439.9
Other police expenditure[10,12]	..	..	..	..	..	13.7
Total police expenditure	347.4	358.4	373.5	401.3	434.1	453.6
Fire operational expenditure	..	..	..	..	..	107.7
Other fire expenditure[10,12]	..	..	..	..	..	2.7
Total fire expenditure	82.1	89.3	95.2	99.1	104.7	110.4
National park operational expenditure	..	..	..	..	..	10.8
Other national park expenditure[10,12]	..	..	..	..	..	2.1
Total national park expenditure	-	5.9	6.9	9.8	11.0	12.9
Gross revenue expenditure	3 509.8	3 644.5	3 776.7	4 010.0	4 232.2	4 618.9
Less specific and special government grants (except council tax benefit grant)	-463.8	-482.1	-433.2	-498.8	-468.5	-644.4
Net revenue expenditure	3 046.0	3 162.4	3 343.5	3 511.2	3 763.7	3 974.5
Putting to (-)/drawing from (+) reserves	-24.1	-0.7	0.1	30.1	-6.7	-16.9
Buget requirement	3 021.9	3 161.7	3 343.5	3 541.3	3 757.0	3 957.6
Plus discretionary non-domestic rate relief	2.3	1.0	1.5	0.7	1.7	1.9
Less revenue support grant	-1 769.1	-1 798.2	-1 890.2	-2 030.9	-2 146.8	-2 339.9
Less police grant	-171.1	-179.5	-180.7	-186.0	-194.6	-196.2
Less re-distributed non-domestic rates income	-584.0	-612.0	-656.0	-638.0	-697.0	-643.0
Less transitional grant	-16.7	-31.2	-22.2	-17.0	-4.0	-4.8
Council tax requirement	483.3	541.8	595.9	670.1	716.4	775.6
of which:						
Paid by council tax benefit grant from the Department for work and pensions	85.1	93.6	99.8	108.2	110.1	113.7
Paid directly by council tax payers	398.3	448.2	496.2	561.9	606.3	661.9
Northern Ireland						
Total expenditure[13]						
Capital	65.2	77.2	..	..	..	..
Other	304.3	324.6	359.1	404.5	..	..
Total income	370.4	407.3	359.1	404.5	..	..

1 For Scotland figure for 2000/2001 is a provisional outurn figure not a budget figure.

2 Adjustments made for transfers of responsibilities of various services out of local authority responsibility, changes of funds between SSAs and specific grants and for changes in the level of specific grants and other minor function changes.

3 Capital Expenditure charged to the Revenue Account

4 Includes:
   (i) Gross expenditure on council tax benefit.
   (ii) Expenditure on council tax reduction scheme.
   (iii) Discretionary (non-domestic) rate relief.
   (iv) Flood defence payments to the National Rivers Authority (now Environment Agency).
   (v) Payments in respect of grant maintained schools (1998/99 only).
   (vi) Bad debt provision.

5 This measure of expenditure is referred to as 'Gross Revenue Expenditure' on local authority returns, but is actually net of expenditure met by sales, fees, charges and interest receipts, and excludes most expenditure on the housing revenue account and on trading services.

6 Service expenditure is shown excluding that financed by sales, fees and and charges, but including that financed by specific and special government grants. For definitions of the below please e-mail: LGFS.Transfer@Wales.gsi.gov.uk

7 Includes housing benefit, and private sector housing costs such as provision for the homeless. Excludes council owned housing.

8 Includes cemeteries and crematoria, community safety, environmental health, food safety, open spaces and waste collection / disposal.

9 Expenditure on council tax benefit expenditure funded by the specific grant from the Department for Work and Pensions is excluded. This amount is part of the financing of the council tax requirement, and would be double counted within gross revenue expenditure if it was also recorded within the line for council tax benefit expendture. As such, this line records only that council tax benefit expenditure funded directly by the local authorities.

10 Includes central administrative costs of corporate management, democratic representation and certain costs, such as those relating to back-year or additional pension contributions which should not be allocated to individual services.

11 Includes agricultural services, central services to the public such as birth registration and elections, coastal and flood defence, community councils, consumer protection and licensing. Also includes capital expenditure charged to the revenue account and are net of any interest expected to accrue on balances.

12 Includes debt financing costs, capital expenditure charged to the revenue account and are net of any interest expected to accrue on balances. The figures cannot be reliably split out from the police, fire and national park total expenditure figures.

13 'Capital' and 'Other' figures cannot be added to give 'Total' figure because of double counting of loan charges, which is recorded as both 'Capital' and 'Other' expenditure.

Sources: Office of the Deputy Prime Minister: 020 7944 4163; Scottish Executive, Economic Advice & Statistics: 0131 244 7033; National Assembly for Wales: 029 2082 5355; Department of the Environment for Northern Ireland: 028 9054 0707

17.15 Funding of revenue expenditure
Years ending 31 March

£ millions

		Community charge system			Council tax system									
		1990 /91	1991[1] /92	1992 /93	1993 /94	1994 /95	1995 /96	1996 /97	1997 /98	1998 /99	1999 /00	2000[2] /01	2001[2] /02	2002[2] /03
England														
Revenue expenditure[3]														
1999/00 prices £m[4]	KRTM	49 068	52 125	53 751	51 812	53 716	53 695	54 024	53 223	55 015	57 419	60 026	62 802	65 252
Cash £m	KRTN	35 851	39 472	42 020	41 506	43 602	44 827	46 532	47 256	50 189	53 651	57 329	61 270	65 252
Government grants[5]														
Cash £m	KRTO	12 927	18 620	20 968	21 685	23 679	23 335	23 003	23 840	25 291	26 421	27 787	30 341	31 343
Per cent	KRTP	36	47	50	52	54	52	49	50	50	49	47	49	48
Non- domestic rates[6]														
Cash £m	KRTQ	10 429	12 408	12 306	11 584	10 692	11 361	12 743	12 034	12 531	13 619	15 407	15 144	16 633
Per cent	KRTR	29	32	29	28	25	25	27	25	25	25	27	25	25
Community charges and council taxes[7]														
Cash £m	KRTS	12 251	8 533	9 521	8 912	9 239	9 777	10 461	11 241	12 332	13 278	14 200	15 245	16 648
Per cent	KRTT	34	22	23	21	21	22	22	24	24	25	25	25	26
Wales[8]														
Revenue expenditure	ZBXH	2 217	2 473	2 644	2 624	2 755	2 932	2 990	3 121	3 257	3 430	3 605	3 865	4 093
General government grants[1,9]	ZBXI	1 250	1 660	1 753	1 807	1 881	1 873	2 001	1 957	2 009	2 093	2 234	2 345	2 541
Specific government grants[1,10]	ZBXG	59	64	69	70	73	70	73	75	95	86	94	102	118
Share of redistributed non- domestic rates	ZBXJ	443	525	536	470	464	520	459	584	612	656	638	697	643
Community charge/council tax income[11]	ZBXK	477	231	299	323	354	394	449	483	542	596	670	716	776
Other[12]	ZBXL	−12	−7	−12	−46	−17	75	9	22	−	−2	−31	5	15

1 In 1991-92, a grant of £140 per taxpayer was given to local authorities in Wales to reduce community charge bills. Although identified separately from general government grants in 1991-92 it has been included under that heading as it was added into revenue support grant in subsequent years.

2 Budget figures

3 'Revenue expenditure to compare with TSS' ie. expenditure financed from revenue support grants, specific grants within Aggregate External Finance, special grants, non domestic rates, community charges/council taxes and balances. Also include spending met by community charge grant (1991-92), and additional grant for teacher pay (1992-93), SSA reduction grant (1994/95 onwards), police grant (1995/96 onwards), Central Support Reduction Grant (1999/00 onwards) and Greater London Local Authority Grant (2000/01 onwards). This series is not the total of the others. The difference is due to funding by balances and other adjustments.

4 Revenue expenditure at 2002/03 prices have been calculated using the GDP deflator. Major function changes include:
(i) Increased responsibilities as a result of care in the community since 1 April 1993.
(ii) Funding for colleges of further education and sixth form colleges transferred to the Further Education Funding Council (FEFC) on 1 April 1993.

5 Revenue support grants, specific and special grants within AEF, community charge grant (1991/92), teachers' pay award additional grant (1995/96 onward) and Greater London Authority Grant (2000/01 onwards).

6 1990/91 onwards: distributables amount from non-domestic rate pool. 1993/94 onwards: includes City Offset.

7 1990/91 to 1992/93: gross of community charge benefit community charge transitional relief/community charge reduction scheme grant. 1993/94 onwards: gross of council tax benefit. 1993/94 to 1995/96: council tax transitional reduction scheme.

8 Revenue expenditure is gross revenue expenditure excluding that funded by specific grants outside AEF. This excludes expenditure on services, which are mainly administered by the local authorities on behalf of local government, for example mandatory students awards, so that the measure is a better reflection of total local authority expenditure. Revenue expenditure is often referred to as expenditure on a total standard spending basis.

9 Includes all hypothecated grants, namely revenue support grant, police grant, council tax reduction scheme grant and the adjustment to reverse the transfer out of nursery voucher monies in 1997-98.

10 Comprises specific and supplementary grants within aggregate external finance, excluding police grant.

11 This includes community council precepts, and income covered by community charge/council tax benefit grant, but excludes council tax reduction scheme grant.

12 This includes use of, or contributions to, local authority reserves and other minor adjustments.

Sources: Department for Transport: 020 7944 4163;
National Assembly for Wales: 029 2082 5355

289

17.16 Local authority capital expenditure and receipts[1]
Years ending 31 March

£ millions

		1996	1997	1998	1999	2000	2001
England		1996/97 final outturn	1997/98 final outturn	1998/99 final outturn	1999/00 final outturn	2000/01 final outturn[2]	2001/02 provisional outturn[2]
Expenditure[3]							
Education	KRUD	807	857	995	1 139	1 533	1 974
Personal Social Services	KRUE	194	150	140	134	156	151
Transport	KRUC	1 194	1 114	1 053	1 086	1 410	1 953
Housing	KRUB	2 529	2 346	2 513	2 406	2 779	3 005
Arts and libraries	GEKZ	69	130	150	195	194	235
Agriculture and fisheries	GELA	64	55	57	48	45	21
Sport and recreation	KRUH	217	205	235	241	291	355
Other[4]	GELB	1 006	1 121	1 140	1 299	1 341	1 554
Fire and civil defence	GELC	49	50	49	50	46	61
Police and probation	GELD	262	253	263	286	291	346
Magistrates courts	GELE	28	19	33	28	22	35
Total	KRUR	6 419	6 298	6 630	6 912	8 109	9 691
Receipts							
Education	KRUT	120	133	82	102	119	142
Personal social services	KRUV	57	43	52	51	63	61
Transport	KRUU	132	34	64	105	98	41
Housing	KRUS	1 169	1 438	1 630	2 249	2 441	2 217
Arts and libraries	GELF	1	2	6	2	19	24
Agriculture and fisheries	GELG	63	64	51	48	44	43
Sport and recreation	KRUX	9	13	10	8	12	9
Other[4]	GELH	545	544	687	960	600	936
Fire and civil defence	GELI	5	9	3	5	8	8
Police and probation	GELJ	82	70	76	118	104	88
Magistrates court	GELK	–	1	–	2	4	9
Total	KRVB	2 183	2 349	2 662	3 651	3 512	3 578

1 'Total capital expenditure' in this table includes acquisition of share or loan capital. Similarly 'Total capital receipts' in this table include the disposal of share or loan capital and disposal of other investments.
2 The figures shown here have been adjusted based on historical differences between provisional and final outturn
3 Expenditure funded by Regeneration (including SRB) resources is included in gross expenditure.
4 'Other' covers other environmental services, consumer protection and employment services.

Source: Department for Transport: 020 7944 4076

17.17 Capital expenditure and income

£ millions

Financial year	Expenditure			Income				
	Expenditure on land works, etc	Capital assigned to repayment of debt	All expenditure	Loans	Government grants	Miscellaneous	All income	Gross debt at end of year
	KRVC	KRVD	KRVE	KRVF	KRVG	KRVH	KRVI	KRVJ
1970/71	1 792	150	1 942	1 516	106	349	1 970	13 384
1971/72	1 938	170	2 109	1 605	116	421	2 143	14 450
1972/73	2 418	213	2 631	2 030	122	531	2 682	16 105
1973/74	3 286	225	3 511	2 781	143	619	3 544	18 300
1974/75[1]	3 712	127	3 839	3 209	128	498	3 835	18 884
1975/76	3 917	198	4 115	3 285	177	647	4 109	21 930
1976/77	3 783	312	4 095	3 097	249	803	4 149	24 534
1977/78	3 487	352	3 839	2 677	255	981	3 913	26 282
1978/79	3 621	390	4 011	2 627	351	1 139	4 117	27 103
1979/80	4 249	331	4 580	2 992	385	1 367	4 745	30 187
1980/81	4 476	413	4 889	2 900	492	1 864	5 256	32 076
1981/82	4 061	563	4 623	2 527	470	2 177	5 174	34 069
1982/83	5 090	634	5 724	3 358	416	3 100	6 874	36 231
1983/84	5 890	562	6 452	3 538	379	3 294	7 211	38 698
1984/85	6 352	515	6 867	3 381	327	3 283	6 991	40 554
1985/86	5 748	348	6 096	3 008	360	3 239	6 607	40 138
1986/87	5 899	328	6 227	2 814	388	3 878	7 081	43 033
1987/88	6 091	486	6 577	2 953	297	4 286	7 536	44 904
1988/89	7 166	658	7 824	2 985	270	6 122	9 376	47 295
1989/90	9 590	474	10 064	2 919	440	6 110	9 469	48 695

Financial year	Gross capital expenditure	Income					Capital receipts set aside[2]	Credit ceiling[3]	Provision for credit liabilities[3]
		Credit approvals used	Government grants	Capital receipts	Other income	Total income			
At 1 April 1990	-	-	-	-	-	-	4 241	42 167	4 241
	KRVK	KRVL	KRVM	KRVN	KRVO	KRVP	KRVQ	KRVR	KRVS
1990/91	6 869	2 786	907	3 165	542	7 400	2 022	41 125	5 677
1991/92	6 572	3 140	1 041	2 251	674	7 106	1 353	41 234	6 502
1992/93	6 567	3 229	1 210	2 110	619	7 168	908	37 051	6 282
1993/94	7 124	2 948	1 279	3 310	651	8 188	356	37 941	6 041
1994/95	6 950	2 722	1 176	2 458	724	7 080	1 409	37 673	6 921
1995/96	6 910	2 264	1 484	1 966	1 278	6 992	1 160	37 103	7 677
1996/97	6 420	2 120	1 388	2 183	1 132	6 823	1 039	37 261	8 520
1997/98	6 298	2 099	1 262	2 349	1 129	6 839	1 186	36 711	8 081
1998/99	6 630	2 334	1 160	2 662	1 413	7 569	1 130	36 782	7 301
1999/00	6 912	2 301	1 168	3 651	1 480	8 600	1 483	36 364	7 470
2000/01	8 109	3 216	2 175	3 512	1 342	10 245	1 642	36 628	7 231

1 Reorganisation of local government in April 1974 transferred responsibility for various services to regional health and water authorities.
2 Excluding Social Housing Grant and European Regional Development Fund (ERDF) grants.
3 At end of year.

Source: Department for Transport: 020 7944 4076

17.18 Expenditure of local authorities
Scotland
Year ending 31 March

£ thousand

Out of revenue [1]

		1991/92	1992/93	1993/94	1994/95	1995/96	1996/97	1997/98	1998/99	1999/00	2000/01
Total	KQTA	7 985 137	8 560 071	8 713 471	9 111 751	9 690 424	9 196 125	9 566 936	10 033 985	10 439 999	10 924 634
General Fund Services:	KQTB	6 093 642	6 542 916	6 589 420	6 904 228	7 324 381	7 151 759	6 679 396	7 021 038	7 429 626	7 884 168
Education	KQTC	2 564 363	2 757 058	2 537 582	2 563 049	2 654 158	2 629 961	2 512 725	2 649 170	2 855 945	3 037 780
Libraries, museums and galleries	KQTD	109 181	117 243	125 791	132 055	149 427	138 483	121 387	124 648	131 696	134 174
Social work	KQTE	733 067	806 613	914 436	1 045 638	1 222 693	1 289 928	1 315 387	1 394 142	1 519 191	1 632 843
Law, order and protective services	KQTF	704 943	763 917	804 616	828 480	866 567	816 315	931 795	952 940	1 006 000	1 047 034
Roads[2]	KQTG	589 564	633 874	650 555	684 452	676 116	716 570	440 712	546 945	527 018	564 738
Environmental services	KQTH	283 968	305 645	322 534	330 039	351 689	329 674	343 565	349 413	373 050	393 333
Planning	KQTI	174 380	188 753	202 027	211 346	226 073	210 827	163 380	179 078	198 285	194 771
Leisure and recreation	KQTJ	362 560	383 081	396 874	405 083	451 952	426 422	364 853	368 023	375 579	387 115
Other services	KQTL	445 968	456 198	516 842	580 561	591 766	562 462	456 219	430 790	435 155	465 612
Other general fund expenditure[3]	KQTM	125 648	130 534	118 163	123 525	133 940	31 117	29 373	25 889	7 707	26 768
Housing	KQTN	1 573 590	1 672 566	1 738 427	1 806 022	1 924 930	2 000 684	1 658 935	1 754 686	1 821 380	1 886 189
Trading services:	KQTO	443 553	475 123	503 787	525 026	575 053	74 799	75 976	79 644	87 321	80 355
Water supply	KQTP	203 847	218 864	239 291	255 081	274 773	–	–	–	–	–
Sewerage	KQTQ	185 216	194 576	200 036	209 323	233 525	–	–	–	–	–
Passenger transport	KQTR	603	859	681	685	794	2 849	1 524	121	336	162
Ferries	KQTS	4 508	8 336	7 203	7 574	7 744	6 831	7 512	8 930	9 709	10 005
Harbours, docks and piers	KQTT	28 008	27 811	16 215	16 804	15 301	13 482	12 884	15 697	15 923	13 604
Road bridges	KQTV	9 629	9 508	10 948	7 579	11 755	12 759	16 064	16 408	8 231	8 606
Slaughterhouses	KQTW	1 427	1 282	985	976	1 000	794	850	228	4	–
Markets	KQTX	6 086	8 145	8 462	8 615	10 336	14 278	13 479	13 161	14 106	23 844
Other trading services	KQTY	4 229	5 742	19 966	18 389	19 825	23 806	23 663	25 099	39 012	24 134
Loan charges:[4] Total	KQTZ	1 327 639	1 343 768	1 346 433	1 383 167	1 451 179	1 121 448	1 126 637	1 152 728	1 109 379	1 100 690
Allocated to : General Fund services	KMHV	607 867	631 479	649 212	677 377	710 801	639 380	651 982	710 371	701 515	708 822
Housing	KMHW	542 248	528 488	505 407	499 904	504 162	475 507	471 274	438 556	402 936	386 512
Trading services	KMHX	177 524	183 801	191 814	205 886	236 216	6 561	3 381	3 801	4 928	5 356

On capital works [5]

		1991/92	1992/93	1993/94	1994/95	1995/96	1996/97	1997/98	1998/99	1999/00	2000/01
Total	KQUA	1 276 006	1 344 250	1 428 545	1 518 362	1 528 167	889 572	813 900	815 981	816 473	802 672
General Fund Services:	KQUB	620 287	650 779	699 250	760 564	767 795	540 127	540 096	541 769	557 119	538 843
Education	KQUC	81 007	92 584	85 619	113 121	114 128	101 898	112 753	125 341	136 508	127 781
Libraries, museums and galleries	KQUD	9 225	15 319	11 077	12 822	16 757	11 602	9 974	13 231	10 261	5 834
Social work	KQUE	26 017	32 940	29 040	29 067	30 298	20 658	19 660	22 554	22 097	21 539
Law, order and protective services	KQUF	19 903	28 230	32 951	33 635	35 847	41 326	37 701	37 727	37 132	35 761
Roads	KQUG	164 333	179 275	189 525	198 178	187 988	116 881	108 227	113 954	108 500	117 485
Environmental services	KQUH	12 798	13 239	18 905	16 595	14 580	10 226	21 193	18 397	14 936	17 944
Planning	KQUI	84 900	69 065	76 477	102 152	103 221	51 182	69 648	50 854	52 045	47 684
Leisure and recreation	KQUJ	51 490	44 774	74 563	65 411	57 243	36 232	29 692	40 926	52 365	44 516
Administrative buildings and equipment	KQUK	29 996	24 980	17 888	23 994	14 693	40 014	45 374	35 107	35 824	34 633
Other services	KQUL	140 618	150 373	163 205	165 589	193 040	110 108	85 814	83 678	87 451	85 666
Housing	KQUM	485 131	460 140	467 811	497 997	517 593	345 713	270 005	268 135	255 019	255 189
Trading Services:	KQUN	170 588	233 331	261 484	259 801	242 779	3 732	3 799	6 077	4 335	8 640
Water supply	KQUO	77 000	109 655	128 081	123 564	107 064	–	–	–	–	–
Sewerage	KQUP	88 035	113 998	127 047	130 634	131 684	–	–	–	–	–
Ferries	KQUR	773	18	–	376	355	521	770	268	1 030	23
Harbours, docks and piers	KQUS	336	5 020	2 300	1 982	1 218	934	1 175	1 626	1 389	6 192
Airports	KQUT	2	2	184	173	763	1 149	439	–	–	607
Road bridges	KQUU	380	694	799	830	805	277	973	2 791	600	964
Slaughterhouses	KQUV	56	87	1 068	139	63	112	69	54	12	–
Other trading services	KMHY	4 006	3 857	2 005	2 103	827	739	373	1 338	1 304	854

1 Gross expenditure less inter-authority and inter-account transfers.
2 Including general fund support for transport (LA and NON-LA).
3 General fund contributions to Housing and Trading services (excluding transport), are also included in the expenditure figures for these services. From 1996/97 water and sewerage are excluded from other general fund expenditure.
4 From 1997/98 loan charges are not included within individual service totals
5 Expenditure out of loans, government grants and other capital receipts.

Source: Scottish Executive, Economic Advice & Statistics: 0131 244 7033

17.19 Income of local authorities: classified according to source
Scotland
Year ending 31 March

£ thousand

		1990 /91	1991 /92	1992 /93	1993 /94	1994 /95	1995 /96	1996 /97	1997 /98	1998 /99	1999 /00	2000 /01
Revenue account												
Rates[1]	KQXA	1 351 627	1 414 346	1 336 395	1 258 863	1 198 575	1 310 721	1 313 531	1 326 129	1 437 646	1 440 522	1 662 691
Community charges	KQXB	890 645	802 005	932 994	–	–	–	–	–	–	–	–
Council tax	KPUC	–	–	–	822 830	918 502	976 465	968 153	1 070 405	1 146 366	1 193 693	1 273 316
Government grants												
RSG:	KQXC	2 495 840	2 706 629	3 546 958	3 582 127	3 741 567	3 716 567	3 649 694	3 520 461	3 483 815	3 537 043	3 440 842
Rate rebate grant	KQXG	30 941	37 304	33 741	41 772	39 860	4 456	496	–	–	–	–
Community charge grant[2]	KIMJ	..	437 105	15 512	–	–	–	–	–	–	–	–
Community charge rebate grants	KQXH	192 378	112 904	153 231	–	–	–	–	–	–	–	–
Council tax rebate grants	KPUD	–	–	–	166 015	186 219	193 937	226 132	260 424	274 940	275 789	279 459
Other grants and subsidies	KQXI	882 296	951 871	1 049 899	1 118 978	1 179 327	1 236 160	1 347 706	1 480 890	1 642 045	1 778 216	1 891 839
Sales	KQXJ	50 001	45 134	54 399	61 970	59 182	64 284	59 059	46 874	39 595	43 660	49 826
Fees and charges	KQXK	1 288 728	1 410 355	1 435 951	1 421 565	1 471 320	1 528 270	1 539 611	1 625 952	1 668 223	1 682 385	1 776 455
Other income[3]	KQXL	132 009	161 791	184 581	194 151	209 819	207 005	238 985	290 427	324 932	398 894	453 458
Capital account												
Sale of fixed assets	KQXM	416 838	415 475	413 083	441 600	529 528	500 838	499 143	327 569	335 037	303 582	149 504
Revenue contributions to capital	KQXP	48 997	73 896	111 710	163 228	134 156	197 606	119 641	149 423	204 982	213 564	210 912
Transfer from special funds	KMHZ	2 196	1 218	1 751	7 902	10 679	9 035	2 652	36 929	26 959	125 365	27 317
Other receipts	KMGV	24 649	23 110	42 631	32 554	38 736	29 571	45 067	32 118	45 028	39 014	45 351

1 Excluding government grants towards rate rebates and domestic element of rate support grant (RSG). Including domestic water rate receipts.
2 Payment to local authorities in respect of the £140 reduction in community charge awarded.

3 From 1996-97 Other Income includes income from Health Boards and Trusts, Other Public Bodies and Interest on Revenue Balances.

Source: Scottish Executive, Economic Advice & Statistics: 0131 244 7033

17.20 Income of local authorities from government grants[1]
Scotland
Year ending 31 March

£ thousand

		1990 /91	1991 /92	1992 /93	1993 /94	1994 /95	1995 /96	1996 /97	1997 /98	1998 /99	1999 /00	2000 /01
General fund services	KQYA	339 619	368 717	403 437	428 927	450 056	468 660	487 734	557 536	690 569	818 537	935 452
Education	KQYB	17 809	17 699	20 439	21 791	17 452	17 186	18 324	61 960	92 368	225 668	324 340
Libraries, museums and galleries	KQYC	80	106	154	108	247	123	137	326	627	507	634
Social work	KQYD	10 561	24 817	32 626	36 734	48 091	50 230	57 576	59 892	62 167	71 611	78 611
Law, order and protective services	KQYE	235 477	253 548	274 149	288 835	295 600	312 812	330 767	359 811	366 961	382 246	401 485
Transport[2]	KQYF	4 580	3 325	3 540	1 993	4 315	4 788	403	237	97 649	68 429	57 702
Environmental services	KQYG	50	56	50	84	82	42	119	159	89	71	301
Planning	KQYH	971	947	785	1 310	867	3 030	3 337	4 885	2 695	4 311	4 375
Leisure and recreation	KQYI	1 739	1 503	1 396	1 476	1 609	1 830	1 509	1 856	1 509	1 491	2 377
Central administration[3]	KQYJ	–	–	–	–	–	–	–	–	–	–	–
Other services	KQYK	68 352	66 716	70 298	76 596	81 793	78 619	75 562	68 410	66 504	64 203	65 627
Housing	KQYL	538 042	577 321	640 127	684 519	723 604	762 172	856 435	920 700	948 232	959 276	956 239
Trading services	KQYM	4 024	4 739	5 405	4 954	4 009	4 557	–	–	–	403	148
Water supply	KQYN	3 998	4 139	4 255	4 823	4 009	4 459	–	–	–	–	–
Ferries	KQYO	–	1	46	47	–	–	–	–	–	–	–
Other trading services	KQYP	26	599	1 104	84	–	98	–	–	–	403	148
Grants not allocated to specific services[4]	KMGY	2 719 159	3 293 942	3 749 442	3 789 914	3 781 426	3 721 023	3 650 190	3 520 461	3 483 815	3 537 043	3 440 842
Total	KMGZ	3 600 844	4 244 719	4 798 411	4 908 314	4 959 095	4 956 412	4 994 362	4 998 697	5 122 616	5 315 259	5 332 681

1 Including grants for capital works.
2 The significant increase in 1998/99 is due to the different reporting of a grant in aid of expenditure on rail passenger services in the Strathclyde Passenger Transport area.
3 From 1990/91 Central Administration income is included in the relevant service income.

4 Revenue support grant, community charge grant and rate and community charge rebate grants.

Source: Scottish Executive, Economic Advice & Statistics: 0131 244 7033

17.21 Expenditure of local authorities
Northern Ireland
Years ending 31 March

£ thousand

		Out of revenue and special funds										
		1990 /91	1991 /92	1992 /93	1993 /94	1994 /95	1995 /96	1996 /97	1997 /98	1998 /99	1999 /00	2000 /01
Total	KQVA	193 450	203 650	214 107	230 666	251 737	252 794	294 563	304 305	413 698	388 419	409 930
Libraries, museums and art galleries	KQVB	3 881	4 030	4 644	5 647	7 214	8 481	10 956	13 928	14 571	19 900	23 097
Environmental health services:												
Refuse collection and disposal	KQVC	29 363	32 131	33 582	39 952	42 109	41 284	52 267	56 246	56 360	62 226	65 289
Public baths	KQVD	1 571	1 808	1 505	1 562	1 648	1 703	1 838	2 585	2 634	1 750	1 724
Parks, recreation grounds, etc	KQVE	68 593	74 439	80 601	91 258	101 319	100 418	111 884	115 302	118 396	158 304	170 999
Other sanitary services	KQVF	24 237	26 251	27 593	32 074	34 582	35 706	39 545	39 682	42 923	44 214	45 552
Housing (grants and small dwellings acquisition)[1]	KQVG	1 130	860	792	873	553	472	489	545	358	37	28
Trading services:												
Gas supply	KQVH	3 472	–	–	–	–	–	..	..	..	..	..
Cemeteries	KQVI	4 492	4 908	5 044	5 352	5 984	5 489	5 120	5 626	5 887	5 973	6 151
Other trading services (including markets, fairs and harbours)	KQVJ	7 340	7 778	7 335	7 123	6 587	4 254	8 672	7 016	10 779	9 366	7 209
Miscellaneous	KQVK	49 371	51 445	53 011	46 825	51 741	54 987	63 792	63 375	161 790	86 649	89 881
Total loan charges	KQVL	19 430	20 226	21 693	19 194	20 797	21 122	24 363	34 823	26 413	..	..
Loan charges included in terms of expenditure above:												
Allocated to rate fund services	KQVM	15 155	16 777	18 785	..	..	..	..	..	..	..	..
Allocated to trading services	KQVN	3 904	3 102	2 689	..	..	..	..	..	..	..	..
Not allocated	KQVO	371	347	219	..	..	..	..	..	..	..	..

1 Expenditure met out of loans, government grants for capital works, sales of property and other capital receipts.

Source: Department of the Environment for Northern Ireland: 028 9054 0707

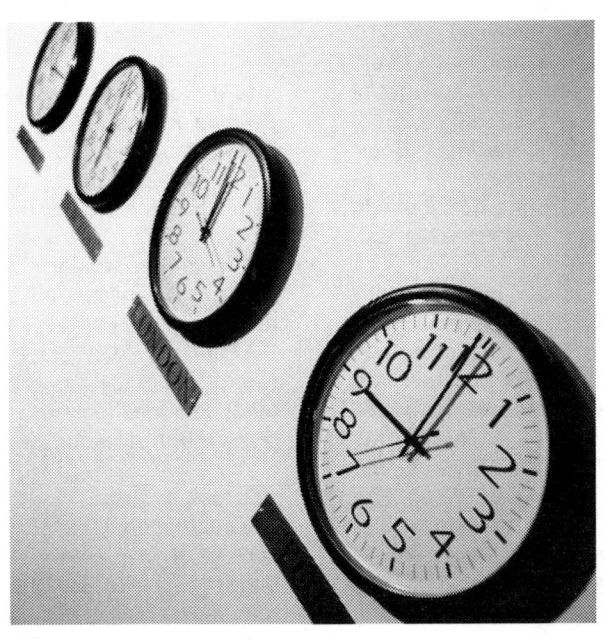

18 External trade and investment

External trade and investment

External trade *(Table 18.1 and 18.3 to 18.6)*
The statistics in Table 18.1 are on a Balance of Payments (BoP) basis; all other statistics in this section are on an Overseas Trade Statistics (OTS) basis, compiled from information provided to HM Customs and Excise by importers and exporters, which values exports 'f.o.b.' (free on board) and imports 'c.i.f.' (including insurance and freight). In addition to deducting these freight costs and insurance premiums from the OTS figures, coverage adjustments are made to convert the OTS data to a BoP basis. Adjustments are also made to the level of all exports and EU imports to take account of estimated under-recording. The adjustments are set out and described in the annual ONS *'Pink Book' (United Kingdom Balance of Payments)*. These adjustments are made to conform to the definitions in the 5th edition of the IMF Balance of Payments Manual.

Aggregate estimates of trade in goods, seasonally adjusted and on a BoP basis are published monthly in the ONS First Release UK Trade. More detailed figures are available from the ONS Databank and are also published in the Monthly Review of External Trade Statistics (Business Monitor MM24). Detailed figures for EU and non-EU trade on an OTS basis are produced by HM Customs and Excise, and published by The Stationery Office in Overseas Trade Statistics of the United Kingdom. HM Customs and Excise provide accurate and up to date information via the website www.uktradeinfo.com.

A fuller description of how trade statistics are compiled can be found in Statistics on Trade in Goods (Government Statistical Service Methodological Series).

Import penetration and export sales ratios *(Table 18.2)*
The ratios were first introduced in the August 1977 edition of *Economic Trends* in an article, 'The Home and Export Performance of United Kingdom Industries'. The article described the conceptual and methodological problems involved in measuring such variables as import penetration.

The industries are grouped according to the 1992 Standard Industrial Classification. The four different ratios are defined as follows:

Ratio 1: percentage ratio of imports to home demand
Ratio 2: percentage ratio of imports to (home demand plus exports)
Ratio 3: percentage ratio of exports to total manufacturers' sales
Ratio 4: percentage ratio of exports to (total manufacturers' sales plus imports)

Home demand is defined as total manufacturers' sales plus imports minus exports. **This is only an approximate estimate as different sources are used for the total manufacturers' sales and the import and export data. Total manufacturers' sales are determined by the ProdCom inquiry and import and export data are provided by HM Customs & Excise.**

Ratio 1 is commonly used to describe the import penetration of the home market. Allowance is made for the extent of a domestic industry's involvement in export markets by using Ratio 2; this reduces as exports increase.

Similarly, Ratio 3 is the measure normally used to relate exports to total sales by UK producers and Ratio 4 makes an allowance for the extent that imports of the same product are coming into the UK.

International trade in services *(Tables 18.7 and 18.8)*
These data relate to overseas trade in services and cover both production and non-production industries (excluding the Public Sector). In terms of types of services traded this equates to trade in royalties, various forms of consultancy, computing and telecommunications services, advertising and market research and other business services. A separate inquiry covers the Film and Television industries. The surveys cover receipts from the provision of services to residents of other countries (exports) and payments to residents of other countries for services rendered (imports).

Sources of data
The International Trade in Services (ITIS) surveys (which consist of a quarterly component addressed to the largest businesses and an annual component for the remainder) are based on a sample of companies derived from the Inter-departmental Business register. The companies are asked to show the amounts for their imports and exports against the geographical area to which they were paid or from which they were received - irrespective of where they were first earned.

The purpose of the ITIS survey is to record international transactions which impact on the UK's Balance of Payments; hence companies are asked to exclude from their earnings trade expenses such as the cost of services purchased abroad. Exports and imports of Services are excluded where they are included within an invoice for the import or export of goods; in this case they will already be counted in the estimate for Trade in Goods. However, earnings from third country trade, i.e. from arranging the sale of goods between two countries other than the UK and where the goods never physically enter the UK (known as merchanting), are included. Earnings from commodity trading are also included. Together these two comprise "Trade Related Services".

"Royalties" are the largest part of the total trade in services collected in the ITIS survey: these cover transactions for items such as printed matter, sound recordings, performing rights, patents, licences, trademarks, designs, copyrights, manufacturing rights, the use of technical "know-how" and technical assistance.

Balance of payments *(Tables 18.9 to 18.12)*
Tables 18.9 to 18.12 are derived from *United Kingdom Balance of Payments 2002 edition* - the ONS *Pink Book*. The following general notes to the tables provide brief definitions and explanations of the figures and terms used. Further notes are included in the *Pink Book*.

Summary of Balance of Payments

The Balance of Payments consists of the current account, the capital account, the financial account and the International Investment Position. The **current account** consists of trade in goods and services, income and current transfers. **Income** consists of investment income and compensation of employees. The **capital account** mainly consists of capital transfers and the **financial account** covers financial transactions. The **International Investment Position** covers balance sheet levels of UK external assets and liabilities. Every credit entry in the balance of payments accounts should, in theory, be matched by a corresponding debit entry so that total current, capital and financial account credits should be equal to, and therefore offset by, total debits. In practice there is a discrepancy termed **net errors and omissions**.

The Current Account

Trade in goods

The goods account covers exports and imports of goods. Imports of motor cars from Japan, for example, are recorded as debits in the trade in goods account whereas exports of vehicles manufactured in the UK are recorded as credits. Trade in goods forms a component of the expenditure measure of Gross Domestic Product (GDP).

Trade in services

The services account covers exports and imports of services (eg, civil aviation). Passenger tickets for travel on UK aircraft sold abroad, for example, are recorded as credits in the services account whereas the purchases of airline tickets from foreign airlines by UK passengers are recorded as debits. Trade in services, along with trade in goods, forms a component of the expenditure measure of Gross Domestic Product (GDP).

Income

The income account consists of compensation of employees and investment income and is dominated by the latter. Compensation of employees covers employment income from cross-border and seasonal workers which is less significant in the UK than in other countries. Investment income covers earnings (eg, profits, dividends and interest payments and receipts) arising from cross-border investment in financial assets and liabilities. For example, earnings on foreign bonds and shares held by financial institutions based in the UK are recorded as credits in the investment income account, whereas earnings on UK company securities held abroad are recorded as investment income debits. Investment income forms a component of Gross National Income (GNI) but not Gross Domestic Product (GDP).

Current transfers

Current transfers are composed of central government transfers (eg, taxes and payments to, and receipts from, the European Union) and other transfers (eg, gifts in cash or kind received by private individuals from abroad or receipts from the EU, where the UK government acts as an agent for the ultimate beneficiary of the transfer). Current transfers do not form a component either of Gross Domestic Product (GDP) or

of Gross National Income (GNI). For example payments to the UK farming industry under the EU Agricultural Guarantee Fund are recorded as credits in the current transfers account while payments of EU agricultural levies by the UK farming industry are recorded as debits in the current transfers account.

Capital Account

Capital account transactions involve transfers of ownership of fixed assets, transfers of funds associated with acquisition or disposal of fixed assets and cancellation of liabilities by creditors without any counterparts being received in return. The main components are migrants transfers, EU transfers relating to fixed capital formation (regional development fund and agricultural guidance fund) and debt forgiveness. Funds brought into the UK by new immigrants would, for example, be recorded as credits in the capital account, while funds sent abroad by UK residents emigrating to other countries would be recorded as debits in the capital account. The size of capital account transactions are quite minor compared with the current and financial accounts.

Financial Account

While investment income covers earnings arising from cross-border investments in financial assets and liabilities, the financial account of the balance of payments covers the flows of such investments. Earnings on foreign bonds and shares held by financial institutions based in the UK are, for example, recorded as credits in the investment income account, but the acquisition of such foreign securities by UK based financial institutions are recorded as net debits in the financial account or portfolio investment abroad. Similarly the acquisitions of UK company securities held by foreign residents are recorded in the financial account as net credits or portfolio investment in the UK.

International Investment Position

While the financial account covers the flows of foreign investments and financial assets and liabilities, the International Investment Position records the levels of external assets and liabilities. While the acquisition of foreign securities by UK based financial institutions are recorded in the financial account, as net debits, the total holdings of foreign securities by UK based financial institutions are recorded as levels of UK external assets. Similarly the holdings of UK company securities held by foreign residents are recorded as levels of UK liabilities.

Foreign direct investment
(Tables 18.13 to 18.18)

Direct investment refers to investment that adds to, deducts from or acquires a lasting interest in an enterprise operating in an economy other than that of the investor, the investor's purpose being to have an effective voice in the management of the enterprise. (For the purposes of the statistical inquiry, an effective voice is taken as equivalent to a holding of 10 per cent or more in the foreign enterprise.) Other investments in which the investor does not have an effective voice in the management of the enterprise are mainly portfolio investments and these are not covered here. Cross-border investment by public corporations or in property

External trade and investment

(which is regarded as direct investment in the national accounts) is not covered here, but is shown in the balance of payments. Similarly foreign direct investment earnings data are shown net of tax in Tables 18.15 and 8.18 but are gross of tax in the balance of payments.

Direct investment is a financial concept and is not the same as capital expenditure on fixed assets. It covers only the money invested in a related concern by the parent company and the concern will then decide how to use the money. A related concern may also raise money locally without reference to the parent company.

The investment figures are published on a net basis, that is, they consist of investments net of disinvestments by a company into its foreign subsidiaries, associate companies and branches.

Definitional changes from 1997
The new European System of Accounts (ESA(95)) definitions were introduced from the 1997 estimates. The changes were as follows:

i)   Previously for the measurement of direct investment, an effective voice in the management of an enterprise was taken as the equivalent of a 20 per cent shareholding. This is now 10 per cent.

ii)   The Channel Islands (Jersey, Guernsey etc.) and the Isle of Man have been excluded from the definition of the economic territory of the UK. Prior to 1987 these islands were considered to be part of the United Kingdom.

iii)   Interest received or paid was replaced by interest accrued in the figures on earnings from direct investment. There is deemed to be little or no impact arising from this definitional change on the estimates.

New register sources available from 1998 have led to revisions for the figures from that year onwards. These sources gave an improved estimate of the population satisfying the criteria for foreign direct investment.

The definitional changes have been introduced from 1997 and the register changes from 1998. The data prior to these years have not been reworked in Tables 18.13 to 18.18. For clarity, the Offshore Islands are identified separately on the tables. The breaks in the series for the other definitional changes are not quantified but are relatively small. More detailed information on the effect of these changes appears in the business monitor, MA4 – Foreign Direct Investment 2000, which was published in February 2002 and is available on the ONS website.

Sources of data
The figures in Tables 18.13 to 18.18 are based on annual inquiries into foreign direct investment for 2000. These were sample surveys which involved sending around 1,050 forms to UK businesses investing abroad and 2,250 forms to UK businesses in which foreign parents and associates had invested. The tables also contain some revisions to 1998 and 1999 as a result of new information coming to light in the course of the latest inquiries. Further details from the latest annual inquiries, including analyses by industry and by components of direct investment, are available in business monitor MA4. Initial figures were published on the ONS website in a first release, "Foreign Direct Investment 2000", in December 2001. Data for 2001 will be published in a first release in December 2002, followed by the full business monitor MA4 in February 2003.

Country allocation
The analysis of inward investment is based on the country of ownership of the immediate parent company. Thus, inward investment in a UK company may be attributed to the country of the intervening overseas subsidiary, rather than the country of the ultimate parent. Similarly, the country analysis of outward investment is based on the country of ownership of the immediate subsidiary. As an example, to the extent that overseas investment in the UK is channelled through holding companies in the Netherlands, the underlying flow of investment from this country is overstated and the inflow from originating countries is understated.

Further information
More detailed statistics on foreign direct investment are available on request from Simon Harrington, Office for National Statistics, Financial & Accounting Surveys Division, Room D.245, Government Buildings, Cardiff Road, Newport, South Wales, United Kingdom, NP10 8XG. Telephone: 01633 813314, Fax: 01633 812855, e-mail simon.harrington@ons.gov.uk.

18.1 Trade in goods United Kingdom
On a balance of payments basis[1]

		1991	1992	1993	1994	1995	1996	1997	1998	1999	2000	2001
Value(£ millions)												
Exports of goods	BOKG	103 939	107 863	122 229	135 143	153 577	167 196	171 923	164 056	166 166	187 936	191 754
Imports of goods	BOKH	114 162	120 913	135 295	146 269	165 600	180 918	184 265	185 869	193 538	218 262	225 295
Balance on trade in goods	BOKI	−10 223	−13 050	−13 066	−11 126	−12 023	−13 722	−12 342	−21 813	−27 372	−30 326	−33 541
Price index numbers 1995 = 100												
Exports of goods	BQKR	82.8	84.5	95.0	96.9	100.0	100.7	95.3	90.3	89.5	92.9	93.1
Imports of goods	BQKS	82.2	82.9	91.2	94.3	100.0	99.8	93.2	87.6	86.4	90.1	89.8
Terms of trade[2]	BQKT	100.7	101.9	104.2	102.8	100.0	100.9	102.3	103.1	103.6	103.1	103.7
Volume index numbers 1995 = 100												
Exports of goods	BQKU	78.0	79.9	83.1	91.3	100.0	107.6	116.7	118.2	123.3	137.5	140.7
Imports of goods	BQKV	81.9	87.3	90.5	94.5	100.0	109.5	120.3	131.1	141.2	158.3	164.4

1 See chapter text. Statistics of trade in goods on a balance of payments basis are obtained by making certain adjustments in respect of valuation and coverage to the statistics recorded in the *Overseas Trade Statistics*. These adjustments are described in detail in *The Pink Book 2002*.

2 Export price index as a percentage of the import price index.

Source: Office for National Statistics: 020 7533 6064

18.2 Import penetration and export sales ratios for products of manufacturing industry [1,2]
United Kingdom: SIC 92

			1998	1999	2000
Ratio 1 Imports/Home Demand					
Description		*SIC Division*			
Total of divisions below	BAZY		47	47	52
Mining of Metal Ores[3]	BAZZ	13	..	..	..
Other Mining and Quarrying	BBAM	14	101	132	166
Food products and beverages	BBAN	15	22	22	22
Tobacco products	BBAO	16	9	8	7
Textiles	BAZJ	17	56	57	60
Wearing Apparel: Dressing and dyeing of fur	BAZK	18	73	80	86
Tanning and dressing of leather:luggage, handbags, saddlery, harness and footwear	BBAP	19	83	88	92
Wood products of wood and cork (except furniture) articles of straw and plaiting materials	BBAQ	20	36	38	39
Pulp, paper and paper products	BBAR	21	38	37	38
Publishing, printing and reproduction of recorded media	BBAS	22	6	6	6
Chemicals and chemical products	BAZL	24	62	62	65
Rubber and plastic products	BBAT	25	28	28	29
Other non metallic mineral products	BBAU	26	20	20	21
Basic metals	BBAV	27	66	62	75
Fabricated metal products (except machinery and equipment)	BBAW	28	20	20	22
Machinery and equipment not elsewhere classified	BBAX	29	59	59	60
Office machinery and computers	BBAY	30	84	88	107
Electrical machinery not elsewhere classified	BBAZ	31	55	57	61
Radio, television and communication equipment and apparatus	BBBA	32	89	88	99
Medical, precision and optical instruments, watches and clocks	BBBB	33	71	71	77
Motor vehicles, trailers and semi-trailers	BBBC	34	60	60	65
Other transport equipment	BBBD	35	64	58	74
Furniture and manufacturing not elsewhere classified	BBBE	36	52	51	52
Ratio 2 Imports/Home Demand plus Exports					
Description		*SIC Division*			
Total of divisions below	BBBF		34	34	37
Mining of Metal Ores[3]	BBBG	13	..	..	..
Other Mining and Quarrying	BBBH	14	53	62	65
Food products and beverages	BBBI	15	19	19	19
Tobacco products	BBBJ	16	6	5	4
Textiles	BAZN	17	43	43	45
Wearing Apparel: Dressing and dyeing of fur	BAZO	18	56	62	68
Tanning and dressing of leather:luggage, handbags, saddlery, harness and footwear	BBBK	19	64	68	71
Wood products of wood and cork (except furniture) articles of straw and plaiting materials	BBBL	20	34	36	37
Pulp, paper and paper products	BBBM	21	32	32	33
Publishing, printing and reproduction of recorded media	BBBN	22	6	6	6
Chemicals and chemical products	BAZP	24	36	36	38
Rubber and plastic products	BBBO	25	23	23	24
Other non metallic mineral products	BBBP	26	17	17	17
Basic metals[2]	BBBQ	27	45	43	47
Fabricated metal products (except machinery and equipment)	BBBR	28	17	17	18
Machinery and equipment not elsewhere classified	BBBS	29	35	37	37
Office machinery and computers	BBBT	30	54	56	60
Electrical machinery not elsewhere classified	BBBU	31	37	37	40
Radio, television and communication equipment and apparatus	BBBV	32	47	48	53
Medical, precision and optical instruments, watches and clocks	BBBW	33	40	41	45
Motor vehicles, trailers and semi-trailers	BBBX	34	42	43	45
Other transport equipment	BBBY	35	37	35	39
Furniture and manufacturing not elsewhere classified	BBBZ	36	40	40	42

18.2 continued

Import penetration and export sales ratios for products of manufacturing industry [1,2]
United Kingdom: SIC 92

			1998	1999	2000
Ratio 3 Exports/Sales					
Description		*SIC Division*			
Total of divisions below	BBCK		42	42	47
Mining of Metal Ores[3]	BBCL	13	..	..	..
Other Mining and Quarrying	BBCM	14	102	140	173
Food products and beverages	BBCN	15	15	14	14
Tobacco products	BBCO	16	42	41	44
Textiles	BAZR	17	42	43	45
Wearing Apparel:Dressing and dyeing of fur	BAZS	18	52	59	66
Tanning and dressing of leather:luggage, handbags, saddlery, harness and footwear	BBCP	19	63	71	80
Wood products of wood and cork (except furniture) articles of straw and plaiting materials	BBCQ	20	7	8	7
Pulp, paper and paper products	BBCR	21	21	20	20
Publishing, printing and reproduction of recorded media	BBCS	22	9	9	8
Chemicals and chemical products	BAZT	24	66	66	68
Rubber and plastic products	BBCT	25	25	24	24
Other non metallic mineral products	BBCU	26	20	18	18
Basic metals	BBCV	27	57	54	71
Fabricated metal products (except machinery and equipment)	BBCW	28	19	18	19
Machinery and equipment not elsewhere classified	BBCX	29	62	60	60
Office machinery and computers	BBCY	30	78	82	109
Electrical machinery not elsewhere classified	BBDK	31	53	55	57
Radio, television and communication equipment and apparatus	BBDL	32	89	87	99
Medical, precision and optical instruments, watches and clocks	BBDM	33	73	72	76
Motor vehicles, trailers and semi-trailers	BBDN	34	50	49	57
Other transport equipment	BBDO	35	66	62	77
Furniture and manufacturing not elsewhere classified	BBDP	36	40	36	34
Ratio 4 Exports/Sales plus Imports					
Description		*SIC Division*			
Total of divisions below	BBDQ		28	28	30
Mining of Metal Ores[3]	BBDR	13	..	..	..
Other Mining and Quarrying	BBDS	14	47	53	61
Food products and beverages	BBDT	15	12	12	12
Tobacco products	BBDU	16	40	39	42
Textiles	BAZV	17	24	24	25
Wearing Apparel: Dressing and dyeing of fur	BAZW	18	23	23	21
Tanning and dressing of leather: luggage, handbags, saddlery, harness and footwear	BBDV	19	23	23	23
Wood products of wood and cork (except furniture) articles and straw and plaiting materials	BBDW	20	5	5	5
Pulp, paper and paper products	BBDX	21	14	13	13
Publishing, printing and reproduction of recorded media	BBDY	22	9	8	8
Chemicals and chemical products	BAZX	24	41	41	42
Rubber and plastic products	BBDZ	25	19	19	19
Other non-metallic mineral products	BBEA	26	17	15	15
Basic metals	BBEB	27	31	31	38
Fabricated metal products (except machinery and equipment)	BBEC	28	16	15	16
Machinery and equipment not elsewhere classified	BBED	29	41	38	38
Office machinery and computers	BBEE	30	36	36	44
Electrical machinery not elsewhere classified	BBEF	31	33	34	35
Radio, television and communication equipment and apparatus	BBEG	32	47	45	46
Medical, precision and optical instruments, watches and clocks	BBEH	33	43	43	42
Motor vehicles, trailers and semi-trailers	BBEI	34	29	28	32
Other transport equipment	BBEJ	35	42	40	47
Furniture and manufacturing not elsewhere classified	BBEK	36	24	22	20

1 See chapter text.
2 Division 23 (coke, refined petroleum products and nuclear fuel) and SIC 24610 (manufacture of explosives) are excluded from the analysis. SIC 27100 (basic iron and steel and ferro-alloys) is not incorporated in PROD-COM and therefore also does not form part of the analysis.
3 Division 13 (mining of metal ores) has not been published since 1995.

Source: Office for National Statistics: 01633 813065

18.3 United Kingdom exports, by commodity[1]

£ million BOP-consistent basis seasonally adjusted

		1992	1993	1994	1995	1996	1997	1998	1999	2000	2001
0. Food and live animals	BOGG	5 276	5 869	6 305	7 079	6 997	6 581	6 279	5 924	5 829	5 545
Of which:											
01. Meat and meat preparations	BOGS	829	997	1 229	1 466	1 081	925	745	659	640	434
02. Dairy products and eggs	BQMS	534	658	692	820	732	745	745	685	657	629
04 & 08. Cereals and animal feeding stuffs	BQMT	1 545	1 600	1 523	1 702	2 008	1 800	1 710	1 562	1 603	1 395
05. Vegetables and fruit	BQMU	332	315	398	456	470	455	407	438	401	420
1. Beverages and tobacco	BQMZ	3 401	3 304	3 734	4 113	4 331	4 522	3 937	4 023	4 079	4 186
11. Beverages	BQNB	2 435	2 656	2 865	2 986	3 138	3 305	2 879	3 004	3 065	3 248
12. Tobacco	BQOW	966	648	869	1 127	1 193	1 217	1 058	1 019	1 014	938
2. Crude materials	BQOX	1 865	2 158	2 397	2 725	2 583	2 489	2 269	2 087	2 447	2 469
Of which:											
24. Wood, lumber and cork	BQOY	25	22	45	46	52	52	57	69	75	72
25. Pulp and waste paper	BQOZ	39	22	50	66	57	64	48	54	79	81
26. Textile fibres	BQPA	486	508	571	636	611	568	493	447	492	446
28. Metal ores	BQPB	458	628	663	771	657	642	556	515	757	849
3. Fuels	BOPN	7 479	9 075	9 492	9 942	11 578	11 016	7 513	9 929	17 057	16 518
33. Petroleum and petroleum products	ELBL	7 172	8 624	9 079	9 384	10 928	10 239	7 018	9 123	15 584	14 934
32, 34 & 35. Coal, gas and electricity	BOQI	307	451	413	558	650	777	495	806	1 473	1 584
4. Animal and vegetable oils and fats	BQPI	85	118	171	221	207	264	243	197	156	152
5. Chemicals	ENDG	14 931	17 742	18 806	20 999	22 166	21 901	22 102	23 071	24 992	28 095
Of which:											
51. Organic chemicals	BQPJ	3 692	4 484	4 731	4 923	5 152	4 974	4 913	5 489	5 716	6 140
52. Inorganic chemicals	BQPK	1 179	1 249	1 120	1 236	1 190	1 183	1 160	1 139	1 495	1 652
53. Colouring materials	CSCE	1 277	1 455	1 479	1 618	1 641	1 578	1 542	1 538	1 565	1 548
54. Medicinal products	BQPL	2 983	3 784	4 010	4 926	5 333	5 416	5 857	6 279	7 219	9 429
55. Toilet preparations	CSCF	1 466	1 702	2 012	2 124	2 409	2 569	2 449	2 466	2 602	2 756
57 & 58. Plastics	BQQA	2 129	2 530	2 800	3 276	3 294	3 166	3 192	3 149	3 366	3 462
6. Manufactures classified chiefly by material	BQQB	15 427	17 760	19 574	22 459	23 142	22 675	21 243	20 302	22 673	22 890
Of which:											
63. Wood and cork manufactures	BQQC	129	133	170	189	228	250	254	278	255	265
64. Paper and paperboard manufactures	BQQD	1 726	1 882	2 049	2 350	2 343	2 309	2 199	2 022	2 098	2 094
65. Textile manufactures	BQQE	2 444	2 661	2 950	3 282	3 471	3 421	3 261	3 018	3 052	3 038
67. Iron and steel	BQQF	2 996	3 220	3 660	4 345	4 059	3 637	3 317	2 577	2 844	2 887
68. Non-ferrous metals	BQQG	1 748	1 955	2 233	2 864	2 680	2 774	2 436	2 133	3 169	3 051
69. Metal manufactures	BQQH	2 192	2 319	2 648	3 086	3 346	3 368	3 586	3 545	3 595	3 877
7. Machinery and transport equipment[2]	BQQI	43 768	49 443	55 852	65 353	73 366	79 002	78 021	78 872	87 821	88 487
71 - 716, 72, 73 & 74. Mechanical machinery	BQQK	13 921	15 179	16 272	18 337	20 481	22 329	22 699	21 885	22 145	24 704
716, 75, 76 & 77. Electrical machinery	BQQL	16 042	21 110	24 900	30 652	32 939	34 252	34 463	36 009	42 685	42 541
78. Road vehicles	BQQM	8 679	8 520	9 654	11 644	14 278	14 811	14 555	15 079	15 602	14 090
79. Other transport equipment	BQQN	5 126	4 634	5 026	4 720	5 668	7 610	6 304	5 899	7 389	7 152
8. Miscellaneous manufactures[2]	BQQO	13 580	15 101	17 315	18 859	20 873	21 530	20 552	20 265	21 197	22 373
Of which:											
84. Clothing	CSCN	2 035	2 377	2 717	3 056	3 356	3 259	2 982	2 808	2 730	2 611
85. Footwear	CSCP	332	417	479	519	595	605	539	536	520	495
87 & 88. Scientific and photographic	BQQQ	4 351	4 824	5 357	5 900	6 594	6 974	6 712	6 738	7 331	7 948
9. Other commodities and transactions	BOQL	2 051	1 659	1 497	1 827	1 953	1 943	1 897	1 496	1 685	1 039
TOTAL UK EXPORTS	BOKG	107 863	122 229	135 143	153 577	167 196	171 923	164 056	166 166	187 936	191 754

1 See chapter text. The numbers on the left hand side of the table refer to the code numbers of the *Standard International Trade Classification*, Revision 3, which was introduced in January 1988.

2 Sections 7 and 8 are shown by broad economic category in table G2 of the *Monthly Review of External Trade Statistics*.

Source: Office for National Statistics: 020 7533 6064

18.4 United Kingdom imports, by commodity[1]

£ million BOP-consistent basis seasonally adjusted

		1992	1993	1994	1995	1996	1997	1998	1999	2000	2001
0. Food and live animals	BQQR	10 701	11 219	11 660	12 923	14 030	13 318	13 185	13 292	13 268	14 429
Of which:											
01. Meat and meat preparations	BQQS	1 920	1 913	1 884	2 237	2 540	2 231	2 003	2 141	2 357	2 743
02. Dairy products and eggs	BQQT	1 060	1 007	1 092	1 077	1 194	1 101	1 107	1 165	1 166	1 246
04 & 08. Cereals and animal feeding stuffs	BQQU	1 628	1 768	1 682	1 781	1 915	1 991	1 807	1 714	1 761	1 980
05. Vegetables and fruit	BQQV	2 919	3 033	3 285	3 820	4 173	3 898	4 008	4 028	3 889	4 158
1. Beverages and tobacco	BQQW	1 912	2 081	2 228	2 638	3 392	3 593	4 065	4 495	4 537	4 356
11. Beverages	EGAT	1 488	1 667	1 829	2 065	2 479	2 610	2 897	3 080	2 958	2 884
12. Tobacco	EMAI	424	414	399	573	913	983	1 168	1 415	1 579	1 472
2. Crude materials	ENVB	4 228	4 620	5 041	5 893	5 859	5 670	5 077	4 860	5 812	5 940
Of which:											
24. Wood, lumber and cork	ENVC	930	1 053	1 300	1 142	1 202	1 239	1 100	1 087	1 195	1 160
25. Pulp and waste paper	EQAH	569	505	578	979	656	572	480	513	760	612
26. Textile fibres	EQAP	435	454	576	636	639	590	448	414	415	401
28. Metal ores	EHAA	1 030	1 053	1 028	1 358	1 474	1 460	1 316	1 307	1 816	2 006
3. Fuels	BQAT	7 123	7 473	6 342	6 161	7 284	6 824	4 892	5 427	10 016	10 799
33. Petroleum and petroleum products	ENXO	5 562	6 012	5 142	5 061	6 118	5 679	3 976	4 674	9 048	9 529
32, 34 & 35. Coal, gas and electricity	BPBI	1 561	1 461	1 200	1 100	1 166	1 145	916	753	968	1 270
4. Animal and vegetable oils and fats	EHAB	388	457	498	561	686	603	554	569	495	524
5. Chemicals	ENGA	11 205	12 980	14 156	17 481	18 095	17 405	17 379	18 619	20 633	23 050
Of which:											
51. Organic chemicals	EHAC	2 695	3 109	3 421	4 670	4 719	4 462	4 512	4 786	5 372	5 646
52. Inorganic chemicals	EHAE	914	983	1 063	1 086	1 233	1 107	1 017	1 051	1 046	1 190
53. Colouring materials	CSCR	661	870	788	930	1 000	975	1 005	958	1 003	986
54. Medicinal products	EHAF	1 603	2 021	2 254	2 785	3 061	3 100	3 308	4 124	4 711	6 218
55. Toilet preparations	CSCS	913	1 014	1 193	1 364	1 477	1 506	1 621	1 774	2 005	2 272
57 & 58. Plastics	EHAG	2 936	3 311	3 672	4 597	4 338	4 168	3 905	3 821	4 147	4 137
6. Manufactures classified chiefly by material	EHAH	19 905	21 697	23 844	27 760	28 700	28 007	27 695	26 930	29 231	30 525
Of which:											
63. Wood and cork manufactures	EHAI	801	872	997	1 037	1 078	1 083	1 086	1 153	1 249	1 354
64. Paper and paperboard manufactures	EHAJ	3 674	3 763	4 180	5 200	4 961	4 550	4 504	4 318	4 406	4 922
65. Textile manufactures	EHAK	3 778	3 974	4 401	4 806	5 075	5 003	4 864	4 383	4 365	4 349
67. Iron and steel	EHAL	2 433	2 574	2 905	3 620	3 604	3 337	3 205	2 474	2 730	3 163
68. Non-ferrous metals	EHAM	2 473	2 848	2 915	3 753	3 720	3 625	3 709	2 946	3 714	3 833
69. Metal manufactures	EHAN	2 460	2 546	2 812	3 239	3 492	3 561	3 738	3 771	4 059	4 369
7. Machinery and transport equipment[2]	EHAO	45 577	53 353	59 993	68 044	76 120	80 518	83 308	88 502	99 622	98 865
71 - 716, 72, 73 & 74. Mechanical machinery	EHAQ	11 142	11 802	13 095	15 148	16 540	17 037	17 155	17 319	17 863	18 885
716, 75, 76 & 77. Electrical machinery	EHAR	19 154	23 559	26 146	31 487	35 299	35 792	36 901	40 727	50 840	44 363
78. Road vehicles	EHAS	11 616	14 463	15 893	17 831	20 238	21 704	22 482	24 009	23 115	26 333
79. Other transport equipment	EHAT	3 665	3 529	4 859	3 578	4 043	5 985	6 770	6 447	7 804	9 284
8. Miscellaneous manufactures[2]	EHAU	18 103	19 989	21 325	22 522	24 987	26 568	27 910	29 043	32 802	35 528
Of which:											
84. Clothing	CSDR	4 256	4 699	4 779	5 178	6 059	6 630	7 026	7 487	8 494	9 214
85. Footwear	CSDS	1 102	1 233	1 427	1 514	1 770	1 912	1 864	2 043	2 000	2 244
87 & 88. Scientific and photographic	EHAW	4 051	4 620	4 837	5 382	6 001	6 067	6 106	6 174	7 272	7 696
9. Other commodities and transactions	BQAW	1 771	1 426	1 182	1 617	1 765	1 759	1 804	1 801	1 846	1 279
TOTAL UK IMPORTS	BOKH	120 913	135 295	146 269	165 600	180 918	184 265	185 869	193 538	218 262	225 295

1 See chapter text. The numbers on the left hand side of the table refer to the code numbers of the *Standard International Trade Classification*, Revision 3, which was introduced in January 1988.

2 Sections 7 and 8 are shown by broad economic category in table G2 of the *Monthly Review of External Trade Statistics*.

Source: Office for National Statistics: 020 7533 6064

18.5 United Kingdom exports, by area[1]

£ million BOP-consistent basis seasonally adjusted

		1992	1993	1994	1995	1996	1997	1998	1999	2000	2001
European Union:	ENOF	64 976	69 402	76 876	89 536	95 758	96 048	95 690	97 860	107 990	111 414
EMU members:	QAKW	60 984	64 884	71 644	83 271	89 124	89 504	89 240	91 771	101 465	105 096
Germany	ENYO	15 185	16 097	17 339	20 242	20 715	20 686	20 593	20 465	22 790	24 009
Greece	CHNT	776	929	933	1 038	1 147	1 046	1 033	1 148	1 234	1 127
France	ENYL	11 493	12 215	13 655	15 265	17 093	16 602	16 451	16 908	18 575	19 537
Italy	CHNO	6 137	6 094	6 836	7 883	8 027	8 214	8 609	7 832	8 428	8 533
Netherlands	CHNP	8 491	8 121	9 593	12 346	13 484	13 923	12 985	13 634	15 163	14 807
Belgium and Luxembourg	CHNQ	5 706	7 150	7 367	8 298	8 522	8 450	8 446	9 241	10 321	10 055
Irish Republic	CHNS	5 733	6 369	7 163	7 794	8 661	9 357	9 605	10 784	12 374	14 061
Portugal	CHNU	1 164	1 376	1 259	1 469	1 677	1 752	1 722	1 712	1 660	1 600
Spain	CHNV	4 509	4 494	5 131	6 098	6 725	6 745	7 172	7 526	8 302	8 490
Finland	CHMZ	995	1 121	1 316	1 716	1 810	1 570	1 434	1 353	1 470	1 633
Austria	CHMY	795	918	1 052	1 122	1 263	1 159	1 190	1 168	1 148	1 244
Non-EMU members	QAKZ	3 992	4 518	5 232	6 265	6 634	6 544	6 450	6 089	6 525	6 318
Sweden	CHNA	2 435	2 900	3 411	4 157	4 420	4 451	4 393	4 034	4 210	4 014
Denmark	CHNR	1 557	1 618	1 821	2 108	2 214	2 093	2 057	2 055	2 315	2 304
Other Western Europe:	HCJD	4 298	5 317	5 772	6 417	7 332	7 850	7 673	6 473	7 430	7 167
Of which:											
Norway	EPLX	1 409	1 505	2 047	2 002	2 051	2 607	2 689	2 052	2 017	1 862
Switzerland	EPLV	1 839	2 282	2 480	2 729	3 185	2 958	2 902	2 732	3 062	3 578
Turkey	EOBA	690	1 047	821	1 149	1 554	1 734	1 614	1 210	1 799	1 179
Iceland	EPLW	92	148	110	138	152	153	161	160	193	154
North America:	HBZQ	14 741	17 779	19 722	20 450	22 357	23 871	24 793	27 801	33 715	33 772
Of which:											
USA	EOBB	12 640	15 403	17 081	17 901	19 761	20 900	21 721	24 238	29 276	29 561
Canada	EOBC	1 637	1 848	1 935	1 804	1 970	2 147	2 178	2 546	3 488	3 239
Mexico	EPJX	302	336	393	277	317	428	545	581	675	689
Other OECD countries:	HCII	5 371	6 677	7 843	9 467	11 121	10 917	8 875	9 261	11 038	10 910
Of which:											
Japan	EOBD	2 172	2 673	3 047	3 814	4 295	4 177	3 151	3 305	3 671	3 743
Australia	EPMA	1 340	1 611	1 957	2 140	2 488	2 457	2 218	2 163	2 699	2 344
South Korea	ERDM	644	805	987	1 162	1 313	1 228	675	948	1 350	1 284
Poland	ERDR	589	732	716	953	1 364	1 355	1 188	1 179	1 304	1 310
New Zealand	EPMB	258	335	422	440	475	409	340	326	305	314
Czech Republic	FKML	..	290	383	571	722	712	699	739	934	1 088
Hungary	QALC	157	209	263	296	349	438	487	489	616	621
Oil exporting countries:	HDII	6 051	6 589	5 811	6 296	7 933	9 404	7 313	5 536	6 030	6 472
Of which:											
Dubai	QALI	548	681	624	701	750	866	833	790	966	1 011
Saudi Arabia	ERDI	1 969	1 844	1 534	1 621	2 436	3 656	2 614	1 485	1 557	1 523
Indonesia[2]	FKMR	315	333	371	518	813	674	368	385	403	313
Kuwait	QATB	264	313	319	548	569	485	327	294	338	358
Nigeria	QATE	625	641	467	430	425	410	454	449	524	686
Rest of the World	HCHW	12 427	16 461	19 122	21 413	22 695	23 829	19 713	19 235	21 733	22 019
Of which:											
Brazil	FKMO	270	422	539	679	851	1 030	927	743	774	819
China	ERDN	425	755	868	832	744	924	861	1 212	1 469	1 735
Egypt	QALL	251	347	378	385	432	501	505	540	498	458
Hong Kong	ERDG	1 597	2 177	2 356	2 664	2 942	3 223	2 680	2 312	2 673	2 717
India	ERDJ	937	1 155	1 340	1 689	1 717	1 575	1 247	1 451	2 058	1 797
Israel	ERDL	583	895	1 060	1 113	1 274	1 180	1 082	1 295	1 516	1 376
Malaysia	ERDK	633	985	1 346	1 192	1 169	1 210	679	936	907	1 045
Pakistan	FKMU	308	336	362	342	347	270	235	223	207	234
Philippines	FKMX	202	313	364	436	397	601	303	241	273	397
Russia	ERDQ	..	561	728	871	1 016	1 234	932	542	668	903
Singapore	ERDH	1 137	1 459	1 811	2 072	2 159	2 049	1 604	1 599	1 624	1 613
South Africa	EPME	1 071	1 149	1 452	1 837	1 892	1 637	1 534	1 281	1 413	1 558
Taiwan	ERDP	552	681	752	965	949	1 035	875	864	1 015	890
Thailand	ERDO	473	677	769	838	981	866	390	464	582	601

1 See chapter text.
2 Includes East Timor.

Source: Office for National Statistics: 020 7533 6064

18.6 United Kingdom imports, by area[1]

£ million BOP-consistent basis seasonally adjusted

		1992	1993	1994	1995	1996	1997	1998	1999	2000	2001
European Union:	**ENOS**	69 910	74 434	82 448	94 059	100 628	100 516	102 261	105 120	111 261	116 617
EMU members	**QAKX**	64 383	68 735	76 082	87 323	93 399	93 514	95 745	98 287	103 976	109 240
Germany	**ENYS**	18 588	19 891	21 860	26 234	27 583	25 602	25 094	26 486	27 800	28 668
Greece	**CHOB**	370	315	348	429	402	398	360	397	432	475
France	**ENYP**	11 945	13 430	15 037	16 457	16 869	18 001	17 957	18 167	18 274	19 390
Italy	**CHNW**	6 609	6 660	7 496	8 264	8 897	9 537	9 743	9 332	9 467	9 883
Netherlands	**CHNX**	9 676	8 973	10 064	11 516	12 592	12 314	13 409	13 414	15 169	15 121
Belgium and Luxembourg	**CHNY**	5 601	6 678	7 121	8 130	9 063	9 491	10 109	10 475	11 411	12 890
Irish Republic	**CHOA**	4 945	5 449	5 897	7 045	7 340	7 384	7 802	8 492	9 538	9 454
Portugal	**CHOC**	1 141	1 235	1 283	1 467	1 685	1 758	1 790	1 817	1 720	1 592
Spain	**CHOD**	2 952	3 266	3 678	4 356	5 115	5 095	5 740	5 894	6 010	6 911
Finland	**CHNC**	1 636	1 880	2 271	2 500	2 681	2 541	2 328	2 361	2 757	2 975
Austria	**CHNB**	920	958	1 027	925	1 172	1 393	1 413	1 452	1 398	1 881
Non-EMU members:	**QALA**	5 527	5 699	6 366	6 736	7 229	7 002	6 516	6 833	7 285	7 377
Sweden	**CHND**	3 201	3 566	4 196	4 537	4 837	4 688	4 360	4 606	4 921	4 692
Denmark	**CHNZ**	2 326	2 133	2 170	2 199	2 392	2 314	2 156	2 227	2 364	2 685
Other Western Europe:	**HBTS**	8 407	9 489	9 374	10 341	11 387	10 801	9 759	10 583	13 099	12 477
Of which:											
Norway	**EPMX**	3 798	4 027	3 711	4 175	4 790	4 687	3 431	3 544	5 562	5 601
Switzerland	**EPMV**	3 830	4 590	4 677	4 981	5 210	4 668	4 770	5 308	5 484	4 606
Turkey	**EOBU**	446	515	610	768	898	993	1 105	1 205	1 448	1 692
Iceland	**EPMW**	233	242	233	244	257	229	250	282	365	286
North America:	**HCRB**	15 298	17 960	19 379	22 293	24 910	27 311	27 919	28 018	33 445	34 989
Of which:											
USA	**EOBV**	13 221	15 886	17 233	19 615	22 069	24 355	24 892	24 355	28 404	29 662
Canada	**EOBW**	1 824	1 805	1 827	2 300	2 407	2 483	2 518	3 014	4 007	3 703
Mexico	**EPJY**	149	160	233	288	322	371	366	395	613	687
Other OECD countries:	**HDJQ**	9 911	11 421	12 312	13 762	13 780	14 659	15 023	15 797	18 236	17 385
Of which:											
Japan	**EOBX**	7 051	8 140	8 584	9 276	8 584	9 040	9 121	9 119	10 212	9 138
Australia	**EPNA**	953	954	1 035	1 068	1 239	1 319	1 366	1 338	1 543	1 790
South Korea	**ERDY**	890	1 029	1 068	1 505	1 949	2 155	2 201	2 784	3 414	2 771
Poland	**ERED**	338	429	533	616	573	596	654	662	904	1 162
New Zealand	**EPNB**	405	474	527	555	604	554	518	565	544	548
Czech Republic	**FKMM**	..	234	271	312	356	449	551	571	800	1 095
Hungary	**QALD**	112	145	232	358	404	467	533	656	683	705
Oil exporting countries:	**HCPC**	2 857	3 600	3 049	2 930	3 263	3 328	3 183	3 241	4 256	3 979
Of which:											
Dubai	**QALJ**	175	123	123	169	207	284	337	433	401	398
Saudi Arabia	**ERDU**	900	1 208	757	649	656	838	789	784	975	933
Indonesia[2]	**FKMS**	501	665	728	814	855	860	868	934	1 081	1 131
Kuwait	**QATC**	116	204	223	133	159	169	165	122	314	297
Nigeria	**QATF**	149	110	117	163	257	101	124	112	89	65
Rest of the World	**HCIF**	14 534	18 391	19 704	22 215	26 948	27 650	27 726	30 779	37 965	39 848
Of which:											
Brazil	**FKMP**	830	872	891	936	941	911	884	965	1 114	1 289
China	**ERDZ**	891	1 279	1 592	1 843	2 112	2 383	2 820	3 384	4 824	5 786
Egypt	**QALM**	130	180	245	235	269	258	278	255	411	409
Hong Kong	**ERDS**	2 242	2 894	2 988	3 364	3 900	4 153	4 370	4 911	5 915	5 799
India	**ERDV**	808	1 050	1 249	1 363	1 542	1 550	1 384	1 423	1 650	1 829
Israel	**ERDX**	454	530	555	659	797	842	875	996	1 025	948
Malaysia	**ERDW**	1 032	1 350	1 166	1 414	2 277	1 933	1 896	1 955	2 287	1 954
Pakistan	**FKMV**	256	312	348	344	372	362	338	318	363	426
Philippines	**FKMY**	225	266	237	335	857	728	855	983	1 155	1 163
Russia	**EREC**	..	792	781	916	1 218	1 418	1 393	1 307	1 472	2 034
Singapore	**ERDT**	1 113	1 558	1 836	2 101	2 463	2 590	2 342	2 349	2 392	2 085
South Africa	**EPNE**	811	964	941	1 058	1 165	1 323	1 352	1 569	2 553	2 866
Taiwan	**EREB**	1 305	1 561	1 535	1 640	2 000	2 237	2 219	2 625	3 559	2 808
Thailand	**EREA**	600	746	884	987	1 137	1 167	1 263	1 291	1 601	1 621

1 See chapter text.
2 Includes East Timor.

Source: Office for National Statistics: 020 7533 6064

18.7 Services supplied (exports) and purchased (imports)[1,2]: 2000

£ millions

	Exports	Imports	Net
Business services			
Legal	1 395	428	968
Accounting	662	209	454
Management consulting	1 046	397	650
Advertising	1 125	649	476
Market research	247	109	138
Research and development	2 319	681	1 638
Insurance: premiums	-	112	-112
claims	18	-	18
Financial Services	1 785	289	1 496
Property	19	28	-9
Other business services	2 970	1 246	1 723
Telecommunications services			
Communications	1 244	1 172	71
Computer	2 071	718	1 353
Information	369	89	280
Technical services			
Architectural	69	14	55
Engineering (consulting, process etc.)	2 386	665	1 721
Surveying	68	56	12
Construction	116	53	63
Agriculture	37	10	27
Other technical[3]	1 106	461	645
Miscellaneous services			
Operational leasing	292	316	-24
Cultural services			
TV and radio services	175	23	152
Music services (excluding royalties)	31	9	22
Other cultural	246	167	79
Royalties	4 111	3 222	889
Trade related services			
Own account earning	497	73	424
Commission	1 155	637	518
Commodity trading	528	183	345
Management services to affiliated companies	1 265	775	491
All other services	1 093	543	550
WORLD TOTAL	28 455	13 332	15 113

1 See chapter text.
2 Due to rounding, the sum of constituent items may not always equal the total shown. Data excludes the following industries: Financial, Film and TV, Travel and Transport, Public Sector (including Education) and Law Society members.

3 Includes data for Mining.

Source: Office for National Statistics

18.8 International trade in services[1,2] by country: 2000

£ millions

	Exports	Imports	Net
European Union	10 612	5 297	5 315
Austria	125	63	62
Belgium/Luxembourg	1 016	509	506
Denmark	361	174	188
Finland	302	76	227
France	1 430	1 030	400
Germany	2 363	1 171	1 192
Greece	124	50	75
Irish Republic	1 383	532	852
Italy	550	330	220
Netherlands	1 859	898	961
Spain	496	242	254
Sweden	490	173	317
Portugal and EU Institutions[3]	113	51	62
EFTA	1 511	950	561
Iceland	14	2	11
Liechtenstein	13	7	6
Norway	410	271	139
Switzerland	1 074	669	404
Other European countries	1 551	613	938
Czech Republic	62	30	32
Poland	80	32	48
Russia	88	39	49
Channel Islands	174	42	132
Isle of Man	9	8	2
Turkey	68	38	30
Rest of Europe	249	119	130
Europe Unallocated	822	305	517
Africa	873	251	622
South Africa	216	56	159
Rest of Africa	598	180	418
Africa Unallocated	60	15	45
America	8 554	4 343	4 211
Brazil	102	39	63
Canada	363	161	203
Mexico	48	43	5
USA	7 112	3 746	3 365
Rest of America	612	313	300
America Unallocated	317	42	275
Asia	4 816	1 660	3 156
China	105	41	65
Hong Kong	236	103	132
India	90	71	19
Indonesia	67	19	48
Israel	116	78	38
Japan	980	411	569
Malaysia	114	23	91
Pakistan	30	35	-6
Phillippines	99	29	70
Singapore	590	70	521
South Korea	139	24	115
Taiwan	53	19	34
Thailand	46	17	30
Rest of Asia[4]	1 677	629	1 048
Asia Unallocated	474	91	383
Australia and Oceania	394	172	221
Australia	301	137	164
New Zealand	37	21	16
Rest of Australia and Oceania	43	7	36
Oceania Unallocated	12	7	5
Rest of World Unallocated	133	45	88
International Orgainisations	-	-	-
WORLD TOTAL	28 444	13 331	15 113
Economic Zones			
OCED	20 853	10 823	10 030
NAFTA	7 300	3 947	3 354
Central and Eastern Europe	293	126	167
OPEC	1 618	497	1 121
ASEAN	938	163	775
CIS	250	129	120
NICs1	1 018	216	802
Offshore Financial centres	1 389	479	909
ACP	544	315	229

1 See chapter text
2 Due to rounding, the sum of constituent items may not always equal the total shown. Data excludes the following industries: Financial, Film and TV, Travel and Transport, Public Sector (including Education) and Law Society members.

3 Portugal and EU Institutions have been merged to avoid disclosure.
4 Includes data for Saudi Arabia for reasons of disclosure.

Source: Office for National Statistics

18.9 Summary of balance of payments[1] in 2001
United Kingdom

£ millions

	Credits	Debits
1. Current account		
A. Goods and services	267 979	290 912
1. Goods	191 754	225 295
2. Services	76 225	65 753
2.1. Transportation	12 220	15 808
2.2. Travel	12 632	26 382
2.3. Communications	1 270	1 754
2.4. Construction	109	46
2.5. Insurance	3 832	764
2.6. Financial	12 807	2 948
2.7. Computer and information	2 573	817
2.8. Royalties and licence fees	5 495	4 104
2.9. Other business	22 859	10 509
2.10. Personal, cultural and recreational	906	648
2.11. Government	1 522	1 973
B. Income	139 920	130 794
1. Compensation of employees	1 049	869
2. Investment income	138 831	129 849
2.1 Direct investment	43 844	28 075
2.2 Portfolio investment	34 897	34 650
2.3 Other investment (including earnings on reserve assets)	60 130	67 076
C. Current transfers	16 374	23 518
1. Central government	4 953	7 584
2. Other sectors	11 421	15 934
Total current account	**424 273**	**445 360**
2. Capital and financial accounts		
A. Capital account	2 686	1 489
1. Capital transfers	2 556	985
2. Acquisition/disposal of non-produced, non-financial assets	130	504
B. Financial account	295 477	281 098
1. Direct investment	43 775	23 710
Abroad		23 710
1.1. Equity capital		19 180
1.2. Reinvested earnings		23 757
1.3. Other capital[2]		−19 227
In United Kingdom	43 775	
1.1. Equity capital	12 893	
1.2. Reinvested earnings	9 628	
1.3. Other capital[3]	21 254	
2. Portfolio investment	42 583	93 351
Assets		93 351
2.1. Equity securities		47 780
2.2. Debt securities		45 571
Liabilities	42 583	
2.1. Equity securities	18 123	
2.2. Debt securities	24 460	
3. Financial derivatives (net)		−8 417
4. Other investment	209 119	175 539
Assets		175 539
4.1 Trade credits		−74
4.2 Loans		48 078
4.3 Currency and deposits		127 779
4.4 Other assets		−244
Liabilities	209 119	
4.1. Trade credits	−	
4.2. Loans	85 904	
4.3. Currency and deposits	122 977	
4.4. Other liabilities	238	
5. Reserve assets		−3 085
5.1. Monetary gold		−786
5.2. Special drawing rights		−22
5.3. Reserve position in the IMF		633
5.4. Foreign exchange		−2 915
Total capital and financial accounts	**298 163**	**282 587**
Total current, capital and financial accounts	**722 436**	**727 947**
Net errors and omissions	5 511	

1 See chapter text.
2 Other capital transaction on direct investment abroad represents claims on affiliated enterprises less liabilities to affiliated enterprises
3 Other capital transactions on direct investment in the United Kingdom represents liabilities to direct investors less claims on direct investors

Source: Office for National Statistics

18.10 Summary of balance of payments[1]
Balances (credits less debits)
United Kingdom

£ millions

				Current account							
	Trade in goods	Trade in services	**Total goods and services**	Compensation of employees	Investment income	**Total income**	**Current transfers**	**Current balance**	Capital account	Financial account	Net errors & omissions
	LQCT	KTMS	KTMY	KTMP	HMBM	HMBP	KTNF	HBOG	FKMJ	HBNT	HHDH
1948	−152	−64	−216	−20	223	203	96	83	−17	−58	−8
1949	−137	−43	−180	−20	206	186	29	35	−12	−103	80
1950	−54	−4	−58	−21	378	357	39	338	−10	−447	119
1951	−692	32	−660	−21	322	301	29	−330	−15	426	−81
1952	−272	123	−149	−22	231	209	169	229	−15	−229	15
1953	−244	123	−121	−25	207	182	143	204	−13	−177	−14
1954	−210	115	−95	−27	227	200	55	160	−13	−174	27
1955	−315	42	−273	−27	149	122	43	−108	−15	34	89
1956	50	26	76	−30	203	173	2	251	−13	−250	12
1957	−29	121	92	−32	223	191	−5	278	−13	−313	48
1958	34	119	153	−34	261	227	4	384	−10	−411	37
1959	−116	118	2	−37	233	196	–	198	−5	−68	−125
1960	−404	39	−365	−35	201	166	−6	−205	−6	−7	218
1961	−144	51	−93	−35	223	188	−9	86	−12	23	−97
1962	−104	50	−54	−37	301	264	−14	196	−12	−195	11
1963	−123	4	−119	−38	364	326	−37	170	−16	−30	−124
1964	−551	−34	−585	−33	365	332	−74	−327	−17	392	−48
1965	−263	−66	−329	−34	405	371	−75	−33	−18	49	2
1966	−111	44	−67	−39	358	319	−91	161	−19	22	−164
1967	−601	157	−444	−39	354	315	−118	−247	−25	179	93
1968	−708	341	−367	−48	303	255	−119	−231	−26	688	−431
1969	−214	392	178	−47	468	421	−109	490	−23	−794	327
1970	−18	455	437	−56	527	471	−89	819	−22	−818	21
1971	205	590	795	−63	481	418	−90	1 123	−23	−1 330	230
1972	−736	665	−71	−52	407	355	−142	142	−35	477	−584
1973	−2 573	803	−1 770	−68	1 074	1 006	−336	−1 100	−39	1 031	108
1974	−5 241	1 118	−4 123	−92	1 184	1 092	−302	−3 333	−34	3 185	182
1975	−3 245	1 447	−1 798	−102	518	416	−313	−1 695	−36	1 569	162
1976	−3 930	2 532	−1 398	−140	1 100	960	−534	−972	−12	507	477
1977	−2 271	3 306	1 035	−152	−280	−432	−889	−286	11	−3 286	3 561
1978	−1 534	3 777	2 243	−140	138	−2	−1 420	821	−79	−2 655	1 913
1979	−3 326	4 076	750	−130	155	25	−1 777	−1 002	−103	864	241
1980	1 329	3 829	5 158	−82	−1 683	−1 765	−1 653	1 740	−4	−2 157	421
1981	3 238	3 951	7 189	−66	−1 058	−1 124	−1 219	4 846	−79	−5 312	545
1982	1 879	3 198	5 077	−95	−1 273	−1 368	−1 476	2 233	6	−1 233	−1 006
1983	−1 618	4 076	2 458	−89	280	191	−1 391	1 258	75	−3 287	1 954
1984	−5 409	4 491	−918	−94	1 284	1 190	−1 566	−1 294	107	−7 130	8 317
1985	−3 416	6 767	3 351	−120	−877	−997	−2 924	−570	185	−1 657	2 042
1986	−9 617	6 403	−3 214	−156	1 850	1 694	−2 094	−3 614	135	−122	3 601
1987	−11 698	6 813	−4 885	−174	1 091	917	−3 570	−7 538	333	10 764	−3 559
1988	−21 553	4 450	−17 103	−64	817	753	−3 500	−19 850	235	17 201	2 414
1989	−24 724	3 643	−21 081	−138	−654	−792	−4 448	−26 321	270	18 001	8 050
1990	−18 707	4 337	−14 370	−110	−2 869	−2 979	−4 932	−22 281	497	15 083	6 701
1991	−10 223	4 102	−6 121	−63	−3 244	−3 307	−1 231	−10 659	290	5 269	5 100
1992	−13 050	5 482	−7 568	−49	177	128	−5 534	−12 974	421	5 089	7 464
1993	−13 066	6 581	−6 485	35	−226	−191	−5 243	−11 919	309	11 330	280
1994	−11 126	6 379	−4 747	−170	3 518	3 348	−5 369	−6 768	33	2 126	4 609
1995	−12 023	8 481	−3 542	−296	2 397	2 101	−7 574	−9 015	533	4 964	3 518
1996	−13 722	9 597	−4 125	93	1 111	1 204	−5 788	−8 709	736	5 515	2 458
1997	−12 342	12 528	186	83	3 823	3 906	−5 812	−1 720	804	−5 066	5 982
1998	−21 813	12 666	−9 147	−10	12 568	12 558	−8 225	−4 814	473	245	4 096
1999	−27 372	11 794	−15 578	201	2 335	2 536	−6 687	−19 729	943	19 735	−949
2000	−30 326	11 838	−18 488	143	9 169	9 312	−10 032	−19 208	1 823	13 993	3 392
2001	−33 541	10 472	−22 461	180	8 982	9 126	−7 144	−21 087	1 197	14 379	5 511

1 See chapter text.

Source: Office for National Statistics

18.11 Balance of Payments[1]: current account
United Kingdom

£ millions

		1991	1992	1993	1994	1995	1996	1997	1998	1999	2000	2001
Credits												
Exports of goods and services												
Exports of goods	LQAD	103 939	107 863	122 229	135 143	153 577	167 196	171 923	164 056	166 166	187 936	191 754
Exports of services	KTMQ	32 001	36 228	41 411	45 365	49 932	55 895	59 699	64 745	70 443	77 199	76 225
Total exports of goods and services	KTMW	135 940	144 091	163 640	180 508	203 509	223 091	231 622	228 801	236 609	265 135	267 979
Income												
Compensation of employees	KTMN	551	551	595	681	887	911	1 007	840	960	1 014	1 049
Investment income	HMBN	75 073	66 153	72 333	73 702	87 132	91 621	95 337	102 945	99 865	134 223	138 831
Total income	HMBQ	75 624	66 704	72 928	74 383	88 019	92 532	96 344	103 785	100 825	135 237	139 920
Current transfers												
Central government	FJUM	4 892	2 180	2 826	2 138	1 730	2 828	2 173	1 943	3 542	2 463	4 953
Other sectors	FJUN	9 281	10 295	9 565	9 454	10 751	16 088	10 929	10 500	10 464	9 810	11 421
Total current transfers	KTND	14 173	12 475	12 391	11 592	12 481	18 916	13 102	12 443	14 006	12 273	16 374
Total	HBOE	**225 737**	**223 270**	**248 959**	**266 483**	**304 009**	**334 539**	**341 068**	**345 029**	**351 440**	**412 645**	**424 273**
Debits												
Imports of goods and services												
Imports of goods	LQBL	114 162	120 913	135 295	146 269	165 600	180 918	184 265	185 869	193 538	218 262	225 295
Imports of services	KTMR	27 899	30 746	34 830	38 986	41 451	46 298	47 171	52 079	58 649	65 361	65 753
Total imports of goods and services	KTMX	142 061	151 659	170 125	185 255	207 051	227 216	231 436	237 948	252 187	283 623	290 912
Income												
Compensation of employees	KTMO	614	600	560	851	1 183	818	924	850	759	871	869
Investment income	HMBO	78 317	65 976	72 559	70 184	84 735	90 510	91 514	90 377	97 530	125 054	129 849
Total income	HMBR	78 931	66 576	73 119	71 035	85 918	91 328	92 438	91 227	98 289	125 925	130 794
Current transfers												
Central government	FJUO	3 450	3 812	4 343	4 977	5 022	5 297	5 260	6 787	7 482	8 015	7 584
Other sectors	FJUP	11 954	14 197	13 291	11 984	15 033	19 407	13 654	13 881	13 211	14 290	15 934
Total current transfers	KTNE	15 404	18 009	17 634	16 961	20 055	24 704	18 914	20 668	20 693	22 305	23 518
Total	HBOF	**236 396**	**236 244**	**260 878**	**273 251**	**313 024**	**343 248**	**342 788**	**349 843**	**371 169**	**431 853**	**445 360**
Balances												
Trade in goods and services												
Trade in goods	LQCT	−10 223	−13 050	−13 066	−11 126	−12 023	−13 722	−12 342	−21 813	−27 372	−30 326	−33 541
Trade in services	KTMS	4 102	5 482	6 581	6 379	8 481	9 597	12 528	12 666	11 794	11 838	10 472
Total trade in goods and services	KTMY	−6 121	−7 568	−6 485	−4 747	−3 542	−4 125	186	−9 147	−15 578	−18 488	−22 461
Income												
Compensation of employees	KTMP	−63	−49	35	−170	−296	93	83	−10	201	143	180
Investment income	HMBM	−3 244	177	−226	3 518	2 397	1 111	3 823	12 568	2 335	9 169	8 982
Total income	HMBP	−3 307	128	−191	3 348	2 101	1 204	3 906	12 558	2 536	9 312	9 126
Current transfers												
Central government	FJUQ	1 442	−1 632	−1 517	−2 839	−3 292	−2 469	−3 087	−4 844	−3 940	−5 552	−2 631
Other sectors	FJUR	−2 673	−3 902	−3 726	−2 530	−4 282	−3 319	−2 725	−3 381	−2 747	−4 480	−4 513
Total current transfers	KTNF	−1 231	−5 534	−5 243	−5 369	−7 574	−5 788	−5 812	−8 225	−6 687	−10 032	−7 144
Total (Current balance)	HBOG	**−10 659**	**−12 974**	**−11 919**	**−6 768**	**−9 015**	**−8 709**	**−1 720**	**−4 814**	**−19 729**	**−19 208**	**−21 087**

1 See chapter text.

Source: Office for National Statistics

18.12 Balance of payments[1]: summary of international investment position, financial account and investment income

United Kingdom

£ billions

		1991	1992	1993	1994	1995	1996	1997	1998	1999	2000	2001
Investment abroad												
International investment position												
Direct investment	HBWD	128.1	151.8	172.6	176.1	203.7	201.6	223.3	299.6	428.1	609.9	645.2
Portfolio investment	HHZZ	260.6	327.2	469.8	429.8	499.3	548.2	651.0	704.6	825.0	900.4	899.0
Other investment	HLXV	528.4	639.7	684.4	708.6	808.1	851.0	1 066.6	1 104.2	1 138.2	1 442.4	1 620.2
Reserve assets	LTEB	26.0	28.3	29.7	30.7	31.8	27.3	22.8	23.3	22.2	28.8	25.6
Total	HBQA	943.1	1 146.9	1 356.5	1 345.2	1 542.9	1 628.1	1 963.7	2 131.8	2 413.5	2 981.5	3 190.0
Financial account transactions												
Direct investment	-HJYP	9.3	11.3	18.2	22.7	28.7	22.3	38.2	73.3	125.0	168.6	23.7
Portfolio investment	-HHZC	32.3	28.6	89.6	-21.8	39.3	59.6	51.9	31.9	20.6	67.3	93.4
Other investment	-XBMM	-20.2	31.7	45.3	27.8	47.5	137.1	168.2	17.2	57.6	265.9	175.5
Reserve assets	-AIPA	2.7	-1.4	0.7	1.0	-0.2	-0.5	-2.4	-0.2	-0.6	7.3	-2.3
Total	-HBNR	24.1	68.9	153.5	27.3	113.6	217.6	254.9	125.4	199.9	504.2	281.1
Investment income												
Direct investment	HJYW	13.2	13.8	17.4	21.9	24.8	28.5	29.4	29.8	33.1	44.6	43.8
Portfolio investment	HLYX	9.7	12.6	16.7	16.4	19.7	20.2	23.8	29.0	25.6	32.9	34.9
Other investment	AIOP	50.5	38.4	36.8	33.8	41.0	41.3	40.7	43.0	40.0	55.8	59.2
Reserve assets	HHCB	1.7	1.5	1.5	1.6	1.7	1.6	1.4	1.1	1.2	1.0	1.0
Total	HMBN	75.1	66.2	72.3	73.7	87.1	91.6	95.3	102.9	99.9	134.2	138.8
Investment in the UK												
International investment position												
Direct investment	HBWI	128.6	130.8	135.9	129.9	146.2	152.6	173.7	213.6	250.3	306.6	347.5
Portfolio investment	HLXW	208.8	247.1	306.9	320.0	406.3	480.0	583.3	694.4	831.1	1 000.9	978.9
Other investment	HLYD	608.3	756.3	882.3	877.4	1 013.0	1 064.9	1 282.1	1 359.0	1 412.7	1 711.1	1 888.5
Total	HBQB	945.7	1 134.2	1 325.1	1 327.3	1 565.5	1 697.5	2 039.1	2 267.0	2 494.0	3 018.6	3 214.8
Financial account transactions												
Direct investment	HJYU	9.2	9.4	10.9	7.1	13.8	17.6	22.8	45.1	55.2	79.1	43.8
Portfolio investment	HHZF	9.8	9.6	28.8	30.7	37.3	43.0	26.7	20.9	115.4	166.4	42.6
Other investment	XBMN	10.3	55.0	125.2	-8.3	67.4	162.5	200.3	59.6	49.0	272.7	209.1
Total	HBNS	29.4	74.0	164.9	29.5	118.6	223.1	249.8	125.6	219.6	518.2	295.5
Investment income												
Direct investment	HJYX	4.9	5.6	11.1	10.6	13.8	16.6	14.9	8.8	17.0	27.1	28.1
Portfolio investment	HLZC	14.4	13.3	14.2	17.2	20.6	23.7	26.6	29.2	31.2	30.8	34.7
Other investment	HLZN	58.9	47.1	47.2	42.5	50.3	50.1	50.0	52.5	49.3	67.1	67.1
Total	HMBO	78.3	66.0	72.6	70.2	84.7	90.5	91.5	90.4	97.5	125.1	129.8
Net investment												
International investment position												
Direct investment	HBWQ	-0.6	20.9	36.7	46.2	57.5	49.0	49.5	85.9	177.8	303.3	297.7
Portfolio investment	CGNH	51.8	80.1	162.9	109.8	93.0	68.2	67.7	10.2	-6.1	-100.4	-79.9
Other investment	CGNG	-79.8	-116.6	-197.9	-168.8	-204.9	-213.9	-215.5	-254.7	-274.4	-268.7	-268.3
Reserve assets	LTEB	26.0	28.3	29.7	30.7	31.8	27.3	22.8	23.3	22.2	28.8	25.6
Net investment position	HBQC	-2.6	12.8	31.4	17.9	-22.6	-69.4	-75.5	-135.2	-80.5	-37.0	-24.8
Financial account transactions												
Direct investment	HJYV	-0.1	-1.8	-7.2	-15.6	-14.9	-4.7	-15.4	-28.3	-69.8	-89.5	20.1
Portfolio investment	HHZD	-22.5	-19.1	-60.8	52.5	-2.0	-16.6	-25.3	-11.0	94.8	99.1	-50.8
Other investment	HHYR	30.6	23.3	79.8	-36.1	19.9	25.4	32.1	42.4	-8.5	6.7	33.6
Reserve assets	AIPA	-2.7	1.4	-0.7	-1.0	0.2	0.5	2.4	0.2	0.6	-7.3	2.3
Net transactions	HBNT	5.3	5.1	11.3	2.1	5.0	5.5	-5.1	0.2	19.7	14.0	14.4
Investment income												
Direct investment	HJYE	8.3	8.2	6.2	11.4	10.9	11.9	14.5	21.1	16.1	17.5	15.8
Portfolio investment	HLZX	-4.8	-0.7	2.5	-0.8	-0.9	-3.5	-2.8	-0.2	-5.6	2.1	0.2
Other investment	CGNA	-8.4	-8.7	-10.4	-8.7	-9.4	-8.8	-9.3	-9.5	-9.3	-11.4	-7.9
Reserve assets	HHCB	1.7	1.5	1.5	1.6	1.7	1.6	1.4	1.1	1.2	1.0	1.0
Net earnings	HMBM	-3.2	0.2	-0.2	3.5	2.4	1.1	3.8	12.6	2.3	9.2	9.0

1 See chapter text.

Source: Office for National Statistics

18.13 Net outward foreign direct investment by UK companies[1] analysed by area and main country [2,3]

£ millions

		1990	1991	1992	1993	1994	1995	1996	1997	1998	1999	2000
Europe	GQBX	5 844	3 978	4 911	6 171	9 241	9 184	13 321	19 964	23 286	44 140	131 554
EU	CAUU	5 103	3 919	4 613	6 146	8 278	9 457	13 432	17 368	11 777	38 821	128 393
Austria	CBJD	58	45	16	13	102	90	102	16	26	−18	192
Belgium and Luxembourg	CAUV	−211	316	−191	160	132	438	991	1 536	−118	151	1 224
Denmark	CAUW	43	66	47	237	64	416	−176	47	−105	111	−52
Finland	CBJE	4	−1	7	10	26	112	28	−5	80	217	−213
France	CAUX	1 158	486	628	471	423	1 515	2 375	2 380	−46	2 171	5 925
Germany	CAUY	187	155	536	1 333	1 261	1 478	1 184	1 078	1 463	1 308	111 215
Greece	CAUZ	42	37	167	44	84	163	106	302	221	−52	149
Irish Republic	CAVA	144	388	895	1 082	100	776	755	450	1 165	..	4 672
Italy	CAVB	548	258	222	282	298	406	421	447	554	190	−3 440
Netherlands	CAVC	2 258	985	1 585	2 436	4 615	2 953	6 577	9 804	7 772	6 781	−2 331
Portugal	CAVD	159	61	237	25	169	159	56	112	6	180	262
Spain	CAVE	699	982	217	−31	460	431	735	864	232	617	9 525
Sweden	CBJG	15	141	249	84	546	522	277	335	529	..	1 268
EFTA of which	CAVG	497	−42	163	−84	645	−594	−12	2 195	8 806	3 251	725
Norway	CBJF	32	35	156	92	662	−255	96	1 997	782	226	−148
Switzerland	CBJH	465	−74	−1	−177	−16	−338	−110	197	8 015	3 024	872
Other European Countries of which	GQBY	244	100	135	110	317	322	−97	402	2 703	2 068	2 436
Russia[4]	GLAA	2	−2	..	11	115	39	132	448	−171	231	141
UK offshore islands	GLAC	−	−	−	−	−	−	−	−933	2 476	1 296	2 076
America of which	GQBZ	2 181	2 628	2 657	8 673	8 464	13 460	3 277	13 953	48 972	73 891	34 132
Bermuda	CBKZ	276	−438	506	586	349	291	142	−43	469	−91	−249
Brazil	CBLA	211	89	121	38	291	473	692	337	323	855	571
Canada	CAVK	894	318	−106	5	−4	244	−159	823	406	849	2 891
Chile	GQCA	19	80	−22	101	76	220	89	168	169	−693	295
Colombia	GQCB	20	−264	..	−245	204	123	100	241	346	340	−468
Mexico	GLAD	27	39	114	44	42	79	110	760	152	106	147
Panama	GLAE	−13	100	211	−100	94	75	103	..	311	153	11
USA	CAVJ	47	2 235	1 321	7 975	6 549	11 840	1 837	10 509	46 116	70 006	29 863
Asia	GQCI	888	853	959	1 596	2 049	1 657	2 823	2 251	1 718	4 572	−1 247
Near and Middle East Countries of which	CBKF	244	489	44	−239	253	154	28	350	1 674	−914	−275
Gulf Arabian countries[5]	GQCC	239	476	27	−236	250	116	30	260	1 620	−677	−443
Other Asian Countries of which	GQCD	644	364	915	1 834	1 796	1 503	2 794	1 901	45	5 486	−971
Hong Kong	CAVN	−250	−245	−18	456	128	734	730	−359	1 554	312	−3 302
India	GLAF	42	2	−27	139	87	61	110	171	209	148	285
Indonesia	GLAG	−46	74	−59	69	92	−28	155	170	97	−31	−139
Japan	CAVM	235	−4	13	−49	245	169	378	383	14	1 929	1 269
Malaysia	CBKN	159	140	272	363	286	28	184	731	619	227	−974
Singapore	CBKQ	344	232	569	528	590	−48	535	352	−2 473	1 373	286
South Korea	GLAH	4	20	37	44	27	47	32	−26	281	172	−113
Thailand	GLAI	40	24	51	103	177	245	194	103	88	28	240
Australasia and Oceania of which	GQCE	999	1 239	1 280	658	959	2 596	1 843	827	208	730	3 027
Australia	CBJO	913	1 089	989	655	625	2 258	1 472	737	221	715	2 923
New Zealand	CBJP	−24	66	110	71	264	67	244	255	−111	78	79
Africa of which	GQCF	196	606	300	262	327	707	561	623	−25	1 175	358
Kenya	GLAJ	47	22	23	33	9	67	24	73	39	51	168
Nigeria	CBJY	−12	227	138	347	−197	−271	−94	234	−145	160	16
South Africa	CAVO	22	151	72	314	170	466	−25	401	−197	386	−333
Zimbabwe	CBKD	52	72	59	36	28	16	25	1	36	74	38
World Total	CDQD	10 108	9 304	10 107	17 358	21 040	27 604	21 823	37 619	74 159	124 508	167 822
OECD	GQCG	7 731	7 673	7 343	14 864	16 880	23 686	17 545	33 212	68 175	115 813	166 744
Central and Eastern Europe[6]	GQCH	2	18	37	41	168	194	201	214	465	111	312

1 See chapter text.
2 Net investment includes unremitted profits.
3 Minus sign indicates net disinvestment overseas.
4 Prior to 1995 Russia covers other former USSR countries, the Baltic States and Albania.
5 Includes Abu Dhabi, Bahrain, Dubai, Iraq, Kuwait, Oman, Other Gulf States, Qatar, Saudi Arabia and Yemen.
6 Includes Albania, Belarus, Bulgaria, Croatia, Czech Republic, Estonia, Hungary, Latvia, Lithuania, Poland, Romania, Serbia and Montenegro, Slovakia and Slovenia.

Sources: ONS Foreign Direct Investment Inquiries: 01633 813314; Bank of England

18.14 UK outward foreign direct international investment[1] position - book value of net assets analysed by area and main country at year end

£ millions

		1990	1991	1992	1993	1994	1995	1996	1997	1998	1999	2000
Europe	GQCJ	34 450	37 272	44 213	57 853	66 705	76 434	87 582	99 263	117 181	170 905	355 579
EU	CDLN	31 610	34 312	40 620	53 914	61 674	72 808	83 902	92 072	96 817	149 804	328 190
Austria	CDLZ	336	384	371	379	454	734	578	461	506	731	765
Belgium and Luxembourg	CDLO	1 590	2 505	3 804	2 687	3 189	3 172	5 326	5 701	5 560	11 062	11 060
Denmark	CDLP	757	739	863	1 301	1 538	2 803	2 273	2 123	2 295	3 048	1 593
Finland	CDMA	102	80	122	104	117	271	215	217	254	390	566
France	CDLQ	6 898	7 290	8 043	8 619	10 357	12 913	13 128	11 368	10 217	12 774	20 575
Germany	CDLR	4 217	3 998	3 804	5 974	8 442	9 215	8 943	8 328	10 319	10 892	121 654
Greece	CDLS	159	156	288	294	203	500	465	366	508	393	607
Irish Republic	CDLT	2 048	2 743	3 333	4 169	4 436	4 587	6 282	6 182	7 792	27 000	33 204
Italy	CDLU	2 093	2 400	2 427	2 287	2 475	2 698	3 196	3 064	3 149	3 035	5 944
Netherlands	CDLV	8 287	8 369	11 980	23 190	25 228	29 906	37 676	48 240	50 175	69 257	106 236
Portugal	CDLW	865	1 032	1 171	1 195	932	1 210	1 190	1 023	1 067	1 074	1 307
Spain	CDLX	3 498	3 796	3 471	2 820	3 157	3 399	3 477	3 748	3 299	3 674	5 564
Sweden	CDMD	761	821	942	894	1 146	1 401	1 154	1 250	1 675	6 475	19 116
EFTA	CDLY	2 511	2 545	2 968	3 303	4 113	2 522	2 161	1 533	10 547	9 298	10 917
of which												
Norway	CDMC	522	542	736	803	1 513	1 244	1 171	1 116	470	3 874	3 936
Switzerland	CDME	1 989	2 003	2 232	2 500	2 594	1 279	988	415	10 072	5 421	6 976
Other European Countries	GQCK	329	415	626	636	918	1 103	1 520	5 658	9 818	11 803	16 472
of which												
Russia[2]	GQAA	9	10	20	7	26	120	238	401	201	247	−123
UK offshore islands	GQAB	–	–	–	–	–	–	–	2 690	6 937	9 057	13 776
America	GQCU	62 381	62 939	74 868	77 003	75 390	83 275	67 592	80 324	139 031	208 078	203 738
of which												
Bermuda	CDOA	4 630	4 628	5 382	4 869	5 403	5 504	5 295	4 942	4 689	5 075	6 071
Brazil	CDOB	1 250	1 345	1 880	1 963	2 059	2 323	2 421	2 214	1 607	2 374	3 098
Canada	CDML	6 219	6 253	6 766	7 162	4 919	5 395	4 563	5 748	4 952	5 627	8 430
Chile	GQCT	207	363	416	481	439	666	670	970	1 101	1 080	1 340
Colombia	GQCS	..	594	1 109	839	1 071	1 207	1 274	1 197	559	986	766
Mexico	GQAC	405	428	504	419	334	350	553	1 327	801	1 036	947
Panama	GQAD	100	232	630	435	507	467	744	..	..	750	220
USA	CDMM	45 532	45 367	54 688	57 380	55 174	62 159	49 170	59 083	121 408	186 410	178 227
Asia	GQCL	8 285	9 633	12 230	14 118	16 095	18 038	19 916	19 389	20 957	24 148	25 823
Near and Middle East Countries	CDNH	314	749	748	698	754	788	676	917	2 675	1 030	1 259
of which												
Gulf Arabian countries[3]	GQCM	229	657	592	617	660	704	586	658	2 374	626	753
Other Asian Countries	GQCR	7 970	8 884	11 482	13 419	15 341	17 250	19 239	18 472	18 283	23 118	24 564
of which												
Hong Kong	CDNN	1 654	1 895	2 753	3 569	3 373	4 033	4 636	4 406	5 330	5 533	4 681
India	GQAE	341	302	245	490	601	498	532	703	705	869	1 246
Indonesia	GQAF	264	316	222	272	295	418	391	801	641	421	285
Japan	CDMP	1 591	1 674	1 998	1 936	2 613	2 397	2 437	1 605	1 855	3 628	4 477
Malaysia	CDNQ	706	845	1 285	1 750	2 119	1 813	2 164	2 411	1 908	2 088	1 741
Singapore	CDNT	2 449	2 691	3 516	3 706	4 445	5 287	5 822	5 186	5 632	6 072	6 300
South Korea	GQAG	57	69	114	155	183	250	238	154	219	603	403
Thailand	GQAH	205	253	359	404	511	920	1 053	1 009	630	375	695
Australasia and Oceania	GQCN	9 951	10 210	11 222	12 287	13 517	13 985	14 636	13 312	12 179	11 652	12 265
of which												
Australia	CDMO	8 924	9 057	9 605	10 299	11 153	11 365	12 213	10 598	9 071	9 475	10 004
New Zealand	CDMQ	696	700	930	1 443	1 689	1 670	1 640	1 663	1 625	1 855	1 919
Africa	GQCQ	3 868	4 039	4 080	4 570	5 409	4 955	4 876	5 873	4 232	9 876	7 173
of which												
Kenya	GQAI	267	233	249	165	673	276	237	361	415	389	430
Nigeria	CDNA	325	419	490	754	681	335	321	1 060	463	508	804
South Africa	CDMR	2 012	2 239	2 311	2 622	2 202	2 827	2 429	2 527	1 698	6 620	3 051
Zimbabwe	CDNF	402	324	411	248	331	262	200	192	114	171	130
World Total	CDOO	118 935	124 093	146 613	165 831	177 116	196 687	194 601	218 162	293 581	424 660	604 579
OECD	GQCO	97 637	100 517	118 430	136 247	142 332	159 476	157 652	175 434	249 340	368 986	545 903
Central & Eastern Europe[4]	GQCP	9	36	123	106	460	427	622	1 782	2 178	1 313	2 091

1 See chapter text.
2 Prior to 1995 Russia covers other former USSR countries, the Baltic States and Albania.
3 Includes Abu Dhabi, Bahrain, Dubai, Iraq, Kuwait, Oman, Other Gulf States, Qatar, Saudi Arabia and Yemen.

4 Includes Albania, Belarus, Bulgaria, Croatia, Czech Republic, Estonia, Hungary, Latvia, Lithuania, Poland, Romania, Serbia and Montenegro Slovakia and Slovenia.

Sources: ONS Foreign Direct Investment Inquiries: 01633 813314;
Bank of England

18.15 Net earnings from foreign direct investment overseas[1] by UK companies analysed by area and main country [2,3]

£ millions

		1990	1991	1992	1993	1994	1995	1996	1997	1998	1999	2000
Europe	GQCV	4 727	4 182	3 315	5 182	7 033	8 289	9 700	10 440	11 349	14 355	21 832
EU	CAWG	4 198	3 721	2 499	4 450	6 138	7 251	8 557	8 994	9 822	11 244	17 288
Austria	CBLQ	49	43	54	35	52	73	82	65	49	45	76
Belgium and Luxembourg	CAWH	165	259	404	412	387	308	358	297	632	401	1 294
Denmark	CAWI	91	71	115	207	115	286	208	191	215	220	256
Finland	CBLR	9	–	24	22	30	43	–	36	58	95	112
France	CAWJ	688	598	279	50	607	619	999	1 036	994	1 222	2 113
Germany	CAWK	623	617	260	381	834	1 032	951	844	828	1 241	2 567
Greece	CAWL	22	12	50	58	−202	−106	172	122	77	162	217
Irish Republic	CAWM	265	414	393	669	516	639	847	1 112	1 245	1 367	1 645
Italy	CAWN	220	175	75	113	219	272	327	268	327	403	1 152
Netherlands	CAWO	1 674	1 141	758	2 459	2 986	3 248	3 748	4 143	4 481	5 246	5 703
Portugal	CAWP	124	93	83	53	162	188	184	96	162	152	261
Spain	CAWQ	219	197	−5	39	234	338	493	561	464	389	1 150
Sweden	CBLT	50	103	12	−48	200	310	188	224	288	300	743
EFTA	CAWS	476	433	740	639	792	899	963	991	848	1 618	2 366
of which												
Norway	CBLS	242	214	281	119	267	224	311	242	134	248	303
Switzerland	CBLU	233	219	459	520	524	675	652	747	705	1 369	2 062
Other European Countries	GQCW	53	28	75	95	103	139	180	454	680	1 494	2 177
of which												
Russia[4]	GQAJ	1	..	..	2	3	12	24	−30	−214	–	44
UK offshore islands	GQAK	–	–	–	–	–	–	–	225	685	1 081	1 178
America	GQCX	6 962	4 624	5 530	6 126	8 007	10 254	10 698	11 867	11 976	12 841	13 601
of which												
Bermuda	CBNK	269	449	562	428	446	509	506	70	440	466	343
Brazil	CBNL	227	87	182	193	348	432	650	380	322	113	246
Canada	CAWW	464	189	175	283	357	374	571	913	844	868	645
Chile	GQCY	35	88	118	139	195	263	265	236	147	143	251
Colombia	GQCZ	64	21	−40	16	−22	28	23	53	2	78	259
Mexico	GQAL	12	−2	41	43	48	52	74	145	95	186	102
Panama	GQAM	54	17	−27	69	51	45	67	..	180	..	46
USA	CAWV	5 402	3 255	4 065	4 621	5 894	7 803	8 034	9 339	9 672	9 681	10 633
Asia	GQDA	2 114	2 355	2 636	2 792	3 449	2 501	3 776	3 249	4 137	2 768	4 838
Near and Middle East Countries	CBMS	235	303	342	283	297	262	241	475	921	485	819
of which												
Gulf Arabian countries[5]	GQDB	249	300	317	273	293	260	212	424	878	443	709
Other Asian Countries	GQDC	1 879	2 053	2 293	2 509	3 152	2 239	3 536	2 774	3 215	2 283	4 019
of which												
Hong Kong	CAYB	439	440	846	972	1 427	1 362	1 463	623	959	881	703
India	GQAN	88	77	−2	−190	121	100	81	124	194	188	336
Indonesia	GQAO	25	71	18	60	48	71	87	143	114	54	61
Japan	CAWY	72	115	182	142	199	212	281	313	167	545	603
Malaysia	CBNA	182	197	229	248	221	248	332	360	247	352	445
Singapore	CBND	967	1 010	839	977	781	−144	883	795	1 291	28	1 207
South Korea	GQAP	7	10	5	8	29	40	34	17	34	13	49
Thailand	GQAQ	34	17	28	78	84	75	101	95	16	130	103
Australasia and Oceania	GQDD	854	541	960	1 233	2 131	2 044	2 269	1 950	1 532	1 434	2 012
of which												
Australia	CBMB	925	535	809	991	1 776	1 587	1 747	1 503	1 092	1 139	1 692
New Zealand	CBMC	−98	5	73	213	302	322	319	278	147	263	278
Africa	GQDE	869	986	844	1 465	737	807	1 055	965	658	1 097	1 580
of which												
Kenya	GQAR	47	36	41	34	41	46	35	94	78	67	68
Nigeria	CBML	159	273	280	498	−27	−35	61	46	49	65	88
South Africa	CAWZ	410	425	280	488	366	438	503	521	399	656	930
Zimbabwe	CBMQ	73	81	77	54	58	58	50	58	53	73	60
World Total	GLAB	15 526	12 688	13 285	16 796	21 355	23 894	27 498	28 470	29 652	32 496	43 862
OECD	GQDF	11 486	8 279	8 624	11 454	15 578	18 567	20 621	22 601	22 810	25 812	34 387
Central & Eastern Europe[6]	GQDG	2	1	7	11	−24	16	15	118	75	252	592

1 See chapter text.
2 A minus sign indicates net losses.
3 Net earnings equal profits of overseas branches plus UK companies' receipts of interest and their share of profits of overseas subsidiaries and associates. Earnings are after deducting provisions for depreciation and overseas tax on profits, dividends and interest.
4 Prior to 1995 Russia covers other former USSR countries, the Baltic States and Albania.

5 Includes Abu Dhabi, Bahrain, Dubai, Iraq, Kuwait, Oman, Other Gulf States, Qatar, Saudi Arabia and Yemen.
6 Includes Albania, Belarus, Bulgaria, Croatia, Czech Republic, Estonia, Hungary, Latvia, Lithuania, Poland, Romania, Serbia and Montenegro, Slovakia and Slovenia.

Sources: ONS Foreign Direct Investment Inquiries: 01633 813314;
Bank of England

18.16 Net inward Foreign direct investment[1] in the UK analysed by area and main country [2,3]

£ millions

		1990	1991	1992	1993	1994	1995	1996	1997	1998	1999	2000
Europe	GQDH	8 042	4 910	4 044	2 202	3 065	4 626	6 931	8 394	22 892	39 398	54 008
EU	CAYO	7 628	4 578	3 433	1 589	3 367	3 555	4 673	6 905	12 654	39 676	51 794
Austria	CBOB	62	11	−45	13	60	21	20	18	154	−13	175
Belgium and Luxembourg	CAYP	296	201	65	−427	357	520	6	174	1 068	551	792
Denmark	CAYQ	154	122	91	97	76	68	151	228	227	398	477
Finland	CBOC	36	8	54	−42	32	−36	2	193	129	228	87
France	CAYR	1 551	1 333	802	−37	310	1 004	1 321	2 647	778	3 217	31 766
Germany	CAYS	1 610	396	1 261	656	71	2 090	835	1 123	484	26 278	10 360
Greece	CAYT	..	..	..	..	..	..	..	..	1	3	..
Irish Republic	CAYU	229	137	−32	49	224	−35	221	1 127	724	78	350
Italy	CAYV	−42	45	−37	80	177	328	−184	−32	99	23	469
Netherlands	CAYW	2 085	2 335	1 135	1 244	1 915	−633	2 610	1 180	9 019	7 860	4 277
Portugal	CAYX	..	..	..	..	..	..	..	..	5	11	−6
Spain	CAYY	3	−11	3	14	21	17	66	71	99	119	..
Sweden	CBOE	1 658	5	129	−56	119	184	−379	147	−132	924	627
EFTA	CAZB	431	327	674	550	−176	1 036	2 211	1 512	9 859	−660	1 401
of which												
Norway	CBOD	201	−71	−34	49	−131	124	1 060	182	−116	−502	−392
Switzerland	CBOF	229	399	710	501	−44	912	1 151	1 320	9 967	−165	1 779
Other European Countries	GQDI	−17	5	−62	64	−125	36	47	−21	379	382	813
of which												
Russia[4]	GQAS	−26	−11	..	49	−	19	61	19	..	..	102
UK offshore islands	GQAT	−	−	−	−	−	−	−	−74	426	325	699
America	GQDJ	6 266	1 898	3 720	5 993	2 344	8 750	7 210	10 615	18 770	17 159	16 331
of which												
Canada	CAZF	−264	265	−45	33	−246	−438	444	374	58	519	1 846
USA	CAZE	5 095	1 879	3 748	5 142	2 138	9 293	6 742	10 045	18 596	15 953	14 061
Asia	GQDK	1 931	255	630	570	186	−189	412	402	1 421	−2 189	4 795
Near and Middle East Countries	GQAU	−54	137	251	115	78	58	64	103	81	137	87
Other Asian Countries	GQAV	1 986	118	380	456	110	−248	348	299	1 340	−2 326	4 708
of which												
Hong Kong	GQAW	10	53	280	106	45	−124	10	15	60	17	927
Japan	CAZH	2 091	48	−21	277	4	−379	209	288	968	−2 646	2 825
Singapore	GQAX	9	7	9	14	2	40	1	41	15	329	807
South Korea	GQAY	..	..	..	43	2	85	−8	−78	187	−112	−18
Australasia and Oceania	GQDL	852	1 328	323	995	387	−647	992	714	986	−133	1 504
of which												
Australia	CBOJ	957	937	340	995	260	−708	1 096	721	1 093	..	1 456
New Zealand	CBOK	−105	391	−17	−	127	60	−104	−6	−107	..	45
Africa	GQAZ	64	27	99	111	63	117	118	170	808	143	390
of which												
South Africa	CAZJ	38	30	85	58	50	125	109	149	585	130	351
World Total	CBDH	17 155	8 418	8 816	9 871	6 046	12 654	15 662	20 296	44 877	54 376	77 029
OECD	GQBA	15 727	8 428	8 221	8 636	5 346	12 511	15 235	19 758	43 306	52 590	73 403
Central & Eastern Europe[5]	GQBB	−	−	−7	−	−141	15	−19	14	−16	2	8

1 See chapter text.
2 Net investment includes unremitted profits.
3 A minus sign indicates net disinvestment in the UK.
4 Prior to 1995 Russia covers other former USSR countries, the Baltic States and Albania.

5 Includes Albania, Belarus, Bulgaria, Croatia, Czech Republic, Estonia, Hungary, Latvia, Lithuania, Poland, Romania, Serbia and Montenegro, Slovakia and Slovenia.

Sources: ONS Foreign Direct Investment Inquiries: 01633 813314; Bank of England

18.17 UK inward foreign direct international investment[1] position - book value of net liabilities analysed by area and main country at year end

£ millions

		1990	1991	1992	1993	1994	1995	1996	1997	1998	1999	2000
Europe	GQDM	40 606	45 205	46 928	47 770	47 281	52 144	55 856	58 037	81 385	118 793	150 226
EU	CDOT	33 707	38 036	39 547	40 266	39 998	43 493	43 774	44 927	69 248	107 249	137 468
Austria	CDPF	104	103	−30	93	428	412	280	79	334	253	601
Belgium and Luxembourg	CDOU	1 634	1 812	1 817	1 801	2 221	2 170	1 233	1 856	2 810	4 143	3 851
Denmark	CDOV	685	701	877	1 339	1 072	1 127	850	927	1 560	1 971	2 818
Finland	CDPG	423	364	437	300	356	352	334	444	729	921	1 042
France	CDOW	7 427	9 000	8 749	7 880	7 728	8 289	9 147	13 880	16 265	19 797	48 938
Germany	CDOX	4 239	4 597	5 627	5 921	5 589	8 854	9 508	10 078	11 573	36 250	25 989
Greece	CDOY	..	..	..	..	..	..	..	..	..	47	..
Irish Republic	CDOZ	1 069	840	865	681	956	686	703	1 837	2 807	3 098	3 475
Italy	CDPA	597	649	845	875	839	1 223	988	824	1 406	1 540	2 423
Netherlands	CDPB	14 182	16 547	16 715	18 477	18 511	17 173	18 692	12 131	28 227	33 891	40 941
Portugal	CDPC	..	..	..	..	..	..	..	..	..	179	..
Spain	CDPD	318	329	356	346	178	164	78	247	463	1 015	2 231
Sweden	CDPI	3 025	3 058	3 274	2 542	2 105	2 908	1 871	2 521	2 910	4 144	3 839
EFTA of which	CDPE	6 794	7 040	7 308	7 225	7 111	8 188	11 735	12 379	9 103	9 203	9 513
Norway	CDPH	748	661	647	701	506	665	1 571	1 866	1 559	560	854
Switzerland	CDPJ	6 044	6 375	6 657	6 519	6 605	7 523	10 164	10 422	7 444	8 516	8 502
Other European Countries of which	GQDN	105	129	73	280	172	463	348	731	3 035	2 341	3 244
Russia[2]	GQBC	18	18	−51	43	24	80	212	..	258	192	..
UK offshore islands	GQBD	−	−	−	−	−	−	−	341	2 465	1 780	2 604
America of which	GQDU	49 721	49 682	50 910	55 209	55 918	59 420	62 253	77 408	101 645	104 331	113 693
Canada	CDPM	4 104	4 427	4 065	4 101	4 593	2 652	3 517	4 129	4 090	7 070	9 819
USA	CDPN	43 784	44 434	46 001	49 537	49 829	55 129	55 956	70 270	93 419	93 469	100 526
Asia	GQDO	7 184	7 378	6 935	7 655	7 782	7 934	8 072	9 166	10 308	7 050	15 124
Near and Middle East Countries	GQBE	1 110	1 372	1 099	1 427	2 027	1 324	1 274	1 450	1 380	1 026	1 369
Other Asian Countries of which	GQBF	6 073	6 006	5 836	6 228	5 755	6 609	6 797	7 715	8 928	6 024	13 754
Hong Kong	GQBG	406	200	422	262	233	19	31	56	331	445	..
Japan	CDPQ	5 648	5 346	4 929	5 427	5 105	5 542	5 888	6 562	7 387	4 174	7 770
Singapore	GQBH	47	..	..	415	421	500	503	757	447	834	1 659
South Korea	GQBI	..	−43	−28	−3	−203	12	−206	−305	−66	−202	−245
Australasia and Oceania of which	GQDP	7 937	8 715	9 135	9 560	9 644	8 527	7 707	7 354	7 839	7 147	11 572
Australia	CDPP	6 799	7 655	8 083	8 598	7 968	7 021	6 169	6 003	5 938	5 450	10 359
New Zealand	CDPR	912	832	824	844	1 676	1 506	1 538	1 351	1 554	1 055	1 208
Africa of which	GQBJ	313	393	501	811	712	861	766	991	1 641	953	1 205
South Africa	CDPS	263	342	438	618	549	665	578	743	1 228	767	862
World Total	CDPZ	105 760	111 373	114 409	121 005	121 336	128 885	134 654	152 956	202 817	238 274	291 820
OECD	GQBK	101 702	107 814	110 816	116 082	116 171	123 761	128 475	145 336	190 717	227 529	276 481
Central & Eastern Europe[3]	GQBL	29	29	24	21	10	258	14	24	63	103	110

1 See chapter text.
2 Prior to 1995 Russia covers other former USSR countries, the Baltic States and Albania.

3 Includes Albania, Belarus, Bulgaria, Croatia, Czech Rebuplic, Estonia, Hungary, Latvia, Lithuania, Poland, Romania, Serbia and Montenegro, Slovakia and Slovenia.

Sources: ONS Foreign Direct Investment Inquiries: 01633 813314; Bank of England

18.18 Net earnings from foreign direct investment in the UK[1] analysed by area and main country [2,3]

£ millions

		1990	1991	1992	1993	1994	1995	1996	1997	1998	1999	2000
Europe	GQDQ	2 007	1 243	2 482	4 833	3 661	5 432	6 401	5 746	1 485	6 643	15 116
EU	CBDJ	1 689	1 025	1 932	3 556	3 659	4 657	5 631	5 231	2 908	6 232	13 770
Austria	CBOR	−8	..	..	−5	94	30	55	13	12	15	72
Belgium and Luxembourg	CBDK	−3	−53	−1	224	272	249	209	139	408	349	151
Denmark	CBDL	88	42	−17	92	18	152	137	171	269	208	369
Finland	CBOS	−43	−71	−36	−52	2	88	74	80	70	106	207
France	CBDM	420	377	340	633	227	836	705	1 239	648	1 871	2 185
Germany	CBDN	169	22	221	576	507	700	706	563	−185	−171	2 106
Greece	CBDO	..	..	..	..	..	..	..	..	23	28	22
Irish Republic	CBDP	−4	−27	−12	74	92	155	141	222	397	251	413
Italy	CBDQ	−73	−55	−24	97	246	196	318	430	249	189	148
Netherlands	CBDR	1 148	927	1 731	1 820	2 076	2 070	3 053	2 034	640	2 947	7 718
Portugal	CBDS	..	..	..	..	..	..	..	..	−5	2	8
Spain	CBDT	−	−29	−5	55	17	42	69	106	85	127	85
Sweden	CBOU	13	−56	−177	46	107	127	146	219	300	309	286
EFTA of which	CBDW	316	146	846	1 188	−33	685	709	408	−1 411	311	1 205
Norway	CBOT	17	−14	−35	27	12	11	−58	121	−171	−212	115
Switzerland	CBOV	301	338	885	1 161	−45	675	768	277	−1 248	518	1 081
Other European Countries of which	GQDR	2	−104	−296	88	36	89	60	108	−9	100	142
Russia[4]	GQBM	2	..	..	55	1	15	31	..	..	12	..
UK offshore islands	GQBN	−	−	−	−	−	−	−	33	42	47	−6
America of which	GQDV	5 131	2 948	2 391	4 917	4 992	5 824	7 589	6 775	6 365	7 857	8 513
Canada	CBEA	273	199	47	234	506	228	281	65	198	368	800
USA	CBDZ	4 602	2 951	2 284	4 441	4 372	5 606	6 986	6 512	5 848	7 586	7 830
Asia	GQDS	102	193	107	106	172	459	300	−332	−597	137	1 115
Near and Middle East Countries	GQBO	−119	−89	−31	16	−8	112	89	96	46	137	79
Other Asian Countries of which	GQBP	222	283	139	90	181	347	211	−428	−643	−	1 036
Hong Kong	GQBQ	−23	47	207	52	4	−2	28	21	−185	26	31
Japan	CBEC	261	246	−41	45	171	334	151	−502	−391	−61	806
Singapore	GQBS	−12	3	−2	4	1	5	−	41	−79	88	231
South Korea	GQBT	..	..	..	7	15	−6	−6	−11	−20	−60	−74
Australasia and Oceania of which	GQDT	−302	74	211	418	327	472	594	860	629	508	219
Australia	CBOZ	−168	92	222	410	330	479	566	830	602	..	189
New Zealand	CBPA	−134	−18	..	8	−1	−6	28	..	85	..	21
Africa of which	GQBU	−6	3	..	19	25	49	44	55	7	127	165
South Africa	CBED	−6	−1	6	9	21	38	35	46	−23	114	148
World Total	CBEV	6 932	4 461	5 197	10 293	9 176	12 235	14 928	13 103	7 889	15 272	25 128
OECD	GQBV	6 831	4 878	5 371	9 998	9 118	12 081	14 388	12 583	7 838	14 905	24 560
Central & Eastern Europe[5]	GQBW	−	−	2	1	24	60	13	18	−12	11	12

1 See chapter text.
2 A minus sign indicates net losses.
3 Net earnings equal profits of UK branches plus overseas investors' receipts of interest and their share of the profits of UK subsidiaries and associates. Earnings are after deducting provisions for depreciation and UK tax on profits and interest.

4 Prior to 1995 Russia covers other former USSR countries, the Baltic States and Albania.
5 Includes Albania, Belarus, Bulgaria, Croatia, Czech Republic, Estonia, Hungary, Latvia, Lithuania, Poland, Romania, Serbia and Montenegro, Slovakia and Slovenia.

Sources: ONS Foreign Direct Investment Inquiries: 01633 813314;
Bank of England

19 Research and development

Research and development

Research and development
(Tables 19.1 to 19.5)
Research and experimental development (R&D) is defined for statistical purposes as 'creative work undertaken on a systematic basis in order to increase the stock of knowledge, including knowledge of man, culture and society, and the use of this stock of knowledge to devise new applications'.

R&D is financed and carried out mainly by businesses, the Government, and institutions of higher education. A small amount is performed by non-profit-making bodies. Gross Expenditure on R&D (GERD) is an indicator of the total amount of R&D performed within the UK: it has been approximately 2 per cent of GDP in recent years. Detailed figures are reported each year in a First Release published in March and the August edition of the ONS's *Economic Trends*. Table 19.1 shows the main components of GERD.

The ONS conducts an annual survey of expenditure and employment on R&D performed by Government, and of Government funding of R&D. The survey collects data on outturn and planning years. Until 1993 the detailed results were reported in the *Annual Review of Government Funded R&D* produced by the Office of Science and Technology (OST). From 1997 the results have appeared in OST's *Science, Engineering and Technology Statistics* publication. Table 19.2 gives some broad totals for gross expenditure by Government (expenditure before deducting funds received by Government for R&D). Table 19.3 gives a breakdown of net expenditure (receipts are deducted).

The ONS conducts an annual survey of R&D in business. Tables 19.4 and 19.5 give a summary of the main trends up to 2002. The latest set of results from the survey will be available in a First Release dated 22 November 2002 and a Business Monitor (MA14) to be published in January 2003.

Statistics on expenditure and employment on R&D in Higher Education Institutions (HEIs) are based on information collected by Higher Education Funding Councils and HESA (Higher Education Statistics Agency). In 1994 a new methodology was introduced to estimate expenditure on R&D in HEIs. This is based on the allocation of various Funding Council Grants. Full details of the new methodology are contained in SET Statistics available on the Office of Science and Technology Web Site at www.ost.gov.uk/setstats/.

The most comprehensive international comparisons of resources devoted to R&D appear in Main Science and Technology Indicators published by the organisation for Economic Co-operation and Development (OECD). The Statistical Office of the European Union and the United Nations also compile R&D statistics based on figures supplied by member states.

To make international comparisons more reliable the OECD have published a series of manuals giving guidance on how to measure various components of R&D inputs and outputs. The most important of these is the Frascati Manual, which defines R&D and recommends how resources for R&D should be measured. The UK follows the Frascati Manual as far as possible.

For information on available aggregated data on Research and Development please contact Jane Morgan on 01633 813109 (e-mail jane.morgan@ons.gov.uk).

19.1 Cost of research and development: analysis by sector[1]
United Kingdom

	Work performed within each sector													
	1994		1995		1996		1997		1998		1999		2000	
	£m	%	£m	%	£m	%	£m	%	£m	%	£m	%	£m	%
Sector carrying out the work (£m cash terms)														
Government	2 051	15	1 462	10	1 495	10	1 427	10	1 487	10	1 450	9	1 489	8
Research Councils	-	-	581	4	575	4	590	4	591	4	622	4	646	4
Business enterprise	8 842	65	9 116	65	9 297	65	9 556	65	10 133	66	11 302	67	11 510	66
Higher education	2 623	19	2 696	19	2 792	19	2 893	20	3 040	20	3 324	20	3 645	21
Private non-profit	168	1	177	1	177	1	190	1	203	1	231	1	255	1
Total	13 684	100	14 034	100	14 336	100	14 657	100	15 454	100	16 929	100	17 543	100

	Finance provided by each sector													
	1994		1995		1996		1997		1998		1999		2000	
	£m	%	£m	%	£m	%	£m	%	£m	%	£m	%	£m	%
Sector providing the funds (£m cash terms)														
Government	4 479	33	2 514	18	2 402	17	2 332	16	2 535	16	2 601	15	2 534	14
Research Councils	-	-	1 078	8	1 092	8	1 135	8	1 117	7	1 185	7	1 259	7
Higher Education Funding Councils	-	-	1 018	7	1 027	7	1 033	7	1 085	7	1 157	7	1 276	7
Higher education	116	1	119	1	120	1	123	1	130	1	142	1	158	1
Business enterprise[2]	6 886	50	6 765	48	6 817	48	7 321	50	7 356	48	8 213	49	8 648	49
Private non-profit	514	4	511	4	545	4	578	4	621	4	701	4	815	5
Abroad	1 689	12	2 029	14	2 331	16	2 136	15	2 610	17	2 929	17	2 854	16
Total	13 684	100	14 034	100	14 336	100	14 657	100	15 454	100	16 929	100	17 543	100

1 See chapter text.
2 Including research associations and public corporations.

Source: Office for National Statistics: 01633 813109

19.2 Gross Central Government expenditure on research and development[1]
United Kingdom

£ millions

	1995/96		1996/97		1997/98		1998/99		1999/00		2000/01	
	Intra-mural	Extra-mural[2]	Intra-mural	Extra-mural[2]	Intra-mural	Extra-mural[2]	Intra-mural	Extra-mural[2]	Intra-mural	Extra-mural[2]	Intra-mural	Extra-mural[2]
Defence	692	1 562	804	1 429	774	1 639	818	1 436	784	1 716	828	1 718
Research councils	599	823	593	851	608	852	608	865	644	894	667	1 024
Higher Education Institutes	-	1 018	-	1 027	-	1 033	-	1 085	-	1 157	-	1 276
Other programmes	374	572	290	628	253	681	266	714	274	810	283	841
Total (excluding NHS)	1 665	3 975	1 686	3 936	1 635	4 205	1 692	4 100	1 703	4 577	1 778	4 859

1 See chapter text.
2 Including work performed overseas and excluding monies spent with other government departments.

Source: Office for National Statistics: 01633 813109

19.3 Net central government expenditure on research and development[1], using European Union objectives for R&D expenditure

United Kingdom

£ millions

		1990 /91	1991 /92	1992 /93	1993 /94	1994 /95	1995 /96	1996 /97	1997 /98	1998 /99	1999 /00	2000 /01
Exploration and exploitation of the earth	KDVP	145.2	143.9	120.5	98.8	106.8	105.2	95.4	81.3	78.5	79.5	85.8
Infrastructure and general planning of land-use	KDVQ	74.1	64.2	85.6	96.7	98.1	94.1	98.8	98.9	103.5	104.4	79.0
Control of environmental pollution	KDVR	70.3	71.9	69.5	108.7	117.2	131.8	128.7	136.2	142.8	147.0	151.1
Protection and promotion of human health (ex NHS)	KDVS	292.0	298.4	341.5	383.1	397.2	416.0	427.4	444.8	450.1	519.5	530.6
Production, distribution and rational utilisation of energy	KDVT	141.7	133.0	120.0	96.8	55.5	52.3	43.2	41.0	28.0	29.0	31.9
Agricultural production and technology	KDVU	198.6	216.2	261.1	284.6	263.4	281.9	257.0	268.9	255.5	260.6	266.6
Industrial production and technology	KDVV	478.8	399.0	394.1	458.7	184.4	165.8	144.6	116.9	61.6	56.5	108.4
Social structures and relationships	KDVW	110.8	115.5	141.9	149.1	141.9	137.1	120.7	113.8	154.7	217.6	270.8
Exploration and exploitation of space	KDVX	155.2	134.2	149.1	187.4	161.5	153.0	164.1	164.4	142.5	142.7	146.3
Research financed from General University Funds	KDVY	835.0	919.1	963.3	968.4	1 017.9	1 018.6	1 027.5	1 033.3	1 085.1	1 157.1	1 276.1
Non-oriented research	KDVZ	287.6	287.6	337.1	267.3	612.5	653.5	680.5	671.0	677.0	700.5	789.3
Other civil research	KDWA	11.0	35.5	23.8	34.0	22.2	24.7	20.5	21.6	25.8	20.6	22.2
Defence	KDWB	2 154.7	2 208.8	2 071.1	2 268.6	2 021.9	2 098.9	2 143.5	2 312.1	2 099.5	2 347.3	2 384.1
Total (excluding NHS)	KDWC	4 955.1	5 027.4	5 078.6	5 402.3	5 200.4	5 332.9	5 351.8	5 504.2	5 304.5	5 782.1	6 142.1

1 See chapter text.

Source: Office for National Statistics: 01633 813109

19.4 Intramural expenditure on business enterprise R&D[1]
At Current Prices and Constant Prices
United Kingdom

£ millions

(i) Current Prices

		Total				Civil				Defence		
		1998	1999	2000		1998	1999	2000		1998	1999	2000
Total	KDWD	10 133	11 302	11 510	KDWN	8 600	9 626	9 838	KDWX	1 533	1 675	1 671
Manufacturing Total	KDWE	8 142	8 995	9 231	KDWO	6 725	7 376	7 582	KDWY	1 417	1 619	1 649
Chemicals	KDWF	2 926	3 253	3 528	KDWP	2 926	3 252	3 527	KDWZ	–	1	–
Mechanical engineering	KDWG	730	712	776	KDWQ	455	434	463	KDXA	276	279	314
Electrical machinery	KJRT	1 320	1 335	1 558	KJTC	916	1 013	1 163	KJUL	404	322	395
Aerospace	KDWJ	1 020	1 235	1 094	KDWT	983	1 159	1 023	KDXD	36	77	71
Transport equipment	KDWK	1 039	1 237	1 091	KDWU	485	535	457	KDXE	554	701	634
Other manufacturing[2]	KDWL	1 108	1 222	1 183	KDWV	960	983	948	KDXF	147	239	235
Services[2]	KDWM	1 668	1 972	1 905	KDWW	1 552	1 915	1 883	KDXG	116	57	22
Other: Total	HFRU	323	335	374	HFRZ	322	335	374	MKFB	–	–	–
Agriculture, hunting and forestry; Fishing	HFRV	102	115	135	HFSA	102	115	135	MKFC	–	–	–
Extractive industries	HFRW	41	42	46	HFSB	41	42	46	MKFD	–	–	–
Electricity, gas and water supply	HFRX	140	137	160	HFSC	140	137	160	MKFE	–	–	–
Construction	HFRY	39	41	34	HFSE	39	41	34	MKFF	–	–	–

(ii) 2000 Prices

		Total				Civil				Defence		
		1998	1999	2000		1998	1999	2000		1998	1999	2000
Total	HFWY	10 569	11 507	11 510	HFXH	8 970	9 801	9 838	HFYM	1 599	1 705	1 671
Manufacturing Total	HFWZ	8 492	9 158	9 231	HFXI	7 014	7 510	7 582	HFYN	1 478	1 648	1 649
Chemicals	HFXA	3 052	3 312	3 528	HFXJ	3 052	3 311	3 527	HFYO	–	1	–
Mechanical engineering	HFXB	761	725	776	HFXK	475	442	463	HFYP	288	284	314
Electrical machinery	HFXC	1 377	1 359	1 558	HFYH	955	1 031	1 163	HFYQ	421	328	395
Aerospace	HFXD	1 064	1 257	1 094	HFYI	1 025	1 180	1 023	HFYR	38	78	71
Transport equipment	HFXE	1 084	1 259	1 091	HFYJ	506	545	457	HFYS	578	714	634
Other manufacturing[2]	HFXF	1 156	1 244	1 183	HFYK	1 001	1 001	948	HFYT	153	243	235
Services[2]	HFXG	1 740	2 208	1 905	HFYL	1 619	1 950	1 883	HFYU	121	58	22
Other: Total	HFSF	337	341	374	HFSK	336	341	374	MKFG	–	–	–
Agriculture, hunting and forestry: Fishing	HFSG	106	117	135	HFSL	106	117	135	MKFH	–	–	–
Extractive industries	HFSH	43	43	46	HFSM	43	43	46	MKFI	–	–	–
Electricity, gas and water supply	HFSI	146	139	160	HFSN	146	139	160	MKFJ	–	–	–
Construction	HFSJ	41	42	34	HFSO	41	42	34	MKFK	–	–	–

1 See chapter text.
2 Data have changed from previous editions of AA due to a product group that was included in services but is now included in other manufacturing.

Source: Office for National Statistics: 01633 813109

19.5 Sources of funds for R&D within Business Enterprises in the United Kingdom[1]

		Total				Civil				Defence		
		1998	1999	2000		1998	1999	2000		1998	1999	2000
Funds for Business Enterprise R&D £m cash terms												
Total	KDYL	10 133	11 302	11 510	KDYT	8 600	9 626	9 838	KDZB	1 533	1 675	1 671
Government funds	KDYM	1 094	1 157	1 013	KDYU	307	316	228	KDZC	787	841	785
Overseas funds	KDYN	2 238	2 570	2 470	KDYV	1 857	2 092	2 003	KDZD	381	478	467
Mainly own funds	KDYO	6 800	7 575	8 026	KDYW	6 435	7 219	7 607	KDZE	365	356	419
Funds for Business Enterprise R&D Percentage												
Total	KDYP	100	100	100	KDYX	100	100	100	KDZF	100	100	100
Government funds	KDYQ	11	10	9	KDYY	4	3	2	KDZG	51	50	47
Overseas funds	KDYR	22	23	21	KDYZ	22	22	20	KDZH	25	29	28
Mainly own funds	KDYS	67	67	70	KDZA	75	75	77	KDZI	24	21	25

1 See chapter text.

Source: Office for National Statistics: 01633 813109

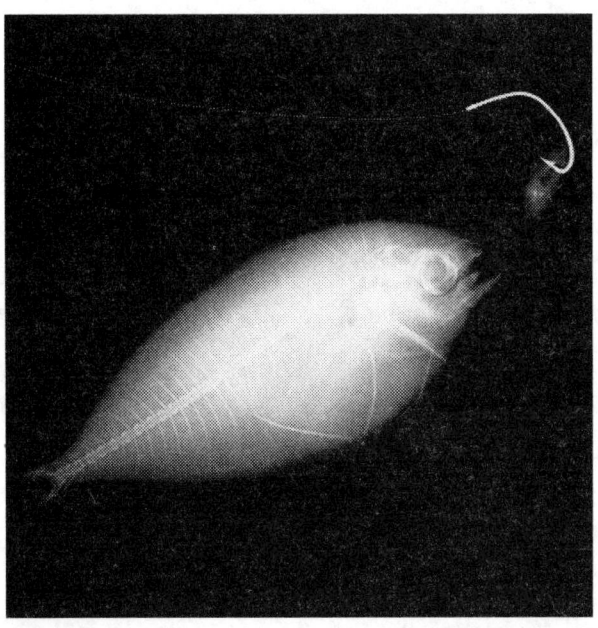

20 Agriculture, fisheries and food

Agriculture, fisheries and food

Output and input *(Tables 20.1 and 20.2)*
For both tables, output is a net of VAT collected on the sale of non-edible products. Figures for total output include subsidies on products, but not other subsidies.

Unspecified crops include turf, other minor crops and arable area payments for fodder maize. Eggs include the value of duck eggs and exports of eggs for hatching. Landlords' expenses are included within farm maintenance, miscellaneous expenditure and depreciation of buildings and works. Also included within "other farming costs" are livestock and crop costs, water costs, insurance premia, bank charges, professional fees, rates, and other farming costs.

Other subsidies
Agri-Environment schemes include Environmentally and Nitrate Sensitive Areas, Countryside Stewardship, Countryside Premium, Tir Cymen, Tir Gofal, Moorland, Habitat, Farm Woodland and Organic Farming Schemes. Included in "other" subsidies are guidance premium for beef and sheep meat production, Pilot Beef and Sheep Extensification Scheme, non-agricultural horse grazing and farm accounts grant as well as historic data for fertiliser and lime grant and payments to small scale cereal producers.

Compensation of employees and interest charges
Total compensation of employees excludes the value of work done by farm labour on own account capital formation in buildings and work. "Interest" relates to interest charges on loans for current farming purposes and buildings and less interest on money held on short-term deposit.

Rent
Rent paid (after deductions) is the rent paid on all tenanted land including "conacre" land in Northern Ireland, less landlords' expenses and the benefit value of dwellings on that land. Rent received (after deductions) is the rent received by farming landowners from renting of land to other farmers, less landlords' expenses and the benefit value of dwellings on that land. Total net rent is the net rent flowing out of the agricultural sector paid to non-farming landowners, including that part of tenanted land in Northern Ireland. (Although there has been some updating of the technical procedures for calculating this figure, it corresponds with the previous net rent variable.)

Agricultural censuses and surveys *(Tables 20.3, 20.5 and 20.13)*
The coverage for holdings includes all main and minor holdings for each country. Scotland now includes minor holdings and Northern Ireland data are now based on all active farm business.

Estimated quantity of crops and grass harvested *(Table 20.4)*
The estimated yields of sugar beet and hops are obtained from production figures supplied by British Sugar plc, and the main hop producers in England and Wales. In Great Britain potato yields are estimated in consultation with the British Potato Council.

Forestry *(Table 20.6)*
Statistics for state forestry are from the Annual Reports and Accounts of Forest Enterprise in Great Britain and the Forest Service in Northern Ireland.

For private forestry in Great Britain, statistics on new planting and restocking are based on records of the Woodland Grant Scheme, and timber removals are estimated from a survey of the largest timber harvesting companies. Productive woodland is based on data obtained from censuses of woodlands and adjusted to reflect subsequent changes. Figures are based on results from the 1995-1999 National Inventory of Woodlands and Trees.

Average weekly earnings and hours of agricultural and horticultural workers *(Tables 20.7 and 20.8)*
Since 1998, data on the Earnings and Hours of Agricultural and Horticultural workers have been collected via an annual telephone survey. This annual survey collects information for a snapshot in time, relating to the month of September. The survey covers seven main categories of workers and in 2001 data were collected on 1,274 workers. Prior to 1998, data were collected from a monthly postal survey, which mainly covered male full-time workers.

The survey provides data which are used by the Agricultural Wages Board when considering wage claims and by the Department for Environment, Food and Rural Affairs in considering the cost of labour in agriculture and horticulture.

Fisheries *(Tables 20.14 and 20.15)*
Data relating to the weight and value of landings of fish in the United Kingdom (Table 20.14) is generally obtained from sales notes completed at fish market auctions.

Fishing fleet information (Table 20.15) is obtained from vessel registers maintained by the Department for Environment, Food and Rural Affairs in England and Wales and the Scottish Executive Agriculture and Fisheries Department.

Estimated average household food consumption in Great Britain - National Food Survey *(Table 20.16)*

The sample
The National Food Survey results are derived from the responses of a random sample of private households throughout Great Britain. Although the survey was extended to include Northern Ireland in 1996, the results given are for Great Britain in order to preserve continuity. The person most responsible for the catering arrangements of the household is designated as the main diary keeper; he or she records details of all items of food for human consumption brought into the home during the course of a week. Until 1997 about 8,000 households in Great Britain participated in the Survey. From 1997 a more efficient sample design was introduced and the sample for Great Britain was reduced to around 6,000 households. A description of the sampling methods is given in the annual reports; the latest is *National Food Survey* 2000.

Household
A group of persons living in the same dwelling and sharing common catering arrangements. The size of

the household is defined in terms of the number of persons who spend at least four nights in the household during the week of the survey and also have at least one meal a day from the household food supply on at least four days. The head of the household and the main diary keeper are regarded as 'persons' in all cases.

Food obtained for consumption

Purchases of selected foods for home consumption during the Survey week (including purchases in bulk and, exceptionally, school milk) plus any garden or allotment produce, etc, consumed during the week. For a few minor miscellaneous items, expenditure is recorded but not the quantity (eg artificial sweeteners). The survey also includes information on confectionery and soft and alcoholic drinks brought home and, published from 1994, on food and drink consumed outside the home.

Although the quantity of food purchased or obtained free during the survey week will differ from the actual consumption of an individual household, the average quantity of food for a large number of households will equal the average consumption if there is no general change in the level of larder stocks.

20.1 Outputs, inputs and income at current prices[1]
United Kingdom
Calendar years

£ millions

		1991	1992	1993	1994	1995	1996	1997	1998	1999	2000	2001[2]
Outputs[3]												
Cereals:												
wheat	KFKA	1 689	1 682	1 782	1 723	2 079	2 315	1 851	1 652	1 525	1 580	1 222
barley	KFKB	715	855	844	847	1 108	1 183	977	781	735	685	726
oats	KFKC	52	58	72	82	89	86	71	61	58	65	64
rye, mixed corn and triticale	KFKD	3	4	6	7	9	9	9	8	8	8	6
1. Total production of cereals	KFKF	2 458	2 599	2 704	2 659	3 285	3 593	2 907	2 502	2 326	2 338	2 019
Other crops:												
oilseed rape	KFKG	362	301	410	377	387	434	406	417	371	246	275
linseed	KIBT	39	84	184	39	41	39	52	68	132	34	16
sugar beet	KFKH	310	386	353	343	355	358	329	298	280	252	255
hops	KFKI	21	18	21	20	17	20	20	14	13	11	10
peas and beans for stockfeed	KFKJ	107	124	186	147	135	129	129	112	115	113	141
hay and dried grass	KFKK	28	24	25	27	29	29	28	23	23	22	23
grass and clover seed	KFKL	15	15	14	16	15	21	23	20	19	11	9
straw	LUJX	165	116	219	249	321	222	169	184	188	218	236
unspecified crops[4]	LUJY	44	33	46	55	56	61	52	51	53	51	51
2. Total production of other crops	KFKN	1 091	1 100	1 458	1 273	1 356	1 313	1 207	1 188	1 194	958	1 017
3. Total production of potatoes	KFKO	527	533	390	710	1 095	636	390	630	750	454	600
Horticulture:												
vegetables	KFKP	980	936	915	998	1 067	1 083	962	989	962	877	970
fruit	KFKQ	283	281	272	247	258	292	199	259	257	228	243
ornamentals	KFKR	524	526	567	605	630	678	671	650	715	672	708
fruit, vegetables and tomato seeds	KFKS	6	9	8	7	7	7	7	7	7	7	7
4. Total production of horticulture	KFKT	1 794	1 753	1 762	1 857	1 962	2 060	1 838	1 905	1 941	1 785	1 928
Livestock												
finished cattle and calves	KFKU	2 051	1 999	2 372	2 468	2 580	2 546	2 276	1 982	2 048	2 000	1 809
finished sheep and lambs	KFKV	1 138	1 159	1 245	1 235	1 334	1 295	1 194	1 130	1 025	960	625
finished pigs	KFKW	1 024	1 150	1 044	1 038	1 179	1 374	1 204	888	788	794	751
poultry	KFKX	1 084	1 128	1 267	1 362	1 353	1 526	1 494	1 365	1 272	1 303	1 317
other livestock	KFKY	119	125	128	130	134	143	148	147	147	150	152
5. Total production of livestock	KFLA	5 416	5 561	6 056	6 233	6 580	6 883	6 316	5 513	5 279	5 206	4 654
Livestock products:												
milk	KFLB	2 790	2 925	3 187	3 310	3 498	3 495	3 154	2 709	2 653	2 393	2 818
eggs[5]	KFLC	398	387	413	412	383	453	415	381	344	371	406
clip wool	KFLD	42	41	30	46	46	40	35	24	21	23	16
unspecified livestock products	KFLE	21	23	24	22	24	24	25	21	26	23	19
6. Total production of livestock products	KFLF	3 251	3 376	3 655	3 791	3 951	4 011	3 629	3 135	3 045	2 810	3 260
Capital formation in livestock												
cattle	KUJZ	265	426	624	568	414	297	391	295	203	191	359
sheep	LUKA	129	139	134	151	149	150	198	154	56	48	75
pigs	LUKB	16	18	14	14	16	20	15	5	7	5	6
poultry	LUKC	110	114	117	111	121	130	130	135	125	131	129
7. Total capital formation in livestock	KFLI	520	698	889	844	701	596	735	588	391	374	569

20.1
continued

Outputs, inputs and income at current prices[1]
United Kingdom
Calendar years

£ millions

		1991	1992	1993	1994	1995	1996	1997	1998	1999	2000	2001[2]
Other agricultural activities												
contract work	LUKD	413	437	471	502	553	608	575	571	614	608	612
leasing out milk quota	LUKE	32	42	104	127	136	169	120	99	99	42	4
leasing out ewe premium	LUKF	–	–	5	6	6	5	4	4	4	3	2
leasing out suckler cow premium	LUKG	–	–	1	1	1	1	1	6	3	4	5
8. Total other agricultural activities	LUOS	445	479	580	635	697	783	699	680	720	657	622
9. Total inseparable non-agricultural activities	LUOT	246	267	294	321	325	360	369	418	426	439	457
10. Gross output at basic prices[6]	KFLT	15 749	16 366	17 788	18 321	19 951	20 236	18 090	16 560	16 071	15 022	15 126
11. Total subsidies (less taxes) on product	LUOU	660	804	1 763	1 686	2 107	2 782	2 588	2 436	2 396	2 180	1 943
12. Output at market prices (10-11)	LUOV	15 089	15 562	16 024	16 635	17 845	17 454	15 502	14 123	13 675	12 842	13 183
of which												
transactions within the agricultural industry	LUNP	..	..	..	..	..	..	..	..	..	..	..
feed wheat	LUNQ	95	114	81	75	55	67	77	79	64	33	38
feed barley	LUNR	255	265	233	201	199	206	193	164	148	136	144
feed oats	LUNS	22	19	21	22	16	16	12	12	14	12	12
seed potatoes	LUNT	17	23	13	14	41	34	9	12	30	9	12
straw	LUNU	156	109	207	236	308	212	160	173	176	205	222
contract work	LUNV	413	437	471	502	553	608	575	571	614	608	612
leasing of quota	LUNW	32	42	109	133	144	175	124	109	106	49	11
total capital formation in livestock	LUNX	520	698	889	844	701	596	735	588	391	374	569
Intermediate consumption (expenditure net of reclaimed VAT)												
Feedingstuffs												
compounds[7]	LUNY	1 734	1 671	1 764	1 689	1 806	1 960	1 772	1 524	1 402	1 285	1 404
straights[7]	LUNZ	763	796	834	888	963	937	750	667	632	642	699
feed purchased from other farms	LUOA	371	399	336	297	271	289	282	254	227	181	194
other costs	LUOB	–	69	72	76	84	80	71	68	69	..	..
13. Total feedingstuffs	KFMB	2 868	2 865	2 934	2 875	3 040	3 185	2 804	2 444	2 261	2 108	2 297
Seeds												
cereals	KFMC	123	114	114	112	121	124	103	84	94	82	94
other	KFMD	189	201	183	213	262	256	233	247	237	189	198
14. Total seeds	KFME	312	315	296	326	384	380	337	331	331	271	292
15. Total fertilisers and lime	KFMM	918	834	763	790	923	1 040	983	827	752	753	785
16. Pesticides	KFMN	545	531	547	557	590	647	675	655	620	611	555
Farm maintenance												
occupier	KCOZ	202	226	248	282	304	297	298	257	251	231	242
landlord[8]	KCPA	64	64	64	64	64	68	72	71	69	68	67
17. Total farm maintenance	KCPB	265	291	312	346	368	365	370	328	320	298	309
Miscellaneous expenditure												
machinery repairs	KFMO	612	601	638	631	722	746	722	700	700	654	676
machinery fuel and oil	KFMP	335	327	349	343	354	400	397	368	402	488	492
veterinary expenses and medicines	KCPC	222	231	253	274	289	298	308	288	271	264	252
power and fuel (mainly electricity)	KCPD	252	245	246	243	237	248	233	231	222	242	224
imported livestock	LUOC	31	37	35	33	25	19	23	15	16	18	12
straw for bedding	LUOD	156	109	207	236	308	212	160	173	176	205	222
contract work	LUOE	413	437	471	502	553	608	575	571	614	608	612
leasing of quota	LUOF	32	42	109	133	144	175	124	109	106	49	11
other farming costs[8,9]	KCPG	1 440	1 593	1 646	1 697	1 718	1 883	2 007	1 959	1 980	1 936	1 980
18. Total miscellaneous expenses	KCPH	2 874	3 012	3 324	3 473	3 734	3 921	3 896	3 800	3 847	3 716	3 751

20.1
continued

Outputs, inputs and income at current prices[1]
United Kingdom
Calendar years

£ millions

		1991	1992	1993	1994	1995	1996	1997	1998	1999	2000	2001[2]
19. Total intermediate consumption	KCPM	8 369	8 420	8 772	8 954	9 629	10 186	9 694	8 983	8 754	8 487	8 707
20. Gross value added at basic prices (10-19)	LUOG	7 380	7 947	9 016	9 367	10 322	10 050	8 395	7 576	7 317	6 535	6 418
Consumption of Fixed Capital												
buildings and works	LUOH	636	568	568	582	640	681	671	683	700	690	679
landlord[8,10]	KCPP	115	105	105	110	120	94	85	83	78	77	76
other	KCPQ	520	463	463	472	520	587	586	600	622	612	603
plant, machinery and vehicles	KCPR	1 098	1 110	1 142	1 180	1 230	1 296	1 327	1 333	1 320	1 285	1 285
cattle	LUOI	318	330	577	529	416	314	393	316	207	288	320
sheep	LUOJ	148	120	137	141	174	189	155	106	68	93	83
pigs	LUOK	16	18	14	15	17	18	15	9	8	7	6
poultry	LUOL	109	118	108	108	121	130	123	147	137	129	127
21. Total Consumption of Fixed Capital	KCPS	2 324	2 263	2 546	2 554	2 598	2 629	2 685	2 594	2 441	2 492	2 499
22. Net value added (at basic prices)(20-21)	KCPT	5 055	5 684	6 470	6 813	7 724	7 422	5 710	4 983	4 877	4 043	3 919
Other subsidies												
animal disease compensation	LUOM	7	6	10	7	7	5	15	24	28	41	29
set-aside	LUON	–	–	142	206	198	159	90	88	170	127	184
Agri-Environment schemes[11]	ZBXC	13	27	38	47	61	73	92	114	131	156	220
less favoured area payments[12]	LUOO	–	–	–	–	–	–	–	–	–	–	164
vehicle licenses	ZBXD	32	34	40	42	46	54	56	59	59	59	48
23. Total other subsidies less taxes	LUOP	–32	–21	126	192	193	157	113	138	238	232	514
24. Net value added at factor cost(22+23)	LUOQ	5 024	5 663	6 596	7 006	7 917	7 578	5 823	5 120	5 114	4 275	4 433
25. Total compensation of employees[13]	LUOR	1 779	1 784	1 787	1 827	1 836	1 881	1 930	1 977	2 028	1 897	1 914
26. Interest[14]	KCPU	837	715	524	536	587	553	622	681	596	633	579
Rent												
net rent paid[15]	ZBXE	161	175	179	182	176	303	336	331	321	310	302
net rent received[16]	ZBXF	..	..	..	..	..	74	80	81	82	79	72
27. Net rent expenditure	KCPV	161	175	179	182	176	229	256	250	238	232	230
28. Total income from farming (24-25-26-27)	KCQB	2 247	2 989	4 107	4 460	5 318	4 915	3 016	2 212	2 252	1 513	1 710

1 See chapter text.
2 Provisional.
3 Output is net of VAT collected on the sale of non-edible products. Figures for total output include subsidies on products, but not other subsidies.
4 Includes turf, other minor crops and arable area payments for fodder maize.
5 Includes the value of duck eggs.
6 Gross Output at basic prices includes subsidies (less taxes) on products.
7 For 1991 the split between compounds and straights has been estimated based on the split present in later years.
8 Landlords' expenses are included within farm maintenance, miscellaneous expenditure and depreciation of buildings and works.
9 Includes livestock and crop costs, water costs, insurance premiums, bank charges, professional fees, rates, and other farming costs.
10 A more empirically based methodology for calculating landlords' depreciation was introduced in 2000. The new series has been linked with the old one using a smoothing procedure for the transition year of 1996.
11 Includes Environmentally and Nitrate Sensitive Areas, Countryside Stewardship, Countryside Premium, Tir Cymen, Tir Gofal, Moorland, Habitat, Farm Woodland and Organic Farming Schemes.

12 From 2001, this is the land area based schemes which replaced the Hill Livestock Compensatory Allowance Scheme in 2001. These are Tir Mynydd in Wales, Less Favoured Area Compensatory Allowances Scheme in Northern Ireland, Less Favoured Areas Support Scheme in Scotland and Hill Farm Allowance in England.
13 Excludes the value of work done by farm labour on own account capital formation in buildings and works.
14 Interest charges on loans for current farming purposes and buildings and works less interest on money held on short term deposit.
15 Rent paid on all tenanted land (including 'conacre' land in Northern Ireland) less landlords' expenses, landlords' depreciation and the benefit value of dwellings on that land.
16 Rent received by farming landowners from renting of land to other farmers less landlords' expenses. This series began in 1996 following a revision to the methodology of calculating net rent.

Source: Department for Environment, Food and Rural Affairs: 01904 455089

20.2 Output and input volume indices[1]
United Kingdom
Calendar years

1995=100

		1991	1992	1993	1994	1995	1996	1997	1998	1999	2000	2001[2]
Outputs[3]												
Cereals:												
wheat	LUKH	103	99	90	93	100	112	104	108	103	116	81
barley	LUKI	95	108	89	87	100	112	113	96	95	94	96
oats	LUKJ	79	82	78	98	100	96	94	95	87	104	99
rye, mixed corn and triticale	LUKK	79	91	86	91	100	97	96	90	106	118	96
1. Total production of cereals	LUKL	100	101	89	91	100	112	107	103	100	109	87
Other crops:												
oilseed rape	LUKM	120	113	96	102	100	118	131	135	137	94	99
linseed	LUKN	202	279	239	116	100	107	132	178	375	53	48
sugar beet	LUKO	103	120	115	103	100	124	131	119	126	108	97
hops	LUKP	146	116	128	108	100	126	120	82	70	63	57
peas and beans for stockfeed	LUKQ	116	120	161	129	100	101	123	116	124	134	159
hay and dried grass	LUKR	119	104	106	103	100	102	98	88	90	87	83
grass and clover seed	LUKS	136	126	116	133	100	98	107	97	105	80	61
straw	LUKT	75	65	74	78	100	85	74	71	63	66	63
unspecified crops[4]	LUKU	112	94	117	115	100	89	74	64	62	54	48
2. Total production of other crops	LUKV	110	111	110	100	100	108	114	110	118	92	90
3. Total production of potatoes	LUKW	97	121	105	98	100	108	102	90	107	94	97
Horticulture:												
vegetables	LUKX	111	113	106	105	100	106	101	99	100	93	90
fruit	LUKY	128	129	122	106	100	105	70	89	93	84	89
ornamentals	LUKZ	104	107	108	103	100	95	98	95	98	101	101
fruit, vegetable and tomato seeds	LULA	111	120	103	98	100	98	96	97	92	94	98
4. Total production of horticulture	LULB	111	113	109	105	100	102	96	97	99	95	94
Livestock												
finished cattle and calves	LULC	106	98	94	100	100	73	79	81	82	80	71
finished sheep and lambs	LULD	107	103	102	99	100	94	94	100	99	94	66
finished pigs	LULE	101	101	102	106	100	101	110	112	102	86	79
poultry	LULF	84	85	90	96	100	104	106	108	106	106	110
other livestock	LULG	98	99	101	100	100	102	102	102	102	102	101
5. Total production of livestock	LULH	99	96	96	100	100	89	94	97	95	91	82
Livestock products:												
milk	LULI	102	101	102	104	100	100	101	99	101	99	101
eggs[5]	LULJ	106	104	102	102	100	100	104	105	101	106	115
clip wool	LULK	105	105	100	97	100	95	97	103	95	92	70
unspecified	LULL	102	112	111	92	100	84	90	79	94	83	69
6. Total production of livestock products	LULM	102	102	102	103	100	100	101	100	101	99	102
Capital formation in livestock:												
cattle	LULN	89	100	101	101	100	98	96	92	94	81	95
sheep	LULO	76	109	95	126	100	88	115	124	93	58	122
pigs	LULP	116	119	114	116	100	110	119	95	100	66	64
poultry	LULQ	94	91	100	100	100	102	108	101	95	100	104
7. Total capital formation in livestock	LULR	86	101	100	105	100	97	105	103	96	85	106
Other agricultural activities												
contract work	LULS	92	91	93	95	100	106	107	113	122	118	119
leasing out milk quota	LULT	65	68	79	91	100	103	112	120	130	125	39
leasing out ewe premium	LULU	83	83	83	92	100	75	53	62	61	57	54
leasing out suckler cow premium	LULV	50	50	50	54	100	81	66	453	242	237	244
8. Total other non-agricultural activities	LULW	88	87	90	94	100	105	108	115	123	119	115
9. Total inseparable non-agricultural activities	LULX	86	91	98	103	100	108	107	117	118	117	118

20.2
continued

Output and input volume indices[1]
United Kingdom
Calendar years

1995=100

		1991	1992	1993	1994	1995	1996	1997	1998	1999	2000	2001[2]
10. **Gross output** (at basic prices)[6]	LULY	100	101	99	100	100	100	101	101	102	98	93
of which												
transactions within the agricultural industry												
feed wheat	LULZ	161	190	141	146	100	122	176	210	175	98	102
feed barley	LUMA	121	124	107	105	100	105	126	124	114	111	115
feed oats	LUMB	113	94	95	119	100	89	82	100	118	107	103
seed potatoes	LUMC	104	132	121	88	100	119	86	79	84	76	56
straw	LUMD	74	64	73	78	100	85	73	70	61	64	61
contract work	LUME	92	91	93	95	100	106	107	113	122	118	119
leasing of quota	LUMF	65	68	79	91	100	101	109	121	127	122	50
total capital formation in livestock	LUMG	86	101	100	105	100	97	105	103	96	85	106
Intermediate Consumption (formerly known as inputs) (Expenditure net of reclaimed VAT)												
Feedingstuffs:												
compounds[7]	LUMH	95	96	98	100	100	101	97	95	98	90	93
straights[7]	LUMI	82	84	85	96	100	89	80	85	86	90	86
feed purchased from other farms	LUMJ	128	135	113	114	100	108	133	140	127	108	112
other costs	LUMK	94	94	97	100	100	99	98	100	..	..	..
13. Total feedingstuffs	LUML	94	96	96	100	100	98	95	95	96	92	92
Seeds:												
cereals	LUMM	107	93	96	95	100	104	95	83	93	84	94
other	LUMN	95	103	97	100	100	102	100	99	96	96	100
14. Total seeds	LUMO	99	99	97	98	100	103	99	94	95	92	98
15. Total fertilisers and lime	LUMP	107	103	100	95	100	103	108	103	97	87	82
16. Pesticides	LUMQ	99	94	96	93	100	104	108	112	108	113	106
Farm maintenance:												
occupier	LUMR	75	83	89	98	100	97	96	82	81	73	76
landlord[8]	LUMS	105	105	104	102	100	97	97	95	93	92	93
17. Total farm maintenance	LUMT	80	87	92	99	100	97	96	85	84	77	79
Miscellaneous expenditure:												
machinery repairs	LUMU	102	93	94	91	100	98	94	91	89	82	82
machinery fuel and oil	LUMV	94	99	98	102	100	96	100	107	104	91	95
veterinary expenses and medicines	LUMW	78	81	88	95	100	102	104	97	91	89	87
power and fuel (mainly electricity)	LUMX	108	99	101	102	100	101	100	109	103	100	94
imported livestock	LUMY	181	209	125	124	100	85	108	76	..	..	..
straw for bedding	LUMZ	74	64	73	78	100	85	73	70	61	64	61
contract work	LUNA	92	91	93	95	100	106	107	113	122	118	119
leasing of quota	LUNB	65	68	79	91	100	101	109	121	127	122	50
other farming costs[8,9]	LUNC	96	101	101	101	100	106	109	104	102	98	100
18. Total miscellaneous expenses	LUND	92	92	94	96	100	102	103	100	99	95	95
19. Total intermediate consumption (formerly known as Gross input)	LUNE	95	95	95	97	100	101	101	99	98	94	93
20. **Gross Value Added** (10-19)	LUNF	107	108	102	102	100	99	101	103	107	104	91
Consumption of fixed capital:												
buildings and works	LUNG	99	100	100	100	100	102	102	101	99	97	94
landlord[8,10]	LUNH	106	96	95	95	100	71	60	57	56	55	55
other	MBGE	98	101	101	102	100	109	111	111	109	107	104
plant, machinery and vehicles	LUNI	102	100	99	99	100	101	102	100	98	96	93
cattle	LUNJ	96	79	88	87	100	105	94	89	91	109	88
sheep	LUNK	77	82	86	102	100	97	79	81	92	96	117
pigs	LUNL	103	104	101	110	100	92	101	111	98	83	53
poultry	LUNM	94	96	92	98	100	103	103	110	104	99	97
21. Total consumption of Fixed Capital	LUNN	97	94	96	97	100	102	99	98	97	97	93
22. **Net value added** (at basic prices)	LUNO	111	114	104	104	100	98	101	106	112	108	88

1 See chapter text.
2 Provisional.
3 Output is net of VAT collected on the sale of non-edible products. Figures for total output include subsidies on products, but not other subsidies.
4 Includes turf, other minor crops and arable area payments for fodder maize.
5 Includes the value of duck eggs.
6 Gross Output at basic prices includes subsidies (less taxes) on products.
7 For 1991 the split between compounds and straights has been estimated based on the split present in later years.

8 Landlords' expenses are included within farm maintenance, miscellaneous expenditure and depreciation of buildings and works.
9 Includes livestock and crop costs, water costs, insurance premiums, bank charges, professional fees, rates, and other farming costs.
10 A more empirically based methodology for calculating landlords' depreciation was introduced in 2000. The new series has been linked with the old one using a smoothing procedure for the transition year of 1996.

Source: Department for Environment, Food and Rural Affairs: 01904 455080

20.3

Agriculture land-use
United Kingdom
Area at the June census[1]

Thousand hectares

		1991	1992	1993	1994	1995	1996	1997	1998	1999	2000	2001
Total Agricultural area	BFAH	18 853	18 849	18 890	18 850	18 746	18 750	18 653	18 604	18 579	18 311	18 555
Crops	BFAA	4 957	4 982	4 520	4 470	4 544	4 722	4 990	4 971	4 709	4 665	4 454
Bare fallow	BFAB	67	53	50	46	43	37	29	34	33	37	43
Total tillage	KIJR	5 024	5 035	4 569	4 516	4 586	4 759	5 020	5 005	4 742	4 702	4 497
All grass under 5 years old	KFEM	1 608	1 584	1 582	1 456	1 407	1 395	1 405	1 301	1 226	1 226	1 205
Total arable land	KFEN	6 632	6 618	6 152	5 972	5 993	6 154	6 425	6 306	5 968	5 928	5 702
All grasses 5 years old and over	KFEO	5 327	5 279	5 274	5 388	5 375	5 354	5 282	5 364	5 449	5 364	5 584
Total tillage and grass	KFEP	11 959	11 897	11 426	11 360	11 368	11 507	11 706	11 671	11 417	11 292	11 286
Sole right rough grazing	BFAD	4 950	4 943	4 879	4 825	4 785	4 760	4 657	4 621	4 575	4 445	4 435
Set aside[2]	DMNF	97	160	677	728	633	509	306	313	572	567	800
All other land on agricultural holdings including woodland	BFAE	614	618	680	712	734	751	763	773	789	780	801
Total land on agricultural holdings	BFAF	17 620	17 619	17 661	17 626	17 520	17 527	17 432	17 377	17 352	17 083	17 323
Common rough grazing (estimated)	BFAG	1 233	1 230	1 229	1 224	1 226	1 223	1 221	1 227	1 227	1 228	1 232
Crops	BFAA	4 957	4 982	4 520	4 470	4 544	4 722	4 990	4 971	4 709	4 665	4 454
Cereals	BFAJ	3 501	3 489	3 033	3 043	3 182	3 359	3 514	3 418	3 141	3 348	3 014
Wheat	BFAK	1 981	2 067	1 759	1 811	1 859	1 976	2 036	2 045	1 847	2 086	1 635
Barley	BFAL	1 395	1 299	1 166	1 108	1 193	1 269	1 359	1 253	1 179	1 128	1 245
Oats	BFAM	104	100	92	109	112	96	100	98	92	109	112
Mixed corn	BFAN	4	4	3	3	3	3	2	2	2	2	3
Rye[3]	BFAO	9	8	6	7	8	8	9	10	8	7	5
Triticale[4]	DMNH	10	11	7	6	7	7	8	11	13	16	14
Other arable crops (excluding potatoes)	DMNI	1 074	1 115	1 128	1 073	993	937	1 125	1 210	1 211	979	1 102
Oilseed rape	BFAP	440	421	377	404	354	356	445	507	417	332	404
Sugar beet not for stock feeding[3]	BFAQ	196	197	197	195	196	199	196	189	183	173	177
Hops[5]	DMNJ	4	4	3	3	3	3	3	3	3	2	1
Peas for harvesting dry and field beans	DMNK	203	208	244	228	195	178	197	213	202	208	276
Linseed[6]	DMNL	92	144	150	58	54	49	73	100	209	71	31
Other crops	DMNM	141	141	157	185	195	204	210	200	197	192	214
Potatoes	BFAR	177	181	171	164	172	178	166	164	178	166	165
Horticultural	BFAV	204	198	188	189	187	189	184	180	179	172	173
Vegetables grown in the open	DMNN	139	135	126	127	130	132	126	125	126	119	120
Orchard fruit	BFBG	34	33	32	32	28	28	30	30	28	28	28
Soft fruit	DMNO	15	14	13	13	12	12	11	10	9	10	9
Ornamentals[7]	DMNP	14	14	14	14	15	14	14	14	13	14	14
Glasshouse crops	DMNQ	2	2	2	2	2	2	2	2	2	2	2

1 Includes estimates for minor holdings for all countries. See chapter text.
2 Figures are for England only in 1991 and Great Britain only in 1992.
3 Figures are for England and Wales only.
4 Figures are for Great Britain only.

5 Figures are for England only
6 Figures are for England and Wales only in 1991 and Great Britain only in 1992
7 Includes non-commercial orchards.

Source: Agricultural Departments: 01904 455332

20.4 Estimated quantity of crops and grass harvested[1,2]
United Kingdom

Thousand tonnes

		1990	1991	1992	1993	1994	1995	1996	1997	1998	1999	2000
Cereals												
Wheat	KFQA	14 035	14 362	14 095	12 890	13 320	14 310	16 100	15 020	15 450	14 870	16 700
Barley	KFQB	7 911	7 632	7 368	6 050	5 950	6 840	7 790	7 830	6 620	6 580	6 490
Oats	KFQC	520	522	503	480	600	615	590	575	585	540	640
Mixed corn for threshing	KFQD	17	15	16	14	13	16	12	11	7	11	13
Rye for threshing	KFQE	40	49	37	30	43	43	51	53	55	43	44
Maize for threshing	KFQF	1 035	1 695	1 975	2 730	..	..	..	..	..	..	..
Potatoes												
Early crop	KFQG	437	359	411	426	337	373	325	386	336	341	..
Main crop	KFQH	6 106	6 000	7 402	6 647	6 203	6 033	6 900	6 739	6 081	6 759	..
Fodder crops												
Beans for stockfeeding	KFQI	474	423	445	612	454	319	318	377	378	397	450
Turnips, swedes	KFQJ	920	835	760	620	..	..	..	..	..	..	..
Fodder beet and mangolds	KFQK	640	715	710	655	..	..	..	..	..	..	..
Maize for threshing or stock-feeding	KFQL	..	..	..	..	..	..	..	..	..	..	..
Kale, cabbage, savoys and kohl rabi	KFQN	535	610	515	485	..	..	..	..	..	..	..
Peas harvested dry for stock-feeding	KFQP	320	224	209	266	246	229	239	297	259	286	253
Other crops												
Sugar beet[3,4]	KFQQ	7 902	8 701	10 148	9 666	8 720	8 431	10 420	11 084	10 002	10 584	9 335
Rape grown for oilseed	KFQR	1 258	1 278	1 166	1 100	1 243	1 224	1 415	1 527	1 566	1 737	1 129
Hops[4]	KFQS	5	6	5	6	5	4	6	5	4	..	..
Horticultural crops												
Vegetables grown in the open												
Brussels sprouts	KFQW	91	100	98	102	93	74	83	74	71	79	63
Cabbage (including savoys and spring greens)	KFQX	406	395	379	381	356	377	348	280	286	268	251
Cauliflowers	KFQY	295	317	309	312	268	247	217	191	192	168	152
Carrots	KFQZ	492	536	532	605	567	525	679	591	626	702	455
Parsnips	KFRA	46	50	56	69	65	66	88	92	99	95	77
Turnips and swedes	KFRB	143	156	161	141	137	124	136	107	121	126	106
Beetroot	KFRC	87	83	104	84	89	72	72	72	66	61	72
Onions, Dry bulb	KFRD	224	231	216	322	245	254	313	329	376	406	379
Onions, Salad	KFRE	23	26	24	25	25	25	30	25	25	27	14
Leeks	KFRF	64	72	66	60	57	61	44	49	55	46	40
Broad beans	KFRG	13	20	17	11	12	11	10	10	13	12	13
Runner beans including French	KFRH	28	37	39	46	36	30	35	35	30	24	22
Peas, Green for market	KFRI	8	8	6	6	6	8	7	8	7	7	7
Peas, Green for processing	KFRJ	238	223	211	209	181	198	216	168	152	143	174
Celery	KFRK	46	49	44	41	42	39	38	39	35	40	36
Lettuce	KFRL	198	193	174	145	179	192	187	158	152	156	138
Rhubarb	KFRM	27	21	20	22	20	20	20	18	21	23	19
Protected crops												
Tomatoes	KFRN	134	133	122	110	108	113	117	115	109	117	113
Cucumbers	KFRO	101	104	90	104	83	88	86	82	84	84	80
Lettuce	KFRP	50	47	44	37	33	30	27	24	21	20	19
Fruit crops												
Total Dessert Apples	KFRQ	179.0	148.3	164.7	167.1	175.9	138.5	105.4	96.0	97.8	133.9	101.3
Total Culinary Apples	KFRR	125.7	157.2	161.8	158.7	130.2	134.9	118.5	91.1	85.9	112.4	99.5
Pears	KFRS	34.1	36.0	30.8	30.7	32.5	29.7	35.8	33.0	26.3	22.7	26.6
Plums	KFRT	7.2	21.5	21.1	11.8	11.0	14.4	19.6	12.1	6.4	9.3	5.3
Cherries	KFRU	1.5	1.0	3.8	2.4	1.3	3.5	3.6	0.6	0.9	1.3	0.4
Soft fruit	KFRV	102.4	102.2	94.1	94.5	77.4	76.5	81.6	59.4	60.5	65.9	60.7

1 For vegetables; output marketed for the calendar year; for horticultural crops output marketed for the crop year.
2 Except for sugar beet and hops, the production area for England and Wales is the area returned at the June census together with estimates for very small holdings (known as minor holdings). In Scotland and Northern Ireland the area returned at June is also the production area, except that estimates for minor holdings are included in Scotland for potatoes and in Nortern Ireland for barley, oats and potatoes.

3 From 1991 figures are adjusted to constant 16% sugar content.
4 See chapter text.

Source: Agricultural Departments: 01904 455332

20.5 Cattle, sheep, pigs and poultry on agricultural holdings[1]
United Kingdom
At June each year

Thousands

		1991	1992	1993	1994	1995	1996	1997	1998	1999	2000	2001
Total cattle and calves	**BFCG**	12 003	11 924	11 851	11 954	11 857	12 040	11 637	11 519	11 423	11 135	10 602
of which:												
dairy cows	**BFCH**	2 771	2 683	2 668	2 716	2 603	2 587	2 478	2 439	2 440	2 336	2 251
beef cows	**BFCI**	1 700	1 731	1 784	1 809	1 840	1 864	1 862	1 947	1 924	1 842	1 708
heifers in calf	**BFCJ**	738	768	803	775	775	818	848	787	763	718	701
Total sheep and lambs	**BFCM**	44 166	44 540	44 436	43 813	43 304	42 086	42 823	44 471	44 656	42 264	36 716
of which:												
ewes and shearlings	**CKUQ**	20 665	20 732	20 881	20 861	20 830	20 550	20 696	21 260	21 458	20 449	17 921
lambs under one year old	**BFCP**	22 213	22 607	22 394	21 758	21 350	20 443	21 032	22 138	22 092	20 857	17 769
Total pigs	**BFCQ**	7 695	7 707	7 853	7 892	7 627	7 590	8 072	8 146	7 284	6 482	5 845
of which:												
sows in pig and other sows for breeding	**CKUU**	690	683	698	691	654	649	683	675	603	537	527
gilts in pig	**CKUR**	109	110	117	106	101	107	116	103	85	73	71
Total fowls	**KPSV**	128 025	124 842	131 093	126 653	127 035	..	..	..	..	..	..
of which:												
table fowls including broilers	**CKUT**	76 111	73 748	79 940	75 696	77 177	..	..	98 244	101 625	105 689	112 531
laying fowls[2]	**CKUV**	33 416	33 348	32 965	32 682	31 837	..	34 286	29 483	29 258	28 687	29 895
growing pullets	**CKUW**	11 102	10 849	10 750	10 388	10 210	..	11 510	9 860	9 583	9 461	9 367

1 Includes estimates for minor holdings for all countries. See chapter text.
2 Excludes fowls laying eggs for hatching.

Source: Department of Agriculture and Rural Development Farming Statistics:
01904 455332

20.6 Forestry[1]
United Kingdom

Area-thousand hectares, volume-thousand m³ overbark standing[2]

	1980	1990	1998	1999	2000	2001	2002
Woodland area[3]							
United Kingdom	2 175	2 400	2 758	2 775	2 793	2 790	2 800
England[4]	948	958	1 093	1 097	1 103	1 100[5]	1 104
Scotland[4]	920	1 120	1 298	1 308	1 318	1 317[5]	1 324
Wales[4]	241	248	286	288	289	289	288
Northern Ireland	67	74	81	82	83	83	84
Forestry Commission / Forest Service	946	956	895	891	886	861[5]	855
Other[6]	1 230	1 443	1 863	1 884	1 907	1 929	1 945
Conifer	1 372	1 576	1 651	1 656	1 663	1 660	1 658
Broadleaved[7]	804	824	1 107	1 120	1 131	1 130	1 143

	1991/92	1992/93	1993/94	1994/95	1995/96	1996/97	1997/98	1998/99	1999/00	2000/01	2001/02
New Planting[8]											
United Kingdom	18.0	19.0	18.6	19.9	16.4	17.2	16.7	16.7	17.4	18.3	13.4
England	4.0	5.1	6.2	5.1	4.4	4.4	4.1	4.9	5.5	5.5	4.5
Scotland	12.7	12.1	10.5	13.4	10.6	11.7	11.4	10.5	10.4	11.7	8.0
Wales	0.4	0.4	0.6	0.6	0.4	0.4	0.5	0.6	0.7	0.4	0.3
Northern Ireland	0.9	1.3	1.3	0.9	1.0	0.8	0.6	0.7	0.8	0.7	0.7
Forestry Commission / Forest Service	3.4	2.8	1.8	1.2	0.6	0.6	0.2	0.2	0.3	0.3	0.3
Other[9]	14.6	16.2	16.8	18.7	15.8	16.6	16.4	16.5	17.2	18.0	13.1
Conifer	11.6	10.1	7.4	9.4	7.4	7.7	7.0	6.6	6.5	5.2	3.8
Broadleaved	6.5	8.9	11.2	10.5	8.9	9.5	9.7	10.1	10.9	13.2	9.7
Restocking[8]											
United Kingdom	16.6	17.0	16.8	14.6	13.9	15.0	14.1	14.0	15.1	15.2	13.7
England	6.9	6.7	6.4	4.9	4.2	4.3	4.3	4.0	3.8	3.8	3.3
Scotland	6.8	7.5	7.6	6.6	6.8	7.2	6.3	6.3	8.0	8.0	7.8
Wales	2.4	2.4	2.4	2.6	2.3	3.0	2.7	3.0	2.6	2.2	1.9
Northern Ireland	0.5	0.5	0.5	0.6	0.6	0.6	0.7	0.6	0.6	1.1	0.8
Forestry Commission / Forest Service	8.7	8.9	8.4	8.4	8.4	8.4	8.5	8.5	8.8	8.9	9.1
Other[9]	7.8	8.1	8.5	6.2	6.6	6.6	5.6	5.6	6.3	6.2	4.6
Conifer	11.8	11.5	11.5	11.0	10.9	11.4	11.2	11.3	11.9	12.2	11.4
Broadleaved	4.8	5.5	5.3	3.6	3.0	3.4	2.9	2.8	3.2	2.9	2.3

	1994	1995	1996	1997	1998	1999	2000	2001
Wood Production (volume)								
United Kingdom	8 540	8 690	8 650	9 340	9 160	9 740	10 430	10 710
Great Britain								
Softwood	7 350	7 440	7 510	8 170	8 070	8 660	9 310	9 600
Forestry Commission	4 320	4 130	4 290	4 570	4 830	5 440	5 530	5 140
Private Woodland	3 030	3 310	3 220	3 600	3 250	3 210	3 780	4 460
Hardwood[10]	950	990	880	910	800	760	740	710
Northern Ireland[11]	250	250	250	260	290	320	380	400

1 See chapter text.
2 Overbark standing is the volume of wood including the bark before trees are felled.
3 Areas as at 31 March.
4 For England, Scotland and Wales, 1980 woodland area figures are the published results from the 1979-1982 Census of Woodlands and Trees and figures for 1990 are adjusted to reflect subsequent changes. From 1998 onwards they are based on results from the 1995-1999 National Inventory of Woodlands and Trees, adjusted to reflect subsequent changes.
5 The apparent fall in woodland cover in 2001 is due to the reclassification of Forestry Commission open land within the forest.
6 "Other" is private woodland and non-Forestry Commission / Forest Service public woodland.

7 Broadleaved includes coppice. For data based on 1979-82 Census, all scrub and other non-plantation woodland have been assumed to be broadleaved.
8 Figures shown are for the areas of new planting and restocking in the year to 31 March.
9 "Other" figures are for grant aided planting on non-Forestry Commission/ Forest Service woodland. They exclude areas planted without the aid of grants.
10 Hardwood is timber from broadleaved species. Most hardwood production comes from private woodlands; the figures are estimates based on reported deliveries to wood processing industries.
11 Most Northern Ireland production is from the Forest Service. The figures shown include Forest Service estimates of private sector production.

Sources: Forest Service Agency;
Department of Agriculture and Rural Development (Northern Ireland);
Forestry Commission: 0131 334 0303

20.7 Average weekly earnings and hours of male agricultural workers[1]
England and Wales
At September in each year

		1996	1997	1998	1999	2000	2001
Average weekly earnings (£)	LQML	288.33	286.01	301.24	301.22	298.24	332.66
95% confidence interval		(+/-£13.59)	(+/-£11.57)	(+/-£12.69)	(+/-£11.88)	(+/-£13.84)	(+/-£15.08)
Average weekly hours worked	LQMM	52.4	50.9	50.7	50.9	49.0	51.9
95% confidence interval		(+/-1.8)	(+/-1.3)	(+/-1.5)	(+/-1.4)	(+/-1.4)	(+/-1.7)
Average earnings/hours (£)	LQMN	5.50	5.62	5.94	5.92	6.09	6.42
95% confidence interval		(+/-£0.12)	(+/-£0.12)	(+/-£0.18)	(+/-£0.15)	(+/-£0.18)	(+/-£0.20)
Number of workers in the sample		172	244	274	292	234	251

1 Total earnings of regular full-time male workers, aged 19 and over. Results include all payments-in-kind, valued where applicable in accordance with the Agricultural Wages Order. Excluded are earnings and hours of hire farm managers. See also chapter text.

Source: Department for Environment, Food and Rural Affairs: 01904 455332

20.8 Average weekly earnings and hours of different types of agricultural workers[1]
England and Wales
At September 2001

	Full-time		Part-time[2]		Casual[3]		
	Male	Female	Male	Female	Male	Female	Managers
Average weekly earnings (£)	332.66	245.54	127.65	116.61	192.93	136.35	436.72
95% confidence interval	(+/-£15.08)	(+/-£16.52)	(+/-£18.84)	(+/-£16.26)	(+/-£18.04)	(+/-£12.43)	(+/-£22.89)
Average weekly hours worked	51.9	44.8	22.8	22.1	35.0	28.7	..
95% confidence interval	(+/-1.7)	(+/-1.6)	(+/-2.5)	(+/-2.2)	(+/-3.1)	(+/-2.4)	
Average earnings/hour (£)	6.42	5.48	5.59	5.27	5.51	4.75	..
95% confidence interval	(+/-£0.20)	(+/-£0.31)	(+/-£0.39)	(+/-£0.45)	(+/-£0.19)	(+/-£0.29)	
Number of workers in the sample	251	62	98	80	231	117	220

1 Total earnings of workers, aged 19 and over, including all payments-in-kind valued where applicable in accordance with the Agricultural Wages order. See also chapter text.

2 Part-time workers are defined as working less than 39 basic hours per week.
3 Casual workers are employed on a temporary basis.

Source: Department for Environment, Food and Rural Affairs: 01904 455332

20.9 Sales for food of agricultural produce and livestock
United Kingdom

		Unit	1991	1992	1993	1994	1995	1996	1997	1998	1999	2000	2001
Cereals:		Thousand											
Wheat[1]	KCQK	tonnes	4 269	4 212	3 865	4 234	4 668	4 842	4 737	4 676	4 826	4 707	..
Barley	KCQL	"	3 849	3 599	2 762	3 190	3 776	3 692	3 411	3 483	3 412	3 750	..
Oats[2]	KCQM	"	215	222	208	215	216	235	259	273	270	263	..
Potatoes[3]	KCQN	"	5 800	6 008	6 382	6 519	5 961	6 146	6 279	5 997	6 210	6 523	6 005
Milk[4]:													
Milk utilised for liquid consumption	KCQO	Million litres	6 893	6 966	7 026	6 926	6 922	6 838	6 748	6 739	6 853	6 768	6 761
Milk utilised for manufacture	KCQP	Million litres	7 022	6 876	6 880	7 134	6 918	6 934	7 059	6 821	6 988	6 550	6 715
Total milk available for domestic use[5]	KCQQ	Million litres	14 282	14 189	14 228	14 420	14 255	14 194	14 258	13 973	14 234	13 737	13 942
Hen eggs in shell	KCQR	Million dozens	818	806	791	787	774	775	794	792	743	747	806
Animals slaughtered:													
Cattle and calves:													
Cattle	KCQS	Thousands	3 568	3 355	2 944	3 089	3 266	2 291	2 264	2 297	2 217	2 280	2 073
Calves	KCQT	"	49	33	19	22	26	24	20	32	75	153	92
Total	KCQU	"	3 617	3 387	2 963	3 112	3 292	2 315	2 284	2 329	2 292	2 433	2 166
Sheep and lambs	KCQV	"	20 918	19 428	18 864	18 962	19 311	18 049	16 660	18 688	19 116	18 381	12 884
Pigs:													
Clean pigs	MBGD	"	14 091	14 143	14 265	14 681	14 021	13 897	15 132	15 872	14 350	12 369	10 449
Sows and boars	KCQZ	"	366	373	356	389	355	324	363	415	379	321	180
Total	KCRA	"	14 457	14 515	14 620	15 069	14 376	14 221	15 496	16 286	14 728	12 691	10 628
Poultry:[6] slaughtered	KCRB	Millions	700	696	721	761	783	823	850	856	848	843	865

Note: The figures for cereals and for animals slaughtered relate to periods of 52 weeks

1 Flour millers' receipts of home-grown wheat.
2 Oatmeal millers' receipts of home-grown oats.
3 Total sales for human consumption in the UK.
4 Data to 1994 sourced from the Milk Marketing Boards. Data from 1995 sourced from surveys run by the agricultural departments. 1994 includes two months of data sourced from the surveys run by the agricultural departments.

5 The totals of liquid consumption and milk used for manufacture may not add up to the total available for domestic use because of adjustments for dairy wastage, stock changes and other uses, such as farmhouse consumption, milk fed to stock and on farm waste.
6 Total fowls, ducks, geese and turkeys.

Source: Department for Environment, Food and Rural Affairs: 01904 455332

20.10 Stocks of food and feedingstuffs[1]
United Kingdom

At end-December in each year

Thousand tonnes

		1991	1992	1993	1994	1995	1996	1997	1998	1999	2000	2001
Wheat and flour (as wheat)	KCRC	1 461	1 839	1 255	1 236	1 036	1 012	984	1 047	848	..	..
Barley (GB only)	KCRD	1 489	2 028	1 401	1 375	1 542	1 502	1 441	1 224	1 373	..	..
Maize	KCRE	36	109	23	32	33	25	45	67	43	..	..
Oilcake and meal[2]	KCRF	93	107	92	108	103	89	79	69	72	..	..
Oilseeds and nuts (crude oil equivalent)	KCRG	18	11	17	28	34	25	18	12	18	..	..
Vegetable oil (as crude oil)	KCRI	89	94	90	109	96	100	99	98	97	..	..
Marine oil (as crude oil)	KCRJ	9	8	8	18	17	10	4	–	–	..	..
Butter[3]	KCRK	65.0	63.0	34.2	19.1	11.3	14.3	7.3	11.0	22.1	17.0	18.0
Meat and offal[4]	KCRL	212.0	218.2	198.7	102.5	76.9	129.5	161.9	156.8	84.1	53.7	53.7
Raw coffee[5]	KCRM	10	10	12	13	11	8	7	8	7	8	13
Tea[6]	KCRN	43	40	44	43	38	39	37	38	38	28	31
Sugar	KCRO	824	888	1 069	1 016	766	807	1 003	928	..	..	..

1 Recorded stocks, including stocks in bond or held by the main processors.
2 Excluding castor meal, cocoa cake and meal.
3 In addition to stocks in public cold stores surveyed by DEFRA, closing stocks include all intervention stocks in private cold stores.

4 Stocks of imported and home-produced meat and offal held in public cold stores, excluding poultrymeat, bacon and ham.
5 Including manufacturers' stocks and additional public warehouses.
6 Covering stocks held by primary wholesalers and held in public/private warehouses.

Source: Department for Environment, Food and Rural Affairs: 01904 455332

20.11 Processed food and animal feedingstuffs: production
United Kingdom

Thousand tonnes

		1991	1992	1993	1994	1995	1996	1997	1998	1999	2000	2001
Flour milling:												
Wheat milling: total[1]	KFTA	4 796	5 022	5 236	5 290	5 338	5 501	5 535	5 707	5 668	5 617	..
Home produced[1]	KFTB	4 185	4 192	3 781	4 106	4 598	4 772	4 667	4 582	4 701	4 609	..
Imported	KFTC	611	830	1 455	1 184	740	729	868	1 125	966	1 008	..
Flour produced[1]	KFTD	3 851	3 975	4 120	4 232	4 294	4 454	4 439	4 526	4 497	4 486	..
Offals produced[1]	KFTE	968	1 045	1 123	1 078	1 079	1 111	1 111	1 221	1 181	1 148	..
Oat milling:												
Oats milled by oatmeal millers	KFTF	216	225	207	209	217	250	259	272	266	261	..
Products of oat milling	KFTG	124	124	105	102	110	123	129	154	157	155	..
Seed crushing:												
Oilseeds and nuts processed	KFTH	1 710	1 807	1 903	2 035	2 122	2 466	2 587	2 683	2 398	2 380	..
Crude oil produced, including production of maize oil	KFTI	583	636	658	739	779	862	909	915	832	820	..
Oilcake and meal produced, excluding castor meal, cocoa cake and meal	KFTJ	1 081	1 125	1 187	1 242	1 305	1 541	1 614	1 687	1 484	1 475	
Production of home-killed meat: total including meat subsequently canned	KFTK	2 454	2 391	2 260	2 380	2 392	2 093	2 161	2 276	2 141	2 068	1 770
Beef	KFTL	1 018	970	858	915	973	701	695	704	675	704	650
Veal	KFTM	2	1	1	1	1	1	1	1	2	4	3
Mutton and lamb	KFTN	385	362	349	352	364	345	321	356	361	359	258
Pork	KFTO	772	786	783	807	761	778	875	937	829	731	611
Offal[2]	KFTP	277	272	268	305	293	268	269	278	272	269	249
Production of poultry meat[3]	KFTQ	1 211	1 226	1 289	1 344	1 397	1 461	1 502	..	..	..	..
Production of bacon and ham, including meat subsequently canned	KFTR	193	189	216	233	245	241	239	236	233	209	197
Production of milk products:												
Butter[4]	KFTS	132	127	141	148	133	130	139	137	141	132	126
Cheese (including farmhouse)	KFTT	309	332	338	341	362	377	377	366	368	340	395
Condensed milk: includes skim concentrate and condensed milk used in manufacture of chocolate crumb	KFTU	198	206	191	196	181	206	214	192	177	162	161
Milk powder: excluding buttermilk and whey powder												
Full cream	KFTV	79	84	71	83	90	83	96	97	102	105	83
Skimmed	KFTW	143	106	132	142	117	108	109	107	102	83	71
Cream, fresh and sterilised; including farm cream[4]	KFTX	254	240	255	274	281	281	268	266	275	270	263
Sugar: production from home-grown sugar-beet (as refined sugar)	KFTY	1 220	1 472	1 433	1 263	1 469	1 324	1 524	1 557	..	..	..
Production of compound fats:												
Margarine and other table spreads	KFTZ	481	477	493	487	490	491	461	448	421	388	..
Solid cooking fats	KFUA	117	116	129	109	110	123	109	131	125	135	..
Production of other processed foods:												
Jam and marmalade	KFUB	..	..	..	..	..	..	..	..	..	..	..
Syrup and treacle[5]	KFUC	51	49	52	50	48	..	..	..	..	..	..
Chocolate confectionery	KSJS	534	532	563	573	592	608	569	567	552	555	550
Sugar confectionery	KSJT	303	300	302	322	322	351	345	337	317	297	312
Cocoa beans excluding re-exports	KFVX	148	159	171	163	160	189	174	172	168	..	..
Soups, canned and powdered	KFUF	..	..	..	..	..	..	..	..	..	..	..
Canned meat	KFUG	147	..	..	..	..	..	..	..	..	..	..
Breakfast cereals, other than oatmeal and oatmeal flakes	KFUJ	290	303	302	325	335	343	359	349	354	334	..
Glucose	KFUM	557	568	580	593	607	642	637	644	630	657	..
Production of soft drinks (million litres):												
Concentrated	KFUN	..	..	..	..	..	..	..	..	..	..	..
Unconcentrated	KFUO	..	..	..	..	..	..	..	..	..	..	..
Compound feedingstuffs: total[1]	KFUP	10 374	10 514	11 141	11 402	11 609	11 801	11 304	11 206	11 404	10 612	..
Cattle food[1]	KFUQ	3 798	4 098	4 271	4 347	4 476	4 430	3 926	3 844	4 264	4 039	..
Calf food[1]	KFUR	280	242	261	286	307	277	227	197	187	190	..
Pig food[1]	KFUS	2 361	2 489	2 561	2 547	2 453	2 566	2 659	2 740	2 435	2 089	..
Poultry food[6]	KFUT	3 062	2 737	3 123	3 179	3 243	3 280	3 324	3 213	3 139	3 063	..
Other compounds[1]	KFUU	873	948	925	1 043	1 130	1 249	1 168	1 210	1 378	1 231	..

Note: The figures relate to periods of 52 weeks (53 weeks in 1992 and 1998) with the following exceptions which are on a calendar year basis: butter, cheese, cream, canned meat, soft drinks, condensed milk and milk powder, canned vegetables, canned and bottled fruit, jam and marmalade, and soups.

Please note production of Poultry Feed by Integrated Poultry Units has been;
1992 = 2,556,000 tonnes
1993 = 2,679,000 tonnes
1994 = 2,767,000 tonnes
1995 = 2,892,000 tonnes
1996 = 3,012,000 tonnes
1997 = 3,072,000 tonnes
1998= 3,105,000 tonnes
1999= 2,940,000 tonnes
2000= 2,974,000 tonnes
These figures have been revised following the receipt of more up-to-date information.

1 Data for 1991 are not strictly comparable with those for later years.
2 Including poultry offal.
3 Total of fowl, ducks, geese and turkeys (carcase weight).
4 Includes cream from the residual elements of low fat milk production.
5 This survey ceased at the end of 1995.
6 It was found that data for Poultry food had previously contained some mills whose production or part of their production should have been recorded against the Integrated Poultry Unit (IPU) series. Production for these sites has now been moved from the Poultry food series to the IPU series. These data were available from 1992 onwards. Data for 1991 have been estimated in order to make the Poultry food series comparable.

Source: Department for Environment, Food and Rural Affairs: 01904 455332

20.12 Food and animal feedingstuffs: disposals

Thousand tonnes

		1991	1992	1993	1994	1995	1996	1997	1998	1999	2000	2001
Flour[1]	KFPU	3 798	3 932	4 076	4 200	4 293	4 457	4 434	4 529	4 487	4 489	..
Sugar (as refined sugar): total disposals	KFPV	2 297	2 319	2 154	2 196	2 177	2 200	2 040	2 143	..	..	..
For food in the United Kingdom[2]	KFPW	2 280	2 292	2 123	2 165	2 157	2 180	2 007	2 106	..	..	..
Syrup and treacle[3]	KFPX	51	49	52	50	48	..	..	..	..	..	..
Meat and fish:												
Fresh and frozen meat and offal, including usage for canning:												
Beef and veal	KFPY	1 130	1 145	1 094	1 228	1 206	804	865	872	942	922	907
Mutton and lamb	KFPZ	511	497	470	474	504	501	468	496	497	494	371
Pork	KFVA	847	877	895	922	926	963	1 039	1 116	1 062	1 001	866
Offal[4]	KFVB	324	335	316	351	354	312	320	315	322	328	305
Poultry-meat[5,6]	KFVC	1 247	1 327	1 361	1 453	1 493	1 581	1 560	1 649	1 696	1 707	1 715
Bacon and ham, including usage for canning	KFVD	446	428	453	457	473	502	477	468	461	477	477
Dairy products:												
Butter	KFVI	245	258	279	284	255	240	256	238	244	255	241
Cheese	KFVJ	509	560	523	559	577	617	614	632	645	595	663
Condensed milk[7]	KFVK	211	218	202	208	195	217	229	205	190	178	172
Milk powder, excluding buttermilk and whey powder:												
Full cream	KFVM	81	91	75	91	97	94	105	107	112	117	88
Skimmed	KFVN	157	136	144	149	138	95	103	91	127	162	86
Hen eggs in shell[8]	KFVO	853	831	821	837	818	833	838	819	795	827	..
Oils (as crude oil):												
Vegetable oil	KFVP	1 465	1 488	1 492	1 567	1 905	1 960	2 010	1 780	2 449	..	..
Marine oil for the manufacture of margarine and compound fat	KFVQ	115	114	95	91	105	100	52	31	8	8	..
Potatoes	KFVR	7 068	7 876	8 288	7 835	7 055	7 661	7 938	7 626	7 584	8 139	7 225
Other foods:												
Chocolate confectionery	KFVT	621	640	667	696	674	698	672	697	670	672	665
Sugar confectionery, excluding medicated	KFVU	362	367	366	382	380	410	420	415	393	393	403
Tea excluding re-exports	KFVV	152	147	157	149	141	148	152	145	133	144	133
Raw coffee	KFVW	101	108	116	119	105	116	118	122	115	109	105
Barley:[9]												
For brewing and distilling and for food	KFVY	3 917	3 436	2 682	3 092	3 574	3 579	3 439	3 502	3 324	3 646	..
Maize (including maize meal): total disposals	KFVZ	1 510	1 433	1 414	1 382	1 409	1 372	1 429	1 445	1 238	..	..
Animal feed	KCRT	145	148	152	173	154	156	174	194	198	206	..
Oilcake and meal	KCRQ	3 470	3 646	3 891	4 152	4 462	4 429	4 041	3 677	4 035	..	..
Wheat milling offals	KCRR	1 064	1 086	1 170	1 121	1 131	1 157	1 158	1 273	1 209	1 176	..
Fish and poultry meal for animal feed,[10] figures relate to sales	KCRS	383	430	382	385	378	257	233	216	194	193	..

Note: The figures relate to periods of 52 weeks with the following exceptions which are on a calendar year basis: fish and potatoes; condensed milk; milk powder; butter and sugar.

1 Data for 1991 are not strictly comparable with those for later years.

2 Including sugar used in the manufacture of other foods subsequently exported. Excluding sugar in imported manufactured foods.

3 This survey ceased at the end of 1995.

4 Including poultry offal.

5 Carcase weight.

6 Total of fowls, ducks, geese and turkeys.

7 Includes skim concentrate and condensed milk used in the manufacture of chocolate crumb.

8 Million dozen eggs.

9 From 1992 figures exclude sales of barley and barley screenings and are not strictly comparable with those from earlier years.

10 Before a ban on 29 March 1996 this included poultry meat as well as mammalian meat and bonemeal.

Source: Department for Environment, Food and Rural Affairs: 01904 455332

20.13 Number of workers employed in agriculture [1,2]
United Kingdom

Thousands

	Regular workers				Seasonal or casual workers			All workers			Salaried managers[3]
		Whole - time		Part - time								
	Total	Male	Female	Male	Female	Total	Male	Female	Total	Male	Female	
	BANC	BAMY	BAMZ	BANA	BANB	BANF	BAND	BANE	BANI	BANG	BANH	KAYG
1990 Jun	183.3	109.7	15.7	29.9	28.0	90.5	55.6	35.0	273.8	195.2	78.6	8.1
1991 Jun	176.9	104.7	15.0	29.7	27.4	86.6	53.8	32.8	263.5	188.2	75.3	7.9
1992 Jun	169.9	99.9	14.8	29.1	26.1	86.2	54.4	31.9	256.2	183.3	72.8	7.8
1993 Jun	165.3	96.5	13.7	29.8	25.3	85.4	55.0	30.4	250.7	181.3	69.4	7.6
1994 Jun	161.0	93.6	13.2	30.0	24.2	82.2	53.9	28.4	243.2	177.5	65.7	7.8
1995 Jun	157.4	90.4	13.0	30.0	24.1	83.7	56.5	27.2	241.2	176.8	64.3	7.7
1996 Jun	156.4	89.2	12.6	31.2	23.4	81.5	55.6	25.8	237.9	176.0	61.9	7.8
1997 Jun	154.4	87.5	12.6	31.2	23.1	80.9	55.3	25.5	235.2	174.0	61.2	7.8
1998 Jun[4,5]	155.6	88.0	13.1	29.7	24.7	79.5	55.6	23.8	235.0	172.8	62.2	12.1
1999 Jun	144.7	82.7	11.9	27.5	22.6	73.0	51.8	21.2	217.7	162.0	55.6	13.8
2000 Jun	128.9	73.4	10.3	24.6	20.6	64.4	45.9	18.5	193.3	143.9	49.4	11.1
2001 Jun	120.8	69.0	10.9	22.0	18.9	63.2	44.6	18.6	184.0	135.6	48.5	13.4

1 Includes estimates for minor holdings for all countries.
2 Figures exclude school children, farmers, partners, directors and their spouses and most trainees.
3 Great Britain only.

4 Results from 1998 onwards are not comparable with previous years, due to changes in the labour questions on the June Agricultural and Horticultural Census in England, Wales and Scotland.
5 From 1998, all farmers managing holdings for limited companies or other institutions in England and Wales were asked to classify themselves as salaried managers.

Sources: Department for Environment, Food and Rural Affairs;
Farming Statistics: 01904 455332

20.14 Landings of fish by United Kingdom vessels: live weight and value[1] into United Kingdom

		Quantity (thousand tonnes)							Value (£ thousand)					
		1996	1997	1998	1999	2000	2001		1996	1997	1998	1999	2000	2001
Total all species	KSJU	635.9	593.3	552.5	506.5	464.7	458.3	KSLN	491 045	467 694	484 005	464 131	422 063	423 687
Total wet fish	KSJV	504.3	467.2	428.3	389.8	337.6	332.1	KSLO	343 045	314 712	323 297	297 831	268 816	256 364
Brill	KSJX	0.5	0.5	0.4	0.3	0.4	0.4	KSLP	2 639	2 244	1 674	1 405	1 839	2 032
Catfish	KSJY	1.1	1.0	0.8	0.7	0.8	0.7	KSLQ	1 449	1 152	1 070	1 006	1 081	896
Cod	KSJZ	75.7	71.0	72.7	46.8	37.0	28.1	KSLR	69 752	67 641	79 450	62 587	50 635	37 368
Dogfish	KSKA	9.7	8.6	7.4	6.9	7.3	7.0	KSLS	7 002	5 586	5 535	5 295	5 862	6 280
Haddock	KSKB	89.1	82.6	82.8	71.3	50.3	42.3	KSLT	54 333	44 778	57 131	59 286	51 181	36 295
Hake	KSKC	2.8	2.7	2.5	3.9	3.5	2.2	KSLU	7 346	6 375	5 117	7 839	6 941	5 303
Lemon Soles	KSKD	5.1	5.2	4.7	4.5	4.0	3.6	KSLV	11 897	11 786	10 620	10 374	9 934	9 937
Ling	KSKE	9.2	9.4	10.0	8.8	7.6	6.9	KSLW	6 945	6 568	8 291	8 502	7 571	7 384
Megrims	KSKF	6.0	6.0	5.3	5.0	5.0	4.3	KSLX	10 430	9 467	8 573	9 326	8 914	7 035
Monks or Anglers	KSKG	29.7	25.6	18.5	15.5	14.7	15.1	KSLY	51 468	45 947	38 540	35 591	33 609	33 789
Plaice	KSKH	12.5	12.9	11.5	9.5	8.6	7.7	KSLZ	16 013	15 484	13 185	12 549	9 869	9 011
Pollack (Lythe)	KSKI	2.9	3.0	2.6	2.3	2.5	2.6	KSMA	2 563	2 491	2 423	2 734	3 197	3 300
Saithe	KSKJ	13.3	12.3	10.1	10.4	10.2	9.7	KSMB	5 674	4 894	4 971	4 878	4 089	4 258
Sand Eels	KSKK	9.3	14.5	11.6	6.8	9.7	1.3	KSMC	505	815	742	283	400	..
Skates and Rays	KSKL	8.3	7.2	6.8	5.6	5.5	5.5	KSMD	7 451	6 215	6 403	5 380	5 677	5 679
Soles	KSKM	2.5	2.3	2.0	2.0	1.9	2.1	KSME	14 068	14 800	13 960	13 829	11 295	13 223
Turbot	KSKN	0.8	0.7	0.6	0.5	0.5	0.5	KSMF	5 006	4 263	3 614	2 918	2 859	3 277
Whiting	KSKO	37.3	34.5	26.7	25.4	23.3	15.1	KSMG	18 962	15 939	13 380	14 010	14 317	9 913
Whiting, Blue	KSKP	3.5	12.4	27.8	38.4	17.7	20.0	KSMH	190	693	2 003	1 476	743	936
Whitches	KSKQ	2.3	2.3	1.9	2.2	2.4	2.7	KSMI	3 068	2 263	1 587	2 202	2 352	2 678
Other Demersal	KSKR	13.3	13.2	12.7	15.7	14.6	17.7	KSMJ	16 614	16 000	15 612	18 559	16 025	19 765
Total Demersal[2]	KSKS	334.8	327.9	319.3	282.6	227.3	195.5	KSMK	313 377	285 402	293 882	280 028	248 392	218 414
Herring[3]	KSKT	72.3	57.4	39.5	45.3	39.5	43.8	KSML	8 742	6 430	4 897	5 057	4 073	10 447
Horse Mackerel	KSKU	22.0	5.5	5.1	2.1	2.7	3.5	KSMM	2 966	878	783	304	440	587
Mackerel[3]	KSKV	60.8	63.2	54.4	41.3	54.6	63.9	KSMN	15 645	19 822	21 754	9 544	13 848	23 877
Pilchards	KSKW	6.8	4.7	4.7	3.5	2.9	6.8	KSMO	959	696	765	550	602	1 665
Sprats	KSKX	7.2	8.3	5.0	14.3	8.3	5.1	KSMP	1 175	1 386	1 112	2 053	1 040	607
Tuna	KSKY	..	..	..	0.1	..	..	KSMQ	66	46	44	111	20	..
Other Pelagic	KSKZ	0.3	0.1	0.2	0.6	2.3	3.6	KSMR	116	52	60	184	401	762
Total Pelagic	KSLA	169.5	139.3	108.9	107.2	110.3	126.7	KSMS	29 668	29 309	29 416	17 803	20 424	37 949
Cockles	KSLB	24.2	19.5	12.1	14.2	20.3	19.0	KSMT	3 266	3 632	4 162	2 526	2 953	3 832
Crabs	KSLC	20.3	22.5	27.2	23.0	25.7	25.0	KSMU	22 226	24 264	32 290	26 983	28 036	27 830
Lobsters	KSLD	1.3	1.5	1.6	1.8	1.2	1.1	KSMV	11 888	13 060	14 489	14 928	12 458	11 436
Mussels	KSLE	12.3	9.6	12.7	8.4	7.5	14.9	KSMW	4 574	3 102	3 502	2 107	1 442	4 835
Nephrops	KSLF	29.0	31.1	28.6	31.1	28.3	28.4	KSMX	57 164	63 480	56 810	74 327	60 778	68 433
Periwinkles	KSLG	2.4	2.9	2.0	1.2	1.1	0.8	KSMY	2 046	2 735	1 892	1 165	1 089	791
Queens	KSLH	2.3	5.6	8.1	5.9	5.3	8.7	KSMZ	1 225	1 954	2 887	2 563	2 292	3 667
Scallops	KSLI	17.1	18.5	20.1	19.1	19.7	19.5	KSNA	27 036	27 576	30 156	29 145	30 741	29 853
Shrimps/Prawns	KSLJ	2.7	1.0	2.2	2.0	1.6	2.6	KSNB	3 257	960	2 594	2 931	2 062	3 566
Squid	KSLK	1.4	1.6	2.2	2.1	1.4	1.4	KSNC	2 987	4 044	4 362	4 190	2 716	3 903
Other shellfish	KSLL	18.7	12.2	7.6	8.0	14.8	14.9	KSND	12 332	8 176	7 564	5 434	8 680	9 177
Total shellfish	KSLM	131.6	126.1	124.2	116.7	127.0	136.2	KSNE	148 001	152 983	160 708	166 299	153 247	167 323

1 See chapter text.
2 Includes fish roes.
3 Includes transshipments, i.e. caught by UK boats but not actually landing at UK ports. These quantities are transshipped to foreign vessels in coastal waters and are later recorded as exports.

Source: Department for Environment, Food and Rural Affairs: 01904 455332

20.15 United Kingdom fishing fleet[1]
At 31 December each year

Numbers

		1993	1994	1995	1996	1997	1998	1999	2000	2001
By size										
10m and under	**KSNF**	7 666	7 195	6 320	5 606	5 474	5 487	5 409	5 273	5 227
10.01 - 12.19m	**KSNG**	1 361	1 167	1 016	800	732	628	577	547	536
12.20 - 17.00m	**KSNH**	751	680	622	540	523	491	468	467	442
17.01 - 18.29m	**KSNI**	220	193	187	164	162	154	154	131	143
18.30 - 24.38m	**KSNJ**	657	610	574	509	471	443	414	406	405
24.39 - 30.48m	**KSNK**	210	211	212	223	227	226	224	219	218
30.49 - 36.58m	**KSNL**	124	126	127	114	104	89	80	77	75
over 36.58m	**KSNM**	119	116	117	117	119	121	122	122	123
Total over 10m	**KSNN**	3 442	3 103	2 855	2 467	2 338	2 152	2 039	1 969	1 942
Total UK fleet (excluding islands)	**KSNO**	11 108	10 297	9 174	8 073	7 812	7 639	7 448	7 242	7 169
By segment										
Pelagic gears	**KSNP**	69	68	67	58	49	50	46	44	47
Beam trawl	**KSNQ**	240	212	220	215	153	123	114	111	116
Demersal trawls and seines	**KXET**	..	..	..	1 040	..	..	..	..	..
Demersal trawls	**KSIX**	988	854	856	..	..	..	..	..	..
Nephrop trawls	**KSIY**	560	593	528	411	..	..	..	..	..
Seines	**KSIZ**	203	197	165	..	..	..	..	..	..
Demersal, Seines and Nephrops	**JZCI**	..	..	..	..	1 428	1 318	1 235	1 208	1 158
Lines and Nets	**KSNR**	329	300	267	224	214	187	172	165	146
Shellfish: mobile	**KSNS**	181	206	194	265	227	241	243	211	229
Shellfish: fixed	**KSNT**	312	305	283	339	352	311	301	297	301
Distant water	**KSNU**	14	13	12	15	13	14	12	13	11
Under 10m	**KSNV**	8 128	7 607	6 757	6 091	6 022	6 027	5 916	5 769	5 713
Non-active/non-TAC	**KSNW**	668	472	371	–	–	–	–	–	–
Other: Mussel Dredgers	**JZCJ**	..	..	..	..	3	2	2	2	7
Total UK fleet[2]	**KSNX**	11 692	10 827	9 720	8 658	8 461	8 273	8 041	7 820	7 728

1 See chapter text.
2 The UK figures here include Channel Islands and Isle of Man.

Source: Department for Environment, Food and Rural Affairs: 01904 455332

20.16 Estimated household food consumption by all households in Great Britain[1]

Grammes per person per week

		1990	1991	1992	1993	1994	1995	1996	1997	1998	1999	2000
Liquid wholemilk[2] (ml)	KPQM	1 232	1 104	995	898	870	812	776	712	693	634	664
Fully skimmed (ml)	KZBH	193	198	213	217	207	204	137	158	164	167	164
Semi skimmed (ml)	KZBI	516	579	752	814	863	899	935	978	945	958	975
Other milk and cream (ml)	KZBJ	228	247	262	249	252	255	259	248	243	248	278
Cheese	KPQO	113	117	114	109	106	108	111	109	104	104	110
Butter	KPQP	46	44	41	40	39	36	39	38	39	37	39
Margarine	KPQQ	91	89	79	70	43	41	36	26	26	20	21
Low and reduced fat spreads	KZBK	45	47	51	52	74	72	79	77	69	71	68
All other oils and fats (ml for oils)	KPQR	67	60	74	69	70	69	71	62	62	58	58
Eggs (number)	KPQS	2.20	2.25	2.08	1.92	1.86	1.85	1.87	1.78	1.74	1.68	1.75
Preserves and honey	KPQT	48	51	45	42	43	39	41	41	38	33	33
Sugar	KPQU	171	167	156	151	144	136	144	128	119	107	105
Beef and veal	KPQV	149	152	141	133	131	121	101	110	109	110	124
Mutton and lamb	KPQW	83	86	71	66	54	54	66	56	59	57	55
Pork	KPQX	84	82	72	80	77	71	73	75	76	69	68
Bacon and ham, uncooked	KPQY	86	85	77	77	77	76	77	72	76	68	71
Bacon and ham, cooked (including canned)	KPQZ	32	33	33	35	38	39	33	41	40	39	41
Poultry uncooked	JZCH	211	202	216	222	209	215	233	221	218	201	214
Cooked poultry (not purchased in cans)	KYBP	15	14	15	16	20	22	23	33	33	35	39
Other cooked and canned meats	KPRB	62	60	68	60	63	63	62	52	49	48	51
Offals	KPRC	14	13	12	11	9	9	7	7	5	5	5
Sausages, uncooked	KPRD	68	62	61	60	61	63	63	63	60	58	60
Other meat products	KPRE	163	173	183	194	203	211	207	209	216	221	239
Fish, fresh and processed (including shellfish)	KPRF	69	65	67	71	71	68	72	70	70	70	67
Canned fish	KPRG	29	30	32	30	30	29	31	31	29	31	32
Fish and fish products, frozen	KPRH	47	43	43	44	44	46	50	46	46	42	44
Potatoes (excluding processed)	KPRI	996	959	901	875	812	803	805	745	715	673	707
Fresh green vegetables	KPRJ	277	259	250	240	245	225	233	251	246	245	240
Other fresh vegetables	KPRK	459	461	475	477	464	470	489	497	486	500	492
Frozen potato products	KYBQ	73	82	92	98	103	99	113	106	111	113	120
Other frozen vegetables	KPRL	112	117	106	105	107	101	94	94	88	87	80
Potato products not frozen	JZCF	62	59	75	80	82	89	92	90	89	86	82
Canned beans	KPRM	124	123	120	112	111	117	125	122	118	112	114
Other canned vegetables (excl. potatoes)	KPRN	117	120	124	114	103	110	113	104	99	92	97
Other processed vegetables (excl. potatoes)	LQZH	41	43	50	52	55	48	55	52	54	59	54
Apples	KPRO	201	190	187	179	180	183	175	179	181	169	180
Bananas	KPRP	125	129	144	151	162	176	185	195	198	202	206
Oranges	KPRQ	81	76	72	62	65	66	63	62	63	50	54
All other fresh fruit	KPRR	198	216	216	224	238	247	263	276	274	290	304
Canned fruit	KPRS	52	52	51	48	46	45	43	44	37	38	38
Dried fruit, nuts and fruit and nut products	KPRT	36	39	38	39	36	34	36	35	34	30	35
Fruit juices (ml)	KPRU	202	250	222	236	240	244	258	277	304	284	303
Flour	KPRV	91	81	81	82	62	57	70	54	55	56	67
Bread	KPRW	797	752	755	757	758	756	752	746	742	717	720
Buns, scones and teacakes	KPRX	34	39	40	39	38	36	47	43	41	40	43
Cakes and pastries	KPRY	70	79	76	79	85	85	87	93	88	87	89
Biscuits	KPRZ	149	147	148	142	138	135	150	138	137	132	141
Breakfast cereals	KPSA	127	134	132	129	134	135	140	135	136	134	143
Oatmeal and oat products	KPSB	15	19	15	14	11	11	13	16	11	13	15
Other cereals and cereal products	JZCG	187	204	217	218	218	251	304	293	270	284	291
Tea	KPSC	43	42	39	36	38	39	38	36	35	32	34
Instant coffee	KPSD	14	15	14	13	13	12	13	11	12	11	11
Canned soups	KPSE	68	69	70	66	68	64	72	70	71	67	71
Pickles and sauces	KPSF	67	69	72	77	77	80	84	92	96	91	107

1 See chapter text.
2 Including also school and welfare milk.

Sources: Department for Environment, Food and Rural Affairs;
(National Food Survey): 020 7270 8563

21 Production

Production

Annual Business Inquiry *(Table 21.1)*

The Annual Business Inquiry (ABI) estimates cover all UK businesses registered for Value Added Tax (VAT) and/ or Pay As You Earn (PAYE), classified to the 1992 Standard Industrial Classification (SIC(92)) headings listed in the tables. The ABI obtains details on these businesses from the ONS Inter-Departmental Business Register (IDBR).

As with all its statistical inquiries, the ONS is concerned to minimise the form-filling burden of individual contributors and as such the ABI is a sample inquiry. The sample was designed as a stratified random sample of about 69,600 businesses, the inquiry population is stratified by SIC(92) and employment using the information from the register.

The inquiry results are grossed up to the total population, so that they relate to all active UK businesses on the IDBR for the sectors covered.

The results meet a wide range of needs for government, economic analysts and the business community at large. In official statistics the inquiry is an important source for the national accounts and input-output tables, but also provides weights for the indices of production and producer prices. Inquiry results also enable the United Kingdom to meet statistical requirements of the European Union.

Data from 1995 and 1996 were calculated on a different basis from those for 1997 and later years. In order to provide a link between the two data series, the 1995 and 1996 data were subsequently reworked to provide estimates on a consistent basis.

Revised Annual Business Inquiry results down to SIC(92) 4 digit class level for 1995-2000, giving both analysis and tabular detail, are now available free of charge from the ONS Website at www.statistics.gov.uk/abi/, with further extracts and bespoke analyses available on request. This service replaces existing publications.

Manufacturers' sales by industry *(Table 21.2)*

This table shows the total manufacturers' sales for products classified to the 1992 Standard Industrial Classification and collected under the PRODCOM (Products of the European Community) Inquiry since its introduction in 1993. Some data are not available for confidentiality reasons or where data have not been published for a given period. Detailed product sales data together with exports and imports data are available in the Product Sales and Trade quarterly and annual reports (PRQ and PRA series).

Number of local units in manufacturing industries in 2002 *(Table 21.3)*

This table shows the number of local units (sites) in manufacturing by employment sizebands. The classification breakdown is at division level (2 digit) as classified to the 1992 Standard Industrial Classification held on the Inter-Departmental Business Register (IDBR). This register became fully operational in 1995 and combines information on VAT traders and PAYE employers in a statistical register comprising 2 million enterprises (businesses), representing nearly 99% of economic activity. Business Monitor PA1003 – Size Analysis of United Kingdom Businesses 2002 provides further details and contains detailed information on enterprises in the UK including size, classification and location. Additionally, this information is available for manufacturing local units.

For further information on the IDBR see the National Statistics website at www.statistics.gov.uk/idbr.

Production of primary fuels *(Table 21.4)*

This table shows indigenous production of primary fuels. It includes the extraction or capture of primary commodities and the generation or manufacture of secondary commodities. Production is always gross; that is, it includes the quantities used during the extraction or manufacturing process. Primary fuels are coal, natural gas (including colliery methane), oil primary electricity (i.e. electricity generated by hydro, nuclear and wind stations and also electricity imported from France through the interconnector) and renewables (includes solid renewables such as wood, straw and waste and gaseous renewables such as landfill gas and sewage gas). The figures are presented on a common basis, expressed in million tonnes of oil equivalent. Estimates of the gross calorific values used for converting the statistics for the various fuels to these are given in the Digest of UK Energy Statistics (published by The Stationery Office and available on the Internet at www.dti.gov.uk/energy/inform/dukes/). Chapter 1 of the Digest of UK Energy Statistics gives more information on these figures.

Total inland energy consumption *(Table 21.5)*

This table shows energy consumption by fuel and final energy consumption by fuel and class of consumer. Primary energy consumption covers consumption of all primary fuels (defined above) for energy purposes. This measure of energy consumption includes energy that is lost by converting primary fuels into secondary fuels, i.e. the energy lost burning coal to generate electricity or the energy used by refineries to separate crude oil into fractions, in addition to losses in distribution. The other common way of measuring energy consumption is to measure the energy content of the fuels supplied to consumers. This is called final energy consumption. It is net of fuel used by the energy industries, conversion, transmission and distribution losses. The figures are presented on a common basis, measured as energy supplied and expressed in million tonnes of oil equivalent. Estimates of the gross calorific values used for converting the statistics for the various fuels to these are given in the *Digest of UK Energy Statistics* (published by The Stationery Office and available on the Internet at www.dti.gov.uk/energy/ inform/dukes/). So far as practicable the user categories have been grouped on the basis of the SIC(92) although the methods used by each of the supply industries to identify end users are slightly different. Chapter 1 of the *Digest of UK Energy Statistics* gives more information on these figures.

Coal *(Table 21.6)*

Since 1995, aggregate data on coal production have been obtained from the Coal Authority. In addition, main coal producers provide data in response to an annual DTI inquiry which covers production (deepmined and opencast), trade, stocks and disposals. HM Customs and Excise also provide trade data for solid fuels. The DTI collects information on the use of coal from UK Iron and Steel Statistics Bureau, and consumption of coal for electricity generation is covered by data provided by the electricity generators.

Gas *(Table 21.7)*
Production figures, covering the production of gas from the UKCS offshore and onshore gas fields and gas obtained during the production of oil, are obtained from returns made under the DTI's Petroleum Production Reporting System. Additional information is used on imports and exports of gas and details from the operators of gas terminals in the UK to complete the picture.

It is no longer possible to present information on fuels input into the gas industry and gas output and sales in the same format as in previous editions of this table. As such, users are directed to Chapter 4 of the 2002 edition of the *Digest of UK Energy Statistics*, where more detailed information on gas production and consumption in the UK is available.

DTI carry out an annual survey of gas suppliers to obtain details of gas sales to the various categories of consumer. Estimates are included for the suppliers with the smallest market share since the DTI inquiry covers only the largest suppliers (i.e. those more than about 0.5% per cent share of the UK market).

Electricity *(Tables 21.8 - 21.10)*
The electricity Tables 21.8 to 21.10 cover all generators and suppliers of electricity in the United Kingdom.

The relationship between generation, supply, availability and consumption is as follows:

Electricity generated
less electricity used on works
equals electricity supplied (gross)

less electricity used in pumping at pumped storage stations
equals electricity supplied (net)

plus imports (net of exports) of electricity
equals electricity available

less losses and statistical differences
equals electricity consumed.

In table 21.8 'major power producers' are those generating companies corresponding to the old public sector supply system, i.e. AES Electric Ltd., American Electric Power., Anglian Power Generation., Barking Power Ltd., BNFL Magnox, British Energy plc., Coolkeeragh Power Ltd., Corby Power Ltd., Coryton Energy Company Ltd., Deeside Power, Derwent Cogeneration Ltd., Edison Mission Energy Ltd., Enfield Energy Centre Ltd., Entergy Power Group Ltd., Fellside Heat and Power Ltd., Fibrogen Ltd., Fibropower Ltd., Fibrothetford Ltd., Fife Power Ltd., Great Yarmouth Power Ltd., Humber Power Ltd., Innogy plc., International Power plc., Killingholme Power Ltd., Lakeland Power

Ltd., London Power Company, Medway Power Ltd., Midlands Power Ltd., NIGEN, Peterborough Power Ltd., PowerGen plc., Premier Power Ltd., Regional Power Generators Ltd., Rocksavage Power Company Ltd., Saltend Co-generation Company Ltd., Sita Tyre Recycling Ltd., Scottish Power plc., Scottish and Southern Energy plc., Seabank Power Ltd., SELCHP Ltd. (South East London Combined Heat & Power Ltd.), South Coast Power Ltd., South Western Electricity, Sutton Bridge Power Ltd., Teesside Power Ltd., TXU Europe Power Ltd.

In Table 21.10 all fuels are converted to the common unit of million tonnes of oil equivalent, i.e. the amounts of oil which would be needed to produce the output of electricity generated from those fuels.

More detailed statistics on energy are given in the *Digest of United Kingdom Energy Statistics 2002*. Readers may wish to note that the production and consumption of fuels are presented using commodity balances. A commodity balance shows the flows of an individual fuel through from production to final consumption, showing its use in transformation and energy industry own use.

Oil and oil products *(Tables 21.11 - 21.13)*
The data on the production of crude oil, condensates and natural gases given in Table 21.11 are collected by the DTI direct from the operators of production facilities and terminals situated on UK territory, either onshore or offshore, ie on the UK Continental Shelf. Data are also collected from the companies on their trade in oil and oil products. These data are used in preference to the foreign trade as recorded by HM Customs & Excise in the Overseas Trade Statistics.

Data on the internal UK oil industry (i.e. on the supply, refining and distribution of oil and oil products in the UK) are collected by the UK Petroleum Industry Association. These data, reported by individual refining companies and wholesalers, and supplemented where necessary by data from other sources, provide the contents of Tables 21.12 and 21.13. The data are presented in terms of deliveries to the inland UK market. This is regarded as an acceptable proxy for actual consumption of products. The main shortcoming is that, whist changes in stocks held by companies in central storage areas are taken into account, changes in the levels of stocks further down the retail ladder (such as stocks held on petrol station forecourts) are not. This is not thought to result in a significant degree of difference in the data.

Iron and steel *(Tables 21.14 - 21.16)*

Iron and steel industry
The general definition of the UK iron and steel industry is based on groups 271 "ECSC iron and steel", 272 "Tubes", and 273 "Primary Transformation" of the UK Standard Industrial Classification (1992), except those parts of groups 272 and 273 which cover cast iron pipes, drawn wire, cold formed sections and Ferro alloys.

The definition excludes certain products which may be made by works within the industry, such as refined iron,

Production

finished steel castings, steel tyres, wheels, axles and rolled rings, open and closed die forgings, colliery arches and springs. Iron foundries and steel stockholders are also considered to be outside of the industry.

Statistics
The statistics for the UK iron and steel industry are compiled by ISSB Ltd. from data collected from UK steel producing companies with the exception of trade data which is based on HM Customs data.

Crude steel is the total of usable ingots, usable continuously cast semi-finished products and liquid steel for castings.

Production of finished products is the total production at the mill of that product after deduction of any material which is immediately scrapped.

Deliveries are based on invoiced tonnages and will include deliveries made to steel stockholders and service centres by the UK steel industry.

For more detailed information on definitions etc please contact ISSB Ltd. on 020 7343 3900.

Minerals (Table 21.19)
Table 21.19 gives, separately for Great Britain and Northern Ireland, the production of minerals extracted from the ground. The figures for chemicals and metals are estimated from the quality of the ore which is extracted. The data come from an annual census of the quarrying industry which, for Great Britain, is conducted by the Office for National Statistics for the Office of the Deputy Prime Minister and the Department of Trade and Industry.

Building Materials (Table 21.20)
Table 21.20 gives the production of a number of building materials which are closely associated with material extracted from the ground. The data come from surveys conducted by the Office for National Statistics on behalf of the Department of Trade and Industry

Construction (Tables 21.21 - 21.22)
Table 21.21 shows the value of contractors' output in the construction industry in Great Britain. Contractors' output is defined as the amount chargeable to customers for building and civil engineering work done in the relevant period. The data come from surveys run by the Department of Trade and Industry (DTI). As well as being an important input to the National Accounts, it is used by the government and the construction industry in their efforts to fully understand the industry, and also by Eurostat.

Table 21.22 shows the value of new orders in the construction industry; this is also collected by DTI. This information relates to contracts for new construction work awarded to main contractors by clients in both the public and private sectors; it also includes speculative work, undertaken on the initiative of the firm, where no contract is awarded. New orders are used as a good indicator of future output.

Motor vehicle production (Table 21.25)
The figures represent the output of United Kingdom based manufacturers classified to Class 34.10 (motor vehicles) of the Standard Industrial Classification 1992. They are derived from the Motor Vehicle Production Inquiry (MVPI).

These figures include vehicles produced in the form of kits for assembly. The value of the kit must be 50% or more of the value of a corresponding complete vehicle.

Drink and tobacco (Tables 21.26 and 21.27)
Data for these tables are derived by Customs and Excise from the systems for collecting excise duties. Alcoholic drinks and tobacco products become liable to duty when released for consumption in the UK. Figures for releases include both home-produced products and commercial imports. Production figures are also available for potable spirits distilled and beer brewed in the UK.

Alcoholic drink (Table 21.26)
The figures for Imported and other spirits released for home consumption include gin and other UK produced spirits, for which a breakdown is not available.

Since June 1993 beer duty has been charged when the beer leaves the brewery or other registered premises. Previously duty was chargeable at an earlier stage (the worts stage) in the brewing process, and an allowance was made for wastage. Figures for years prior to 1994 include adjustments to bring them into line with current data. The change in June 1993 also led to the availability of data on the strength; a series in hectolitres of pure alcohol is shown from 1994.

Made wine with alcoholic strength from 1.2% to 5.5% is termed 'coolers'. Included in coolers are alcoholic lemonade and similar products of appropriate strength.

Tobacco Products (Table 21.27)
Releases of cigarettes and other tobacco products tend to be higher in the period before a Budget. Products may then be stocked, duty paid, before being sold.

21.1 Production and construction[1]: summary table
United Kingdom

	Estimates for all firms (£ million)					
			Stocks and work in progress		Capital expenditure	
	Total turnover	Gross value added	At end of year	Change during year	*less* disposals	Total employment costs

Standard Industrial Classification: Revised 1992

Production and construction
Sections C-F[3]

	Total turnover	Gross value added	At end of year	Change during year	Capital expenditure less disposals	Total employment costs
	ZIYQ	KSCD	KSCE	KSCF	KSCG	AWKC
1996	617 803	209 942	71 573	605	29 363	101 392
1997	635 402	215 385	71 978	−138	32 024	108 034
1998	631 146	213 097	70 058	361	34 108	112 326
1999	644 806	220 202	66 436	1 527	30 178	114 586
2000	675 961	228 998	67 368	4 028	28 069	116 699

Production industries (Revised definitions)
Sections C-E[3]

	ZIYR	KSCL	KSCM	KSCN	KSCO	AWKH
1996	523 632	179 432	56 675	122	27 943	85 213
1997	538 678	181 569	58 371	−1 150	30 149	89 323
1998	528 705	178 497	55 342	−605	32 289	93 690
1999	533 441	181 053	54 903	192	28 309	93 776
2000	557 224	188 044	55 833	3 275	26 018	95 002

Mining and quarrying
Section C[3]

	ZIYS	KSCT	KSCU	KSCV	KSCW	AWKI
1996	27 507	18 633	658	14	4 977	2 533
1997	26 791	16 530	1 214	17	4 799	2 577
1998	23 953	13 120	1 138	55	6 303	2 542
1999	26 270	15 245	1 138	−5	4 058	2 469
2000	36 648	23 012	909	−56	3 040	2 541

Mining and quarrying of energy producing materials
Subsection CA[3]

	ZIYT	KSDB	KSDC	KSDD	KSDE	KSDF
1996	23 320	16 796	372	−13	4 597	1 829
1997	22 961	14 759	926	−9	4 537	1 929
1998	19 866	11 512	732	23	5 985	1 862
1999	21 975	13 615	850	−19	3 738	1 765
2000	31 726	21 177	604	−81	2 801	1 763

Mining and quarrying except energy producing materials
Subsection CB

	ZIYU	KSDJ	KSDK	KSDL	KSDM	KSDN
1996	4 187	1 837	285	26	380	703
1997	3 830	1 771	288	26	262	647
1998	4 087	1 609	406	32	318	680
1999	4 295	1 630	289	14	320	704
2000	4 921	1 835	305	25	239	778

Manufacturing (Revised definition)
Section D

	ZIYV	KSDR	KSDS	KSDT	KSDU	AWKL
1996	450 177	144 001	54 560	129	18 565	78 764
1997	468 525	148 691	55 701	−1 143	20 248	82 894
1998	460 563	149 906	52 663	−647	20 399	87 077
1999	461 829	150 313	52 041	297	18 295	87 336
2000	474 459	151 096	53 100	3 274	17 313	88 403

21.1
Production and construction[1]: summary table
United Kingdom
continued

			Estimates for all firms (£ million)			
			Stocks and work in progress			
	Total turnover	Gross value added	At end of year	Change during year	Capital expenditure less disposals	Total employment costs

Standard Industrial Classification: Revised 1992

Manufacture of food; beverages and tobacco
Subsection DA

	ZIYW	KSDZ	KSEA	KSEB	KSEC	AWKM
1996	76 868	19 610	7 049	517	2 429	8 593
1997	77 320	20 041	7 616	259	2 665	9 243
1998	73 482	19 351	8 023	−221	2 763	9 333
1999	73 655	19 977	7 958	−62	2 725	9 885
2000	74 105	20 628	7 625	−78	2 296	9 925

Manufacture of textile and textile products
Subsection DB

	ZIYX	KSEH	KSEI	KSEJ	KSEK	AWKN
1996	18 135	7 182	2 911	17	584	4 341
1997	18 874	7 664	3 046	29	506	4 607
1998	17 364	6 699	2 906	−140	552	4 476
1999	16 137	5 930	2 610	−67	460	4 035
2000	14 309	5 412	2 289	−22	275	3 567

Manufacture of leather and leather products
Subsection DC

	ZIYY	KSEP	KSEQ	KSER	KSES	AWKO
1996	2 395	900	389	5	53	487
1997	2 152	787	409	45	49	478
1998	2 005	689	410	−10	42	461
1999	1 837	687	243	−2	38	360
2000	1 747	616	231	−18	9	331

Manufacture of wood and wood products
Subsection DD

	ZIYZ	KSEX	KSEY	KSEZ	KSFA	AWKP
1996	6 010	1 930	675	−7	169	1 233
1997	6 145	2 218	667	15	237	1 267
1998	5 797	2 270	593	6	255	1 360
1999	5 838	2 101	508	−14	238	1 246
2000	6 186	2 304	612	31	227	1 292

Manufacture of pulp, paper and paper products; publishing and printing
Subsection DE

	ZIZA	KSFF	KSFG	KSFH	KSFI	AWKQ
1996	42 637	17 495	2 947	−207	1 843	9 403
1997	42 166	17 717	3 035	−44	2 087	9 762
1998	42 721	18 296	2 660	−28	1 957	10 277
1999	43 387	19 280	2 608	71	1 719	10 260
2000	45 077	19 575	2 628	222	1 826	11 154

Manufacture of coke, refined petroleum products and nuclear fuel
Subsection DF

	ZIZB	KSFN	KSFO	KSFP	KSFQ	AWKR
1996	24 755	2 442	1 076	−94	738	828
1997	25 593	2 024	1 171	−175	704	787
1998	23 322	2 289	885	−196	730	923
1999	25 310	3 087	1 333	449	766	912
2000	31 376	3 007	1 271	71	715	960

21.1
continued

Production and construction[1]: summary table
United Kingdom

			Estimates for all firms (£ million)			
			Stocks and work in progress			
	Total turnover	Gross value added	At end of year	Change during year	Capital expenditure *less* disposals	Total employment costs

Standard Industrial Classification: Revised 1992

Manufacture of chemicals, chemical products and man-made fibres
Subsection DG

	ZIZC	KSFV	KSFW	KSFX	KSFY	AWKS
1996	44 988	15 392	5 692	267	2 779	6 589
1997	46 722	14 582	5 595	−44	2 917	6 852
1998	44 800	14 388	5 671	116	3 174	7 372
1999	46 264	14 763	5 947	63	2 899	7 709
2000	47 404	14 918	6 234	471	2 712	7 534

Manufacture of rubber and plastic products
Subsection DH

	ZIZD	KSGD	KSGE	KSGF	KSGG	AWKT
1996	19 347	7 187	1 911	28	995	4 349
1997	20 323	7 834	1 908	34	1 072	4 631
1998	20 420	8 062	2 021	54	1 102	4 855
1999	19 520	7 554	1 898	24	1 088	4 940
2000	19 795	7 636	1 817	52	975	4 781

Manufacture of other non-metallic mineral products
Subsection DI

	ZIZE	KSGL	KSGM	KSGN	KSGO	AWKU
1996	11 565	5 102	1 471	98	672	2 730
1997	11 866	5 092	1 527	17	571	2 798
1998	11 346	4 904	1 420	29	656	2 771
1999	11 710	4 865	1 364	−106	747	2 759
2000	11 994	5 136	1 454	97	621	2 826

Manufacture of basic iron and of ferro-alloys
Subsection DJ

	ZIZF	KSGT	KSGU	KSGV	KSGW	AWKV
1996	45 158	15 878	4 624	14	1 749	10 066
1997	43 401	16 335	4 289	−23	1 744	9 988
1998	44 399	17 030	4 255	−203	2 024	10 713
1999	40 879	15 941	4 047	99	1 464	10 450
2000	41 623	16 275	4 226	258	1 321	10 694

Manufacture of machinery and equipment not elsewhere specified
Subsection DK

	ZIZG	KSHB	KSHC	KSHD	KSHE	AWKW
1996	35 118	12 591	5 277	63	1 223	7 780
1997	36 045	13 373	5 483	96	1 109	8 345
1998	35 580	13 414	5 084	46	982	8 637
1999	33 306	12 254	5 044	−230	954	8 356
2000	33 990	12 319	4 862	−19	858	8 546

Manufacture of electrical and optical equipment
Subsection DL

	ZIZH	KSHJ	KSHK	KSHL	KSHM	AWKX
1996	56 485	18 069	7 180	−224	2 386	10 147
1997	61 008	18 964	7 337	16	2 792	10 766
1998	61 037	19 203	6 832	−10	2 688	11 568
1999	64 949	19 613	7 014	119	1 962	11 884
2000	69 217	21 137	8 894	1 702	2 386	12 527

21.1
continued

Production and construction[1]: summary table
United Kingdom

	Total turnover	Gross value added	Stocks and work in progress		Capital expenditure *less* disposals	Wages and salaries
			At end of year	Change during year		

Estimates for all firms (£ million)

Standard Industrial Classification: Revised 1992

	Total turnover	Gross value added	At end of year	Change during year	Capital expenditure *less* disposals	Wages and salaries
Manufacture of transport equipment Subsection DM						
	ZIZI	KSHR	KSHS	KSHT	KSHU	AWKY
1996	52 714	14 991	11 716	−437	2 488	9 020
1997	61 465	16 204	11 729	−1 427	3 237	9 876
1998	62 933	17 157	10 330	−200	2 948	10 840
1999	63 239	17 955	9 648	−128	2 749	10 866
2000	61 366	15 968	9 276	445	2 608	10 731
Manufacture not elsewhere classified Subsection DN						
	ZIZJ	KSHZ	KSIA	KSIB	KSIC	AWKZ
1996	14 001	5 231	1 641	88	457	3 199
1997	15 443	5 856	1 890	62	557	3 494
1998	15 356	6 153	1 574	110	528	3 493
1999	15 798	6 306	1 820	82	485	3 674
2000	16 270	6 165	1 683	61	484	3 536
Electricity, gas and water supply Section E						
	ZIZK	KSIH	KSII	KSIJ	KSIK	AWLA
1996	45 948	16 797	1 458	−21	4 402	3 916
1997	43 361	16 348	1 456	−25	5 102	3 852
1998	44 189	15 471	1 542	−14	5 586	4 071
1999	45 342	15 496	1 723	−100	5 955	3 970
2000	46 117	19 935	1 824	57	5 665	4 057
Construction Section F						
	ZIZL	KSIP	KSIQ	KSIR	KSIS	AWLB
1996	94 171	30 510	14 898	483	1 420	16 179
1997	96 724	33 816	13 607	1 012	1 875	18 711
1998	102 441	34 600	14 716	966	1 819	18 636
1999	111 365	39 150	11 533	1 335	1 869	20 810
2000	118 738	40 954	11 534	753	2 052	21 697

1 See chapter text.

Source: Office for National Statistics: 01633 812435

21.2
Manufacturers' sales by industry[1]
United Kingdom

£ millions

Industry	SIC (92)	1998	1999	2000	2001
Other mining and quarrying					
Quarrying of stone for construction	KSPF	14110	31	..	37	..
Quarrying of limestone, gypsum and chalk	KSPG	14120	319	222	209	..
Quarrying of slate	KSPH	14130	3	3	3	..
Operation of gravel and sand pits	KSPJ	14210	1 605	1 615	..	..
Mining of clays and kaolin	KSPK	14220	..	..	306	..
Mining of chemical and fertilizer minerals	KSPL	14300	62	59	64	..
Production of salt	KSPM	14400	..	..	158	..
Other mining and quarrying not elsewhere classified	KSPN	14500	63	60	56	..
Manufacture of food products and beverages					
Production and preserving of meat	KSPO	15110	3 380	3 412	3 334	..
Production and preserving of poultry meat	KSPP	15120	1 577	1 709	1 872	..
Bacon and ham production	KSPQ	15131	..	870	887	..
Other meat and poultry meat processing	KSPR	15139	3 695	3 794	4 008	..
Processing and preserving of fish and fish products	KSPS	15200	1 347	1 542	1 534	1 673
Processing and preserving of potatoes	KSPT	15310	..	..	..	..
Fruit and vegetable juice	KSPU	15320	..	543	546	547
Processing and preserving of fruit and vegetables not elsewhere classified	KSPV	15330	1 933	1 922	2 009	..
Crude oils and fats	KSPW	15410	635	508	425	531
Refined oils and fats	KSPX	15420	489	467	488	..
Margarine and similar edible fats	KSPY	15430	462	470	434	..
Operation of dairies	KTEH	15510	5 758	5 640	5 570	..
Ice cream	KSPZ	15520	530	553	498	..
Grain mill products	KSQA	15610	2 809	2 770	2 615	..
Starches and starch products	KSQB	15620	375	379	376	..
Prepared feeds for farm animals	KSPI	15710	2 046	1 903	2 002	..
Prepared pet foods	KSQC	15720	1 303	1 160	1 189	..
Bread; fresh pastry goods and cakes	KSQD	15810	4 190	4 007	4 035	3 916
Rusks and biscuits; preserved pastry goods and cakes	KSQE	15820	2 974	..	..	3 107
Sugar	KSQF	15830	1 204	1 127	1 047	1 140
Cocoa; chocolate and sugar confectionery	KSQG	15840	3 323	..	3 414	3 356
Macaroni, noodles, couscous and similar farinaceous products	KSQH	15850	..	..	476	555
Processing of tea and coffee	KSQI	15860	1 484	..	..	..
Condiments and seasonings	KSQJ	15870	..	..	..	..
Homogenised food preparations and dietetic foods	KSQK	15880	..	..	100	..
Manufacture of other food products not elsewhere classified	KSQL	15890	1 848	1 942	2 111	..
Distilled potable alcoholic beverages	KSQM	15910	2 108	2 171	2 031	..
Production of ethyl alcohol from fermented materials	KSQN	15920	104	101	..	..
Wines	KSQO	15930	159	98	85	..
Cider and other fruit wines	KSQP	15940	466	565	475	505
Other non-distilled fermented beverages	KSQQ	15950	–	–	–	..
Beer	KSQR	15960	4 722	4 660	3 685	3 627
Malt	KSQS	15970	295	264	234	250
Mineral waters and soft drinks	KSQT	15980	..	2 776	..	..
Manufacture of tobacco products					
Tobacco products	KSQU	16000	2 482	2 443	2 282	1 796
Manufacture of textiles					
Preparation and spinning of textile fibres	KSQV	17100	1 000	891	798	673
Textile weaving	KSQW	17200	1 073	972	902	836
Finishing of textiles	KSQX	17300	715	629	575	516
Soft furnishings	KSQY	17401	492	444	458	554
Canvas goods, sacks etc	KSQZ	17402	123	161	137	141
Household textiles	KSRA	17403	896	942	987	909
Carpets and rugs	KSRB	17510	1 083	1 029	973	904
Cordage, rope, twine and netting	KSRC	17520	82	80	79	103

21.2
continued

Manufacturers' sales by industry[1]
United Kingdom

£ millions

Industry	SIC (92)	1998	1999	2000	2001
Manufacture of textiles continued					
Nonwovens and articles made from nonwovens, except apparel	KSRD 17530	145	158	..	172
Lace	KSRE 17541	62	39	34	28
Narrow fabrics	KSRF 17542	233	223	210	190
Other textiles not elsewhere classified	KSRG 17549	519	498	516	497
Knitted and crocheted fabrics	KSRH 17600	..	..	374	
Knitted and crocheted hosiery	KSRI 17710	452	363	..	284
Knitted and crocheted pullovers, cardigans and similar	KSRJ 17720	759	664	582	413
Manufacture of wearing apparel; dressing and dyeing of fur					
Leather clothes	KSRK 18100	17	14	16	14
Workwear	KSRL 18210	290	279	261	252
Men's outerwear	KSRM 18221	763	613	421	343
Other women's outerwear	KSRN 18222	1 297	1 001	915	805
Men's underwear	KSRO 18231	553	437	294	230
Women's underwear	KSRP 18232	911	779	737	618
Hats	KSRQ 18241	70	63	..	55
Other wearing apparel and accessories	KSRR 18249	652	604	568	496
Dressing/dyeing of fur; articles of fur	KSRS 18300	7	6	5	3
Tanning and dressing of leather; manufacture of luggage, handbags, saddlery, harness and footwear					
Tanning and dressing of leather	KSRT 19100	362	304	309	310
Luggage, handbags and the like, saddlery and harness	KSRU 19200	238	256	242	..
Footwear	KSRV 19300	905	760	610	624
Manufacture of wood and of products of wood and cork, except furniture; manufacture of articles of straw and plaiting materials					
Sawmilling and planing of wood, impregnation of wood	KSRW 20100	622	678	636	..
Veneer sheets	KSRX 20200	686	722	719	710
Builders' carpentry and joinery	KSRY 20300	2 030	1 797	2 673	2 817
Wooden containers	KSRZ 20400	499	455	423	..
Other products of wood	KSSA 20510	381	375	309	..
Articles of cork, straw and plaiting materials	KSSB 20520	14	15	15	13
Manufacture of pulp, paper and paper products					
Paper and paperboard	KSSC 21120	3 521	3 337	3 339	..
Corrugated paper and paperboard, sacks and bags	KSSD 21211	..	556	597	..
Cartons, boxes, cases and other containers	KSSE 21219	3 463	3 340	3 254	3 399
Household and sanitary goods and toilet requisites	KSSF 21220	..	1 484	1 544	1 611
Paper stationery	KSSG 21230	683	669	693	697
Wallpaper	KSSH 21240	302	268	..	..
Other articles of paper and paperboard not elsewhere classified	KSSI 21250	798	743	822	798
Publishing, printing and reproduction of recorded media					
Publishing of books	KSSJ 22110	2 913	3 067	3 240	3 362
Publishing of newspapers	KSSK 22120	3 577	3 659	3 883	..
Publishing of journals and periodicals	KSSL 22130	6 172	6 666	6 985	..
Publishing of sound recordings	KSSM 22140	..	165	181	..
Other publishing	KSSN 22150	476	502	453	..
Printing of newspapers	KSSO 22210	..	..	181	..
Printing not elsewhere classified	KSSP 22220	9 263	9 361	9 732	..
Bookbinding and finishing	KSSQ 22230	422	433	492	461
Composition and plate-making	KSSR 22240	538	543	614	..
Other activities related to printing	KSSS 22250	655	734	700	..
Reproduction of sound recording	KSST 22310	336	..	429	..
Reproduction of video recording	KSSU 22320	193	..	173	184
Reproduction of computer media	KSSV 22330	118	..	..	..
Manufacture of chemicals and chemical products					
Industrial gases	KSSW 24110	625	530	..	539
Dyes and pigments	KSSX 24120	1 017	1 049	1 095	1 071
Other inorganic basic chemicals	KSSY 24130	1 369	1 251	1 155	1 160
Other organic basic chemicals	KSSZ 24140	4 013	4 151	5 412	5 747
Fertilizers and nitrogen compounds	KSTA 24150	617	737	714	592

21.2
continued

Manufacturers' sales by industry[1]
United Kingdom

£ millions

Industry	SIC (92)	1998	1999	2000	2001
Manufacture of chemicals and chemical products continued					
Plastics in primary forms	KSTB 24160	3 305	3 500	3 775	3 745
Synthetic rubber in primary forms	KSTC 24170	346	..	351	322
Pesticides and other agro-chemical products	KSTD 24200	..	725	1 049	1 138
Paints, varnishes and similar coatings, printing ink and mastic	KSTE 24300	2 468	2 627	2 600	2 536
Basic pharmaceutical products	KSTF 24410	508	521	666	692
Pharmaceutical preparations	KSTG 24420	6 030	7 298	7 264	8 107
Soap and detergents, cleaning and polishing preparations	KSTH 24510	1 827	1 922	1 917	1 961
Perfumes and toilet preparations	KSTI 24520	2 465	2 529	2 656	2 660
Explosives	KSTJ 24610	123	107	109	..
Glues and gelatines	KSTK 24620	380	353	318	376
Essential oils	KSTL 24630	461	526	..	589
Photographic chemical material	KSTM 24640	1 204	..	605	347
Prepared unrecorded media	KSTN 24650	134	141	131	..
Other chemical products not elsewhere classified	KSTO 24660	2 206	2 315	2 382	2 097
Man-made fibres	KSTP 24700	754	673	739	659
Manufacture of rubber and plastic products					
Rubber tyres and tubes	KSTQ 25110	1 014	970	859	811
Retreading and rebuilding of rubber tyres	KSTR 25120	..	120	..	..
Other rubber products	KSTS 25130	1 814	1 742	1 704	..
Plastic plates, sheets, tubes and profiles	KSTT 25210	3 171	3 108	3 182	..
Plastic packing goods	KSTU 25220	2 677	2 677	2 615	..
Builders' ware of plastic	KSTV 25230	3 211	3 141	3 550	3 993
Other plastic products	KSTW 25240	3 914	4 214	4 314	..
Manufacture of other non-metallic mineral products					
Flat glass	KSTX 26110	159	187	231	..
Shaping and processing of flat glass	KSTY 26120	838	766	774	..
Hollow glass	KSTZ 26130	721	712	676	..
Glass fibres	KSUA 26140	298	292	280	..
Manufacturing and processing of other glass including technical glassware	KSUB 26150	317	283	333	297
Ceramic household and ornamental articles	KSUC 26210	655	563	563	515
Ceramic sanitary fixtures	KSUD 26220	..	213	222	200
Ceramic insulators and insulating fittings	KSUE 26230	..	29	..	..
Other technical ceramic products	KSUF 26240	..	27	28	26
Other ceramic products	KSUG 26250	22	..	16	..
Refractory ceramic products	KSUH 26260	476	446	437	..
Ceramic tiles and flags	KSUI 26300	103	97	87	100
Bricks, tiles and construction products in baked clay	KSUJ 26400	592	627	618	632
Cement	KSUK 26510	..	..	..	..
Lime	KSUL 26520	..	..	70	..
Plaster	KSUM 26530	..	105	..	113
Concrete products for construction purposes	KSUN 26610	1 611	..	1 799	1 777
Plaster products for construction purposes	KSUO 26620	267	..	321	..
Ready mixed concrete	KSUP 26630	1 134	1 224	1 216	1 301
Mortars	KSUQ 26640	..	92	104	..
Fibre cement	KSUR 26650	91	88	..	..
Other articles of concrete, plaster and cement	KSUS 26660	..	96	97	103
Cutting, shaping and finishing of stone	KSUT 26700	141	169	178	..
Abrasive products	KSUU 26810	230	218	208	194
Other non-metallic mineral products not elsewhere classified	KSUV 26820	747	712	660	..
Manufacture of basic metals					
Cast iron tubes	KSUW 27210	244	..	207	..
Steel tubes	KSUX 27220	1 290	1 028	1 053	..
Cold drawing	KSUY 27310	..	..	108	..

21.2 Manufacturers' sales by industry[1]
United Kingdom
continued

£ millions

Industry		SIC (92)	1998	1999	2000	2001
Manufacture of basic metals continued						
Cold rolling of narrow strip	KSUZ	27320	126	104	106	97
Cold forming or folding	KSVA	27330	149	..	..	122
Wire drawing	KSVB	27340	334	294	266	..
Other first processing of iron and steel not elsewhere classified	KSVC	27350	83	78	83	87
Precious metals production	KSVD	27410	228	259	277	326
Aluminium production	KSVE	27420	2 148	2 018	2 194	..
Lead, zinc and tin production	KSVF	27430	389	368	351	372
Copper production	KSVG	27440	867	755	..	..
Other non-ferrous metal production	KSVH	27450	604	521	583	594
Casting of iron	KSVI	27510	757	655	663	..
Casting of steel	KSVJ	27520	186	152	160	160
Casting of light metals	KSVK	27530	316	283	290	289
Casting of other non-ferrous metals	KSVL	27540	465	..	..	..
Manufacture of fabricated metal products, except machinery and equipment						
Metal structures and parts of structures	KSVM	28110	4 750	5 267	4 791	5 140
Builders' carpentry and joinery of metal	KSVN	28120	803	860	854	964
Tanks, reservoirs and containers of metal	KSVO	28210	..	..	..	..
Central heating radiators and boilers	KSVP	28220	631	624	595	545
Steam generators, except central heating hot water boilers	KSVQ	28300	533	569	574	457
Forging, pressing, stamping and roll forming of metal	KSVR	28400	2 313	2 199	2 116	..
Treatment and coating of metals	KSVS	28510	1 143	1 109	1 055	1 116
General mechanical engineering	KSVT	28520	2 837	2 942	2 777	2 862
Cutlery	KSVU	28610	219	..	..	..
Tools	KSVV	28620	1 042	950	1 011	..
Locks and hinges	KSVW	28630	673	633	621	595
Steel drums and similar containers	KSVX	28710	165	141	..	138
Light metal packaging	KSVY	28720	1 258	..	..	..
Wire products	KSVZ	28730	570	552	524	..
Fasteners, screw machine products, chain and spring	KSWA	28740	781	702	671	..
Other fabricated metal products not elsewhere classified	KSWB	28750	1 712	1 627	1 530	..
Manufacture of machinery and equipment not elsewhere classified						
Engines and turbines, except aircraft, vehicles and cycle engines	KSWC	29110	..	1 556	1 635	..
Pumps	KSWD	29121	1 013	1 025	1 031	986
Compressors	KSWE	29122	1 210	1 224	1 352	1 263
Taps and valves	KSWF	29130	1 349	1 171	1 193	1 169
Bearings, gears, gearing and driving elements	KSWG	29140	1 117	1 011	1 027	..
Furnaces and furnace burners	KSWH	29210	412	311	299	..
Lifting and handling equipment	KSWI	29220	2 907	2 852	2 679	..
Non-domestic cooling and ventilation equipment	KSWJ	29230	2 637	2 526	..	..
Other general purpose machinery not elsewhere classified	KSWK	29240	2 164	2 101	2 220	..
Agricultural tractors	KSWL	29310	1 060	919	..	..
Other agricultural and forestry machinery	KSWM	29320	616	538	545	..
Machine tools	KSWN	29400	2 026	1 924	1 792	1 593
Machinery for metallurgy	KSWO	29510	95	81	91	..
Machinery for mining	KSWP	29521	575	452	381	..
Earth-moving equipment	KSWQ	29522	996	..	..	983
Equipment for concrete crushing and screening and roadworks	KSWR	29523	503	..	..	..
Machinery for food, beverage and tobacco processing	KSWS	29530	661	643	606	..
Machinery for textile, apparel and leather production	KSWT	29540	679	251	233	..
Machinery for paper and paperboard production	KSWU	29550	329	239	200	..
Other special purpose machinery not elsewhere classified	KSWV	29560	2 152	1 975	2 004	..
Weapons and ammunition	KSWW	29600	1 720	1 511	1 383	..

21.2
continued

Manufacturers' sales by industry[1]
United Kingdom

£ millions

Industry	SIC (92)	1998	1999	2000	2001
Manufacture of machinery and equipment not elsewhere classified continued					
Electric domestic appliances	KSYR 29710	1 882	1 745	1 817	..
Non-electric domestic appliances	KSWX 29720	..	531	501	..
Manufacture of office machinery and computers					
Office machinery	KSWY 30010	1 152	1 173	1 168	..
Computers and other information processing equipment	KSWZ 30020	9 981	9 858	11 661	..
Manufacture of electrical machinery and apparatus not elsewhere classified					
Electric motors, generators and transformers	KSXA 31100	2 298	2 229	2 428	..
Electricity, distribution and control apparatus	KSXB 31200	2 735	2 726	2 662	..
Insulated wire and cable	KSXC 31300	1 365	1 243	1 323	..
Accumulators, primary cells and batteries	KSXD 31400	489	499	548	..
Lighting equipment and electric lamps	KSXE 31500	1 301	1 273	1 215	1 125
Electrical equipment for engines and vehicles not elsewhere classified	KSXF 31610	1 156	1 103	..	..
Other electrical equipment not elsewhere classified	KSXG 31620	1 649	1 611	1 865	..
Manufacture of radio, television and communication equipment and apparatus					
Electronic valves and tubes and other electronic components	KSXH 32100	4 245	3 577	4 542	..
Telegraph and telephone apparatus and equipment	KSXI 32201	3 952	4 887	5 467	4 231
Radio and electronic capital goods	KSXJ 32202	2 805	4 007	4 895	..
Television and radio receivers, sound or video recording etc	KSXK 32300	3 399	3 169	3 457	..
Manufacture of medical, precision and optical instruments, watches and clocks					
Medical and surgical equipment and orthopaedic appliances	KSXL 33100	1 643	1 656	1 643	..
Instruments and appliances for measuring, checking, testing etc	KSXM 33200	4 930	4 943	5 053	..
Industrial process control equipment	KSXN 33300	866	779	681	..
Optical instruments and photographic equipment	KSXO 33400	957	1 028	996	..
Watches and clocks	KSXP 33500	85	90	74	..
Manufacture of motor vehicles, trailers and semi-trailers					
Motor vehicles	KSXQ 34100	21 102	22 353	19 689	20 040
Bodies (coachwork) for motor vehicles (excluding caravans)	KSXR 34201	876	797	838	853
Trailers and semi-trailers	KSXS 34202	980	907	862	..
Caravans	KSXT 34203	340	380	412	391
Parts and accessories for motor vehicles and their engines	KSXU 34300	..	..	8 365	..
Manufacture of other transport equipment					
Building and repairing of ships	KSXV 35110	1 594	2 442	1 557	..
Building and repairing of pleasure and sporting boats	KSXW 35120	437	459	492	..
Railway and tramway locomotives and rolling stock	KSXX 35200	..	932	1 221	..
Aircraft and spacecraft	KSXY 35300	..	13 958	12 794	..
Motorcycles	KSXZ 35410	..	..	..	..
Bicycles	KSYA 35420	115	112	114	103
Invalid carriages	KSYB 35430	..	123	116	120
Other transport equipment not elsewhere classified.	KSYC 35500	..	89	81	85
Manufacture of furniture; manufacturing not elsewhere classified					
Chairs and seats	KSYD 36110	2 458	2 458	2 532	2 678
Other office and shop furniture	KSYE 36120	1 259	1 278	1 432	1 333
Other kitchen furniture	KSYF 36130	908	1 065	975	927
Other furniture	KSYG 36140	1 967	2 170	2 072	2 107
Mattresses	KSYH 36150	501	524	542	566
Striking of coins and medals	KSYI 36210	..	..	..	..
Jewellery and related articles not elsewhere classified	KSYJ 36220	540	565	599	490
Musical instruments	KSYK 36300	60	51	52	42
Sports goods	KSYL 36400	269	252	257	275
Games and toys	KSYM 36500	467	447	492	..
Imitation jewellery	KSYN 36610	31	32	29	28
Brooms and brushes	KSYO 36620	168	166	167	..
Miscellaneous stationers' goods	KSYP 36631	270	250	217	..
Other manufacturing not elsewhere classified	KSYQ 36639	504	521	474	..

1 See chapter text. ProdCom data is published on the ONS website in the PRA and PRQ series of reports. Data not yet available for 2002 may eventually become available on the website.

Source: Office for National Statistics: 01633 813065

21.3 Number of local units in manufacturing industries in 2002[1]
United Kingdom
Standard Industrial Classification 1992 Division by Employment Sizeband

				Employment size					
	1 - 9	10 - 19	20 - 49	50 - 99	100 - 199	200 - 499	500 - 999	1,000+	Total

Number of local units

Division

	1 - 9	10 - 19	20 - 49	50 - 99	100 - 199	200 - 499	500 - 999	1,000+	Total
15/16 Food products; beverages and tobacco	5 855	1 580	1 180	600	490	430	130	40	10 305
17 Textiles and textile products	3 485	690	640	345	195	95	10	-	5 465
18 Wearing apparel; dressing and dyeing of fur	3 815	735	550	160	80	55	10	-	5 405
19 Leather and leather products	635	120	105	55	35	15	-	-	965
20 Wood and wood products	6 565	975	655	165	70	25	-	-	8 455
21 Pulp, paper and paper products	1 430	335	425	245	185	80	10	-	2 705
22 Publishing, printing and reproduction of recorded media	23 885	2 930	1 865	655	330	200	35	15	29 920
23 Coke, refined petroleum products and nuclear fuel	150	30	45	30	10	10	15	-	285
24 Chemicals, chemical products and man-made fibres	2 215	580	610	365	270	185	70	20	4 315
25 Rubber and plastic products	4 135	1 260	1 240	575	325	165	25	5	7 730
26 Other non-metallic mineral products	5 015	790	645	315	160	100	15	-	7 050
27 Basic metals	1 350	320	365	205	140	80	20	5	2 485
28 Fabricated metal products, except machinery and equipment	20 830	4 145	2 950	935	340	130	25	-	29 360
29 Machinery and equipment not elsewhere classified	8 435	2 095	1 850	745	375	235	45	20	13 805
30 Office machinery and computers	915	125	110	65	50	35	10	10	1 310
31 Electrical machinery and apparatus not elsewhere classified	3 455	725	710	340	210	155	40	5	5 635
32 Radio, television and communication equipment and apparatus	1 720	275	310	150	105	70	40	20	2 690
33 Medical, precision and optical instruments, watches and clocks	2 990	690	615	295	180	75	25	5	4 880
34 Motor vehicles, trailers and semi-trailers	1 500	360	400	225	155	155	40	30	2 860
35 Other transport equipment	1 590	250	220	120	100	75	35	35	2 420
36/37 Manufacturing not elsewhere classified	16 230	1 810	1 125	420	200	110	20	5	19 920
Total manufacturing (15/37)	116 205	20 825	16 620	7 015	4 005	2 470	615	215	167 970

1 See chapter text. The data in this table are taken from the NS publication, Business Monitor *PA1003 - Size Analysis of United Kingdom Businesses* 2002 edition. The count of units refers to local units, i.e. individual sites, rather than whole businesses. All counts have been rounded to avoid disclosure.

Source: Office for National Statistics: 01633 812293

21.4 Production of primary fuels[1]
United Kingdom

Million tonnes of oil equivalent

		1990	1991	1992	1993	1994	1995	1996	1997	1998	1999	2000	2001
Coal	HFZQ	56.4	57.6	51.5	41.6	29.7	32.8	31.1	30.3	25.8	23.2	19.6	20.0
Petroleum[2]	HGCY	100.1	99.9	103.7	109.6	138.9	142.7	142.1	140.4	145.3	150.2	138.3	127.8
Natural Gas[3]	HGDB	45.5	50.6	51.5	60.5	64.6	70.8	84.2	85.9	90.2	99.1	108.3	105.8
Primary electricity[4]	HGDN	16.7	17.8	18.9	22.0	21.7	21.7	22.4	23.5	24.0	22.9	20.2	21.2
Renewables	HGDO	0.7	0.7	0.8	1.2	1.6	1.7	1.8	1.9	2.1	2.2	2.4	2.7
Total Production	HGDP	219.4	226.7	226.5	234.9	256.6	269.7	281.6	282.1	287.2	297.7	288.7	277.6

1 See chapter text.
2 Crude oil plus all condensates and petroleum gases extracted at gas seperation plants.
3 Includes colliery methane.
4 Nuclear, natural flow hydro electricity excluding generation of pumped storage stations and generation at wind stations.

Source: Depatment of Trade and Industry: 020 7215 5187

21.5 Total inland energy consumption[1]
United Kingdom
Heat supplied basis

Million tonnes of oil equivalent

		1991	1992	1993	1994	1995	1996	1997	1998	1999	2000	2001
Inland energy consumption of												
primary fuels and equivalents[2]	KLWA	219.5	216.7	220.7	217.5	218.4	230.0	226.8	230.8	231.4	233.4	237.7
Coal[3]	KLWB	67.1	63.0	55.0	51.3	48.9	45.7	40.8	40.9	36.7	38.1	41.5
Petroleum[4]	KLWC	77.1	77.5	78.1	76.7	75.4	77.8	75.5	76.1	76.0	76.1	76.5
Primary electricity	KLWD	19.2	20.4	23.5	23.0	23.1	23.8	25.0	25.0	24.2	21.4	22.1
Natural gas	KLWE	55.4	55.1	62.9	64.9	69.2	81.0	83.5	86.9	92.5	95.5	95.1
Renewables and waste	GYUY	0.7	0.8	1.2	1.6	1.7	1.8	1.9	2.1	2.2	2.4	2.7
less Energy used by fuel producers and losses in conversion and distribution	KLWF	67.7	65.7	68.0	64.9	68.0	73.0	72.9	75.0	74.2	74.7	76.9
Total consumption by final users[2]	KLWG	151.8	151.1	152.7	152.5	150.4	157.0	153.9	155.8	157.1	158.7	160.8
Final energy consumption by type of fuel												
Coal (direct use)	KLWH	8.6	8.1	7.6	6.9	5.3	4.4	4.3	3.7	3.5	2.0	3.2
Coke and breeze	KLWI	4.0	3.9	3.8	3.9	3.9	1.0	0.8	0.9	1.0	1.0	0.8
Other solid fuel[5]	KLWJ	0.8	0.7	0.8	0.8	0.7	0.8	0.7	0.7	0.5	0.5	0.5
Coke oven gas	KLWK	0.6	0.5	0.6	0.6	0.6	0.4	0.5	0.4	0.2	0.2	0.1
Natural gas (direct use)	KLWL	49.7	48.4	49.3	49.9	50.1	56.5	54.2	55.9	55.1	56.8	57.6
Electricity	KLWM	24.2	24.2	24.6	24.4	25.3	26.5	26.8	27.1	27.8	28.3	28.7
Petroleum (direct use)[6]	KLWN	63.5	64.6	65.4	65.2	63.7	66.1	65.4	66.0	65.7	66.6	66.8
Renewables	GYVA	0.5	0.7	0.7	0.9	1.0	1.0	0.9	0.9	0.7	0.6	0.6
Final energy consumption by class of consumer												
Agriculture	KLWP	1.4	1.4	1.4	1.4	1.3	1.4	1.3	1.4	1.3	1.2	1.2
Iron and steel industry	KLWQ	6.6	6.5	7.0	6.9	6.9	4.2	4.2	4.0	3.8	3.7	3.5
Other industries	KLWR	31.6	30.2	29.5	30.8	29.4	30.3	30.4	30.5	30.9	30.8	31.6
Railways[6]	KLWS	1.1	1.2	1.3	1.3	1.3	1.3	1.2	1.3	1.2	1.2	1.2
Road transport	KLWT	38.5	39.4	39.5	39.7	39.3	40.8	41.3	41.0	41.4	41.6	41.5
Water transport	KLWU	1.4	1.4	1.3	1.2	1.2	1.3	1.3	1.2	1.1	1.0	0.8
Air transport	KLWV	6.9	7.4	7.9	8.1	8.5	8.9	9.3	10.2	11.0	12.0	11.4
Domestic	KLWW	44.8	44.1	45.5	43.9	42.7	48.1	44.8	46.1	46.1	46.9	48.6
Public administration	KLWX	8.2	8.7	8.1	8.3	8.5	8.8	8.4	8.1	8.4	8.2	8.1
Commercial and other services	KLWY	11.3	10.9	11.2	11.0	11.3	11.9	11.7	12.0	11.9	12.0	12.7

1 See chapter text.
2 Includes heat sold from 1999.
3 Includes net trade and stock change in other solid fuels.
4 Refinery throughput of crude oil, *plus* net foreign trade and stock change in petroleum products. Petroleum products not used as fuels (chemical feedstock, industrial and white spirits, lubricants, bitumen and wax) are excluded.

5 Includes manufactured liquid fuels from 1994.
6 Includes fuel used at transport premises.

Source: Department of Trade and Industry: 020 7215 5187

21.6 Coal: supply and demand[1]
United Kingdom

Million tonnes

			1991	1992	1993	1994	1995	1996	1997	1998	1999	2000	2001
Supply													
Production of deep-mined coal	KLXA		73.4	65.8	50.5	31.9	35.2	32.2	30.3	25.7	20.9	17.2	17.3
Production of opencast coal	KLXB		18.6	18.2	17.0	16.8	16.4	16.3	16.7	14.3	15.3	13.4	14.2
Total	KLXC		92.0	84.0	67.5	48.7	51.5	48.5	47.0	40.0	36.2	30.6	31.5
Recovered slurry, fines, etc	KLXD		2.2	0.5	0.7	0.1	1.5	1.7	1.5	1.1	0.9	0.6	0.4
Imports	KLXE		19.6	20.3	18.4	15.1	15.9	17.8	19.8	21.2	20.3	23.4	35.5
Total	KLXF		113.8	104.8	86.6	64.9	68.9	68.0	68.3	62.4	57.4	54.6	67.5
Change in colliery stocks	KLXG	KSOL	2.8	2.2	1.8	−4.2	−4.2	−3.0	0.7	−0.2	0.6	−3.5	−0.1
Change in stocks at opencast sites	KLXH		−0.8	0.6	0.5	−0.5							
Total supply	KLXI		111.8	102.0	84.5	69.6	73.1	70.9	67.6	62.7	56.8	58.2	67.5
Home consumption													
Total home consumption	KLXW		107.5	100.6	86.6	81.7	76.9	71.4	63.1	63.2	55.7	58.9	64.5
Overseas shipments and bunkers	KLXX		1.7	1.0	1.1	1.2	0.9	1.0	1.1	1.0	0.8	0.7	0.6
Total consumption and shipments	KLXY		109.2	101.6	87.7	82.9	77.8	72.4	64.2	64.1	56.5	59.5	65.1
Change in distributed stocks[2]	KLXZ		3.6	1.2	−3.6	−13.9	−4.4	−0.9	3.0	−1.2	0.6	−1.2	2.6
Balance[3]	KLYA		−1.0	−0.8	0.4	0.6	−0.3	−0.5	0.3	−0.3	−0.3	−0.2	−0.2
Stocks at end of year													
Distributed[2]	KLYB		32.3	33.5	29.9	16.0	11.6	10.8	13.8	12.6	13.2	12.0	14.6
At collieries	KLYC	KSOM	8.8	10.9	12.7	8.5	7.1	4.2	4.8	4.6	5.2	1.6	1.6
At opencast sites	KLYD		2.2	2.8	3.3	2.8							
Total stocks	KLYE		43.3	47.2	45.9	27.3	18.7	14.9	18.6	17.2	18.3	13.7	16.2

1 See chapter text. Figures relate to periods of 52 weeks. For 1998, figures relate to 52 weeks estimate for period ended 26 December 1998.
2 Excludes distributed stocks held in merchant yards etc, mainly for the domestic market, and stocks held by the industrial sector.

3 This is the balance between supply and consumption, shipments and changes in known distributed stocks.

Source: Department of Trade and Industry: 020 7215 2717

21.7

Fuel input and gas output: gas sales[1]
United Kingdom
Public supply

Giga-watt hours

		1991	1992	1993	1994	1995	1996	1997	1998	1999	2000	2001
Analysis of gas sales												
Fuel producers												
Power stations[2]	KIKK	6 561	17 894	81 778	114 575	145 790	201 929	251 787	267 703	315 400	324 679	311 545
Coal extraction and manufacture of solid fuels	KIKL	630	1 042	415	266	368	344	193	67	14	6	4
Coke ovens	KIKM	62	108	191	1	1	–	–	–	–	–	–
Petroleum refineries	KIKN	279	1 940	2 449	1 933	2 922	2 907	3 002	3 753	4 155	3 641	4 192
Nuclear fuel production	KIKO	496	508	565	550	467	874	923	989	1 021	1 272	1 210
Production and distribution of other energy	KIKP	270	447	178	114	352	437	487	549	629	619	451
Total final producers	KIKQ	8 298	21 939	85 576	117 439	149 900	206 491	256 392	273 061	321 219	330 217	317 402
Final users:												
Iron and steel industry	KIKR	12 565	13 908	15 577	20 327	19 988	20 940	20 577	20 105	21 622	21 118	20 972
Other industries	KIKS	139 488	132 936	132 719	143 979	150 697	12 646	13 429	14 415	13 905	14 387	12 568
Domestic	KIKT	333 963	330 100	340 162	329 710	326 010	375 841	345 532	355 895	358 066	369 909	379 163
Public administration	KIKU	40 030	43 817	38 725	41 119	46 308	51 411	52 315	51 976	43 253	44 088	45 455
Agriculture	KIKV	1 087	1 286	1 277	1 227	1 210	1 417	1 440	953	1 155	1 315	1 327
Miscellaneous	KIKW	59 394	54 769	58 917	58 790	61 502	65 080	59 022	64 695	62 079	63 477	64 724
Total final users	KIKX	586 527	576 816	587 377	595 152	605 715	527 335	492 315	508 039	500 080	514 294	524 209
Total sales	KIKY	594 825	598 755	672 952	712 592	755 615	733 826	748 707	781 100	821 299	844 511	841 611

1 See chapter text. The breakdown of consumption by industrial users is made according to the 1980 Standard Industrial Classification.
2 Includes auto-production of electricity.

Source: Department of Trade and Industry: 020 7215 2717

21.8 Electricity: generation, supply and consumption[1]
United Kingdom

Gigawatt-hours

		1991	1992	1993	1994	1995	1996	1997	1998	1999	2000	2001
Electricity generated												
Major power producers: total	KLUA	301 490	300 177	305 434	306 726	313 958	326 235	324 133	333 764	336 608	341 783	352 985
Conventional thermal and other[2]	AWLC	..	..	..	175 187	170 056	160 791	133 591	134 009	118 762	131 062	139 409
Combined cycle gas turbine stations	KJCS	312	2 991	22 811	36 971	48 720	65 880	86 974	93 832	114 620	117 935	117 183
Nuclear stations	KLUC	70 543	76 807	89 353	88 282	88 964	94 671	98 146	99 486	95 133	85 063	90 093
Hydro-electric stations:												
Natural flow	KLUE	3 777	4 591	3 522	4 317	4 096	2 801	3 337	4 237	4 431	4 331	3 216
Pumped storage	KLUF	1 523	1 697	1 437	1 463	1 552	1 556	1 486	1 624	2 902	2 694	2 356
Renewables other than hydro	KLUG	3	45	165	506	570	536	599	576	760	698	728
Other generators: total	KLUH	21 385	20 864	17 669	18 252	20 084	24 632	26 534	28 938	31 544	35 525	32 841
Conventional thermal and other[2]	AWLD	..	..	..	14 263	15 387	18 334	18 629	19 091	19 434	18 796	17 854
Combined cycle gas turbine stations	KJCT	310	409	607	1 505	2 126	3 535	4 412	5 428	7 127	11 304	8 833
Hydro-electric stations (natural flow)	KLUK	847	840	780	777	742	592	832	881	905	755	840
Renewables other than hydro	KILA	784	1 028	1 417	1 707	1 829	2 171	2 661	3 538	4 078	4 671	5 314
All generating companies: total	KLUL	322 875	321 043	323 102	324 978	334 042	350 867	350 667	362 702	368 152	377 309	385 826
Conventional thermal and other[2]	AWYH	..	..	..	189 451	185 443	179 125	152 220	153 100	138 196	149 858	157 263
Combined cycle gas turbine stations	KJCU	622	3 400	23 418	38 475	50 846	69 415	91 386	99 260	121 747	129 239	126 016
Nuclear stations	KLUN	70 543	76 807	89 353	88 282	88 964	94 671	98 146	99 486	95 133	85 063	90 093
Hydro-electric stations:												
Natural flow	KLUP	4 624	5 431	4 302	5 094	4 838	3 393	4 169	5 118	5 336	5 086	4 056
Pumped storage	KLUQ	1 523	1 697	1 437	1 463	1 552	1 556	1 486	1 624	2 902	2 694	2 356
Renewables other than hydro	KLUR	787	1 073	1 582	2 213	2 399	2 707	3 260	4 114	4 838	5 369	6 042
Electricity used on works: Total	KLUS	20 111	20 237	19 287	17 491	17 411	16 078	16 560	17 408	16 707	16 333	17 376
Major generating companies	KLUT	18 424	18 485	17 391	16 696	16 510	14 967	15 411	16 140	15 462	14 952	15 994
Other generators	KLUU	1 687	1 752	1 896	795	901	1 111	1 149	1 268	1 245	1 381	1 382
Electricity supplied (gross)												
Major power producers: total	KLUV	283 066	281 692	287 264	290 780	299 000	311 268	308 722	317 624	321 146	326 831	336 991
Conventional thermal and other[2]	AWYI	..	..	..	167 866	163 818	155 086	127 419	127 788	112 919	124 828	132 655
Combined cycle gas turbine stations	KJCV	309	2 964	22 611	36 815	48 525	65 604	86 682	93 005	112 768	116 110	115 124
Nuclear stations	KLUX	62 761	69 135	80 979	79 962	80 598	85 820	89 341	90 590	87 672	78 334	82 985
Hydro-electric stations:												
Natural flow	KLUZ	3 767	4 579	3 513	4 265	4 051	2 763	3 299	4 225	4 409	4 316	3 204
Pumped storage	KLVA	1 465	1 635	1 388	1 417	1 502	1 507	1 439	1 569	2 804	2 603	2 340
Renewables other than hydro	KLVB	3	37	136	455	506	488	542	447	574	640	683
Other generators: total	KLVC	19 698	19 112	16 522	18 207	20 909	23 521	25 385	27 670	30 299	34 144	31 459
Conventional thermal and other[2]	AWYJ	..	..	..	14 333	16 338	17 492	17 815	18 250	18 655	18 217	17 180
Combined cycle gas turbine stations	KJCW	298	394	584	1 466	2 100	3 358	4 192	5 157	6 771	10 741	8 393
Hydro-electric stations (natural flow)	KLVF	839	832	772	769	733	584	822	869	894	743	829
Renewables other than hydro	KIKZ	753	987	1 360	1 639	1 738	2 085	2 555	3 393	3 978	4 443	5 058
All generating companies: total	KLVG	302 764	300 804	303 815	308 987	319 909	334 789	334 107	345 294	351 445	360 975	368 450
Conventional thermal and other[2]	AWYK	..	..	..	182 199	180 156	172 578	145 234	146 038	131 574	143 045	149 835
Combined cycle gas turbine stations	KJCX	607	3 358	23 195	38 281	50 625	68 962	90 874	98 162	119 539	126 851	123 517
Nuclear stations	KLVI	62 761	69 135	80 979	79 962	80 598	85 820	89 341	90 590	87 672	78 334	82 985
Hydro-electric stations:												
Natural flow	KLVK	4 666	5 411	4 285	5 034	4 784	3 347	4 121	5 094	5 303	5 059	4 033
Pumped storage	KLVL	1 465	1 635	1 388	1 417	1 502	1 507	1 439	1 569	2 804	2 603	2 340
Renewables other than hydro	KLVM	756	1 024	1 496	2 094	2 244	2 573	3 097	3 840	4 552	5 083	5 741
Electricity used in pumping												
Major power producers	KLVN	2 109	2 257	1 948	2 051	2 282	2 430	2 477	2 594	3 774	3 499	3 210
Electricity supplied (net): Total	KLVO	300 654	298 547	301 868	306 936	317 627	332 359	331 630	342 700	347 671	357 476	365 240
Major power producers	KLVP	280 956	279 435	285 316	288 729	296 718	308 838	306 245	315 030	317 372	323 332	333 781
Other generators	KLVQ	19 698	19 112	16 552	18 207	20 909	23 521	25 385	27 670	30 299	34 144	31 459
Net imports	KGEZ	16 408	16 694	16 716	16 887	16 313	16 755	16 574	12 468	14 244	14 174	10 399
Electricity available	KGIZ	317 062	315 241	318 584	323 830	333 940	349 114	348 203	355 168	361 915	371 650	375 640
Losses in transmission etc	KGKW	26 221	23 788	22 838	31 000	30 020	29 335	27 138	29 818	29 862	31 241	32 213
Electricity consumption: Total	KGKX	290 841	291 453	295 746	292 830	303 920	319 779	321 065	325 350	332 053	340 409	343 427
Fuel industries	KGKY	9 794	9 984	9 615	7 518	8 070	9 211	8 624	8 406	8 037	9 702	8 463
Final users: total	KGKZ	281 048	281 468	286 130	285 310	295 849	310 567	312 441	316 944	324 016	330 707	334 964
Industrial sector	KGLZ	99 570	95 277	96 842	96 120	101 780	107 631	108 102	108 443	112 250	114 915	113 589
Domestic sector	KGMZ	98 098	99 482	100 456	101 407	102 210	107 513	104 455	109 410	110 308	111 842	115 336
Other sectors	KGNZ	83 380	86 711	88 833	87 790	91 860	95 423	99 884	99 091	101 458	103 950	106 039

1 See chapter text.
2 Includes electricity supplied by gas turbines and oil engines and plants producing electricity from renewable resources other than hydro.

Source: Department of Trade and Industry: 020 7215 5190

21.9 Electricity: plant capacity and demand
United Kingdom

Megawatts

		At end of March					At end of December[1]					
		1993	1994	1995	1996		1996	1997	1998	1999	2000	2001
Major power producers[2]:												
Total declared net capability	KGON	63 997	64 901	64 923	66 100	GUFY	69 090	68 288	68 390	70 058	72 030	73 219
Conventional steam stations	KGOO	44 860	41 143	38 453	38 242	GUFZ	38 230	37 395	35 081	35 427	34 640	34 640
Combined cycle gas turbine stations	KJCZ	1 129	5 463	8 364	9 034	GUGA	12 052	12 252	14 638	16 110	19 349	20 517
Nuclear stations[3,4]	KGOP	11 353	11 894	12 037	12 762	GUGB	12 916	12 946	12 956	12 956	12 486	12 486
Gas turbines and oil engines	KGOQ	2 539	2 248	1 895	1 890	GUGC	1 721	1 526	1 492	1 333	1 323	1 323
Hydro-electric stations:												
Natural flow	KGOR	1 314	1 314	1 314	1 314	GUGD	1 313	1 311	1 327	1 327	1 327	1 348
Pumped storage	KGOS	2 787	2 787	2 788	2 788	GUGE	2 788	2 788	2 788	2 788	2 788	2 788
Renewables other than hydro	KGOT	15	52	72	71	GUGF	70	70	108	117	117	117
Other generators:												
Total capacity of own generating plant[5]	KGOU	3 502	3 622	3 818	4 025	GUGG	4 181	4 625	4 990	5 388	6 303	6 343
Conventional steam stations[6]	KGOV	3 037	3 096	3 257	3 234	GUGH	3 192	3 240	3 251	3 317	3 509	3 504
Combined cycle gas turbine stations	KJDA	150	150	153	343	GUGI	410	757	1 002	1 241	1 789	1 776
Hydro-electric stations (natural flow)	KGOX	110	111	111	118	GUGJ	142	145	148	150	158	160
Renewables other than hydro	KILB	205	265	297	330	GUGK	437	483	589	680	847	903
All generating companies: Total capacity[5]	KGOY	67 499	68 523	68 741	70 126	GUGL	73 271	72 913	73 380	75 446	78 333	79 562
Conventional steam stations[6]	KGOZ	47 897	44 239	41 710	41 476	GUGM	41 422	40 635	38 332	38 744	38 149	38 144
Combined cycle gas turbine stations	KJDC	1 279	5 613	8 517	9 377	GUGN	12 462	13 009	15 640	17 351	21 138	22 293
Nuclear stations[3]	KGPM	11 353	11 894	12 037	12 762	GUGO	12 916	12 946	12 956	12 956	12 486	12 486
Gas turbines and oil engines	KGPN	2 539	2 248	1 895	1 890	GUGP	1 721	1 526	1 492	1 333	1 323	1 323
Hydro-electric stations:												
Natural flow	KGPO	1 424	1 425	1 425	1 432	GUGQ	1 455	1 456	1 475	1 477	1 485	1 508
Pumped storage	KGPP	2 787	2 787	2 788	2 788	GUGR	2 788	2 788	2 788	2 788	2 788	2 788
Renewables other than hydro	KGPQ	220	317	369	401	GUGS	507	553	697	797	964	1 020
Major power producers[2]:												
Simultaneous maximum load met [7]	KGPR	51 663	54 848	52 362	55 611	GUGT	56 815	56 965	56 312	57 849	58 452	57 052
System load factor[8] (percentage)	KGQY	66.6	63.8	67.3	65.4	GUGU	66.3	66.2	67.4	66.6	67.8	70.8

1 From 1996 data are on a calendar year basis.
2 See chapter text.
3 The 1995 figure includes 300 MW of the 1,188 MW capacity of Sizewell B which began to produce electricity in March 1995.
4 Nuclear generators are now included under "major power producers" only.
5 Capacity figures for other generators are as at end-December of the previous year.

6 For other generators, conventional steam stations cover all types of stations not separately listed.
7 Maximum load in year to end of March.
8 The average hourly quantity of electricity available during the year ended March expressed as a percentage of the maximum demand.

Source: Department of Trade and Industry: 020 7215 5190

21.10 Electricity: fuel used in generation
United Kingdom

Million tonnes of oil equivalent

		1991	1992	1993	1994	1995	1996	1997	1998	1999	2000	2001
Major power producers[1]: total all fuels	KGPS	72.90	71.30	72.32	71.65	72.72	74.61	71.48	74.94	73.62	74.41	77.48
Coal	FTAJ	49.0	46.0	38.3	35.9	35.0	32.4	27.1	28.7	24.5	27.8	30.6
Oil[2]	FTAK	5.9	5.0	4.4	3.6	3.1	3.0	1.2	0.8	0.8	0.8	0.8
Gas[3]	KGPT	–	1.0	6.3	9.1	11.4	15.2	19.3	20.3	24.2	24.4	23.8
Nuclear[4]	FTAL	17.4	18.5	21.6	21.2	21.3	22.2	22.0	23.4	22.2	19.6	20.8
Hydro (natural flow)	FTAM	0.3	0.4	0.3	0.4	0.4	0.2	0.3	0.4	0.4	0.4	0.3
Other fuels used by UK companies[3]	KGPU	–	–	0.1	0.1	0.1	0.1	0.2	0.2	0.2	0.3	0.3
Net imports	KGPV	1.4	1.4	1.4	1.5	1.4	1.4	1.4	1.1	1.2	1.2	0.9
Other generators: total all fuels	KGPW	5.4	6.7	4.5	3.5	5.8	6.0	6.7	7.1	7.3	8.1	7.7
Transport undertakings												
Gas	KGPX	0.2	0.2	0.2	0.2	0.2	0.2	0.2	0.2	0.2	0.2	0.2
Undertakings in industrial sector												
Coal	KGPY	1.0	1.0	1.3	1.2	1.3	1.2	1.2	1.2	1.0	0.9	1.0
Oil	KGPZ	1.7	3.1	1.4	0.5	1.0	1.0	0.8	0.7	0.7	0.8	0.6
Gas	KGQM	0.3	0.3	0.8	0.6	1.6	1.8	2.2	2.5	2.7	3.3	2.8
Hydro (natural flow)	KGQO	0.1	0.1	0.1	0.1	0.1	0.1	0.1	0.1	0.1	0.1	0.1
Other fuels	KGQP	1.9	1.1	1.0	1.0	1.7	1.8	2.2	2.4	2.6	2.8	3.0
All generating companies: total fuels	KGQQ	78.3	78.0	76.8	75.2	78.6	80.6	78.2	82.0	80.9	82.5	85.2
Coal	KGQR	50.0	46.9	39.6	37.1	36.3	33.6	28.3	29.9	25.5	28.7	31.7
Oil	KGQS	7.6	8.1	5.8	4.1	4.1	4.0	2.0	1.5	1.5	1.6	1.4
Gas[3]	KGQT	0.6	1.5	7.0	9.9	13.3	17.2	21.7	23.0	27.1	27.9	26.8
Nuclear[4]	KGQU	17.4	18.5	21.6	21.2	21.3	22.2	22.0	23.4	22.2	19.6	20.8
Hydro (natural flow)	KGQV	0.4	0.5	0.4	0.4	0.4	0.3	0.4	0.4	0.5	0.4	0.3
Other fuels used by UK companies[3,5]	KGQW	0.9	1.1	1.0	1.1	1.8	1.9	2.4	2.6	2.9	3.1	3.3
Net imports	KGQX	1.4	1.4	1.4	1.5	1.4	1.4	1.4	1.1	1.2	1.2	0.9

1 See chapter text.
2 Includes oil used in gas turbine and diesel plant for lighting up coal fired boilers and Orimulsion.
3 For 1991 gas used by major power producers was included with other fuels for reasons of confidentiality.

4 Nuclear generators are now included under "major power producers" only.
5 Main fuels included are coke oven gas, blast furnace gas, waste products from chemical processes and sludge gas.

Source: Department of Trade and Industry: 020 7215 5190

Production

21.11 Indigenous production, refinery receipts, imports and exports of oil[1]

Thousand tonnes

		1991	1992	1993	1994	1995	1996	1997	1998	1999	2000	2001
Total indigenous petroleum production[2]	KMBA	91 260	94 251	100 188	126 812	129 894	129 742	128 234	132 363	137 099	126 245	116 679
Crude petroleum[3]:												
Refinery receipts total	KMBB	92 523	92 789	97 400	93 771	93 572	96 660	97 023	93 797	88 286	88 014	84 503
Foreign trade[4]												
Imports	KMBF	57 084	57 683	61 701	53 096	48 749	50 099	49 994	47 958	44 869	54 387	53 551
Exports	AXRB	55 131	57 627	64 415	83 205	84 578	81 563	79 400	84 610	91 797	92 918	86 746
Net imports	AXRC	1 953	56	−2 714	−30 109	−35 829	−31 464	−29 406	−36 652	−46 928	−38 531	−33 195
Petroleum products												
Foreign trade												
Imports[4]	BHMI	10 140	10 567	10 064	10 441	9 878	9 315	8 705	11 327	13 896	14 212	16 978
Exports[4]	AXRD	19 351	20 250	23 060	22 157	21 614	23 681	26 755	24 375	21 730	20 677	19 080
Net imports[4]	AXRE	−9 211	−9 683	−12 996	−11 716	−11 736	−14 366	−18 049	−12 957	−7 834	−6 465	−2 102
International marine bunkers	BHMK	2 486	2 546	2 478	2 313	2 465	2 664	2 961	3 080	2 329	2 079	2 274

1 See chapter text. The term 'indigenous' is used in this table to cover oil produced on the UK Continental Shelf. This includes small amounts produced onshore.
2 Crude oil *plus* condensates and petroleum gases derived at onshore treatment plants.

3 Includes process (partly refined) oils.
4 Foreign trade as recorded by the petroleum industry and may differ from figures published in *Overseas Trade Statistics*.

Source: Department of Trade and Industry: 020 7215 5184

21.12 Throughput of crude and process oils and output of refined products from refineries[1]

United Kingdom

Thousand tonnes

		1991	1992	1993	1994	1995	1996	1997	1998	1999	2000	2001
Throughput of crude and process oils	KMAU	92 001	92 334	96 274	93 162	92 743	96 661	97 024	93 797	88 285	88 013	84 503
less: Refinery fuel:	KMAA	6 058	6 080	6 383	6 256	6 481	6 623	6 572	6 468	5 976	5 402	5 162
Losses	KMAB	467	471	308	261	129	152	86	233	324	−128	2 409
Total output of refined products	KMAC	85 476	85 783	89 583	86 645	86 133	89 885	90 366	87 096	81 985	82 739	76 931
Gases:												
Butane and propane	KMAE	1 664	1 583	1 575	1 605	1 815	1 828	1 950	1 978	2 002	1 957	1 764
Other petroleum	KMAF	134	172	162	132	133	144	139	200	209	169	92
Naphtha and other feedstock	KMAG	2 515	3 040	2 696	2 794	2 711	2 824	2 854	2 335	2 465	3 145	3 428
Aviation spirit	KMAH	–	–	–	–	–	–	–	–	16	31	101
Motor spirit	KMAJ	27 793	27 980	28 394	27 562	27 254	28 046	28 260	27 392	25 587	23 929	21 455
Industrial and white spirit	KMAK	136	150	159	143	143	136	128	136	130	124	121
Kerosene:												
Aviation turbine fuel	KMAL	7 037	7 681	8 341	7 697	7 837	8 305	8 342	7 942	7 352	6 620	5 910
Burning oil	KMAM	2 446	2 450	2 707	2 967	2 924	3 510	3 336	3 471	3 603	3 141	3 088
Gas/diesel oil	KMAN	26 057	25 650	27 361	27 137	27 169	28 903	28 778	27 859	26 226	28 879	26 794
Fuel oil	KMAO	13 205	12 388	13 183	11 378	10 969	11 479	11 747	11 066	10 289	10 302	9 941
Lubricating oil	KMAP	973	1 163	1 264	1 296	1 261	1 111	1 231	1 134	920	717	656
Bitumen	KMAQ	2 302	2 336	2 450	2 569	2 459	2 189	2 258	2 190	1 667	1 468	1 707
Petroleum wax	KMAR	37	62	59	64	46	41	65	59	264	445	416
Petroleum coke	KMAS	555	535	621	679	759	714	598	694	648	857	765
Other products	KMAT	620	593	613	623	653	655	680	640	607	955	692

1 See chapter text. Crude and process oils comprise all feedstocks, other than distillation benzines, for treatment at refinery plants. Refinery production does not cover further treatment of finished products for special grades such as in distillation plant for the preparation of industrial spirits.

Source: Department of Trade and Industry: 020 7215 5184

21.13 Deliveries of petroleum products for inland consumption[1]
United Kingdom

Thousand tonnes

		1991	1992	1993	1994	1995	1996	1997	1998	1999	2000	2001
Total (including refinery fuel)	KMCA	80 564	81 550	82 173	81 213	80 175	82 013	79 073	78 437	77 985	76 635	76 077
Total (excluding refinery fuel)	KMCB	74 506	75 470	75 970	74 957	73 694	75 390	72 501	71 969	72 009	71 233	70 915
Butane and propane	ECAQ	2 272	1 890	1 992	2 486	2 481	2 439	2 426	2 368	2 249	2 070	2 155
Other Petroleum Gases (includes Ethane)	ECAR	986	1 201	1 261	1 459	1 489	1 482	1 561	1 534	1 829	1 707	1 873
Naphtha	ECAS	3 299	3 281	3 117	2 866	2 885	3 010	2 640	2 882	3 100	2 344	1 594
Aviation spirit	KMCI	24	27	27	29	29	32	37	36	45	52	59
Motor spirit:												
Retail deliveries:												
Leaded Premium / Lead Replacement Petrol	KMCK	13 793	12 481	11 046	9 503	7 993	7 043	6 138	4 595	2 629	1 462	837
Super Premium Unleaded	KMCL	1 158	1 401	1 439	1 323	925	698	506	409	473	403	420
Premium Unleaded	KMCM	8 429	9 541	10 754	11 536	12 603	14 228	15 188	16 432	18 307	19 208	19 095
Total Retail Deliveries	ECAT	23 380	23 423	23 239	22 362	21 521	21 969	21 832	21 436	21 409	21 073	20 352
Commercial consumers:												
Leaded Premium / Lead Replacement Petrol	KMCO	360	294	217	178	149	135	112	91	61	44	34
Super Premium Unleaded	KMCP	15	22	25	26	17	11	9	4	6	6	9
Premium Unleaded	KMCQ	267	304	286	277	285	294	298	318	311	480	538
Total Commercial Consumers	ECAU	642	620	528	481	451	440	419	413	378	530	581
Total Motor spirit	BHOD	24 022	24 043	23 767	22 843	21 972	22 409	22 251	21 849	21 787	21 603	20 933
Industrial and white spirits	KMCS	162	159	164	170	178	184	195	179	174	170	149
Kerosene:												
Aviation turbine fuel	BHOE	6 176	6 666	7 106	7 284	7 660	8 049	8 411	9 241	9 939	10 698	10 297
Burning oil	KMCT	2 383	2 472	2 625	2 655	2 774	3 336	3 343	3 575	3 633	3 748	4 244
Gas/diesel oil:												
Derv fuel:												
Retail Deliveries	ECAV	3 145	3 449	3 765	4 345	4 814	5 537	6 127	6 602	7 137	7 713	8 198
Commercial Consumers	ECAW	7 549	7 683	8 041	8 569	8 643	8 828	8 849	8 541	8 371	8 168	8 220
Total Derv fuel	BHOI	10 694	11 132	11 806	12 914	13 457	14 365	14 976	15 143	15 508	15 881	16 418
Other gas/diesel oil (includes Mdf)	ECAX	8 684	8 616	8 516	8 167	7 879	8 349	8 053	8 005	7 196	7 036	7 008
Fuel oil	BHOK	11 948	11 481	10 770	9 275	7 975	6 854	3 936	2 935	2 415	1 833	2 202
Lubricating oils	BHOL	759	786	806	795	895	864	872	813	790	801	796
Bitumen	BHOM	2 514	2 555	2 523	2 595	2 420	2 146	2 015	1 967	1 928	1 975	1 923
Petroleum wax	KMCU	49	47	48	47	44	44	44	18	37	32	32
Petroleum coke	KMCV	154	682	778	911	1 008	1 210	1 095	887	660	776	760
Miscellaneous products	KMCW	378	431	661	461	548	617	646	537	719	507	472

1 See chapter text.

Source: Department of Trade and Industry: 020 7215 5184

21.14 Iron and steel[1]
Summary of steel supplies, deliveries and stocks
United Kingdom

		Finished product weight - thousand tonnes										
		1991	1992	1993	1994	1995	1996	1997	1998	1999	2000	2001
Supply, disposal and consumption												
UK producers' home deliveries	KLTA	7 951	7 315	7 567	7 827	8 257	8 383	8 626	8 260	7 652	7 255	6 762
Imports excluding steelworks receipts	KLTB	4 509	4 418	4 132	5 012	5 384	5 147	5 894	6 466	6 014	6 387	6 978
Total deliveries to home market (a)	KLTC	12 460	11 733	11 698	12 839	13 641	13 530	14 520	14 726	13 666	13 642	13 740
Total exports (producers, consumers, merchants)	KLTD	7 444	7 718	7 621	8 120	8 228	8 917	9 060	8 008	7 623	7 446	6 512
Exports by UK producers	KLTE	7 082	7 587	7 536	7 873	7 828	8 305	8 534	7 876	7 416	7 163	6 182
Derived consumers' and merchants' exports (b)	KLTF	362	131	85	247	400	612	526	132	207	283	330
Net home disposals (a)-(b)	KLTG	12 098	11 602	11 614	12 592	13 241	12 918	13 994	14 594	13 460	13 359	13 410
Consumers' and merchants' stock change	KLTH	−400	60	60	390	..	..	..	..	..	..	..
Estimated home consumption	KLTI	12 498	11 542	11 554	12 202	13 241	12 918	13 994	14 594	13 460	13 359	13 410
Stocks												
Producers												
- ingots & semis	KLTJ	1 035	933	1 005	946	1 068	767	946	717	747	755	705
- finished steel	KLTK	1 719	1 573	1 425	1 389	1 274	1 515	1 358	1 495	1 318	1 039	977
Consumers	KLTL	1 400	1 410	1 300	1 470	..	..	..	..	..	..	..
Merchants	KLTM	840	890	1 060	1 280	..	..	..	..	..	..	..

		Crude steel equivalent - million tonnes										
		1991	1992	1993	1994	1995	1996	1997	1998	1999	2000	2001
Estimated home consumption												
Crude steel production[2]	KLTN	16.47	16.21	16.62	17.28	17.60	17.99	18.50	17.32	16.28	15.16	13.54
Producers' stock change	KLTO	−0.07	−0.30	−0.09	−0.12	0.01	−0.07	0.03	−0.11	−0.19	−0.33	−0.14
Re-usable material	KLTP	0.07	0.06	0.08	0.09	0.08	0.07	0.06	0.02	..	..	..
Total supply from home sources	KLTQ	16.61	16.57	16.79	17.49	17.67	18.13	18.53	17.45	16.47	15.48	13.68
Total imports[3]	KLTR	6.21	5.99	5.44	6.58	7.05	7.01	7.49	8.38	7.81	8.43	9.11
Total exports[3]	KLTS	8.72	9.07	8.95	9.55	9.63	10.26	10.43	9.25	8.70	8.61	7.53
Net home disposals	KLTT	14.10	13.49	13.28	14.52	15.09	14.88	15.59	16.58	15.58	15.30	15.26
Consumers' and merchants' stock change	KLTU	−0.50	0.07	0.07	0.48	..	..	..	..	..	..	..
Estimated home consumption	KLTV	14.60	13.42	13.21	14.04	15.09	14.88	15.59	16.58	15.58	15.30	15.26

1 See chapter text. The figures relate to periods of 52 weeks (53 weeks in 1992).
2 Includes liquid steel for castings.
3 Based on HM Customs Statistics, reflecting total trade rather than producers' trade.

Source: Iron and Steel Statistics Bureau: 020 8686 9050 ext 126

21.15

Iron and steel[1]
Iron ore, manganese ore, pig iron and iron and steel scrap
United Kingdom

Thousand tonnes

		1991	1992	1993	1994	1995	1996	1997	1998	1999	2000	2001
Iron ore												
Jurassic	KLOA	57	29	–	–	–	–	–	–	–	–	–
Hematite	KLOB	–	–	–	–	–	–	–	–	–	–	–
Production: total	KLOC	57	29	–	–	–	–	–	–	–	–	–
Home produced	KLOD	57	29	–	–	–	–	–	–	–	–	–
Imported	KLOE	17 833	17 235	17 507	18 161	18 670	19 720	20 820	19 532	18 739	16 928	15 113
Consumption: total	KLOF	17 890	17 264	17 507	18 161	18 670	19 720	20 820	19 532	18 739	16 928	15 113
Manganese ore												
Consumption	KLOG	383	308	152	64	32	48	37	22	14	36	4
Pig iron (and blast furnace ferro-alloys)												
Average number of furnaces in blast during period	KLOH	*8*	*8*	*8*	*8*	*8*	*9*	*9*	*9*	*9*	*8*	*8*
Production												
Steelmaking iron	KLOI	11 834	11 469	11 534	11 943	12 236	12 830	13 054	12 746	12 139	10 890	9 870
Foundry iron	KLOJ	50	73	–	–	–	–	–	–	–	–	–
Speigeleisen and ferro-manganese	KLOK	178	137	45	–	–	–	–	–	–	–	–
In blast furnaces: total	KLOL	12 062	11 679	11 579	11 943	12 236	12 830	13 054	12 746	12 139	10 890	9 870
In steel works and steel foundries	KLOM	11 836	11 463	11 554	11 889	12 121	12 753	13 044	12 746	12 139	10 890	9 870
In iron foundries	KLON	181	214	..	..	..	..	..	..	..	..	..
Consumption of pig iron: total	KLOO	12 017	11 677	11 554	11 889	12 121	12 753	13 044	12 746	12 139	10 890	9 870
Iron and steel scrap												
Steelworks and steel foundries												
Circulating scrap	KLOQ	2 332	2 449	2 303	2 326	2 390	2 639	2 459	2 380	2 488	2 287	2 019
Purchased receipts	KLOR	3 694	3 739	4 149	4 533	4 688	4 130	5 418	4 045	3 433	3 327	3 001
Consumption	KLOS	6 085	6 190	6 550	6 874	7 012	6 828	7 207	6 408	5 884	5 675	5 026
Stocks (end of period)	KLOT	365	365	267	253	319	260	236	253	290	229	224
Iron foundries												
Arisings	KLOU	582	587	..	..	..	..	..	..	..	..	..
Consumption	KLOV	1 457	1 556	..	..	..	..	..	..	..	..	..

1 See chapter text. The figures relate to periods of 52 weeks (53 weeks in 1992).

Source: Iron and Steel Statistics Bureau: 020 8686 9050 ext 126

21.16

Iron and steel[1]
Number of furnaces and production of steel
United Kingdom

			1991	1992	1993	1994	1995	1996	1997	1998	1999	2000	2001
Steel furnaces													
(Number in existence at end of period)[2]													
Total	KLPA		209	206	202	202	192	192	192	190	181	181	181
Oxygen converters	KLPC		14	11	11	11	11	11	11	11	11	11	11
Electric	KLPD		195	195	191	191	181	181	181	179	170	170	170
Production of crude steel													
(thousand tonnes)													
Total	KLPF		16 474	16 212	16 625	17 286	17 604	17 992	18 499	17 315	16 284	15 155	13 543
by process													
Oxygen converters	KLPH		12 540	12 092	12 330	12 909	13 082	13 758	13 986	13 426	12 634	11 551	10 271
Electric	KLPI		3 934	4 120	4 295	4 377	4 522	4 234	4 513	3 889	3 650	3 604	3 272
by cast method													
Cast to ingot	KLPK		2 201	2 083	2 140	2 033	2 174	1 892	1 660	784	534	539	369
Continuously cast	KLPL		14 085	13 958	14 319	15 079	15 250	15 912	16 653	16 346	15 637	14 470	13 024
Steel for castings	KLPM		189	171	166	174	180	188	186	185	127	146	150
by quality													
Non alloy steel	KLPN		15 496	15 195	15 558	16 062	16 243	16 708	17 193	16 145	15 263	14 004	12 482
Stainless and other alloy steel	KLPO		978	1 017	1 067	1 224	1 361	1 284	1 306	1 170	1 035	1 151	1 061
Production of finished steel products													
(all quantities)[3] (thousand tonnes)													
Rods and bars for reinforcement (in coil and lengths)	KLPP		1 151	1 130	1 229	1 269	1 154	1 182	1 118	1 133	893	812	755
Wire rods and other rods and bars in coil	KLPQ		1 272	1 327	1 427	1 524	1 642	1 536	1 565	1 492	1 407	1 408	1 389
Hot rolled bars in lengths	KLPR		1 192	1 178	1 140	1 275	1 311	1 499	1 716	1 791	1 542	1 545	1 449
Bright steel bars[4]	KLPS		257	281	295	363	424	357	385	336	311	337	296
Light sections other than rails	KLPT		324	349	294	306	286	298	302	318	264	183	201
Heavy and light rails and accessories	KGQZ	KLPU	2 297	2 361	2 408	2 412	2 549	2 557	2 397	2 346	2 303	1 915	1 931
Other heavy sections		KLPV											
Hot rolled plates, sheets and strip in coil and lengths	KLPW		7 270	7 145	7 230	7 715	8 077	8 512	8 956	8 454	7 893	7 278	5 821
Cold rolled plates and sheets in coil and lengths	KLPX		3 592	3 532	3 635	3 835	4 100	4 221	4 437	4 288	3 914	3 612	2 944
Cold rolled strip[4]	KLPZ		286	222	229	243	267	246	255	259	233	218	201
Tinplate	KLQW		742	805	829	767	791	739	754	772	736	753	602
Other coated sheet	KLQX		1 647	1 795	1 865	2 021	2 306	2 366	2 534	2 610	2 475	2 471	1 773
Tubes and pipes[4]	KLQY		1 260	1 187	1 155	1 136	1 183	1 317	1 310	1 276	1 100	1 061	1 096
Forged bars[4]	KLQZ		7	4	2	2	3	3	3	3	2	1	1

1 See chapter text. The figures relate to periods of 52 weeks (53 weeks in 1992).
2 Includes steel furnaces at steel foundries.

3 Includes material for conversion into other products listed in the table.
4 Based on producers' deliveries.

Source: Iron and Steel Statistics Bureau: 020 8686 9050 ext 126

21.17 Non-ferrous metals
United Kingdom

		1990	1991	1992	1993	1994	1995	1996	1997	1998	1999	2000
Copper												
Production of refined copper:												
Primary	KLAA	47.0	16.6	10.4	10.7	11.1	12.0	13.0	9.1	6.4	1.7	–
Secondary	KLAB	74.6	53.5	31.7	35.9	35.6	43.0	43.6	51.3	47.4	48.6	–
Home consumption:												
Refined	KLAC	317.2	269.4	308.3	325.0	377.3	397.9	396.0	408.3	374.1	305.3	322.8
Scrap (metal content)	KLAD	126.3	118.5	83.2	77.9	88.0	81.0	81.0	69.0	64.6	112.5	132.4
Stocks (end of period)[1,2]	KLAE	11.7	9.3	9.7	9.3	8.1	7.5	6.6	12.8	7.5	7.3	10.4
Analysis of home consumption												
(refined and scrap):[3] total	KLAF	443.5	387.9	391.5	403.0	468.0	493.2	477.3	477.4	438.7	417.7	455.2
Wire[4]	KLAG	220.2	191.9	247.0	253.9	306.2	321.4	309.4	312.5	287.2	276.1	310.0
Rods, bars and sections	KLAH	54.4	52.7	51.5	53.2	54.9	59.0	58.3	58.3	53.6	46.9	43.6
Sheet, strip and plate	KLAI	54.4	37.1	31.0	30.7	33.0	37.1	34.0	36.5	30.5	27.7	32.3
Tubes	KLAJ	73.0	65.5	62.0	65.2	73.9	75.7	75.6	70.1	67.4	67.1	69.4
Castings and miscellaneous	KLAK	41.5	40.7	..	..	..	..	..	..	..	..	..
Zinc												
Slab zinc:												
Production	KLAL	93.3	100.7	96.8	102.4	101.3	106.0	96.9	107.7	99.6	132.8	99.6
Home consumption	KLAM	193.0	183.7	190.1	195.9	196.5	198.4	195.7	194.8	187.9	198.9	205.7
Stocks (end of period)	KLAN	12.2	11.2	11.4	11.4	10.5	9.8	10.5	10.1	10.6	10.9	11.3
Other zinc (metal content):												
Consumption	KLAO	52.4	49.5	46.7	45.4	45.0	46.8	41.3	41.5	37.3	41.6	46.3
Analysis of home consumption												
(slab and scrap): total	KLAP	245.4	233.2	236.8	241.3	241.5	245.2	237.1	236.3	226.2	236.7	242.5
Brass	KLAQ	51.4	47.2	40.9	41.6	42.6	45.2	39.1	41.6	36.6	33.6	34.4
Galvanized products	KLAR	104.7	96.6	103.4	105.1	107.4	110.7	110.3	108.4	103.8	116.6	120.9
Zinc sheet and strip	KLAS	3.6	3.6	4.1	4.0	4.6	3.0	3.0	3.3	3.3	3.3	3.3
Zinc alloy die castings	KLAT	44.4	45.4	45.2	46.5	46.5	46.5	46.5	46.5	46.5	46.5	46.5
Zinc oxide	KLAU	21.1	20.3	22.5	20.7	21.6	21.6	20.7	20.6	20.4	21.1	21.8
Other products	KLAV	20.2	20.2	20.8	23.4	18.8	18.2	17.5	16.1	11.0	11.0	11.0
Refined lead												
Production[5,6]	KLAW	329.4	311.0	346.8	363.8	352.5	320.7	351.4	384.1	349.7	347.6	334.2
Home consumption[6,7]												
Refined lead	KLAX	301.6	263.8	263.6	263.6	267.6	285.4	272.8	270.4	275.5	283.3	300.6
Scrap and remelted lead[6]	KLAY	32.5	33.6	38.7	35.2	38.5	41.6	43.4	39.1	38.4	32.2	40.9
Stocks (end of period)[8]												
Lead bullion	KLAZ	18.0	22.8	36.3	20.7	10.2	9.5	32.9	15.5	20.9	17.1	10.0
Refined soft lead at consumers	KLBA	22.3	21.8	24.5	25.0	23.5	24.9	28.8	29.1	27.4	25.7	25.8
In LME Warehouses (UK)	KLBB	12.1	8.0	9.0	9.5	6.1	0.4	3.0	2.4	–	0.1	–
Analysis of home consumption												
(refined and scrap): total	KLBC	334.0	297.4	302.3	298.8	306.1	327.0	316.2	309.5	313.9	315.5	333.5
Cables	KLBD	10.4	8.6	9.3	8.9	9.3	9.8	9.8	9.7	9.7	9.7	9.6
Batteries (excluding oxides)	KLBE	51.0	51.9	53.4	48.7	52.5	52.7	52.3	54.7	51.6	47.4	50.5
Oxides and compounds:												
Batteries	KLBF	52.8	54.2	53.1	53.9	55.2	56.2	54.9	56.1	54.4	53.1	55.9
Other uses	KLBG	73.7	55.0	55.6	56.3	53.9	53.8	56.1	54.5	56.4	57.0	56.8
Sheets and pipes	KLBH	96.8	79.8	82.8	82.7	84.6	101.2	94.1	91.1	96.1	94.9	102.3
Solder	KLBJ	8.0	7.7	7.4	7.4	7.4	7.4	7.4	7.4	7.4	7.4	7.4
Alloys	KLBK	14.0	12.2	14.7	14.1	15.3	15.9	12.1	9.4	9.4	11.9	15.2
Other uses	KLBL	27.5	28.0	26.2	26.8	27.9	30.0	29.5	26.6	28.9	34.1	37.1

21.17
Non-ferrous metals
United Kingdom

Thousand tonnes

		1990	1991	1992	1993	1994	1995	1996	1997	1998	1999	2000	2001
Tin													
Tin ore (metal content):													
Production	KLBM	3.4	2.3	2.0	2.2	1.9	2.1	2.3	0.4	–	–	..	..
Tin metal[9]:													
Production[10]	KLBO	12.0	5.2	–	–	–	–	–	–	..	..	..	..
Home consumption[10]	KLBT	10.4	10.3	10.4	10.4	10.4	10.5	10.5	9.8	9.6	10.0	..	..
Exports and re-exports[11]	KLBQ	5.7	2.9	0.2	0.3	1.2	2.7	0.6	0.3	0.1	0.1	..	..
Stocks (end of period):													
Consumers	KLBR	1.0	1.0	1.0	1.0	1.0	1.0	1.0	1.0	1.0	1.0	..	..
Analysis of home consumption													
(excluding scrap): total	KLBT	10.4	10.3	10.4	10.4	10.4	10.5	10.5	9.8	9.6	10.0	..	..
Tinplate	KLBU	3.6	3.6	3.6	3.6	3.6	3.6	3.6	2.8	2.6	3.0	..	..
Alloys	KLBV	3.4	3.3	3.4	3.4	3.3	3.4	3.5	3.6	3.6	3.6	..	..
Solder	KLBW	1.0	1.1	1.1	1.1	1.1	1.1	1.1	1.1	1.1	1.1	..	..
Other uses	KLBX	2.4	2.3	2.3	2.3	2.4	2.4	2.3	2.3	2.3	2.3	..	..
Primary aluminium[12]													
Production	KLBY	289.8	293.5	244.2	239.1	231.2	237.9	240.0	247.7	258.4	269.7	305.1	340.8
Despatches to consumers	KLBZ	520.2	485.4	587.2	815.3	610.6	459.4	593.7	456.4	648.5	480.1	234.4	450.7
Secondary aluminium													
Production	KLCA	201.4	195.1	197.3	236.2	224.3	229.7	261.0	242.7	274.8	258.3	237.7	248.6
Exports	KLCC	59.7	64.8	83.5	98.3	124.8	145.8	152.2	153.3	156.6	143.1	84.2	59.9
Fabricated aluminium													
Total despatches[13]	KLCD	547.7	518.0	598.2	592.0	643.1	648.3	633.5	663.2	668.5	668.7	738.7	690.9
Rolled products[14]	KLCE	261.0	269.4	328.9	309.3	346.4	359.2	327.9	350.4	352.5	349.7	419.1	384.8
Extrusions and tubes[15]	KLCF	157.9	129.1	132.8	136.2	142.7	142.1	149.6	160.8	168.0	181.7	184.7	177.1
Castings	KLCH	111.3	97.3	116.3	133.0	143.4	147.0	156.0	152.0	148.0	137.3	134.9	129.0
Refined nickel													
Production (including ferro-nickel)	KLCM	26.5	28.6	28.0	28.0	28.4	35.1	42.0	36.6	39.1	39.5	..	..

1 Unwrought copper (electrolytic, fire refined and blister).
2 Reported stocks of refined copper held by consumers and those held in London Metal Exchange (LME) warehouses in the United Kingdom.
3 Copper content.
4 Consumption for high-conductivity copper and cadmium copper wire represented by consumption of wire rods, production of which for export is also included.
5 Lead reclaimed from secondary and scrap material and lead refined from bullion and domestic ores.
6 Figures for production and consumption of refined lead include antimonial lead, and for scrap and remelted lead, exclude secondary antimonial lead.
7 Including toll transactions involving fabrication.
8 Excluding goverment stocks.

9 Including production from imported scrap and residues refined on toll.
10 Primary and secondary metal.
11 Including re-exports on toll transactions.
12 Including primary alloys. Despatches to consumers are calculated as the despatches by UK industry plus imports, minus exports but deliveries to LME warehouses are not included.
13 Includes wrought, cast products, and excludes foil products.
14 Includes foil stock and excludes foil products.
15 Excluding forging bars, wirebars, and almost two-thirds of despatches of hot rolled rod.

Sources: World Bureau of Metal Statistics: 01920 461274;
Aluminium Federation: 0121 456 1103

21.18 Fertilisers
Deliveries to UK agriculture by Members of the Fertiliser Manufacturers' Association
Years ending 30 June

Thousand tonnes

		1991	1992	1993	1994	1995	1996	1997	1998	1999	2000	2001
Nutrient Content												
N (nitrogen):												
Straight	KGRM	628	587	537	553	602	685	615	664	618	637	479
Compounds	KGRN	462	378	377	413	449	444	420	406	430	398	400
P_2O_5 (phosphate)	KGRO	278	227	218	236	272	284	287	296	291	253	228
K_2O (potash)	KGRP	364	287	284	299	343	353	356	360	357	309	269
Compounds - total product	KGRQ	2 742	2 254	2 216	2 378	2 656	2 688	2 664	2 620	2 727	2 523	2 228

Source: Fertiliser Manufacturers' Association: 01780 720422

21.19 Minerals: production[1]

Thousand tonnes

		Great Britain										
		1991	1992	1993	1994	1995	1996	1997	1998	1999	2000	2001
Limestone	KLEA	91 999	86 000	90 069	102 844	90 933	82 442	84 252	85 382	82 714	80 810	83 492
Sandstone	KLEB	12 928	11 586	12 100	13 494	15 017	12 581	12 457	13 545	11 870	12 056	11 897
Igneous rock	KLEC	46 008	48 630	49 209	50 014	49 641	43 731	42 370	39 838	45 294	44 633	45 053
Clay/shale	KLED	13 038	12 155	10 891	12 464	13 930	11 804	11 322	12 230	11 355	10 838	10 426
Industrial sand	KLEE	4 201	3 615	3 587	4 038	4 344	4 861	4 704	4 662	4 092	4 095	3 848
Chalk	KLEF	10 317	9 171	9 076	10 236	9 949	9 239	9 550	9 934	9 667	9 213	8 205
Fireclay	KLEG	867	572	479	679	708	536	338	577	545	595	459
Barium sulphate	KLEH	86	77	33	34	74	93	57	64	59	54	70
Calcium fluoride	KLEI	78	76	70	50	46	..	58	52	46	21	46
Copper	KLEJ	0.2	–	–	–	–	–	–	–	–	–	–
Lead	KLEK	..	..	..	2	..	..	..	1	1	..	1
Tin	KLEL	2.3	2.0	2.2	1.9	2.0	2.1	2.0	–	–	–	–
Zinc	KLEM	1.0	..	..	..	..	..	–	–	–	–	–
Iron ore: crude	KLEN	..	4	..	2	2	1	2	2	1	1	1
Iron ore: iron content	KLEO	..	2	1	1	1	1	1	1	1	1	..
Calcspar	KLEP	8	4	3	..	..	..	13	15	..	..	12
China clay	KLEQ / KILC	3 744	2 732	2 852	2 977	3 076	2 654	2 798	2 866	2 841	2 779	2 804
Ball clay	KIMS	..	..	..	913	..	..	..	..	..	..	..
Chert and flint	KLER	5	..	..	..	..	..	..	..	6	..	2
Fuller's earth	KLES	202	203	153	193	150	183	162	111	83	103	..
Lignite	KLET	3	3	3	2	–	–	–	–	–	–	–
Rock salt	KLEU	2 088	..	..	..	..	..	..	..	..	..	..
Salt from brine	KLEV	1 319	..	..	..	..	..	..	..	..	..	..
Salt in brine	KLEW	..	3 401	4 076	4 009	3 548	3 512	3 561	..	..	..	..
Anhydrite	KLEX	..	..	..	..	..	..	..	..	–	–	–
Dolomite	KLEY	19 454	18 539	17 985	17 616	17 966	16 555	17 282	15 632	13 698	13 069	14 314
Gypsum	KLEZ	..	..	..	..	..	..	..	..	..	..	..
Slate[2]	KLFA	360	326	462	402	275	408	347	425	361	479	551
Soapstone and talc	KLFB	11	5	5	5	4	5	5	5	6	5	5
Sand and gravel (land-won)	KLFC	85 479	78 341	79 380	86 341	78 031	70 489	74 362	73 016	74 785	74 877	74 599
Sand and gravel (marine dredged)	KLFD	12 439	10 557	10 090	11 331	11 625	11 508	12 004	12 952	13 424	14 356	13 611

		Northern Ireland										
		1991	1992	1993	1994	1995	1996	1997	1998	1999	2000	2001
Sand and gravel	KLFG	3 832	3 697	4 318	5 109	5 262	7 684	5 138	5 300	5 517	5 073	6 194
Basalt and igneous rock (other than granite)	KLFH	7 787	9 024	8 557	6 480	7 564	6 974	6 286	6 107	7 861	9 480	6 448
Limestone	KLFI	2 861	3 398	3 236	..	3 703	4 122	3 500	3 892	4 219	3 538	4 746
Sandstone[3]	KLFJ	3 679	3 304	3 959	5 480	4 779	4 941	6 042	6 584	3 615	2 844	8 070
Granite	KLFL	..	..	..	..	..	–	–	–	–	–	–
Others[4]	KLFN	..	..	647	896	812	1 392	625	473	1 579	3 098	753

1 See chapter text.
2 Includes waste used for constructional fill, and powder and granules used in manufacturing.

3 Prior to 1993 the 'Sandstone' heading was called 'Grit and conglomerate'. The new heading is all encompassing and was confirmed as correct with the Geological Survey in Northern Ireland.
4 Rock salt, Chalk, Diatomite and Fireclay.

Source: Office for National Statistics: 01633 812082

21.20 Building materials and components: production[1]
Great Britain

		Unit	1991	1992	1993	1994	1995	1996	1997	1998	1999	2000	2001
Building bricks[2]	KLGA	Millions	3 212	3 000	2 639	3 114	3 256	3 046	2 997	3 000	2 939	2 864	2 754
Common bricks	GRTD	"	642	497	436	464	480	401	422	385	367	342	320
Facing bricks	GRTE	"	2 340	2 266	1 978	2 421	2 546	2 430	2 386	2 411	2 369	2 287	2 211
Engineering bricks	GRTF	"	230	237	225	229	230	216	190	204	204	235	223
Clay bricks (including sand-lime)	GRTG	"	2 999	2 819	2 447	2 900	3 065	2 880	2 828	2 830	2 759	2 694	2 595
Concrete bricks	GRTH	"	213	181	192	214	191	166	169	171	180	170	159
Cement (grey Portland)[3]	KLGB	Thousand tonnes	12 297	11 006	11 039	12 307	11 805	12 214	12 638	12 409	12 697	12 452	11 854
Sand and gravel	GRTI	"	97 918	88 898	89 470	97 672	89 656	81 997	86 366	85 968	88 209	89 234	88 210
Building sand[4]	KLGC	"	18 079	16 769	17 406	18 534	17 389	14 655	15 337	13 810	13 941	14 219	13 772
Concreting sand	KLGD	"	31 239	28 573	28 021	30 977	29 390	28 659	30 130	30 244	31 730	31 167	31 656
Gravel[5]	KLGE	"	48 598	43 557	44 043	48 162	42 877	38 683	40 899	41 914	42 538	43 847	42 782
Crushed rock	GRTJ	"	148 007	143 967	149 576	161 757	150 838	132 894	133 787	131 716	132 598	130 307	133 759
Coated roadstone	KLGF	"	26 387	26 647	27 238	28 512	28 972	26 270	23 906	23 131	22 260	21 785	23 340
Uncoated roadstone	KLGG	"	60 748	53 471	54 412	51 121	49 307	40 893	40 186	36 816	38 114	36 509	34 638
Fill and ballast	KLGH	"	45 669	48 919	52 141	65 779	56 140	50 982	51 396	51 623	52 144	53 417	47 225
Concrete aggregate	KLGI	"	15 203	14 929	15 786	16 345	16 419	14 748	18 300	20 146	20 080	18 595	28 556
Ready mixed concrete[3]	GRXA	Thousand m³	22 527	20 776	20 771	22 931	21 676	20 892	22 327	22 983	23 550	23 043	23 008
Concrete building blocks	GRTK	Thousand m²	74 631	68 194	74 287	87 548	78 287	75 866	82 537	84 662	87 767	90 219	87 922
Dense aggregate	KLGN	"	32 456	29 732	30 116	36 997	36 933	34 996	37 250	39 439	38 439	37 629	36 598
Lightweight aggregate	KLGO	"	18 581	17 479	19 235	22 048	18 147	16 316	17 783	19 110	20 830	22 991	22 684
Aerated concrete	KLGP	"	23 594	20 984	24 936	28 503	23 207	24 554	27 505	26 113	28 497	29 599	28 639
Concrete roofing tiles	KLGM	"	26 359	21 490	24 574	28 149	26 118	24 651	24 958	24 981	25 972	26 765	24 825
Roofing & architectural slates	GRXB	tonnes	41 025	41 615	37 321	44 910	42 030	48 474	44 578	46 159	46 998	41 214	45 604
Fibre cement products	KLGK	Thousand tonnes	133.7	121.1	128.7	154.1	160.5	146.2	163.5	160.9	156.2	..	..

1 See chapter text.
2 Excluding refractory and glazed bricks.
3 United Kingdom.
4 Includes sand and gravel used for coating.
5 Includes hoggin.

Source: Department of Trade & Industry: 020 7215 1555

21.21 Construction: Value of output in Great Britain[1]

£ millions

		1991	1992	1993	1994	1995	1996	1997	1998	1999	2000	2001
All work: total	FGAY	51 115	47 472	46 323	49 439	52 643	55 243	58 352	62 060	65 704	69 676	74 690
New work: total	BLAB	27 726	24 814	23 556	25 086	26 672	27 926	29 928	32 491	35 587	37 660	39 970
New housing: total	KLQA	5 796	6 084	6 628	7 417	7 135	7 013	7 983	8 430	8 418	9 985	10 233
For public sector	BLAC	793	1 243	1 415	1 671	1 660	1 421	1 232	1 069	1 012	1 319	1 437
For private sector	BLAD	5 003	4 841	5 213	5 746	5 475	5 592	6 751	7 361	7 406	8 666	8 796
Infrastructure: total	KIAM	6 062	5 716	5 544	5 149	5 660	6 338	6 311	6 182	6 200	6 453	7 146
Other new work: total (excluding infrastructure)	KLQB	15 867	13 015	11 384	12 521	13 877	14 575	15 635	17 878	20 968	21 223	22 591
For public sector	BLAE	4 142	4 181	4 045	4 384	4 661	4 441	3 756	4 151	4 919	4 854	5 330
For private sector	KLQC	11 725	8 834	7 339	8 137	9 217	10 134	11 879	13 727	16 049	16 369	17 261
Private Industrial	BLAF	2 622	2 234	2 208	2 489	3 008	3 119	3 491	3 810	3 973	3 716	3 701
Private Commercial	BLAG	9 103	6 600	5 131	5 648	6 209	7 015	8 388	9 917	12 076	12 653	13 560
Repair and maintenance: total	BLAH	23 389	22 658	22 767	24 353	25 971	27 317	28 423	29 569	30 117	32 016	34 720
Housing: total	KLQD	13 001	12 586	12 809	13 767	14 595	15 035	15 755	16 202	16 370	16 906	17 620
For public sector	BLBK	4 938	4 991	5 439	5 963	6 465	6 637	6 629	6 506	6 485	6 552	6 630
For private sector	BLBL	8 063	7 595	7 370	7 804	8 130	8 398	9 126	9 696	9 885	10 354	10 990
Public other work	BLAJ	5 291	5 087	4 916	5 211	5 398	5 252	5 079	5 220	5 371	5 685	6 110
Private other work	BLAK	5 098	4 985	5 042	5 375	5 978	7 030	7 590	8 147	8 376	9 424	10 991

1 See chapter text. Output by contractors, including unrecorded estimates by small firms and self-employed workers, and output by public sector direct labour departments - classified to construction in the *1992 Standard Industrial Classification.*

Source: Department of Trade and Industry: 020 7215 1953

21.22 Construction: Value of new orders obtained by contractors[1]
Great Britain

£ millions

		1991	1992	1993	1994	1995	1996	1997	1998	1999	2000	2001
New work: total	FHAA	19 455	17 493	19 965	21 285	22 065	22 834	24 806	27 477	26 079	28 120	29 643
Public housing	BLBC	875	1 246	1 668	1 386	1 182	1 073	995	933	969	910	1 084
Private housing[2]	BLBD	4 552	4 016	4 874	5 721	4 905	5 416	6 253	5 997	5 901	6 085	6 525
New housing: total	FGAU	5 427	5 263	6 542	7 106	6 087	6 487	7 248	6 930	6 869	6 995	7 610
Infrastructure:												
Water	KIBV	509	669	421	412	500	640	733	957	760	1 084	531
Sewerage	KIBW	429	469	447	389	394	481	656	737	789	380	540
Electricity	KIBX	301	281	211	170	218	294	382	359	254	244	279
Roads	KIBY	1 415	1 322	1 435	1 356	1 531	1 710	928	821	957	1 445	1 572
Gas, communications, air	KIBZ	441	554	642	494	904	745	693	745	713	1 085	584
Railways	KIDP	125	200	623	412	351	524	416	573	471	539	1 271
Harbours	KIDQ	203	252	220	218	273	270	182	287	250	215	377
Total	BAWT	3 423	3 746	3 998	3 451	4 170	4 664	3 991	4 479	4 195	4 992	5 154
of which												
- Public	KIDS	2 090	1 690	2 472	2 211	2 327	1 671	1 352	1 505	1 495	1 430	2 085
- Private	KIDT	1 333	2 056	1 525	1 240	1 843	2 993	2 639	2 974	2 700	3 562	3 068
Other public non-housing:												
Factories	KIDU	89	128	111	111	94	91	72	84	72	64	30
Warehouses	KIDV	14	54	23	38	29	14	27	20	24	12	10
Oil, steel, coal	KIDW	13	47	30	12	13	4	4	2	5	1	8
Schools and colleges	KIDX	584	584	655	658	710	707	749	770	791	986	1 498
Universities	KIDY	150	203	353	376	373	355	273	405	345	329	378
Health	KIDZ	578	644	697	752	717	681	491	769	635	685	813
Offices	KIFP	492	499	684	469	393	379	391	292	390	291	395
Entertainment	KIFQ	250	189	281	308	285	259	342	432	435	359	392
Garages	KIFR	44	28	42	49	51	28	34	19	36	44	30
Shops	KIFS	25	23	26	14	21	12	35	35	29	34	38
Agriculture	KIFT	17	14	44	22	12	8	33	17	9	12	46
Miscellaneous	KIFU	421	351	450	844	508	418	441	660	503	999	479
Total	BAWU	2 677	2 763	3 397	3 654	3 206	2 956	2 894	3 504	3 273	3 815	4 117
Private industrial:[2]												
Factories	KIFW	1 830	1 006	1 221	1 451	2 055	1 603	2 184	1 878	1 698	1 444	1 588
Warehouses	KIFX	438	426	429	498	594	663	901	1 014	821	1 110	911
Oil, steel, coal	KIFY	79	72	27	51	76	71	64	79	38	34	43
Total	BAWV	2 347	1 503	1 677	1 999	2 725	2 337	3 149	2 971	2 558	2 589	2 542
Private commercial:[2]												
Schools, universities	KIHP	175	121	134	115	105	156	189	351	393	577	702
Health	KIHQ	369	193	179	255	288	277	356	651	411	455	349
Offices	KIHR	2 215	1 691	1 471	1 777	2 123	2 169	2 506	3 472	3 566	4 384	4 748
Entertainment	KIHS	1 111	747	751	928	940	1 407	1 847	2 244	2 224	1 873	1 674
Garages	KIHT	261	234	308	300	301	265	344	315	266	169	190
Shops	KIHU	1 222	1 034	1 278	1 453	1 871	1 795	1 937	2 154	1 901	1 889	2 212
Agriculture	KIBN	105	94	108	120	124	123	148	146	100	77	105
Miscellaneous	KIBO	123	103	122	127	126	198	198	259	321	305	242
Total	BAWW	5 581	4 218	4 351	5 075	5 877	6 390	7 525	9 593	9 184	9 729	10 221

1 See chapter text. Classified to construction in the *1992 Standard Industrial Classification.*
2 Figures for private sector include work to be carried out by contractors on their own initiative for sale.

Source: Department of Trade and Industry: 020 7215 1953

21.23 Total engineering
Total turnover of UK based manufacturers[1]
Standard Industrial Classification 1992 Not seasonally adjusted.

£ millions

Activity heading Product group		1996	1997	1998	1999	2000	2001
Class 29: Manufacture of machinery and equipment not elsewhere classified							
2911 Manufacture of engines and turbines except aircraft, vehicle and cycle engines	FMJM	1 708	1 498	1 577	1 435	1 525	2 018
2912 Manufacture of pumps and compressors	FMJN	2 359	2 324	2 495	2 393	2 466	2 338
2913 Manufacture of taps and valves	FMJO	1 324	1 297	1 392	1 127	1 245	1 256
2914 Manufacture of bearings, gears, gearing and driving elements	FMJP	1 692	1 548	1 541	1 403	1 338	1 280
2922 Manufacture of lifting and handling equipment	FMJR	4 005	3 603	3 667	3 793	3 603	3 345
2923 Manufacture of non-domestic cooling and ventilation equipment	FMJS	3 314	3 541	3 629	3 329	3 414	3 673
2924 Manufacture of other general purpose machinery not elsewhere classified	FMJT	2 619	2 824	2 813	3 061	3 037	3 328
2940 Manufacture of machine tools	BBET	2 136	950	1 002	867	937	908
2952 Manufacture of machinery for mining, quarrying and construction	FMJY	2 096	2 375	2 450	2 339	2 435	2 372
2953 Manufacture of machinery for food, beverage and tobacco processing	FMJZ	998	967	860	723	760	834
2954 Manufacture of machinery for textile, apparel and leather production	FMKA	408	372	339	230	236	220
2956 Manufacture of other special purpose machinery not elsewhere classified	FMKC	2 626	2 395	2 289	2 148	1 960	1 955
2971 Manufacture of electric domestic appliances	FMKD	2 139	2 173	2 186	2 093	2 132	2 231
Total	LMDA	34 262	34 151	34 052	32 146	31 867	31 992
Class 30 : Manufacture of electrical and optical equipment							
3001 Manufacture of office machinery	FMGS	1 406	1 241	1 314	1 405	1 523	1 476
3002 Manufacture of computers and other information processing equipment	FMGT	12 166	13 518	13 745	13 713	12 651	12 355
Total	LMGA	13 615	14 796	15 099	15 161	14 221	13 850
Class 31 : Manufacture of electrical machinery and apparatus not elsewhere classified							
3110 Manufacture of electric motors, generators and transformers	FMDN	2 420	2 447	2 414	2 629	2 785	2 744
3120 Manufacture of electricity distribution and control apparatus	FMDW	3 863	3 657	3 561	3 814	4 226	4 090
3130 Manufacture of insulated wire and cable	FMEF	2 490	2 077	1 808	1 650	1 663	1 467
3140 Manufacture of accumulators, primary cells and primary batteries	FMEO	695	685	632	588	606	494
3150 Manufacture of lighting equipment and electric lamps	FMEX	1 998	1 927	1 817	1 848	1 803	1 654
3161 Manufacture of other electrical equipment for engines and vehicles not otherwise classified	FMPU	1 457	1 364	1 266	1 069	1 031	1 030
3162 Manufacture of other electrical equipment not elsewhere classified	FMPV	3 247	3 178	3 527	3 544	2 840	2 811
Total	LMGB	15 949	15 287	14 949	15 056	14 900	14 191
Class 32 : Manufacture of radio, television and communication equipment and apparatus							
3210 Manufacture of electronic valves and tubes and other electronic components	FMFG	5 698	5 546	5 552	4 653	6 696	4 458
3220 Manufacture of television and radio transmitters and apparatus for line telephony and line telegraphy	FMHI	6 815	7 029	7 786	11 799	15 242	10 543
3230 Manufacture of television and radio receivers, sound or video recording or reproducing apparatus and associated goods	FMFP	4 921	4 654	4 375	4 243	4 485	4 478
Total	LMGC	17 768	17 552	18 037	20 967	26 815	19 478
Class 33 : Manufacture of medical, precision and optical instruments, watches and clocks							
3310 Manufacture of medical and surgical equipment and orthopaedic appliances	FMFY	2 263	2 039	1 974	2 199	2 279	2 510
3320 Manufacture of instruments and appliances for measuring, checking, testing, navigating and other purposes, except industrial process control equipment	FMHR	7 114	6 844	6 533	6 262	6 541	7 102
3340 Manufacture of optical instruments and photographic equipment	FMIJ	1 263	1 297	1 371	1 207	1 289	1 291
Total	LMGD	11 785	11 651	11 449	11 140	11 498	11 780

1 The figures shown represent the output of UK based manufacturers classified to Subsections DK and DL of the Standard Industrial Classification 1992. The figures shown are derived from the monthly production inquiry (MPI) and include estimates for non-responders and for establishments which are not sampled. Orders on hand figures are given for the end of the period to which they relate.

Source: Office for National Statistics: 01633 812786

21.24 Volume index numbers of turnover and orders for the engineering industries
United Kingdom

	Total			Home			Export		
	Orders on hand end of period (1995 average = 100)	1995 average monthly sales = 100		Orders on hand end of period (1995 average = 100)	1995 average monthly sales = 100		Orders on hand end of period (1995 average = 100)	1995 average monthly sales = 100	
		New orders[1]	Turnover		New orders[1]	Turnover		New orders[1]	Turnover
Total Engineering industries *SIC 1992 Class 29, 30, 31,32 and 33*									
	FGWA	FGWB	FGVT	FGVU	FGVV	FGVW	FGVX	FGVY	FGVZ
1993	95.9	87.8	87.6	93.0	92.9	92.5	100.2	80.5	80.7
1994	105.2	98.3	95.5	106.2	103.3	99.2	103.6	91.1	90.2
1995	98.3	97.9	100.0	99.8	98.0	100.0	96.0	97.8	100.0
1996	94.5	103.4	104.5	94.9	99.3	100.8	93.9	109.3	109.9
1997	97.6	108.6	107.7	98.4	103.8	102.7	96.3	115.4	114.8
1998	94.9	112.0	112.8	90.4	102.6	105.1	101.8	125.4	123.8
1999	106.6	122.8	119.3	105.1	117.3	112.8	108.9	130.6	128.6
2000	120.3	133.1	129.0	120.0	124.3	119.6	120.9	145.7	142.4
2001	107.4	119.6	123.4	118.7	119.7	120.2	89.9	119.3	128.1
Manufacture of Machinery and Equipment *SIC 1992 Class 29*									
	FGVB	FGVD	FGVF	FGVH	FGVJ	FGVL	FGVN	FGVP	FGVR
1993	94.9	96.3	96.0	86.0	100.9	100.3	109.9	88.3	88.6
1994	107.1	104.2	99.9	108.1	111.0	103.3	105.2	92.3	94.0
1995	97.8	96.7	100.0	97.7	96.4	100.0	97.9	97.3	100.0
1996	96.1	98.6	99.2	99.8	97.1	96.4	89.8	101.2	104.1
1997	100.6	99.4	97.8	106.0	97.3	95.1	91.4	102.9	102.3
1998	85.9	92.5	97.7	86.7	86.8	93.5	84.4	102.5	105.1
1999	88.1	93.6	92.8	92.0	92.6	90.7	81.6	95.4	96.4
2000	92.8	94.0	92.3	94.4	88.2	87.4	90.2	104.0	100.9
2001	88.2	90.8	92.5	90.5	89.0	90.3	84.3	94.1	96.2
Manufacture of Electrical and Optical Equipment *SIC 1992 Class 30, 31,32 and 33*									
	FGVC	FGVE	FGVG	FGVI	FGVK	FGVM	FGVO	FGVQ	FGVS
1993	96.6	82.7	82.6	99.0	87.5	87.2	93.2	76.7	76.7
1994	103.7	94.7	92.8	104.5	98.0	96.4	102.5	90.6	88.3
1995	98.7	98.7	100.0	101.5	99.2	100.0	94.6	98.1	100.0
1996	93.3	106.3	107.7	90.8	100.8	103.8	96.9	113.3	112.7
1997	95.2	114.1	113.6	92.0	108.2	107.8	99.9	121.7	120.9
1998	102.1	123.7	121.8	93.4	113.4	112.9	114.6	136.7	133.1
1999	121.3	140.3	135.2	116.2	134.2	127.8	128.9	148.1	144.6
2000	142.4	156.6	151.0	141.8	148.8	141.6	143.3	166.4	162.9
2001	122.8	136.8	142.0	142.6	140.7	140.5	94.0	131.8	143.9

1 Net of cancellations.

Source: Office for National Statistics: 01633 812786

21.25 Motor vehicle production[1]
United Kingdom

Numbers

		1991	1992	1993	1994	1995	1996	1997	1998	1999	2000	2001
Motor vehicles												
SIC 1992, Class 34-10 Passenger cars: total	JCYM	1 236 900	1 291 880	1 375 524	1 466 823	1 532 084	1 686 134	1 698 001	1 748 258	1 786 623	1 641 452	1 492 365
1 000 c.c. and under	GKAB	26 621	22 037	98 034	98 178	95 198	108 645	119 894	112 044	113 204	96 043	93 695
Over 1 000 c.c. but not over 1 600c.c.	GKAD	830 530	793 307	709 615	729 397	814 873	845 084	829 079	814 595	776 111	676 438	632 747
Over 1 600 c.c. but not over 2 800 c.c.	GKAF	338 877	437 951	515 487	573 357	528 444	635 861	653 147	720 556	758 478	723 294	634 573
Over 2 800 c.c.	GKAH	40 872	38 585	52 388	65 891	93 569	96 544	95 881	101 063	138 830	145 677	131 350
Commercial vehicles: total	JCYG	217 141	248 453	193 467	227 815	233 001	238 314	237 706	227 379	185 905	172 442	192 873
Of which: Light commercial vehicles Trucks:	GKDH	184 005	216 477	171 141	197 285	199 346	205 372	210 942	203 629	162 176	145 655	169 705
Under 7.5 tonnes	GKDJ	8 773	9 558	4 755	8 154	9 523	8 913	6 254	5 006	4 107	5 160	5 003
Over 7.5 tonnes	GKDL	11 766	11 113	8 269	10 016	11 727	10 128	7 932	7 002	6 443	6 849	7 356
Motive units for articulated vehicles	GKCV	2 700	2 788	2 283	2 794	3 476	2 631	2 574	2 492	2 739	2 673	2 539
Buses, coaches and mini buses	GKDN	9 837	8 517	7 019	9 566	8 939	11 270	10 004	9 250	10 440	12 105	8 270

1 See chapter text. Figures for motor vehicles relate to periods of 52 weeks (53 weeks in 1993).

Source: Office for National Statistics: 01633 812963

21.26 Alcoholic drink[1]
United Kingdom

			1991	1992	1993	1994	1995	1996	1997	1998	1999	2000	2001
Spirits[2]		Thousand hectolitres of alcohol											
Production	KMEA	"	4 476	4 219	3 974	4 106	4 507	4 868	5 297	5 145	4 705	4 210	4 368
Released for home consumption													
Home produced whisky	KMEE	"	383	356	374	383	310	321	312	289	323	314	321
Imported and other	KMEG	"	529	505	504	531	481	495	533	505	596	615	647
Total	KMEH	"	912	861	878	914	791	815	845	794	919	929	968
Beer[3]		Thousand hectolitres											
Production	BFNK	"	59 552	57 616	56 746	58 333	56 800	58 072	59 139	56 652	57 854	55 279	56 802
Released for home consumption	BAYL	"	63 038	60 973	59 177	60 575	59 129	59 894	61 114	58 835	58 917	57 007	58 234
		Thousand hectolitres of pure alcohol											
Production	JYXJ		..	..	..	2 345	2 298	2 360	2 406	2 333	2 364	2 299	2 358
Released for home consumption	JYXK		..	..	..	2 453	2 410	2 448	2 504	2 439	2 428	2 382	2 429
Wine of fresh grapes													
Released for home consumption		Thousand hectolitres											
Fortified	KMEM	"	357	345	335	329	330	331	323	370	316	289	287
Still table	KMEN	"	5 910	6 166	6 471	6 759	6 576	6 995	7 653	7 979	8 391	8 864	9 534
Sparkling	KMEO	"	316	292	296	297	315	358	382	416	576	543	515
Total	KMEP	"	6 583	6 803	7 102	7 385	7 221	7 684	8 358	8 765	9 284	9 696	10 336
Made-wine													
Released for home consumption													
Other than coolers	KMEQ	"	436	439	505	470	516	513	485	406	416	431	364
Coolers[4]	KJDD	"	263	433	485	549	903	1 781	1 153	1 244	1 802	2 800	3 712
Cider and perry													
Released for home consumption	KMER	"	3 713	4 398	4 496	4 811	5 575	5 656	5 513	5 548	6 022	6 006	5 911

1 See chapter text.
2 Potable spirits distilled.
3 A new system was introduced for beer duty in June 1993. The figures in this table include adjustments to data prior to this date to bring them into line with current data.

4 Made wine with alcoholic strength 1.2% to 5.5%. Includes alcoholic lemonade of appropriate strength and similar product.

Source: HM Customs and Excise: 020 7865 5323

21.27 Tobacco products: released for home consumption[1]
United Kingdom

			1991	1992	1993[2]	1994	1995	1996	1997	1998	1999	2000	2001
Cigarettes:		Thousand million											
Home produced	KMFA	"	85.3	76.4	85.8	82.4	70.8	73.8	71.1	67.8	28.2	49.3	47.7
Imported	KMFB	"	10.3	9.3	9.5	10.2	9.5	9.5	9.9	7.5	6.0	7.3	6.8
Total	KMFC	"	95.6	85.7	95.2	92.6	80.3	83.3	81.0	75.3	34.2	56.6	54.5
Cigars:		Million kg.											
Home produced	KMFD	"	1.9	1.8	1.7	1.6	1.5	1.4	1.3	1.2	0.9	1.0	0.9
Imported	KMFE	"	0.1	0.1	0.1	0.1	0.1	0.1	0.1	0.1	0.1	0.1	0.1
Total	KMFF	"	2.1	1.9	1.8	1.7	1.6	1.5	1.4	1.3	1.0	1.1	1.0
Hand-rolling tobacco:													
Home produced	KMFG	"	4.1	3.7	3.5	3.0	2.4	2.1	1.8	1.7	2.0	2.1	2.8
Imported	KMFH	"	0.1	0.1	0.1	0.1	0.1	0.1	0.1	0.1	–	–	–
Total	KMFI	"	4.2	3.8	3.6	3.2	2.6	2.3	1.9	1.8	2.0	2.2	2.8
Other smoking and chewing tobacco:													
Home produced	KMFJ	"	2.0	1.8	1.8	1.5	1.3	1.2	1.1	1.0	0.6	0.7	0.7
Imported	KMFK	"	0.1	0.2	0.1	0.1	0.1	0.1	0.1	0.1	0.1	0.1	0.1
Total	KMFL	"	2.1	2.0	1.9	1.6	1.4	1.3	1.2	1.1	0.7	0.8	0.8

1 See chapter text.
2 1993 contained two Budgets, in March and November.

Source: HM Customs and Excise: 020 7865 5323

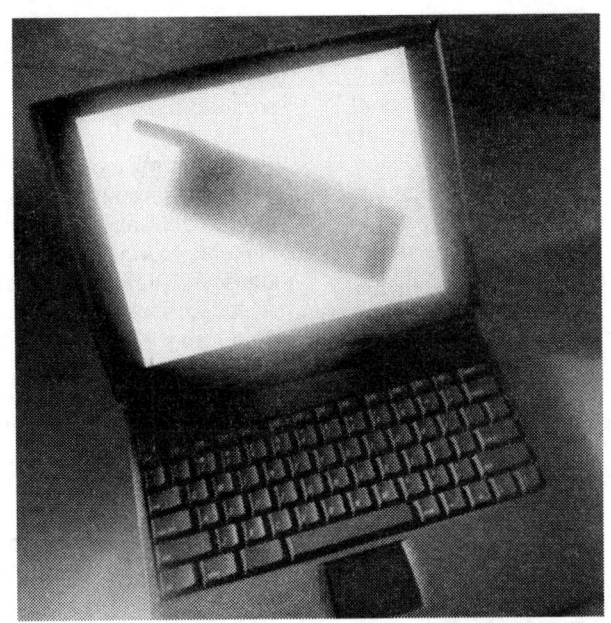

22 Banking, insurance etc

Banking, insurance etc

Other banks' balance sheet *(Table 22.3)*
The implementation of the review of banking statistics at end-September 1997 has resulted in several changes to this table:

(a)   The table now includes the business of all monthly and quarterly reporting banks in the UK; it formerly covered only the business of monthly reporting institutions.

(b)   The Channel Islands and Isle of Man are no longer treated as part of the UK for statistical purposes. Banking institutions in the Channel Islands and Isle of Man no longer have the option of being within the UK banking sector and their business, along with the business of offshore island branches of UK mainland banks, is now excluded from the figures within this table. Additionally, the business of the UK banking sector with offshore island residents and entities has been reclassified from UK residents to non-residents.

(c)   The table now contains more comprehensive detail of business with building societies. This business was previously included indistinguishably within the UK private sector elements of the table.

(d)   The aggregate balance sheet of the banking sector has been inflated because it is now reported on an accrual basis rather than a cash basis (accrued amounts payable/ receivable are shown under liabilities and assets respectively). Additionally, acceptances have been brought onto the balance sheet and are shown under both liabilities and assets.

With effect from 1998, the balance sheet of the Banking Department of the Bank of England is excluded from this table, and other banks' business with the Issue Department is reclassified from "UK public sector" to "UK banks".

Bank lending to, and bank deposits from, UK residents *(Tables 22.4 and 22.5)*
These are series of statistics based on the Standard Industrial Classification 1992.

Table 22.4 comprises loans, advances (including under reverse repos), finance leasing, acceptances, facilities and holdings of sterling and euro commercial paper. It includes lending under the Department of Trade and Industry special scheme for domestic shipbuilding. Holdings of investments and bills and adjustments for transit items are not included.

Table 22.5 includes borrowing under sale and repurchase agreements (repro). Adjustments for transit items are not included.

Figures for both tables are supplied by monthly reporting banks and grossed to cover quarterly reporters. They exclude lending to building societies and to residents of the Channel Islands and Isle of Man.

Capital issues and redemptions *(Table 22.14)*
The estimates in this table relate to new money raised on the stock market by issues of ordinary, preference and loan capital (public issues, offers for sale, issues by tender, placings and issues to shareholders and employees) by non-resident borrowers split between central government, state and local governments and companies.

The estimates include UK local government negotiable bonds (of not less than one year) issue to or through the agency of banks, discount houses, issuing houses or brokers. Mortgages, bank advances and any other loans redeemable in less than twelve months are excluded; so also are loans from UK government funds (including the former Industrial Reorganisation Corporation and the National Enterprise Board) but not government subscriptions to company issues made *pari passu* with the market. Issues to shareholders are included only if the sole or principal share register is maintained in the United Kingdom.

Estimates of issues are based on the prices at which securities are offered to the market. Subscriptions are recorded under the periods in which they are due to be paid. Redemptions exclude share buy-backs. They relate to fixed interest securities of the kinds included as issues; conversion issues in lieu of cash repayment are included in the gross figures of both issues and redemptions. These figures include issues of debentures and loan stock carrying the right of conversion into, or subscription to, equity capital.

The division between the United Kingdom and non-resident company borrowers is determined by the location of the registered office. The industrial classification of companies is according to the primary occupation of the borrowing company or group. Until 1982 it is based on the Standard Industrial Classification (SIC) 1968, from 1983 to 1995 on SIC 1983 and subsequently on SIC 92.

The estimates exclude issues on the unlisted securities market which was launched by the Stock Exchange in November 1980. These issues are mainly of ordinary shares by industrial and commercial companies. Estimates of new money raised are: 1990 364; 1991 261.

Consumer credit *(Table 22.16)*
Figures for net lending refer to changes in amounts outstanding adjusted to remove distortions caused by revaluations of debt outstanding, such as write-offs. Lending by retailers refers to self-financed credit advanced by food retailers, clothing retailers, household

goods retailers, mixed business retailers (other than co-operative societies) and general mail order houses. Class 3 loans are advanced under the terms of the Building Societies' Act 1986. Loans on personal accounts exclude loans for house purchase and bridging finance.

Data relating to the narrower coverage cover finance houses and other specialist credit grantors, bank credit cards (operated under the VISA and Mastercard systems), and secured loans by building societies. A high proportion of credit advanced in certain types of agreement, notably on credit cards, is repaid within a month. This reflects use of such agreements as a method of payment rather than a way of obtaining credit.

22.1 Bank of England

£ millions

		December										
		1991	1992	1993	1994	1995	1996	1997	1998	1999	2000	2001
Issue Department												
Liabilities:												
Notes in circulation	AEFA	17 466	17 542	18 218	20 055	21 262	22 407	23 715	24 573	27 232	29 412	32 226
Notes in Banking Department	AEFB	4	8	12	5	7	12	5	7	8	8	4
Assets:												
Government securities[1]	AEFC	11 791	7 808	6 816	11 468	14 552	16 524	16 416	15 826	17 264	13 498	13 996
Other securities[2]	AEFD	5 679	9 742	11 414	8 592	6 717	5 896	7 304	8 754	9 976	15 921	18 234
Banking Department												
Liabilities:												
Total[3]	AEFE	5 825	5 623	11 095	6 192	7 114	6 229	7 221	6 802	52 072	10 397	12 639
Public deposits[4]	AEFF	104	97	6 205	938	1 159	1 001	1 192	237	195	391	437
Bankers' deposits[5]	AEFH	1 813	1 553	1 700	1 855	2 001	2 021	2 800	1 388	1 357	1 520	2 354
Reserves and other accounts[6]	AEFI	3 894	3 959	3 175	3 385	3 941	3 193	3 214	5 163	50 506	8 471	9 834
Assets:												
Total	KCYT	5 825	5 623	11 095	6 192	7 114	6 229	7 221	6 802	52 071	10 397	12 640
Government securities	AEFJ	1 346	1 237	1 174	1 050	1 090	1 232	1 373	1 352	1 444	1 504	1 795
Advances and other accounts	AEFK	2 443	3 935	9 411	4 696	5 499	2 339	5 388	3 302	46 895	6 533	6 413
Premises, equipment and other securities[6]	AEFL	2 031	443	498	441	518	2 646	455	2 141	3 724	2 352	4 428
Notes and coin	AEFM	5	8	12	5	7	12	5	7	8	8	4

1 Including the historic liability of the Treasury of £11 million until 1993.
2 Including gilt and Treasury bill repurchase agreements from 1994 (previously in "Government securities").
3 The only liability not shown separately is the Bank's capital (held by the Treasury) which has been constant at £14.6 million.
4 Excluding local government and public corporations' deposits which are included under Reserves and other accounts.

5 These consist of operational deposits held mainly by the clearing banks and non-operational cash ratio deposits for which institutions authorised under the Banking Act, deposit - taking UK branches of "European Authorised Institutions" and (from 1998) building societies are liable.
6 Large increases from 1999 arise from the Bank of England's role in TARGET, as a result of which other European central banks may hold substantial credit balances or overdrafts with the Bank.

Source: Bank of England: 020 7601 3236

22.2 Value of inter-bank clearings[1]

£ billions

		1991	1992	1993	1994	1995	1996	1997	1998	1999	2000	2001
Bulk paper clearings												
Cheque (formerly general)	KCYY	1 084	1 052	1 065	1 075	1 097	1 161	1 196	1 214	1 225	1 214	1 210
Credit (formerly credit clearing)	KCYZ	104	101	97	93	92	94	94	92	88	82	80
High-value clearings												
Town	KCZA	2 228	1 387	1 069	681	59	–	–	–	–	–	–
CHAPS	KCZB	19 050	20 929	23 545	25 052	26 719	28 881	36 032	41 501	44 704	49 146	52 913
Electronic clearing	KCZC	772	803	836	941	1 055	1 251	1 432	1 602	1 761	1 922	2 166

1 Excludes inter-branch clearings and clearings in Scotland and Northern Ireland.

Source: Association of Payment Clearing Services (APACS): 020 7711 6323

22.3 Other banks' balance sheet[1]

£ millions

		1992	1993	1994	1995	1996	1997	1998	1999[2]	2000	2001
Sterling liabilities											
Notes outstanding & cash loaded cards	TBFA	2 084	2 186	2 456	2 576	2 717	2 832	2 929	3 311	3 359	3 866
Sight deposits											
UK banks	TBFB	14 243	14 768	16 222	16 983	20 138	44 573	37 839	33 463	40 054	59 573
UK building societies	TBFC	..	..	..	..	..	950	1 277	841	1 168	1 466
UK public sector	TBFD	2 952	3 335	3 301	3 824	3 641	3 781	3 003	3 450	3 403	4 283
Other UK residents	TBFE	148 011	161 907	164 451	192 297	211 179	271 233	295 068	325 392	372 725	415 969
Non-residents	TBFF	15 094	15 075	16 425	18 690	17 707	37 730	43 528	44 581	55 489	55 837
Time deposits											
UK banks	TBFG	78 640	68 531	75 629	90 044	95 798	99 782	111 970	112 530	110 955	125 261
UK building societies	TBFH	–	–	–	–	–	5 682	4 361	4 253	4 688	4 856
UK public sector	TBFI	3 193	4 223	4 908	7 896	6 087	9 059	9 748	8 064	8 241	8 306
Other UK residents	TBFJ	157 979	162 053	166 505	190 707	210 045	284 629	295 924	282 789	301 007	301 926
of which TESSAs	TBFK	4 331	5 896	7 517	10 314	9 389	20 394	21 568	22 868	24 265	9 752
of which SAYE	TBFL	–	–	–	–	–	2 254	2 604	2 840	2 726	2 439
Non-residents	TBFM	58 550	58 583	62 905	68 274	63 995	91 040	97 953	116 967	134 844	150 964
Acceptances granted	TBFN	–	–	–	–	–	19 952	16 658	12 854	10 012	10 627
Liabilities under sale and repurchase agreements											
of which British govt. securities	TBFU	–	–	–	–	22 668	47 297	55 561	56 145	83 819	83 330
UK banks	TBFP	–	–	–	–	13 718	29 089	43 314	48 213	56 408	60 551
UK building societies	TBFQ	..	..	..	..	..	20	32	200	36	–
UK public sector	TBFR	–	..	–	–	2 279	6 044	–	–	14 351	5 127
Other UK residents	TBFS	–	–	–	–	7 703	18 114	20 918	17 165	22 974	25 732
Non-residents	TBFT	–	–	–	–	683	5 664	5 469	5 542	9 849	8 643
CDs and other short-term paper issued	TBFV	50 912	52 783	63 880	70 277	96 390	119 266	138 248	158 826	151 153	153 768
Total sterling deposits	TBFW	529 575	541 260	574 224	658 993	749 364	1 046 609	1 125 311	1 175 130	1 297 356	1 392 890
Sterling items in suspense and transmission	TBFX	10 317	11 011	8 412	10 423	12 120	16 054	15 714	17 307	15 261	16 702
Net derivatives	TBFY	..	..	..	..	..	8 186	8 342	8 324	10 992	4 029
Accrued amounts payable	TBFZ	..	..	..	..	..	20 713	24 632	22 122	23 726	22 836
Sterling capital and other internal funds	TBGA	68 640	71 833	78 775	82 160	90 464	103 462	103 868	100 575	133 436	148 294
Total sterling liabilities	TBGB	610 616	626 290	663 868	754 152	854 666	1 197 856	1 280 796	1 326 769	1 484 130	1 588 618
Foreign currency liabilities											
Sight and time deposits											
UK banks	TBGC	89 532	95 921	105 813	104 769	91 314	90 858	77 128	77 684	99 447	106 368
UK building societies	TBGD	..	..	..	..	..	1 027	639	681	233	279
UK public sector	TBGE	..	..	..	..	..	226	149	126	1 808	926
Other UK residents	TBGF	..	..	..	..	..	64 188	60 513	65 203	79 627	95 666
Non-residents	TBGG	543 883	580 951	618 769	696 380	605 439	716 573	766 934	736 792	914 888	1 001 394
Acceptances granted	TBGH	..	..	..	..	..	743	729	619	689	638
Sale and repurchase agreements											
UK banks	TBGJ	–	–	–	–	17 114	21 311	30 669	25 170	38 901	54 499
UK building societies	TBGK	..	..	..	..	..	–	–	–	–	–
UK public sector	TBGL	..	..	..	..	..	22	–	–	468	1
Other UK residents	TBGM	..	..	..	..	..	25 716	26 742	21 997	35 145	52 438
Non-residents	TBGN	..	..	–	..	61 307	100 936	118 909	115 357	139 656	154 976
CDs and other short-term paper issued	TBGO	73 814	61 017	67 869	89 032	101 005	131 620	124 151	151 009	199 510	224 225
Total foreign currency deposits	TBGP	754 851	790 361	851 856	972 832	975 619	1 153 220	1 206 562	1 194 637	1 510 373	1 691 409
Items in suspense and transmission	TBGQ	11 261	20 714	14 779	13 881	21 272	35 713	25 026	30 548	46 678	47 363
Net derivatives	TBGR	..	..	..	..	..	8 654	2 656	3 704	–4 472	–3 854
Accrued amounts payable	TBGS	..	..	..	..	..	21 996	25 184	18 080	18 568	17 756
Capital and other internal funds	TBGT	20 833	21 581	21 081	26 430	25 535	31 676	46 952	69 798	89 359	85 416
Total foreign currency liabilities	TBGU	786 945	832 656	887 716	1 013 143	1 022 426	1 251 258	1 306 380	1 316 767	1 660 506	1 838 090
Total liabilities	TBGV	1 397 561	1 458 946	1 551 584	1 767 295	1 877 092	2 449 114	2 587 177	2 643 536	3 144 636	3 426 708

22.3 Other banks' balance sheet[1]

continued

£ millions

		1992	1993	1994	1995	1996	1997	1998	1999[2]	2000	2001
Sterling assets											
Notes and coins	TBGW	4 454	4 711	4 983	5 357	4 812	5 225	6 699	9 047	8 007	6 566
With UK central bank											
Cash ratio deposits	TBGX	1 402	1 415	1 490	1 682	1 888	2 566	1 068	1 141	1 275	1 386
Other	TBGY	−42	183	103	113	533	216	383	676	117	143
Market loans											
UK banks	TBGZ	87 691	79 281	88 582	103 006	109 500	139 996	148 138	144 537	149 174	181 350
UK bank CDs	TBHB	20 620	19 028	23 632	26 767	36 922	62 584	65 510	75 071	65 156	68 868
UK bank commercial paper	TBHC	..	..	..	..	..	29	130	208	8	52
UK building societies CDs etc and deposits	TBHD	4 433	5 360	5 358	4 387	4 891	4 242	4 505	5 093	4 748	3 933
Non-residents	TBHE	33 734	43 571	44 582	47 470	50 585	79 368	84 162	74 403	94 381	102 413
Acceptances granted											
UK building societies	TBHF	..	..	..	..	..	−	−	−	−	−
UK public sector	TBHG	..	..	..	..	..	−	−	−	−	−
Other UK residents	TBHH	..	..	..	..	..	18 573	15 394	11 933	9 496	9 992
Non-residents	TBHI	..	..	..	..	..	1 379	1 264	920	516	635
Bills											
Treasury bills	TBHJ	1 952	1 561	4 166	10 404	1 652	554	779	2 749	1 612	8 474
UK bank bills	TBHA	..	..	..	..	..	18 221	14 110	11 426	7 011	8 098
UK building societies	TBHK	..	..	..	..	..	−	−	−	−	−
Other UK	TBHL	..	..	..	..	..	1 116	1 221	818	1 202	1 601
Non-residents	TBHM	..	..	..	..	..	309	207	206	287	744
Claims under sale and repurchase agreements											
of which British govt. securities	TBHT	−	−	−	−	26 030	47 158	56 639	64 943	86 362	84 068
UK banks	TBHO	−	−	−	−	16 853	27 611	41 969	39 667	46 088	46 585
UK building societies	TBHP	..	..	..	..	..	345	134	91	116	327
UK public sector	TBHQ	..	..	..	..	..	−	−	−	9 067	4 692
Other UK residents	TBHR	..	..	..	..	..	21 283	23 803	30 338	35 058	36 222
Non-residents	TBHS	..	..	..	..	..	6 873	5 907	6 310	7 266	7 010
Advances											
UK public sector	TBHU	2 397	3 309	3 526	3 549	2 912	3 872	3 403	2 567	2 746	2 442
Other UK residents	TBHV	366 096	371 086	380 615	426 936	460 107	636 162	672 812	732 649	823 787	891 790
Non-residents	TBHW	12 336	12 268	12 163	13 403	16 759	21 102	21 039	23 364	24 494	29 483
Banking dept. lending to central govt. (net)	TBNU	1 277	−5 407	−947	−1 801	948	−2 741	−	..	..	..
Investments											
British government stocks	TBHX	4 848	13 753	14 366	17 135	19 910	23 078	14 714	9 243	2 867	499
Other public sector	TBHY	236	204	303	409	303	283	215	124	88	116
UK banks	TBHZ	..	..	..	..	..	11 922	13 415	13 584	22 935	23 965
UK building societies	TBIA	4 767	5 492	4 769	4 639	4 898	2 875	2 223	2 506	2 251	2 099
Other UK residents	TBIB	..	..	..	..	..	45 134	48 781	57 391	77 647	82 013
Non-residents	TBIC	..	..	..	..	..	9 343	11 834	13 775	20 572	23 462
Items in suspense and collection	TBID	16 426	17 135	16 477	17 613	19 830	23 526	23 888	23 441	21 982	24 024
Accrued amounts receivable	TBIE	..	..	..	..	..	15 003	17 352	15 173	15 919	13 528
Other assets	TBIF	11 724	11 146	10 242	10 525	10 267	12 218	12 593	13 036	12 654	12 876
Total sterling assets	TBIG	617 158	630 527	668 960	755 937	852 075	1 192 264	1 257 652	1 321 486	1 468 527	1 595 380
Foreign currency assets											
Market loans and advances											
UK banks	TBIH	87 596	96 129	99 885	98 305	83 920	90 367	72 263	74 250	93 269	104 107
UK banks' CDs etc.	TBII	11 239	8 642	7 226	9 345	7 793	13 633	11 065	14 364	13 171	13 298
UK building societies CDs etc. and deposits	TBIJ	..	..	..	..	..	83	259	451	173	354
UK public sector	TBIK	4 061	3 421	28	38	36	25	45	20	30	13
Other UK residents	TBIL	65 836	71 326	76 538	102 061	72 213	76 356	83 968	88 847	107 707	118 106
Non-residents	TBIM	504 567	489 439	534 589	604 783	505 953	598 541	616 832	599 146	743 781	783 057
Claims under sale and repurchase agreement											
UK banks	TBIO	−	−	−	−	21 189	24 184	31 900	28 008	41 801	61 188
UK building societies	TBIP	..	..	..	..	..	−	−	−	737	23
UK public sector	TBIQ	..	..	..	..	..	22	−	−	−	−
Other UK residents	TBIR	..	..	..	..	..	55 945	39 764	33 027	57 876	73 237
Non-residents	TBIS	−	−	−	−	75 376	121 101	147 562	146 756	199 990	219 449
Acceptances granted	TBIT	..	..	..	..	..	743	729	619	689	638
Bills	TBIU	11 784	15 398	10 490	14 429	9 660	12 728	15 239	19 508	21 878	25 399
Investments											
British government stocks	TBIV	..	..	..	..	..	3 453	4 755	4 473	3 518	890
Other public sector	TBIW	..	..	..	..	..	−	−	−	−	4
UK banks	TBIX	..	..	..	..	..	2 850	4 310	8 607	11 706	10 633
UK building societies	TBIY	701	889	997	728	701	414	526	631	939	850
Other UK residents	TBIZ	..	..	..	..	..	4 055	4 584	5 679	12 298	18 129
Non-residents	TBJA	79 547	114 904	128 507	154 398	161 045	186 288	234 563	243 147	297 404	324 073
Items in suspense and collection	TBJB	9 981	19 371	15 572	17 598	21 664	40 175	30 229	29 706	44 885	55 026
Accrued amounts receivable	TBJC	..	..	..	..	..	23 673	27 821	20 163	21 279	18 969
Other assets	TBJD	1 586	2 791	1 868	1 817	1 809	2 215	3 111	4 648	2 978	3 880
Total foreign currency assets	TBJE	780 403	828 419	882 624	1 011 358	1 025 017	1 256 850	1 329 525	1 322 050	1 676 109	1 831 322
Total assets	TBJF	1 397 561	1 458 946	1 551 584	1 767 295	1 877 092	2 449 114	2 587 177	2 643 536	3 144 636	3 426 702
Holdings of own sterling acceptances	TBJG	21 988	21 814	18 274	18 721	21 521	1 823	2 137	1 725	1 231	916
Holdings of own FC acceptances	TBJH	1 439	914	640	1 153	1 031	291	170	150	135	118
Eligible banks' total sterling acceptances	TBJI	21 812	21 726	18 168	18 476	21 220	21 366	18 722	14 523	10 597	11 320
Eligible liabilities	TBJJ	406 885	425 353	440 032	507 279	564 648	766 683	807 803	849 289	952 062	1 012 194

1 See chapter text.

2 Data for 1999 reflect the acquisition of Birmingham Midshires Building Society by Halifax plc during that year.

Source: Bank of England: 020 7601 3236

22.4 Industrial analysis of bank lending to UK residents[1]
Not seasonally adjusted

£ millions

	UK residents		Agriculture, hunting and forestry	Fishing	Mining & quarrying	Manufacturing	Food, beverages & tobacco	Textiles & leather	Pulp, paper, publishing & printing
	Total to	of which sterling				Total			
Amounts outstanding (sterling & other currencies)									
Loans & advances (including under repo & sterling commercial paper)									
	TBOA	TBOB	TBOC	TBOD	TBOE	TBOF	TBOG	TBOH	TBOI
2000	1 037 887	871 099	7 735	401	4 182	58 368	11 014	1 849	8 055
2001	1 126 933	935 369	7 493	463	3 911	57 028	9 729	1 749	7 008
Acceptances									
	TBQA	TBQB	TBQC	TBQD	TBQE	TBQF	TBQG	TBQH	TBQI
2000	9 528	9 185	27	–	683	2 694	1 100	89	131
2001	5 553	5 265	23	–	151	1 472	480	85	72
Total									
	TBSA		TBSC	TBSD	TBSE	TBSF	TBSG	TBSH	TBSI
2000	1 047 415		7 761	401	4 866	61 062	12 114	1 938	8 186
2001	1 132 486		7 516	463	4 061	58 500	10 209	1 834	7 079
of which in sterling									
	TBUA		TBUC	TBUD	TBUE	TBUF	TBUG	TBUH	TBUI
2000	880 284		7 674	370	3 188	41 026	9 446	1 568	5 567
2001	940 635		7 434	425	2 527	37 200	7 783	1 394	4 870
Facilities granted									
	TCAA		TCAC	TCAD	TCAE	TCAF	TCAG	TCAH	TCAI
2000	1 299 185		9 919	487	10 084	114 560	26 504	3 120	13 761
2001	1 403 406		9 609	544	12 031	107 175	23 399	2 832	12 627
of which in sterling									
	TCCA		TCCC	TCCD	TCCE	TCCF	TCCG	TCCH	TCCI
2000	1 049 450		9 800	439	4 410	67 411	15 250	2 628	8 599
2001	1 125 620		9 501	496	3 987	62 321	13 616	2 271	7 694

	Manufacturing					Electricity, gas and water supply		Construction
	Chemicals, man-made fibres, rubber & plastics	Non-metallic mineral products & metals	Machinery, equipment & transport equipment	Electrical, medical & optical equipment	Other manufacturing	Electricity, gas & heated water	Cold water purification & supply	
Amounts outstanding (sterling & other currencies)								
Loans & advances (including under repo & sterling commercial paper)								
	TBOJ	TBOK	TBOL	TBOM	TBON	TBOO	TBOP	TBOQ
2000	6 846	7 715	9 204	7 207	6 477	11 593	1 379	11 518
2001	6 328	7 319	10 309	8 239	6 347	7 135	1 266	13 471
Acceptances								
	TBQJ	TBQK	TBQL	TBQM	TBQN	TBQO	TBQP	TBQQ
2000	323	239	486	199	127	185	10	187
2001	237	116	225	169	88	350	10	105
Total								
	TBSJ	TBSK	TBSL	TBSM	TBSN	TBSO	TBSP	TBSQ
2000	7 170	7 954	9 689	7 406	6 605	11 778	1 389	11 705
2001	6 565	7 435	10 534	8 409	6 434	7 485	1 276	13 576
of which in sterling								
	TBUJ	TBUK	TBUL	TBUM	TBUN	TBUO	TBUP	TBUQ
2000	4 474	5 225	6 558	3 766	4 423	8 194	1 178	10 725
2001	4 282	4 636	6 019	4 012	4 203	6 178	1 029	12 726
Facilities granted								
	TCAJ	TCAK	TCAL	TCAM	TCAN	TCAO	TCAP	TCAQ
2000	15 842	12 922	17 566	14 083	10 760	21 928	4 531	20 089
2001	14 321	11 811	18 505	13 402	10 277	18 807	3 707	21 299
of which in sterling								
	TCCJ	TCCK	TCCL	TCCM	TCCN	TCCO	TCCP	TCCQ
2000	8 131	8 484	11 376	6 149	6 794	13 575	3 022	18 031
2001	7 695	7 436	10 891	6 292	6 426	11 453	2 534	19 533

22.4 Industrial analysis of bank lending to UK residents[1]
Not seasonally adjusted
continued

£ millions

	Wholesale and retail trade					Real estate, renting, computer and other business activities		
Total	Sale & repair of motor vehicles & fuel	Other wholesale trade	Other retail trade & repair	Hotels and restaurants	Transport, storage & communication	Total	Development, buying, selling, renting of real estate	Renting of machinery & equipment

Amounts outstanding (sterling & other currencies)

Loans & advances (including under repo & sterling commercial paper)

	TBOR	TBOS	TBOT	TBOU	TBOV	TBOW	TBOX	TBOY	TBPA
2000	36 365	8 745	13 642	13 978	15 410	19 092	81 047	56 525	5 797
2001	34 936	8 896	13 490	12 550	17 810	23 260	99 596	71 025	7 243

Acceptances

	TBQR	TBQS	TBQT	TBQU	TBQV	TBQW	TBQX	TBQY	TBRA
2000	1 573	169	886	517	11	58	897	707	26
2001	957	133	620	204	5	80	454	258	14

Total

	TBSR	TBSS	TBST	TBSU	TBSV	TBSW	TBSX	TBSY	TBTA
2000	37 938	8 914	14 529	14 495	15 421	19 150	81 945	57 232	5 823
2001	35 892	9 028	14 110	12 754	17 815	23 340	100 050	71 282	7 257

of which in sterling

	TBUR	TBUS	TBUT	TBUU	TBUV	TBUW	TBUX	TBUY	TBVA
2000	30 373	8 542	8 566	13 265	13 952	14 892	77 382	56 121	5 426
2001	28 447	8 502	8 531	11 414	15 366	18 539	95 227	70 330	6 376

Facilities granted

	TCAR	TCAS	TCAT	TCAU	TCAV	TCAW	TCAX	TCAY	TCBA
2000	58 280	12 263	21 829	24 188	19 681	57 005	108 913	72 877	6 848
2001	56 933	11 989	21 614	23 330	21 761	50 343	131 233	89 705	8 261

of which in sterling

	TCCR	TCCS	TCCT	TCCU	TCCV	TCCW	TCCX	TCCY	TCDA
2000	45 906	11 316	13 912	20 678	16 856	32 958	100 629	70 490	6 215
2001	43 965	10 993	14 083	18 888	18 055	29 751	121 838	87 541	7 032

Real estate, renting, computer and other business activities					Recreational, personal & community service activities		Financial intermediation (excl. insurance & pehsion funds)	
Computer & related activities	Legal, accountancy, consultancy & other business activities	Public administration & defence	Education	Health & social work	Recreational, cultural & sporting activities	Personal & community services activities	Total	Financial leasing corporations

Amounts outstanding (sterling & other currencies)

Loans & advances (including under repo & sterling commercial paper)

	TBPB	TBPC	TBPD	TBPE	TBPF	TBPH	TBPG	TBPI	TBPJ
2000	2 950	15 775	12 199	3 102	6 934	7 242	4 429	251 141	35 568
2001	3 453	17 876	7 253	3 545	7 350	8 280	3 966	273 579	36 315

Acceptances

	TBRB	TBRC	TBRD	TBRE	TBRF	TBRH	TBRG	TBRI	TBRJ
2000	22	143	–	–	–	69	6	2 872	635
2001	7	175	–	–	–	72	3	1 655	152

Total

	TBTB	TBTC	TBTD	TBTE	TBTF	TBTH	TBTG	TBTI	TBTJ
2000	2 972	15 918	12 199	3 102	6 934	7 311	4 435	254 013	36 203
2001	3 460	18 051	7 253	3 545	7 350	8 352	3 969	275 234	36 467

of which in sterling

	TBVB	TBVC	TBVD	TBVE	TBVF	TBVH	TBVG	TBVI	TBVJ
2000	2 359	13 476	11 432	3 072	6 835	6 611	4 087	144 389	35 086
2001	2 810	15 711	7 225	3 517	7 245	7 611	3 672	148 272	34 871

Facilities granted

	TCBB	TCBC	TCBD	TCBE	TCBF	TCBH	TCBG	TCBI	TCBJ
2000	4 777	24 411	14 366	3 734	8 427	12 011	5 770	278 606	39 854
2001	5 681	27 586	8 978	4 612	8 986	12 418	5 142	311 029	38 997

of which in sterling

	TCDB	TCDC	TCDD	TCDE	TCDF	TCDH	TCDG	TCDI	TCDJ
2000	3 789	20 135	13 446	3 693	8 249	9 771	5 247	159 858	38 017
2001	4 359	22 907	8 576	4 552	8 786	10 623	4 655	170 105	37 046

22.4
continued

Industrial analysis of bank lending to UK residents[1]
Not seasonally adjusted

£ millions

	Financial intermediation (excl. insurance & pension funds)								
	Non-bank credit grantors, excl. credit unions	Credit unions	Factoring corporations	Mortgage & housing credit corporations	Investment & unit trusts excl. money market mutual funds	Money market mutual funds	Bank holding companies	Securities dealers (f)	Other financial intermediaries
Amounts outstanding (sterling & other currencies)									
Loans & advances (including under repo & sterling commercial paper)									
	TBPK	TBPL	TBPM	TBPN	TBPO	TBPP	TBPQ	TBPR	TBPS
2000	11 989	3	2 416	15 344	7 286	–	12 519	118 815	47 202
2001	10 468	3	2 790	17 558	8 552	182	16 290	124 505	56 917
Acceptances									
	TBRK	TBRL	TBRM	TBRN	TBRO	TBRP	TBRQ	TBRR	TBRS
2000	661	–	125	14	133	–	13	126	1 166
2001	591	–	153	14	8	–	36	52	649
Total									
	TBTK	TBTL	TBTM	TBTN	TBTO	TBTP	TBTQ	TBTR	TBTS
2000	12 650	3	2 541	15 357	7 418	–	12 532	118 941	48 368
2001	11 059	3	2 942	17 572	8 560	182	16 326	124 557	57 566
of which in sterling									
	TBVK	TBVL	TBVM	TBVN	TBVO	TBVP	TBVQ	TBVR	TBVS
2000	11 527	3	2 236	15 357	4 225	–	11 578	33 750	30 627
2001	9 431	3	2 691	17 512	5 027	158	13 107	33 478	31 993
Facilities granted									
	TCBK	TCBL	TCBM	TCBN	TCBO	TCBP	TCBQ	TCBR	TCBS
2000	14 416	62	2 688	16 907	12 075	36	12 732	124 173	55 662
2001	12 483	18	3 074	19 190	20 741	187	17 066	132 997	66 277
of which in sterling									
	TCDK	TCDL	TCDM	TCDN	TCDO	TCDP	TCDQ	TCDR	TCDS
2000	12 834	45	2 356	16 897	7 612	–	11 779	35 504	34 815
2001	10 533	6	2 808	19 056	14 260	158	13 429	35 542	37 267

	Activities auxiliary to financial intermediation			Individuals & individual trusts		
	Insurance companies & pension funds	Fund management activities	Other	Total	Lending secured on dwellings inc. bridging finance	Other loans & advances
Amounts outstanding (sterling & other currencies)						
Loans & advances (including under repo & sterling commercial paper)						
	TBPT	TBPU	TBPV	TBPW	TBPX	TBPY
2000	19 759	4 384	10 332	471 274	377 065	94 209
2001	16 116	6 777	18 495	515 204	407 406	107 798
Acceptances						
	TBRT	TBRU	TBRV			
2000	207	40	8			
2001	202	–	14			
Total						
	TBTT	TBTU	TBTV	TBTW	TBTX	TBTY
2000	19 966	4 423	10 340	471 274	377 065	94 209
2001	16 318	6 777	18 509	515 204	407 406	107 798
of which in sterling						
	TBVT	TBVU	TBVV	TBVW	TBVX	TBVY
2000	18 441	3 225	2 322	470 917	377 028	93 888
2001	14 792	4 287	4 111	514 802	407 365	107 437
Facilities granted						
	TCBT	TCBU	TCBV	TCBW	TCBX	TCBY
2000	26 757	6 916	11 566	505 556	390 349	115 207
2001	27 481	8 705	19 636	562 977	432 258	130 719
of which in sterling						
	TCDT	TCDU	TCDV	TCDW	TCDX	TCDY
2000	22 933	4 837	3 257	505 123	390 310	114 813
2001	22 281	5 338	4 827	562 441	432 164	130 277

1 See chapter text.

Source: Bank of England: 020 7601 3236

22.5 Industrial analysis of bank deposits from UK residents[1]

£ millions

	Total from UK residents	Agriculture, hunting and forestry	Fishing	Mining & quarrying	Manufacturing Total	Food, beverages & tobacco	Textiles & leather	Pulp, paper, publishing & printing
Amounts outstanding (sterling & other currencies)								
Deposit liabilities (including under repos)								
	TDAA	TDAB	TDAC	TDAD	TDAE	TDAF	TDAG	TDAH
2000	839 750	3 049	103	4 317	33 126	3 453	1 257	4 538
2001	910 267	3 667	113	3 730	33 673	3 599	1 126	4 111
of which in sterling								
	TDCA	TDCB	TDCC	TDCD	TDCE	TDCF	TDCG	TDCH
2000	722 701	3 003	94	1 853	24 774	2 666	1 070	3 863
2001	761 236	3 554	100	1 844	24 752	2 868	961	3 455

	Manufacturing				Electricity, gas and water supply		
	Chemicals, man-made fibres, rubber & plastics	Non-metallic mineral products & metals	Machinery, equipment & transport equipment	Electrical, medical & optical equipment	Other manufacturing	Electricity, gas & heated water	Cold water purification & supply	Construction
Amounts outstanding (sterling & other currencies)								
Deposit liabilities (including under repos)								
	TDAI	TDAJ	TDAK	TDAL	TDAM	TDAN	TDAO	TDAP
2000	5 094	3 273	6 383	5 715	3 413	3 813	1 178	8 855
2001	4 329	3 577	6 855	6 695	3 381	5 095	1 558	9 915
of which in sterling								
	TDCI	TDCJ	TDCK	TDCL	TDCM	TDCN	TDCO	TDCP
2000	3 156	2 719	4 754	3 937	2 609	3 512	853	8 544
2001	2 700	2 857	5 097	3 984	2 829	3 968	1 261	9 701

	Wholesale and retail trade					Transport, storage & communication	Real estate, renting, computer and other business activities		
	Total	Sale & repair of motor vehicles & fuel	Other wholesale trade	Other retail trade & repair	Hotels and restaurants		Total	Development, buying, selling, renting of real estate	Renting of machinery & equipment
Amounts outstanding (sterling & other currencies)									
Deposit liabilities (including under repos)									
	TDAQ	TDAR	TDAS	TDAT	TDAU	TDAV	TDAW	TDAX	TDAY
2000	22 153	2 694	10 101	9 358	3 192	16 691	60 348	15 366	1 307
2001	24 972	2 819	10 987	11 166	3 658	17 836	63 558	17 484	1 089
of which in sterling									
	TDCQ	TDCR	TDCS	TDCT	TDCU	TDCV	TDCW	TDCX	TDCY
2000	18 684	2 470	7 439	8 775	3 100	13 737	55 688	15 106	1 180
2001	21 834	2 729	8 748	10 357	3 558	14 709	59 038	17 239	1 037

22.5 Industrial analysis of bank deposits from UK residents[1]

continued

£ millions

	Real estate, renting, computer and other business activities					Recreational, personal & community service activities		Financial intermediation (excl. insurance & pension funds)	
	Computer & related activities	Legal, accountancy, consultancy & other business activities	Public administration & defence	Education	Health & social work	Recreational, cultural & sporting activities	Personal & community services activities	Total	Financial leasing corporations
Amounts outstanding (sterling & other currencies)									
Deposit liabilities (including under repos)									
	TDAZ	TDBA	TDBB	TDBC	TDBD	TDBF	TDBE	TDBG	TDBH
2000	7 621	36 054	27 046	4 552	6 307	6 852	10 262	147 247	2 485
2001	7 012	37 973	16 834	4 829	6 809	7 074	10 494	173 421	3 130
of which in sterling									
	TDCZ	TDDA	TDDB	TDDC	TDDD	TDDF	TDDE	TDDG	TDDH
2000	6 698	32 703	24 822	4 427	6 059	6 262	9 905	80 354	1 970
2001	5 836	34 925	15 951	4 705	6 687	6 596	10 008	87 363	2 458

	Financial intermediation (excl. insurance & pension funds)								
	Non-bank credit grantors, excl. credit unions	Credit unions	Factoring corporations	Mortgage & housing credit corporations	Investment & unit trusts excl. money market mutual funds	Money market mutual funds	Bank holding companies	Securities dealers	Other financial intermediaries
Amounts outstanding (sterling & other currencies)									
Deposit liabilities (including under repos)									
	TDBI	TDBJ	TDBK	TDBL	TDBM	TDBN	TDBO	TDBP	TDBQ
2000	3 511	302	390	1 367	17 596	403	7 494	68 040	45 660
2001	3 410	169	279	2 247	17 626	528	9 589	78 036	58 406
of which in sterling									
	TDDI	TDDJ	TDDK	TDDL	TDDM	TDDN	TDDO	TDDP	TDDQ
2000	2 525	302	349	1 366	14 337	400	5 860	24 341	28 904
2001	2 747	169	216	2 247	13 757	505	7 991	28 119	29 155

	Insurance companies & pension funds	Activities auxiliary to financial intermediation		Individuals & individual trusts
		Placed by fund managers	Other	
Amounts outstanding (sterling & other currencies)				
Deposit liabilities (including under repos)				
	TDBR	TDBS	TDBT	TDBU
2000	57 517	29 423	14 287	379 431
2001	56 199	34 096	28 009	404 727
of which in sterling				
	TDDR	TDDS	TDDT	TDDU
2000	50 142	21 704	7 382	377 802
2001	49 089	24 927	8 596	402 998

1 See chapter text.

Source: Bank of England: 020 7601 3236

22.6 Public sector net cash requirement and other counterparts to changes in money stock during the year

Not seasonally adjusted

£ millions

		1991	1992	1993	1994	1995	1996	1997	1998	1999	2000	2001
Public sector net cash requirement (surplus-)	ABEN	6 959	28 436	43 358	39 344	35 446	24 690	11 827	−6 412	−1 791	−37 339	−2 861
Sales(-) of public sector debt to M4 private sector	KHGZ	−5 686	−20 268	−30 800	−23 426	−21 659	−18 993	−16 122	1 508	−1 265	13 591	−11 853
M4 lending[1]	AVBS	37 066	25 537	22 680	31 604	57 744	59 130	68 208	64 137	78 087	111 233	82 446
External and foreign currency finance of the public sector	KHJP	−3 058	−12 647	−10 768	654	−3 640	−10 884	−2 453	−4 717	6 199	3 614	23 557
Other external and foreign currency flows[2]	AVBW	1 253	8 830	14 266	−8 074	−3 443	18 020	25 952	14 028	−46 411	6 843	−22 158
Net non-deposit liabilities (increase-)	AVBX	−8 452	−12 046	−14 859	−14 545	−8 563	−12 626	−7 050	−8 426	−1 552	−30 487	−10 803
Money stock (M4)	AUZI	28 082	17 843	23 877	25 557	55 885	59 337	80 362	60 118	33 268	67 455	58 329

1 Bank and building society lending, plus holdings of commercial bills by the Issue Department of the Bank of England.
2 Including sterling lending to non-residents sector.

Source: Bank of England: 020 7601 5468

22.7 Money stock and liquidity

£ millions

		1991	1992	1993	1994	1995	1996	1997	1998	1999	2000	2001
Amounts outstanding at end-year												
Notes and coin in circulation with the M4 private sector[1]	VQKT	15 628	16 698	17 716	18 661	19 847	20 642	22 242	23 705	26 269	28 185	30 482
UK private sector sterling non-interest bearing sight deposits[2,3]	AUYA	29 405	28 667	34 521	33 502	35 450	38 447	38 937	37 262	43 011	46 604	50 205
Money stock (M2)[3,4]	VQXV	335 883	373 179	394 438	410 396	436 957	460 108	484 593	515 005	559 214	598 271	649 668
Money stock M4[3]	AUYM	504 133	517 883	544 055	567 157	623 385	682 786	721 977	783 240	816 427	884 957	942 012
Changes during the year[5]												
Notes and coin in circulation with the M4 private sector[1]	VQLU	428	1 066	1 023	956	1 177	797	1 611	1 501	2 582	1 968	2 305
UK private sector sterling non-interest bearing sight deposits[2,3]	AUZA	−774	−327	4 203	1 092	1 782	3 530	5 349	−631	5 759	3 364	3 830
Money stock (M2)[3,4]	AUZE	22 987	9 807	18 851	17 624	26 491	24 323	35 963	30 968	42 397	38 964	51 751
Money stock M4[3]	AUZI	28 082	17 843	23 877	25 557	55 885	59 337	80 362	60 118	33 268	67 455	58 329

1 The estimates of levels of coin in circulation include allowance for wastage, hoarding, etc.

2 Non-interest bearing deposits are confined to those with institutions included in the United Kingdom banks sector (See Table 22.3).

3 Revised rules on netting of customers' credit balances against their borrowing increased the UK private sector's outstanding balances of deposits and borrowing by £2.5bn at end-December 1993. Within retail deposit, £1.7bn of the increase was in NIB bank deposits. Re-netting during 1994 amounted to £1.7bn. Changes data have been adjusted to exclude these effects. Building societies' data from 1992 onwards are affected by the revised treatment of building society transit items within M4.

4 With effect from the flow for December 1992, M2 comprises the UK non-monetary financial institutions and non-public sector, i.e. M4 private sector's holdings of notes and coin together with its sterling denominated retail deposits with UK monetary financial institutions.

5 As far as possible the changes exclude the effect of changes in the number of contributors to the series, and also of the introduction of new statistical returns. Changes are not seasonally adjusted.

Source: Bank of England: 020 7601 5468

22.8 Selected retail banks' base rate[1]

Percentage rates operative between dates shown

Rates

Date of change	New rate	Date of change	New rate	Date of change	New rate
1986 Jan 9	12.50	Jul 5	10.00	Feb 3	6.75
Mar 19	11.50	Jul 18	10.00-10.50	Dec 13	6.50
Apr 8	11.00-11.50	Jul 19	10.50		
Apr 9	11.00	Aug 8	10.50-11.00	1996 Jan 18	6.25
Apr 21	10.50	Aug 9	11.00	Mar 8	6.00
May 23	10.00-10.50	Aug 25	11.00-12.00	Jun 6	5.75
May 27	10.00	Aug 26	12.00	Oct 30	5.75-6.00
Oct 14	10.00-11.00	Nov 25	13.00	Oct 31	6.00
Oct 15	11.00				
		1989 May 24	14.00	1997 May 6	6.25
		Oct 5	15.00	Jun 6	6.25-6.50
1987 Mar 10	10.50			Jun 9	6.50
Mar 18	10.00-10.50	1990 Oct 8	14.00	Jul 10	6.75
Mar 19	10.00			Aug 7	7.00
Apr 28	9.50-10.00	1991 Feb 13	13.50	Nov 6	7.25
Apr 29	9.50	Feb 27	13.00		
May 11	9.00	Mar 22	12.50	1998 Jun 4	7.50
Aug 6	9.00-10.00	Apr 12	12.00	Oct 8	7.25
Aug 7	10.00	May 24	11.50	Nov 5	6.75
Oct 23	9.50-10.00	Jul 12	11.00	Dec 10	6.25
Oct 29	9.50	Sep 4	10.50		
Nov 4	9.00-9.50			1999 Jan 7	6.00
Nov 5	9.00			Feb 4	5.50
Dec 4	8.50	1992 May 5	10.00	Apr 8	5.25
		Sep 16[1]	12.00	Jun 10	5.00
1988 Feb 2	9.00	Sep 17[1]	10.00-12.00	Sep 8	5.00-5.25
Mar 17	8.50-9.00	Sep 18	10.00	Sep 10	5.25
Mar 18	8.50	Sep 22	9.00	Nov 4	5.50
Apr 11	8.00	Oct 16	8.00-9.00		
May 17	7.50-8.00	Oct 19	8.00	2000 Jan 13	5.75
May 18	7.50	Nov 13	7.00	Feb 10	6.00
Jun 2	7.50-8.00				
Jun 3	8.00	1993 Jan 26	6.00	2001 Feb 8	5.75
Jun 6	8.00-8.50	Nov 23	5.50	Apr 5	5.50
Jun 7	8.50			May 10	5.25
Jun 22	8.50-9.00	1994 Feb 8	5.25	Aug 2	5.00
Jun 23	9.00	Sep 12	5.75	Sep 18	4.75
Jun 28	9.00-9.50	Dec 7	6.25	Oct 4	4.50
Jun 29	9.50			Nov 8	4.00
Jul 4	9.50-10.00	1995 Feb 2[1]	6.25-6.75		

1 Data obtained from Barclays Bank, Lloyds TSB Bank, HSBC and National Westminster Bank whose rates are used to compile this series. Where all the rates did not change on the same day a spread is shown.

Source: Bank of England: 020 7601 4342

22.9 Average three month sterling money market rates[1]

Rate per cent

	1992	1993	1994	1995	1996	1997	1998	1999	2000	2001	2002
Treasury bills:[2] KDMM											
January	9.97	6.05	4.88	5.93	6.08	6.01	6.84	5.28	5.72	5.49	3.83
February	9.80	5.37	4.76	6.16	5.96	5.81	6.88	5.04	5.83	5.46	3.87
March	10.10	5.38	4.83	6.09	5.81	5.92	6.95	4.92	5.86	5.23	3.97
April	9.97	5.33	4.88	6.30	5.80	6.09	7.02	4.90	5.90	5.12	3.97
May	9.42	5.30	4.81	6.20	5.82	6.15	6.99	4.93	5.95	4.98	3.95
June	9.42	5.19	4.88	6.37	5.58	6.37	7.29	4.76	5.85	4.99	3.98
July	9.43	5.13	5.09	6.62	5.49	6.60	7.22	4.76	5.83	5.01	3.84
August	9.65	5.06	5.34	6.59	5.54	6.81	7.19	4.85	5.80	4.72	3.77
September	9.16	5.16	5.39	6.52	5.54	6.88	6.94	5.08	5.80	4.43	..
October	7.47	5.15	5.44	6.57	5.55	6.94	6.54	5.25	5.75	4.16	..
November	6.49	4.95	5.63	6.44	6.02	7.09	6.31	5.20	5.69	3.78	..
December	6.39	4.87	5.87	6.21	6.08	7.04	5.72	5.49	5.63	3.83	..
Eligible bill: KDMY											
January	10.08	6.43	5.07	6.41	6.18	6.15	7.28	5.63	5.90	5.64	3.91
February	9.87	5.59	4.95	6.54	6.00	5.99	7.24	5.28	6.01	5.56	3.92
March	10.14	5.62	4.90	6.40	5.87	6.01	7.25	5.11	5.98	5.37	3.99
April	10.18	5.66	4.93	6.44	5.83	6.26	7.24	5.02	6.05	5.21	4.04
May	9.56	5.67	4.92	6.54	5.85	6.31	7.20	5.08	6.09	5.06	4.01
June	9.52	5.62	4.94	6.44	5.66	6.50	7.41	4.94	6.03	5.08	4.04
July	9.59	5.63	5.01	6.66	5.57	6.80	7.49	4.89	5.97	5.07	3.94
August	9.80	5.59	5.44	6.64	5.60	6.95	7.40	4.94	5.97	4.82	3.86
September	9.43	5.58	5.54	6.55	5.63	7.02	7.20	5.16	5.95	4.57	..
October	7.78	5.50	5.74	6.58	5.76	7.10	6.91	5.42	5.92	4.26	..
November	6.70	5.31	5.89	6.49	6.10	7.27	6.52	5.43	5.88	3.85	..
December	6.69	5.04	6.12	6.29	6.18	7.31	6.05	5.59	5.78	3.88	..
Interbank rate: AMIJ											
January	10.65	6.94	5.39	6.56	6.36	6.32	7.48	5.80	6.06	5.76	3.98
February	10.37	6.16	5.22	6.75	6.16	6.19	7.46	5.43	6.15	5.69	3.98
March	10.62	5.98	5.16	6.66	6.05	6.20	7.48	5.30	6.15	5.47	4.06
April	10.62	5.98	5.21	6.67	6.00	6.38	7.44	5.23	6.21	5.33	4.11
May	10.06	5.97	5.17	6.72	6.02	6.45	7.41	5.25	6.23	5.17	4.08
June	9.98	5.89	5.13	6.64	5.85	6.66	7.63	5.12	6.14	5.19	4.11
July	10.15	5.95	5.20	6.80	5.73	6.96	7.71	5.07	6.11	5.19	3.99
August	10.35	5.84	5.53	6.79	5.75	7.15	7.66	5.18	6.14	4.93	3.92
September	9.99	5.91	5.67	6.72	5.77	7.21	7.38	5.32	6.12	4.65	..
October	8.32	5.76	5.91	6.73	5.94	7.26	7.14	5.94	6.08	4.36	..
November	7.21	5.57	6.06	6.64	6.30	7.54	6.89	5.78	6.00	3.93	..
December	7.15	5.33	6.37	6.49	6.35	7.62	6.38	5.97	5.89	3.99	..
Certificate of deposits: KOSA											
January	10.53	6.82	5.29	6.48	6.31	6.27	7.44	5.74	6.02	5.73	3.96
February	10.27	6.00	5.14	6.67	6.11	6.14	7.42	5.38	6.10	5.66	3.96
March	10.51	5.87	5.09	6.59	6.01	6.15	7.43	5.26	6.09	5.44	4.04
April	10.50	5.84	5.12	6.62	5.96	6.33	7.40	5.19	6.17	5.30	4.08
May	9.95	5.86	5.10	6.66	5.98	6.39	7.37	5.22	6.19	5.15	4.06
June	9.89	5.77	5.06	6.56	5.79	6.62	7.59	5.09	6.10	5.16	4.09
July	10.04	5.81	5.11	6.72	5.69	6.92	7.66	5.03	6.08	5.17	3.97
August	10.21	5.71	5.45	6.73	5.71	7.12	7.61	5.14	6.09	4.90	3.90
September	9.83	5.79	5.58	6.66	5.74	7.17	7.34	5.28	6.08	4.62	..
October	8.17	5.65	5.81	6.68	5.89	7.22	7.09	5.86	6.05	4.33	..
November	7.04	5.46	5.97	6.58	6.25	7.50	6.82	5.72	5.98	3.91	..
December	7.02	5.23	6.25	6.44	6.29	7.57	6.32	5.89	5.85	3.96	..
Local authority deposits: KDPX											
January	10.61	6.84	5.30	6.52	6.31	6.27	7.43	5.76	6.03	5.73	3.85
February	10.34	6.09	5.12	6.69	6.13	6.15	7.40	5.38	6.09	5.62	3.88
March	10.57	5.93	5.08	6.59	6.02	6.14	7.40	5.27	6.08	5.39	4.01
April	10.59	5.95	5.14	6.60	5.98	6.33	7.38	5.17	6.12	5.26	4.05
May	10.02	5.94	5.12	6.68	6.00	6.38	7.34	5.19	6.14	5.13	4.06
June	9.94	5.86	5.08	6.58	5.80	6.57	7.56	5.07	6.09	5.10	4.05
July	10.10	5.90	5.18	6.76	5.69	6.90	7.64	5.01	6.04	5.12	3.95
August	10.24	5.80	5.44	6.74	5.71	7.11	7.55	5.11	6.06	4.86	3.87
September	9.82	5.85	5.62	6.65	5.72	7.19	7.35	5.19	6.05	4.58	..
October	8.28	5.70	5.84	6.68	5.86	7.21	7.08	5.83	6.03	4.29	..
November	7.17	5.51	5.99	6.60	6.24	7.49	6.85	5.64	5.96	3.82	..
December	7.08	5.26	6.32	6.43	6.30	7.56	6.35	5.88	5.80	3.87	..

1 A full definition of these series is given in Section 7 of the ONS Financial
  Statistics Explanatory Handbook.
2 Average rate of discount at weekly (Friday) tender.

Source: Bank of England: 020 7601 4342

22.10 Average foreign exchange rates[1]

	1992	1993	1994	1995	1996	1997	1998	1999	2000	2001	2002
Sterling exchange rate index (1990 = 100) AJHX											
January	99.6	88.8	92.0	88.5	83.2	95.9	104.7	99.6	108.5	104.4	106.9
February	99.7	84.7	90.4	87.4	83.8	97.4	104.7	100.8	108.4	104.1	107.4
March	98.9	86.4	89.8	85.6	83.5	97.4	106.8	102.8	108.4	105.0	106.5
April	100.2	88.9	89.2	84.5	83.8	99.5	107.1	103.4	110.1	105.8	107.1
May	101.7	89.0	88.9	84.3	84.6	99.0	103.4	104.2	108.5	106.6	105.3
June	101.7	88.3	89.1	84.1	86.0	100.4	105.4	104.7	104.6	106.8	103.6
July	101.2	90.5	87.9	83.6	85.7	104.5	105.3	103.5	105.6	107.2	105.3
August	100.5	90.3	87.8	84.4	84.7	102.5	104.6	103.3	107.4	105.1	105.4
September	96.5	89.8	88.1	84.8	86.1	100.4	103.3	104.7	106.2	106.1	..
October	88.7	89.4	89.1	84.3	88.4	101.1	100.7	105.4	109.2	105.8	..
November	86.2	90.2	89.1	83.3	92.0	103.8	100.6	105.7	107.3	106.1	..
December	88.2	91.0	89.1	82.9	93.8	104.4	100.4	106.7	106.4	106.5	..
Sterling/US Dollar AJFA											
January	1.8127	1.5325	1.4939	1.5747	1.5306	1.6587	1.6353	1.6509	1.6402	1.4769	1.4323
February	1.7781	1.4386	1.4799	1.5720	1.5364	1.6246	1.6407	1.6276	1.5998	1.4529	1.4231
March	1.7238	1.4625	1.4917	1.6005	1.5271	1.6063	1.6620	1.6220	1.5802	1.4454	1.4225
April	1.7576	1.5472	1.4837	1.6074	1.5145	1.6295	1.6733	1.6105	1.5837	1.4350	1.4434
May	1.8109	1.5481	1.5029	1.5868	1.5152	1.6334	1.6366	1.6154	1.5075	1.4259	1.4593
June	1.8556	1.5099	1.5252	1.5949	1.5418	1.6446	1.6507	1.5950	1.5089	1.4014	1.4863
July	1.9186	1.4963	1.5463	1.5953	1.5539	1.6702	1.6437	1.5747	1.5088	1.4139	1.5546
August	1.9412	1.4911	1.5427	1.5681	1.5502	1.6034	1.6320	1.6073	1.4910	1.4365	1.5377
September	1.8559	1.5261	1.5651	1.5584	1.5597	1.6015	1.6822	1.6243	1.4355	1.4635	..
October	1.6577	1.5037	1.6057	1.5779	1.5862	1.6329	1.6952	1.6572	1.4511	1.4517	..
November	1.5275	1.4806	1.5886	1.5623	1.6626	1.6890	1.6620	1.6214	1.4256	1.4358	..
December	1.5536	1.4904	1.5595	1.5398	1.6647	1.6597	1.6705	1.6132	1.4625	1.4409	..
Sterling/Euro THAP											
January	1.3731	1.2383	1.3295	1.2525	1.1631	1.3559	1.5166	1.4236	1.6201	1.5753	1.6222
February	1.3808	1.1884	1.3082	1.2331	1.1707	1.3906	1.5196	1.4534	1.6266	1.5786	1.6348
March	1.3742	1.2164	1.2915	1.2038	1.1692	1.3944	1.5507	1.4902	1.6377	1.5901	1.6224
April	1.3881	1.2453	1.2840	1.1890	1.1763	1.4243	1.5490	1.5051	1.6730	1.6084	1.6282
May	1.4047	1.2493	1.2719	1.1893	1.1923	1.4217	1.4834	1.5185	1.6655	1.6304	1.5914
June	1.3979	1.2522	1.2709	1.1828	1.2094	1.4499	1.5110	1.5374	1.5882	1.6434	1.5515
July	1.3732	1.2969	1.2455	1.1693	1.2007	1.5247	1.5091	1.5204	1.6052	1.6433	1.5665
August	1.3550	1.2977	1.2420	1.1836	1.1845	1.5043	1.4912	1.5146	1.6478	1.5955	1.5723
September	1.3093	1.2735	1.2469	1.1903	1.2066	1.4591	1.4617	1.5458	1.6471	1.6060	..
October	1.2192	1.2727	1.2563	1.1759	1.2407	1.4623	1.4200	1.5491	1.6994	1.6024	..
November	1.1992	1.2958	1.2613	1.1612	1.2873	1.4914	1.4290	1.5706	1.6664	1.6166	..
December	1.2234	1.3076	1.2672	1.1589	1.3192	1.5053	1.4254	1.5953	1.6302	1.6151	..

1 Working day average. A full definition of these series is given in Section 7 of the ONS Explanatory Handbook.

Source: Bank of England: 020 7601 4342

22.11 Average FTSE Actuaries share indices[1]

	1992	1993	1994	1995	1996	1997	1998	1999	2000	2001	2002
FT 30 AJMT											
(1 July 1935=100)											
January	1 937.55	2 161.96	2 620.12	2 314.26	2 749.65	2 816.35	3 316.29	3 533.15	3 894.87	3 550.35	2 706.04
February	1 974.94	2 195.20	2 615.71	2 318.80	2 748.04	2 851.43	3 466.66	3 662.63	3 583.41	3 488.73	2 556.21
March	1 946.12	2 252.83	2 523.40	2 354.84	2 759.32	2 878.24	3 704.62	3 760.35	3 667.74	3 258.51	2 624.81
April	1 983.89	2 213.18	2 485.27	2 438.47	2 827.87	2 844.17	3 805.78	3 996.92	3 638.75	3 200.29	2 568.64
May	2 123.50	2 207.04	2 455.02	2 495.93	2 800.40	2 978.86	3 874.65	3 964.51	3 634.60	3 275.60	2 518.05
June	2 027.33	2 249.20	2 343.28	2 520.49	2 762.43	3 000.31	3 829.91	4 042.05	3 705.09	3 233.31	2 273.42
July	1 856.49	2 242.42	2 370.69	2 566.60	2 721.55	3 074.31	3 872.48	4 083.59	3 702.08	2 997.61	2 015.27
August	1 741.10	2 371.00	2 485.86	2 618.07	2 801.45	3 155.89	3 556.16	4 024.71	3 688.48	2 946.34	1 919.40
September	1 794.52	2 348.43	2 404.62	2 632.99	2 823.96	3 222.33	3 199.89	3 913.54	3 483.90	2 481.82	..
October	1 899.13	2 363.62	2 342.27	2 598.68	2 844.23	3 346.83	3 043.19	3 700.20	3 395.04	2 444.83	..
November	2 023.15	2 357.95	2 367.99	2 618.81	2 790.12	3 146.25	3 398.12	3 886.71	3 595.55	2 670.72	..
December	2 115.20	2 492.46	2 327.92	2 647.33	2 779.80	3 256.86	3 437.49	4 021.40	3 589.67	2 699.78	..
FTSE 100 AJNO											
(1 January 1984=1000)											
January	2 520.19	2 790.29	3 431.29	3 028.27	3 715.78	4 166.48	5 242.10	5 975.84	6 471.60	6 193.48	5 186.27
February	2 543.31	2 840.17	3 396.40	3 051.68	3 738.08	4 316.57	5 657.73	6 010.79	6 178.51	6 118.41	5 126.80
March	2 495.24	2 897.07	3 206.10	3 078.24	3 697.50	4 349.78	5 861.80	6 168.55	6 541.46	5 713.40	5 252.56
April	2 549.44	2 837.45	3 130.94	3 198.38	3 792.32	4 312.51	5 974.51	6 459.86	6 312.71	5 767.89	5 206.33
May	2 702.34	2 830.13	3 089.23	3 288.31	3 758.41	4 622.62	5 936.72	6 322.04	6 210.24	5 877.82	5 167.79
June	2 604.44	2 874.70	2 980.32	3 351.55	3 734.02	4 649.40	5 847.04	6 425.82	6 450.25	5 753.06	4 732.34
July	2 443.25	2 850.73	3 036.57	3 426.50	3 707.21	4 843.16	5 987.19	6 422.83	6 433.31	5 462.43	4 238.08
August	2 344.11	3 019.28	3 178.50	3 486.95	3 841.75	4 945.56	5 555.77	6 210.91	6 480.01	5 444.36	4 255.80
September	2 452.41	3 028.12	3 098.35	3 534.27	3 927.10	5 010.35	5 171.92	6 116.94	6 462.63	4 887.19	..
October	2 587.09	3 125.15	3 046.77	3 531.80	4 020.99	5 145.13	5 063.84	6 071.20	6 293.60	5 060.03	..
November	2 712.92	3 111.59	3 086.85	3 580.31	3 969.54	4 846.24	5 595.58	6 487.49	6 362.19	5 242.32	..
December	2 777.08	3 313.68	3 026.62	3 650.05	4 038.89	5 087.53	5 695.61	6 718.34	6 243.13	5 181.27	..
FTSE 250 HSDY											
(31 December 1985=1 412.60)											
January	2 416.60	2 911.16	3 982.73	3 442.44	4 064.09	4 555.58	4 827.40	4 904.94	6 433.85	6 640.09	5 972.32
February	2 483.96	3 025.33	4 043.22	3 415.44	4 173.78	4 612.14	5 007.04	5 192.55	6 227.49	6 720.57	5 790.71
March	2 464.98	3 110.07	3 863.01	3 380.00	4 267.75	4 654.82	5 396.04	5 430.80	6 639.72	6 299.23	6 072.47
April	2 543.71	3 105.83	3 787.30	3 492.65	4 460.37	4 516.06	5 554.73	5 689.94	6 235.96	6 187.58	6 158.57
May	2 796.13	3 147.15	3 715.69	3 599.70	4 512.56	4 512.02	5 799.26	5 760.77	6 227.50	6 533.12	6 129.29
June	2 705.19	3 206.75	3 508.83	3 656.27	4 442.75	4 488.19	5 739.27	5 829.07	6 511.06	6 463.31	5 717.89
July	2 412.63	3 229.30	3 537.07	3 751.14	4 281.41	4 455.37	5 595.92	6 019.49	6 719.79	6 111.88	4 999.59
August	2 241.03	3 441.33	3 736.79	3 877.61	4 356.08	4 628.92	5 173.36	5 996.57	6 855.46	6 145.25	4 790.13
September	2 283.05	3 450.16	3 643.98	3 944.57	4 417.69	4 691.23	4 657.92	5 907.51	6 873.12	5 432.80	..
October	2 430.38	3 493.16	3 496.27	3 931.11	4 436.44	4 839.20	4 516.20	5 630.98	6 549.05	5 328.41	..
November	2 599.44	3 456.16	3 529.07	3 924.12	4 408.96	4 639.14	4 885.03	5 965.43	6 661.71	5 761.06	..
December	2 736.30	3 662.08	3 447.33	3 964.00	4 414.07	4 735.67	4 766.50	6 306.32	6 486.66	5 896.11	..
FTSE 350 HSDZ											
(31 December 1985=682.94)											
January	1 217.25	1 371.71	1 727.07	1 516.86	1 845.10	2 068.86	2 515.13	2 814.00	3 139.34	3 036.97	2 566.51
February	1 233.21	1 402.36	1 719.55	1 523.13	1 864.31	2 133.08	2 694.81	2 852.95	3 003.39	3 009.92	2 530.96
March	1 212.79	1 432.87	1 627.45	1 529.79	1 857.35	2 149.97	2 812.26	2 936.53	3 183.90	2 812.11	2 600.65
April	1 241.34	1 409.41	1 591.09	1 587.54	1 912.92	2 122.15	2 871.66	3 075.23	3 060.19	2 828.61	2 585.72
May	1 326.02	1 410.73	1 566.38	1 633.07	1 904.66	2 242.88	2 880.53	3 025.51	3 017.11	2 895.80	2 567.27
June	1 283.90	1 433.98	1 504.97	1 663.19	1 888.45	2 251.03	2 839.93	3 073.04	3 136.08	2 838.58	2 356.63
July	1 187.91	1 426.89	1 529.57	1 701.71	1 862.53	2 323.26	2 881.50	3 087.31	3 143.57	2 693.78	2 104.07
August	1 131.99	1 513.47	1 604.51	1 737.88	1 922.50	2 380.26	2 672.02	2 999.44	3 172.37	2 687.98	2 100.43
September	1 179.00	1 517.78	1 564.18	1 762.92	1 960.31	2 411.60	2 472.77	2 954.26	3 166.18	2 408.31	..
October	1 240.77	1 558.17	1 531.81	1 760.62	2 000.47	2 478.65	2 417.18	2 913.51	3 073.86	2 477.00	..
November	1 307.83	1 550.67	1 548.23	1 778.73	1 977.68	2 342.66	2 661.39	3 109.10	3 109.40	2 579.29	..
December	1 349.36	1 648.53	1 516.74	1 809.73	2 005.29	2 445.93	2 690.25	3 231.63	3 048.54	2 560.26	..
FTSE All-share AJMA											
(10 April 1962=100)											
January	1 203.08	1 351.60	1 710.35	1 501.87	1 818.72	2 041.99	2 455.05	2 715.41	3 072.11	2 979.84	2 513.48
February	1 218.70	1 384.99	1 709.09	1 506.17	1 839.78	2 105.82	2 624.19	2 757.57	2 947.10	2 955.31	2 476.01
March	1 199.04	1 415.40	1 619.80	1 511.04	1 836.04	2 121.89	2 740.51	2 841.78	3 126.10	2 759.72	2 543.59
April	1 225.16	1 393.70	1 582.06	1 566.98	1 892.47	2 092.74	2 799.69	2 976.58	3 000.08	2 771.56	2 531.10
May	1 310.73	1 397.10	1 559.27	1 614.69	1 889.96	2 203.40	2 814.73	2 935.82	2 959.31	2 841.85	2 514.06
June	1 260.28	1 419.94	1 497.44	1 643.59	1 875.05	2 207.24	2 775.66	2 982.44	3 076.22	2 786.32	2 309.21
July	1 171.62	1 413.38	1 517.70	1 680.80	1 844.67	2 269.94	2 804.19	3 000.90	3 085.70	2 640.55	2 060.92
August	1 114.82	1 498.55	1 591.47	1 718.13	1 899.46	2 324.27	2 597.71	2 920.81	3 114.63	2 633.13	2 055.28
September	1 156.91	1 505.06	1 554.01	1 743.26	1 938.37	2 357.80	2 397.79	2 880.46	3 112.47	2 356.57	..
October	1 221.44	1 544.80	1 516.65	1 739.84	1 973.94	2 422.75	2 338.00	2 835.95	3 015.93	2 418.85	..
November	1 284.96	1 535.11	1 533.46	1 755.17	1 951.91	2 293.45	2 571.19	3 024.26	3 050.28	2 522.94	..
December	1 324.08	1 628.88	1 502.42	1 783.30	1 976.41	2 388.17	2 595.88	3 146.68	2 989.69	2 507.59	..

1 Working day average. A full definition of these series is given in Section 7 of
the ONS Explanatory Handbook.

Source: Bank of England: 020 7601 4342

393

Banking, insurance etc.

22.12 Average Zero Coupon Yields[1]

	1992	1993	1994	1995	1996	1997	1998	1999	2000	2001	2002
Nominal Five Year Yield ZBRG											
January	9.54	7.46	5.89	8.63	6.85	7.15	6.18	4.30	6.28	5.07	4.90
February	9.34	7.06	6.23	8.53	7.12	6.82	6.10	4.46	6.13	5.04	4.94
March	9.71	6.94	6.96	8.45	7.45	7.07	6.09	4.69	5.89	4.86	5.22
April	9.53	7.23	7.58	8.25	7.52	7.28	5.93	4.66	5.80	4.96	5.21
May	9.08	7.47	7.97	7.95	7.53	6.94	5.95	4.95	5.82	5.14	5.22
June	9.10	7.34	8.45	7.77	7.46	6.96	6.04	5.28	5.61	5.25	5.05
July	9.08	7.02	8.27	7.89	7.30	7.01	6.12	5.49	5.58	5.26	4.88
August	9.45	6.62	8.47	7.70	7.19	6.97	5.80	5.75	5.65	5.03	4.54
September	9.18	6.59	8.71	7.47	7.18	6.72	5.32	6.00	5.65	4.90	..
October	8.06	6.43	8.64	7.56	6.97	6.51	4.94	6.25	5.46	4.74	..
November	7.46	6.35	8.49	7.21	7.18	6.69	4.92	5.86	5.33	4.55	..
December	7.65	5.89	8.49	6.88	7.20	6.46	4.51	5.90	5.14	4.88	..
Nominal Ten Year Yield ZBRH											
January	9.21	8.51	6.39	8.57	7.46	7.52	5.96	4.24	5.62	4.75	4.85
February	9.08	8.25	6.78	8.50	7.80	7.15	5.91	4.39	5.44	4.90	4.90
March	9.40	7.95	7.43	8.45	8.08	7.41	5.85	4.60	5.18	4.64	5.18
April	9.15	8.06	7.79	8.31	8.06	7.58	5.69	4.53	5.14	4.90	5.19
May	8.82	8.32	8.24	8.07	8.10	7.08	5.73	4.83	5.23	5.05	5.22
June	8.90	8.11	8.65	8.04	8.09	7.04	5.60	5.07	5.05	5.11	5.05
July	8.79	7.74	8.47	8.20	7.96	6.92	5.65	5.24	5.09	5.10	4.95
August	9.04	7.23	8.54	8.07	7.86	6.97	5.41	5.25	5.18	4.88	4.68
September	8.99	7.09	8.77	7.93	7.86	6.70	5.03	5.51	5.25	4.91	..
October	8.78	7.00	8.64	8.09	7.56	6.37	4.93	5.68	5.09	4.77	..
November	8.42	6.97	8.51	7.78	7.56	6.46	4.83	5.11	4.98	4.58	..
December	8.46	6.45	8.43	7.52	7.52	6.22	4.44	5.19	4.80	4.83	..
Nominal Twenty Year Yield ZBRI											
January	..	9.19	6.57	8.23	7.89	7.74	5.94	4.36	4.45	4.33	4.69
February	8.67	8.97	6.88	8.16	8.19	7.39	5.88	4.44	4.38	4.42	4.72
March	8.94	8.67	7.45	8.15	8.37	7.59	5.78	4.60	4.25	4.45	4.99
April	8.81	8.63	7.69	8.09	8.30	7.73	5.61	4.53	4.35	4.76	5.02
May	8.57	8.74	7.98	7.92	8.38	7.16	5.67	4.75	4.40	4.87	5.08
June	8.61	8.51	8.18	7.98	8.41	7.08	5.42	4.77	4.37	4.98	4.93
July	8.43	8.12	8.08	8.24	8.34	6.80	5.45	4.67	4.38	4.90	4.82
August	8.55	7.56	8.15	8.14	8.26	6.86	5.30	4.53	4.49	4.69	4.57
September	8.72	7.37	8.29	8.05	8.27	6.64	4.91	4.62	4.63	4.88	..
October	9.37	7.27	8.23	8.30	7.98	6.36	4.87	4.56	4.61	4.92	..
November	9.09	7.20	8.18	7.98	7.81	6.37	4.73	4.07	4.39	4.53	..
December	9.00	6.63	8.08	7.80	7.67	6.17	4.47	4.20	4.30	4.65	..
Real Ten Year Yield ZBRJ											
January	4.29	3.56	2.73	3.87	3.42	3.45	3.10	2.00	2.10	2.22	2.52
February	4.22	3.19	2.86	3.86	3.54	3.27	3.06	1.91	2.17	2.27	2.50
March	4.33	3.01	3.09	3.87	3.67	3.43	3.00	1.85	2.05	2.33	2.53
April	4.51	3.07	3.25	3.79	3.63	3.56	2.91	1.70	2.08	2.56	2.43
May	4.43	3.23	3.48	3.57	3.72	3.57	2.92	1.91	2.14	2.58	2.43
June	4.38	3.25	3.76	3.56	3.77	3.66	2.85	1.89	2.12	2.54	2.33
July	4.50	3.19	3.84	3.58	3.70	3.62	2.77	1.90	2.14	2.56	2.42
August	4.77	3.15	3.78	3.48	3.58	3.60	2.65	2.19	2.25	2.42	2.33
September	4.67	3.09	3.81	3.45	3.57	3.52	2.59	2.31	2.28	2.51	..
October	3.77	3.02	3.82	3.63	3.41	3.23	2.67	2.26	2.33	2.53	..
November	3.42	2.95	3.81	3.52	3.43	3.25	2.40	2.05	2.34	2.39	..
December	3.67	2.79	3.83	3.43	3.42	3.11	2.11	1.98	2.23	2.58	..
Real Twenty Year Yield ZBRK											
January	..	3.84	3.07	3.89	..	3.67	3.06	2.07	2.01	1.88	2.26
February	..	3.68	3.23	3.89	3.79	3.49	3.05	1.99	1.95	1.88	2.30
March	..	3.53	3.45	3.88	3.81	3.59	2.98	1.93	1.78	1.99	2.32
April	4.52	3.54	3.51	3.80	3.75	3.68	2.85	1.81	1.84	2.25	2.25
May	4.40	3.63	3.68	3.64	3.82	3.66	2.83	1.99	1.91	2.32	2.25
June	4.32	3.59	3.91	3.69	3.86	3.69	2.63	1.97	1.87	2.27	2.17
July	4.40	3.52	3.93	3.71	3.81	3.57	2.58	2.00	1.90	2.24	2.24
August	4.55	3.35	3.84	3.62	3.75	3.57	2.53	2.14	1.96	2.16	2.15
September	4.48	3.25	3.88	3.61	3.76	3.48	2.49	2.26	1.96	2.31	..
October	3.98	3.19	3.87	3.73	3.61	3.22	2.59	2.22	1.99	2.32	..
November	3.82	3.21	3.85	3.61	3.62	3.18	2.36	1.92	1.94	2.12	..
December	3.96	3.08	3.87	3.56	3.62	3.06	2.14	1.87	1.87	2.24	..

1 Working day average. Calculated using the Variable Roughness Penalty (VRP) model.

Source: Bank of England: 020 7601 4342

22.13 Average Rates on Representative British Government Stocks[1]

	1992	1993	1994	1995	1996	1997	1998	1999	2000	2001	2002
5 Year Conventional Rate KORP											
January	9.57	6.88	5.76	8.61	6.78	7.19	6.33	4.25	6.36	5.17	4.94
February	9.34	6.72	6.05	8.52	7.02	6.86	6.24	4.41	6.23	5.13	4.96
March	9.75	6.62	6.72	8.44	7.56	7.08	6.26	4.65	6.01	4.94	5.23
April	9.54	6.91	7.33	8.26	7.43	7.30	6.11	4.66	5.95	4.97	5.26
May	9.09	7.10	7.74	7.96	7.61	6.98	6.14	4.93	5.97	5.15	5.48
June	9.12	7.01	8.22	7.79	7.52	7.01	6.31	5.27	5.78	5.32	5.10
July	9.13	6.70	8.06	7.90	7.35	7.09	6.14	5.49	5.75	5.34	4.92
August	9.50	6.35	8.31	7.69	7.21	7.02	5.84	5.80	5.81	5.09	4.57
September	9.13	6.34	8.61	7.45	7.20	6.78	5.34	6.04	5.81	4.94	..
October	7.80	6.17	8.57	7.54	7.01	6.59	4.88	6.24	5.66	4.78	..
November	7.15	6.09	8.44	7.16	7.22	6.79	4.86	5.89	5.50	4.59	..
December	7.38	5.66	8.49	6.83	7.26	6.60	4.45	5.91	5.27	4.88	..
10 year Conventional Rate KORQ											
January	9.47	8.22	6.23	8.66	7.42	7.53	6.07	4.16	5.75	4.86	4.84
February	9.32	7.91	6.61	8.59	7.75	7.17	6.02	4.32	5.56	4.88	4.91
March	9.67	7.66	7.29	8.53	8.05	7.41	5.97	4.54	5.29	4.75	5.15
April	9.43	7.82	7.68	8.39	8.05	7.60	5.81	4.48	5.25	4.95	5.23
May	9.06	8.06	8.13	8.12	8.08	7.13	5.85	4.77	5.35	5.13	5.51
June	9.14	7.87	8.54	8.08	8.04	7.10	5.77	5.02	5.15	5.09	5.06
July	9.08	7.49	8.37	8.23	7.91	7.01	5.67	5.20	5.18	5.16	4.94
August	9.35	6.98	8.52	8.10	7.81	7.05	5.56	5.24	5.27	4.92	4.66
September	9.17	6.90	8.80	7.92	7.80	6.77	5.10	5.52	5.32	4.92	..
October	8.68	6.81	8.70	8.08	7.51	6.47	4.93	5.70	5.15	4.76	..
November	8.26	6.77	8.57	7.75	7.56	6.59	4.87	5.16	5.06	4.58	..
December	8.38	6.29	8.53	7.45	7.54	6.34	4.49	5.24	4.88	4.88	..
20 Year Conventional Rate KORR											
January	9.23	8.74	6.53	8.45	7.73	7.71	6.04	4.36	4.91	4.52	4.81
February	9.12	8.44	6.88	8.43	8.04	7.35	5.98	4.47	4.80	4.58	4.83
March	9.44	8.19	7.49	8.40	8.28	7.58	5.90	4.64	4.64	4.56	5.12
April	9.25	8.42	7.81	8.30	8.26	7.74	5.73	4.58	4.71	4.84	5.14
May	8.93	8.58	8.18	8.09	8.31	7.21	5.79	4.83	4.77	4.98	5.45
June	8.99	8.36	8.48	8.08	8.31	7.15	5.59	4.92	4.68	5.10	5.03
July	8.85	7.98	8.35	8.30	8.21	6.93	5.63	4.88	4.70	5.05	4.92
August	9.06	7.46	8.46	8.19	8.12	6.98	5.43	4.82	4.79	4.83	4.65
September	9.08	7.31	8.65	8.06	8.11	6.74	5.02	4.97	4.90	4.94	..
October	9.15	7.18	8.56	8.26	7.84	6.45	4.92	4.97	4.84	4.80	..
November	8.78	7.12	8.46	7.93	7.77	6.50	4.79	4.46	4.64	4.55	..
December	8.78	6.57	8.39	7.70	7.67	6.32	4.49	4.56	4.51	4.75	..
10 Year Index-Linked Rate KORS											
January	4.29	3.60	2.70	3.89	3.42	3.44	3.01	2.00	2.11	2.21	2.61
February	4.18	3.23	2.81	3.87	3.57	3.23	2.94	1.94	2.16	2.30	2.53
March	4.29	3.07	3.07	3.86	3.70	3.41	2.89	1.90	2.06	2.34	2.55
April	4.47	3.11	3.25	3.79	3.66	3.55	2.80	1.74	2.08	2.55	2.45
May	4.41	3.30	3.51	3.58	3.74	3.52	2.83	1.96	2.15	2.61	2.58
June	4.40	3.31	3.78	3.58	3.80	3.62	2.81	1.93	2.13	2.56	2.35
July	4.51	3.22	3.85	3.61	3.82	3.68	2.67	1.93	2.14	2.57	2.46
August	4.76	3.16	3.82	3.52	3.59	3.59	2.55	2.20	2.25	2.45	2.37
September	4.68	3.09	3.85	3.46	3.57	3.47	2.59	2.32	2.29	2.56	..
October	3.82	3.03	3.84	3.65	3.41	3.17	2.66	2.26	2.33	2.55	..
November	3.40	2.96	3.84	3.54	3.42	3.23	2.39	2.03	2.32	2.42	..
December	3.61	2.75	3.85	3.45	3.41	3.01	2.11	1.99	2.20	2.65	..
20 Year Index-Linked rate KORT											
January	4.34	3.84	2.96	3.91	3.58	3.62	3.01	2.06	2.01	1.96	2.35
February	4.32	3.64	3.11	3.89	3.70	3.43	3.01	1.97	1.98	1.99	2.36
March	4.49	3.50	3.35	3.89	3.82	3.55	2.92	1.93	1.83	2.09	2.39
April	4.59	3.51	3.45	3.81	3.77	3.65	2.80	1.81	1.90	2.35	2.32
May	4.42	3.62	3.64	3.64	3.84	3.61	2.79	1.99	1.97	2.41	2.43
June	4.35	3.57	3.88	3.67	3.88	3.65	2.61	1.97	1.94	2.38	2.23
July	4.42	3.48	3.90	3.71	3.72	3.68	2.56	1.97	1.96	2.36	2.30
August	4.61	3.32	3.83	3.62	3.75	3.54	2.51	2.12	2.03	2.25	2.21
September	4.55	3.22	3.87	3.60	3.74	3.43	2.51	2.23	2.04	2.39	..
October	4.00	3.15	3.86	3.74	3.60	3.17	2.58	2.18	2.08	2.38	..
November	3.77	3.14	3.85	3.62	3.59	3.16	2.35	1.91	2.02	2.19	..
December	3.94	2.98	3.86	3.55	3.58	3.02	2.12	1.88	1.94	2.33	..

1 Working day average.

Source: Bank of England: 020 7601 4342

22.14 Capital issues and redemptions[1]

£ millions

		1991	1992	1993	1994	1995	1996	1997	1998	1999	2000	2001
Total issues and redemptions												
Gross issues	KDSF	26 735	20 649	40 615	37 110	25 929	38 354	38 217	33 000	54 989	75 891	73 612
Gross redemptions	KDSG	3 765	7 011	11 399	11 866	10 367	14 123	14 579	11 607	12 661	10 472	11 281
Issues *less* redemptions: total	KDSH	22 970	13 638	29 216	25 244	15 562	24 231	23 638	21 393	42 328	65 419	62 331
Loan capital	KDSI	11 498	12 744	22 560	24 640	20 788	29 493	29 960	28 624	37 639	55 409	50 461
Preference shares	DEDO	1 245	589	1 700	603	2 875	710	−881	−330	−438	275	1 816
Ordinary shares	DEDF	10 849	6 224	16 671	14 620	9 777	10 273	8 614	4 637	10 127	19 517	18 734
UK borrowers: total	DEDX	22 970	13 638	29 216	25 244	15 562	24 231	23 638	21 393	42 328	65 419	62 331
Local government	DEEA	1	1	−1	–	–	–	–	–	–	–	–
Listed public companies	KDSN	22 969	13 637	29 217	25 244	15 562	24 231	23 638	21 393	42 328	65 419	62 331
Non-resident borrowers: total	KDSO	5 132	1 829	9 237	3 285	2 153	9 452	10 790	3 935	3 356	7 390	71
Central government[2] Non-resident central and local government[2]	KIMI KDSP KDSQ	2 956	2 001	5 525	749	652	1 929	2 724	2 889	2 080	5 766	3 336
Companies[3]	KHDR	2 176	−172	3 712	2 536	1 501	7 523	8 066	1 046	1 276	1 624	−3 265
UK listed public companies												
All companies: total	KDSN	22 969	13 637	29 217	25 244	15 562	24 231	23 638	21 393	42 328	65 419	62 331
Loan capital	KDSS	10 875	6 824	10 846	10 021	2 910	13 248	15 905	17 086	32 639	45 627	41 781
Preference shares	KDST	1 245	589	1 700	603	2 875	710	−881	−330	−438	275	1 816
Ordinary shares	KDSU	10 849	6 224	16 671	14 620	9 777	10 273	8 614	4 637	10 127	19 517	18 734
Financial corporations: total	DEEC	7 815	5 427	12 523	11 774	−341	11 030	6 711	6 830	16 104	26 120	28 549
Loan capital	KDSW	6 027	3 898	7 455	6 972	−4 005	7 508	4 142	6 190	13 191	22 267	22 970
Preference shares	KDSX	660	459	1 221	138	1 538	868	−536	175	−438	292	1 773
Ordinary shares	DELC	1 128	1 070	3 847	4 664	2 126	2 654	3 105	465	3 351	3 561	3 806
Other companies: total	DEEB	15 154	8 210	16 694	13 470	15 903	13 201	16 927	14 563	26 224	39 299	33 782
Loan capital	KDTA	4 848	2 926	3 391	3 049	6 915	5 740	11 763	10 896	19 448	23 360	18 811
Preference shares	KDTB	585	130	479	465	1 337	−158	−345	−505	–	−17	43
Ordinary shares	DEEY	9 721	5 154	12 824	9 956	7 651	7 619	5 509	4 172	6 776	15 956	14 928
UK listed public companies												
Financial companies: total	KDTD	7 817	5 426	12 519	11 774	−342	11 032	8 172	6 828	16 106	26 119	28 549
Monetary financial institutions	KDTE	2 856	1 972	4 764	3 763	−648	9 618	22	2 161	2 312	14 231	14 911
Insurance corporations	DELR	63	394	1 694	501	578	1 007	1 805	617	1 843	85	2 591
Investment trust companies	DELS	841	709	3 027	4 118	1 415	1 537	927	427	231	2 396	1 723
Other[4]	KDTH	4 057	2 351	3 034	3 392	−1 687	−1 130	5 418	3 623	11 720	9 407	9 324
Other companies: total	DEEB	15 154	8 210	16 694	13 470	15 903	13 201	16 927	14 563	26 224	39 299	33 782
Manufacturing industries: total	KDTJ	5 611	4 460	7 133	4 814	9 536	1 888	1 849	−413	3 637	6 129	3 566
Minerals and metal manufacture	DEKN	1 170	1 116	447	76	534	−947	−549	−325	637	822	−3
Chemicals and allied industries	DEKO	338	51	2 043	283	1 759	1 124	854	−295	393	−419	1 142
Metal goods, engineering and vehicles	DEKP	1 165	1 197	1 441	1 535	1 097	365	676	94	987	498	338
Electrical and electronic engines	DEKQ	219	339	119	376	868	447	451	145	167	4 086	342
Food, drink and tobacco	DEKR	1 289	561	1 136	1 242	3 730	−112	−279	−474	876	−396	295
Other manufacturing	DEKS	1 430	1 196	1 947	1 302	1 548	1 011	696	442	577	1 538	1 452
Energy	DEKT	817	539	1 413	1 173	948	1 821	1 781	1 829	3 255	1 409	3 456
Water	DEKU	724	168	212	251	648	354	509	1 025	1 642	210	643
Construction	DEKV	852	238	662	1 284	53	623	703	54	258	203	23
Distribution, hotels and repairs	DEKW	3 121	1 064	2 191	1 137	901	854	1 481	1 242	1 291	2 603	1 603
Transport and communications	DEKX	843	418	872	912	1 134	3 744	4 769	6 946	10 220	16 381	15 124
Property companies	DEKY	1 402	212	2 007	1 873	1 370	1 907	2 798	1 196	1 605	1 704	4 853
Services	DEKZ	1 782	1 118	2 207	2 025	1 310	2 011	3 039	2 689	4 322	10 660	4 519

1 See chapter text. Components of aggregated series may not always sum to the total due to rounding discrepancies.
2 The main issuers within the non-resident central/ local government sectors appear to have been raising finance from programme bond issues. Therefore, there have been few stand alone bond issues. Conversely, the bonds they have previously issued are now beginning to mature. Hence the reason for the low figures for 2001.

3 Non-resident companies including public corporations.
4 'Other' includes special finance agencies (listed public companies engaged in the provision of medium and long-term finance to industry, eg ICFC) and those finance houses and other consumer credit grantors not included under banks and building societies.

Source: Bank of England: 020 7601 5949

22.15 Building societies[1]
United Kingdom

		1992	1993	1994	1995[2]	1996[2]	1997[2]	1998[2]	1999[2]	2000[3]	2001
Number and balance sheets											
Societies on register (number)	KRNA	105	101	96	94	88	82	78	72	68	65
Share investors (thousands)	KRNB	37 533	37 809	38 150	38 998	37 768	19 234	21 195	21 774	22 237	20 311
Depositors (thousands)	KRNC	3 879	3 686	5 369	6 143	6 718	882	820	642	660	501
Borrowers (thousands)	KRND	7 055	7 140	7 222	6 906	6 586	2 703	2 934	2 868	2 925	2 579
Assets and liabilities (£ million)											
Liabilities:											
Shares	KRNE	187 108.4	194 975.1	201 812.2	200 682.0	196 546.4	90 092.8	103 289.8	109 137.7	119 298.5	119 815.2
Deposits and loans	KRNF	57 067.5	62 301.2	69 925.2	67 513.8	73 919.1	31 033.7	33 311.2	34 746.6	44 262.4	37 358.9
Taxation and other	KRNG	2 559.5	2 565.7	2 939.2	3 306.2	3 727.4	1 338.8	1 586.4	1 665.4	1 664.0	1 244.9
General reserves	KRNH	12 634.4	14 269.5	16 312.3	17 218.3	17 940.3	7 331.2	7 926.4	8 301.5	8 987.1	8 511.2
Other Capital	KRNI	3 144.7	3 900.9	4 125.7	3 498.0	4 762.3	1 643.9	1 550.7	1 529.2	1 861.0	1 416.1
Assets: total	KRNJ	262 514.5	278 012.4	295 114.6	292 218.3	296 895.5	131 440.4	147 664.5	155 380.4	176 073.0	168 346.2
Mortgages	KRNK	210 994.5	221 237.6	240 297.2	236 841.0	241 472.9	107 531.5	118 288.4	123 183.4	137 072.3	130 229.6
Investments	KHVZ KRNL	42 909.1	47 174.2	50 786.7	50 894.1	51 016.7	21 869.8	27 102.0	29 917.8	36 574.2	35 925.9
Cash	KRNM										
Other	KRNN	8 610.1	9 600.6	4 030.7	4 483.2	4 405.9	2 039.1	2 274.1	2 279.2	2 426.6	2 190.7
Current transactions (£ million)											
Mortgage advances	KRNU	34 989.0	32 259.0	34 829.0	34 673.0	38 488.0	28 771.7	21 988.3	23 997.9	28 233.6	29 320.0
Management expenses	KRNX	2 723.7	2 952.5	3 136.7	3 352.6	3 555.3	2 270.5	1 501.7	1 573.8	1 640.7	1 528.0

1 The figures for each year relate to accounting years ending on dates between 1 February of that year and 31 January of the following year.
2 The societies which have converted to the banking sector, namely Cheltenham & Gloucester (August 1995), National & Provincial (August 1996), Alliance & Leicester (April 1997), Halifax (June 1997), Woolwich (July 1997), Bristol & West (July 1997), Northern Rock (October 1997), and Birmingham Midshires (April 1999) have been included in flow figures (using flows up to the date of conversion), but have been excluded from the end of year balances.

3 Bradford & Bingley, which converted to the banking sector in December 2000, is included within flow figures and the end of year balances.

Source: Financial Services Authority: 020 7676 1000

22.16 Consumer credit[1]

£ millions

		1991	1992	1993	1994	1995	1996	1997	1998	1999	2000	2001
Total amount outstanding	AILA	53 555	52 609	52 330	..	..	..	..	..	..	..	..
	VZRD	54 416	53 486	53 295	58 051	68 205	77 494	88 098	102 222	116 155	128 037	141 715
Total net lending	-AIKL	2 245	284	2 423	..	..	..	..	..	..	..	..
	VZQC	2 318	484	2 653	5 743	8 234	11 215	12 013	14 489	14 857	14 231	17 731
Retailers	AAPP	37	25	69	83	−133	75	208	7	103	−285	−27
Building societies' class 3 loans	ALPY	−45	−69	46	89	238	383	120	−22	11	111	68
Banks	AIKN	2 523	792	843	3 704	5 606	7 682	9 027	11 711	10 999	13 195	16 181
of which												
Credit cards	VTFY	774	126	700	..	..	..	..	..	..	..	..
	VZQS	774	138	719	1 483	2 103	3 029	3 507	4 858	5 676	6 686	6 229
Loans on personal accounts	VTGA	1 805	615	156	..	..	..	..	..	..	..	..
Other	VZQT	1 544	346	1 934	4 260	6 132	8 186	8 507	9 634	9 181	7 546	11 504
Insurance companies	-AIKQ	68	29	165	..	..	..	..	..	..	..	..
	RSBK	69	29	170	−178	39	−81	4	−16	223	−269	−9
Non-bank credit companies	-AGSJ	−417	−483	1 332	1 856	2 222	2 805	2 287	2 409	2 928	676	980
Other specialist lenders	VZQQ	−266	−297	1 525	2 045	2 485	3 156	2 654	2 810	3 521	1 478	1 518
Total gross lending	VZQG	12 530	11 913	54 094	75 039	89 114	103 215	116 079	133 710	147 014	158 713	175 102
Narrower coverage[2]												
Total amount outstanding	RLWE	30 624	30 120	32 204	37 027	..	..	..	..	..	..	..
Total net lending	RLWF	1 060	367	3 042	5 515	..	..	..	..	..	..	..
Total new credit advanced	RLBY	47 098	48 865	54 859	62 050	..	..	..	..	..	..	..

1 See chapter text.
2 Data no longer available from 1995.

Source: Office for National Statistics: 01633 812789

22.17 End-year assets and liabilities of investment trust companies, unit trusts[1] and property unit trusts[2]

£ millions

		1991	1992	1993	1994	1995	1996	1997	1998	1999	2000	2001
Investment trust companies												
Short-term assets and liabilities (net):	CBPL	730	390	623	273	627	1 076	1 157	2 263	71	423	161
Cash and UK bank deposits	AHAG	789	820	992	1 006	1 660	1 424	1 577	2 647	1 227	2 202	2 513
Other short-term assets	CBPN	711	645	1 030	772	738	794	1 445	1 734	1 097	1 082	656
Short-term liabilities	-CBPS	-378	-595	-794	-942	-1 120	-805	-1 865	-2 118	-2 253	-2 861	-3 008
Medium and long-term liabilities and capital:	-CBPO	-23 417	-28 895	-36 140	-40 180	-43 882	-50 911	-54 117	-49 985	-57 616	-60 412	-54 630
Issued share and loan capital	-CBPQ	-5 076	-4 827	-8 286	-10 978	-13 250	-8 330	-8 625	-8 837	-8 565	-8 934	-8 796
Foreign currency borrowing	-CBPR	-135	-407	-473	-354	-1 061	-638	-658	-607	-880	-994	-933
Other borrowing	-CBQA	-733	-802	-849	-1 354	-622	-823	-1 296	-1 723	-1 716	-2 503	-3 251
Reserves and provisions, etc	-AHBC	-17 473	-22 859	-26 532	-27 494	-28 949	-41 120	-43 538	-38 818	-46 455	-47 981	-41 650
Investments:	CBPM	22 392	28 586	35 300	39 586	43 410	50 034	53 076	46 313	56 491	59 948	54 822
British government securities	AHBF	415	996	1 013	2 490	1 194	1 422	1 052	815	1 217	821	645
UK company securities:												
Loan capital and preference shares	CBGZ	720	814	854	1 000	846	832	1 320	1 351	1 425	1 654	1 516
Ordinary and deferred shares	CBGY	10 637	12 825	14 892	15 926	19 384	25 046	29 082	24 729	28 010	33 456	30 338
Overseas company securities:												
Loan capital and preference shares	CBHA	355	514	533	896	740	279	1 165	768	979	963	1 143
Ordinary and deferred shares	AHCC	9 105	11 943	16 886	17 873	19 485	21 047	17 747	17 741	23 330	21 355	19 476
Other investments	CBPT	1 160	1 494	1 122	1 401	1 761	1 408	2 868	1 051	1 530	1 699	1 704
Unit trusts												
Short-term assets and liabilities:	CBPU	1 698	2 099	2 673	3 266	3 116	3 822	5 048	6 883	5 894	8 340	7 979
Cash and UK bank deposits	AGYE	1 318	1 793	2 579	3 102	3 326	3 895	4 731	6 020	4 797	6 969	5 748
Other short-term assets	CBPW	628	920	1 013	1 364	986	1 201	869	1 343	1 545	2 319	2 763
Short-term liabilities	-CBPX	-248	-614	-919	-1 200	-1 196	-1 274	-552	-480	-448	-948	-532
Foreign currency borrowing	-AGYK	-47	-8	-39	-21	-1	–	–	–	–	–	–
Investments:	CBPZ	50 459	58 785	88 479	83 495	104 069	125 841	144 038	162 929	213 553	222 844	204 899
British government securities	CBHT	523	664	959	1 414	1 774	2 716	3 087	3 771	3 627	4 693	4 690
UK company securities:												
Loan capital and preference shares	CBHU	1 337	1 664	2 906	2 970	3 298	5 029	6 494	9 290	13 322	14 654	16 318
Ordinary and deferred shares	RLIB	29 546	33 356	49 657	43 335	59 122	67 509	85 742	93 291	119 496	116 808	103 704
Overseas company securities:												
Loan capital and preference shares	CBHV	516	570	864	1 001	2 145	1 288	1 834	1 801	3 032	3 212	4 046
Ordinary and deferred shares	RLIC	18 124	21 862	32 904	33 473	36 062	47 346	42 898	51 119	70 256	79 601	71 341
Other assets	CBQE	413	669	1 189	1 302	1 668	1 953	2 518	3 657	3 820	3 876	4 800
Property unit trusts												
Short-term assets and liabilities (net)	AGVC	86	103	237	119	280	255	328	254	205	285	247
Property	CBQG	1 241	1 373	1 492	2 197	1 807	2 582	3 895	2 740	2 722	3 488	2 078
Other assets	AGVL	–	34	60	11	11	11	168	197	436	380	151
Long-term borrowing	-AGVM	-8	-42	-42	–	-131	-45	-247	-106	-75	-391	-90

Note: Assets are shown as positive: liabilities as negative.
1 Including open ended investment companies (OEICs).
2 Investments are at market value.

Source: Office for National Statistics: 01633 812789

22.18 Self-administered pension funds: market value of assets
United Kingdom

End year

£ millions

		1993	1994	1995	1996	1997	1998	1999	2000
Total pension funds[1]									
Total net assets	AHVA	480 547	443 467	508 581	543 879	656 874	699 191	812 228	765 199
Short-term assets	RYIQ	20 279	22 617	26 114	31 521	35 368	39 005	32 703	36 638
British government securities	AHVK	34 279	41 854	52 659	57 783	80 533	91 084	98 882	92 458
UK local authority long-term debt	AHVO	81	250	83	89	156	183	133	177
Overseas government securities	AHVT	11 044	11 092	11 721	11 800	13 079	15 493	16 684	19 206
UK company securities									
Ordinary shares	AHVP	251 099	219 189	256 625	276 001	339 687	334 648	357 230	299 318
Other	AHVQ	5 758	3 935	7 064	6 180	5 618	8 168	9 258	16 978
Overseas company securities									
Ordinary shares	AHVR	84 118	74 813	82 164	84 163	104 187	108 884	148 335	135 514
Other	AHVS	2 103	3 045	1 184	4 909	3 851	3 842	5 099	12 736
UK loans and mortgages	RLDQ	260	44	34	83	160	22	14	7
UK land, property and ground rent	AHWA	21 932	24 353	21 317	21 637	24 176	24 355	31 107	32 945
Authorised unit trust units	AHVU	13 188	13 345	15 212	21 767	21 979	30 596	33 731	34 587
Property unit trusts	AHVW	1 905	2 463	2 485	2 666	3 219	3 211	5 498	4 835
Other assets	RKPL	38 761	31 318	36 352	30 628	32 978	47 136	82 273	90 841
Total liabilities	GQFX	4 261	4 852	4 412	5 347	8 118	7 436	8 719	11 041

1 These figures cover funded schemes only and therefore exclude the main superannuation arrangements in the central government sector.

Source: Office for National Statistics: 01633 812729

22.19 Insurance companies: balance sheet
Market values
End year

£ millions

		1992	1993	1994	1995	1996	1997	1998	1999	2000
Long-term insurance companies										
Assets										
Total current assets (gross)	RYEW	18 101	16 925	16 690	24 171	31 699	42 795	46 165	56 360	62 937
Agents' and reinsurance balances (net)	AHNY	799	457	−209	−157	−232	155	1 383	508	384
Other debtors[1]	RKPN	4 198	4 368	4 562	7 565	12 982	15 708	18 210	18 613	21 045
British government securities	AHNJ	50 970	72 575	64 921	80 268	90 996	107 847	127 903	126 223	116 734
UK local authority securities etc	AHNN	667	772	815	1 322	1 088	914	1 722	1 456	1 170
UK company securities[2]	RKPO	172 204	237 020	217 034	272 554	304 587	386 734	438 666	539 834	557 293
Overseas company securities	RKPP	32 101	49 087	48 195	59 950	62 378	73 428	82 122	120 665	107 439
Overseas government securities	AHNS	8 793	8 874	6 871	8 793	7 554	8 471	17 515	18 494	18 004
Loans and mortgages	RKPQ	8 345	7 885	6 833	7 305	6 653	8 271	11 027	10 914	9 687
UK land, property and ground rent	AHNX	30 074	33 939	35 914	35 596	36 209	42 275	45 903	50 387	49 705
Overseas land, property and ground rent	RGCP	124	144	151	118	114	98	252	206	1 975
Other investments	RKPR	2 663	3 096	4 644	2 162	3 886	3 416	5 654	8 334	8 385
Total	RFXN	329 039	435 142	406 421	499 647	557 914	690 112	796 522	951 994	954 760
Net value of direct investment in:										
Non-insurance subsidiaries and associate companies in the United Kingdom	RYET	2 569	2 288	2 547	2 773	3 033	3 426	3 035	3 045	6 133
UK associate and subsidiary insurance companies and insurance holding companies	RYEU	639	1 186	504	701	575	−239	148	2 245	3 586
Overseas subsidiaries and associates	RYEV	773	1 016	1 034	987	986	1 104	1 087	3 638	4 002
Total assets	RKBI	333 020	439 632	410 506	504 108	562 508	694 403	800 792	960 922	968 481
Liabilities										
Borrowing:										
Borrowing from UK banks	RGDF	1 162	1 234	1 570	1 907	2 234	3 027	3 252	6 064	8 272
Other UK borrowing	RGDE	1 007	553	982	796	1 349	786	1 040	3 070	2 823
Borrowing from overseas	RGDD	603	381	176	79	90	104	148	159	38
Long-term business:										
Funds	RKDC	280 276	354 711	357 263	424 866	470 893	581 009	669 301	800 184	838 485
Claims admitted but not paid	RKBM	951	1 035	1 085	1 419	1 441	1 436	1 712	2 032	2 249
Provision for taxation net of amounts receivable:										
UK authorities	RYPI	−1 119	−141	−470	502	2 568	4 207	5 443	6 344	5 381
Overseas authorities	RYPJ	−14	−20	29	−11	9	25	67	314	67
Provision for recommended dividends	RYPK	46	83	76	195	276	368	359	201	183
Other creditors and liabilities	RYPL	3 763	4 020	4 399	5 979	6 303	8 083	12 509	17 042	19 031
Excess of assets over above liabilities:										
Excess of value of assets over liabilities in respect of long-term funds	RKBR	43 511	74 160	42 608	63 255	71 817	89 790	96 456	116 951	79 173
Minority interests in UK subsidiary companies	RKTI	30	30	−	3	−	2	−	25	−
Shareholders' capital and reserves in respect of general business	RKBS	1 952	890	1 143	2 050	2 576	3 862	6 299	6 139	10 287
Other reserves including profit and loss account balances	RKBT	852	2 696	1 645	3 068	2 952	1 704	4 206	2 396	2 492
Total liabilities	RKBI	333 020	439 632	410 506	504 108	562 508	694 403	800 792	960 922	968 481

399

22.19
continued

Insurance companies: balance sheet
Market values
End year

£ millions

		1992	1993	1994	1995	1996	1997	1998	1999	2000
Other than long-term insurance companies										
Assets										
Total current assets (gross)	RYME	6 523	6 467	7 426	8 318	11 559	12 628	8 524	10 468	8 772
Agents' and reinsurance balances (net)	AHMX	6 380	5 887	6 123	7 494	11 569	9 405	10 528	12 177	8 362
Other debtors[1]	RKPS	1 765	1 847	2 118	3 403	6 097	5 998	6 277	7 059	7 179
British government securities	AHMJ	8 378	11 474	12 320	14 363	16 893	15 666	16 409	15 938	14 561
UK local authority securities etc	AHMN	49	59	50	56	42	16	14	10	8
UK company securities[2]	RKPT	10 480	14 533	14 312	17 425	17 825	18 845	18 440	18 800	18 585
Overseas company securities	RKPU	3 747	4 163	3 578	4 422	5 072	6 594	8 676	6 284	8 190
Overseas government securities	AHMS	4 660	5 324	5 064	6 511	9 546	8 215	10 459	7 980	6 849
Loans and mortgages	RKPV	1 147	1 234	1 321	1 337	1 593	1 385	1 335	1 070	1 429
UK land, property and ground rent	AHMW	2 398	2 375	2 121	2 100	2 077	2 842	1 146	1 085	1 069
Overseas land, property and ground rent	RYNK	185	80	89	128	120	149	107	83	45
Other investments	RKPW	633	418	536	665	716	2 465	2 366	2 638	2 294
Total	RKAL	46 345	53 861	55 058	66 222	83 106	84 208	84 281	84 027	77 343
Net value of direct investment in:										
Non-insurance subsidiaries and associate companies in the United Kingdom	RYNR	2 617	2 214	2 474	2 449	3 195	6 950	5 553	7 074	7 038
UK associate and subsidiary insurance companies and insurance holding companies	RYNS	1 087	1 835	1 738	1 642	7 170	4 204	6 424	5 617	5 400
Overseas subsidiaries and associates	RYNT	9 908	12 275	11 854	15 485	14 859	16 402	14 239	17 775	15 993
Total assets	RKBY	59 957	70 185	71 124	85 798	108 330	111 764	110 497	114 493	105 774
Liabilities										
Borrowing:										
Borrowing from UK banks	RYMB	434	721	1 382	1 584	1 524	3 029	1 825	1 392	783
Other UK borrowing	RYMC	1 677	1 989	2 354	2 370	2 536	2 996	1 551	3 186	4 239
Borrowing from overseas	RYMD	1 296	1 103	1 626	1 876	1 976	1 202	1 600	3 045	1 867
General business technical reserves	RKCT	38 005	39 746	42 374	47 493	58 618	59 527	60 775	59 455	60 236
Long-term business:										
Funds	RKTF	–	–	–	–	–	–	–	–	–
Claims admitted but not paid	RKTK	–	–	–	–	–	–	–	–	–
Provision for taxation net of amounts receivable:										
UK authorities	RYPO	−295	235	397	841	807	1 253	1 197	939	874
Overseas authorities	RYPP	24	14	22	16	22	7	11	11	11
Provision for recommended dividends	RYPQ	650	794	874	1 098	1 407	2 048	1 318	1 817	2 682
Other creditors and liabilities	RYPR	1 921	1 987	2 551	2 955	3 886	3 873	3 793	4 981	6 293
Excess of assets over above liabilities:										
Excess of value of assets over liabilities in respect of long-term funds	RKCG	–	–	–	–	–	–	–	–	–
Minority interests in UK subsidiary companies	RKCH	33	80	52	22	24	60	68	29	33
Shareholders' capital and reserves in respect of general business	RKCI	14 552	21 355	17 628	25 545	35 069	35 172	34 397	35 372	24 699
Other reserves including profit and loss account balances	RKCJ	1 660	2 161	1 864	1 998	2 461	2 597	4 215	4 265	4 056
Total liabilities	RKBY	59 957	70 185	71 124	85 798	108 330	111 764	110 497	114 493	105 774

1 Including outstanding interest, dividends and rents (net).
2 Including authorised unit trust units.

Source: Office for National Statistics: 01633 812729

22.20 Individual insolvencies

Numbers

		1990	1991	1992	1993	1994	1995	1996	1997	1998	1999	2000	2001
England and Wales													
Bankruptcies[1]	AIHW	12 058	22 632	32 106	31 016	25 634	21 933	21 803	19 892	19 647	21 611	21 550	23 447
Individual voluntary arrangements[2,3]	AIHI	1 929	3 008	4 688	5 687	5 105	4 386	4 468	4 549	4 902	7 195	7 978	6 298
Total	AIHK	13 987	25 640	36 794	36 703	30 739	26 319	26 271	24 441	24 549	28 806	29 528	29 775
Scotland													
Sequestrations[4]	KRHA	4 350	7 665	10 845	6 828	2 182	2 188	2 503	2 502	3 016	3 195	2 965	3 048
Northern Ireland													
Bankruptcies[5]	KRHB	286	367	406	474	438	399	415	393	394	401	347	292
Individual voluntary arrangements[3,6]	KJRK	..	2	42	67	84	64	101	84	122	173	260	177
Total	KRHD	286	369	448	541	522	463	516	477	516	574	607	469

1 Comprises receiving and administration orders under the Bankruptcy Act 1914 and bankruptcy orders under the Insolvency Act 1986. Orders later consolidated or rescinded are included in these figures.
2 Introduced under the Insolvency Act 1986.
3 For statistical purposes deeds of arrangement are now included with individual voluntary arrangements.
4 Sequestrations awarded but not brought into operation are included in these figures.

5 Comprises bankruptcy adjudication orders, arrangement protection orders and orders for the administration of estates of deceased insolvents. Orders later set aside or dismissed are included in these figures.
6 Introduced under the Insolvency Northern Ireland order 1989.

Source: Department of Trade and Industry: 020 7215 3291/3305

22.21 Company insolvencies

Numbers

		1990	1991	1992	1993	1994	1995	1996	1997	1998	1999	2000	2001
England and Wales													
Compulsory liquidations	AIHR	5 977	8 368	9 734	8 244	6 597	5 519	5 080	4 735	5 216	5 209	4 925	4 675
Creditors' voluntary liquidations	AIHS	9 074	13 459	14 691	12 464	10 131	9 017	8 381	7 875	7 987	9 071	9 392	10 297
Total	AIHQ	15 051	21 827	24 425	20 708	16 728	14 536	13 461	12 610	13 203	14 280	14 317	14 972
Scotland													
Compulsory liquidations	KRGA	251	304	310	286	242	252	266	254	338	364	344	378
Creditors' voluntary liquidations	KRGB	219	312	360	265	202	189	175	223	228	208	239	224
Total	KRGC	470	616	670	551	444	441	441	477	566	572	583	602
Northern Ireland													
Compulsory liquidations	KRGD	73	112	79	73	69	72	68	60	53	58	83	60
Creditors' voluntary liquidations	KRGE	55	71	77	85	52	37	54	53	46	45	53	40
Total	KRGF	128	183	156	158	121	109	122	113	99	103	136	100

Source: Department of Trade and Industry: 020 7215 3291/3305

22.22 Industry analysis: bankruptcies
England and Wales

Numbers

		1991	1992	1993	1994	1995	1996	1997	1998	1999	2000	2001
Industry												
Self-employed												
Agriculture and horticulture	KRFY	266	313	277	231	218	168	155	157	183	173	183
Manufacturing:												
Food, drink and tobacco	KRFZ	48	56	34	33	30	31	18	21	17	18	10
Chemicals	KRLA	12	9	7	23	8	5	5	7	4	2	2
Metals and engineering	KRLB	424	634	612	523	396	411	413	378	385	306	339
Textiles and clothing	KRLC	152	174	160	95	114	91	76	81	87	81	75
Timber and furniture	KRLD	233	317	207	176	158	118	98	96	94	90	88
Paper, printing and publishing	KRLE	143	205	161	142	142	117	104	101	112	80	75
Other	KRLF	120	125	169	133	146	117	116	110	111	84	79
Total	KRLG	1 132	1 520	1 350	1 125	994	890	830	794	810	661	668
Construction and transport:												
Construction	KRLH	3 812	4 692	4 361	3 362	2 783	2 713	2 182	1 919	1 911	1 741	1 783
Transport and communication	KRLI	1 620	2 038	1 754	1 402	1 138	1 227	1 162	1 060	1 187	1 120	1 134
Total	KHGP	5 432	6 730	6 115	4 764	3 921	3 940	3 344	2 979	3 098	2 861	2 917
Wholesaling:												
Food, drink and tobacco	KRLJ	68	114	114	94	103	77	62	53	45	49	40
Motor vehicles	KRLK	21	48	21	28	33	36	28	20	22	29	20
Other	KRLL	122	220	191	160	122	101	78	92	83	83	61
Total	KHGQ	211	382	326	282	258	214	168	165	150	161	121
Retailing:												
Food, drink and tobacco	KRLM	895	1 001	1 107	981	782	662	546	514	438	424	347
Motor vehicles and filling stations	KRLN	362	399	412	343	316	327	276	238	241	237	199
Other	KRLO	1 442	2 159	2 087	1 615	1 566	1 268	1 048	971	1 032	801	792
Total	KHGR	2 699	3 559	3 606	2 939	2 664	2 257	1 870	1 723	1 711	1 462	1 338
Services:												
Financial institutions	KRLP	247	266	292	241	185	125	105	79	54	45	39
Business services	KRLQ	1 284	1 859	1 843	1 537	1 354	1 176	1 117	1 057	1 162	1 127	1 107
Hotels and catering	KRLR	1 481	2 366	2 437	2 102	1 956	1 736	1 603	1 309	1 376	1 263	1 187
Total	KHGS	3 012	4 491	4 572	3 880	3 495	3 037	2 825	2 445	2 592	2 435	2 333
Other	KHGT	1 857	2 530	2 315	1 893	1 732	2 161	2 077	2 157	2 179	2 199	2 279
Total: self-employed	KRLT	14 609	19 525	18 561	15 114	13 282	12 667	11 269	10 420	10 723	9 952	9 839
Other individuals												
Employees	KRLU	1 639	2 588	2 507	2 279	1 981	2 471	2 625	3 141	4 357	4 601	5 525
No occupation and unemployed	KRLV	2 811	4 325	4 816	3 696	2 859	3 294	3 051	3 384	4 457	4 856	5 848
Directors and promoters of companies	KRLW	667	965	862	628	484	368	310	272	330	296	328
Occupation unknown	KRLX	2 906	4 703	4 270	3 917	3 327	3 003	2 637	2 430	1 744	1 845	1 937
Total: other individuals	KRLY	8 023	12 581	12 455	10 520	8 651	9 136	8 623	9 227	10 888	11 598	13 638
Total bankruptcies	KRLZ	22 632	32 106	31 016	25 634	21 933	21 803	19 892	19 647	21 611	21 550	23 477

Source: Department of Trade and Industry: 020 7215 3291/3305

22.23 Industry analysis: company insolvencies[1]
England and Wales

Numbers

		1991	1992	1993	1994	1995	1996	1997	1998	1999	2000	2001
Industry												
Agriculture and horticulture	KRMA	135	191	157	166	99	89	51	65	75	67	90
Manufacturing:												
Food, drink and tobacco	KRMB	171	215	213	142	130	163	93	89	67	104	71
Chemicals	KRMC	134	141	91	108	69	65	31	57	35	61	37
Metals and engineering	KRMD	1 344	1 621	1 381	932	681	658	591	594	698	683	704
Textiles and clothing	KRME	1 052	1 120	917	736	567	568	596	526	419	423	320
Timber and furniture	KRMF	527	508	333	252	267	249	181	149	190	187	199
Paper, printing and publishing	KRMG	856	830	777	579	452	438	364	426	387	386	484
Other	KRMH	939	1 014	878	859	681	599	613	652	780	678	717
Total	KRMI	5 023	5 449	4 590	3 608	2 847	2 740	2 469	2 493	2 576	2 522	2 532
Construction and transport:												
Construction	KRMJ	3 373	3 830	3 189	2 401	1 844	1 610	1 419	1 325	1 529	1 474	1 509
Transport and communication	KRMK	1 246	1 261	1 082	774	706	682	540	504	443	526	481
Total	KHGU	4 619	5 091	4 271	3 175	2 550	2 292	1 959	1 829	1 972	2 000	1 990
Wholesaling:												
Food, drink and tobacco	KRML	287	388	231	244	205	183	158	139	187	150	125
Motor vehicles	KRMM	152	186	142	112	83	95	41	60	38	29	24
Other	KRMN	841	672	639	638	678	429	340	364	394	391	363
Total	KHGV	1 280	1 246	1 012	994	966	707	539	563	619	570	512
Retailing:												
Food, drink and tobacco	KRMO	291	406	388	299	246	236	219	186	193	200	114
Motor vehicles and filling stations	KRMP	245	339	229	226	195	227	132	120	142	141	172
Other	KRMQ	1 578	1 732	1 388	1 186	1 127	956	891	847	919	853	833
Total	KHGW	2 114	2 477	2 005	1 711	1 568	1 419	1 242	1 153	1 254	1 194	1 119
Services:												
Financial institutions	KRMR	394	563	421	259	198	222	111	101	118	57	28
Business services	KRMS	2 396	2 788	2 415	1 807	1 525	1 500	1 528	1 617	1 831	1 605	1 618
Hotels and catering	KRMT	748	1 010	912	777	692	708	609	626	562	530	538
Total	KJRS	3 538	4 361	3 748	2 843	2 415	2 430	2 248	2 344	2 511	2 192	2 184
Other	KHGX	5 118	5 610	4 925	4 231	4 091	3 784	4 102	4 756	5 273	5 772	6 545
Total company insolvencies	KHGY	21 827	24 425	20 708	16 728	14 536	13 461	12 610	13 203	14 280	14 317	14 972

1 Including partnerships.

Source: Department of Trade and Industry: 020 7215 3291/3305

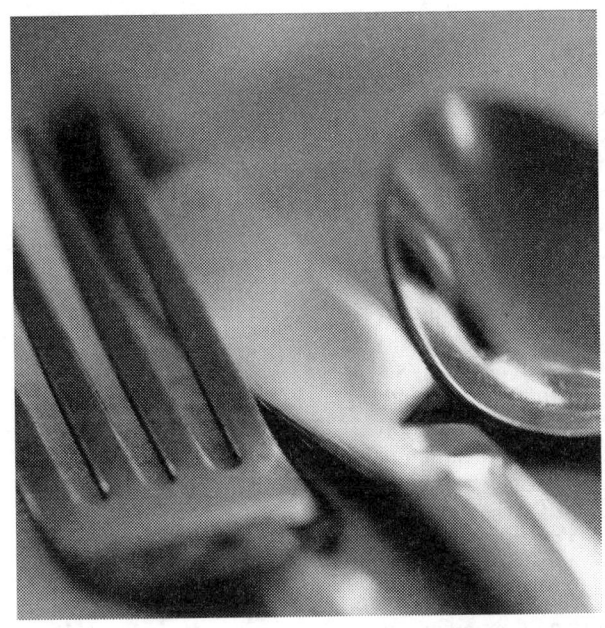

23 Service industry

Service industry

Annual Business Inquiry *(Tables 23.1, 23.3 and 23.4)*
For details of the Annual Business Inquiry, see the text accompanying table **21.1**.

Retail trade: index numbers of value and volume *(Table 23.2)*
The main purpose of the Retail Sales Inquiry (RSI) is to provide up to date information on short period movements in the level of retail sales. In principle, the RSI covers the retail activity of every business classified in the retail sector (Division 52 of the 1992 Standard Industrial Classification) in Great Britain. A business will be classified to the retail sector if its main activity is one of the individual 4 digit SIC categories within Division 52. The retail activity of a business is then defined by its retail turnover, i.e. the sale of all retail goods (note that petrol, for example, is not a retail good).

The RSI is compiled from the information returned to the statutory monthly retail trades inquiry. The inquiry is addressed to a stratified sample of 5000 businesses classified to the retail sector, the stratification being by 'type of store' (the individual 4 digit SIC categories within Division 52) and by size. The sample structure is designed to ensure that the inquiry estimates are as accurate as possible. In terms of the selection, this means that:

- each of the individual 4 digit SIC categories are represented, their coverage depending upon the relative size of the category and the variability of the data.

- within each 4 digit SIC category, the larger retailers tend to be fully enumerated with decreasing proportions of medium and smaller retailers.

The structure of the inquiry is updated periodically, by reference to the more comprehensive results of the Annual Retail Inquiry (ARI). The monthly inquiry also incorporates a rotation element for the smallest retailers. This helps to spread the burden more fairly, as well as improving the representativeness between successive benchmarks.

During 1998, the retail sales index was rebased using detailed information from the 1995 annual retailing inquiry. The reference year is now set at 1995=100. Details of the work, together with revised figures for January 1990 to December 1997, were published in *ONS News Release* (98) 349 on 21 October 1998.

The latest summary statistics are published each month by *First Release*. More disaggregated value indices (not seasonally adjusted) are published each month in *Business Monitor SDM28*, via the National Statistics Website: www.statistics.gov.uk.

23.1 Retail businesses[1]
United Kingdom
All currency values are £ million

		1997	1998	1999	2000
Number of businesses	ZABE	218 333	216 000	216 826	215 373
Total turnover[2]	ZABL	207 489	221 267	230 822	241 363
Value added tax in total turnover	ZABM	20 410	21 778	22 494	23 797
Retail turnover[2]	ZABN	193 928	202 538	209 962	218 967
Non-retail turnover[2]	ZABO	13 561	18 729	20 860	22 395
Other income					
Value of commercial insurance claims received	ZABP	..	117	85	96
Subsidies received from UK government sources and the EC	ZAEN	..	13	19	6
Employment costs[3]	ZABQ	21 178	22 958	25 072	26 699
Gross wages and salaries	ZABR	19 165	20 552	22 430	24 068
Redundancy and severance payments	ZABS	..	145	329	145
Employers' National Insurance contributions	ZABT	2 013	1 514	1 547	1 657
Contributions to pension funds[4]	ZABU	..	747	767	829
Stocks					
Increase during year	ZABV	1 387	1 204	1 271	831
Value at end of year	ZABW	19 593	19 849	21 095	21 246
Total turnover[3] divided by end-year stocks (Quotient)	ZABX	9.5	10.1	9.9	10.2
Purchases of goods, materials and services[3]	ZABY	148 254	157 694	161 841	169 145
Goods bought for resale without processing	ZABZ	126 833	134 241	135 830	142 099
Energy and water products for own consumption[5]	ZACA	2 568	1 832	1 826	1 895
Goods and materials[5]	ZACB	..	3 035	3 484	3 426
Hiring, leasing or renting of plant, machinery and vehicles	ZACC	677	662	761	812
Commercial insurance premiums	ZACD	617	554	582	593
Road transport services	ZACE	2 051	1 847	1 627	1 789
Telecommunication services	ZACF	468	474	506	550
Computer and related services	ZACG	484	534	636	659
Advertising and marketing services	ZACH	2 491	2 429	2 771	2 827
Other services	ZACI	12 066	12 085	13 818	14 495
Taxes, duties and levies	ZACJ	3 534	3 823	3 987	4 171
National non-domestic (business) rates	ZACK	2 965	3 116	3 253	3 373
Other amounts paid for taxes, duties and levies	ZACL	569	707	734	798
Capital expenditure					
Cost of acquisitions	ZACM	7 722	8 264	8 215	8 270
Proceeds from disposals	ZACN	1 438	1 141	2 270	1 670
Net capital expenditure	ZACO	6 284	7 123	5 945	6 600
Amount included in acquisitions for assets under finance leasing arrangements	ZACP	..	284	498	642
Work of a capital nature carried out by own staff (included in acquisitions)	ZACQ	77	80	78	75
Gross margin					
Amount	ZACR	61 633	65 837	72 655	75 007
As a percentage of adjusted turnover[6]	ZACS	32.9	33.0	34.9	34.5
Approximate gross value added at basic prices	ZACT	39 719	42 502	47 287	48 712

23.1

Retail businesses[1]
United Kingdom
All currency values are £ million

£ million

		1997	1998	1999	2000
Total turnover	ZABL	207 489	221 267	230 822	241 363
Retail turnover	ZABN	193 928	202 538	209 962	218 967
1 Fruit (including fresh, chilled, dried, frozen, canned and processed)	DSSX	3 523	3 851	3 960	4 033
2 Vegetables (including fresh, chilled, dried, frozen, canned and processed)	DSSY	4 945	5 425	5 404	5 551
3 Meat (including fresh, chilled, smoked, frozen, canned and processed)	DSSZ	10 951	11 736	11 405	10 794
4 Fish, crustaceans and molluscs (including fresh, chilled, frozen, canned and processed)	DSTA	2 044	2 083	2 092	2 175
5 Bakery products and cereals (including rice and pasta products)	DSTC	7 837	8 279	8 419	8 649
6 Sugar, jam, honey, chocolate and confectionery (including ice-cream)	DSTD	5 831	5 793	5 977	6 237
7 Alcoholic drink	DSTE	8 569	9 116	9 947	10 495
8 Non-alcoholic beverages (including tea, coffee, fruit drinks and vegetable drinks)	DSTF	5 244	5 368	5 561	5 565
9 Tobacco (excluding smokers requisites, eg pipes, lighters, etc)	DSTG	8 603	8 720	8 823	8 135
10 Milk, cheese and eggs (including yoghurts and cream)	DSTH	6 580	6 795	6 911	6 970
11 Oils and fats (including butter and margarine)	DSTI	1 089	1 163	1 115	1 244
12 Food products not elsewhere classified (including sauces, herbs, spices and soups)	DSTJ	9 100	10 217	10 110	10 403
13 Pharmaceutical products	DSTK	1 666	1 791	1 930	2 457
14 National Health Receipts	DSTL	5 262	5 588	5 799	6 418
15 Other medical products and therapeutic appliances and equipment	DSTN	2 566	2 008	2 268	2 760
16 Other appliances, articles and products for personal care	DSTO	6 641	6 925	7 538	8 212
17 Other articles of clothing, accessories for making clothing	DSTP	1 185	1 237	1 371	1 484
18 Garments	DSTQ	23 458	24 382	26 044	25 912
19 Footwear (excluding sports shoes)	DSTR	4 673	4 474	4 297	4 417
20 Travel goods and other personal effects not elsewhere classified	DSTT	705	771	750	782
21 Household textiles (including furnishing fabrics, curtains, etc)	DSTV	2 993	3 230	3 478	3 358
22 Household and personal appliances whether electric or not	DSUA	5 127	5 279	5 261	5 366
23 Glassware, tableware and household utensils (including non-electric)	DSUB	2 773	2 874	3 117	2 684
24 Furniture and furnishings	DSUC	9 772	9 773	10 294	10 491
25 Audio and visual equipment (including radios, televisions and video recorders)	DSUE	3 774	3 655	3 770	4 076
26 Recording material for pictures and sound (including audio and video tapes, blank and pre-recorded records, etc)	DSUG	3 215	3 088	3 332	3 655
27 Information processing equipment (including printers, software, calculators and typewriters)	DSUL	2 530	2 743	2 839	3 222
28 Decorating and DIY supplies	DSUM	4 634	4 655	5 051	5 470
29 Tools and equipment for house and garden	DSUN	1 928	2 104	2 171	2 425
30 Books	DSUP	2 209	2 230	2 221	2 339
31 Newspapers and periodicals	DSUQ	3 528	3 382	3 467	3 541
32 Stationery and drawing materials and miscellaneous printed matter	DSUW	3 441	3 398	3 634	3 897
33 Carpets and other floor coverings (excluding bathroom mats, rush and door mats)	DSUX	2 578	2 803	2 944	3 135
34 Photographic and cinematographic equipment and optical instruments	DSUZ	878	762	873	1 064
35 Telephone and telefax equipment (including mobile phones)	DSVA	1 169	1 418	1 698	2 214
36 Jewellery, silverware and plate; watches and clocks	DSVB	3 246	2 809	2 806	3 441
37 Works of art and antiques (including furniture, floor coverings and jewellery)	DSVF	1 311	1 583	1 629	1 626
38 Equipment and accessories for sport, camping, recreation and musical instruments	DSVH	2 613	3 277	3 337	4 035
39 Spare part and accessories for all types of vehicle and sales of bicycles	DSVI	526	819	593	665
40 Games, toys, hobbies (including video game software, video game computers that plug into the tv, video-games cassettes and CD-ROMs)	DSVM	3 126	3 302	3 426	4 045
41 Other goods not elsewhere classified (including sale of new postage stamps and sales of liquid and solid fuels)	DSVN	4 377	5 001	5 308	5 952
42 Non-durable household goods (including household cleaning, maintenance products) and paper products and other non-durable household goods	DSVO	2 874	3 140	3 270	3 531
43 Natural or artificial plants and flowers	DSVQ	1 975	2 274	2 241	2 701
44 Pets and related products (including pet food)	DSVR	1 925	2 221	2 186	2 335
45 Repair of household and personal items	DSVS	935	998	1 294	1 008

1 See chapter text.
2 Inclusive of VAT.
3 Exclusive of VAT.
4 Previously combined with employers' National Insurance contributions for 1997.

5 Previously combined with purchases of energy, water and materials for 1997.
6 Turnover is adjusted to take out VAT.

Source: Office for National Statistics: 01633 812435

23.2 Retail trade: Index numbers of value and volume of sales[1]
Great Britain

Weekly average 1995 = 100, not seasonally adjusted

Value		Sales in 1995 £million	1991	1992	1993	1994	1995	1996	1997	1998	1999	2000	2001
All retailing: total	EAFY	166 681	84.1	87.3	92.0	96.3	100.0	105.4	112.0	116.4	120.3	124.7	132.6
All retailing: large	EAFZ	119 937	78	83	89	94	100	107	115	121	126	132	141
All retailing: small	EAGA	46 743	100	100	101	102	100	102	103	104	104	106	112
Predominantly food stores: total	EAFS	74 914	80.2	85.7	90.1	94.4	100.0	105.3	110.7	116.3	120.3	124.4	132.9
Predominantly food stores: large	EAGK	57 713	75	82	87	93	100	107	113	120	125	129	138
Predominantly food stores: small	EAGL	17 201	102	102	102	100	100	100	102	103	105	109	116
Non specialised food stores: total	EAGB	60 602	75	81	87	93	100	107	113	119	124	128	137
Non specialised food stores: large	EAGC	54 878	73	80	86	92	100	107	114	121	125	130	139
Non specialised food stores: small	EAGD	5 724	95	96	97	98	100	102	104	104	108	112	120
Specialised food stores	EAPP	14 311	103	105	105	102	100	100	101	103	105	107	114
Retail sale of fruit and vegetables	EAOZ	1 283	115	108	102	98	100	100	102	112	104	108	127
Retail sale of meat and meat products	EAPA	2 515	129	122	116	107	100	97	92	89	91	96	101
Retail sale of fish, crustaceans and molluscs	EAPB	266	147	128	123	109	100	95	91	78	61	61	66
Retail sale of bread cakes and confectionery	EAPC	1 796	95	99	102	102	100	100	103	109	108	111	114
Retail sale of alcohol and other beverages	EAPD	3 208	90	95	95	96	100	101	104	105	110	100	102
Retail sale of tobacco products	EAPE	3 944	102	108	109	106	100	100	103	106	111	118	128
Other specialised food stores	EAPF	1 296	108	105	110	105	100	97	100	102	111	117	117
Predominantly non-food stores: total	EAFT	83 184	85.8	87.2	92.4	97.0	100.0	105.8	113.5	116.8	120.7	126.0	134.1
Predominantly non-food stores: large	EAGM	55 351	81	83	89	95	100	107	118	122	128	136	146
Predominantly non-food stores: small	EAGN	27 832	97	96	100	102	100	104	105	107	106	106	111
Non specialised predominantly non-food stores: total	EAGE	15 035	84.5	88.1	93.4	96.4	100.0	108.2	115.5	116.9	120.2	126.6	133.3
Non specialised predominantly non-food stores: large	EAGF	12 070	84	87	92	95	100	108	115	117	121	128	135
Non specialised predominantly non-food stores: small	EAGG	2 964	91	98	106	103	100	109	116	115	115	120	124
Pharmaceutical, medical, cosmetic and toilet goods	EAPQ	3 165	81	89	97	97	100	102	109	113	116	120	125
Textiles, clothing, footwear and leather: total	EAFU	26 100	85.8	87.2	91.2	96.8	100.0	104.2	111.8	112.4	114.9	118.4	126.2
Textiles clothing footwear and leather: large	EAGO	20 352	80	84	89	95	100	106	116	118	121	125	133
Textiles clothing footwear and leather: small	EAGP	5 746	111	101	102	103	100	97	96	93	92	94	102
Retail sale of textiles	EAPG	699	105	106	127	117	100	99	105	106	108	113	112
Retail sale of clothing: total	EAGH	21 535	85	87	90	96	100	106	113	115	118	122	129
Retail sale of clothing: large	EAGI	17 606	80	84	89	95	100	108	118	120	124	128	136
Retail sale of clothing: small	EAGJ	3 928	106	99	99	101	100	95	92	92	91	92	100
Retail sale of footwear and leather goods	EAPH	3 864	91	87	92	100	100	97	105	98	99	101	110
Household goods stores: total	EAFV	19 770	85.9	86.9	92.9	97.0	100.0	107.9	118.3	124.8	130.3	138.4	148.0
Household goods stores: large	EAGQ	13 273	75	81	87	94	100	109	122	130	138	150	161
Household goods stores: small	EAGR	6 496	108	101	106	104	100	106	112	114	115	115	121
Retail sale of furniture, lighting, etc	EAPI	6 400	94	94	101	103	100	108	122	128	127	133	142

23.2 Retail trade: Index numbers of value and volume of sales[1]
Great Britain

Weekly average 1995 = 100, not seasonally adjusted

		Sales in 1995 £million	1991	1992	1993	1994	1995	1996	1997	1998	1999	2000	2001
Retail sale of electrical household appliances	EAPJ	7 727	80	79	86	91	100	108	119	124	132	141	150
Retail sale of hardware paint and glass	EAPK	5 642	87	91	96	100	100	107	114	122	131	141	152
Other specialised non-food stores: total	EAFW	22 280	86.3	87.1	92.5	97.3	100.0	104.1	110.0	114.8	119.3	123.4	131.6
Other specialised non-food stores: large	EAGS	9 655	85	81	89	94	100	103	119	124	137	150	164
Other specialised non-food stores: small	EAGT	12 624	87	92	95	100	100	105	103	108	106	103	107
Retail sale of books newspapers and periodicals	EAPL	4 078	88	92	97	99	100	104	109	117	118	118	123
Retail sale of floor covering	EAPM	1 045	91	92	98	99	100	107	116	99	90	94	95
Photo, optical and precision equipment office supplies and equipment	EAWH	2 676	112	111	97	97	100	104	103	104	115	124	136
Other retail sale in specialised stores not elsewhere specified	EAWK	10 201	87	83	90	95	100	105	112	120	128	130	139
Second-hand goods stores	EAQA	1 112	67	68	74	105	100	94	104	102	97	117	139
Other retail sale (non-store) and repair: total	EAFX	8 583	99.0	99.3	102.1	104.3	100.0	102.8	107.7	113.9	115.9	114.0	116.3
Other retail sale (non-store) and repair: large	EAGU	6 872	90	91	97	102	100	104	112	122	126	122	123
Other retail sale (non-store) and repair: small	EAGV	1 710	119	118	114	110	100	96	90	82	75	80	91
Retail sale via mail order houses	EAPN	6 629	89	92	98	103	100	103	109	117	123	121	120
Non-store retail excl. mail order	EAPO	1 544	113	110	107	106	100	100	102	101	87	88	95
Repair of personal and household goods	EAPR	408	99	106	115	106	100	104	110	110	106	105	131
Volume													
All retailing	EAHC	166 681	91.8	92.4	95.3	98.8	100.0	103.1	108.5	111.7	115.6	120.8	128.0
Predominantly food stores	EAGW	74 914	90.4	93.1	95.0	98.1	100.0	101.9	105.9	108.8	110.8	113.6	117.7
Predominantly non-food stores	EAGX	83 184	91.0	90.3	94.2	98.4	100.0	104.4	111.2	114.3	119.9	127.9	138.1
Non specialised predominantly non-food stores	EAHI	15 035	92.9	93.6	97.0	99.0	100.0	106.0	111.5	111.5	114.7	122.2	129.0
Textiles, clothing, footwear and leather	EAGY	26 100	88.0	89.1	92.3	97.5	100.0	104.3	111.2	112.0	117.1	124.7	137.3
Household goods stores	EAGZ	19 770	87.0	86.5	92.2	97.3	100.0	106.8	117.2	125.2	135.2	148.6	161.6
Other specialised non-food stores	EAHA	22 280	97.1	93.8	96.7	100.1	100.0	101.4	105.7	109.2	113.2	117.0	124.4
Other retail sale (non-store) and repair	EAHB	8 583	105.7	103.8	105.0	106.1	100.0	101.4	105.7	111.6	115.2	115.6	119.2

1 See chapter text.

Source: Office for National Statistics: 01633 812609

23.3 Motor trades[1,2]
United Kingdom

| | Number of businesses | Total turnover | Motor trades turnover | Retail sales of | | Sales to other dealers of | | Gross sales of used motor vehicles and motorcycles | Turnover from sales of petrol, diesel, oil and other petroleum products | Other motor trades sales and receipts (including parts and accessories, workshop receipts) | Non-motor trades turnover |
| | | | | New cars | Other new motor vehicles and motorcycles | New cars | Other new motor vehicles and motorcycles | | | | |
	Number	£ million	£ million	£ million	£ million	£ million	£ million	£ million	£ million	£ million	£ million
Sale, maintenance and repair of motor vehicles and motorcycles; retail sale of automotive fuel (SIC 92 50.00)											
	MKEQ	CMRH	CMRI	CMRJ	CMRK	CMRL	CMRM	CMRN	CMRO	CMRP	CMRQ
1996	71 119	108 805	105 489	19 888	3 246	16 085	2 328	25 558	11 698	26 686	3 316
1997	72 527	119 065	115 442	23 119	3 311	15 762	2 395	28 328	12 871	29 656	3 623
1998	72 105	123 130	119 816	24 492	3 626	16 922	2 547	27 327	13 445	31 457	3 314
1999	72 298	128 956	125 752	25 992	3 598	16 780	2 936	28 233	15 448	32 765	3 204
2000	71 568	129 838	126 524	24 597	3 596	15 887	3 102	30 205	17 225	31 911	3 314
Sale of motor vehicles (SIC 92 50.10)											
	MKER	EWRI	FDFZ	FDGA	FDGB	FDGC	FDGD	FDGE	FDGF	FDGG	FDHJ
1996	36 383	76 920	76 009	18 877	2 878	16 053	2 225	23 793	1 271	10 912	911
1997	34 664	84 394	83 548	22 554	2 890	15 737	2 255	26 910	1 182	12 020	847
1998	31 196	87 035	86 122	23 897	3 125	16 896	2 435	26 124	1 379	12 266	913
1999	29 761	88 644	87 918	25 073	2 977	16 752	2 622	26 063	1 335	13 095	726
2000	28 018	86 743	86 154	23 371	2 494	15 874	2 743	28 379	1 114	12 178	589
Maintenance and repair of motor vehicles (SIC 92 50.20)											
	MKES	FDHK	FDHL	FDHM	FDHN	FDHO	FDHP	FDHQ	FDHR	FDHS	FDHT
1996	19 709	8 263	8 147	796	129	19	1	1 021	550	5 631	116
1997	22 027	8 008	7 829	417	78	20	5	662	286	6 361	179
1998	24 680	8 976	8 862	297	54	17	–	312	343	7 839	114
1999	26 089	11 118	10 951	724	61	22	8	1 416	656	8 063	167
2000	27 226	11 240	10 936	1 020	567	12	32	1 103	445	7 755	305
Sale of motor vehicle parts and accessories (SIC 92 50.30)											
	MKET	FDIW	FDIX	FDIY	FDIZ	FDJA	FDJB	FDJC	FDJD	FDJE	FDJF
1996	5 829	10 066	9 806	70	24	9	–	118	78	9 507	260
1997	6 583	10 741	10 567	9	21	–	–	70	79	10 388	174
1998	7 187	10 962	10 808	8	5	–	–	89	111	10 595	154
1999	7 630	11 128	11 085	46	34	1	–	112	73	10 819	44
2000	7 771	11 098	11 077	–	83	–	–	82	60	10 852	21
Sale, maintenance and repair of motorcycles and related parts and accessories (SIC 92 50.40)											
	MKEU	FDKI	FDKJ	FDKK	FDKL	FDKM	FDKN	FDKO	FDKP	FDKQ	FDKR
1996	1 231	1 019	996	15	214	–	102	342	3	320	23
1997	1 522	1 248	1 225	–	322	–	135	344	2	422	23
1998	1 782	1 274	1 196	–	441	–	112	281	1	361	78
1999	2 077	1 665	1 626	17	526	–	306	342	3	432	40
2000	2 281	1 946	1 938	22	451	–	328	416	1	721	8
Retail sale of automotive fuel (SIC 92 50.50)											
	MKEV	FDLV	FDLW	FDLX	FDLY	FDLZ	FDMA	FDMB	FDMC	FDMD	FDME
1996	7 967	12 537	10 531	130	1	4	–	284	9 796	316	2 006
1997	7 701	14 673	12 273	139	–	5	–	342	11 322	465	2 400
1998	7 260	14 883	12 828	290	1	9	–	521	11 611	396	2 055
1999	6 741	16 401	14 173	130	–	5	1	300	13 382	356	2 228
2000	6 272	18 811	16 420	184	1	–	–	224	15 605	406	2 391

23.3 Motor trades[1,2]
United Kingdom
continued

	Purchases of goods, materials and services											
	Total purchases	Energy, water and materials	Used motor vehicles and motorcycles	Parts used solely in repair and servicing activities	Other goods for resale	Hiring, leasing and renting of plant, machinery and vehicles	Commercial insurance premiums	Road transport services	Telecommun- ication services	Computer and related services	Advertising and marketing services	Other services
	£ million	£ million	£ million	£ million	£ million	£ million	£ million	£ million	£ million	£ million	£ million	£ million

Sale, maintenance and repair of motor vehicles and motorcycles; retail sale of automotive fuel (SIC 92 50.00)

	CMNR	CMRS	COBU	CMRT	CMRU	CMRV	CMRW	CMRX	CMRY	CMRZ	CMSA	CMSB
1996	94 753	505	23 001	5 739	59 599	183	328	299	226	132	1 316	3 425
1997	102 471	643	25 327	5 614	64 809	245	361	327	245	130	1 190	3 580
1998	106 431	1 638	24 673	6 236	67 545	228	343	326	249	185	1 464	3 545
1999	111 324	1 280	25 223	6 249	71 895	247	360	356	282	232	1 713	3 488
2000	112 325	1 387	27 047	5 136	72 025	282	397	402	280	229	1 633	3 508

Sale of motor vehicles (SIC 92 50.10)

	FDGH	FDGI	FDGJ	FDGK	FDGL	FDGM	FDGN	FDGO	FDGP	FDGQ	FDGR	FDGS
1996	68 655	248	21 483	3 048	39 869	86	163	202	123	88	1 110	2 235
1997	74 663	298	24 065	2 803	43 307	106	179	191	133	88	998	2 495
1998	77 395	975	23 604	2 592	46 218	90	156	205	126	99	1 233	2 097
1999	78 607	632	23 444	2 720	47 629	74	177	196	151	142	1 462	1 979
2000	76 973	631	25 463	2 063	44 677	64	164	241	137	141	1 376	2 016

Maintenance and repair of motor vehicles (SIC 92 50.20)

	FDHU	FDHV	FDHW	FDHX	FDHY	FDHZ	FDIA	FDIB	FDIC	FDID	FDIE	FDIF
1996	5 703	115	900	2 266	1 583	59	89	21	45	17	89	519
1997	5 102	176	604	2 291	1 235	97	102	37	49	18	70	423
1998	5 667	292	300	3 171	846	86	112	23	54	21	74	688
1999	7 236	298	1 150	3 080	1 590	115	116	33	66	35	92	661
2000	7 402	364	957	2 562	2 411	137	145	21	70	41	89	606

Sale of motor vehicle parts and accessories (SIC 92 50.30)

	FDJG	FDJH	FDJI	FDJJ	FDJK	FDJL	FDJM	FDJN	FDJO	FDJP	FDJQ	FDJR
1996	8 107	69	101	291	7 044	31	42	69	40	21	82	317
1997	8 336	74	68	328	7 186	31	46	89	46	21	92	355
1998	8 624	169	144	346	7 089	43	50	88	53	42	111	489
1999	8 825	257	103	290	7 359	49	36	76	46	39	118	452
2000	8 904	290	71	266	7 421	58	52	92	49	31	89	485

Sale, maintenance and repair of motorcycles and related parts and accessories (SIC 92 50.40)

	FDKT	FDKU	FDKV	FDKW	FDKX	FDKY	FDKZ	FDLA	FDLB	FDLC	FDLD	FDLE
1996	856	3	271	29	489	1	5	4	2	2	14	36
1997	1 060	17	293	43	629	1	8	4	4	1	11	49
1998	1 088	46	226	29	731	1	4	3	2	1	21	24
1999	1 423	10	314	55	958	1	7	6	4	3	22	44
2000	1 611	30	366	138	948	1	11	6	6	3	26	75

Retail sale of automotive fuel (SIC 92 50.50)

	FDMF	FDMG	FDMH	FDMI	FDMJ	FDMK	FDML	COBV	COBW	COBX	COBY	COBZ
1996	11 432	70	246	105	10 614	6	29	3	16	4	21	318
1997	13 310	78	297	149	12 452	10	26	6	13	2	19	258
1998	13 657	154	399	98	12 661	8	21	7	14	23	25	247
1999	15 232	82	213	105	14 357	8	24	46	15	13	18	351
2000	17 435	71	190	108	16 568	22	26	43	17	12	53	326

	Taxes, duties and levies			Capital Expenditure			
	Total taxes and levies	National (non-domestic business) rates	Other amounts paid for taxes, duties and levies	Cost of acquisitions	Cost of disposals	Net capital expenditure	Work of a capital nature carried out by own staff (included in acquisitions)
	£ million	£ million	£ million	£ million	£ million	£ million	£ million

Sale, maintenance and repair of motor vehicles and motorcycles; retail sale of automotive fuel (SIC 92 50.00)

	CMSC	CMSD	CMSE	CMSF	CMSG	CMSH	CMSI
1996	598	467	131	827	354	473	7
1997	692	500	192	1 550	570	980	14
1998	951	496	455	2 026	836	1 190	39
1999	904	535	369	1 964	685	1 280	21
2000	868	534	334	1 948	658	1 290	8

Sale of motor vehicles (SIC 92 50.10)

	FDGT	FDGU	FDGV	FDGW	FDGX	FDGY	FDGZ
1996	330	216	114	617	311	306	5
1997	373	277	96	934	398	536	7
1998	610	240	370	1 225	655	570	27
1999	543	246	297	1 211	461	749	13
2000	476	222	254	1 115	464	651	6

Maintenance and repair of motor vehicles (SIC 92 50.20)

	FDIG	FDIH	FDII	FDIJ	FDIK	FDIL	FDIM
1996	106	103	3	72	14	58	1
1997	142	84	58	266	38	228	4
1998	142	114	28	437	97	340	2
1999	172	132	39	389	86	303	7
2000	184	140	44	366	75	291	2

Sale of motor vehicle parts and accessories (SIC 92 50.30)

	FDJS	FDJT	FDJU	FDJV	FDJW	FDJX	FDJY
1996	111	104	7	92	15	77	1
1997	105	80	25	238	81	157	3
1998	100	73	27	180	43	137	6
1999	97	85	13	193	67	126	1
2000	104	87	18	211	50	162	1

Sale, maintenance and repair of motorcycles and related parts and accessories (SIC 92 50.40)

	FDLF	FDLG	FDLH	FDLI	FDLJ	FDLK	FDLL
1996	8	6	2	11	2	9	–
1997	12	11	1	24	6	18	–
1998	16	10	6	26	10	16	4
1999	18	7	11	23	3	20	1
2000	22	11	11	28	11	17	–

Retail sale of automotive fuel (SIC 92 50.50)

	COCA	COCB	COCC	COCD	COCE	COCF	COCG
1996	43	38	5	35	12	23	–
1997	60	48	12	88	47	41	–
1998	83	59	24	158	31	127	–
1999	73	65	9	149	67	82	–
2000	81	74	8	228	59	169	–

	Stocks			Employment costs			Gross margin		Approximate gross value added at basic prices
	Increase during year	Value at end of year	Total turnover divided by end-year stocks	Total employment costs	Gross wages and salaries paid	National insurance and pension contributions	Amount	As a percentage of adjusted turnover	
	£ million	£ million	Quotient	£ million	£ million	£ million	£ million	Percentage	£ million

Sale, maintenance and repair of motor vehicles and motorcycles; retail sale of automotive fuel (SIC 92 50.00)

	Increase during year	Value at end of year	Total turnover divided by end-year stocks	Total employment costs	Gross wages and salaries paid	National insurance and pension contributions	Amount	As a percentage of adjusted turnover	Approximate gross value added at basic prices
	CMSJ	CMSK	CMSL	CMSM	COBP	COBQ	COBR	COBS	COBT
1996	888	11 127	9.8	6 206	5 564	642	21 354	20,6	14 816
1997	1 388	12 079	9.9	6 981	6 229	752	24 703	21.6	17 804
1998	1 133	12 862	9.6	7 660	6 802	858	25 809	21.7	17 464
1999	1 042	13 738	9.4	8 179	7 295	884	26 398	21.5	18 726
2000	658	13 461	9.6	8 307	7 417	890	25 981	20.8	18 249

Sale of motor vehicles (SIC 92 50.10)

	FDHA	FDHB	FDHC	FDHD	FDHE	FDHF	FDHG	FDHH	FDHI
1996	748	8 786	8.8	3 381	3 024	357	13 268	17.8	8 904
1997	1 213	9 494	8.9	3 766	3 349	417	15 433	18.8	10 856
1998	948	10 233	8.5	4 048	3 594	454	15 569	18.0	10 274
1999	995	10 797	8.2	4 285	3 815	469	15 676	18.2	11 064
2000	594	10 491	8.3	4 375	3 889	486	14 921	17.6	10 364

Maintenance and repair of motor vehicles (SIC 92 50.20)

	FDIN	FDIO	FDIP	FDIQ	FDIR	FDIS	FDIT	FDIU	FDIV
1996	30	558	14.8	1 366	1 230	136	3 544	59.1	2 588
1997	46	544	14.7	1 435	1 273	162	3 924	67.7	2 898
1998	28	515	17.4	1 718	1 517	201	4 687	80.4	3 317
1999	−3	747	14.9	1 930	1 725	205	5 283	65.7	3 898
2000	−43	670	16.8	1 917	1 714	204	5 213	60.1	3 876

Sale of motor vehicle parts and accessories (SIC 92 50.30)

	FDJZ	FDKA	FDKB	FDKC	FDKD	FDKE	FDKF	FDKG	FDKH
1996	81	1 231	8.2	1 018	911	107	2 711	27.7	2 034
1997	66	1 329	8.1	1 231	1 104	127	3 225	30.8	2 449
1998	53	1 332	8.2	1 292	1 142	150	3 436	32.2	2 373
1999	31	1 403	7.9	1 295	1 151	144	3 401	31.4	2 332
2000	43	1 450	7.7	1 354	1 210	144	3 370	31.1	2 229

Sale, maintenance and repair of motorcycles and related parts and accessories (SIC 92 50.40)

	FDLM	FDLN	FDLO	FDLP	FDLQ	FDLR	FDLS	FDLT	FDLU
1996	16	216	4.7	69	61	8	246	24.6	177
1997	25	263	4.7	93	83	10	309	25.6	213
1998	77	333	3.8	101	90	11	365	29.1	262
1999	−24	291	5.7	128	115	13	313	19.5	218
2000	30	364	5.3	102	92	10	514	28.4	368

Retail sale of automotive fuel (SIC 92 50.50)

	COCH	COCI	COCJ	COCK	COCL	COCM	COCN	CMQN	CMQO
1996	13	336	37.3	372	338	34	1 585	12.7	1 113
1997	37	449	32.7	456	420	36	1 812	12.4	1 388
1998	27	449	33.1	501	459	42	1 752	11.7	1 238
1999	43	502	32.7	541	488	53	1 725	10.6	1 215
2000	35	487	38.7	557	512	45	1 964	10.5	1 412

1 See chapter text. Figures are exclusive of VAT.
2 Data for 1996 were collected on a different basis from those for 1997 onwards.

Source: Office for National Statistics: 01633 812435

23.4 Catering and allied trades[1]
United Kingdom

			Taxes and levies[2]			Capital expenditure[2]			
Number of businesses	Total turnover[3]	Total taxes and levies	National (non-domestic business) rates	Other amounts paid for taxes duties and levies	Capital acquisitions	Capital disposals	Net capital expenditure	Work of a capital nature carried out by your own staff (included in acquisitions)
Number	£ million	£ million	£ million	£ million	£ million	£ million	£ million	£ million

Total catering and allied trades (SIC 92 55.00)

	MKEK	CMKX	CMLM	CMLJ	CMLL	CMLP	CMLQ	CMLK	CMLR
1996	110 583	41 666	979	787	192	2 991	445	2 546	14
1997	110 245	45 844	1 082	899	183	3 909	465	3 444	14
1998	111 815	48 680	1 215	1 053	162	4 453	519	3 934	30
1999	114 353	51 315	1 295	1 156	139	4 793	649	4 144	49
2000	116 753	55 506	1 342	1 249	93	4 933	485	4 448	37

Hotels and motels (SIC 92 55.11 and 55.12)

	MKEL	CMLW	CMML	CMMI	CMMK	CMMO	CMMP	CMMJ	CMMQ
1996	12 163	8 933	244	226	18	782	195	587	3
1997	11 555	9 589	255	228	28	1 116	99	1 018	8
1998	11 374	10 333	259	254	5	1 221	105	1 116	3
1999	11 381	10 970	269	260	9	1 333	203	1 130	8
2000	11 195	11 629	301	293	8	1 403	106	1 297	10

Camping sites and other provision of short-stay accommodation (SIC 92 55.21 to 55.23)

	MKEM	CMMV	CMNK	CMNH	CMNJ	CMNN	CMNO	CMNI	CMNP
1996	3 094	1 620	43	43	..	159	15	144	1
1997	3 289	1 945	59	50	9	253	36	216	2
1998	3 435	2 071	67	62	6	261	37	224	2
1999	3 688	1 932	61	53	8	274	38	236	7
2000	3 857	2 153	69	63	6	229	46	182	5

Restaurants or cafes, take-away food shops (SIC 92 55.30)

	MKEN	CMNU	CMOJ	CMOG	CMOI	CMOM	CMON	CMOH	CMOO
1996	46 379	11 643	246	225	21	625	66	559	1
1997	46 984	12 660	272	250	22	720	62	657	2
1998	48 362	13 710	305	290	15	971	122	849	1
1999	49 955	14 618	386	360	26	1 048	137	911	7
2000	51 472	16 950	406	383	23	1 302	129	1 174	2

Licensed clubs with entertainment, independent, tenanted, managed public houses or wine bars (SIC 92 55.40)[4]

	MKEO	CMOT	CMPI	CMPF	CMPH	CMPL	CMPM	CMPG	CMPN
1996	45 134	15 484	423	270	153	1 364	164	1 200	8
1997	44 198	16 792	451	336	115	1 734	265	1 470	2
1998	44 283	17 820	559	429	130	1 910	251	1 658	12
1999	44 647	18 423	551	460	92	2 032	263	1 769	25
2000	45 230	18 899	535	481	54	1 852	197	1 655	20

Canteen operator, catering contractor (SIC 92 55.51 and 55.52)

	MKEP	CMPS	CMQH	CMQE	CMQG	CMQK	CMQL	CMQF	CMQM
1996	3 813	3 986	23	23	..	61	5	56	1
1997	4 219	4 858	44	35	9	86	3	83	–
1998	4 361	4 748	24	19	5	91	5	87	12
1999	4 682	5 372	28	23	5	106	8	99	2
2000	4 999	5 876	31	28	3	147	7	140	–

23.4 Catering and allied trades[1]
United Kingdom
continued

	Stocks[2]		Purchases of goods and services[2]									
	Increase during year	Value at end of year	Total purchases	Energy, water and materials	Goods for resale	Hiring, leasing of plant, machinery etc.	Commercial insurance premiums	Road transport services	Telecommun- ication services	Computer and related services	Advertising and marketing services	Other services
	£ million	£ million	£ million	£ million	£ million	£ million	£ million	£ million	£ million	£ million	£ million	£ million
Total catering and allied trades (SIC 92 55.00)												
	CMLN	CMLO	CMLI	CMKZ	CMLA	CMLB	CMLC	CMLD	CMLE	CMLF	CMLG	CMLH
1996	38	787	19 966	6 108	7 971	208	281	62	154	36	477	4 669
1997	48	840	21 371	8 053	7 338	234	285	89	187	50	546	4 589
1998	43	969	22 702	9 335	7 094	273	271	51	189	62	581	4 846
1999	60	1 067	23 856	8 848	8 028	306	272	100	213	105	608	5 377
2000	40	1 087	25 587	10 128	8 088	346	372	101	232	129	625	5 566
Hotels and motels (SIC 92 55.11 and 55.12)												
	CMMM	CMMN	CMMH	CMLY	CMLZ	CMMA	CMMB	CMMC	CMMD	CMME	CMMF	CMMG
1996	−10	130	3 413	1 211	548	66	83	14	64	15	173	1 239
1997	−1	137	3 532	1 487	506	68	73	27	60	17	162	1 132
1998	1	157	3 702	1 663	512	54	72	11	58	17	169	1 178
1999	−5	208	3 817	1 667	450	65	67	25	60	36	167	1 280
2000	3	181	3 966	1 804	386	65	72	28	57	29	183	1 343
Camping sites and other provision of short-stay accommodation (SIC 92 55.21 to 55.23)												
	CMNL	CMNM	CMNG	CMMX	CMMY	CMMZ	CMNA	CMNB	CMNC	CMND	CMNE	CMNF
1996	4	65	761	165	252	8	27	6	10	3	47	243
1997	8	87	887	172	278	11	23	5	10	5	55	327
1998	−1	91	932	212	265	11	22	3	15	6	76	321
1999	3	85	852	184	220	5	28	10	12	6	66	321
2000	−4	84	901	202	243	9	35	10	14	23	57	308
Restaurants or cafes, take-away food shops (SIC 92 55.30)												
	CMOK	CMOL	CMOF	CMNW	CMNX	CMNY	CMNZ	CMOA	CMOB	CMOC	CMOD	CMOE
1996	6	185	5 725	2 212	1 679	21	66	15	30	5	119	1 578
1997	14	206	6 175	2 926	1 538	27	78	22	41	7	159	1 376
1998	16	231	6 683	3 197	1 611	49	66	10	43	11	159	1 537
1999	26	291	7 079	3 183	1 934	53	70	29	61	19	200	1 530
2000	9	276	7 965	3 784	2 130	46	92	36	64	29	231	1 552
Licensed clubs with entertainment, independent, tenanted, managed public houses or wine bars (SIC 92 55.40)[4]												
	CMPJ	CMPK	CMPE	CMOV	CMOW	CMOX	CMOY	CMOZ	CMPA	CMPB	CMPC	CMPD
1996	29	338	8 203	1 298	5 143	86	93	17	41	4	125	1 396
1997	15	340	8 665	2 042	4 800	95	96	17	64	13	158	1 379
1998	21	408	9 147	2 796	4 389	96	96	15	62	17	160	1 517
1999	24	392	9 386	2 028	4 924	147	91	15	67	28	161	1 925
2000	40	440	9 811	2 380	4 715	194	153	15	79	34	135	2 106
Canteen operator, catering contractor (SIC 92 55.51 and 55.52)												
	CMQI	CMQJ	CMQD	CMPU	CMPV	CMPW	CMPX	CMPY	CMPZ	CMQA	CMQB	CMQC
1996	9	69	1 864	1 222	349	27	12	10	9	9	13	213
1997	12	71	2 111	1 427	216	32	14	18	11	9	11	374
1998	7	82	2 237	1 497	317	63	16	12	11	10	18	293
1999	12	92	2 721	1 785	500	35	17	21	14	15	14	321
2000	−1	105	2 944	1 959	613	31	21	13	18	14	20	256

23.4 Catering and allied trades[1]
continued United Kingdom

| | Employment costs[2] | | | Gross margin[5] | | | Accommodation | |
	Total employment costs	Gross wages and salaries paid	National insurance and pension contributions	Amount	As a percentage of turnover	Value added at basic prices[5]	Number of establishments	Letting bedplaces
	£ million	£ million	£ million	£ million	Percentage	£ million	Number	Number

Total catering and allied trades (SIC 92 55.00)

	CMKY	CMKV	CMKW	CMQP	CMQQ	CMQR	CMLS	CMLT
1996	8 214	7 570	644	27 634	77.3	15 639	..	..
1997	9 200	8 493	707	32 088	81.1	18 055	23 207	1 591 979
1998	10 261	9 461	799	34 870	82.9	19 333	23 038	1 481 204
1999	11 012	10 169	844	36 159	81.5	20 568	23 667	1 731 601
2000	11 673	10 781	892	39 613	82.8	22 285	26 833	1 802 778

Hotels and motels (SIC 92 55.11 and 55.12)

	CMLX	CMLU	CMLV	CMQS	CMQT	CMQU	CMMR	CMMS
1996	2 179	1 998	181	7 047	92.5	4 182	–	–
1997	2 257	2 071	186	7 663	93.6	4 636	13 505	727 016
1998	2 460	2 251	209	8 284	94.2	5 101	12 907	701 488
1999	2 605	2 392	213	8 922	95.0	5 595	12 583	757 491
2000	2 770	2 535	235	9 568	95.9	6 022	14 772	792 812

Camping sites and other provision of short-stay accommodation (SIC 92 55.21 to 55.23)

	CMMW	CMMT	CMMU	CMQV	CMQW	CMQX	CMNQ	CMRR
1996	255	235	20	1 181	82.7	672	–	–
1997	312	293	19	1 456	84.0	846	4 598	770 397
1998	350	326	24	1 574	85.4	913	4 396	669 423
1999	355	325	30	1 460	85.3	865	4 913	844 311
2000	405	370	35	1 615	85.4	989	5 092	861 661

Restaurants or cafes, take-away food shops (SIC 92 55.30)

	CMNV	CMNS	CMNT	CMQY	CMQZ	CMRA	CMOP	CMOQ
1996	2 095	1 946	149	8 316	83.1	4 270	..	..
1997	2 404	2 231	174	9 352	85.8	4 715	655	29 815
1998	2 787	2 590	196	10 258	86.5	5 223	692	31 680
1999	2 985	2 762	223	10 665	84.5	5 592	1 033	45 449
2000	3 318	3 071	247	12 377	85.2	6 573	1 055	60 444

Licensed clubs with entertainment, independent, tenanted, managed public houses or wine bars (SIC 92 55.40)[4]

	CMOU	CMOR	CMOS	CMRB	CMRC	CMRD	CMPO	CMPP
1996	2 418	2 227	191	7 937	60.1	4 877	..	–
1997	2 657	2 451	205	9 494	66.0	5 629	4 449	64 751
1998	2 982	2 752	230	10 793	70.6	6 052	5 044	78 614
1999	3 206	2 975	231	10 762	68.1	6 383	5 137	84 351
2000	3 150	2 934	216	11 441	70.7	6 396	5 914	87 860

Canteen operator, catering contractor (SIC 92 55.51 and 55.52)

	CMPT	CMPQ	CMPR	CMRE	CMRF	CMRG		
1996	1 267	1 164	103	3 153	90.3	1 638		
1997	1 569	1 447	122	4 132	95.1	2 228		
1998	1 681	1 541	140	3 962	93.0	2 044		
1999	1 861	1 715	146	4 349	89.9	2 133		
2000	2 030	1 872	159	4 611	88.1	2 304		

1 See chapter text. Data for 1996 were collected on a different basis from those for 1997 onwards.
2 Exclusive of VAT.
3 Inclusive of VAT.
4 Includes figures for managed public houses owned by breweries.
5 The total turnover figure used to calculate these data excludes VAT.

Source: Office for National Statistics: 01633 812435

417

SOURCES

This index of sources gives the titles of official publications or other sources containing statistics allied to those in the tables of this *Annual Abstract*. These publications provide more detailed analyses than are shown in the *Annual Abstract*. This index includes publications to which reference should be made for short-term (monthly or quarterly) series. No entry is made in this index for items where the data have been obtained from departmental records. Further advice on published statistical sources is available from the National Statistics Public Enquiry Service on the numbers provided on page ii.

Subject	Table number in *Abstract*	Government department or other organisation	Official publication or other source
1. Area			
	1.1	Ordnance Survey Ordnance Survey of Northern Ireland Office for National Statistics	Regional Trends (annual, The Stationery Office (TSO))
2. Parliamentary elections			
Elections	2.1	University of Plymouth for the Electoral Commission	British Electoral Facts 1832-1999 (Ashgate) Dod's Parliamentary Companion (annual)
By-elections	2.2	University of Plymouth for the Electoral Commission	Vachers Parliamentary Companion (quarterly) Social Trends (annual, TSO)
3. International development			
	3.1, 3.2	Department for International Development	Statistics on International Development (annual)
4. Defence			
	4.1 - 4.11	Ministry of Defence/ DASA	UK Defence Statistics 2002 (TSO)
5. Population and vital statistics			
Population	5.1 - 5.3, 5.5, 5.6	Office for National Statistics	*England and Wales*: Census reports 1911, 1921, 1931, 1951, 1961, 1971, 1981 and 1991 Census 1991, Key Population and Vital Statistics; Great Britain Digest of Welsh Statistics (annual, National Assembly for Wales)
		General Register Office (Scotland)	*Scotland*: Census reports 1951, 1961, 1971, 1981 and 1991 Census 1991, Key statistics for urban areas: Scotland
		Northern Ireland Statistics and Research Agency	*Northern Ireland*: Census of population 1951, 1961, 1966 and 1971, 1981 and 1991
		Office for National Statistics	*England and Wales*: Series FM (Family statistics), DH (Deaths), MB (Morbidity), PP (Population estimates and projections), MN (Migration) and VS (Key population and vital statistics) Series PP1, Population estimates: The Registrar General's estimates of the population of regions and local government areas of England and Wales Population Trends (quarterly TSO) Health Statistics Quarterly (TSO)
		General Register Office (Scotland)	*Scotland*: Annual report of the Registrar General for Scotland Annual estimate of the population of Scotland
		Northern Ireland Statistics and Research Agency	*Northern Ireland*: Annual report of the Registrar General
Projections	5.1 - 5.3	Government Actuary's Department Office for National Statistics	Series PP2, Population projections - national figures
Migration	5.7 5.8, 5.9	Office for National Statistics	International Migration 2001 - interim revised estimates (first release) Series MN (International migration) Population Trends (quarterly, TSO)
	5.10, 5.11	Home Office	Control of immigration statistics United Kingdom (annual)
Vital statistics	5.4, 5.12 - 5.22	Office for National Statistics	*England and Wales*: Series FM (Births, marriages and divorce statistics), DH (Deaths), MB (Morbidity), PP (Population estimates and projections), MN (International migration) and VS (Key population and vital statistics) Population Trends (quarterly, TSO)

SOURCES

Subject	Table number in *Abstract*	Government department or other organisation	Official publication or other source
	5.4, 5.12 - 5.21	General Register Office (Scotland)	*Scotland*: Annual report of the Registrar General for Scotland Quarterly return of births, deaths and marriages
		Northern Ireland Statistics and Research Agency	*Northern Ireland*: Annual report of the Registrar General Quarterly return of births, deaths and marriages
	5.14	Northern Ireland Court Service	Northern Ireland Judicial Statistics (annual)
	5.18	Scottish Executive	
	5.22	Government Actuary's Department	*England and Wales*: Interim Life Table *Scotland*: Interim Life Table *Northern Ireland*: Annual Report of the Registrar General

6. Education

Subject	Table number in *Abstract*	Government department or other organisation	Official publication or other source
	6.1 - 6.11	Department for Education and Skills	Education and Training Statistics for the United Kingdom (annual,TSO)
		National Assembly for Wales	Digest of Welsh Statistics (annual) Statistics of education and training in Wales (annual and ad-hoc, NAfW)
		Scottish Executive	Scottish educational statistics (annual and ad-hoc, SE) Scottish Social Statistics (annual)
		Northern Ireland Department of Education	Annual Abstract of Statistics, Northern Ireland (annual,DENI) Northern Ireland education statistics (annual and ad-hoc, DENI)
		Northern Ireland Department for Employment and Learning	Northern Ireland further and higher education statistics (annual and ad-hoc, DELNI)

7. Labour market

Subject	Table number in *Abstract*	Government department or other organisation	Official publication or other source
Labour Force Survey	7.1 - 7.3, 7.6, 7.9, 7.10, 7.12, 7.15 - 7.17	Office for National Statistics	Labour Market Trends (monthly, TSO)
	7.4, 7.5	Office for National Statistics	
	7.7	Cabinet Office	Civil Service Statistics (annual) Monthly Digest of Statistics (TSO)
	7.8	Office for National Statistics Home Office Scottish Executive	Labour Market Trends (monthly, TSO)
Claimant count	7.11, 7.13 7.14, 7.27	Office for National Statistics	Labour Market Trends (monthly, TSO)
	7.18	Office for National Statistics	Labour Market Trends (monthly TSO) Monthly Digest of Statistics (TSO)
New Earnings Survey	7.19, 7.20, 7.23, 7.25	Office for National Statistics	New Earnings Survey (annual, ONS)
Average Earnings Index	7.21, 7.22	Office for National Statistics	Labour Market Trends (monthly, TSO) Monthly Digest of Statistics (TSO)
	7.24	Department of Enterprise, Trade and Investment (Northern Ireland)	New Earnings Survey Northern Ireland (annual) (some details in Northern Ireland Annual Abstract of Statistics)
	7.26	Department of Trade and Industry	Labour Market Trends (monthly, TSO)

8. Personal income, expenditure and wealth

Subject	Table number in *Abstract*	Government department or other organisation	Official publication or other source
	8.1 8.2	Office for National Statistics Board of Inland Revenue	Economic Trends, March (monthly, TSO) Inland Revenue Statistics (annual, TSO) Economic Trends (monthly, TSO)
	8.3 - 8.5	Office for National Statistics	Expenditure and Food Survey, (annual) (1990 onwards edition-Family Spending)(annual, TSO)

9. Health

Subject	Table number in *Abstract*	Government department or other organisation	Official publication or other source
National health service	9.1	Department of Health	Appropriation Accounts (annual) Health and Personal Social Services Statistics for England (annual)

Subject	Table number in *Abstract*	Government department or other organisation	Official publication or other source
		National Assembly for Wales	Health Statistics Wales (annual)
	9.2	Scottish Health Service, Common Services Agency	
	9.3	Central Services Agency, Department of Health, Social Services and Public Safety (Northern Ireland)	Summary of Health and Personal Social Services (Northern Ireland) Accounts (annual) Hospital Statistics (annual)
	9.4	Department of Health Scottish Health Service, Common Services Agency National Assembly for Wales	Health and Personal Social Services Statistics for England (annual)
Public health	9.5	Office for National Statistics	
		General Register Office (Scotland)	
		General Register Office (Northern Ireland)	
	9.6	PHLS Communicable Disease Surveillance Centre	Communicable Disease Statistics Series MB2 (annual) Annual Review of Communicable Diseases
		Scottish Health Service, Common Services Agency	Scottish Health Statistics (annual)
		General Register Office (Northern Ireland)	Annual report of the Registrar General Northern Ireland Quarterly return of births, deaths and marriages
	9.7 - 9.9	Health and Safety Executive	Health and Safety Statistics (annual)

10. Social protection

Subject	Table number in *Abstract*	Government department or other organisation	Official publication or other source
Social security pensions, benefits and allowances	10.1, 10.2,	Department for Work and Pensions	National Insurance Fund Account (annual)
	10.4	Board of Inland Revenue	
	10.3, 10.5, 10.6 - 10.16	Department for Work and Pensions, Information and Analysis Unit	
Working Family Tax Credit	10.12	Board of Inland Revenue	Quarterly Enquiry United Kingdom (quarterly)
Social services	10.17 - 10.21	Office for National Statistics Department for Education and Skills	Appropriation Accounts (annual) Northern Ireland Annual Abstract of Statistics
Housing	10.22	Office for National Statistics	

11. Crime and justice

Subject	Table number in *Abstract*	Government department or other organisation	Official publication or other source
	11.1	Home Office	Crime in England and Wales 2001/02
	11.2	Home Office	
		Scottish Executive Justice Department The Police Service of Northern Ireland	*Scotland*: Report of Her Majesty's Chief Inspector of Constabulary for Scotland (annual) The Chief Constable's Annual Report
	11.3 - 11.11	Home Office	Criminal Statistics, England and Wales (annual) (TSO) Prison statistics, England and Wales (annual) Digest of Welsh Statistics (annual, Welsh Office)
	11.12	Home Office	HM Prison Service Annual Report and Accounts April 2001 - March 2002
	11.13	Scottish Executive Justice Department	Recorded Crime in Scotland, 2001
	11.14- - 11.17	Scottish Executive Justice Department	Criminal Proceedings in Scottish Courts

SOURCES

Subject	Table number in *Abstract*	Government department or other organisation	Official publication or other source
	11.18, 11.19	Scottish Executive Justice Department	Prison Statistics Scotland, 2001 Scottish Prison Service Annual Report and Accounts 2001-02
	11.21 - 11.23	Northern Ireland Office	

12. Lifestyles

	12.1	Department for Culture, Media and Sport	Department for Culture, Media and Sport Annual Report 2002
	12.2	Department for Culture, Media and Sport	Table B17 – Labour Market Trends
	12.3	Office for National Statistics	GB Cinema Exhibitors News Release Monthly Digest of Statistics (TSO)
	12.4	Department for Culture, Media and Sport	British Film Institute Film and Television Handbook
	12.5	Office for National Statistics	Travel Trends (annual, TSO) Overseas Travel and Tourism First Release Monthly Digest of Statistics (TSO)
		English Tourism Council	The UK Tourist: Statistics (annual) Sightseeing in the UK (annual) Visits to Visitor Attractions (annual) www.staruk.org.uk The national tourism statistics website
		Wales Tourist Board/ VisitScotland/Northern Ireland Tourist Board	
	12.6	English Tourism Council/ Wales Tourist Board/ VisitScotland/Northern Ireland Tourist Board	Sightseeing in the UK (annual)
	12.7	Department for Culture, Media and Sport	Camelot - National Lottery Press Releases
		Gaming Board for Great Britain	The Gaming Board for Great Britain Annual Report www.gbgb.org.uk The Gaming Board website

13. Environment, water and housing

Subject			
Environment	13.1, 13.19	Office for National Statistics	United Kingdom National Accounts (annual, TSO)
	13.2 - 13.7 13.9 -13.18	Department for Environment, Food and Rural Affairs	Digest of Environmental Statistics (annual, www.defra.gov.uk/environment/statistics/des) The Environment in your Pocket (annual)
	13.10	Scottish Environmental Protection Agency	
Water	13.8	Office of Water Services (OFWAT)	Companies 2002 June Return to OFWAT (annual)
Housing	13.20	Office of the Deputy Prime Minister National Assembly for Wales Scottish Executive Department for Social Development, Northern Ireland	www.housing.odpm.gov.uk/statistics Live Tables 241-247 Welsh Housing Statistics (annual, NAfW) Statistical Bulletins on Housing (SE) Northern Ireland Housing Statistics (annual)
	13.21	Office of the Deputy Prime Minister	www.housing.odpm.gov.uk/statistics Live Table 111

14. Transport and communications

Subject			
General	14.1, 14.2, 14.4	Department for Transport	
	14.3	Office for National Statistics	
Road transport	14.5 - 14.11	Department for Transport	Transport Statistics Great Britain (annual, TSO) Vehicle Licensing Statistics (annual, TSO) Monthly Digest of Statistics (TSO) Road accidents in Great Britain (annual, TSO) Road accidents Wales (annual, National Assembly for Wales)

Subject	Table number in *Abstract*	Government department or other organisation	Official publication or other source
`	14.12, 14.13	Department of the Environment for Northern Ireland	Transport Statistics NI
Rail transport	14.19, 14.20	Department for Transport	Transport Statistics Great Britain (annual, TSO) Health and Safety Executive: Industry and Services (annual) Bulletin of Rail Statistics (quarterly)
	14.21, 14.22	Department of the Environment for Northern Ireland	Transport Statistics NI
Air transport	14.23 - 14.27	Civil Aviation Authority	Monthly Digest of Statistics (TSO) Civil Aviation Authority; Annual Statements of Movements, Passengers and Cargo Civil Aviation Authority; Monthly Statements of Movements, Passengers and Cargo Accidents to aircraft on the British Register (annual)
Sea transport	14.28, 14.29	Department for Transport	Maritime Statistics (annual, TSO) Monthly Digest of Statistics (TSO)
Passenger movement	14.30	Department for Transport Civil Aviation Authority	Monthly Digest of Statistics (TSO)
Communications	14.31	Royal Mail Parcel Force Capita Business Services Ltd. Post Office Counters Ltd	Monthly Digest of Statistics (TSO) Post Office report and accounts (annual)

15. National accounts

Subject	Table number in *Abstract*	Government department or other organisation	Official publication or other source
	15.1 - 15.22	Office for National Statistics	United Kingdom National Accounts (annual, TSO) Monthly Digest of Statistics (TSO) Economic Trends (monthly, TSO) UK Economic Accounts (quarterly, TSO) Consumer Trends (quarterly, TSO)

16. Prices

Subject	Table number in *Abstract*	Government department or other organisation	Official publication or other source
Producer prices	16.1, 16.2	Office for National Statistics	Producer Price Index Press Notice (monthly) Business Monitor MM22, Producer Price Indices (monthly, TSO) Monthly Digest of Statistics (TSO)
Consumer prices	16.3 - 16.5	Office for National Statistics	Monthly Digest of Statistics (TSO) Labour Market Trends (monthly, TSO) Focus on Consumer Price Indices (monthly, National Statistics website)
	16.6, 16.7	Department for Environment, Food and Rural Affairs	Agriculture in the UK (annual) Agricultural Price Indices (Monthly Statistical Notice) Monthly Digest of Statistics (TSO)
	16.8	Department for Environment, Food and Rural Affairs	Agriculture in the UK (annual)

17. Government finance

Subject	Table number in *Abstract*	Government department or other organisation	Official publication or other source
Central government	17.1 - 17.3	Office for National Statistics	Financial Statistics (monthly, TSO)
	17.4	Office for National Statistics	Financial Statistics (monthly, TSO)
	17.5	Office for National Statistics	Blue Book (annual)
	17.6 - 17.7	HM Treasury Office for National Statistics	Consolidated Fund and National Loans Fund Accounts Financial Statistics (monthly, TSO)
	17.8	Bank of England	
Saving	17.9	Department for National Savings	Accounts of National Savings Bank Investment Deposit Accounts (annual) Ordinary Deposit Accounts (annual)
Central government	17.10, 17.11	Board of Inland Revenue	Inland Revenue website
Rateable values	17.12	Board of Inland Revenue	Inland Revenue website
Local authorities	17.13, 17.14	Office of the Deputy Prime Minister National Assembly for Wales	Local government financial statistics (England) (annual) Welsh local government financial statistics (annual)

SOURCES

Subject	Table number in *Abstract*	Government department or other organisation	Official publication or other source
		Public Works Loan Board	Annual report of the Public Works Loan Board
		Scottish Executive, Economic Advice and Statistics	Local financial returns (Scotland) (annual)
		Department of the Environment for Northern Ireland	
		Chartered Institute of Public Finance and Accountancy	
	17.15, 17.16	Department for Transport, National Assembly for Wales	Local government financial statistics (England) (annual) Welsh local government financial statistics (annual)
	17.17	Department for Transport,	Local government financial statistics (England) (annual)
	17.18 - 17.20	Scottish Executive, Economic Advice and Statistics	Local financial returns (Scotland) (annual)
	17.21	Department of the Environment for Northern Ireland	District Council - Summary of Statement of Accounts (annual)

18. External trade and investment

Subject	Table number in *Abstract*	Government department or other organisation	Official publication or other source
	18.1 - 18.8	HM Customs and Excise	OTS1 Overseas Trade Statistics, (formerly MM20), monthly publication Extra EC OTS2 Overseas Trade Statistics, (formerly MM20A), monthly publication Intra EC and World OTSQ Overseas Trade Statistics, (formerly MQ20), quarterly publication Intra EC OTSA Overseas Trade Statistics, (formerly MA20), annual publication Extra and Intra EC
		Office for National Statistics	Business Monitor MM24, Monthly Review of External Trade Statistics (monthly, TSO) Overseas Trade Analysed in Terms of Industries MQ10 (quarterly, TSO) Monthly Digest of Statistics (monthly, TSO)
	18.9 - 18.18	Office for National Statistics Bank of England	United Kingdom Balance of Payments (annual, TSO) Quarterly figures: UK Economic Accounts Financial Statistics (monthly, TSO) Foreign Direct Investment MA4 (annual, National Statistics website)

19. Research and development

Subject	Table number in *Abstract*	Government department or other organisation	Official publication or other source
	19.1 - 19.5	Office for National Statistics	Business Monitor MA14, Research and Development in UK Business (annual, ONS)

20. Agriculture, fisheries and food

Subject	Table number in *Abstract*	Government department or other organisation	Official publication or other source
Agriculture	20.1, 20.2	Department for Environment, Food and Rural Affairs	Agriculture in the United Kingdom (annual)
	20.3 - 20.5	Department for Environment, Food and Rural Affairs	Agricultural Statistics; United Kingdom (annual) Scottish Agricultural Economics (annual) Welsh Agricultural Statistics (annual, National Assembly for Wales)
	20.6	Forestry Commission	Great Britain: Annual Report and Accounts of the Forestry Commission
		Department of Agriculture and Rural Development (Northern Ireland)	Northern Ireland Annual Abstract of Statistics
	20.7, 20.8	Department for Environment, Food and Rural Affairs	DEFRA Statistical Notice
Food	20.9 - 20.12	Department for Environment, Food and Rural Affairs	Monthly Digest of Statistics (TSO)
	20.13	Department for Environment, Food and Rural Affairs	Agricultural Statistics, United Kingdom (annual) As for notes 20.3 - 20.5

Subject	Table number in *Abstract*	Government department or other organisation	Official publication or other source
Fisheries	20.14, 20.15	Department of Environment, Food and Rural Affairs; Scottish Executive Agricultural Departments	*England and Wales*: Sea fisheries statistical tables (annual) *Scotland*: Fisheries of Scotland report (annual) Scottish Sea fisheries statistics (annual, TSO)
Food consumption	20.16	Department for Environment, Food and Rural Affairs	National Food Survey

21. Production
Production and construction

Subject	Table	Dept	Source
Production and construction	21.1	Office for National Statistics	Annual Business Inquiry (www.statistics.gov.uk/abi/)
Manufacturers sales	21.2	Office for National Statistics	ProdCom Product Sales and Trade PRA and PRQ series of reports
	21.3	Office for National Statistics	Size analysis of United Kingdom Businesses (Business Monitor PA1003) (annual, ONS)
Energy	21.4 - 21.12	Department of Trade and Industry (Energy Market Units)	Digest of United Kingdom Energy Statistics (annual) Energy Trends (monthly and quarterly) Annual Business Inquiry (www.statistics.gov.uk/abi/)
Iron and steel	21.13 - 21.15	Iron and Steel Statistics Bureau	Iron and steel industry: annual statistics published by the Iron and Steel Statistics Bureau Corporation Regional Trends (annual, TSO)
Industrial materials	21.16	World Bureau of Metal Statistics Aluminium Federation	World Metal Statistics (monthly) Annual Business Inquiry (www.statistics.gov.uk/abi/)
	21.17	Fertiliser Manufacturers' Association	Monthly Digest of Statistics (TSO) Annual Business Inquiry (www.statistics.gov.uk/abi/)
Minerals	21.18	Office of the Deputy Prime Minister Department of Trade and Industry Department of Economic Development (Northern Ireland)	Minerals (Business Monitor PA 1007) (annual, ONS) Natural Environment Research Council: United Kingdom Minerals Yearbook Northern Ireland Annual Abstract of Statistics
Building Materials	21.19	Department of Trade and Industry	Mionthly Statistics of Building Materials and Components (DTI) Monthly Digest of Statistics (TSO)
Construction (output)	21.20	Department of Trade and Industry	Construction Statistics Annual (DTI)
Construction (new orders)	21.21	Department of Trade and Industry	Construction Statistics Annual (DTI)
Engineering	21.22, 21.23	Office for National Statistics	Annual Business Inquiry (www.statistics.gov.uk/abi/)
Motor vehicle production	21.24	Office for National Statistics	Business Monitor PM 34.10, (monthly, ONS) Annual Business Inquiry (www.statistics.gov.uk/abi/) Sector Review- Motor Trades (formerly Business Monitor SDA27) (annual, TSO)
Drink and tobacco	21.25, 21.26	HM Customs and Excise	Annual report of the Commissioners of HM Customs
		Office for National Statistics	Monthly Digest of Statistics (TSO)

22. Banking, insurance, etc

Subject	Table	Dept	Source
Banking	22.1	Bank of England	Bank of England Annual Report and Accounts
	22.2	Association of Payment Clearing Services	Annual report of the Bankers' Clearing House
	22.3 - 22.5	Bank of England	Bank of England Quarterly Bulletin
	22.6	Bank of England	Financial Statistics (monthly, TSO)
	22.7	Bank of England	Bank of England Quarterly Bulletin
	22.8	Bank of England	Bank of England Quarterly Bulletin
	22.9 - 22.13	Bank of England	Monthly Digest of Statistics (TSO) Financial Statistics (monthly, TSO)
	22.14	Bank of England	Financial Statistics (monthly, TSO), tables E2.1 to E2.10
Other financial institutions	22.15	Financial Services Authority	Building Societies: Statistical Tables

Subject	Table number in *Abstract*	Government department or other organisation	Official publication or other source
	22.16	Office for National Statistics	Business Monitor SDQ7, Assets and Liabilities of Finance Houses and Other Credit Companies (quarterly, ONS)
	22.17	Office for National Statistics	Financial Statistics (monthly, TSO) Monthly Digest of Statistics (TSO) Business Monitor MQ5, Insurance Companies; Pension Funds and Trusts Investments (quarterly, ONS) First Release
	22.18, 22.19	Office for National Statistics	Financial Statistics (monthly, TSO) Business Monitor MQ5, Insurance Companies; Pension Funds and Insolvency Trusts Investments (quarterly, ONS)
	22.20 - 22.23	Department of Trade and Industry	Insolvency Annual Report (DTI) Companies (DTI) Financial Statistics (monthly, TSO)

23. Service industry

Subject	Table number in *Abstract*	Government department or other organisation	Official publication or other source
Retail trades	23.1	Office for National Statistics	Annual Business Inquiry (www.statistics.gov.uk/abi/)
	23.2	Office for National Statistics	Business Monitor SDM 28, via National Statistics Website: www.statistics.gov.uk
Motor trades	23.3	Office for National Statistics	Annual Business Inquiry (www.statistics.gov.uk/abi/)
Catering	23.4	Office for National Statistics	Annual Business Inquiry (www.statistics.gov.uk/abi/)

INDEX

Figures indicate table numbers

Figures indicate table numbers

INDEX

Figures indicate table numbers

Figures indicate table numbers

INDEX

Figures indicate table numbers

Figures indicate table numbers

INDEX